Black Theater, U.S.A.

FORTY-FIVE PLAYS
BY BLACK AMERICANS
1847-1974

JAMES V. HATCH, Editor
TED SHINE, Consultant

The Free Press

A DIVISION OF MACMILLAN PUBLISHING CO., INC.

NEW YORK

Copyright © 1974 by The Free Press
A Division of Macmillan Publishing Co., Inc.

All rights reserved. No part of this book may be reproduced or transmitted in any form or by any means, electronic or mechanical, including photocopying, recording, or by any information storage and retrieval system, without permission in writing from the Publisher.

CAUTION: Professionals and amateurs are hereby warned that all the plays in this volume, being fully protected under the copyright laws of the United States of America, the British Empire, including the Dominion of Canada, and all other countries of the Berne and Universal Copyright Conventions, are subject to royalty. These plays are for the reading public only, and all performance rights, including professional, amateur, motion picture, recitation, lecturing, public reading, radio and television broadcasting, and the rights of translation into foreign languages, are strictly reserved. Anyone disregarding the authors' rights renders himself liable to prosecution. Inquiries concerning these rights should be addressed to the author or agent named in the acknowledgments appearing after the copyright notices. All other inquiries should be addressed to the publishers named.

The Free Press
A Division of Macmillan Publishing Co., Inc.
866 Third Avenue, New York, N.Y. 10022

Library of Congress Catalog Card Number: 75-169234

Printed in the United States of America

printing number

20 19 18 17 16 15 14 13 12

The Brown Overcoat, by Victor Séjour, is reprinted by permission of the translator, Mrs. Pat Hecht. All performance rights are the property of Mrs. Hecht.

Appearances, by Garland Anderson, was copyrighted originally in 1924 under the title *Judge Not According to Appearances*.

Mine Eyes Have Seen, by Alice Dunbar Nelson, is reprinted by permission of Crisis Publishing Company, Inc., New York City.

For Unborn Children, by Myrtle Livingston, is reprinted by permission of the author and Crisis Publishing Company, Inc., New York City.

The Church Fight, by Ruth Gaines-Shelton, is reprinted by permission of Crisis Publishing Company, Inc., New York City.

Undertow, by Eulalie Spence, is reprinted by permission of the author.

The Purple Flower, by Marita Bonner, is reprinted by permission of Crisis Publishing Company, Inc., New York City.

Balo, by Jean Toomer, is reprinted by permission of Mrs. Marjorie Content Toomer.

'Cruiter, by John Matheus, is reprinted by permission of the author and the National Urban League.

The Idle Head, by Willis Richardson, is reprinted by permission of the author.

Bad Man, by Randolph Edmonds, is reprinted by permission of the author.

Job Hunters, by H. F. V. Edward, is reprinted by permission of the author and Crisis Publishing Company, Inc., New York City.

Don't You Want To Be Free?, by Langston Hughes, is reprinted by permission of Harold Ober Associates, Inc., 40 East 49th St., New York, N.Y. 10017; copyright 1938 by Langston Hughes; copyright renewed. The poetry in the play is reprinted by permission of Alfred A. Knopf, Inc., from *Selected Poems*, by Langston Hughes: "Negro," "Danse Africaine," "Dream Variations," "Cross," "The Weary Blues," and "When Sue Wears Red" are copyright 1926 by Alfred A. Knopf, Inc., renewed 1954 by Langston Hughes; "Song for a Dark Girl," "Bound No'th Blues," "Bad Luck Card," and "Cora" are copyright 1927 by Alfred A. Knopf, Inc., renewed 1955 by Langston Hughes; "Share-Croppers" and "Morning After" are copyright 1942 by Alfred A. Knopf, Inc., renewed 1970 by Arna Bontemps and George Houston Bass; "The Negro Mother" is copyright 1938 and renewed 1966 by Langston Hughes; copyright 1959 by Langston Hughes.

Big White Fog, by Theodore Ward, is printed by permission of the author.

The quotation in the introduction to Owen Dodson's *Divine Comedy* is from "Father Divine" in *The Negro in New York*, copyright The New York Public Library, and is reprinted by permission.

Divine Comedy, by Owen Dodson, is printed by permission of the author.

Graven Images, by May Miller, is reprinted by permission of the author.

Natural Man, by Theodore Browne, is printed by permission of the author.

Flight of the Natives, by Willis Richardson, is reprinted by permission of the author.

Native Son, by Richard Wright and Paul Green, is reprinted by permission of Samuel French, Inc., 25 West 45th St., New York, N.Y. 10036. Copyright 1941 by Paul Green and Richard Wright; renewed 1968 by Paul Green and Ellen Wright.

District of Columbia, by Stanley Richards, is reprinted by permission of the author and the National Urban League. Inquiries concerning performance or publication should be addressed to the author's agent: Warren Bayless, W. B. Agency, Inc., 551 Fifth Ave., New York, N.Y. 10017.

Walk Hard, by Abram Hill, is printed by permission of the author.

The Tumult and the Shouting, by Thomas Pawley, is printed by permission of the author.

The Amen Corner, by James Baldwin, is reprinted by permission of the Robert Lantz-Candida Donadio Literary Agency, Inc., 111 West 57th St., New York, N.Y. 10019. Copyright © 1968 by James Baldwin.

Take a Giant Step, by Louis Peterson, is reprinted by permission of International Famous Agency, Inc., 1301 Avenue of the Americas, New York, N.Y. 10019. Copyright © 1954 by Louis Peterson.

In Splendid Error, by William Branch, is printed by permission of the author and the Ann Elmo Agency, Inc., 52 Vanderbilt Ave., New York, N.Y. 10017. Copyright © 1953 by William Branch under the title of *Frederick Douglass*.

Star of the Morning, by Loften Mitchell, music and lyrics by Louis Mitchell and Romare Bearden, is printed by permission of the author. Copyright 1961 by Loften Mitchell.

Limitations of Life, by Langston Hughes, is printed by permission of Harold Ober Associates Inc., 40 East 49th St., New York, N.Y. 10017. Copyright 1938 by Langston Hughes; copyright renewed.

Dry August (*Mrs. Patterson*), by Charles Sebree, is printed by permission of the author.

Fly Blackbird, by C. Bernard Jackson and James V. Hatch, is printed by permission of the authors.

Day of Absence, by Douglas Turner Ward, is reprinted by permission of Curtis Brown, Ltd., 60 East 56th St., New York, N.Y. 10022.

The Drinking Gourd, by Lorraine Hansberry, is reprinted from *Les Blancs and the Last Plays*, by Lorraine Hansberry, by permission of Random House, Inc. Copyright © 1969, 1972 by Robert Nemiroff, executor of the estate of Lorraine Hansberry.

Wine in the Wilderness, by Alice Childress, is reprinted by permission of the author and her representative, Flora Roberts, Inc., 116 East 59th St., New York, N.Y. 10022. Copyright 1969 by Alice Childress.

The Owl Answers, by Adrienne Kennedy, is reprinted by permission of the William Morris Agency, Inc., 1350 Avenue of the Americas, New York, N.Y. 10019.

Job Security, by Martie Charles, is printed by permission of The New Lafayette Theater Agency, 2439 Seventh Ave., Harlem, New York, N.Y. 10030.

Little Ham, by Langston Hughes, is reprinted by permission of Harold Ober Associates Inc., 40 East 49th St., New York, N.Y. 10017. Copyright 1935 by Langston Hughes; copyright renewed.

The Slave, by Imamu Amiri Baraka, is reprinted by permission of The Sterling Lord Agency, 600 Madison Ave., New York, N.Y. 10021. Copyright © 1964 by LeRoi Jones.

Goin' a Buffalo, by Ed Bullins, is reprinted by permission of The New Lafayette Theater Agency, 2349 Seventh Ave., Harlem, New York, N.Y. 10030.

Herbert III, by Ted Shine, is printed by permission of the author and his representative, Flora Roberts, Inc., 116 East 59th St., New York, N.Y. 10022.

Blk Love Song #1, by Val Ferdinand, is printed by permission of the author.

For William R. Reardon
whose scholarship and encouragement inspired this book

Table of Contents

Foreword
   TED SHINE   ix

1. Those Who Left and Those Who Stayed   1

The Black Doctor (1847)
   IRA ALDRIDGE   3
The Brown Overcoat (1858)
   VICTOR SÉJOUR   25
The Escape; or, A Leap for Freedom (1858)
   WILLIAM WELLS BROWN   34

2. Yes We Must, Yes We Can   59

Caleb the Degenerate (1901)
   JOSEPH S. COTTER, SR.   61
Appearances (1925)
   GARLAND ANDERSON   100

3. Early Plays by Black Women   135

Rachel (1916)
   ANGELINA GRIMKE   137
Mine Eyes Have Seen (1918)
   ALICE DUNBAR NELSON   173
They That Sit in Darkness (1919)
   MARY BURRILL   178
For Unborn Children (1926)
   MYRTLE SMITH LIVINGSTON   184
The Church Fight (1925)
   RUTH GAINES-SHELTON   188
Undertow (1929)
   EULALIE SPENCE   192
The Purple Flower (1928)
   MARITA BONNER   201

4. Black Folk Plays of the 1920's   209

A Sunday Morning in the South (1925)
   GEORGIA DOUGLAS JOHNSON   211
Balo (1924)
   JEAN TOOMER   218
'Cruiter (1926)
   JOHN MATHEUS   225
The Idle Head (1929)
   WILLIS RICHARDSON   233
Bad Man (1934)
   RANDOLPH EDMONDS   241

5. From the Depression   253

Job Hunters (1931)
   H. F. V. EDWARD   255
Don't You Want To Be Free? (1937)
   LANGSTON HUGHES   262
Big White Fog (1938)
   THEODORE WARD   278
Divine Comedy (1938)
   OWEN DODSON   320

6. Plays of Black History   351

Graven Images (1929)
   MAY MILLER   353
Natural Man (1937)
   THEODORE BROWNE   360
Flight of the Natives (1927)
   WILLIS RICHARDSON   382

7. Social Protest of the 1940's   391

Native Son (1941)
   RICHARD WRIGHT and PAUL GREEN   393
District of Columbia (1945)
   STANLEY RICHARDS   432
Walk Hard (1944)
   ABRAM HILL   437

8. Black Family Life   473

The Tumult and the Shouting (1969)
   THOMAS PAWLEY   475

The Amen Corner (1954)
JAMES BALDWIN   514
Take A Giant Step (1953)
LOUIS PETERSON   547

9. Biography   585

In Splendid Error (1954)
WILLIAM BRANCH   587
Star of the Morning (1964)
LOFTEN MITCHELL   618

10. Comedy as Protest   653

Limitations of Life (1938)
LANGSTON HUGHES   655
Dry August (1949)
CHARLES SEBREE   658
Fly Blackbird (1960)
C. BERNARD JACKSON and JAMES V. HATCH   671
Day of Absence (1965)
DOUGLAS TURNER WARD   695

11. Modern Black Women   711

The Drinking Gourd (1960)
LORRAINE HANSBERRY   713
Wine in the Wilderness (1969)
ALICE CHILDRESS   737
The Owl Answers (1965)
ADRIENNE KENNEDY   756
Job Security (1970)
MARTIE CHARLES   765

12. Black Theater for Black People   773

Little Ham (1935)
LANGSTON HUGHES   775
The Slave (1964)
IMAMU AMIRI BARAKA (LEROI JONES)   812
Goin' A Buffalo (1966)
ED BULLINS   826
Herbert III (1974)
TED SHINE   854
Blk Love Song #1 (1969)
VAL FERDINAND   864
Bibliographies   875

Index   881

Foreword

This anthology is the outgrowth of need and neglect: the desperate *need* for a single volume with enough plays by black writers so that they might be read and evaluated historically and the neglect of editors and publishers who have ignored the works of all but a few playwrights. A number of anthologies of black plays have recently been published, but the purpose has been either the introduction of new talent (handling only those plays professionally produced) or the compilation of the works of a single author. Earlier anthologies are useful as historical sources, but they obviously do not include current works and are often out of print. In anthologizing black playwrights, there has been, until recently, a tendency to use the same playwrights and the same plays over and over again. Certainly the familiar works merit attention, but there are other writers whose works are of equal merit—Alice Childress, William Branch, Loften Mitchell, Theodore Ward, Owen Dodson, Theodore Browne, Thomas Pawley, and Val Ferdinand, to mention a few. Teachers are perplexed because there has been no single volume devoted exclusively to the evolution of the black playwright in America, except Darwin T. Turner's *Black Drama in America: An Anthology* (1971), which includes works by black playwrights between 1923 and 1968. Students are perplexed because it is often impossible to locate some of the plays that they have heard about. This indifference to black playwrights is perhaps best illustrated by the anthology *Fifty Best Plays of the American Theater*, (compiled by the late John Gassner and Clive Barnes), which does not include a *single* play by a black writer—not even Lorraine Hansberry's *A Raisin in the Sun*, which won the New York Drama Critics' Circle Award as the best play of the 1958–1959 season. Instead, black characters are poorly represented by white playwrights in *Uncle Tom's Cabin, Green Pastures*, and *Porgy*.

The plays in this anthology represent a historical approach to black drama that, it is hoped, will give the reader some idea of what black playwrights think and feel about themselves, their people, and their country. These plays were selected because they represent stages in the evolution of black dramaturgy in America; in many instances they have not been previously published.

Black playwrights were slow to emerge in our society because of slavery and racial injustice. When they did begin to write, their plays were seldom, if ever produced, and only a few were published. No matter what the quality of their works may be, they do give us an opportunity to examine ideas, characters, and life from *primary* sources. Black characters appeared in American dramas as early as 1767, beginning with Raccoon in Andrew Barton's (Thomas Forrest's) *The Disappointment*: or, *The Force of Credulity*. With few exceptions the plays that followed used blacks mostly for comic relief or as "contented" servants. This stereotyping was sustained and climaxed by the minstrel show, which sprang up in the early 1840's. Not until 1852, when Harriet Beecher Stowe's novel, *Uncle Tom's Cabin*, was adapted for the stage, was there a major attempt in American drama to treat black characters and the problem of slavery with sympathy.

The popularity of Mrs. Stowe's play prompted numerous imitations, both pro and con, dealing with the theme. It was within this atmosphere that William Wells Brown composed *The Escape; or, A Leap to Freedom*. The play contains melodrama characteristic of the period, but is all the more remarkable because it is autobiographical and perhaps the first protest play by a black American playwright.

Joseph S. Cotter's *Caleb, the Degenerate: A Study in Types, Customs, and Needs of the American Negro*, was the first play to deal with the problem of finding a place for blacks within American society some thirty-eight years after the Emancipation Proclamation. A half century after the Emancipation, a new generation of talented blacks emerged, and their creative efforts, along with the "discovery" of black music, art, dance, literature, and life of the past, were to alter greatly the direction of the arts in America.

Beginning in 1917, white playwrights made earnest efforts to try to present a less calumnious picture of blacks and black life on stage. A new folk drama was born. Ridgeley Torrence, Eugene O'Neill, Paul Green, and Dorothy and DuBose Heyward were among the pioneers in this area. Even today someone interested in plays dealing with black life or folklore is usually referred to these writers. The integrity of their intentions is unquestionable, but they lacked a true knowledge of the black experience. Ironically, at the same time that works of these white playwrights were being produced, an amazingly large number of black playwrights were recording a truer black experience in numerous unproduced plays. These plays have been virtually ignored, except for a few scattered productions in black colleges, community theatres, high schools, and churches.

The professional theatre has been reluctant to produce plays by black playwrights. Had Garland Anderson been less aggressive, *Appearances*, in all probability, would not have been the first full-length play by a black writer to reach Broadway. Since its production in 1925, fewer than thirty-five plays by blacks have been produced on the Great White Way. Over the last thirty years there have been fewer than sixty-five plays by blacks presented off-Broadway.

Producers argue that blacks don't support the commercial theater. They fail to realize that most blacks who would attend simply cannot afford the exorbitant price of tickets; and, too, more and more blacks have discovered that much of what is presented in the commercial theatre has little relevance to them. This feeling is especially strong among young blacks, as many black colleges with drama programs or departments are discovering. Their audiences no longer want to be *entertained* with popular Broadway successes; instead, they are demanding to be *instructed* by black writers such as Ed Bullins and Imamu Baraka (LeRoi Jones).

It is a fallacy that blacks do not need and enjoy theater. They do. The African Grove Company, The Lafayette Theatre, The Rose McClendon Players, The American Negro Theatre, The Howard Players, and other college drama groups; The Negro Ensemble, The New Lafayette Theatre, The Free Southern Theater, The Performing Arts Society, and The Inner City Repertory (both in Los Angeles) are but a few examples from the past and present. In black communities across the country a new and vital theater of relevance is developing.

The plays in this volume include a wide variety of themes, styles, and approaches to dramaturgy. Many of them are "problem" or "protest" plays; others are merely concerned with an aspect of black life. Some are comic, some tragic. They have been compiled as testimony to the brilliant accomplishments of black Americans under the most adverse circumstances and in a relatively short period of time.

TED SHINE

1

Those Who Left and Those Who Stayed

Ira Aldridge   Victor Séjour   William Wells Brown

In William Dunlap's play, *A Trip to Niagara*, which opened in 1828, the black gentleman, Job Jerryson, tells a fellow servant, "If you would like to see our theater, I can give you an order. I am one of the managers. We rehearse every club night—the Shakespeare Club." In all likelihood Mr. Jerryson is referring to The African Grove, a theater founded in the season of 1820–21 by a Mr. Brown (his first name is not known) and a group of black actors for their own recreation. This stage, located in lower Manhattan at Bleecker and Mercer Streets, had a capacity of three or four hundred persons. Newspapers of the time contain accounts of the theater's success, especially their Shakespearean productions. The popularity of the company was such that the management "graciously made a partition at the back of their house for the accommodation of the whites." The African Grove was the first professional black theater in America.

In this theater, the drama *King Shotaway*, based on "the Insurrection of the Caravs on the Island of St. Vincent," was performed. Although the script is not extant, *King Shotaway* is probably the first play written and performed by Afro-Americans. Here in this theater, James Hewlett, the West Indian actor, performed. Here Ira Aldridge made his stage debut in the part of Rolla in *Pizarro*. The African Grove was closed in 1822 by the Constable after white rowdies "out for a lark brought disorder and wanton mischief."

The remainder of the nineteenth century offered one major opportunity for black actors: blackface minstrelsy. In 1865, Charles Hicks, an Afro-American, organized the Georgia Minstrels, a company of black actors and musicians. In order for these men to obtain bookings they had to have a white manager. They also were required to wear minstrel makeup: the face was covered with burnt cork, with the mouth and eyes circled in red and white. In the 1890's some black actors stopped wearing this disguise; a number turned to writing and producing their own musical variety shows (e.g., *A Trip to Coon Town*).

Faced with a theatrical desert, some Afro-Americans left to work in Europe—Louis Gottschalk, Billy Kersands, Elizabeth Taylor Greenfield, James Bland, Ira Aldridge, Victor Séjour. All were successful abroad. Others—William Easton, Sissieretta Jones, Bob Cole, Will Marion Cook, Sam Lucas—elected to work in the

United States. Beyond personal preference and opportunity to travel, the decision to stay in America may often have depended on whether the artist was in minstrelsy or not. If the artist were "serious"—that is, if he wished to write or perform drama or concert music *sans* blackface, his hopes lay outside the country.

Of the four black American playwrights of the nineteenth century whose work is extant, two—Ira Aldridge and Victor Séjour—left; two others—William Wells Brown and William Easton—stayed to use dramaturgy in their struggle against racism. In 1893, William Easton wrote, "Indeed we have had excellent caricaturists of the Negro, in his only recognized school of legitimate drama, i.e., buffoonery. But the author of this work [*Dessalines*] hopes to see a happier era inaugurated by the constant production of legitimate drama written exclusively for Negro players." To support his proposal, Mr. Easton wrote two black militant verse plays: *Dessalines* and *Christophe*. However, the "happier era" he hoped for did not begin to develop for another thirty years.

William Wells Brown, although he traveled widely in Europe lecturing on American slavery, wrote plays that he read to abolitionist audiences in the United States in the 1850's. *The Escape*, is printed here.

Of the three playwrights printed in this section, two concerned themselves with "the problem," one did not. Yet all shared one common irony—none directly influenced the black American theater that blossomed in the twentieth century.

Ira Aldridge (1807–1867)

The Black Doctor   1847

The white handerkerchief in the dark hand of the Moor, the dark face in a cloak of white marble, the eyes fastened on the handkerchief: this is the Pietro Calvi bust of Othello that stands inside the entrance of the Schomburg Research Library in Harlem.

Of the visitors who pause to glance at the statue, a few recognize the bronze plaque's legend: *Ira Aldridge, the Tragedian*. The names, if not the accomplishments, of great nineteenth-century actors (Booth, Kean, Bernhardt) are known to many Americans. The name of the African Roscius, whom Herbert Marshall calls "a dark star whose brilliance has been dimmed by sins of omission and commission of the white world," was nurtured through a hundred years of silence by a few writers who would remind America during Negro History Week that Mr. Aldridge was the first black American honored by the Republic of Haiti for service to his race. They remembered that the actor had received the Prussian Gold Medal for Arts and Science from King Frederick, and that he had been awarded the Medal of Ferdinand from Franz Joseph of Austria for his performance of Othello. But an accurate and complete account of his life and times became available only in 1958, when Herbert Marshall and Mildred Stock published *Ira Aldridge, the Negro Tragedian*.

Ira Aldridge claimed descent from the Fulah princes of Senegal. Although there are conflicting stories, the evidence indicates that he was born in about 1807 in New York City, where he attended the African Free School on Mulberry Street. In 1820–21, young Aldridge saw plays at the African Grove Theater and watched the fine West Indian actor, James Hewlett, perform. Ira Aldridge at 17 faced the same choices that other black men who wished to be theater artists faced: to stay and find some kind of work in black-face song and dance, or to leave America. In 1824, Mr. Aldridge sailed for London, never to return.

The story of his life in Europe is one of struggle, recognition, and success. Billing himself as The African Roscius, a native of Senegal, he established himself not only in the black roles of Othello and Titus Andronicus, but as King Lear, Macbeth, Shylock, and Richard III.

Nor did he limit himself to Shakespeare. His repertoire included *The Padlock*, a comedy in which he played Mungo, a disobedient servant; the role of Ginger Blue, a waiter, in *The Virginia Mummy*, a farce; and Fabian in *The Black Doctor*. This play, originally written in French by Anicet-Bourgeois, opened in London in 1846. The version printed here was adapted for the English stage by Ira Aldridge.

The plot is a romantic tale of the black physician who heals, falls in love with, and marries (secretly) the daughter of a French aristocrat. There follows the inevitable family conflict, imprisonment, insanity, and a predictable denouement. However, the racial statement Mr. Aldridge made in the play's main character presents the doctor with dignity—a dignity marred by his acceptance of European standards of culture at the expense of his own color.

As described by Mr. Aldridge, Fabian "is not a black man, but a handsome Mulatto, yellow and brown." This description may have been intended as a portrait of the author. (One critic compared Mr. Aldridge to "a new half penny.") Quite possibly he is also indicating to white men who blackened themselves for Negro roles with ham fat and burnt cork that the term "black" includes shades other than charcoal.

Mr. Aldridge's color irritated those English critics who could not endure to see a "slave" perform Shakespeare. Other critics came to the actor's defense. Perhaps the tragedian's situation was akin to the black doctor's in the play: his color sometimes provoked hostility, but his talent was so in evidence that his detractors could not hold the field. Like Fabian, he married a white woman; but unlike the fictional character, Ira Aldridge lived to the age of sixty, and enjoyed children, honors, property, and British citizenship. Whatever Europe's prejudices, they did not prevent the artist from developing and living by his talent.

The Black Doctor

CAST OF CHARACTERS
(in order of appearance)

HANNIBAL GRIMAUD, *wine shop owner*
LIZETTE GRIMAUD, *his wife*
SUSANNE GRIMAUD, *his daughter*
PIERRE BRIQUET, *valet to St. Luce*
JACQUES FILS, *suitor to Susanne*
CHRISTIAN, *old Negro servant to Fabian*
FABIAN, *the black doctor*
PAULINE REYNERIE, *beloved of Fabian*
LIA, *mulatto servant to Pauline*
CHEVALIER ST. LUCE, *cousin and fiancé to Pauline*
MARCHIONESS DE LA REYNERIE, *Pauline's mother*
ANDRE, *loyal friend to Fabian*
AURELIA, *sister to St. Luce*
LORDS, LADIES, SOLDIERS, JAILORS, *etc.*

ACT ONE

Scene One

(*The Wine-shop of* HANNIBAL GRIMAUD, *at the town of St. Louis, in the Isle of Bourbon.—Enter* GRIMAUD, LIZETTE, *and* SUSANNE, *right*)

GRIMAUD   Don't talk, woman, but hear me! I'm Commander-in-Chief: as the great Louis said, "I'm France"—which means, I'm everything and everybody.
LIZETTE   But now, husband, consider—
GRIMAUD   Don't waste your breath by husbanding me! I'm firm, inflexible! A solid square! There's no breaking through me.
SUSANNE   But, dear father—
GRIMAUD   Don't father me you jade; or rather, don't get anybody else to father me. I tell you, when you do marry, it shall be to a man of my choosing. Do you imagine that I, Hannibal Grimaud, who have served seventeen campaigns, will condescend to marry my daughter to a common barber?
LIZETTE   Pierre Briquet isn't a common barber; he keeps as good a shop as any in the town, and is well to do in the world beside.
GRIMAUD   Not a common barber! Look at my chin; how dare you contradict me? Didn't he shave me yesterday with his own hand?
SUSANNE   That was out of friendship; for, you know, your own hand shook so with—
GRIMAUD   Silence, you impudent baggage, or I'll shake you. Once for all, I tell you I'm not to be shaved into any such connections; and as for that other suitor of yours—that threadpaper fellow, Jacques Fils, why, he's a fool.
LIZETTE   He's as good a young man as any in town.
GRIMAUD   Good! Good for nothing.
LIZETTE   Sober, steady and industrious.
SUSANNE   And an excellent workman.
LIZETTE   Two such suitors are not to be despised.
SUSANNE   And I'm sure men are scarce enough in the colony, unless you'd have me marry a blackamoor.
GRIMAUD   You shall marry whom I please, you jade, and he shall be as black as I like. I tell you Pierre Briquet and Jacques Fils are very well in their way; but be prudent, girl; give your best smiles to the best customers. Remember you're a soldier's daughter; and though your post may be a wine-shop, let your heart be surrounded with a *chevaux de frize* of pride, which shall render it impervious to the puffs of a barber, or all the finedrawn compliments of a tailor.
LIZETTE   I'm sure Susanne has all the proper pride of her mother's family.
GRIMAUD   Lather and soapsuds, what do you mean? Why, you were only a laundress when I raised you to the honorable distinction of a soldier's wife! Her mother's family indeed—she has little to boast of on that score.
LIZETTE   Score, indeed! Your washing-score was long enough when I married you, and you were only a—
GRIMAUD   Silence, woman! (*looking round*) Here comes some neighbors; order, to your post. And remember, I'm commander. (*enter* PIERRE

BRIQUET *and* JACQUES FILS, *left*) Welcome neighbors, welcome.

BRIQUET   Good morning, friend Grimaud; I've some news for you; so just step in, though I'm in a terrible hurry.

GRIMAUD   Ay; good, I hope?

BRIQUET   For me, at any rate; but first, some wine; my throat's as dry as the high road.

JACQUES   And so is mine.

GRIMAUD   Susanne, some wine. Ah, this is a fine country.

BRIQUET   Do you say so?

GRIMAUD   Ay, for wine's cheap, and one's always thirsty—ha, ha!

ALL   Ha, ha! very cool. (SUSANNE *brings wine*)

GRIMAUD   Well, Master Briquet, now for your news.

BRIQUET   Well, first and foremost, my shop's to let.

SUSANNE   Your shop?

BRIQUET   Yes, my shop, pretty one; I'm this very day engaged by the Chevalier St. Luce, as his valet and confidential attendant.

SUSANNE   What! Mademoiselle de la Reynerie's cousin, and who they say is to be her husband?

BRIQUET   So they say; and now she's her own mistress, the death of her mother having removed all restraint.

GRIMAUD   But is the death of the Marchioness authenticated?

BRIQUET   Why, seeing the vessel she was to have sailed to France in was wrecked, and every soul has perished, there's very little doubt of the matter. Ah, poor Mademoiselle de la Reynerie! She has had two narrow escapes, for grief and anxiety had nearly killed her.

GRIMAUD   Ay, but the Black Doctor saved her both times.

LIZETTE   Only, to think now, that a mulatto, and a slave, should have become the most eminent physician in all the island!

GRIMAUD   The Black Doctor isn't a slave.

LIZETTE   Well, but he was before he was free.

GRIMAUD   Don't you run down people, wife of mine. Remember what you were before I married you.

BRIQUET   But the strangest thing of all is, that after the Black Doctor had saved the life of Mademoiselle de la Reynerie, and become domiciled in the family, he should suddenly disappear, and now nearly six months have elapsed since he was seen here in St. Louis, though some of the negroes say he has been observed wandering on the cliffs, but always avoiding anyone who appeared to seek him.

GRIMAUD   Well, everybody likes the Black Doctor, and so they should, if it were only for the services he has rendered Mademoiselle de la Reynerie; she'll be a treasure to the man that wins her.

BRIQUET   And she's so rich, too, plenty of gold and jewels; plantations here, and estates in France.

GRIMAUD   Unexceptionable and desirable plunder, friend Briquet, and worth leading a forlorn hope for.

SUSANNE   I suppose we may look soon, then for a wedding?

BRIQUET   Why, can't exactly say, though the Chevalier will shortly honor me with his entire confidence, and I'll let you know as soon as we arrange affairs.

GRIMAUD (*goes upstage;* LIZETTE *follows*)   We, indeed.

BRIQUET   I say, Susanne, what pleasure I should have in curling you up for a certain day.

SUSANNE   Curling me up, indeed! What do you mean?

BRIQUET   Though art couldn't improve you, Susanne. Macassar oil, bergamot, and eau de Cologne would be only adding perfumery to the violet.

SUSANNE   La! Briquet, how you do talk.

JACQUES (*aside, very melancholy*)   I see my suit cut on the cross; soft soap carries it.

SUSANNE   What's the matter, Jacques? You seem dull today.

JACQUES (*very spoony*)   Not particular.

BRIQUET   It's only the thoughts of losing my company, Susanne; quite natural, you know! The needle always inclines to the pole—but I must be off.

JACQUES (*joyfully*)   What! Are you going?

BRIQUET   Yes, and I'm going to take you with me; you don't think I'd leave you here with Susanne?

JACQUES (*going up*)   Heigho!

BRIQUET   Besides, I must attend the Chevalier; he will be expecting me. Good bye, Susanne, I shall see you again soon; good day, Grimaud; good day Madame Grimaud.

GRIMAUD   If you hear any news of the Black Doctor, mind you let us know.

BRIQUET It's likely I shall; for little Lia, the foster sister of Mademoiselle de la Reynerie, is very ill, and as he can't have left the island, no doubt he'll be found to attend upon her; but I must say goodbye once more, Susanne. (*aside*) I shall see you again this evening. Come along, Jacques.

JACQUES (*sorrowfully*) Goodbye all. (*looking at* SUSANNE) Heigho! (*exit at the door*)

GRIMAUD That Briquet's a greater puppy than ever; and as for the other, why he's a perfect idiot. Come hustle about, it's near dinner time.

SUSANNE Puppy, indeed! I'm sure Briquet's not at all a puppy.

LIZETTE Nor poor Jacques half such a fool as he looks to be; but nobody is good enough for you.

GRIMAUD Yes, you're good enough for me, but don't dare dispute with me; I'll teach you to mutiny; to the right about, march! (*they go off*, he follows, right)

Scene Two

(*Fabian's Hut, constructed of bamboo, an opening right, facing the audience, and leading to a garden. In the garden is seen a green bank, another opening at the back, which is the entrance to the hut, from which wild rocky scenery is visible. Second-entrance, left, a door leading to the interior of the hut; at the back, right, of the entrance, a small trunk, a hatchet hanging on a nail just over it. Rude couch, covered with tiger skin—a few wooden chairs left, and facing the audience. As scene opens,* CHRISTIAN, *an old Negro, is seen watching at the entrance, as if looking for someone*)

CHRISTIAN How long he stays! Well, I must prepare his meal, though I fear he will not taste it. (*looking out*) Ah! he comes at last; how unhappy he looks; when he's that way, my presence here seems to oppress him; so I'll retire, and wait till he calls me. (*exit, left*)

(*Enter* FABIAN, *slowly, right, holding in his hand a little cross of gold, hanging from his neck; places his hat on the little trunk, and his gun near the entrance*)

FABIAN Sacred relic, worn by my mother, and which, after I had closed her eyes in death, I took from her cold breast—when evil thoughts cross me, I press you to my lips, and all my anger is absorbed in tears. Can this little relic, so powerful against evil, avail nothing to my sufferings? In vain I place it on my burning heart; it cannot quench the passion that consumes it. To it alone I breathe my fearful secret; that I, a mulatto, and late a slave, dare to love the daughter of a white man—the daughter of him who was my master! It is madness—madness! (*falls on his knees, his hand on the foot of the couch*) Pray for me, my mother!

(CHRISTIAN *appears at the entrance, looks in, and signs to* PAULINE *to enter. She enters with* LIA, *who is leaning on her arm, and appears ill; places her on a seat near the entrance, and comes down alone*)

PAULINE (*after an effort to speak*) Monsieur Fabian.

FABIAN (*quickly turning at the sound of her voice*) Heavens! (*rises*)

PAULINE (*advancing*) Monsieur Fabian!

FABIAN Is it indeed you, mademoiselle, and here?

PAULINE (*with great gentleness*) When death threatened, you came to my assistance; when life and health returned, you left me; but you did not impose on me forgetfulness nor ingratitude. (*offers a purse*)

FABIAN (*with emotion*) And it is for this you are here? Oh, mademoiselle, I thought you were good—generous—

PAULINE The gold I have brought you, I wish you to distribute among your poor patients—

FABIAN (*taking the purse*) You are an angel. (*looking at* LIA *with happiness*) I bless heaven for seconding my endeavors; again I see you, whom death has twice so nearly snatched away—I am happy, I am proud!

PAULINE Good Fabian! But this mystery that cause me to—

FABIAN Mystery!

PAULINE Yes, which perhaps you can help me to unravel. Since you have ceased to come to the Reynerie, a man has been seen at night wandering about the dwelling, near my window; he has eluded all search—all pursuit; one night the negro on duty fired at him quite at random, and next morning, at the foot of a large tree, traces of blood were found. Fabian, I cannot tell you my feelings at the sight of that blood.

(*looking earnestly at him*) You had not always that scar on your forehead.

FABIAN That scar? A fall I had on the rock.

PAULINE (*aside, agonized*) 'Twas his blood!

FABIAN Mademoiselle, what is the matter?

PAULINE Fabian, the desire to thank you was not the only motive that brought me here; I have come to claim your assistance for my poor foster-sister, Lia.

FABIAN Lia! Once so happy and so gay!

PAULINE But now so ill, so spirit-broken! Yes, Fabian, poor Lia is sinking beneath sorrows I am ignorant of; she will die if you do not save her. (*brings* LIA *forward*) Look at her. Courage, dear Lia; he restored me, and will give you health and strength.

FABIAN (*gives her a seat, takes her hand, and looks at her*) What is the matter, Lia?

LIA (*without raising her head*) Nothing.

PAULINE Dear Lia, tell Fabian the cause of your suffering.

LIA I do not suffer.

PAULINE (*to* FABIAN) Always the same answer; you cannot assist, if she persists in the silence; she will die, and none will ever know the grief that killed her.

FABIAN Yes, I know it.

LIA (*alarmed*) Heavens!

FABIAN I know her malady, but cannot save her.

PAULINE (*alarmed*) What do you say?

FABIAN The sickness that oppresses her is of the heart.

LIA (*rising in terror*) Fabian, Fabian! Oh, be silent. (*falls back in her seat*)

PAULINE (*aside*) This mystery!

FABIAN You love.

LIA Oh, no, no, no, no, no.

FABIAN Do not try to deceive me; the budding passion which brightened to your eyes during your mistress's convalescence, since then I see has grown, and consumed the heart in which you strived to stifle it.

LIA (*hiding her face in her hands*) Have pity, Fabian, have pity!

FABIAN And this love, pure and chaste, you would hide from all, as if it were a shame for you to love one whom you have no right to love, and who despises you.

PAULINE Oh no! 'Tis impossible.

FABIAN Because he is not of your accursed race; because he is a European.

PAULINE What do I hear?

FABIAN And yet is Monsieur Bertrand a good and worthy young man.

LIA Do not mention that name.

PAULINE Bertrand, the young Frenchman? Mr. Barbantine's clerk?

FABIAN Yes, mademoiselle, yes! He is a good and worthy young man; but his skin is white (*to* LIA) and yours is dark, as mine; therefore you have not the right to love him. Suffer, poor sister, suffer and despair, for yours is a malady for which there is no remedy.

PAULINE Oh, heavens! Ought I to understand?

LIA (*weeping*) I wish to die; 'tis all I desire.

PAULINE Unhappy girl, but you must not, shall not; I will save you. (*looking at* FABIAN) You say he is not of her race; what is that to me, since she loves him—would die for him? You hear me, Fabian; I say she shall live, she shall be his wife.

LIA (*joyfully*) His wife!

FABIAN (*astonished*) 'Tis impossible.

PAULINE It shall be my work, my secret care, known only to us three; he loves you?

LIA But if he marries me, he is lost.

FABIAN Yes, he will be proscribed, driven out by the man who has fostered him.

PAULINE No matter, I am rich; I know it now, and for the first time feel proud of it. He shall be free, and you shall be happy. (*looking at* FABIAN) I know not what gives me strength and resolution, before unknown to me; by-and-by we will go to Barbantine's residence; I will see Bertrand, he shall hear me, he will understand; but you, Lia, weak and suffering, must not go with me, and I will not confide our secret to another; (*with firmness*) I will go alone.

FABIAN (*sorrowfully*) Alone!

PAULINE (*with gentleness*) No, Fabian, you shall go with me; when it strikes three at St. Louis, be at the end of the avenue of palms. Come, Lia, my sister, look cheerfully, all will be well. Look, Fabian, she is better already; her eyes are brighter; thanks to you, she feels the blessings of hope, and hope is life. Come, Lia, come. (*exit hurriedly:* LIA *kisses his hand, and exits after her*)

FABIAN He is of another race—what is that to me? She loves him—would die for him! She said so, here but now, and to me, who would die for her. Oh, mother, mother, bless you; I asked you, you prayed for me, and in an instant heaven has sent me a moment of joy—of bliss. (*the report of a gun heard, and* ST. LUCE *calling without*)

ST. LUCE (*without*) Help! Help!

(CHRISTIAN *appears at the entrance, and points, left*)

CHRISTIAN Master! Master! Yonder a hunter! A Serpent! (*takes down hatchet, is going*)

FABIAN You are not strong enough; give me the weapon. (*takes hatchet from him, and rushes out*)

CHRISTIAN (*following to entrance*) No, master, no, let me go; my life is worthless, but your— (*enter* ST. LUCE, *conducted by* FABIAN) Ha, he was in time.

FABIAN (*to* ST. LUCE) Lean on me, sir.

ST. LUCE (*a gun in his hand*) No thank you, Doctor; I am not much hurt. (CHRISTIAN *takes* ST. LUCE'S *hat and gun and places them in a corner*)

FABIAN (*gives hatchet to* CHRISTIAN, *who replaces it*) Some water. (*exit* CHRISTIAN. FABIAN *gives* ST. LUCE *a seat*)

ST. LUCE I have many times seen death as near, but have never been on such intimate terms with a serpent before; 'tis an indigenous produce which does little honor to your country. (CHRISTIAN *returns with coconut-shell full of water and gives it to* FABIAN, *who hands it to* ST. LUCE)

ST. LUCE (*returns it to* FABIAN. *after drinking*) Thank you.

FABIAN (*looking at his left hand*) You are wounded.

ST. LUCE O, 'tis nothing.

FABIAN Allow me. (*taking from the little trunk the necessaries to dress the wound*) What could bring you to this isolated spot? (*exit* CHRISTIAN, *who returns immediately with more water;* FABIAN *washes and dresses* ST. LUCE'S *wounded hand*)

ST. LUCE Only curiosity! You must know I was stretched out under a banana tree, enjoying that dreamy repose, which, while it transports us to an ideal world, still allows us to hear what is passing in this. I dreamt I was hunting at Marly, when suddenly the foliage near me became agitated, and thinking it was a rabbit, I seized my gun, and fired, as near as I could judge, upon the spot of his hiding place, when all of a sudden I saw the grey head of an enormous serpent rise up before me; so I called out lustily for help, and my kind stars sent you to my assistance, when there was no more space between me and my enemy than just enough for your hatchet. By my faith, Doctor, you are a wonderful man, and your exact manner of amputation is complete.

FABIAN Sir, if you ever seek rest, this miserable dwelling is at your service; but if you desire to return to St. Louis, allow me to offer a guide.

ST. LUCE (*rising*) A thousand thanks for your proffered hospitality; but I must not give my sister time to be uneasy at my absence; therefore, will only accept the guide you offer.

FABIAN (*to* CHRISTIAN) Prepare to conduct the Chevalier by the road through St. Hane.

ST. LUCE Doctor, you are decidedly the good genius of our family; without your assistance, lovely eyes might this night have been drowned in tears; yes, my cousin would again have hid her sweet face in the grief of mourning, which is soon to smile on her affianced husband.

FABIAN (*at the back of the stage, turns suddenly round*) Affianced husband: of whom do you speak?

ST. LUCE Of my cousin, who is to—

FABIAN Of Mademoiselle de la Reynerie?

ST. LUCE Certainly.

FABIAN No, it is impossible.

ST. LUCE Impossible: and why?

FABIAN (*embarrassed*) Because I know no one in Bourbon worthy to possess such a treasure.

ST. LUCE True; but then I do not belong to the Isle.

FABIAN You!

ST. LUCE Yes, I am in love, my dear sir—seriously in love; you are astonished to hear it, they would not believe it at Versailles; but I repeat it, I'm in love, and intend to marry; our union was first projected by Madame de la Reynerie, and Pauline but waited the end of her mourning, in order to obey her mother's wish.

FABIAN (*overpowered*) She!

ST. LUCE And though the aristocracy of Bourbon should blame me ever so, I shall insist on your presence at my marriage, which, but for you, death had twice prevented. Farewell, Doctor, or rather, goodbye for the present. (*to* CHRISTIAN, *who is standing at the entrance, and presents* CHEVALIER *with hat and gun*) Go on before me friend, and heaven protect us from sun and serpents. Goodbye, Fabian. (*exit* ST. LUCE *and* CHRISTIAN)

FABIAN (*with a sudden burst*) She loves that man, he will be her husband! And yet but now I have saved him! I have allowed him to go from me with life. (*seizes his gun, is about to rush out, and suddenly stops*) Kill him! Assassinate him! No, no, 'tis not he who should die! It is, ah—I; water! Air! I shall suffocate! (*falls at the end of the couch, his hand falls on his chest, he seizes the little cross suspended round his neck*) Again that dreadful idea crossed my brain, and my hand unintentionally falls on this little relic—O, my mother, 'tis your voice I hear, 'tis heaven commands I should avoid a crime, and still drag on this wretched life of suffering! (*three o'clock strikes*) Three o'clock; she is waiting for me—she, St. Luce's bride! (*rises with a sudden burst*) No, no, it shall not be! I will not die alone. (*throws away cross*) Mother, I hear you not, you shall not save her—together, together, we will die together! (*rushes out*)

Scene Three

(*The High Road near Reynerie. Enter* BRIQUET *and* JACQUES, *right; they are both a little elevated*)

BRIQUET Capital stuff that, wasn't it, Jacques? That's the house to live in! Long life to the Chevalier and his intended bride. I say, Jacques, my boy, why don't you laugh?

JACQUES I can't laugh, Briquet: I'm melancholy.

BRIQUET It's a professional failing; tailors are naturally melancholy; sedentary employment produces thoughts, therefore it's natural.

JACQUES You've called me a natural three times.

BRIQUET Don't interrupt me Jacques, but listen,—what was I saying? O, I remember; long life to the Chevalier and his intended bride! Talking of brides I intend to be married myself shortly.

JACQUES You be married! And pray who is to be the bride?

BRIQUET Who's to be the bride? Why, whom do you think but Susanne, the lovely charming little Susanne?

JACQUES Have you got her consent?

BRIQUET Not yet.

JACQUES Have you got her father's consent?

BRIQUET Not exactly, but I've got the consent of one party.

JACQUES What, her mother?

BRIQUET No (*hiccup*) myself.

JACQUES Well, that's something towards it, but I should like to see you propose it to old Grimaud, he'd—

BRIQUET What do I care about old Grimaud? Do you think I'm afraid of old Grimaud? I'm afraid of nobody, when my blood's up. I fear neither man nor—(*turning round*) the devil! (*enter* CHRISTIAN, *the old negro, right*)

CHRISTIAN Your master waits for you at the Reynerie.

BRIQUET What do you know about my master?

CHRISTIAN But little! I have just acted as his guide—he met with a slight accident in the woods.

BRIQUET An accident?

CHRISTIAN Yes, which delayed him beyond the time appointed to his return. But all danger is past, thanks to the timely assistance of my master.

BRIQUET And who is your master?

CHRISTIAN The Black Doctor. (*exit, right*)

BRIQUET (*turns from him as he speaks*) I say, Jacques. (*looks round, finds* CHRISTIAN *gone*) Why, he's gone; so the Black Doctor's come to hand at last. I was going down to Grimaud's, but as my new master wants me I can't, so do you tell him. Do you hear that the Black Doctor's still in the land of the living? None of your nonsense now with Susanne. I feel rather queer, but the Chevalier will attribute that to my anxiety on his account. Good-bye Jacques; keep steady, my boy; I shall see you tomorrow; keep steady—and keep me always in your eye as an example. (*they exit differently*)

Scene Four

(*Enormous rocks, left. A rock, right forming a grotto; near which, on one side is a stone bench, a rock in which steps are rudely cut, descending to the sea in the center of the stage; with a rock in which a seat appears rudely cut. A pathway, left, a little elevated, and overhanging the steep cliffs. The whole scene is wild and gloomy in the extreme; the sea at back. As the scene opens* PAULINE *and* FABIAN *appear at the very top of the rock, right*)

PAULINE This path seems unfrequented; why have we come this way?

FABIAN The inhabitants rarely visit this bay, which they have called the mulatto's grotto; there is a popular legend attached to it.

PAULINE Shall we reach the Reynerie before Bertrand? I wish to be first, to tell Lia of the success of our enterprise.

FABIAN He is going round in the boat; the wind and tide will be against him, so we have the advantage. Rest yourself here a moment to recruit your strength.

PAULINE (*sits on rock, center of stage*) This is a wild and gloomy spot.

FABIAN Did you not desire me to take the most retired route? Mademoiselle de la Reynerie wished to avoid anyone whilst walking beside the mulatto Fabian. 'Twas otherwise in your childhood; then you did not disdain to lean on my arm.

PAULINE (*after a moment's silence as if to change the conversation*) Fabian, I think you have my fan.

FABIAN (*takes it from his bosom, and presents it to her respectfully*) 'Tis here, Mademoiselle.

PAULINE But, you too must be tired, Fabian, for your hand trembles so as it did just now; are you ill?

FABIAN No, lady.

PAULINE Ah, I shall be so happy to tell Lia the obstacles that separated her from Bertrand no longer exist; in a month she shall leave the colony with her affianced husband; they shall live in a country where prejudice will not condemn their union—will not crush their mutual affection; Lia, my sister you at least shall be happy. (*sighing*)

FABIAN Happy! Yes, in the love of her husband! For without his love of what avail would have been my penetration or your generous friendship?

PAULINE Bertrand has a noble heart.

FABIAN He loves her.

PAULINE He was not born under your sky; had he been a creole, he would have hid his passion in the utmost depths of his heart.

FABIAN And Lia would have perished; and had Bertrand been a creole he dared not have shed one tear to her memory; is it not so?

PAULINE (*rising with calm dignity*) Fabian, we will continue our walk; the Countess and her brother will be waiting for me.

FABIAN (*endeavoring to contain himself*) He loves you, lady.

PAULINE (*embarrassed*) He has told me so.

FABIAN He is to be your husband.

PAULINE 'Twas my mother's dearest wish. (FABIAN *staggers against the rock, right;* PAULINE *is going, turns round and looks at him*) Fabian, I am waiting for you. (*he passes his hand across his forehead, appears to be looking attentively at two crosses carved in one of the rocks*)

FABIAN Those two crosses carved in the rock, and which appertain to the legend I told you of just now.

PAULINE What legend?

FABIAN Shall I tell you?

PAULINE Yes, tell me the history of this legend.

FABIAN (*goes back, looks at the sea which is seen gradually to rise, then returns to* PAULINE) Listen, then. There lived in St. Louis, a poor mulatto—a slave, who (I have forgotten for what good service rendered to his master) received his freedom! The generous gift should have made him happy, but it was otherwise; for once free he was compelled to leave his master's dwelling, and under that roof dwelt his better angel. At length he went forth, more wretched in his freedom than in his slavery! For he loved—yes madly loved—adored that master's daughter. (*wind heard*)

PAULINE (*alarmed*) How dreadfully the wind howls.

FABIAN (*not heeding her*) He would have buried his love in his heart, though it had crushed it; but the young and noble lady, who used to converse with him, in few kind words, completed the delusion. He thought himself beloved—and though respect to the pride of her race forbade her to be his, he thought at least she would never be another's. The fool was dreaming; one word awoke him, she was about to marry—to marry! She had deceived him, had sported with his agony; she should not have done so—it was imprudent for then the wretched man took an oath to unite himself to her by the solemn, dreadful, awful tie of death.

PAULINE (*rising agitated, looks at the sea, which is gradually surrounding them*) Fabian! Fabian! Not now; the sea rises. (*going*) Let us go. Come, come, Fabian!

The Black Doctor

FABIAN (*detains her*) Go! (*smiles*) No, the mulatto had calculated every chance; in his turn he had deceived the young girl—he had led her into a snare—they both stood here—on the spot we now occupy; the tide was rising fast, only one path was free—but the sea continued to gain on them. (*seizes both her hands*) The young girl entreated the mulatto to try to save her; but he, without pity for her terror or her tears, held her with hands of iron. At last he told her he loved her. (*looking round*) Still the sea was gaining ground; every chance of escape was gone, and yet death has less of horror for the young girl than the mulatto's love.

PAULINE (*in much terror*) Fabian, for pity's sake, save me!

FABIAN Save you! And is it not possible you guess I love you?

PAULINE (*struggling with her feelings*) No, no! You are deceiving me; you would not—could not see me die here before your eyes!

FABIAN (*pointing to sea*) Look, Pauline, before we should reach the rocks which we now but descended together, the sea would dash us to atoms against their rugged points! I feared my own weakness, and closed every avenue to the road of repentance or pity; death surrounds us, but we shall perish together! How! You no longer tremble, will you not call down heaven's curses on your destroyer's head?

PAULINE (*solemnly*) Fabian!

FABIAN (*pointing to sea*) No earthly power can save us!

PAULINE (*rushing to pathway, which the sea has not yet reached*) Then let me beg my mother's forgiveness and pray to heaven for you. (*falls on her knees against the rock*)

FABIAN For me!

PAULINE Yes, for you! Now I am sure of death, I may acknowledge, without shame or remorse, that I understand you, Fabian, and I forgive you, for I have long, long loved you!

FABIAN Did I hear aright? Love me! And I—I am her murderer! Oh, heavens, (*rushes to her and supports her in his arms*) you will not allow it! Kill me! But save her! (*looks around*) Ah! 'Tis too late! She is already dying. (*carries her up the rock, lays her down, takes off his vest, waves it, shouting for help. The sea reaches them, curtain falls as he is still struggling with her in the water. Bertrand is seen at the back in a boat. Curtain*)

ACT TWO

Scene One

(*A handsome drawing-room in the Marchioness's Home in Paris, elegantly furnished. At the back, large folding doors, opening to a gallery; on each side, at the back, a large window, with hangings, a door left and right; handsome bookcase and bureau on each side; canopy, left, arm chairs right and left; a handbell on the bookcase. Enter* BRIQUET *and* JACQUES, *very handsomely and foppishly dressed, and rather grotesquely*)

BRIQUET And so, friend Jacques, you have followed us to Paris?

JACQUES Yes, I felt so dull when you left, that I made up my mind to come too; but what a grand house to be sure!

BRIQUET (*offers snuff*) Yes, we are pleasantly situated. Do you still operate? (*makes sign of cutting with shears*)

JACQUES Yes, I cut out.

BRIQUET Ah, you rogue, you have cut me out; and how does Madame Fils?

JACQUES Oh, she's quite well.

BRIQUET Delighted to hear it—shall be still more delighted to see her. I bear no ill-will; but how the deuce you managed it, I never could guess.

JACQUES Why, you see, I didn't talk of marrying until I got more than my own consent in the business.

BRIQUET Ha, ha, I recollect; but really, in Paris, a wife is rather an incumbrance, and you see my situation brings me so much in contact with the fashionable world, that one don't miss the little comforts, as they are termed, of matrimony; strange things have happened since we rusticated in St. Louis.

JACQUES Strange, indeed, to think that the Marchioness, whom we all supposed drowned, should be alive after all.

BRIQUET Yes, and she is gone to Versailles, to present her daughter, Madame Pauline, to her Majesty, the Queen, upon her return from the colonies; she'll be back in an hour.

JACQUES And the Black Doctor?

BRIQUET Oh, he's with us—couldn't do without him; though, by-the-by, the Marchioness doesn't much relish his being here; but the circumstance of his having twice saved her daughter's life, and her still delicate health, in some way reconcile her to his presence.

JACQUES That was a fearful business, too, when Monsieur Bertrand saved them both; there was a sort of mystery in that affair!

BRIQUET No doubt, no doubt, friend Jacques; there are more mysteries than we can fathom in this world; it was, as you say, a close shave.

JACQUES Rather too fine-drawn an affair for me, I own; and the marriage with the Chevalier!

BRIQUET Why, there seems some reluctance on her part, but the Marchioness is positive. I suppose, eventually, she must marry; but come into my room, and we will take a glass to old times, and our future acquaintance. (*as they are going, enter* ANDRE *at the door in back, which is open*) And what do you want, friend?

ANDRE The Doctor, if you please.

BRIQUET This is not a doctor's shop, friend; you are in the house of the Marchioness de la Reynerie.

ANDRE Yes, I know; but he I seek lives here.

BRIQUET Who is it you mean?

ANDRE The Doctor; the good worthy man I have come to thank; he's well-known in our quarter, ever since he attended my poor mother; everybody gave her up, even the hospital doctors; and today, thanks to him, she's quite well again! Oh, he's got plenty of practice; but he always gives the poor the preference; and when he passes our way, men, women, and children bless the Black Doctor.

BRIQUET The Black Doctor! Oh, now I know who you mean. He means Fabian.

ANDRE Is that his name?

BRIQUET Yes, he's a mulatto, an enfranchised slave, whom Mademoiselle de la Reynerie brought over from Bourbon, a curiosity.

(FABIAN *appears at door, dressed in court suit, sword, etc.*)

ANDRE A curiosity, indeed! Goodness and charity are, no doubt, a curiosity to you; take care how you speak about him before me!

FABIAN (*comes down*) Noble heart!

ANDRE Ah, is that you, Doctor?

BRIQUET Come along, Jacques.

ANDRE Why, Doctor, how dares that powdered monkey—

FABIAN (*calmly*) How is your mother, today, Andre?

ANDRE Well, quite well; she sent me, though strong enough to come herself, but she was afraid—

FABIAN Afraid!

ANDRE This is how it is, Doctor; we took it into our heads that, as everybody must live by their trade, a doctor can't give away his time to everybody for nothing; so I worked double tides, and have brought you a fortnight's wages; it isn't much, but such as it is there it is.

FABIAN I accept your offer, good friend, but you must be my banker, and when you meet with a fellow-creature who needs it more than yourself, give it to him.

ANDRE From you?

FABIAN As you please.

ANDRE I'll do as you desire! Farewell, Mr. Fabian; don't forget Andre. In a few months I am going to my brother in Bretagne—'tis our country.

FABIAN Bretagne?

ANDRE Yes, if you should ever come there you shall have the best place at our fireside, as you already have in our hearts. Farewell, Mr. Fabian. (*exit at door, first shaking* FABIAN's *hand*)

FABIAN (*seats himself, and finishes reading a letter, which he has in his hand*) "Yes, Fabian, with Bertrand, my husband, who loves me more than ever, in the bosom of his family, who welcomed me as another child; I am happy, very happy; when you hear of this, ah, let us hear of your happiness, too." (*refolds the letter ironically*) Happy! yes, my good Lia, I live in a noble house, am head lackey to the Marchioness de la Reynerie—distinguished honor! True, I am waited on by my fellow servants, in my own apartment. Oh, yes, I am happy, very happy! (*rising*) Heavens! Whence comes this patience, this resignation? For six long months have I endured this, and yet I have not roused my sleeping energies, and cried aloud to them all. She whom you surround with such homage, such flattery, she is mine, my own, my wife! No, I am silent. Shut up the livelong day, I endeavor to forget my condition in study, and only when I hear the carriage which conveys the Marchioness from the door, do I venture to exchange a look—a word with Pauline, then a stranger comes, and I must needs retire, a smile and a tear—(*noise of carriage, he runs to window and looks out*) 'Tis she! I shall see her, I shall see her. Oh, this is the secret of my resignation. (*a servant opens the folding doors, the* CHEVALIER, *in court-dress, enters, conducting* PAULINE, *who is also in court-dress.* ST. LUCE *does not notice* FABIAN, *who stands aside, and is not seen by* PAULINE. *Aside*) Still that man forever at her side!

ST. LUCE Now, cousin! Cannot the gracious reception you met with at Versailles, raise a smile in that beautiful face? For my part, like the Marchioness, I was delighted as I observed the looks of our charming Queen wander from yourself to rest on me—she doubtless guessed what I could poorly conceal.

PAULINE Your pardon, Chevalier, my mother, I believe, is waiting for you.

ST. LUCE May I not be excused for forgetting her, when by your side? (*aside*) Ever cold and constrained! I cannot understand it. Adieu, for the present my lovely cousin! Do try to think a little of me until I see you again, I shall think of no one else. (*he is about to kiss her hand, she withdraws it, he signifies his mortification; as he is going, stops on seeing* FABIAN) So, you were here, were you?

PAULINE (*surprised*) Fabian!

ST. LUCE In the drawing room, we may readily discern we are not in Bourbon, and are making rapid strides towards equality, as the commons have it. (*aside*) This is very strange, but doubtless you have come for mademoiselle's order—you should have knocked sir. If there are no longer slaves in Paris, I believe we still have lackeys. (*exit at door*)

FABIAN True, a slave in Bourbon! here a lackey.

PAULINE (*in a supplicating voice*) But the slave! The lackey! Is he not my lord—my husband in the sight of heaven, and in mine, who lives for him? Is he not great, is he not noble, has he not a right to be proud of himself? Do you not bear next your heart a sacred deed, signed by a minister of heaven—a deed that plainly says "That the lackey—the slave—is my master?"

FABIAN Our marriage, blessed by an unknown minister, in an isolated corner in the Isle of Bourbon, your mother will have power to break, by a simple motion of her fan. (*drawing a paper from his breast*) Since this may not be the passport of happiness for either, at least it can be made the instrument of revenge.

PAULINE (*calmly*) Yes, Fabian, you can show it to my mother; you can say to her, your daughter has changed her proud name of La Reynerie for that of Fabian; your daughter has even given herself to me. You can do all this, and I should forgive you; but my mother would curse the memory of her child!

FABIAN Oh, forgive me, Pauline, forgive me; you know not what I suffer, you know not my wretchedness; but fear not, I will bear up against the grief that is killing me, against the jealousy that consumes me.

PAULINE What, Fabian, jealousy?

FABIAN No, no doubt ever entered my heart, it would kill me at once. Pauline, I will be confiding, calm! I shall see you daily go to those fetes where so many temptations surround you, but I will be silent; you will accept his arm for your escort, that man who is ever at your side, that man who loves you, I shall see him, as I did but now, gaze on you with admiration, raise that hand to his lips, which is mine—I say, I shall see all this, and yet I shall be silent.

MARCHIONESS (*without*) Pauline, 'tis I, open the door.

PAULINE My mother, and she will find me here, and with you.

FABIAN (*rushes to window*) No, though I should be dashed to atoms on the pavement below.

PAULINE Stay! (*pointing to the chamber*) There, in that room, by the back staircase, hasten.

MARCHIONESS (*without*) Pauline! Pauline, I say!

FABIAN (*going by direction, right*) You see I am obedient. I am going; I shall be silent. (*Exit*)

(*Enter the* MARCHIONESS, *center*)

MARCHIONESS (*looking round*) Were you alone, Pauline?

PAULINE (*embarrassed*) Yes, yes, mother, alone.

MARCHIONESS When the Chevalier left you, Fabian was here.

PAULINE He was.

MARCHIONESS How did the man presume to enter here, without your express order?

PAULINE (*hesitating*) He came to tell me of a visit he had paid to some poor pensioners of mine, as I had desired him.

MARCHIONESS (*haughtily*) And I desire you

may have no such explanations in the future; tomorrow he shall leave this house, and in three days quit France.

PAULINE   He! Fabian?

MARCHIONESS   I am about to send him back to the colony, there he will henceforth enjoy independence. I will reward him, as I ought, for his faithful servitude to you; but let us speak no more of the man, but come at once to the business that brings me here now. The Queen was pleased with you, my daughter, and in order to have you one of her ladies of honor, her Majesty wishes you to marry.

PAULINE   What do I hear?

MARCHIONESS   The Chevalier St. Luce will this evening receive letters patent that will confer on him the title of Count, and tomorrow the King will add to the obligations I already owe him, by himself signing your contract.

PAULINE   No, no, I did not hear aright; mother, 'tis impossible!

MARCHIONESS   Impossible! Listen to me, Pauline; I have determined to have you a noble protector, and a defender; I could not confide my child to one more noble or more worthy than St. Luce, already almost my son. I repeat, 'tis my determination you should marry him, and by the memory of your father, it shall be as I say. (*goes to bookcase and rings bell*)

PAULINE   (*aside*)   Then 'tis heaven's will I should die! (*enter servant, center*)

MARCHIONESS   Tell Fabian I have an important command for him; show all visitors into this apartment, I will receive him here. (*exit servant. To* PAULINE) You will for the future receive the Chevalier as your intended husband. (PAULINE *kneels to her, kisses her hand, and weeps*) Pauline, you cannot make me alter my determination! Your resistance would be as useless as your prayers.

PAULINE   Mother, heaven is my witness, I would have devoted to you the life you gave me. I asked, I sought, but to live in your heart, and you drive me from you!

MARCHIONESS   To give you to the arms of a husband.

PAULINE   Before your will excludes me and separates us, my mother, gaze on me as you used to do; when a child I looked for and found all, all my joys in your eyes; bless me as you used to do, when I prayed to heaven that I might live and die for my mother's love.

MARCHIONESS   (*raising her*)   Tomorrow, Pauline, at the altar, I will bless both my children.

PAULINE   (*aside*)   Tomorrow you will have no daughter! (*servant opens door at back*)

MARCHIONESS   Calm yourself, Pauline; we are no longer alone.

(*Servant announces the following ladies and gentlemen:* COUNTESS DE RESADEUC, MDLLE. *and* CHEVALIER DE ST. LUCE, MADAME DE BEAUMEAL, MONSIEUR *and* MADAME DE LA FRERAGE, MARCHIONESS L'AMBERVILLE, COUNCILLOR OMMISSOR. *All the company is received by the* MARCHIONESS, *who presents them to* PAULINE *as they enter; she curtsies to them all; the* MARCHIONESS *conducts the ladies to the canopy, and places herself in an armchair beside it;* PAULINE, *struggling with emotion, conducts one of the ladies right; one chair remains unoccupied between her and the lady; the gentlemen remain standing in groups behind the ladies right and left; the* COUNTESS DE RESADEUC *alone remains standing for a moment by the* MARCHIONESS)

AURELIA ST. LUCE   My good aunt, at length the dearest wish of my heart will be fulfilled. St. Luce has just told me—

MARCHIONESS   (*smiling*)   That I am a very humble and obedient subject. It is my intention it should be known at Versailles this very evening, that I have presented the Countess de St. Luce, lady of honor to her Majesty, the Queen, to all my friends.

ALL   Lady of honor! (*the gentlemen compliment* ST. LUCE)

AURELIA ST. LUCE   At length, then you are my sister. (*taking* PAULINE'*s hand*)

PAULINE   (*aside*)   Heaven! Give me one hour more of strength and courage!

ST. LUCE   My dear aunt, I know not how to thank you; but believe me, I will prove worthy of the treasure you confide to me. (*kisses the hand of* REYNERIE, *approaches* PAULINE, *who remains motionless*) How! not one look? (*enter servant, center*)

SERVANT   Monsieur Fabian, Madam.

PAULINE   Fabian!

ST. LUCE   She starts at the name!

MARCHIONESS   Very well, tell him to wait.

AURELIA ST. LUCE (*to* MARCHIONESS *de la Reynerie*) Poor Fabian, I have scarcely seen him since his arrival, and I have talked so much

The Black Doctor

about him to these ladies that they are as anxious to see him as I was at the Isle of Bourbon.

MARCHIONESS In this apartment! You forget.

AURELIA (*laughing*) O, they won't know of it in Bourbon.

PAULINE (*aside*) Before so many he will betray himself.

ST. LUCE (*aside*) Pale, trembling. 'Twas the same this morning, and always so at the question of his name! By heaven! I will know how far she is interested in this man. My dear aunt, allow me to join in my sister's entreaty; besides, I owe Fabian a debt.

MARCHIONESS You!

ST. LUCE Yes, of honor.

MARCHIONESS Well, dear Count, today I cannot refuse you anything. (*to servant*) Tell Fabian he may come in. (*exit servant*)

PAULINE (*aside*) We are lost!

ST. LUCE (*laughing*) Quite a presentation, I declare.

(*Enter* FABIAN: *at sight of company he stops; upon a sign from the* MARCHIONESS *bows and addresses her*)

FABIAN You sent for me, madam; what are your commands?

AURELIA (*to a lady*) What do you think of him?

MARCHIONESS You are about to quit my house to leave France.

AURELIA Why? Where is he going?

MARCHIONESS To Bourbon.

FABIAN (*quickly*) Madam, I— (*catches* PAULINE's *eye, stops*)

ST. LUCE (*aside*) How she watches him!

FABIAN When am I to depart, madam?

MARCHIONESS Tomorrow; the steward has received my orders. You will find that I have not forgotten past services, nor been unmindful of your future welfare; you may now retire.

ST. LUCE (*to* MARCHIONESS) Not yet, my dear aunt; you must allow me to beg you will delay his departure for a few days. Fabian, we are no longer at Bourbon; therefore I can and will reward you for the service you there rendered me; the invitation I there gave you I hold good here, and repeat, I wish you to be present at my marriage with Mademoiselle de la Reynerie, (*looks from* FABIAN *to* PAULINE) which will be celebrated in three days. (FABIAN *suddenly starts*.)

PAULINE *instantly rises, and takes her eyes from him.* FABIAN, *struggling with his feelings, endeavours to be calm and silent. Aside*) Again! At all hazard I will know the worst.

AURELIA You will grant my brother's request, will you not, dear aunt? Fabian, you do not thank my brother.

ST. LUCE (*smiles contemptuously*) No, I remember; 'tis very natural; he does not like to own himself so bad a prophet. Fabian has declared all marriage impossible for Mademoiselle de la Reynerie.

MARCHIONESS He!

ST. LUCE Yes, my dear aunt; doubtless he was afraid of losing so profitable and unexpected a source of patronage and favor. (*looks at* PAULINE) What other motive could there be? I am afraid our cousin's protection has been thoughtless, and perhaps may be fatal to our Doctor.

MARCHIONESS How?

ST. LUCE No doubt, in Bourbon 'twill be necessary to duff these trappings of a gentleman which appear rather strange; here 'tis only laughed at, but in Bourbon 'twould be otherwise; there his insolence would be chastised, particularly the sword, which sits but ill on a mulatto, who could not dare to raise it even to ward off the planter's whip!

PAULINE (*without taking her eyes from* FABIAN) Ah!

AURELIA Brother, you are cruel!

ST. LUCE (*haughtily*) No, sister; 'tis not I, but reason that says every man in his station. Look! Fabian already pays dearly for the ridiculous dreams to which an imputed benevolence has given birth; he suffers, for he cannot forget what he was—what he is! See how he plays with the hilt of the sword! That hand, which still wears the impression of the chain—

FABIAN (*in a fury*) Ah! (*draws the sword and with a sudden expression breaks it, throws it at his feet, and covering his face with his hands, weeps*)

ST. LUCE Why, what's the matter?

AURELIA (*coming between them*) Brother, you are very cruel; you have wounded his feelings.

PAULINE (*rushing forward*) I can endure this no longer; 'tis cowardly—infamous! (*goes to her mother and speaks in a voice choked with passion and sobs*) Mother, dismiss these people; I must speak to you alone!

MARCHIONESS (*rising*) This agitation!

PAULINE Have pity on me—on yourself! Dismiss them!

MARCHIONESS (*aside to her*) You alarm me, Pauline! Friends, my daughter is ill; it alarms me!

AURELIA Indeed! (*to* PAULINE) Are you ill?

MARCHIONESS Leave us to ourselves! Chevaliers, adieu until tomorrow! (*exit guests*)

ST. LUCE (*aside*) If you have indeed favored this unruly rival, cousin, I have at least paid your insult by insult. Come, sister. (*takes her hand; as he is leading her off gives a look of scorn at* FABIAN, *who is following him*)

PAULINE No, no—stay, Fabian!

MARCHIONESS Why do you detain him?

PAULINE Because if you drive him forth, you must also drive me forth; because if he goes, 'tis my duty to follow him.

MARCHIONESS To follow Fabian!

PAULINE Yes, mother, my love—my lord—my husband!

MARCHIONESS He!

PAULINE (*to him*) Look up, loved and injured Lord; heaven, that gives you resignation, has at last given me courage; can you forgive me?

MARCHIONESS Fabian's wife! No, you did not say that?

PAULINE I have said it, mother, and my husband shall not be dishonoured.

MARCHIONESS Wretched girl, take then—

FABIAN (*coming between them*) Be not in such haste to curse, lady! Your malediction would be impious and could not reach to heaven. She, who now humbles herself, who weeps, is pure as the angels. True, she loved me, a poor slave—because I had staked my life to save her mother's; but I tell you your blood runs in her veins. She was ashamed of her love, and only on the brink of a precipice, death surrounding us, when help appeared impossible, as with her last breath, her secret escaped her.

MARCHIONESS Heavens, was I restored to life but to be witness of this dishonor? This infamous marriage shall be dissolved.

FABIAN Dissolve my marriage! You cannot do it, madam; call your servants—they shall make way for your daughter's husband; recall the Chevalier St. Luce, who so insolently crushed me with his aristocracy, and whom but for Pauline's imploring look, I would have annihilated as I did that weapon; call him, and I will tell my insolent rival 'tis now his turn to feel the torments of jealousy and rage, for his betrothed is my lawful wedded wife!

MARCHIONESS I will invoke the judge, the magistrate, the King himself!

FABIAN All slaves who set foot on European ground are free; therefore am I, before affranchised, now doubly so; and the law makes no distinction of rank or colony.

MARCHIONESS (*to* PAULINE) You hear him—you hear this man proclaim our shame! If your father could rise from his grave, he would strike you dead! He would rather see you in your grave than so degraded, so dishonored!

PAULINE (*takes a small phial from her bosom*) Then let him judge me! Father, I come! (FABIAN *rushes to her, seizes phial, throws it away*)

FABIAN Pauline!

MARCHIONESS What does this mean?

FABIAN It means, madam, that she was about to swallow poison.

MARCHIONESS Poison!

FABIAN Yes, which she had concealed, that your curse might fall upon her corpse!

MARCHIONESS (*sinking overpowered into a chair*) Pauline!

PAULINE (*kneeling*) I cannot live under my mother's malediction.

FABIAN Then 'tis for me to complete this act of devotion. What neither your King nor your laws can do, Fabian himself will act. This marriage—consecrated by a holy minister of heaven, who will reveal the secret to no one—this inviolable—this indissoluble marriage, I myself will annul.

PAULINE You!

MARCHIONESS How say you?

FABIAN (*struggling with his grief*) Madam, I restore to you your daughter. Pauline, this one act has repaid me hours of grief and misery, and anguish; you would have died for me, you shall live for your mother! (*forces her to* Marchioness) Farewell, Pauline; you cannot be mine till we meet again in heaven! (*at the door*) Not mine, Pauline, but never another's! Farewell! (*exit*)

PAULINE Mother, he leaves me but to seek comfort in death! (*tries to follow him.* MARCHIONESS *detains her*)

MARCHIONESS (*to servants, who enter*) Follow Fabian, see you do not let him leave the house. Should it be necessary, use force; but on no account let him depart.

ACT THREE

Scene One

(*The stage is divided horizontally in two parts, each part again divided into two portions. The portion right, above, forms a well-lighted apartment, splendidly furnished; at back, a window with curtains; left, a toilet-table, dressing-glass, center, a table with an arm-chair on each side; a door leading to staircase, which forms left of upper portion; at foot of staircase, a trap-door leading to dungeon below. The staircase is not seen, but forms left lower portion; lower portion, right, is the dungeon; a large stone pillar, behind which, is straw; in front of and right of pillar, a stone bench; left of pillar, at back, a window, with iron bars; on front pillar, on block of stone, a lighted lamp.* BRIQUET *is discovered in the upper apartment reading a newspaper.*)

BRIQUET Eleventh of July—then I have been as an inhabitant of the Royal Chateau, the Bastille, two months and six days exactly, and why? "Briquet," said my master, Monsieur de St. Luce, "you are my valet, I give you twelve hundred francs a year to wait upon me, shave me, dress me and powder my wig, in whatever corner of France I may be. The King sends me to the Bastille, therefore you must follow me, to dress, shave, and powder me, in the Bastille." (*rises*) And here we are, lodged in the tower of the chapel, just above the moat. This apartment is not so bad, nor the bedroom either; the furniture is good, I may say, elegant; in short, 'tis a gentlemanly prison, but still it is a prison! (*drums without*) Hallo! What does that mean? First time I've heard them since we've been here; perhaps the King's coming to see us and give us our liberty. (*drums again*) *Enter* ST. LUCE, *in drawing-gown*)

ST. LUCE Briquet! What, rascal! Didn't you hear me?

BRIQUET Yes sir; did you say the carriage, sir?

ST. LUCE Eh?

BRIQUET I beg your pardon, sir; I'm always forgetting we are in "status quo."

ST. LUCE (*Laughing*) We must accustom ourselves to it, Briquet. (*sits*) Come, dress my hair.

BRIQUET (*getting comb, etc.*) But sir, aren't you going to try to get out of here?

ST. LUCE (*looking in a hand mirror*) I beg pardon? Never! I've done the King great service and he has punished me! So much the worse for him.

BRIQUET (*combing his hair*) And me too! I beg your pardon, but it seems to me you did—

ST. LUCE My duty, sir! I was breakfasting at the "cafe de joie"; facing me were three citizens. I should have known the plebians a mile off, by the smell of them. (Take care what you are about.) They were members of the new assembly of deputies of the States General, chatting on public affairs. (*looks in glass*) A little more powder on that side. At the mention of a proposition, which I did not approve of, I rose and addressed them, and flatly told them I thought everything of the aristocracy, very little of the clergy, and nothing of the people; so we warmed upon the subject until we quarreled. I offered to fight one of them; he accepted! "My name," said I, "is the Chevalier de St. Luce." "Sir," says the fellow, "my name is Barnaby." "Never heard of it," said I. Then the bystanders threw themselves between us, and separated Barnaby and me; but the adventure reached the ears of the court. Well, thinks I, Barnaby will be arrested; but instead of that they arrested me.

BRIQUET Yes, sir, I understand; but I never offended Barnaby, so I—

ST. LUCE What do you complain of? The lodging's well enough, the table is well served, the wine excellent, and the air of captivity a fine thing for the appetite. Ring for my dinner.

BRIQUET (*taking glass from* ST. LUCE) Yes, sir, but then you didn't leave your heart at the gate of the Bastille, while I—but, perhaps I haven't told you I was just going to be married?

ST. LUCE Oh, yes, you did; I thought it a capital joke.

BRIQUET Not for my intended, though—poor little Runnette, I appointed to meet her by the third tree on the left-hand side of the park, and she's been waiting there two months and six days exactly; how impatient she must be.

ST. LUCE Oh, don't make yourself uneasy; she's found amusements, I dare say; a great many of the national guards pass through the park.

BRIQUET Sir, don't talk in that way, or I shall be capable of setting fire to the Bastille.

ST. LUCE Well, I won't prevent you; but first see after the dinner.

BRIQUET Yes, sir, I'll get the table ready. Poor Runnette, how tired she must be. (*exit*)

ST. LUCE Poor fellow! He also is jealous. My suspicion is right. Pauline loved Fabian, and must have owned it to her mother; for when I presented myself at the house I was informed he had departed for the Isle of Bourbon and would never return to France. The Marchioness had left Paris, taking Pauline with her; she was to become a nun! By my faith, to be trifled with, deceived, and sacrificed for a mulatto! I know not where to hide my shame; fortunately the King came to my assistance, and hid me and my blushes in the Bastille. (*drums heard*) What the devil's the matter today? Briquet!

BRIQUET Perhaps it is some fete day. (*heavy bell heard*) Hark to the great bell of Notre Dame! (*both look out of window*)

(*Enter Jailor, left, followed by Cook with the dinner. They place it on the table.* COOK *exits, and* JAILOR *locks the door*)

ST. LUCE (*at window*) Oh, here's my dinner. (*to* JAILOR) What have you brought me?

JAILOR (*giving* BRIQUET *a basket*) Everything we could get of the best, Chevalier, and, as usual, wine from the governor's cellar.

ST. LUCE You are a capital fellow, and full of little delicate attentions. (*looks into basket*) What! No ice? I must have some ice, or I shall send a complaint to the King.

BRIQUET Dine without ice! Impossible!

JAILOR It isn't our fault, sir; an express was sent off this morning to procure some, but it isn't come yet. The parks and public places are crowded with people, and every place is very difficult of access.

ST. LUCE What's their difficulty of movement to me?

BRIQUET Certainly not, we see not so much room to move about. (*exit right with basket.* JAILOR *goes to window*)

ST. LUCE They ought to have an ice house in the place, but they have no consideration for state prisoners. By-the-by, I sent a request to the ministers; I have asked for a room where I can have better air. Can anything be more scandalous than to lodge a gentleman even with the moat, in the very cellar, for I suppose there can be nothing underneath us!

JAILOR (*at window*) No sir, nothing underneath.

ST. LUCE What are you staring at, eh?

JAILOR (*leaving window quickly*) Me, sir!

ST. LUCE (*at window*) I am not mistaken—they are arranging cannon on the rampart, to the left.

JAILOR Possibly.

ST. LUCE Can these plebeians have begun their system? (*drum*) Yes, that's the call to arms! By heaven, if I were but free, I could wish for nothing better than the command of a company of musketeers to sweep the path clean of these rascals!

BRIQUET (*at door*) Dinner, ready, sir.

ST. LUCE Bravo! Let but the King give these gentlemen of Paris a good lesson, and the minister send them a few leaden sugar plums, I'll forgive them both for making me dine without ice! (*exit. Enter* SECOND JAILOR *from staircase*)

SECOND JAILOR The storm threatens! They are only waiting for the cannon from the Invalids, to attack the Bastille. The governor fears the insurgents may gain some communication with the prisoners! come, quick! (*exit both, left door, and lock it*)

(*The straw behind the pillar in dungeon, compartment right, is seen to move, and* FABIAN, *pale and haggard, raises himself, passes his hand over his forehead, and rises with difficulty; takes the lamp, approaches window, looks out, listens, then retires discouraged; puts lamp on stone*)

FABIAN (*shaking his head*) Nothing! Still nothing! (*shivering*) The damp has penetrated my very limbs! I asked them for a little fresh straw, and they said it would cost too much! Straw! Your hatred and revenge are well obeyed here, proud Marchioness! it would have been more merciful to let me die than bury me alive. While I thought to purchase Pauline's pardon by my exile, they threw me into this tomb! Why should I complain? Death will come quicker here; but Pauline, what has become of her? (*warms his hands over lamp*) My limbs are frozen, but here, (*places hand on heart*) here I am on fire! Kind heaven, preserve my reason till Andre's return; but why should I expect him? May not what I fancy to be recollection, be but a dream? For now I doubt everything! My memory, my thoughts, my existence; and yet, no, I remember well, yesterday I was sitting there—there, when a voice struck upon my ear, and that voice was Andre's; yes, Andre, who was at work in that gloomy gallery. I called, whispered my name, but he could not understand that the voice of a man proceeded from the bowels of the earth! (*listens again*) Nothing! Nothing! (*falls, overwhelmed*) Andre will not come! (*a stone falls at this moment through the window, a letter attached to it*) What's that? (*picks up letter*) A letter from him; yes, yes, it is; thanks Andre! Thank heaven! (*weeps, at last he opens letter. At this moment,* JAILOR *is seen, descending staircase; he opens trap, carries a loaf of bread and a jug of water.* FABIAN *reads letter by lamp, while* JAILOR *descends into left division, below*) "My dear benefactor, I know not if I shall be fortunate enough to see you; all Paris is in arms, and they are firing on all who approach the Bastille; but you shall have the letter, though they take my life." My good Andre! "I have been to the Marchioness's house, and it was filled with mourning; the hall was hung with black. (*he is almost choked with emotion*) A priest was in prayer beside an escutcheoned coffin, covered with velvet. I asked who was dead in the house, and they answered—(*enter* JAILOR *quickly;* FABIAN *has just time to hide the letter*)

JAILOR (*puts bread and water on stone*) Here!

FABIAN   Thank you.

JAILOR   Yesterday, while a man was at work in that gallery (*pointing to window*) you approached that opening; the sentinel saw the light from your lamp and also your signs. (*seizes lamp*) You won't do it again!

FABIAN   What are you going to do?

JAILOR   Take away the lamp; 'tis the governor's order.

FABIAN (*on his knees*) O, no, no, not now, for mercy's sake!

JAILOR   We know nothing here but obedience. (*puts out lamp, exits, and locks door*)

FABIAN (*still on his knees*) Heavens! I cannot see, and my letter! (*goes to window, and then to place where lamp stood*) All is darkness, all is night; the coffin—those mourners; who, who could it be? (*with a cry of despair*) Ah, she—she is dead! (*falls senseless on the straw. The cannonading begins; noise of musketry.* JAILOR *appears through trap—gets on staircase*)

JAILOR   They have commenced the attack! Luckily the Bastille is impregnable. (*goes upstairs, and exit, left door. Reports of cannon at end of scene*)

(*Enter* BRIQUET, *right*)

BRIQUET   The cannon! Merciful powers! Why, it's the cannon. (*enter* ST. LUCE, *right*)

ST. LUCE (*going to window*) Yes, the artillary of the fortress are firing on the Place St. Antoine; but, by heaven; the Place St. Antoine answers them in their own way!

BRIQUET   Heavens! Is it possible? (*shouts without*)

ST. LUCE   This is becoming serious! Listen! Those confused cries—that dreadful clamor!

BRIQUET (*at window*) And yonder on the ramparts, what a crowd! O, sir, they are no longer soldiers—it is the people!

(*Shouts without, "Victory! Victory!"*)

ST. LUCE   'Tis impossible; why they'll never take the Bastille like a cockle-shell! (*shouts without, "Victory! Victory!" Last discharge of musketry; and the doors are bent in with hatchets; the one at top of stairs falls—several men and soldiers hurry in, some carrying torches, all shouting "Victory!" Listening at door*) They are coming at us! (*the doors are broken in, and several persons enter the* CHEVALIER's *apartments; a soldier of the French Guard is at the head of them*) What is this?

ALL   Liberty! Liberty!

ST. LUCE   How long has it been the fashion to enter the Bastille thus?

SOLDIER   There is no longer a Bastille; tomorrow it will be levelled to the ground; citizen, you are free!

ST. LUCE (*astonished*) Nonsense!

BRIQUET (*quickly*) Free! The people fought for us; hurrah for the people!

SOLDIER   Citizens, you are free!

ALL   Liberty! Liberty! (*all leave room and remain outside*)

ST. LUCE   Certainly, I shall go out, but not this figure! Briquet, quick, my coat and hat! (BRIQUET *enters inner room.* ST. LUCE *takes off dressing gown;* BRIQUET *reenters with necessaries for toilet*)

BRIQUET   Here they are, sir. (*dresses him*)

(*Entre* ANDRE *down staircase, gets amongst crowd, looks about*)

ANDRE Yes, I'm sure it was in this tower.
SOLDIER Who are you looking for?
ANDRE A poor prisoner.
SOLDIER There is no one else here; there's nothing beneath. Come, let us go.
ALL Ay, ay.
ANDRE Nay, stay; I'm sure I'm not mistaken; I am sure beneath our feet a wretched man is perishing, for whom but now I risked my life.
SOLDIER Look yourself and be satisfied.
ANDRE (*pointing to trap*) This trap, perhaps it may be raised; let us try.
ALL Yes, yes. (*they all assist with hatchets, etc.*)
ANDRE Pull it up. (*they raise it*) There, look!
SOLDIER And do you mean to say there is a living being down there?
ANDRE Yes, a fellow-creature; a good and worthy man. (*goes down followed by others; one bears a torch*)
ST. LUCE Now my gloves and my hat. (BRIQUET *gives them*) My sword—ha! I haven't one. Now then, I'll soon to Versailles.
BRIQUET And I to the Park. (*both exit up staircase;* BRIQUET *shouting* "Hurrah for the people!" *At this moment* ANDRE *and others break into dungeon below, and, by the torchlight, discover* FABIAN)
ANDRE Fabian! Fabian! 'Tis I, Andre! (*raises him*)
FABIAN (*reviving*) Andre! Andre! Are you, too, a prisoner?
ANDRE No, no; you are free.
FABIAN (*joyfully*) Free! (*rises, is rushing out, suddenly returns to* ANDRE) Fool that I am! If they have restored my liberty it is because she is dead—Pauline is dead!
ANDRE No, no; it was not she—'tis the Marchioness.
FABIAN And I am free?
ALL Yes, you are—you are! (*shouts*) Liberty! Liberty!

(FABIAN *rushes to staircase, then stops suddenly, looks at* ANDRE *and those who surround him; then breaks into a loud fit of laughter; they look sorrowfully at him. 'Tis apparent his reason is gone. At last he falls senseless and exhausted. He is raised by* ANDRE. *Cannon again. The whole back of upper part of scene falls in, and discovers the city, the ramparts, and various groups with torches, etc. Women, citizens, soldiers; red fire, etc.*)

ACT FOUR

Scene One

(*An immense gothic apartment in the old Castle of Resadeuc in Bretagne; at the back, a high and vast fireplace; left of fireplace, a large window, opening on a balcony; right of fireplace, a gallery, which is lighted by two painted windows; doors right and left, two each, by side of which hang portraits of the Marquis and Marchioness de la Reynerie, that of the Marchioness is right; left, a small table with writing materials, beside it an armchair; right, a sofa; at back, by fireplace, a gothic stool.* BRIQUET *watching at window,* ST. LUCE. *standing by fireplace;* AURELIA *and* PAULINE *seated, warming themselves*)

ST. LUCE (*to* BRIQUET) Do you see anything strange or suspicious about the chateau?
BRIQUET No, sir, I see nothing but the snow and ice. (*through open window snow is seen falling*) If you will allow me, sir, I'll close the window. (*shuts it*) Oh, dear! What a precious year is the year 1793!
ST. LUCE Go, hasten to the fisherman who promised to let me have his boat to cross to Noman-Mere. Once at sea, either by his own will or by force, he shall take us to England. My sister and my cousin Pauline will not be safe until then. Quick! Quick!
BRIQUET I'm gone, sir. (*exit*)
AURELIA (*rising*) Why take us from this asylum, which the devotion of our tenentry has hitherto rendered so secure.
PAULINE (*rising*) My dear friends, why did you expose yourselves for me? Why did you not leave me to die?
AURELIA Pauline, we may await death in a cell or at the foot of the cross; but to die on a scaffold, exposed to insult from an enraged mob—to die by the hand of the executioner—O, 'tis too dreadful to think of!
PAULINE Those tortures would be but momentary, and my life is one continued agony—you know that my dying mother never forgave poor Fabian, who suddenly disappeared, since when we could never learn if he still lived or had ceased to suffer.
ST. LUCE When my sister confided your secret to me, I did all in my power to discover

him; I wrote to Bourbon, but none had seen or heard of him; the enraged people disbelieve your marriage, and consider Fabian was sacrificed through your connivance.

AURELIA O, could the late Marchioness see death thus hovering around you, she would call on Fabian to preserve her child; for the proof of the marriage, which is in his possession, would now save her life!

ST. LUCE Yes, that certificate, signed by the Abbe L'Audrey, who performed the ceremony, would prove her innocence. (*Enter* BRIQUET)

BRIQUET I could not find the fisherman, sir; but I have brought his brother, who knew all about it.

ST. LUCE (*to* AURELIA) 'Till I have test of this man's fidelity, it would be imprudent to let him see our cousin.

AURELIA (*pointing to door*) We will wait in the library. Come, Pauline.

ST. LUCE Bring the man in. (*exit* BRIQUET)

PAULINE (*looking at portrait*) Mother, mother! Why should we separate again? Here, at the foot of this dear but dreadful image, I would be content to die. (*exit with* AURELIA, *right door. Enter* BRIQUET *with* ANDRE; *he points to* ST. LUCE)

BRIQUET There is the gentleman. (*exit at back*)

ST. LUCE (*at table with papers*) Why is it your brother has not come?

ANDRE He is on a jury at Nantz; I am informed of the business. Bless you, sir, I soon got my hand in again to the old trade; I'll take you quite as safely as my brother.

ST. LUCE Are you sure of that?

ANDRE I shall have a steady comrade.

ST. LUCE Discreet and silent.

ANDRE Poor fellow, he never speaks to anyone, never remembers anyone! His complaint is all in his brain, and in his heart—so, at least, the doctor says, but his arms are stiff and strong, and the sea breeze does him good. He often spends whole days in the boat, and loves to be rocked by the waves in the clear sunshine; it brings his own country to recollection. He is very wretched, and I have often heard him mention the names of those who have caused all his sorrows. Then at times he weeps over, and hides again in his bosom, a timeworn discolored paper, which he treasures as a precious relic.

ST. LUCE (*busy with papers and scarce hearing the latter part of Andre's speech*) You will be answerable for this man?

ANDRE As for myself, sir.

ST. LUCE (*putting papers in pocket*) 'Tis well; have you brought him with you?

ANDRE Yes sir; he was delighted when he saw me prepare the boat, and I told him we were going for a sail as soon as the tide served.

ST. LUCE Where is he?

ANDRE Sitting yonder, under the chestnut tree.

ST. LUCE Now I'll give you the sum agreed for by your brother.

ANDRE I am at your service, sir.

ST. LUCE Follow me, then. (*exit left door, followed by* ANDRE)

(*Enter* FABIAN, *from gallery, right, walks slowly, looking on all sides*)

FABIAN Andre! Andre! The tide is up; we must go. It is still rising—rising! (*fancying himself surrounded by the waves*) O, save her! Save her! Leave me to perish, I ought to perish—the Abbe L'Audrey! Yes, the poor mulatto will love you—cherish you, even as the mariner does his distant home! (*sees portrait of* MARCHIONESS) There—there is your mother! (*supplicating*) Do not curse! No—no, do not curse her! I will go, I will leave her! (*holds out his arms*) Take her, bind me—send me to a dungeon—to the Bastille, ha! (*a pause*) Hark! The cannon—they are coming! Free! Yes—yes, I am free—free! (*puts hand to head, closes his vest*) How I tremble! I am very cold—ha! Some fire, fire! (*sits by fire. Enter* ST. LUCE *and* ANDRE, *left door*)

ST. LUCE Well, then, now we understand each other, I'll fetch the ladies.

ANDRE And I'll bring my comrade. (*going, sees* FABIAN) Ha! There he is, poor fellow! (*speaks kindly to him*) We are coming on board—don't you hear me? Ha! I see, he has forgotten me again. Come, 'tis I, Andre!

(*Enter* AURELIA *and* PAULINE, *right door*)

AURELIA Courage, Pauline, courage! (*enter* ST. LUCE, *right door*)

ST. LUCE Come, let us be quick. (*enter* BRIQUET, *in terror*)

BRIQUET O, sir! O, my lady!

ST. LUCE What's the matter?
BRIQUET It's all over with us!
ALL What?
BRIQUET I was keeping a lookout as you desired me, sir, when on a sudden, I saw a number of armed men coming by the Nantz road.
ALL Nantz!
BRIQUET They are led on by two ill-looking fellows, one of whom I heard say to the rest, pointing to the chateau, "'Tis there she is hid—there you will find the *ci-devant* Marchioness de la Reynerie!"
ANDRE (*suddenly*) Reynerie!
ST. LUCE They cannot enter but by force. Come, come—we may yet escape! (*they are going*)
ANDRE (*aside*) 'Tis she then, the Marchioness, I was about to save!
ST. LUCE (*to* ANDRE) Why do you pause?
ANDRE (*comes down centre*) Take back your money—I recall my promise!
ST. LUCE How say you?
ANDRE (*throws down purse*) I say that for a million of gold I would not guide you!
PAULINE Heavens! What do you mean?
ANDRE I mean, lady, I will not aid in the escape of Mademoiselle de la Reynerie—I will not save her whom I have denounced!
ST. LUCE You wretch!
ANDRE Justice is for all.
PAULINE What have I ever done to you?
ANDRE To me, lady, nothing; had you been my enemy, I could have forgiven you; but you and your family consigned my friend, my benefactor, the best of men, to the foul dungeons of the Bastille!
ST. LUCE Dare you accuse her?
ANDRE Yes, and to prove my accusation, I had the jailor's book in my hand, from which I tore a leaf, and there read these words following after my friend's name: "At the request of the family of de Reynerie this man is to be forgotten." I kept that leaf, and have placed it in the hands of the tribunal of Nantz.
ST. LUCE Wretch! (*places hand on sword*)
ANDRE Take my life, but I will not be your guide.
AURELIA (*to* ANDRE) This is a dreadful error; believe me when I swear she is innocent—O, have pity on her.
ANDRE Pity for her; look at her victim! (*points to* FABIAN)

ALL Here!
ANDRE Yes, there is the martyred victim to the pride of the de la Reynerie.
PAULINE (*with energy, and looking at* FABIAN) Why does he not, then accuse me? Why does he not look at me? I am Pauline de la Reynerie, and before Heaven declare I never injured you. (FABIAN *raises his head, she recognizes him*)
PAULINE Fabian! (*chord*)
ANDRE You know him, then?
PAULINE Fabian!
ANDRE Yes, look at him; see what the Bastille has done for him.
ALL The Bastille.
PAULINE (*looking at portrait*) O, mother, mother.
ANDRE I brought him from there myself; and when I told him he was free, he no longer understood me—his reason had fled. (FABIAN *comes down, right*)
ALL Mad.
PAULINE No, no, I'll not believe it; he will know me. My friend, my husband. Heaven has had pity on us—if but for a day, an hour, it has united us. Heavens! Not one look of joy—not an expression of love in his eyes.
AURELIA The Bastille, he was in the Bastille.
ANDRE Yes. When I brought him away they wanted to put him in the madhouse; but then he would but have exchanged his prison; so I took him, and I have shared my crust with him ever since.
PAULINE Did you do this? (*takes his hand*) O, may heaven bless you for it. If riches are still left to us, all shall be yours. If I am permitted to live, you shall be our friend, our brother! And if I am to die, my last prayer upon the scaffold shall be for you and for him. (*turns to* FABIAN)
ANDRE What says she? Was Fabian, then—
ST. LUCE Her husband.
ANDRE Her husband.
AURELIA When Fabian was in the Bastille, she too was a prisoner; and now you have destroyed her!
ANDRE You are not deceiving me? No, no; falsehood has not such accents. Sir, when you are ready we will go. (*distant shouts*)
AURELIA (*to* ST. LUCE) Come, come.
ANDRE Nay, 'tis too late! But fear not, lady, fear not! (*goes to window*) My brother is amongst them. (*to* AURELIA) Come with me, lady; you

are known and respected by all here; they will hear you, and believe you; and you can assist me to repair the wrong I have done.

AURELIA   Yes, yes. Come brother, come. (*exit all but* PAULINE *and* FABIAN)

PAULINE (*looking at* FABIAN) Still that dreadful insensibility—still dumb! Heavens! Cannot my tears, my grief, find a way to his heart. (*falls on her knees before him*)

FABIAN (*looking at her*) Poor Lia! You suffer much! Why do you weep?

PAULINE (*quickly*) You remember Lia! O, then you cannot forget Pauline!

FABIAN   Pauline! Yes—the affianced wife of the Chevalier St. Luce. (*clock strikes three—he rises*) Three o'clock—she is waiting for me.

PAULINE   Where are you going?

FABIAN   To the Palmtree walk. I will not suffer and die alone. I'll—hush—yes—I'll take her to the Grotto by the sea—we will die together!

PAULINE   Horrible thought.

FABIAN   Hush, the tide is up—at five o'clock. (*shouts without*)

PAULINE (*rushes to window*) They are here—they do not believe Andre.

FABIAN (*to himself*) I know the way.

PAULINE   They are coming—they will soon force an entrance. (*returns to* FABIAN) Fabian! One effort to restore his reason—the moment is propitious. You remember the Grotto by the sea?

FABIAN (*to himself*) The tide was rising.

PAULINE   I was resigned, for I thought to die with you, and for you.

FABIAN (*still the same*) The tide was higher. (*shouts without*)

PAULINE   They approach. Fabian, do you hear those shouts; today, as in Bourbon, the tempest surrounds us, but much more terrible than the ocean. It is a dreadful mob, thirsting for human blood. (*now nearer, and she clings to him*) O, Fabian! Save me! Save me!

FABIAN   Now, now, it rises higher, higher.

PAULINE (*looking at him*) Still the same! Heaven, thy will be done. Fabian, when at Bourbon I believed myself dying. I owned I loved you! Fabian, my husband, I love you now. Death is indeed at hand, and my last sigh shall breathe a blessing on your name.

FABIAN (*half recollecting*) Yes, yes; you are Pauline.

PAULINE (*falls on knees*) Merciful heaven, receive my thanks.

(*Noise. Enter* AURELIA *and* ST. LUCE)

AURELIA   They are here, Pauline, they are here.

ST. LUCE   They will see Fabian.

PAULINE (*joyfully*) He has recognized me.

FABIAN (*recognizing* ST. LUCE, *and relapsing immediately*) Still that man forever at her side. (*enter* ANDRE, *followed by Citizens, armed, from balcony and garden*)

PAULINE   Andre! Andre! He has recognized me.

ANDRE (*to all*) Look: brother! See, all, I have not deceived you.

FABIAN (*wildly*) What do these men mean?

AURELIA   Speak, Fabian; tell them Mademoiselle de la Reynerie was ignorant of your captivity in the Bastille.

FABIAN (*in a low voice*) In the Bastille. (*movement in crowd*)

ANDRE   Tell them she is your wife.

FABIAN (*looking at* MARCHIONESS's *portrait*) No, no, the Marchioness would kill her; 'tis false, I am not her husband. (*murmurs of indignation from mob*)

PAULINE   O, heaven, (*to* FABIAN) you will destroy me.

FABIAN   No, no, hush; I will save you.

PIERRE (*fiercely*) You hear him; he himself accuses her! To Nantz with the aristocrat!

ALL   To Nantz! to Nantz!

ANDRE (*restraining them.—to* PIERRE) Brother, brother! (*a man in gallery, armed with gun, steps forward*)

MAN   We may as well settle it here. (*he fires at* PAULINE, FABIAN *rushes forward, receives the shot, staggers, and falls*)

ANDRE   Wretch, what have you done?

PAULINE (*falls on her knees beside* FABIAN) Murdered—murdered him! (*people retire confused.* FABIAN *is raised by* CHEVALIER *and* ANDRE; *his reason is returning*)

FABIAN   Pauline, dear Pauline, it is indeed you? (*trying to recollect*) Ha, ha, again I—

PEOPLE (*rushing forward*) Death to the house of Reynerie.

ANDRE (*in terror*) They will kill her!

FABIAN (*struggling to his feet*) Kill her! (*his reason returns*) Stand off! She is my wife!

ALL   His wife!

ST. LUCE   Yes, his wife.

PIERRE (*advancing*)   Show us the proof.

ALL   Ay, ay; the proof.

FABIAN   The proof? 'tis here. (FABIAN *is supported by* ST. LUCE, ANDRE *holding* PAULINE *before him;* AURELIA *is on right hand; he opens his vest and produces the marriage certificate, gives it to* PIERRE, *who shows it to people, and they retire up, expressing silent regret. As he opens his vest, blood flows*)

PAULINE (*shuddering*)   Ha! There is blood upon his breast! (*falls on his neck*) They have murdered him!

FABIAN (*sinking fast*)   Pauline, the blow that struck me, was intended for you, and I—I bless heaven, who has granted me to die for—you, for—you! (*dies in their arms*)

(*Curtain*)

Victor Séjour (1817–1874)

The Brown Overcoat   1858

The parents of Juan Victor Séjour Marcou et Ferrand sent their son to Paris at the age of nineteen, to complete his education and "to remove him from the wretched conditions to which his people were then a prey." For the remaining thirty-eight years of his adult life, Mr. Séjour lived and worked in the Parisian theatre. He returned home to New Orleans but once, to see his ailing mother. "Tall, handsome and distinguished, with sparkling brown eyes and with a complexion too dark and lips too large for him to be mistaken for Caucasian, Séjour was an impressive figure at Paris in the heyday of his glory" (Charles Rousseve, *The Negro in Louisiana*, 1937).

Beginning in 1844, with the performance of his verse drama *Diégarias* by the Théâtre Français, Mr. Séjour saw twenty-one of his plays staged in Paris. Here he was an active member of the literary social life. He knew Alexander Dumas, also a mulatto. He was friend and private secretary to Louis Napolean.

Mr. Séjour wrote full-length romantic-historical dramas in the manner of Victor Hugo, whom he admired. The reports that he wrote one play with blacks as characters, *The Volunteers of 1814*, are false. This play does not concern itself with the siege of New Orleans but with Napolean in Europe. He probably wrote no plays with black characters.

The Brown Overcoat was produced the same year that W. W. Brown published *The Escape*. It is a typical artificial comedy in what was by 1858 the degenerated tradition of Molière and Beaumarchais. The dialogue is sometimes witty, often depending on puns that cannot be duplicated in translation. The play has nothing to do with race, and has little to do with the world.

Yet the play is significant in a collection of this kind, for here is the only black American playwright who led a successful nonracial artistic life. Unlike Mr. Aldridge, he seems to have left the "problem" behind in America. Mr. Séjour seems to have accomplished complete integration into a society where he might practice his art as he pleased.

A contemporary of Séjour's, Louis Gottschalk, a pianist, composer, and a Creole from New Orleans, also escaped to Paris. Here at eighteen years of age he wrote *La Bamboula, Danse des Negres* (1847).

Victor Séjour wrote no play with the equivalent power of Mr. Gottschalk's *La Bamboula*. Indeed, few of his plays have been produced since his death (although *The Brown Overcoat*, translated by Townsend Brewster, was produced off-Broadway on December 6, 1972). The relationship between an artist's roots, his conflicts, and his creative genius is complex. How much beauty does the black playwright owe to his marriage to the "problem?"

The Brown Overcoat

CAST OF CHARACTERS

ANNA, *servant to the Countess*
THE COUNTESS
THE BARON, *her lover*

Translated by PAT HECHT, *1970*

SCENE *A small elegant drawing room with a table in the middle; a window on the right, opening out onto the street; flowers in vases on the fireplace.*

Scene One   The Countess, Anna

(ANNA *is tidying up. The* COUNTESS *is stretched out on a chaise longue, a bouquet of flowers in her hand*)

ANNA (*indicating a book*) Yes, Madame, a book entitled *Love* by Monsieur de Stendhal.
COUNTESS Put it there. Madame de Montville claims that it is a ridiculous book.
ANNA Perhaps she is no longer young enough to believe in it.
COUNTESS So, the Baron came...
ANNA Yes, madame, yesterday, after dark...
COUNTESS (*indicating the mantlepiece*) Take away those flowers; they must be wilted.
ANNA Wilted?... no, not at all, Madame, they are the ones the Baron brought.
COUNTESS You are unaware, I imagine, that certain flowers wilt more quickly than others... Take them away.
ANNA (*aside*) That poor baron... Can it be the beginning of the end already? (*she leaves*)
COUNTESS (*alone*) To break off a relationship is nothing; it is the manner of going about it that is everything. A man who could guess the exact moment when he inspires indifference would be indeed precious. Yes, but where can you find this phoenix... The least conceited imagines himself adored—adored! A day, a year passes, but always... (*she shrugs her shoulders, smiling.* ANNA *returns*)
ANNA (*aside*) The execution is complete.
COUNTESS I will dine at six o'clock.
ANNA Yes, Madame.
COUNTESS Have the carriage harnessed, I am going out this evening.
ANNA (*straightening*) Yes, Madame.
COUNTESS (*aside*) That young man thinks about me, I know it. Why else should I encounter his large eyes every time I go to the window... especially in such weather! (*at the window*) George... a lovely name! George Duroi... a great artist... however, I can't shout at him across the rooftops, nor make signals to him like a frustrated virgin....
ANNA (*to the* COUNTESS) Madame is going to catch cold. (*aside*) She doesn't hear me... my word, that's astonishing... is it because of the little musician across the way? Oh, no, she doesn't like music. (*aloud*) If Madame believes me, she will come in, the wind is cold.
COUNTESS (*angrily*) Cold... then close the window. (*a bell outside rings*) Someone is ringing. (ANNA *exits*) That girl sees everything... Bah! I am a widow, thank God, and free. (*picking up her bouquet*) Dear little bouquet!... everyday, on my window or on the seat of my carriage, I find one like it. Certainly the Baron would not take such pains... he is becoming dull. (*to* ANNA, *who returns*) Well?
ANNA It's the seamstress delivering Madame's negligees.
COUNTESS What sort of air do they have?
ANNA A babbling and coquetish air, which should please Madame.
A VALET (*from the upstage door*) Monsieur the Baron of Precy, Madame?...
COUNTESS (*aside*) He is certainly tactful, this time. Usually he enters unannounced.... I have half a mind to say I am not in... no, I would make an enemy.... I prefer to strangle him with kid gloves. (*aloud*) Show him in. (*to* ANNA) I must look like an escaped prisoner....
ANNA Madame the Countess has never been more beautiful.

COUNTESS Flatterer. (*aside*) In fact, so much the better, at least I will not frighten him when I send him away. (*the* BARON *enters;* ANNA *exits*)

Scene Two   The Baron, the Countess

BARON (*kissing her hand*) Good day, Countess! . . .
COUNTESS Good day, Baron. . . . —But why are you here, it's only two o'clock?
BARON I've come too early?
COUNTESS My word! . . . How are you?
BARON Very well.
COUNTESS And your horses?
BARON Poorly: my little mare broke her knee this morning.
COUNTESS You have had your hair cut?
BARON No.
COUNTESS You have curious air about you. . . . Ah, it's your collar. It's not flattering.
BARON The time of Adonises is past. (*offering her a bouquet*) Countess?
COUNTESS You couldn't be more gallant. (*she stuffs it into one of the vases on the mantle*)
BARON How cold it is.—Have you been out?
COUNTESS (*sitting*) No. Why?
BARON It's freezing here . . . the fire must have been allowed to go out.
COUNTESS (*picking up a newspaper*) I haven't stirred, I have letters to write. (*she reads*)
BARON It's amazing.
COUNTESS Oh, how awful! . . . A young girl has just killed her father!
BARON (*warming himself*) I saw that. . . . Turn the page, you'll see a man who was hacked up like a piece of beef.
COUNTESS What did you think of Frezzolini?
BARON The same as everyone else—ravishing!
COUNTESS And that lovely big family of bourgeois we had in front of us?
BARON Which ones?
COUNTESS In wedding clothes, piled on top of each other like a stack of sheets; they had red hands, were ecstatic about everything, and stuffed their bouquets between their legs so they could applaud.
BARON Ah, that's true.—Yesterday I was at Madame de Montville's. . . . I spent my night chasing after seats.
COUNTESS I would love to have seen you, you who love to take your time . . . then, what are you doing?
BARON (*taking off his overcoat*) I don't want to make you lie, Countess. (*he throws it on a piece of furniture*)
COUNTESS That's it, act like you're at an inn, don't bother yourself, do as you like. She visited me this morning.
BARON Who? The inn?*
COUNTESS Charming. A little French lesson which you give me in passing. . . . What is the price?
BARON I will tell you later, Countess.
COUNTESS (*shrugging her shoulders*) I had a visit from Madame de Montville. Her blond hair was blazing.
BARON (*sitting*) A beautiful incendiary . . . a real forest fire.
COUNTESS That woman is flighty, don't you think so? She seemed as startled as a lark.
BARON Oh, good God . . . why? . . . does she have problems of the heart?
COUNTESS She came from the sea, it's possible. Oh, by the way . . . Ah, but is it possible?
BARON Some gossip, tell me?
COUNTESS She noticed that Paul had brown eyes, she thought they were black until now, and she broke off their relationship.
BARON Paul expected it.
COUNTESS For a long time?
BARON For six months.
COUNTESS But they've only known each other three.
BARON What do you expect, he's a cautious man.
COUNTESS (*indicating the overcoat*) Baron, just what is that?
BARON That? It's my overcoat.
COUNTESS Ah! Yes, your maroon overcoat.
BARON Yes, my brown overcoat. . . .
COUNTESS How can you like maroon? You bought it?
BARON Someone might have given it to me, who knows. (*aside*) She has her nerve.
COUNTESS You were saying?
BARON Nothing, nothing. (*he takes a few steps toward the mantle*)
COUNTESS Are you bored?
BARON Once a week, Countess.

* A play on words based on the use of the possessive in French. It does not translate well into English.

COUNTESS Is this your day?
BARON Perhaps tomorrow.
COUNTESS You know, your friend Paul is a generous man. At least he has enough pride to anticipate certain things.
BARON Unless one is conceited, one always does. It is in good taste to save a woman the confusion and embarrassment of those things.
COUNTESS But still, must one guess them?
BARON A witty woman shows them in her attitude.
COUNTESS You think so?
BARON A timid or false woman in her opinions.
COUNTESS Look at me Baron—what do you see?
BARON That new coiffeur suits you.
COUNTESS And?
BARON You are charming!
COUNTESS That's all?...
BARON (*kissing her hand*) A thousand pardons, Countess, you are adorable.
COUNTESS (*aside*) My attitude says nothing, it seems. I'll have to open his eyes.
BARON (*taking the book*) Love! (*throwing it on the table*)... These authors are delightful.... They find a thousand little things in love.... Me, I would compare love to a box of matches. That's not poetic, but it's true—and the termination of a relationship to a railway system; that's even less poetic, but no less true. There are trains and trains, I tell you, convoys and convoys—of certain women—you've seen them go by. You say to them: "I know everything!"... they turn their back laughing... rupture at full speed.... Others... you encounter them when you are attired any old way, with your cravat badly tied; they look at you over their fans as if you were a curiosity, and there they are, cured... a pleasure train! As for those frantic virgins, it's different:—three o'clock strikes, you arrive with a story which I've heard told twenty times with success. You have lost on the rise or the fall of the stock exchange. She opens her eyes wide, shaking.... But you slowly take out the most elegant little wallet in Russian leather... emotion stifled.... You delicately reveal the five or six thousand franc notes that you have slipped inside... her eyes soften... and you offer it all, crying: I am ruined; arrange to live your life with this, or find another lover. She throws her arms around your neck, which means she has already made her choice, and, after all is said, you are the right sort of man.
COUNTESS At a cheap price.
BARON At the current price—a merchandise train.
COUNTESS You are in the mood for absurdities, Baron, continue....
BARON I'm finished.
COUNTESS Then your train has no branch lines?
BARON To where?
COUNTESS Why, to the country of love which is true, profound, eternal.
BARON Ah! Heroines of novels. They are deadly; they have hollow eyes, a pale complexion; little hands which have claws, little teeth which bite, little knives which kill, little cups of tea which poison. But you are loved for yourself alone—to be a slave, it's nothing; a galley slave, it's little.... "Don't complain, silly, you are loved for yourself." Finally the chain is broken... you breathe... but too late! Unhappy creature!... She was jealous, and you have swallowed arsenic without suspecting it... thus the victim pants, his teeth chatter, his eyes roll, his hair falls, he is going to die, he dies; the locomotive explodes!...
COUNTESS You have been loved like that, Baron?
BARON Perhaps by you, Countess.
COUNTESS What time is it?
BARON (*taking out his watch*) My watch has stopped!... look, your clock too!
COUNTESS (*yawning*) And if we did the same, Baron?
BARON (*sitting down*) I'm agreeable.
COUNTESS (*aside*) He's settling in!
BARON (*reading a newspaper*) Ah! What a comment!... Arthur has a genius for flexible relationships. You think of putting him out the door, it's too late, he has already jumped out the window.
COUNTESS But that's very shrewd!
BARON You think so?... It's possible!... In fact, why not?... I am of that school myself! I always jump out the window.
COUNTESS (*offering her hand*) Goodbye, Baron.
BARON (*astonished*) Are you going out?
COUNTESS Me? No, I'm staying. (*she sits*)
BARON (*rising, aside*) What's the matter with

her? (*leaning on her chair*) Shall we dine together?

COUNTESS   I had a little bouquet.... What have you done with it?

BARON   A bouquet?

COUNTESS   Look for it, I'm attached to it.

BARON   Flowers, Countess, none.... (*as if remembering*) But wait....

COUNTESS   You sat on them?

BARON   Ah, Countess.... But what is the matter with you today?

COUNTESS   The Marquis of Lorman sat in a wash basin. He never noticed it until the water started running down his legs.

BARON   The Marquis is sixty years old.

COUNTESS   Age has nothing to do with it. Well, my flowers, where are they? They couldn't have flown away.

BARON   I thought I saw them under my overcoat.

COUNTESS   My poor flowers.... Why, your overcoat is a monument! They must be crushed.

BARON (*producing the flowers*)   It's true. See here, Countess, it's a little thing.

COUNTESS   A little thing! And do you also undress in a drawing room!... You have no respect for anything! Baron, I already told you that I was irritated by your overcoat, your abominable maroon overcoat... what more do you want?

BARON   Brown, Countess!

COUNTESS   You know very well that maroon fades.

BARON   But brown, Countess, brown?

COUNTESS   It's ugly and heavy!

BARON   Heavier than gray?

COUNTESS   Well, just because you were in the Crimean and at the assault of Sebastopol, you think you can do anything... you were a zouave!... Oh, how well I understand Madame de Montville, who hated her husband's outfit with yellow buttons... there are certain things that get on your nerves and you wish they were a hundred miles away.

BARON (*laughing*)   Poor Montville!... Ah! Let us speak of him... it was neither his outfit nor his buttons she detested, it was him.

COUNTESS   Well, Madame de Montville fled green, I flee maroon.

BARON (*picking up his overcoat*)   There, there, Countess.... Yes, my overcoat is maroon... yes, it has faded... but I'll have your furniture recovered... is that agreed?

COUNTESS (*aside, exasperated*)   Oh! (*aloud*) But you are not going to have my furniture recovered—you sit on it, that's all.... Save that for your little dancers from the Opera.

BARON   I'll take my overcoat away, I'll hang my overcoat elsewhere. (*striking his forehead with his hand*) Ah! (*he fumbles through all his pockets*)

COUNTESS   What is the matter with you? What? Are you going to assassinate me, like in *Antony*?*

BARON (*emphatically, gesturing with his overcoat*)   If she resists me, I have her... but no, that would not be appropriate....

COUNTESS (*aside*)   Conceited!

BARON   Besides, you are a widow. Your ticket for the box, I forgot it.

COUNTESS   What box?

BARON   The box you asked me to get for the Théâtre Français. Today is Friday.

COUNTESS   I asked you for a box at the Théâtre Français? But what can you be thinking of? I have known all their idiocies for the past ten years. I am going to the concert.

BARON   To the concert? You?

COUNTESS   Yes, me. So?

BARON   You hate music, you've told me so twenty times.

COUNTESS   Military music, yes.

BARON   Bravo. Then when the evenings are long and you become bored, we can play together. I love my dear violin... but I didn't dare tell you about it.... I have neglected it, that dear friend; it has been in its case for the past ten months.

COUNTESS   What... what are you saying... you have your friends in cases?

BARON (*laughing*)   Why, no, Countess... I'm speaking of my violin.

COUNTESS   Fine, you will play for me... from a distance. (*piano music is heard in the distance*) Here, listen... there, that passage... oh, how beautiful, how admirable!

BARON (*warming himself*)   I believe Litz or Thalberg whipped through their melodies in a much different manner.

COUNTESS   Vandal! But listen! That's genius!

BARON   Genius! Nowadays everyone has

---

* Probably a reference to *Julius Caesar*, with confusion about both the title and the assassin.

genius, even my porter. He has the genius to bring me my newspapers and my letters.

COUNTESS Go ahead, scoff! but in the field of art you are as advanced as a Chinaman.

BARON The Chinese, Countess, invented gunpowder before us.

COUNTESS Yes, but they are Chinese.

BARON If the whole world became ecstatic about a note of music, that would be quite a concert.

COUNTESS To be brief, tonight I am going to Hertz's.

BARON You have tickets?

COUNTESS No!... I counted on you to find them for me.... But, truly, am I asking too much, Baron?

BARON How many seats?

COUNTESS Two... as close to the orchestra as possible.... Run quickly, and thank you in advance. When you decide to be amiable, you do it better than anyone.

BARON (*putting on his overcoat*) You'll hear Monsieur George Duroi... a talented man, that one.

COUNTESS Ah!

BARON Very talented... do you want me to take you?

COUNTESS You know him?

BARON Not at all, but should I meet him so I may introduce you?

COUNTESS You are too kind.

BARON I shall return. (*he leaves*)

Scene Three The Countess (*alone*)

COUNTESS At last!... (*the sound of a carriage is heard*) Bon voyage!... At least he'll exercise his horses.... (*she opens the window*) He is at his window!... It is his eyes that please me most of all!... How different they are from the Baron's dull, dead eyes. Ah! these artists, their breath embraces the air, the habit of fame illuminates them, near or far, they dazzle like the sun. (ANNA *enters and gives the* COUNTESS *a letter and a bouquet on a silver platter*)

Scene Four The Countess, Anna

COUNTESS (*turning*) What is it?

ANNA A letter, Madame!

COUNTESS (*opening the letter, aside*) It's from him!... (*while reading*) What a charming thought... he asks me to attend his concert and sends me tickets.... Oh, yes, I'll go... and he will see in my eyes the certainty and the pride of his triumph!... I am going to thank him!... (*she sits at her table and searches... looking at a paper*) An old draft of a letter to the Baron... (*throwing it away*) Two months already! Was I such a fool then? (*she finds her pen*) Ah! (*as soon as she begins to write, she stops*) No!... he will see me, that will be enough—Anna!

ANNA (*coming nearer*) Madame?

COUNTESS Straighten my hair. Has my gown come?

ANNA Yes, Madame.

COUNTESS My blue gown?

ANNA Yes, Madame.

COUNTESS What do you think of it?

ANNA It is the most beautiful blue. Madame will make more than one person jealous, they will be so envious of the Baron.

COUNTESS Ah! (*aside*) It's true, he loves blue... they'll think it's for him. (*aloud*) Arrange my hair with fresh violets... with these, for instance. (*she indicates the bouquet which accompanied the letter*) I'll wear my white gown.

ANNA Perhaps these violets won't be sufficient; if Madame wants more, she can choose from the ones the Baron brought.

COUNTESS Why no... they are already faded, see....

ANNA (*aside, finishing the coiffeur*) Already!... she must have boiled them... (*aloud*) There, it's done, Madame.

COUNTESS (*primping in front of her mirror*) Not too bad. (*the* BARON *enters*)

Scene Five The Baron, the Countess

BARON (*entering*) It's me, Countess.... I have been gone a long time... but you must blame only the congestion of the streets... the road thronged with curious spectators... they were pushing about the wheels of my carriage, and all that for a mere chimney fire. (*he removes his overcoat and starts to put it on the chair*)

COUNTESS Again?

BARON Oh, pardon me, I forgot.... Habit, what can you expect? (*he goes toward the room on the right*)

COUNTESS Where are you going?
BARON Nurtured in the seraglio....
COUNTESS Into my bedroom?... Is this a bet, Baron?
BARON Is there nothing left but the anteroom?
COUNTESS And so? Isn't that enough for the maroon?
BARON (*his overcoat in his hand*) You know the proverb, Countess....
COUNTESS (*indicating the overcoat*) Get rid of that furnishing.
BARON A brutal but true proverb....
COUNTESS You haven't left?
BARON When you want to kill your dog....* Never mind. I'll take my "furnishing" away. (*he exits*)
COUNTESS (*alone, irritated*) He will never understand! Oh! Men! Until they are twenty, they are idiots, after thirty, they are absurd!... (*to the* BARON, *who returns*) How old are you, Baron?
BARON Thirty-two.
COUNTESS (*aside*) That's it.
BARON Why?
COUNTESS I am twenty-eight, and you are younger than I am.
BARON How do you make that out?
COUNTESS Me? I don't. (*she sits*)
BARON (*aside*) But what is the matter with her today? (*aloud*) Here are your tickets for the concert.
COUNTESS (*aside, with irritation*) He found some. (*aloud*) I am going to write to Madame de Montville, we will go together.
BARON I will pick you up.
COUNTESS No, don't bother. (*she writes*)
BARON Say what you like, I'm freezing in your house.
COUNTESS That's an idea.
BARON (*warming himself*) Yes, it's also the thermometers' idea, they all show fifteen degrees below zero.
COUNTESS In Russia?
BARON In Paris.
COUNTESS Along the waterfront?...
BARON In this room.
COUNTESS (*rising*) Last year's thermometer,

it might have frozen in this weather, that's possible. (*she rings for* ANNA, *who enters*) Have this note taken to Madame de Montville immediately; I would like an answer.
BARON Now I have it on my legs. (*stamping*)
COUNTESS What?
BARON The wind... no wonder, the window is open.
COUNTESS Oh, that's right... it was smoky.
BARON (*going to close the window*) Undoubtedly it was also smoky at your neighbor's, his window is yawning wide open.
COUNTESS That's because it's bored.
BARON (*closing the window*) And yours too ... is bored?
COUNTESS That's its prerogative... isn't that permitted?... your overcoat really exasperates me!
BARON Women are strange, admit it. I am not speaking about swollen women who chew charcoal... that only proves one thing, that swelling is an unnatural condition.*
COUNTESS (*laughing*) There is a singularly idiotic paradox.
BARON Paradox is the fertilizer of truth. There is a world down there, said Columbus, paradox; the world turns, cried Galileo, paradox.... Who would dare to think and say the contrary today?
COUNTESS What are you getting at?
BARON As for wit, it's an exercise for hunchbacks. I have been told Voltaire wasn't one. Who knows. Who will prove to me that he didn't have Aesop's hump inside himself and that one was not the cover of the other.
COUNTESS Conclude, Baron... what are you getting at, finally?
BARON What am I getting at? Well, Countess, in asking you have done me a service... I have lost my train of thought.
COUNTESS You are irritating. You speak of the strangeness of women. But be brief. You have wit, I agree; but you act too much as if you know it and are waiting to be admired.
BARON I must be as stupid as a goose to justify the description you've given of me.
COUNTESS Women are strange, you say... which women?
BARON You, for example!... Yes, you! My

---

* Here one of the Countess' lines has been omitted. In the original there is a play upon the word *marron*, which has multiple meanings. The English *maroon*, lacks this richness and the joke is therefore not translatable.

* The French word "grosse" means not only swollen, but both fat and pregnant. The play on words in the original is a clever one.

overcoat is brown, and you know it; for three months I have had the bad habit, I admit, to put that garment on this chair; for three months that thing has come and gone without horrifying you ... and today, all of a sudden, my overcoat attracts your attention ... you become edgy when you see it ... it becomes maroon ... it is ugly, it is heavy, it fades ... and all that for a wicked little cheap bouquet of violets that I touched by mistake! ...

COUNTESS Crushed!

BARON Crushed, so be it! But that, come now—

COUNTESS There, your friend Paul is passing under my window on horseback.

BARON Invite him up, he will judge us.

COUNTESS Do you believe that someone can look without seeing, Baron?

BARON Yes, blind men.

COUNTESS Listen without hearing? ...

BARON Yes, deaf men.

COUNTESS Very well! I know such a man, who neither sees nor hears, although he has eyes as open as doors, and ears ... well! ... I wouldn't say that about your friend, Paul. No, he is basically Parisian from head to foot. And in addition, he has something about him which assures you that he will never care for you more than is appropriate. His whole personality is arranged for that. He spies your looks, observes your bearing, convinced that a woman will always know that he is willing to guess her thoughts. A smile, it's enough; half a word, it's too much. He enters a boudoir as one does a mechanized theater. He fears what is underneath. You might pity him if he ignored the fact that that is where the mysterious mirror of our dreams, I might even say the inventory of our weaknesses, is found. This Chinese curio is there, why? this faded bouquet, why? this tear drop on the leaf of a half-opened book, why? yesterday you like blue, today you like pink, why? And finally, this window is open when it ought to be closed, why?

BARON (*laughing*) But on that account, Amelie, your window was open and I asked you why.

COUNTESS What a curious thing man is! You invent an entire mass of delicate revelations to enlighten him; half lights to show your soul; muted colors to betray your thoughts. ... But bah! the former man of wit looks at you through his past triumphs. His vanity is eternal, he considers your love eternal. Here the comparison becomes absurd. Rupture at full speed,* that's false: nothing is more torturous and less prompt ... the ties tighten with the efforts you make to break them. However, what is more painful to say than: "I no longer love you," or else, "I love another," or yet "I have been unfaithful to you." At the confessional, it is good, you have a grill in between, and, if necessary, little curtains that you can close ... but to have there, under your eyes, in front of you, near you, a man you have forgotten and whom you must make understand, it, it's horrible! Oh, what a stupid thing vanity is. I am furious with these conceited idiots who have a triple blindfold over their eyes. Unless you put a hundred guards at your door to keep them from coming in, they will never understand. Don't you agree?

BARON It's possible.

COUNTESS I am going to dress. (*aside*) I believe he has understood. (*she exits*)

Scene Six   The Baron (*alone*)

BARON Have I been anticipated? I am afraid I have. It seems I am beginning to decrease in value. Now the important thing is to salvage an honorable retreat ... a retreat of illusions. (*he looks at himself in the mirror*) Still, I'm not getting too much of a stomach yet. ...
(ANNA *enters and starts towards the mantle*)

Scene Seven   The Baron, Anna

BARON Come here, Anna.

ANNA (*aside*) Here comes the critical moment, my girl, you are going to be questioned.

BARON Will your mistress be ready soon?

ANNA In ten minutes, Baron.

BARON I have acted like a fool here; thinking too much of the Countess and not enough of you. We have an account to settle, here! ...

ANNA Five louis! Baron, here are five louis which could, if necessary, be very eloquent.

BARON You are mistaken ... and just in case you want to speak, here is another louis to keep you silent. Go on, go.

---

* A reference to the Baron's earlier train analogy. The connection is no clearer in the original.

Scene Eight — The Baron (*alone*)

BARON I am satisfied with myself. I would also like to teach the Countess a little lesson. (*noticing the draft of the letter*) What is this? (*he picks it up*) A draft of a letter, from the Countess.... Perhaps this will tell me more than I want to know. Bah! For what purpose. (*he throws the paper on the table*) But it is always good to know these things, if only to be the first to laugh. (*he picks up the letter and reads*) "Dear Baron!" She is writing to me ... to announce my disaster. At least she is courteous about it. (*reading*) "I was in a state of despair because they didn't have you wait yesterday evening." Yesterday evening?... (*he reads*) "Like an idiot, that stupid Anna let you leave." It's true, she didn't say anything to me. (*reading*) "I have a thousand things in my heart," A thousand things leading up to a dismissal; she is charming! (*reading*) "A thousand things in my heart. First, I love you like a madwoman..." (*looking*) Like a madwoman! Dear Amelie! (*reading*) "Next..." Nothing more! ... next ... like a madwoman, that's certain! I too am amazed!... that poor Countess! Here she is!... (*the* COUNTESS *enters in evening dress*)

Scene Nine — The Countess, the Baron

COUNTESS (*aside*) Still here!
BARON (*looking at her hair. Aside*) My violets!... I must not mention them to her, she would be capable of persuading me that they are not mine!... (*aloud*) Do you know you are charming to no longer be angry with me, Countess.
COUNTESS From what do you conclude that?
BARON From what?... from nothing!... You are angry at me, so be it. Then I beg your pardon on my knees! (*he kneels at her feet*)
COUNTESS This is the first time I have ever seen you like that.
BARON (*trying to kiss her hand*) There is a beginning to everything, Countess.
COUNTESS (*withdrawing her hand*) No!
BARON (*rising, wounded*) Ah!... has my overcoat bitten you this time?
COUNTESS It's as if ... it sprawls out in this anteroom as if it were at an old clothes shop ... one might even say it swells.*
BARON Perhaps it is sick ... you must send your doctor to cure it.
COUNTESS (*dryly*) Ah! charming.
BARON It does annoy you, doesn't it.
COUNTESS It irritates me.
BARON It is, however, close to the door ... but perhaps not close enough.
COUNTESS Not at all ... however ...
BARON However, it ought to be on my shoulders, shouldn't it?
COUNTESS I didn't say that.
BARON Come, I agree that I am a fool, Countess. Here we have been strolling for two hours, my overcoat and me, me and my overcoat, from room to room, and I didn't notice it until just now. (*six o'clock strikes*) Six o'clock! (*kissing her hand*) Your dinner hour, Countess, farewell!
COUNTESS Your place is set, you know.
BARON Yes ... yes ... later ... tomorrow. (*the piano is heard*)
COUNTESS (*aside, happily*) Ah! (*the* BARON *observes her*)
BARON (*aside*) What, music impassions her to this degree? Her?.... But wait! the musician, perhaps! (*he goes to the window and looks. Softly*) Countess?
COUNTESS What?
BARON But your neighbor, that's George Duroi!
COUNTESS Really?
BARON You didn't know?... Well! I've told you ... His overcoat is handsome.
COUNTESS And?
BARON (*kissing her hand*) It is blue.
COUNTESS What do you mean by that?
BARON In two months, Countess, let me know if blue fades.—Farewell, Countess, farewell! (*he exits. A moment of silence;—then, the Countess rings; to* ANNA, *who appears*)
COUNTESS Have dinner served!

---

* In French the word for overcoat is masculine. Thus, in the original the possessive pronoun in this speech and the next few lines could refer to the Baron as well as the overcoat.

William Wells Brown (1814–1884)

The Escape; or, A Leap for Freedom   1858

In 1857, the United States Supreme Court held that a man once defined as property could not shed the title of property merely by walking about in "free territory", but had to be returned to his original owner. The Dred Scott decision reaffirmed the sanctity of property.

In 1859, John Brown, angered and impatient with federal law and order, attacked Harper's Ferry in what he hoped would be the beginning of protracted guerilla warfare—protracted until the conscience of America could distinguish men from property.

Taking his plot from man-as-property and his viewpoint from abolitionism, William Wells Brown published *The Escape* in 1858. This play was based on personal experience, an experience as bizarre as it was common: birth into slavery.

> I was born in Lexington, Ky. The man who stole me as soon as I was born recorded the birth of all the infants which he claimed to be born his property.... My father's name as I learned from my mother, was George Higgins. He was a white man, a relative of my master, and connected with some of the first families in Kentucky.

With these sentences Mr. Brown begins his autobiography, *Narrative of William Wells Brown, a Fugitive Slave* (1847), a story that traces his life from his unhappy childhood to his escape in 1834 at the age of twenty. Mr. Brown's rage against the humiliations of slavery began early:

> my master, Dr. Young, had no children of his own, but had a nephew, the son of his brother. When this boy was brought to Dr. Young, his name being William, the same as mine, my mother was ordered to change mine to something else. This, at the time, I thought to be one of the most cruel acts that could be committed upon my rights; and I received several very severe whippings for telling people that my name was William.

Later the author not only reassumed his given name, but chose his own surname, Wells Brown, after the Ohio Quaker who befriended him on his last flight for freedom.

His two previous attempts to escape had failed. His first recapture resulted in "Virginia play," a punishment in which the slave was tied in the smokehouse, flogged, then smoked by setting piles of tobacco stems afire. After the slave had coughed his lungs out, he was untied and sent back to work.

The Escape parallels the author's autobiography in a number of incidents. The "melodramatic" ending, where Glen and Melinda fight off their pursuers to "jump into the boat as it leaves the shore" for Canada, is more than a great theatrical climax; it is a rendering of a real battle near Buffalo in which Brown, with black and white friends, fought off the sheriff and a posse to save slaves from recapture.

Relentlessly, through humor and pathos, Mr. Brown records "rottened" virtue. The master, his wife, the clergyman, the overseer ("the Yankees were the most cruel"), and the slave speculator claim virtue but demonstrate that they do not have it. *The Escape* is a documentation of the thesis that *power corrupts*.

The play deserves to be read for more reasons than the gratuity that "William Wells Brown was the first Negro to . . .". *The Escape* is an insightful study of the white institution of slavery. Our bookshelves groan under white studies of the Negro "problem." Mr. Brown provides us with a firsthand empirical black study of the white "problem." The script is a refutation of the southern romantic tradition of antebellum chivalry and *noblesse oblige*. It reveals the South as a corrupt society.

The play was written for the abolitionists of the North. Mr. Brown read the play aloud to these white liberals, hoping—one must assume—to outrage their consciences. The author employed the devices that made his audience feel comfortable; for example, he created Cato, the darkey dialect comic. But Cato, when he sees his opportunity, makes his leap for freedom—an action that no white playwright of that period ever considered for a low comedy character. By this leap for freedom, Cato becomes a human being.

"The [Negro] stereotype," writes Sterling Brown, "is very flattering to a [white] race which for all its self-assurance seems to stand in great need of flattery." This great need, which spun a thousand stories and plays, oozed up from the festering conscience of the New World where God—if not the framers of the Constitution—recognized all men as equal.

To possess the riches of the virgin continent, to make it possible for future politicians to boast of an economy that provided greater material gifts than those of any other place in the world, the land had to be seized from the red man—justified by the "cowboy'n'indian" myths. The land had to be worked by the black man—justified by "nigger" myths. This need to justify began an unbroken chain of American stereotypes. From *The Candidates* (1770) to the present, each stereotype helped to smother the American conscience.

But for all the constant reassurance the New World democrat took from his playwrights, the truth that he was a racist killer burst out into his everyday encounters. If the slaves were happy, why did the plantation's overseer need dogs?

As a piece of theater, Mr. Brown's play deserves our attention. The author knew what his audience liked—melodrama! *Uncle Tom's Cabin*, already six years old in 1858, clearly demonstrated what the public would listen to: plays that moved in a succession of short scenes arranged for maximum variety of emotions—from the lover's tryst, to dialect comedy, to a fight, to a song. The "box" set had not yet made its appearance: painted scenic drops, dioramas, and sliding wings mounted on tracks enabled these epics to lurch forward at a cinematic pace.

Evaluations of Mr. Brown's play have varied over the years, perhaps reflecting the individual critic's own time as much as an objective appraisal of the play. The abolitionists liked it when the author gave dramatic readings in the late 1850's.

Mr. Brown's Drama is, in itself, a masterly refutation of all apologies for slavery, and abounds in wit, satire, philosophy, arguments and facts, all ingeniously interwoven into one of the most interesting dramatic compositions of modern times. [Auburn N.Y., *Daily Advertiser*]

Or again,

Mr. Brown exhibits a dramatic talent possessed by few who have under the best instructions, made themselves famous on the stage. [*Seneca Falls Courier*]

After the Civil War the play was neglected—as *Uncle Tom's Cabin* was not. In 1937, Sterling Brown noted in his book *Negro Poetry and Drama* that the play was a "hodge-podge with some humor and satire and much melodrama." Playwright Loften Mitchell, in his history, *Black Drama* (1967), writes, "[Brown's] scenes, unfortunately, are close to blackface minstrelsy, much more so than the author's personal slave experiences should have permitted." In her study *Negro Playwrights in the American Theater, 1925-1959* (1969), Doris Abramson, who is to be thanked for uncovering a copy of the play in the Boston Athenaeum Library, summarizes her evaluation by calling it "an interesting document both from a social and theatrical point of view". Louis Phillips, in a preface to a published edition of *The Escape* (1969), praises the script: "As a play it can certainly hold its own with *Uncle Tom's Cabin*." Yet, as James Weldon Johnson states in *Black Manhattan* (1930) Brown's career was "in no degree a direct factor in the Negro's theatrical development". The North's victories in battle did not admit black playwrights onto the American stage.

The Escape; or, A Leap for Freedom

PLAYWRIGHT'S PREFACE

This play was written for my own amusement, and not with the remotest thought that it would ever be seen by the public eye. I read it privately, however, to a circle of my friends, and through them was invited to read it to a Literary Society. Since then, the drama has been given in various parts of the country. By the earnest solicitation of some in whose judgment I have the greatest confidence, I now present it in a printed form to the public. As I never aspired to be a dramatist, I ask no favor for it, and have little or no solicitude for its fate. If it is not readable, no word of mine can make it so; if it is, to ask favor for it would be needless.

The main features in the drama are true. Glenn and Melinda are actual characters, and still reside in Canada. Many of the incidents are drawn from my own experience of eighteen years at the South. The marriage ceremony, as performed in the second act, is still adhered to in many of the southern states, especially in the farming districts.

The ignorance of the slave, as seen in the case of Big Sally, is common wherever chattel slavery exists. The difficulties created in the domestic circle by the presence of beautiful slave women, as found in Dr. Gaines's family is well understood by all who have ever visited the valley of the Mississippi.

The play, no doubt, abounds in defects, but as I was born in slavery, and never had a day's schooling in my life, I owe the public no apology for errors.

W. W. B.

CHARACTERS REPRESENTED

DR. GAINES, *proprietor of the farm at Muddy Creek*
MR. CAMPBELL, *a neighboring slave owner*
REV. JOHN PINCHEN, *a clergyman*
DICK WALKER, *a slave speculator*
MR. WILDMARSH, *neighbor to Dr. Gaines*
MAJOR MOORE, *a friend of Dr. Gaines*
MR. WHITE, *a citizen of Massachusetts*
BILL JENNINGS, *a slave speculator*
JACOB SCRAGG, *overseer to Dr. Gaines*
MRS. GAINES, *wife of Dr. Gaines*
MR. AND MRS. NEAL, AND DAUGHTER, *Quakers, in Ohio*
THOMAS, *Mr. Neal's hired man*
GLEN, *slave of Mr. Hamilton, brother-in-law of Dr. Gaines*
CATO, SAM, SAMPEY (BOB), MELINDA, DOLLY, SUSAN, AND BIG SALLY, *slaves of Dr. Gaines*
PETE, NED, BILL, AND TAPIOCA, *slaves*
OFFICERS, LOUNGERS, BARKEEPER, *etc.*

ACT ONE

Scene One

(*A Sitting-Room.* MRS. GAINES, *looking at some drawings*—SAMPEY, *a white slave, stands behind the lady's chair. Enter* DR. GAINES, *right*)

DR. GAINES Well, my dear, my practice is steadily increasing. I forgot to tell you that neighbor Wyman engaged me yesterday as his family physician; and I hope that the fever and ague, which is now taking hold of the people, will give me more patients. I see by the New Orleans papers that the yellow fever is raging there to a fearful extent. Men of my profession are reaping a harvest in that section this year. I would that we could have a touch of the yellow fever here, for I think I could invent a medicine that would cure it. But the yellow fever is a luxury that we medical men in this climate can't expect to enjoy; yet we may hope for the cholera.

MRS. GAINES Yes, I would be glad to see it more sickly here, so that your business might prosper. But we are always unfortunate. Everybody here seems to be in good health, and I am afraid that they'll keep so. However, we must hope for the best. We must trust in the Lord. Providence may possibly send some disease among us for our benefit.

(*Enter* CATO, *right*)

CATO Mr. Campbell is at de door, massa.
DR. GAINES Ask him in, Cato.

(*Enter* MR CAMPBELL, *right*)

DR. GAINES Good morning, Mr. Campbell. Be seated.

MR. CAMPBELL Good morning, doctor. The same to you, Mrs. Gaines. Fine morning, this.

MRS. GAINES Yes, sir; beautiful day.

MR. CAMPBELL Well, doctor, I've come to engage you for my family physician. I am tired of Dr. Jones. I've lost another very valuable nigger under his treatment; and, as my old mother used to say, "change of pastures makes fat calves."

DR. GAINES I shall be most happy to become your doctor. Of course, you want me to attend to your niggers, as well as to your family?

MR. CAMPBELL Certainly, sir. I have twenty-three servants. What will you charge me by the year?

DR. GAINES Of course, you'll do as my other patients do, send your servants to me when they are sick, if able to walk?

MR. CAMPBELL Oh, yes; I always do that.

DR. GAINES Then I suppose I'll have to lump it, and say $500 per annum.

MR. CAMPBELL Well, then, we'll consider that matter settled; and as two of the boys are sick, I'll send them over. So I'll bid you good day, doctor. I would be glad if you would come over some time, and bring Mrs. Gaines with you.

DR. GAINES Yes, I will; and shall be glad if you will pay us a visit, and bring with you Mrs. Campbell. Come over and spend the day.

MR. CAMPBELL I will. Good morning, doctor. (*exit* MR CAMPBELL, *right*)

DR. GAINES There, my dear, what do you think of that? Five hundred dollars more added to our income. That's patronage worth having! And I am glad to get all the negroes I can to doctor, for Cato is becoming very useful to me in the shop. He can bleed, pull teeth, and do almost anything that the blacks require. He can put up medicine as well as any one. A valuable boy, Cato!

MRS. GAINES But why did you ask Mr. Campbell to visit you, and to bring his wife? I am sure I could never consent to associate with her, for I understand that she was the daughter of a tanner. You must remember, my dear, that I was born with a silver spoon in my mouth. The blood of the Wyleys runs in my veins. I am surprised that you should ask him to visit you at all; you should have known better.

DR. GAINES Oh, I did not mean for him to visit me. I only invited him for the sake of compliments, and I think he so understood it; for I should be far from wishing you to associate with Mrs. Campbell. I don't forget, my dear, the family you were raised in, nor do I overlook my own family. My father, you know, fought by the side of Washington, and I hope some day to have a handle to my own name. I am certain Providence intended me for something higher than a medical man. Ah! by-the-by, I had forgotten that I have a couple of patients to visit this morning. I must go at once. (*exit* DR. GAINES, *right*)

(*Enter* HANNAH, *left*)

MRS. GAINES Go, Hannah, and tell Dolly to to kill a couple of fat pullets, and to put the biscuit to rise. I expect brother Pinchen here this afternoon, and I want everything in order. Hannah, Hannah, tell Melinda to come here. (*exit* HANNAH, *left*) We mistresses do have a hard time in this world; I don't see why the Lord should have imposed such heavy duties on us poor mortals. Well, it can't last always. I long to leave this wicked world, and go home to glory. (*enter* MELINDA) I am to have company this afternoon, Melinda. I expect brother Pinchen here, and I want everything in order. Go and get one of my new caps, with the lace border, and get out my scolloped-bottomed dimity petticoat, and when you go out, tell Hannah to clean the white-handled knives, and see that not a speck is on them; for I want everything as it should be while brother Pinchen is here. (*exit* MRS. GAINES, *left*, MELINDA, *right*)

Scene Two

(*Doctor's shop*—CATO *making pills. Enter* DR. GAINES, *left*)

DR. GAINES Well, Cato, have you made the batch of ointment that I ordered?

CATO Yes, massa; I dun made de intment, an' now I is making the bread pills. De tater pills is up on the top shelf.

DR. GAINES I am going out to see some patients. If any gentlemen call, tell them I shall be in this afternoon. If any servants come, you attend to them. I expect two of Mr. Campbell's boys over. You see to them. Feel their pulse, look at their tongues, bleed them, and give them each a dose of calomel. Tell them to drink no cold water, and to take nothing but water gruel.

CATO Yes, massa; I'll tend to 'em. (*exit* DR. GAINES, *left*) I allers knowed I was a doctor, an' now de ole boss has put me at it, I muss change my coat. Ef any niggers comes in, I wants to look suspectable. Dis jacket don't suit a doctor; I'll change it. (*exit* CATO—*immediately returning in a long coat*) Ah! now I looks like a doctor. Now I can bleed, pull teef, or cut off a leg. Oh! well, well, ef I aint put de pill stuff an' de intment stuff togedder. By golly, dat ole cuss will be mad when he finds it out, won't he? Nebber mind, I'll make it up in pills, and when de flour is on dem, he won't know what's in 'em; an' I'll make some new intment. Ah! yonder comes Mr. Campbell's Pete an' Ned; dems de ones massa sed was comin'. I'll see ef I looks right. (*goes to the looking-glass and views himself*) I em some punkins, ain't I? (*knock at the door*) Come in.

(*Enter* PETE *and* NED, *right*)

PETE Whar is de doctor?
CATO Here I is; don't you see me?
PETE But whar is de ole boss?
CATO Dat's none you business. I dun tole you dat I is de doctor, an' dat's enuff.
NED Oh! do tell us whar de doctor is. I is almos dead. Oh me! oh dear me! I is so sick. (*horrible faces*)
PETE Yes, do tell us; we don't want to stan here foolin'.
CATO I tells you again dat I is de doctor. I larn de trade under massa.
NED Oh! well, den, give me somethin' to stop dis pain. Oh dear me! I shall die. (*he tries to vomit, but can't—ugly faces*)
CATO Let me feel your pulse. Now put out your tongue. You is berry sick. Ef you don't mine, you'll die. Come out in de shed, an' I'll bleed you. (*exit all—re-enter*) Dar, now take dese pills, two in de mornin' and two at night, and ef you don't feel better, double de dose. Now, Mr. Pete, what's de matter wid you?
PETE I got de cole chills, an' has a fever in de night.
CATO Come out, an' I'll bleed you. (*exit all re-enter*) Now take dese pills, two in de mornin' and two at night, an' ef dey don't help you, double de dose. Ah! I like to forget to feel your pulse and look at your tongue. Put out your tongue. (*feels his pulse*) Yes, I tells by de feel ob your pulse dat I is gib you de right pills. (*enter Mr. Parker's* BILL, *left*) What you come in dat door widout knockin' for?
BILL My toof ache so, I didn't tink to knock. Oh, my toof! my toof! Whar is de doctor?
CATO Here I is; don't you see me?
BILL What! you de doctor, you brack cuss! You looks like a doctor! Oh, my toof! my toof! Whar is de doctor?
CATO I tells you I is de doctor. Ef you don't believe me, ax dese men. I can pull your toof in a minnit.
BILL Well, den, pull it out. Oh, my toof! how it aches! Oh, my toof! (CATO *gets the rusty turnkeys*)
CATO Now lay down on your back.
BILL What for?
CATO Dat's de way massa does.
BILL Oh, my toof! Well, den, come on. (*lies down,* CATO *gets astraddle of* BILL's *breast, puts the turnkeys on the wrong tooth, and pulls—* BILL *kicks, and cries out*)—Oh, do stop! Oh! oh! oh! (CATO *pulls the wrong tooth—* BILL *jumps up*)
CATO Dar, now, I tole you I could pull your toof for you.
BILL Oh, dear me! Oh, it aches yet! Oh me! Oh, Lor-e- massy! You dun pull de wrong toof. Drat your skin! ef I don't pay you for this, you brack cuss! (*they fight, and turn over table, chairs and bench—* PETE *and* NED *look on. Enter* DR. GAINES, *right*)
DR. GAINES Why, dear me, what's the matter? What's all this about? I'll teach you a lesson, that I will. (*the* DOCTOR *goes at them with his cane*)
CATO Oh, massa! he's to blame, sir. He's to blame. He struck me fuss.
BILL No, sir; he's to blame; he pull de wrong toof. Oh, my toof! oh, my toof!
DR. GAINES Let me see your tooth. Open your mouth. As I live, you've taken out the wrong tooth. I am amazed. I'll whip you for this; I'll whip you well. You're a pretty doctor. Now lie down, Bill, and let him take out the right tooth; and if he makes a mistake this time, I'll cowhide him well. Lie down, Bill. (BILL *lies down, and* CATO *pulls the tooth*) There now, why didn't you do that in the first place?
CATO He wouldn't hole still, sir.

BILL   He lies, sir. I did hole still.

DR. GAINES   Now go home, boys; go home. (*exit* PETE, NED *and* BILL, *left*)

DR. GAINES   You've made a pretty muss of it, in my absence. Look at the table! Never mind, Cato; I'll whip you well for this conduct of yours today. Go to work now, and clear up the office. (*exit* DR. GAINES, *right*)

CATO   Confound dat nigger! I wish he was in Ginny. He bite my finger and scratch my face. But didn't I give it to him? Well, den, I reckon I did. (*he goes to the mirror, and discovers that his coat is torn—weeps*) Oh, dear me! Oh, my coat—my coat is tore! Dat nigger has tore my coat. (*he gets angry, and rushes about the room frantic*) Cuss dat nigger! Ef I could lay my hands on him, I'd tare him all to pieces,—dat I would. An' de ole boss hit me wid his cane after dat nigger tore my coat. By golly, I wants to fight somebody. Ef ole massa should come in now, I'd fight him. (*rolls up his sleeves*) Let 'em come now, ef dey dare—ole massa, or any body else; I'm ready for 'em.

(*Enter* DR. GAINES, *right*)

DR. GAINES   What's all this noise here?

CATO   Nuffin', sir; only jess I is puttin' things to rights, as you tole me. I didn't hear any noise except de rats.

DR. GAINES   Make haste, and come in; I want you to go to town. (*exit* DR. GAINES, *right*)

CATO   By golly, de ole boss like to cotch me dat time, didn't he? But wasn't I mad? When I is mad, nobody can do nuffin' wid me. But here's my coat, tore to pieces. Cuss dat nigger! (*weeps*) Oh, my coat! oh, my coat! I rudder he had broke my head den to tore my coat. Drat dat nigger! Ef he ever comes here agin, I'll pull out every toof he's got in his head—dat I will. (*exit, right*)

Scene Three

(*A room in the quarters. Enter* GLEN, *left*)

GLEN   How slowly the time passes away. I've been waiting here two hours, and Melinda has not yet come. What keeps her, I cannot tell. I waited long and late for her last night, and when she approached, I sprang to my feet, caught her in my arms, pressed her to my heart, and kissed away the tears from her moistened cheeks. She placed her trembling hand in mine, and said, "Glen, I am yours; I will never be the wife of another." I clasped her to my bosom, and called God to witness that I would ever regard her as my wife. Old Uncle Joseph joined us in holy wedlock by moonlight; that was the only marriage ceremony. I look upon the vow as ever binding on me, for I am sure that a just God will sanction our union in heaven. Still, this man, who claims Melinda as his property, is unwilling for me to marry the woman of my choice, because he wants her himself. But he shall not have her. What he will say when he finds that we are married, I cannot tell; but I am determined to protect my wife or die. Ah! here comes Melinda. (*enter* MELINDA, *right*) I am glad to see you, Melinda. I've been waiting long, and feared you would not come. Ah! in tears again?

MELINDA   Glen, you are always thinking I am in tears. But what did master say today?

GLEN   He again forbade our union.

MELINDA   Indeed! Can he be so cruel?

GLEN   Yes, he can be just so cruel.

MELINDA   Alas! alas! how unfeeling and heartless! But did you appeal to his generosity?

GLEN   Yes, I did; I used all the persuasive powers that I was master of, but to no purpose; he was inflexible. He even offered me a new suit of clothes, if I would give you up; and when I told him that I could not, he said he would flog me to death if I ever spoke to you again.

MELINDA   And what did you say to him?

GLEN   I answered, that, while I loved life better than death, even life itself could not tempt me to consent to a separation that would make life an unchanging curse. Oh, I would kill myself, Melinda, if I thought that, for the sake of life, I could consent to your degradation. No, Melinda, I can die, but shall never live to see you the mistress of another man. But, my dear girl, I have a secret to tell you, and no one must know it but you. I will go out and see that no person is within hearing. I will be back soon. (*exit* GLEN, *left*)

MELINDA   It is often said that the darkest hour of the night precedes the dawn. It is ever thus with the vicissitudes of human suffering. After the soul has reached the lowest depths of despair, and can no deeper plunge amid its rolling, fœtid shades, then the reactionary forces of man's nature begin to operate, resolution takes the place of despondency, energy succeeds instead of apathy, and an upward tendency is felt and exhibited. Men then hope against power, and smile in defiance of despair. I shall never forget when first I saw Glen. It is now more than a year since he came here with his master, Mr. Hamilton. It was a glorious moonlight night in autumn. The wide and fruitful face of nature was silent and buried in repose. The tall trees on the borders of Muddy Creek waved their leafy branches in the breeze, which was wafted from afar, refreshing over hill and vale, over the rippling water, and the waving corn and wheat fields. The starry sky was studded over with a few light, flitting clouds, while the moon, as if rejoicing to witness the meeting of two hearts that should be cemented by the purest love, sailed triumphantly along among the shifting vapors.

Oh, how happy I have been in my acquaintance with Glen! That he loves me, I do well believe it; that I love him, it is most true. Oh, how I would that those who think the slave incapable of the finer feelings, could only see our hearts, and learn our thoughts,—thoughts that we dare not utter in the presence of our masters! But I fear that Glen will be separated from me, for there is nothing too base and mean for master to do, for the purpose of getting me entirely in his power. But, thanks to Heaven, he does not own Glen, and therefore cannot sell him. Yet he might purchase him from his brother-in-law, so as to send him out of the way. But here comes my husband.

(*Enter* GLEN, *left*)

GLEN I've been as far as the overseer's house, and all is quiet. Now, Melinda, as you are my wife, I will confide to you a secret. I've long been thinking of making my escape to Canada, and taking you with me. It is true that I don't belong to your master, but he might buy me from Hamilton, and then sell me out of the neighborhood.

MELINDA But we could never succeed in the attempt to escape.

GLEN We will make the trial, and show that we at least deserve success. There is a slave trader expected here next week, and Dr. Gaines would sell you at once if he knew that we were married. We must get ready and start, and if we can pass the Ohio river, we'll be safe on the road to Canada. (*exit, right*)

Scene Four

(*Dining-room.* REV. MR. PINCHEN *giving* MRS. GAINES *an account of his experience as a minister*—HANNAH *clearing away the breakfast table*—SAMPEY *standing behind* MRS. GAINES' *chair*)

MRS. GAINES Now, do give me more of your experience, brother Pinchen. It always does my soul good to hear religious experience. It draws me nearer and nearer to the Lord's side. I do love to hear good news from God's people.

MR. PINCHEN Well, sister Gaines, I've had great opportunities in my time to study the heart of man. I've attended a great many camp-meetings, revival meetings, protracted meetings, and death-bed scenes, and I am satisfied, sister Gains, that the heart of man is full of sin, and desperately wicked. This is a wicked world, sister Gaines, a wicked world.

MRS. GAINES Were you ever in Arkansas, brother Pinchen? I've been told that the people out there are very ungodly.

MR. PINCHEN Oh, yes, sister Gaines. I once spent a year at Little Rock, and preached in all the towns round about there; and I found some hard cases out there, I can tell you. I was once spending a week in a district where there were a great many horse thieves, and one night, somebody stole my pony. Well, I knowed it was no use to make a fuss, so I told brother Tarbox to say nothing about it, and I'd get my horse by preaching God's everlasting gospel; for I had faith in the truth, and knowed that my Savior would not let me lose my pony. So the next Sunday I preached on horse-stealing, and told the brethren to come up in the evenin' with their hearts filled with the grace of God. So that night the house was crammed brim full with anxious souls, panting for the bread of life. Brother Bingham opened with prayer, and brother Tarbox followed, and I saw right off that we were gwine to have a blessed time. After I got 'em pretty well warmed up, I jumped on to one of the seats, stretched out my hands, and said, "I know who stole my pony; I've found out; and you are in here tryin' to make people believe that you've got religion; but you ain't got it. And if you don't take my horse back to brother Tarbox's pasture this very night, I'll tell your name right out in meetin' tomorrow night. Take my pony back, you vile and wretched sinner, and come up here and give your heart to God." So the next mornin', I went out to brother Tarbox's pasture, and sure enough, there was my bob-tail pony. Yes, sister Gaines, there he was, safe and sound. Ha, ha, ha.

MRS. GAINES Oh, how interesting, and how fortunate for you to get your pony! And what power there is in the gospel! God's children are very lucky. Oh, it is so sweet to sit here and listen to such good news from God's people! You Hannah, what are you standing there listening for, and neglecting your work? Never mind, my lady, I'll whip you well when I am done here. Go at your work this moment you lazy huzzy! Never mind, I'll whip you well. (*aside*) Come, do go on, brother Pinchen, with your godly conversation. It is so sweet! It draws me nearer and nearer to the Lord's side.

MR. PINCHEN Well, sister Gaines, I've had some mighty queer dreams in my time, that I have. You see, one night I dreamed that I was dead and in heaven, and such a place I never saw before. As soon as I entered the gates of the celestial empire, I saw many old and familiar faces that I had seen before. The first person that I saw was good old Elder Pike, the preacher that first called my attention to religion. The next person I saw was Deacon Billings, my first wife's father, and then I saw a host of godly faces. Why, sister Gaines, you knowed Elder Goosbee, didn't you?

MRS. GAINES Why, yes; did you see him there? He married me to my first husband.

MR. PINCHEN Oh, yes, sister Gaines, I saw the old Elder, and he looked for all the world as if he had just come out of a revival meetin'.

MRS. GAINES Did you see my first husband there, brother Pinchen?

MR. PINCHEN No, sister Gaines, I didn't see brother Pepper there; but I've no doubt but that brother Pepper was there.

MRS. GAINES Well, I don't know; I have my doubts. He was not the happiest man in the world. He was always borrowing trouble about something or another. Still, I saw some happy moments with Mr. Pepper. I was happy when I made his acquaintance, happy during our courtship, happy a while after our marriage, and happy when he died. (*weeps*)

HANNAH Massa Pinchen, did you see my ole man Ben up dar in hebben?

MR. PINCHEN No, Hannah; I didn't go amongst the niggers.

MRS. GAINES No, of course brother Pinchen didn't go among the blacks. What are you asking questions for? Never mind, my lady, I'll whip you well when I'm done here. I'll skin you from head to foot. (*aside*) Do go on with your heavenly conversation, brother Pinchen; it does my very soul good. This is indeed a precious moment for me. I do love to hear of Christ and Him crucified.

MR. PINCHEN Well, sister Gaines, I promised sister Daniels that I'd come over and see her this morning, and have a little season of prayer with her, and I suppose I must go. I'll tell you more of my religious experience when I return.

MRS. GAINS If you must go, then I'll have to let you; but before you do, I wish to get your advice upon a little matter that concerns Hannah. Last week, Hannah stole a goose, killed it, cooked it, and she and her man Sam had a fine time eating the goose; and her master and I would never have known a word about it, if it had not been for Cato, a faithful servant, who told his master. And then, you see, Hannah had to be severely whipped before she'd confess that she stole the goose. Next Sabbath is sacrament day, and I want to know if you think that Hannah is fit to go to the Lord's supper after stealing the goose.

MR. PINCHEN Well, sister Gaines, that depends on circumstances. If Hannah has confessed that she stole the goose, and has been sufficiently whipped, and has begged her master's pardon, and begged your pardon, and thinks she'll never do the like again, why then I suppose she can go to the Lord's supper; for

> While the lamp holds out to burn,
> The vilest sinner may return.

But she must be sure that she has repented, and won't steal any more.

MRS. GAINS Now, Hannah, do you hear that? For my own part, I don't think she's fit to go to the Lord's supper, for she had no occasion to steal the goose. We give our niggers plenty of good wholesome food. They have a full run to the meal tub, meat once a fortnight, and all the sour milk about the place, and I'm sure that's enough for anyone. I do think that our niggers are the most ungrateful creatures in the world, that I do. They aggravate my life out of me.

HANNAH I know, missis, dat I steal de goose, and massa whip me for it, and I confess it, and I is sorry for it. But, missis, I is gwine to de Lord's supper, next Sunday, kase I ain't agwine to turn my back on my bressed Lord an' Massa for no old tough goose, dat I ain't. (*weeps*)

MR. PINCHEN Well, sister Gaines, I suppose I must go over and see sister Daniels; she'll be waiting for me. (*exit* MR. PINCHEN, *center*)

MRS. GAINS Now, Hannah, brother Pinchen is gone, do you get the cowhide and follow me to the cellar, and I'll whip you well for aggravating me as you have today. It seems as if I can never sit down to take a little comfort with the Lord, without you crossing me. The devil always puts it into your head to disturb me, just when I am trying to serve the Lord. I've no doubt but that I'll miss going to heaven on your account. But I'll whip you well before I leave this world, that I will. Get the cowhide and follow me to the cellar. (*exit* MRS. GAINES *and* HANNAH, *right*)

ACT TWO

Scene One

(*Parlor.* DR. GAINES *at a table, letters and papers before him. Enter* SAMPEY, *left*)

SAMPEY Dar's a gemman at de doe, massa, dat wants to see you, seer.

DR. GAINES Ask him to walk in, Sampey. (*exit* SAMPEY, *left*)

(*Enter* WALKER)

WALKER Why, how do you do, Dr. Gaines? I em glad to see you, I'll swear.

DR. GAINES How do you do, Mr. Walker? I did not expect to see you up here so soon. What has hurried you?

WALKER Well, you see, doctor, I comes when I em not expected. The price of niggers is up, and I em gwine to take advantage of the times. Now, doctor, ef you've got any niggers that you wants to sell, I em your man. I am paying the highest price of anybody in the market. I pay cash down, and no grumblin'.

DR. GAINES I don't know that I want to sell any of my people now. Still, I've got to make up a little money next month, to pay in bank; and another thing, the doctors say that we are likely to have a touch of the cholera this summer, and if that's the case, I suppose I had better turn as many of my slaves into cash as I can.

WALKER Yes, doctor, that is very true. The cholera is death on slaves, and a thousand dollars in your pocket is a great deal better than a nigger in the field, with cholera at his heels. Why, who is that coming up the lane? It's Mr. Wildmarsh as I live! Jest the very man I wants to see. (*enter* MR. WILDMARSH) Why, how do you do, Squire,? I was jest a thinkin' about you.

WILDMARSH How are you, Mr. Walker? and how are you, doctor? I am glad to see you both looking so well. You seem in remarkably good health, doctor?

DR. GAINES Yes, Squire, I was never in the enjoyment of better health. I hope you left all well at Licking?

WILDMARSH Yes, I thank you. And now, Mr. Walker, how goes times with you?

WALKER Well, you see, Squire, I em in good spirits. The price of niggers is up in the market, and I am lookin' out for bargains; and I was jest intendin' to come over to Lickin' to see you, to see if you had any niggers to sell. But it seems as ef the Lord knowed that I wanted to see you, and directed your steps over here. Now, Squire, ef you've got any niggers you wants to sell, I em your man. I am payin' the highest cash price of anybody in the market. Now's your time, Squire.

WILDMARSH No, I don't think I want to sell any of my slaves now. I sold a very valuable gal to Mr. Haskins last week. I tell you, she was a smart one. I got eighteen hundred dollars for her.

WALKER Why, Squire, how you do talk! Eighteen hundred dollars for one gal? She must have been a screamer to bring that price. What sort of a lookin' critter was she? I should like to have bought her.

WILDMARSH She was a little of the smartest gal I've ever raised; that she was.

WALKER Then she was your own raising, was she?

WILDMARSH Oh, yes; she was raised on my place, and if I could have kept her three or four years longer, and taken her to the market myself,

I am sure I could have sold her for three thousand dollars. But you see, Mr. Walker, my wife got a little jealous, and you know jealousy sets women's heads a teetering, and so I had to sell the gal. She's got straight hair, blue eyes, prominent features, and is almost white. Haskins will make a spec, and no mistake.

WALKER Why, Squire, was she that pretty little gal that I saw on your knee the day that your wife was gone, when I was at your place three years ago?

WILDMARSH Yes, the same.

WALKER Well, now, Squire, I thought that was your daughter; she looked mightily like you. She was your daughter, wasn't she? You need not be ashamed to own it to me, for I am mum upon such matters.

WILDMARSH You know, Mr. Walker, that people will talk, and when they talk, they say a great deal; and people did talk, and many said the gal was my daughter; and you know we can't help people's talking. But here comes the Rev. Mr. Pinchen; I didn't know that he was in the neighborhood.

WALKER It is Mr. Pinchen, as I live; jest the very man I wants to see. (*enter* MR. PINCHEN, *right*) Why, how do you do, Mr. Pinchen? What in the name of Jehu brings you down here to Muddy Creek? Any camp-meetins, revival meetins, death-bed scenes, or anything else in your line going on down here? How is religion prosperin' now, Mr. Pinchen? I always like to hear about religion.

MR. PINCHEN Well, Mr. Walker, the Lord's work is in good condition everywhere now. I tell you, Mr. Walker, I've been in the gospel ministry these thirteen years, and I am satisfied that the heart of man is full of sin and desperately wicked. This is a wicked world, Mr. Walker, a wicked world, and we ought all of us to have religion. Religion is a good thing to live by, and we all want it when we die. Yes, sir, when the great trumpet blows, we ought to be ready. And a man in your business of buying and selling slaves needs religion more than anybody else, for it makes you treat your people as you should. Now, there is Mr. Haskins,— he is a slave-trader, like yourself. Well, I converted him. Before he got religion, he was one of the worst men to his niggers I ever saw; his heart was as hard as stone. But religion has made his heart as soft as a piece of cotton. Before I converted him, he would sell husbands from their wives, and seem to take delight in it; but now he won't sell a man from his wife, if he can get any one to buy both of them together. I tell you, sir, religion has done a wonderful work for him.

WALKER I know, Mr. Pinchen, that I ought to have religion, and I feel that I am a great sinner; and whenever I get with good pious people like you and the doctor, and Mr. Wildmarsh, it always makes me feel that I am a desperate sinner. I feel it the more, because I've got a religious turn of mind. I know that I would be happier with religion, and the first spare time I get, I am going to try to get it. I'll go to a protracted meeting, and I won't stop till I get religion. Yes, I'll scuffle with the Lord till I gets forgiven. But it always makes me feel bad to talk about religion, so I'll change the subject. Now, doctor, what about them thar niggers you thought you could sell me?

DR. GAINES I'll see my wife, Mr. Walker, and if she is willing to part with Hannah, I'll sell you Sam and his wife, Hannah. Ah! here comes my wife; I'll mention it. (*enter* MRS. GAINES, *left*) Ah! my dear, I am glad you've come. I was just telling Mr. Walker, that if you were willing to part with Hannah, I'd sell him Sam and Hannah.

MRS. GAINES Now, Dr. Gaines, I am astonished and surprised that you should think of such a thing. You know what trouble I've had in training up Hannah for a house servant, and now that I've got her so that she knows my ways, you want to sell her. Havn't you niggers enough on the plantation to sell, without selling the servants from under my very nose?

DR. GAINES Oh, yes, my dear; but I can spare Sam, and I don't like to separate him from his wife; and I thought if you could let Hannah go, I'd sell them both. I don't like to separate husbands from their wives.

MRS. GAINS Now, gentlemen, that's just the way with my husband. He thinks more about the welfare and comfort of his slaves, than he does of himself or his family. I am sure you need not feel so bad at the thought of separating Sam from Hannah. They've only been married eight months, and their attachment can't be very strong in that short time. Indeed, I shall be glad if you do sell Sam, for then I'll make Hannah *jump the broomstick* with Cato, and I'll have them both here under my eye. I never will again let one of my house servants marry a field hand—never! For when night comes on, the servants are off to the quarters, and I have to holler and holler enough to split my throat before I can make them hear. And another thing: I want you to sell Melinda. I don't intend to keep that mulatto wench about the house any longer.

DR. GAINES My dear, I'll sell any servant from the place to suit you, except Melinda. I can't think of selling her—I can't think of it.

MRS. GAINES I tell you that Melinda shall leave this house, or I'll go. There, now you have it. I've had my life tormented out of me by the presence of that yellow wench, and I'll stand it no longer. I know you love her more than you do me, and I'll—I'll—I'll write—write to my father. (*weeps*). (*Exit* MRS. GAINES, *left*)

WALKER Why, doctor, your wife's a screamer, ain't she? Ha, ha, ha. Why, doctor, she's got a tongue of her own, ain't she? Why, doctor, it was only last week that I thought of getting a wife myself; but your wife has skeered the idea out of my head. Now, doctor, if you wants to sell the gal, I'll buy her. Husband and wife ought to be on good terms, and your wife won't feel well till the gal is gone. Now, I'll pay you all she's worth, if you wants to sell.

DR. GAINES No, Mr. Walker; the girl my wife spoke of is not for sale. My wife does not mean what she says; she's only a little jealous. I'll get brother Pinchen to talk to her, and get her mind turned upon religious matters, and then she'll forget it. She's only a little jealous.

WALKER I tell you what, doctor, ef you call that a little jealous, I'd like to know what's a heap. I tell you, it will take something more than religion to set your wife right. You had better sell me the gal; I'll pay you cash down, and no grumblin'.

DR. GAINES The girl is not for sale, Mr. Walker; but if you want two good, able-bodied servants, I'll sell you Sam and Big Sally. Sam is trustworthy, and Sally is worth her weight in gold for rough usage.

WALKER Well, doctor, I'll go out and take a look at 'em, for I never buys slaves without examining them well, because they are sometimes injured by over-work or underfeedin'. I don't say that is the case with yours, for I don't believe it is; but as I sell on honor, I must buy on honor.

DR. GAINES Walk out, sir, and you can examine them to your heart's content. Walk right out, sir.

Scene Two

(*View in front of the Great House. Examination of* SAM *and* BIG SALLY.—DR. GAINES, WILDMARSH, MR. PINCHEN *and* WALKER *present*)

WALKER Well, my boy, what's your name?

SAM Sam, sir, is my name.

WALKER How old are you, Sam?

SAM Ef I live to see next corn plantin' time, I'll be 27, or 30, or 35, or 40—I don't know which, sir.

WALKER Ha, ha, ha. Well, doctor, this is rather a green boy. Well, mer feller, are you sound?

SAM Yes, sir, I spec I is.

WALKER Open your mouth and let me see your teeth. I allers judge a nigger's age by his teeth, same as I dose a hoss. Ah! pretty good set of grinders. Have you got a good appetite?

SAM Yes, sir.

WALKER Can you eat your allowance?

SAM Yes, sir, when I can get it.

WALKER Get out on the floor and dance; I want to see if you are supple.

SAM I don't like to dance; I is got religion.

WALKER Oh, ho! you've got religion, have you? That's so much the better. I likes to deal in the gospel. I think he'll suit me. Now, mer gal, what's your name?

SALLY I is Big Sally, sir.

WALKER How old are you, Sally?

SALLY I don't know, sir; but I heard once dat I was born at sweet pertater diggin' time.

WALKER Ha, ha, ha. Don't know how old you are! Do you know who made you?

SALLY I hev heard who it was in de Bible dat made me, but I dun forget de gentman's name.

WALKER Ha, ha, ha. Well, doctor, this is the greenest lot of niggers I've seen for some time. Well, what do you ask for them?

DR. GAINES You may have Sam for $1000, and Sally for $900. They are worth all I ask for them. You know I never banter, Mr. Walker. There they are; you can take them at that price, or let them alone, just as you please.

WALKER Well, doctor, I reckon I'll take

'em; but it's all they are worth. I'll put the handcuffs on 'em, and then I'll pay you. I likes to go accordin' to Scripter. Scripter says ef eatin' meat will offend your brother, you must quit it; and I say, ef leavin' your slaves without the handcuffs will make 'em run away, you must put the handcuffs on 'em. Now, Sam, don't you and Sally cry. I am of a tender heart, and it ollers makes me feel bad to see people cryin'. Don't cry, and the first place I get to, I'll buy each of you a great big *ginger cake*,—that I will. Now, Mr. Pinchen, I wish you were going down the river. I'd like to have your company; for I allers likes the company of preachers.

MR. PINCHEN. Well, Mr. Walker, I would be much pleased to go down the river with you, but it's too early for me. I expect to go to Natchez in four or five weeks, to attend a camp-meetin', and if you were going down then, I'd like it. What kind of niggers sells best in the Orleans market, Mr. Walker?

WALKER Why, field hands. Did you think of goin' in the trade?

MR. PINCHEN Oh, no; only it's a long ways down to Natchez, and I thought I'd just buy five or six niggers, and take 'em down and sell 'em to pay my travellin' expenses. I only want to clear my way.

Scene Three

(*Sitting-room—table and rocking-chair. Enter* MRS. GAINES, *right, followed by* SAMPEY)

MRS. GAINES I do wish your master would come; I want supper. Run to the gate, Sampey, and see if he is coming. (*exit* SAMPEY, *left*) That man is enough to break my heart. The patience of an angel could not stand it.

(*Enter* SAMPEY, *left*)

SAMPEY Yes, missis, master is coming.

(*Enter* DR. GAINES, *left. The Doctor walks about with his hands under his coat, seeming very much elated*)

MRS. GAINES Why, doctor, what is the matter?

DR. GAINES My dear, don't call me *doctor*.

MRS. GAINES What should I call you?

DR. GAINES Call me Colonel, my dear—Colonel. I have been elected Colonel of the Militia, and I want you to call me by my right name. I always felt that Providence had designed me for something great, and He has just begun to shower His blessings upon me.

MRS. GAINES Dear me, I could never get to calling you Colonel; I've called you Doctor for the last twenty years.

DR. GAINES Now, Sarah, if you will call me Colonel, other people will, and I want you to set the example. Come, my darling, call me Colonel, and I'll give you anything you wish for.

MRS. GAINES Well, as I want a new gold watch and bracelets, I'll commence now. Come, Colonel, we'll go to supper. (*aside*) Ah! now for my new shawl. Mrs. Lemme was here today, Colonel, and she had on, Colonel, one of the prettiest shawls, Colonel, I think, Colonel, that I ever saw, Colonel, in my life, Colonel. And there is only one, Colonel, in Mr. Watson's store, Colonel; and that, Colonel, will do, Colonel, for a Colonel's wife.

DR. GAINES Ah! my dear, you never looked so much the lady since I've known you. Go, my darling, get the watch, bracelets and shawl, and tell them to charge them to Colonel Gaines; and when you say "Colonel," always emphasize the word.

MRS. GAINES Come, Colonel, let's go to supper.

DR. GAINES My dear, you're a jewel,—you are! (*exit, right*)

(*Enter* CATO, *left*)

CATO Why, whar is massa and missis? I tought dey was here. Ah! by golly, yonder comes a mulatter gal. Yes, its Mrs. Jones's Tapioca. I'll set up to dat gal, dat I will. (*enter* TAPIOCA, *right*) Good ebenin', Miss Tappy. How is your folks?

TAPIOCA Pretty well, I tank you.

CATO Miss Tappy, dis wanderin' heart of mine is yours. Come, take a seat! Please to squze my manners; love discommodes me. Take a seat. Now, Miss Tappy, I loves you; an ef you will jess marry me, I'll make you a happy husband, dat I will. Come, take me as I is.

TAPIOCA But what will Big Jim say?

CATO Big Jim! Why, let dat nigger go to Ginny. I want to know, now, if you is tinkin' about dat common nigger? Why, Miss Tappy,

I is surstonished dat you should tink 'bout frowin' yoursef away wid a common, ugly lookin' cuss like Big Jim, when you can get a fine lookin', suspectable man like me. Come, Miss Tappy, choose dis day who you have. Afore I go any furder, give me one kiss. Come, give me one kiss. Come, let me kiss you.

TAPIOCA No you shan't—dare now! You shan't kiss me widout you is stronger den I is; and I know you is dat. (*he kisses her. Enter* DR. GAINES, *right, and hides*)

CATO Did you know, Miss Tappy, dat I is de head doctor 'bout dis house? I beats de ole boss all to pieces.

TAPIOCA I hev hearn dat you bleeds and pulls teef.

CATO Yes, Miss Tappy; massa could not get along widout me, for massa was made a doctor by books; but I is a natral doctor. I was born a doctor, jess as Lorenzo Dow was born a preacher. So you see I can't be nuffin' but a doctor, while massa is a bunglin' ole cuss at de bissness.

DR. GAINES (*in a low voice*) Never mind; I'll teach you a lesson, that I will.

CATO You see, Miss Tappy, I was gwine to say—Ah! but afore I forget, jess give me anudder kiss, jess to keep company wid de one dat you give me jess now,—dat's all. (*kisses her*) Now, Miss Tappy, duse you know de fuss time dat I seed you?

TAPIOCA No, Mr. Cato, I don't.

CATO Well, it was at de camp-meetin'. Oh, Miss Tappy, dat pretty red calliker dress you had on dat time did de work for me. It made my heart flutter—

DR. GAINES (*low voice*) Yes, and I'll make your black hide flutter.

CATO Didn't I hear some noise? By golly, dar is teves in dis house, and I'll drive 'em out. (*takes a chair and runs at the* DOCTOR, *and knocks him down. The* DOCTOR *chases* CATO *round the table*) Oh, massa, I didn't know 'twas you!

DR. GAINES You scoundrel! I'll whip you well. Stop! I tell you. (*curtain falls*)

ACT THREE

Scene One

(*Sitting-room.* MRS. GAINES, *seated in an arm chair, reading a letter. Enter* HANNAH, *left*)

MRS. GAINES You need not tell me, Hannah, that you don't want another husband, I know better. Your master has sold Sam, and he's gone down the river, and you'll never see him again. So, go and put on your calico dress, and meet me in the kitchen. I intend for you to *jump the broomstick* with Cato. You need not tell me that you don't want another man. I know that there's no woman living that can be happy and satisfied without a husband.

HANNAH Oh, missis, I don't want to jump de broomstick wid Cato. I don't love Cato; I can't love him.

MRS. GAINES Shut up, this moment! What do you know about love? I didn't love your master when I married him, and people don't marry for love now. So go and put on your calico dress, and meet me in the kitchen. (*exit* HANNAH, *left*) I am glad that the Colonel has sold Sam; now I'll make Hannah marry Cato, and I have them both here under my eye. And I am also glad that the Colonel has parted with Melinda. Still, I'm afraid that he is trying to deceive me. He took the hussy away yesterday, and says he sold her to a trader; but I don't believe it. At any rate, if she's in the neighborhood, I'll find her, that I will. No man ever fools me. (*exit* MRS. GAINES, *left*)

Scene Two

(*The kitchen—slaves at work. Enter* HANNAH, *right*)

HANNAH Oh, Cato, do go and tell missis dat you don't want to jump de broomstick wid me,—dat's a good man! Do, Cato; kase I nebber can love you. It was only las week dat massa sold my Sammy, and I don't want any udder man. Do go tell missis dat you don't want me.

CATO No, Hannah, I ain't a gwine to tell missis no such think, kase I dose want you, and I ain't a-gwine to tell a lie for you ner nobody else. Dar, now you's got it! I don't see why you need to make so much fuss. I is better lookin' den Sam; an' I is a house servant, an' Sam was only a fiel hand; so you ought to feel proud of a change. So go and do as missis tells you. (*exit* HANNAH, *left*) Hannah needn't try to get me to tell a lie; I ain't a-gwine to do it, kase I dose want her, an' I is bin wantin' her dis long time, an' soon as massa sold Sam, I knowed I would get her. By golly, I is gwine to be a married man. Won't I be happy! Now, ef I could only jess run away from ole massa, an' get to Canada wid Hannah, den I'd show 'em who I was. Ah! dat reminds me of my song 'bout ole massa and Canada, an' I'll sing it fer yer. Dis is my moriginal hyme. It comed into my head one night when I was fass asleep under an apple tree, looking up at de moon. Now for my song:—

AIR—"*Dandy Jim*"

Come all ye bondmen far and near,
Let's put a song in massa's ear,
It is a song for our poor race,
Who're whipped and trampled with disgrace.

CHORUS
My old massa tells me, Oh,
This is a land of freedom, Oh;
Let's look about and see if it's so,
Just as massa tells me, Oh.

He tells us of that glorious one,
I think his name was Washington,
How he did fight for liberty,
To save a threepence tax on tea.
CHORUS

But now we look about and see
That we poor blacks are not so free;
We're whipped and thrashed about like fools,
And have no chance at common schools.
CHORUS

They take our wives, insult and mock,
And sell our children on the block,
They choke us if we say a word,
And say that "niggers" shan't be heard.
CHORUS

Our preachers, too, with whip and cord,
Command obedience in the Lord;
They say they learn it from the big book,
But for ourselves, we dare not look.
CHORUS

There is a country far away,
I think they call it Canada,
And if we reach Victoria's shore,
They say that we are slaves no more.

Now haste, all bondmen, let us go,
And leave this *Christian* country, Oh;
Haste to the land of the British Queen,
Where whips for negroes are not seen.

Now, if we go, we must take the night,
And never let them come in sight;
The bloodhounds will be on our track,
And wo to us if they fetch us back.

Now haste all bondmen, let us go,
And leave this *Christian* country, Oh;
God help us to Victoria's shore,
Where we are free and slaves no more!

(*Enter* MRS. GAINES, *left*)

MRS. GAINES Ah! Cato, you're ready, are you? Where is Hannah?

CATO Yes, missis; I is bin waitin' dis long time. Hannah has bin here tryin' to swade me to tell you dat I don't want her; but I telled her dat you sed I must jump de broomstick wid her, an' I is gwine to mind you.

MRS. GAINES That's right, Cato; servants should always mind their masters and mistresses, without asking a question.

CATO Yes, missis, I allers dose what you and massa tells me, an' axes nobody.

(*Enter* HANNAH, *right*)

MRS. GAINES Ah! Hannah; come, we are waiting for you. Nothing can be done till you come.

HANNAH Oh, missis, I don't want to jump de broomstick wid Cato; I can't love him.

MRS. GAINES Shut up, this moment. Dolly, get the broom. Susan, you take hold of the other end. There, now hold it a little lower—there, a little higher. There, now, that'll do. Now Hannah, take hold of Cato's hand. Let Cato take hold of your hand.

HANNAH Oh, missis, do spare me. I don't want to jump de broomstick wid Cato.

MRS. GAINES Get the cowhide, and follow me to the cellar, and I'll whip you well. I'll let you know how to disobey my orders. Get the cowhide, and follow me to the cellar. (*exit* MRS. GAINES *and* HANNAH, *right*)

DOLLY Oh, Cato, do go an' tell missis dat you don't want Hannah. Don't you hear how she's whippin' her in de cellar? Do go an' tell missis dat you don't want Hannah, and den she'll stop whippin' her.

CATO No, Dolly, I ain't a-gwine to do no such a thing, kase ef I tell missis dat I don't want Hannah, den missis will whip me; an' I ain't a-gwine to be whipped fer you, ner Hannah, ner nobody else. No, I'll jump de broomstick wid every woman on de place, ef missis wants me to, before I'll be whipped.

DOLLY Cato, ef I was in Hannah's place, I'd see you in de bottomless pit before I'd live wid you, you great big wall-eyed, empty-headed, knock-kneed fool. You're as mean as your devilish old missis.

CATO Ef you don't quit dat busin' me, Dolly, I'll tell missis as soon as she comes in, an' she'll whip you, you know she will.

(*Enter* MRS. GAINES *and* HANNAH, *right*. MRS. GAINES *fans herself with her handkerchief, and appears fatigued*)

MRS. GAINES You ought to be ashamed of yourself, Hannah, to make me fatigue myself in this way, to make you do your duty. It's very naughty in you, Hannah. Now, Dolly, you and Susan get the broom, and get out in the middle of the room. There, hold it a little lower—a little higher; there, that'll do. Now, remember that this is a solemn occasion; you are going to jump into matrimony. Now, Cato, take hold of Hannah's hand. There, now, why couldn't you let Cato take hold of your hand before? Now get ready, and when I count three, do you jump. Eyes on the *broomstick!* All ready. One, two, three, and over you go. There, now you're husband and wife, and if you don't live happy together, it's your own fault; for I am sure there's nothing to hinder it. Now, Hannah, come up to the house, and I'll give you some whiskey, and you can make some apple toddy, and you and Cato can have a fine time. (*exit* MRS. GAINES *and* HANNAH, *left*)

DOLLY I tell you what, Susan, when I get married, I is gwine to have a preacher to marry me. I ain't a-gwine to jump de broomstick. Dat will do for fiel' hands, but house servants ought to be 'bove dat.

SUSAN Well, chile, you can't speck any ting else from ole missis. She come from down in Carlina, from 'mong de poor white trash. She don't know any better. You can't speck nothin' more dan a jump from a frog. Missis says she is one of de akastocacy; but she ain't no more of an akastocacy dan I is. Missis says she was born wid a silver spoon in her mouf; ef she was, I wish it had a-choked her, dat's what I wish. Missis wanted to make Linda jump de broomstick wid Glen, but massa ain't a-gwine to let Linda jump de broomstick wid anybody. He's gwine to keep Linda fer heself.

DOLLY You know massa took Linda 'way las' night, an' tell missis dat he has sold her and sent her down de river; but I don't b'lieve he has sold her at all. He went ober towards de poplar farm, an' I tink Linda is ober dar now. Ef she is dar, missis'll find it out, fer she tell'd massa las' night, dat ef Linda was in de neighborhood, she'd find her. (*exit* DOLLY *and* SUSAN)

Scene Three

(*Sitting room—chairs and table. Enter* HANNAH, *right*)

HANNAH I don't keer what missis says; I don't like Cato, an' I won't live wid him. I always love my Sammy, an' I loves him now. (*knock at the door—goes to the door. Enter* MAJ. MOORE, *center*) Walk in, sir; take a seat. I'll call missis, sir; massa is gone away. (*exit* HANNAH, *right*)

MAJ. MOORE So I am here at last, and the Colonel is not at home. I hope his wife is a good-looking woman. I rather like fine looking-women, especially when their husbands are from home. Well, I've studied human nature to some purpose. If you wish to get the good will of a man, don't praise his wife, and if you wish to gain the favor of a woman, praise her children, and swear that they are the picture of their father, whether they are not not. Ah! here comes the lady.

(*Enter* MRS. GAINES, *right*)

MRS. GAINES Good morning, sir!

MAJ. MOORE Good morning, madam! I am Maj. Moore, of Jefferson. The Colonel and I had seats near each other in the last Legislature.

MRS. GAINES Be seated, sir. I think I've heard the Colonel speak of you. He's away, now; but I expect him every moment. You're a stranger here, I presume?

MAJ. MOORE Yes, madam, I am. I rather like the Colonel's situation here.

MRS. GAINES It is thought to be a fine location. (*enter* SAMPEY, *right*) Hand me my fan, will you, Sampey?

(SAMPEY *gets the fan and passes near the* MAJOR, *who mistakes the boy for the Colonel's son. He reaches out his hand*)

MAJ. MOORE How do you do, Bob? Madam I should have known that this was the Colonel's son, if I had met him in California; for he looks so much like his papa.

MRS. GAINES (*to the boy*)   Get out of here this minute. Go to the kitchen. (*exit* SAMPEY, *right*) That is one of the niggers, sir.

MAJ. MOORE   I beg your pardon, madam; I beg your pardon.

MRS. GAINES   No offence, sir; mistakes will be made. Ah! here comes the Colonel.

(*Enter* DR. GAINES, *center*)

DR. GAINES   Bless my soul, how are you, Major? I'm exceedingly pleased to see you. Be seated, be seated, Major.

MRS. GAINES   Please excuse me, gentlemen; I must go and look after dinner, for I've no doubt that the Major will have an appetite for dinner, by the time it is ready. (*exit* MRS. GAINES, *right*)

MAJ. MOORE   Colonel, I'm afraid I've played the devil here today.

DR. GAINES   Why, what have you done?

MAJ. MOORE   You see, Colonel, I always make it a point, wherever I go, to praise the children, if there are any, and so today, seeing one of your little servants come in, and taking him to be your son, I spoke to your wife of the marked resemblance between you and the boy. I am afraid I've insulted madam.

DR. GAINES   Oh! don't let that trouble you. Ha, ha, ha. If you did call him my son, you didn't miss it much. Ha, ha, ha. Come, we'll take a walk, and talk over matters about old times. (*exit, left*)

Scene Four

(*Forest scenery. Enter* GLEN, *left*)

GLEN   Oh, how I want to see Melinda! My heart pants and my soul is moved whenever I hear her voice. Human tongue cannot tell how my heart yearns toward her. Oh, God! thou who gavest me life, and implanted in my bosom the love of liberty, and gave me a heart to love, Oh, pity the poor outraged slave! Thou, who canst rend the veil of centuries, speak, Oh, speak, and put a stop to this persecution! What is death, compared to slavery? Oh, heavy curse, to have thoughts, reason, taste, judgment, conscience and passions like another man, and not have equal liberty to use them! Why was I born with a wish to be free, and still be a slave? Why should I call another man master? And my poor Melinda, she is taken away from me, and I dare not ask the tyrant where she is. It is childish to stand here weeping. Why should my eyes be filled with tears, when my brain is on fire? I will find my wife—I will; and wo to him who shall try to keep me from her!

Scene Five

(*Room in a small cottage on the Poplar Farm, ten miles from Muddy Creek, and owned by* DR. GAINES. *Enter* MELINDA, *right*)

MELINDA   Here I am, watched, and kept a prisoner in this place. Oh, I would that I could escape, and once more get with Glen. Poor Glen! He does not know where I am. Master took the opportunity, when Glen was in the city with his master, to bring me here to this lonely place, and fearing that mistress would know where I was, he brought me here at night. Oh, how I wish I could rush into the arms of sleep!—that sweet sleep, which visits all alike, descending, like the dews of heaven, upon the bond as well as the free. It would drive from my troubled brain the agonies of this terrible night.

(*Enter* DR. GAINES, *left*)

DR. GAINES   Good evening, Melinda! Are you not glad to see me?

MELINDA   Sir, how can I be glad to see one who has made life a burden, and turned my sweetest moments into bitterness?

DR. GAINES   Come, Melinda, no more reproaches! You know that I love you, and I have told you, and I tell you again, that if you will give up all idea of having Glen for a husband, I will set you free, let you live in this cottage, and be your own mistress, and I'll dress you like a lady. Come, now, be reasonable!

MELINDA   Sir, I am your slave; you can do as you please with the avails of my labor, but you shall never tempt me to swerve from the path of virtue.

DR. GAINES   Now, Melinda, that black scoundrel Glen has been putting these notions into your head. I'll let you know that you are my property, and I'll do as I please with you. I'll teach you that there is no limit to my power.

MELINDA   Sir, let me warn you that if you

compass my ruin, a woman's bitterest curse will be laid upon your head, with all the crushing, withering weight that my soul can impart to it; a curse that shall cling to you throughout the remainder of your wretched life; a curse that shall haunt you like a spectre in your dreams by night, and attend upon you by day; a curse, too, that shall embody itself in the ghastly form of the woman whose chastity you will have outraged. Command me to bury myself in yonder stream, and I will obey you. Bid me do anything else, but I beseech you not to commit a double crime,—outrage a woman, and make her false to her husband.

DR. GAINES You got a husband! Who is your husband, and when were you married?

MELINDA Glen is my husband, and I've been married four weeks. Old Uncle Joseph married us one night by moonlight. I see you are angry; I pray you not to injure my husband.

DR. GAINES Melinda, you shall never see Glen again. I have bought him from Hamilton, and I will return to Muddy Creek, and roast him at the stake. A black villain, to get into my way in that manner! Here I've come ten miles tonight to see you, and this is the way you receive me!

MELINDA Oh, master, I beg you not to injure my husband! Kill me, but spare him! Do! do! he is my husband!

DR. GAINES You shall never see that black imp again, so good night, my lady! When I come again, you'll give me a more cordial reception. Good night! (*exit* DR. GAINES, *left*)

MELINDA I shall go distracted. I cannot remain here and know that Glen is being tortured on my account. I must escape from this place,—I must,—I must!

(*Enter* CATO, *right*)

CATO No, you ain't a-gwine to 'scape, nudder. Massa tells me to keep dese eyes on you, an' I is gwine to do it.

MELINDA Oh, Cato, do let me get away! I beg you, do!

CATO No; I tells you massa telled me to keep you safe; an' ef I let you go, massa will whip me. (*exit* CATO, *left*)

(*Enter* MRS. GAINES, *right*)

MRS. GAINES Ah, you trollop! here you are! Your master told me that he had sold you and sent you down the river, but I knew better; I knew it was a lie. And when he left home this evening, he said he was going to the city on business, and I knew that was a lie too, and determined to follow him, and see what he was up to. I rode all the way over here tonight. My side-saddle was lent out, and I had to ride ten miles bare-back, and I can scarcely walk; and your master has just left here. Now deny that, if you dare.

MELINDA Madam, I will deny nothing which is true. Your husband has just gone from here, but God knows that I am innocent of anything wrong with him.

MRS. GAINES It's a lie! I know better. If you are innocent, what are you doing here, cooped up in this cottage by yourself? Tell me that!

MELINDA God knows that I was brought here against my will, and I beg that you will take me away.

MRS. GAINES Yes, Melinda, I will see that you are taken away, but it shall be after a fashion that you won't like. I know that your master loves you, and I intend to put a stop to it. Here, drink the contents of this vial,—drink it!

MELINDA Oh, you will not take my life,—you will not!

MRS. GAINES Drink the poison this moment!

MELINDA I cannot drink it.

MRS. GAINES I tell you to drink this poison at once. Drink it, or I will thrust this knife to your heart! The poison or the dagger, this instant! (*she draws a dagger;* MELINDA *retreats to the back of the room, and seizes a broom.*)

MELINDA I will not drink the poison! (*they fight;* MELINDA *sweeps off* MRS. GAINES,—*cap, combs and curls. Curtain falls*)

ACT FOUR

Scene One

(*Interior of a dungeon—*GLEN *in chains*)

GLEN When I think of my unmerited sufferings, it almost drives me mad. I struck the doctor, and for that, I must remain here loaded with chains. But why did he strike me? He takes my wife from me, sends her off, and then comes and beats me over the head with his cane. I did right to strike him back again. I would I had killed him. Oh! there is a volcano pent up in the hearts of the slaves of these Southern States that will burst forth ere long. When that day comes, wo to those whom its unpitying fury may devour! I would be willing to die. if I could smite down with these chains every man who attempts to enslave his fellow-man.

(*Enter* SAMPEY, *right*)

SAMPEY Glen, I jess bin hear massa call de oberseer, and I spec somebody is gwine to be whipped. Anudder ting: I know whar massa took Linda to. He took her to de poplar farm, an' he went away las' night, an' missis she follow after massa, an' she ain't come back yet. I tell you, Glen, de debil will be to pay on dis place, but don't you tell anybody dat I tole you. (*exit* SAMPEY, *right*)

Scene Two

(*Parlor.* DR. GAINES, *alone*)

DR. GAINES Yes, I will have the black rascal well whipped, and then I'll sell him. It was most fortunate for me that Hamilton was willing to sell him to me. (*enter* MR. SCRAGG, *left*) I have sent for you, Mr. Scragg. I want you to take Glen out of the dungeon, take him into the tobacco house, fasten him down upon the stretcher, and give him five hundred lashes upon his bare back; and when you have whipped him, feel his pulse, and report to me how it stands, and if he can bear more, I'll have you give him an additional hundred or two, as the case may be.

SCRAGG I tell you, doctor, that suits me to a charm. I've long wanted to whip that nigger. When your brother-in-law came here to board, and brought that boy with him, I felt bad to see a nigger dressed up in such fine clothes, and I wanted to whip him right off. I tell you, doctor, I had rather whip that nigger than go to heaven, any day,—that I had!

DR. GAINES Go, Mr. Scragg, and do your duty. Don't spare the whip!

SCRAGG I will, sir; I'll do it in order. (*exit* SCRAGG, *left*)

DR. GAINES Everything works well now, and when I get Glen out of the way, I'll pay Melinda another visit, and she'll give me a different reception. But I wonder where my wife is? She left word that she was going to see her brother, but I am afraid that she has got on my track. That woman is the pest of my life. If there's any place in heaven for her, I'd be glad if the Lord would take her home, for I've had her too long already. But what noise is that? What can that be? What is the matter?

(*Enter* SCRAGG, *left, with face bloody*)

SCRAGG Oh, dear me! oh, my head! That nigger broke away from me, and struck me over the head with a stick. Oh, dear me! Oh!

DR. GAINES Where is he, Mr. Scragg?

SCRAGG Oh! sir, he jumped out of the window; he's gone. Oh! my head; he's cracked my skull. Oh, dear me, I'm kilt! Oh! oh! oh!

(*Enter* SLAVES, *right*)

DR. GAINES Go, Dolly, and wash Mr. Scragg's head with some whiskey, and bind it up. Go at once. And Bob, you run over to Mr. Hall, and tell him to come with his hounds; we must go after the rascal. (*exit all except the* DOCTOR, *right*) This will never do. When I catch the scoundrel, I'll make an example of him; I'll whip him to death. Ah! here comes my wife. I wonder what she comes now for? I must put on a sober face, for she looks angry. (*enter* MRS. GAINES, *left*) Ah! my dear, I am glad you've come, I've been so lonesome without you. Oh! Sarah, I don't know what I should do if the Lord should take you home to heaven. I don't think that I should be able to live without you.

MRS. GAINES Dr. Gaines, you ought to be ashamed to sit there and talk in that way. You know very well that if the Lord should call me home to glory tonight, you'd jump for joy. But you need not think that I am going to leave this world before you. No; with the help of the Lord, I'll stay here to foil you in your meanness. I've been on your track, and a dirty track it is, too. You ought to be ashamed of yourself. See what promises you made me before we were married; and this is the way you keep your word. When I married you, everybody said that it was a pity that a woman of my sweet temper should be linked to such a man as you. (*she weeps and wrings her hands*)

DR. GAINES Come, my dear, don't make a fool of yourself. Come, let's go to supper, and a strong cup of tea will help your head.

MRS. GAINES Tea help my head! tea won't

help my head. You're a brute of a man; I always knew I was a fool for marrying you. There was Mr. Comstock, he wanted me, and he loved me, and he said I was an angel, so he did; and he loved me, and he was rich; and mother always said that he loved me more than you, for when he used to kiss me, he always squeezed my hand. You never did such a thing in your life. (*she weeps and wrings her hands*)

DR. GAINES Come, my dear, don't act so foolish.

MRS. GAINES Yes; everything I do is foolish. You're a brute of a man; I won't live with you any longer. I'll leave you—that I will. I'll go and see a lawyer, and get a divorce from you—so I will.

DR. GAINES Well, Sarah, if you want a divorce, you had better engage Mr. Barker. He's the best lawyer in town; and if you want some money to facilitate the business, I'll draw a check for you.

MRS. GAINES So you want me to get a divorce, do you? Well, I won't have a divorce; no, I'll never leave you, as long as the Lord spares me. (*exit* MRS. GAINES, *right*)

Scene Three

(*Forest at night—large tree. Enter* MELINDA, *left*)

MELINDA This is indeed a dark night to be out and alone on this road. But I must find my husband, I must. Poor Glen! if he only knew that I was here, and could get to me, he would. What a curse slavery is! It separates husbands from their wives, and tears mothers from their helpless offspring, and blights all our hopes for this world. I must try to reach Muddy Creek before daylight, and seek out my husband. What's that I hear?—footsteps? I'll get behind this tree.

(*Enter* GLEN, *right*)

GLEN It is so dark, I'm afraid I've missed the road. Still, this must be the right way to the poplar farm. And if Bob told me the truth, when he said that Melinda was at the poplar farm, I will soon be with her; and if I once get her in my arms, it will be a strong man that shall take her from me. Aye, a dozen strong men shall not be able to wrest her from my arms. (MELINDA *rushes from behind the tree*)

MELINDA Oh, Glen! It is my husband,—it is!

GLEN Melinda! Melinda! it is, it is. Oh God! I thank Thee for this manifestation of Thy kindness. Come, come, Melinda, we must go at once to Canada. I escaped from the overseer, whom Dr. Gaines sent to flog me. Yes, I struck him over the head with his own club, and I made the wine flow freely; yes, I pounded his old skillet well for him, and then jumped out of the window. It was a leap for freedom. Yes, Melinda, it was a leap for freedom. I've said "master" for the last time. I am free; I'm bound for Canada. Come, let's be off, at once, for the negro dogs will be put upon our track. Let us once get beyond the Ohio river, and all will be right. (*exit, right*)

ACT FIVE

Scene One

(*Bar-room in the American Hotel—travellers lounging in chairs, and at the bar. Enter* BILL JENNINGS, *right*)

BARKEEPER Why, Jennings, how do you do?

JENNINGS Say Mr. Jennings, if you please.

BARKEEPER Well, Mr. Jennings, if that suits you better. How are times? We've been expecting you, for some days.

JENNINGS Well, before I talk about the times, I want my horses put up, and want you to tell me where my niggers are to stay tonight. Sheds, stables, barns, and everything else here, seems pretty full, if I am a judge.

BARKEEPER Oh! I'll see to your plunder.

FIRST LOUNGER I say, Barkeeper, make me a brandy cocktail, strong. Why, how do you do, Mr. Jennings?

JENNINGS Pretty well, Mr. Peters. Cold evening, this.

FIRST LOUNGER Yes, this is cold. I heard you speak of your niggers. Have you got a pretty large gang?

JENNINGS No, only thirty-three. But they are the best that the country can afford. I shall clear a few dimes, this trip. I hear that the price is up.

(*Enter* MR. WHITE, *right*)

WHITE Can I be accommodated here tonight, landlord?
BARKEEPER Yes, sir; we've bed for man and beast. (*to the waiter*) Go, Dick, and take the gentleman's coat and hat. You're a stranger in these parts, I rec'on.
WHITE Yes, I am a stranger here.
SECOND LOUNGER Where mout you come from, ef it's a far question?
WHITE I am from Massachusetts.
THIRD LOUNGER I say, cuss Massachusetts!
FIRST LOUNGER I say so too. There is where the fanatics live; cussed traitors. The President ought to hang 'em all.
WHITE I say, landlord, if this is the language that I am to hear, I would like to go into a private room.
BARKEEPER We ain't got no private room empty.
FIRST LOUNGER Maybe you're mad 'bout what I said 'bout your State. Ef you is, I've only to say that this is a free country, and people talks what they please; an' ef you don't like it, you can better yourself.
WHITE Sir, if this is a free country, why do you have slaves here? I saw a gang at the door, as I came in.
SECOND LOUNGER He didn't mean that this was a free country for niggers. He meant that it's free for white people. And another thing, ef you get to talking 'bout freedom for niggers, you'll catch what you won't like, mister. It's right for niggers to be slaves.
WHITE But I saw some white slaves.
FIRST LOUNGER Well, they're white niggers.
WHITE Well, sir, I am from a free State, and I thank God for it; for the worst act that a man can commit upon his fellow-man, is to make him a slave. Conceive of a mind, a living soul, with the germs of faculties which infinity cannot exhaust, as it first beams upon you in its glad morning of existence, quivering with life and joy, exulting in the glorious sense of its developing energies, beautiful, and brave, and generous, and joyous, and free,—the clear pure spirit bathed in the auroral light of its unconscious immortality,—and then follow it in its dark anddreary passage through slavery, until oppression stifles and kills, one by one, every inspiration and aspiration of its being, until it becomes a dead soul entombed in a living frame!
THIRD LOUNGER Stop that; stop that, I say.

That's treason to the country; that's downright rebellion.
BARKEEPER Yes, it is. And another thing,— this is not a meeting-house.
FIRST LOUNGER Yes, if you talk such stuff as that, you'll get a chunk of cold lead in you, that you will.

(*Enter* DR. GAINES *and* SCRAGG, *followed by* CATO, *right*)

DR. GAINES Gentlemen, I am in pursuit of two valuable slaves, and I will pay five hundred dollars for their arrest. (*exit* MR. WHITE, *left*)
FIRST LOUNGER I'll bet a picayune that your niggers have been stolen by that cussed feller from Massachusetts. Don't you see he's gone?
DR. GAINES Where is the man? If I can lay my hands on him, he'll never steal another nigger. Where is the scoundrel?
FIRST LOUNGER Let's go after the feller. I'll go with you. Come, foller me. (*exit all, left, except* CATO *and the* WAITER)
CATO Why don't you bring in massa's saddle-bags? What de debil you standin' dar for? You common country niggers don't know nuffin', no how. Go an' get massa's saddle-bags and bring 'em in. (*exit* SERVANT, *right*) By golly! ebry body's gone, an' de bar-keeper too. I'll tend de bar myself now; an' de fuss gemman I waits on will be dis gemman of color. (*goes behind the counter, and drinks*) Ah, dis is de stuff fer me; it makes my head swim; it makes me happy right off. I'll take a little more.

(*Enter* BARKEEPER, *left*)

BARKEEPER What are you doing behind the bar, you black cuss?
CATO I is lookin' for massa's saddle-bags, sir. Is dey here?
BARKEEPER But what were you drinking there?
CATO Me drinkin'! Why, massa, you muss be mistaken. I ain't drink nuffin'.
BARKEEPER You infernal whelp, to stand there and lie in that way!
CATO Oh, yes, seer, I did tase dat coffee in dat bottle; dat's all I did.

(*Enter* MR. WHITE, *left, excited*)

MR. WHITE I say, sir, is there no place of concealment in your house? They are after me, and my life is in danger. Say, sir, can't you hide me away?

BARKEEPER Well, you ought to hold your tongue when you come into our State.

MR. WHITE But, sir, the Constitution gives me the right to speak my sentiments, at all times and in all places.

BARKEEPER We don't care for Constitutions nor nothin' else. We made the Constitution, and we'll break it. But you had better hide away; they are coming, and they'll lynch you, that they will. Come with me; I'll hide you in the cellar. Foller me. (*exit* BARKEEPER *and* WHITE, *left*)

(*Enter the mob, right*)

DR. GAINES If I can once lay my hands on that scoundrel, I'll blow a hole through his head.

JENNINGS Yes, I say so too; for no one knows whose niggers are safe, now-a-days. I must look after my niggers. Who is that I see in the distance? I believe it's that cussed Massachusetts feller. Come, let's go after him. (*exit the mob, right*)

Scene Two

(*Forest at night. Enter* GLEN *and* MELINDA, *right*)

MELINDA I am so tired and hungry, that I cannot go further. It is so cloudy that we cannot see the North Star, and therefore cannot tell whether we are going to Canada, or further South. Let's sit down here.

GLEN I know that we cannot see the North Star, Melinda, and I fear we've lost our way. But, see! the clouds are passing away, and it'll soon be clear. See! yonder is a star; yonder is another and another. Ah! yonder is the North Star, and we are safe!

> Star of the North! though night winds drift
>   The fleecy drapery of the sky
> Between thy lamp and me, I lift,
>   Yea, lift with hope my sleepless eye,
> To the blue heights wherein thou dwellest,
> And of a land of freedom tellest.
>
> Star of the North! while blazing day
>   Pours round me its full tide of light,
> And hides thy pale but faithful ray,
>   I, too, lie hid, and long for night:
> For night: I dare not walk at noon,
> Nor dare I trust the faithless moon—
>
> Nor faithless man, whose burning lust
>   For gold hath riveted my chain,—
> Nor other leader can I trust
>   But thee, of even the starry train;
> For all the host around thee burning,
> Like faithless man, keep turning, turning.
>
> I may not follow where they go:—
>   Star of the North! I look to thee
> While on I press; for well I know,
>   Thy light and truth shall set me free:—
> Thy light, that no poor slave deceiveth;
> Thy truth, that all my soul believeth.
>
> Thy beam is on the glassy breast
>   Of the still spring, upon whose brink
> I lay my weary limbs to rest,
>   And bow my parching lips to drink.
> Guide of the friendless negro's way,
> I bless thee for this quiet ray!
>
> In the dark top of southern pines
>   I nestled, when the Driver's horn
> Called to the field, in lengthening lines,
>   My fellows, at the break of morn.
> And there I lay till thy sweet face
> Looked in upon "my hiding place."
>
> The tangled cane-brake, where I crept
>   For shelter from the heat of noon,
> And where, while others toiled, I slept,
>   Till wakened by the rising moon,
> As its stalks felt the night wind free,
> Gave me to catch a glimpse of thee.
>
> Star of the North! in bright array
>   The constellations round thee sweep,
> Each holding on its nightly way,
>   Rising, or sinking in the deep,
> And, as it hangs in mid heaven flaming,
> The homage of some nation claiming.
>
> *This* nation to the Eagle cowers;
>   Fit ensign! she's a bird of spoil:—
> Like worships like! for each devours
>   The earnings of another's toil.
> I've felt her talons and her beak,
> And now the gentler Lion seek.
>
> The Lion, at the Monarch's feet
>   Crouches, and lays his mighty paw
> Into her lap!—an emblem meet
>   Of England's Queen, and English law:
> Queen, that hath made her Islands free!
> Law, that holds out its shield to me!
>
> Star of the North! upon that shield
>   Thou shinest,—Oh, for ever shine!
> The negro, from the cotton field
>   Shall, then, beneath its orb recline,
> And feed the Lion, crouched before it,
> Nor heed the Eagle, screaming o'er it!

The Escape; or, A Leap for Freedom

With the thoughts of servitude behind us, and the North Star before us, we will go forward with cheerful hearts. Come, Melinda, let's go on. (*exit, left*)

Scene Three

(*A street. Enter* MR. WHITE, *right*)

MR. WHITE I am glad to be once more in a free State. If I am caught again south of Mason and Dixon's line, I'll give them leave to lynch me. I came near losing my life. This is the way our constitutional rights are trampled upon. But what care these men about Constitutions, or anything else that does not suit them? But I must hasten on. (*exit, left*)

(*Enter* CATO, *in disguise, right*)

CATO I wonder if dis is me? By golly, I is free as a frog. But maybe I is mistaken; maybe dis ain't me. Cato, is dis you? Yes, seer. Well, now it is me, an' I em a free man. But, stop! I muss change my name, kase ole massa might foller me, and somebody might tell him dat dey seed Cato; so I'll change my name, and den he won't know me ef he sees me. Now, what shall I call myself? I'm now in a suspectable part of de country, an' I muss have a suspectable name. Ah! I'll call myself Alexander Washington Napoleon Pompey Cæsar. Dar, now, dat's a good long, suspectable name, and everybody will suspect me. Let me see; I wonder ef I can't make up a song on my escape? I'll try.

AIR—"*Dearest Mae*"

Now, freemen, listen to my song, a story I'll relate,
It happened in de valley of de ole Kentucky State:
Dey marched me out into de fiel', at every break of day,
And work me dar till late sunset, widout a cent of pay.

Dey work me all de day,
Widout a bit of pay,
And thought, because dey fed me well,
I would not run away.

Massa gave me his ole coat, an' thought I'd happy be,
But I had my eye on de North Star, an' thought of liberty;
Ole massa lock de door, an' den he went to sleep,
I dress myself in his bess clothes, an' jump into de street.

CHORUS
Dey work me all de day,
Widout a bit of pay,
So I took my flight, in the middle of de night,
When de sun was gone away.

Sed I, dis chile's a freeman now, he'll be a slave no more;
I travell'd faster all dat night, dan I ever did before.
I came up to a farmer's house, jest at de break of day,
And saw a white man standin' dar, sed he, "You are a runaway."
CHORUS

I tole him I had left de whip, an' bayin' of de hound,
To find a place where man is man, ef sich dar can be found;
Dat I had heard, in Canada, dat all mankind are free,
An' dat I was going dar in search of liberty.
CHORUS

I've not committed any crime, why should I run away?
Oh! shame upon your laws, dat drive me off to Canada.
You loudly boast of liberty, an' say your State is free,
But ef I tarry in your midst, will you protect me?
CHORUS

Scene Four

(*Dining-room.—table spread.* MRS. NEAL *and* CHARLOTTE)

MRS. NEAL Thee may put the tea to draw, Charlotte. Thy father will be in soon, and we must have breakfast. (*enter* MR. NEAL, *left*) I think, Simeon, it is time those people were called. Thee knows that they may be pursued, and we ought not to detain them long here.

MR. NEAL Yes, Ruth, thou art right. Go, Charlotte, and knock on their chamber door, and tell them that breakfast is ready. (*exit* CHARLOTTE, *right*)

MRS. NEAL Poor creatures! I hope they'll reach Canada in safety. They seem to be worthy persons.

(*Enter* CHARLOTTE, *right*)

CHARLOTTE I've called them, mother, and they'll soon be down. I'll put the breakfast on the table.

(*Enter* NEIGHBOR JONES, *left*)

Mr. NEAL Good morning, James. Thee has

heard, I presume, that we have two very interesting persons in the house?

JONES Yes, I heard that you had two fugitives by the Underground road, last night; and I've come over to fight for them, if any persons come to take them back.

(*Enter* THOMAS, *right*)

MR. NEAL Go, Thomas, and harness up the horses and put them to the covered wagon, and be ready to take these people on, as soon as they get their breakfast. Go, Thomas, and hurry thyself. (*exit* THOMAS, *right*) And so thee wants to fight, this morning, James?

JONES Yes; as you belongs to a society that don't believe in fighting, and I does believe in that sort of thing, I thought I'd come and relieve you of that work, if there is any to be done.

(*Enter* GLEN *and* MELINDA, *right*)

MR. NEAL Good morning, friends. I hope thee rested well, last night.

MRS. NEAL Yes, I hope thee had a good night's rest.

GLEN I thank you, madam, we did.

MR. NEAL I'll introduce thee to our neighbor, James Jones. He's a staunch friend of thy people.

JONES I am glad to see you. I've come over to render assistance, if any is needed.

MRS. NEAL Come, friends, take seats at the table. (*to* GLEN *and* MELINDA) Thee'll take seats there. (*all take seats at the table*) Does thee take sugar and milk in thy tea?

MELINDA I thank you, we do.

JONES I'll look at your *Tribune*, Uncle Simeon, while you're eating.

MR. NEAL Thee'll find it on the table.

MRS. NEAL I presume thee's anxious to get to thy journey's end?

GLEN Yes, madam, we are. I am told that we are not safe in any of the free States.

MR. NEAL I am sorry to tell thee, that that is too true. Thee will not be safe until thee gets on British soil. I wonder what keeps Thomas; he should have been here with the team.

(*Enter* THOMAS, *left*)

THOMAS All's ready; and I've written the prettiest song that was ever sung. I call it "The Underground Railroad."

MR. NEAL Thomas, thee can eat thy breakfast far better than thee can write a song, as thee calls it. Thee must hurry thyself, when I send thee for the horses, Thomas. Here lately, thee takes thy time.

THOMAS Well, you see I've been writing poetry; that's the reason I've been so long. If you wish it, I'll sing it to you.

JONES Do let us hear the song.

MRS. NEAL Yes, if Thomas has written a ditty, do let us hear it.

MR. NEAL Well, Thomas, if thee has a ditty, thee may recite it to us.

THOMAS Well, I'll give it to you. Remember that I call it, "The Underground Railroad."

AIR—"*Wait for the Wagon*"

Oh, where is the invention
  Of this growing age,
Claiming the attention
  Of statesman, priest, or sage,
In the many railways
  Through the nation found,
Equal to the Yankees'
  Railway under-ground?

CHORUS
No one hears the whistle,
  Or rolling of the cars,
While negroes ride to freedom
  Beyond the stripes and stars.

On the Southern borders
  Are the Railway stations,
Negroes get free orders
  While on the plantations;
For all, of ev'ry color,
  First-class cars are found,
While they ride to freedom
  By Railway under-ground.
CHORUS

Masters in the morning
  Furiously rage,
Cursing the inventions
  Of this knowing age;
Order out the bloodhounds,
  Swear they'll bring them back,
Dogs return exhausted,
  Cannot find the track.
CHORUS

Travel is increasing,
  Build a double track,
Cars and engines wanted,
  They'll come, we have no lack.
Clear the track of loafers,
  See that crowded car!
Thousands passing yearly,
  Stock is more than par.
CHORUS

JONES Well done! That's a good song. I'd like to have a copy of them verses. (*knock at the door.* CHARLOTTE *goes to the door, and returns.* Enter CATO, *left, still in disguise*)

MR. NEAL Who is this we have? Another of the outcasts, I presume?

CATO Yes, seer; I is gwine to Canada, an' I met a man, an' he tole me dat you would give me some wittals an' help me on de way. By golly! ef dar ain't Glen an' Melinda. Dey don't know me in dese fine clothes. (*goes up to them*) Ah, chillen! I is one wid you. I golly, I is here too! (*they shake hands*)

GLEN Why, it is Cato, as I live!

MELINDA Oh, Cato, I am so glad to see you! But how did you get here?

CATO Ah, chile, I come wid ole massa to hunt you; an' you see I get tired huntin' you, an' I am now huntin' for Canada. I leff de ole boss in de bed at de hotel; an' you see I thought, afore I left massa, I'd jess change clothes wid him; so, you see, I is fixed up,—ha, ha, ha. Ah, chillen! I is gwine wid you.

MRS. NEAL Come, sit thee down, and have some breakfast.

CATO Tank you, madam, I'll do dat. (*sits down and eats*)

MR. NEAL This is pleasant for thee to meet one of thy friends.

GLEN Yes, sir, it is; I would be glad if we could meet more of them. I have a mother and sister still in slavery, and I would give worlds, if I possessed them if by so doing I could release them from their bondage.

THOMAS We are all ready, sir, and the wagon is waiting.

MRS. NEAL Yes, thee had better start.

CATO Ef anybody tries to take me back to ole massa, I'll pull ebry toof out of dar heads, dat I will! As soon as I get to Canada, I'll set up a doctor shop, an' won't I be poplar? Den I rec'on I will. I'll pull teef fer all de people in Canada. Oh, how I wish I had Hannah wid me! It makes me feel bad when I tink I ain't a-gwine to see my wife no more. But, come, chillen, let's be makin' tracks. Dey say we is most to de British side.

MR. NEAL Yes, a few miles further, and you'll be safe beyond the reach of the Fugitive-Slave Law.

CATO Ah, dat's de talk fer dis chile. (*exit, center*)

Scene Five

(*The Niagara River—a ferry.* FERRYMAN, *fastening his small boat*)

FERRYMAN (*advancing, takes out his watch*) I swan, if it ain't one o'clock. I thought it was dinner time. Now there's no one here, I'll go to dinner, and if anybody comes, they can wait until I return. I'll go at once. (*exit, left*)

(*Enter* MR. WHITE, *right, with an umbrella*)

MR. WHITE I wonder where that ferryman is? I want to cross to Canada. It seems a little showery, or else the mist from the Falls is growing thicker. (*takes out his sketch-book and pencils,—sketches*)

(*Enter* CANE PEDLAR, *right*)

PEDLAR Want a good cane today, sir? Here's one from Goat Island,—very good, sir,—straight and neat,—only one dollar. I've a wife and nine small children,—youngest is nursing, and the oldest only three years old. Here's a cane from Table Rock, sir. Please buy one! I've had no breakfast today. My wife's got the rheumatics, and the children's got the measles. Come, sir, do buy a cane! I've a lame shoulder, and can't work.

MR. WHITE Will you stop your confounded talk, and let me alone? Don't you see that I am sketching? You've spoiled a beautiful scene for me, with your nonsense.

(*Enter* SECOND PEDLAR, *right*)

SECOND PEDLAR Want any bead bags, or money purses? These are all real Ingen bags, made by the Black Hawk Ingens. Here's a pretty bag, sir, only 75 cents. Here's a money purse, 50 cents. Please, sir, buy something! My wife's got the fever and ague, and the house is full of children, and they're all sick. Come, sir, do help a worthy man!

MR. WHITE Will you hold your tongue? You've spoiled some of the finest pictures in the world. Don't you see that I am sketching? (*exit* PEDLARS, *right, grumbling*) I am glad those fellows have gone; now I'll go a little further up the shore, and see if I can find another boat. I want to get over. (*exit, left*)

(*Enter* DR. GAINES, SCRAGG, *and an* OFFICER)

OFFICER I don't think that your slaves have

crossed yet, and my officers will watch the shore below here, while we stroll up the river. If I once get my hands on them all the Abolitionists in the State shall not take them from me.

DR. GAINES I hope they have not got over, for I would not lose them for two thousand dollars, especially the gal.

(*Enter* FIRST PEDLAR)

PEDLAR Wish to get a good cane, sir? This stick was cut on the very spot where Sam Patch jumped over the falls. Only 50 cents. I have a sick wife and thirteen children. Please buy a cane; I ain't had no dinner.

OFFICER Get out of the way! Gentlemen, we'll go up the shore. (*exit, left*)

(*Enter* CATO, *right*)

CATO I is loss fum de cumpny, but dis is de ferry, and I spec dey'll soon come. But didn't we have a good time las' night in Buffalo? Dem dar Buffalo gals make my heart flutter, dat dey did. But, tanks be to de Lord, I is got religion. I got it las' night in de meetin.' Before I got religion, I was a great sinner; I got drunk, an' took de name of de Lord in vain. But now I is a conwerted man; I is bound for hebben; I toats de witness in my bosom; I feel dat my name is rote in de book of life. But dem niggers in de Vine Street Church las' night shout an' make sich a fuss, dey give me de headache. But, tank de Lord, I is got religion, an' now I'll be a preacher, and den dey'll call me de Rev. Alexander Washinton Napoleon Pompey Cæsar. Now I'll preach and pull teef, bofe at de same time. Oh, how I wish I had Hannah wid me! Cuss ole massa, fer ef it warn't for him, I could have my wife wid me. Ef I hadn't religion, I'd say "Damn ole massa!" but as I is a religious man, an' belongs to de church, I won't say no sich a thing. But who is dat I see comin'? Oh, it's a whole heap of people. Good Lord! what is de matter?

(*Enter* GLEN *and* MELINDA, *left, followed by* OFFICERS)

GLEN Let them come; I am ready for them. He that lays hands on me or my wife shall feel the weight of this club.

MELINDA Oh, Glen, let's die here, rather than again go into slavery.

OFFICER I am the United States Marshal. I have a warrant from the Commissioner to take you, and bring you before him. I command assistance.

(*Enter* DR. GAINES, SCRAGG, *and* OFFICER, *right*)

DR. GAINES Here they are. Down with the villain! down with him! but don't hurt the gal!

(*Enter* MR. WHITE, *right*)

MR. WHITE Why, bless me! these are the slaveholding fellows. I'll fight for freedom! (*takes hold of his umbrella with both hands.— The fight commences, in which* GLEN, CATO, DR. GAINES, SCRAGG, WHITE, *and the* OFFICERS, *take part.—*FERRYMAN *enters, and runs to his boat.—* DR. GAINES, SCRAGG *and the* OFFICERS *are knocked down,* GLEN, MELINDA *and* CATO *jump into the boat, and as it leaves the shore and floats away,* GLEN *and* CATO *wave their hats, and shout loudly for freedom.—Curtain falls*)

2

Yes We Must, Yes We Can

Joseph S. Cotter, Sr. Garland Anderson

It is no accident that the two plays in this section were written by self-made men. Each man was responsible for himself by the age of eleven. Each had less than four years of school. Each was driven to write a play in order to espouse a personal philosophy that can be traced to Booker T. Washington, although twenty-five years separated the two plays. Each believed that hard work plus initiative equals success. And for these men, it did.

The work ethic has received continuous enunciation, from the essays of Thomas Carlyle to those of Ayn Rand. The belief in individual initiative and rugged individualism was institutionalized in the Declaration of Independence and in the Constitution, was credited with "taming" the new continent, and was part of the American Dream. One of the nineteenth-century exponents of individualism was Elbert Hubbard, who in 1898 wrote in his pamphlet *Message to Garcia* (40 million copies sold): "The world bestows its big prizes both in money and honors, for but one thing, and that is Initiative. What is Initiative? I'll tell you: It is doing the right thing without being told."

An Andrew Carnegie did not need to be told why he should work. God and Herbert Spenser knew that it was a clear case of survival of the fittest.

In this atmosphere of unopposed capitalism it is not surprising to find American black men who believed they could do whatever they set their hearts to. The long list of "He was the first Negro to . . ." is witness not only to America's racism but to the individual initiative of men like Joseph S. Cotter, Sr. and Garland Anderson. Both men were heavily influenced by Booker T. Washington, but at the same time they express the general American optimism of "Yes, I Can!" It is in reference to their time that they should be judged, and for the dues they paid.

Joseph S. Cotter, Sr. (1861–194?)

Caleb the Degenerate

1901

The close of the nineteenth century saw a cocky white America. The Spanish had been defeated with the easy bravado of William Randolph Hearst and Teddy Roosevelt. Andrew Carnegie proved that a poor boy with God on his side could produce *The Gospel of Wealth*. The Wright brothers took to wings at Kitty Hawk. In the Gay Nineties the Supreme Court declared the Separate but Equal Doctrine of education. A decade later the newly founded NAACP totalled the annual number of lynchings by hanging, shooting, burning, drowning, beating, and cutting at more than 100 per year. As a climax to these murders, the Reverend Thomas Dixon published his Christian defense of the KKK in a novel, *The Clansman*, which was made into a play and finally into a popular film, *The Birth of a Nation*.

In this milieu Booker T. Washington sought ways to prevent the complete social, political and economic reenslavement of the Negro people. His method was not militancy but accommodation. He reassured white southerners that "Your families will be surrounded by the most patient, faithful, law-abiding and unresentful people that the world has seen." The means toward creating these "unresentful people" was to be Industrial Education: "the very best service is to teach the present generation to provide a material or industrial foundation. On such a foundation will grow habits of thrift, a love of work, economy, ownership of property, bank accounts."

One of Dr. Washington's disciples, Joseph S. Cotter, addressed a poem to his master entitled "Dr. Booker T. Washington to the National Negro Business League."

> What deeds have sprung from plow and pick!
> What bank-rolls from tomatoes.
> No dainty crop of rhetoric
> Can match one of potatoes.

Born in 1861 in Bardstown, Kentucky (where Stephen Foster wrote some of his minstrel melodies), young Joseph Cotter was reputed to be reading at four years of age. He did not go to school, but from age ten to age twenty-two labored in brickyards and as a teamster on the levee. Then in a burst of ten short months he put himself through night school and became a teacher. He published his first book in 1901, at his own expense. He was then the father of six-year-old Joseph, Jr., who later was to become a recognized poet in his own right.

In the tradition of many self-made men, Joseph Cotter, Sr. gave over much of his writing to urging others to emulate his own success. The first of "The Negro's Ten Commandments," he wrote, is "Thy fathers' God forsake not and thy manhood debase not, and thou shalt cease to say 'I am a Negro, therefore I cannot.'" And toward this end he published poems, stories and, in 1901, one full-length play: *Caleb, the Degenerate: A Study of the Types, Customs, and Needs of the American Negro*.

Caleb, the main character, is a degenerate and a villain by the standards of 1900. He sells his father's corpse to medical students; he pushes his mother to her death; he smokes, drinks, bullies, lies, steals, and takes cocaine. He raves against God and church:

> They rather worship God whose cruel laws
> are made up wholly of mistakes and flaws.
> The time shall be when they will cease to follow
> Views that are so disgusting and so hollow.
> Let blinded Christians, ere they think or stir,
> Confer with me, their great philosopher.

Caleb's philosophy is to vehemently spurn the Establishment in all its aspects. There is something in his perpetual anger, his bitter wit, his hopelessly destructive life, that makes him a rebel in the modern sense—much as Johnny Williams in *No Place To Be Somebody* becomes a hero as antihero.

Opposed to Caleb's satanic nature are the Bishop, his stepdaughter, Olivia, and the faculty and children of the Industrial School. These "good Negroes" represent the true course the race is to take—learn a trade, save money, be Christian, and don't get involved in any Back-to-Our-African-Homeland movements. From this simplistic interpretation, it is no wonder that most critics—among those who have bothered to read the play—have not many good words to say for it.

They attack Mr Cotter's verse: "It is dull in the writing," says Fannin S. Belcher, Jr., "chaotic in treatment and unactable" (Ph.D. dissertation, Yale University, 1945). They attack Cotter's characters: "*Caleb* . . . is filled with unbelievable characters spouting incredible lines. There is no moment when they touch reality," comments Doris Abramson.

When the play has been praised, it is often in a tone of condescension. Alfred Austin, poet laureate of England, responded by letter when the play was sent to him: "It affords yet further evidence of the latent capacity of your long maltreated race for mental development." Author Israel Zangwill did not manage much better: "I do not profess to understand it all, but I desire to express my appreciation of the passages of true poetry in which you express the aspirations of the Negro race for salvation by labor."

Before these evaluations are accepted, a question needs to be answered: what audience was Mr. Cotter writing for? Was he simply showing his black brothers a pathway toward economic salvation? Was he showing his white brothers that they need not fear the black man? Finally, was Mr. Cotter writing two plays, an overt and a covert one?

The answer to all these questions is "Yes." Yes, Mr. Cotter is urging the black man to follow Dr. Washington's work ethic. As has been suggested, the race virulence of America was at a crest in Cotter's time. Solutions for survival had to be found. Yes, the play was written with an eye to the white reader. The preface to the play was composed by Thomas Watkins, financial editor of the Louisville *Courier-Journal*, who wrote, "The author is one of a race that has given scarcely anything of literature to the world." How pleased Mr. Watkins must have been to help a good nigra. But although the surface features of the play were meant for the white and black readers who already believed, there is a subsurface that commands the attention of those aware of the black experience.

The failure of the critics to find much merit in *Caleb* is a failure to recognize this subsurface of black experience, a powerful intensity created out of Joseph Cotter's own growing up in America. Nowhere is this intensity greater than in the character of Caleb.

For the reader who is attracted by the emotional drive of Caleb, it is intriguing to note the author's belated attempt in the fourth act to explain Caleb's degeneracy by shifting the blame to another man.

DOCTOR . . . His mother sinned ere he was born. This tainted him, therefore his wicked course.

BISHOP No! No! She did not sin. Caleb was led To that belief.

DOCTOR Was led?

BISHOP Rahab's the man!

The blame is Rahab's, but the motivation for the crime has only been pushed back, not explained. The nature of the "mother's sin" is not clear. Ten years later, Mr. Cotter made it more explicit when he published a collection of short stories. The lead story is entitled "Caleb," and follows the plot of the play in many respects—except that the mother and father of Caleb were married twice: once before and once after emancipation (the slave marriage presumably was not sanctified by church and state). Caleb was born between the marriages, ergo a bastard. When Caleb learns this in the story, he strikes his father "violently over the heart." The father falls dead.

This story of patricide is followed by a tale entitled "Rodney." Mr. Cotter writes:

Rodney was an illegitimate child. He knew not what this meant, but the sting of it embittered his young life.

The Negro has as much prejudice as the white man. Under like conditions the Negro would make the same laws against the white. This crept out in the treatment of Rodney. His worst enemies were always Negroes. The Anglo-Saxon blood in his veins made scoffers of some and demons of others.

To be pitied is the boy who has never framed the

word "father" upon his lips. Rodney attempted it once, but failed, and never tried again. He stood before his father bareheaded and with the coveted word on his lips.

"You have a fine head of hair," said the father.

"That's what people say." replied Rodney.

"Are you proud of it?"

"Should I be, Sir?"

"Well, my little man, it's a disgrace to you."

This was the first and last meeting of Rodney and his father. Joseph Cotter himself was the bastard son of a black mother and her "employer," a Scotch-Irishman, "a prominent citizen of Louisville." The fact that young Joseph was not sent to school but put to menial work at the age of ten suggests that the "prominent citizen" did not rejoice in his Negro son. It is fair to speculate that Cotter's black experience as the bastard black son of a white father speaks through both Rodney and Caleb.

There are three fathers in the play: Grandison, who is dead when the play opens; the Bishop, Olivia's adopted father, a man who has a lecherous itch for his ward; and Noah, whose beard Caleb pulls out. Speeches are given over to the value of mother love, but no praises are given to fathers—nor is one ever allowed to merit praise. The Industrial School is saved by Olivia. Joseph Cotter hated his Anglo-Saxon father, and by extension, the country he attempts to praise in act three. A comparison of the Old Man's speeches, as he urges his followers to leave "a country that is one ignoble grave," with those of the Bishop, who is defending America as a paradise, makes the latter appear vacuous. The Back-to-Our-African-Homeland section is powerful. It is of small consequence that the Old Man is slipped into the final tableau to show that he has acquiesced to the Bishop's America.

In his own preface to the play, the author states: "The Negro needs very little politics, much industrial training, and a dogged settledness as far as going to Africa is concerned. To this should be added clean, intelligent fireside leadership. Much of any other kind is dangerous for the present. I am a Negro and speak from experience."

This is hardly a denunciation of those who wish to return to Africa. Militancy is not rejected: it is rejected "only for the present."

How much Mr. Cotter is aware of his own dual attitude regarding white America must be left to the reader—with one final hint. What is the real allegory of the scene in act two between the Bishop, Olivia, and the ministers? Is this a "realistic" scene, or did Mr. Cotter write a surrealistic scene of associative visual and aural images? If the scene were transferred to *Alice in Wonderland* (and it could easily be done), would it not become "significant?"

Perhaps the case that the author was consciously disguising his material can never be proved. Indeed, it may not be possible to show that some of the best scenes of the play sprang "unintended" from his unconscious. However, a fair and sensitive reading will reveal that Joseph Cotter is a black man whose total being is writing out the anguish of his life. It may be enough that he saw early that for the black man to have power he must own the means of distribution and production. And perhaps the fairytale ending was Mr. Cotter's final note of satire on what might be expected from the great white fathers.

Caleb, the Degenerate: A Study of the Types, Customs, and Needs of the American Negro

CAST OF CHARACTERS

(all are American Negroes)

THE BISHOP, *adopted father to Olivia*
NOAH, *father to Olivia*
CALEB, *son to Patsy and Grandison*
GRANDISON
RAHAB, *a minister, politician, and teacher to Caleb*
UNDERTAKER
DOCTOR
HIRED MAN
DUDE
OLIVIA
FRONY, *friend to Olivia*
PATSY
A WAIF
A WOMAN
NEIGHBORS, MINISTERS, OFFICERS, CANDIDATES FOR AFRICA, MEDICAL STUDENTS, BOYS AND GIRLS OF INDUSTRIAL SCHOOL.

ACT ONE

Scene One

(*Hall in the* BISHOP's *house. Enter* OLIVIA, *playing a violin. The* BISHOP *follows quickly and seizes the bow*)

BISHOP   Reflect, my child, reflect! You should not wed
This Caleb, this hell-builder upon earth.
You counsel well when others are in need.
Yourself you counsel not, or in such wise
Your steps are led not heavenward. No! No!
At times your thoughts have made mine error-proof.
Your views, thrice wedded to occasion, raise
The neighborhood above its ancient self.
Yourself you counsel not. My child, reflect!

(*She begins to play, but stops when he goes on*)

My darling Margaret is still in mind.
That night! That night! 'T is day, but here it is.
The rain, the thunder, and the lightning's flash,
The twisted timbers and the flooded streams,
The cattle's lowing and the horses' neigh,
Come back to me. I stand beside her bed,
My Margaret's bed. The storm disturbs me not;
For Margaret, my darling Margaret,
Is eying me and whispering my name.
She shall be mine again! Disease's hold
Is lessening. She shall be mine again!
Strength comes! She rises, staggers to the door;
And, ere I am aware of what she means,
Darts out into the storm. I follow her!
"My Margaret! My Margaret!" I cry.
"Health! Health! I go to health!" she answers me.
I cannot see. I feel my way about.
The lightning's angry flashing shows her form.
"My Margaret! My Margaret!" I cry.
"'T is health! 'T is health!" cries back my Margaret.

Caleb the Degenerate

I blunder on and on. The day has come,
And dead and mangled lies my Margaret.
I have one more. 'T is you, Olivia!
You wed a brute, my child?

OLIVIA   Caleb's the man!

(*exit, playing softly*)

BISHOP My child, come back! Storms! Lightning! Plague! Come back!
Better be dead with these—Come back! Come back!—
Than living death with Caleb! Child, come back!

OLIVIA (*without*) What profits it? A child is never grown.

(*she breaks chord on violin*)

A broken chord! Chords break so easily.

(*Enter* FRONY)

BISHOP Frony!
FRONY You have the news?
BISHOP Frony, what news?
FRONY Rahab and Caleb met two nights ago.
BISHOP The Devil's peace-making is God's despair.
Rahab was preaching nonsense, was he not?
FRONY He dealt in facts and logic, strange to say.
BISHOP His prayers?
FRONY His prayers! They change with changeless things.
BISHOP He prays them full; then kills them with amen.
He preached in praise of Caleb's evil deeds?
FRONY He rated him at what he's really worth.
BISHOP As enemies they hold each other now.
I took it that the meeting made them friends.
FRONY It did.
BISHOP You may explain. I wait to learn.
FRONY "You are my subject, Caleb!" Rahab said.
"I see you sailing, sailing, sailing round Perdition—begging, begging to be damned!
Tarry no longer! Hear the preached word!
Tarry no longer, lest the brink be passed!
Be saved! Be saved! Polluted man, be saved!"
BISHOP Friends after that?
FRONY Listen! Some more remains!
BISHOP (*he hears violin. Aside*) I listen! Child! My child!

(*music stops*)

Go on! I hear!
FRONY "Be saved?" asked Caleb. "Let us both be saved.
You drunkard, gambler, hidden libertine!"
A look! Three steps! A clinch! A fall! A groan!
Caleb was victor! Rahab raised him up,
Grasped Caleb's hand and said: "We must be friends!"
BISHOP 'Tis strange!
FRONY 'Tis true!
BISHOP The end of it?
FRONY Murder!
BISHOP Which killed the other?
FRONY Caleb—
BISHOP A murderer?
FRONY What else? A saint?
BISHOP This Rahab lived too long.
FRONY You understand?
BISHOP I do!
FRONY Rahab's alive.
BISHOP I do not understand. Explain! Explain!
FRONY Grandison's dead!
BISHOP A horse's kick, or bite?
I often cautioned him of silly risks.
FRONY You understand?
BISHOP Do I?
FRONY 'Twas Caleb's hand That slew his father.
BISHOP Daughter! Daughter! Come! Caleb's a parricide! Come! Come! Come! Come!

(*re-enter* OLIVIA)

OLIVIA Caleb's the man, Bishop!
BISHOP He is the—the—
(*to* FRONY) You saw. Tell how it was.
FRONY His course was wrong.
BISHOP His father chided?
OLIVIA Fathers love to chide!
BISHOP Give us the full of it! (*to* OLIVIA) Listen! Profit!

FRONY Sharp words! Hard blows! A dead man's stare to heaven!

(BISHOP *breathes hard, staggers and starts to go*)

OLIVIA Bishop! (*she looks pale and staggers toward him*)
FRONY Olivia! (*takes hold of* OLIVIA)
BISHOP (*in a rage*) Caleb's the man!
FRONY Your daughter, sir!
BISHOP (*pathetically*) My daughter is in love! She needs no father.
OLIVIA (*she starts to him*) Bishop!
BISHOP (*holds hand to heart*) Parricide! I go! Your father may return with me. (*exit slowly*)
FRONY To see how woman's wit can cudgel man's?
(*to* OLIVIA) The Bishop's wrath—
OLIVIA The Bishop's wrath is his.
FRONY This Caleb is—
OLIVIA Not here to damn you back.
FRONY Is this a case of love?
OLIVIA How worketh love?
FRONY I know it well, and know it not at all.
OLIVIA Let each explain the other's ignorance.
FRONY It were a nobler task than wedding brutes.
OLIVIA A woman you?
FRONY (*surprised*) Why, yes!
OLIVIA Have loved a man?
FRONY Well—yes! (*this reservedly*)
OLIVIA Have had an only son?
FRONY (*sorrowfully*) Yes! yes!

(Re-enter BISHOP *with* NOAH, *unseen*)

OLIVIA How many women may undo one's son?
FRONY Mine was so marred by one and dragged to death.
OLIVIA One kills his body! Two may save his soul! Patsy and I—
FRONY Advance you on defeat!

(*On seeing the* BISHOP *and* NOAH *they examine and measure their hands*)

NOAH I see.
BISHOP What now?
NOAH A word perchance—
BISHOP (*faint heartedly*) Perchance A word.
NOAH Occasion's ripe.
BISHOP Not for success.
NOAH See you clearly?
BISHOP Clearly enough. Know you I've dealt with women!
NOAH Think you more than I?
BISHOP The case is ours. You may conduct affairs.
NOAH Go on! Go on!
BISHOP My way?
NOAH Well—yes—your way.
OLIVIA The way of hands—well—yes—the way of hands—
FRONY Go on! Go on! We'll measure them again.

(FRONY *measures her own hands and then compares her foot with* OLIVIA'*s.* OLIVIA *looks at* BISHOP)

BISHOP I'll see this Caleb in his mother's house.
NOAH You'll see a buzzard wooing God's elect; A serpent strangling love and fanging peace.
BISHOP 'Twill be an argument that I can use. On now to Patsy's. Grandison lies dead. We'll soothe the mother while we watch the son.
NOAH The plan is good. Let's hasten. Come you on.

(*He goes out quickly and motions the* BISHOP *to follow.* OLIVIA *has been watching the* BISHOP *earnestly. She looks down and sees* FRONY *comparing their feet.* FRONY *touches* OLIVIA'*s foot with hers*)

FRONY A healthy foot! Mine's smaller. Think you so?
OLIVIA Unfair, Frony! Ours is a game of hands.

(*The* BISHOP *bows as he calls their names. They bow in return*)

BISHOP Frony!
FRONY Bishop!
BISHOP Olivia!
OLIVIA Bishop!

(*The* BISHOP *goes out slowly, bowing to one and then to the other*)

FRONY (*sarcastically*) Lover! Buzzard! Serpent! Caleb's the man?

OLIVIA A woman loves—
FRONY   A buzzard?
OLIVIA   May be so.

(FRONY *snaps her fingers*)

 Caleb's the man! All things combine to show
 His viciousness and prove that he is low.
 Caleb's the man! The world's experience
 Says: "Trust no man who throttles innocence!"

(*Exit* FRONY. *Curtain rises on the next scene as* OLIVIA *goes out*)

Scene Two

(*A room in* PATSY's *cottage. One door leads to yard from end of room. At other end steps lead to room where* GRANDISON *lies dead. In rear is a long, high window. Two chairs and table are in room. Poverty is stamped on all*)

(*Enter* RAHAB *from death-chamber. He is followed closely by* FRONY. PATSY's *groans come from room. He walks around room, turns pages of Bible for text.* FRONY *follows and looks over his shoulder*)

RAHAB Grandison's death is no ill-wind to me.
 I'll preach his funeral. 'Twill open ways
 Whereby I may regain a step or two.
 Here is a text that suits the subject well.

(*He reads aloud*)

 "Man born of woman is of few days and—"

FRONY A skunk like you should preach no funeral.
RAHAB Why? Why? I am a minister! Now, why?
FRONY You are a scamp, a thief, a devil! a—!

(NOAH *and the* BISHOP *enter hurriedly from yard.* RAHAB, *seeing the* BISHOP, *runs to chair, sits and turns up coat-collar to hide his face*)

BISHOP Frony, we come! Does Patsy bear it well?
FRONY She does! She groans! She swoons! She is nigh death!

(FRONY *leads them toward death-chamber. The* BISHOP *stops on steps and looks at* RAHAB, *whose face is still hidden*)

BISHOP That man?
FRONY   Rahab!
NOAH   'Tis Caleb's devil's man!

(*They enter death-chamber.* PATSY's *groans are heard. When the door is slammed,* RAHAB *springs up as from a trap and runs to middle of floor. He shouts half-circularly. He puffs like a little steam engine the while. At end he stretches himself and breathes hard*)

RAHAB I move me thus, when I am glad at heart.
 Who would I be? Myself—my own sweet self!

(*He opens Bible and sits at table.* CALEB *enters from yard unseen with whip and spurs in hand*)

 Now, to this goodly text. The sermon will—
CALEB There is no need of sermon.
RAHAB (*startled*)   Think you not?
CALEB No sermon!
RAHAB (*he rises*) Why?
CALEB (*moves about*) Money! Money! Money!

(*He goes to window and calls hired man*)

 You, there! Your laziness is wanted here!

RAHAB (*he slams Bible on table. Aside* Worthless! Worthless! I've missed my chance in life!

(*Hired man comes to window*)

CALEB (*gives him spurs*) Here take my spurs and stick yourself with them!

(*Hired man stands at window and looks at spurs.* CALEB *goes to door and calls the hired man*)

 You, there! Your laziness is wanted here!

RAHAB (*to* CALEB) You are a trainer!
CALEB   I?
HIRED MAN (*at door. Hands spurs to* CALEB)
 Your spurs?
CALEB (*shoves whip into hired man's face*) My whip
 Be off! Your laziness needs stirring up!

(HIRED MAN *goes*)

RAHAB Your spurs are fine! Your whip is good enough
To flog a fellow such as you had here.
CALEB The law is all that saves his scaly back.
RAHAB What need have you for whip and spurs?
CALEB   My horse!
RAHAB Your horse?
CALEB   My horse must clip it! Flesh is naught!
A little breeding serves a righteous end.
RAHAB You have money! Explain! I am your friend.
CALEB (*points to death-chamber*) Five hundred dollars were upon his life.

(*Door of chamber is opened.* PATSY *groans.* FRONY *rushes out.* NOAH *stands on steps.* BISHOP *stands in door*)

FRONY (*as she rushes out*) Camphor!
NOAH (*on steps*)   Camphor!
BISHOP (*in door*)   Camphor!
FRONY (*hands bottle to* NOAH) Here!
NOAH (*hands bottle to* BISHOP) Here!

(NOAH *and* BISHOP *rush in.* FRONY *rushes to door and turns to* CALEB *and* RAHAB)

FRONY (*scornfully*)   Devils!

(*She enters*)

RAHAB Five hundred dollars?
RAHAB You've bought him?
CALEB   Yes! Money flies!
RAHAB (*makes motion raking in money*)
                      Meward fly!
You said you'd buy no horse without a tale.
CALEB He has a tale about him that's a tale.
RAHAB Tell it!

(NOAH *in door of death-chamber*)

NOAH (*to* CALEB) Your mother swoons!
CALEB (*to* NOAH)   I tell a tale!
NOAH Come! Come!
CALEB (*to* NOAH) Remain and hear the tale! 'Tis smart!

(NOAH *goes in quickly*)

RAHAB His cost?
CALEB   I though you wished the tale.
RAHAB   The cost!
CALEB He cost a quacking duck and a torn apron.
RAHAB The tale! The tale!
CALEB Jasper, the shoemaker, would not be a hatter lest his handiwork treat heads to a sweat, which treats eyes to a smarting, which fills the mind with hard thoughts, which sharpen as they leave the tongue. He would not be a glover lest there be more clapping than wearing. To wear is to prove greatness. To clap is to hand-bawl! A bawler! A bawler! Jasper would not be a bawler! He was—
RAHAB A shoemaker! Go on with the tale!
CALEB He was too humane to kill a chinch which circled his neck time and again and ended on the tip of his nose before the whole congregation.
RAHAB Neither you nor I can understand such humanity. The tale!
CALEB He was too honest to drink water in which the king's shoepegs had been soaked lest he thrive on stolen substance.
RAHAB The King should have thriven on his blood!
CALEB Now, Jasper owned a quacking duck that was clock to him in the morning, servant at meal-time, and that feathered his bed at night. A neighbor-woman, who was thirty and nine—and who should have had nine and thirty on her bare back—who talked the neighborhood into confusion, her husband into murder, her sons into theft, and her daughters into ill-marriages, stole the duck and hid it in a barrel.
RAHAB Woman and mystery always make a good tale. Go on!
CALEB "Woman," said Jasper, as she was feeding her ducks, "I suspect you of theft!" "Man," said the woman, "I suspect you of insolence! Let's see! Ducky! Ducky! I scatter you honest corn!" "Quack! Quack!" came from the barrel. "There's life in the barrel!" said Jasper. "There's a dream in your head!" replied the woman, and placed her apron over the barrel. "I'll have my duck!" said Jasper, and thrust his hand through the apron and seized the duck. As he held up the apron and duck a stranger rode up on the horse in question. "Fine morning!" said the stranger. "Quack!" Quack!" went the duck. Off! went the horse, leaving the stranger to take his fall as he had it, and his revenge as he could get it. Jasper was affrighted and said: "Who'll own the apron and

Caleb the Degenerate

the duck?" "I own the apron and the duck!" said I to the stranger. "I'll pay the damages!" said Jasper. "I'll buy the horse!" said I. "Who'll pay for the apron?" bawled the woman. "I," answered the man and sprang to his feet. Ere I could pay the money the man and woman eloped. They perished in a storm. Jasper buried their bodies by way of damages; and I kept the horse as a matter of business.

RAHAB A quacking duck and a torn apron! When will a fairy tale be given flesh and blood again?

CALEB Never! The horse cost me two hundred dollars. I'm feeling gay! When in such moments I am bound to tell a sprightly lie.

BISHOP (*in door*) Your mother is better!

CALEB (*he frowns*) I'm worse!

(*The* BISHOP *shakes his head and goes in*)

RAHAB Did you not say the sermon should not be?

CALEB I did! No sermon! Students will be here!
An undertaker, too! A sham affair! You understand?

RAHAB I do! The sermon's out!

CALEB I rode the horse to find the student's place.

RAHAB Your father's horse!

CALEB The horse his death-fees bought. Two hundred dollars of the five! You see?

RAHAB You are so modern in your filial views.

CALEB "Weaker and wiser" is the ancient saw.

(HIRED MAN *appears at the window*. FRONY *enters from death-chamber*)

FRONY (*to* CALEB) Your mother sleeps!

CALEB That sleep will be too short!

HIRED MAN The undertaker, sir! Five other men!
Four bear a litter!

CALEB (*to* RAHAB *as he passes out*) It will bear the dead!

(*exit hurriedly to the yard*)

FRONY What said he?

RAHAB Nothing that amuses you!

FRONY Beware!!

RAHAB Of what? Hell-fire?

FRONY You seem to know!

(*re-enter* CALEB *with* UNDERTAKER)

CALEB (*to* UNDERTAKER) You know your trade?

UNDERTAKER I do!

CALEB (*points to death-chamber*)
Make estimate!

(*Exit* CALEB *quickly*. UNDERTAKER *stops and looks around*)

RAHAB (*roughly*) That way, death-worm!

FRONY (*kindly*) This way, kind sir! (*opens door*)
Walk in! (*enter* UNDERTAKER. *She closes door*)
Grandison's blood!

RAHAB What know I of his blood?

FRONY You shed it!

RAHAB Caleb shed it!

FRONY Your thought helped!

(CALEB *leads five men with a litter past window*. RAHAB *sees*. FRONY *does not*)

You taught him doctrine that will ruin youth.

(*He throws up Bible, catches it and whistles*)

You sinned so well he loved sin's charming gilt.

RAHAB I am a master then! Hurrah for me!

(*Enter* CALEB *from death-chamber with* UNDERTAKER)

CALEB (*to* FRONY) The doctor enters! Have all come in here!

(FRONY *enters chamber*. CALEB *and* RAHAB *talk aside*. UNDERTAKER *approaches several times to speak, but is waved back by* CALEB. *Enter* PATSY. *She groans. She hobbles in, leaning on* NOAH *and the* BISHOP. *She holds money in hand*. FRONY *follows and fans her. She is seated. They stand by her chair*. RAHAB *hugs Bible and looks solemn*)

CALEB (*to* UNDERTAKER) A thirty-dollar coffin! I say no!
Five dollars for a robe? No, death-worm, no!
Four carriages? No, undertaker, no!
Think you a son must curb his appetite
Because a pauper father breathes no more?
The living must have money! I'm alive!
Cold dignity is all the dead require.
The living must have money! Hear you that!

He was my father! I am—well—his heir!
Forgetfulness, I bid you hide the first!
I own the other for its luxury!
Five hundred dollars were upon his life!
I have it all save a few paltry dimes!
(*to* PATSY) Old woman, you have that? Ah, cigarettes.

(*He takes money from her*)

Now, undertaker—sober business man!
You see conditions! Make your estimate!
You think about your trade? Drink! Cigarettes!
You'd rob me, sir? Drink! Cocaine! Cigarettes!
I'd stake them, sir, against your trade—your life!
Out! Out! death-worm! Out! Out! You wont? You will!
Offend not living men to serve the dead!
Out! Out! (UNDERTAKER *hurries out*)
He went! (*to* PATSY)—Old woman, why those tears?

PATSY (*faintly*) Caleb, my boy, where is your heart?
CALEB Patsy,
Your husband has it in his pauper breast.
He boasted of a hide-bound honesty.
I boast me of my liberty and wit.
BISHOP (*to* CALEB) Are you a human being?
CALEB Look me o'er!
BISHOP You have a soul?
CALEB What mean you by that word?
BISHOP I mean—
CALEB I would not know your meaning! You
Would make sense senseless in explaining it!
BISHOP You are a monster!
CALEB You have spoken truth!
BISHOP You know not God!
CALEB You mean God knows not me!
BISHOP You are an infidel?
CALEB I am! I am!
BISHOP You move without a current, sail, or creed!
CALEB My current is myself! My wit's my sail!
BISHOP Your creed?
CALEB I have a creed! It suits you not!

BISHOP What is it?
CALEB Here it is! Prepare your ire!
Men stagger in my light, yet are too dull
To see that my creed is infallible.
They rather worship God whose cruel laws
Are made up wholly of mistakes and flaws.
The time shall be when they will cease to follow
Views that are so disgusting and so hollow.
Let blinded Christians, ere they think or stir,
Confer with me, their great philosopher.
When they have steeped their souls in blasphemy,
And trodden under foot theology,
They will be fit to teach true piety,
As I have searched for light should Christians search,
They'll find that faith in God the soul will smirch,
And know that hell's another name for church.
Therefore, my fellow-men, on you I call.
I am your friend, and heartily extol
My creed of life to save you, one and all.
There is my creed!
BISHOP It is no creed!
CALEB What then?
BISHOP 'Tis soulful nothing with a dash of brain
That sees itself polluted through itself.
FRONY Our demon!
NOAH Hell's forerunner!
PATSY (*motherly. She rises*) Caleb—son—
This mother's breast of mine would feed you still!

(STUDENT *taps on window-pane.* CALEB *goes to window.* RAHAB *holds door leading to yard.* STUDENT *gives* CALEB *money*)

STUDENT (*to* CALEB) Here is your money, sir!
We have the corpse!
'Tis decomposed a little, but'twill do.
FRONY Students!

(GRANDISON's *body is borne by window on a litter*)

BISHOP My heavens! Can it be?
FRONY   Students!
PATSY Caleb, your father! Oh— (*falls into* NOAH's *arms*)
CALEB Be patient, fools!

(BISHOP *peers out window.* FRONY *tries death-chamber door and finds it fastened.* CALEB *looks at money and smiles.* RAHAB *motions to him to divide. Curtain*)

ACT TWO

Scene One

(OLIVIA's *library. Enter* OLIVIA)

OLIVIA 'Twas horrible! 'Twas horrible! Caleb
    Did prove a demon! 'Tis my sober thought
    Great God will hear no prayers that he will make.

(*Enter* FRONY *hurriedly*)

FRONY You should have seen! You should—
OLIVIA   I heard enough.
FRONY Are satisfied?
OLIVIA   That I should strive the more.
FRONY I'd give my life to lead you out of this.
OLIVIA Lend me your wit. 'Twill stand the better watch.
FRONY Upon which side? Explain! I'll take a breath!

(*She sits on chair*)

OLIVIA An urchin stretches him upon the ground;
    And, dog-like, laps the water from the spring.
    He fears no ill. He thinks: "I am, therefore,
    I am protected." Life's too full of life
    To shake his faith. So Patsy trusts in God.
    One tells a story till the plot grows dear.
    Men clamor for a change. He says: "Not so!
    I've put my joys and sorrows into it
    After this fashion." Patsy scorns to change
    Her worship's rule. 'Tis life through joy and pain.
    Such constancy is life in league with God.
    She sees no penury in wanting bread
    When that want comes from giving, crumb by crumb,
    One's little store to such as toil for naught.
    A little sock or kerchief or a hood
    Is dearer unto her than volumes filled
    With deeds of men who slay the God in man
    For pen and ink to libel nature with.
    She serves her day by serving her hearth-stone.
FRONY She is so worthy! Speak the truth of her!
OLIVIA A button's dropped by some one in a crowd.
    One passes it and scarcely sees its form.
    Another comes and sees it's what it is,
    But goes his way unmindful of its worth.
    Another, curious and prudent-wise,
    Stores it about him for a future need.
    The need may come a score of times, but he
    Bethinks him not he has it near at hand.
    A wiser one will use it in his need,
    Perchance, with others of no kindred. Then
    Another, with fine sense of fitness, will
    Seek out its fellows somewhere and salute
    The seeing eye with wholeness. So we think.
    Thoughts face us as we move. We see them not;
    Or see them simply recognizably,
    And plod along unburdened by their aid;
    Or press them to us but ne'er think to use
    Such trifles when a serious moment comes;
    Or use them in connection where no trace
    Of fellowship or kindred may be found.
    Few use their thoughts as wisely as a child
    Uses the buttons it has found in play.
    Patsy is such a thinker. She can think

	A thought into the world, and thereby guard
	It with the destinies that save the world.
	She'll soon give back to earth and air and sky
	Her mortal dust, immortal in its trend.
FRONY	She is so worthy!
OLIVIA	You would help her then?
FRONY	I would!
OLIVIA	Help me!
FRONY	To wed—?
OLIVIA	No argument!
	The Bishop comes!
FRONY	I heard! I know! I'll help!

(*She rises*)

	He would invite you to an argument,
	Making this Caleb serve as central point.
	He boasts him that if you will listen well
	Your thoughts of Caleb shall be spears to prick
	Your wild affections into haggardness.
	I'll go to meet him! You've a starting point?
	His sermons! He is pleased to hear from them.
	I like not Caleb, but I'll help you out,
	We women must be women! Men are men! (*exit*)
OLIVIA	I do remember some well-timed remarks
	Concerning genius and the fear of hell.
	They're from a sermon I once heard him preach.
	These will I cite and wed to argument.
	I'll at him first! The rule of courtesy
	Will steel his patience. (*steps are heard*)
	I do hear his step.

(*Re-enter* FRONY)

FRONY	Some ministers will seek the Bishop here
	To say good-bye. Can you make use of them?
OLIVIA	I know them well. Each one is practiced well.
	I had it done bethinking of this hour.
	The Bishop?
FRONY	In his garden!
OLIVIA	Doing what?
FRONY	Consulting with your father. (*exit*)
OLIVIA	Plotting still!
	These ministers will play a little part.
	'Twill break monotony and give me rest.
	What if the Bishop knew? Appointments? No!

(*Re-enter* FRONY *with* BISHOP)

FRONY	You saw this Caleb and remember him.
BISHOP	I did! I do!
FRONY	You think him vile? And thought him worthy of death?
BISHOP	I do! I did!
FRONY	Think you a sermon would be remedy?
BISHOP	No one remembers sermons!
OLIVIA	I do!
FRONY	She does and often speaks to me of yours.
BISHOP	Of mine?
FRONY	Your text, your sermon and your very voice
	She oft repeats to me, and I say true.
	Provoke her, Bishop, and she'll gladly preach
	A part of your own sermon. Try her once!
OLIVIA	As Frony says your sermons cling to me.
BISHOP	As you to Caleb?
OLIVIA	I have no mind to make comparisons.
	Besides the ancient rule of courtesy
	Forbids that you bring up a second point
	When I have introduced a sober first.
BISHOP	'Tis true! Go on!
OLIVIA	I heard you preach, and seem to hear you still.

(*The* BISHOP *takes it for a compliment*)

	It was on "Genius and the Fear of Hell."
	"The fear of hell doth lift man heavenward."
	This was the gist of half of your discourse.
	I think not so!
FRONY	I think not so! Bishop,
	You think not so since you have older grown?

(The BISHOP *is silent and buries his head in his hands*)

OLIVIA 'Twould edge my temper and unwing my hope.

FRONY (*to* BISHOP) Make that a text and preach the sermon o'er.

(BISHOP *takes Bible from pocket and opens it*)

OLIVIA Whenever man is taught the fear of hell,
He seeks it in the living and the dead.
See how the ages all do sanction this!

FRONY You see it, Bishop! Sanction what you see!

OLIVIA No longer do the airs of Paradise
Exist for him to hearten and assure.
No longer does he know that God must still
O'ermaster Satan ere the soul be dumb.
Man's ever doomed to woe and death in life,
To make his faith the tutor to his fear,
To crush his God and elevate an Imp,
So long as he does hold such savagery.
His wild audacity will lead him on
To smite with slavering hand an angel's face.
Then straight his witlessness would wonder how
So pure a stroke could leave so foul a stain.

FRONY That stroke hit home. Some sparks should be in sight.

OLIVIA The tragedy of tragedies must be:
To teach the laws of Heaven so that they cross
And smite each other till the sons of men
Know not the voice of God from that of him
Who sits in Hell, but reigns not anywhere.

FRONY That is theology. (*to* BISHOP) Speak I the truth?

(*The* BISHOP *looks through his glasses at the ceiling*)

OLIVIA Past ages toyed with man. He knew it not,
And made their jest the altar of his praise.
They thorned his soul with fear, yet asked him why
He was so slow to sniff the Rose of Life.
They dulled his sight by bringing Hell so close,
Then scorned him for not seeing Heaven afar.
The Present should be loath to fellowship
A Past whose creed made life's sweet peace a dirge.

BISHOP (*dryly and slowly*) Somewhat fatigued, Frony?

FRONY (*quickly*) Are you?

BISHOP (*quickly*) Are you?

(*He listens attentively*)

OLIVIA As some strong man, in firm and joyous mood,
Plants a small seed beside his cabin door,
And without thought of fear or future ill,
Tends it by day and croons o'er it by night
Until the vine springs up and bears a gourd,
The which he takes, all famishing of thirst,
And, step by step, climbs up a shaggy steep
Where from a stream so small it comes in drops
He fills it to the brim; but ere he drinks,
Hears cries from a poor, thirsty traveler
Who pants and groans upon the plain below;
And then, forgetting his own ease and weal,
Bears down the water and so saves a life;
Then as he dies from bruises and of thirst
Thinks all is well since he has humbly served
His gracious Maker in a simple act;
So you, O, child of Heaven and of Earth,

	Must tend your life, making your daily prayer
	An ardent wish to gain that you may give;
	Feeling no fear, firmly believing that
	Nearness to duty, not to burning Hell,
	Must ever be the voice that leads to Heaven.
FRONY	Good thought is that! Some seem to think not so.
BISHOP	Duty is ever right. Fear plays its part. (*to* OLIVIA) I spoke of genius. Now, speak you of it.
	What did I say? Do you remember it?
OLIVIA	Yes! You said naught, and I remember it.
FRONY	She told me of it, and I—. (*to* OLIVIA) Did I laugh? Speak on, Olivia!
BISHOP	Yes! Say your say.
	I worship thought though feminine in garb.
OLIVIA	You lead by questioning. 'Twill draw me out.
BISHOP	I question? I?
FRONY	O, question anything!

(*Loud coughing without*)

	Some ministers would say goodbye to you.
	I go to let them in. Now, question on! (*exit* FRONY)
BISHOP	I question? I? Let's hear your questioning.
OLIVIA	I'd hear your answering.
BISHOP	No! No! No! Ask You on and on and answer when you will.
OLIVIA	Is genius feminine?
BISHOP	The question's good.
OLIVIA	Your man of genius is not masculine.
	There's much of woman in him. He prefers
	To keep the secret and the worth of it.
	Is it bred of disease?
BISHOP	The question's good.
OLIVIA	Eloquence proves not that the vocal chords
	Are in sad plight. So genius and the brain.
	The one who's dull has a diseased brain.
	One's birthright is fine feeling and a true thought
	Is genius satisfied?
BISHOP	The question's good.
OLIVIA	Rarely, if ever, is it ours to see A thinker who is trained harmoniously.
	He who has genius in a certain line
	Allies himself, or may, with the divine.
	But mostly is this done at the expense
	Of a well-planned and rounded excellence.
	The gods proclaim that he is doubly blessed.
	He cries: "Begone, ye gods! I am distressed!"

(FRONY *shows two ministers in*)

FRONY	(*at door*) In! In! The Bishop waits. He's in a mood!

(*They enter and whisper aside.* FRONY *goes back. Enter* NOAH)

NOAH	I'll in myself! What's going to happen here?
BISHOP	Remain and see!
NOAH	(*to* BISHOP) You've been successful, eh?
FRONY	(*looks in*) Remain and see! (*she comes in*)
NOAH	I will!
BISHOP	(*to* NOAH) Come to my side. (*he goes*)

(*The* MINISTERS *stand on either side of table and toss ball to each other.* OLIVIA *and* FRONY *let their hair so fall that it covers back of head and face. They stand with arms around each other's neck and rock to and fro.*)

OLIVIA	Ball! Ball!
FRONY	That means a little game. Ha! ha!

(*They continue to rock and measure first hands and then feet. Ball rolls under table.* MINISTERS *upset table in getting it.* BISHOP'*s hat falls.* FIRST MINISTER *rubs his head with one hand and hands hat to* SECOND MINISTER, *who does same and hands hat to* NOAH. NOAH *takes it and wipes it reluctantly.* MINISTERS *whisper again*)

BISHOP	My hat! Is this a game of ball? My hat!
NOAH	Stay, Bishop, stay! You see just what you see!
BISHOP	I stay! Is this a trick? Then let me learn!
	Even a sober man may smile at whims.

Caleb the Degenerate

FIRST MINISTER (*lays ball on table*) Here, Bishop!
SECOND MINISTER (*puts down doll-shoes*) Here, Bishop!
THIRD MINISTER (*enters hurriedly, lays on table doll-toys and loaf of bread*) Bishop, look well!
FRONY The game! The game!
OLIVIA Who'll live to see it out?

(FIRST *and* SECOND MINISTERS *run to* OLIVIA *and* FRONY *and fan them with their beavers.* NOAH *puts* BISHOP's *beaver on table and goes to door*)

BISHOP Noah, you go?
NOAH My wits won't let me stay. (*exit* NOAH)

(OLIVIA *and* FRONY *put up their hair*)

BISHOP Things seem to say: "Be philosophical."
You'd have a game? Let each one take a part.

(FIRST *and* SECOND MINISTERS *give their hats to* THIRD MINISTER *to hold. He bows and holds them with dignity*)

Draw near! (*all draw near*) Olivia, take you the ball!
Good Ministers, take each a little shoe!
The loaf of bread, Frony! (*to* THIRD MINISTER) Some of the toys?
THIRD MINISTER Bishop, I'm toying now with this headwear
That wears so well a score of years might fail
To see its gloss in need of hatter's aid.
Suppose my grandfather had owned these hats;
Suppose they came to me as his estate;
Suppose I brought them to a place like this;
Suppose I fanned two ladies, side by side;
Suppose I gave them to a friend to hold;
Suppose he held them in his sturdy left; (*holds them so*)
Suppose he drew his right and poised it thus; (*he draws as though to strike*)
Suppose—
MINISTERS We take our beavers back again.

(*They take them and lay them aside*)

BISHOP (*to* THIRD MINISTER) What would you have?
We would not slight you, sir.
THIRD MINISTER (*walks to* FRONY *and points to bread*)
A slight division of the honors here.
OLIVIA I'll squeeze. (*she squeezes the ball.*
FIRST MINISTER *points to* SECOND MINISTER's *feet and to little shoes*)
FIRST MINISTER How many pairs will make a pair?

(FRONY *looks at bread as though she would eat it*)

FRONY My teeth are many years younger than I.
THIRD MINISTER (*aside*) I do not ask for a division there.
BISHOP These trinkets seem to tell a sober tale.
I see a people, friendless, ignorant,
Living from hand to mouth, from jail to grave.
They wander here and there, scorning the moss
That clutches to the heel of industry.
They swarm into the towns with empty heads,
With idle hands that know not handicraft,
With vicious appetites that lead to death,
With views of life a child might scorn to hold.
They know the past but as a burial ground.
No friendly spectre rises up therefrom.
A thousand years of life glare in their face.
They glare again and mock their seriousness.
When God turns politician they are saints.
Philosophy is made to lag behind.
A childish intuition's asked to point
A certain finger toward the times to be.
How poor, how helpless, how misguided they!
MINISTERS Bishop, these trinkets tell a sober tale.

OLIVIA (*aside to* FRONY) The secret's out! How happened it?
FRONY I guess!
OLIVIA Your guess?
FRONY (*aloud*) The Ministers kept not their word.
MINISTERS The Bishop makes appointments! That means much!
OLIVIA Bishop, we would explain the whole affair.
FRONY It shall be plain.
BISHOP Let it come further on!
MINISTERS The Bishop knows, and he'll explain it well.
BISHOP These people, my beloved people, must
    Be wise to know, be skilled to seize the shaft
    That sets in motion life's unnumbered wheels.
    The head! The hand! The hand! The head! These two
    Will save the noble remnant. Let us act!
OLIVIA Let us act!
FRONY Let us act now!
MINISTERS Let us act!
BISHOP The ball means progress.
OLIVIA (*tries to make the ball bigger*) I'll not squeeze it more.
BISHOP It means the progress that draws after it
    The things we eat and wear and use in life.
FIRST MINISTER These little shoes are very small. How's that?
BISHOP The smallness shows how scant our footing is.
    We are a baby that's too small to shoe.
    Ages ago the white man's effort dropped
    A pebble in the sea of progress. Now,
    Circles that gird the universe are seen.
    We drop a pebble in today. We see
    Our pebble but the white man's circle. Strange!
FRONY My teeth are younger far than I, but I
    Can see you see the game we wished to play.
THIRD MINISTER (*aside*) Each speech is seasoned with her younger teeth.
OLIVIA The bread means what?
BISHOP The Bible tells us that
    In our own brow's sweat shall we eat our bread.
FRONY The doll-toys, Bishop?
BISHOP They are models of
    The many things we need to learn to make.
OLIVIA (*to* MINISTER) You told!
FRONY (*to* MINISTER) You told!
FIRST MINISTER We did!
SECOND MINISTER We did!
BISHOP They did!
OLIVIA We meant to play and then explain the game.
    We train the hand. Our boys and girls find books
    Are good to make, to guide, to let alone.
    Making a book is caging life's best life.
    Go, cage life's life before you pause to read.
    Books guide you when you own their soul and thought.
BISHOP Industrial training is the thing at last.
FRONY How dull we were!
OLIVIA How far we looked to learn
    A truth that's taught by jingling pots and pans.
MINISTER (*to* OLIVIA) Are we excused?
OLIVIA Address the Bishop there!
MINISTERS Goodbye, Bishop!
BISHOP Frony, they say goodbye!
FRONY I'll go with them and talk the matter o'er.
THIRD MINISTER I'll go with you. The bread is tempting still.

(FRONY *goes out. The* MINISTERS *follow with toys in their beaver hats. Enter* NOAH *slowly*)

BISHOP Well! Well! Noah! Your wits won't let you stay?

(*Exit* NOAH *quickly.* OLIVIA *holds the* BISHOP'*s beaver and motions him to toss the ball. He does. She catches it in hat*)

OLIVIA My hat! Is this a game of ball? My hat!
BISHOP Olivia, my child, it is a game
    Of progress that I riddled out for you.

(*She puts hat on table*)

OLIVIA Tomorrow night at our industrial school
My pupils show their work. Be there on time!
BISHOP I learned your little game.
OLIVIA You learned it well.
What think you of the force of handicraft?
BISHOP God's love and handicraft must save the world.
OLIVIA You've seen my book—"The Negro and His Hands?"
BISHOP I have not read it.
OLIVIA I will give you one.

(*She goes out to get book*)

BISHOP How she evades! Ha! ha! That little game!
That little riddle on industrial work!
She thought to puzzle me and then explain.
The ministers would blab! I did the rest.
She cunningly evades at every point.
Caleb's my theme. Directness wins her scorn.
There am I weak.

(*Re-enter* OLIVIA)

OLIVIA Somehow I have misplaced
The book. 'Twas my last copy.
BISHOP (*aside*) I see now!
You gave the book to Caleb?
OLIVIA I did not.
BISHOP 'Twas in his hands. He said it was your last.
You have one copy of yourself. Beware!
OLIVIA The rule of courtesy is potent still.
Caleb is not the subject.

(*She looks at books on shelf*)

BISHOP (*aside*) Books! Books! Books!

(*He looks at books on another shelf, holds one up and reads lead-pencil writing on back. She thinks he reads title*)

"The Negro and His Hands."—Olivia.

(*She starts to him*)

OLIVIA You've found it? Now, take back your hasty charge.

(*He still holds up book*)

BISHOP 'Tis written plainly with a lead-pencil.
(*she returns to book-shelf*)
(*aside*) Another indirection, win or lose!
(*to* OLIVIA) Your ideal man
OLIVIA I have him.
BISHOP Let me hear.
OLIVIA He is a man who lives a peaceful life
Which kills from a continual round with strife.
His being born without a single fear
Makes him of course an abject coward here.
He grows so fast the growing duly stunts,
And breathes so smoothly that he always grunts.
The more he learns, the more he sees 'tis needed
To keep his empty mental-garden weeded.
When men are killed outright and resurrected
He holds such little things should be expected.
And to become, thinks he, extremely wise
One simply has to misapply his eyes.
And seeing things as they will never be
Leads ever on to true philosophy.
By placing twilight at the early dawn
He stops his motion while he still goes on.
Humility in him is two-edged pride,
And what's in glory is not glorified.
He makes an everlasting truce with death,
Then straightway turns and draws his latest breath.
BISHOP That character's impossible. Again!
OLIVIA His is an eye that runs compassion's length.
His is a tongue that snares the simplest words
Round simplest thoughts in beauty's fadeless mesh.
Such art as his the soul of man endears.
Through all the silences of all the years.

	Right-fettered and full-faced he halts him by
	Each column wrong has builded to the sky.
	He flaws each flaw until proof-laden runs
	Faith's highest hope past earth and stars and suns.
BISHOP	That is not Caleb—
OLIVIA	Well you know 'tis not.
BISHOP	Again!
OLIVIA	How many think you I possess?
BISHOP	Enough to banish Caleb.
OLIVIA	He's secure.
BISHOP	What think you of his creed—his atheist's creed.
	He thundered it into his mother's ears.
	He blurted it above his father's corpse.
OLIVIA	I think not of it now. I do not wish.
	Accept the creed of strenuous modern life?
BISHOP	Of strenuous modern life? Well, let me hear.
OLIVIA	God makes a man. Conditions make his creed.
	When reason's torch has once been kindled by
	The vicious fancies of the ignorant
	And fueled by the greed and soullessness
	That stamp eternal vengeance everywhere,
	The human in us often scoffs and says:
	"There is no God nor Heaven to be found.
	Hope is the star that lights self unto self.
	Faith is the hand that clutches self's decree.
	Mercy is oil self keeps for its own ills.
	Justice is hell made present by a blow.
	Conditions, therefore, make this creed I hold:
	God-like I strive, but man-like I rebel!"
	Man is most man, and, therefore, most like God
	When he does weigh life's actions in such scales
	As balance not for his sufficiency,
	But quiver till the All-intelligence
	Applies a power whose name is very truth.

	Great men, not creeds, will have the right of way.
BISHOP	(*he calls as to one afar off*) Caleb! Caleb! You have the right of way.
	A great man, you? (*takes up his hat*) Ha! ha! (*starts to door*) Ha! ha! (*bows to* OLIVIA) Ha! ha! (*he raises hat to put it on. Ball falls to floor. He hurries out. She begins with last line pronounced*)
OLIVIA	Great men, not creeds, will have the right of way.
	They clash in every age; and clashing strip
	Some worn-out garment from the limbs of Truth.
	Should one put forth his eager hand and touch
	Truth's perfect robes they would entangle it
	And hold it captive till God's reckoning time. (*exit*)

(*Curtain*)

Scene Two

(PATSY's *orchard. At the rising of the curtain* PATSY *is lying on a couch. Her head is bandaged and slightly elevated.* CALEB *sits in a chair, nodding and holding in his mouth a partly-consumed cigarette.* PATSY *claps her hands to arouse him.*)

PATSY	(*clapping her hands*) Caleb, my boy! My breath! My breath! Caleb! Come! Come! A kiss! A touch! Caleb! My breath!

(*she tries to clap her hands, but simply beats the air*)

O, God, forgive my boy! My—breath—is—short. (*she dies*)

(*Enter* BISHOP *and* FRONY. *They go to the bed and examine* PATSY. CALEB *awakes*)

FRONY	(*to* CALEB *softly*) Patsy is dead.
CALEB	(*after lighting his cigarette*) She is? Then bury her.

(*He remains in the chair and smokes with dignity.* FRONY *arranges bed, crosses* PATSY's *hands and feels her forehead*)

BISHOP	(*pointing to bandage*) That bandage on your mother's head!

CALEB I see!
BISHOP How came it there?
CALEB She fell.
BISHOP How happened it?
CALEB You know? Then tell. I do not deal in dreams.
BISHOP (*coming closer*) You tell me you could listen?
CALEB Yes! Why not?
  'Tis but a serious trifle. Speak! I hear!

(BISHOP *steps aside, rubs his hands and looks puzzled*)

FRONY (*points to chair in which* CALEB *sits*)
  'Twas in that very chair she sat.
CALEB (*playfully*) And dreamed.
BISHOP Of you!
CALEB You fear to tell a dream? Then speak!
FRONY 'Twas from that chair she fell!
BISHOP Her bandaged head!
FRONY Her death has followed.
BISHOP How she did cry out: "My baby! My Caleb! Perdition!"
CALEB Whew!
  You are so easily excited! Whew!

BISHOP (*takes hold of chair.* CALEB *nods in answer to each question*)

  'Twas in this chair she sat? From it she fell?
  Her head was cut? She suffered days and months?
  Her death came from that fall?
CALEB (*nods several times*) I'll nod and nod!
  Your other questions now are answered.
  Whew!
  The dream!
FRONY I heard her tell it oft. I wept Each time.
BISHOP Who could refrain?
CALEB Tell it and see.
BISHOP After this manner did she speak.
CALEB (*lightly*) Come on!
BISHOP "Methought my Caleb was a babe again.
  I pressed his head to mine and crooned and crooned
  A baby ditty—old, nonsensical—
  Yet ever sweet to each true mother's heart.
  When he said 'dad' I kissed his chin, mouth, nose,
  Eyes, forehead; breathed and kissed them o'er again.
  Five years passed by. He sat upon my knee
  While I placed roses on his tender brow.
  Ten years passed by. I saw him stand above
  His school-mates in their studies and their games.
  Again I looked and saw a man full-grown—
  I, bent and gray, leaning upon his arm—
  Loved by the just, respected by the wise.
  Swift Time, the robber, beckoned to my babe.
  I pinched his chin and kissed it o'er and o'er.
  I clapped his hands and kissed until he laughed.
  I rubbed his feet and kissed and kissed and kissed.
  I fell asleep. When I awoke my babe
  Was lying on the floor. Thinking 'twas hurt,
  I screamed 'my babe.' Straightway it was a man—
  Caleb, the heartless. 'Caleb,' then I called.
  A flame of fire sprang up. It circled him.
  I cried: 'Perdition! Save! O, God! O, God!'
  I leaped to help him. O, this head of mine!
  'Twill be my death! A mother's love is all
  Of God's great love and all the million pangs
  Of mother-hood can drive into her soul."
CALEB I have refrained. Come, Frony, with your tears.

(FRONY *removes bandage from* PATSY'*s head and shows scar across forehead*)

FRONY This scar will place the word ingratitude
  'Cross Heaven's gate. Your doom—
CALEB To hear tame speech.

BISHOP Your mother told this dream. You heard! You scoffed!
You came one morning, hungry, barefooted.
"Shoes, Patsy! Money, Patsy!" This you said.
She leaned to kiss you and—
CALEB I shoved her off.
That scar is ugly. My fine taste rebelled.
BISHOP She saw your feet. She thought of how she kissed
Them in her dream. She stooped—
CALEB I coldly said:
"Tis not caresses. It is shoes I want."
BISHOP You got them?
CALEB Yes! It was her place to give.

(FRONY *looks upon* PATSY)

FRONY Her eye-lids quiver! She's alive—alive!
Patsy's alive!

(BISHOP *runs to bed.* CALEB *is undisturbed*)

BISHOP Let's see! No! No! She's gone!
CALEB You are so easily excited. Whew!
BISHOP You slew your father. Now, I understand.
You have all God condemns the Devil for.
CALEB Sink not good manners in fine eloquence.
BISHOP Look on your father through your mind's eye.
CALEB No!
He's gone! Let him continue! Speak! I sleep!

(*He pretends to sleep. He snores*)

BISHOP You turn yourself into a spurious coin
And boast that it has naught that recommends.
Bad, worse, worst, worsted you!
Naught can come next!

(*He snores more loudly. The* BISHOP *shakes him roughly*)

You sleep? The slaying of your father wins
A blissful rest? You sleep? Defaming her
Who gave you life—
CALEB (*tries to rise*) Let me confess!
BISHOP Is just?
You sleep?
CALEB (*on his feet*) I would confess!
BISHOP (*forcing him to his knees*) No! No! Sleep on!
CALEB I will confess! I'd wed your foster-child!
BISHOP You'd wed? I'd slay!
(*throws him to ground. Lifts his foot to stamp him in face*)
I'd slay!
(*lowers his foot*)
Oh, I forgot!
Your mother's dead, and I'm a man of God.

(*He kneels at* CALEB'S *side in attitude of prayer.* CALEB *groans.* FRONY *looks into* PATSY'S *face. Curtain falls. It rises immediately.* CALEB *stands aside and looks dignified. The* BISHOP *still kneels and looks toward Heaven. Many neighbors have come to see* PATSY. *As* OLIVIA *enters* CALEB *looks abashed and runs out. The curtain falls. It rises immediately on next scene*)

Scene Three

(PATSY'S *orchard. Enter* NOAH, *chased in by* CALEB)

CALEB (*yells in* NOAH'S *ear*) Hello, graybeard!
Would have good company?
Have mine and answer as I question you.
Olivia and I— You see the point?
Too dull to see? You need a shaking up! (*shakes him*)
Olivia and I would— (NOAH *shows disgust*) How you frown
It pleases me. Ho, blessed privilege!
Olivia and I would wed.
NOAH (*scornfully*) No! No!
CALEB You say no, no! I say yes, yes, Graybeard!
You need a son-in-law. Now, listen well!
I am a gambling man. Have heard of it?
Have not? You should know all my noble parts.
Confusion halts for me. Peace hastens by.
God I reject. Woman I may accept.

Graybeard, you need a son-in-law like me.
I prophesy for you. Now, listen well!
A thief you'll be. (*makes movements of picking chickens*)
Chickens! chickens! chickens!
You've stolen one. You have it in the pot.
Your thumb and finger grip a steaming leg.
Some of the meat is sizzling in your mouth.
A voice without says: "Noah, let me in.
I fear my chicken's feeding in your coop."
"No! no!" you say, and take another bite.
The voice goes on without, and you within.
You need a son-in-law to prophesy.
I see you sitting there beside a post.
Soap, water, brushes, combs are set aside.
Your color's that of dirt. Your lice are fat.
They and your finger nails have scabbed your back.
What's in your hand? A pair of ancient dice.
You shake them thus and thus. (*makes motion of shaking*)
You throw them thus. (*makes motion of throwing*)
You frown and curse. You rub your back and smile.
No fellow-player? Money is at stake?
No! No! Graybeard! You gamble with yourself,
Or rather with the lice upon your back.
They bite a hundred places all at once.
You'd season pain with fun. Therefore, you cast
The dice to see where first to make attack.

(NOAH *starts to leave.* CALEB *leads him back by his beard*)

I'll tell you when to shun a bit of truth.

(NOAH *leans against a tree and trembles*)

You need my sense. I prophesy again.
Drunk! drunk! Graybeard? 'Tis a most natural thing.
Drunk! Drunk! You sit beside an ancient fire.
The back-log sputters. You reply to it:
"I'll be with you when you do come to me."
I laugh and take you for my cuspidor.
The back-log sputters. You say: "Wait a bit,
Or come my way. I am a sober man,
A gentleman who never— Drinks you say?
Three full ones, if you please! I come! I come!"
You jump behind the log. I laugh and spit.
You are a crackling now. I say amen.
You need a son-in-law. Olivia
And I would wed. What think you of the match?

(NOAH *starts to go.* CALEB *holds him by the beard*)

Answer!
NOAH   I go to bury Patsy.
CALEB   I
Would wed Olivia. The exchange is fair.
Your beard is long enough. A little pull
Will give you speech. (*pulls it*)
NOAH   My beard!
CALEB   Answer, I say!
NOAH   I go to dig your mother's grave.
CALEB   You must
Remain awhile to please that mother's son.
NOAH   She must be buried.
CALEB   I must have a wife.

(*pulls out beard and throws it down*)

NOAH   My beard is being wasted.
CALEB   What of that?
My strength is not.
NOAH   Oh! Oh!
CALEB   Ha! Ha! Answer!
NOAH   Ye-es.
CALEB (*mimics*) Ye-es! (*evens up beard with knife*)
You are adorned. Your son-in-law
Would thank you, but he has not heart enough.

(*Exit* CALEB. NOAH *picks up scattered beard and*

puts it into pocket-book. He looks for more beard as BISHOP *enters unseen*)

NOAH (*on all-fours looking for beard*) Olivia!
BISHOP (*softly, beckoning*) Olivia!
NOAH   Quickly!

(*Enter* OLIVIA)

BISHOP Quickly! (*points to* NOAH) A mystery I can not solve! (*exit* BISHOP)
OLIVIA A mystery this is I fain would solve. Father!
NOAH   O, loss! O, precious loss!
OLIVIA (*takes hold of him*)   Rise! Rise!
NOAH (*pulls back*) I'm nearer to my loss.
OLIVIA   What is the loss?
NOAH Who wrought it better ask.
OLIVIA   Please tell it me!
NOAH (*rises*) I would acquaint you of my morning's work.
I take a hand in Patsy's burial.

(*He kisses her three times*)

The first is for your mother who was wise.
OLIVIA In wedding you? I never heard her say
So much when she did curtain lecture you.
You should have said my mother who was brave.
NOAH That's lightly said.
OLIVIA   Its truth has weight enough.
NOAH The second, child, is for your innocence.
(*kisses her again*)
The third—the third—
OLIVIA   Is what? Now, let me hear.
NOAH It is my dying kiss—my curse! Go! Go!
OLIVIA That extra kiss? I see! It would commend—
NOAH This Caleb to the jaws of hungry dogs.
OLIVIA Your views are human—
NOAH   When my foes are less. Go!
OLIVIA I go not alone. No parting kiss? None? I go not alone.
NOAH   Alone? No! No! The woes of earth condensed will be your guide.

(*Re-enter* BISHOP)

Go! Go!
BISHOP   Wait yet awhile.
NOAH   Go! Go!
BISHOP   Wait yet.
NOAH You compromise!
BISHOP   You speak unwittingly!
Her views are wrong, but who does not applaud
A will like hers that brooks no veering wind?
A brain that blots out custom's diary?
NOAH Good sense applauds the workings of good sense.
Call nonsense what you please. I take my leave.

(*Opens pocket-book and looks at beard as he goes out*)

BISHOP Your way is yours, and you will see it through.
Now, tell me plainly why you take this course.
'Tis not a case of love?
OLIVIA   What think you, sir? (*exit* OLIVIA)

(*Curtain*)

ACT THREE

Scene One

(*Working-room of Industrial School. On one side are anvil, hammer, forge, benches for shoemakers and carpenters. On the other are tables and chairs for sewing-girls. Rocking-chair, desk, and other things made by carpenters are on exhibition. Walls are lined with work by blacksmiths, shoemakers, and sewing-girls. A screen stands off aside. A small blackboard hangs on rear wall. There is empty space on wall where horse-shoes are to be hung. Boys and girls are uniformed. On the rising of the curtain the* BISHOP *stands alone. He strikes the anvil with a hammer and lays it aside.*)

BISHOP That sound is the password to Negro enfranchisement. Muscle woos the field. Brain woos the market. Wedded they conquer the world. He, in whom they unite, may issue the contract for running all things and award it to himself.

(*Enter* OLIVIA *examining a piece of sewing. The* BISHOP *follows her and tries to steal a kiss*)

OLIVIA (*turning*) As many as you wish, Bishop-father.

BISHOP (*kisses her*) Some boys came to steal my roses. I tapped upon the window-pane and frightened them away. They came again. Again I tapped. Again they fled. I bethought me of some such trick my boyhood's follies knew. I said: "Come, boys! Roses, boys! Have your fill!" Said one: "Thanks, sir! If we can't have the pleasure of stealing your roses, we don't want them." My dear Olivia, 'tis sometimes so with kisses.

OLIVIA You are not all theologian. You are part man.

BISHOP The boys and girls?

OLIVIA They will enter soon.

BISHOP How pass the time?

OLIVIA Speech-making!

BISHOP The speaker?

OLIVIA You!

BISHOP The subject?

OLIVIA Let the occasion suggest. Look! Real anvil, real shoes, real everything!

BISHOP Real work!

OLIVIA Yes!

BISHOP Real life then!

OLIVIA Yes! How tardy it is!

BISHOP How unreal has been the Negro's past! We are a primitive people.

OLIVIA Very!

BISHOP With civilized ideas.

OLIVIA That are mostly borrowed.

BISHOP What a damning combination!

OLIVIA Why, Bishop! You speak truthfully though.

BISHOP 'Tis like a monkey among clocks and watches. The clocks seem to say: "Stop!" The watches say: "Go on!" The watches are hurled at the clocks, and both are ruined. When silence reigns, the monkey says: "I have set progress a foot." 'Tis a damning combination.

OLIVIA Emphasize it, Bishop.

BISHOP Many a naked African is superior to the Negro American collegian. His simple thought is his own, and he can give it an original setting. Witness the proverbs and fables among the wild Africans. Witness the vast amount of undigested thought in the other case.

(*Enter four girls who examine tools and other things on boys' side*)

OLIVIA How make the Negro more original?

BISHOP He must follow the laws of inquisitiveness and necessity. Till then he is a puppet where there is no material for laughter, and is straightway silenced out of court.

OLIVIA Give an example.

BISHOP I am alone. I see the heavens, the earth, and a wild boar. The boar would pierce me, but I seize a rock and break off its tusks. When hungry I slay the boar and eat. As I lie upon the ground old age creeps through me. I arise and build me a house in the boughs of the trees. As I look down upon the damp earth and the bones of the boar I see what lessons I have learned from necessity. As I look from my house and behold the moon, stars, and blue expanse above I grow inquisitive. Gratitude and inquisitiveness wed, and from them I spring a child of song to sing and sing of what I have seen and felt.

OLIVIA How cultivate his own style?

BISHOP His thought must spring from action, and his words from sheer necessity. He who has a thought has a style. Start a handful of snow down a hill. At the foot it is a huge ball. Thus thought finds words for its utterance.

OLIVIA Give an example of thought and style.

BISHOP A dog attacks a cat. The cat claws not, bites not. It simply humps its back, and the dog retires.

OLIVIA What will you draw from that?

BISHOP A proverb showing thought and style.

OLIVIA Give it.

BISHOP The hump in the back, rather than the sharpness of the claws, protects the cat.

OLIVIA One more!

BISHOP A person with rheumatism is undignified in movements.

OLIVIA Now, for that.

BISHOP Few cultivate dignity and rheumatism at the same time.

OLIVIA The Negro would be literary.

BISHOP He would. Let him put his brain into his muscle and both into the world around him, and he will be.

OLIVIA Industrial training makes—

BISHOP For health, wealth, morals, literature, civilization.

(*Two* GIRLS *lift a hammer with difficulty and strike an anvil. The others stand by and go through same motions. When hammer strikes all breathe hard. They stop and rub each other's arms.*

BISHOP *examines rocking-chair.* BOYS *and* GIRLS *enter with tools.* OLIVIA *directs them to places.* BLACKSMITHS, CARPENTERS, *and* SHOEMAKERS *take their places.* GIRLS *go to their side for sewing.* BOY *and* GIRL *stand aside with pencils and pads. All hold up tools and stand ready to begin work*)

BISHOP Congratulations, boys and girls! Again
Congratulations! This is life—real life.
The brow's pure sweat has kept the world God-like.
A hatchet, saw, or hammer in your hand
Is far more eloquent than learned words,
If there be skill to use, spirit to dare.
Each man unto his sphere. The laws of God
Will have it so. Agree with law and live.
Sloth marshalled yesterday to destiny,
A destiny that makes today a death,
A death that's resurrected by the clang
Of tools in brawny hands, of energy,
Thought-pointed, in the markets of the world.
Agree with law and live. You have been told
A silver tongue can steer a nation's bark.
Look at the idle prattle of the past.
Unreal has been our life. We sought with straws
To leverage what others did with steel.
We turned our hopes to bubbles, proudly blew
And wondered why they sent no answer back.
Agree with law and live. 'Tis yours to send
A thrill progressive through the race's heart.
'Tis yours to realize God's ancient way
Of taming savagery through handicrafts.
Let clang the anvil! (BLACKSMITH *strikes shoe*)
          Let the saw's sharp teeth
Gnaw passways through and through rebellious wood.

(CARPENTERS *begin to saw*)

          Progress can not outstrip the needle's point,
Therefore, your needles, girls—your needles, girls.

(GIRLS *begin to sew*)

          Attend, my boys—you of the awl and pegs.
Be clear of sight! Cut straight! Sew well! Know that
Man is but little better than his shoes.

(SHOEMAKERS *begin to work. All are ready to begin*)

          Ready?
ALL   Ready!
BISHOP   To earn your bread?
ALL   Aye! Aye!
BISHOP To do the right?
ALL   Always!
BISHOP   To help mankind?
ALL 'Till life shall end!
BISHOP   Let go! You lead the race!

(*All work vigorously. Enter* FRONY *and* WOMAN *with* OLIVIA'S *book. They sit back to back and search books.* BOY *and* GIRL *with pencils and pads watch workers and write compositions.* BISHOP *and* OLIVIA *move about and examine work.* BOYS *hold up work and examine it.* GIRLS *sew on.* OLIVIA *directs them*)

FRONY (*to* WOMAN) What seek you?
WOMAN   What seek you?
FRONY   A laugh!
WOMAN   Find it!

(*They search books*)

BISHOP (*to* BOY *and* GIRL) I'll read your compositions, little ones.
BOY Mine first!
GIRL   Mine first!
BISHOP   Both first. Each sentence shall Draw from both compositions.
GIRL (*points to* BOY) His thoughts!
BOY (*points to* GIRL)   Her words!
BISHOP What shall the gender of the sentence be?
BOY Don't know. I'll think.
GIRL   Don't know. I'll pray not to.
FONY Ha! ha!
WOMAN   You found the laugh? Where? Where?

FRONY	Nowhere! I laughed to cheer me up to find the laugh.
WOMAN	You might have made me laugh a real laugh.
GIRL	Do laugh!
BOY	A real laugh!
GIRL	'Twill bring again The bloom—

(FRONY *and* WOMAN *spring from their seats and face each other*)

FRONY AND WOMAN (*pointing to each other*)	You lost some twenty years ago.

(BOYS *resume their work quietly*)

OLIVIA	That ring is better than the ring of words.

(GIRLS *hold up work and examine it*)

FRONY (*holds up book*)	The laugh is here.
WOMAN	How know you that?
FRONY	The book Was written by Olivia.
WOMAN (*holds up book and strikes it*)	'Tis here.

(WOMAN *sits and nods.* FRONY *consults* OLIVIA *about book.* BISHOP *reads children's composition*)

BISHOP	"They sew my heart into the fabrics there."
GIRL	My words! Your thoughts! 'Tis masculine!
BOY	No! no!
BISHOP	"He thrones my heart upon the anvil there."
BOY	Your words! Your thought! It is so feminine.
GIRL	How read you that?
BOY	'Tis what I wish to know.
BISHOP	Explain it to yourselves some far on day When you have lived and learned.

(BISHOP *sits in chair and rocks*)

BOY	And we have wed.

(GIRL *covers her face with pad*)

GIRL	Go shame yourself for speaking as you feel.
BOY	Go think of it and shame me with consent.

(WOMAN *drops book, laughs, and runs out.* GIRLS *laugh.* BOYS *keep time working with their tools.* BOY *and* GIRL *strike heads together. Enter* RAHAB *and* DUDE, *magnificently dressed. All stop work.* BOYS *whisper to each other.* GIRLS *shake garments they are working upon and grunt*)

RAHAB	Hewers of wood and drawers of water! No Latin, Greek, or mathematics. None To wear the badge of haughty leadership. Hewers of wood and drawers of water! We men should organize for faith and prayer. Heaven is just. A little faith and prayer, And all the luxuries of earth are ours. (*to* DUDE) Let us be gentlemen and serve the race As politicians.
DUDE	That's the very thing.
RAHAB	'Twill match our dignity.
DUDE	And swell our purse.
GIRLS	Go, simpletons!
DUDE	The girls would have us go.
BOYS	Go, simpletons!
DUDE	The boys would have us go. Suppose we go ere trouble lends us speed.
FRONY	Say, man, why don't you go?
DUDE	Explain and go.

(RAHAB *draws* DUDE *aside and whispers to him.* GIRL *and* BOY *go to them, look them over and write on pads.* BOYS *and* GIRLS *examine each other's work. Two* GIRLS *smell a shoe and turn up their noses. Another* GIRL *holds up handkerchief she has made.* BOY *pretends to blow his nose and motions for it.* GIRL *whips him over the head with it.* OLIVIA *takes horseshoe from* BLACKSMITH *and holds it up.* BLACKSMITH *hangs shoes on wall.* CARPENTER *begins working-design on board.* SHOEMAKER *puts finishing touches on shoe.* GIRLS *measure each other for a dress. Two other* GIRLS *take dirty, ragged little girl, who has entered, behind screen, and dress her in clothes taken from wall. Other* GIRLS *sew on*)

OLIVIA (*holds up horseshoe*)	This is well made. 'Tis perfect, or near so.
BISHOP	How best define perfection?
OLIVIA	In this case 'Tis best done with a hammer.

BISHOP 'Tis the way.
OLIVIA It is not Rahab's way.
BISHOP He counts for naught.
OLIVIA The crowd he represents is troublesome.

(BLACKSMITH *has placed horseshoes on the wall so as to form the word "Work." He taps them gently with a piece of iron to attract attention*)

BLACKSMITH (*to* RAHAB) Out! out!
GIRL Let's shake him out!
 (GIRLS *shake garments*)
BOY AND GIRL Let's rhyme him out!
DUDE Good sense dictates—
BLACKSMITH Good sense dictates.
RAHAB What? What?
DUDE You see the people you've induced to leave
 For Africa.
OLIVIA (*to* RAHAB) They go and you remain?
RAHAB They go, and I remain.
FRONY To live at ease
 On stolen fare.
DUDE They may come here, and then?
RAHAB Let's go! (*they start.* FRONY, GIRL *and* BOY *stand near the door and stop them*)
TWO GIRLS Let's go! (*they walk up against wall and look back*)
 Rahab, a wall! Let's go!
BLACKSMITH (*raises hammer*) A wall's a wall.
 I think he doesn't choose.

(*Re-enter* WOMAN, *laughing*)

WOMAN Such silly things! Rahab, they wait for you.
 'Tis pitiful to see such silly things.
 They must be silly when a thing like you
 Can make them sell their cotton and their mules.
 What cloth you wear! What shoes! You roguish rogue!
 Their hard-earned dollars weight your pockets now.
 They will be here. Beware!
BLACKSMITH (*to* RAHAB) Suppose you go.

(GIRL *and* BOY *draw ugly picture of* RAHAB)

FRONY (*to* BOY *and* GIRL) Now, draw him well.
 We want a hearty laugh.

OLIVIA They would be gentlemen and serve the race
 As politicians.
BISHOP Rahab, politics
 Has been a game with you. Blindly you led.
 As blindly were you followed.
RAHAB I saw well.
 If they did not, they have a chance to learn.
OLIVIA They may learn yet. Think you it possible?
RAHAB When did you bargain for the needed sense?
OLIVIA Simplicity in them breeds theft in you.
 A vote to them is life and death. You take
 The vote and live. They give it you and die.
RAHAB It is a game of sense. I play. They sleep.
OLIVIA You love the race?
RAHAB I love the race? I lead.
 Others may do the loving. I look up.
OLIVIA I love Rahab. (*he turns toward her*)
 I love Rahab.
RAHAB Woman,
 That spurs me on to action.
OLIVIA That's your speech
 Upon yourself. It spurs you on—
BISHOP To death.
BLACKSMITH Sharpen the spurs, Rahab.
FRONY Rahab! (*he turns*)
WOMAN Rahab! (*he turns*)
BLACKSMITH Rahab, the Blacksmith gives you good advice.
FRONY Rahab, we think of you as one would think
 Of—of—
WOMAN This picture here. (GIRL *shows picture.* BOY *is delighted.* GIRLS *throw sewing at* RAHAB)
A GIRL O, we forgot.
 Rahab, you did not earn the cloth you wear.
 Thief! Thief! (GIRLS *pick up sewing*)
BLACKSMITH Thief! Thief!
WOMAN A silly thief!
FRONY A fool!
BLACKSMITH (*goes to* RAHAB) My clothes are plain but paid for with my sweat. (*he rubs against* RAHAB, *who rubs off dirt with his hand*)

Caleb the Degenerate

FRONY Be not so careful of your cloth, Rahab.
WOMAN Your ruling passion will supply your need.
RAHAB Ladies and gentlemen, a gentleman
Like me—
DUDE (*straightens up and steps out*) Like me!
RAHAB (*to* DUDE) I am the orator!
DUDE I am the gentleman.
RAHAB A gentleman
Like me should have the treatment—
DUDE I should have.
RAHAB Let us unite in this!
DUDE United we!
I am the whole. Shadow me as I move. (*he moves about*)
OLIVIA A shadow asks a shadow to unite.
A combination that combines two naughts!
DUDE (*goes to* RAHAB) Are we two naughts?
RAHAB I am the orator.
DUDE I am the other that will equal it.
RAHAB Stand off a pace!
DUDE I fear!
RAHAB What fear you?
DUDE I
Fear you—
RAHAB 'Tis spoken well.
DUDE Will play the fool
And leave me out of it.
OLIVIA You wrangle well.
Rahab, you are a leader?
RAHAB Yes!
DUDE Your name!
My answer! Yes!
RAHAB Does this fine Dude disturb?

(*All cry yes*)

Suppose we put him out. (*all cry no*)
Why not? He helps—
OLIVIA To show what Rahab is.
BISHOP He is—
BLACKSMITH (*strikes anvil*) A sound!

(DUDE *stands beside* BLACKSMITH. GIRLS *put hands to ears as though to listen.* FRONY *goes up to* RAHAB. *She puts hand to ear as though to listen. She goes back to* WOMAN *and pretends to tell her something.* WOMAN *plays dumb.* GIRL *and* BOY *play same and run to* BISHOP. RAHAB *is alone. He turns around and seems lost.* BLACKSMITH *shouts as* RAHAB *did in first act, and blows hard*)

I move me thus when I am glad at heart.

A GIRL Who would I be?
BOY Myself!
WOMAN My own—
FRONY Sweet self!

(*All bow and retire to corners of room, leaving the* BISHOP, OLIVIA, *and* RAHAB *in center of floor.* OLIVIA *opens her book*—"*The Negro and His Hands*")

Now, find the laugh. Rahab might relish it.
RAHAB Ladies and gentlemen, don't laugh at me.
I might commit—
BISHOP You mean might suicide?
RAHAB I might. The strain is hard. I might. Ladies,
I might. Good gentlemen, I might. Don't laugh!

(*All laugh save* BISHOP *and* OLIVIA)

BLACKSMITH (*striking shoe with hammer*) Rahab, I liken this unto your brain.
SHOEMAKER (*driving pegs into shoe*) Rahab, I liken pegs unto your teeth. (*works on a shoe*)
CARPENTER (*sawing board*) Thus would I honor your smooth tongue, Rahab. (*planes a board*)
FRONY Let's laugh again.
OLIVIA No! no! I fear his tears.
BLACKSMITH They might come rushing, rushing. Yes, they might.
RAHAB (*loudly*) Ladies and gentlemen— (BOYS *stop up ears with fingers.* GIRLS *stamp and hiss*)
FRONY (*runs to* RAHAB) Do you not see
They have no mind to listen? You are dull. (*runs back*)
RAHAB (*to* DUDE) Let us combine!
DUDE That is the word. Let us Combine—
RAHAB One friend! One friend!
DUDE To lesson you.
OLIVIA Two fools at outs! One dulls the other's wits.
Two scamps that dare not kiss the lip of Truth!
RAHAB (*looking around, baring his throat*) Give me an instrument.
The end must be!

Give me an instrument! Life's cheating death!

(BOYS *hide tools*)

BISHOP   There is no need of fear. Each give him one.

(*All offer tools*)

RAHAB (*he motions them off*)   My misery may yet cream o'er my life.
WOMAN   I wonder if the Dude is seeking ends.
FRONY   Not to his nonsense, lying, trickery.
OLIVIA   Cowardly Dude, be brave awhile. Lesson
Your friend in suicidal ends. Be quick!

(DUDE *shakes his head*)

BISHOP (*rises from chair*)   The Negro is no suicide as yet.
Some think it shows a most reserved strength.
It is a weakness. Mark my words and heed.
A race that is not suicidal has
Not wit enough—not pluck enough to rule.
WOMAN   Now, find the laugh. Rahab is Rahab still.

(OLIVIA *reads from her book*)

OLIVIA   "There is a man who takes his daily fare
From such as know not life as life."
FRONY (*pointing to* RAHAB)   The man!
OLIVIA   "Who talks for votes and votes to suit his purse."
FRONY   The very man!
WOMAN   He stands the charges well.
RAHAB   Had you not me in mind in writing that?
OLIVIA   I had nothing in mind.
BISHOP   Are you the man?
FRONY   Let us not laugh. It grows too serious.
BISHOP   You are the man. You are the nothing. You—
The politician on whom politics
Casts witchery until your feet are set
In rapid motion. Peril follows then.
You have no light save that ambition lends,
And no man yet did ever walk by it
To a sure destiny. You have no thought
Save that which springs from trifling with itself.
You can not help a saucy whirlwind. Why?
You seldom know just when it will appear.
'Tis here. 'Tis there. 'Tis spent in whirligigs.
If you approach it, woe unto your eyes.
'Tis so with your poor thinking. Who can tell
When you indulge in moments serious?
Who ever saw you spend a silent hour
In linking what is now with what was then?
Thinking with you would be so out of place
That all your organism would rebel.
You might essay it for a moment, but
'Twould be a moment filled with levity.
Offer a helping hand? No man of sense
Would so transgress. 'Tis very dangerous.
A leader you? Laugh at yourself and quit.
OLIVIA   A little laugh would so improve his face.
BISHOP   A leader, you?
OLIVIA   Do ask that tenderly.
He has a past he fain would bolster up.
BISHOP (*tenderly*)   A leader you?
RAHAB   Who says that I am not?

(DUDE *stands behind* BLACKSMITH *and views him disgustingly.* BOY *and* GIRL *stand behind the* BISHOP *and applaud him gently.* FRONY *and the* WOMAN *hold book and seem to read as* BISHOP *talks.* GIRLS *stand together and rock to and fro, holding work in hands.* BOYS *hold tools ready for work.* OLIVIA *pats them on heads. The* BISHOP *holds string attached to a dirty bottle*)

BISHOP   The conjurer of anti-bellum days
Would bottle up a few indifferent herbs,
Mixed with a little sugar, salt, and oil.
He called the bottle Jack. A foot of string

Attached it to his hand. He swayed and groaned.

(BOYS, GIRLS, *and* WOMEN *sway and groan*)

He kissed it, patted it, and spoke to it.

(BOYS, GIRLS, *and* WOMEN *so treat things in their hands*)

"Now, are you ready, Jack? Let's see! Let's see!"

(*They examine things and nod*)

"Let us begin. I start. You follow, Jack.

(*They begin to swing things in their hands*)

Now, this way! That way! Any way you please!

(*They swing in keeping with words*)

You swung your way and thereby told the truth.
Let all who are in doubt or love or fear
Consult with you, good Jack, and fortune fate."

OLIVIA Rahab, consult with Jack and fortune fate.
BISHOP You are as simple as that conjurer.
You hold a vote is ample remedy
For all the ills a backward race may have.
You say: "My people, vote your sentiments.
Be sure they are not yours. You must not think
Of things political. It spoils the drift
Of ancient teachings. Vote your sentiments
The while you taste the drink that buys the vote.
Your sentiments are good as gold. Therefore,
Be certain that you get a fair exchange.
Neglect your work to foster sentiments.
Neglect your family to cast a vote.
Be sure the man who feeds and shelters you
Shall feel the weight of all your sentiments
Advancing his opponent. Simply vote,
And you are great beyond all measurement.
Naught else can equal voting. Simply vote,
And all the past is as it had not been.
Voting is magical. The present holds
No paradise this key can not unlock!'

OLIVIA A leader you?
RAHAB Who says—
OLIVIA The Bishop says—
BISHOP Your votes and follies are an equal twain.
A leader you?
RAHAB Who—?
DUDE (*to* RAHAB) Save your breath.
RAHAB I will.
OLIVIA Observe your thumb and finger. (*he looks at them*) Make them fit Your nose.
FRONY 'Twill save your breath. A book! Observe!

(*She holds book before him. He folds his arms and looks at ceiling*)

WOMAN Observe the men that I bring back with me. (*exit quickly*)
BISHOP Observe the worth of manhood's simple ways.
Observe your carelessness and root it out.
Observe your roughness and the cure for it.
Observe your ignorance and wisdom it.
Observe your savagery—

(*Enter* OLD MAN *and* FOLLOWERS, *men and women, whom* RAHAB *is about to send to Africa*)

OLD MAN To savage parts
We soon set sail. Rahab, we wait on you

(RAHAB *moves among them and bows. Re-enter* WOMAN *with two* OFFICERS)

OFFICER Rahab, we wait on you. (*they lead him out*)
FRONY What of the Dude?
DUDE I am converted.
BLACKSMITH Take a hammer then.
(*he takes one*)
DUDE I feel like growing eloquent.
OLIVIA Proceed
Upon the basis of the anvil there.

OLD MAN   Our leader's gone.
BISHOP   To pay for robbing you.
OLD MAN   The proof?
BISHOP   There's proof enough. His clothes are part.

(*Re-enter* OFFICER *with beaver hat, coat, and vest*)

OFFICER   The rest we will secure when he's in jail.
DUDE   Secure what I have on when I'm in jail.

(OFFICER *leads* DUDE *out*)

OLD MAN (*to* FOLLOWERS)   Let's try again. We must to Africa.
WOMEN FOLLOWERS   We must.

(*Little American flags are passed to members of school*)

OLD MAN   That is our home.
MEN FOLLOWERS   Our home!
WOMEN FOLLOWERS   Our home!
OLD MAN   "My Country 'Tis of Thee" I can not sing.

(*The* BLACKSMITH *sings the three first lines of hymn.* BISHOP, OLIVIA, *and rest of school wave flags*)

OLD MAN   Hush! hush! It means not anything to me.
MEN FOLLOWERS   Not anything!
WOMEN FOLLOWERS   Not anything.
ALL   Nothing.
OLD MAN   What have we given to this goodly land?
BISHOP   A little muscle and a world of sighs.
OLD MAN   We won no victories on bloody fields?
BISHOP   Full many, and we have their heritage.
OLD MAN   Their heritage! A little space to breathe—
          A fruitless hour to feel one's loneliness—
          A country that is one ignoble grave.
BISHOP   Old Man, you wrong the land in which we dwell.
          As you have said it is a goodly land.
          The race is not the unit. It is man.
          The individual eclipses all.
          Who rules his fireside with kindly tact,
          Who robs his neighborhood of ancient sloth,
          Will have no fruitless hour, no loneliness.

(OLIVIA *offers flags to* OLD MAN *and* FOLLOWERS. *They refuse them*)

BISHOP   Ignoble graves but hide ignoble dead.
OLD MAN (*points to flag in* BISHOP'*s hand*) Ignoble you to touch so foul a rag.
          It flaunts a lie in Heaven's trustful face.
          You would be loyal? Negro loyalty
          Is paid in shot and flame. Disloyal we!

(FOLLOWERS *move about and bow assent*)

          Be wise! Join us! Kindle our hated race!
          To Africa! To Africa with them!
          Expansion may expand to Uncle Sam's
          Discomfiture. Our moment then! Be wise!
          A foreign foe may ask our sturdy arm.
          Our moment then! We'll strike! We'll Strike! We'll strike!
          Be wise! Kindle the race! A man? Lead on!

(BISHOP, OLIVIA, *and* SCHOOL *wave flags*)

BISHOP   Disloyal to my native land?
          A traitor to the stripes and stars?
          I lift this tried and sturdy hand
          To forge my brother's prison bars?
          Perish the hellish thought!
          My all shall go as a true patriot's ought.

(FOLLOWERS *shake baggage at* BISHOP)

          Justice at times may slightly swerve
          And turn the course of freedom back.
          Her blinded presence tend to nerve
          The mob that puts me to the rack,
          Yes I am what I am—
          A force to guard the rights of Uncle Sam.

(FOLLOWERS *start to rush out.* PUPILS *wave flags and start to follow.* OLD MAN *beckons, and* FOLLOWERS *return.* PUPILS *wave flags and resume places*)

My faith looks up through blood and tears,
And tarries at the golden dawn
Whose beams slant out across the years
Proclaiming Freedom fully born.
I must do what I can
To hasten on this boon to struggling man.

FOLLOWERS No, no.
PUPILS Yes, yes.

(OLD MAN *starts to go out but stops*)

BISHOP (*pointing to* OLD MAN) He who complains is but a laggard born,
A simpleton, a coward. Mark him well!
He prays of his complaints, and straight complains
Him of his prayers. To him all lands are hells.

(OLD MAN *starts to rush out.* BLACKSMITH *dances before him and stops him*)

BLACKSMITH Abrupt your course! List to a random thought!
Stir up a dust somehow! Squeeze out a sigh!
Bethink you of some trick to murder peace!
Pass on! Pass on! Your mood is moody still!

(*Exit* OLD MAN. FOLLOWERS *start to rush out, but return when the* BISHOP *speaks*)

BISHOP Why chafe you so, my brothers, O, my brothers?
Why strain you ever at a weight you bear not?
Why cloak yourselves against occasion's breezes
That waft to you the perfumes whose inhaling
Divorces Truth from her false cousin, Fancy?
Why form a helmet 'gainst some dreamy evil
That blinds you ever-madly, madly blinds you?
Why gather troubles chance has left around you
As one would gather pebbles by the wayside?
Why with these airy troubles storm the Present
That bird-like comes singing your sure redemption?
Why of these airy troubles raise a bulwark
That severs you from God and God's anointed?

(*They draw nearer and strain to hear*)

Know you the eye that makes a mark of vengeance
Fathers a soul warped by its degradation?
Know you the soul that ever glows and triumphs
Must harbor naught of malice or of envy?
My brothers, O, my brothers, be not wanting
In the clear vision that has led the nations
From life barbaric unto life whose oneness
Proves, as naught else can prove, God's hand in nature.
There is a chance. It lies in the discretion
That hails no spectre-past to thwart the present,
That slays no happy future for the slaying.
There is a chance. It springs from out the wedding
Of native thought to universal triumph.
Too hard you say? Think you a world is conquered
By blowing bubbles on a bed of lilies?

(*They back out slowly in a body*)

The wine of life is brewing, O, my brothers!
The hand of God upholds and tilts the chalice.
Quaff quickly, brothers, quaff! You won't? Your failing
Deserves the wrath of God, the scourge of nations.
Their cudgel, use-inured and anger-pointed,
Is all-sufficient in the day of trial.

Beware its stroke, my brothers, O, my brothers!

(*They disappear as last words are uttered.* PUPILS *wave flags, approach* BISHOP, *bow and retire*)

(*to* PUPILS)   Let us be true to worship, trained in toil,
A standing menace to what gives offense,
And this our land shall be our paradise.
Know you, my faithful children, that the man
Of toil best honored is. His sweaty brow
Is his well-done in life, his grace in death.
The cross and handicrafts are God and man
Revealing each to each. Remember that!

(*All bow assent. Enter* GIRL *from behind screen, holding dirty, ragged clothes in hand*)

GIRL   I am so clean! I feel so good! Thanks! thanks!
Look at my clothes! They fit! They fit! They fit!
Such darling girls you are! Thanks! thanks! thanks! thanks!

(GIRL *moves about while talking.* PUPILS *move and wave flags*)

BISHOP   Work is the basis of life's heritage.
It is the mountain, bottoming at sea,
And rising far above the angry waves
Whereon a people's hopes may fruit in life.
It is the slayer of full many boasts,
The wiper-out of dream-encompassed ends.
The Negro of the past had faith in faith.
Henceforward he must rise to faith in sight.
He visions what is clearly tangible,
And tangles visions with reality.
He needs the wisdom that is won of toil,
The patience that is bred of constant aim,
The hopefulness that stales not out of use,
A sense of worth that slays all else but worth,
A view of God that lets God regulate
Life's devious ways without the prayers of fools.
Work is the basis of life's heritage.

ALL   Thanks! thanks! thanks! thanks! thanks! thanks! (*wave flags*)

BISHOP (*looking up*)   Thanks, Master, thanks! (*Curtain*)

ACT FOUR

Scene One

(*A narrow street. Enter* NOAH *slowly, stroking his beard. The* BISHOP *and* FRONY *follow him at a distance*)

FRONY   Noah! (*he looks back and grunts*)
BISHOP   Noah! (*he looks back, clears his throat and goes out.* FRONY *follows him*) A man of few words and much beard! May be unpleasant dreams of his beard have added to his melancholy. 'Tis often so reported. Such a beard costs fifty years of toil, tears, and expectations. It is worth, in this case, all but the life of the owner. He might exchange it for the undoing of Caleb. The end! The ungodly end! Caleb has disappeared. Now, Olivia goes. The ungodly end! No no! Be thwarted, logic! I would have no image of that end. (*Re-enter* FRONY) The report, Frony?
FRONY   It is true. Caleb went weighted with baggage.
BISHOP   What of Olivia?
FRONY   She comes this way, baggage in hand and good-by on lip.
BISHOP   Has Noah found tongue?
FRONY   No!
BISHOP   He may.
FRONY   When he loses his beard.
BISHOP   Or Caleb finds his reward.

(*Enter* OLIVIA, *baggage in hand, followed by* NOAH)

OLIVIA   Caleb shall soon find his reward.
ALL   Olivia!
OLIVIA   Good-by!
FRONY (*removing* OLIVIA's *hat*)   Good-by!
BISHOP (*taking baggage*)   Good-by!
NOAH   Say good-by for me.

BISHOP AND FRONY Good-by!
OLIVIA This is a serious company.
NOAH Yes! Say good-by for me.
BISHOP AND FRONY Good-by!
OLIVIA This is misguided company.
BISHOP "Caleb's the man! Caleb's secure. Caleb shall soon find his reward!" These are your speeches.
OLIVIA Yes! As Frony says: "Woman's wit may cudgel man's." Caleb's the man for what? He's secure in what? His reward shall be what?
BISHOP I might have questioned thus.
FRONY (*going to* BISHOP) Yes! Why did you not?
OLIVIA He is the man to expiate his crimes. He is secure in the coils of retribution. His reward shall be death.
NOAH Death!
FRONY (*to* OLIVIA, *patting her on shoulder*) We make progress.
BISHOP Why this suspense?
OLIVIA Why your charge? Your speeches are: "Reflect, my child! You should not wed this hell-builder upon earth. Your steps are led not heavenward. My daughter is in love. She needs no father." You charged—
FRONY On and on!
OLIVIA I balanced it with suspense.
NOAH Caleb! Suspense! Death! (*looks at beard in pocket-book*)
OLIVIA Good nature writhes under such charges. Sharpened wits though are the remedy.
FRONY Your answer, Bishop?
BISHOP You saw! You heard! You know!
NOAH No, not what I know.
BISHOP You were so kind—
OLIVIA To Caleb?
BISHOP Yes!
OLIVIA I was kind to Patsy.
BISHOP There was I misled.
NOAH There was I—but death!
OLIVIA Our school first lived in Patsy's mind. I came with views unsuited to our people. She was my teacher. I built upon her thought. Now, see the result. Her wish was I speak well of Caleb until her taking off. I did so. You misjudged.
BISHOP My child, Caleb asked me for your hand.

(NOAH *is greatly agitated*)

OLIVIA Perchance he heard how you charged. He then countercharged for fun in his fiendish way.
NOAH Fiendish? Yes, fiendish! Death!
OLIVIA You remember how he ran when I appeared?
BISHOP Yes!
OLIVIA You remember my ideal man?
BISHOP Yes!
OLIVIA What more was needed?
BISHOP Yes! yes! But your speeches were— Well— Your pardon—your pardon! (*he embraces and kisses her*)
FRONY Bishop! (*he turns her loose.* FRONY *embraces her*) A part of her pardon's mine.
NOAH Take my pardon, too. (BISHOP *and* FRONY *embrace her*)
BISHOP What of Caleb's reward?
NOAH Death!
OLIVIA In a sane hour his conscience mastered him.
NOAH Conscience! (*shakes his head*)
OLIVIA He went to yon lone wood with a piece of meat, a jug of water, and a dagger.
FRONY (*aside*) Ah, the baggage!
OLIVIA The meat and water come first. Then comes the dagger.
NOAH Quickly! Surely!
BISHOP Poor lad!
NOAH What said you, Bishop?
OLIVIA Poor crazed lad!
NOAH Sympathy misplaced is hope hopeless.
BISHOP He was crazed, you say? How?
OLIVIA Drink! Cocaine! Cigarettes!
BISHOP (*to* NOAH) Can you forgive?
NOAH Can I forget my loss, my beard?
BISHOP (*aside*) I think not!
OLIVIA Your loss, father? You did not explain it.
NOAH Explain it? No!
FRONY Hereafter let us exchange wedding mysteries for bearded ones.
OLIVIA Must I be off to Boston without hat or baggage?
FRONY To Boston?
BISHOP To Boston?
OLIVIA I go to speak for the school.

(NOAH *grunts and breathes in a way that shows he is relieved*)

BISHOP (*gives her baggage*) Good-by! My prayers are yours.

FRONY (*puts on hat*) Good-by! I'll to the train with you.
OLIVIA Good-by! Good-by, father!
NOAH Good-by! Woo business! (*exit* OLIVIA *and* FRONY)
BISHOP Noah, can you—?
NOAH Forgive? No! (*exit looking at beard*)
BISHOP Woman's wit did cudgel man's. Her speeches! My witlessness! 'Twas fair enough! I should have known. Poor crazed lad! Rahab is responsible. Well, I have no beard to mourn and revenge, and I may render the poor lad service. I will search him out. (*exit*)

(*The curtain rises on next scene immediately*)

Scene Two

(*A wood. Before* CALEB's *hut. At the rising of the curtain* CALEB *is seated on a rock with his back to the hut. He looks like a wild man. His hair is unkept. He is nigh shirtless. His legs are bare from knees down. They have been broken by a fall, and are bloody from the attack of a dog. It is a dreary wood. A piece of meat hangs from a tree. A jug of water hangs from roof of hut. The moon and stars give light. He hugs his legs, looks from side to side, pants and lolls his tongue like a dog.*)

CALEB My legs! My legs! (*points to meat*) Meat! (*to drink*) Drink!
This—this means death.
Three days, three days and nights, I've suffered thus.
In putting up that meat I fell. My legs
Were broken. I crawled here. I here remain.
A stray dog found me here. (*points to sores*) Here! here! here! here!
He bit me, tore my flesh. Here! here! here! here!
He left no flesh upon the bones. Here! here—!
My legs! My legs! Death woos! I fear? No! no!

(*He tries to rise, but falls back*)

I must, therefore I will. My dagger's keen! (*holds it up*)
I have not strength of heart to use it yet.
If I could sleep a little, I might wake
With strength enough—enough. I'll try! My legs!

(*He tries to sleep. He pants and lolls his tongue. Enter* BISHOP *and* DOCTOR *unseen*)

BISHOP (*to* DOCTOR) That's Caleb—
DOCTOR The degenerate?
BISHOP Yes! yes!
CALEB (*faintly*) My legs! My legs!
DOCTOR He is a parricide?
BISHOP That drove him here—
CALEB (*very faintly*) My legs! My legs!
BISHOP To die.
A little daily.
DOCTOR Why his many crimes?
BISHOP He claims his mother sinned ere he was born.
This tainted him. Therefore his wicked course.
CALEB I can't! Off, sleep! My legs! My legs! Meat! Drink!

(*Takes up dagger and kisses it*)

My only friend! I kiss you! Oh! My legs!
She sinned ere I was born. Therefore I am
My present self. She sinned! I am—! My legs!

(*He tries to grasp dagger tightly*)

Have I the strength? Have I the heart? I'll try!

(*He trembles. His teeth chatter*)

I'm cold! I'm hot! I'm sad! I'm woe-begone!
I have a mind that puts me out of mind.
The stars shall set, shall set and rise, and I—
Be true, good blade—shall be as cold as they.
BISHOP You heard?
DOCTOR His mother sinned! A dog's excuse!
BISHOP Pure mother-love, consoling mother-love
Is the one balm that long-lost Eden gave
To guilty man and could not take away.
By mother-love man is whate'er he is.

CALEB
For mother-love he struggles, conquers, dies.
Through mother-love the stars his kindred are.
Shall anything that evil man calls guilt
Dry up this love within the breast of him
Whose bone, whose sinue, and whose blood are hers?
No! No! She did not sin. She loved! She loved!
Are we not taught love is the law fulfilled?

CALEB O, God, if I have sinned because the blood
Thou gavest me was tainted ere my birth,
Whose is the wrong? Whose is the reckoning?
Master, I leave it all with Thee—with Thee.
Men sneer and say: "Be guided by your will!"
I have no will! I never had a will!
Thy fate, O God, did rob me of my will!

BISHOP A babe was he whose soft and dimpled cheeks
Invited kisses from a seraph's lips.
A gentle mother thought his coo a prayer.
Old seers beheld in him God's messenger.
But he through Rahab sank and sank and sank,
And cheers him with the thought—
God made him so.

CALEB The stars shall set, shall set and rise, and I—
Begin, good blade—shall be as cold as they.

(*He tries to stab himself. They take dagger from him. He does not recognize them. He hugs his legs more tightly and snaps at them dog-fashion. They examine his legs*)

DOCTOR His legs are broken.
BISHOP Oh, what savage bites!
The flesh is gone! The bones stare out at us!
DOCTOR They must be taken off. The hospital—
BISHOP That's death! That's death?

CALEB My legs! My legs! The morgue!
The morgue! I see! How cold it is! My legs!
Gentlemen, are you gentlemen? My legs!
BISHOP His mind! It wavers now.
DOCTOR 'Ts better so.
Its weakness is far stronger than its strength.
CALEB I'm at the hospital! You've cut them off!
You brutes cut off my legs! Off! off! I say!
I see! They're coming back! Come on, good legs!
Off! Off! You butchers, off! Your knives are sharp!
Come on, good legs, and take me from the morgue.
Off! off! you brutes! You'd butcher me again!
Come, my right leg! Come, my left leg! That's it!
On, good right leg? On, good left leg? (*he feels*) Yes! Yes!
Welcome, tried friends! Let's from this cursed place!
Back! back! you brutes! Your knives are sharp. Back! Back!
Let's down the steps! Back! back! you brutes! Right on!
Down—down the steps! Now, we are half-way down.
My right foot, you shall not, shall not turn round.
'Tis done! The toes are where the heel should be.
I now go up a step and down a step.
Back! back! you brutes! Your knives! Your knives! My legs!
My right leg's off and hops up, step by step.
My left leg's off and hops down, step by step.
My body falls! You'll take it to the morgue.
The morgue's so cold—so cold—so—
What—is—this? (*falls*)
DOCTOR (*looks at him*) 'Tis death!

(*He walks off.* BISHOP *looks down on him*)

His mother sinned ere he was born.

	This tainted him, therefore his wicked course.
BISHOP	No! no! She did not sin. Caleb was led To that belief.
DOCTOR	Was led?
BISHOP	Rahab's the man.
DOCTOR	Rahab? His sin is great. I would know all.
BISHOP	His evil genius wrought this ruin here.
DOCTOR	Eternal vengeance should pursue him then.
BISHOP	It does pursue. Perhaps his spirit now Is mingling with— (*he hesitates*)
DOCTOR	The damned! A spade's a spade.
BISHOP	I know the man, his life. But yesterday He did confess to me. Noah was there. His gloomy cell and gloomier deeds are weights He can not bear. He takes no food, no drink.
DOCTOR	How wrought he such a ruin?
BISHOP	Rahab's speech Charmed Caleb when a youth.
DOCTOR	Many were charmed.
BISHOP	Then followed teachings that few youths could stand. His love for parents dwindled day by day. Restraint was not for him who knew so much. He hated work and all who favored it. His ideal gentleman must ever eat The bread another earns and wear the clothes He picks up, borrows, steals. He hated God Because he saw his fellows prosperous.
DOCTOR	This came from Rahab's teaching?
BISHOP	All of it. A living lesson eats into the soul.
DOCTOR	Caleb's belief was strong. How was it shaped?
BISHOP	When he was thwarted of some luxury Rahab would say: "This is your mother's sin." And quote the text that seems to bear it out.
DOCTOR	I wonder if he's dead.
BISHOP	Who's dead?
DOCTOR	Rahab!
BISHOP	Noah is with him. He will bring us word.
DOCTOR	Rahab was satisfied?
BISHOP	Are devils?
DOCTOR	No!
BISHOP	Caleb must drink, become a bondless slave To cigarettes.
DOCTOR	Noah delays—delays.
BISHOP	While Caleb slept Rahab would hold cocaine So that he'd sniff it as he breathed.
DOCTOR	The end Was then in sight. (*aside*) Noah, report the end.
BISHOP	This ruin here was not responsible.
DOCTOR	Rahab thinks what? Or what thought he? Past tense For him.
BISHOP	Past tense? Ah, yes! "Fool, fool was I. O, pardon Caleb, God. I should be damned."
DOCTOR	He so confessed?
BISHOP	He did.

(*Enter* NOAH, *hurriedly*)

DOCTOR (*to* NOAH)	He is—? Let's hear!
NOAH	Dead! Dead!
BISHOP	His last words were—?
NOAH	"Fool, fool was I. O, pardon Caleb, God. I should be damned."

(*He sees* CALEB)

	Dead? (*he kneels by him*) I'll forgive. God help me to forgive.
DOCTOR	Man is a mystery.
BISHOP	He started pure. But now? What of the best man now? Virtue In some mysterious way has mothered sin. Evil may back-step till it ends in good.
DOCTOR	The proverb saith: "We have all been born, But not interred." The thought's worth thinking on.
BISHOP	Another saith: "Man is like the grass."

(DOCTOR *puts his arm around* BISHOP *and looks at* CALEB. NOAH *remains kneeling. Curtain. It rises on next scene as quickly as possible*)

Caleb the Degenerate

Scene Three

(*Grounds of industrial school. On the rising of the curtain* NOAH *is embracing and kissing* OLIVIA, *who holds bank-checks in her hand. The* BISHOP *and* FRONY *stand apart and point to them. Boys and girls of the Industrial School eye* DUDE, *who is now United States' soldier. He is so uniformed. He stands erect in rear and holds large flag.* OLD MAN *and* FOLLOWERS *look up at flag and wave little flags.* GIRLS *and* BOYS *wave flags*)

NOAH My Olivia was right.
OLIVIA Thanks!
BISHOP My Olivia will ever be right.
OLIVIA Thanks!
NOAH My Olivia—
BISHOP My Olivia—
OLIVIA A daughter's thanks to both!
FRONY Out with your checks, Olivia! A hundred thousand, did you say?
OLIVIA Yes! More is to follow.
FRONY Thanks to the givers!
DUDE Thanks! Let's use the gifts. More grounds, workshops, dormitories.
OLD MAN Thanks, Olivia!
FOLLOWERS Yes, thanks!
BISHOP You did it all yourself?
NOAH Is she not Olivia?
OLD MAN Have faith in Olivia.
FOLLOWERS Do!
BLACKSMITH (*to* FOLLOWERS) How changed you are!
DUDE And I?
GIRLS (*pointing to* DUDE) The Dude!
DUDE (*indignantly*) No! The soldier.
FRONY (*goes to* DUDE) Your clothes have a brave front.

(GIRLS *approach* DUDE, *clap hands and retire*)

BLACKSMITH (*to* DUDE) They may applaud you next.
BISHOP (*to* OLIVIA) Give us the story of your enterprise.
OLIVIA Chance threw me with a group of millionaires.
  I doubted, fretted, feared. At last I spoke.
  The speech was short and simple. See the checks!
BISHOP They lost no time in writing them?
OLIVIA   A tale
  Our folks oft slumber o'er drew tears from them.
FRONY And they left checks with you.
OLD MAN   The difference!
DUDE 'Tis plainly seen.
OLD MAN   Appreciation sends
  A hundred thousand us-ward. Therefore we
  Should have—
BISHOP   Ten million bank accounts.
OLD MAN   Yes! yes!
  We have appreciation now.
FOLLOWERS   We have.
BISHOP Greatness holds trust with you, Olivia.
  Your stock in trade? Grit, health, and breathing space.
  Your spirit mutinies 'gainst time and tide.
  You see no inch that may not make an ell.
  You woo no aim you do not wed in time.
NOAH Why do you pause? True words and precious words
  Are these you speak. Why do you pause, I say?
  Speak on! Pause not!
OLD MAN   Now pause he must; for time
  And praise entrap her not.
NOAH (*stroking his beard*)   Good! Good!
                              'Tis true!
FRONY You speak like men. Redeem a faulty past.

(GIRLS *embrace and kiss* OLIVIA)

BLACKSMITH A woman's way!
FRONY   'Tis more sincere than speech.
  Redeem a faulty past.
BLACKSMITH (*to* MEN)   Suppose we do.

(MEN *start to* OLIVIA)

OLIVIA Good sirs, I need a rest. (*they stop*)
FRONY (*kisses her*)   She needs a rest.

(FOLLOWERS *laugh and pat each other*)

OLD MAN (*to* FOLLOWERS) Redeem the past we must.
FOLLOWERS   We must.
DUDE   We must.
BISHOP The change was sudden.
OLD MAN   And sincere.
BISHOP   The cause?

OLD MAN   Your speech did warn.
BISHOP   What then?
OLD MAN   We found Rahab
   An evil influence.
DUDE   His death paid not
   The havoc that he wrought.

(FOLLOWERS *move about and look at their ragged clothes*)

OLD MAN (*pointing to* FOLLOWERS)   Behold his work!
   The homes he ruined shall condemn him here.
NOAH   The soul he ruined shall condemn him there.
OLD MAN   Henceforth we labor with Olivia.

(OLIVIA *bows.* FOLLOWERS *bow*)

BISHOP (*to* DUDE)   You look the man that's needed in the wars.
DUDE   I will remember me to be a man.

(BOY *holds flag.* GIRLS *turn* DUDE *around and examine his clothes*)

BISHOP   Let each remember him to be a man.
   Who is down-trodden? He who thorns his course.
   Who is a weakling? He who weds with sloth.
   Who fails ignobly? He who cultivates
   The aims that grovel and the wits that shame.
   Let each remember him to be a man;
   And, brothers mine, the world has naught to give
   That may not nestle in your willing hands.
OLD MAN   I like that speech, my brother. Speak right on!
FOLLOWERS   Right on!
DUDE   Right on!
BISHOP   What say you girls?
GIRLS   Right on!
OLIVIA   Right on to work! 'Tis well enough to stir
   One's blood with talk. 'Tis better still to make
   That talk a text and work the sermon out.
   I go to work. (*Exit quickly*)
OLD MAN   We go to work. (*Exit* OLD MAN *with* FOLLOWERS)
BLACKSMITH   To work!

(BLACKSMITH, BOYS, *and* GIRLS *run out*)

DUDE   I go to war. Some say the Negro shirks
   The tasks of peace. Who says he will not fight?
   I go to war. (*Exit, bearing flag with dignity*)

(FRONY *starts to run after* DUDE. BISHOP *and* NOAH *stop her*)

BISHOP (*to* FRONY)   To war?
FRONY (*after freeing herself*)   To work. (*exit quickly*)
NOAH (*very solemnly*)   At last!
   Your words! My beard! Olivia's success!
   At last! (*exit slowly*)
BISHOP   How safe and handy is plain truth!
   My words! His beard! Olivia's success!
   Hers is success. Failure? 'Tis a misfit.
   To coincide is life. One measures not
   His native force. He sees no chains that bind
   His ready out-put to a waiting need.
   He tries. He fails. He tries and fails again.
   Each trial curbs him in the onward race.
   Each failure veers him from a happy goal.
   "Upon such terms," says he, "life is not life.
   False Life and I are dwelling by a stream.
   I thirst. Life tosses water on the shore.
   The shore is sand, and I am thirsty still.
   Away, false Life, away! I'll drink! I'll lave
   My thirsty limbs! I've drunk! Where is the ground?
   My limbs are awkward. They belong on shore.
   They splash! My mouth! My nose! My ears! I sink!
   My head is up! False legs! False arms! I sink!
   Up once again! I—choke! I—I—sink!"

Failure? 'Tis a misfit. Success is what?
'Tis a measurement of self. 'Tis measurement
Of all the forces that encounter self.
'Tis fitting these together day by day.
'Tis seeing goals with eyes that never blink.
'Tis finding desert spots and changing them
So that their fruitage stars man's ancient lot,
And links his freedom with the linked spheres. (*exit*)

(*Curtain*)

Garland Anderson (1886–1939)

Appearances

1925

Garland Anderson may be remembered in London as the black man who introduced Nu-Snack, the cold malted milk, to England in the 1930's. In America he was the first black to have a full-length play produced on Broadway.

The life story of Mr. Anderson is nearly as dramatic as the plot of his own play. Born in Wichita, Kansas, circa 1886, he had completed four years of schooling before his father moved and took a job as janitor in the Sacramento, California, Post Office. At this time Garland Anderson's mother died. "I was eleven and I ran away from home."

The early 1920's found Mr. Anderson, now in his mid-thirties, working as a bellhop in a San Francisco hotel. After viewing *The Fool*, a moralistic drama by Channing Pollack, Garland Anderson decided to write his own play.

At first the idea seemed absurd.... No one realized more than myself that though I wanted to write this play, I had no training in the technique of dramatic construction; but I also realized that to shirk what I wanted to do could be likened to the outer shell of the acorn after it was planted in the ground saying to the inner stir of life for expression, "What are you stirring for? Surely you don't expect to become a great oak tree?"

With this firm conviction I determined to write a play.

In three weeks of writing between calls at the switchboard at the hotel he had completed the story of a black bellhop falsely accused of rape. He entitled it *Don't Judge by Appearances*. The title was later abbreviated to *Appearances*.

At a friend's suggestion he sent the play to the actor Al Jolson, who gave the novice playwright a trip to New York City to seek his fortune. A backer's audition was arranged at the Waldorf; the name of Governor Al Smith appeared on the invitation. Richard Harrison (de Lawd in *Green Pastures*, 1930) read *Appearances* to 600 guests while Mr. Anderson "sat near by in his bellhop uniform." One hundred forty dollars was raised.

Garland Anderson was not discouraged. "You can have what you want if you want it hard enough." He wrote to President Coolidge. When an appointment was refused, he went to the White House and persuaded the President's secretary to allow him an interview. "It was due in no small measure to his interest in my work that my play was produced in New York."

Lester A. Sagar took over the production of *Appearances*, a script that had "three colored characters." They were cast black.

Broadway policy in 1925 was to play "colored" roles in blackface to avoid mixed casts. The exception had been the introduction of the black comedian, Bert Williams, into the Ziegfeld Follies (see *Star of the Morning*). Rehearsals had hardly begun when a headline appeared "Nedda Harrigan Quits Play with Negro in the Cast":

Miss Harrigan emphasized the fact that her decision must not be construed as indicative of race prejudice, but said that the production of a play called for so close an association with other players she felt that she could not be happy under the circumstances.

In the year previous, 1924, the press had demanded that the off-Broadway production of *All God's Chillun Got Wings* be banned because Paul Robeson kissed the hand of the white actress. But the times were in transition. Because *Appearances* succeeded with a mixed cast, David Belasco took courage and produced *Lulu Belle* (1926) with white actors as mulattos but the rest of the company Negro.

Appearances opened at the Frolic Theater on October 13, 1925, and ran twenty-three performances. In 1927–1929 the play toured Los Angeles, Seattle, Chicago, and San Francisco, playing several weeks or months in each city. On April 1, 1929, *Appearances* opened again in New York City at the Hudson Theater. This time it ran twenty-four performances.

By the time the production arrived in

London, in March 1930, a black comedian named Doe Doe Green (playing the role of Rufus) had so delighted the English as a *succès de curiosité* that Mr. Green was billed in headlines larger than the play's title.

Despite the distortion that made Rufus the star, the theme of *Appearances*—"as a man thinketh, so is he"—is clearly carried by Carl the bellhop. This sober, hardworking, cheerful, and very self-possessed character was certainly an advance in dignity over any black image on the professional stage at that time. It is in sharp contrast to Rufus, who is no fool.

Mr. Anderson's statement was a brave one for 1925: a black man is *falsely* accused by a white woman. How did he dare present a white woman whose virtue was inferior to that of a black man? Mr. Anderson had to create a *dénouement* for Broadway's satisfaction, and he did.

To make moral judgments about Mr. Anderson and his play is perhaps to lose sight of an amazing black phenomenon, one that has always been present in America: the black man who believes that personal hard work can triumph over social obstacles. Because white America subscribed to this triumph-of-the-will tenet, the society has (on occasion) made room for the Garland Andersons—as examples of the theorum that a man born in a log cabin can become president.

Garland Anderson wrote for a white audience, attempting to give them something better than what they usually saw of the black man. That he had little or no influence on the black theater is true although Mr. Anderson claimed to have written three other plays. The last years of his life (he died in 1939) were spent as an ordained minister of Constructive Thinking at the Truth Center. He published a book on his beliefs, *Uncommon sense*, and traveled widely.

A newspaper in Regina, Canada reported on one of Mr. Anderson's lectures (in 1936), that "He is the first Negro since Booker T. Washington to tour the country speaking to white people only. Seldom, he admitted, does a Negro ever appear to hear him. 'They are not interested,' he said rather sadly."

Appearances

CAST OF CHARACTERS

FRANK THOMPSON
CARL
MRS. GLADYS THOMPSON
FRED KELLARD
ELSIE BENTON
LOUISE THORNTON
JUDGE TOHRNTON
RUFUS JONES
ELLA
JACK WILSON
POLICE OFFICER
JUDGE ROBINSON
CLERK OF COURT
COURT STENOGRAPHER
GERALD SAUNDERS
HIRAM MATTHEWS
A. A. ANDREWS
BAILIFF

PROLOGUE

(SCENE: *lobby of the Hotel Mount Shasta. A small residential hotel in San Francisco. There is a desk, a partition left of the desk that partially masks door to an office. In centre of left wall is a staircase going up and off left. The main entrance is right. Entrance back of desk by lifting section of desk. Service 'phone back of desk, a cigar, cigarette case. Left and below stairs door to service quarters. Other furniture to suit.*
TIME: *7:30 evening.*
DISCOVERED: *at rise:* JUDGE ROBINSON *and* JUDGE THORNTON *both seated. Lights up*)

JUDGE ROBINSON   Same old topics, nothing new. Can't find anything in the paper.
JUDGE THORNTON   Tell me, Judge Robinson, do you believe this man whom you were forced to sentence to-day was guilty.
JUDGE ROBINSON   Why—yes, I do.
JUDGE THORNTON   Sorry I can't agree with you, but I don't think he was.
JUDGE ROBINSON   How can you say that, Judge Thornton, when you were in court yourself, for surely you could see that all the appearances were against him.
JUDGE THORNTON   I know, but I have come to believe we cannot judge entirely by appearances.
JUDGE ROBINSON   You're getting sentimental in your old age. Why not only the appearances, but the testimony, the evidence, in fact everything was against him.
JUDGE THORNTON   Admitting all of that, it was only circumstantial at the best and all during this trial to-day there was going over in my mind something which Carl (the bell-boy here) told me the other day. He described to me the most beautiful and realistic dream I ever heard, in this dream there was a trial scene which in many ways was similar to the case before you to-day.
JUDGE ROBINSON   The bell-boy. Oh, yes, he is the one who thinks a man can do anything he believes he can. What is he delving in, some kind of creed or religion?
JUDGE THORNTON   Oh, he says it is just simple faith and no particular creed or religion.
JUDGE ROBINSON   If he believes a man can do anything, then why don't he make something of himself? Why is he working as a bell-hop?
JUDGE THORNTON   That is just what I was going to tell you, be believes that his dream is coming true, for he intends to work it out himself and in doing it he will prove that any man can do what he believes he can, if his purpose is right.
JUDGE ROBINSON   How will this prove his point?
JUDGE THORNTON   He reasons this way. That if he, with color, lack of education, lack of money and all against him, can work his dream out in real life, it will prove that other people with greater advantages can naturally do greater things.
JUDGE ROBINSON   What is this dream all about?

JUDGE THORNTON   I wouldn't want to spoil the effect by trying to tell you. I'd like him to tell it to you just as he did to me, for his description is so realistic that you can almost see and hear each character.

JUDGE ROBINSON   Well, you have me interested now. I want to hear it.

(*Enter* CARL)

JUDGE THORNTON   Carl! I want you to tell Judge Robinson your unusual dream just as you told it to me.

CARL   Judge, it would take too long, and maybe Judge Robinson wouldn't want to listen.

JUDGE ROBINSON   Go right ahead, Carl, I haven't a thing in the world to do.

CARL   It's all so wonderful that when I think of it I just fill up, but I believe it will come true. You know my dream began right here in the lobby of this hotel, and both you, Judge Robinson and Judge Thornton were in it, and a lot of other people you both know. There was Mrs. Thornton, Mr. Wilson, Mrs. Thompson, Mr. Thompson, Mr. Kellard, and other people. Do you know I seem to see it now, just as real, just as plain . . . first I heard the telephone ring, then I saw someone appear in the distance, not so plain at first, but it seemed to grow clearer and clearer until I heard Mr. Thompson say:

(*Fade out into Act One*)

ACT ONE

(*Scene: same as Prologue. Discovered at rise:* CARL *standing center.* MR. THOMPSON *answering 'phone*)

THOMPSON   Yes sir . . . Mr. Morie wants his mail, Carl.

CARL   Yes, sir. I'll take it right up, sir.

(MRS. THOMPSON *comes down stairs. Goes to desk*)

THOMPSON (*as she passes him*)   Still angry, my dear?

MRS. THOMPSON   Who? I?—What's the use of being angry?

THOMPSON   I know I have my faults, but I don't deserve this.

MRS. THOMPSON   Maybe it's because of your faults, you still keep up the semblance. A wife sometimes is a very good protection.

THOMPSON   It's a good thing I've got a sense of humor.

(FRED KELLARD *enters from swing doors*)

KELLARD (*goes to desk*)   How d'ye.

THOMPSON   How do you do, sir. (*turns register and offers pen*) Nice evening, isn't it?

KELLARD   Yeh—fine—oh, I ain't expecting to stay here. I'm looking for Mr. Jack Wilson.

(CARL *enters down stairs*)

THOMPSON   Mr. Wilson's out. (*to* CARL) Did Mr. Wilson leave any message?

CARL   He said if a gentleman named Kellard called to tell him he would be back by eight o'clock. (*sits on bench*) He had to go to his office. It's almost that now.

KELLARD   Thank you. That's me. I'm Kellard. (*takes out watch*) Guess my Ingersoll's mite fast.

THOMPSON   Won't you take a seat and wait?

KELLARD   Thanks. (*sits on settee*) Great city, this.

THOMPSON   Ah, yes. San Francisco is the greatest city on the Pacific Coast, bar none.

KELLARD   Did you say bar one?

THOMPSON   I said bar none—guess you're from the East.

KELLARD   Well I was born in England, but I've been a cowpuncher so long I've almost forgotten it, the place I come from now is known as Hell's Hole, and it is. (*rises*) You got seegars there?

THOMPSON   Yes, sir.

KELLARD (*turns to* MRS. THOMPSON)   Does the lady mind if I smoke?

MRS. THOMPSON   Not at all.

KELLARD   Thanks. (*goes to desk*) I got a particular good taste in cigars.

THOMPSON (*takes a box of cigars from case*) Yes. Well, here's one I can recommend.

KELLARD (*reaches in box*)   Yes, sir. A particular good taste.

THOMPSON   Three for a dollar.

KELLARD (*takes hand away suddenly*)   Yeh —but my pocketbook limits my taste to about two for a quarter.

THOMPSON (*gets another box and offers it*) Here you are. A very good cigar.

KELLARD (*takes two. Puts one in pocket, lights other*) Business rushin'.

THOMPSON Saturday night is our off night. Most of our guests spend a week end in the country.

KELLARD Must be nice to be rich. (*to* CARL) What's that you're reading, son? (CARL *stands up*) Oh! Kinder deep, ain't it?

CARL No, sir. I don't find it so.

KELLARD Yeh! I tried to read it, once, couldn't make a thing out of it.

CARL You read it, sir?

KELLARD Yes, sir. A school teacher we had up our way from Los Angeles had this book among others. Well, she was a nice cheerful little body, but somehow I couldn't get interested in her.

(THOMPSON *goes across, looks at* MRS. THOMPSON, *then looks out door left, then exits office door*)

CARL Her. Oh!! I see! I suppose if you could have got interested in her, you might have worked up an interest in *her* books.

KELLARD (*goes to chair right of table, sits*) You said a mouthful, son. But she certainly was a nice cheerful little body.

(ELSIE *enters door left, hesitates, then goes to desk*)

ELSIE I beg pardon, but do you have cigarettes?

CARL (*goes behind desk*) Yes, ma'am. Any particular brand?

ELSIE Have you the Deities with the cork tips?

CARL Yes, miss.

ELSIE (*pays for cigarettes, looks all round lobby*) So sorry to trouble you, but I forgot to get a package in town and I thought you might possibly keep them. It's nice to know a place where a lady may purchase cigarettes without going into a regular tobacco shop.

CARL (*offers coin*) Your change, miss.

ELSIE Keep the change. (*exits door left*)

(CARL *returns to bench* THOMPSON *enters, looks out door left*)

KELLARD Yes, sir. Must be plum embarrassing for that lady to go into a real tobacco shop. Yes, sir. Say don't you serve meals here?

THOMPSON Yes, sir, but dinner's over.

KELLARD Only asked ya to make talk. I had dinner down the street, in the Oriental Cafe.

That boy's got a mighty good head on him. I tried that book he's reading. Someways I think I'm plain thick.

THOMPSON Carl not only understands it, but I am sure he practices it, eh, Carl?

CARL Yes, sir.

KELLARD (*sits*) And it works?

CARL Yes, sir.

KELLARD Yeah, always?

CARL It has never failed me yet.

KELLARD As I remember it, it worked mighty well for that little school teacher, exceptin' it was kinder slow in one thing.

THOMPSON What was that?

KELLARD She was trying to get a husband.

THOMPSON A husband? Wouldn't a single man do? (*both laugh*)

MRS. THOMPSON Apparently not nowadays.

(THOMPSON *exits office*)

KELLARD Well, you know what I mean.

CARL Did she get one, sir?

KELLARD Married the biggest crook and liar in the country.

CARL Crook?

KELLARD Yes, sir, and made him so durned honest, that cheatin' him is like stealing candy from a baby. He's still a right smart liar. We call him A. A. Alias Ananias.

CARL Who was Ananias?

KELLARD Ananias? Why, he's the granddaddy of all the liars. Yes, sir! He could lie . . .

(LOUISE THORNTON *enters stairs right, looks at* KELLARD, *goes to desk*)

LOUISE Stamp, Carl?

CARL (*goes behind desk*) Yes, Miss Thornton. How many, Miss, one, one two. I mean one two-cent stamp?

KELLARD (*removes hat*) I beg your pardon, ma'am. I really have better manners than to stare at a lady that way. I beg your pardon.

(THOMPSON *enters*)

THOMPSON The man is waiting to see Mr. Wilson.

KELLARD Yes, ma'am! Kellard is the name, miss, Fred Kellard.

LOUISE (*goes to* KELLARD) Oh, yes. Mr. Wilson spoke of you. You have a mine or something that he is interested in.

KELLARD Yes, miss. That's just what it is. A mine or something.

THOMPSON This is Miss Louise Thornton, daughter of Judge Thornton—and a—well, a close friend of Mr. Wilson.

(*They shake hands*)

KELLARD I am pleased to meet you, miss.

CARL (*comes from behind desk*) Shall I mail it for you Miss Louise?

LOUISE No. Thank you, Carl. (*starts to door left*) I'll mail it myself. It's only a little way and I'll enjoy the walk.

(CARL *goes back to seat*)

KELLARD Gosh! I just thought of something.

THOMPSON What?

KELLARD I was so interested talking to the proprietor of that Capital Cafe, that I plum forgot to tip the waiter.

THOMPSON Oh, I guess it'll be all right.

KELLARD No, sir. My conscience wouldn't let me sleep. I just gotta go to put myself right with that waiter.

LOUISE Oh, well, the mailbox is on the way to the Cafe.

KELLARD (*goes to door left*) Yeh, I was hoping it was.

THOMPSON But how about Mr. Wilson?

KELLARD Tell him we'll be back shortly. (*exit*)

THOMPSON Mr. Jack Wilson better look out with that chap around.

MRS. THOMPSON It might be a good thing for him. It isn't good for a man to be too sure.

THOMPSON What do you mean by that?

MRS. THOMPSON Oh . . . Just what I said.

THOMPSON Wait a minute.

MRS. THOMPSON Well?

THOMPSON Just what did you mean by that?

MRS. THOMPSON I said, "It isn't good for a man to be too sure"; if you don't understand, I can't explain. (*exits*)

THOMPSON (*sits on settee*) Carl!

CARL Yes, sir.

THOMPSON You know pretty nearly everything that goes on in this hotel.

CARL Yes, sir.

THOMPSON You must know that everything isn't as it should be between Mrs. Thompson and myself.

CARL I'm sorry to say I do.

THOMPSON I've heard you talk about these ideas you have and I've seen some of them work. Now what would you do, if you were in my place? Forget your color, what would you do?

CARL (*looks at book*) This little book says, first put myself right, sir, and everything else would be right.

THOMPSON Suppose *she's* wrong?

CARL I'd put myself right, sir, and everything else would be all right.

THOMPSON Easier said than done.

CARL No, sir, it's just as easy to do if you believe and know you can. Mrs. Thompson is a very fine lady, sir.

THOMPSON (*goes back of desk*) You bet she is. None better.

(JUDGE THORNTON *enters. Goes directly to stairs*)

JUDGE Hello!

CARL Good evening, Judge.

THOMPSON Miss your dinner, Judge?

JUDGE No, I had it at the Club. Where is Louise?

THOMPSON She went to mail a letter. I had a bite put up in your room.

JUDGE Oh, thanks, you're not only a good manager, Thompson, you're a fine host.

THOMPSON The customer is always right, even when he praises us.

JUDGE I guess you're right. Well, tell Louise when she returns that I'm up in my room. (*exits*)

(RUFUS *enters*)

RUFUS Please, Mister, can I use your telephone?

THOMPSON Go ahead. (RUFUS *looks at 'phone, holding it at several angles*) What's the matter?

RUFUS I'se looking to see where I drops the nickel.

THOMPSON That's all right, make your call and pay me after.

RUFUS Yes, sir. Thank you, Boss. Hello, Central, I want Main 806, yes, Ma'm, that's it. Hello, is dis Main 806? Mrs. Harper, please. I see you had an ad. in the paper Tuesday for a colored boy. Did you get the boy? Is he satisfactory? No, he isn't satisfactory? What's the matter with that boy? Lody me. Could a boy be as bad as that. What's that? You say you're going to fire that boy to-morrow morning? Yes, ma'm, I'll be there to-morrow morning. Sure you can depend on me. (*starts for door left*)

THOMPSON Well, Sam, it looks as though you would get that job.

RUFUS Get it—I just lost it. I had my suspicion, I was going to get fired. Now I know it, yes, sir, I knows it. (*goes back to desk. Hands* THOMPSON *coin*) But here's your nickel. Thank you, boss.

THOMPSON Just a minute. What's your name?

RUFUS My name is Rufus George Washington Jones.

THOMPSON And what kind of work are you doing for Mrs. Harper?

RUFUS Mrs. Harper's running a boarding house. And I was hired as janitor, but I spent most of my time washing dishes and scrubbing floors.

THOMPSON What did she pay you?

RUFUS Fourteen dollars a week is all I get.

THOMSON Well, Rufus, I need a porter and if you are willing to work I'll give you eighteen to work for me.

(*'phone rings*)

RUFUS How much did you say, boss?

THOMPSON Fifteen dollars a week.

RUFUS I heard you the first time, boss.

THOMPSON (*at 'phone*) Hello! Sure! Delighted. (*crosses to stairs*) Take care of this boy, Carl, and look after the desk. Judge wants to see me.

CARL Yes, sir.

(THOMPSON *exits stairs right*)

RUFUS Did he say "Judge?"

CARL Yes.

RUFUS Jest call him Judge. He ain't a regular honest-to-goodness Judge is he?

CARL Oh, yes, he's a regular Judge. Why?

RUFUS I just wanted to know, in case sometime I have to say *good morning*, Judge.

CARL That's no way to think. Don't think about the thing you don't want to happen. Only think about what you want.

RUFUS Think! What has "thinking" got to do with what I get?

CARL Everything, because what you think most about is what you get the most of.

RUFUS Oh, yes. I see! What you thinking about, Master Carl?

CARL Oh, I have a great theory. I believe a man can become anything he thinks he can. You wouldn't understand. Are you ready to start work? (*crosses to door right and rings bell*)

RUFUS Nothin' else but!

CARL I've rung for Miss Buford. She'll show you your *duties*.

RUFUS Show me what . . .

CARL Your *duties*. Your *work*.

RUFUS Work? Oh, yes. When you said "show me my duties," I thought you meant something else entirely different.

(ELLA BUFORD *enters service door.* CARL *rises*)

ELLA You rang, Carl?

RUFUS Look at that, a colored girl, and a high yaller.

CARL Yes, Miss Ella. I wish to introduce you to Mr. Rufus George Washington Jones. Have I the right name?

RUFUS You sure has, but I'se generally called jest Rufus.

ELLA (*comes to* RUFUS) How do you do, Rufus?

RUFUS (*shakes hands with her*) I'm very well, Miss, and I thanks yuh for asking.

CARL This is Miss Ella Buford, who is the acting housekeeper. Mrs. Thompson herself being the regular one.

RUFUS Buford! Did you say Buford?

CARL Yes.

RUFUS I know some Bufords. It wouldn't be that you is relations to the Bufords of Gadsden, Alabama, ma home town?

ELLA No, sir, my family came from Ohio.

RUFUS Oh, which reminds me of a story, if I may exude. Well, one darkey meets another darkey and says, "Ain't you the darkey I met in Chicago last spring?" And the other darkey says, "I ain't never been in Chicago my whole life." Then the first darkey says, "I ain't never been in Chicago my own self," so it must have been two other darkeys.

CARL (*comes between* ELLA *and* RUFUS) What was the name of that *story-telling* porter we had about a year ago, Ella?

ELLA Oh, you mean Mr. Percival Caldwell.

CARL That boy just *storied* himself right out of his job, Rufus.

RUFUS I perceive your point, Mr. Carl, yes, sir, I perceive it clearly.

CARL Miss Buford is a law student at the University. Mrs. Thompson allows her off for her classes.

RUFUS A law student! If I ever gets in trouble and use a lawyer, I suttinly avail myself of your professional proclivities. No jury could ever resist the charms of such a delightful defender.

CARL Miss Ella and I are also engaged to be married, Rufus.

RUFUS I gives yuh my firmest condemnations. I gives 'em for both of you each.

(WILSON *enters door left*)

WILSON What is this? A colored convention?

CARL I beg your pardon, Mr. Wilson, I didn't hear you come in. Miss Ella will show you your duties.

ELLA This way, Rufus . . .

RUFUS Show me my duties? Yes, sir, I know what you mean. First time he tells me duties, I think it's something entirely different. (*exit with* ELLA *service door*)

WILSON Did anyone call?

CARL (*goes behind desk*) Yes, sir, a Mr. Fred Kellard. He forgot something and went to attend to it. Said he would be right back.

WILSON What did he forget? His gun?

CARL No, sir, he forgot to tip the waiter at the Capital Cafe and he went back to attend to it.

WILSON (*goes to desk*) Miss Louise in?

CARL No, sir. Her father, the Judge, is in. Miss Louise went to mail a letter.

WILSON Give me a package of Melachrinos.

CARL (*gives him cigarettes*) Yes, sir. Charge them?

WILSON Yes. Carl, give me a light. Hurry up Carl . . . (CARL *gives him a light*)

CARL Yes, sir.

WILSON About three weeks ago you and I had a heart-to-heart talk about Miss Louise.

CARL Yes, sir.

WILSON I told you to cut out this bunk that you have been handing her.

CARL Yes, sir.

WILSON The stuff you read in those books. This good in everyone and God within everything comes to pass as a result of the law. And I promised something bad would happen to you if you didn't cut it out.

CARL Yes, sir.

WILSON Some of the people around here seem to think you're all right. But to me you're just a slick proposition. Repeating a lot of stuff that you don't believe in yourself in order to put yourself in *good* with a lot of fool white folks.

CARL Yes, sir.

WILSON And I'll tell the world you seem to be getting away with it.

CARL Yes, sir.

WILSON Now, for some reason Miss Louise is trying to postpone our wedding for a year. "Something from within" tells her to wait, "an inner voice," and I know where she got that "inner voice" and "something from within," because I've heard you use it.

CARL Yes, sir.

WILSON And the thought struck me—this is a slick nigger. And naturally the big thing he's after is money.

CARL Yes, sir. It would be natural for *you* to think that.

WILSON (*rises and goes to* CARL) Now, last time I threatened, but I didn't seem to scare you at all.

CARL No, sir, you didn't scare me.

WILSON Oh, figured you were in so solid there wasn't anything I could do that would bother you?

CARL Nothing you could do would bother me, sir.

WILSON Yeh? Well . . . er . . . here's a better proposition. If Miss Louise changes her mind and the wedding takes place, say within a month, there's five hundred dollars in it for you.

CARL Yes, sir.

WILSON And you'll do it?

CARL No, sir.

WILSON You won't?

CARL No, sir, I will not.

WILSON (*back to settee, sits*) Oh! All right, we'll see what happens.

CARL You call me a "slick nigger" and say these things I work so hard to believe in are "bunk." You're wrong, Mr. Wilson. You're wrong when you say I'm slick, wrong when you call my ideas "bunk." Mr. Wilson, I'll admit that I'm just a negro servant, a good servant to everyone, even to you.

WILSON I was wrong, Carl. You're not a slick nigger. You're just a damn fool nigger.

CARL But there's no color in words, in ideas, Mr. Wilson. They belong to anyone who asks for them.

THOMPSON (*comes downstairs*) Hello Jack!

WILSON Hello, Frank!

THOMPSON Just up having a little drink—"Apollinaris Water" with your future father-in-law. He has a good brand.

WILSON Oh, yes. Come over and sit down.

THOMPSON Sure! (*to* CARL) Anything?

CARL No, sir.

WILSON That damned nigger gets my goat.

THOMPSON Don't do that, Wilson! He can hear you. If you knew how hard it is to get as good a boy as he is ... you think of me, damn it. You're always picking on him. Sometimes I think because you *know* he won't fight back.

WILSON All anybody has to do to get a rise out of you is to say something against Carl. Forget it. I was just kidding. (*'phone rings*) Listen, this chap Kellard, I told you about.

(CARL *answers 'phone*)

THOMPSON Yes, he was in.

WILSON Well, he has a selenium mine.

THOMPSON Yes.

WILSON And there's a lot of money in it for someone to get out.

CARL (*from 'phone*) Mr. Thompson!

THOMPSON What is it?

CARL Mrs. Thompson says to send up the porter. The bathroom door is stuck in Mrs. French's room. (*goes to service door right*)

THOMPSON All right. Attend to it ... and ... check up those grocery bills Carl.

CARL I'll do it, sir. (*exits service door*)

THOMPSON All right, now, shoot!

WILSON This chap, Kellard, has been working this mine called "Hell's Hole" and he needs about a hundred and fifty thousand dollars to develop it.

THOMPSON And he's here to try and get it?

WILSON Yeh. The minute he came to me I wired East and I've got an offer of one hundred thousand dollars for the property as it stands.

THOMPSON Good boy.

WILSON Yes, but the damn fool won't sell.

THOMPSON Did you show him the offer?

WILSON I did *not*. I sounded him out and found he was dead set, that he wouldn't sell for—for half a million.

THOMPSON I see.

WILSON You want a piece of it?

THOMPSON What, the mine?

WILSON No, the cash offer.

THOMPSON I don't get yuh!

WILSON I've got a contract drawn up, that he's going to sign giving me power of attorney to handle everything with no time limit. Now, if you've got ten thousand to spare, I'll declare you in.

THOMPSON Say! Have you stopped to think how this guy Kellard might act if he got riled?

WILSON Handling roughnecks like him is one of the best things I do. Well, how about it?

THOMPSON I haven't got the money.

WILSON Your wife has.

THOMPSON Yes, but there's a slight coldness there.

WILSON What about?

THOMPSON I don't exactly know, but I think that someone has tipped her off about something.

WILSON You think she's wise about Elsie?

THOMPSON No, I guess her suspicions are just general, but I wish you'd suggest to Elsie to keep away from here.

WILSON Has she been here?

THOMPSON Came in here to-night. Pulled a bum story about forgetting to buy some cigarettes. You gotta tell her to keep away from here.

WILSON I'll do that all right. But did your wife see her?

THOMPSON No. She was sitting there writing a letter, but didn't look up.

WILSON Oh, I see. So this doesn't interest you.

(JUDGE THORNTON *comes downstairs*)

THOMPSON No, unless I can fix up things with Gladys.

JUDGE Did I understand you to say that Louise went out to mail a letter?

THOMPSON Yes.

JUDGE She must have gone to Oakland to do it.

WILSON Was she alone?

THOMPSON No. She left here with Mr. Kellard.

WILSON With whom?

THOMPSON Kellard, she came in while he was here and I presented her.
JUDGE Kellard! Who is Mr. Kellard?
WILSON A client of mine. Hardly a chap I would introduce to Louise however, a roughneck miner.

(*'Phone rings*)

THOMPSON That's so? He didn't strike me that way.
JUDGE No?

(*Enter* CARL *from service door. Crosses to desk at once to answer 'phone*)

THOMPSON No. A rough, breezy sort of a chap. From the height of his heels I should say an ex-cowpuncher.
CARL (*at 'phone*) Yes, ma'am. Someone for you Mr. Wilson.
WILSON Thanks.
JUDGE Maybe that's Louise.
WILSON (*at 'phone.* JUDGE *goes to writing desk*) Hello! Yes! Yes! Well, all you've got to do is to go through with it. Do as you're told! If there's any trouble I'll take care of you. (*goes down to* JUDGE)

(RUFUS *comes downstairs*)

THOMPSON (*from behind desk*) Did you fix that bathroom door, Rufus?
RUFUS Yes, sir. Sure did! She gives me thirty cents to get some ice cream for my own self.... (RUFUS *starts to door*)
THOMPSON All right, Rufus, you can go and get it. And Rufus ...
RUFUS (*stops*) Yes, sir.
THOMPSON Be sure you get *ice cream*.
RUFUS Yes, sir, boss. I know what you mean, but the place I could get that dun got raided by the government. I'se going to get me a strawberry nut sundae just drippin' with chocolate juice. (*exits*)
LOUISE (*enters left*) Hello, Jack. Daddy.

(KELLARD *enters*)

WILSON Where were you?
KELLARD (*to* WILSON) She was with me. But don't shoot me until you hear the end of it. It is all my fault.
LOUISE Oh, it was not your fault.
KELLARD Mr. Wilson, to set your mind at rest, before I had time to tell her that her eyes were like the skies over Mount Shasta or that her hair was like the sun-kissed wheat tossed in the wind, she held up her hand so that I could see that she had been corralled by a better man.
LOUISE Oh, er ... Daddy, this is Mr. Kellard, a friend of Jack's. Mr. Kellard, my father, Judge Thornton.
KELLARD I throw myself on the mercy of the Court, your Honor.
JUDGE Perhaps it isn't the first time, Mr. Kellard.
KELLARD Well, I will admit that good luck and smart lying has saved me several times.
WILSON Where were you?
KELLARD May I explain?
WILSON (*to* KELLARD) No, no, thank you. (*to* LOUISE) I think you should explain. Your father and I were worried and we were just going out to find you.
JUDGE Jack, being an ardent young lover, may have been worried, my dear, but I can hardly say I was.
WILSON You left to mail a letter—the mail box is two blocks from here and you're away nearly half an hour.
KELLARD I can explain everything, Mr. Wilson, and when I have you will see it was all my fault.
LOUISE It was not your fault any more than it was mine.
WILSON (*to* KELLARD) You'll understand my feelings, Kellard, when I tell you that there have been several attacks recently around this neighborhood on young and unprotected women.
JUDGE Is that so? I haven't heard of it.
WILSON (*to* JUDGE) The police have kept it out of the papers.
JUDGE Well, you're the District Attorney, you'd have to prosecute these cases, so you ought to know.
WILSON (*to* KELLARD) The girls claim it was a colored man who annoyed them. So naturally, you understand, Kellard.
KELLARD Certainly, but I can't figure out what danger Miss Louise would be in from anybody if she was with me.
THOMPSON Well, perhaps he thinks you're the danger!
KELLARD I beg your pardon, sir, but that

remark might be interpreted several ways.

THOMPSON I meant that you're young and not hard to look at and haven't any trouble expressing yourself.

KELLARD That last crack of yours—that no trouble in expressing yourself, sometimes referred to by my friends as gabbing, that really is what delayed Miss Louise.

WILSON Miss Thornton. You'll pardon my calling your attention to your little slip—Miss Thornton, not Miss Louise.

LOUISE I like the way he drawls "Miss Louise," and when he corrected himself I told him not to.

WILSON I suppose he liked the way you said Fred and that's what you call him.

LOUISE Oh, don't be silly!

JUDGE Now suppose we change the subject. Mr. Kellard, I understand that you are a miner, or an owner of a mine.

KELLARD Yes, I have a selenium mine. (*takes document from pocket*) Here's the prospectus.

LOUISE If you want to know he started telling me about his mine and your interest in it, and that was why *I* was so interested and didn't notice how far we were walking.

WILSON All right, I accept your apology.

LOUISE But I'm not apologizing. I have nothing to apologize for. Really, Jack, you're awfully aggravating!

JUDGE Reckon my way of changing the subject wasn't a happy one. I'll try again.

KELLARD Better not, Judge. I'm sorry and I'll ease myself right out.

(KELLARD *starts for door* WILSON *goes up and stops him*)

WILSON I have that contract here for you to sign, Kellard.

KELLARD Yeah? I reckon it can wait. Yes, sir. I reckon I'd rather let it wait.

WILSON (*takes a hold of* KELLARD) Just a minute. You have me wrong, Kellard. Listen, just a minute. In the first place I'm very much in love and perhaps a little jealous, and as Thompson says—you're young and not hard to look at. You understand.

LOUISE It is because you're angry at me for something else that you're scolding me for this.

WILSON All right. I'm sorry, I apologize.

LOUISE You should.

WILSON Well, I do.

(KELLARD goes to CARL and takes book he's reading)

KELLARD Reckon I'll try changing the subject, Judge. Once some cowboys nursing a grudge decided to settle it, and set to. It was a cruel wicked fight... when suddenly a little school marm from Los Angeles with ideas like is in this book, hove in sight....

WILSON Oh, I see, one of those good stories you heard.

KELLARD No, sir. I was there.

LOUISE You were in the fight?

KELLARD Yes, ma'am. I was in the middle of it and on the bottom. Well, the first thing I know... I see that little school marm on with a hose and she said, "If you galouts will stand where you are, still, and close your eyes I'll demonstrate peace." Well, there wasn't much choice so we did as she said. Everything was quiet for about a minute, then she said "Amen."

THOMPSON Did it stop you?

KELLARD Sure did. We got laughing so much, we just laughed all the fight out of us, and the little school marm laughed with us.

JUDGE (*picks up book and looks at it*) That's one of Carl's books, isn't it?

KELLARD Yes, sir.

JUDGE Carl.

CARL Yes, Judge?

JUDGE Could anybody do that?

CARL Yes, Judge.

JUDGE Well, we seem to be trying to have a battle royal.

CARL Yes, Judge.

JUDGE Could I do it?

CARL Yes, Judge, that is if you believe you can.

JUDGE Well, I believe, I believe I can!

WILSON Darn silly bunk!

LOUISE I don't think it bunk!

WILSON All right, my eyes are closed.

JUDGE Now, everybody who has rancour in their hearts, close their eyes until I say "Amen." (LOUISE *motions to* WILSON *to close his eyes. Pause. Everyone laughs*) Amen!

WILSON Darned silly bunk.

LOUISE Yes, but it worked. I couldn't look at you without laughing to save my life.

JUDGE Well, Carl. It's manner of working rather surprised me but as Louise says—"It worked."

KELLARD The fact is, Wilson, this young lady and I started in the same general direction from here and in an unguarded or thoughtless moment she asked me about the selenium mine, and you know how it is when I get going. Did you say you had those contracts?

WILSON Yes. Want to look them over?

KELLARD Sure I do.

WILSON Oh, Frank, can we use your office?

THOMPSON Of course, Go through here, Mr. Kellard.

(WILSON *exits*)

KELLARD Sure does work, don't it?

CARL Yes, sir.

KELLARD Wish I could understand the darned thing. (*exits*)

(JUDGE *takes out cigar and matches and lights match*)

JUDGE Explain yourself young lady. Explain this playing fast and loose with a young man's affections.

LOUISE (*runs to* JUDGE, *blows out match, and runs to bottom of stairs. Turns to* THOMPSON) Yes, I will. Is Mrs. Thompson in her room?

THOMPSON Yes.

LOUISE Anyone with her?

THOMPSON I don't think so.

LOUISE I'll go up and explain to her.

JUDGE But, Louise, you listen to me...

LOUISE (*goes up a step*) But... we walked so far that we had to get a taxi to get us back. (*step*) And the waiter is still waiting for his tip! (*step*) And here is the letter I went out to mail. (*exits*)

WILSON (*comes from office*) Judge Thornton, will you witness this signature?

JUDGE Why, certainly (*they exit*)

(MRS. THOMPSON *and* LOUISE *come downstairs.* THOMPSON *sees them and goes into office*)

MRS. THOMPSON (*goes to settee*) Carl, will you ask Ella to make some lemonade?

CARL Yes, madam, I will. (*exits*)

LOUISE (*runs up to office door, listens, then comes back*) Yes, he's with them.

MRS. THOMPSON Who, Jack?

LOUISE Oh, yes, Jack's there too. Did you notice the drawly way he has?

MRS. THOMPSON All I noticed was... that he seemed to be rather a fast worker.

LOUISE Fast. Why, he's chain lightning! He has mentioned every nice thing about me that I know of and a lot more I never thought of. (*looks at office door*) He said my giggle sounded like the silvery mountain stream laughing its way over moss-covered rocks. Now... you... listen to it. Do you hear any silvery mountain stream?

MRS. THOMPSON No, it would seem to me that your drawling gentleman has had a lot of practice at that kind of conversation.

LOUISE Certainly. But how do you explain the fact that one of the one's he has practiced on hasn't gobbled him up?

MRS. THOMPSON Perhaps one of them has.

LOUISE There you go trying to spoil it all, but I don't think so. Help me find out.

MRS. THOMPSON Of course I will.

WILSON (*coming from office*) Well, that's that.

LOUISE Is... your... business finished?

(KELLARD *comes from office.* WILSON *takes* KELLARD'*s hand, shakes it and tries to start him to door*)

WILSON Signed, sealed and delivered. Now, we won't keep you any longer, Kellard.

MRS. THOMPSON Mr. Kellard surely has no desire to tear himself away so quickly?

(KELLARD *stops. Throws hat down on sofa*)

KELLARD No, ma'am. I never give going away a thought.

MRS. THOMPSON You're probably thirsty, after your long, dry talk. I've ordered some lemonade.

KELLARD Lemonade? Lady, you saved my life! Anything I adore... is a nice cold glass of lemonade. (*to* LOUISE) Don't you?

LOUISE I love it!

MRS. THOMPSON *Mrs. Kellard* probably prepares it nicely.

KELLARD There ain't no Mrs. Kellard yet, but I hope Mrs. Kellard when I get her likes lemonade the way you do, Miss Thornton.

WILSON Sounds to me like a put-up job. (*goes up to desk*)

LOUISE (*to* WILSON) What do you mean dear?

WILSON You know what I mean.

LOUISE No, I don't really.

(*Enter* ELLA *and* CARL *from Service door*)

MRS. THOMPSON Put it there, Carl. Sit down, Mr. Kellard.
KELLARD (*sits on setee*) Yes, ma'am.
MRS. THOMPSON Interrupt your studies, Ella?
ELLA No, ma'am. Shall I serve it?

(LOUISE *gives* KELLARD *a glass of lemonade*)

MRS. THOMPSON No, Ella. We'll serve ourselves.
WILSON I beg your pardon, Kellard, but really gentlemen do not seat themselves while ladies stand.
KELLARD No? Well . . . Perhaps you're right, but I learned my manners in England from my grandma, and when a lady invites me to sit, I jest naturally sit.
WILSON Oh, I didn't understand. Sorry.
ELLA Will that be all, Mrs. Thompson?
MRS. THOMPSON Yes, that's all. Good-night.

(ELLA *goes upstairs*)

CARL Good night, Ella.
ELLA Good night, Carl.
LOUISE (*turns to* CARL) Oh, Carl, aren't you and Ella engaged?
CARL Yes, Miss Louise, why?
LOUISE Is that the way you say good-night?
CARL We said good night before we came in.
ELLA (*from head of stairs*) That's why it took so long to make the lemonade. (*exits*)
CARL (*to* THOMPSON) Albert is here. May I go?
THOMPSON Of course. And if you see that boy Rufus tell him to hurry with that ice cream. He must be freezing it. Good night, Carl. (*exits*)
CARL I will, sir. Good night. (*exits*)

(JUDGE THORNTON *enters*. WILSON *goes up to 'phone and makes a call*)

MRS. THOMPSON Here we are, won't you have a glass of lemonade, Judge?
JUDGE Thanks.
LOUISE Jack, here's your lemonade. Here, dad.
JUDGE Business all settled up, Mr. Kellard.
KELLARD Yes, sir. I figure a month from now I ought to have enough money to start operations.
WILSON (*from 'phone*) I hope to interest the Judge, Kellard.
JUDGE Perhaps. Just a little. Speculation is bad at my time of life.
KELLARD See here, Judge. You're not speculating when you invest your money in my mine. No, sir, I'd rather like to tell you about it.
JUDGE And I'd like to hear about it.
KELLARD (*talks very fast*) Well, this is a selenium mine up here at Hell's Hole, the ore is about 90 per cent real stuff . . . .
JUDGE But not to-night . . . some other time.
KELLARD Just as you say, Judge. I reckon it *is* getting late.

(*'Phone rings*)

JUDGE No, not late for young folks, but I guess I'll wander upstairs. Good night.

(THOMPSON *comes from office and answers 'phone*)

LOUISE Good-night, dad.
THOMPSON Oh, yes, Mrs. French. Why, I don't know. Should have been back long ago? I'll send him up with the ice cream the minute he comes. (*exits office*)
JUDGE Mr. Kellard, if you are not otherwise engaged, I should be pleased to have you come here to-morrow and have dinner with me.
KELLARD Thank you, sir.
WILSON Fine! Be company for *you*, Judge. Louise and I are going to spend the day motoring.
LOUISE Oh, I've forgotten that.
WILSON I haven't.
KELLARD You wouldn't.
WILSON What?
KELLARD I didn't say anything.
WILSON Thought you did.
KELLARD No, sorry.
JUDGE Well, good night. (*exits*)
MRS. THOMPSON Now, Mr. Kellard, you told Miss Thornton all about your mine. Mr. Wilson knows all about it, suppose you and I go out on the verandah and you tell me all about it.
KELLARD Yes, ma'am.
LOUISE Oh, I think I can stand hearing it again myself.
MRS. THOMPSON Yes, but you can hardly

Appearances

expect Jack to, and I want to hear. You do want to tell me, don't you? (*exits*)

KELLARD Yes, ma'am, sure do. (*to* LOUISE) Well, do we say good night now, Miss Thornton.

LOUISE Good night, sir. I'm really, really glad to have met you.

KELLARD Yeah, I'll probably be in town for two or three weeks.

WILSON Thought you said you were going right back after we signed up?

KELLARD I won't lie. I did say that, but since then something very, very important has come up. Something I hope will detain me. Goodnight, Miss Louise. I beg your pardon, Miss Thornton. (*exits right*)

LOUISE Good night.

WILSON What's the idea?

LOUISE If you are going to start that sort of talk I'm going right upstairs.

WILSON I suppose I haven't any right to talk this way? I suppose I haven't any reason to feel hurt or abused?

LOUISE I don't know whether you have or not, yet.

WILSON Just when I should be feeling happy; just when I close the deal that would make me a barrel of money, so I can marry you and support you, you turn on me and act this way. Do you think you are giving me a square deal?

LOUISE No, I don't. And I know I ought to be ashamed of myself, but I'm not.

WILSON What have I done?

LOUISE Perhaps it's the things you haven't done. I don't know, but for quite a while now you seem to enjoy rubbing me the wrong way. First you didn't like the way I combed my hair, then my skirts might have been longer.

WILSON Oh, I say! You didn't take me seriously.

LOUISE You didn't say it, but you might just as well have, and then when I became interested in Carl's books you not only made fun of them, but you tried to make fun of me and developed a positive hatred of Carl.

(WILSON *has been pacing up and down center all during this speech. He stops and almost yells*)

WILSON That damn nigger is back of it all! He's got you hypnotized.

LOUISE Don't talk like an idiot and for goodness' sake sit down. Pacing up and down like a bear in its cage.

(*Woman screams offstage*).

WILSON My God! What was that? (*runs to door right. Looks out*)

(*Enter* MRS. THOMPSON *and* KELLARD. KELLARD *exits.*)

LOUISE That's a woman screaming.

(*Offstage*: "HELP . . . HELP")

MRS. THOMPSON Louise, there's some woman in trouble.

LOUISE Where's Mr. Kellard?

(*Enter* THOMPSON *from office*)

THOMPSON What's the matter? Guess I'll go and find out. (*exits*)

LOUISE I'm going.

MRS. THOMPSON You can do no good there. People are running from every direction.

(JUDGE *comes downstairs*)

JUDGE I saw a mob forming. What's the matter?

MRS. THOMPSON We don't know.

LOUISE We heard a woman scream.

MRS. THOMPSON There is someone coming this way, running. He's coming in here.

(RUFUS *enters door left*)

RUFUS I didn't do nothin'. I didn't do nothin', Carl called me. They ain't going to lynch me. I didn't do nothing'. 'Fore God, I didn't. Let me go.

WILSON What's the matter?

RUFUS Get out of my way! Get out of my way! . . . They ain't going to get me. They ain't going to lynch me. And . . . (*rushes off*)

JUDGE We should have held him.

(*Cries offstage*: "Lynch him. String him up. Lynch him. Lynch the damn nigger. Get a rope," etc.)

THOMPSON The mob is coming this way. Bring the lady here.

(ELSIE BENTON *is brought in by* SAUNDERS *and* MATTHEWS. ELLA *enters*)

MRS. THOMPSON A glass of water.

(THOMPSON *exits*)

ELLA What is it? What is it, Miss Louise?
LOUISE We don't know.
ELLA Carl! (CARL *is dragged on by a Policeman*, ELLA *kneels by* CARL) Carl, boy, what have they done to you?
MRS. THOMPSON Mrs. Benton!
JUDGE I'm Judge Thornton, Officer, what happened?
ELSIE (*hysterically*) I was walking along the street when this negro attacked me and when I fought him off he called another negro, but that's the one ... look, he almost tore my waist off my body!
ELLA What have they done to you? What is it, boy? Tell your Ella.
WILSON So they got you at last, did they, Carl? This is a good chance to try that "bunk" of yours.
CARL Bunk, that bunk, as you call it, is always with me. I've done nothing wrong and have nothing to fear.

(*Curtain*)

ACT TWO

(*A courtroom, one week later*)

JUDGE Is that all?
WILSON That's all.
JUDGE (*to witness*) Then step down.
CLERK Next witness.
WILSON Mrs. Elsie Benton ...

(*General murmur from witnesses, saying* "Now the case will start. So that's the woman," *etc.*)

CLERK (*to bailiff*) Mrs. Elsie Benton.
BAILIFF (*calls*) Mrs. Elsie Benton. (ELSIE BENTON *rises and goes to witness stand*)
CLERK Name?
ELSIE Elsie Benton.
CLERK Address?
ELSIE 869 Pine Street.
CLERK Raise your right hand. Do you solemnly swear that the evidence you are about to give will be the truth, the whole truth, and nothing but the truth, so help you, God?
ELSIE I do. (*she sits*)
WILSON Mrs. Benton, will you please explain in your own words, just what happened.
ELSIE About nine o'clock on the evening of the sixteenth....
JUDGE Mrs. Benton, you will kindly address your remarks to the jury.
ELSIE On the evening of the sixteenth about 9 o'clock I was going to post a letter. Just as I was walking past a vacant lot this ... the Negro stepped out behind me, then turned suddenly and said to me "White girl, I want you to go with me." I told him to go along about his business or I would scream and started to hurry along as it was dark and I was afraid, then he took hold of me and tried to put his hand over my mouth, I screamed, trying to get away, when I heard him call "Rufus, Rufus, come help me," and I twisted in his grasp long enough to see another man come out of the vacant lot. I fought, fought desperately, fought as any woman will fight in defense of her honor, but I could feel myself being drawn nearer and nearer to that vacant lot, then I heard shouts; and before the other Negro could help, men came and rescued me.
JUDGE Then what happened?
ELSIE They captured the first man ... but the other one ... after a fight ... got away. What happened directly after that I don't know. Everything went black. When I came to ... two men were supporting me ... and the first man ... the one who accosted me ... was in the hands of the police.... Everything after that is a sort of blur.... All I know is I awoke in my own apartment in the care of a nurse.
WILSON Is that all you remember, Mrs. Benton?
ELSIE Yes, sir.
WILSON That's all, your Honor.
JUDGE ROBINSON Does the defendant's lawyer care to question the witness?
CLERK Your Honor, the attorney for the defendant is not present.
JUDGE ROBINSON (*to* CARL) Where is your attorney?
CARL Your Honor, I have no attorney. I do not feel that one is necessary.
JUDGE ROBINSON Young man, you are here charged with a very serious offence. If you are convicted it means a long term of imprisonment.
CARL Your Honor, I am innocent of this charge. I shall tell nothing but the truth, and the truth needs no defense.

Appearances

ELLA Your Honor, I am here to defend Carl Sanderson.

WILSON I object.

ELLA But your Honor.

JUDGE ROBINSON The objection sustained. The defendant has waived his rights to an attorney.

JUDGE THORNTON Your Honor.

JUDGE ROBINSON Judge Thornton.

JUDGE THORNTON Your Honor, the defendant, Carl Sanderson, has certain ideas regarding the power of truth that we, of perhaps more mature experience, do not have, having met the power of lies. I did not know until yesterday that the defendant intended to take this stand. In fact I had been led, or perhaps misled, into the idea that his defense had been taken care of. As Carl Sanderson doesn't wish Counsel I shall respect his belief—but his co-defendant, Rufus Jones, hasn't any such scruples and it is as his attorney that I appear in the case.

JUDGE ROBINSON It has been many years since you have been in this court, Judge Thornton. A court whose bench you so ably graced. I welcome you.

JUDGE THORNTON I thank you, Judge Robinson.

WILSON (*rises. To* JUDGE THORNTON) Well, now the usual courtesies from one Judge to another having been attended to, do you wish to question the witness?

JUDGE THORNTON No. (ELSIE *rises*)

WILSON One moment before you leave the stand, Mrs. Benton. (*looks at papers, then to stand*) Mrs. Benton, are you a native of California?

ELSIE No, sir. I was born in Utah.

WILSON You are a married woman?

ELSIE A widow, sir.

WILSON A widow? Have you been a widow long?

ELSIE About two years. Please don't ask me how my husband died; if he'd been alive this couldn't have happened. . . .

WILSON One moment. (*goes to table. Picks up dress. Back to stand*) Is this the garment you wore on the night of the attack?

ELSIE Yes.

WILSON And it was damaged in this manner during the assault?

ELSIE Yes.

WILSON Your Honor, I wish to offer this in evidence.

JUDGE ROBINSON Mark it for identification, Exhibit A.

(CLERK *takes dress, marks it, then gives it to a stenographer*)

WILSON That is all, Mrs. Benton.

(WILSON *sits.* ELSIE *leaves stand, back to seat*)

CLERK Next witness.

WILSON Arresting officer.

CLERK Officer Calahan.

BAILIFF Officer Calahan.

(CALAHAN *rises and takes the stand*)

CLERK Do you solemnly swear the evidence you are about to give to be the truth, the whole truth, and nothing but the truth, so help you God?

POLICEMAN I do.

WILSON State to the Court what you know of the case.

OFFICER I was walking along Howard Street about 9 o'clock on Saturday evening, the sixteenth, when my attention was attracted by people running on Seventh Street. I immediately ran and arrived just in time to rescue the prisoner from the mob.

JUDGE ROBINSON Then what happened?

OFFICER I had considerable trouble keeping the crowd under control. They were shouting "Lynch him" and, "Get a rope." The complainant identified the prisoner and I made the arrest, charging him with assault.

JUDGE ROBINSON Is that all you know about the case?

OFFICER There was talk of another negro who was concerned in the assault, but I didn't see him.

JUDGE ROBINSON But the other man was apprehended?

OFFICER Well, your Honor, I was so hot on his trail that he gave himself up. He knew he didn't have a chance. He's here in court.

WILSON That's all, your Honor.

JUDGE ROBINSON Do you wish to question the witness?

CARL No, your Honor.

JUDGE ROBINSON You, Judge Thornton?

JUDGE THORNTON No questions, your Honor.

JUDGE ROBINSON That's all.

(CALAHAN *goes back to seat*)

CLERK Next witness.
WILSON Gerald Saunders.
CLERK Gerald Saunders.
BAILIFF Gerald Saunders.

(WILSON *beckons to* SAUNDERS, *who points to himself, as though to ask "You mean me?"* WILSON *nods and* SAUNDERS *beams an acknowledgment.* SAUNDERS *takes stand*)

CLERK Your name?
SAUNDERS Gerald Saunders.
STENOGRAPHER I didn't get that.
CLERK Sanders.
SAUNDERS I beg your pardon, but the name is pronounced "Sawnders."
CLERK All right... Your address?
SAUNDERS Number eleven Poinsettia Place.
CLERK Raise your right hand! Do you solemnly swear that the evidence you are about to give shall be the truth, the whole truth and nothing but the truth, so help you God?
SAUNDERS I certainly do! (*sits*)
WILSON State to the Court just what you know about the case.
SAUNDERS Well, it was about 9 o'clock on the evening of the sixteenth....
JUDGE ROBINSON (*gavel*) A little louder, please.
SAUNDERS Well, it was about 9 o'clock on the evening of the sixteenth; while strolling along Seventh Street I was going to make whoopee, I was startled by a woman's scream about a block away. I turned and saw a woman struggling to free herself from a man and heard her screams. Always responding to the calls of the weaker sex when in danger (*loud laugh. Gavel*), I turned and rapidly ran to the rescue. As I approached I saw another man going to join the struggle. Then other men came, but I... I... was the first on the scene.
JUDGE ROBINSON Yes, yes, go on.
SAUNDERS But when... this other man... this other black fellow saw me, he turned and ran away, but this one... was still struggling with the lady... the charming lady who is sitting there. I immediately launched myself into the fray and struck the Negro. Others joined me and only the arrival of the Officer, saved the man from the expression of my just wrath.
CLERK Your Honor, I didn't get that.

JUDGE ROBINSON His just wrath. Is that all you know?
SAUNDERS Yes, your Honor.
JUDGE ROBINSON I thought so. (*to* CARL) Do you wish to question the witness?
CARL No, your Honor.
JUDGE ROBINSON You, Judge Thornton?
JUDGE THORNTON No, your Honor.
JUDGE ROBINSON That's all. (*gavel*) Step down!
SAUNDERS Oh, but your Honor, no matter what may be said here....
CLERK His Honor said "That's all."
WILSON Hiram Matthews.
CLERK Hiram Matthews.
BAILIFF Hiram Matthews.

(MATTHEWS *takes stand*)

CLERK Your name?
MATTHEWS Hiram Matthews.
CLERK Your address?
MATTHEWS 425 Bush Street.
CLERK Raise your right hand. Do you solemnly swear that the evidence you are about to give shall be the truth, the whole truth, and nothing but the truth, so help you God?
MATTHEWS Well, yes...
CLERK Say "I do."
MATTHEWS Well, well, I do.
WILSON State to the court anything that you may know about this case.
MATTHEWS Well, about 9 o'clock in the evening, on the evening of the sixteenth...
JUDGE ROBINSON (*gavel*) We can hear you.
MATTHEWS Oh, well! I was going along Seventh Street, on my way home... having been to see Mr. Lewis on Eighth Street about a job of work... being a first-class painter... as you know, Judge.
JUDGE ROBINSON Proceed.
MATTHEWS Well, I was walking along when I heard a woman scream. And looking up the street I saw a man and a woman struggling.
JUDGE ROBINSON Proceed.
MATTHEWS Well, I immediately started running and I passed this feller Sanders, as I run.
SAUNDERS (*rises*) Saunders!

(BAILIFF *puts him down*)

JUDGE ROBINSON I trust you run faster than

Appearances

you can talk, Matthews.

MATTHEWS Well if Sanders can run as fast as he can talk he'd a beat me to it.

JUDGE ROBINSON Proceed.

MATTHEWS Well, as I got close, I could see what the trouble was. I see the complaintiff a-strugglin' to free herself from the grasp of the prisoner.

JUDGE ROBINSON Proceed.

MATTHEWS Well, getting up (*rises*), I grabbed the prisoner and separated him from the complaintiff and took a healthy punch at him like this (*takes wild punch at air*) and I caught him on the nose! (*sits*)

JUDGE ROBINSON Did you see the other defendant, Rufus Jones?

MATTHEWS Well, yes and no. Ya see I was too busy helpin' the crowd, with the one that I punched to notice much, but seems to me as there was another one for somebody give me a hell... a hell (*gavel*) healthy kick and I got the bruise to show for it yit, but I ain't swearing to nothin' I ain't sure of, and I ain't *sure* I seen him.

JUDGE ROBINSON Is that all?

MATTHEWS Well, yes, your Honor.

JUDGE ROBINSON Do you wish to question the witness?

CARL (*rises*) No, your Honor. (*sits*)

JUDGE ROBINSON Judge Thornton?

JUDGE (*rises*) Mr. Matthews, there seems to be some difference of opinion between you and Mr. Saunders.

SAUNDERS (*rises*) Thank you. (*sits*)

MATTHEWS Well, to tell you the truth, I never seen this man Sanders in the mix-up until after it was all over, and then I see he was the man who was trying to help me support her when she fainted.

JUDGE THORNTON That's all. (*sits*)

JUDGE ROBINSON Questions? (WILSON *shakes head negative*) Step down.

CLERK Next witness.

WILSON (*rises. To Judge*) If it pleases the court we rest here. I have thirty witnesses who will testify as to the later events of the assault, but... it seems to be wasting the time of your Honor, and members of the jury to put them on the stand. (*sits*)

JUDGE ROBINSON Witnesses for the defense.

CARL (*rises*) May I take the stand, your Honor?

JUDGE ROBINSON Certainly. (CARL *takes stand*)

CLERK Your name?

CARL Carl Sanderson.

CLERK Your address?

CARL 861 Sutter Street.

CLERK Raise your right hand. Do you solemnly swear that the evidence you are about to give shall be the truth, the whole truth, and nothing but the truth?

CARL I swear that what I am about to say is the truth and nothing else but the truth, so help me God!

CLERK Say "I do."

CARL I do.

JUDGE ROBINSON Will you tell this court what you know about what happened on the night in question?

CARL May I be allowed to tell my story in my own way, Judge?

JUDGE ROBINSON Certainly.

CARL (*sits*) Thank you... Members of the Jury, I firmly believe that when a man tells the truth, the whole truth and nothing but the truth, knowing in his heart that it will be re-acted to as the truth, no other result possibly can follow. I am speaking now simply to tell the truth.... On the night of Saturday the sixteenth, about 9 o'clock, I was walking up Seventh Street when I noticed a lady.... Just as I passed her she said, "Just a minute"... I looked round, and as there was no one else in sight, I asked her if she was speaking to me, and she replied "I certainly am," and added, "Give me that ten dollars you owe me." I insisted that she must be mistaken, as I was certain that she had never laid eyes on me until that night.

JUDGE ROBINSON Just a minute. You admit then that you were on Seventh Street that night?

CARL Yes, your Honor.

JUDGE ROBINSON And you admit that you saw this woman, Mrs. Benton?

CARL Yes, your Honor.

JUDGE ROBINSON You also admit that you spoke to her?

CARL Yes, your Honor, but only after...

JUDGE ROBINSON That's enough, go on with your story.

CARL She said: "I just got out of jail, and I don't mind going back. If you don't give me that ten dollars now I will scream and say that you assaulted me"... I tried to reason with her... but she insisted... and said: "I'll give you just one second to produce the money"; then I tried to walk away from her, but she stayed right even with me. She took a firm grip on my coat. At that time we were just beside the vacant lot, and she let out a piercing scream, and I tried to free myself from her, then I pulled myself away—I turned and saw Rufus Jones and I called him, then someone hit me and I was knocked down; then someone kicked me and jumped on me. Then someone pulled me up on my feet and pushed me back to the fence. It was Kellard, and he held the crowd off, till the Officer came up and put me under arrest.

ELSIE (*rises*) He's a liar, your Honor. How dare he say I held his coat!

(*Gavel.* BAILIFF *puts* ELSIE *down*)

JUDGE ROBINSON Have you any witnesses to verify what you have told the court?

CARL Your Honor the truth is the only evidence I need.

JUDGE ROBINSON Young man, you are here charged with a terrible crime. It has been entered as assault. It might have been entered under another name that would have meant, if convicted, the penitentiary for practically your life. At best, conviction will mean a long sentence. You may believe that truth has the power you think it has, but your belief doesn't coincide with the facts as they appear to a Judge sitting in court. I admit it should, but I am sorry to say it does not.

CARL It must stand with me, your Honor. It's my most treasured possession. It's all I have, and I stake my all on it.

WILSON (*rises*) Your Honor, this man is just a clever crook.

JUDGE THORNTON (*rises*) I object, your honor.

WILSON You're not appearing for this defendant, Judge Thornton.

JUDGE ROBINSON There has been nothing here introduced as evidence that the defendant is a crook, and even though Judge Thornton is not this boy's lawyer the Court, in the interests of law, and its proper administration, must order your statement to be stricken from the record.

WILSON Exception, your Honor.

(WILSON *and* JUDGE THORNTON *sit*)

JUDGE ROBINSON Note the exception. Is that all?

CARL Yes your Honor.

JUDGE ROBINSON Step down.

(CARL *goes to seat.* JUDGE THORNTON *rises, comes to bench*)

JUDGE THORNTON Your Honor, I appreciate the wisdom of your statement to the defendant, Carl Sanderson, regarding the truth, and I could wish with you that it would prevail, especially in our courts, but I have also seen the power of truth exemplified by the defendant whom I have known for the last two years, and such has been his proof that I feel he has a certain right to his faith. In defending Rufus Jones, my client, naturally my defenses must include Carl Sanderson, but such is my respect for him and his philosophy of life that if I could I would limit my defense solely to that of my client, but that is impossible. (*back to table. Looks through papers. Calls*) Mr. Frederick Kellard, will you take the stand?

CLERK Frederick Kellard.

BAILIFF Frederick Kellard.

(KELLARD *takes stand*)

CLERK Your name?

KELLARD Frederick L. Kellard.

CLERK Your address?

KELLARD I'm stopping at the Hotel Mount Shasta now.

CLERK Raise your right hand. Do you solemnly swear that the evidence you are about to give shall be the truth, the whole truth, and nothing but the truth, so help you God?

KELLARD I do.

JUDGE THORNTON Mr. Kellard, will you tell the court what you know about the case.

KELLARD Yes, sir. On the evening of the trouble, and at the time it happened, I was sittin' talking to Mrs. Thompson, wife of the proprietor of the Hotel Mount Shasta, on the porch of that hotel. I heard a scream and lookin' down the street, which I could see from where I was sittin', I saw a man and a woman ... now—it seems to me the *man* was tryin' to get away from the woman.

Appearances

ELSIE (*rises*) How can you tell such a lie.

JUDGE ROBINSON You must not interrupt, Madam.

ELSIE But when I hear him say . . .

MATTHEWS (*rises*) That wasn't nothing like it at all.

SAUNDERS (*rises*) No such thing happened, I swear.

ELSIE But when I hear . . .

JUDGE ROBINSON (*gavel*) Order in court. Proceed Mr. Kellard.

(*Everyone quiet immediately*)

KELLARD Yes, your Honor. Then I saw another man approach, then the lady cried "Help, help, murder," and I jumped off the porch and started on my way there, but before I could reach them quite a crowd had assembled and there was a fight goin' on. I found this man Matthews sittin' on the back of a man on the ground and the other gentleman, Mr. Sanders, heroically kickin' the fallen man in the face.

SAUNDERS (*rises*) Certainly I kicked him, and I'd do it again.

(*Gavel*—BAILIFF *puts him down*)

KELLARD Yes, Ma'am, I reckon you would, if he was lyin' down with somebody on his back.

WILSON (*rises*) I object.

JUDGE ROBINSON Object! One of your own witnesses started it. Proceed Mr. Kellard.

(WILSON *sits*)

KELLARD Yes, your Honor. Well, there was Sanders . . .

SAUNDERS (*rises*) Saunders is my name.

(BAILIFF *puts him down*)

KELLARD . . . and Matthews and six or seven more tryin' to join 'em. I knocked the heroic Mr. Sanders down and Mr. Matthews is mistaken about the colored boy kickin' him. It was me.

MATTHEWS I don't believe it.

KELLARD I can tell you the exact place I landed, if you want me to.

(*General laugh. Gavel*)

JUDGE ROBINSON Proceed, Mr. Kellard.

KELLARD Well, then, I lifted the man to his feet, for he was hurt, and for the first time realized it was Carl, the colored boy from the hotel. I pushed him back against the fence and battled with the mob till the police officer came, and then stood by with the officer as he took him to the hotel to wait for the wagon.

JUDGE ROBINSON Is that all?

KELLARD Yes, your Honor.

JUDGE THORNTON (*rises—to* WILSON) Your witness. (*sits*)

WILSON (*rises—to bench*) Your Honor, Mr. Kellard and I are friends and interested in business. I wish you would explain to him that our friendship and business relationship must not be allowed to interfere with my professional duties.

JUDGE ROBINSON I'm quite sure Mr. Kellard will understand. Proceed with your examination.

WILSON Mr. Kellard, in your description of things, aren't you sometimes inclined to . . . well . . . er . . . amplify them a bit?

KELLARD Well . . . I'm rather fond of using what you might term "a little local color."

WILSON Exactly! And isn't your inclination to do that likely to cause you to use a little "color" in your description of the assault?

KELLARD No—sir! When a feller man is facin' a long term in prison I take no chance on "color"—I speak the facts, facts as I see 'em.

WILSON In your testimony you stated that "the *man* seemed to be tryin' to get away from the *lady*."

KELLARD Yes, sir.

WILSON And you heard the witnesses, Saunders and Matthews, testify under oath. Now they say the lady was struggling to get away from the man.

KELLARD Yeah, I heard 'em.

WILSON Have you good eyesight, Mr. Kellard?

KELLARD Ain't takin' to wearin' specks yet.

SAUNDERS (*rises*) Oh, is that so?

JUDGE ROBINSON Kindly remove the witness Saunders from the Court. (*loud laugh from* MATTHEWS) Also Mr. Matthews. (BAILIFF *takes each one to door right and policeman puts them out*)

WILSON Perhaps you only "seemed" to see this to keep from testifying to what you really saw.

KELLARD The inference bein'?

WILSON Never mind about the inference. Isn't it a fact that you really saw the same as the other witnesses?

KELLARD No, sir, I did not.
WILSON And these two witnesses *saw* and you only "seemed to see."
KELLARD They didn't see.
WILSON Are you sure of that?
KELLARD Yes, sir.
WILSON And why are you so sure, Mr. Kellard?
KELLARD Because I can see in the dark better than either of 'em. And *I* couldn't see.
WILSON Oh, you can see in the dark, can you? Are you a "Nictolops?"
KELLARD Well, if you'll tell me what that is, I'll tell you if I am.
WILSON It's the technical name for a person who sees in the dark.
KELLARD Oh—there's lots of them where I come from. But I never heard them called that.
WILSON What do you call them?
KELLARD Night herders. We herd thousands of cattle night after night an' ye learn to see mighty well in the dark, an' I'm particular good at it. And that's why I say they didn't see what they claimed; when we get a herder that's *sure* he sees things in the dark, we generally bed him down in the booby hatch.
WILSON You have heard this lady testify? Now you wouldn't infer that she lies, you're a man, aren't you?
KELLARD Yes, sir.
WILSON With a man's heart? And a man's respect for women?
KELLARD Yes, sir.
WILSON Then why do you sit there and lie—what can be your object?
KELLARD That's what's worrying me—and somethin' I can't git through my head.
WILSON (*quickly*) You mean you can't understand your object in telling this lie?
KELLARD No, sir. I can't understand *hers*.
WILSON (*pause—then to bench*) I object to that answer.
JUDGE ROBINSON If I strike out this answer from the record I'll have to strike out all the matter you have used in leading up to it.
WILSON (*goes back to table*) Withdraw the objection.
JUDGE ROBINSON Through with the witness?
WILSON Yes, your Honor. (*sits*)
JUDGE THORNTON (*rises*) Mr. Kellard, did you ever see my defendant Rufus Jones?
KELLARD I couldn't swear to that, but I did see something black pass me on the way to the fight!
JUDGE THORNTON When did you first meet the defendant, Carl Sanderson?
KELLARD In the early part of the evening on which the trouble took place.
JUDGE THORNTON How did you meet him?
KELLARD He was the bell-hop at the hotel and seein' him around I spoke to him.
JUDGE THORNTON You were not a friend of his?
KELLARD No, sir, never laid eyes on him till that night.
JUDGE THORNTON Then your interest in coming here is purely to see justice done?
KELLARD Yes, Judge.

(JUDGE THORNTON *goes back to table*)

JUDGE ROBINSON Is that all?
JUDGE THORNTON Yes, your Honor. All right, Mr. Kellard. (JUDGE ROBINSON *motions* KELLARD *to step down*) Mr. Frank Thompson.
CLERK Frank Thompson.
BAILIFF Frank Thompson.

(THOMPSON *takes stand*)

CLERK Your name?
THOMPSON Frank Thompson.
CLERK Your address?
THOMPSON Hotel Shasta.
CLERK Raise your right hand. Do you solemnly swear that the evidence you are about to give shall be the truth, the whole truth, and nothing but the truth, so help you God?
THOMPSON I do. (*sits*)
JUDGE THORNTON (*rises and comes to stand*) Do you know the other defendant? My client Rufus Jones?
THOMPSON Yes, sir. He came in the night of the trouble, he wanted work and I liked his looks and hired him as porter.
JUDGE THORNTON The defendant, Carl Sanderson, is in your employ is he not?
THOMPSON Yes, sir.
JUDGE THORNTON Will you tell the court what you know about him?
THOMPSON Carl Sanderson has been in my employ for the past two years and a half and I've always found him conscientious and faithful in the discharge of his duty, trustworthy, and honest. I never had or heard any complaint regarding his conduct while in my employ.

JUDGE THORNTON   That's all.
JUDGE ROBINSON   Any questions?
WILSON (*rises*)   No questions. (*sits*)
JUDGE ROBINSON   Step down.
JUDGE THORNTON   Rufus Jones.
CLERK   Rufus Jones.
BAILIFF   Rufus Jones.

(RUFUS *rises, starts to put hat on.* JUDGE THORNTON *stops him.* RUFUS *then starts for stand, sees* JUDGE ROBINSON, *stops*)

RUFUS   Good morning Judge. (*finally gets to stand*) You ain't goin' to leave me, Judge?
JUDGE THORNTON   No, no, Rufus.
CLERK   Name?
RUFUS   My name is . . . my name is . . . where is my name?
CLERK   Yes?
RUFUS   Yes, sir.
JUDGE ROBINSON   Just give him your full name Rufus.
RUFUS   My full name is Rufus George Washington Jones, sir.
CLERK   Address?
RUFUS   Sir?
CLERK   Where . . . are . . . you . . . staying?
RUFUS   I'm in jail now.
CLERK   All right . . . Raise your right hand.
(RUFUS *raises left hand*) [JUDGE THOMPSON Other hand, Rufus] . . .
CLERK   Do you solemnly swear that the evidence you are about to give shall be the truth, the whole truth, and nothing but the truth, so help you God?
RUFUS   I don't know what the gentleman says he says it so fast.
JUDGE ROBINSON   He is asking you to tell the truth on the Bible, Rufus.
RUFUS   Sure I tell the truth, so help me God.
JUDGE ROBINSON   Proceed with your examination, Judge Thornton.

(RUFUS *goes to sit down, keeping tight grip on Bible.* CLERK *pulls it away from him*)

JUDGE THORNTON   Will you tell the court anything you know about this alleged assault?
RUFUS   Sir?
JUDGE THORNTON   About the trouble.
RUFUS   Oh. Well, the night of the trouble, I goes in the hotel to telephone. And the boss man there, Mr. Thompson, he tell me he has got a job of work for me, as porter, and he introduces me to Mr. Carl and Mr. Carl introduces me to Miss Ella Buford. I thought she was related to some Bufords I knows in Gadsden, Alabama, but she says she came from . . . oh . . .
JUDGE ROBINSON (*gavel*)   Just a minute. Is this necessary?
JUDGE THORNTON (*up to bench*)   I have tried to get this witness down to facts. I have tried leading him a little, but the minute I interrupt, while he is trying to figure out the meaning of my question he loses all idea of any answer. It was a night of horror to this boy and every little incident of that night stands out to him doubly magnified.
JUDGE ROBINSON   All right, go ahead.

(JUDGE THORNTON *back to stand*)

RUFUS   Yes, sir. Judge, your Honor—where was I, Mr. Judge?
JUDGE THORNTON   Miss Ella Buford didn't come from Gadsden, Alabama.
RUFUS   No, siree, she come from Ohio. Well, Miss Buford she explains to me my duties. That means my work, your Honor.
JUDGE ROBINSON   Proceed.
RUFUS   Yes, your Honor, I is proceeding. Where was I at, Mr. Judge?
JUDGE THORNTON   Miss Ella Buford had explained your duties.
RUFUS   Yes, Judge. Well, the first thing in my duties was—the surface bell rings and Mr. Thompson, the gentleman sittin' there he says —"Boy go to room forty-eight—Mrs. French— her bathroom door is dum stuck—you go fix it!" Well, I goes up . . .
JUDGE THORNTON   All right, Rufus. Now after you fixed Mrs. French's bathroom door, what did she say to you?
RUFUS   But Mr. Judge, I ain't fixed that door yet.
JUDGE THORNTON   I know, but omit the fixing and come to what she said to you *after* you had fixed it.
RUFUS   She couldn't say nothing to me, judge, till after I fixed that door . . . and I ain't fixed it yet.
JUDGE THORNTON   All right, Rufus.
JUDGE ROBINSON   Why is this necessary? And what bearing does it have on the case?
JUDGE THORNTON (*to bench*)   It explains the movement of the witness and will *prove* that there could not have been collusion between this

boy and Carl Sanderson as inferred in the charge.

JUDGE ROBINSON   All right. Proceed.

(JUDGE THORNTON *back to stand*)

RUFUS   Yes, Judge. Well I . . . Where was I, Judge?

JUDGE THORNTON   Mrs. French was giving you money.

RUFUS   Yes, Judge, No, Judge. She ain't givin' me no money yet.

JUDGE THORNTON   All right then; you went up to Mrs. French's room—go ahead.

RUFUS   Yes, sir, Judge. Well I'se goes up to room foorty-eight and I knocks on the door, and I can't hear nothin', then I knocks agin. Then I hears a voice, my . . . way off. And it says "Come in—the outside door is unlocked." Well I goes in. Then a voice says: "I'm here in the bathroom and the door is stuck," and I could tell by the lady's voice that the lady is real mad. And I says, "Lady, jes' a minute, and I bust this door right ofen its hingus." Well, before I can bust, that lady says "Boy, I got this cake of soap in my hand and it's a big one and if you bust in that door, I'll bust you in the head." Well I does! I turns the knob way round and the door loosens . . . she had done forgot to turn the knob . . . And the lady laughs and says, "Boy, I'd give a dollar for a plate of ice-cream," and I says "Give me the dollar and I get it for you," and she gives me thirty cents to buy some ice cream for my ownself, then I comes downstairs, tell the boss man, Mr. Thompson, and he says I can go and get the ice cream.

JUDGE THORNTON   About what time was that, Rufus?

RUFUS   About 8:30, Judge.

JUDGE THORNTON   Will you tell the court where you were between that time and 9 o'clock, the time of the alleged assault?

RUFUS   Yes, sir, Judge. I knows these places around here don't sell ice cream to no colored folks, so I goes way down South, take me ten minutes on the car and I go to Carlins drug store. (*to* JUDGE ROBINSON) That's the colored drug store, your Honor.

JUDGE THORNTON   Yes, go on.

RUFUS   And I gets myself a strawberry nut sundae with chocolate juice. It costs me fifteen cents. And it tastes so good I gets myself a coffee nut sundae smothered in with more chocolate juice. Then I comes back, to Drews, that big store on Howard Street, that place just jammed and packed and them clerks all busy, so I sees the boss man in the back and I tells him, and he gits it for me his ownself all done up in a box; so I starts for the hotel. I'se hurrying. When somebody says: "Rufus—Rufus," and I sees it's Carl, and I see the lady's got hold of him and he's trying to get away. And I starts towards him. Then it seems that the ground opens up and there's nothin' but white folks all around me, and I gets a club on the back of my head and I falls down and somebody jumps on me. So I pulls myself up and I fights myself out. I jumps a fence, goes through the hotel, gets to the next street. I goes down a block, then down Seventh Street. I'se all in, so I lands in a hole in the street where's they is fixing a colvert. A big piece of the drain pipe, just big enough for I can crawl in, and I does lie there.

JUDGE THORNTON   How long did you lie there, Rufus?

RUFUS   I *don't* know, Judge. A long time. Then I hear folks come to that hole, and I sees lights flashin'— . . . and I hear somebody say, they is tryin' to get dogs. When I hears them say dogs—I jus' like to die.

JUDGE THORNTON   You have been chased by dogs, Rufus?

RUFUS   Yes, sir, Mr. Judge.

JUDGE ROBINSON   Does the fact of him being chased by dogs have any bearing on *this* case?

JUDGE THORNTON   Only that it shows the blind hatred that seems to inflame certain types of white minds where a Negro is concerned; and will explain to the jury why some of the testimony may have been influenced by this hatred.

JUDGE ROBINSON   You wouldn't wish to infer that the *Court* has been influenced by that, Judge?

JUDGE THORNTON (*to bench*)   No, your Honor, but the *jury* have to decide this case on *evidence* perhaps influenced by this prejudice.

JUDGE ROBINSON   All right, proceed.

JUDGE THORNTON   Come, Rufus, I want you to tell the court all about those dogs.

RUFUS (*terrified*)   Dogs?

JUDGE THORNTON (*quietly*)   Yes, Rufus, the dogs.

RUFUS   Well, I was workin' for a lady back home and she 'cused me of stealin' a ring, so they takes and locks me in the smoke house till the Constable can come. So I digs myself out and gets away an' into a swamp and hides myself. In the middle of the night the baying of the dogs wakes me up and I knows they got the scent by the way they bays, and I starts travellin', but 'tain't no use, so I climbs a big old stump and soon the dogs is all round me, then the white folks come and they want to string me up, but the constable wouldn't let them; and they drags me back to the house, when we gets there, the lady she finds her ring where she lost it, and tell the folks I didn't steal it at all.

JUDGE ROBINSON Did they arrest her?

RUFUS No, sir. She gave me two dollars and give me my job back agin.

JUDGE ROBINSON And you took them?

RUFUS Yes, sir. First time I ever had a whole two dollars in my whole life.

JUDGE THORNTON Your witness. (RUFUS *rises*) Stay right there, Rufus.

WILSON (*rises, comes to center*) I congratulate Judge Thornton. Altho' he has not been practicing in court for years he has lost none of his ability to keep one eye on the jury. So members of the jury if Rufus suddenly develops an inability to understand or answer any questions, the Judge has prepared you to believe that it is ignorance and not his desire to evade the questions I put to him.

JUDGE ROBINSON Time enough to talk of that when the witness fails to answer.

WILSON Because his Honor seems to reprove me at times, doesn't mean that his Honor wishes *you* to confuse *me* with the case I'm prosecuting.

JUDGE ROBINSON (*gavel*) You will ask me to strike that off the record of this court, Wilson, or I'll hold you in contempt.

WILSON Will your Honor have my remark stricken from the record?

JUDGE ROBINSON Strike it out.

(STENOGRAPHER *does so*)

WILSON You say that no store in the neighborhood or near the place of the assault will serve a colored man with ice cream?

RUFUS No sir, I didn't say that.

WILSON Don't you know that it's against the law to refuse to serve a colored person?

RUFUS I never said they refused to serve you, sir.

WILSON Oh, then, you could have bought the ice cream around there?

RUFUS Yes, sir.

WILSON Then why didn't you?

RUFUS Well, they will serve you, sir, but they put some flavor on that ice cream that just spoils it for eatin', sir.

(*Laugh*—WILSON *walks away right, disgusted*)

WILSON That's preposterous.

RUFUS Is that so, sir? I never hears with what they calls it before. It sure taste worse than it sounds—

WILSON Don't try to be funny.

RUFUS Lord God, boss, I ain't tryin' to be funny. This ain't no place for me to try to be funny in.

WILSON (*back to stand*) How near were you to Sanderson when he *claimed* he called to you?

RUFUS Well, Ah think it was—

WILSON How near were you to Carl Sanderson when he claimed he called to you?

RUFUS Well, I think . . .

WILSON Don't think. Answer my question.

RUFUS Boss, I gotta think, I ain't no lawyer.

WILSON Don't try to evade my question. How near were you to Carl Sanderson when he claimed he called to you?

RUFUS About thirty-five or forty yards, sir.

WILSON Didn't you testify in the police court that you were fifty or sixty yards away?

RUFUS I don't remember what I said—I was too scared.

WILSON You mean you don't want to remember?

RUFUS No, sir.

WILSON And because you don't want to remember you're unable to remember? Answer yes or no.

RUFUS Yes or no.

WILSON What do you mean by "yes or no?"

RUFUS I don't know, sir—you *told* me to say "yes or no" and I does it.

WILSON Your Honor, this isn't a dumb or ignorant witness, but a smart or instructed witness trying to evade the questions I put to him.

JUDGE ROBINSON I think his answers are made in all seriousness; proceed.

WILSON You say you saw the defendant, Carl Sanderson, and the lady struggling? And the lady was screaming—now then, wasn't it because the lady's screams had interfered with your dastardly intentions that Carl Sanderson was trying to get away?

RUFUS Sir?

WILSON Didn't you hear me?

RUFUS Yes, sir.

WILSON Then answer me.

RUFUS I hears you talking, sir, but I don't know what you say.

WILSON (*to bench*) I appeal to your Honor.

JUDGE ROBINSON Mr. Wilson, would you *like* the court to conduct the case for you?

WILSON (*back to stand*) Wasn't Carl Sanderson trying to get away, because the lady's screams had frightened him?

RUFUS I don't know, sir. All I know is he sure was trying to get away.

WILSON You're certain of that?

RUFUS Yes, sir. *Certain sure.*

WILSON And wasn't it the same reason you tried to get away?

RUFUS No, sir, I didn't run till I gets hit in the head and kicked.

WILSON Ah! If you are innocent as you claim you are, why did you run?

RUFUS What did you say?

WILSON I said, if you are innocent, why did you run?

RUFUS Because you're innocent ain't goin' ter do yer no good if you're hangin' from a telegram pole.

WILSON (*walks away right*) You don't mean to say that in a civilized city like San Francisco that you were afraid of being lynched?

RUFUS When I hears somebody say "lynch"—I knows that ain't no place for me to be in.

WILSON (*back to stand*) You admit that it was after the lady screamed that Carl Sanderson tried to get away?

RUFUS When I sees him, he sure was tryin' to git away from that lady.

WILSON And she was screaming and calling for help?

RUFUS Yes, sir.

WILSON That's all. (*back to seat*)

JUDGE THORNTON (*rises*) That's all Rufus, you may step down.

(RUFUS *back to table*)

JUDGE THORNTON Louise Thornton.

CLERK Louise Thornton.

BAILIFF Louise Thornton.

CLERK Name?

LOUISE Louise Thornton.

CLERK Address?

LOUISE Hotel Shasta.

CLERK Raise your right hand. Do you solemnly swear that the evidence you are about to give shall be the truth, the whole truth, and nothing but the truth, so help you God?

LOUISE I do. (*sits*)

JUDGE THORNTON (*rises—comes to center*) Will you tell the court what you know about this case?

LOUISE The morning after the trouble I remembered that Rufus said he had a package containing ice cream. After this I walked down to the place where the trouble happened and found—

(JUDGE *goes to table. Gets ice cream box, comes back to stand*)

JUDGE This?

LOUISE Yes. On it is printed "Drew's Confectionery and Ice Cream Store." I took this down to Mr. Drew and asked him if he remembered the colored boy purchasing the ice cream and he said he did, that he himself had waited on the boy and the time was about 9 o'clock. That's all.

JUDGE THORNTON (*holds box up*) I desire to offer this in evidence, your Honor.

JUDGE ROBINSON Mark it for identification—Exhibit A for the defense. Is that all?

(CLERK *takes box. Marks it*)

JUDGE THORNTON That's all, your Honor.

JUDGE ROBINSON Do you care to question the witness?

WILSON No questions. (*rises and goes to stand to help* LOUISE *down. She walks right by him.* WILSON *back to table, sits*)

JUDGE THORNTON Your Honor, inasmuch as there has been no evidence introduced in this case which in any way connects my client, Rufus Jones, with the alleged assault, I move that he is discharged.

WILSON (*rises*) I object.

JUDGE ROBINSON Overruled. I find no evidence against Rufus Jones and order his discharge. Rufus Jones . . .

RUFUS Sir?

JUDGE ROBINSON Rufus Jones, you may go.

Appearances

RUFUS Yes, sir. Alabama Bound. (*exits right*)

(JUDGE THORNTON *goes to table, sits*)

WILSON (*rises*) Your client having been discharged, Judge Thornton, that ends your connection with this case. (*sits*)

JUDGE THORNTON (*rises*) Your Honor, I throw myself on the mercy of the court and beg that I be allowed to remain.

JUDGE ROBINSON Your request is granted.

WILSON (*rises*) But your Honor . . .

JUDGE ROBINSON Judge Thornton, will you join me on the Bench?

JUDGE THORNTON I thank you, your Honor.

(WILSON *sits*)

JUDGE ROBINSON How long will it take the prosecution to prepare its case for the jury?

WILSON I'm ready now, your Honor.

JUDGE ROBINSON Proceed.

(WILSON *rises—goes to center of stage*)

WILSON Your Honor and members of the Jury. There are many crimes committed by hypocrites who mask their crimes under the cloak of religion. In my brief career before the courts I have found most criminals claim innocence, even those caught redhanded, as the defendant in this case was. Imagine, members of the jury, a young woman leaves her apartment in the city at 9 o'clock to mail a letter, when suddenly out of the dark of a vacant lot a black man jumps. And taking hold of her he tries to drag her into the lot. A place covered with great high weeds. She resists, screaming, and is rescued from this man who would have despoiled her. The law says there must be one law for white and the same law for the black, and I subscribe to the law, but there is something that the law cannot control and that is the honor of a white woman when attacked by a black man. Some of you have wives and daughters; all of you have had mothers; just imagine a woman, a widow; does not your blood boil at this dastardly attack, this dastardly thing that happened to her? The defendant has made no defense; he has refused counsel. Why? Do I need to ask why? You know why he refused to defend himself; because he had no defense to offer. Don't believe this nonsense about good, and truth, the greatest criminal tried in the courts of this city quoted that holy book, the Bible, every time he opened his mouth. You know who I mean, and the only reason this man doesn't stand charged with rape and murder was because he was interrupted before he could put into execution his fiendish desire. In his own testimony on the stand, he admits he was on Seventh Street the night of the attack. He admits he saw Mrs. Benton, he admits he *spoke* to her. Those were his admissions,—you know the rest. Now I ask you, Members of the Jury, to bring in a verdict of guilty, for that's the only verdict you, as men, can bring in, for by it you will prove your humanity; by it you will prove your protection of your own homes, your daughters, your wives, your sweethearts. . . . So I ask you Members of the Jury to bring in a verdict of guilty. (*back to table. Sits*)

JUDGE ROBINSON Carl Sanderson. Do you wish to address the jury? It's your right.

CARL (*rises*) Yes, your Honor. Your Honor, and Members of the Jury, I have made no defense because I need none. I have done no wrong and that's why I believe harm cannot come to me. Even if you find me guilty and send me to prison I will still believe that good will still be good and truth more powerful than prison bars. I feel nothing but good to this lady who has so falsely accused me and in my heart there is a great sorrow for her; for as good will come from good, so evil comes from evil; it is as one thinks in his heart. I have told the truth —there is nothing more to say. (*sits*)

JUDGE ROBINSON (*rises*) Members of the Jury, it is now my duty to charge you as to the law or the laws governing this case. Laws are made for the protection of the people, with suitable penalties for those who break these laws. Everyone is entitled to this protection and anyone breaking them must be punished. The plaintiff claims that the defendant wantonly attacked her on the public highway. The defendent claims that he was the one attacked. Therefore you must seek among the evidence for a motive—for back of every action there must be a motive. You will weigh the evidence carefully. The defendant has the same rights in this court as the plaintiff . . . The attorney for the plaintiff has tried to infer that the rulings of this court were induced by some personal animus on the part of the court. This you will take no cognizance of . . . It is a trick some lawyers descend to just for that purpose... that is to give you the impression that the court bears malice. (MRS. THOMPSON *writes note, gives it to* LOUISE, *who starts for bench*. BAILIFF *stops her, then takes note and gives it to* JUDGE THORNTON) I merely tell you this so that you may judge impartially. You will now retire to the Jury Room and report to me when you have reached a verdict.

(JUDGE THORNTON *leaves bench, comes down center*)

JUDGE THORNTON   Your Honor, I move that this case be re-opened on the ground of new evidence.
WILSON (*rises*)   I object. This is a trick to confuse the court and the jury.
JUDGE THORNTON   Your Honor knows me well enough to know that I would not ask this without some powerful reason.
WILSON   You cannot interfere with the rules of the law in this way. The court cannot allow it. This case has gone to the jury.
JUDGE THORNTON   If your Honor please, the jury can retire while this evidence is being submitted and your Honor decides its bearing on this case.
JUDGE ROBINSON   Your request is granted.
WILSON   I object.
JUDGE ROBINSON   Over-ruled.
WILSON   Your client has been discharged. You have no rights in this case.
JUDGE THORNTON (*turns to Wilson*)   I have the right of every man to see justice done.
JUDGE ROBINSON   Members of the Jury. I request that you do not start your deliberations until you hear from me.
WILSON   I object.
JUDGE ROBINSON   Over-ruled.
WILSON   This is a trick to confuse you, Members of the Jury.
JUDGE ROBINSON   Mr. Bailiff, you will place under arrest anyone holding speech with the jury.
WILSON   I object to the whole proceeding.
JUDGE ROBINSON   Over-ruled.
WILSON   I take exception to that ruling. (*sits*)
JUDGE ROBINSON   Note the exception—proceed, Judge Thornton.
JUDGE THORNTON   Mrs. Thompson, will you take the stand?

(MRS. THOMPSON *takes stand*)

CLERK   Your name?
MRS. THOMPSON   Gladys Thompson.
CLERK   Your address?
MRS. THOMPSON   Hotel Mount Shasta.
CLERK   Raise your right hand. Do you solemnly swear that the testimony you are about to give shall be the truth, the whole truth, and nothing but the truth, so help you God?
MRS. THOMPSON   I do. (*sits*)
JUDGE ROBINSON   Mrs. Thompson, if you have testimony to offer which has a vital bearing on this case, as your action suggests, you will state to the court why you waited until this time to introduce it.
MRS. THOMPSON   I was hoping against hope that I wouldn't have to tell, but when I heard what your Honor said to the jury about "motive," I knew what the jury's verdict would be, and some irresistible force compelled me to write this note, and hand it to Louise, and she had it passed to her father.
JUDGE ROBINSON   You have not given me a motive yet, Mrs. Thompson.
MRS. THOMPSON   I knew that it would let someone who is very near to me and very dear to me know something that I didn't want him to know.
JUDGE ROBINSON   Yes.
MRS. THOMPSON   I am speaking of my husband.

(THOMPSON *rises*)

JUDGE ROBINSON   What has your husband to do with it?
MRS. THOMPSON   Oh, nothing directly... but I found that he was spending a great deal of his time with another woman and I engaged a detective to watch him.
WILSON (*rises*)   I object.
JUDGE ROBINSON   Over-ruled. (WILSON *sits*) Proceed, Mrs. Thompson.
MRS. THOMPSON   And I asked the detective to find out for me all he could about that woman.
WILSON (*rises*)   This is immaterial, and irrelevant, and I object to it.
JUDGE ROBINSON   Over-ruled.
WILSON   Exception.
JUDGE ROBINSON   Noted. (WILSON *sits*) Proceed.
MRS. THOMPSON   Mrs. Elsie Benton is not a widow. Her husband is alive and lives in Provo

Appearances

City, Utah, with her little boy whom she deserted nearly two years ago.

(ELSIE *rises, startled, comes down to table*)

WILSON (*rises*) Which, even if true, has nothing to do with the fact that she was assaulted.

JUDGE ROBINSON (*gavel*) Quiet! Proceed.

MRS. THOMPSON She has been enamored and living with another man ever since that time.

ELSIE Stop her, for God's sake, can't you stop her?

(WILSON *quiets her*)

MRS. THOMPSON Six months ago, in Oakland, where she and this man had an apartment, she accused another man of practically the same thing that she has charged Carl with, but this man suspected and instead of having him arrested, he had her arrested, charging blackmail.

ELSIE Can't you stop her?

(WILSON *quiets her again*)

MRS. THOMPSON Her counsel made such a fine plea for her that the Judge remanded her in custody. And another thing—Mrs. Benton is not a white women. I have positive proof that she is a Negress. If Mr. Wilson wants me to go on I will.

WILSON (*comes to bench*) Wait, wait. Your Honor knows that all I have ever asked from the Court was justice and if Mrs. Thompson can prove these things, I'll be only too . . .

MRS. THOMPSON The detective with the affidavits is waiting.

JUDGE ROBINSON Who is the detective?

MRS. THOMPSON Ex-chief McAuliffe. Shall I go on, your Honor?

WILSON No, no, your Honor . . . all I asked was justice. I am quite satisfied. The plaintiff has misled me. (*back to table*)

ELSIE (*rises*) But you said . . . you promised.

WILSON Shut up or you'll end in prison yourself.

ELSIE I won't shut up. You said . . .

WILSON Quiet!

ELSIE Wait! It wasn't my fault, he planned it all—he wanted to get rid of Carl. It's all his fault.

WILSON Will you be still?

ELSIE I don't want to go to jail again.

WILSON Quiet! Your Honor.

ELSIE He made me do it, your Honor. He wanted to get rid of Carl. He planned it all.

WILSON Your Honor, I can explain. . . .

JUDGE ROBINSON (*rises*) *You* will explain to the Bar Association—The witness, Mrs. Benton, will remain in the custody of this court. Carl Sanderson . . .

(ELSIE *collapses*)

CARL Yes, sir.

JUDGE ROBINSON It is evident from the testimony of Mrs. Thompson and the quarrel between Attorney Wilson and Mrs. Benton that you have been the victim of a plot . . . What its objects were, and why it was planned, this court will find out. You will pass out of this court completely exonerated. The case against you is dismissed. *You are discharged.*

(*Gavel. Curtain*)

ACT THREE

(*At rise:* CARL, *behind hotel desk in uniform. Short pause. Enter* RUFUS *from porch*)

RUFUS (*goes to desk. Gives mail to* CARL) Mail, Mr. Carl.

CARL Thanks.

RUFUS If you're busy on your work, Mr. Carl, I can rack 'em for you.

CARL That's all right, Rufus, I'm finished writing for the time being. I've got to dream some more.

RUFUS Ever since we 'scapes from bein' put in jail you does nothin' but write. Does it all come out of your own head?

CARL It all comes from the source of infinite supply.

RUFUS Sometimes I got dreams too.

CARL Yes?

RUFUS Oh yes, sur, but they's all about chicken and gin.

CARL If you would dream something good for you, Rufus, you would realize that dream, if you have faith in yourself.

RUFUS Faith! What is that?

CARL I believe I read something in the Bible about "Faith being the substance of the thing hoped for, the evidence of the thing not seen."

RUFUS That 'minds me of when I was a pickaninny runnin' around our cabin in Alabama.

CARL How's that?

RUFUS We never had much *ham*, but I always dreamed and hoped that one day we get a lot.

CARL Did you get it?

RUFUS Sure, one night my pappy came home with two whole pounds.

CARL Where did he get it?

RUFUS I reckon he got it from the source of infinite supply . . . when the store-keeper had his back turned . . . Well, my mammy ate one pound and my pappy ate the other and when I gets the dish there's nothing left but faith . . .

CARL Faith?

RUFUS No! I means gravy.

CARL Why do you call faith "gravy," Rufus?

RUFUS 'Cause it's the substance of the thing hoped for and the evidence of the thing not seen.

CARL Go 'way from here, boy!

(RUFUS *exits left*. THOMPSON *enters from stairs*)

THOMPSON (*goes back of desk*) Is the mail in, Carl?

CARL Yes, sir.

THOMPSON I suppose I deserve all I am getting, eh Carl?

CARL You know better than I do, sir.

THOMPSON Mrs. Thompson might write and let me know where she is.

CARL (*sits on bench*) No news is good news, sir.

(*Enter* ANDREWS)

THOMPSON Good evening. Want your key, Mr. Andrews?

ANDREWS (*goes directly to stairs*) I have it, thank you.

THOMPSON Here is a letter for you.

ANDREWS (*he stops and takes letter from* THOMPSON) Thanks.

(LOUISE *enters*)

LOUISE Good evening, Mr. Andrews.

ANDREWS How do you do?

THOMPSON Oh, you two have met?

ANDREWS Oh, yes indeed. (*exit upstairs*)

LOUISE (*goes to desk left, picks up papers*) Oh, yes, indeed . . . Did Fred get back?

THOMPSON Carl, did you see Mr. Kellard?

CARL Yes, sir. He said he had a date with a policeman and went out.

LOUISE He wandered off with my vanity case . . . put it in his pocket and walked off with it.

THOMPSON That is a tragedy, isn't it?

LOUISE It will be for him when I get my hands on him.

THOMPSON Do you know, I wouldn't be surprised if Wilson is trying to frame Fred Kellard with this fellow's assistance. There is nothing too rotten for that bird to try.

LOUISE You think that Andrews may be helping Jack Wilson?

THOMPSON I think he will stand watching.

LOUISE Tell me when Fred gets back. I'll talk to him.

THOMPSON Everything is all right?

LOUISE (*crosses to stairs*) I promised Ella that I would look over her accounts.

THOMPSON I don't know what I should have done if you hadn't helped out, Miss Louise, since Gladys went away.

(*'Phone rings*)

LOUISE It is no more than Gladys would have done for me. Besides I am glad for the chance to learn a little something about housekeeping.

(LOUISE *exits upstairs*)

CARL Hello! Yes ma'am. No, Mrs. French, no mail. Nothing but your bill. No, ma'am. It isn't due till the fifteenth.

(THOMPSON *goes to desk left, sits*. CARL *exits service door*. ELSIE *appears at door left. Crosses to right*)

THOMPSON (*rises, sees* ELSIE) What are you doing here?

ELSIE Your wife asked me to come.

THOMPSON (*goes over to her*) My wife wouldn't have anything to do with a woman like you.

ELSIE Your wife has had a great deal to do with a woman like me. If you'll listen, perhaps you'll understand. You know your wife's story at the trial was true... Do you know who the man was?... Jack Wilson... I came here on a visit about two years ago... met him... fell madly in love with him, and finally went to live with him, sending word to my husband that I had gone to Los Angeles.

THOMPSON What has all this to do with Mrs. Thompson?

ELSIE After that trial Wilson lied himself out of it... he's clever... he put it all on me... and that judge simply tore me to bits... then let me go on the condition that I leave San Francisco at once.

THOMPSON But you are here.

ELSIE Ella told your wife of my trouble. I was sick, body and soul. When I was strong enough she urged me to go back to my husband and boy... and she even went with me— back home.

THOMPSON Where *is* my wife? Will you take me to her?

ELSIE I can't. I'd like to speak to Carl.

THOMPSON (*goes to service door*) Carl? (CARL *enters*) Mrs. Benton wishes to speak to you. (THOMPSON *exits to office*)

ELSIE Carl, when you realize that great dream of yours and you're famous...

(*Enter* WILSON)

CARL Famous; my dream hasn't anything in it about being famous, all I ask is to realize it for the good it will bring to others.

ELSIE Carl, here's a letter from Mrs. Thompson. She asked me to give it to you secretly.

CARL From Mrs. Thompson? Oh, thank you.

(THOMPSON *enters from office*)

WILSON Well? What are you doing here?

THOMPSON None of your damn business.

WILSON I'll make it my business.

THOMPSON (*steps between* WILSON *and 'phone*) You keep away from that 'phone.

(CARL *exits*)

WILSON The police have an order to pick up this woman any time she is found in San Francisco.

THOMPSON She came to see me. She is under my protection, and nobody is going to touch her.

(RUFUS *enters*)

WILSON (*starts for door, left*) I don't need your 'phone. I'll get a policeman.

THOMPSON If this man tries to leave here, Rufus, you stop him.

RUFUS Yes, sir. Sure will.

WILSON Before you go out of this town I'll have the police after you, and your husband no doubt will be also glad to know where you are.

ELSIE And my husband, who is waiting for me in Oakland, will be after you, Mr. Jack Wilson. He is crazy to meet you, for he knows everything you did to me.

WILSON How interesting?

THOMPSON Rufus. I am going to take Mrs. Benton out and put her in a taxi. If Wilson tries to 'phone or follow us, I leave you to stop him.

(THOMPSON *goes to door, waits*)

RUFUS Yes, sir, Mr. Boss, I sure will.

ELSIE (*starts for door, and stops near* WILSON) I *am* glad to see you again, Jack.

WILSON Yes?

ELSIE Yes. They say Love is blind, after seeing you again I'll tell the world it is not only blind, but deaf and dumb... particularly dumb. (*exit with* THOMPSON)

WILSON Get away from that 'phone.

RUFUS No, sir. Mr. Boss man says you shouldn't use it.

WILSON Give me that 'phone before I take it away from you.

RUFUS Mr. Wilson, did you ever hear of Alabama Jones—the prize-fighter?

WILSON Yes, why?

RUFUS My name's Jones, and I come from Alabama.

WILSON Give me that 'phone.

RUFUS Now, wait a minute, the Boss man says you can't use it. This one is named "lightnin'." And this one's named "dynamite." When Lightnin' jabs... Dynamite crosses over and busts... Ooze away from me white man... ooze on away.

WILSON You can't bluff me.

RUFUS Lord God, man, I ain't tryin' to bluff you. I'se just stating facts. If you think I'm bluffin', just call my bluff.

WILSON You wouldn't dare strike a white man.

RUFUS Ain't never did it yet, outside the

ring, but the Boss man told me to watch that 'phone.

WILSON (*starts for 'phone*) Get out of my way.

RUFUS (*stops him*) Mr. Wilson, if you like your face don't start nothing, because if you does you ain't going to recognize you' own self for months and months.

WILSON (*sits*) You damn orang-outang, you!

RUFUS What's that you called me?

WILSON An orang-outang.

RUFUS I don't know what that is, but if you don't take it back I'se going to lam you one for luck. Now is I what you said, or isn't I? Answer yes or no.

WILSON No.

RUFUS What? What you say?

WILSON No, I mean—yes.

RUFUS What you mean—No, I mean yes.

WILSON You stay in your place!

RUFUS One of the rules of the prize ring is ... never hit a man when he's down ... and you're safe while you're setting ... But don't rise, white boy ... don't rise.

(THOMPSON *enters*)

THOMPSON All right, Rufus.

RUFUS Oh Boss; don't never give me no more job like that.

THOMPSON Why?

RUFUS He's nervous and I'm scared to death.

THOMPSON Did you have your dinner yet?

RUFUS No, sir, but God and this gentleman has given me a fine appetite.

THOMPSON Then run along and eat.

RUFUS Yes, sir. If they is one word in the English language that spells more to me than any other, it is that one word E. T. E. Eat. (*exit*)

THOMPSON Now, Wilson, you can get out. And God help you if anyone interferes with Mrs. Benton.

WILSON I came here to see Mr. Andrews. He is a guest here, and I have the right to call on him.

THOMPSON He can get out with you. I am running this hotel.

(ANDREWS *enters*)

ANDREWS Oh, Wilson.

WILSON Andrews, I came here to see you.

ANDREWS What's the matter?

WILSON This fool, Thompson, is trying to put me out.

THOMPSON Mr. Andrews, you are a guest here. It is none of my business what my guests do or with whom they associate, but this man Wilson is a crook.

ANDREWS I guess I can take care of myself. I don't need a wet nurse yet.

THOMPSON All right. Your week is up tomorrow. I should need your room.

ANDREWS All right. You'll get it.

(THOMPSON *exits to office*)

WILSON I offered him a chance to come in on the selenium mine, and he is sore because he didn't.

ANDREWS Some people are that way, aren't they?

WILSON World's full of them.

ANDREWS Well, the check arrived. Here it is. (*shows check*) "Pay to the Order of John Wilson" ... pay to you personally ... that's right, isn't it? You own the property?

WILSON Yes.

ANDREWS You have the bill of sale—assignments and everything with you?

WILSON Yes.

ANDREWS You bought this mine from Kellard, didn't you?

WILSON Yes, sure.

ANDREWS Well that's O.K. Well, I'm going down the street. Like to come?

WILSON Yes.

ANDREWS All right! Wait 'til I get my hat and I'll go with you. (*exit upstairs*)

(CARL *enters service door, goes up to desk*)

WILSON You're a pretty slick proposition, but you've slipped a cog this time.

CARL What do you mean, sir?

WILSON You know what I mean—How long has this little affair been going on ... Oh, don't look so dumb. (*grabs letter from* CARL'*s pocket. Enter* THOMPSON) The affair between you and Mrs. Thompson.

THOMPSON Wilson, will you please leave my wife's name out of your discussion.

WILSON Perhaps you would rather let your bell-hop discuss her. He is apparently on more intimate terms with her.

THOMPSON (*rushes at* WILSON) Damn you—you ...

Appearances

WILSON (*stops him*) Wait a minute! Ask your little "good-within" boy to explain the letter Elsie Benton gave him from your wife.

THOMPSON Letter! Did you receive a letter from Mrs. Thompson?

CARL Nothing personal, sir.

WILSON Not personal! Listen to this. "Carl, I have decided to do what you asked. Although I didn't think I could ever bring myself to it. . . . By all means let no one at the hotel know of our plans, especially my husband," and it is signed "Gladys Thompson."

THOMPSON And I trusted you—you dirty rat. Corresponding with my wife. (*grasps Carl by neck, chokes him, throws him down.* ELLA *enters right*)

ELLA (*rushes to* THOMPSON, *takes his arm*) Mr. Thompson, Mr. Thompson! What are you doing? You are killing him, please . . .

THOMPSON He's been secretly corresponding with my wife.

ELLA Oh, I know, I know! Carl has been corresponding with Mrs. Thompson. Why, only to-night Mrs. Benton brought him a letter from your wife saying she would return to you.

THOMPSON Return . . . to me?

ELLA Why, yes, Mr. Thompson. She came in through the servants entrance. We had planned to surprise you. Your wife is upstairs now waiting for you.

(THOMPSON *looks at* CARL, *then exits upstairs*)

WILSON As somebody once said, "The Devil can quote Scripture." If anybody wants me, I'll be in Mr. Andrews' room. (*exit upstairs*)

ELLA (*helps* CARL *get up*) Carl—Carl boy! (RUFUS *enters*) Rufus!

RUFUS Yes, Miss Ella.

ELLA Take this laundry up to Room 48.

RUFUS Yes, ma'am.

CARL What was that song you were singing, Rufus?

RUFUS Song? Oh! That was a spiritual—an old convict song.

CARL Sing some more.

RUFUS Sure. (*sings until off upstairs.* CARL *sits*)

ELLA (*kneels beside* CARL) Carl.

CARL Yes, dear!

ELLA Have you thought of where you are going and what you are going to do when you've realized your great ambition?

CARL You mean, where are *we* going, and what are *we* going to do, don't you, dear? We are going back among our own people. For I realize now how much we need them, and they need us.

ELLA Oh, I'm so proud of you. You're going up and up—and will take your place along with Frederick Douglass and Booker T. Washington.

CARL We are going up together dear. For any success I might attain will be due to the inspiration I receive from you. For I firmly believe that any man who ever succeeded must have been inspired by some good woman.

ELLA It makes me so happy to hear that I've been an inspiration to you.

CARL You've been that, and more dear. I have a wonderful idea—(THOMPSON *and* MRS. THOMPSON *enter down stairs*) Now when we get back to Savannah, we are first going to . . .

THOMPSON *Ella!* Check up that new linen.

ELLA Yes sir. (*they jump up*)

CARL I didn't hear him come in, did you?

ELLA Nugh-nugh! (*exits right. Enter* JUDGE THORNTON *from stairs*)

JUDGE Has anyone seen Mr. Kellard?

CARL Yes, sir. He's out on the porch with Miss Louise. Shall I look for him?

JUDGE No, don't look for him . . . better page him.

CARL Yes, sir . . . Paging Mr. Fred Kellard . . . Paging Mr. Fred Kellard . . . (*exits door left*)

JUDGE Well, Mrs. Thompson, I suppose we'll get some service now you're back. This good man of yours has been wandering round like a ghost with a silent sorrow. Mighty glad to see you back and so will everyone else be.

(THOMPSON *exits office*)

MRS. THOMPSON I know about everything. Louise has been writing to me.

(CARL *enters, paging* "Mr. Frederick Kellard," *and exits to office. Enter* KELLARD *left*)

KELLARD Who's paging me? Look who's here! (*goes down to* MRS. THOMPSON) Glad to see you.

(*Enter* LOUISE)

JUDGE I want to see you, Fred.

LOUISE Gladys, when did you get back?

JUDGE You're in this too, Louise.

(*They go to porch entrance*)

LOUISE I'm busy.

JUDGE I've been all over your case, Fred. You gave Wilson Power of Attorney to practically do as he likes, but who gave you the right to give that Power of Attorney?

KELLARD Why, my partners did.

JUDGE Did they give it you in writing?

KELLARD No, sir. There isn't a speck of writing between us. Share and share alike, three ways.

JUDGE But legally, that doesn't count, without their written signatures. Mr. Wilson hasn't a leg to stand on.

KELLARD Listen, Judge, they gave me the right—told me whatever I did would go with them.

JUDGE I know. But you got tied up with a crook.

KELLARD You see, Judge, it's like this; one of my partners has been East and he's trying to work it another way. He's got a customer who will take over the whole thing, promote it on the same terms, but absolutely refuses to let Wilson have anything to do with it. Now if this partner fails, we'll see if we can work it out some other way.

JUDGE Well, you don't mind if I go after him, do you?

KELLARD No, sir, you go just as far as you like.

(WILSON *and* ANDREWS *come down stairs talking*)

WILSON But I can't see the necessity of it.

ANDREWS (*goes to above table*) No doubt, but you must remember we are an old Boston firm, and do business accordingly.

WILSON Ah! The two-handed gunman.

KELLARD Who told you that Wilson?

WILSON My friend, Mr. Andrews.

KELLARD Did he tell you I was a good two-handed gunman?

WILSON Yes.

KELLARD And did he tell you I was a good shot with either hand?

WILSON He did.

KELLARD Well, I'm sorry he told you that Wilson, because if you don't settle that business pretty quick, you're going to learn it personally.

WILSON You can't get away with that rough stuff here.

KELLARD I can't, eh? Now you listen to me, and you wait 'til I'm through. I worked for two whole years in Hell's Hole, and believe me it was Hell without any drinking water. But you can get out of there, but no man yet has ever come out of the Hell I'll send you to.

ANDREWS Aw! This stuff doesn't get us anywhere. Let's get our business over with. Oh, Judge Thornton!

JUDGE Yes.

ANDREWS Pardon me, but will you witness a little business transaction for me?

JUDGE Why not?

ANDREWS (*shows* JUDGE *check*) Thank you. I want you to witness that I have passed to Mr. Wilson a certified check for one hundred thousand dollars.

JUDGE I will.

ANDREWS And here, Mr. Wilson, is the check.

WILSON (*starts for door*) Thanks. I'm late. You'll have to excuse me.

JUDGE (*stops him*) Just a minute, Jack. I have a little business to transact with you.

(KELLARD *goes in front of door left*)

WILSON Some other time.

JUDGE Some other time won't do, it's now.

WILSON (*walks by Judge*) You can't detain me if I want to go.

KELLARD Perhaps I can.

JUDGE First, the assignment, signed by Fred Kellard, assigning the property to you isn't worth the paper it's written on.

ANDREWS What's that you say, Judge?

WILSON It's good enough for me.

JUDGE It happens that he has two partners.

WILSON That's a lie.

JUDGE Have you their signatures in your Incorporation papers?

ANDREWS Do you mean that Wilson doesn't own the property?

JUDGE He never owned it. He was only empowered to incorporate, issue and sell the stock.

ANDREWS Wilson, you sold me something you do not own. You received our money under false pretences. That's criminal, isn't it, Judge?

JUDGE Yes, sir.

WILSON (*comes to center*) Well, if you are going to make a fuss, here's your check. Give me back those contracts.

ANDREWS But we want the mine! You were a witness, Judge.

WILSON (*starts back to door*) Well, if you won't take the check, I'll keep it.

KELLARD Just a minute. Payment on that check is stopped.

WILSON Why? It's certified.

KELLARD Obtained under false pretences. And, before you can cash it in the morning, I'll get out an injunction and every bank in California will know about it.

WILSON What do you mean?

KELLARD This is what I mean. Meet my partner, Andrew Andrews—better known as Alias Ananias Andrews.

LOUISE He's your partner?

KELLARD Yes, ma'am.

WILSON It's a frameup. You can't get away with it.

JUDGE You'll be lucky Wilson if these men don't telephone to the police and put you under arrest as a common swindler.

WILSON Yes, perhaps you're right, Judge. I say, perhaps you're right. Looks as though I'm in a bit of a mess, all through this damned check. (*gives check to* CARL) Carl, here's a tip for you for the black page in your book of converts. Something to talk about from me. It isn't worth anything, you might have it framed. I'll remember the time I gave a bell-boy a certified check for one hundred grand, but it does look like a jam. Doesn't it, Judge?

JUDGE Certainly does, Wilson.

WILSON (*turns to* ANDREWS) So you're Mr. Andrews from Boston are you?

ANDREWS I never even saw Boston.

WILSON And I thought you were from the East.

ANDREWS Sure I been East... all the way to Omaha. Carl, will you ask that gentleman outside to step in?

(CARL *exits*)

WILSON Well, you certainly put it over.

(POLICEMAN *enters left*)

ANDREWS Yes, sir. We planned this little party for your special benefit, and just so you won't forget it, here is a little souvenir for you.

(POLICEMAN *hands* WILSON *a warrant*)

WILSON Well, what's this?

ANDREWS It's a warrant for your arrest for taking money under false pretences and other things ... issued by Judge Robinson.

WILSON I never did like that Judge.

OFFICER Reckon you remember me, Mr. Wilson. I'm the policeman that arrested that colored boy you framed.

WILSON Oh, yes, I remember you perfectly.

OFFICER Will you come quietly, or shall I use these? (*shows a pair of handcuffs*)

WILSON Quietly—very—very quietly. Well, things seem to have broken pretty badly for me folks.

ANDREWS So Wilson, you turned out to be a first-class crook.

WILSON Crook, yes—but not first class. I was caught.

CARL You can't fight good, sir.

WILSON Good... hell. The only good that any of you have that I haven't is good luck. Well, don't do anything till you hear from me. (*exit with* OFFICER)

CARL But what will I do with this check?

JUDGE Too bad it isn't any good, Carl. If it was you'd be rich and able to realize any ambition you might have.

CARL But I have realized my ambition, Judge.

LOUISE Realized it, how?

KELLARD What is the ambition you realized?

CARL You don't know—but you, even Mr. Wilson and Mrs. Benton and Judge Robinson, you've all helped me to realize it.

KELLARD How come?

(*Lights start dimming*)

CARL A few years ago I dreamed I was going to do something big in life. It seemed too wonderful to be true, but that dream was with me night and day; it would give me no rest, so I said, "If God has given me this dream, he'll give me the power and knowledge by which to realize it, for its message was good, good for my own people, good for everyone it could reach."

LOUISE I'm dying to know what it is. Aren't you, Fred?

KELLARD Just jumpin' right out of my skin.

CARL I dreamed a play; first, it was just a jumble of thoughts that gradually straightened itself out, then characters came into being and they began to think and then to talk, and as they talked I put it down on paper. For all my thoughts and all they said were filled with a big message.

JUDGE What's the message, Carl?

CARL If a black bell-boy with not much schooling could imagine himself a playwright; that by believing and working he could write a play that was interesting and entertaining enough to hold an audience, it would prove to the world beyond the shadow of a doubt that any man can do what he desires to do, can become anything he desires to be. For you see you are all characters that I have dreamt.

(*All lights out, but blues and overhead spot*)

KELLARD How come? Wait a minute. You mean I'm a dream? And not real?

CARL No. You're real now.

LOUISE Am I engaged to marry him?

(*Blues dim out slowly*)

CARL Yes.

LOUISE Oh ... then that's all right.

THOMPSON What about me? Am I a dream hotel manager or a real one?

CARL You're all real now.

ALL Real! Real!

CARL (*steps into spot. Blues out*) And as my dream came to an end, I could hear Mr. Kellard say, "Wait a minute! You mean to say I'm a dream?" And then Miss Thornton said, "Am I engaged to marry him?" Then Mr. Thompson spoke—all I could hear was "Real—Real" —Then I knew my dream had ended in a wonderful reality, for they were dreams, and now they are real people. And I thank God my dream has come true.

(*Their voices became fainter and fainter. Curtain.*)

3

Early Plays by Black Women

**Angelina Weld Grimke   Alice Dunbar-Nelson
Mary Burrill   Myrtle Smith Livingston   Eulalie Spence
Ruth Gaines-Shelton   Marita Bonner**

The six one-act plays and the one full-length play gathered here were published between April 1918 and April 1929; from the end of World War I to the stock market crash. This decade was variously named the Harlem Renaissance, The Negro Awakening, and The Decade of the New Negro. This decade saw the Garvey Universal Negro Improvement Association enroll two million dues-paying members before its leader's arrest and deportation in 1927 (see Introduction to *Big White Fog*). It was a decade of black rebellions in Omaha, Chicago, Knoxville, Tulsa, Washington, D.C. It was a decade of black writers: DuBois, McKay, Brawley, Johnson, Woodson, Toomer, Fauset, Locke, White, Hughes. It was a decade of Black musicals on Broadway: *Shuffle Along, Keep Shufflin', From Dixie to Broadway, The Black Birds, The Blackberries, Chocolate Dandies, Running Wild, Brown Buddies*. It was a decade that saw twenty plays on Negro themes presented on Broadway, five of them written by blacks. It was a decade that began with barely twenty one-act plays on Negro themes and ended with over eighty.

W. E. B. DuBois, editor of *Crisis Magazine* and a tireless promoter of black artists, wrote in 1926,

If a man writes a play, and a good play, he is lucky if he earns first class postage upon it. Of course he may sell it commercially to some producer on Broadway; but in that case it would not be a Negro play or if it is a Negro play it will not be about the kind of Negro you and I know or want to know. If it is a Negro play that will interest us and depict our life, experience and humor, it can not be sold to the ordinary theatrical producer, but it can be produced in our churches and lodges, and halls.

The seven plays reprinted here were never intended for Broadway. Six appeared in periodicals: *Birth Control Review, Carolina, Crisis, Opportunity*. All were written by women, who have always been well represented in black dramaturgy. Some of these plays were prize winners in contests sponsored by *Crisis* and *Opportunity* magazines. All are original voices that were unwelcome in the commercial theater of the 1920's, voices that "depict our life, experience and humour."

The reader might keep in mind Eldridge Cleaver's observation about the myth of the strong black woman. "He [the white man] turned the black woman into a strong self-reliant Amazon and deposited her in his kitchen—that's the secret of Aunt Jemima's bandana." Question: Do these women playwrights paint true portraits of black women?

Angelina Weld Grimke (1880–1958)

Rachel   1916

In 1915, Dr. Booker T. Washington died. America prepared for her first Great War to Save Civilization. Some 737,626 black men were inducted into the armed services. Thousands of others, with the promise of high wages before them, migrated from the rural South to industrial cities of the North (see *'Cruiter*). In 1916 James W. Johnson became Secretary of the NAACP.

The Drama Committee of the NAACP in Washington, D.C., decided to make its "first attempt to use the stage for race propaganda in order to enlighten the American people relative to the lamentable condition of ten millions of Colored citizens in this free republic."

The seriousness of the pressures upon blacks in the cities at this time can be partially judged by the extent of the black "rebellions" in St. Louis in 1917, in Chicago and Washington in 1919, and in Tulsa in 1921. Routinely, the American white dramatists of this period were presenting an exotic picture of Negro city life, an image that was to culminate in Heyward's *Porgy* in 1927.

Ernest Culbertson, a white journalist, wrote a play *Goat Alley*, the title taken from a black community in Washington, D.C. The advertisements for the production in 1921 read in part: "a new play of primitive love and life," exhibiting "a red hot crap game." Although the script itself is less exotic than its publicity, it nevertheless indicates the prevailing white image of Negro life. And it is in part this image of razor-wielding that Angelina Grimke seems to have set out to correct with her play, *Rachel*.

Some critics have said that *Rachel* is the first play to be written by a black that was publicly performed by black actors. This is true only if musicals are ignored—and if Mr. Brown's *King Shotaway* of 1823 is disregarded.

Miss Grimke (not to be confused with the abolitionist, her great-aunt of the same name), was born in 1880. She, like the heroine of her play, was an English teacher in Washington, D.C. Her father, a prominent journalist, Archibald Grimke, served as U.S. Council in Santo Domingo, and was Vice-President of the NAACP.

When the NAACP presented *Rachel*, on March 3 and 4, 1916, at the Myrtill Miner Normal School, the results were mixed. "A minority section of the Committee dissented from this propaganda platform and were instruments," Montgomery Gregory reports, "in founding the Howard Players organization, promoting the purely artistic approach...." (*Plays of Negro Life*, 1927).

Those who favored "the purely artistic approach" versus those who elected "to use the stage for race propaganda" had joined in an ancient and honored struggle in the arts: is theatre primarily for teaching or for entertainment? In contemporary black theater these two positions have sometimes been redefined as "don't rock the boat" versus "tell it like it is."

For the reader who does not like the message play, *Rachel* is unwelcome news. Fannin Belcher, Jr. writes, "The drama is a morbid sermon on the after-effects of lynching and the innumerable humiliations to which Negro Americans are subjected." Morbid for Mr. Belcher, but not for those who in 1916 were interested in stopping lynching. It is perhaps unfair to judge a play for what it never intended to be.

It is likely that the play was produced for two audiences: a white audience that needed to know and to suffer empathically the injustices of the characters in *Rachel* and a black audience that needed to see an image of its members not only as they conceived themselves to be, but as they wished themselves to be.

The black audience was divided in its reaction to the play in much the same fashion that it would be today. What is the ideal for the black reader: to relate deeply to his ethnic roots or to strive toward a more generalized American culture? In addition, *Rachel* must be judged in terms of another question: How much of the black image will the writer permit the white audience to see? For it is a fact that if the black man gives the white man one inch toward a stereotype, he will take a mile.

Is there any way an objective evaluation can be made of *Rachel*? Perhaps, if the reader will concede two things: theatrical production and a style relevant to 1916.

Certainly some sections that read poorly play better on stage. An important case in point is the use of children. Anyone who attends the theater knows how a child on the stage seizes the attention. Generally, the younger the child, the more the audience is fascinated with that double awareness that the child is acting but also acknowledging the presence of the audience. The frequent use of children in *Rachel* would be a director's nightmare but, if done well, would create a powerful emotional force. Count the kisses given. Note the number of times characters are addressed by endearments.

This leads to the second concession the modern reader must make: acceptance of the sentimental style. *Rachel* is in the Louisa May Alcott tradition. Miss Grimke is writing with true feeling, but the four wars since the writing make her tender feelings seem Victorian and precious.

The Lovings, the family of the play, could be embraced by every American who ever described his origins as "poor but honest and clean." (Isn't Lorraine Hansberry writing of the same family?) Rachel inspects the ears and fingernails for any trace of dirt. She corrects grammar: "You ran the water too, boy, not 'runned' it." The author sees no conflict between the middle class virtues and the beauties of being black.

I love little black and brown babies best of all. . . . Ma dear, I think their white teeth and the clear whites of their big eyes and their dimples everywhere are—are—(breaks off) And Ma dear, because I love them best, I pray God every night to give me when I grow up, little black and brown babies to protect and guard.

When Rachel's brother Tom is told that there is a surprise treat, he guesses dill pickles, tripe, hog's jowl, pig's feet, and chitlings. Nor is Tom Loving emasculated by the bourgeois standards of routine work, thrift, and cleanliness: "If being a *gentleman* means not being a *man*, I don't wish to be one." He blackens the eye of a white classmate who calls him "nigger." The only words spoken against blackness come from the angry, courageous, and bitter Mrs. Lane: "My husband and I are poor, and we're ugly, and we're black." And she is speaking ironically, giving white America's opinion of herself.

A reader who approaches *Rachel* with historical perspective and an open heart should not be ashamed if occasional lumps rise in his throat. Angelina Grimke was a sensitive and delicate artist. She wrote poetry about herself.

UNDER THE DAYS

The days fall upon me
one by one they fall,
Like leaves—
They are black,
They are gray,
They are white;
They are shot through with gold and fire.
They fall,
They fall,
Ceaselessly,
They cover me,
They crush
They smother.
Who will ever find me under the days?

Rachel

CAST OF CHARACTERS

MRS. LOVING, *mother*
RACHEL LOVING, *her daughter*
TOM LOVING, *her son*
JOHN STRONG, *Tom's friend*
JIMMY, *the neighbor's small boy*
MRS. LANE, *a black woman*
ETHEL, *her daughter*
EDITH, LOUISE, NANCY, MARY, MARTHA, JENNY, *children*

ACT ONE

(*The scene is a room scrupulously neat and clean and plainly furnished. The walls are painted green, the woodwork, white. In the rear at the left* (left *and* right *are from the spectator's point of view*) *an open doorway leads into a hall. Its bare, green wall and white baseboard are all that can be seen of it. It leads into the other rooms of the flat. In the center of the rear wall of the room is a window. It is shut. The white sash curtains are pushed to right and left as far as they will go. The green shade is rolled up to the top. Through the window can be seen the red bricks of a house wall, and the tops of a couple of trees moving now and then in the wind. Within the window, and just below the sill, is a shelf upon which are a few potted plants. Between the window and the door is a bookcase full of books and above it, hanging on the wall, a simply framed, inexpensive copy of Millet's "The Reapers." There is a run extending from the right center to just below the right upper entrance. It is the vestibule of the flat. Its open doorway faces the left wall. In the right wall near the front is another window. Here the sash curtains are drawn together and the green shade is partly lowered. The window is up from the bottom. Through it street noises can be heard. In front of this window is an open, threaded sewing-machine. Some frail, white fabric is lying upon it. There is a chair in front of the machine and at the machine's left a small table covered with a green cloth. In the rear of the left wall and directly opposite to the entrance to the flat is the doorway leading into the kitchenette, dishes on shelves can be seen behind glass doors.*

In the center of the left wall is a fireplace with a grate in it for coals; over this is a wooden mantel painted white. In the center is a small clock. A pair of vases, green and white in coloring, one at each end, complete the ornaments. Over the mantel is a narrow mirror; and over this, hanging on the wall, Burne-Jones' "Golden Stairs," simply framed. Against the front end of the left wall is an upright piano with a stool in front of it. On top is music neatly piled. Hanging over the piano is Raphael's "Sistine Madonna." In the center of the floor is a green rug, and in the center of this, a rectangular dining-room table, the long side facing front. It is covered with a green table-cloth. Three dining-room chairs are at the table, one at either end and one at the rear facing front. Above the table is a chandelier with four gas jets enclosed by glass globes. At the right front center is a rather shabby arm-chair upholstered in green.

Before the sewing-machine, MRS. LOVING *is seated. She looks worried. She is sewing swiftly and deftly by hand upon a waist in her lap. It is a white, beautiful thing and she sews upon it delicately. It is about half-past four in the afternoon; and the light is failing. Mrs. Loving pauses in her sewing, rises and lets the window-shade near her go up to the top. She pushes the sash-curtains to either side, the corner of a red brick house wall being thus brought into view. She shivers slightly, then pushes the window down at the bottom and lowers it a trifle from the top. The street noises become less distinct. She takes off her thimble, rubs her hands gently, puts the thimble on again, and looks at the clock on the mantel. She then reseats herself, with her chair as close to the window as possible and begins to sew. Presently a key is heard, and the door opens and shuts noisily.*
RACHEL *comes in from the vestibule. In her left arm she carries four or five books strapped*

together; under her right, a roll of music. Her hat is twisted over her left ear and her hair is falling in tendrils about her face. She brings into the room with her the spirit of abounding life, health, joy, youth. MRS. LOVING *pauses, needle in hand, as soon as she hears the turning key and the banging door. There is a smile on her face. For a second, mother and daughter smile at each other. Then* RACHEL *throws her books upon the dining-room table, places the music there also, but with care, and rushing to her mother, gives her a bear hug and a kiss.*)

RACHEL Ma dear! dear, old Ma dear!

MRS. LOVING Look out for the needle, Rachel! The waist! Oh, Rachel!

RACHEL (*on her knees and shaking her finger directly under her mother's nose*) You old, old fraud! You know you adore being hugged. I've a good mind . . .

MRS. LOVING Now, Rachel, please! Besides, I know your tricks. You think you can make me forget you are late. What time is it?

RACHEL (*looking at the clock and expressing surprise*) Jiminy Xmas! (*whistles*) Why, it's five o'clock!

MRS. LOVING (*severely*) Well!

RACHEL (*plaintively*) Now, Ma dear, you're going to be horrid and cross.

MRS. LOVING (*laughing*) Really, Rachel, that expression is not particularly affecting, when your hat is over your ear, and you look, with your hair over your eyes, exactly like some one's pet poodle. I wonder if you are ever going to grow up and be ladylike.

RACHEL Oh! Ma dear, I hope not, not for the longest time, two long, long years at least. I just want to be silly and irresponsible, and have you to love and torment, and, of course, Tom, too.

MRS. LOVING (*smiling down at Rachel*) You'll not make me forget, young lady. Why are you late, Rachel?

RACHEL Well, Ma dear, I'm your pet poodle, and my hat is over my ear, and I'm late, for the loveliest reason.

MRS. LOVING Don't be silly, Rachel.

RACHEL That may sound silly, but it isn't. And please don't "Rachel" me so much. It was honestly one whole hour ago when I opened the front door down stairs. I know it was, because I heard the postman telling some one it was four o'clock. Well, I climbed the first flight, and was just starting up the second, when a little shrill voice said, "Lo!" I raised my eyes, and there, half-way up the stairs, sitting in the middle of a step, was just the dearest, cutest, darlingest little brown baby boy you ever saw. "Lo! yourself," I said. "What are you doing, and who are you anyway?" "I'm Jimmy; and I'm widing to New York on the choo-choo tars." As he looked entirely too young to be going such a distance by himself, I asked him if I might go too. For a minute or two he considered the question and me very seriously, and then he said, "Es," and made room for me on the step beside him. We've been everywhere: New York, Chicago, Boston, London, Paris and Oshkosh. I wish you could have heard him say that last place. I suggested going there just to hear him. Now, Ma dear, is it any wonder I am late? See all the places we have been in just one "teeny, weeny" hour? We would have been traveling yet, but his horrid, little mother came out and called him in. They're in the flat below, the new people. But before he went, Ma dear, he said the "cunningest" thing. He said, "Will you tum out an' p'ay wif me aden in two minutes?" I nearly hugged him to death, and it's a wonder my hat is on my head at all. Hats are such unimportant nuisances anyway!

MRS. LOVING Unimportant nuisances! What ridiculous language you do use, Rachel! Well, I'm no prophet, but I see very distinctly what is going to happen. This little brown baby will be living here night and day. You're not happy unless some child is trailing along in your rear.

RACHEL (*mischievously*) Now, Ma dear, who's a hypocrite? What? I suppose you don't like children! I can tell you one thing, though, it won't be my fault if he isn't here night and day. Oh, I wish he were all mine, every bit of him! Ma dear, do you suppose that "she woman" he calls mother would let him come up here until it is time for him to go to bed? I'm going down there this minute. (*rises impetuously*)

MRS. LOVING Rachel, for Heaven's sake! No! I am entirely too busy and tired today without being bothered with a child romping around in here.

RACHEL (*reluctantly and a trifle petulantly*) Very well, then. (*for several moments she watches her mother, who has begun to sew again. The displeasure vanishes from her face*) Ma dear!

MRS. LOVING Well.

RACHEL Is there anything wrong today?

MRS. LOVING I'm just tired, chickabiddy, that's all.

RACHEL (*moves over to the table. Mechanically takes off her hat and coat and carries them out into the entryway of the flat. She returns and goes to the looking glass over the fireplace and tucks in the tendrils of her hair in rather a preoccupied manner. The electric doorbell rings. She returns to the speaking tube in the vestibule. Her voice is heard answering*) Yes!—Yes!—No, I'm not Mrs. Loving. She's here, yes!—What? Oh! come right up! (*appearing in the doorway*) Ma dear, it's some man, who is coming for Mrs. Strong's waist.

MRS. LOVING (*pausing and looking at Rachel*) It is probably her son. She said she would send for it this afternoon. (RACHEL *disappears. A door is heard opening and closing. There is the sound of a man's voice. Rachel ushers in* MR. JOHN STRONG) STRONG (*bowing pleasantly to* MRS. LOVING) Mrs. Loving? (MRS. LOVING *bows, puts down her sewing, rises and goes toward* STRONG) My name is Strong. My mother asked me to come by and get her waist this afternoon. She hoped it would be finished.

MRS. LOVING Yes, Mr. Strong, it is all ready. If you'll sit down a minute, I'll wrap it up for you. (*she goes into hallway leading to other rooms in flat*)

RACHEL (*manifestly ill at ease at being left alone with a stranger; attempting, however, to be the polite hostess*) Do sit down, Mr. Strong. (*they both sit*)

RACHEL (*nervously after a pause*) It's a very pleasant day, isn't it, Mr. Strong?

STRONG Yes, very. (*he leans back composedly, his hat on his knee, the faintest expression of amusement in his eyes*)

RACHEL (*after a pause*) It's quite a climb up to our flat, don't you think?

STRONG Why, no! It didn't strike me so. I'm not old enough yet to mind stairs.

RACHEL (*nervously*) Oh! I didn't mean that you are old! Anyone can see you are quite young, that is, of course, not too young, but,— (STRONG *laughs quietly*) There! I don't blame you for laughing. I'm always clumsy just like that.

MRS. LOVING (*calling from the other room*) Rachel, bring me a needle and the sixty cotton, please.

RACHEL All right, Ma dear! (*rummages for the cotton in the machine drawer, and upsets several spools upon the floor. To* STRONG) You see! I can't even get a spool of cotton without spilling things all over the floor. (STRONG *smiles,* RACHEL *picks up the spools and finally gets the cotton and needle*) Excuse me! (*goes out door leading to other rooms.* STRONG, *left to himself, looks around casually. The "Golden Stairs" interests him and the "Sistine Madonna"*)

RACHEL (*reenters, evidently continuing her function of hostess*) We were talking about the climb to our flat, weren't we? You see, when you're poor, you have to live in a top flat. There is always a compensation, though; we have bully—I mean nice air, better light, a lovely view, and nobody "thud-thudding" up and down over our heads night and day. The people below have our "thud-thudding," and it must be something *awful*, especially when Tom and I play "Ivanhoe" and have a tournament up here. We're entirely too old, but we still play. Ma dear rather dreads the climb up three flights, so Tom and I do all the errands. We don't mind climbing the stairs, particularly when we go up two or three at a time,—that is— Tom still does. I can't, Ma dear stopped me. (*sighs*) I've got to grow up it seems.

STRONG (*evidently amused*) It is rather hard being a girl, isn't it?

RACHEL Oh, no! It's not hard at all. That's the trouble; they won't let me be a girl. I'd love to be.

MRS. LOVING (*reentering with* parcel. *She smiles*) My chatterbox, I see, is entertaining you, Mr. Strong. I'm sorry to have kept you waiting, but I forgot, I found, to sew the ruching in the neck. I hope everything is satisfactory. If it isn't, I'll be glad to make any changes.

STRONG (*who has risen upon her entrance*) Thank you, Mrs. Loving, I'm sure everything is all right.

(*He takes the package and bows to her and* RACHEL. *He moves towards the vestibule,* MRS. LOVING *following him. She passes through the doorway first. Before leaving,* STRONG *turns for a second and looks back quietly at* RACHEL. *He goes out too.* RACHEL *returns to the mirror, looks at her face for a second, and then begins to touch and pat her hair lightly and delicately here and there.* MRS. LOVING *returns*).

RACHEL (*still at the glass*) He *was* rather nice, wasn't he Ma dear?—for a man? (*laughs*) I guess my reason's a vain one,—he let me do all the talking. (*pauses*) Strong? Strong? Ma dear, is his mother the little woman with the sad, black eyes?

MRS. LOVING (*resuming her sewing; sitting before the machine*) Yes. I was rather curious, I confess, to see this son of hers. The whole time I'm fitting her she talks of nothing else. She worships him. (*pauses*) It's rather a sad case, I believe. She is a widow. Her husband was a doctor and left her a little money. She came up from the South to educate this boy. Both of them worked hard and the boy got through college. Three months he hunted for work that a college man might expect to get. You see he had the tremendous handicap of being colored. As the two of them had to live, one day, without her knowing it, he hired himself out as a waiter. He has been one now for two years. He is evidently goodness itself to his mother.

RACHEL (*slowly and thoughtfully*) Just because he is *colored!* (*pauses*) We sing a song at school, I believe, about "The land of the free and the home of the brave." What an amusing nation it is.

MRS. LOVING (*watching* RACHEL *anxiously*) Come, Rachel, you haven't time for "amusing nations." Remember, you haven't practised any this afternoon. And put your books away; don't leave them on the table. You didn't practise any this morning either, did you?

RACHEL No, Ma dear,—didn't wake up in time. (*goes to the table and in an abstracted manner puts books on the bookcase; returns to the table; picks up the roll of sheet music she has brought home with her; brightens; impulsively*) Ma dear, just listen to this lullaby. It's the sweetest thing. I was so "daffy" over it, one of the girls at school lent it to me. (*she rushes to the piano with the music and plays the accompaniment through softly and then sings, still softly and with great expression, Jessie Gaynor's "Slumber Boat"*)

> Baby's boat's the silver moon;
>   Sailing in the sky,
> Sailing o'er the sea of sleep,
>   While the clouds float by.
>
> Sail, baby, sail,
>   Out upon that sea,
> Only don't forget to sail
>   Back again to me.
>
> Baby's fishing for a dream,
>   Fishing near and far,
>
> His line a silver moonbeam is,
>   His bait a silver star.
>
> Sail, baby, sail,
>   Out upon that sea,

Listen, Ma dear, right here. Isn't it lovely? (*plays and sings very softly and slowly*)

> Only don't forget to sail
>   Back again to me.

(*pauses; in hushed tones*) Ma dear, it's so beautiful—it—it hurts.

MRS. LOVING (*quietly*) Yes, dear, it is pretty.

RACHEL (*for several minutes watches her mother's profile from the piano stool. Her expression is rather wistful*) Ma dear!

MRS. LOVING Yes, Rachel.

RACHEL What's the matter?

MRS. LOVING (*without turning*) Matter! What do you mean?

RACHEL I don't know. I just *feel* something is not quite right with you.

MRS. LOVING I'm only tired—that's all.

RACHEL Perhaps. But—(*watches her mother a moment or two longer; shakes her head; turns back to the piano. She is thoughtful; looks at her hands in her lap*) Ma dear, wouldn't it be nice if we could keep all the babies in the world—always little babies? Then they'd be always little, and cunning, and lovable; and they could never grow up, then, and—and—be bad. I'm so sorry for mothers whose little babies—grow up—and—and—are bad.

MRS. LOVING (*startled; controlling herself, looks at Rachel anxiously, perplexedly. Rachel's eyes are still on her hands. Attempting a light tone*) Come, Rachel, what experience have you had with mothers whose babies have grown up to be bad? You—you talk like an old, old woman.

RACHEL (*without raising her eyes, quietly*) I *know* I'm not old; but, just the same I know that is true. (*softly*) And I'm so sorry for the mothers.

MRS. LOVING (*with a forced laugh*) Well, Miss Methuselah, how do you happen to know all this? Mothers whose babies grow up to be bad don't, as a rule, parade their faults before the world.

RACHEL That's just it—that's *how* you know. They don't talk at all.

MRS. LOVING (*involuntarily*) Oh! (*ceases to sew; looks at* RACHEL *sharply; she is plainly worried. There is a long silence. Presently* RACHEL *raises her eyes to Raphael's 'Madonna" over the piano. Her expression becomes rapt; then, very softly, her eyes still on the picture, she plays and sings Nevin's "Mighty Lak A Rose"*)

> Sweetest li'l feller,
>   Ev'rybody knows;
> Dunno what to call him,
>   But he mighty lak' a rose!
> Lookin' at his Mammy
>   Wid eyes so shiny blue,
> Mek' you think that heav'n
>   Is comin' clost ter you!
>
> W'en his dar a sleepin'
>   In his li'l place
> Think I see de angels
>   Lookin' thro' de lace.
> W'en de dark is fallin',
>   W'en de shadders creep,
> Den dey comes on tip-toe,
>   Ter kiss him in his sleep.
>
> Sweetest li'l feller, etc.

(*with head still raised, after she has finished, she closes her eyes. Half to herself and slowly*) I think the loveliest thing of all the lovely things in this world is just (*almost in a whisper*) being a mother!

MRS. LOVING (*turns and laughs*) Well, of all the startling children, Rachel! I am getting to feel, when you're around as though I'm shut up with dynamite. What next? (RACHEL *rises, goes slowly to her mother, and kneels down beside her. She does not touch her mother*) Why so serious, chickabiddy?

RACHEL (*slowly and quietly*) It is not kind to laugh at sacred things. When you laughed, it was as though you laughed—at God!

MRS. LOVING (*startled*) Rachel!

RACHEL (*still quietly*) It's true. It was the best in me that said that—it was God! (*pauses*) And, Ma dear, if I believed that I should grow up and not be a mother, I'd pray to die now. I've thought about it a lot, Ma dear, and once I dreamed, and a voice said to me—oh! it was so real—"Rachel, you are to be a mother to little children." Wasn't that beautiful? Ever since I have known how Mary felt at the "Annunciation." (*almost in a whisper*) *God spoke to me through some one, and I believe*. And it has explained so much to me. I know now why I just can't resist any child. I have to love it—it calls me—it—draws me. I want to take care of it, wash it, dress it, live for it. I want the feel of its little warm body against me, its breath on my neck, its hands against my face. (*pauses thoughtfully for a few moments*) Ma dear, here's something I don't understand: I love the little black and brown babies best of all. There is something about them that—that—clutches at my heart. Why—why—should they be—oh!—pathetic? I don't understand. It's dim. More than the other babies, I feel that I must protect them. They're in danger, but from what? I don't know. I've tried so hard to understand, but I can't. (*her face radiant and beautiful*) Ma dear, I think their white teeth and the clear whites of their big black eyes and their dimples everywhere—are—are—(*breaks off*) And, Ma dear, because I love them best, I pray God every night to give me, when I grow up, little black and brown babies—to protect and guard. (*wistfully*). Now, Ma dear, don't you see why you must never laugh at me again? Dear, dear, Ma dear? (*buries her head in her mother's lap and sobs*)

MRS. LOVING (*for a few seconds, sits as though dazed, and then instinctively begins to caress the head in her lap. To herself*) And I suppose my experience is every mother's. Sooner or later—of a sudden she finds her own child a stranger to her. (*to* RACHEL, *very tenderly*) Poor little girl! Poor little chickabiddy!

RACHEL (*raising her head*) Why do you say, "Poor little girl," like that? I don't understand. Why, Ma dear, I never saw tears in your eyes before. Is it—is it—because you know the things I do not understand? Oh! it *is* that.

MRS. LOVING (*simply*) Yes, Rachel, and I cannot save you.

RACHEL Ma dear, you frighten me. Save me from *what*?

MRS. LOVING Just life, my little chickabiddy!

RACHEL Is life so terrible? I had found it mostly beautiful. How can life be terrible, when the world is full of little children?

MRS. LOVING (*very sadly*) Oh, Rachel! Rachel!

RACHEL Ma dear, what have I said?

MRS. LOVING (*forcing a smile*) Why, the

truth, of course, Rachel. Life is not terrible when there are little children—and you—and Tom—and a roof over our heads—and work—and food—and clothes—and sleep at night. (*pauses*) Rachel, I am not myself today. I'm tired. Forget what I've said. Come, chickabiddy, wipe your eyes and smile. That's only an imitation smile, but it's better than none. Jump up now, and light the lamp for me, will you? Tom's late, isn't he? I shall want you to go, too, for the rolls and pie for supper.

RACHEL (*rises rather wearily and goes into the kitchenette. While she is out of the room* MRS. LOVING *does not move. She sits staring in front of her.* MRS. LOVING *can just be seen when* RACHEL *reenters with the lamp. She places it on the small table near her mother, adjusts it, so the light falls on her mother's work, and then lowers the window shades at the windows. She still droops.* MRS. LOVING, *while* RACHEL *is in the room, is industrious.* RACHEL *puts on her hat and coat listlessly. She does not look in the glass*) Where is the money, Ma dear? I'm ready.

MRS. LOVING Before you go, Rachel, just give a look at the meat and see if it is cooking all right, will you, dearie?

RACHEL (*goes out into the kitchenette and presently returns*) It's all right, Ma dear.

MRS. LOVING (*while* RACHEL *is out of the room, she takes her pocket-book out of the machine-drawer, opens it, takes out money and gives it to* RACHEL *upon her return*) A dozen brown rolls, Rachel. Be sure they're brown! And, I guess,—an apple pie. As you and Tom never seem to get enough apple pie, get the largest she has. And here is a quarter. Get some candy—any kind *you* like, Chickabiddy. Let's have a party tonight, I feel extravagant. Why, Rachel! why are you crying?

RACHEL Nothing, dear Ma dear. I'll be all right when I get in the air. Goodbye! (*rushes out of the flat.* MRS. LOVING *sits idle. Presently the outer door of the flat opens and shuts with a bang, and* TOM *appears.* MRS. LOVING *begins to work as soon as she hears the banging door*).

TOM 'Lo, Ma! Where's Sis,—out? The door's off the latch. (*kisses his mother and hangs hat in entryway*)

MRS. LOVING (*greeting him with the same beautiful smile with which she greeted* RACHEL) Rachel just went after the rolls and pie. She'll be back in a few minutes. You're late, Tommy.

TOM No, Ma—you forget—it's pay day. (*with decided shyness and awkwardness he hands her his wages*) Here, Ma!

MRS. LOVING (*proudly counting it*) But, Tommy, this is every bit of it. You'll need some.

TOM Not yet! (*constrainedly*) I only wish—. Say, Ma, I hate to see you work so hard. (*fiercely*) Some day—some day—. (*breaks off*)

MRS. LOVING Son, I'm as proud as though you had given me a million dollars.

TOM (*emphatically*) I may some day,—you see. (*abruptly changing the subject*) Gee! Ma, I'm hungry. What's for dinner? Smell's good.

MRS. LOVING Lamb and dumplings and rice.

TOM Gee! I'm glad I'm living—and a pie too?

MRS. LOVING Apple pie, Tommy.

TOM Say, Ma, don't wake me up. And shall "muzzer's" own little boy set the table?

MRS. LOVING Thank you, Son.

TOM (*folds the green cloth, hangs it over the back of the arm-chair, gets white table-cloth from kitchenette and sets the table. The whole time he is whistling blithely a popular air. He lights one of the gas jets over the table*) Ma!

MRS. LOVING Yes, Son.

TOM I made "squad" today,—I'm quarter-back. Five other fellows tried to make it. We'll all have to buy new hats, now.

MRS. LOVING (*with surprise*) Buy new hats! Why?

TOM (*makes a ridiculous gesture to show that his head and hers are both swelling*) Honest, Ma, I had to carry my hat in my hand tonight,—couldn't even get it to perch aloft.

MRS. LOVING (*smiling*) Well, I for one, Son, am not going to say anything to make you more conceited.

TOM You don't *have* to say anything. Why, Ma, ever since I told you, you can almost look down your own back your head is so high. What? (MRS. LOVING *laughs. The outer door of the flat opens and shuts.* RACHEL'S *voice is heard*)

RACHEL (*without*) My! that was a "dreful" climb, wasn't it? Ma, I've got something here for you. (*appears in the doorway carrying packages and leading a little boy by the hand. The little fellow is shy but smiling*) Hello, Tommy! Here, take these things for me. This is Jimmy. Isn't he a dear? Come, Jimmy. (TOM *carries the packages into the kitchenette.* RACHEL *leads* JIMMY *to* MRS. LOVING) Ma dear, this is my brown baby. I'm going to take him right down stairs again. His mother is as sweet as can be, and let me bring him up just to see you. Jimmy, this is Ma dear. (MRS. LOVING *turns expectantly to see the child. Standing before her, he raises his face to hers with an engaging smile. Suddenly, without word or warning, her body stiffens; her hands grip her sewing convulsively; her eyes stare. She makes no sound*)

RACHEL (*frightened*) Ma dear! What is the matter? Tom! Quick! (TOM *reenters and goes to them*)

MRS. LOVING (*controlling herself with an effort and breathing hard*) Nothing, dears, nothing. I must be—I am—nervous tonight. (*with a forced smile*) How do-you-do, Jimmy? Now, Rachel—perhaps—don't you think—you had better take him back to his mother? Goodnight, Jimmy! (*eyes the child in a fascinated way the whole time he is in the room.* RACHEL, *very much perturbed, takes the child out*) Tom, open that window, please! There! That's better! (*still breathing deeply*) What a fool I am!

TOM (*patting his mother awkwardly on the back*) You're all pegged out, that's the trouble—working entirely too hard. Can't you stop for the night and go to bed right after supper?

MRS LOVING I'll see, Tommy dear. Now I must look after the supper.

TOM Huh! Well, I guess not. How old do you think Rachel and I are anyway? I see; you think we'll break some of this be-au-tiful Hav-i-land china, we bought at the "Five and Ten Cent Store." (*to* RACHEL *who has just reentered wearing a puzzled and worried expression. She is without hat and coat*) Say, Rachel, do you think you're old enough?

RACHEL Old enough for what, Tommy?

TOM To dish up the supper for Ma.

RACHEL (*with attempted sprightliness*) Ma dear thinks nothing can go on in this little flat unless she does it. Let's show her a thing or two. (*they bring in the dinner.* MRS. LOVING *with trembling hands tries to sew.* TOM *and* RACHEL *watch her covertly. Presently she gets up*)

MRS. LOVING I'll be back in a minute, children. (*goes out the door that leads to the other rooms of the flat.* TOM *and* RACHEL *look at each other*)

RACHEL (*in a low voice keeping her eyes on the door*) Why do you suppose she acted so strangely about Jimmy?

TOM Don't know—nervous, I guess,—worn out. I wish—(*breaks off*)

RACHEL (*slowly*) It may be that; but she hasn't been herself this afternoon. I wonder—Look out! Here she comes!

TOM (*in a whisper*) Liven her up. (RACHEL *nods.* MRS. LOVING *reenters. Both rush to her and lead her to her place at the right end of the table. She smiles and tries to appear cheerful. They sit down,* TOM *opposite* MRS. LOVING *and* RACHEL *at the side facing front.* MRS. LOVING *asks grace. Her voice trembles. She helps the children bountifully, herself sparingly. Every once in a while she stops eating and stares blankly into her plate; then, remembering where she is suddenly, looks around with a start and goes on eating.* TOM *and* RACHEL *appear not to notice her*)

TOM Ma's "some" cook, isn't she?

RACHEL Is she! Delmonico's isn't in it.

TOM (*presently*) Say, Rachel, do you remember that Reynolds boy in the fourth year?

RACHEL Yes. You mean the one who is flat-nosed, freckled, and who squints and sneers?

TOM (*looking at* RACHEL *admiringly*) The same.

RACHEL (*vehemently*) I hate him!

MRS. LOVING Rachel, you do use such violent language. Why hate him?

RACHEL I do—that's all.

TOM Ma, if you saw him just once, you'd understand. No one likes him. But, then, what can you expect? His father's in "quod" doing time for something, I don't know just what. One of the fellows says he has a real decent mother, though. She never mentions him in any way, shape or form, he says. Hard on her, isn't it? Bet I'd keep my head shut too;—you'd never get a yap out of me. (RACHEL *looks up quickly at her mother;* MRS. LOVING *stiffens perceptibly, but keeps her eyes on her plate.* RACHEL *catches* TOM's *eye; silently draws his attention to their mother; and shakes her head warningly at him*)

TOM (*continuing hastily and clumsily*) Well, anyway, he called me "Nigger" today. If his face isn't black, his eye is.

RACHEL Good! Oh! Why did you let the other one go?

TOM (*grinning*) I knew he said things

behind my back; but today he was hopping mad, because I made quarter-back. He didn't!

RACHEL Oh, Tommy! How lovely! Ma dear, did you hear that? (*chants*) Our Tommy's on the team! Our Tommy's on the team!

TOM (*trying not to appear pleased*) Ma dear, what did I say about er—er "capital" enlargements?

MRS. LOVING (*smiling*) You're right, Son.

TOM I hope you got that "capital," Rachel. How's that for Latin knowledge? Eh?

RACHEL I don't think much of your knowledge, Tommy dear; but (*continuing to chant*) Our Tommy's on the team! Our Tommy's on the team! Our—(*breaks off*) I've a good mind to kiss you.

TOM (*threateningly*) Don't you dare.

RACHEL (*rising and going toward him*) I will! I will! I will!

TOM (*rising, too, and dodging her*) No, you don't, young lady. (*a tremendous tussle and scuffle ensues*)

MRS. LOVING (*laughing*) For Heaven's sake! children, do stop playing and eat your supper. (*they nod brightly at each other behind her back and return smiling to the table*)

RACHEL (*sticking out her tongue at Tom*) I will!

TOM (*mimicking her*) You won't!

MRS. LOVING Children! (*they eat for a time in silence*)

RACHEL Ma dear, have you noticed Mary Shaw doesn't come here much these days?

MRS. LOVING Why, that's so, she doesn't. Have you two quarreled?

RACHEL No, Ma dear. (*uncomfortably*). I—think I know the reason—but I don't like to say, unless I'm certain.

TOM Well, I know. I've seen her lately with those two girls who have just come from the South. Twice she bowed stiffly, and the last time made believe she didn't see me.

RACHEL Then you think—? Oh! I was afraid it was that.

TOM (*bitterly*) Yes—we're "niggers"—that's why.

MRS. LOVING (*slowly and sadly*) Rachel, that's one of the things I can't save you from. I worried considerably about Mary, at first— you do take your friendships so seriously. I knew exactly how it would end. (*pauses*) And then I saw that if Mary Shaw didn't teach you the lesson—some one else would. They don't want you, dearies, when you and they grow up. You may have everything in your favor—but they don't *dare* to like you.

RACHEL I know all that is generally true— but I had hoped that Mary— (*breaks off*)

TOM Well, I guess we can still go on living even if people don't speak to us. I'll never bow to *her* again—that's certain.

MRS. LOVING But, Son, that wouldn't be polite, if she bowed to you first.

TOM Can't help it. I guess I can be blind, too.

MRS. LOVING (*wearily*) Well—perhaps you are right—I don't know. It's the way I feel about it too—but—but I wish my son always to be a *gentleman*.

TOM If being a *gentleman* means not being a *man*—I don't wish to be one.

RACHEL Oh! well, perhaps we're wrong about Mary—I hope we are. (*sighs*) Anyway, let's forget it. Tommy guess what I've got. (*rises, goes out into entryway swiftly, and returns holding up a small bag*) Ma dear treated. Guess!

TOM Ma, you're a thoroughbred. Well, let's see—it's—a dozen dill pickles?

RACHEL Oh! stop fooling.

TOM I'm not. Tripe?

RACHEL Silly!

TOM Hog's jowl?

RACHEL Ugh! Give it up—quarter-back.

TOM Pig's feet?

RACHEL (*in pretended disgust*) Oh! Ma dear —send him from the table. It's CANDY!

TOM Candy? Funny, I never thought of that! And I was just about to say some nice, delicious chitlings. Candy! Well! Well! (RACHEL *disdainfully carries the candy to her mother returns to her own seat with the bag and helps herself. She ignores* TOM)

TOM (*in an aggrieved voice*) You see, Ma, how she treats me. (*in affected tones*) I have a good mind, young lady to punish you, er—er corporeally speaking. Tut! Tut! I have a mind to master thee—I mean—you. Methinks that if I should advance upon you, apply, perchance, two or three digits to your glossy locks and extract—aha!—say, a strand—you would no more defy me. (*he starts to rise*)

MRS. LOVING (*quickly and sharply*) Rachel! give Tom the candy and stop playing. (RACHEL *obeys. They eat in silence. The old depression returns. When the candy is all gone,* RACHEL *pushes her chair back, and is just about to rise, when her mother, who is very evidently nerving herself for something, stops her*) Just a moment, Rachel. (*pauses, continuing slowly and very seriously*) Tom and Rachel! I have been trying to make up my mind for some time whether a certain thing is my duty or not. Today—I have decided it is. You are old enough, now,—and I see you ought to be told. Do you know what day this is? (*both* TOM *and* RACHEL *have been watching their mother intently*) It's the sixteenth of October. Does that mean anything to either of you?

TOM and RACHEL (*wonderingly*) No.

MRS. LOVING (*looking at both of them thoughtfully, half to herself*) No—I don't know why it should. (*slowly*) Ten years ago—today—your father and your half-brother died.

TOM I do remember, now, that you told us it was in October.

RACHEL (*with a sigh*) That explains—today.

MRS. LOVING Yes, Rachel. (*pauses*) Do you know—how they—died?

TOM and RACHEL Why, no.

MRS. LOVING Did it ever strike you as strange—that they—died—the same day?

TOM Well, yes.

RACHEL We often wondered, Tom and I; but—but somehow we never quite dared to ask you. You—you—always refused to talk about them, you know, Ma dear.

MRS. LOVING Did you think—that—perhaps —the reason—I—I—wouldn't talk about them —was—because, because—I was ashamed—of them? (TOM *and* RACHEL *look uncomfortable*)

RACHEL Well, Ma dear—we—we—did—wonder.

MRS. LOVING (*questioningly*) And you thought?

RACHEL (*haltingly*) W-e-l-l—

MRS. LOVING (*sharply*) Yes?

TOM Oh! come, now, Rachel, you know we haven't bothered about it at all. Why should we? We've been happy.

MRS. LOVING But when you have thought— you've been ashamed? (*intensely*) Have you?

TOM Now, Ma, aren't you making a lot out of nothing?

MRS. LOVING (*slowly*) No. (*half to herself*) You evade—both—of you. You *have* been ashamed. And I never dreamed until today you could take it this way. How blind—how almost criminally blind, I have been.

RACHEL (*tremulously*) Oh! Ma dear, don't! (TOM *and* RACHEL *watch their mother anxiously and uncomfortably.* MRS. LOVING *is very evidently nerving herself for something*)

MRS. LOVING (*very slowly, with restrained emotion*) Tom—and Rachel!

TOM Ma!

RACHEL Ma dear! (*a tense, breathless pause*)

MRS. LOVING (*bracing herself*) They—they— were lynched!!

TOM and RACHEL (*in a whisper*) Lynched!

MRS. LOVING (*slowly, laboring under strong but restrained emotion*) Yes—by Christian people —in a Christian land. We found out afterwards they were all church members in good standing —the best people. (*a silence*) Your father was a man among men. He was a fanatic. He was a Saint!

TOM (*breathing with difficulty*) Ma—can you—will you—tell us—about it?

MRS. LOVING I believe it to be my duty. (*a silence*). When I married your father I was a widow. My little George was seven years old. From the very beginning he worshiped your father. He followed him around—just like a little dog. All children were like that with him. I myself have never seen anybody like him. "Big" seems to fit him better than any other word. He was big-bodied—big-souled. His loves were big and his hates. You can imagine, then, how the wrongs of the Negro—ate into his soul. (*pauses*) He was utterly fearless. (*a silence*) He edited and owned, for several years, a small Negro paper. In it he said a great many daring things. I used to plead with him to be more careful. I was always afraid for him. For a long time, nothing happened—he was too important to the community. And then—one night—ten years ago—a mob made up of the respectable people in the town lynched an innocent black man—and what was worse— they knew him to be innocent. A white man was guilty. I never saw your father so wrought up over anything: he couldn't eat; he couldn't sleep; he brooded night and day over it. And then—realizing fully the great risk he was running, although I begged him not to—and all his friends also—he deliberately and calmly went to work and published a most terrific denunciation of that mob. The old prophets in the Bible were not more terrible than he. A day or two later, he received an anonymous letter, very evidently from an educated man, calling upon him to retract his words in the next issue. If he refused his life was threatened. The next week's issue contained an arraignment as frightful, if not more so, than the previous one. Each word was white-hot, searing. That night, some dozen masked men came to our house.

RACHEL (*moaning*) Oh, Ma dear! Ma dear!

MRS. LOVING (*too absorbed to hear*) We were not asleep—your father and I. They broke down the front door and made their way to our bedroom. Your father kissed me—and took up his revolver. It was always loaded. They broke down the door. (*a silence. She continues slowly and quietly*) I tried to shut my eyes—I could not. Four masked men fell—they did not move any more—after a little. (*pauses*). Your father was finally overpowered and dragged out. In the hall—my little seventeen-year-old George tried to rescue him. Your father begged him not to interfere. He paid no attention. It ended in their dragging them both out. (*pauses*) My little George—was—a man! (*controls herself with an effort*) He never made an outcry. His last words to me were: "Ma, I am glad to go with Father." I could only nod to him. (*pauses*) While they were dragging them down the steps, I crept into the room where you were. You were both asleep. Rachel, I remember, was smiling. I knelt down by you—and covered my ears with my hands—and waited. I could not pray—I couldn't for a long time—afterwards. (*a silence*) It was very still when I finally uncovered my ears. The only sounds were the faint rustle of leaves and the "tap-tapping of the twig of a tree" against the window. I hear it still—sometimes in my dreams. *It was the tree—where they were.* (*a silence*) While I had knelt there waiting —I had made up my mind what to do. I dressed myself and then I woke you both up and dressed you. (*pauses*) We set forth. It was a black, still night. Alternately dragging you along and carrying you—I walked five miles to the house of some friends. They took us in, and we remained there until I had seen my dead laid comfortably at rest. They lent me money to come North—I couldn't bring you up—in the South. (*a silence*) Always remember this: There never lived anywhere—or at any time— any two whiter or more beautiful souls. God gave me one for a husband and one for a son and I am proud. (*brokenly*) You—must—be— proud—too. (*a long silence.* MRS. LOVING *bows her head in her hands.* TOM *controls himself with an effort.* RACHEL *creeps softly to her mother kneels beside her and lifts the hem of her dress to her lips. She does not dare touch her. She adores her with her eyes*)

MRS. LOVING (*presently raising her head and glancing at the clock*) Tom, it's time, now, for you to go to work. Rachel and I will finish up here.

TOM (*still laboring under great emotion goes out into the entryway and comes back and stands in the doorway with his cap. He twirls it around and around nervously*) I want you to know, Ma, before I go—how—how proud I am. Why, I didn't believe two people could be like that— and live. And then to find out that one—was your own father—and one—your own brother. —It's wonderful! I'm—not much yet, Ma, but —I've—I've just got to be something now. (*breaks off. His face becomes distorted with passion and hatred*) When I think—when I think—of those devils with white skins—living somewhere today—living and happy—I—see— red! I—I—goodbye! (*rushes out, the door bangs*)

MRS. LOVING (*half to herself*) I was afraid— of just that. I wonder—if I did the wise thing— after all.

RACHEL (*with a gesture infinitely tender, puts her arm around her mother*) Yes, Ma dear, you did. And, hereafter, Tom and I share and share alike with you. To think, Ma dear, of ten years of this—all alone. It's wicked! (*a short silence*)

MRS. LOVING And, Rachel, about that dear, little boy, Jimmy.

RACHEL Now, Ma dear, tell me tomorrow. You've stood enough for one day.

MRS. LOVING No, it's better over and done with—all at once. If I had seen that dear child suddenly any other day than this—I might have borne it better. When he lifted his little face to me—and smiled—for a moment—I thought it was the end—of all things. Rachel, he is the image of my boy—my George!

RACHEL Ma dear!

MRS. LOVING And, Rachel—it will hurt— to see him again.

RACHEL I understand, Ma dear. (*a silence. Suddenly*) Ma dear, I am beginning to see—to understand—so much. (*slowly and thoughtfully*) Ten years ago, all things being equal, Jimmy might have been—George? Isn't that so?

MRS. LOVING Why—yes, if I understand you.

RACHEL I guess that doesn't sound very clear. It's only getting clear to me, little by little. Do you mind my thinking out loud to you?

MRS. LOVING No, chickabiddy.

RACHEL If Jimmy went South now—and grew up—he might be—a George?

MRS. LOVING Yes.

RACHEL Then, the South is full of tens, hundreds, thousands of little boys, who, one day may be—and some of them with certainty—Georges?

MRS. LOVING Yes, Rachel.

RACHEL And the little babies, the dear, little, helpless babies, being born today—now—and those who will be, tomorrow, and all the tomorrows to come—have *that* sooner or later to look forward to? They will laugh and play and sing and be happy and grow up, perhaps, and be ambitious—just for *that*?

MRS. LOVING Yes, Rachel.

RACHEL Then, everywhere, everywhere, throughout the South, there are hundreds of dark mothers who live in fear, terrible, suffocating fear, whose rest by night is broken, and whose joy by day in their babies on their hearts is three parts—pain. Oh, I know this is true—for this is the way I should feel, if I were little Jimmy's mother. How horrible! Why—it would be more merciful—to strangle the little things at birth. And so this nation—this white Christian nation—has deliberately set its curse upon the most beautiful—the most holy thing in life—motherhood! Why—it—makes—you doubt—God!

MRS. LOVING Oh, hush! little girl. Hush!

RACHEL (*suddenly with a great cry*) Why, Ma dear, *you know. You* were a *mother, George's mother*. So, this is what it means. Oh, Ma dear! Ma dear! (*faints in her mother's arms*)

ACT TWO

(TIME: *October sixteenth, four years later; seven o'clock in the morning.*

SCENE: *The same room. There have been very evident improvements made. The room is not so bare; it is cosier. On the shelf, before each window, are potted red geraniums. At the windows are green denim drapery curtains covering fresh white dotted Swiss inner curtains. At each doorway are green denim portieres, On the wall between the kitchenette and the entrance to the outer rooms of the flat, a new picture is hanging, Millet's "The Man With the Hoe." Hanging against the side of the run that faces front is Watts's "Hope." There is another easy-chair at the left front. The table in the center is covered with a white table-cloth. A small asparagus fern is in the middle of this. When the curtain rises there is the clatter of dishes in the kitchenette. Presently* RACHEL *enters with dishes and silver in her hands. She is clad in a bungalow apron. She is noticeably all of four years older. She frowns as she sets the table. There is a set expression about the mouth. A child's voice is heard from the rooms within*)

JIMMY (*still unseen*) Ma Rachel!

RACHEL (*pauses and smiles*) What is it, Jimmy boy?

JIMMY (*appearing in rear doorway, half-dressed, breathless, and tremendously excited over something. Rushes toward* RACHEL) Three guesses! Three guesses! Ma Rachel!

RACHEL (*her whole face softening*) Well, let's see—maybe there is a circus in town.

JIMMY No siree! (*in a sing-song*) You're not right! You're not right!

RACHEL Well, maybe Ma Loving's going to take you somewhere.

JIMMY No! (*vigorously shaking his head*) It's—

RACHEL (*interrupting quickly*) You said I could have three guesses, honey. I've only had two.

JIMMY I thought you had three. How many are three!

RACHEL (*counting on her fingers*) One! Two! Three! I've only had one! two!—See? Perhaps Uncle Tom is going to give you some candy.

JIMMY (*dancing up and down*) No! No! No! (*catches his breath*) I leaned over the bath-tub, way over, and got hold of the chain with the button on the end, and dropped it into the little round place in the bottom. And then I runned lots of water in the tub and climbed over and fell in splash! just like a big stone; (*loudly*) and took a bath all by myself alone.

RACHEL (*laughing and hugging him*) All by yourself, honey? You ran the water, too, boy, not "runned" it. What I want to know is, where was Ma Loving all this time?

JIMMY I stole in "creepy-creep" and looked at Ma Loving and she was awful fast asleep. (*proudly*) Ma Rachel, I'm a "nawful," big boy now, aren't I? I are almost a man, aren't I?

RACHEL Oh! Boy, I'm getting tired of correcting you—"I am almost a man, am I not?" Jimmy, boy, what will Ma Rachel do, if you grow up? Why, I won't have a little boy any more! Honey, you mustn't grow up, do you hear? You mustn't.

JIMMY Oh, yes, I must; and you'll have me just the same, Ma Rachel. I'm going to be a policeman and make lots of money for you and Ma Loving and Uncle Tom, and I'm going to buy you some trains and fire-engines, and little, cunning ponies, and some rabbits, and some great 'normous banks full of money—lots of it. And then, we are going to live in a great, big castle and eat lots of ice cream, all the time, and drink lots and lots of nice pink lemonade.

RACHEL What a generous Jimmy boy! (*hugs him*) Before I give you "morning kiss," I must see how clean my boy is. (*inspects teeth, ears and neck*) Jimmy, you're sweet and clean enough to eat. (*kisses him; he tries to strangle her with hugs*) Now the hands. Oh! Jimmy, look at those nails! Oh! Jimmy! (JIMMY *wriggles and tries to get his hands away*) Honey, get my file off of my bureau and go to Ma Loving; she must be awake by this time. Why, honey, what's the matter with your feet?

JIMMY I don't know. I thought they looked kind of queer, myself. What's the matter with them?

RACHEL (*laughing*) You have your shoes on the wrong feet.

JIMMY (*bursts out laughing*) Isn't that most 'normously funny? I'm a case, aren't I— (*pauses thoughtfully*) I mean—am I not, Ma Rachel?

RACHEL Yes, honey, a great big case of molasses. Come, you must hurry now, and get dressed. You don't want to be late for school, you know.

JIMMY Ma Rachel! (*shyly*) I—I have been making something for you all the morning—ever since I waked up. It's awful nice. It's—stoop down, Ma Rachel, please—a great, big (*puts both arms about her neck and gives her a noisy kiss.* RACHEL *kisses him in return, then pushes his head back. For a long moment they look at each other; and, then, laughing joyously, he makes believe he is a horse, and goes prancing out of the room.* RACHEL, *with a softer, gentler expression, continues setting the table. Presently,* MRS. LOVING, *bent and worn-looking, appears in the doorway in the rear. She limps a trifle*)

MRS. LOVING Good morning, dearie. How's my little girl, this morning? (*looks around the room*). Why, where's Tom? I was certain I heard him running the water in the tub, sometime ago. (*limps into the room*)

RACHEL (*laughing*) Tom isn't up yet. Have you seen Jimmy?

MRS. LOVING Jimmy? No. I didn't know he was awake, even.

RACHEL (*going to her mother and kissing her*) Well! What do you think of that! I sent the young gentleman to you, a few minutes ago, for help with his nails. He is very much grown up this morning, so I suppose that explains why he didn't come to you. Yesterday, all day, you know, he was a puppy. No one knows what he will be by tomorrow. All of this, Ma dear, is preliminary to telling you that Jimmy boy has stolen a march on you, this morning.

MRS. LOVING Stolen a march! How?

RACHEL It appears that he took his bath all by himself and, as a result, he is so conceited, peacocks aren't in it with him.

MRS. LOVING I heard the water running and thought, of course, it was Tom. Why, the little rascal! I must go and see how he has left things. I was just about to wake him up.

RACHEL Rheumatism's not much better this morning, Ma dear. (*confronting her mother*) Tell me the truth, now, did you or did you not try that liniment I bought you yesterday?

MRS. LOVING (*guiltily*) Well, Rachel, you see—it was this way, I was—I was so tired, last night,—I—I really forgot it.

RACHEL I thought as much. Shame on you!

MRS. LOVING As soon as I walk around a bit it will be all right. It always is. It's bad, when I first get up—that's all. I'll be spry enough in a few minutes. (*limps to the door; pauses*) Rachel, I don't know why the thought should strike me, but how very strangely things turn out. If any one had told me four years ago that Jimmy would be living with us, I should have laughed at him. Then it hurt to see him; now it would hurt not to. (*softly*) Rachel, sometimes—I wonder—if, perhaps, God—hasn't relented a little—and given me back my boy,—my George.

RACHEL The whole thing was strange, wasn't it?

MRS. LOVING Yes, God's ways are strange and often very beautiful; perhaps all would be beautiful—if we only understood.

RACHEL God's ways are certainly very mysterious. Why, of all the people in this apartment-house, should Jimmy's father and mother be the only two to take the smallpox, and the only two to die. It's queer!

MRS. LOVING It doesn't seem like two years ago, does it?

RACHEL Two years, Ma dear! Why it's three the third of January.

MRS. LOVING Are you sure, Rachel?

RACHEL (*gently*) I don't believe I could ever forget that, Ma dear.

MRS. LOVING No, I suppose not. That is one of the differences between youth and old age—youth attaches tremendous importance to dates,—old age does not.

RACHEL (*quickly*) Ma dear, don't talk like that. You're not old.

MRS. LOVING Oh! yes, I am, dearie. It's sixty long years since I was born; and I am much older than that, much older.

RACHEL Please, Ma dear, please!

MRS. LOVING (*smiling*) Very well, dearie, I won't say it any more. (*a pause*) By the way,—how—does Tom strike you, these days?

RACHEL (*avoiding her mother's eye*) The same old, bantering, cheerful Tom. Why?

MRS. LOVING I know he's all that, dearie, but it isn't possible for him to be really cheerful. (*pauses; goes on wistfully*) When you are little, we mothers can kiss away all the trouble, but when you grow up—and go out—into the world—and get hurt—we are helpless. There is nothing we can do.

RACHEL Don't worry about Tom, Ma dear, he's game. He doesn't show the white feather.

MRS. LOVING Did you see him, when he came in, last night?

RACHEL Yes.

MRS. LOVING Had he had—any luck?

RACHEL No. (*firmly*) Ma dear, we may as well face it—it's hopeless, I'm afraid.

MRS. LOVING I'm afraid—you are right. (*shakes her head sadly*) Well, I'll go and see how Jimmy has left things and wake up Tom, if he isn't awake yet. It's the waking up in the mornings that's hard. (*goes limping out rear door.* RACHEL *frowns as she continues going back and forth between the kitchenette and the table. Presently* TOM *appears in the door at the rear. He watches* RACHEL *several moments before he speaks or enters.* RACHEL *looks grim enough*).

TOM (*entering and smiling*) Good-morning, "Merry Sunshine"! Have you, perhaps, been taking a—er—prolonged draught of that very delightful beverage—vinegar? (RACHEL, *with a knife in her hand, looks up unsmiling. In pretended fright*) I take it all back, I'm sure. May I request, humbly, that before I press my chaste, morning salute upon your forbidding lips, that you—that you—that you—er—in some way rid yourself of that—er—knife? (*bows as* RACHEL *puts it down*). I thank you. (*he comes to her and tips her head back; gently*) What's the matter with my little Sis?

RACHEL (*her face softening*) Tommy dear, don't mind me. I'm getting wicked, I guess. At present I feel just like—like curdled milk. Once upon a time, I used to have quite a nice disposition, didn't I, Tommy?

TOM (*smiling*) Did you, indeed! I'm not going to flatter you. Well, brace yourself, old lady. Ready, One! Two! Three! Go! (*kisses her, then puts his hands on either side of her face, and raising it, looks down into it*). You're a pretty, decent little sister, Sis, that's what T. Loving thinks about it; and he knows a thing or two. (*abruptly looking around*) Has the paper come yet?

RACHEL I haven't looked, it must have, though, by this time. (TOM, *hands in his pockets, goes into the vestibule. He whistles. The outer door opens and closes, and presently he saunters back, newspaper in hand. He lounges carelessly in the arm-chair and looks at* RACHEL)

TOM May T. Loving be of any service to you?

RACHEL Service! How?

TOM May he run, say, any errands, set the table, cook the breakfast? Anything?

RACHEL (*watching the lazy figure*) You look like working.

TOM (*grinning*) It's at least—polite—to offer.

RACHEL You can't do anything; I don't trust you to do it right. You may just sit there, and read your paper—and try to behave yourself.

TOM (*in affectedly meek tones*) Thank you, ma'am. (*opens the paper, but does not read.* JIMMY *presently enters riding around the table on a cane.* RACHEL *peeps in from the kitchenette and smiles.* TOM *puts down his paper*) 'Lo! Big Fellow, what's this?

JIMMY (*disgustedly*) How can I hear? I'm miles and miles away yet. (*prances around and around the room; presently stops near* TOM, *attempting a gruff voice*) Good-morning!

TOM (*lowering his paper again*) Bless my stars! Who's this? Well, if it isn't Mr. Mason! How-do-you-do, Mr. Mason? That's a beautiful horse you have there. He limps a trifle in his left, hind, front foot, though.

JIMMY He doesn't!

TOM He does!

JIMMY (*fiercely*) He doesn't!

TOM (*as fiercely*) I say he does!

MRS. LOVING (*appearing in the doorway in the rear*) For Heaven's sake! What is this? Good-morning, Tommy.

TOM (*rising and going toward his mother,* JIMMY *following astride of the cane in his rear*) Good-morning, Ma. (*kisses her; lays his head on her shoulder and makes believe he is crying; in a high falsetto*) Ma! Jimmy says his horse doesn't limp in his hind, front right leg, and I says he does.

JIMMY (*throws his cane aside, rolls on the floor and kicks up his heels. He roars with laughter*) I think Uncle Tom is funnier than any clown in the "Kickus."

TOM (*raising his head and looking down at* JIMMY; RACHEL *stands in the kitchenette doorway*) In the *what*, Jimmy?

JIMMY In the "kickus," of course.

TOM "Kickus"! "Kickus"! Oh, Lordy! (TOM *and* RACHEL *shriek with laughter;* MRS. LOVING *looks amused;* JIMMY, *very much affronted, gets upon his feet again.* TOM *leans over and swings* JIMMY *high in the air*) Boy, you'll be the death of me yet. Circus, son! Circus!

JIMMY (*from on high, soberly and with injured dignity*) Well, I thinks "Kickus" and circus are very much alike. Please put me down.

RACHEL (*from the doorwasy*) We laugh, honey, because we love you so much.

JIMMY (*somewhat mollified, to* TOM) Is that so, Uncle Tom?

TOM Surest thing in the world! (*severely*) Come, get down, young man. Don't you know you'll wear my arms out? Besides, there is something in my lower vest pocket, that's just dying to come to you. Get down, I say.

JIMMY (*laughing*) How can I get down? (*wriggles around*)

TOM How should I know? Just get down, of course. (*very suddenly puts* JIMMY *down on his feet.* JIMMY *tries to climb up over him*).

JIMMY Please sit down, Uncle Tom?

TOM (*in feigned surprise*) Sit down! What for?

JIMMY (*pummeling him with his little fists, loudly*) Why, you said there was something for me in your pocket.

TOM (*sitting down*) So I did. How forgetful I am!

JIMMY (*finding a bright, shiny penny, shrieks*) Oh! Oh! Oh! (*climbs up and kisses* TOM *noisily*).

TOM Why, Jimmy! You embarrass me. My! My!

JIMMY What is 'barrass?

TOM You make me blush.

JIMMY What's that?

MRS. LOVING Come, come, children! Rachel has the breakfast on the table. (TOM *sits in* JIMMY'*s place and* JIMMY *tries to drag him out*).

TOM What's the matter, now?

JIMMY You're in *my* place.

TOM Well, can't you sit in mine?

JIMMY (*wistfully*) I wants to sit by my Ma Rachel.

TOM Well, so do I.

RACHEL Tom, stop teasing Jimmy. Honey, don't you let him bother you; ask him please prettily.

JIMMY Please prettily, Uncle Tom.

TOM Oh! well then. (*gets up and takes his own place. They sit as they did in Act I only* JIMMY *sits between* TOM, *at the end, and* RACHEL)

JIMMY (*loudly*) Oh, goody! goody! goody! We've got sau-sa-ges.

MRS. LOVING Sh!

JIMMY (*silenced for a few moments;* RACHEL *ties a big napkin around his neck, and prepares his breakfast. He breaks forth again suddenly and excitedly*) Uncle Tom!

TOM Sir?

JIMMY I took a bath this morning, all by

myself alone, in the bath-tub, and I ranned, no (*doubtfully*) I runned, I think—the water all in it, and got in it all by myself; and Ma Loving thought it was you; but it was *me*.

TOM (*in feignedly severe tones*) See here, young man, this won't do. Don't you know I'm the only one who is allowed to do that here? It's a perfect waste of water—that's what it is.

JIMMY (*undaunted*) Oh! no, you're not the only one, 'cause Ma Loving and Ma Rachel and me—alls takes baths every single morning. So, there!

TOM You 'barrass me. (JIMMY *opens his mouth to ask a question;* TOM *quickly*) Young gentleman, your mouth is open. Close it, sir; close it.

MRS. LOVING Tom, you're as big a child exactly as Jimmy.

TOM (*bowing to right and left*) You compliment me. I thank you, I am sure.

(*They finish in silence*)

JIMMY (*sighing with contentment*) I'm through, Ma Rachel.

MRS. LOVING Jimmy, you're a big boy, now, aren't you? (JIMMY *nods his head vigorously and looks proud.*) I wonder if you're big enough to wash your own hands, this morning?

JIMMY (*shrilly*) Yes, ma'am.

MRS. LOVING Well, if they're beautifully clean, I'll give you another penny.

JIMMY (*excitedly to* RACHEL) Please untie my napkin, Ma Rachel! (RACHEL *does so*) "Excoose" me, please.

MRS. LOVING AND RACHEL Certainly. (JIMMY *climbs down and rushes out at the rear doorway*)

MRS. LOVING (*solemnly and slowly; breaking the silence*) Rachel, do you know what day this is?

RACHEL (*looking at her plate; slowly*) Yes, Ma dear.

MRS. LOVING Tom.

TOM (*grimly and slowly*) Yes, Ma.

(*A silence*)

MRS. LOVING (*impressively*) We must never —as long—as we live—forget this day.

RACHEL No, Ma dear.

TOM No, Ma.

(*Another silence*)

TOM (*slowly; as though thinking aloud*) I hear people talk about God's justice—and I wonder. There, are you, Ma. There isn't a sacrifice—that you haven't made. You're still working your fingers to the bone—sewing— just so all of us may keep on living. Rachel is a graduate in Domestic Science; she was high in her class; most of the girls below her in rank have positions in the schools. I'm an electrical engineer—and I've tried steadily for several months—to practice my profession. It seems our educations aren't of much use to us: we aren't allowed to make good—because our skins are dark. (*pauses*) And, in the South today, there are white men—(*controls himself*). They have everything; they're well-dressed, well-fed, well-housed; they're prosperous in business; they're important politically; they're pillars in the church. I know all this is true—I've inquired. Their children (our ages, some of them) are growing up around them; and they are having a square deal handed out to them—college, position, wealth, and best of all, freedom, without galling restrictions, to work out their own salvations. With ability, they may become— anything; and all this will be true of their children's children after them. (*a pause*) Look at us—and look at them. We are destined to failure—they, to success. Their children shall grow up in hope; ours, in despair. Our hands are clean;—theirs are red with blood—red with the blood of a noble man—and a boy. They're nothing but low, cowardly, bestial murderers. The scum of the earth shall succeed. —God's justice, I suppose.

MRS. LOVING (*rising and going to* TOM; *brokenly*) Tom, promise me—one thing.

TOM (*rises gently*) What is it, Ma?

MRS. LOVING That—you'll try—not to lose faith—in God. I've been where you are now— and it's black. Tom, we don't understand God's ways. My son, I know, now—He is beautiful. Tom, won't you try to believe, again?

TOM (*slowly, but not convincingly*) I'll try, Ma.

MRS. LOVING (*sighs*) Each one, I suppose, has to work out his own salvation. (*after a pause*) Rachel, if you'll get Jimmy ready, I'll take him to school. I've got to go down town shopping for a customer, this morning. (RACHEL *rises and goes out the rear doorway;* MRS. LOVING, *limping very slightly now, follows. She turns and looks back yearningly at* TOM, *who has seated himself again, and is staring unseeingly at his plate. She goes out.* TOM *sits without moving until he hears* MRS. LOVING'S *voice within and* RACHEL'S *faintly; then he gets the paper, sits in the arm-chair and pretends to read*)

MRS. LOVING (*from within*) A yard, you say, Rachel? You're sure that will be enough. Oh! you've measured it. Anything else?—What?—Oh! all right. I'll be back by one o'clock, anyway. Good-bye. (*enters with* JIMMY. *Both are dressed for the street.* TOM *looks up brightly at* JIMMY)

TOM Hello! Big Fellow, where are you taking *my* mother, I'd like to know? This is a pretty kettle of fish.

JIMMY (*laughing*) Aren't you funny, Uncle Tom! Why, I'm not taking her anywhere. She's taking me. (*importantly*) I'm going to school.

TOM Big Fellow, come here. (JIMMY *comes with a rush*). Now, where's that penny I gave you? No, I don't want to see it. All right. Did Ma Loving give you another? (*vigorous noddings of the head from* JIMMY) I wish you to promise me solemnly—Now, listen! Here, don't wriggle so! not to buy—Listen! too many pints of ice-cream with my penny. Understand?

JIMMY (*very seriously*) Yes, Uncle Tom, cross my "tummy"! I promise.

TOM Well, then, you may go. I guess that will be all for the present. (JIMMY *loiters around looking up wistfully into his face*) Well?

JIMMY Haven't you—aren't you—isn't you —forgetting something?

TOM (*grabbing at his pockets*) Bless my stars! what now?

JIMMY If you could kind of lean over this way. (TOM *leans forward*) No, not that way. (TOM *leans toward the side away from* JIMMY) No, this way, this way! (*laughs and pummels him with his little fists*) This way!

TOM (*leaning toward* JIMMY) Well, why didn't you say so, at first?

JIMMY (*puts his arms around* TOM'S *neck and kisses him*) Good-bye, dear old Uncle Tom. (TOM *catches him and hugs him hard*) I likes to be hugged like that—I can taste—sau-sa-ges.

TOM You 'barrass me, son. Here, Ma, take your boy. Now remember all I told you, Jimmy.

JIMMY I 'members.

MRS. LOVING God bless you, Tom, Good luck.

JIMMY (*to* TOM) God bless you, Uncle Tom. Good luck!

TOM (*much affected, but with restraint, rising*) Thank you—Good-bye. (MRS. LOVING *and* JIMMY *go out through the vestibule.* TOM *lights a cigarette and tries to read the paper. He soon sinks into a brown study. Presently* RACHEL *enters humming.* TOM *relights his cigarette; and* RACHEL *proceeds to clear the table. In the midst of this, the bell rings three distinct times*)

RACHEL *and* TOM John!

TOM I wonder what's up—It's rather early for him.—I'll go. (*rises leisurely and goes out into the vestibule. The outer door opens and shuts. Men's voices are heard.* TOM *and* JOHN STRONG *enter. During the ensuing conversation* RACHEL *finishes clearing the table, takes the fern off, puts on the green table-cloth, places a doily carefully in the centre, and replaces the fern. She apparently pays no attention to the conversation between her brother and* STRONG. *After she has finished, she goes to the kitchenette. The rattle of dishes can be heard now and then*)

RACHEL (*brightly*) Well, stranger, how does it happen you're out so early in the morning?

STRONG I hadn't seen any of you for a week, and I thought I'd come by, on my way to work, and find out how things are going. There is no need of asking how you are, Rachel. And the mother and the boy?

RACHEL Ma dear's rheumatism still holds on.—Jimmy's fine.

STRONG I'm sorry to hear that your mother is not well. There isn't a remedy going that my mother doesn't know about. I'll get her advice and let you know. (*turning to* TOM) Well, Tom, how goes it? (STRONG *and* TOM *sit*)

TOM (*smiling grimly*) There's plenty of "go," but no "git there."

(*There is a pause*).

STRONG I was hoping for better news.

TOM If I remember rightly, not so many years ago, you tried—and failed. Then, a colored man had hardly a ghost of a show; —now he hasn't even the ghost of a ghost.

STRONG That's true enough. (*a pause*) What are you going to do?

TOM (*slowly*) I'll do this little "going act" of mine the rest of the week; (*pauses*) and then, I'll do anything I can get to do. If necessary,

I suppose, I can be a "White-wing."

STRONG Tom, I came— (*breaks off; continuing slowly*) Six years ago, I found I was up against a stone wall—your experience, you see, to the letter. I couldn't let my mother starve, so I became a waiter. (*pauses*) I studied waiting; I made a science of it, an art. In a comparatively short time, I'm a head-waiter and I'm up against another stone wall. I've reached my limit. I'm thirty-two now, and I'll die a head-waiter. (*a pause*) College friends, so-called, and acquaintances used to come into the restaurant. One or two at first—attempted to commiserate with me. They didn't do it again. I waited upon them—I did my best. Many of them tipped me. (*pauses and smiles grimly*) I can remember my first tip, still. They come in yet; many of them are already powers, not only in this city, but in the country. Some of them make a personal request that I wait upon them. I am an artist, now, in my proper sphere. They tip me well, extremely well—the larger the tip, the more pleased they are with me. Because of me, in their own eyes, they're philanthropists. Amusing, isn't it? I can stand their attitude now. My philosophy—learned hard, is to make the best of everything you can, and go on. At best, life isn't so very long. You're wondering why I'm telling you all this. I wish you to see things exactly as they are. There are many disadvantages and some advantages in being a waiter. My mother can live comfortably; I am able, even, to see that she gets some of the luxuries. Tom, it's this way—I can always get you a job as a waiter; I'll teach you the art. If you care to begin the end of the week—all right. And remember this, as long as I keep my job—this offer holds good.

TOM I—I— (*breaks off*) Thank you. (*a pause; then smiling wryly*) I guess it's safe enough to say, you'll see me at the end of the week. John you're— (*breaking off again. A silence interrupted presently by the sound of much vigorous rapping on the outer door of the flat.* RACHEL *appears and crosses over toward the vestibule*).

RACHEL Hear the racket! My kiddies gently begging for admittance. It's about twenty minutes of nine, isn't it? (TOM *nods*). I thought so. (*Goes into the entryway; presently reappears with a group of six little girls ranging in age from five to about nine. All are fighting to be close to her; and all are talking at once. There is one exception: the smallest tot is self-possessed and self-sufficient. She carries a red geranium in her hand and gives it her full attention*).

LITTLE MARY It's my turn to get "Morning kiss" first, this morning, Miss Rachel. You kissed Louise first yesterday. You said you'd kiss us "alphebettically." (*ending in a shriek*) You promised! (RACHEL *kisses* MARY, *who subsides*)

LITTLE NANCY (*imperiously*) Now, me. (RACHEL *kisses her, and then amid shrieks, recriminations, pulling of hair, jostling, etc., she kisses the rest. The small tot is still oblivious to everything that is going on*).

RACHEL (*laughing*) You children will pull me limb from limb; and then I'll be all dead; and you'll be sorry—see, if you aren't. (*they fall back immediately.* TOM *and* JOHN *watch in amused silence.* RACHEL *loses all self-consciousness, and seems to bloom in the children's midst*). Edith! come here this minute, and let me tie your hair-ribbon again. Nancy, I'm ashamed of you, I saw you trying to pull it off. (NANCY *looks abashed but mischievous*). Louise, you look as sweet as sweet, this morning; and Jenny, where did you get the pretty, pretty dress?

LITTLE JENNY (*snuffling, but proud*) My mother made it. (*pauses with more snuffles*) My mother says I have a very bad cold. (*there is a brief silence interrupted by the small tot with the geranium*)

LITTLE MARTHA (*in a sweet, little voice*) I—have—a—pitty—'ittle flower.

RACHEL Honey, it's beautiful. Don't you want "Morning kiss" too?

LITTLE MARTHA Yes, I do.

RACHEL Come, honey. (RACHEL *kisses her*). Are you going to give the pretty flower to Jenny's teacher? (*vigorous shakings of the head in denial*) Is it for—mother? (*more shakings of the head*) Is it for—let's see—Daddy? (*more shakings of the head*) I give up. To whom are you going to give the pretty flower, honey?

LITTLE MARTHA (*shyly*) "Oo."

RACHEL You, darling!

LITTLE MARTHA Muzzer and I picked it—for "oo." Here 't is. (*puts her finger in her mouth, and gives it shyly*)

RACHEL Well, I'm going to pay you with three big kisses. One! Two! Three!

LITTLE MARTHA I can count, One! Two!

Free! Tan't I? I am going to school soon; and I wants to put the flower in your hair.

RACHEL (*kneels*) All right, baby. (LITTLE MARTHA *fumbles and* RACHEL *helps her*).

LITTLE MARTHA (*dreamily*) Miss Rachel, the 'ittle flower loves you. It told me so. It said it wanted to lie in your hair. It is going to tell you a pitty 'ittle secret. You listen awful hard—and you'll hear. I wish I were a fairy and had a little wand, I'd turn everything into flowers. Wouldn't that be nice, Miss Rachel?

RACHEL Lovely, honey!

LITTLE JENNY (*snuffling loudly*) If I were a fairy and had a wand, I'd turn you, Miss Rachel, into a queen—and then I'd always be near you and see that you were happy.

RACHEL Honey, how beautiful!

LITTLE LOUISE I'd make my mother happy—if I were a fairy. She cries all the time. My father can't get anything to do.

LITTLE NANCY If I were a fairy, I'd turn a boy in my school into a spider. I hate him.

RACHEL Honey, why?

LITTLE NANCY I'll tell you sometime—I hate him.

LITTLE EDITH Where's Jimmy, Miss Rachel?

RACHEL He went long ago; and chickies, you'll have to clear out, all of you, now, or you'll be late. Shoo! Shoo! (*she drives them out prettily before her. They laugh merrily. They all go into the vestibule*)

TOM (*slowly*) Does it ever strike you—how pathetic and tragic a thing—a little colored child is?

STRONG Yes.

TOM Today, we colored men and women, everywhere—are up against it. Every year, we are having a harder time of it. In the South, they make it as impossible as they can for us to get an education. We're hemmed in on all sides. Our one safeguard—the ballot—in most states, is taken away already, or is being taken away. Economically, in a few lines, we have a slight show—but at what a cost! In the North, they make a pretense of liberality: they give us the ballot and a good education, and then—snuff us out. Each year, the problem just to live, gets more difficult to solve. How about these children—if we're fools enough to have any? (RACHEL *reenters. Her face is drawn and pale. She returns to the kitchenette*)

STRONG (*slowly, with emphasis*) That part—is damnable! (*a silence*)

TOM (*suddenly looking at the clock*) It's later than I thought. I'll have to be pulling out of here now, if you don't mind. (*raising his voice*) Rachel! (RACHEL *still drawn and pale, appears in the doorway of the kitchenette. She is without her apron*) I've got to go now, Sis. I leave John in your hands.

STRONG I've got to go, myself, in a few minutes.

TOM Nonsense, man! Sit still. I'll begin to think, in a minute, you're afraid of the ladies.

STRONG I am.

TOM What! And not ashamed to acknowledge it?

STRONG No.

TOM You're lots wiser than I dreamed. So long! (*gets hat out in the entry-way and returns; smiles wryly*) "Morituri Salutamus." (*they nod at him*—RACHEL *wistfully. He goes out. There is the sound of an opening and closing door.* RACHEL *sits down. A rather uncomfortable silence, on the part of* RACHEL, *ensues.* STRONG *is imperturbable*)

RACHEL (*nervously*) John!

STRONG Well?

RACHEL I—I listened.

STRONG Listened! To what?

RACHEL To you and Tom.

STRONG Well,—what of it?

RACHEL I didn't think it was quite fair not to tell you. It—it seemed, well, like eavesdropping.

STRONG Don't worry about it. Nonsense!

RACHEL I'm glad—I want to thank you for what you did for Tom. He needs you, and will need you. You'll help him?

STRONG (*thoughtfully*) Rachel, each one—has his own little battles. I'll do what I can. After all, an outsider doesn't help much.

RACHEL But friendship—just friendship—helps.

STRONG Yes. (*a silence*) Rachel, do you hear anything encouraging from the schools? Any hope for you yet?

RACHEL No, nor ever will be. I know that now. There's no more chance for me than there is for Tom,—or than there was for you—or for any of us with dark skins. It's lucky for me that I love to keep house, and cook, and sew. I'll never get anything else. Ma dear's sewing, the little work Tom has been able to get, and the little sewing I sometimes get to do—keep us from the poorhouse. We live. According to your philosophy, I suppose, make the best of it—it might be worse.

STRONG (*quietly*) You don't want to get morbid over these things, you know.

RACHEL (*scornfully*) That's it. If you see things as they are, you're either pessimistic or morbid.

STRONG In the long run, do you believe, that attitude of mind—will be—beneficial to you? I'm ten years older than you. I tried your way. I know. Mine is the only sane one. (*goes over to her slowly; deliberately puts his hands on her hair, and tips her head back. He looks down into her face quietly without saying anything*)

RACHEL (*nervous and startled*) Why, John, don't! (*he pays no attention, but continues to look down into her face*)

STRONG (*half to himself*) Perhaps—if you had—a little more fun in your life, your point of view would be—more normal. I'll arrange it so I can take you to some theatre, one night, this week.

RACHEL (*irritably*) You talk as though I were a—a jelly-fish. You'll take me, how do you know *I'll* go?

STRONG You will.

RACHEL (*sarcastically*) Indeed! (STRONG *makes no reply*) I wonder if you know how—how—maddening you are. Why, you talk as though my will counts for nothing. It's as if you're trying to master me. I think a domineering man is detestable.

STRONG (*softly*) If he's, perhaps, *the* man?

RACHEL (*hurriedly, as though she had not heard*) Besides, some of these theatres put you off by yourself as though you had leprosy. I'm not going.

STRONG (*smiling at her*) You know I wouldn't ask you to go, under those circumstances. (*a silence*) Well, I must be going now. (*he takes her hand, and looks at it reverently.* RACHEL, *at first resists; but he refuses to let go. When she finds it useless, she ceases to resist. He turns his head and smiles down into her face*) Rachel, I am coming back to see you, this evening.

RACHEL I'm sure *we'll* all be very glad to see you.

STRONG (*looking at her calmly*) I said—*you*. (*very deliberately, he turns her hand palm upwards, leans over and kisses it; then he puts it back into her lap. He touches her cheek lightly*) Good-bye—little Rachel. (*turns in the vestibule door and looks back, smiling*) Until tonight. (*He goes out.* RACHEL *sits for some time without moving. She is lost in a beautiful day-dream. Presently she sighs happily, and after looking furtively around the room, lifts the palm* JOHN *has kissed to her lips. She laughs shyly and jumping up, begins to hum. She opens the window at the rear of the room and then commences to thread the sewing-machine. She hums happily the whole time. A light rapping is heard at the outer door.* RACHEL *listens. It stops, and begins again. There is something insistent, and yet hopeless in the sound.* RACHEL *looking puzzled, goes out into the vestibule. . . . The door closes. Rachel, and a black woman, poorly dressed, and a little ugly, black child come in. There is the stoniness of despair in the woman's face. The child is thin, nervous, suspicious, frightened*)

MRS. LANE (*in a sharp, but toneless voice*) May I sit down? I'm tired.

RACHEL (*puzzled, but gracious; draws up a chair for her*) Why, certainly.

MRS. LANE No, you don't know me—never even heard of me—nor I of you. I was looking at the vacant flat on this floor—and saw your name—on your door,—"Loving!" It's a strange name to come across—in this world. —I thought, perhaps, you might give me some information. (*the child hides behind her mother and looks around at* RACHEL *in a frightened way*)

RACHEL (*smiling at the woman and child in a kindly manner*) I'll be glad to tell you anything, I am able Mrs.—

MRS. LANE Lane. What I want to know is, how do they treat the colored children in the school I noticed around the corner? (*the child clutches at her mother's dress*).

RACHEL (*perplexed*) Very well—I'm sure.

MRS. LANE (*bluntly*) What reason have you for being sure?

RACHEL Why, the little boy I've adopted goes there; and he's very happy. All the children in this apartment-house go there too; and I know they're happy.

MRS. LANE Do you know how many colored children there are in the school?

RACHEL Why, I should guess around thirty.

MRS. LANE I see. (*pauses*) What color is this little adopted boy of yours?

RACHEL (*gently*) Why—he's brown.

MRS. LANE Any black children there?

RACHEL (*nervously*) Why—yes.

MRS. LANE Do you mind if I send Ethel over by the piano to sit?

RACHEL N—no, certainly not. (*places a chair by the piano and goes to the little girl holding out her hand. She smiles beautifully. The child gets farther behind her mother*)

MRS. LANE She won't go to you—she's afraid of everybody now but her father and me. Come Ethel. (MRS. LANE *takes the little girl by the hand and leads her to the chair. In a gentler voice*) Sit down, Ethel. (ETHEL *obeys. When her mother starts back again toward* RACHEL, *she holds out her hands pitifully. She makes no sound*) I'm not going to leave you, Ethel. I'll be right over here. You can see me. (*the look of agony on the child's face, as her mother leaves her, makes* RACHEL *shudder*) Do you mind if we sit over here by the sewing-machine? Thank you. (*they move their chairs*)

RACHEL (*looking at the little, pitiful figure watching its mother almost unblinkingly*) Does Ethel like apples, Mrs. Lane?

MRS. LANE Yes.

RACHEL Do you mind if I give her one?

MRS. LANE No. Thank you, very much.

RACHEL (*goes into the kitchenette and returns with a fringed napkin, a plate, and a big, red apple, cut into quarters. She goes to the little girl, who cowers away from her; very gently*) Here, dear, little girl, is a beautiful apple for you. (*the gentle tones have no appeal for the trembling child before her*)

MRS. LANE (*coming forward*) I'm sorry, but I'm afraid she won't take it from you. Ethel, the kind lady has given you an apple. Thank her nicely. Here! I'll spread the napkin for you, and put the plate in your lap. Thank the lady like a good little girl.

ETHEL (*very low*) Thank you. (*they return to their seats.* ETHEL *with difficulty holds the plate in her lap. During the rest of the interview between* RACHEL *and her mother, she divides her attention between the apple on the plate and her mother's face. She makes no attempt to eat the apple, but holds the plate in her lap with a care that is painful to watch. Often, too, she looks over her shoulder fearfully. The conversation between* RACHEL *and her mother is carried on in low tones*)

MRS. LANE I've got to move—it's *Ethel*.

RACHEL What is the matter with that child? It's—it's heartbreaking to see her.

MRS. LANE I understand how you feel,—I don't feel anything, myself, any more. (*a pause*) My husband and I are poor, and we're ugly and we're black. Ethel looks like her father more than she does like me. We live in 55th Street—near the railroad. It's a poor neighborhood, but the rent's cheap. My husband is a porter in a store; and, to help out, I'm a caretaker. (*pauses*) I don't know why I'm telling you all this. We had a nice little home—and the three of us were happy. Now we've got to move.

RACHEL Move! Why?

MRS. LANE It's Ethel. I put her in school this September. She stayed two weeks. (*pointing to* ETHEL) That's the result.

RACHEL (*in horror*) You mean—that just two weeks—in school—did that?

MRS. LANE Yes. Ethel never had a sick day in her life—before. (*a brief pause*) I took her to the doctor at the end of the two weeks. He says she's a nervous wreck.

RACHEL But what could they have done to her?

MRS. LANE (*laughs grimly and mirthlessly*) I'll tell you what they did the first day. Ethel is naturally sensitive and backward. She's not assertive. The teacher saw that, and, after I had left, told her to sit in a seat in the rear of the class. She was alone there—in a corner. The children, immediately feeling there was something wrong with Ethel because of the teacher's attitude, turned and stared at her. When the teacher's back was turned they whispered about her, pointed their fingers at her and tittered. The teacher divided the class into two parts, divisions, I believe, they are called. She forgot all about Ethel, of course, until the last minute, and then, looking back, said sharply: "That little girl there may join this division," meaning the group of pupils standing around her. Ethel naturally moved slowly. The teacher called her sulky and told her to lose a part of her recess. When Ethel came up—the children drew away from her in every direction. She was left standing alone. The teacher then proceeded to give a lesson about kindness to animals. Funny, isn't it, *kindness* to *animals*? The children forgot Ethel in the excitement of talking about their pets. Presently, the teacher turned to Ethel and said disagreeably: "Have you a pet?" Ethel said, "Yes," very low. "Come, speak up, you sulky child, what is it?" Ethel said: "A blind puppy." They all laughed, the teacher and all. Strange, isn't it, but Ethel loves that puppy. She spoke up: "It's mean to laugh at a little blind puppy. I'm glad he's blind." This remark brought forth more laughter. "Why are your glad," the teacher asked curiously. Ethel refused to say. (*pauses*) When I asked her why, do you know what she told me? "If he saw me, he might not love me any more." (*a pause*) Did I tell you that Ethel is only seven years old?

RACHEL (*drawing her breath sharply*) Oh! I didn't believe any one could be as cruel as that —to a little child.

MRS. LANE It isn't very pleasant, is it? When the teacher found out that Ethel wouldn't answer, she said severely: "Take your seat!" At recess, all the children went out. Ethel could hear them playing and laughing and shrieking. Even the teacher went too. She was made to sit there all alone—in that big room—because God made her ugly—and black. (*pauses*) When the recess was half over the teacher came back. "You may go now," she said coldly. Ethel didn't stir. "Did you hear me!" "Yes'm." "Why don't you obey?" "I don't want to go out, please." "You don't, don't you, you stubborn child! Go immediately!" Ethel went. She stood by the school steps. No one spoke to her. The children near her moved away in every direction. They stopped playing, many of them, and watched her. They stared as only children can stare. Some began whispering about her. Presently one child came up and ran her hand roughly over Ethel's face. She looked at her hand and Ethel's face and ran screaming back to the others, "It won't come off! See!" Other children followed the first child's example. Then one boy spoke up loudly: "I know what she is, she's a nigger!" Many took up the cry. God or the devil interfered—the bell rang. The children filed in. One boy boldly called her "Nigger!" before the teacher. She said, "That isn't nice,"—but she smiled at the boy. Things went on about the same for the rest of the day. At the end of school, Ethel put on her hat and coat—the teacher made her hang them at a distance from the other pupils' wraps; and started for home. Quite a crowd escorted her. They called her "Nigger!" all the way. I *made* Ethel go the next day. I complained to the authorities. They treated me lightly. I was determined not to let them force my child out of school. At the end of two weeks—I had to take her out.

RACHEL (*brokenly*) Why,—I never—in all my life—heard anything—so—pitiful.

MRS. LANE Did you ever go to school here?

RACHEL Yes. I was made to feel my color— but I never had an experience like that.

MRS. LANE How many years ago were you in the graded schools?

RACHEL Oh!—around ten.

MRS. LANE (*laughs grimly*) Ten years! Every year things are getting worse. Last year wasn't as bad as this. (*pauses*) So they treat the children all right in this school?

RACHEL Yes! Yes! I know that.

Mrs. Lane I can't afford to take this flat here, but I'll take it. I'm going to have Ethel educated. Although, when you think of it,—it's all rather useless—this education! What are our children going to do with it, when they get it? We strive and save and sacrifice to educate them—and the whole time—down underneath, we know—they'll have no chance.

RACHEL (*sadly*) Yes, that's true, all right.— God seems to have forgotten us.

MRS. LANE God! It's all a lie about God. I know.—This fall I sent Ethel to a white Sunday-school near us. She received the same treatment there she did in the day school. Her being there, nearly broke up the school. At the end, the superintendent called her to him and asked her if she didn't know of some nice colored Sunday-school. He told her she must feel out of place, and uncomfortable there. That's your Church of God!

RACHEL Oh! how unspeakably brutal. (*controls herself with an effort; after a pause*) Have you any other children?

MRS. LANE (*dryly*) Hardly! If I had another —I'd kill it. It's kinder. (*rising presently*) Well, I must go, now. Thank you, for your information—and for listening. (*suddenly*) You aren't married, are you?

RACHEL No.

MRS. LANE Don't marry—that's my advice. Come, Ethel. (ETHEL *gets up and puts down the things in her lap, carefully upon her chair. She goes in a hurried, timid way to her mother and clutches her hand*). Say good-bye to the lady.

ETHEL (*faintly*) Good-bye.

RACHEL (*kneeling by the little girl—a beautiful smile on her face*) Dear little girl, won't you let me kiss you good-bye? I love little girls. (*the child hides behind her mother; continuing brokenly*) Oh!—no child—ever did—that to me—before!

MRS. LANE (*in a gentler voice*) Perhaps, when we move in here, the first of the month, things may be better. Thank you, again. Good-morning! You don't belie your name. (*all three go into the vestibule. The outside door opens and closes.* RACHEL *as though dazed and stricken returns. She sits in a chair, leans forward, and clasping her hands loosely between her knees, stares at the chair with the apple on it where* ETHEL LANE *has sat. She does not move for some time. Then she gets up and goes to the window in the rear center and sits there. She breathes in the air deeply and then goes to the sewing-machine and begins to sew on something she is making. Presently her feet slow down on the pedals; she stops; and begins brooding again. After a short pause, she gets up and begins to pace up and down slowly, mechanically, her head bent forward. The sharp ringing of the electric bell breaks in upon this.* RACHEL *starts and goes slowly into the vestibule. She is heard speaking dully through the tube*)

RACHEL Yes!—All right! Bring it up! (*presently she returns with a long flower box. She opens it listlessly at the table. Within are six, beautiful crimson rosebuds with long stems.* RACHEL *looks at the name on the card. She sinks down slowly on her knees and leans her head against the table. She sighs wearily*) Oh! John! John!—What are we to do?—I'm—I'm—afraid! Everywhere—it is the same thing. My mother! My little brother! Little, black, crushed Ethel! (*in a whisper*) Oh! God! You who I have been taught to believe are so good, so beautiful how could—You permit—these—things? (*pauses, raises her head and sees the rosebuds. Her face softens and grows beautiful, very sweetly*) Dear little rosebuds—you—make me think—of sleeping, curled up, happy babies. Dear beautiful, little rosebuds! (*pauses; goes on thoughtfully to the rosebuds*) When—I look—at you—I believe—God is beautiful. He who can make a little exquisite thing like this, and this can't be cruel. Oh! He can't mean me—to give up—love—and the hope of little children. (*there is the sound of a small hand knocking at the outer door.* RACHEL *smiles*) My Jimmy! It must be twelve o'clock. (*rises*) I didn't dream it was so late. (*starts for the vestibule*) Oh! the world can't be so bad. I don't believe it. I won't. I *must* forget that little girl. My little Jimmy is happy—and today John—sent me beautiful rosebuds. Oh, there are lovely things, yet. (*goes into the vestibule. A child's eager cry is heard; and* RACHEL *carrying* JIMMY *in her arms comes in. He has both arms about her neck and is hugging her. With him in her arms, she sits down in the armchair at the right front*).

RACHEL Well, honey, how was school today?

JIMMY (*sobering a trifle*) All right, Ma Rachel. (*suddenly sees the roses*) Oh! look at the pretty flowers. Why, Ma Rachel, you forgot to put them in water. They'll die.

RACHEL Well, so they will. Hop down this minute, and I'll put them in right away. (*gathers up box and flowers and goes into the kitchenette.* JIMMY *climbs back into the chair. He looks thoughtful and serious.* RACHEL *comes back with the buds in a tall, glass vase. She puts the fern on top of the piano, and places the vase in the center of the table*) There, honey, that's better, isn't it? Aren't they lovely?

JIMMY Yes, that's lots better. Now they won't die, will they? Rosebuds are just like little "chilyun," aren't they, Ma Rachel? If you are good to them, they'll grow up into lovely roses, won't they? And if you hurt them, they'll die. Ma Rachel do you think all peoples are kind to little rosebuds?

RACHEL (*watching Jimmy shortly*) Why, of course. Who could hurt little children? Who would have the heart to do such a thing?

JIMMY If you hurt them, it would be lots kinder, wouldn't it, to kill them all at once, and not a little bit and a little bit?

RACHEL (*sharply*) Why, honey boy, why are you talking like this?

JIMMY Ma Rachel, what is a "Nigger?"

(RACHEL *recoils as though she had been struck*).

RACHEL Honey boy, why—why do you ask that?

JIMMY Some big boys called me that when I came out of school just now. They said: "Look at the little nigger!" And they laughed. One of them runned, no ranned, after me and threw stones; and they all kept calling "Nigger! Nigger! Nigger!" One stone struck me hard in the back, and it hurt awful bad; but I didn't cry, Ma Rachel. I wouldn't let them make me cry. The stone hurts me there, Ma Rachel; but what they called me hurts and hurts here. What is a "Nigger," Ma Rachel?

RACHEL (*controlling herself with a tremendous effort. At last she sweeps down upon him and hugs and kisses him*) Why, honey, boy, those boys didn't mean anything. Silly, little, honey boy! They're rough, that's all. How *could* they mean anything?

JIMMY You're only saying that, Ma Rachel, so I won't be hurt. I know. It wouldn't ache here like it does—if they didn't mean something.

RACHEL (*abruptly*) Where's Mary, honey?

JIMMY She's in her flat. She came in just after I did.

RACHEL Well, honey, I'm going to give you two big cookies and two to take to Mary; and you may stay in there and play with her, till I get your lunch ready. Won't that be jolly?

JIMMY (*brightening a little*) Why, you never give me but one at a time. You'll give me two? —One? Two?

RACHEL (*gets the cookies and brings them to him.* JIMMY *climbs down from the chair*) Shoo! now, little honey boy. See how many laughs you can make for me, before I come after you. Hear? Have a good time, now.

(JIMMY *starts for the door quickly; but he begins to slow down. His face gets long and serious again.* RACHEL *watches him*)

RACHEL (*jumping at him*) Shoo! Shoo! Get out of here quickly, little chicken. (*she follows him out. The outer door opens and shuts. Presently she returns. She looks old and worn and grey; calmly. Pauses*) First, it's little, black Ethel— and then's it's Jimmy. Tomorrow, it will be some other little child. The blight—sooner or later—strikes all. My little Jimmy, only seven years old poisoned! (*through the open window comes the laughter of little children at play.* RACHEL, *shuddering, covers her ears*). And once I said, centuries ago, it must have been: "How can life be so terrible, when there are little children in the world?" Terrible! Terrible! (*in a whisper, slowly*) That's the reason it *is* so terrible. (*the laughter reaches her again; this time she listens*) And, suddenly, some day, from out of the black, the blight shall descend, and shall still forever—the laughter on those little lips, and in those little hearts. (*pauses thoughtfully*) And the loveliest thing—almost, that ever happened to me, that beautiful voice, in my dream, those beautiful words: "Rachel, you are to be the mother to little children." (*pauses, then slowly and with dawning surprise*) Why, God, you were making a mock of me; you were laughing at me. I didn't believe God could laugh at our sufferings, but He can. We are accursed, accursed! We have nothing, absolutely nothing. (STRONG's *rosebuds attract her attention. She goes over to them, puts her hand out as if to touch them, and then shakes her head, very sweetly*) No, little rosebuds, I may not touch you. Dear, little, baby rosebuds,—I am accursed. (*gradually her whole form stiffens, she breathes deeply; at last slowly*) You God!— You terrible, laughing God! Listen! I swear— and may my soul be damned to all eternity, if I do break this oath—I swear—that no child of mine shall ever lie upon my breast, for I will not have it rise up, in the terrible days that are to be—and call me cursed. (*a pause, very wistfully; questioningly*). Never to know the loveliest thing in all the world—the feel of a little head, the touch of little hands, the beautiful utter dependence—of a little child? (*with sudden frenzy*) You can laugh, Oh God! Well, so can I. (*bursts into terrible, racking laughter*) But I can be kinder than You. (*fiercely she snatches the rosebuds from the vase, grasps them roughly, tears each head from the stem, and grinds it under her feet. The vase goes over with a crash; the water drips unheeded over the table-cloth and floor*) If I kill, You Mighty God, I kill at once—I do not torture. (*falls face downward on the floor. The laughter of the children shrills loudly through the window*)

ACT THREE

TIME: *Seven o'clock in the evening, one week later.*

(PLACE: *The same room. There is a coal fire in the grate. The curtains are drawn. A lighted oil lamp with a dark green porcelain shade is in the center of the table.* MRS. LOVING *and* TOM *are sitting by the table,* MRS. LOVING *sewing,* TOM *reading. There is the sound of much laughter and the shrill screaming of a child from the bedrooms. Presently* JIMMY *clad in a flannelet sleeping suit, covering all of him but his head and hands, chases a pillow, which has come flying through the doorway at the rear. He struggles with it, finally gets it in his arms, and rushes as fast as he can through the doorway again.* RACHEL *jumps at him with a cry. He drops the pillow and shrieks. There is a tussle for possession of it, and they disappear. The noise grows louder and merrier.* TOM *puts down his paper and grins. He looks at his mother*)

TOM Well, who's the giddy one in this family now?

MRS. LOVING (*shaking her head in troubled manner*) I don't like it. It worries me. Rachel— (*breaks off*)

TOM Have you found out, yet—

MRS. LOVING (*turning and looking toward the rear doorway, quickly interrupting him*) Sh! (RACHEL, *laughing, her hair tumbling over her shoulders, comes rushing into the room.* JIMMY *is in close pursuit. He tries to catch her, but she dodges him. They are both breathless*)

MRS. LOVING (*deprecatingly*) Really, Rachel, Jimmy will be so excited he won't be able to sleep. It's after his bedtime, now. Don't you think you had better stop?

RACHEL All right, Ma dear. Come on, Jimmy; let's play "Old Folks" and sit by the fire. (*she begins to push the big armchair over to the fire.* TOM *jumps up, moves her aside, and pushes it himself.* JIMMY *renders assistance*)

TOM Thanks, Big Fellow, you are "sure some" strong. I'll remember you when these people around here come for me to move pianos and such things around. Shake! (*they shake hands*)

JIMMY (*proudly*) I am awful strong, am I not?

TOM You "sure" are a Hercules. (*hurriedly, as* JIMMY's *mouth and eyes open wide*). And see here! don't ask me tonight who that was. I'll tell you the first thing tomorrow morning. Hear? (*returns to his chair and paper*)

RACHEL (*sitting down*) Come on, honey boy, and sit in my lap.

JIMMY (*doubtfully*) I thought we were going to play "Old Folks."

RACHEL We are.

JIMMY Do old folks sit in each other's laps?

RACHEL Old folks do anything. Come on.

JIMMY (*hesitatingly climbs into her lap, but presently snuggles down and sighs audibly from sheer content;* RACHEL *starts to bind up her hair*) Ma Rachel, don't please! I like your hair like that. You're—you're pretty. I like to feel of it; and it smells like—like—oh!—like a barn.

RACHEL My! how complimentary! I like that. Like a barn, indeed!

JIMMY What's "complimentary"?

RACHEL Oh! saying nice things about me. (*pinching his cheek and laughing*) That my hair is like a barn, for instance.

JIMMY (*stoutly*) Well, that is "complimentary." It smells like hay—like the hay in the barn you took me to, one day, last summer. 'Member?

RACHEL Yes honey.

JIMMY (*after a brief pause*) Ma Rachel!

RACHEL Well?

JIMMY Tell me a story, please. It's "story-time," now, isn't it?

RACHEL Well, let's see. (*they both look into the fire for a space; beginning softly*) Once upon a time, there were two, dear, little boys, and they were all alone in the world. They lived with a cruel, old man and woman, who made them work hard, very hard—all day, and beat them when they did not move fast enough, and always, every night, before they went to bed. They slept in an attic on a rickety, narrow bed, that went screech! screech! whenever they moved. And, in summer, they nearly died with the heat up there, and in winter, with the cold. One wintry night, when they were both weeping very bitterly after a particularly hard beating, they suddenly heard a pleasant voice saying: "Why are you crying, little boys?" They looked up, and there, in the moonlight, by their bed, was the dearest, little old lady. She was dressed all in grey, from the peak of her little pointed hat to her little, buckled shoes. She held a black cane much taller than her little self. Her hair fell about her ears in tiny, grey corkscrew curls, and they bobbed about as she moved. Her eyes were black and bright—as bright as—well, as that lovely, white light there. No, there! And her cheeks were as red as the apple I gave you yesterday. Do you remember?

JIMMY (*dreamily*) Yes.

RACHEL "Why are you crying, little boys?" she asked again, in a lovely, low, little voice. "Because we are tired and sore and hungry and cold; and we are all alone in the world; and we don't know how to laugh any more. We should so like to laugh again." "Why, that's easy," she said, "it's just like this." And she laughed a little, joyous, musical laugh. "Try!" she commanded. They tried, but their laughing boxes were very rusty, and they made horrid sounds. "Well," she said, "I advise you to pack up, and go away, as soon as you can, to the Land of Laughter. You'll soon learn there, I can tell you." "Is there such a land?" they asked doubtfully. "To be sure there is," she answered the least bit sharply. "We never heard of it," they said. "Well, I'm sure there must be plenty of things you never heard about," she said just the "leastest" bit more sharply. "In a moment you'll be telling me flowers don't talk together, and the birds." "We never heard of such a thing," they said in surprise, their eyes like saucers. "There!" she said, bobbing her little curls. "What did I tell you? You have much to learn." "How do you get to the Land of Laughter?" they asked. "You go out of the eastern gate of the town, just as the sun is rising; and you take the highway there, and follow it; and if you go with it long enough, it will bring you to the very gates of the Land of Laughter. It's a long, long way from here; and it will take you many days." The words had scarcely left her mouth, when, lo! the little lady disappeared, and where she had stood was the white square of moonlight—nothing else. And without more ado these two little boys put their arms around each other and fell fast asleep. And in the grey, just before daybreak, they awoke and dressed; and, putting on their ragged caps and mittens, for it was a wintry day, they stole out of the house and made for the eastern gate. And just as they reached it, and passed through, the whole east leapt into fire. All day they walked, and many days thereafter, and kindly people, by the way, took them in and gave them food and drink and sometimes a bed at night. Often they slept by the roadside, but they didn't mind that for the climate was delightful—not too hot, and not too cold. They soon threw away their ragged little mittens. They walked for many days, and there was no Land of Laughter. Once they met an old man, richly dressed, with shining jewels on his fingers, and he stopped them and asked: "Where are you going so fast, little boys?" "We are going to the Land of Laughter," they said together gravely. "That," said the old man, "is a very foolish thing to do. Come with me, and I will take you to the Land of Riches. I will cover you with garments of beauty, and give you jewels and a castle to live in and servants and horses and many things besides." And they said to him: "No, we wish to learn how to laugh again; we have forgotten how, and we are going to the Land of Laughter." "You will regret not going with me. See, if you don't," he said; and he left them in quite a huff. And they walked again, many days, and again they met an old man. He was tall and imposing-looking and very dignified. And he said: "Where are you going so fast, little boys?" "We are going to the Land of Laughter," they said together very seriously. "What!" he said, "that is an extremely foolish thing to do. Come with me, and I will give you power. I will make you great men: generals, kings, emperors. Whatever you desire to accomplish will be permitted you." And they smiled politely: "Thank you very much, but we have forgotten how to laugh, and we are going there to learn how." He looked upon them haughtily, without speaking, and disappeared. And they walked and walked more days; and they met another old man. And he was clad in rags, and his face was thin, and his eyes were unhappy. And he whispered to them: "Where are you going so fast, little boys?" "We are going to the Land of Laughter," they answered, without a smile. "Laughter! Laughter! that is useless. Come with me and I will show you the beauty of life through sacrifice, suffering for others. That is the only life. I come from the Land of Sacrifice." And they thanked him kindly, but said: "We have suffered long enough. We have forgotten how to laugh. We would learn again." And they went on; and he looked after them very wistfully. They walked more days, and at last they came to the Land of Laughter. And how do you suppose they knew this? Because they could hear, over the wall, the sound of joyous laughter, —the laughter of men, women, and children. And one sat guarding the gate, and they went to her. "We have come a long, long distance; and we would enter the Land of Laughter." "Let me see you smile, first," she said gently. "I sit at the gate; and no one who does not know how to smile may enter the Land of Laughter." And they tried to smile, but could not. "Go away and practice," she said kindly, "and come back tomorrow." And they went away, and practiced all night how to smile; and in the morning they returned, and the gentle lady at the gate said: "Dear little boys, have you learned how to smile?" And they said: "We have tried. How is this?" "Better," she said, "much better. Practice some more, and come back tomorrow." And they went away obediently and practiced. And they came the third day. And she said: "Now try again." And tears of delight came into her lovely eyes. "Those were very beautiful smiles," she said. "Now, you may enter." And she unlocked the gate, and kissed them both, and they entered the Land— the beautiful Land of Laughter. Never had they seen such blue skies, such green trees and grass; never had they heard such birds songs. And people, men, women and children, laughing softly, came to meet them, and took them in, and made them at home; and soon, very soon, they learned to sleep. And they grew up here, and married, and had laughing, happy children. And sometimes they thought of the Land of Riches, and said: "Ah! well!" and sometimes of the Land of Power, and sighed a little; and sometimes of the Land of Sacrifice—and their eyes were wistful. But they soon forgot, and laughed again. And they grew old, laughing. And then when they died—a laugh was on their lips. Thus are things in the beautiful Land of Laughter. (*there is a long pause*)

JIMMY I like that story, Ma Rachel. It's nice to laugh, isn't it? Is there such a land?

RACHEL (*softly*) What do you think, honey?

JIMMY I thinks it would be awful nice if there was. Don't you?

RACHEL (*wistfully*) If there only were! If there only were!

JIMMY Ma Rachel.

RACHEL Well?

JIMMY It makes you think—kind of— doesn't it—of sunshine medicine?

RACHEL Yes, honey,—but it isn't medicine there. It's always there—just like—well—like our air here. It's *always* sunshine there.

JIMMY Always sunshine? Never any dark?

RACHEL No, honey.

JIMMY You'd—never—be—afraid there, then, would you? Never afraid of nothing?

RACHEL No, honey.

JIMMY (*with a big sigh*) Oh!—Oh! I *wisht* it was here—not there. (*puts his hand up to* RACHEL'*s face; suddenly sits up and looks at her*) Why, Ma Rachel dear, you're crying. Your face is all wet. Why! Don't cry! Don't cry!

RACHEL (*gently*) Do you remember that I told you the lady at the gate had tears of joy in her eyes, when the two, dear, little boys smiled that beautiful smile?

JIMMY Yes.

RACHEL Well, these are tears of joy, honey, that's all—tears of joy.

JIMMY It must be awful queer to have tears of joy, 'cause you're happy. I never did. (*with a sigh*) But, if you say they are, dear Ma Rachel, they must be. You knows everything, don't you?

RACHEL (*sadly*) Some things, honey, some things. (*a silence*)

JIMMY (*sighing happily*) This is the beautiful-est night I ever knew. If you would do just one more thing, it would be lots more beautiful. Will you, Ma Rachel?

RACHEL Well, what, honey?

JIMMY Will you sing—at the piano, I mean, it's lots prettier that way—the little song you used to rock me to sleep by? You know, the one about the "Slumber Boat"?

RACHEL Oh! honey, not tonight. You're too tired. It's bedtime now.

JIMMY (*patting her face with his little hand; wheedlingly*) Please! Ma Rachel, please! pretty please!

RACHEL Well, honey boy, this once, then. Tonight, you shall have the little song—I used to sing you to sleep by (*half to herself*) perhaps, for the last time.

JIMMY Why, Ma Rachel, why the last time?

RACHEL (*shaking her head sadly, goes to the piano; in a whisper*) The last time. (*she twists up her hair into a knot at the back of her head and looks at the keys for a few moments; then she plays the accompaniment of the "Slumber Boat" through softly, and, after a moment, sings. Her voice is full of pent-up longing, and heartbreak, and hopelessness. She ends in a little sob, but attempts to cover it by singing, lightly and daintily, the chorus of "The Owl and the Moon,"... Then softly and with infinite tenderness, almost against her will, she plays and sings again the refrain of "Slumber Boat"*)

  Sail, baby, sail
   Out from that sea,
  Only don't forget to sail
   Back again to me.

(*Presently she rises and goes to* JIMMY, *who is*

Rachel

lolling back happily in the big chair. During the singing, TOM *and* MRS. LOVING *apparently do not listen; when she sobs, however,* TOM's *hand on his paper tightens;* MRS. LOVING's *needle poises for a moment in mid-air. Neither looks at* RACHEL. JIMMY *evidently has not noticed the sob*).

RACHEL (*kneeling by* JIMMY) Well, honey, how did you like it?

JIMMY (*proceeding to pull down her hair from the twist*) It was lovely, Ma Rachel. (*yawns audibly*) Now, Ma Rachel, I'm just beautifully sleepy. (*dreamily*) I think that p'r'aps I'll go to the Land of Laughter tonight in my dreams. I'll go in the "Slumber Boat" and come back in the morning and tell you all about it. Shall I?

RACHEL Yes, honey. (*whispers*)

> Only don't forget to sail
> Back again to me.

TOM (*suddenly*) Rachel! (RACHEL *starts slightly*). I nearly forgot. John is coming here tonight to see how you are. He told me to tell you so.

RACHEL (*stiffens perceptibly, then in different tones*) Very well. Thank you. (*suddenly with a little cry she puts her arms around Jimmy*) Jimmy! honey! don't go tonight. Don't go without Ma Rachel. Wait for me, honey. I do so wish to go, too, to the Land of Laughter. Think of it, Jimmy; nothing but birds always singing, and flowers always blooming, and skies always blue—and people, all of them, always laughing, laughing. You'll wait for Ma Rachel, won't you, honey?

JIMMY Is there really and truly, Ma Rachel, a Land of Laughter?

RACHEL Oh! Jimmy, let's hope so; let's pray so.

JIMMY (*frowns*) I've been thinking—(*pauses*) You have to smile at the gate, don't you, to get in?

RACHEL Yes, honey.

JIMMY Well, I guess I couldn't smile if my Ma Rachel wasn't somewhere close to me. So I couldn't get in after all, could I? Tonight, I'll go somewhere else, and tell you all about it. And then, some day, we'll go together, won't we?

RACHEL (*sadly*) Yes, honey, some day—some day. (*a short silence*) Well, this isn't going to "sleepy-sleep," is it? Go, now, and say good-night to Ma Loving and Uncle Tom.

JIMMY (*gets down obediently, and goes first to* MRS. LOVING. *She leans over, and he puts his little arms around her neck. They kiss; very sweetly*) Sweet dreams! God keep you all the night!

MRS. LOVING The sweetest of sweet dreams to you, dear little boy! Good-night! (RACHEL *watches, unwatched, the scene. Her eyes are full of yearning*)

JIMMY (*going to* TOM, *who makes believe he does not see him*) Uncle Tom!

TOM (*jumps as though tremendously startled;* JIMMY *laughs*) My! how you frightened me. You'll put my gizzard out of commission, if you do that often. Well, sir, what can I do for you?

JIMMY I came to say good-night.

TOM (*gathering* JIMMY *up in his arms and kissing him; gently and with emotion*) Good-night, dear little Big Fellow! Good-night!

JIMMY Sweet dreams! God keep you all the night! (*goes sedately to* RACHEL, *and holds out his little hand*). I'm ready, Ma Rachel. (*yawns*) I'm so nice and sleepy.

RACHEL (*with* JIMMY's *hand in hers, she hesitates a moment, and then approaches* TOM *slowly. For a short time she stands looking down at him; suddenly leaning over him*) Why, Tom, what a pretty tie! Is it new?

TOM Well, no, not exactly. I've had it about a month. It is rather a beauty, isn't it?

RACHEL Why, I never remember seeing it.

TOM (*laughing*) I guess not. I saw to that.

RACHEL Stingy!

TOM Well, I am—where my ties are concerned. I've had experience.

RACHEL (*tentatively*) Tom!

TOM Well?

RACHEL (*nervously and wistfully*) Are you—will you—I mean, won't you be be home this evening?

TOM You've got a long memory, Sis. I've that engagement, you know. Why?

RACHEL (*slowly*) I forgot; so you have.

TOM Why?

RACHEL (*hastily*) Oh! nothing—nothing. Come on, Jimmy boy, you can hardly keep those little peepers open, can you? Come on, honey. (RACHEL *and* JIMMY *go out the rear doorway. There is a silence*)

MRS. LOVING (*slowly, as though thinking aloud*) I try to make out what could have happened; but it's no use—I can't. Those four days, she lay in bed hardly moving, scarcely speaking. Only her eyes seemed alive. I never saw such a wide, tragic look in my life. It was as though her soul had been mortally wounded. But how? how? What could have happened?

TOM (*quietly*) I don't know. She generally tells me everything; but she avoids me now. If we are alone in a room—she gets out. I don't know what it means.

MRS. LOVING She will hardly let Jimmy out of her sight. While he's at school, she's nervous and excited. She seems always to be listening, but for what? When he returns, she nearly devours him. And she always asks him in a frightened sort of way, her face as pale and tense as can be: "Well, honey boy, how was school today?" And he always answers, "Fine, Ma Rachel, fine! I learned—"; and then he goes on to tell her everything that has happened. And when he has finished, she says in an uneasy sort of way: "Is—is that all?" And when he says "Yes," she relaxes and becomes limp. After a little while she becomes feverishly happy. She plays with Jimmy and the children more than ever she did—and she played a good deal, as you know. They're here, or she's with them. Yesterday, I said in remonstrance, when she came in, her face pale and haggard and black hollows under her eyes: "Rachel, remember you're just out of a sick-bed. You're not well enough to go on like this." "I know," was all she would say, "but I've got to. I can't help myself. This part of their little lives must be happy—it just must be." (*pauses*) The last couple of nights, Jimmy has awakened and cried most pitifully. She wouldn't let me go to him; said I had enough trouble, and she could quiet him. She never will let me know why he cries; but she stays with him, and soothes him until, at last, he falls asleep again. Every time she has come out like a rag; and her face is like a dead woman's. Strange isn't it, this is the first time we have ever been able to talk it over? Tom, what could have happened?

TOM I don't know, Ma, but I feel, as you do; something terrible and sudden has hurt her soul; and, poor little thing, she's trying bravely to readjust herself to life again. (*pauses, looks at his watch and then rises, and goes to her. He pats her back awkwardly*) Well, Ma, I'm going now. Don't worry too much. Youth, you, know, gets over things finally. It takes them hard, that's all—. At least, that's what the older heads tell us. (*gets his hat and stands in the vestibule doorway*) Ma, you know, I begin with John tomorrow. (*with emotion*) I don't believe we'll ever forget John. Good-night! (*exit.* MRS. LOVING *continues to sew.* RACHEL, *her hair arranged, reenters through the rear doorway. She is humming*).

RACHEL He's sleeping like a top. Aren't little children, Ma dear, the sweetest things, when they're all helpless and asleep? One little hand is under his cheek; and he's smiling. (*stops suddenly, biting her lips. A pause*) Where's Tom?

MRS. LOVING He went out a few minutes ago.

RACHEL (*sitting in* TOM's *chair and picking up his paper. She is exceedingly nervous. She looks the paper over rapidly; presently trying to make her tone casual*) Ma,—you—you—aren't going anywhere tonight, are you?

MRS. LOVING I've got to go out for a short time about half-past eight. Mrs. Jordan, you know. I'll not be gone very long, though. Why?

RACHEL Oh! nothing particular. I just thought it would be cosy if we could sit here together the rest of the evening. Can't you—can't you go tomorrow?

MRS. LOVING Why, I don't see how I can. I've made the engagement. It's about a new reception gown; and she's exceedingly exacting, as you know. I can't afford to lose her.

RACHEL No, I suppose not. All right, Ma dear. (*presently, paper in hand, she laughs, but not quite naturally*) Look! Ma dear! How is that for fashion, anyway? Isn't it the "limit"? (*rises and shows her mother a picture in the paper. As she is in the act, the bell rings. With a startled cry*) Oh! (*drops the paper, and grips her mother's hand*)

MRS. LOVING (*anxiously*) Rachel, your nerves are right on edge; and your hand feels like fire. I'll have to see a doctor about you; and that's all there is to it.

RACHEL (*laughing nervously, and moving toward the vestibule*) Nonsense, Ma dear! Just because I let out a whoop now and then, and have nice warm hands? (*goes out, is heard talking through the tube*) Yes! (*her voice emitting tremendous relief*) Oh! bring it right up! (*appearing in the doorway*) Ma dear, did you buy anything at Goddard's today?

MRS. LOVING Yes; and I've been wondering why they were so late in delivering it. I bought it early this morning. (RACHEL *goes out again. A door opens and shuts. She reappears with a bundle*)

MRS. LOVING Put it on my bed, Rachel, please. (*exit* RACHEL *rear doorway; presently returns empty-handed; sits down again at the table with the paper between herself and mother; sinks in a deep revery. Suddenly there is the sound of many loud knocks made by numerous small fists.* RACHEL *drops the paper, and comes to a sitting posture, tense again. Her mother looks at her, but says nothing. Almost immediately* RACHEL *relaxes*).

RACHEL My kiddies! They're late, this evening. (*goes out into the vestibule. A door opens and shuts. There is the shrill, excited sound of childish voices.* RACHEL *comes in surrounded by the children, all trying to say something to her at once.* RACHEL *puts her finger on her lip and points toward the doorway in the rear. They all quiet down. She sits on the floor in the front of the stage, and the children all cluster around her. Their conversation takes place in a half-whisper. As they enter they nod brightly at* MRS. LOVING, *who smiles in return*) Why so late, kiddies? It's long past "sleepy-time."

LITTLE NANCY We've been playing "Hide and Seek," and having the mostest fun. We promised, all of us, that if we could play until half-past seven tonight we wouldn't make any fuss about going to bed at seven o'clock the rest of the week. It's awful hard to go. I *hate* to go to bed!

LITTLE MARY, LOUISE and EDITH So do I! So do I! So do I!

LITTLE MARTHA I don't. I love bed. My bed, after my muzzer tucks me all in, is like a nice warm bag. I just stick my nose out. When I lifts my head up I can see the light from the dining-room come in the door. I can hear my muzzer and fazzer talking nice and low; and then, before I know it, I'm fast asleep, and I dream pretty things, and in about a minute it's morning again. I love my little bed, and I love to dream.

LITTLE MARY (*aggressively*) Well, I guess I love to dream too. I wish I could dream, though, without going to bed.

LITTLE NANCY When I grow up, I'm never going to bed at night! (*darkly*) You see.

LITTLE LOUISE "Grown-ups" just love to poke their heads out of windows and cry, "Child'run, it's time for bed now; and you'd better hurry, too, I can tell you." They "sure" are queer, for sometimes when I wake up, it must be about twelve o'clock, I can hear my big sister giggling and talking to some silly man. If it's good for me to go to bed early—I should think—

RACHEL (*interrupting suddenly*) Why, where is my little Jenny? Excuse me, Louise dear.

LITTLE MARTHA Her cold is awful bad. She coughs like this (*giving a distressing imitation*) and snuffles all the time. She can't talk out loud, and she can't go to sleep. Muzzer says she's fev'rish—I thinks that's what she says. Jenny says she knows she could go to sleep, if you would come and sit with her a little while.

RACHEL I certainly will. I'll go when you do, honey.

LITTLE MARTHA (*softly stroking* RACHEL'*s arm*) You're the very nicest "grown-up," (*loyally*) exept my muzzer, of course, I ever knew. You knows all about little chil'run and you can be one, although you're all grown up. I think you would make a lovely muzzer. (*to the rest of the children*) Don't you?

ALL (*in excited whispers*) Yes, I do.

RACHEL (*winces, then says gently*) Come, kiddies, you must go now, or your mothers will blame me for keeping you. (*rises, as do the rest.* LITTLE MARTHA *puts her hand into* RACHEL'*s*) Ma dear, I'm going down to sit a little while with Jenny. I'll be back before you go, though. Come, kiddies, say good-night to my mother.

ALL (*gravely*) Good-night! Sweet dreams! God keep you all the night.

MRS. LOVING Good-night dears! Sweet dreams, all!

(*Exeunt* RACHEL *and the children.* MRS. LOVING *continues to sew. The bell presently rings three distinct times. In a few moments,* MRS. LOVING *gets up and goes out into the vestibule. A door opens and closes.* MRS. LOVING *and* JOHN STRONG *come in. He is a trifle pale but his imperturbable self.* MRS. LOVING, *somewhat nervous, takes her seat and resumes her sewing. She motions* STRONG *to a chair. He returns to the vestibule, leaves his hat, returns, and sits down*).

STRONG Well, how is everything?

MRS. LOVING Oh! about the same, I guess. Tom's out. John, we'll never forget you—and your kindness.

STRONG That was nothing. And Rachel?

MRS. LOVING—She'll be back presently. She went to sit with a sick child for a little while.

STRONG And how is she?

MRS. LOVING She's not herself yet, but I think she is better.

STRONG (*after a short pause*) Well, what *did* happen—exactly?

MRS. LOVING That's just what I don't know.

STRONG When you came home—you couldn't get in—was that it?

MRS. LOVING Yes. (*pauses*) It was just a week ago today. I was down town all the morning. It was about one o'clock when I got back. I had forgotten my key. I rapped on the door and then called. There was no answer. A window was open, and I could feel the air under the door, and I could hear it as the draught sucked it through. There was no other sound. Presently I made such a noise the people began to come out into the hall. Jimmy was in one of the flats playing with a little girl named Mary. He told me he had left Rachel here a short time before. She had given him four cookies, two for him and two for Mary, and had told him he could play with her until she came to tell him his lunch was ready. I saw he was getting frightened, so I got the little girl and her mother to keep him in their flat. Then, as no man was at home, I sent out for help. Three men broke the door down. (*pauses*) We found Rachel unconscious, lying on her face. For a few minutes I thought she was dead. (*pauses*). A vase had fallen over on the table and the water had dripped through the cloth and onto the floor. There had been flowers in it. When I left, there were no flowers here. What she could have done to them, I can't say. The long stems were lying everywhere, and the flowers had been ground into the floor. I could tell that they must have been roses from the stems. After we had put her to bed and called the doctor, and she had finally regained consciousness, I very naturally asked her what had happened. All she would say was, "Ma dear, I'm too—tired—please." For four days she lay in bed scarcely moving, speaking only when spoken to. That first day, when Jimmy came in to see her, she shrank away from him. We had to take him out, and comfort him as best we could. We kept him away, almost by force, until she got up. And, then, she was utterly miserable when he was out of her sight. What happened, I don't know. She avoids Tom, and she won't tell me. (*pauses*) Tom and I both believe her soul has been hurt. The trouble isn't with her body. You'll find her highly nervous. Sometimes she is very much depressed; again she is feverishly gay—almost reckless. What do you think about it, John?

STRONG (*who has listened quietly*) Had anybody been here, do you know?

MRS. LOVING No, I don't. I don't like to ask Rachel; and I can't ask the neighbors.

STRONG No, of course not. (*pauses*) You say there were some flowers?

MRS. LOVING Yes.

STRONG And the flowers were ground into the carpet?

MRS. LOVING Yes.

STRONG Did you happen to notice the box? They must have come in a box, don't you think?

MRS. LOVING Yes, there was a box in the kitchenette. It was from "Marcy's." I saw no card.

STRONG (*slowly*) It is rather strange. (*a long silence during which the outer door opens and shuts.* RACHEL *is heard singing. She stops abruptly. In a second or two she appears in the door. There is an air of suppressed excitement about her*)

RACHEL Hello! John. (STRONG *rises, nods at her, and brings forward for her the big arm-chair near the fire*) I thought that was your hat in the hall. It's brand new, I know—but it looks—"Johnlike." How are you? Ma! Jenny went to sleep like a little lamb. I don't like her breathing, though. (*looks from one to the other; flippantly*) Who's dead? (*nods her thanks to* STRONG *for the chair and sits down*)

MRS. LOVING Dead, Rachel?

RACHEL Yes. The atmosphere here is so funereal,—it's positively "crapey."

STRONG I don't know why it should be—I was just asking how you are.

RACHEL Heavens! Does the mere inquiry into my health precipitate such an atmosphere? Your two faces were as long, as long—(*breaks off*) Kind sir, let me assure you, I am in the very best of health. And how are you, John?

STRONG Oh! I'm always well. (*sits down*)

MRS. LOVING Rachel, I'll have to get ready to go now. John, don't hurry. I'll be back shortly, probably in three-quarters of an hour—maybe less.

RACHEL And maybe more, if I remember Mrs. Jordan. However, Ma dear, I'll do the best I can—while you are away. I'll try to be a credit to your training. (MRS. LOVING *smiles and goes out the rear doorway*) Now, let's see—in

Rachel

the books of etiquette, I believe, the properly reared young lady, always asks the young gentleman caller—you're young enough, aren't you, to be classed still as a "young gentleman caller?" (*no answer*) Well, anyway, she always asks the young gentleman caller sweetly something about the weather. (*primly*) This has been an exceedingly beautiful day, hasn't it, Mr. Strong? (*No answer from* STRONG, *who, with his head resting against the back of the chair, and his knees crossed is watching her in an amused, quizzical manner*) Well, really, every properly brought up young gentleman, I'm sure, ought to know, that it's exceedingly rude not to answer a civil question.

STRONG (*lazily*) Tell me what to answer, Rachel.

RACHEL Say, "Yes, very"; and look interested and pleased when you say it.

STRONG (*with a half-smile*) Yes, very.

RACHEL Well, I certainly wouldn't characterize that as a particularly animated remark. Besides, when you look at me through half-closed lids like that—and kind of smile—what are you thinking? (*no answer*) John Strong, are you deaf or—just plain stupid?

STRONG Plain stupid, I guess.

RACHEL (*in wheedling tones*) What were you thinking, John?

STRONG (*slowly*) I was thinking—(*breaks off*)

RACHEL (*irritably*) Well?

STRONG I've changed my mind.

RACHEL You're not going to tell me?

STRONG No.

(MRS. LOVING *dressed for the street comes in*)

MRS. LOVING Goodbye, children. Rachel, don't quarrel so much with John. Let me see—if I have my key. (*feels in her bag*) Yes, I have it. I'll be back shortly. Good-bye. (STRONG *and* RACHEL *rise. He bows*)

RACHEL Good-bye, Ma dear. Hurry back as soon as you can, won't you? (*exit* MRS. LOVING *through the vestibule.* STRONG *leans back again in his chair, and watches* RACHEL *through half-closed eyes.* RACHEL *sits in her chair nervously*)

STRONG Do you mind, if I smoke?

RACHEL You know I don't.

STRONG I am trying to behave like—Reginald—"the properly reared young gentleman caller." (*lights a cigar; goes over to the fire, and throws his match away.* RACHEL *goes into the kitchenette, and brings him a saucer for his ashes. She places it on the table near him*) Thank you. (*they both sit again,* STRONG *very evidently enjoying his cigar and* RACHEL) Now this is what I call cosy.

RACHEL Cosy! Why?

STRONG A nice warm room—shut in—curtains drawn—a cheerful fire crackling at my back—a lamp, not an electric or gas one, but one of your plain, old-fashioned kerosene ones—

RACHEL (*interrupting*) Ma dear would like to catch you, I am sure, talking about *her* lamp like that. "Old-fashioned! plain!"—You have nerve.

STRONG (*continuing as though he had not been interrupted*) A comfortable chair—a good cigar—and not very far away, a little lady, who is looking charming, so near, that if I reached over, I could touch her. You there—and I here.—It's living.

RACHEL Well! of all things! A compliment—and from *you*! How did it slip out, pray? (*no answer*) I suppose that you realize that a conversation between two persons is absolutely impossible, if one has to do her share all alone. Soon my ingenuity for introducing interesting subjects will be exhausted; and then will follow what, I believe, the story books call, "an uncomfortable silence."

STRONG (*slowly*) Silence—between friends—isn't such a bad thing.

RACHEL Thanks awfully. (*leans back; cups her cheek in her hand, and makes no pretense at further conversation. The old look of introspection returns to her eyes. She does not move*)

STRONG (*quietly*) Rachel! (RACHEL *starts perceptibly*) You must remember I'm here. I don't like looking into your soul—when you forget you're not alone.

RACHEL I hadn't forgotten.

STRONG Wouldn't it be easier for you, little girl, if you could tell—some one?

RACHEL No (*a silence*)

STRONG Rachel,—you're fond of flowers,—aren't you?

RACHEL Yes.

STRONG Rosebuds—red rosebuds—particularly?

RACHEL (*nervously*) Yes.

STRONG Did you—dislike—the giver?

RACHEL (*more nervously; bracing herself*) No, of course not.

STRONG Rachel,—why—why—did you—kill the roses—then?

RACHEL (*twisting her hands*) Oh, John! I'm so sorry, Ma dear told you that. She didn't know, you sent them.

STRONG So I gathered. (*pauses and then leans forward; quietly*) Rachel, little girl, why—did you kill them?

RACHEL (*breathing quickly*) Don't you believe —it—a—a—kindness—sometimes—to kill?

STRONG (*after a pause*) You—considered—it —a—kindness—to kill them?

RACHEL Yes. (*another pause*)

STRONG Do you mean—just—the roses?

RACHEL (*breathing more quickly*) John!—Oh! must I say?

STRONG Yes, little Rachel.

RACHEL (*in a whisper*) No. (*there is a long pause.* RACHEL *leans back limply, and closes her eyes. Presently* STRONG *rises, and moves his chair very close to hers. She does not stir. He puts his cigar on the saucer*)

STRONG (*leaning forward; very gently*) Little girl, little girl, can't you tell me why?

RACHEL (*wearily*) I can't.—It hurts—too much—to talk about it yet,—please.

STRONG (*takes her hand; looks at it a few minutes and then at her quietly*) You—don't—care, then? (*she winces*) Rachel!—Look at me, little girl! (*as if against her will, she looks at him. Her eyes are fearful, hunted. She tries to look away, to draw away her hand; but he holds her gaze and her hand steadily*) Do you?

RACHEL (*almost sobbing*) John! John! don't ask me. You are drawing my very soul out of my body with your eyes. You must not talk this way. You mustn't look—John, don't! (*tries to shield her eyes*)

STRONG (*quietly takes both of her hands, and kisses the backs and the palms slowly. A look of horror creeps into her face. He deliberately raises his eyes and looks at her mouth. She recoils as though she expected him to strike her. He resumes slowly*) If—you—do—care, and I know now—that you do—nothing else, *nothing should count.*

RACHEL (*wrenching herself from his grasp and rising. She covers her ears; she breathes rapidly*) No! No! No!—You *must* stop. (*laughs nervously; continues feverishly*) I'm not behaving very well as a hostess, am I? Let's see. What shall I do? I'll play you something, John. How will that do? Or I'll sing to you. You used to like to hear me sing; you said my voice, I remember, was sympathetic, didn't you? (*moves quickly to the piano*). I'll sing you a pretty little song. I think it's beautiful. You've never heard it, I know. I've never sung it to you before. It's Nevin's "At Twilight." (*pauses, looks down, before she begins, then turns toward him and says quietly and sweetly*) Sometimes—in the coming years—I want—you to remember—I sang you this little song.—Will you?—I think it will make it easier for me—when I—when I— (*breaks off and begins the first chords.* STRONG *goes slowly to the piano. He leans there watching intently.* RACHEL *sings*)

> The roses of yester-year
>   Were all of the white and red;
> It fills my heart with silent fear
>   To find all their beauty fled.
>
> The roses of white are sere,
>   All faded the roses red,
> And one who loves me is not here
>   And one that I love is dead.

(*A long pause. Then* STRONG *goes to her and lifts her from the piano-stool. He puts one arm around her very tenderly and pushes her head back so he can look into her eyes. She shuts them, but is passive*).

STRONG (*gently*) Little girl, little girl, don't you know that suggestions—suggestions—like those you are sending yourself constantly—are wicked things? You, who are so gentle, so loving, so warm—(*breaks off and crushes her to him. He kisses her many times. She does not resist, but in the midst of his caresses she breaks suddenly into convulsive laughter. He tries to hush the terrible sound with his mouth; then brokenly*) Little girl—don't laugh—like that.

RACHEL (*interrupted throughout by her laughter*) I have to.—God is laughing.—We're his puppets.—He pulls the wires,—and we're so funny to Him.—I'm laughing too—because I can hear—my little children—weeping. They come to me generally while I'm asleep,—but I can hear them now.—They've begged me—do you understand?—begged me—not to bring them here;—and I've promised them—not to. —I've promised. I can't stand the sound of their crying.—I have to laugh—Oh! John! laugh!—laugh too!—I can't drown their weeping.

(STRONG *picks her up bodily and carries her to the armchair*)

STRONG (*harshly*) Now, stop that!

RACHEL (*in sheer surprise*) W-h-a-t?

STRONG (*still harshly*) Stop that!—You've lost your self-control.—Find yourself again!

(*He leaves her and goes over to the fireplace, and stands looking down into it for some little time.* RACHEL, *little by little, becomes calmer.* STRONG *returns and sits beside her again. She doesn't move. He smoothes her hair back gently, and kisses her forehead—and then, slowly, her mouth. She does not resist; simply sits there, with shut eyes, inert, limp*)

STRONG Rachel! (*pauses*) There is a little flat on 43rd Street. It faces south and overlooks a little park. Do you remember it?—it's on the top floor?—Once I remember your saying—you liked it. That was over a year ago. That same day—I rented it. I've never lived there. No one knows about it—not even my mother. It's completely furnished now—and waiting—do you know for whom? Every single thing in it, I've bought myself—even to the pins on the little bird's eye maple dresser. It has been the happiest year I have ever known. I furnished it—one room at a time. It's the prettiest, the most homelike little flat I've ever seen. (*very low*) Everything there—breathes love. Do you know for whom it is waiting? On the sitting-room floor is a beautiful, Turkish rug—red, and blue and gold. It's soft—and rich—and do you know for whose little feet it is waiting? There are delicate curtains at the windows and a bookcase full of friendly, eager, little books.—Do you know for whom they are waiting? There are comfortable leather chairs, just the right size and a beautiful piano—that I leave open—sometimes, and lovely pictures of Madonnas. Do you know for whom they are waiting? There is an open fireplace with logs of wood, all carefully piled on gleaming andirons—and waiting. There is a bellows and a pair of shining tongs—waiting. And in the kitchenette painted blue and white, and smelling sweet with paint is everything: bright pots and pans and kettles, and blue and white enamel-ware, and all kinds of knives and forks and spoons—and on the door—a roller-towel. Little girl, do you know for whom they are all waiting? And somewhere—there's a big, strong man—with broad shoulders. And he's willing and anxious to do anything—everything, and he's waiting very patiently. Little girl, is it to be—yes or no?

RACHEL (*during* STRONG's *speech life has come flooding back to her. Her eyes are shining; her face, eager. For a moment she is beautifully happy*) Oh! you're too good to me and mine, John. I—didn't dream any one—could be—so good. (*leans forward and puts his big hand against her cheek and kisses it shyly*)

STRONG (*quietly*) Is it—yes—or no, little girl?

RACHEL (*feverishly, gripping his hands*) Oh, yes! yes! yes! and take me quickly, John. Take me before I can think any more. You mustn't let me think, John. And you'll be good to me, won't you? Every second of every minute, of every hour, of every day, you'll have me in your thoughts, won't you? And you'll be with me every minute that you can? And, John, John!—you'll keep away the weeping of my little children. You won't let me hear it, will you? You'll make me forget everything everything—won't you?—Life is so short, John. (*shivers and then fearfully and slowly*) And eternity so—long. (*feverishly again*) And, John, after I am dead—promise me, promise me you'll love me more. (*shivers again*) I'll need love then. Oh! I'll need it. (*suddenly there comes to their ears the sound of a child's weeping. It is monotonous, hopeless, terribly afraid. Rachel recoils*) Oh! John!—Listen!—It's my boy, again.—I—John—I'll be back in a little while. (*goes swiftly to the door in the rear, pauses and looks back. The weeping continues. Her eyes are tragic. Slowly she kisses her hand to him and disappears.* JOHN *stands where she has left him looking down. The weeping stops. Presently* RACHEL *appears in the doorway. She is haggard, and grey. She does not enter the room. She speaks as one dead might speak—tonelessly, slowly*)

RACHEL Do you wish to know why Jimmy is crying?

STRONG Yes.

RACHEL I am twenty-two—and I'm old; you're thirty-two—and you're old; Tom's twenty-three—and he is old. Ma dear's sixty—and she said once she is much older than that. She is. We are all blighted; we are all accursed—all of us—, everywhere, we whose skins are dark—our lives blasted by the white man's prejudice. (*pauses*) And my little Jimmy—seven years old, that's all—is blighted too. In a year or two, at best, he will be made old by suffering.

(*pauses*) One week ago, today, some white boys, older and larger than my little Jimmy, as he was leaving the school—called him "Nigger"! They chased him through the streets calling him, "Nigger! Nigger! Nigger!" One boy threw stones at him. There is still a bruise on his little back where one struck him. That will get well; but they bruised his soul—and that—will never—get well. He asked me what "Nigger" meant. I made light of the whole thing, laughed it off. He went to his little playmates, and very naturally asked them. The oldest of them is nine!—and they knew, poor little things—and they told him. (*pauses*) For the last couple of nights he has been dreaming—about these boys. And he always awakes—in the dark—afraid—afraid—of the now—and the future—I have seen that look of deadly fear—in the eyes—of other little children. I know what it is myself.—I was twelve—when some big boys chased me and called me names.—I never left the house afterwards—without being afraid. I was afraid, in the streets—in the school—in the church, everywhere, always, afraid of being hurt. And I—was not—afraid in vain. (*the weeping begins again*) He's only a baby—and he's blighted. (*to* JIMMY) Honey, I'm right here. I'm coming in just a minute. Don't cry. (*to* STRONG) If it nearly kills me to hear my Jimmy's crying, do you think I could stand it, when my own child, flesh of my flesh, blood of my blood—learned the same reason for weeping? Do you? (*pauses*) Ever since I fell here—a week ago—I am afraid—to go—to sleep, for every time I do—my children come—and beg me—weeping—not to—bring them here—to suffer. Tonight, they came—when I was awake. (*pauses*) I have promised them again, now—by Jimmy's bed. (*in a whisper*) I have damned—my soul to all eternity—if I do. (*to* JIMMY) Honey, don't! I'm coming. (*to* STRONG) And John,—dear John—you see—it can never be—all the beautiful, beautiful things—you have—told me about. (*wistfully*) No—they—can never be—now. (STRONG *comes toward her*) No,—John dear,—you—must not—touch me—any more. (*pauses*) Dear, this—is—"Good-bye."

STRONG (*quietly*) It's not fair—to you, Rachel, to take you—at your word—tonight. You're sick; you've brooded so long, so continuously,—you've lost—your perspective. Don't answer, yet. Think it over for another week and I'll come back.

RACHEL (*wearily*) No,—I can't think—any more.

STRONG You realize—fully—you're sending me—for always?

RACHEL Yes.

STRONG And you care?

RACHEL Yes.

STRONG It's settled, then for all time—"Good-bye!"

RACHEL (*after a pause*) Yes.

STRONG (*stands looking at her steadily a long time, and then moves to the door and turns, facing her; with infinite tenderness*) Good-bye, dear, little Rachel—God bless you.

RACHEL Good-bye, John! (STRONG *goes out. A door opens and shuts. There is finality in the sound. The weeping continues. Suddenly; with a great cry*) John! John! (*runs out into the vestibule. She presently returns. She is calm again. Slowly*) No! No! John. Not for us. (*a pause; with infinite yearning*) Oh! John,—if it only—if it only— (*breaks off, controls herself. Slowly again; thoughtfully*) No—No sunshine—no laughter—always—darkness. That is it. Even our little flat— (*in a whisper*) John's and mine—the little flat—that calls, calls us—through darkness. It shall wait—and wait—in vain—in darkness. Oh, John! (*pauses*) And my little children! my little children! (*the weeping ceases; pauses*) I shall never—see—you—now. Your little, brown, beautiful bodies—I shall never see.—Your dimples—everywhere—your laughter—your tears—the beautiful, lovely feel of you here. (*puts her hands against her heart*) Never—never—to be. (*a pause, fiercely*) But you are somewhere—and wherever you are you are mine! You are mine! All of you! Every bit of you! Even God can't take you away. (*a pause; very sweetly; pathetically*) Little children!—My little children!—No more need you come to me—weeping—weeping. You may be happy now—you are safe. Little weeping, voices, hush! hush! (*the weeping begins again. To* JIMMY, *her whole soul in her voice*) Jimmy! My little Jimmy! Honey! I'm coming.—Ma Rachel loves you so. (*sobs and goes blindly, unsteadily to the rear doorway; she leans her head there one second against the door; and then stumbles through and disappears. The light in the lamp flickers and goes out.... It is black. The terrible, heartbreaking weeping continues.*)

Alice Dunbar-Nelson (1875–1935)

Mine Eyes Have Seen

1918

Published in the last months of World War I by the widow of the poet Paul Lawrence Dunbar, *Mine Eyes Have Seen* is an examination of the loyalty the Negro owes to a nation that offers no loyalty to him.

The appearance of this play during wartime certainly had a double edge. On one hand Mrs. Dunbar-Nelson is warning white America that black soldiers will fight only for a "do right" nation. On the other hand, she is assuring America that the black soldier will revenge German atrocities (crucifying children, raping girls, and so on). The author does not mention one war rumor—that the "Huns" were cutting off the hands of Belgian children.

In 1973 the author's niece, Pauline Young, recalled in an interview that her aunt "taught us English in the high school. She produced her play and we all took parts. The audience loved it . . . but nobody would publish it."

Alice Dunbar-Nelson, in addition to her poetry and fiction, wrote a column in the Pittsburg *Courier*. A member of the American Friends Peace Committee, she traveled the country delivering militant political speeches.

Nonetheless, she must have felt frustration with the traditional role of women in wartime, which is reflected in her poem "I Sit and Sew."

. . .

The little useless seam, the idle patch;
Why dream I here beneath my homely thatch,
When there they lie in sodden mud and rain,
Pitifully calling me, the quick ones and the slain?
You need me, Christ! It is no roseate dream
That beckons me—this pretty futile seam,
It stifles me—God, must I sit and sew?

The ending of the play has been left open for the reader to supply. Has the author "loaded" the play so the reader must supply the ending that the author wishes?

Mine Eyes Have Seen

CAST OF CHARACTERS

DAN, *the cripple*
CHRIS, *the younger brother*
LUCY, *the sister*
MRS. O'NEILL, *an Irish neighbor*
JAKE, *a Jewish boy*
JULIA, *Chris' sweetheart*
BILL HARVEY, *a muleteer*
CORNELIA LEWIS, *a settlement worker*

TIME *Now*
PLACE *A manufacturing city in the northern part of the United States.*

(SCENE: *Kitchen of a tenement. All details of furnishing emphasize sordidness—laundry tubs, range, table covered with oil cloth, pine chairs. Curtain discloses* DAN *in a rude imitation of a steamer chair, propped by faded pillows, his feet covered with a patch-work quilt.*

LUCY *is bustling about the range preparing a meal. During the conversation she moves from range to table, setting latter and making ready the noon-day meal.*

DAN *is about thirty years old; face thin, pinched, bearing traces of suffering. His hair is prematurely grey; nose finely chiselled; eyes wide, as if seeing BEYOND. Complexion brown.*

LUCY *is slight, frail, brown-skinned, about twenty, with a pathetic face. She walks with a slight limp.*)

DAN Isn't it most time for him to come home, Lucy?
LUCY It's hard to tell, Danny, dear; Chris doesn't come home on time any more. It's half-past twelve, and he ought to be here by the clock, but you can't tell any more—you can't tell.
DAN Where does he go?
LUCY I know where he doesn't go, Dan, but where he does, I can't say. He's not going to Julia's any more lately. I'm afraid, Dan, I'm afraid!
DAN Of what, Little Sister?
LUCY Of everything; oh, Dan, it's too big, too much for me—the world outside, the street —Chris going out and coming home nights moody-eyed; I don't understand.
DAN And so you're afraid? That's been the trouble from the beginning of time—we're afraid because we don't understand.
LUCY (*coming down front, with a dish cloth in her hand*) Oh, Dan, wasn't it better in the old days when we were back home—in the little house with the garden, and you and father coming home nights and mother getting supper, and Chris and I studying lessons in the dining-room at the table—we didn't have to eat and live in the kitchen then, and—
DAN (*grimly*) —And the notices posted on the fence for us to leave town because niggers had no business having such a decent home.
LUCY (*unheeding the interruption*) —And Chris and I reading the wonderful books and laying our plans—
DAN —To see them go up in the smoke of our burned home.
LUCY (*continuing, her back to* DAN, *her eyes lifted, as if seeing a vision of retrospect*) —And everyone petting me because I had hurt my foot when I was little, and father—
DAN —Shot down like a dog for daring to defend his home—
LUCY —Calling me "Little Brown Princess," and telling mother—
DAN —Dead of pneumonia and heartbreak in this bleak climate.
LUCY —That when you—
DAN —Maimed for life in a factory of hell! Useless—useless—broken on the wheel. (*his voice breaks in a dry sob*)
LUCY (*coming out of her trance, throws aside the dish-cloth, and running to* DAN, *lays her cheek against his and strokes his hair*) Poor Danny, poor Danny, forgive me, I'm selfish.

DAN Not selfish, Little Sister, merely natural.

(*Enter roughly and unceremoniously* CHRIS. *He glances at the two with their arms about each other, shrugs his shoulders, hangs up his rough cap and mackinaw on a nail, then seats himself at the table, his shoulders hunched up; his face dropping on his hand.* LUCY *approaches him timidly*)

LUCY Tired, Chris?
CHRIS No.
LUCY Ready for dinner?
CHRIS If it is ready for me.
LUCY (*busies herself bringing dishes to the table*) You're late to-day.
CHRIS I have bad news. My number was posted today.
LUCY Number? Posted? (*pauses with a plate in her hand*)
CHRIS I'm drafted.
LUCY (*drops plate with a crash.* DAN *leans forward tensely, his hands gripping the arms of his chair*) Oh, it can't be! They won't take you from us! And shoot you down, too? What will Dan do?
DAN Never mind about me, Sister. And you're drafted, boy?
CHRIS Yes—yes—but—(*he rises and strikes the table heavily with his hand*) I'm not going.
DAN Your duty—
CHRIS —Is here with you. I owe none elsewhere, I'll pay none.
LUCY Chris! Treason! I'm afraid!
CHRIS Yes, of course, you're afraid, Little Sister, why shouldn't you be? Haven't you had your soul shrivelled with fear since we were driven like dogs from our home? And for what? Because we were living like Christians. Must I go and fight for the nation that let my father's murder go unpunished? That killed my mother—that took away my chances for making a man out of myself? Look at us—you—Dan, a shell of a man—
DAN Useless—useless—
LUCY Hush, Chris!
CHRIS —And me, with a fragment of an education, and no chance—only half a man. And you, poor Little Sister, there's no chance for you; what is there in life for you? No, if others want to fight, let them. I'll claim exemption.
DAN On what grounds?

CHRIS You—and Sister. I am all you have; I support you.
DAN (*half rising in his chair*) Hush! Have I come to this, that I should be the excuse, the woman's skirts for a slacker to hide behind?
CHRIS (*clenching his fists*) You call me that? You, whom I'd lay down my life for? I'm no slacker when I hear the real call of duty. Shall I desert the cause that needs me—you—Sister—home? For a fancied glory? Am I to take up the cause of a lot of kings and politicians who play with men's souls, as if they are cards—dealing them out, a hand here, in the Somme—a hand there, in Palestine—a hand there, in the Alps—a hand there, in Russia—and because the cards don't match well, call it a misdeal, gather them up, throw them in the discard, and call for a new deal of a million human, suffering souls? And must I be the Deuce of Spades?

(*During the speech, the door opens slowly and* JAKE *lounges in. He is a slight, pale youth, Hebraic, thin-lipped, eager-eyed. His hands are in his pockets, his narrow shoulders drawn forward. At the end of* CHRIS' *speech he applauds softly*)

JAKE Bravo! You've learned the patter well. Talk like the fellows at the Socialist meetings.
DAN and LUCY Socialist meetings!
CHRIS (*defiantly*) Well?
DAN Oh, nothing; it explains. All right, go on—any more?
JAKE Guess he's said all he's got breath for. I'll go; it's too muggy in here. What's the row?
CHRIS I'm drafted.
JAKE Get exempt. Easy—if you don't want to go. As for me—

(*Door opens, and* MRS. O'NEILL *bustles in. She is in deep mourning, plump, Irish, shrewd-looking, bright-eyed*)

MRS. O'NEILL Lucy, they do be sayin' as how down by the chain stores they be a raid on the potatoes, an' ef ye're wantin' some, ye'd better be after gittin' into yer things an' comin' wid me. I kin kape the crowd off yer game foot—an' what's the matter wid youse all?
LUCY Oh, Mrs. O'Neill, Chris has got to go to war.
MRS. O'NEILL An' ef he has, what of it? Ye'll starve, that's all.
DAN Starve? Never! He'll go, we'll live.

(LUCY *wrings her hands impotently.* MRS. O'NEILL *drops a protecting arm about the girl's shoulder*)

MRS. O'NEILL   An' it's hard it seems to yer? But they took me man from me year before last, an' he wint afore I came over here, an' it's a widder I am wid me five kiddies, an' I've niver a word to say but—

CHRIS   He went to fight for his own. What do they do for my people? They don't want us, except in extremity. They treat us like—like—like—

JAKE   Like Jews in Russia, eh? (*he slouches forward, then his frame straightens itself electrically*) Like Jews in Russia, eh? Denied the right of honor in men, eh? Or the right of virtue in women, eh? There isn't a wrong you can name that your race has endured that mine has not suffered, too. But there's a future, Chris—a big one. We younger ones must be in that future—ready for it, ready for it— (*his voice trails off, and he sinks despondently into a chair*)

CHRIS   Future? Where? Not in this country? Where?

(*The door opens and* JULIA *rushes in impulsively. She is small, slightly built, eager-eyed, light-brown skin, wealth of black hair; full of sudden shyness.*)

JULIA   Oh, Chris, someone has just told me—I was passing by—one of the girls said your number was called. Oh, Chris, will you have to go? (*she puts her arms up to* CHRIS' *neck; he removes them gently, and makes a slight gesture toward* DAN's *chair*)

JULIA   Oh, I forgot. Dan, excuse me. Lucy, it's terrible, isn't it?

CHRIS   I'm not going, Julia.

MRS. O'NEILL   Not going!

DAN   Our men have always gone, Chris. They went in 1776.

CHRIS   Yes, as slaves. Promised a freedom they never got.

DAN   No, gladly, and saved the day, too, many a time. Ours was the first blood shed on the altar of National liberty. We went in 1812, on land and sea. Our men were through the struggles of 1861—

CHRIS   When the Nation was afraid not to call them. Didn't want 'em at first.

DAN   Never mind; they helped work out their own salvation. And they were there in 1898—

CHRIS   Only to have their valor disputed.

DAN   —And they were at Carrizal, my boy, and now—

MRS. O'NEILL   An' sure, wid a record like that—ah, 'tis me ould man who said at first 'twasn't his quarrel. His Oireland bled an' the work of thim divils to try to make him a traitor nearly broke his heart—but he said he'd go to do his bit—an' here I am.

(*There is a sound of noise and bustle without, and with a loud laugh,* BILL HARVEY *enters. He is big, muscular, rough, his voice thunderous. He emits cries of joy at seeing the group, shakes hands and claps* CHRIS *and* DAN *on their backs.*)

DAN   And so you weren't torpedoed?

HARVEY   No, I'm here for a while—to get more mules and carry them to the front to kick their bit.

MRS. O'NEILL   You've been—over there?

HARVEY   Yes, over the top, too. Mules, rough-necks, wires, mud, dead bodies, stench, terror!

JULIA (*horror-stricken*)   Ah—Chris!

CHRIS   Never, mind, not for mine.

HARVEY   It's a great life—not. But I'm off again, first chance.

MRS. O'NEILL   They're brutes, eh?

HARVEY   Don't remind me.

MRS. O'NEILL (*whispering*)   They maimed my man, before he died.

JULIA (*clinging to* CHRIS)   Not you, oh, not you!

HARVEY   They crucified children.

DAN   Little children? They crucified little children.

CHRIS   Well, what's that to us? They're little white children. But here our fellow-countrymen throw our little black babies in the flames—as did the worshippers of Moloch, only they haven't the excuse of a religious rite.

JAKE (*slouches out of his chair, in which he has been sitting brooding*)   Say, don't you get tired sitting around grieving because you're colored? I'd be ashamed to be—

DAN   Stop! Who's ashamed of his race? Ours the glorious inheritance; ours the price of achievement. Ashamed! I'm *proud*. And you, too, Chris, smouldering in youthful wrath, you, too, are proud to be numbered with the darker ones, soon to come into their inheritance.

MRS. O'NEILL   Aye, but you've got to fight to

keep yer inheritance. Ye can't lay down when someone else has done the work, and expect it to go on. Ye've got to fight.

JAKE If you're proud, show it. All of your people—well, look at us! Is there a greater race than ours? Have any people had more horrible persecutions—and yet—we're loyal always to the country where we live and serve.

MRS. O'NEILL And us! Look at us!

DAN (*half tears himself from the chair, the upper part of his body writhing, while the lower part is inert, dead*) Oh, God! If I were but whole and strong! If I could only prove to a doubting world of what stuff my people are made!

JULIA But why, Dan, it isn't our quarrel? What have we to do with their affairs? These white people, they hate us. Only today I was sneered at when I went to help with some of their relief work. Why should you, my Chris, go to help those who hate you?

(CHRIS *clasps her in his arms, and they stand, defying the others*)

HARVEY If you could have seen the babies and girls—and old women—if you could have— (*covers his eyes with his hand*)

CHRIS Well, it's good for things to be evened up somewhere.

DAN Hush, Chris! It is not for us to visit retribution. Nor to wish hatred on others. Let us rather remember the good that has come to us. Love of humanity is above the small considerations of time or place or race or sect. Can't you be big enough to feel pity for the little crucified French children—for the ravished Polish girls, even as their mothers must have felt sorrow, if they had known, for *our* burned and maimed little ones? Oh, Mothers of Europe, we be of one blood, you and I!

(*There is a tense silence.* JULIA *turns from* CHRIS, *and drops her hand. He moves slowly to the window and looks out. The door opens quietly, and* CORNELIA LEWIS *comes in. She stands still a moment, as if sensing a difficult situation*)

CORNELIA I've heard about it, Chris, your country calls you. (CHRIS *turns from the window and waves hopeless hands at* DAN *and* LUCY) Yes, I understand; they do need you, *don't* they?

DAN (*fiercely*) No!

LUCY Yes, we do, Chris, we do need you, but your country needs you more. And, above that, your race is calling you to carry on its good name, and with that, the voice of humanity is calling to us all—we can manage without you, Chris.

CHRIS You? Poor little crippled Sister. Poor Dan—

DAN Don't pity me, pity your poor, weak self.

CHRIS (*clenching his fist*) Brother, you've called me two names today that no man ought to have to take—a slacker and a weakling!

DAN True. Aren't you both? (*leans back and looks at* CHRIS *speculatively*)

CHRIS (*makes an angry lunge towards the chair, then flings his hands above his head in an impatient gesture*) Oh, God! (*turns back to window*)

JULIA Chris, it's wicked for them to taunt you so—but Chris—it *is* our country—our race—(*outside the strains of music from a passing band are heard. The music comes faintly, gradually growing louder and louder until it reaches a crescendo. The tune is "The Battle Hymn of the Republic," played in stirring march time*)

DAN (*singing softly*) "Mine eyes have seen the glory of the coming of the Lord!"

CHRIS (*turns from the window and straightens his shoulders*) And mine!

CORNELIA "As He died to make men holy, let us die to make them free!"

MRS. O'NEILL An' ye'll make the sacrifice, me boy, an' ye'll be the happier.

JAKE Sacrifice! No sacrifice for him, it's those who stay behind. Ah, if they would only call me, and call me soon!

LUCY We'll get on, never fear. I'm proud! Proud! (*her voice breaks a little, but her head is thrown back*)

(*As the music draws nearer, the group breaks up, and the whole roomful rushes to the window and looks out.* CHRIS *remains in the center of the floor, rigidly at attention, a rapt look on his face.* DAN *strains at his chair, as if he would rise, then sinks back, his hand feebly beating time to the music, which swells to a martial crash. Curtain.*)

Mary Burrill

They That Sit in Darkness — 1919

A parenthesis below the title of the play in its original printing states that the play was "written for the *Birth Control Review*," where it appeared in September, 1919.

This periodical was a monthly platform for progressive men and women of that time who lobbied for the right of women to have birth control information—a struggle that did not end until fifty years later. The right of birth control was a part of the struggle for women's liberation: the nineteenth amendment, equal pay, opportunity for equal employment, the right of abortion. The *Review* did not devote itself to Negro population control. The movement was concerned with all women, but especially the poor who were victimized by the cycle of poverty—children—poverty.

The author, a woman who taught English in Washington, D.C., presents women, not men. Her theme is birth control. The author does not blame the husband, not does she even bring him on stage.

Some of the characterization of this play is done by the speech idiom. A careful comparison of this dialect rendering with that of the white man's "darkey" dialect of the same period will reveal that there is more to capturing folk language than a substitution of d's for t's. Note how the dialect transcription of white playwright Ridgley Torrence approaches cryptography:

—Oh, whuffo dee drag me out an' hilt me back? I bo'one man an' him dee tuk'n bu'nt. An' 'e slep' right 'n dis room w'en de man wuz shot w'ich dee 'cuze 'im er!

They That Sit in Darkness

CHARACTERS

MALINDA JASPER, *the mother*
LINDY, MILES, ALOYSIUS, MARY ELLEN, JIMMIE, JOHN HENRY, A WEEK-OLD INFANT, *her children*
ELIZABETH SHAW, *a visiting nurse*

The action passes in a small country town in the South in our own day.

(*It is late afternoon of a day in September. The room, which does a three-fold duty as kitchen, dining room, and living room for the Jasper family, is dingy and disorderly. Great black patches as though from smoke are on the low ceilings and the walls. To the right is a door leading into a bedroom. In the opposite wall another door leads into a somewhat larger room that serves as bedroom for six Jasper children. In the rear wall a door opens into a large yard. A window is placed to the left of the door while against the wall to the right there stands an old, battered cow-hide trunk. The furniture, which is poor and dilapidated, consists of a table in the center of the room, a cupboard containing a few broken cups and plates, a rocker, and two or three plain chairs with broken backs and uncertain legs. Against the wall to the left there is a kitchen stove on which sit a tea-kettle and a wash-boiler. Near the window, placed upon stools, are two large laundry tubs. Through open window and door one gets a glimps of snowy garments waving and glistening in the sun.* MALINDA JASPER, *a frail, tired-looking woman of thirty-eight, and* LINDY, *her seventeen-year-old daughter, are bending over the tubs swirling their hands in the water to make sure that their task is completed. From the yard come the constant cries of children at play.*)

MRS. JASPER (*straightening up painfully from the tubs*) Lor', Lindy, how my side do hurt! But thank goodnis, dis job's done! (*she sinks exhausted into the rocker*) Run git me one them tablits de doctor lef' fo' dis pain! (LINDY *hurries into the adjoining room and returns with the medicine*)

MRS. JASPER (*shaking her head mournfully*) Dis ole pain goin' be takin' me 'way f'om heah one o' dese days!

LINDY (*looking at her in concern*) See, Ma, I tole yuh not to be doin' all this wuk! Whut's Miss 'Liz'beth goin' er say when she comes heah this evenin' an' fine out you done all this wuk after she tole yuh pertic'lar yestiddy that she wuz'n goin' let yuh out'n bed 'fo' three weeks—an' here 't'ain't been a week sence baby wuz bawn!

MRS. JASPER Ah ain't keerin' 'bout whut Mis' 'Liz'beth say! Easy nuf, Lindy, fo' dese nurses to give dey advice—dey ain't got no seben chillern to clothe an' feed—but when dis washin' git back Ah kin nevah ketch up!

LINDY (*reprovingly*) But I could 'a done it all mys'f.

MRS. JASPER An' been all day an' night doin' it—an' miss gittin' you'se'f off in de mawnin' tuh Tuskegee—no indeedy!

LINDY (*hesitatingly*) P'rhaps I oughtn' be goin' erway an' leavin' yuh wid all dis washin' to do ever' week, an' de chillern to look after—an' the baby an' all. Daddy he gits home so late he cain't be no help.

MRS. JASPER (*wearily*) Nebber you mind, Lindy, Ah'm going be gittin' aw-right bime-by. Ah ain't a-goin' be stan'in' in de way yo' gittin' dis edicashun. Yo' chance don' come, Lindy, an' Ah wants ter see yuh tek it! Yuh been a good chile, Lindy, an' Ah wants ter see yuh git mo'e out'n life dan Ah gits. Dem three yeah at Tuskegee warn't seem long.

LINDY (*her face brightening up*) Yassum, an' ef Mister Huff, the sup'inten'ent meks me county teacher lak he sez he'll do when I git back, I kin do lots mo'e fo' you an' the chillern!

(*The cry of a week-old infant comes from the adjoining room*)

MRS. JASPER Dar now! Ah'm mighty glad he

didn' wake up 'tel we git dis washin' done! Ah reckon he's hongry. Ain't Miles come back wid de milk yet? He's been gawn mos' 'en hour—see ef he's took dat guitar wid 'im.

LINDY (*going to the door and looking out*) I doan see it nowheres so I reckon he's got it.

MRS. JASPER Den Gawd knows when we'll see 'im! Lak es not he's some'airs settin' by de road thumpin' dem strings—dat boy 'ud play ef me or you wuz dyin'! Ah doan know whut's goin' come o' 'im—he's just so lazy en shif'lis!

LINDY Doan yuh go werrin' 'bout Miles, Ma He'll be aw-right ef he kin only learn music. an' do whut he likes. (*the cry of the infant becomes insistent*) No, Ma, you set still—I'll git his bottle an' 'tend to him. (*she goes into the bedroom*)

(*The shrieks of the children in the yard grow louder. A shrill cry of anger and pain rises above the other voices, and* MARY ELLEN, *age six, appears crying at the door.*)

MARY ELLEN (*holding her head*) Ma! Ma! Mek Aloysius b'have hisse'f! He hit me on de haid wid all his might!

MRS. JASPER (*rushing to the door*) Aloysius! Yuh Aloysius! It warn't do yuh no good ef Ah 'ave to come out'n dere to yuh! John Henry, git down f'om dat tree, 'fo yuh have dem clo'es in de durt! Yo' chillern 'nuf to worry me to death!

(*As* LINDY *returns with the baby's empty bottle*, MILES *enters the rear door. He is a good-natured but shiftless looking boy of sixteen. A milk pail is swinging on his arm, leaving his hands free to strum a guitar*)

LINDY Have yuh brought the milk, Miles? An' the bread?

MILES (*setting down the milk pail*) Nup! Mister Jackson say yuh cain't have no milk, an' no nothin' 'tel de bill's paid.

MRS. JASPER Den Gawd knows we'll starve, 'cause Ah see'd yo' daddy give de doctor ebery cent o' his wages las' week. An' dey warn't be no mo'e money comin' in 'tel Ah kin git dis wash out to de Redmon's.

LINDY Well, baby's gawn back to sleep now, and p'rhaps Miss 'Liz'beth will bring some milk fo' de baby when she come in lak she did yestiddy—but they ain't nothing heah fo' de other chillern.

(*The shrieks of the children at play in the yard grow louder.*)

ALOYSIUS (*calling from without*) Ma! Ma! John Henry done pull' down de clo'es line!

MRS. JASPER (*rushing again to the door*) Come in heah! Ever' single one o' yuh! Miles, run fix 'em up an' see ef any o' 'em got in de durt!

(*The Jasper children, four in number, a crestfallen, pathetic looking little group—heads unkempt, ragged, undersized, under-fed, file in terrified.*)

JOHN HENRY (*terror-stricken*) It warn't me, Ma, it was Aloysius!

MRS. JASPER Heish yo' mouf'! March yo'se'f ever' one o' yuh an' go to baid!

MARY ELLEN (*timidly*) We's ain't had no suppah.

MRS. JASPER An' whut's mo'e, yuh ain't goin' git no suppah 'tel yuh larns to b'have yo'se'f!

ALOYSIUS (*in a grumbling tone*) Cain't fool me—Ah heerd Lindy say dey ain't no suppah fo' us!

MRS. JASPER (*calling to the children as they disappear in the room to the left*) Ef Ah heahs one soun' Ah'm comin' in dere an' slap yuh into de middle o' nex' week! (*as she sinks again exhausted into the rocker*) Them chillern's goan ter be de death o' me yit!

MILES (*appearing at the door*) De clo'es ain't dirty. I fo'git to tell yuh—I stopp't by Sam Jones an' he say he'll be 'round fo' Lindy's trunk 'bout sun-down.

MRS. JASPER Ah reckons yu'd bettah git yo' clo'es an' pack up 'cause it warn't be long fo' sun-down.

LINDY (*dragging the old trunk to the center of the room*) I ain't a-goin' less'n you git bettah, Ma. Yuh look right sick to me!

(*As* LINDY *is speaking*, MISS ELIZABETH SHAW, *in the regulation dress of a visiting nurse and carrying a small black bag, appears at the rear door*)

MISS SHAW (*looking in consternation at Mrs. Jasper*) Malinda Jasper! What are you doing out of bed! You don't mean to say that you have washed all those clothes that I see in the yard?

MRS. JASPER Yassum, me an' Lindy done 'em.

MISS SHAW (*provoked*) And you look completely exhausted! Come you must get right to bed!

MRS. JASPER (*leaning her head wearily against the back of the rocker*) Lemme res' myse'f jes a minute—Ah'll be goin' 'long to-rectly.

MISS SHAW It's a wonder in your condition that you didn't die standing right at those tubs! I don't mean to scare you but—

MRS. JASPER (*with extreme weariness*) Lor', Mis' 'Liz'beth, it ain't *dyin'* Ah'm skeer't o', its *livin'*—wid all dese chillern to look out fo'. We ain't no Elijahs, Mis' 'Lis'beth, dey ain't no ravens flyin' 'roun' heah drappin' us food. All we gits, we has to git by wukin' hard! But thanks be to Gawd a light's dawnin'! My Lindy's gittin' off to Tuskegee to school tomorrer, Mis' 'Liz'beth!

MISS SHAW (*surprised*) I didn't know that Lindy was thinking about going away to school.

MRS. JASPER Thinkin' 'bout it! Lindy ain't been thinkin' an' dreamin' 'bout nothin' else sence Booker Washin'ton talked to de farmers down youder at Shady Grove some ten yeah ergo. Did yo' know Booker Washin'ton, Mis' 'Liz'beth?

MISS SHAW I saw him once a long time ago in my home town in Massachusetts. He was a great man.

MRS. JASPER Dat he wuz! Ah kin see him now—him an' Lindy, jes a teeny slip o' gal—after de speakin' wuz ovah down dere at Shady Grove, a-standin' under de magnolias wid de sun a-pou'in' through de trees on 'em—an' he wid his hand on my li'l Linly's haid lak he wuz givin' huh a blessin', an' a-sayin': "When yuh gits big, li'l gal, yuh mus' come to Tuskegee an' larn, so's yuh kin come back heah an' he'p dese po' folks!" He's daid an' in his grave but Lindy ain't nevah fo'git dem words.

MISS SHAW Just think of it! And ten years ago! How glad I am that her dream is coming true. Won't it cost you quite a bit?

MRS. JASPER Lor', Lindy 'ud nevah git dere ef we had to sen' huh! Some dem rich folks up yonder in yo' part de world is sen'in' huh.

LINDY (*entering with her arms laden with things for her trunk*) Good evenin', Mis' 'Liz'beth.

MISS SHAW Well, Lindy, I've just heard of your good fortune. How splendid it is! But what will the baby do without you! How is he this afternoon?

LINDY He's right smart, Mis' 'Liz'beth. I been rubbing his leg lack you showed me. Do yoh think it'll evah grow ez long ez the other'n?

MISS SHAW I fear, Lindy, those little withered limbs seldom do; but with care it will grow much stronger. I have brought him some milk—there in my bag. Be careful to modify it exactly as I showed you, and give what is left to the other children.

LINDY (*preparing to fix the milk*) Yes Mis' 'Liz'beth.

MISS SHAW (*nodding at Lindy*) What *will you do*, Malinda, when she goes? You will have to stop working so hard. Just see how exhausted you are from this heavy work!

MRS. JASPER Lor', Mis' 'Liz'beth, Ah'll be awright torectly. Ah did de same thing after my li'l Tom was bawn, an' when Aloysius wuz bawn Ah git up de nex' day—de wuk had to be done.

MISS SHAW (*very gravely*) But you must not think that you are as strong now as you were then. I heard the doctor tell you very definitely that this baby had left your heart *weaker than ever*, and that you *must* give up this laundry work.

MRS. JASPER (*pleadingly*) 'Deed, Mis' 'Liz'beth, we needs dis money whut wid all dese chillern, an' de sicknis' an' fune'ul 'spenses of li'l Tom an' Selena—dem's de chillern whut come 'tween John Henry an' dis las' baby. At'er dem bills wuz paid heah come Pinkie's trouble.

MISS SHAW Pinkie?

MRS. JASPER (*sadly*) Yuh nevah seed Pinkie 'cause she lef' 'fo' yuh come heah. She come 'tween Miles an' Aloysius—she warn't right in de haid—she wuked ovah tuh Bu'nett's place—Ah aint nevah been much on my gals wukin' round dese white men but Pinkie *mus' go*; an' fus thing we know Bu'nett got huh in trouble.

MISS SHAW Poor, poor girl! What did you do to the Burnett man?

MRS. JASPER (*with deep feeling*) Lor', Mis' 'Liz'beth, cullud folks cain't do nothin' to white folks down heah! Huh Dad went on sumpin awful wid huh ever' day, an' one mawnin' we woked up and Pinkie an' huh baby wuz gawn! We ain't nevah heerd f'om huh tuh dis day—(*she closes her eyes as if to shut out the memory of Pinkie's sorrow*) Me an' Jim 'as allus put ouah tru's in de Lawd, an' we wants tuh raise up dese chillern to be good, hones' men an' women but we has tuh wuk so hard to give 'em de li'l de gits dat we ain't got no time tuh look at'er dey sperrits. When Jim go out to wuk—chillern's sleepin'; when he comes in late at night—chillern's sleepin' When Ah git through scrubbin' at dem tubs all Ah kin do is set in dis cheer an' nod—Ah doan wants tuh see no chillern! Ef it warn't fo' Lindy—huh got a mighty nice way wid 'em—Gawd he'p 'em!

MISS SHAW Well, Malinda, you have certainly your share of trouble!

MRS. JASPER (*shaking her head wearily*) Ah wonder whut sin we done that Gawd punish me an' Jim lak dis!

MISS SHAW (*gently*) God is not punishing you, Malinda, you are punishing yourselves by having children every year. Take this last baby—you knew that with your weak heart that you should never have had it and yet—

MRS. JASPER But whut kin Ah do—de chillern *come!*

MISS SHAW You must be careful!

MRS. JASPER Be keerful! Dat's all you nu'ses say! You an' de one whut come when Tom wuz bawn, an' Selena! Ah been keerful all Ah knows how but whut's it got me—ten chillern, eight livin' an' two daid! You got'a be tellin' me sumpin' better'n dat, Mis' 'Liz'beth!

MISS SHAW (*fervently*) I wish to God it were lawful for me to do so! My heart goes out to you poor people that sit in darkness, having, year after year, children that you are physically too weak to bring into the world—children that you are unable not only to educate but even to clothe and feed. Malinda, when I took my oath as nurse, I swore to abide by the laws of the State, and the law forbids my telling you what you have a right to know!

MRS. JASPER (*with the tears trickling from her closed eyes*) Ah ain't blamin' you, Mis' 'Liz'beth, but—

MISS SHAW Come, come, Malinda, you must not give away like this. You are worn out—come, you must get to bed.

LINDY (*entering with more things for her trunk*) I'm glad yuh gittin' huh to bed, Mis' 'Liz'beth, I been tryin' to all day.

MRS. JASPER (*as she walks unsteadily toward her room*) Lindy, honey, git yo' trunk pack't. Thank Gawd yo' chance done come! Give dat (*nodding toward the partially filled bottle of milk*) to de chillern. Mis' 'Liz'beth say dey kin have it.

LINDY All right, Ma. Mis' 'Liz'beth, ef you needs me jes call.

(MALINDA *and the* NURSE *enter the bedroom.* LINDY *is left packing her trunk.* MILES *can be heard from without strumming upon his guitar*)

MARY ELLEN (*poking her head out of the door to the children's room*) Lindy, Lindy, whut wuz dat Ma say we all kin have?

LINDY Some milk—it ain't much.

(*The* CHILDREN *bound into the room.* MARY ELLEN, *first at the table, seizes the bottle and lifts it to her lips*)

ALOYSIUS (*snatching the bottle from* MARY ELLEN) Yuh got 'a be las', 'cause Mis' 'Liz'beth say we mus'n' nebber eat or drink at'er yuh! Did'n' she, Lindy?

LINDY (*as* MARY ELLEN *begins to cry*) Ef yo' all git to fussin' I ain't goan to bring yuh nothin' when I comes back!

MARY ELLEN (*as the children crowd about Lindy*) Whut yuh goan 'a bring us, Lindy?

LINDY (*as she puts her things carefully into her trunk*) When I comes back I'm goan to bring yuh all some pretty readin' books, an' some clo'es so I kin tek yuh to school ever' day where yuh kin learn to read 'em!

JOHN HENRY (*clapping his hands*) Is we all goin', Lindy? Miles too?

LINDY Yes indeedy! An' whut's mo'e I'm goan 'a git Miles a fine new guitar an' let him learn music. An' some day ever' body'll be playin' an' singin' his songs!

ALOYSIUS (*glowing with excitement*) Some day he might have his own band! Might'n' he, Lindy? Lak dat big white one whut come fru heah f'om 'Lanta! Ole Miles'll come struttin' down de road.

(ALOYSIUS *seizes the broom, and in spite of the handicap of bow legs, gives a superb imitation of a drum-major leading his band*)

LINDY (*watching* ALOYSIUS' *antics*) An' I'm goin' tuh have Aloysius' li'l legs straightened. (*as the children roll in merriment*) 'Sh! 'sh! Mus'n' mek no noise 'cause Ma ain't well! An' in de evenin' we'll have a real set-down-to-de table suppah—Dad he won't have to wuk so hard so he kin git home early—an' after suppah we all kin set 'round de fiah lak dey do ovah to Lawyer Hope's an' tell stories an' play games—

(*The* CHILDREN, *radiant as though these dreams were all realities, huddle closer about* LINDY *who, packing done, now sits enthroned upon her battered trunk*)

LINDY 'Sh—sh! Wuz that Mis' 'Liz'beth callin'? (*They listen intently but can hear nothing save the sweet, plaintive notes of an old Spiritual that* MILES *is playing upon his guitar*) Then we'll git some fine Sunday clo'es, an' a hoss an' wagun, an' when Sunday come we'll all climb in an' ride to Shady Grove to Meetin'—an' we'll set under de trees in de shade an' learn 'bout li'l Joseph an' his many-cullud coat; an' li'l Samu'l whut de Lawd called while he wuz sleepin'; an' de li'l baby whut wuz bawn in de stable an' wuz lots poor'n me an' you. An' on Sunday evenin' we'll—

MISS SHAW (*appearing at the bedroom door and speaking hurriedly*) Send the children to bed quickly, Lindy, I need you.

(*The children run into their room*)

ALOYSIUS (*wistfully, at the door*) Ef we's good, Lindy, let us git up when Sam Jones come an' see de trunk go?

LINDY (*quickly*) Mebbe—hurry up!

MISS SHAW (*very seriously*) Lindy, your mother's condition has grown suddenly very, very serious. The exertion of today is beginning to tell on her heart. Bring me some boiling water immediately for my hypodermic. (*calling from the rear door*) Miles, Miles! Run to the Hope's as fast as you can and ask them to telephone for the doctor—your mother is very ill. Tell him the nurse says it is urgent!

(MISS ELIZABETH *hurries into the bedroom, followed soon after by* LINDY *with the water. In a few minutes the sobbing of* LINDY *can be heard, and the* NURSE *re-enters the kitchen. She leans against the frame of the rear door as though exhausted and stares out into the yard at the clothes fluttering like white spirits in the gathering dusk. Then sighing deeply, she puts on her bonnet and cape and turns to go*)

MILES (*rushing in breathlessly, with his guitar under his arm*) De Hopes ain't—

MISS SHAW (*placing her hand tenderly on his shoulder*) Never mind, now, Miles, your mother is dead.

MILES (*his guitar crashing to the floor*) Dead!

MISS SHAW Yes, and you must help Lindy all you can. I would not leave but I have a case up the road that I must see tonight. I'll be back tomorrow. (*as* MILES *walks with bowed head toward his mother's room*) Come, Miles, you had better bring in the clothes before it gets dark.

(*As* MILES *follows her out,* LINDY *enters the kitchen. The light has gone from her face for she knows that the path now stretching before her and the other children will be darker even than the way that they have already known.*)

MILES (*awkwardly, as he struggles in with the hamper piled high with the snowy clothes*) Anything mo' Ah kin do, Lindy?

LINDY (*as she sits on the edge of her trunk and stares in a dazed, hopeless way at the floor*) I reckon yu'd bettah walk up de road a piece to meet Dad an' hurry him erlong. An' stop in de Redmon's an' tell 'em dey cain't have de wash tomorrer 'cause—(*gulping back her tears*) 'cause Ma's dead; but I'll git 'em out myself jes ez soon ez I kin. An', Miles, leave word fo' Sam Jones 'at he need'n' come fo' de trunk.

Myrtle Smith Livingston (1901–)

For Unborn Children   1926

Myrtle Smith Livingston was twenty-five and newly married in 1926 when she won third prize in a magazine contest for her play. Born in Holly Grove, Arkansas, she attended Howard University before becoming a school teacher in Colorado. She now teaches at Lincoln University in Missouri.

For Unborn Children deals with a popular race theme: miscegenation. This play reverses the usual stage pairing of white man (southern) and black woman. The use of the black man and the white woman may be related to the fact that the play was written by a woman. Marion, the black sister in the play, clearly voices her anger: "What is to become of us when our own men throw us down?" Perhaps Mrs. Livingston's anger at the black man taking a white woman is reflected in the play's incredible ending, LeRoy's acceptance of his "punishment." The reader should also keep in mind that "any Negro blood" made a person a Negro—some state laws required only one drop.

Miscegenation is the one racial theme on which black and white playwrights have always agreed: mixing is bad.

The official white myth ran like this: Mixing of the races was bad for whites although it might improve the Negro. Nevertheless, on stage, persons of mixed blood must die, even if the black blood be but one drop. The most well-known of this genre was Dion Boucicault's *The Octoroon* (1859).

The tragic-mulatto tradition continued down through Edward Shelton's *The Nigger* (1909), where the hero is about to be elected governor when he discovers his black past, to Eugene O'Neill's serious attempt to examine the issues in *All God's Chillun Got Wings* (1924). A generation later the American audience watched Jack Johnson climb into bed with his white woman in Howard Sackler's *Great White Hope*, but any objections were nicely taken care of by her death before curtain time.

The black tradition was similar. Langston Hughes' first play on Broadway, *Mulatto* (1935), presented the mixed son of a white plantation owner and his black house servant. The son kills his father and is killed in return. Important modifications to this trend are Alice Childress' lovely, human play *Wedding Band* (1966) and Adrienne Kennedy's intense examination of miscegenation in *Funnyhouse of a Negro* (1964) and *The Owl Answers* (1965).

It is interesting to speculate as to why American playwrights, black and white, have denied the reality of thousands of mixed marriages and romances and instead have continued to confirm the stage myth of the tragic-mulatto.

For Unborn Children

CAST OF CHARACTERS

LEROY CARLSON, *a young lawyer*
MARION CARLSON, *his sister*
GRANDMA CARLSON, *his grandmother*
SELMA FRAZIER, *a young white girl*
A MOB

(*The scene of the play is somewhere in the South; the characters are all of Negro descent except the young white girl and the members of the mob. The time is the present.*

A living room is tastefully, though not richly, furnished, denoting the occupancy of a refined family, evidently of the middle class. There is a sofa to one side, a table in the center, and a leather comfort-chair in the corner; another leather chair sits in the upper part of the room. A window is in the rear. There are two entrances, one right and one left. MARION *is seen sitting on the sofa reading the evening paper as the curtain rises. After perusing it quietly for a minute, she throws it down and goes to the window, peering out into the night.*

Her grandmother, a gentle, well-bred, old lady enters)

GRANDMA CARLSON Hasn't Roy come yet, Marion?

MARION No, he hasn't, grandmother; and I'm beginning to get worried; it's almost 9 o'clock now and he said he'd be here by 6.

GRANDMA CARLSON Did you telephone the office for him?

MARION Yes; he left about 5:30, they said.

GRANDMA CARLSON (*with a sigh sits in the comfort-chair*) I suppose he's somewhere with that girl again.

MARION Oh! If he would only let her alone! He knows what it will mean if they find it out; it's awful for him to keep us in this terrible suspense!

GRANDMA CARLSON Do you suppose talking to her would do any good? Do you know her?

MARION Yes, by sight; a nice enough girl all right, but then she's white and she ought to stay in her own race; she hasn't any right to be running around after our men. I know it wouldn't be of any use to talk to her; and Roy—!

GRANDMA CARLSON Yes, dear, I know; we hardly dare to say anything to him about it; but, Marion, we've got to do something!

MARION But, grandmother, what? I'm at my wit's end! Since they can't be married here, they're going to run away and go north someplace where they can, and (*despairingly*) I don't see anything we can do to stop them!

GRANDMA CARLSON (*sadly and preoccupied*) I suppose I'll have to tell him; well, if it will stop him—

MARION Tell him what?

GRANDMA CARLSON (*with a start as she realizes that she said more than she intended to*) Oh, nothing, child; look again; don't you see him yet?

MARION No. Oh! it's terrible not knowing whether he's all right or if some mob has— (*buries her face in her hands*)

GRANDMA CARLSON (*wincing*) No,—no—don't say that!

MARION But you know that's what will happen if it's found out before they get away!

GRANDMA CARLSON (*moaning*) Oh, my child! I don't know which would be the hardest to bear! I'd almost rather that he should die now than to marry a white woman, but O! Dear Lord! Not such a death as that!

(*The noise of a door being unlocked is heard outside; it is opened and then shut*)

MARION (*relieved*) Here he is now; well, thank goodness, it hasn't happened yet. (*her nervous tension relaxes and her anger rises throughout the following scene*)

(LEROY *enters*)

LEROY (*throws cap on table*) Hello; (*smiles sheepishly*) been giving me "Hail Columbia," I guess, haven't you?

MARION (*sarcastically*) This is what you call 6 o'clock, I suppose, is it?

LEROY I'm sorry, sis; I had an engagement and I couldn't make it here by then; I meant to call you and let you know, but,—well, I'm sorry.

GRANDMA CARLSON We were just worried; you know we can't feel very easy these days, Roy, when we don't know where you are; you know the sentiment down here.

MARION (*bitterly*) What does he care about how we feel? His family and his career too, for that matter, mean nothing to him now; and his whole heart and soul are wrapped up in his girl, —a white girl! I guess your engagement this evening was with her; I know it was!

LEROY (*trying to control his temper*) Yes, it was; I still have the liberty of making an engagement with anyone I choose, Marion.

GRANDMA CARLSON But you haven't the right, son, to cause us unnecessary worry and pain. You know how much your sister and I both care about you, and it wouldn't be much to just let us know where you are.

LEROY (*contritely*) I didn't mean to worry, you, Granny; I was on my way home when—her note was brought to me, and I didn't have time to call you then. You won't have to worry much longer now, anyway; we've decided to leave tomorrow night.

MARION (*shocked*) Tomorrow night? Good Heavens, Roy! You can't go through with it! Have you lost all your manhood?

GRANDMA CARLSON (*her voice throbs with pain*) Ah, boy, you've forgotten us! Don't you love us at all anymore since she came into your life?

LE ROY O, Granny, I hate to leave you and sis; but you know we can't stay here and marry, confound these laws! It will be better for us to go some place where we aren't known, anyway. I wish you and Marion could go with us.

MARION (*almost hysterical*) I wouldn't go a step with you and your white woman if I was going to be killed for it! If you've lost your self-respect, I still have mine! I wouldn't spit on a woman like her! There must be something terribly wrong with her, for white women don't marry colored men when they can get anybody else! You poor fool! If it's color you want, why couldn't you stay in your own race? We have women who are as white as any white person could be! My God! What is to become of us when our own men throw us down? Even if you do love her can't you find your backbone to conquer it for the sake of your race? I know they're as much to blame as we are, but inter-marriage doesn't hurt them as much as it does us; laws would never have been passed against it if the states could have believed white women would turn Negro men down, but they knew they wouldn't; they can make fools out of them too easily, and you're too much of a dupe to see it! Well, if you marry her, may God help me never to breathe your name again! (*runs from the room sobbing*)

LEROY (*sorrowfully and pleadingly*) Oh, Granny, you don't feel that way too, do you? Selma and I can't help it because we don't belong to the same race, and we have the right to be happy together if we love each other, haven't we?

GRANDMA CARLSON (*sadly*) We have the right to be happy, child, only when our happiness doesn't hurt anybody else; and when a colored man marries a white woman, he hurts every member of the Negro race!

LEROY (*perplexed*) But,—I don't understand;—how?

GRANDMA CARLSON He adds another link to the chain that binds them; before we can gain that perfect Freedom to which we have every right, we've got to prove that we're better than they! And we can't do it when our men place white women above their own!

LEROY (*imploringly*) But, Grandmother, I love her so much! Not because she's white, but just for herself alone; I'd love her just the same if she were black! And she loves me too! Oh! I can't believe it would be wrong for us to marry!

GRANDMA CARLSON Sometimes we best prove our love by giving up the object of it. You can't make her happy, Roy; she'll be satisfied for a while, but after that the call of her blood will be stronger than her love for you, and you'll both be miserable: she'll long for her own people; you won't be enough.

LEROY (*miserably*) What shall I do? Oh, Lord, have mercy! Granny, I can't give her up! I couldn't live without her!

GRANDMA CARLSON (*with tears in her eyes*)

Think of the unborn children that you sin against by marrying her, baby! Oh, you can't know the misery that awaits them if you give them a white mother! Every child has a right to a mother who will love it better than life itself; and a white woman cannot mother a Negro baby!

LEROY But, Granny—

GRANDMA CARLSON (*pathetically*) I know, Honey! I've never told you this,—I didn't want you to know,—but your mother was a white woman, and she made your father's life miserable as long as he lived. She never could stand the sight of you and Marion; she hated you because you weren't white! I was there to care for you, but I'm getting old, Honey, and I couldn't go through it again! Boy, you can't make the same mistake your father did!

LEROY (*in repugnance*) Oh, Granny, why didn't you tell me before? My mother, white! I've wondered why you never spoke of her! And she hated us! My God! That makes it different!

(GRANDMA CARLSON *rises and kisses him on the forehead, holding his face between her hands, and looking deep into his eyes*)

GRANDMA CARLSON I'll leave you alone with God and your conscience, and whatever you decide, I'll be satisfied. (*goes out*)

(LEROY *sits with his head bowed in his hands; presently a light tapping is heard at the window, which finally attracts his attention; he crosses to it, and seeing who is there, motions toward the door, going to open it;* SELMA *enters, almost exhausted*)

SELMA (*breathless and terrorized*) A mob!—Hurry!—They're—coming—here—after—you.—You—must—go!—Hurry!

LEROY (*in amazement*) A mob—after me?

SELMA Hurry and go!—They're coming now! (*a rumble of voices is heard in the distance. Despairingly*) Oh! It's too late! (*sobs*) What shall I do? Oh, they'll—they'll—kill you!

(*The rumble grows louder as it nears the house; cries of* "Lynch him!" "The dirty nigger!" "We'll show him how to fool around a white woman!" *are heard.* GRANDMA CARLSON *and* MARION *enter, fearfully apprehensive*)

MARION (*seeing* SELMA) What's the matter? What's that noise?

GRANDMA CARLSON (*as realization dawns upon her; clutches her heart*) Oh! It can't be! (*falls on her knees and prays*) Dear God! have mercy! Oh, Father in Heaven! Do not desert us now! Hear my prayer and save my boy!

LEROY (*a light breaks over his face and he is transfigured; a gleam of holiness comes into his eyes; looking heavenward*) Thy will be done, O Lord! (*he turns and takes* SELMA's *hands in his*) It has to be, sweetheart, and it is the better way; even though we love each other we couldn't have found happiness together. Forget me, and marry a man of your own race; you'll be happier, and I will too, up there. Goodbye. (*he turns to* MARION) Forgive me, sis, if you can.

MARION (*sobs heartbrokenly*) There isn't anything to forgive, Roy! It's I you should forgive! I'm sorry for everything I said! Oh, God! I can't stand this!

LEROY (*soothingly*) Don't cry, sis; what you said was right; and I want you to know that even if this hadn't happened, I was going to give her up. (*kisses her tenderly. Picks* GRANDMA CARLSON *up from the floor and holds her close in his arms*) It's better this way, Granny; don't grieve so; just think of it as a sacrifice for UNBORN CHILDREN!

VOICE OUTSIDE Come out, you damned nigger, or we'll burn the house down!

MARION (*clings to him, sobbing*) Don't go, Roy! We'll all die together!

LEROY (*puts her from him gently*) No. (*loud and clear*) I'm coming, gentlemen! (*with a last, long, loving look at the three of them he walks out to his death victorious and unafraid*)

Ruth Gaines-Shelton (1873–)

The Church Fight   1925

Ruth Gaines-Shelton was a grandmother when she won second prize ($40.00) for this play in *Crisis* magazine contest of 1925.

The play has two distinctions. It is not about the race "problem," but rather concerns itself with an experience that was apparently universal enough to allow the author to use allegorical names for satirical purposes—church politics. No doubt a number of staunch church members who read the play when it was published in 1926 recognized themselves and their friends.

The play's second distinction is that it is a comedy, one of the few written by black playwrights of the period. And those few involve themes of an in-group nature (life in the church, in the lodge, the struggle to climb socially). The use of comedy and satire to expose the "problem" in interracial situations does not appear until contemporary times. Why so late?

The Church Fight

CHARACTERS

ANANIAS
INVESTIGATOR
JUDAS
PARSON PROCRASTINATOR } the brethren

SAPPHIRA
INSTIGATOR
MEDDLER
EXPERIENCE
TAKE-IT-BACK
TWO-FACE } the sisters

(SCENE: *In the kitchen of* SISTER SAPPHIRA's *home. A small kitchen table with red table cloth on it and breakfast dishes for two; kitchen chair; cupboard with dishes in it; pans and skillets hanging up.*

TIME: 7:30 *in the morning.*

BROTHER ANANIAS *and* SISTER SAPPHIRA *have just finished their breakfast.* ANANIAS *has on overalls and jumper ready for day's work.* SAPPHIRA *is in neat house dress, gingham apron, with dust cap on*)

BROTHER ANANIAS (*lighting pipe*) Well wife, I must go, it's 7:30 and I'll have to skip along; but I want you to remember if that committee meets here today tell them that we ain't going to pay another cent into the Church until Parson Procrastinator leaves. Tell them Parson Shoot, from Rocky-town, says he'll come and take our Church any time.

SISTER SAPPHIRA Don't you worry, Ananias, I ain't going to pay no more money to that man. Why he has plumb robbed the treasury. Why it's just a shame for a preacher to stay at a Church until he kills it plumb dead. Here honey, take your dinner bucket.

(ANANIAS *takes his bucket, says goodbye as he goes out the door*)

SISTER SAPPHIRA (*cleaning up table*) I do hope they can git Brother Procrastinator moved by night. I've got so much work today it looks like I just ain't got time to fool with all them people a-coming here. But we've got to attend to God's work first. (*knock at door; opens door*) Why, you all are here before I've got my house cleaned up; but come right in. I'm so glad you all mean business. (*Enter* SISTER INSTIGATOR *with glasses on, looking over them;* SISTER MEDDLER, *chewing gum.* SISTER EXPERIENCE *with book and pencil looking very important.* SISTER TAKE-IT-BACK, *with head down as if afraid of being discovered.* SISTER TWO-FACE, *smiling sweetly with pretty hat and veil on;* BROTHER INVESTIGATOR, *with Bible;* BROTHER JUDAS, *leaning on cane. All ladies are dressed in house dresses except* SISTER TWO-FACE, *who has a street dress on.* SISTER SAPPHIRA *shakes hands with each one calling the name as she does so*) Just sit right down and let us see what can be done. I'm just all on fire about it.

BROTHER INVESTIGATOR (*sits down at table, takes off glasses and wipes them*) Well, Sister Sapphira, I'll tell you in the beginning, it's no easy task to move a Minister. You see, in the first place, we got to have a "charge" against him; now what charge have we against Parson Procrastinator?

SISTER INSTIGATOR Well Brother Investigator, we ain't got no particular charge agin him, only he's been here thirteen years and we are tired looking at him.

BROTHER INVESTIGATOR That won't do, Sister Instigator; you must have sufficient evidence and proof that he has broken the law, or lived unrighteously.

SISTER MEDDLER Couldn't we make up some kind of a charge agin him?

SISTER EXPERIENCE Better not do that sisters, you'll get into trouble!

SISTER SAPPHIRA There's no danger of that; we could just simply say that Brother Procrastinator has not walked in the straight and narrow path since he's been here.

BROTHER INVESTIGATOR Well, Sister Sapphira, you can't say that unless you tell just *wherein* he failed to walk in the path.

BROTHER JUDAS   Well, I'll just tell you the truth, Brother Investigator; you know I know him. He and I have been arm and arm ever since he's been here. He's a pretty crooked sort of a fellow. Of course I wouldn't like for him to know I squealed on him.

SISTER TAKE-IT-BACK   Well I know one thing, and I saw this with my own eyes: I saw him hold on to Sister Holy's hand so long one night at prayer meeting until Brother Two-Face had to speak to him about it!

SISTER SAPPHIRA   There now! Do you hear that? I've been watching them two, for some time. You know Sister Holy was the one what gave him that gold pencil.

SISTER EXPERIENCE   Sisters you all had better listen to me; you know I've been in one church fight, and I promised God that I'd never be in another. Now in the first place, no church fight can be built on a lie. It's better to let the preacher stay, than damn our souls trying to get rid of him.

BROTHER JUDAS (*singing*) "We want no cowards in our band."

SISTER EXPERIENCE   If there's anybody here, that's afraid to come out and fight in the open, let them get out at once.

SISTER TAKE-IT-BACK   Well I'm one that's not afraid; you all know me. You know what I say first, I say last; and I started out to move Brother Procrastinator and I don't expect to stop until he's gone.

BROTHER JUDAS   That's the way to win out; Sisters, you got to have that fighting spirit.

SISTER INSTIGATOR   I tell you, we just must git rid of this man. Why none of the young people will come to Church because he can't read so anybody can understand him. If he don't go, this Church is going to destruction and ruin.

BROTHER INVESTIGATOR   Now sisters and brothers, I have listened careful to every word you said and I ain't yet had sufficient evidence to ask Parson Procrastinator to go.

SISTER EXPERIENCE   Brother Investigator, I wish to drop this word of warning. When I was in the fight against Parson Hard-head, some of the sisters told so many stories that the Bishop had to turn them out of the Church for lying. Now I don't think we ought to tear the Church all to pieces just to git the Minister to go. If he ain't doing right, let the officers see that he does do right; if he ain't a good man, let the Church get together and pray for God to touch his sinful heart, and convert him. For after all, we are serving God, not man. Men may come and men may go, but God stays forever.

SISTER INSTIGATOR   I see Sister Experience ain't with us in this fight. Of course I ain't never been in a church fight before, but I am in this one heart and hand.

SISTER MEDDLER   I think we ought to find out where Brother Procrastinator got his money from to buy that $7,000 house on 6th Street.

SISTER SAPPHIRA   Oh yes! I forgot that. That does seem funny when we poor creatures can't hardly get a crust of bread to eat; now, there's a charge agin him right there.

SISTER MEDDLER   That's so, I never thought of that. That is a good charge agin him.

BROTHER INVESTIGATOR   What's that, Sister Meddler?

SISTER SAPPHIRA   Why he bought a big house on 6th Street and paid a whole lot of money spot cash for it.

BROTHER INVESTIGATOR   Well what can you do about it? That was his own affair so long as he does not infringe on ours.

SISTER INSTIGATOR   I don't know why it ain't a charge against him. It gives our church a bad name to have the parson flashing money around like he was a rich man and then agin where did he git all that money anyway? I know Morning Glory Baptist Church didn't give it to him, because we only pay him $10 a week.

SISTER MEDDLER   He don't deserve but $5 a week.

BROTHER JUDAS (*looks out window*) Sisters, here comes Brother Procrastinator now.

BROTHER INVESTIGATOR (*goes to door*) Come in Parson Procrastinator, I am glad you came.

(PARSON PROCRASTINATOR *enters with long Prince Albert coat, stove-pipe hat and gold-headed cane; a big gold watch chain is prominent.*)

PARSON PROCRASTINATOR   Yes, Brother Investigator, I just got back from Conference, and heard a church fight was on agin me and that they didn't want me to come back again another year. Now I am here; what charge have you all agin me? (*silence*)

BROTHER INVESTIGATOR   I just told them,

Brother Procrastinator, that they would have to have some charge agin you.

PARSON PROCRASTINATOR That's correct; now let me see who's here. (*puts on glasses; looks around*) Why here's my old friend who will die by me I know. Ain't that so Brother Judas?

BROTHER JUDAS Oh yes, Parson, you can always depend on me.

SISTER EXPERIENCE Parson Procrastinator you know I am your friend; I told them there was no charge agin you, but some of them said they had a charge.

PARSON PROCRASTINATOR Had a charge aginst me? Now who was it who said so?

SISTER TAKE-IT-BACK It wasn't me, Brother Procrastinator, I've never seen nothing wrong out of you.

SISTER SAPPHIRA I never said it, Parson.

PARSON PROCRASTINATOR Well, somebody *must* have said it. Look it up in the minutes, Brother Investigator.

SISTER MEDDLER I know who said it, cause I was looking right in their mouth when they said it.

SISTER SAPPHIRA I know I never had no charge agin Brother Procrastinator 'cause I don't know nothing about him only something good.

SISTER TWO-FACE Parson Procrastinator you do look so fine since you came back from Conference, and we is all just crazy about you.

BROTHER INVESTIGATOR (*who has been searching minutes*) It says here in the minutes that you bought a $7,000 house on 6th Street, but I failed to put down who said it.

PARSON PROCRASTINATOR So that's it, is it? Well, I wants the one who said it, to git right up and tell me why they call it a "charge" agin me.

SISTER EXPERIENCE Well I never said it but I know who did say it. But it's none of my business.

PARSON PROCRASTINATOR Yes it is your business, Sister Experience, you know from your past experience what it means to have a church fight. Now I want the one what said that charge to own it.

SISTER MEDDLER I think it was sister,—

PARSON PROCRASTINATOR That will do, Sister Meddler. We want the sister what said it to speak for herself and if she can't say last what she said first, she is a prevaricator by the law. Now Brother Investigator since nobody will own the charge agin me, just scratch it out, and I wants all them what's for me to stand, and Brother Investigator you count 'em.

BROTHER INVESTIGATOR All what's in the favor of Parson Procrastinator staying with us this year, stand. (*all stand except Sister Experience*) What's your objection Sister Experience?

SISTER EXPERIENCE I was just sitting here counting the liars.

PARSON PROCRASTINATOR Well that will do. That vote is carried. If it is carried by liars, just put it down, Brother Investigator; and I will meet you all at prayer meeting Friday night. (*goes out*)

SISTER TWO-FACE Ain't he a wonderful man. I don't think we could ever get another one like him.

SISTER INSTIGATOR Well I had intended to tell him just what I thought of him if he had stayed.

BROTHER JUDAS Well, he's a good man, and we can't afford to let him go.

SISTER SAPPHIRA I said that in the first place. The trouble with our people is they never stop to think.

SISTER TAKE-IT-BACK That's just it, Sister Sapphira. Now I thank God I've never said a harmful word agin the man in my life.

SISTER MEDDLER (*who has been standing serenely all the time with a look of disgust on her face*) You ought all to be ashamed of yourselves after starting all this fuss and then denying it. Never mind I'm going to tell Parson Procrastinator.

SISTER TWO-FACE I'm glad I didn't say a word agin him. You all know I always did love Parson Procrastinator. I was the one what gave him that gold pencil, but I didn't want everybody to know it.

SISTER EXPERIENCE Sisters, do let us go home, before we defy the law any longer.

BROTHER INVESTIGATOR Yes, all stand please, (*with uplifted hands*) Lord, smile down in tender mercies upon those who have lied, and those who have not lied, close their lips with the seal of forgiveness, stiffen their tongues with the rod of obedience, fill their ears with the gospel of truth, and direct Parson Procrastinator's feet toward the railroad track.

BROTHER JUDAS (*in hard voice*) "Amen."

(*All break up in confusion each saying that* PARSON PROCRASTINATOR *should be moved and they weren't going to put up with him. Curtain.*)

Eulalie Spence (1894–)

Undertow
1929

In April 1929, the *Carolina Magazine* published four short plays by black playwrights: *The Idle Head* by Willis Richardson, *Black Damp* by John F. Matheus, *Scratches* by May Miller, and *Undertow* by Eulalie Spence.

Undertow is set in a Harlem rooming house. All the characters are Negro, and the author uses details (Lenox Avenue, the numbers) to establish the locale. The story, however, is a melodramatic triangle that belongs to no particular culture. Not many black playwrights attempted what Eulalie Spence did: to write a play whose characters were undeniably black, but whose problem within the play was not ethnic.

This observation should not be interpreted as "the characters only happen to be Negro," a comment that critics use to praise the universality of a character, and one that all too often implies that the character is not black but white, painted black. Eulalie Spence's characters are black, but she may be one of the first to write black characters into a non-racial plot. Should she be praised for extending the black experience on the stage, or censored for avoiding it?

Miss Spence entered the United States from the West Indies through Ellis Island at the age of eight with her seven sisters and her father. She received her B.A. from Teachers College in 1937 and her M.A. from Columbia in 1939, majoring in speech. She taught at Eastern District High School until her retirement. Her full length play, *The Whipping*, was optioned by Paramount Productions but was never produced. This option represented "the only money that I've ever made by writing plays."

Undertow

PERSONS IN THE PLAY

DAN, *the man*
HATTIE, *the man's wife*
CHARLEY, *their son*
CLEM, *the other woman*
MRS. WILKES, *a lodger*

(SCENE *Harlem. The dining room in* HATTIE'S *private house. It is a cheerful room, never sunny, but well furnished and spotless from shining floor to snowy linen. The supper dishes have been cleared away, but the table is still set for one who did not appear. Double doors opening upon the hall are at center back. At right there is a door leading to the kitchen. At the left there are two windows facing the street.*

TIME *About 8 o'clock one winter's night.*

AT RISE HATTIE *is sitting at the head of the table frowning heavily at the place of the one who did not appear. She drums impatiently with her fingers for a few seconds then pushing her chair back with more violence than grace, rises.* HATTIE'S *dark face is hard and cold. She has a disconcerting smile—a little contempt and a great deal of distrust. Her body is short and spreads freely in every direction. Her dark dress is covered by an apron which makes her look somewhat clumsy.* CHARLEY, *dressed in an overcoat and hat of the latest mode bursts noisily into the room. He is a slender fellow, about the same complexion of his mother, but possessing none of her strength of character. His good-looking face is weak, with a suggestion of stubbornness about it. His manner is arrogant and somewhat insolent*)

CHARLEY   Ah'm off, Ma.
HATTIE   So Ah see.
CHARLEY (*his glance falls on the table*)   Say, Ma—Gee whiz! Ain't Dad bin home fer supper yet?
HATTIE (*shortly*)   No.
CHARLEY (*with a low whistle*)   Dat's funny, he ain't never stayed out befo' has he?
HATTIE   Not sence Ah married him—'cept—
CHARLEY (*curiously*)   'Cept whut, Ma?
HATTIE   'Cept wunce 'fo yuh was born.
CHARLEY (*with an uproarious laugh*)   An' the old man ain't tried it sence! Reckon yuh fixed him, didn't yuh, Ma! (*he sits down beside the table and laughs once more*)
HATTIE (*sharply*)   Ah ain't trained yuh half's as well's Ah's trained yo' Dad. (*she resumes her seat*) Ah shoulda made yuh stay in school fer one thing.
CHARLEY   Yuh had mo' sense Ma! If yuh'd a bossed me lak yuh's bossed Dad, Ah'd runned away long 'fo now.
HATTIE   Thar ain't no danger uh Dan runnin' off. He ain't got de nerve. Sides, nobuddy'd want him.
CHARLEY   Now doan' fool yuhself, Ma! An easy simp lak Dad'd be snapped up soon 'nuff ef he ever got it intuh his head dat he could do sech a thing.
HATTIE   Dan's a fool, but he knows which side his bread's buttered on.
CHARLEY (*giving his thigh a loud slap*)   Holy smoke!
HATTIE (*irritably*)   Whut's eatin' yuh?
CHARLEY   Nuthin'.
HATTIE (*impatiently*)   Never mind lyin'! Whut's on yuh mind?
CHARLEY   Oh, nuthin'! Ah jes' thought er sumpth'n dat's all. Say, Ma—
HATTIE   Well?
CHARLEY   Ah gotta have five bucks ter-night,—Need 'em bad.
HATTIE   It doan do no harm tuh need 'em. Thar's a plenty things Ah's wanted dat Ah ain't never got.
CHARLEY (*roughly*)   Where the devil do yuh think Ah kin git it, ef Ah doan ask yuh?
HATTIE   Yuh might wuk 'cassionally. Dan ain't bin home a day dese twenty-five years.
CHARLEY (*with a sneer*)   An' yuh's jes' done

callin' him a fool, ain't yuh? The guys in mah crowd doan do no work see? We lives by our brains.

HATTIE   Not by exercisin' 'em, Lawd knows!

CHARLEY   How come yuh think we hits de Number ev'y week? Brain work!

HATTIE   Ef yuh hits so often whut yuh allus comin' ter me 'bout money fer?

CHARLEY   Ef dat ain't lak a woman! It takes money ter make money!

HATTIE   Charley, yuh's gotta cut out dis gamblin'. Ah ain't goin' give yuh no mo' money.

CHARLEY   (*insolently*) Yuh think Ah'm Dad, doan' yuh? Well, Ah ain't! Ah wish ter Gawd Ah knew whut yuh's got over on him. No free man would er stood yuh naggin' all dese years.

HATTIE   (*coldly*) Dem whut can't stan' fer mah ways knows whut dey kin do.

CHARLEY   Wouldn't 'sprise me none ef Dad has walked off—

HATTIE   (*quickly*) Whut makes yuh think so?

CHARLEY   Reckon yu'd like tuh know, wouldn't yuh?

HATTIE   'Tain't likely whut yuh could say's wurth five dollars tuh hear.

CHARLEY   Whut Ah seen wouldn't ah bin wuth nuthin' las' week, but sence Dad ain't showed up, fer supper, it's wuth a damn sight mo'. Yuh'd never guess whut Ah seen him doin' one night las' week up on Lenox Avenue.

HATTIE   Well, yuh might's well say it. Yuh kin have dat five, but lemme tell yuh dat yuh'll be de loser, later, if yuh's lied tuh me.

CHARLEY   Whut Ah's gotta lie fer? (*he stretches his hand across the table, palm upturned*) Hand it over, Ma. (HATTIE *takes a bill, from her stocking and puts it on the table, beside her. She places her closed fist upon the money.* CHARLEY *frowns and draws his hand back*)

HATTIE   Ah ain't never refused tuh pay fer whut Ah gits.

CHARLEY   Oh, all right. Here goes. Me an' Nat Walker was strollin' up Lenox Avenue one night las' week 'bout half past six. Right ahead uh me Ah seen Dad. He was walkin' 'long, slow ez usual wid his head bent, not seein' nobuddy. All uv a sudden, a woman comin' down de Avenue, went up tuh him an' stops him. He looked up kinda dazed like an' stared at her lak he'd seen a ghost. She jes' shook him by de arm an' laughed. By dat time, we come along side an' Ah got a good look at her. She warn't young an' she warn't old. But she looked—well—As jes' doan know how she did look—all laughin' an' happy an' tears in her eyes. Ah didn't look at her much fer starin' at Dad. He looked—all shaken up—an' scared like—Not scared like neither fer Ah seen him smile at her, after a minute. He ain't never smiled lak that befo'—not's Ah kin remember. Nat said— "Reckin yuh Dad's met an' ole gal 'er his"— But Ah only laughed—Struck me kinda funny —that! Dad meetin' an 'ole flame uh his—Ah meant tuh ask Dad 'bout her but it went clean outa mah head. (*he reaches once more for the money. This time he takes it easily, enough.* HATTIE *has forgotten it*)

HATTIE   (*after a pause*) Was she tall?

CHARLEY   Kinda. Plenty taller'n you. (*he rises and takes his hat from the table*)

HATTIE   (*after a pause*) Light?

CHARLEY   So—So,—lighter'n you. (*he moves toward the door*)

HATTIE   Pretty?

CHARLEY   Mebbe. She warn't no chicken— but she was good tuh look at. Tain't no use mopin', Ma. Dad ain't de fus' husban' tuh take dinner wid his girl friend. Funny, though his never doin' it befo'. Well, s'long!

(*he goes out and the door slams noisily.* HATTIE *rouses up at that and starts clearing the table. She has just left the room with the last handful of dishes when the hall door is opened quietly and* DAN *enters. He is a dark man of medium height, slender of build. He looks a little stooped. There is a beaten look about his face—a tired, patient look. He takes off his overcoat and still stands there hesitating.* HATTIE *re-enters, frowns darkly but does not speak. She places a scarf upon the table and a little silver-plated basket from the sideboard*)

DAN   (*dropping his coat and hat upon a chair*) Sorry, Ah'm late, Hattie. (*she does not answer*) Ah ain't had no supper. Reckon Ah'll get it an' eat in de kitchen.

HATTIE   (*icily*) Reckon yuh'll hang dat coat an' hat in de hall whar dey belongs.

DAN   (*apologetically*) Sure. Dunno how Ah come tuh ferget. (*he goes out with his clothes and returns almost immediately. He looks timidly at* HATTIE, *then passes on toward the kitchen door*)

HATTIE (*fiercely*) Keep outa dat kitchen!

DAN But Ah'm hungry, Hattie. Ah ain't had nuthin' tuh eat.

HATTIE Whar yuh bin, dat yur ain't had nuthin 'tuh eat? (DAN *doesn't answer*) Yuh kain't say, kin yuh?

DAN Ah went tuh see a friend uh mine.

HATTIE Half past six ain't callin' hours! (DAN *looks unhappily at the floor*) Less'n yuh's asked ter dine!

DAN It was important! Ah had tuh go.

HATTIE Had tuh go whar? Yuh ain't said whar yuh's bin. (DAN *does not answer*) An yuh ain't got no intention uh saying, has yuh? (DAN *does not answer. He moves once more toward the kitchen*)

HATTIE (*in a shrill voice*) Yuh keep outa thar! Keep outa mah kitchen! Ah kep yuh supper till eight o'clock. Yuh didn' come, an Ah's throwed it out!

DAN Ah'll fix sumpth'n else. Ah doan want much.

HATTIE Yuh ain't goin' messin' in mah kitchen! Yuh's hidin' sumpth'n, Dan Peters, and Ah's gwine fine it out 'fo' long. Yuh ain't gonna trow no dust in mah eyes no second time —not ef Ah knows it!

DAN All right, Ah doan' want no fuss, Hattie. Ah'll go out an' git sumpth'n.

HATTIE Yuh kin fix de furnace 'fo' yuh go. Ah's got 'nuff tuh do runnin' a lodgin' house, 'thout fixin' fires day an' night.

DAN Charley was home. Yuh coulda asked Charley tuh do it.

HATTIE Charley doan' never fix no furnace. It's yo' job when yuh's home an' Ah ain't got no reason tuh wish it on Charley.

DAN Ah'll fix it when Ah gits back. Ah'm hungry, now an' Ah's gwine tuh git sumpth'n tuh eat.

(*he goes out.* HATTIE *listens for the click of the iron gate, then hurries to the window and peers after him. The door is opened softly and a little brown woman sidles in. Her eyes rove constantly always seeking—seeking.* HATTIE *turns around and glares fiercely at her*)

HATTIE What yuh want?

MRS. WILKES (*startled slightly at the grimness of the other's voice*) Ah declare, Mis' Peters, yuh sho' does look put out! Anything de matter?

HATTIE (*shortly*) Did yuh come down here tuh tell me dat?

MRS. WILKES (*with an uneasy laugh*) C'ose not, Mis' Peters! . . . It's pretty cold upstairs. Ah s'pose de fire's goin' ez usual?

HATTIE Yes.

MRS. WILKES It's gettin' colder, Ah reckon. (HATTIE *does not answer*) It's warmer down here. As Ah always tells Mr. Wilkes, gimme a parlor floor an' basement any time. Ef thar's any heat goin' yuh's sure tuh git it—Co'se, Ah ain't complainin', Mis' Peters—

HATTIE H'm!

MRS. WILKES See Mr. Peters got home pretty late tuh-night, didn' he? (HATTIE *answers only with a venomous glance*) Thar's a man with reg'lar habits. Ah often tells Mr. Wilkes dat Ah wish tuh goodness he was a home lovin' man lak Mr. Peters. . . . Well, reckon Ah'll be gwine up again' seein' ez yuh's got comp'ny.

HATTIE (*with a puzzled frown*) Comp'ny?

MRS. WILKES Thar's a lady tuh see yuh. She's upstairs settin' in de parlor.

HATTIE Who let her in?

MRS. WILKES Mr. Wilkes did. He seen her on de stoop. She was jes' gwine tuh ring de bell when Mr. Wilkes come up wid his key. She ask tuh see Mis' Peters an' he tole her tuh set in de parlor. Ef thar's ever a stupid man it sure is mah husban'. 'Stead uh goin' down an tellin' yuh, 'er hollerin' tuh yuh, 'er sendin' her on down, he comes up-stairs an' tells *me* ter go down an' tell yuh. He'd oughta sent her down de basement do' fust place.

HATTIE Send her down, will yuh? Some fine day, Ah 'spec we'll be cleaned out, ef yuh all's gwine let strangers in de house that 'a way.

MRS. WILKES (*with a little cough*) Thought yuh might want tuh see her in de parlor. Ah reckon she ain't no thief, not judgin' from her looks.

HATTIE H'h! Whut she look lak?

MRS. WILKES She's tall—but not too tall.

HATTIE (*forcing her stiffening lips to move*) Light?

MRS. WILKES Lighter'n yuh an' me—

HATTIE (*with a supreme effort*) Pretty?

MRS. WILKES Well, yuh knows her all right! She ain't never bin here befo' ez Ah knows—but yuh knows her frum de way yuh's 'scribed her. Well, 'slong! Ah'll send her down. (*she opens the hall door*) B'r! (*she shivers*) Dis hall cert'nly is cold!

(*The door closes after her. For a moment* HATTIE *looks bewildered. But only for a moment. With a sudden harsh laugh she rips the apron from about her waist and pushes it quickly into the side-board drawer. She goes up to the mirror over the mantle, but one look at herself is all that she can bear. As she turns sharply away the door opens and* CLEM *enters. In one glance* HATTIE's *burning eyes take in the tall, well-dressed figure. The graying hair, the youthful face. If* CLEM's *glance is less piercing, it is nevertheless, just as comprehensive*)

CLEM (*softly*) It's bin a long time, Hattie. (HATTIE *opens her lips to speak, but she doesn't. She sits, rather heavily, and continues to stare at* CLEM) Ah doan' wonder yuh's 'sprised Hattie. (*She hesitates and then drawing up a chair facing* HATTIE, *she too, sits.*) Ah know yuh's waitin' tuh hear whut brought me . . . It's a long story, Hattie. (*at that,* HATTIE *moves impatiently*)

HATTIE Yuh kin start—at de end—

CLEM At de end?

HATTIE At de end. Whut yuh come fer? Yuh's come ter git sumpth'n—Is it—Dan?

CLEM (*leaning back in her chair with a sigh*) De same ole Hattie! De years ain't changed yuh, none.

HATTIE (*with a bitter laugh*) An' de years ain't changed *you*, none.

CLEM Yes. Ah reckon they has, Hattie, Ah's suffered a-plenty.

HATTIE (*with a curl of her lip*) An' yuh think dat yuh's de only one?

CLEM Oh no! Ah kin see yuh's not bin over happy, Hattie, an' Ah knows dat Dan ain't bin happy.

HATTIE Whut reason yuh got ter bring up all dis talk 'bout suff'rin'? Yuh bin seein' Dan agin', ain't yuh?

CLEM Yes. Ah met him jes' by accident one night las' week.

HATTIE An' yuh's bin seein' him sence?

CLEM Yes, ev'y night. Ah's bein' gwine down town ter meet him 'roun six o'clock an' Ah's ride home wid him in de "L."

HATTIE An' tuh-night yuh had him out tuh dinner. (HATTIE's *voice has a deadly calm*)

CLEM No. Tuh-night Ah couldn' go tuh meet him. Ah was called away on business. Ah ain't seen him tuh-night.

HATTIE Did he know yuh was comin' here?

CLEM No.

HATTIE Why'nt yuh tell him, yuh was comin'.

CLEM He wouldn' 'er let me come.

HATTIE Well, say whut yuh's come fer, an' go. It ain't easy settin' here an' listenin' tuh yuh talkin' 'bout Dan.

CLEM (*abruptly*) Yuh's almost driv' him crazy. An' yuh said yuh loved him. (HATTIE's *fingers clench slowly*)

HATTIE Whar'd yuh go to? Whar you bin all dese years?

CLEM South—Virginia, whar I come frum.

HATTIE H'm!

CLEM Ef Ah'd knowed yuh was gwine tuh be unkind tuh him, Ah'd never let him go! Dan ain't knowed a day's happiness sence Ah went away.

HATTIE He—he tole yuh dat?

CLEM Yes! Ah kin fergive yuh fer takin' him 'way frum me—an' de way yuh done it—but it ain't easy fergivin' yuh fer makin' him suffer.

HATTIE An' dat's whut yuh's come here tuh tell me?

CLEM (*passionately*) Dan's dyin' here, right under yo' eyes, an' yo' doan see it. He's dyin' fer kindness—He's dyin' frum hard wuk. He's dyin' frum de want uv love. Ah could allus read him lak a book. He won't talk 'gainst yuh, Hattie, but Ah kin see it all in de way he looks—in de way he looks at me. (CLEM *dabs at her eyes with her handkerchief*)

HATTIE Go on. (*she marvels at her own quietness*)

CLEM (*accusingly*) He's shabby—all uv him —hat an' shoes an coat. Ef he had one suit fer ev'y five dat yuh son has, he'd be pretty well dressed.

HATTIE (*slowly*) Yuh fergit, Charley is Dan's son ez well ez mine.

CLEM An' yuh's set him 'gainst his dad. He sides with yuh ev'y time, doan' he?

HATTIE (*with a faint sneer*) Did yuh read dat too, in de way Dan—looked—at yuh?

CLEM Ef yuh had a brought Charley up diff'rent yuh mighta held on tuh Dan. 'Stead uh dat, yuh's brought him up tuh look down on him.

HATTIE (*she is breathing heavily, her voice comes thick and choked*) Is yuh tru? (*rises*)

CLEM Yuh doan' need Dan an yo' son doan' need him. Well, sence yuh ain't got no use fer him, Ah's gwine take him frum yuh, Hattie. Now yuh knows why Ah's come. (*she rises also and looks down at* HATTIE, *much to the latter's disadvantage*)

HATTIE (*forcing the words out, as though each one pains her*) Funny—how—thoughtful yuh's got sence Ah's las' seen yuh. Yuh come inta mah house twenty years ago as a frien'—an' yuh took Dan when Ah hadn't bin married ter him a year. Yuh didn' give no 'nouncement den 'bout whut yuh was gwine ter do. Yuh jes' took him—an' me expectin' tuh be de mother uv his chile. Gawd! (*a deep shudder runs through her body*) But now—dat yuh's got mo' stylish—mo' lady-like in yuh ways yuh come tuh tell me ve'y politely, dat yuh's gwine tuh take him agin. Is it mah blessin' yuh's waitin' fer? Yuh doan' need no permission.

CLEM Yuh, yuh doan' un'erstan'—Yuh never did un'erstan' Hattie.

HATTIE Mebbe not. Some things is hard tuh un'erstan'.

CLEM Co'se Dan an' me could go off tergether, 'thout yuh permission Yuh knows dat well 'nuff. It's bein' done ev'y day. But we doan' want ter go lak dat.

HATTIE Yuh mean Dan doan' want ter go that 'a-way!

CLEM Yuh's wrong, Hattie. Dan ain't thinkin' 'er nuthin' 'er nobuddy but me. He's fer quittin' an' never sayin' a word tuh yuh but jes' goin' off, me an' him together. But Ah ain't gwine tuh go lak dat. Dis time it's gotta be diff'rent.

HATTIE Diff'rent—how?

CLEM Hattie, Ah wants yuh tuh free Dan. Yuh owes it tuh him. He ain't never bin free sence he's knowed yuh. Will yuh free him?

HATTIE Free him—how?

CLEM Give him a divo'ce.

HATTIE A divo'ce—tuh marry you?

CLEM (*pleadingly*) Yes. 'Taint lak yuh loved him Hattie. Ef yuh loved him Ah couldn' ask yuh. But yuh only holds onta him tru spite—Yuh hates him, mebbe—Yuh treats him lak yuh does.

HATTIE Yuh knows Ah kain't keep him ef he wants tuh go. Reckon Ah knows it, too. Well, ef he wants tuh go he kin go.

CLEM (*with an exclamation of relief*) Thank Gawd! Ah didn' think yuh'd do it, Hattie.

HATTIE Yuh coulda spared yuhself de trubble comin' here—an jes' gone off. It woulda bin more lak yuh.

CLEM But—but—how? Yuh'd have ter know 'bout de devo'ce, Hattie.

HATTIE Devo'ce? Ah ain't said nuthin' 'bout gettin' no devo'ce!

CLEM But — but — yuh — Ah thought — Whut yuh mean, Hattie?

HATTIE Yuh didn' need no devo'ce de fust time, did yuh?

CLEM (*biting her lips to keep back the tears*) Dat—Dat was diff'rent.

HATTIE Ah doan' see it.

CLEM Well, it was. It's gotta be a divo'ce dis time.

HATTIE Ah see Dan's morals has improved some sence *you* went away.

CLEM It ain't Dan whut's holdin' out fer devo'ce—It's—it's me.

HATTIE (HATTIE's *laugh has a bitter edge*) Den it's yo' morals dat's bin improvin'—Well, dey could stan' improvin' a-plenty. (*the fierce edge returns suddenly to her voice*) Yuh's wastin' yo' time an' mine an Dan's! 'Bout lettin' him go—He coulda gone all dese years—Ah warn't holdin' him back! He'd gone too, ef he'd knowed whar to find yuh. Ah knowed ef he ever found yuh, he'd leave me. Well, he didn' find yuh tell now. But long's Ah's got breaf tuh breathe, Ah ain't gwine say "Yes!" 'bout no divo'ce. Ef he kin git one 'thout me, let him git it! Yuh hear me? Now ef yuh's tru, yuh better get outa here. Ah ain't 'sponsible' fer whut Ah says frum now on!

CLEM Hattie, 'fore Gawd, yuh's hard!

HATTIE Ah was soft 'nuff, when yuh fust stepped on me. Ef Ah's hard now, 'tis yo' fault!

CLEM Hattie—Ah ain't tole yuh de real reason why Ah wants dat di'voce—(*a note of despair has crept into her voice*)

HATTIE No? Well, Ah ain't in'trested none.

CLEM Still Ah wants yuh tuh hear! It's sumpthin' dat Ah ain't tole Dan. (*The door is opened quietly and* DAN *enters. He starts—looks fearfully from* CLEM *to* HATTIE *and then back again to* CLEM) Come in, Dan. Ah hope yuh doan' mind ma comin' tuh see Hattie. Ah jes' had tuh come.

DAN (*swallowing painfully*) It won' do no good. (HATTIE *is gazing at him curiously*)

CLEM Mebbe not, but Ah had tuh come.

DAN Ah'm sorry, Hattie. We—we—(*he turns away as if ashamed*)

CLEM Hattie knows ev'ything Dan. Ah's tole her. (DAN *turns toward her*)

DAN Clem, whut was yuh sayin' when Ah come on in? Ah heard yuh—

CLEM (*embarrassed*) Ah didn' want tuh tell yuh—lak dis—

DAN (*gently*) We kain't go back now, Clem. Sence we's in de middle we's gotta git tru, somehow.

CLEM (*turning from him to* HATTIE) Ah didn' mean tuh beg, 'less'n Ah had tuh—

HATTIE (*coldly*) Yuh doan' have tuh—

CLEM Ef 'twas only me—but it ain't. It's fer mah Lucy,—Dan's chile (*there is a terrible silence*) Dan's chile—Ah didn' tell yuh, Hattie, an' Ah didn' tell Dan. Whut woulda bin de use? She's a woman now an' good—an' pretty. She thinks her dad died when she was a baby an' she thinks—she thinks—Ah'm a good woman. She's proud uh me. (*as if unconscious of* HATTIE's *presence*, DAN *grips* CLEM's *hands. They look at each other*)

HATTIE (*as if to herself. She seems to be trying to get it all quite clear*) She thinks yuh's a good woman! An' dat's why yuh expects me tuh give Dan a divo'ce.

CLEM (*eagerly*) Yes, Yes! Yuh see, doan' yuh?

HATTIE Yes, Ah see. Gawd, ef dat ain't funny! She thinks yuh's a good woman. (*she laughs loudly,—hysterically*) Oh, my Gawd!

DAN (*sharply*) Hattie!

HATTIE (*ignoring him*) Tell me mo'—'bout dis—dis new relation, uh Dan's.

CLEM Ah's wuked hard tuh git her de chances Ah didn' have. She's bin tuh school—she's got an' eddication. An' now she's goin' tuh git married tuh a fine feller whut'll be able tuh take care uv her. Now yuh see dat Ah kain't jes' go off wid Dan. It's got tuh be proper—a divo'ce an' all. Yuh see, doan' yuh, Hattie?

HATTIE (*nodding*) Mother an' daughter—double weddin'.

CLEM (*anxiously*) An yuh'll do it, Hattie? Gawd'll bless yuh, Hattie.

HATTIE (*derisively*) How come *you's* passin' on blessins? Yuh knows a lot, doan' yuh 'bout blessins? Wonder ef yuh knows ez much 'bout curses?

CLEM Now, Hattie—

HATTIE (*darkly*) Yuh doan know nuthin' much 'bout curses, does yuh? Well, yuh's cursed, Clem Jackson! Cursed! Yuh's allus bin cursed sence de day yuh cast yuh eyes on Dan!

DAN (*harshly*) Hattie, yuh ain't got no call tuh go on lak dat.

HATTIE (*who does not seem to hear him*) Dan was cursed when he set eyes on yuh. An' Ah was cursed when Ah took yuh fer a frien'.

CLEM (*hurriedly*) Ah'm goin', Hattie! Ah see yuh ain't gwine give in.

HATTIE Whut's yuh hurry? Yuh better hear whut Ah's gwine tuh say . . . Curses. Yes, we's all bin cursed, Clem. Mah Charley's cursed an' yo' Lucy—too bad.

CLEM (*angrily*) Doan' yuh call mah Lucy's name 'long uv yours.

HATTIE (*with a sneer*) Too bad. Wonder how she'll feel when she hears whut a good woman yuh is?

CLEM (*shrinking as if from a blow*) Whut? Yuh—yuh wouldn'—yuh wouldn'—

HATTIE Wouldn' — wouldn' — (*she laughs again—crazily*) Sure, Ah'll fine her! Ef it takes de rest uh mah life, Ah'll fine her. It's too good—tuh keep. How she'll stare when she knows her ma was a prostitute an' her dad—

DAN (*hoarsely*) Damn yuh, Hattie! Doan yuh say no mo'.

HATTIE Ah'll tell her all—all—leavin' out nuthin'.

CLEM (*pleading as if for life*) Yuh couldn', Hattie! Yuh couldn'! Hattie—Hattie—

HATTIE How she play me false—when Ah trusted her—an' how she lie tuh me—How she ruin' mah life—an' come on back tuh take de leavin's once more—

DAN Doan yuh say no mo, Hattie!

HATTIE Yuh'd shut mah mouf' wouldn' yuh? How? How—

DAN Let's go, Clem. Let's go—

HATTIE (*shrilly*) G'wan. Is Ah keepin' yuh? Take yuh street walker back whar she come frum. Yuh kin give Lucy mah regahds. Tell her dat a frien's gwine call on her—real soon—an' ole frien' uv her ma's.

DAN (*with a cry of rage, grips Hattie by the shoulder and shakes her*) Yoh'll shut yo' mouf, Hattie. Promise, 'er fo' Gawd-A-Mighty.

Undertow

HATTIE (*scornfully*) How yuh's thinkin' 'er shuttin' mah mouf, Dan Peters?

DAN Yuh'll keep 'way frum Lucy. Yuh'll promise not tuh say nuthin' 'bout Clem. (DAN *shakes her again roughly*)

HATTIE (*her speech broken with little gasping cries*) Never! An' yuh kain't make me! Ah'll tell her 'bout dis good woman! Dis thief! Dis dirty minded whore! (*without a word,* DAN *grips her by the throat and forces her back—back against the table. Her arms claw awkwardly and then drop to her sides.* CLEM *utters a low cry and springs upon* DAN, *tearing wildly at his fingers.*)

CLEM Dan! Leggo! Leggo, fer Gawd's sake! Dan! (*with a violent movement of disgust he thrusts* HATTIE *from him. She falls heavily from the chair, her head striking the marble base of the mantle—an ugly sound. She lies very still.* DAN *looks at her stupidly.* CLEM *throws her arms about his neck, sobbing hysterically*) Dan! Dan! Yuh come near killin' her!

DAN (*breathing heavily*) Ah'd a done it too, ef yuh hadn't bin thar.

CLEM (*stooping over* HATTIE) She hit her head an awful crack!

DAN Hattie's head's harder'n mos'. Come on, Clem. We kain't stay here, now. She'll be comin' to, 'fo' long! An raisin' de roof.

CLEM (*who is still peering at* HATTIE) Dan, thar's blood comin' out de corner uv her mouf.

DAN She'll be waggin' it again' fo' yuh knows it.

CLEM (*going up to* DAN *and putting her hand on his shoulder*) Dan, Ah wish yuh hadn't done it! 'Twon' do no good!

DAN Ah couldn' stan' it no longer. Ah clean los' mah head when she call yuh—whut she did.

CLEM Yes, Ah know. Poor Danny boy! Ah doan see how yuh's stood it all dese years.

DAN (*putting his arms about her*) Ah was allus thinkin' uv yuh, Clem. Yuh shouldn' 'a lef' me behin'. Yuh'd oughta tole me whar tuh fine yuh. Yuh shoulda tole me 'bout Lucy.

CLEM Yes, Ah see dat now. But yuh b'longed tuh Hattie 'n Ah thought—

DAN Ah never b'longed tuh Hattie. (*he kisses her*) Let's go, Clem. (*she draws away from him*) Why, whut's wrong?

CLEM Ah's gotta think uh Lucy.

DAN Lucy?

CLEM Yes, Lucy. She's yo' chile Dan, an' she doan' know—'bout us.

DAN An' me—Whut 'bout me, an you—Clem—Clem—

CLEM Ah you musn'. Then thar's Hattie. Yuh's gotta think uv Hattie—(*they both turn and look at the figure huddled there on the floor*) Dan, we'd better try'n bring her to. Get some water, Dan.

DAN Ah won't touch her!

CLEM It ain't human leavin' her lak dat. Help me lif' her, Dan. She'll catch her death uh cold on dat flo'! (*very unwillingly* DAN *assists. Together he and* CLEM *get* HATTIE *into a chair. Her head lolls persistently to one side.* CLEM *rubs her hands*) Lak ice! Why, Dan, her fingers all stiff! An'—an' Dan! Feel her pulse! Dan!

(*She draws back terrified.* HATTIE'*s body, unsupported, sags awkwardly against the table.* DAN *quickly seizes her hands, feeling her pulse. He tilts her head backward, looks into her face—feels her heart, then straightens up—his face distorted, his eyes blank.*)

CLEM (*in a whisper*) Dan—she ain't—dead?

DAN Dead. (*he looks down at his hands in horror*)

CLEM (*wildly*) Dan! Whut'll we do! Whut'll we do!

DAN Yuh'll go back tuh Lucy. She needs yuh.

CLEM You needs me mo', Dan!

DAN Yuh kain't help none! Ah doan stan' no chance—reckon Ah owes it tuh Lucy tuh send yuh back tuh her. Ah ain't never had de chance tuh do nuthin' fer her—but dis.

CLEM Ah kain't go, Dan! Doan' mek me. (*her body is wracked with sobs*)

DAN (*taking her in his arms and kissing her*) We's gotta think 'bout Lucy—We's brung each other bad luck, Clem. Hattie was right.

CLEM But Ah loved yuh Dan, an' yuh loved me.

DAN: Ah ain't never loved nobuddy else.

CLEM Whut'll dey do tuh yuh Dan? Dey won't kill yuh? (*she clings tightly to him*) Will dey, Dan?

DAN Co'se not, Honey! Reckon Ah'll git twenty—er fifteen years—mebbe ten—(*he buttons her coat and draws her firmly toward the door*)

CLEM Ten years! (*she wrings her hands with a low moaning cry*)

DAN Ah'll spend 'em all dreamin' 'bout yuh,

Clem, an'—an' Lucy! Yuh musn' grieve, Honey. Go, now, fer Gawd's sake! Ah hears sombuddy comin' down! (*he pushes her out, forcibly. And then the door is shut. The outer door slams.* DAN *listens for the click of the gate. Finally he turns and looks down at* HATTIE) Ah'm sorry, Hattie! 'Fore Gawd, Ah didn' mean tuh do it!

(*Curtain.*)

Marita Bonner (1905–)

The Purple Flower   1928

The 1960's have seen a number of plays by black writers calling for or describing the blood revolution: *The Slave, Experimental Death Unit #1, We Righteous Bombers,* and *Black Terror.* These plays have been seen by white and black audiences.

For the reader who believes that the concepts of the White Devils and Us, and the Call to Revolution have developed since the burning of Watts, *The Purple Flower*, published in *Crisis* in 1928, will be a revelation.

The author uses allegory to tell it like it is. The Leader (Dr. Washington) was mistaken! Work won't do it! Book learning won't do it! Money won't do it! Only blood will pay for blood! Marita Bonner isn't asking, "Will there be a revolution?" but, "Is it time?"

Marita Bonner was born and educated in Massachusetts. She attended Radcliffe College where she studied creative writing with Professor Copeland. After graduation she taught English in Washington, D.C. From 1925 to 1928 a number of her essays, short stories, and plays appeared in *Crisis.*

The first of these, an essay entitled *On Being Young—A Woman—And Colored*, appeared in December, 1925. She discusses what it feels like to be a woman in a male-dominated world and what it is to be black in white America:

> But—"In Heaven's name, do not grow bitter. Be bigger than they are," exhort white friends who have never had to draw breath in a Jim Crow train. Who have never had petty putrid insult dragged over them—drawing blood—like pebbled sand on your body where the skin is tenderest.
>
> You long to explode and hurt everything white; friendly; unfriendly. But you know that you cannot live with a chip on your shoulder.... For chips make you bend your body to balance them. And once you bend, you lose your poise, your balance, and the chip gets into you. The real you. You get hard.
>
> So—being a woman—you can wait.
>
> You must sit quietly without a chip. Not sodden—and weighted as if your feet were cast in iron of your soul. Not wasting strength in enervating gestures as if two hundred years of bonds and whips had really tricked you into nervous uncertainty.
>
> But quiet; quiet. Like Buddha... perhaps Buddha is a woman....
>
> So you too. Still; quiet; with a smile ever so slight, at the eyes, so that Life will flow into and not by you. And you can gather, as it passes, the essences, the overtones, the tints, the shadows; draw understanding to your self.
>
> And then you can, when Time is ripe, swoop to your feet—at your full height—at a single gesture.
>
> Ready to go where?
>
> Why... Wherever God motions.

And where did God motion? For Marita Bonner, it was up the mountain toward the Purple Flower.

The Purple Flower

(TIME   The Middle-of-Things-as-They-are.

[Which means the End-of-Things for some of the characters and the Beginning-of-Things for others.]

PLACE   Might be here, there or anywhere—or even nowhere.

CHARACTERS   SUNDRY WHITE DEVILS.

[They must be artful little things with soft wide eyes such as you would expect to find in an angel. Soft hair that flops around their horns. Their horns glow red all the time—now with blood—now with eternal fire—now with deceit—now with unholy desire. They have bones tied carefully across their tails to make them seem less like tails and more like mere decorations. They are artful little things full of artful movements and artful tricks. They are artful dancers too. You are amazed at their adroitness. Their steps are intricate. You almost lose your head following them. Sometimes they dance as if they were men—with dignity—erect. Sometimes they dance as if they were snakes. They are artful dancers on the Thin-Skin-of-Civilization.]

THE US'S. [They can be as white as the White Devils, as brown as the earth, as black as the center of a poppy. They may look as if they were something or nothing.]

SETTING   The stage is divided horizontally into two sections, upper and lower, by a thin board. The main action takes place on the upper stage. The light is never quite clear on the lower stage; but it is bright enough for you to perceive that sometimes the action that takes place on the upper stage is duplicated on the lower. Sometimes the actors on the upper stage get too vociferous—too violent—and they crack through the boards and they lie twisted and curled in mounds. There are any number of mounds there, all twisted and broken. You look at them and you are not quite sure whether you see something or nothing; but you see by a curve that there might lie a human body. There is thrust out a white hand—a yellow one—one brown—a black. The Skin-of-Civilization must be very thin. A thought can drop you through it.

SCENE   An open plain. It is bounded distantly on one side by Nowhere and faced by a high hill—Somewhere.

ARGUMENT   The WHITE DEVILS live on the side of the hill. Somewhere. On top of the hill grows the purple Flower-of-Life-At-Its-Fullest. This flower is as tall as a pine and stands alone on top of the hill. The US's live in the valley that lies between Nowhere and Somewhere and spend their time trying to devise means of getting up the hill. The WHITE DEVILS live all over the sides of the hill and try every trick, known and unknown, to keep the US's from getting to the hill. For if the US's get up the hill, the Flower-of-Life-at-Its-Fullest will shed some of its perfume and then and there they will be Somewhere with the WHITE DEVILS. The US's started out by merely asking permission to go up. They tilled the valley, they cultivated it and made it as beautiful as it is. They built roads and houses even for the WHITE DEVILS. They let them build the houses and then they were knocked back down into the valley.

SCENE   When the curtain rises, the evening sun is shining bravely on the valley and hillside alike.

The US's are having a siesta beside a brook that runs down the Middle of the valley. As usual they rest with their backs toward Nowhere and their faces toward Somewhere. The WHITE DEVILS are seen in the distance on the hillside. As you see them, a song is borne faintly to your ears from the hillside.

The WHITE DEVILS are saying:

> You stay where you are!
> We don't want you up here!
> If you come you'll be on par
> With all we hold dear.
> So stay—stay—stay—
> Yes stay where you are!

The song rolls full across the valley)

The Purple Flower

A LITTLE RUNTY US   "Hear that, don't you?

ANOTHER US (*lolling over on his back and chewing a piece of grass*)   I ain't studying 'bout them devils. When I get ready to go up that hill —I'm going! (*he rolls over on his side and exposes a slender brown body to the sun*) Right now, I'm going to sleep. (*and he forthwith snores*)

OLD LADY (*an old dark brown lady who has been lying down rises suddenly to her knees in the foreground. She gazes toward the hillside*) I'll never live to see the face of that flower! God knows I worked hard to get Somewhere though. I've washed the shirt off of every one of them White Devils' backs!

A YOUNG US   And you got a slap in the face for doing it.

OLD LADY   But that's what the Leader told us to do. "Work," he said. "Show them you know how." As if two hundred years of slavery had not showed them!

ANOTHER YOUNG US   Work doesn't do it. The Us who work for the White Devils get pushed in the face—down off of Somewhere every night. They don't even sleep up there.

OLD LADY   Something's got to be done though! The Us ain't got no business to sleep while the sun is shining. They'd ought to be up and working before the White Devils get to some other tricks.

YOUNG US   You just said work did not do you any good! What's the need of working if it doesn't get you anywhere? What's the use of boring around in the same hole like a worm? Making the hole bigger to stay in?

(*There comes up the road a clatter of feet and four figures, a middle-aged well-browned man, a lighter-browned middle-aged woman, a medium light brown girl, beautiful as a browned peach and a slender, tall, bronzy brown youth who walks with his head high. He touches the ground with his feet as if it were a velvet rug and not sun-baked, jagged rocks*)

OLD LADY (*addressing the* OLDER MAN) Evenin', Average. I was just saying we ain't never going to make that hill.

AVERAGE   The Us will if they get the right leaders.

THE MIDDLE-AGED WOMAN—CORNERSTONE   Leaders! Leaders! They've had good ones looks like to me.

AVERAGE   But they ain't led us anywhere!

CORNERSTONE   But that is not their fault! If one of them gets up and says, "Do this," one of the Us will sneak up behind him and knock him down and stand up and holler, "Do that," and then he himself gets knocked down and we still sit in the valley and knock down and drag out!

A YOUNG US (*aside*)   Yeah! Drag Us out, but not White Devils.

OLD LADY   It's the truth Cornerstone. They say they going to meet this evening to talk about what we ought to do.

AVERAGE   What is the need of so much talking?

CORNERSTONE   Better than not talking! Somebody might say something after while.

THE YOUNG GIRL—SWEET (*who just came up*) I want to talk too!

AVERAGE   What can you talk about?

SWEET   Things! Something, father!

THE YOUNG MAN—FINEST BLOOD   I'll speak too.

AVERAGE   Oh you all make me tired! Talk—talk—talk—talk! And the flower is still up on the hillside!

OLD LADY   Yes and the White Devils are still talking about keeping the Us away from it, too.

(*A drum begins to beat in the distance. All the* US *stand up and shake off their sleep. The drummer, a short, black, determined looking* US, *appears around the bushes beating the drum with strong, vigorous jabs that make the whole valley echo and re-echo with rhythm. Some of the* US *begin to dance in time to the music*)

AVERAGE   Look at that! Dancing!! The Us will never learn to be sensible!

CORNERSTONE   They dance well! Well!!

(*The* US *all congregate at the center front. Almost naturally, the Young* US *range on one side, the Old* US *on the other.* CORNERSTONE *sits her plump brown self comfortably in the center of the stage. An Old* US *tottering with age and blind comes toward her*)

OLD US   What's it this time, chillun? Is it day yet? Can you see the road to that flower?

AVERAGE   Oh you know we ain't going to get up there! No use worrying!

CORNERSTONE   No it's not day! It is still dark. It is night. (*for the sun has gone and purple blackness has lain across the Valley. Somehow, though, you can see the shape of the flower on top of Somewhere. Lights twinkle on the hill*)

OLD US (*speaking as if to himself*) I'm blind from working—building for the White Devils in the heat of the noon-day sun and I'm weary!

CORNERSTONE Lean against me so they won't crowd you.

(*An old man rises in the back of the ranks; his beard reaches down to his knees but he springs upright. He speaks*)

OLD MAN I want to tell you all something! The Us can't get up the road unless we work! We want to hew and dig and toil!

A YOUNG US You had better sit down before someone knocks you down! They told us that when your beard was sprouting.

CORNERSTONE (*to* YOUTH) Do not be so stupid! Speak as if you had respect for that beard!

ANOTHER YOUNG US We have! But we get tired of hearing "you must work" when we know the Old Us built practically every inch of that hill and are yet Nowhere.

FIRST YOUNG US Yes, all they got was a rush down the hill—not a chance to take a step up!

CORNERSTONE It was not time then.

OLD MAN (*on the back row*) Here comes a Young Us who has been reading in the books! Here comes a Young Us who has been reading in the books! He'll tell us what the books say about getting Somewhere.

(*A* YOUNG MAN *pushes through the crowd. As soon as he reaches the center front, he throws a bundle of books*)

YOUNG MAN I'm through! I do not need these things! They're no good!

OLD MAN (*pushes up from the back and stands beside him*) You're through! Ain't you been reading in the books how to get Somewhere? Why don't you tell us how to get there?

YOUNG MAN I'm through I tell you! There isn't anything in one of these books that tells Black Us how to get around White Devils.

OLD MAN (*softly—sadly*) I thought the books would tell us how!

YOUNG MAN No! The White Devils wrote the books themselves. You know they aren't going to put anything like that in there!

YET ANOTHER OLD MAN (*throwing back his head and calling into the air*) Lord! Why don't you come by here and tell us how to get Somewhere?

A YOUNG MAN (*who had been idly chewing grass*) Aw, you ought to know by now that isn't the way to talk to God!

OLD MAN It ain't! It ain't! It ain't! It ain't! Ain't I been talking to God just like that for seventy years? Three score and ten years—Amen!

THE GRASS CHEWER Yes! Three score and ten years you been telling God to tell you what to do. Telling Him! And three score and ten years you been wearing your spine double sitting on the rocks in the valley too.

OLD US He is all powerful! He will move in his own time!

YOUNG US Well, if he is all powerful, God does not need you to tell Him what to do.

OLD US Well what's the need of me talkin' to Him then?

YOUNG US Don't talk so much to Him! Give Him a chance! He might want to talk to you but you do so much yelling in His ears that He can't tell you anything.

(*There is a commotion in the back stage.* SWEET *comes running to* CORNERSTONE *crying*)

SWEET Oh—oo—!

CORNERSTONE What is it, Sweet?

SWEET There's a White Devil sitting in the bushes in the dark over there! There's a White Devil sitting in the bushes over in the dark! And when I walked by—he pinched me!

FINEST BLOOD (*catching a rock*) Where is he, sister? (*he starts toward the bushes*)

CORNERSTONE (*screaming*) Don't go after him son! They will kill you if you hurt him!

FINEST BLOOD I don't care if they do. Let them. I'd be out of this hole then!

AVERAGE Listen to that young fool! Better stay safe and sound where he is! At least he got somewhere to eat and somewhere to lay his head.

FINEST BLOOD Yes I can lay my head on the rocks of Nowhere.

(*Up the center of the stage toils a new figure of a square set middle-aged* US. *He walks heavily for in each hand he carries a heavy bag. As soon as he reaches the center front he throws the bags down groaning as he does so*)

The Purple Flower

AN OLD MAN 'Smatter with you? Ain't them bags full of gold.
THE NEW COMER Yes, they are full of gold!
OLD MAN Well why ain't you smiling then? Them White Devils can't have anything no better!
THE NEW COMER Yes they have! They have Somewhere! I tried to do what they said. I brought them money, but when I brought it to them they would not sell me even a spoonful of dirt from Somewhere! I'm through!
CORNERSTONE Don't be through. The gold counts for something. It must!

(*An* OLD WOMAN *cries aloud in a quavering voice from the back*)

OLD LADY Last night I had a dream.
A YOUNG US Dreams? Excuse me! I know I'm going now! Dreams!!
OLD LADY I dreamed that I saw a White Devil cut in six pieces—head here, (*pointing*) body here—one leg here—one there—an arm here—an arm there.
AN OLD MAN Thank God! It's time then!
AVERAGE Time for what? Time to eat? Sure ain't time to get Somewhere!
OLD MAN (*walking forward*) It's time! It's time! Bring me an iron pot!
YOUNG US Aw don't try any conjuring!
OLD MAN (*louder*) Bring me a pot of iron. Get the pot from the fire in the valley.
CORNERSTONE Give him the pot!

(*Someone brings it up immediately*)

OLD MAN (*walking toward pot slowly*) Old Us! Do you hear me. Old Us that are here do you hear me?
ALL THE OLD US (*cry in chorus*) Yes, Lord! We hear you! We hear you!
OLD MAN (*crying louder and louder*) Old Us! Old Us!! Old Us that are gone, Old Us that are dust do you hear me? (*his voice sounds strangely through the valley. Somewhere you think you hear—as if mouthed by ten million mouths through rocks and dust—"Yes!—Lord!—We hear you! We hear you"!) And you hear me—give me a handful of dust! Give me a handful of dust! Dig down to the depths of the things you have made! The things you formed with your hands and give me a handful of dust!

(*An* OLD WOMAN *tottering with the weakness of old age crosses the stage and going to the pot, throws a handful of dust in. Just before she sits down again she throws back her head and shakes her cane in the air and laughs so that the entire valley echoes*)

A YOUNG US What's the trouble? Choking on the dust?
OLD WOMAN No child! Rejoicing!
YOUNG US Rejoicing over a handful of dust?
OLD WOMAN Yes. A handful of dust! Thanking God I could do something if it was nothing but make a handful of dust!
YOUNG US Well dust isn't much!
OLD MAN (*at the pot*) Yes, it isn't much! You are dust yourself; but so is she. Like everything else, though, dust can be little or much, according to where it is.

(*The* YOUNG US *who spoke subsides. He subsides so completely that he crashes through the Thin-Skin-of-Civilization. Several of his group go too. They were thinking*)

OLD MAN (*at the pot*) Bring me books! Bring me books!
YOUNG US (*who threw books down*) Here! Take all these! I'll light the fire with them.
OLD MAN No, put them in the pot (YOUNG US *does so*) Bring me gold!
THE MAN OF THE GOLD BAGS Here take this! It is just as well. Stew it up and make teething rings!! (*he pours it into the pot*)
OLD MAN Now bring me blood! Blood from the eyes, the ears, the whole body! Drain it off and bring me blood! (*No one speaks or moves*) Now bring me blood! Blood from the eyes, the ears, the whole body! Drain it off! Bring me blood!! (*No one speaks or moves*) Ah hah, hah! I knew it! Not one of you willing to pour his blood in the pot!
YOUNG US (*facetiously*) How you going to pour your own blood in there? You got to be pretty far gone to let your blood run in there. Somebody else would have to do the pouring.
OLD MAN I mean red blood. Not yellow blood, thank you.
FINEST BLOOD (*suddenly*) Take my blood! (*he walks toward the pot*)
CORNERSTONE O no! Not my boy! Take me instead!
OLD MAN Cornerstone we cannot stand without you!

AN OLD WOMAN What you need blood for? What you doing anyhow? You ain't told us nothing yet. What's going on in that pot?

OLD MAN I'm doing as I was told to do.

A YOUNG US Who told you to do anything?

OLD MAN God. I'm His servant.

YOUNG US (*who spoke before*) God? I haven't heard God tell you anything.

OLD MAN You couldn't hear. He told it to me alone.

OLD WOMAN I believe you. Don't pay any attention to that simpleton! What God told you to do?

OLD MAN He told me take a handful of dust—dust from which all things came and put it in a hard iron pot. Put it in a hard iron pot. Things shape best in hard molds!! Put in books that Men learn by. Gold that Men live by. Blood that lets Men live.

YOUNG US What you suppose to be shaping? A man?

OLD US I'm the servant. I can do nothing. If I do this, God will shape a new man Himself.

YOUNG MAN What's the things in the pot for?

OLD MAN To show I can do what I'm told.

OLD WOMAN Why does He want blood?

OLD MAN You got to give blood! Blood has to be let for births, to give life.

OLD WOMAN So the dust wasn't just nothing? Thank God!

YOUTH Then the books were not just paper leaves? Thank God!

THE MAN OF THE GOLD BAGS Can the gold mean something?

OLD MAN Now I need the blood.

FINEST BLOOD I told you you could take mine.

OLD MAN Yours!

FINEST BLOOD Where else could you get it? The New Man must be born. The night is already dark. We cannot stay here forever. Where else could blood come from?

OLD MAN Think child. When God asked a faithful servant once to do sacrifice, even his only child, where did God put the real meat for sacrifice when the servant had the knife upon the son's throat?

OLD US (*in a chorus*)

> In the bushes, Lord!
> In the bushes, Lord!
> Jehovah put the ram
> In the bushes!

CORNERSTONE I understand!

FINEST BLOOD What do you mean?

CORNERSTONE Where were you going a little while ago? Where were you going when your sister cried out?

FINEST BLOOD To the bushes! You want me to get the White Devil? (*he seizes the piece of rock and stands to his feet*)

OLD MAN No! No! Not that way. The White Devils are full of tricks. You must go differently. Bring him gifts and offer them to him.

FINEST BLOOD What have I to give for a gift?

OLD MAN There are the pipes of Pan that every Us is born with. Play on that. Soothe him—lure him—make him yearn for the pipe. Even a White Devil will soften at music. He'll come out, and he only comes to try to get the pipe from you.

FINEST BLOOD And when he comes out, I'm to kill him in the dark before he sees me? That's a White Devil trick!

OLD MAN An Old Us will never tell you to play White Devil's games! No! Do not kill him in the dark. Get him out of the bushes and say to him: "White Devil, God is using me for His instrument. You think that it is I who play on this pipe! You think that is I who play upon this pipe so that you cannot stay in your bushes. So that you must come out of your bushes. But it is not I who play. It is not I, it is God who plays through me—to you. Will you hear what He says? Will you hear? He says it is almost day, White Devil. The night is far gone. A New Man must be born for the New Day. Blood is needed for birth. Blood is needed for the birth. Come out, White Devil. It may be your blood—it may be mine—but blood must be taken during the night to be given at the birth. It may be my blood—it may be your blood—but everything has been given. The Us toiled to give dust for the body, books to guide the body, gold to clothe the body. Now they need blood for birth so the New Man can live. You have taken blood. You must give blood. Come out! Give it." And then fight him!

FINEST BLOOD I'll go! And if I kill him?

OLD MAN Blood will be given!

FINEST BLOOD And if he kills me?

OLD MAN Blood will be given!

FINEST BLOOD Can there be no other way—cannot this cup pass?

OLD MAN No other way. It cannot pass.

They always take blood. They built up half their land on our bones. They ripened crops of cotton, watering them with our blood. Finest Blood, this is God's decree: "You take blood—you give blood. Full measure—flooding full—over—over!"

FINEST BLOOD I'll go. (*he goes quickly into the shadow. Far off soon you can hear him—his voice lifted, young, sweet, brave and strong*) White Devil! God speaks to you through me!—Hear Him!—Him! You have taken blood; there can be no other way. You will have to give blood! Blood!

(*All the* US *listen. All the valley listens. Nowhere listens. All the* WHITE DEVILS *listen. Somewhere listens.*

Let the curtain close leaving all the US, *the* WHITE DEVILS, *Nowhere, Somewhere, listening, listening. Is it time?*)

4

Black Folk Plays of the 1920's

**Georgia Douglas Johnson   Jean Toomer   John Matheus
Willis Richardson   Randolph Edmonds**

Concurrent with the growth of nationalism is the growth of interest in folk and folk materials. (The Black Nationalism of the late 1960's saw a rediscovery of soul food, nits and grits, and street talk—to the point that "in" food, language, music, dress, and hair became commercial). A considerable number of one-act plays written in the 1920's are subtitled "a folk tragedy," or "a folk comedy," despite the fact that to some black theater people "folk" theater connoted minstrelsy and "darkey comedies." In 1923, the Ethiopian Players (the first group to present a black playwright on Broadway) called themselves "folk theater." Folk plays were a part of black pride—a black pride stimulated into consciousness largely by Marcus Garvey's Universal Negro Improvement Association (see introduction to *Big White Fog*).

Writers of the Negro Renaissance—like Jean Toomer and Alain Locke—sometimes referred to the southern country Negro as a "peasant." This term, apart from whatever connotations it may have had for intellectuals, was borrowed from the rising nationalisms of Europe, particularly the Irish. "Harlem has the same role to play for the New Negro," wrote Alain Locke, in *The New Negro* (1925) "as Dublin has had for the New Ireland. . . ." In 1899 Lady Gregory and William Butler Yeats had formed a "native and poetic" theater where the "living language of the folk" would drive the artificial stage Irishman from the boards. Tragedy need no longer be the property of kings; comedy need no longer be subject to artificiality.

The Irish folk theater impetus entered the Negro theater through the plays of Ridgley Torrence, a white writer. On the eve of the United States' entry into World War I, April 5, 1917, at the Old Garden Theater in New York City, Mrs. Emily Hapgood presented Torrence's *Three Plays for a Negro Theater*. The *New York Post* noted the importance of the event as

the beginnings of something like a folk theater, entirely domestic if not altogether national, and of an indisputable, if as yet incalculable, racial significance. Should it persist, and thrive, it will find within its own peculiar domain many great opportunities, and before long it will be doing better work in better plays. It might even rival the achievements of the Abbey Theatre of Dublin, which had a less propitious start.

A close look at Mr. Torrence's plays, and those of other white playwrights (Culbertson, O'Neill, Heyward, Connelly) reveals these "Negro" plays to be synthetic folk plays, seeking the exotic Negro rather than the real Afro-American—a being whom whites had no way of knowing.

It remained for Afro-American playwrights—Willis Richardson, Jean Toomer, Eulalie Spence, Randolph Edmonds, Georgia D. Johnson, John Matheus—to take a fresh look at Negro life: at its conflicts, its people, and its idiom. An effort to record the poetry of natural speech was made. Certainly there was the hope that if true black characters could be presented on stage, the old Negro stereotypes could be driven off the boards. However, for another twenty years a kind of Gresham's law of the theater was to prevail: bad characterization will drive out good.

Georgia Douglas Johnson (1886–1966)

A Sunday Morning in the South
c. 1925

Georgia Douglas Johnson wrote a number of one-act plays, but she is best known for her poetry. Her modest home on S Street in the Northwest section of Washington, D.C., christened "Halfway House," was for four decades the Mecca for such black artists and intellectuals as Langston Hughes, May Miller, Owen Dodson, Sterling Brown, Alain Locke, and Charles Sebree. During the 1950's, when she was well into her sixties, she watched her street undergo a strange metamorphosis. Old neighbors vanished into suburbia and their homes were converted into rooming houses or apartment houses, charging exorbitant rents to poor blacks who had migrated to Washington from the South or who had been uprooted by urban renewal projects in other sections of the city. The street became a vast slum except for the few homeowners who decided to remain and keep up their property. Mrs. Johnson was one of those who remained, and her home was open to anyone at any time. No problem was too large or too small for her to share. She was a beautiful, down-to-earth woman, who had no concern for appearances or material things. Rosey Poole records this impression in *Beyond the Blues* (1962): "Georgia Douglas Johnson . . . lives in Washington amidst the most chaotic amassment of usable and broken-down typewriters, television sets, radios, furniture and piles of books and papers, among which she finds any single one with unerring instinct. Her gait and talk make one think of an ancient Greek oracle . . ."

Passers-by came to know her as "the old woman with the headband and the tablet around her neck." And indeed she did wear a black headband and, attached to a ribbon around her neck, a pencil and a small, tattered notebook, which she seldom, if ever, removed—"so that when an idea, a word, a line for a poem comes, I can jot it down." She was not above stopping and reprimanding people on the street if she considered their conduct offensive to the race. One day, two young men, their processed hair held by greasy scarves and their backs bent as if they were weary travelers, sullenly walked in front of her house cursing. She stopped them with her pointed cane: "Such filth!" she shouted. "Get those rags off your heads, and walk with your shoulders back! You're black men—you should be proud!" The young men were as startled as Mrs. Johnson's neighbors. They looked at her for a moment; then, embarrassed, they removed the scarves and moved on, shoulders back and heads high. "That's more like it!" she shouted, as they crossed the street. Mrs. Johnson might have seemed eccentric to some, but to those who knew her she was a lovable old woman, and above all a true artist, who continued to write and publish her poetry until her death at the age of eighty.

A Sunday Morning in the South is not one of Mrs. Johnson's best plays (it was never published), but the emotional impact of the piece cannot be ignored. There is a tenseness throughout the work that will anger blacks and, perhaps, appall some whites. The plot is predictable, just as the conclusion is inevitable. An innocent black man is murdered by an angry white mob—*fictionalized*, but in reality Tom could easily have been "Shap" Curry, Moses Jones, or John Cornish, whose bodies were mutilated and burned on May 6, 1922 in Kirvin, Texas, for a murder that they did not commit; or Samuel Carter, who was lynched in 1923 for aiding his son's escape from a mob in Bronson, Florida; or Len Hart, lynched in August that same year for allegedly peeping into the window of a white woman's home near Jacksonville, Florida; or any of the hundreds of blacks who have innocently suffered the same fate. (C. Eric Lincoln lists 1,886 lynchings between 1900 and 1931 in *The Negro Pilgrimage in America* [1967].) This is a protest play by a woman who wants to believe in law and order, but finds this belief more and more difficult to achieve when at every level the law has been unjust or unenforced. As a writer she remains objective; she presents her problem and lets the solution rest within the guilty conscience of her audience. Nevertheless, the atmosphere of the play functions as an ironic comment on the action.

A Sunday Morning in the South

CHARACTERS

SUE JONES, *the grandmother, aged seventy*
TOM GRIGGS, *her grandson, aged nineteen*
BOSSIE GRIGGS, *her grandson, aged seven*
LIZA TRIGGS, *a friend, aged sixty*
MATILDA BROWN, *a friend, aged fifty*
A WHITE GIRL
FIRST OFFICER
SECOND OFFICER

PLACE   *A town in the South.*
TIME   *1924.*

(SCENE: *Kitchen in* SUE JONES' *two room house. A window on left, a door leading to back yard and another leading to front room. A stove against the back wall, a table near it, four chairs, an old time safe with dishes and two bottles—one clear and one dark—a wooden water bucket with shiny brass bales, and a tin dipper hanging near it on a nail.*

As the curtain rises SUE JONES *is seen putting the breakfast on the kitchen table. She wears a red bandanna handkerchief on her grey head, a big blue gingham apron tied around her waist and big wide old lady comfort shoes. She uses a stick as she has a sore leg, and moves about with a stoop and a limp as she goes back and forth from the stove to the table*)

SUE (*calling*) Tom, Tom, you and Bossie better come on out here and git your breakfast before it gits cold; I got good hot rolls this mornin!

TOM (*from next room*) All right grannie, we're coming.

SUE   You better ef you know whut's good for you (*opens stove door, looks at rolls, then begins humming and singing*)

> Eugh...eu...eugh...
> Jes look at the morning star
> Eugh...eu...eugh...
> We'll all git home bye and bye...

(*as she finishes the song* TOM *and* BOSSIE *come hurrying into the kitchen placing their chairs at the table; there is one already at the table for* SUE. SUE *takes rolls out of stove with her apron and brings them to the table*) It's as hard to git yawll out of the bed on Sunday morning as it is to pull hen's teeth.

TOM (*eating. The Church bell next door is heard ringing*) Eugh—there's the church bell. I sho meant to git out to meeting this morning but my back still hurts me. Remember I told you last night how I sprained it lifting them heavy boxes for Mr. John?

SUE (*giving* BOSSIE *a roll and a piece of sausage*) You hadn't oughter done it; you oughter ast him to let somebody hep you—you aint no hoss!

TOM   I reckin I oughter had but I didn't know how heavy they was till I started and then he was gone.

SUE   You oughter had some of my snake oil linament on it last night, that's whut?

TOM   I wish I hader but I was so dead tired I got outer my clothes and went straight to bed. I muster been sleep by nine er clock I reckin.

SUE   Nine er clock! You is crazy! Twant no moren eight when I called you to go to the store and git me a east cake fur my light rolls and you was sleeping like a log of wood; I had to send Bossie fur it.

BOSSIE   Yes, and you snored so loud I thought you would a choked. (*holding out his plate and licking his lips with his tongue*) Grannie kin I have some more?

SUE   Whut? Where is all thot I jest give you?

BOSSIE (*rubbing his stomach with his other hand and smiling broadly*) It's gone down the red lane struttin'.

SUE   Well this is all you gointer git this mornin. (*helping him to more rolls and sausage*) When you git big and work like Tom you kin stuff all you wants to.

BOSSIE   I aint never gointer break my back like Tom working hard—I'm a gointer be a—a preacher that's whut and...

SUE (*catching sight of someone passing the window as she approached the back door*) I bleve that's Liza Twiggs must be on her way to church and smelled these light rolls and coffee. (*a knock is heard at the back door*) Let her in, Bossie!

(BOSSIE *jumps up from the table, hurries to the door and opens it*)

LIZA (*enters sniffling*) Mawning yawll.

SUE Morning Liza—on your way to church?

LIZA Yes the first bell just rung and I thought I'd drop in a minute. (*whiffs again*) Coffee sho smells good!

SUE Tastes better'n it smells—Pull up a cheer and swaller a cupful with one of these light rolls.

LIZA (*drawing up a chair*) Dont keer if I do. (*she is helped to coffee and rolls while* BOSSIE *looks at her disapprovingly. To* SUE) How is your leg gitting on?

SUE Well as I kin expect. I won't never walk on it good no mo. It eats and eats. She is lucky I'm right here next door to church (*to* TOM) Open that winder Tom so I kin hear the singing. (TOM *opens window. To* LIZA) Folks don't like to set next to me in church no mo. Tinks its ketching—a cancer or somethin'. (*then brightly*) Whut you know good?

(*From the church next door is heard the hymn, drifting through the window:* "Amazing grace how sweet the sound / That saves a wretch like me . . .")

LIZA (*listening*) They done started "Amazing grace." (*music continues as a background for their talk*) (*still eating*) That music she is sweet but I got to finish eatin first, then I'll go . . .

SUE I ast you whut you know good.

LIZA Well, I don't know nothin tall good, but I did hear as how the police is all over now trying to run down some po Nigger they say that's tacked a white woman last night right up here near the Pine Street market. They says as how the white folks is shonuff mad too, and if they ketch him they gointer make short work of him.

SUE (*still drinking coffee*) Eugh, eugh, eugh, you don't say. I don't hold wid no rascality and I bleves in meeting out punishment to the guilty but they fust ought to fine out who done it tho and then let the law hanel 'em. That's what I says.

LIZA Me too. I thinks the law oughter hanel 'em too, but you know a sight of times they gits the wrong man and goes and strings him up and don't fin out who done it till it's too late!

SUE That's so. And sometimes the white uns been knowed to blackin they faces and make you bleve some po Nigger done it.

TOM They lynch you bout anything too, not jest women. They say Zeb Brooks was strung up because he and his boss had er argiment.

LIZA Sho did. I says the law's the law and it ought er be er ark uv safty to pertect the weak and not some little old flimsy shack that a puff of wind can blow down.

TOM I been thinking a whole lot about these things and I mean to go to night school and git a little book learning so as I can do something to help—help change the laws . . . make em strong . . . I sometimes get right upset and wonder whut would I do if they ever tried to put something on me . . .

LIZA Pshaw . . . everybody knows you . . . nobody would bother you . . .

SUE No sonnie, you won't never hafter worry bout sich like that but you kin hep to save them po devels that they do git after.

(*Singing comes from the church next door*:

Shine on me, shine on me.
Let the light from the lighthouse shine on me,
Shine on me, shine on me,
Let the light from the lighthouse shine on me.

TOM It takes a sight of learning to understand the law and I'm a gointer . . . (*a quick rap is heard at the door and it is almost immediately pushed open and an* OFFICER *enters as the four at table look up at him in open mouthed amazement*)

FIRST OFFICER Tom Griggs live here?

SUE (*starting up excitedly*) Yes Sir (*stammering*)

FIRST OFFICER (*looking at* TOM) You Tom Griggs?

TOM (*puzzled*) Yes sir.

FIRST OFFICER (*roughly*) Where were you last night at ten o'clock?

SUE (*answering quickly for* TOM) Right here sir, he was right here at home. Whut you want to know fer?

FIRST OFFICER (*to* SUE) You keep quiet, old woman. (*to* TOM) Say, you answer up. Can't you

A Sunday Morning in the South

talk? Where were you last night at ten o'clock.

TOM (*uneasily*) Gramma told you. I was right here at home—in bed at eight o'clock.

FIRST OFFICER That sounds fishy to me—in bed at eight o'clock! And who else knows you were here?

SUE Say Mr. Officer, whut you trying to do to my granson. Shore as God Amighty is up in them heabens he was right here in bed. I seed him and his little brother Bossie there saw him, didn't you Bossie?

BOSSIE (*in a frightened whisper*) Yessum, I seed him and I heered him!

FIRST OFFICER (*to* BOSSIE) Shut up. Your word's nothing. (*looking at* SUE) Nor yours either. Both of you'd lie for him. (*steps to back door and makes a sign to someone outside, then comes back into the room taking a piece of paper from his vest pocket and reads slowly, looking at* TOM *critically as he checks each item*) Age around twenty, five feet five or six, brown skin . . . (*he folds up the paper and puts it back into his vest*) Yep! fits like a glove. (SUE, LIZA *and* TOM *look from one to the other with growing amazement and terror as* SECOND OFFICER *pushes open the door and stands there supporting a young white girl on his arm*)

SECOND OFFICER (*to girl*) Is this the man?

WHITE GIRL (*hesitatingly*) I—I'm not sure . . . but . . . but he looks something like him . . . (*holding back*)

FIRST OFFICER (*encouragingly*) Take a good look, Miss. He fits your description perfect. Color, size, age, everything. Pine Street Market ain't no where from here, and he surely did pass that way last night. He was there all right, all right! We got it figgered all out. (*to* GIRL, *who looks down at her feet*) You say he looks like him?

WHITE GIRL (*looking at him again quickly*) Y-e-s (*slowly and undecidedly*) I think so. I . . . I . . . (*then she covers her face with her arm and turns quickly and moves away from the door, supported by* SECOND OFFICER. FIRST OFFICER *makes a step toward* TOM *and slips handcuffs on him before any one is aware what is happening*)

SUE (*holding on to her chair and shaking her cane at the* OFFICER, *while* BOSSIE *comes up close to her and snivels in her apron*) Whut you doing? What you doing? You can't rest my granson—he ain't done nothing—you can't rest him!

FIRST OFFICER Be quiet, old woman. I'm just going to take him along to the sheriff to question him and if he's telling the truth he'll be right back home here in no time.

SUE But you can't rest him; he don't know no mo bout that po little white chile than I do—You can't take him!

TOM (*utterly bewildered*) Granma, don't take on so. I'll go long with him to the sheriff. I'll splain to him how I couldn't a done it when I was here sleep all the time—I never laid eyes on that white lady before in all my life.

SUE (*to* TOM) Course you ain't. (*to* OFFICER) Mr. Officer, that white chile ain't never seed my granson before—All Niggers looks alike to her; she so upset she don't know whut she's saying.

FIRST OFFICER (*to* SUE *as he pulls* TOM *along*) You just keep cool Grannie, he'll be right back—if he's innocent. (*to* TOM) And the quieter you comes along the better it will be for you.

TOM (*looking back at his grandma from the doorway with terror in his eyes*) I'll be right back granny—don't cry—don't cry—Jest as soon as I see—(*the* OFFICER *pulls him out of the doorway*)

LIZA (*standing with her hands clasped together, her head bowed and swaying from side to side with emotion. She prays*) Sweet Jesus, do come down and hep us this mornin. You knows our hearts and you knows this po boy ain't done nothing wrong. You said you would hep the fatherless and the motherless; do Jesus bring this po orphan back to his ole cripple grannie safe and sound, do Jesus!

BOSSIE (*crying and pulling at his grandma's apron*) Grannie, grannie, whut they gointer do to my brother? Whut they gointer do to him?

SUE (*brokenly*) The good Jesus only knows, but I'm a talking to the Lord now asting Him to . . . (*a rap is heard at the door; it is almost immediately pushed open and* MATILDA BROWN *enters hurriedly and excitedly*)

MATILDA (*breathlessly*) Miss Liza, as I was coming long I seed Tom wid the police and there was some white mens wid guns a trying to take him away from the police—said he'd done been dentified and they want gointer be cheated outen they Nigger this time. I, I flew on down here to tell you, you better do somethin'.

SUE (*shaking nervously from side to side as she leans on her cane for support*) Oh my God, whut kin I do?

LIZA (*alertly*) You got to git word to some of your good white folks, that's whut and git em to save him.

SUE Yes... That's whut... Lemme see... (*she stands tense thinking a moment*) I got it... Miss Vilet... I got to git to Miss Vilet... I nused her when she was a baby and she'll do it ... Her pa's the Jedge.

LIZA That's right! I'll go. You can't go quick.

MATILDA No. Lemme go; I kin move in a hurry, lemme go!

SUE All right Tildy. Tell Miss Vilet her ole nuse Sue is callin on her and don't fail me; tell her they done took Tom and he is perfect innercent, and they gointer take him away from the police, and ax her to ax her pa the Jedge to go git Tom and save him fur God's sake. Now hurry, Tildy, fly!

BOSSIE (*to* SUE) Lemme go long; I knows how to git there quick cutting through the ole field.

LIZA Yes they knows Bossie and he kin hep tell.

SUE Yes Bossie, gone, yawll hurry, hurry! (MATILDA *and* BOSSIE *hurry out of the back door and* SUE *sinks down into a chair exhausted while* LIZA *comes over to her and pats her on the back*)

LIZA Now, now evrything's gointer be all right... Miss Vilet 'll fix it... she ain't gointer let her ole mammy call on her for nothing... she'll make her pa save him.

SUE Yes, she's a good chile... I knows she'll save him.

(SUE *moves her lips in prayer. From the church next door comes the sound of singing; the two women listen to the words with emotion*

> Alas and did my savior bleed
> And did my sovereign die
> Would he devote his sacred head
> For such a worm as I.
>
> Must Jesus bear the cross alone
> And all the world go free,
> No, there's a cross for every one
> And there's a cross for me.

SUE *rocks back and forth in chair, head buried in her apron.* LIZA *walks up and down the floor, throws her hands up imploringly now and then*)

LIZA Oh Lord, hep us to bear our cross! Hep us!

SUE (*drooping*) Liza I'm feeling sorter fainty lack; git me my bottle of camphor out of the safe yonder.

LIZA (*going to safe*) Yes chile, I'll git it. You done gone through a whole lot this mornin, God knows. (*takes up a bottle and holds it up for* SUE *to see*) This it?

SUE (*shaking her head*) Eugh eugh, that's my sweet oil. It's the yuther one in the black bottle ... see it?

LIZA (*taking out bottle and smelling it*) Yes here it is. Strong too. It'll do you good. I has them sinking spells too sometimes (*comes over to* SUE *with stopper out of bottle and holds it to her nose*) There draw a deep bref of it; feel better?

SUE I'll feel better tereckly. My old heart is gittin weak.

LIZA Set back comfortable in your cheer and listen to the singin; they all sho talkin to the Lord fur you in that church this mornin. Listen!

(*The church is singing*):

I must tell Jesus, I cannot bear my burdens alone
In my distress he surely will help me
I cannot bear my burdens alone.

I must tell Jesus, I cannot bear my burdens alone
Jesus my Lord he surely will help me
Jesus will help me, Jesus alone

LIZA That's all, that's all we kin do jes tell Jesus! Jesus! Jesus please bow down your ear! (*walks up and down mumbling a soft prayer as the singing continues mournfully*)

SUE I reckin Tildy's bout on her way back now. I knows Miss Vilet done got her pa by now, don't you reckin, Liza.

LIZA (*sympathetically*) Course; I spects Tom'll be coming back too any minit now. Everybody knows he ain't done no harm.

SUE (*listening to running feet at the door and sitting up straight in chair*) Who dat coming? (MATILDA *pushes open the door and comes in all excited and panting while* BOSSIE *follows her crying*) Whut's the matter? Didn't you find Miss Vilet?

MATILDA (*reluctantly*) It want no use.

SUE No use?

LIZA Whut you mean?

MATILDA I mean—I mean—

LIZA For God's sake Tildy, whut's happened?

A Sunday Morning in the South

MATILDA They—they done lynched him.

SUE (*screams*) Jesus! (*gasps and falls limp in her chair. Singing from church begins.* BOSSIE *runs to her, crying afresh.* LIZA *puts the camphor bottle to her nose again as* MATILDA *feels her heart; they work over her a few minutes, shake their heads and with drooping shoulders, wring their hands. While this action takes place the words of this song pour forth from church:*

>   Lord have mercy.
>   Lord have mercy,
>   Lord have mercy over me.

Sung first time with words and repeated in a low hum as curtain slowly falls)

Jean Toomer (1894–1967)

Balo   1924

In 1922, Jean Toomer wrote:

A visit to Georgia last fall was the starting point of almost everything of worth that I have done. I heard folk-songs come from the lips of Negro peasants. I saw the rich dusk beauty . . . a deep part of my nature . . . sprang suddenly to life and responded to them.

He might have been speaking of the people of *Balo*, which he subtitled "A Sketch of Negro Life." If *Balo* is more a sketch than a play, it is also more honest than most folk drama. Mr. Toomer does not burden his characters or himself with plot. He shows the country life of Georgia black folks. Into this life, or more accurately because of it, the young man, Balo, moves toward his own mystic vision.

Many playwrights, white and black, have presented the "gettin' happy" scene in a Negro church (*Porgy; Run Chillin, Run; Amen Corner*). Many of these scenes work in spite of the artifice imposed by the stage, because of the emotion implicit in the scene, plus the support of music. Observation shows that a real person who "gets happy" (unlike a stage character) may throw her hat, gloves and hymnal into the air, but never her purse or her spectacles—suggesting that in the ecstasy rests a double vision.

It is difficult to believe that the young Balo has this double vision. Balo sees God. Like first love, his religious ecstasy is pure, overwhelming, complete—so much so that although Mr. Toomer wrote the play to be performed by the Howard Players in 1924, it is difficult to imagine a flesh-and-blood actor achieving the sensitivity and the tenderness that Balo has in the theater of our imagination.

Balo

CAST OF CHARACTERS

WILL LEE, *a Negro farmer*
SUSAN LEE, *his wife*
TOM, *his elder son*
BALO, *another son*
JENNINGS, *a white neighbor*
COUSIN BOB
COUSIN MAMIE, *his wife*
UNCLE NED
SAM, *Uncle Ned's companion*
CHILDREN

SCENE *Georgia, 1924.*
TIME *Harvest time.*

(*Autumn dawn. Any week day. Outside, it is damp and dewy, and the fog, resting upon the tops of pine trees, looks like fantastic cotton bolls about to be picked by the early morning fingers of the sun. As the curtain rises, the scene is that of a Negro farmhouse interior. The single room, at all times used for sleeping and sitting, on odd occasions serves as a kitchen, this latter due to the fact that a great fireplace, with hooks for pots and kettles, occupies, together with a small family organ, the entire space of the left-hand wall. This huge hearth suggests that perhaps the place might once have been a plantation cookroom. This is indeed the case, and those who now call it home (having added two rooms to it) remember the grandmother—in her day Marsa Harris' cook—telling how she contrived to serve the dishes hot despite the fact that the big house was some hundred yards away. The old frame mansion still stands, or rather, the ghost of it, in the direct vision of the front door, its habitable portion tenanted by a poor-white family who farm the land to the south of it and who would, but for the tradition of prejudice and the coercion of a rural public opinion, be on terms of a frank friendship with their colored neighbors, a friendship growing out of a similarity of occupations and consequent problems. As it is, there is an understanding and bond between them little known or suspected by northern people. The colored family farms the land to the north, The dividing line, halfway between the two homes, has no other mark save one solid stake of oak. Both farmers did well last year, resisted the temptation to invest in automobiles and player-pianos, saved their money, and so, this season, though their cotton crop failed with the rest, they have a nest egg laid away, and naturally are more conscious of their comparative thrift and prosperity than if the times were good. As was said, the curtain rises upon the general room of the Negro farmhouse. The man himself, in rough gray baggy trousers and suspenders showing white against a gray flannel shirt, is seen whittling a board for shavings and small kindling sticks to start a fire with. As he faces the audience, the half light shades his features, giving but the faint suggestion that they are of a pleasing African symmetry. Having enough kindling, he arranges it in the hearth, strikes a match, and, as the wood catches, tends and coaxes it, squatting on his hams. The flames soon throw his profile into relief. It is surprisingly like that of an Indian. And his hair (lack of hair, really), having been shaved close, completes the illusion. A quick glance around the room will now reveal a closed door (to the left) in the back wall, underneath which a narrow strip of light shows. To the right of the door, against the wall, is a heavy oak bed which has been perfectly made even at this early hour. In the right wall, by the bed, a curtained window lets in at first the gray, and then, as the mist lifts, the yellow light of morning. This side of the curtain is a magnificent oak dresser, a match for the bed, but otherwise out of place and proportion in the room. Both of these are gifts to the family (and have become heirlooms) from old Marsa. A window may be understood to be in the wall facing the audience. Likewise, in this wall, to the left, a door opens on the outside. The walls are plastered and whitewashed. They are sprinkled with calendars, one or two cheap pictures of fruit* (*such as are supposed to befit a dining room*), *and one or two inevitable deathlike family portraits. Chairs are here and there about a central table, in the middle of which, resting on a white covering, is a wooden tray for nut picks and crackers. The floor is covered with a good quality carpet. The fire in the hearth now burns brightly, but fails to fill all but a small portion of it, and so, gives one the impression of insufficiency. While* WILL LEE *is still crouching down, the rear door swings open as his wife comes in. Her complexion is a none too healthy yellow, and her large, deep-set, sad and weary eyes are strangely pathetic, haunted, and almost unearthly in the flamelight. With such a slim and fragile body it is surprising how she manages to carry on her part of the contract.*)

SUSAN LEE (*her voice is high and somewhat cracked*) Come on in. (*she turns about, and re-enters the kitchen.* WILL, *satisfied with his fire, rises and, as he follows her, speaks*)

WILL Whar's Bob an' Bettie Kate?

SUSAN (*through the half-open door*) Sent them for to catch an' milk th' cows.

WILL Whar's th' boys?

SUSAN You-all know they was up all night a-grindin' an' a-boilin' cane. Come on in. (WILL *passes out, and soon his voice is heard in blessing*)

WILL We thanks thee, Heavenly Father, fo' yo' blessin's of th' night. Once more thou hast kept yo' children thru' th' time of Satan an' of sin. Bless us, O Lord. Thou hast brought us like th' dew thru' temptations of th' evil darkness inter th' glory of th' mornin' light. Have mercy, Lord. Keep us, an' give us strength t'do yo' will terday. An' every day. An' we asks you t' bless this yere food prepared in His dear name. Amen. Amen. (*just as* WILL *begins his prayer, two young fellows enter through the front door, but on hearing the blessing in progress, stop, and wait with bowed heads until it is over. Whereupon they advance, and are heard by* WILL)

WILL That you, Tom?

TOM (*the larger of the two boys. A Negro farm hand with a smiling face and easy gait, distinguished at first from* BALO *only by his taller figure and the fact of a seedy black coat which he wears over his patched blue faded overalls*) Yassur.

WILL How much you git?

TOM Mighty nigh eighty gallons.

WILL That's right. Had yo' breakfast?
TOM Yassur.
WILL That you thar, Balo?
BALO Yassur, dat's me.
WILL Reckon you had yo breakfast too?
BOTH Yassur we done et.
WILL Slept any?
BOTH Nasur, dat we ain't.
WILL Well, git yo' Bibles down an' read fo' fifteen minutes, then you-all jes' stretch yo'selfs befo' th' fire an' I'll wake you up by an' by.
BOTH Yassur.

(*they get their Bibles from the organ, stretch out in front the hearth, and begin to read.* BALO *is nearer the audience. As he reads he mumbles his words aloud, and, by the twitching of his face and the movements of his hands, is seen to be of a curious nervous texture beneath his surface placidity.* TOM *soon falls asleep, and begins to breathe deeply and rhythmically. The monotony of this respiration, together with the sound of his own voice seems to excite* BALO *peculiarly. His strange, half-closed eyes burn with a dancing light, and his entire body becomes animated and alive. At this juncture, young voices and young feet enter the room to the rear.* SUSAN *has trouble in getting them seated, and* WILL *in blessing the food. Laughs, shouts, and admonitions, in reality, continue all during the following scene, but, as* BALO *does not hear them, and as the audience is absorbed in* BALO, *all sound from the kitchen ceases on the stage.* BALO *by this time has risen to his feet. Facing the audience, he continues to read, and his words become audible. He is reading St. Matthew VII, 24*)

BALO

Therefore whosoever heareth these sayings of mine, and doeth them, I will liken him unto a wise man, which built his house upon a rock: And the rain descended, and the floods came, and the winds blew, and beat upon that house; and it fell not; for it was founded upon a rock. And everyone that heareth these sayings of mine, and doeth them not, shall be likened unto a foolish man, which built his house upon the sand: And the rain descended, and the floods came, and the winds blew, and beat upon that house; and it fell: and great was the fall of it.

(*here* BALO'S *excitement is so considerable that he leaves off the Bible and chants, with additions, certain passages of it from memory*)

An' th' floods came, an' th' winds blew,
An' th' floods came, an' th' winds blew,
An' th' floods came, an' th' winds blew,
O Lord, have mercy, Lord, O Lord
Have mercy on a soul what sins,
O Lord, on a darky sinner's soul.

(*he repeats this two or three times and is almost beside himself when the tumult from the rear room breaks in on him. He is at first entirely bewildered, but then, with an instinctive rapidity, and before the children enter, stretches himself beside* TOM *on the hearth, and pretends to be asleep. Before so very long, this pretended sleep passes into the real thing.* BOB *and* BETTIE KATE *run through, take a whack at both of them, and go out the front door.* WILL *and* SUSAN *follow them into the front room, and, after they have gone, seat themselves before the fire*)

WILL (*in substance, this is repeated each morning, so that* SUSAN *almost knows it now by heart*) Ain't much t' do this mornin', Susan. Farmin's gittin' p'oly down this way when a man what's used t' work can set afo' th' fire handlin' han's, an' it's yet a month t' Christmas. Money ain't t' be made when syrup can be bought fer what it takes t' haul th' cane, an' git it ground an' biled. An' corn at fifty cents a bushel. Cotton's th' crop fer Georgia. Weevils or no weevils. An' God will took them away when people ain't so sinful (*he indicates the boys*) when folks goes t' sleep with Bibles in their han's. Susan, whar is that there theology book? Mus' be studyin'. Can't afford t' waste no time when I's in th' service of th' Lord. Sho' can't.

SUSAN It's around somewheres, Will. You-all still studyin' seriously t' be a preacher? Thought I changed you back a week ago.

WILL That I is, sho', an' there's lots worse a heap. Sin is stompin' up an' down th' world an' Satan's drivin' with loose reins. Needs a righteous man t' grab them from him 'round this way. Wouldn't let you had that frolic here t'night but what I thought 'twould be as good a chance as any t' turn th' people t' His ways. An' that I wouldn't . . . Cousin Bob an' Mamie comin' early.

(*Outside, a voice is heard calling* WILL)

WILL That you, Mr. Jennings? Come in, sir.

JENNINGS (*coming in. He is their white neighbor—a well-built man with ruddy cheeks and pointed nose, dressed like* WILL *but for his shirt which is of khaki*) Nothin' ter do, eh, Will, but hold yer hands afore th' fire? Lucky last year put a few dollars in th' bank.

WILL Yassur, lucky sho'. (*both remain standing, a little awkwardly despite the friendly greeting.* SUSAN *has kept her seat, and says nothing until directly spoken to*)

JENNINGS (*pointing to the sleeping boys*) Nothin' fer them ter do, eh, sleepin' away th' days an' it ain't yet Christmas.

WILL Nasur. Them's been up all night tho', grindin' cane.

JENNINGS Saw Balo there a while back actin' like he was crazy. An' what do yer think he said? An' kept on repeatin' it, "White folks ain't no more'n niggers when they gets ter heaven, white folks ain't no more'n niggers when they gets ter heaven." (*laughs*) How much you get?

WILL 'Bout eighty gallons.

JENNINGS Not bad from that little biddie piece of land, eh?

WILL Nasur, not bad 'tall. But us has more'n we can use, an' 'twouldn't pay t' ship it at th' present price they pays fer it.

JENNINGS Trade?

WILL Fer what?

JENNINGS Corn; turnips.

WILL Nasur, got too many of them myself. Too much syrup, too. Take some along with you; don't want nothin', sir.

JENNINGS All right, Will. Noticed yer ax handle was busted. I'll send th' boy over with a new one fer yer. An' anything else you want, just ask. Heard someone sayin' somethin' 'bout you goin' north ter live. I told 'em, na,—preachin' an' farmin' is th' line fer you. An' there's only one place fer them an' that's in Georgia, eh, Will?

WILL Yassur, that's right, sho'.

JENNINGS What you got ter say 'bout it, Susan?

SUSAN I don't want him t' preach, Mr. Jennings. Preachin' means neglect th' farm. Up north they say there's lots of things you don't get here. An' I don't know, Mr. Jennings, but I'd like t' get somethin'.

JENNINGS Wall, what do yer call somethin' if money in th' bank ain't somethin' when th' times are hard?

SUSAN Yassur, money, but there's somethin' more'n life besides all th' money in th' world.

I want that somethin' else; an' folks say I might could get it if I went up north.

JENNINGS   How 'bout that, Will?

WILL   Dunno, sir. Maybe so, but I knows this place, an' I don't know that. 'Specks Georgia's big enuf 't hold me till I dies.

JENNINGS   Me, too, Will. Wall, mus' be goin'. I'll send a can here fer that there syrup. An' th' handle.

WILL   Don't mind th' can, Mr. Jennings, sir, jest roll a barrel over, an' roll it back when you is thru'.

JENNINGS   All right. Thanks, Will—return th' same some day. So long.

WILL (*seeing him to the door*)   Yassur, good evenin', Mr. Jennings. (*he closes the door and returns to* SUSAN. *The boys are still sleeping soundly*)

WILL   Wish you'd root me out that book, Susan. (SUSAN *gets up, rummages around, and finds the book.* WILL *immediately drops into his chair, and is at once absorbed. Like* BALO, *though in not quite so pronounced a manner, he too mumbles as he reads.* SUSAN *enters the rear room. At this point the curtain descends for a moment to indicate the passing of the morning, and of the first five hours of the afternoon. When it ascends,* WILL *is seated as before, in front of the fire which now burns briskly and with a sizzling sound in thankful contrast to the dull gray light that filters through the windows. It has clouded up outside, and threatens rain. The boys have left the hearth.* WILL *has exchanged his theology book for the Bible. His eyes seem to be in a concentrated daze, focused on the glowing ashes. A voice coming from the outside arouses him.*)

VOICE   Whoo thar, you, Will?

WILL (*collecting himself*)   That you, Cousin Bob? Come on in. Don't need no ceremonies t' enter this yer house. Come in. Come in. (COUSIN BOB *and his wife, Negro country folks, and six small children from twelve to two and a half years old enter through the rear door by way of the kitchen.* COUSIN MAMIE *carries a large basket covered with a spotless white napkin.*)

WILL   What's that fer on yo' arm, Cousin Mamie?

MAMIE   Supper, Cousin Will. Know'd you'd hab enuf t' share with us-all, but reckoned I'd jes' tote it wid me, 'kase dese hungry mouths don't nebber git enuf t' eat, does you, honey? (*addressing the oldest, who shakes his head bashfully in negation*)   I'll jes warm 'tup over yo' fire dar when you-all goes in t' eat. (*the family all group themselves in a semicircle around the hearth, the older folks on chairs, the younger ones on the floor or standing, shifting ill at ease from foot to foot, uncomfortable in their Sunday shoes*)

COUSIN BOB   Cotton po' wid you dis year I 'specks, Will.

WILL   P'oly, Cousin Bob, p'oly. Three bales at th' outset, an' doin' good at that.

BOB   Any corn?

WILL   More'n I know what t' do with.

BOB   Pigs?

WILL   Doin' well on hogs, Cousin Bob, doin' well. (*the conversation dies out. They sit in perfect silence. Then* SUSAN *and the children come in from somewhere.* SUSAN *greets the new arrivals, kissing each child.* BOB *and* BETTIE KATE *are boisterous and demonstrative, and take delight in their more backward playmates. By the time* SUSAN's *ritual is through with, the front door opens and a middle-aged Negro comes in, assisting an old* (*no one knows how old he is*), *gray-haired, bearded fellow who is blind. This old man has a dignity and a far-away, other-worldly expression such as might have characterized a saint of old. Indeed one immediately thinks of him as some hoary Negro prophet, who, having delivered his message, waits humbly and in darkness for his day to come. He is called* UNCLE NED, *and is so greeted by all as he enters. He returns the greeting*)

UNCLE NED (*deep and low, and remarkably clear for one of his infirmities*)   Chillun, chillun. Blind eyes ain't supposed t' see an' ain't supposed t' cry, but, chilluns, voices allus seem t' be so sad, an' I had reckoned as if th' Lord had minded Him t' make sech reservations fer th' old. An' Uncle Ned has had his chillun since th' days befo' th' war. 'Tain't now like it used t' be—he could see 'em with his two eyes then, an' now he has t' see 'em with his heart. An' 'tain't easy any more. Hearts ain't all a-shinin' as they used t' be. (*abruptly*) God bless an' keep you all.

WILL   Th' kind Lord bless an' preserve you, Uncle Ned.

SAM (UNCLE NED's *companion*)   Amen. Amen. (UNCLE NED *is seated in the center, before the fire.* SUSAN *goes out; and presently calls to* WILL. WILL *beckons to* BOB *and* BETTIE KATE, *and then asks all to have a bite with him*)

WILL   Some supper, folks?

ALL   No, Will, no. Thank y' jest th' same.

MAMIE   I'll take t' feed all those that wants t' eat in here.

WILL   Reckon you will at that. (*he and the children go out.* TOM *comes in with an armful of wood, then follows* WILL. WILL *is heard blessing the food. Everyone in the front room bows his head*)

WILL   Give us this day, our daily bread, O Lord, an' hearts filled up with thanks for Him in whose dear name all food an' goodness is prepared in. Amen. Amen.

SAM (*after* WILL)   Amen. Amen. (MAMIE *sets about warming up some sweet potatoes, meat, and corn bread. She gets a dish or two from the kitchen, and fixes one for* UNCLE NED. *The children eat from one large pan. The grown-ups talk in undertones*)

SAM   What's got inter Will he lettin' Susan have a frolic?

BOB   Dunno.

MAMIE   'Deed I dunno neither. Queer goin's on fer him sho'.

SAM   Ef I was a bettin' man I'd lay a dollar t' a cotton stalk Will'll turn this yer frolic inter a preacher's meetin' afo' he's thru'.

UNCLE NED   That's right, that's true. Will has got t' fear o' God in 'im as sho's you're born.

MAMIE.   Ain't many comin' on a night like this.

SAM   That's right; niggers is sho' funny 'bout gettin' theyself wet. (BALO *comes in, but finding no seat around the fire, installs himself before the organ. His feet begin to pump, and his fingers to touch a key here and there. The sequence of notes finally arranges itself into a Negro melody. It is the one called "Steal Away." As his ear catches the tune, he begins to play in earnest. The folks all join in, at first by humming, and then they sing the words.* UNCLE NED's *gray head swings slowly, and with his right hand he seems to be conducting.* TOM *enters from the kitchen. Likewise* WILL *and* SUSAN *and the children. They all sing. As most everyone knows, the words are:*

CHORUS
Steal away, steal away, steal away to Jesus,
Steal away, steal away home,
I ain't got long to stay here.

VERSE
My Lord calls me, He calls me by the thunder,
I ain't got long to stay here.

My Lord calls me, He calls me by the lightning,
The trumpet sounds within my soul,
The trumpet sounds within my soul,
I ain't got long to stay here.

This is repeated several times. At each repetition the emotional excitation becomes greater. At about the third round, the ordered sequence of words is interrupted at will with such phrases as, "O Lord," "Have Mercy," yet the rhythm and the tune are maintained. Thus is achieved one of the striking, soul-stirring effects of Negro melody. The song reaches its climax, and then gradually sinks and fades away. After the singers once get well under way, BALO *stops playing, except that now and then he emphasizes a passage by a full chord. He sings, and his own emotion grows greater than the rest. As the song dies out, this seems to diminish also. And when all is still, he seems more quiet than the others. But then, after a pause of some seconds, and utterly without warning, he bursts forth*)

BALO (*Rising from his seat and going to the center of the room as if in a somnambulistic trance*)

An' th' floods came, an' th' winds blew,
An' th' floods came, an' th' winds blew,
An' th' floods came, an' th' winds blew,
Have mercy, Lord, have mercy, Lord,
On me, O yes, on me, on me,
Have mercy, Lord, on me, on me.

(*The folks do not seem at all surprised at this outburst. A head or two are slowly nodded while it lasts*)

SAM (*as* BALO *finishes*)—Amen. Amen.

UNCLE NED   Have mercy, Lord, have mercy.

WILL   Amen. Amen.

(*And now voices and raps on the door announce new arrivals. Two couples. They are strikingly similar both in looks and in dress. Black faces that in repose are sad and heavy, but when they break in smiles become light-hearted and gay. The men have on white shirts and collars, loose black coats, pressed dark trousers, and polished black shoes. The two women are in white shirt waists and plain dark skirts. The room, of course, is now quite crowded. The group around the fire breaks up to greet them.* BALO *is again left to compose himself. "Good evenin's" and "hellos" are exchanged, and by the time the wraps are disposed of on the bed,* SAM *has proposed a game of "kyards," They all look suspiciously, as if undecided, at* WILL. *He, however, turns his gaze into the fire, and by his silence gives consent. Two tables are arranged. Seated around them are the two recent couples,* SAM *and* SUSAN, BOB *and* MAMIE. *They begin to play, and, as they forget* WILL's *presence, become quite lively. Some of the children watch the games. Some are still around the fire.* WILL, *with* BALO, TOM, *and* UNCLE NED *hug the hearth. Their conversation is audible, for the players on the stage reduce their jollity to gestures, etc., though of course in fact such is not the case*)

UNCLE NED Cotton drapped this year as wus' as I ever seed it. An' in every weevil I see sho' th' fingers of th' Lord. Reckon you farmers better drap down on your knees an' pray, an' pray ter th' Lord fer ter free you fom yo' sins. White folks hit th' same as black this time.

WILL They sho' is.

UNCLE NED Boll weevils come ter tell us that it's time ter change our ways. Ain't satisfied with sinnin', but gettin' wus'. An' th' Lord looks down an' is angry, an' he says, "Stop," says he, "ken you stop now? If you ken you ken be saved. I'm a-warnin' yer. An' them what heeds my warnin' has time befo' th' Judgment ter repent their sins an' ter be born again. Ter be born again."

WILL Amen, Uncle Ned, Amen. An' true, true. Like Saul y'know, Saul of Tarsus, we is all on our way t' Damascus, an' breathin' out threatnin's an' slaughter 'gainst th' Lord. But we can be born again. We can be born again an' see th' light that Saul saw when he fell down t' th' earth, an' hear th' voice that Saul heard when he lay there kickin' on th' ground an' stirrin' up th' dust on th' road that led inter Damascus. We can be born again, that's sho'. Brother, we can be born again an' go out like Saul an' preach th' gospel of th' Lord. O Lord.

(*they all, that is, all around the hearth, slip immediately and easily into humming an indefinite air derived from a melody. As this increases in volume,* BALO *is seen to tilt back in his chair, and his eyes roll ecstatically upward. Even more suddenly than before he jumps to his feet*)

BALO

Jesus, Jesus, I've found Jesus,
  Th' light that came t' Saul when he was born again,
  Th' voice that spoke t' Saul when he was born again,
  Jesus, Jesus, I've found Jesus,
  One mo'sinner is a-comin' home.

(*Here he falls to his knees, face raised in pain and exaltation, hands clasped in supplication above his head*)

  O Jesus, Jesus, savior of my soul,
  One mo'sinner is a-comin' home,
  One mo' sinner is a-comin' home.

Th' light that came t' Saul when he was born again,
  Th' voice that spoke t' Saul when he was born again,
  Th' light that came t' Saul when he was born again,

  O Jesus, Jesus, savior of my soul,
  Jesus, Jesus, I've found Jesus,
  One mo' sinner is a-comin' home.

(BALO *stops, and gives a desperate glance around the room. Seeing* UNCLE NED, *who has turned to face him, he throws himself into his arms, and breaks into a violent and spasmodic sobbing.* UNCLE NED *raises one arm in blessing, while with the other he encircles him in love. The card players, having become uneasy when* UNCLE NED *first began to talk, stopped their game entirely at* BALO's *outburst, and now file out, heads lowered, in sheepishness and guilt. And as the curtain descends, the others, with the exception of* UNCLE NED *and* BALO, *are seen leaving*). Curtain.

John Matheus (1887–)

'Cruiter
1926

Upwards of 750,000 Southern blacks migrated North in the years 1915-1918. This movement, though accelerated by industrial demand for labor, was not a sudden one, but rather part of a continuous migration beginning in 1879, when the withdrawal of Federal troops from the South allowed the reinstitution of slavery conditions—disenfranchisement, forced labor, and complete social segregation.

The Great War To Save Democracy created a labor shortage that sent Northern industry's recruiters South. White southerners, fearing a permanent Day of Absence for their cheap labor, tried to prevent blacks from leaving. One hundred blacks taken from a train in Savannah were arrested and detained for loitering. Jacksonville City Council required agents to buy a thousand dollar permit for recruiting labor to be sent outside the state. Macon Georgia raised the fee to $25 thousand.

Professor John Matheus first heard these stories while teaching at Florida A & M. "From Chicago, Detroit the recruiters of black labor would surreptitiously appear to take scores of farm hands in trucks to Northern centers. I knew about this from talking to country folk. '*Cruiter* is the result."

'*Cruiter* won the prize in the *Opportunity* magazine contest of 1926. It is one of three published plays by Mr. Matheus, who has taken great care to transcribe the regional speech of lower Georgia. Beyond careful attempts to record the actual sounds of words ("We moght a sont auah chickens tuh Sis Ca'line"), Professor Matheus has recorded idioms that were preserved by the folk culture from Middle English ("Ah jest as leef die a fightin.").

John Matheus has written twenty-four stories, many based in the tri-state area of West Virginia, Ohio, and Pennsylvania where he was born and grew up. He writes, "Through all this section of our nation, even as the black coal seams run under hills, mountains and deep into the ground, so runs that other black seam of race and color."

'*Cruiter* exposes one of the black seams in a touching and dramatic fashion, but at the curtain the seam has not run out. It is to be picked up in Chicago, Detroit, and New York by Richard Wright and others.

'Cruiter

CHARACTERS

GRANNY *aged seventy-seven, a typical Negro "Mammy"*
SONNY, *her grandson, aged twenty-three*
SISSY, *his wife, aged twenty*
A WHITE MAN, *a recruiting agent for a Northern munitions factory*

SCENE *A farm cottage in lower Georgia.*

TIME *Just after the entry of the United States into the World War.*

(*Early morning and Spring, 1918, in lower Georgia. The rising of the curtain reveals the large room of a Negro cabin. The walls are the reverse of the outside weatherboarding. A kerosene lamp is on a shelf. At the end of the room looking toward the audience is a door leading to a bedroom, where the starchy whiteness of a well-made bed is visible. In front of the spectators, at the rear of the room, is a window without glass, half-closed by a heavy wooden shutter. Four feet from the window is a door, wide open, leading to a garden. Rows of collards are seen, an old hoe, and in the background a path to the big road.*
  On the right is a wide, old-fashioned fireplace, where a big pine log makes a smoldering blaze. GRANNY, *her head swathed in a blue bandanna, is bending over the fire, stirring the contents of a huge iron kettle. In the center of the room is a rough table. A hunk of salt pork is on the table and a rusty knife. Under the window is another table supporting a fifteen quart galvanized iron bucket. A gourd dipper is hanging on the wall between the window and the door. Under the gourd a tin washpan is suspended. Below the basin a box in which oranges have been crated. A backless chair is under the center table. A mongrel dog is curled under it.*

Scene One

GRANNY *with her profile to the audience, stirring the kettle and singing*)

Nobody knows de trouble Ah've seen,
Nobody knows but Jesus;
Nobody knows de trouble Ah've seen—

(*stopping abruptly*)—Ah mus' put some mo' watah to dese plague-taked grits. (*walks to the water bucket, takes down the gourd dipper and fills it with water. Returning to the kettle she slowly pours in the water, stirring as she pours and singing*) "Nobody knows de trouble Ah've seen"—dah now! (*hobbles to the open door and looks across the big road toward the east*) 'Pears like Sonny and Sissy ought to be hyar. It is (*squinting at the sun*) it's mighty nigh onto six o'clock. (*a rooster crows lustily beyond the door. She claps her hands and stamps her feet*)— Skat! Skat, sir. Yo' honery rascal—bringin' me company so early in the mornin'. Ah ain't wantin' to see nobody wid all Ah got tuh do. (*a mocking bird sings*) Jes' listen tuh dat bird. Hallelujah! Praise de Lam'. (*sings*)

Oh, when de world's on fiah,
Ah wants God's bosom
Fo' mah piller.

(*goes to the table in the center of the room and begins to slice the bacon*) "Fo' mah piller." (*voice is heard outside*)

SONNY Whoa, mule, whoa, Ah say.
GRANNY (*putting the bacon in a large iron spider*) Ah knowed dey'd be a-gwine fum de field. (*sound of two pairs of shoes is heard; the heavy tread of* SONNY, *the lighter tread of* SISSY)
SONNY (*wearing brogans and overalls*) Mo'in', Granny. Dat bacon sho' smells good.
SISSY (*enters, wearing a blue calico wrapper*) How yo' feelin', Granny?
GRANNY Ah ain't feelin' so peart dis mo'in'. Mus' be needin' some spring tonic.

SONNY (*taking down the washpan and dipping water from the bucket into the pan*) Well, us done planted a haf'n acre co'n. (*washing his face vigorously*) Ah don't know whut Ah'm goin' to do 'bout de cotton dis yeah, ef Ah don't go tuh wah.

SISSY (*dropping down in the doorsil*) Phew! Mah back is sho' breakin'—stoopin' an' stoopin', drappin' dat co'n.

GRANNY Well, yo' know yo' po' pappy allus use tuh put in de cotton tuh pay Mistah Bob fo' he's rations fum de Commissary.

SONNY But dere warn't nary a pesky ole weevil then neither. 'Sides Mistah Bob done tol' me de guv'ment wanted somethin' t'eat. Say dat de Germans ah goin' to sta've us out an' we mus' plant co'n an' 'taters an' sich. He lows, too, Ah got tuh gi' 'em all us maks dis yeah, 'scusin' ouh keep, tuh he'p him fo' not sendin' me to camp.

GRANNY How come? He ain't no sheriff.

SONNY Don't kere, he somethin' t'other wif dis here Draftin' Bo'd. Yo know dey done sent off Aunt Ca'line's crazy Jim?

GRANNY Mah Jesus! Mah Jesus! Yo'se all Ah's lef', Sonny. Gi' it tuh him. Yo' sho'll git kilt ef yo' has to go off fightin'; like yo' gran'-pappy bruder, Samuel, was kilt, when he jined de Yankee Army.

SONNY But 'tain't his'n an' Ah jest as leef die a fightin' dan stay heah an' tek his sass an 'uptiness an' gi' him all Ah mak, lak Ah was on de chain gang.

SISSY (*coming in from the doorsill and throwing out the dirty water in the basin*) Sonny, Sonny, don't yo' know dese hyar whi' fo'ks?

SONNY (*wiping his hands on his overalls*) Don't Ah know 'em? Co'se Ah knows 'em. When Ah was in town Sat'day didn't Ah see Mistah Bob 'sputin' wif ol' Judge Wiley. Didn't Ah heah him say dis wah was raisin' hell wid his business, takin' all de niggahs fum de plantations?

GRANNY Ah knowed dis here disturbance was comin', 'cause Ah seed a light in de sky eb'ry night dis week.

SISSY (*washing her hands and wiping them on her dress*) Where's dey takin' 'em to, Sonny? Do yo' think dey goin' to take yo'?

SONNY How does Ah know? Whatevah whi' fo'ks wants o' we-all, we-all jes' nacherly got tuh do, Ah spose, but Ah ain't ter gwine tuh give Mistah Bob all my wuk an' Sissy's fo' tuh keep me out a wah. Ah ain't skeered.

GRANNY Boy, yo' don't know whut yo' talkin' 'bout. Ah done seed one wah. Men kilt, heads shot off—all de whi' fo'ks in dey big houses, de wimmins, cryin' dey eyes out an' ol' Gen'ral Sherman shootin' an' sottin' on fiah evahthing waht 'ud bu'n. (*mechanically takes the spider off the fire, then the kettle of grits, dishing up both on a large, heavy crockery platter*)

SISSY (*looking at* GRANNY *with tenderness. She and* SONNY *exchange glances, showing appreciation of her*) Heah, Granny, lemme he'p yo' fix breakfas'.

GRANNY Go 'way chile. Yo' got a heap to do he'pin' Sonny all day in de field.

SISSY Oh, that ain't nothin'. (*pulling out the backless chair, then bringing up the orange box and turning it lengthwise so that she and* SONNY *can sit upon it*)

SONNY (*patting* SISSY's *hand*) Po' chile, Ah ain't gwine to have yo' wukin' dis er-way. 'Tain't right.

SISSY Hush, chile, Granny's askin' de blessin'.

GRANNY (*bowing her head*) Bress dis food we'se 'bout tuh receive fo' Christ's sake. Amen. (*she serves their plates generously of the bacon and grits and some gravy made with the bacon*)

SONNY (*eating with his knife*) Er, ah, Granny—

GRANNY Sonny, de co'n meal's 'bout gone. Dere's enough fo' co'npone to-day.

SONNY (*laying down his knife*) Sissy, don't lemme fergit to take some co'n meal when Ah goes tuh town to-morrow, Sat'day, ef us is heah.

SISSY Ef us is heah? Whut yo' mean, Sonny?

GRANNY He mean ef de Lawd's willin'. How come, chile yo' don't tek Him into yo' plannin'?

SONNY (*absent-mindedly*) No, Granny, Ah means jes' whut Ah say, ef all o' us is heah.

SISSY AND GRANNY (*looking at* SONNY *in amazement*) Wha' we gwine tuh be?

SONNY (*hangin' his head*) Ah don't know how to tell yo' 'bout it. Ah been a-thinkin' an' a-plannin' an' skeered to let on.

SISSY (*impatiently*) Whut's yo' talkin' 'bout?

SONNY (*doggedly*) Ah'm talkin' 'bout leavin' heah.

GRANNY How we goin' tuh leave? Wha' to? Hit teks heaps o' money to git away.

SONNY Yo' don't have tuh have no money, no nuthin'. Jes' git away.

SISSY (*incredulous*) How?

GRANNY What's ailin' yo' boy?

SONNY When Ah was in town las' Sat'day a whi' man done tol' me he was lookin' fo' wukers.

GRANNY Whut whi' man?

SONNY He said he was a 'cruiter. Lots a fo'ks ah talkin' 'bout him. Yo' all out heah in de country, yo' don't know nothin' 'bout whut's goin' on. Ah'm tellin' yo'. He sez tuh me ez Ah was standin' in de Gen'ral Sto', kin' o' whisperin' lak: "Do yo' wan' tuh mek some money?"

GRANNY Be keerful o' dese heady fo'ks. Dey ain't out fuh no good.

SONNY But, Granny, he talked hones'.

GRANNY Ah know dey ain't no mo' wuk roun' heah dan whut we all is doin'.

SONNY But dis ain' 'round heah.

SISSY Wha' is ut, Sonny?

SONNY Up No'th.

SISSY (*lighting up*) Up No'th!

GRANNY (*with scorn*) UP NO'TH!

SONNY (*bubbling with enthusiasm*) Yes. Up No'th—wha' we kin be treated lak fo'ks. He told me he would tek us all, tek us an' put us on de train at River Station below town, 'cause a deputy sheriff done 'rested a pa'cel o' niggahs, whut was tryin' tuh follow some other 'cruiter.

SISSY Wha' he now? When could he come?

SONNY He say he was comin' tuh see 'bout ut Friday, today. (*with hesitation*) Dat's why Ah had to tell yo' all.

GRANNY Up No'th? Sonny, dey tell me it's too col' up No'th.

SONNY No, Granny, de 'cruiter say us kin live ez wa'm ez down heah—houses all het by steam. An' Sissy won't have to wuk in no fields neither, ner yo'.

GRANNY But Ah done been down heah seventy-seven yeahs.

SONNY (*triumphantly*) But, Granny, Ah won't have tuh leave yo' tuh fight de wa' 'gin dem Germans.

GRANNY Who say so?

SONNY De 'cruiter.

GRANNY How he know?

SONNY Oh—Ah jes' knows he knows. He sounds lak it when he talks.

SISSY Sonny, why wouldn't yo' have to go tuh wa'?

SONNY He say somethin' Ah don't quite git de meanin' ob, but Ah 'membahs dis. He say Ah could wuk in some kin' o' a—a 'nition factory, wha' dey meks guns an' things, tuh fight de Germans. Dat's why Ah wouldn't have to go.

GRANNY (*looking off into space and tapping her foot slowly*) But yo' can't believe dese whi' fo'ks. Dey're sich liars.

SONNY But he's tellin' de troof.

SISSY Ah hope he's tellin' de troof.

SONNY (*emphatically*) He *is*. He's talkin' sense.

GRANNY Eat yo' breakfus', chillun. Hit's gittin' col'. 'Spec yo'll nebbah heah any mo' fum dat 'cruiter. (*they begin to eat.* GRANNY *gets up to get some hot grits, carrying the pot around and replenishing each plate*)

SONNY (*his mouth full*) We wuk—wuk—wuk. Whut does us git fo' ut? Ouah victuals an' keep. De mules git dat. We ain't no bettern de mules down heah.

GRANNY Yo' ain't seen no slavery days, Sonny.

SONNY Why, slavery days ah right heah now.

GRANNY Dey can't sell yo'.

SONNY But dey kin buy us. Ole Mistah Bob thinks he's done bought us. Dey put bloodhounds on some po' niggah who was tryin' tuh leave ol' man Popperil's plantation. Whut's dat but slavery?

SISSY But, Sonny, Lincum done sot us free. Didn't he, Granny?

GRANNY 'Course he did. Sonny know dat.

SONNY He ain't sot me free. (*an automobile horn is heard at a distance*)

SONNY (*jumping from the orange crate and speaking joyfully*) Dere now. Whut did Ah say? Ah bet dat's him, de 'cruiter.

GRANNY Comin' on Friday. No day to mek new business on Friday. Bad luck's bound to follow yo'.

SISSY 'Pears lak tuh me bad luck's been follering us. (*the horn sounds near. They all go to the door to look*) There 'tis, comin' down de road lickity-split.

SONNY Sho' nuf! Sissy, da hit is, an' hit sho' looks lak de 'cruiter's cah.

GRANNY Looks say nuthin'.

SONNY See. He's stoppin' right by ouah place.

SISSY Sho' is. (*a brisk voice is heard*) Hey there!—

(*Steps sound.* THE WHITE MAN *is seen coming down the path. He stops in front of the open door, hat on and wearing gloves. He talks rapidly and with finality*)

THE WHITE MAN This woman your wife?

SONNY Yas, this is her, Mr. 'Cruiter, an' hyah is mah Granny. (GRANNY *nods her head coldly*)

THE WHITE MAN Well, everything is ready. I came through the country early this morning to avoid other cars on the road. If you say the word I will be back here after you about eleven o'clock to-night. Don't miss this opportunity, folks.

GRANNY Yo' don't know whut yo're axin', Mistah 'Cruiter.

THE WHITE MAN Why, Missus, I am giving this boy a chance to get out, to be a man, like anybody else, make plenty money and have time to enjoy it. (*turning to* SISSY) What do you say? Don't you want to live like a lady and wear fine clothes?

SISSY (*grinning bashfully*) Yas, sir.

SONNY 'Course, Mr. 'Cruiter, Ah sho' wants tuh go.

THE WHITE MAN You know there are many jumping at the chance.

GRANNY Honey, yo' can't tell him now. Whut yo' gwine tuh do wif yo' things?

SONNY Us ain't got nothin' nohow, Granny.

THE WHITE MAN (*looking at his watch*) Well, I must hurry. Tell you what I'll do. I have to come down the road to-night anyway as far as the adjoining plantation.

SISSY (*turning to* GRANNY) Mistah Popperil's place.

THE WHITE MAN I'll blow the horn three times. If you want to come I'll take you. Don't miss this chance of your lifetime. Good wages, transportation to Detroit straight, a good job waiting for you and freedom. (*he leaves hastily*)

GRANNY (*sinks down on the steps*) Huh! (SISSY *looks at* SONNY *expectantly.* SONNY *stands undecided, scratching his head. The automobile is heard leaving in the distance, down the big road*)

GRANNY (*singing*)

Nobody knows de trouble Ah've seen,
Nobody knows but Jesus.

(SISSY *and* SONNY *stand looking on the ground*) 'Twon't be right fo' tuh run dat er-way—widout tellin' nobody. 'Tain't Christian, Sonny.

SONNY Ah ain't stud'in' 'bout Christian.

GRANNY Yo' talk lak a po' sinnah, boy.

SISSY Well, Granny, let us try it. Come on.

GRANNY Ef we leave dis place dis a-way, we dasn't come back, even ef yo' didn't lak it.

SONNY Ah wish Ah knowed whut tuh do.

GRANNY Yo' ain't got no faith, son. Yo' ought tuh trust God, lak us did way back dar in slavery days. An' He heard ouah prayahs.

SISSY Sonny prays, Granny.

SONNY But Ah neveh gits no answer.

SISSY Mebbe dis is an answer.

SONNY (*looking at the heavens*) De sun's risin'. Even ef we go we got tuh keep on wukin' to-day, 'cause ol' Mistah Bob's liable to come heah any time.

GRANNY Sonny, Sissy, Ah can't leave dis place. Why, bress me, my mammy's died heah, ol' Missus is buried heah, yo' gran'daddy crossed ovah Jordan in dis ve'y house, yo' own po' mammy, atter yo' worthless pappy was kilt in de cotton mill, died heah too. Ah'm too puny to leave heah now, too far gone mahself.

SONNY Granny, ain't Ah allus wuked and he'p to tek kere o' yo' evah sence Ah been big enough to hoe a row?

GRANNY Yo' has been a mighty dutiful chile, Sonny. Ah ain't sayin' nutin' 'gin yo' honey. Ah ain't wantin' tuh stan' in yo' light. But Ah can't he'p ut. Ah can't beah tuh leave heah, wha all ma fo'ks ah a-layin' an' go 'way 'mongst heathen people.

SISSY But, Granny, you'd be happy wif us, won't yo'?

GRANNY Yas, chile, Ah'd be happy all right, but Ah'm lak Ephraim Ah reckon, wedded to mah idols. (*forcing the words*) Yo'-all go' long an' lemme stay heah.

SONNY (*fiercely*) But, Granny, yo' know how Mistah Bob's gwine tuh tek it, when he fin's us done gone. Ah nevah 'd feel safe leavin' yo' behin'.

GRANNY Dat's a'right. Ain't Ah wuked fo' he's pappy?

SONNY He ain't keerin' fo' 'at. He's liable to th'ow yo' out wif nuttin'.

GRANNY Ain't dis mah cabin? (*looks around tenderly*) Ain't Ah lived heah fo' fifty yeahs?

SONNY But it's on Mistah Bob's lan'.

GRANNY Yo' kin sen' me some money an' excusin' de asthma an' de misery in mah head Ah kin keep a youngah 'oman dan me pantin', when it come tuh wuk.

SISSY Granny, yo' *mus'* come wid us.

SONNY Ah can't think o' leavin' yo' behin'.

GRANNY (*getting up from the steps and walking wearily into the kitchen*) Don't pester me now. Mebbe—mebbe—Ah knowed trouble was comin', seein' dem lights in de elements.

SISSY (*whispers to* SONNY) She say "Mebbe."

SONNY (*whispering*) Ah wished Ah knowed what tu do.

GRANNY (*looking up and seeing them whispering*) Go long, chillun, yo' needn't be keepin' secrets fum yo' ol' Granny. Mebbe yo're right; mebbe Ah'm right. Dis is a cu'ios worl' anyhow. But dat whi' man ain't come back yit. Dey ain't tekin' niggahs on steam cahs fo' nuttin'. Whi' fo'ks *is* whi' fo'ks.

SONNY Well, Granny, we'll see.

GRANNY Ah'll fix yo'-all's dinner an' bring it down yander to de bottom tree.

SONNY (*to* SISSY) Come on, Sissy, us'll put in one day more anyhow. (*they leave. As the sound of their footsteps ceases the rooster is heard to crow again*)

GRANNY (*going to the door*) Plague tek yo' honery self. (*picks up a spoon and throws in direction of the sound*) Cl'ar out a heah—crowin' up company. Ah don't need no 'cruiters. (*she becomes silent and then sings*)

Down in de Valley—couldn't heah mah Jesus,
Couldn't heah nobody pray, O Lord!—

(*Curtain.*)

Scene Two

(*Same place 10:45 that night. The faint glow of the kerosene lamp accentuates the desolate shadows.* GRANNY *is sitting on the backless chair, her hands folded.* SISSY *is packing clothes in an old dress suitcase. A big bag with a string tied around it rests beside* GRANNY. SONNY, *dressed in overalls and a gray coat, walks back and forth as he talks*)

GRANNY He ain't comin'.

SONNY 'Tain't time yit. (*looking at his dollar watch*) It's only a quarter tuh 'leven.

GRANNY He ain't comin', Ah say.

SONNY Don't put a bad mouf on us, Granny.

SISSY (*to* SONNY) Come heah, he'p me shet dis thing. (SONNY *helps her close the stuffed suitcase*)

GRANNY Bad mouf, chile, Ah's been sittin' heah prayin' fo' yo-all. We ain't nuttin', but wif de ol' Marster we ah pow'ful strong.

SISSY (*holding her head*) Mah head's turnin' 'round all in a whirl.

SONNY Ah yo' ready, Granny?

GRANNY Reckon so.

SISSY Do yo' think he's comin.?

SONNY Sho'.

GRANNY (*shaking her head*) Can't keep fum thinkin' 'bout yo' mammy, how she wouldn't wan' yo' tuh leab heah dis a-way.

SONNY Ah believe she'd wan' us tuh go.

SISSY Whut yo' all talkin' 'bout sich fo'? Yo' mak me skeert.

GRANNY 'Tain't no use bein' skeert. Yo' got tuh face de ol' Marster some o' dese times.

SISSY Oh, Ah ain't skeert o' no ol' Marster, but yo' mek me think o' ghos'es.

SONNY Ah'm skeert o' de clutches o' ol' Mistah Bob. He don't mean us no good. Ah jes' know ef mammy an' pappy could speak dey'd shoo us on.

GRANNY How yo' know so much?

SONNY Ain't Ah done seed de way he looked at niggahs—wicked lak he could swallow 'em whole?

GRANNY (*sighs*) —Lordy! Lordy!

SISSY Whut time is it, Sonny?

SONNY (*looking at his watch*) —Ten tuh 'leven.

GRANNY (*singing*) "—O Lordy, Lordy, won't yo' ketch mah groan".

SONNY Us ain't goin' tuh no funeral, Granny. Ah feels lak it's a picnic—a 'Mancipation Celebration picnic.

SISSY Ah'm rarin' tuh go, too, 'specially sence yo' tol' me 'bout de schools up yander. Ouah chillun kin go tuh whi' fo'ks school.

GRANNY Whi' fo'ks ain't goin' treat niggahs wif book learnin' any bettern we-all.

SONNY We kin treat each othah bettah den. Ah kin treat mahself bettah. An' so kin mah chillun.

GRANNY Yo' young niggahs ah sho' uppity, but Ah hope yo' ain't got no wool ovah yo' eyes.

GRANNY We mought a sont ouah chickens tuh Sis Ca'line.
SISSY She mought a tol' somebody, too, an' dere we'd be.
GRANNY Yo' got dat box fixed for Berry?
SONNY He's already in ut. He ain't used tuh bein' shut up lak dat, de lazy varmint.
GRANNY (*walks to the door and looks out*) The stars ah shinin'. (*comes back and gets a drink from the bucket*)
SISSY (*excitedly*) SAKES ALIVE! Ah see de lights a-comin', 'mobile lights.
SONNY (*running to the door*) She is. We goin' fum heah.
GRANNY (*moodily silent. The glare from the headlights of the automobile lights up the room, shining in through the open door.* GRANNY *looks in wonder at the light*) Ah, chillun, de Lawd is wif us. (*sings*) "Shine on me. Let de light fum de lighthouse, shine on me." (*the chug of the engine is heard and the grinding of the brakes, as the car pulls up. The horn blows three times.* THE WHITE MAN *runs down the walk*)
THE WHITE MAN Are you ready? We have no time to lose.
SONNY We's waitin'. (*gathers up bag, suitcase and hat and starts towards the door*)
SISSY Don't forget Berry.
THE WHITE MAN Who's Berry?
SISSY De dog.
THE WHITE MAN What do you mean? We can't take dogs on this trip.
GRANNY Whut's de mattah wif yo', man? Think we're goin' tuh leave Berry?
THE WHITE MAN See here. It is impossible to take any dog. He'll make too much noise and besides I can't be bothered looking out for him.
SONNY Well, Berry 'll have tuh stay heah, dat's all.
GRANNY Den Ah stays too.
SONNY Whut yo' say?
GRANNY (*stubbornly*) Ah ain't goin' tuh leave Berry.
THE WHITE MAN Ah, come on—cut the argument. We got to make that train.
SISSY (*worried*) He kin fend fo' hisself.
GRANNY Go on yo' chillun, go on. Ah don't wan' tuh go nowhow. Ah jes' been a-pretendin' tuh git yo' started. Ah kin git along. Ain't Ah got along wif whi' fo'ks fo' seventy yeahs an' mo'?
SONNY (*angrily*) Whut yo' wan' tuh act dis a-way fo'?
THE WHITE MAN Well, come on or stay, people. Time's passing.
SONNY Ah'm goin', Granny. Don't yo' see Ah can't stay heah? Ef Ah stay Ah'm goin' tuh git kilt fo' sassin' dese whi' fo'ks; ef Ah go tuh wa', Ah hastuh leave yo' jes' de same an' mebbe git kilt. Ef Ah go No'th and die, Ah'll be a dead free man. (*he puts down bundles and embraces* GRANNY) Mah po' ol' Granny. Ah'm goin' tuh send yo' plenty a money an' Ah'll be back, come Christmas, mebbe to tek yo' atter we gits settled.
GRANNY (*frightened*) Don't, don't come back, not heah. Promise me dat, chile. Yo' know Mistah Bob. He git yo'.
SONNY No, he won't, Ah'll show him.
THE WHITE MAN (*impatiently*) We must be going.
SISSY Fo' God, Granny, come on.
GRANNY (*firmly*) Ah done said mah say.
SONNY Den, good-bye, Granny. (*gives her money*) Ah send yo' plenty mo' fust pay day an' Ah'm goin' tuh have a payday ebery week.
SISSY (*kissing* GRANNY) Good-bye.
GRANNY (*her arms around them both*) Mah po' chillun. Mah po' chillun. (*they tear themselves from her embrace.* THE WHITE MAN *leads the way to the car.* SONNY *takes up the suitcase, but leaves the bag.* SISSY *follows. The sound of the three pairs of footsteps dies away*)
SONNY *and* SISSY (*calling from the car*) Granny?
GRANNY (*standing in the doorway*) Chillun.
SISSY Pray fo' us, Granny. (*the car is heard lurching ahead. The light disappears. The sounds die away.* GRANNY *stands for a minute in the deep silence, looking in the direction of the vanished car. A whining is heard. She looks out in the darkness*)
GRANNY Bress mah soul! Berry! (*she pulls in a crated box, containing the cur. She gets a poker and pries the box open. The dog is wild with appreciation*) Come heah, Berry. (*pulls up the backless chair by the table and sits down, patting the dog*) Berry, you'se all Ah got lef' now. (*rests her elbow on the table, shuts her eyes*) Lordy, Ah'm so tiahed, so tiahed. (*she sits up suddenly, listening attentively*) Who dat knockin' at mah do'? (*she gets up slowly and looks out. Nothing. Shuts the door and bolts it. Sits down again and buries her face in her hands. Again she raises up and listens*) Who dat, knockin' agin?

(*once more she gets up more painfully, unbolts and opens the door. Nothing. Closing it she totters feebly to the chair*) Berry, Ah'm tuckered out. (*croons*) "Somebody knockin' at mah do'!" (*stops. Listens*) Come in. (*falls back in chair, her head rests on the table, her arms limp. She mumbles*) Come in, 'Cruiter. Reckon Ah'm all ready.

(*Curtain.*)

Willis Richardson (1889–)

The Idle Head 1927

Willis Richardson is a pioneer in black drama. He was the first to write plays about Crispus Attucks and Antonio Maceo. He was the first to have a play (one act) produced on Broadway—*The Chip Woman's Fortune*, 1923. He was the first to edit collections of black plays for school children: *Plays and Pageants of Negro Life* (1930) and *Negro History in Thirteen Plays* (1935). He may have become the first to write plays for children when Dr. Du Bois requested him to write five plays for *The Brownies Book*, a children's magazine, 1920–21. (Mr. Richardson is also represented by *Flight of the Natives* in this volume.)

In March, 1972, Mr. Richardson recalled in an interview that he came to write plays after he had seen *Rachel* by Angelina Grimke in 1916, and he had decided that he could do as well. He wrote three one-act plays and took them to the librarian at Howard University.

> Alain Locke and Montgomery Gregory were in charge of the Howard Players, and I was put in touch with them and they liked my writing and they wanted to put on a play of mine but you see the President of Howard was a white man at that time and they couldn't get his consent....
>
> So in Chicago the Ethiopian Art Players was organized and they put on Negro plays, but they didn't know any Negro playwrights, or black playwrights, or whatever you want to call them, so they wrote to *Crisis* and Dr. DuBois put me in touch. They put on Oscar Wilde's *Salome* and my play *The Chip Woman's Fortune*. They went to New York and played at the Frazier Theater and the reviews were so good that they sold lots of tickets. Then at the end of the week the manager made a big mistake. People bought tickets for these two plays but when they came the next week, he put on another play and the people objected so much that they had to give them their money back. The manager left New York and went somewhere and left all the players stranded.... Then finally we had an agreement to put on a play of mine at Howard University; that was the first play by one of our people that was staged there.
>
> (Hatch-Billops Oral Black Theatre History Collection, City College of New York)

The Idle Head first appeared in *Carolina Magazine* in 1929. One critic has dismissed the play as a homily: "Don't steal no matter for what purpose." To accept this terse summary is to ignore Mr. Richardson's concern with the black man who wishes to provide for his family but cannot find work because he will not grin and scratch his head. Which white dramatists had such basic insight into their black male characters in the 1920's?

Mr. Richardson is the author of nearly thirty plays, most of which have been produced in black schools and colleges. He is winner of a Spingarn and two *Crisis* prizes and the Schwab Cup at Yale University. At this writing he lives in Washington, D.C. He is one of a number of theater people, writers, directors, and teachers who long have worked in Southern schools to build black drama: Randolph Edmonds, Thomas Poag, Juanita Oubre, Thomas Pawley, John Ross, Owen Dodson, Melvin Tolson, Clifford Lamb, Darwin Turner, Carlton Molette and Ted Shine are but a few of those whom hundreds of black students honor.

The Idle Head

CAST OF CHARACTERS

MRS. BROADUS, *a washerwoman*
GEORGE BROADUS, *her son*
ALICE BROADUS, *her daughter*
BRO. HARRIS
A CHAUFFEUR
A POLICEMAN

(*The scene is the sitting room in the* BROADUS *home. In the center of the rear wall is a fireplace below a mantel, and on the mantel are a clock and two vases. At the right of the fireplace is a low rocker in which* GEORGE BROADUS *is lying back with his hat drawn over his eyes. At the left of the fireplace in the rear wall is a window. At the left side a door leads to the kitchen and at the right side there are two doors, the one below leading to the hall and the one above leading to the other rooms. Between these doors is a table against the wall and upon the table a large Bible. There are three straight chairs in the room and a few faded pictures about the walls.* GEORGE BROADUS *is a young man about eight and twenty, a little above medium height and very robust. He is wearing worn out clothes and no collar. He leans back in the chair asleep until* MRS. BROADUS *enters from the kitchen. She is a woman of fifty with mixed gray hair, and the facial expression of one who looks forward to nothing but the next day's work. She is wearing a calico dress and gingham apron, and it seems as if she has just left the wash tub. She stops and looks at* GEORGE *a moment and shakes her head before speaking*)

MRS. BROADUS George! George!
GEORGE (*sitting up*) Ma'am?
MRS. BROADUS What you doin' sleep this time o' day? You'll sleep your brains out, boy.
GEORGE There ain't much else to do.
MRS. BROADUS Ain't you goin' to look for a job no more?
GEORGE (*carelessly*) What's the use? Everything's against me.
MRS. BROADUS You don't never expect to find one if you don't look for it, do you?
GEORGE What's the use o' lookin'? Everywhere Ah go they ask me where Ah worked last, and time Ah tell 'em they telephone to find out about me, and soon as they find out Ah don't get the job. Ah'm on the black list, that's all. And Ah've got sense enough to know Ah won't get nothin' to do as long as Ah stay in this town.
MRS. BROADUS Well, Ah don't want you to leave town, Ah tell you right now.

(ALICE, *a young woman of five and twenty has entered the room from the kitchen*)

ALICE George is right, Ma. He never will get another job in this town. All the boys say he ought to been gone long ago.
MRS. BROADUS He won't go long as Ah've got anything to say about it.
ALICE Why? What you want to hang to him so hard for?
MRS. BROADUS Cause Ah want a man in the house. A house ain't nothin' without a man in it. We wouldn't have no protection if it wasn't for George. Ah wouldn't live in no house if it didn't have a man in it.
ALICE Ah don't see a thing in that.
GEORGE (*to* ALICE) You seem mighty anxious to get me away, but you ain't half as anxious to get me away as Ah am to go. Ah want to go where Ah can work.
ALICE Ah don't blame you.
MRS. BROADUS You can work. Ah got a job for you right now. Go and get Mrs. Ross' clothes.
GEORGE Ah'll go, but Ah don't care much about goin' to that house. That ain't the kind of work Ah mean.
MRS. BROADUS If you'll do like Ah tell you you'll get along all right.
GEORGE What is it you want me to do to get along all right?
MRS. BROADUS When you go there be sure to take your hat off and go in the back way. And don't look so mad all the time.

The Idle Head

GEORGE You mean for me to grin, but Ah don't grin.

MRS. BROADUS It might pay you if you did.

GEORGE Then Ah'll never get paid if grinnin's goin' to pay me.

MRS. BROADUS They been complainin' about you comin' in the front way all the time.

GEORGE Who's been complainin'?

MRS. BROADUS The chauffeur said Mrs. Ross didn't like it.

GEORGE Aw, damn the chauffeur!

MRS. BROADUS Don't use that kind o' language in here!

GEORGE Ah'll fix him some o' these days.

MRS. BROADUS (*becoming anxious*) Don't you go out o' here and get in no trouble, George.

GEORGE Ah ain't goin' out lookin' for trouble, but some o' these days he's goin' to catch me wrong. Seems like somebody's always tryin' to do somethin' to make me disagreeable. If it ain't him it's Alice, and if it ain't Alice it's somebody else.

ALICE What did Ah do?

GEORGE You been searchin' ma pockets. You better keep out o' ma pockets if you don't want to have trouble.

ALICE Who's been in your pockets?

GEORGE You! You know you been in 'em!

ALICE Ah don't want nothin' you've got.

GEORGE Ah know you don't. That's because Ah ain't got nothin'. But just the same you take a fool's advice and keep out o' ma pockets.

MRS. BROADUS Go on, George, and stop your quarrellin'.

GEORGE You better make her keep out o' ma pockets. (*pulling his hat tightly on his head he goes out*)

MRS. BROADUS That's right, Alice, you keep out o' his pockets; it might cause trouble. Yo know George's got a mighty mean temper when he gets mad, and you can't tell what he might do.

ALICE (*defiantly*) Ah know he's got better sense than to lay his hands on me. He ain't gone crazy yet.

MRS. BROADUS No, he ain't goin' to lay his hands on you. George wouldn't hit no woman, but he'd raise such a rumpus in the house that all the neighbors ud think he was beatin' us both to death.

ALICE Who cares about him? Ah ain't scared of him.

MRS. BROADUS Ah know you ain't; but just keep out o' his pockets and we won't have trouble. You know a lot o' men think it's the worse thing in the world to have a woman searchin' their pockets. (*there is a knock on the door*) Open the door and see who it is.

(ALICE *opens the door and* BRO. HARRIS *enters. He is a tall servile looking man with side whiskers*)

BRO. HARRIS (*bowing*) Good mornin', sisters.

MRS. BROADUS *and* ALICE Good mornin', Brother Harris.

BRO. HARRIS How you sisters this mornin'?

ALICE Ah'm well.

MRS. BROADUS Ah ain't much, Brother Harris; how you do?

BRO HARRIS Ah'm well, thanks the Lord.

ALICE Have a seat.

BRO. HARRIS (*drawing a memorandum from his pocket*) Ah ain't got that much time. Ah got to be gettin' along. Ah see you sisters wasn't to church last Sunday, and you wasn't to class meetin' last night. You ain't turnin' backsliders, is you?

ALICE No, seh.

MRS. BROADUS Ah tell you, Brother Harris, Ah wasn't feelin' so good Sunday, and the reason Ah didn't come to class meetin' last night, Ah didn't have ma dues.

BRO. HARRIS That's just what Ah'm here to see about. Ah'm collectin' class dues and rally money for the church. You all owe five dollars together on your class, and Ah got you down here for two apiece on this rally. That makes nine dollars.

MRS. BROADUS Nine dollars and we ain't got a cent.

BRO. HARRIS Workin' every day and ain't got a cent?

MRS. BROADUS It takes everything we can make to get somethin' to eat and keep a roof over our heads.

BRO. HARRIS Well, you know this church money's got to be paid. The church can't go on if the members don't pay.

MRS. BROADUS But we ain't been able to spare the money.

BRO. HARRIS You ought to lay aside a little at a time.

MRS. BROADUS People's got to eat, and wear clothes, and live in houses, Brother Harris.

BRO. HARRIS Ah know that, but you all don't manage right.

MRS. BROADUS We do the best we can.

BRO. HARRIS No you don't; you don't do the best you can.

MRS. BROADUS How you mean?

BRO. HARRIS There's that boy o' yours ain't struck a lick o' work in six months.

MRS. BROADUS It ain't his fault.

BRO. HARRIS Whose fault is it?

MRS. BROADUS Ah don't know whose fault it is, but Ah know it ain't his'n. He's been tryin' to get work, but everything's against him.

BRO. HARRIS Don't you believe it. Anybody can get a job that wants one.

MRS. BROADUS He tries and tries, but everywhere he goes they turn him away.

BRO. HARRIS Everybody wouldn't turn him away.

MRS. BROADUS That's what he says, and Ah don't believe he'd lie about it.

BRO. HARRIS Ah can't see how it can be true.

MRS. BROADUS It's a mighty funny thing, but it is true.

BRO. HARRIS And you takin' his word for it?

MRS. BROADUS Ah would take his word; but he ain't the only one that's told me. Men what's worked places where he went has told me the same thing.

BRO. HARRIS How did he get down and out like that?

MRS. BROADUS Ah reckon George is too fiery. He won't stand for nothin'.

BRO. HARRIS He ought'n to be too fiery. He won't get nothin' like that.

MRS. BROADUS He comes by it honest, he gets it from his daddy.

BRO. HARRIS Well, if he ever 'spects to get along he'll have to change his ways.

MRS. BROADUS He can't change his ways, he was born like that.

BRO. HARRIS And another thing, Ah wouldn't be takin' his word so much; if you keep on like you goin' you never will have nothing'.

MRS. BROADUS You don't know George like Ah do. He don't belong to church, but he wouldn't lie to me for nothin'. The most of the things Ah'm tellin' you was told to me by other people.

BRO. HARRIS What did he do to make 'em put him on the black list?

MRS. BROADUS Well, Ah'll tell you what they told me and what he said too: The last job he got was a waiter's job; and you know George never was used to that kind o' work; he was always mighty independent. He gets that from his daddy too. Ma husband never did work for nobody but hisself.

BRO. HARRIS Ah know he didn't.

MRS. BROADUS So this last job George got was at a club. He was comin' by with a tray and a young smart alec throwed a quarter to him and says: "Here, Sambo, here's a tip for you." George didn't make no move to catch the quarter. He just let it hit him and roll on the floor; and then he stood there lookin' that young feller straight in the eyes for a whole minute before he bawls him out. Then George says to him: "Ah ain't workin' for you and ma name ain't Sambo. Ah'm workin' for this club and they pay me by the month for ma work. Ah don't want tips from nobody that calls me Sambo." Some other men told me that was right there and seen it. They said the young feller turned red as a beet. So that night George was fired.

BRO. HARRIS And he ain't had a job since, has he?

MRS. BROADUS No, seh.

BRO. HARRIS He was a fool for actin' like that.

MRS. BROADUS Maybe he was and maybe he wasn't. Ah know he never would take nothin' off nobody, and Ah don't blame him.

BRO. HARRIS Ah don't mean to try go get into your family affairs, Sister Broadus; Ah was just givin' you a little advice about how you might get along better. Course Ah wouldn't like to take this roll of honor in without you all's names on it, so Ah'm goin' down the street to collect some more money, and on ma way back Ah'll drop in to see if you changed your mind. (*going to the door*) You know we can't have people stayin' on the class if they can't pay the dues.

MRS. BROADUS Ah'm sorry, Brother Harris, but Ah don't see how we can do a thing today.

BRO. HARRIS Ah'm comin' back by and look you over anyhow. You all might change your minds. (*he goes out*)

MRS. BROADUS This is the worst pickle we ever been in, Alice.

ALICE Ah reckon it is, Ma. What we goin' to do?

MRS. BROADUS God knows Ah don't know what we goin' to do.

ALICE   We got to do somethin'. If we don't do somethin' they'll put us out o' church. And then we'll be the talk of the town.

MRS. BROADUS   (*her eyes filled with tears*) There ain't nothin' to do but pray.

ALICE   But there ain't no use o' cryin', Ma; cryin' won't do no good.

(*The door is pushed open and* GEORGE *enters with a basket of clothes*)

GEORGE   Ah just seen your class leader goin' down the street? What did he want, money?

MRS. BROADUS   Yes.

GEORGE   He always wants money. He never comes around if it ain't for that. It's the same way with all of 'em.

MRS. BROADUS   Don't be so bitter, George.

GEORGE   Ah ain't bitter, Ah'm tellin' the truth. (*he notices her eyes*) What you been doin', cryin'?

ALICE   Brother Harris said somethin' about puttin' us off the class if we didn't pay our dues, and Ma don't want the whole town talkin' about her.

GEORGE   How much do you owe?

ALICE   Nine dollars.

GEORGE   Nine dollars! Helpin' to get a new suit for the preacher? Suits must be gone up.

ALICE   Ah reckon you're right. (*she goes out*)

MRS. BROADUS   You all ought'nt to talk like that.

GEORGE   He'll be waitin' a long time before he gets it. Even at that Ah know you ought to have the money to give him. And when Ah say that Ah ain't thinkin' so much about him as Ah am about you—you and Alice. You all been doin' things for me all ma life and now it's almost time for me to be doin' somethin' for you all—somethin' you want done.

MRS. BROADUS   That's all right, Ah know you'd do it if you could.

GEORGE   Ah'm goin' to do somethin' too. There ain't nothin' Ah wouldn't do for you all, cause Ah don't care half as much about all the rest of the world as Ah do about you two.

MRS. BROADUS   Don't keep that on your mind. Did you do what Ah told you when you went after them clothes?

GEORGE   What you mean?

MRS. BROADUS   You didn't have no trouble with that chauffeur, did you?

GEORGE   Ah went in the front way, but Ah didn't see him.

MRS. BROADUS   But you mustn't go in the front way, George. Them people don't like it.

GEORGE   It ain't nobody but him.

MRS. BROADUS   The madam don't like it neither. She don't say nothin' but Ah know she don't like it. (GEORGE *is silent*) Ah hopes you don't make me lose this wash, George; it's the best one Ah got.

GEORGE   That chauffeur'll lose somethin' if he keeps on after me.

MRS. BROADUS   If you get in trouble and go to jail, you needn't expect me to get you out.

GEORGE   Ah reckon Ah'd be just as well off in jail, then you and Alice wouldn't have nobody to work for but yourselves.

MRS. BROADUS   Go on, George, and don't talk so foolish. Look through them clothes and see if you see any valuables. She's always leavin' somethin' in her clothes.

GEORGE   All right. Now don't go out there and do a lot o' worryin' about that church money. Let it go.

MRS. BROADUS   Ah can't help it, George. It works on ma mind. Ma name's been on that roll of honor for the last twenty years.

GEORGE   And if Ah wasn't such a burden on you all it ud be on there now.

MRS. BROADUS   Oh, stop your foolishness and look through them clothes.

(*She goes out. He sits staring at the fire for a moment, then takes a knife from his pocket, picks up a stick and begins to whittle it. After a few moments he throws the stick into the fire and spits in after it. He then brings the basket over and begins looking through the clothes. He finds a gold bar pin sticking in a waist, and looking at it closely he puts it upon the mantel and continues to look through the clothes. Finally he comes across a diamond pin. He looks at this carefully, ponders over it then puts it into his pocket. After putting the other clothes back into the basket he takes both pins and examines them more closely. At last after coming to some conclusion he puts the bar pin back upon the mantel and the diamond into his pocket*)

GEORGE   (*calling*)   Ma!

MRS. BROADUS   (*from the kitchen*)   What?

GEORGE   Ah found a pin.

MRS. BROADUS   (*appearing*)   Where is it?

GEORGE (*rising and stretching*)   On the mantel.

(MRS. BROADUS *takes the pin and looks at it.* GEORGE *starts out*)

MRS. BROADUS (*putting the pin down*) Where you goin'?

GEORGE Ah'm goin' out to see if Ah can scrape up enough for you all's church money.

MRS. BROADUS How you goin' to scrape up nine dollars?

GEORGE Ah don't know.

MRS. BROADUS Be careful. You know what they say about the idle head bein' the devil's workshop.

GEORGE Ah ain't goin' to do nothin' to nobody. (*he goes out*)

MRS. BROADUS (*calling*) Alice!

ALICE Ma'am?

MRS. BROADUS Come here. (ALICE *enters wiping water from her hands with her apron*) George found one pin in the clothes.

ALICE Ah wonder what she wants to leave things in her clothes for?

MRS. BROADUS She's mighty careless.

ALICE After a while she'll be losin' somethin' and sayin' she left it in her clothes.

MRS. BROADUS Ah hope not. Ah wouldn't want to be accused o' stealin'.

ALICE Did George look through 'em good?

MRS. BROADUS Ah reckon he did.

ALICE Let's look again. (*there is a knock on the door*)

MRS. BROADUS Come in! (*the door is pushed open and the* CHAUFFEUR *enters.*)

CHAUFFEUR Good mornin'.

MRS. BROADUS *and* ALICE Good mornin'.

CHAUFFEUR Mrs. Ross sent me to ask you all to look through the clothes and see if you could find two pins she had left in 'em.

MRS. BROADUS Ma son just looked through 'em. (*taking the pin from the mantel*) Here's one pin he found.

CHAUFFEUR She said there was two pins, this one and a diamond.

ALICE We ain't seen no diamond. That's the only pin was in there.

CHAUFFEUR Did you all look through the clothes good?

MRS. BROADUS Ma son did.

CHAUFFEUR Where's he?

MRS. BROADUS He's gone out.

CHAUFFEUR Well, Mrs. Ross ain't so much bothered about this pin; it was the other one she was worried about. She said it cost five hundred dollars.

ALICE Five hundred dollars!

CHAUFFEUR (*hoping to add to his own importance*) That ain't nothin', Ah've worked for people that owned pins worth a thousand.

MRS. BROADUS We ain't seen nothin' of it.

CHAUFFEUR Ah'll go back and tell her what you said. You don't know where your son's gone, do you?

MRS. BROADUS (*becoming angry*) Look a here, mister; ma son ain't got nothin' to do with no pin. He ain't seen no pin.

CHAUFFEUR Ah didn't say your son had it; but if it ain't found somebody's goin' to have trouble.

MRS. BROADUS You just as well get your mind off ma boy, cause he's just as honest as the days is long.

CHAUFFEUR All right, we'll see about it. (*he goes out closing the door behind him*)

ALICE There! What did Ah tell you. They're ready to blame that on us right now.

MRS. BROADUS They sha'n't lay it on us.

ALICE How you goin' to stop 'em?

MRS. BROADUS Ah don't know; but Ah know Ah ain't goin' to stand for no pin.

ALICE Ah reckon we better look through them clothes again; maybe George did miss it. (*they begin to search the clothes*)

MRS. BROADUS Ah'd rather find it in here than to have her thinkin' we stole it.

ALICE Ah would too. Ah told you they'd be wantin' to blame us.

MRS. BROADUS They ain't blamed us yet.

ALICE They ain't far from it. Couldn't you tell by the way he talked that he had his mind on George?

MRS. BROADUS (*looking anxiously at each piece as she takes it out*) Ah don't know. Ah don't know. Look careful, gal. (GEORGE *enters*)

GEORGE Didn't Ah look through them clothes good enough?

MRS. BROADUS The Chauffeur's been here and says Mrs. Ross left a diamond pin in these clothes.

GEORGE (*calmly taking off his coat*) He must be crazy.

ALICE (*as they finish searching*) Ah don't see nothin'.

MRS. BROADUS Me neither.

The Idle Head

(GEORGE *hangs his coat on the back of the chair and sits*)

GEORGE Don't worry, Ma. Let her find it where she lost it. Ah bet she'll come across it sooner or later.

MRS. BROADUS Ah don't like for nobody to lose nothin' around me. Ah reckon you're right just the same.

GEORGE Let her do the worryin'.

(MRS. BROADUS *sits and gazes sadly into the fire place*)

GEORGE (*breaking the silence*) Ah did run across some money while Ah was out.

MRS. BROADUS Money?

ALICE Where?

GEORGE Ah borrowed some for you all's church dues.

MRS. BROADUS Who's goin' to lend you nine dollars?

GEORGE Don't you think Ah've got some friends?

ALICE Where is it?

GEORGE (*handing some bills to each of them*) Here.

MRS. BROADUS Ah'm mighty glad to get it. This'll put us on the roll again.

ALICE Indeed it will.

GEORGE (*rising*) Ah reckon Ah'll go in and take a nap.

MRS. BROADUS All right. We'll be ready for Brother Harris when he comes back. (GEORGE *goes into the next room*)

ALICE George might be fiery, but he's got some good friends somewhere.

MRS. BROADUS He sure is.

ALICE Brother Harris'll be kinder surprised, won't he?

MRS. BROADUS Ah bet Ah can knock him down with a feather when he sees these bills. (ALICE *begins to search the pockets of* GEORGE's *coat*)

MRS. BROADUS What you doin'?

ALICE Ah just want to see what he's got.

MRS. BROADUS You better stop that. He'll catch you at it some o' these days and there'll be trouble.

ALICE (*drawing a card from* GEORGE's *pocket*) Look, Ma, a pawn ticket.

MRS. BROADUS A what?

ALICE A pawn ticket. (*there is a knock on the door*)

MRS. BROADUS (*all smiles*) Ah reckon that's Brother Harris now. Come in!

(*The* CHAUFFEUR *enters, followed by a* POLICEMAN. MRS. BROADUS *is so surprised she cannot speak.* ALICE *quickly puts the ticket behind her*)

CHAUFFEUR Ah'm back to see about that pin. Did you find it?

MRS. BROADUS (*frightened*) No. We just got through lookin' in the clothes.

POLICEMAN And you're sure you ain't seen the pin at all?

MRS. BROADUS No, seh, Ah ain't seen it. She didn't send it in these clothes.

POLICEMAN (*to the* CHAUFFEUR *indicating* MRS. BROADUS) Is this the woman that takes in the wash?

CHAUFFEUR Yes.

POLICEMAN (*to* MRS. BROADUS) Ah wouldn't like to see you in trouble, so you better tell where the pin is.

MRS. BROADUS Ah ain't seen no pin, Mister.

CHAUFFEUR Where's your son?

MRS. BROADUS (*pointing to the door*) He's in there sleep.

POLICEMAN (*starting towards the door*) In this room?

MRS. BROADUS (*stopping him*) Wait a minute, mister; don't go in there! If you don't want to get in trouble, don't go in there!

CHAUFFEUR We want to see him.

MRS. BROADUS Ah'll go after him. (*she goes into the next room. The* POLICEMAN *looks upon the mantel while the* CHAUFFEUR *shakes the clothes out of the basket*)

POLICEMAN (*to* ALICE) Do you know anything about that pin?

ALICE No, seh.

CHAUFFEUR What you got behind you? (*just at this moment* MRS. BROADUS *enters followed by* GEORGE. GEORGE *has been asleep and is looking very unpleasant*)

CHAUFFEUR (*starting towards* ALICE) Let's see what you got behind you.

GEORGE (*going forward*) If you put your hands on her Ah'll break your neck!

CHAUFFEUR (*stopping*) What's she got behind her.

GEORGE That's her business.

CHAUFFEUR (*pointing to the coat*) Is this your coat?

CHAUFFEUR (*to the policeman*) Search it.

(the POLICEMAN *takes the coat, but* GEORGE *snatches it from him*)

GEORGE No, you don't! You sha'n't search ma clothes! You can't search me without a warrant! You ain't got no business in here nohow! (*he rolls the coat up and puts it under his arm confident that he has the ticket in the pocket*)

CHAUFFEUR (*pointing to* ALICE) Ah believes she's got that pin behind her.

POLICEMAN What's that behind you?

GEORGE (*laughing*) Let 'em see what you got, Alice. (ALICE *makes no move to do so*) Let 'em see so they can get out o' here. (ALICE *still keeps her hand behind her*)

GEORGE (*still laughing*) Show 'em the pin, Alice.

ALICE He ain't got nothin' to do with what's in ma hand.

CHAUFFEUR She's got it in her hand. Ah'll bet on it.

GEORGE Show 'em what you got in your hand so they can go home and look for the pin.

ALICE No, Ah won't show 'em nothin'.

GEORGE (*going towards her*) Stop your foolishness, gal; so they can get out o' here. (*he pulls her hand from behind her showing the pawn ticket.* GEORGE *is too surprised to speak*)

CHAUFFEUR Oh, Ah know where that pin is now.

POLICEMAN (*taking the ticket*) Who's been to the pawn shop today?

GEORGE (*to* ALICE) You fool! Didn't Ah tell you to keep out o' ma pockets?

POLICEMAN (*Putting his hand on* GEORGE'S *shoulder*) Ah'll have to take you. You pawned the pin, didn't you?

MRS. BROADUS Let 'em take me, George; let 'em take me! Ah'm the cause of it! Ah sent you to pawn that pin!

POLICEMAN (*to* GEORGE) Did you pawn it, or did she?

GEORGE (*pulling on his coat*) Ah done it, you fool; can't you see she's ma mother!

MRS. BROADUS Let 'em take me, George; please let 'em take me! Ah'm old and Ah won't live long nohow! You got a long time to live!

GEORGE That's all right; you didn't do it. They ain't got no right to take you.

CHAUFFEUR Let's take 'em both.

GEORGE (*angrily*) No, you won't take us both, you lackey; you'll take me or none!

POLICEMAN Come on, then, let's be goin'.

MRS. BROADUS (*making a last appeal*) Wait a minute, mister; for God's sake, wait a minute! (*she takes the money from* ALICE *and putting it with what she has offers it to the* POLICEMAN) Here, here's the money! Take it and get the pin out and leave George alone! He didn't mean to steal the pin! He pawned it cause we needed the money! He didn't think about what he was doin'! He's a good boy! He wouldn't steal nothin' from nobody! Honest to God he wouldn't!

POLICEMAN You'll have to tell that to the judge.

GEORGE (*with a fling at* ALICE) If you had kept out o' ma pockets like Ah told you, this wouldn't 've happened!

ALICE How did Ah know you had pawned the pin?

GEORGE It wasn't none o' your business! (*to the* POLICEMAN) Let's go.

(MRS. BROADUS, *who has followed them to the door wringing her hands, falls on her knees as the door closes behind them. She kneels there swaying from one side to the other while* ALICE *stands in the center of the floor with her hands hanging limp at her sides and her lips quivering. Curtain.*)

Randolph Edmonds (1900–)

Bad Man 1934

Estill Springs, Tenn.
February 12, 1918

Jim McIllheron, the Negro who shot and killed Pierce Rodgers and Jessie Tigert, two white men at Estill Springs last Friday and wounded Frank Tigert, was tortured with a red-hot crowbar and then burned to death here tonight at 7:40 by twelve masked men. A crowd of approximately 2000 persons, among whom were women and children, witnessed the burning.

McIllheron, who was badly wounded and unable to walk, was carried to the scene of the murder, where preparation for a funeral pyre was begun.

The captors proceeded to a spot about a quarter of a mile from the railroad station and prepared the death fire. The crowd followed and remained throughout the horrible proceedings. The Negro was led to a hickory tree, to which they chained him. After securing him to the tree a fire was laid. A short distance away another fire was kindled, and into it was put an iron bar to heat.

When the bar became red hot a member of the mob jabbed it toward the Negro's body. Crazed with fright, the black grabbed hold of it, and as it was pulled through his hands the atmosphere was filled with the odor of burning flesh. This was the first time the murderer gave evidence of his will being broken. Scream after scream rent the air. As the hot iron was applied to various parts of his body yells and cries for mercy could be heard in the town.

After torturing the Negro several minutes one of the masked men poured coal oil on his feet and trousers and applied a match to the pyre. As the flames rose, enveloping the Black's body, he begged that he be shot. Yells of derision greeted his request. The angry flames consumed his clothing and little blue blazes shot upward from his burning hair before he lost consciousness. *Chattanooga Daily Times*

This account differs little from hundreds that are available to the student of Americana. In 1918 a Federal antilynch law was hundreds of burnings away.

The dramatic appeal of such incidents attracted white playwrights. Some, like the Reverend Thomas Dixon, favored the lynchings. Others, like Edward Shelton (author of *The Nigger*) portrayed a "good" white man attempting to save the guilty Negro from the mob. Later plays allowed the Negro to be innocent, but still insisted that he be killed. This "pity-the-poor-nigger" genre reached its climax in Jean Paul Sartre's *The Respectful Prostitute*, in which the Negro is seen on his knees to the white whore, begging for his life.

Early black playwrights wrote plays about lynchings too, but with important distinctions: the black man refused to compromise his rights (*Rachel*); the black man was always innocent (*A Sunday Morning in the South*); the black man died with dignity (*Bad Man*).

The inescapable death, aside from being an attempt to tap the conscience of the audience, is related to a stereotype. The Brute Negro, Professor Sterling Brown tells us, is one of the seven classic stereotypes created by white authors. This huge black beast drinks, gambles, cuts, riots, and lusts after white women.

In the hands of black playwrights this stereotype undergoes a transformation: he becomes courageous, a rebel, a fighter against Whitey. The first gentle stirrings of this character in black drama are found in the person of George Broadus of *The Idle Head*. Perhaps the climax of this genre appears in LeRoi Jones' *The Slave*, where Walker Vessels, the revolutionary leader, executes the white man and gets away. Thea Dugger, the bad man of Mr. Edmond's play, is an intermediate step toward developing this modern black rebel. Thea is a romantic denial of the Brute Negro. Although the play's ending will anger a revolutionary, Thea Dugger is an important transitional figure.

Randolph Edmonds is himself an important theater pioneer and playwright. His *Denmark Vesey* and *Nat Turner* were written in the 1920's. He published three anthologies of his own plays in the 1930's and 40's: *Shades and Shadows*, *Six Plays for a Negro Theater*, and *The Land of Cotton and Other Plays*. He has written 47 plays. They are produced by black schools and colleges—primarily in the South, where he has spent his life as an educator. His full length drama *Earth and Stars* has received over 100 performances.

Until his retirement, Professor Edmonds served as Chairman of the Drama Department at Florida A & M University. He has been a prime mover in organizing the study of drama in Southern schools, working as an official in the American Educational Theatre Association, the Southeastern Theater Conference, and the Department of Health, Education, and Welfare. Author of some forty articles on theater and theater research, he is currently writing a history of the Negro in the theater.

Bad Man

CAST OF CHARACTERS

TOM JOINER
TED JAMES
HUBBARD BAILEY
PERCY HARDY
JACK BURCHARD
BURT ROSS
MAYBELLE JOINER
THEA DUGGER

(SCENE: *The interior of a shanty house located at a sawmill camp in a remote section of Alabama. The walls are very rough and crude, giving the impression of weather boards nailed up on the outside without any finishing material on the inside.*
The furniture is very crude and primitive. There are two home-made cots, one along the side to the left and another on the right. The rest of the furniture consists of a crude table, several dilapidated chairs and home-made stools. An upright home-made box is placed conveniently with cooking utensils on top of it.
One door in the back, left, leads to the outside, and another, on the right side, leads to another room in the shanty. One window is in the back, right, and another on the left side. Both have dirty, ragged curtains hung before them. Old coats and overalls hang on nails on the wall, and everything is in an untidy condition.
The people who inhabit these shanties are peasant Negroes who work at the sawmill. Many types are usually found at these camps, ranging from pious church goers to gamblers, murderers, and escaped convicts. All are, generally speaking, illiterate; but some possess a keen native wit, and worthy ambitions.
The opening curtain shows TOM, MAYBELLE, *and* TED. TOM *is a typical sawmill hand, just under forty, and a hard worker. He is dressed in dirty blue overalls, and a ragged shirt.* TED, *who is about twenty, is dressed in dirty, dark trousers, and a white shirt which is beginning to get dirty.* MAYBELLE *is dressed in a loud checked calico dress in rural style. She is about eighteen and is inclined somewhat to coquetry.* TOM *has been looking anxiously out of the window in the rear.* MAYBELLE *is seated at the crude table downstage, somewhat to the left. An oil lamp in the middle shines in her face.* TED *is seated on a bench on the right trying to read a book, and is eating peanuts. The season is early fall, and the time is early dusk*)

TOM (*turning away from the window*) Hit don't look like Pa is comin' back fuh yuh. Hit's dust o' dark now.
MAYBELLE (*anxiously*) He said he would be back at least an hour befo' sunset.
TOM Ah hopes he hurries up and come on.
MAYBELLE He's bound to be 'long in a little while. Don't worry yose'f so much.
TOM Dat's easy tuh say; but shanty houses at sawmill camps ain't no place fuh women, least of all ma own sister.
MAYBELLE Hit don't seem all dat bad.
TOM (*earnestly*) Yuh never can tell whut is gwine tuh happen, and anyt'ing is liable tuh happen 'tween sundown and sunup. Ah don't see why Pa left yuh heah nohow.
MAYBELLE Ah wanted tuh see de place, so he left me heah while he druv five miles out in de country tuh git a possum dawg.
TED (*looking up*) Ah noticed dat one wheel on de buggy was bad. Mayby he gut broke down.
TOM (*moving about anxiously*) Hit would be jes' lak dat ole buggy tuh break down on a night when hit shouldn't.
MAYBELLE Well, ef he don't git back to-night, maybe yuh can find me a place tuh stay.
TOM Naw! Dere ain't no place 'round heah fuh women tuh stay. Ef he don't come back soon we starts walkin'.
MAYBELLE (*looking at her shoes*) Dese shoes don't want me tuh do no walkin'. Dese men

heah ain't so bad Ah's gut tuh walk ten miles in de dark.

TOM Yuh don't know whut yuh is talkin' 'bout. A sawmill camp is de worse place in de world. Sompen bad is always happenin' heah. A man gits killed in de woods or at de mill, or gits shot or cut tuh death each an' every month. We's gut men heah dat will stay 'round de shanty house and gamble from de time de whistle blow Sattiday at noon, 'til Monday mawning. Plenty dese men heah done 'scaped from de chain gang, or killed one or two men. And de white folks dat live up de road at dat little village is wus dan pisen. Ah tells yuh too much happen roun' heah fuh a woman tuh be mixed up in hit.

MAYBELLE Maybe nothin' won't happen to-night.

TOM (*slightly peeved*) Yuh nevah can tell when hit's gwine tuh happen. Ah told yuh not tuh stay heah nohow. Yuh should 'a' gone on wid him tuh git dat dawg. Well, ef he don't come pretty soon, we starts walkin'.

TED (*looking up again*) Ah wouldn't walk way home to-night in de dark, Tom. Ef yo' pa don't come back, Hubbard and me can make a pallet on de floor, and stay in heah wid yuh and Thea.

TOM Ah'll think 'bout hit. Ef yuh is gwine tuh be in heah a minute, Ted, Ah'se gut tuh go over to de commissary and git some blood hound chewin' tobacca. When Ah gits back Ah'll decide what tuh do.

TED Ah'll be heah. Ah ain't gwine nowhar. (TOM *goes out.* TED *throws the book aside and comes over to where* MAYBELLE *is*) Well, yuh might got Tom worried, but yuh ain't got me. Yuh could stay heah a whole week, and Ah'd see dat nothin' bothers yuh.

MAYBELLE (*coquettishly*) Dat's sweet of yuh tuh say so anyhow.

TED (*trying to put his arms around her*) Dat ain't nothin'. Ah wish Ah could say sompen sweet, as Ah is crazy 'bout yuh.

MAYBELLE (*pulling away*) Not now. Ah want yuh tuh tell me sompen 'bout de place heah. Tom is always telling me 'bout how bad de men is. Ah saw some by de commissary, and dey didn't look so bad tuh me.

TED Dey is bad enough. Tom told yuh 'bout right. All dey do jes' as soon as de whistle blow is tuh eat, shoot crap or play gawgie skin. Dey is shootin' and cuttin' all de time. Dey kill a man pretty often heah. Sometime dey git killed in de log woods or at de mill shad.

MAYBELLE Whar is Thea Dugger? Ah's heard Tom talk so much 'bout how bad he is.

TED He is a bad man in many ways all right. He's done killed six men in gamblin' games. He always keep five or six pistols, and five or ten boxes of cottriges. He won't run from nobody. He ain't scared o' de debbil. Ah ain't never seed a man who wa'n't scared of nobody like he.

MAYBELLE He mus' be brave all right.

TED He is. Dey say once when he was workin' in a steel mill in Birmingham, he went into a pool parlor where dey was gamblin'. One man started tuh pull a gun on him. He picked up a cue ball and hit him in de temple and killed him daid as a goat. Den he picked up de man's Smith and Weston and shot up de place. Everybody ran out in de street. Thea ran out arter dem but didn't see nothin' but a mule. So he poured de lead into de mule. Dey say de mule jumped up and fell down daid.

MAYBELLE Hit's a wonder dey didn't 'rest him way up dere in de city.

TED (*proudly*) De police ain't gwine bother Thea Dugger. Nobody 'round heah ain't neither. Dey all giv' him plenty o' elbow room. He kinder like me dough.

MAYBELLE Will Ah git a chance tuh see him?

TED Ef yuh pa don't come 'long pretty quick. He and some de boys is over at de slab fire cookin' and eatin'. Dey'll drift up heah in a little while tuh play gawgie skin or shoot dice.

MAYBELLE Ah's glad Ah is gwine tuh git a chance tuh see him. Ah always wanted to see an honest tuh goodness bad man.

TED (*moving closer*) Ain't Ah bad nuff fuh yuh?

MAYBELLE (*smiling*) Yuh ain't jealous, is yuh?

TED (*putting his arm around her waist*) Who wouldn't be jealous of a fine lookin' gal lak yuh?

MAYBELLE (*pushing him away*) Don't, Ted. Not in heah. Tom will be back in a minute.

TED (*slightly crestfallen*) Is yo' pa softened up on yuh any? Ah'd lak tuh see yuh at yo' house some time.

MAYBELLE Naw, not a bit. He is so set on my gwine away tuh boardin' school nex' week. He don't want me tuh marry no sawmill han'.

He wants me tuh marry a school teacher or doctor or sompen.

TED Well, Ah hopes yuh don't think Ah is gwine be a sawmill han' all ma life. Ah's readin' books. Ah's gwine away tuh de city and be a business man. Ah's already done saved fifty dollars.

MAYBELLE Dat sure is good.

TED (*meditating*) Ah 'spect we's gut tuh run away ef we ever gits married.

MAYBELLE Maybe so.

TED Ah'se started many times tuh tell Tom 'bout our love. Ah'se tired of meetin' yuh in secret.

MAYBELLE (*alarmed*) Don't do dat. He'd git mad as de debbil. Tom is jes' as bad as Pa 'bout ma goin' tuh school. Ef he thought Ah stopped heah mainly tuh see yuh, he'd have a fit.

TED (*pulling her to him*) Fit or no fit, Ah's gwine tuh kiss yuh, dat's all. (*she pulls away but he manages to kiss her*)

MAYBELLE Don't, Ted! Ah's scared in heah.

TED Wid yuh in ma arms, Ah ain't scared of nobody. Yuh don't realize how yuh makes me feel.

MAYBELLE (*coquettishly*) How does Ah makes yuh feel, Ted?

TED Ah don't know. Ah can't tell yuh. Ah'se gut tuh read many mo' books befo' Ah'll be able tuh find words 'nuff. All Ah knows is dat when Ah's wid yuh dere is some kind of feelin' dat runs through me dat makes me feel glad. Sometimes ma heart seems lak hit's gwine tuh bust; other times Ah feel lak shoutin' lak dey do at de Sanctified Church. Ah can't keep meetin' yuh in secret, and den come way up heah in de woods and leave yuh fuh a week. Ah can't do hit much longer, Maybelle. Let's run away and git married.

MAYBELLE Sometime, maybe.

TED Let's make hit next week when yuh is supposed tuh go off tuh boardin' school. We could both go tuh de city, and wurk and go tuh night school. Ah could open up some kind of business. Ah'd do anyt'ing in de wurld ef Ah had yuh wid me all de time.

MAYBELLE All right. Next week, den.

TED Yuh really mean dat? (MAYBELLE *shakes her head in the affirmative. He pulls her to him; but before he can kiss her,* TOM *comes in. They look confused and break away*)

TOM (*scowling*) Whut yuh all doin' in heah?

MAYBELLE Ah...ah...was jes' showin' Ted ma ring. (*holding it up for him to see*)

TOM (*not looking*) Hit looked mighty lak yuh was kissin'.

MAYBELLE Naw we wa'n't. Honest we wa'n't.

TOM (*glaring at* TED, *slowly*) Dis is ma youngest sis, Ted; Ah laks yuh all right, but ef Ah catches any sawmill han' kissin' huh, dat man don't live no mo'. Do yuh understand?

TED (*sulkily*) Ah heah yuh. 'Tain't no use tuh git so mad 'bout hit, dough.

MAYBELLE (*excited and wishing to change the subject*) Ain't yuh seed pa, yit?

TOM Naw, so Ah s'pose we'd better start walkin'.

MAYBELLE (*pouting*) Ah don't feel lak walkin' no ten miles.

TOM Ah done tell yuh yuh can't stay heah!

TED Yuh'd save yose'f a lot o' trouble ef yuh let huh sleep in de next room. Ah'm sure Hubbard don't mind sleepin' on a pallet heah on de floor, and Ah know Ah don't mind.

(*Before* TOM *can answer,* HUBBARD BAILEY *and* JACK BURCHARD *enter. They are typical sawmill workers, dirty, grimy and unkempt.* HUBBARD *has on blue overalls spotted with resin, a tattered khaki shirt, and a dirty grey cap.* JACK *has on a pair of grey trousers and a tan shirt. He wears a cap with the brim turned around in the back. A red bandanna handkerchief is tied around his neck*)

HUBBARD (*before he enters*) Comin' in, Tom.

TOM Come on in ef yuh nose is clean.

JACK Hit ain't clean 'cause hit's full o' sawdust. (*Both are surprised when they see a woman in the shanty.*)

HUBBARD Didn't know yuh had company, Tom.

TOM Jes' ma sistah. Set down, we's gwine in a minute.

TED Whar's Thea?

JACK Comin' up de path right behind us. Heah he is now.

THEA (*as he opens the door*) Back up in heah everybody, Thea Dugger comin' in! (*he opens the door and lumbers in, but stops suddenly when he sees a girl in the shanty.* THEA *is a veritable giant, mean and hard looking. He is dressed in brown overalls, and a dirty white shirt. A crumpled brown hat sets on a head of hair that has needed cutting for a month. Long sideburns come down his jaws. He is a domineering type, and everybody is afraid of him. They hasten to do whatever he says. In a slow draggy manner*) So we's gut a gal visitin' us to-night. Whut she doin' heah, Tom?

TOM (*apologetically*) Dis is ma youngest sistah, Miss Maybelle Joiner, Mr. Thea Dugger. And Ah forgot, Mr. Jack Burchard and Mr. Hubbard Bailey.

MAYBELLE Ah'm glad tuh meet yuh gentlemen.

THEA Ah'm surprised at yuh, Tom, bringin' yo' sistah into a hell hole lak dis.

TOM Ah didn't exactly bring huh. She jes' stopped off heah. Pa was s'posed tuh have been heah and gut huh. We was jes' startin' tuh leave when yuh come in.

THEA Well, don't let me stop yuh. A skin game is gwine on heah to-night, not no Sunday School fuh no woman tuh teach.

TOM (*hurrying* MAYBELLE) All right, Thea. Come on, Maybelle! Let's git gwine.

TED (*coming up to* THEA) Listen, Thea. Ah thought, or er was thinkin' dat since Tom's pa's buggy 'bout broke down, and dey would hab tuh walk 'bout ten miles befo' dey gits home, maybe, somehow we could fix hit up so Maybelle could stay heah.

THEA Ah don't git yo' drift, kid. Yuh is gut tuh snow again. What does yuh want me tuh do? Give up ma bunk?

TED (*backing away*) Naw, not yuh, Thea. Ah thought ef hit's all right wid Hubbard, we could bring some quilts in from de other room and make a pallet on de floor when we git ready tuh go tuh bed, and let huh have our room.

THEA Dat suits me ef hit's all right wid de res'. (*to* MAYBELLE) But, Miss, yuh had better stop yo' ears up wid cotton, 'cause Ah can't play gawgie skin and talk Sunday School talk.

HUBBARD Hit's all right wid me, Tom.

MAYBELLE Ah thank yuh all, and 'tickler yuh, Mr. Thea. (TOM, TED *and* MAYBELLE *go into the next room.* JACK *and* HUBBARD *look at the door through which they have departed*)

JACK Ain't she a good looker, dough?

HUBBARD She's a peach all right. Ef Ah was ten years younger, Ah'd give all de boys a run fuh dere money.

THEA Whut yuh two dumb bells standin' dere fuh? Git de cards and de table. 'Tain't no usen lettin' yo' mouth water 'cause Tom would kill both yuh ef yuh made one pass tuh git huh.

HUBBARD He can't stop us from lookin', dough.

THEA (*yelling*) Come on, git de things straight and stop talkin' so much wid yo' mouth. (THEA *pulls out a pack of worn cards from under his bunk. They sit around the table and* HUBBARD *starts to deal*) Dis deck is too thick. Git de other deck, Hubbard; you'll find hit right under de bunk dere.

HUBBARD Dis deck is all right.

THEA Ah ain't never had no luck wid a thick deck.

HUBBARD We'll play wid dis one jes a little while anyway.

THEA (*standing up and looking at* HUBBARD) Git dat deck, Ah say! (HUBBARD *doesn't move fast enough.* THEA *knocks him out of his chair to the floor*) Is yuh gwine tuh git dat deck?

HUBBARD (*getting up submissively*) All right, Thea. (*before he can sit down,* PERCY HARDY *comes in. He is very nervous and excitable. He is dressed in a pair of patched overalls with a grey shirt*)

JACK Yuh is jes' in time fuh a lil game, Percy. Dat is, providin' yuh is gut some money.

PERCY Ah's gut a little left.

HUBBARD (*sitting down dealing. Money is put up*) Ah thought we cleaned yuh out las' night.

PERCY (*sitting down nervously*) Aw, yuh didn't clean me out. Luck was runnin' 'gainst me so Ah left.

JACK Well, yuh won't hab hit long, 'cause Ah's gwine tuh carry de cub tuh everybody.

(TED *comes into the room and walks around meditatively as if in deep thought*)

THEA Whut's de matter, kid? Sompen on yo' mind?

TED Nothin' in particler, Thea. Ma mind mus' be wanderin' round, dat's all.

JACK (*teasing him*) Mus' be de swell gal in de next room?

THEA Lay off dat kid, Jack. Nobody is s'pose tuh bother him 'long as Thea Dugger is 'round.

JACK (*submissively*) All right, Thea.

PERCY (*he takes a deck and starts to deal. He is nervous and fidgety. His card turns up quickly*) Well, Ah'll be—

THEA (*sternly*) Hold dat, Percy. Dere ain't gwine be no cussin' in heah to-night. Dere is a woman in de next room.

PERCY (*submissively*) Well, Ah'll carry de deal on down.

THEA (*pointing to his card*) Well, dis king will go on down tuh de bottom wid yuh. (*money changes hands several times.* THEA *changes cards, too*)

PERCY Wal, Ah sho' lost on dat deal.

HUBBARD Aw, stop belly achin'.

THEA Deal, Jack! Maybe Percy'll do better.

(TED *sits down hard on one of the bunks,* PERCY *jumps*)

JACK Whut yuh jumpin' 'bout? Yuh seems mighty nervous to-night.

PERCY Ah ain't felt right ever since Ah heard old man Sam was killed.

HUBBARD Any time a white man lives out in de woods by hisse'f, somebody ought tuh knock him in de haid.

PERCY Ah don't know nothin' 'bout hit; but Ah don't believe we's heard de las' of hit yit.

JACK Naw, we don't know nothin' 'bout hit, so we ain't gut nothin' tuh worry 'bout.

THEA Gimme dem pasteboards. Lemme deal. (THEA *takes the cards and shuffles them expertly*) Cut dem, Jack.

HUBBARD Ef Ah don't win dis time Ah gives up.

THEA (*dealing*) Don't give up. Nobody never win nothin' by givin' up. (*he plucks them off one by one*) Fall card, fall jes' lak de leaves in de winter time.

(*Everybody is tense.* THEA *takes the money from first one of them then the other. They select other cards and lose again. The deal goes down*)

HUBBARD Ah's never seen de beat. Two nights in a row he done carried de cub tuh us.

THEA Jes' a little streak o' luck, boys. Yuh'll do de same thing in a minute.

JACK (*disgusted. Gets up*) Ah'm stoppin'. Ah'm through playin' cards when dey fall lak dat.

THEA (*glaring sternly at* JACK) Whut do yuh mean fallin' lak dat? Yuh ain't hintin' dat Ah fixed de cards, is yuh?

JACK (*becoming reckless because of his luck*) Well dey fell mighty funny!

THEA (*rising*) Den yuh is meanin' Ah's cheated.

JACK Ah ain't saying nothin'. (*the others spring up and back away to the wall expecting a fight.* PERCY *is frightened throughout*)

THEA Oh, yes yuh is; and nobody never said dat Thea Dugger cheated at cards and lived.

(JACK *reaches in his pocket for his gun. Before he can bring it out,* THEA *hits him and knocks him down. He springs up and holds the gun on Thea*)

JACK Yuh's been bullyin' us long 'nuff now; and Ah fuh one ain't gwine tuh stand hit no mo'.

THEA (*glancing at the drawn gun*) Well, go on and shoot, yuh white livered chicken; Ah don't believe yuh'se got nerve 'nuff.

HUBBARD Don't shoot, Jack!

THEA Yuh needn't say nothin'. He ain't gut guts 'nuff tuh shoot. (*he walks toward* JACK. JACK *backs away*)

JACK Don't yuh come any closer! Don't yuh come any closer, Ah'll shoot!

THEA (*laughing and going toward him*) Yuh wouldn't shoot ef yuh had de nerve.

JACK Don't yuh come any closer or Ah'll shoot!

(*Suddenly* THEA *makes a spring forward and knocks* JACK's *arm up.* MAYBELLE *and* TOM *come in just in time to see* THEA *wrench the gun from* JACK. *Then he covers* JACK. MAYBELLE *screams, but is quickly stopped by* TOM)

THEA (*holding the gun on* JACK) Six men has tried tuh draw guns on me in ma life, and six men is layin' somewhar in de graveyard,—yuh is de seventh one. Ef yuh knows any prayers tuh say, yuh'd better start sayin' dem.

JACK (*getting down on his knees, moaning*) Have mercy, Thea! Have mercy, Ah didn't mean nothin'.

THEA Yes, yuh did too. Yuh mean Ah cheated at cards. No man is gwine tuh say dat and live.

JACK Ah takes hit back, Thea. Ah takes hit back. Ah didn't mean nothin'.

THEA Ef dere's anything in dis wurl Ah hates, hit's a coward. Since yuh is down on yo' knees, yuh'd better say yo' prayers, 'cause when Ah counts three Ah's gwine tuh shoot.

JACK Please spare ma life, Thea! For Gawd's sake don't shoot me!

THEA One!

JACK (*looking around wildly*) He'p me! He'p me somebody!

THEA Two!

JACK For Gawd's sake don't shoot, think whut yuh is doin'! (*as* THEA *is about to say three* MAYBELLE *screams*)

MAYBELLE For Gawd's sake don't shoot dat man in cold blood!

THEA Yuh'd better keep outer dis, lady. Don't yuh meddle wid things dat don't concern yuh.

TOM Don't say anything tuh him, Maybelle.

MAYBELLE (*getting down on her knees and pulling on* THEA'*s free arm*) Please! Please! Don't shoot him fuh mah sake!

THEA (*gun still drawn on* JACK) Yuh is in de wrong place, lady. Women ain't gut no business 'round sawmill camps; but since yuh is heah, yuh will have de pleasure of seein' yo' fust man die.

MAYBELLE Please, please don't shoot him!

THEA Yuh don't understand, Miss. Ef a man draws a gun on yuh and yuh let him off 'cause he ain't got de nerve tuh shoot, de next time he will git dat nerve. Well, if yuh kill him, dere can't be no next time.

MAYBELLE (*pleading*) Tom always told me how bad yuh was, and Ah always wanted tuh see yuh 'cause Ah didn't believe him. Ah knows dere is a good streak in yuh somewhar. Yuh ain't never 'lowed hit tuh come out. Ah believes yuh is a good man, and won't shoot nobody down in cold blood.

THEA Me, a good man! Nobody never told me dat befo'. Me, a good man! Dat's funny. (*he lowers his gun, speaks to* JACK) Aw, git up offen yo' knees, and thank dis gal fuh savin' yo' life.

JACK (*profuse in his thanks*) Thank yuh, Miss. Thank yuh. Ah thank yuh, too, Thea. Ah didn't mean no harm. Losin' ma money jes' made me furgit.

THEA (*handing the gun back*) Don't do hit no mo', 'cause de next time, dis good man won't be so good. Let's furgit whut happened.

JACK Hit's furgottened.

PERCY Ah's glad dat's over.

(BURT ROSS *breaks into the door hurriedly. He is the foreman of the mills. He has on dirty wrinkled trousers and a clean blue shirt*)

BURT (*excitedly*) Run for your lives everybody! Be quick about it. I've warned the other shanties and they've already gone.

HUBBARD Whut's matter, Cap'n Ross?

BURT Somebody found old man Sam, the old white man who lives by himself over on the hill, with his head split in two with an axe. They said somebody working at the mill did it. The mob is coming down here to get somebody. You'd all better scatter to the woods. I'll join the mob and do what I can to save you.

PERCY (*general confusion*) Oh, my Gawd!

MAYBELLE Whut'll we do, Tom? Whut'll we do, Ted?

TOM Come on, let's make a break fuh de woods.

PERCY Ah knowed sompen would happen. Ah jes' knowed hit. Let's git gwine befo' hit's too late. (*goes out*)

JACK Yes, let's git gwine. Ef dey catch us in dis shanty we ain't gut a chance wid a river in de back, a marsh on one side, and a steep hill on de other.

TOM Come on, Maybelle. Let's git goin'.

MAYBELLE Come on, Ted! (*they hurry out*)

JACK Come along, Hubbard. Dey'll be heah in a minute.

HUBBARD Ain't yuh comin' 'long, Thea?

THEA (*calmly looking out the window*) Naw!

JACK Ah'll see yuh later. (*he starts to go out, but stops*)

HUBBARD Why ain't yuh goin' tuh de woods, Thea?

THEA Yuh go on, Hubbard, ef yuh wants tuh. All ma life Ah's hated a coward, folks dat run away. When Ah was ten years old Ah made up ma mind dat Ah wa'n't gwine tuh run from nothing dat lives, man nor beast; and I ain't never did hit yit, and Ah's too old tuh change. Ain't no man livin' gwine make me run nowhar.

HUBBARD Dese po' whites will shoot yuh down lak a dog.

THEA Ef dey shoot me, dey is gwine tuh shoot me standin' up and facin' dem. Dey ain't gwine tuh shoot me runnin' through no bushes lak no rabbit.

HUBBARD Ah'll stay heah wid yuh, Thea.

JACK Ah s'pose Ah'd jes' as well stay, too.

(TED, MAYBELLE, *and* TOM *come back*)

TOM We heard dem comin'! We was scared tuh cut across de clearin' tuh git tuh de woods.

TED All de other shanty houses is empty. Cap'n Ross told dem befo' he did us.

MAYBELLE Ef Pa had only come back Ah wouldn't 'a' been in all dis.

(PERCY *comes crawling in like a whipped dog*)

PERCY Dey done reached de upper end ob de clearin'. We is cut off from de woods. Dey is gut blood hounds wid dem, too.

HUBBARD Whut'll we all do? . . . Dem po' whites will stop at nothin'.

JACK Whut is we tuh do, Thea? Yuh is de boss.

THEA (*calmly*) We'd better prepare to die.

MAYBELLE Ain't dere nothing we can do? Is we all gut tuh die heah lak rats in a trap?

TED Dat's de way hit looks.

THEA Naw, we don' exactly has tuh die lak no rats. How many gut guns?

JACK I has.

THEA (*gets his box*) Nobody but Jack. Ah'se gut six guns in dis box. Each one has already killed da man who tried to draw hit on me. Each one ought to do some mo' duty wurk. (*he gives one to* TOM, HUBBARD, TED, *and* PERCY) Yuh's gut tuh take one, too, Miss, dis small one.

MAYBELLE Ah's skeered of dem pistols.

THEA Hit's too small tuh be skeered of. Yuh'd better tak hit, Miss. (MAYBELLE *reluctantly takes it*)

TED Dat's right, take hit.

(*The barking of dogs can be heard far off through the woods. Everyone becomes tense.* THEA *tries to break it*)

THEA Ah wonder who killed de old man anyhow.

PERCY (*hysterically*) Nobody knows; hit's certain nobody heah killed him.

(*The barking of the dogs is very near now. Confused voices are also heard.* THEA *is the only one who appears calm. He is looking out of the window*)

TOM (*nervously*) Well, dey is gittin' near heah.

TED (*to* MAYBELLE) Since we don't know whut's gwine tuh happen, don't yuh think we ought tuh tell Tom?

MAYBELLE Umph, humph, yuh tell him.

TED Tom, we's gut sumpin' tuh tell yuh. Wal, er . . . since we don't know whut might happen, we thought—er—would, er . . . tell yuh dat Maybelle and Ah love each other, and we had planned tuh git married sometime even ef we had tuh run away.

TOM I sorta suspicioned dat; but ef yuh'd told me dat four hours ago, Ah would 'a' knocked de daylight outer yuh. We wanted Maybelle tuh go tuh school and git some larnin' and not marry no sawmill han'; but now when hit seems—Well, hit jes' don't matter now 'bout yo' love.

TED (*softly*) Thank yuh, Tom.

(*Noise from the mob and a crash of broken glass*)

MAYBELLE (*running to* TED) Ah's skeered! Whut is we gwine do? (*puts her arms around his neck.* THEA *looks at them*)

TED Don't git skeered, honey. Try tuh be brave lak Thea.

MAYBELLE Don't mind me when Ah say things. Ah really don't mind dying jes' so Ah is wid yuh.

(*Barking dogs.* THEA, *who has been watching the window, wheels around*)

THEA (*wheeling and taking on new life*) Ah thought maybe dey wouldn't come up heah, but heah dey come!

(*Groans. A tense strain is evident*)

PERCY (*whining*) My Gawd! Whut is we gwine tuh do?

THEA We's gwine tuh fight and fight lak hell! Yuh, Tom and Jack, go into de next room, rip off a board in de back so yuh can see ef anybody comes up from de river. Yuh can see who's coming from de swamp through de window. Shoot ef yuh see anybody sneakin' up. Ted, yuh and Hubbard guard dat window. (*one to left*) Shoot ef you see anyone sneakin' up. Me and Percy'll take dis one. (*he goes back to window in the rear*)

TED (*shouting*) Dere dey come 'round de front, Thea.

THEA Let dem come, Ah's ready!

MAYBELLE Ted! (*going over to him*)

TED Git away from befo' dat window! Do yuh want tuh git shot? Git back over dere in de corner!

THEA (*raising his pistol, shouting*) Don't come any further up dat path or Ah'll shoot.

VOICE They're in there, fellows!

ANOTHER VOICE Burn the shanty down! (*a

rock comes in through the window at the left. MAYBELLE *screams*)

VOICES Get the niggers! Lynch 'em.

PERCY (*crawling away down stage*) Ah's skeered, Thea. Ah's skeered tuh death.

THEA (*angrily*) Git back up dere and help me guard dat window or I'll plug yuh mase'f.

VOICE Come on, fellows, let's get 'em. (*barking of dogs*)

ANOTHER VOICE All right, let's go! (THEA *raises his gun and fires*)

VOICES Get de niggers! Burn de shanty! They got guns. Get dem!

THEA Don't come no closer. De next time I ain't goin' tuh miss. Ah's goin' tuh shoot tuh kill.

VOICE They got guns!

ROSS Listen! You're destroying my property. Don't kill all my men; they didn't do it.

VOICE Kill all the niggers! Burn them up!

ROSS (*shouting*) Let's tell them that if the one that did it comes out, we'll let the others go. I can't run my mill if you kill all my hands.

VOICE (*shouting above the noise*) If the one that did the murder comes out we won't do nothin' to the rest. We'll give you five minutes to make up your mind.

ANOTHER VOICE If you don't come out by then we'll burn the shanty down on top of you.

THEA (*walking over to the door on the right*) Tom, Jack, did yuh hear whut dey said? (TOM *and* JACK *come in.* THEA *goes up center*)

TOM Yeah. Dey's give us five minutes.

JACK Dey said de one dat done hit. Who is de one dat done hit, Ah'd lak tuh know.

HUBBARD Dey don't care who done hit jes' so dey git one man.

PERCY (*whining*) But who is goin' tuh bedat one man?

THEA (*in middle of stage*) Heah's yo' chance, boys. One man's gut to go out dere and die. Speak up. We ain't gut long.

TOM Ah would go but Ah's gut tuh he'p pay off Pa's mortgage, and he'p Maybelle heah tuh go tuh school.

JACK Ef Ah had ever seed de old man, Ah wouldn't mind.

PERCY (*whining*) Ah can't go! Ah can't, dat's all! Ah's scared.

HUBBARD Ain't nobody done nothin' heah. Ah don't see why dey have tuh go.

TED Ah suppose Ah's de only one left.

MAYBELLE (*throwing her arms around him*) Ah can't let yuh go! Ah jes' can't!

THEA Ah wouldn't let yuh go, neither, kid. Dat's all right, Ah'll go!

TOM Yuh can't go out dere, Thea.

THEA (*changing tone*) 'Tain't no usen all us gittin' killed; and somebody gut tuh go.

TOM Yuh can't go, Thea! Let's cut de cards. Dat'll settle it 'bout who is to go.

THEA 'Tain't no usen doin' dat. All o' yuh gut fam'lies tuh look out fuh. Ah ain't gut nobody but mase'f; and when Ah'm gone, nothin' much'll be lost.

TED Dat don't make no diff'rence. Yuh has as much right tuh live as any of us.

THEA Hit do make a diff'rence. All ma life Ah's been a bad man, driftin' from one camp tuh another, and one mill tuh another, shootin' and cuttin' and fightin'. Ah s'pose Ah wasn't cut out tuh mount tuh much. (*to* MAYBELLE) Young miss, yuh said Ah had a good streak in me somewhar. Maybe ef yuh wasn't heah, Ah'd feel better and know better whut tuh do. Ah's killed many men in ma life, but Ah ain't never stood 'round and seed no woman die. Somehow Ah can't bring mase'f tuh do hit. Ah hopes yuh and de kid will be happy. Tom ain't gwine do nothin' tuh stop yuh. (*he wheels and walks out of the house leaving everybody stunned and tense.*)

TOM Thea! Thea! Come back!

VOICE Here he is, fellows! Grab him!

VOICE Burn him. (*dogs bark*)

ROSS You didn't do it, Thea! I've seen you all day.

THEA Ah did hit all right.

VOICE He's confessed! That's enough.

VOICE String him up!

VOICE Make a fire! (*voices and barking of the dogs*)

TOM (*looking out of the window at the blazing fire*) Dey is tying him up ... and he ain't doing nothing.... Dey is lighting a fire to him now. He's burning! (*in wild agony*) He's burning! And he ain't even groaning! (*dogs bark. There is a confusion of voices*)

PERCY (*coming back from peeping out of the window. He swings wildly and sinks on the bed*) Ah'se gwine crazy!

TED (*rushing toward the door*) Let me outer heah! Ah can't stand hit!

TOM (*grabbing him and holding him back*) Yuh can't do nothing, Ted. Yuh might as well stay on de inside!

TED (*shouting*) But Thea is burning up out dere, Ah'm tellin' yuh!

TOM Yuh can't do nothin' 'bout hit! None of us can't do nothin' 'bout hit!

TED (*turning dejectedly*) Yuh is right, dead right. We ain't nothin' but sawmill hands. All we is s'posed tuh do is to cut logs, saw lumber, live in dingy shanties, cut, fight, and kill each other. We ain't s'posed tuh pay no 'tention tuh a burnin' man . . . but ef de people wid larnin' can't do nothin' 'bout hit, 'tain't nothin' we can do. 'Tain't nothing we can do. (*he lowers his head in dejection.* MAYBELLE *bursts into tears and faints in a chair. The others are staring wildly or swaying with tears. Outside the fire is burning and the dogs are barking. Voices of the mob come in confused sounds as they ask for souvenirs, and ask each other to pile wood upon the burning body. Curtain.*)

5

From the Depression

H. F. V. Edward Langston Hughes Theodore Ward
Owen Dodson

No statistics quite capture the fear, anger, and despair of the Great Depression of the 1930's. The theater sometimes reflected it in a *Waiting for Lefty* or a *One-Third of a Nation*; Hollywood circumvented it with movies like Busby Berkeley's *Gold Diggers* series and the songs—"We're in the Money"; "With Plenty of Money and You."

White playwrights continued to write of exotic Negroes—*Green Pastures, Savage Rhythm, Scarlet Sister Mary, Brass Ankle, Mamba's Daughters, Porgy and Bess.* Black playwrights discovered that they were not excepted from the rule, "last hired, first fired." The cascade of black musicals that had showered the 1920's—*Runnin' Wild, Shuffle Along, Keep Shufflin', From Dixie to Broadway, Rang Tang, Chocolate Dandies, The Blackbirds*—dribbled to a trickle in the 1930's.

During this period Langston Hughes saw his poetic tragedy *Mulatto* sexed up by the producer for Broadway consumption. But for the majority of Afro-American playwrights, only the Negro Unit of the Federal Theater (under the government Works Progress Administration) gave them a chance to work. In this group were Hughes Allison, Rudolph Fisher, J. A. Smith, Theodore Browne (*see Natural Man*), and Theodore Ward.

Several black theater groups formed in the 1930's: The Harlem Suitcase Theater, Negro People's Theater, The Rose McClendon Players—followed in 1940 by the American Negro Theater and the Negro Playwrights Company. Only now in the 1970's are some of the plays that these groups premiered being published.

The four plays in this section all were written during the Depression. *Job Hunters* is a documentary written by a man who recorded what he saw daily in the unemployment office. *Divine Comedy* is a poetic drama about sick and hungry people turning to false messiahs and supernatural solutions. *Don't You Want To Be Free?* and *Big White Fog* are political plays that offer solutions based on the unity of the black and white working class. All the plays breathe the despair of a society gone wrong. And all offer hope.

H. F. V. Edward (1898–1973)

Job Hunters
1931

The cold of the Depression had been settling into the homes and hearts of Harlem for two years when *Job Hunters* appeared in *Crisis* in December 1931. "Jesus will Lead Me and Welfare will Feed Me" was more bravado than fact. The Home Relief Bureau allowed eight cents per meal for food—if one could get it.

In 1933, one-half of Harlem's 350,000 residents were on relief. This statistic can be understood only in light of other statistics: (1) the average monthly wage of a Negro working man had been $89.60, compared to $110.10 for whites in Harlem; (2) 60 per cent of Negro married women worked, compared to 15 per cent of white women; (3) the average population density of Harlem was 233 persons per acre, compared to 133 for the rest of Manhattan; (4) Negro families paid 40–50 per cent of their incomes for rent, compared to 25 per cent for whites; (5) the mortality rate of Harlem hospital (maintained by a predominately white staff) was more than twice that of Bellevue or Coney Island hospitals.

In 1970, H. F. V. Edward had this to say about the origin of *Job Hunters*:

I worked for six months in the New York State Employment Service as a temporary interviewer, paid by one of the State's work relief projects. At that time the national rate of unemployment was 27 per cent; for Negroes it must have been approximately 40 per cent. Half of my working time was spent in the field in an attempt to locate job vacancies, a discouraging task, but work in the dingy Harlem office on Lenox Avenue at 132nd Street was even more depressing.

After that temporary assignment I joined the staff of *The Crisis* as bookkeeper and advertising manager. Stimulated by the presence of Dr. William E. B. DuBois and the visits by young writers of that period, I tried my hand at that discipline and gave vent to my experience in the seeming hopelessness of the Hoover era.

Job Hunters ends with a warning: the news of the Chicago riots. What must happen was very clear to Mr. Edward. It did—on March 19, 1935. By the next day, 200 stores had been smashed, with an estimated $2 million in damages. Three blacks were dead, hundreds of others were wounded and arrested.

Job Hunters is not so much a play as a document and a warning.

Job Hunters

CAST OF CHARACTERS

WILLIAM JOHNSON, *official of Public Employment Office*
WARREN THOMAS, *a student of sociology and volunteer worker*
CLARENCE WHITE,
GEORGE WASHINGTON,
FRANCIS TAYLOR, } *unemployed*
A CHAUFFEUR,
A MECHANIC,
FIRST UNEMPLOYED
SECOND UNEMPLOYED
THIRD UNEMPLOYED
FOURTH UNEMPLOYED
FIFTH UNEMPLOYED
REPRESENTATIVE OF THE "HEAVENLY MESSENGER"
DISTRIBUTOR OF THE "WORKMEN'S DAILY"
A WOMAN SPEAKER OF THE WORKERS' LEAGUE
A GROUP OF UNEMPLOYED

SCENE *the office of a public employment office in Harlem.*

TIME *July, 1931.*

OFFICIAL (*as he dusts desks and opens blinds. Line of men can be seen standing outside window*) It is three minutes to eight. I must hurry; government employment offices must be punctual and Harlem's Office must keep its good reputation. No C.P.T. here! (*pause*) Another day when I must listen to people's troubles and moanings. Yes, (*recites*) The fever and the fret, here is where men sit and hear each other groan.

(*knock at the door. Shouts*) Be patient, two more minutes. (*more knocks at door. Louder*) Stop knocking! (*looks at his watch*) It isn't eight o'clock yet. (*continued knocking and rattling. Angry*) What's the matter with that impatient bunch! (*goes to the door, unlocks and opens it*)

STUDENT VISITOR (*entering*) Good morning, Mr. Johnson. My name is Thomas, Warren Thomas. The director of public employment offices asked me to report to you.

OFFICIAL Oh, yes, Mr. Brady 'phoned me about you. You are a student working as a volunteer, aren't you? (*relocks door*)

STUDENT VISITOR (*talkative and enthusiastic*) Yes, I am studying sociology at the University of Pennsylvania. I am tremendously interested in government employment service, old age pension, unemployment insurance and such social legislation. You see, I am a socialist. I believe public employment offices are essential. It is the duty of the community to see that men get work and if they cannot find it, they should get unemployment insurance benefits, ...

OFFICIAL (*interrupting*) Well, you can sit here near my desk, (*moving a chair to his desk*) and watch our system of registrations and placements. You'll learn a lot about life's problems here.

STUDENT VISITOR I didn't see a single white man in the line outside. Does the law here demand segregation?

OFFICIAL Oh no, but the law is one thing and the prejudices of the officials enforcing it,— that's another.

STUDENT VISITOR Have a cigar?

OFFICIAL (*smiling*) Well, we don't permit smoking in this office, but—I'll be glad to smoke it at home tonight after I have had supper. (*puts cigar carefully into his pocket—looks at his watch*) It's eight now, I must open the door. (*goes across stage, opens door, men enter and sit down on benches, official returns to his desk. A chauffeur walks to the gate, stands there with a letter in his hand looking at the official*)

CHAUFFEUR Mr. Johnson, you sent me a letter, said you had a job for me?

OFFICIAL Come in, let me see the letter— (*looks at the letter*) Oh yes, take a seat, please? (*motions him to sit on chair in front of desk*) We have a job here for a hackman, must be experienced and have licenses. Now, I know you have driven a taxi here for five years. This job pays 40 per cent of the earnings. What do you think of it?

CHAUFFEUR (*evidently disappointed*) Oh,—why yes, I was in the taxi business for some time, but nowadays, mister, there ain't no money in it. And (*hesitating*) well, to tell you the truth, when I was in the taxi business, I got in with the sportin' crowd. You know how it is. Then with drinkin' and gamblin' I didn't bring any money home.—(*pause*) No,—I guess I don't take it. I promised the missus to quit the taxi game. Gee, I'd like to have sump'n steady, anything like chauffeurin' or truckin'.

OFFICIAL I am sorry, that's all I have in the chauffeuring line today. Stay around or call again tomorrow, will you?

(CHAUFFEUR *leaves desk, but stays in the office for a while*)

OFFICIAL (*picks up slip of paper from desk, stands up, walks toward gate while reading*) Just a minute of quiet! (*reads*) I want an experienced car-washer, eight hours shift, nightwork, $25 per week, no Sunday night work. (*four men rush up through the gate*) Are you experienced with high pressure hose? (*all nod affirmatively*) I am sorry I have only one job, I have to pick one from among you. Let me have your names. (*men give names to official, who writes them down and then looks up their cards*)

FIRST UNEMPLOYED (*sitting on front bench reading newspaper*) Here one banker says prosperity is just around the corner.

SECOND UNEMPLOYED Yea, but he didn't say what street.

THIRD UNEMPLOYED Sure ain't in Harlem.

OFFICIAL Mr. Jackson, your experience seems to fit best into that job. Here is your card, good luck. (*addressing the others*) I am sorry, men. (*they walk back to the waiting room dejectedly*)

OFFICIAL (*again addressing men*) I have another job here, if it can be called a job. Bell Hop wanted, small hotel, no wages, tips only, must bring own uniform.

(*Group of unemployed are amused, laugh*)

SECOND UNEMPLOYED Now, aint that sump'n.

THIRD UNEMPLOYED Got to take your sandwich to work too?

OFFICIAL Is there anybody here, who wants to register? Anyone here who has not registered?

(CLARENCE WHITE *and* GEORGE WASHINGTON *come through gate and are seated, official motions* CLARENCE WHITE *to take seat near desk*)

OFFICIAL What is your name? (*writing particulars on card*)

CLARENCE WHITE Clarence White.

OFFICIAL Address?

(FOURTH UNEMPLOYED *snores loudly. The others look at him*)

OFFICIAL (*to* CLARENCE WHITE) Education?

(FOURTH UNEMPLOYED *snores again, unemployed laugh*)

OFFICIAL (*looks up*) Please wake that man up.

(FOURTH UNEMPLOYED *after much shaking by other unemployed awakens, looks drowsy*)

OFFICIAL (*to* FOURTH UNEMPLOYED) Are you registered here?

FOURTH UNEMPLOYED No Sir.

OFFICIAL Will you come in here and be seated.

(FOURTH UNEMPLOYED *stretches, walks slowly, takes a bite of chewing tobacco, group of unemployed is amused. He slumps down on chair inside gate*)

OFFICIAL A little less noise please! (*addressing* CLARENCE WHITE) Why did you leave the job you held for three years after being graduated from high school?

CLARENCE WHITE (*doubting, hesitating, faltering*) Well, I guess I can tell you. (*drawing closer to official*) You see, I had some trouble with the boss about my wages. You know, always overtime and no extra pay. Well, I got sore and took it out in goods and—I was caught.

OFFICIAL I am glad you told me about that. Now when I am asked about references I shall be informed about the situation. Call here every day, will you? Something will turn up that will suit you. (CLARENCE WHITE *gets up and joins the waiting unemployed*) Next please!

GEORGE WASHINGTON (*taking seat at desk*) Good mornin', how are yo'?

OFFICIAL Good morning.

GEORGE WASHINGTON Very well, thank yo suh.

OFFICIAL What's your name and address?

GEORGE WASHINGTON George Washington, 56 West 137th Street. Apartment 33.

OFFICIAL In what State were you born?

GEORGE WASHINGTON Georgia, Suh, Gordon County.

OFFICIAL How old are you?

GEORGE WASHINGTON Sixty-nine, comin' seventy on de 25th of next month, if de Lord spares me.

OFFICIAL How far did you go in school—what grade?

GEORGE WASHINGTON We ain't had much schoolin' in dem days in Georgia, no suh—jes about a year.

OFFICIAL What kind of work did you do then—farming?

GEORGE WASHINGTON Sho, farmin', den I went to Miami, Florida, worked on construction. Yo know, jes after dat big fire dey had dere about forty years ago.

OFFICIAL (*amused*) Listen, Grandpop, I am not as old as all that.

GEORGE WASHINGTON (*laughing heartily*) Sho, yo ain't—sho, yo ain't.

OFFICIAL (*after having laughed heartily*) How long have you been in New York?

GEORGE WASHINGTON Goin' on thirty-five years.

OFFICIAL What was your last steady job?

GEORGE WASHINGTON Longshoreman wid de Ward line. Worked dere ten years till last August. De boss came 'long and said: George, he said, listen, yo better take a rest. Yo gettin' too old for de job. Dat's what he said. Ain't worked since, steady. 'Couse, I'd saved a few dollars. So, I helped de missus wid de washin'. She's my second wife, a good woman, yes, suh. She's been doin' de washin' for Mrs. Epstein for years. Mrs. Epstein, she live on Jerome Avenue, corner of 170th Street.—I always take de wash up to her. So, about October ob last year she said to me: George, when things don't go so good, come and see me. Well, things got kind-a-tight. So, I went to see Mrs. Epstein. She's a fine lady, always talk good to me. She gave me a letter to some society down town and den I got de three-days-a-week job. But yo know, dat's finished now.

OFFICIAL Have you ever registered for Old Age Pension?

GEORGE WASHINGTON What is dat?

OFFICIAL Don't you know that the State pays people over seventy about $30 per month?

GEORGE WASHINGTON No, Suh.

OFFICIAL (*writing on slip*) You go to this office, tell them, that I sent you,—here is my card—and register for Old Age Pension.

GEORGE WASHINGTON (*overwhelmed*) Oh, yo sure do me good, thank yo suh, thank yo suh, goodby suh, thank yo. (*leaves office bowing out*)

STUDENT VISITOR Social legislation is certainly a blessing.

OFFICIAL Yes, but what can those men do, who are too young for Old Age Pension and too old for industry?

REPRESENTATIVE OF THE "HEAVENLY MESSENGER" (*enters, jovial*) Good morning, good morning, Mr. Johnson, may I leave some copies of the 'Heavenly Messenger' here?

OFFICIAL Go ahead, you know where the rack is!

SECOND UNEMPLOYED Better give us sump'n to eat.

REPRESENTATIVE But you need a strong spirit to face adversity.

OFFICIAL Hey, don't let us have any sermons and arguments.

(REPRESENTATIVE *leaves copies in the rack and goes out, some men pick up copies*)

STUDENT VISITOR How can we have Christan fellowship in this world as long as we have to fight one another for jobs, for bread?

OFFICIAL Yes, you are right. (*pause*) Well, (*to* FOURTH UNEMPLOYED) you are next. Why were you so sleepy?

FOURTH UNEMPLOYED I've been hikin' all the way from North Carolina. Came to see my married brother here, day befo' yisteday. But mah brother lost his job, an' his wife don't want to keep 'm no longer. So they bust up house-keepin'. I've been lookin' round two days, but couldn't catch nuthin'. Ah got no place to sleep an' that piece of apple 'bacci is all keeps me from starvin'.

OFFICIAL (*to* THIRD UNEMPLOYED) Say, Joe, come here a moment! (*comes over to desk*) You know what church is giving out food today? Take this man over and see that he gets something to eat and a place to sleep, will you?

THIRD UNEMPLOYED Sure, come along,

brother. Today it is the Saint Peter, they don't feed you so good no,—tomorrow, let me see, it's Mother Nazareth, you sure get a good square meal there ... (*as they go walking out*)

DISTRIBUTOR OF "WORKMAN'S DAILY" (*enters, carrying copies*) Anybody here want the Workman's Daily, the fighter for the working classes?

OFFICIAL   Please, this is no market place or public thoroughfare, besides, the men want food and jobs and not newspapers.

DISTRIBUTOR   If the men read this paper they will know how to get food and jobs.

OFFICIAL   Please, no selling in here, I say.

DISTRIBUTOR   All right, boss. (*leaves*)

MECHANIC (*leaving group of unemployed and walking to gate*)   Have you anything for me, sir? I have been looking everywhere, can't find a thing to do. Rent is behind, the landlord is getting nasty, the grocer's bill is overdue.

OFFICIAL   I am sorry, I have no inquiry for a mechanic.

MECHANIC   Anything will do, haven't you got anything?

OFFICIAL   Hang around a bit, I may have something soon.

MECHANIC   I cannot sit around quiet. I must have something soon. (*leaves apparently greatly troubled*)

OFFICIAL (*to* STUDENT VISITOR)   This man is an expert auto mechanic. Had his own shop for fifteen years in a small town in Alabama. Somehow, he got into a fight with a white man, his life was threatened and he came up here with his family, leaving all his property behind.

STUDENT VISITOR   Probably escaped a lynching—shocking.

(*Telephone rings, unemployed's attention centers on* OFFICIAL)

OFFICIAL (*answering telephone*)   Public Employment Office.—What is the name? Yes, I have it. What are the hours? Six days a week. How much? $70 per month and room. What is your telephone number? Sure, I'll have a man there in about an hour. Yes, thank you, sir. (*writes out order. To the men*) I want a porter, a light colored porter for an apartment house, experienced, work from 7 to 7, six days a week, $70 per month and room.

(FIFTH UNEMPLOYED *walks up*)

OFFICIAL   Are you single?

FIFTH UNEMPLOYED   Yes Sir.

OFFICIAL   Have you done porter work?

FIFTH UNEMPLOYED   Sure.

OFFICIAL   What is your name? (*conversation continues*)

FIRST UNEMPLOYED (*reading newspaper*)   Here is a white man, a broker, shoot his'self 'cause he's broke.

SECOND UNEMPLOYED (*stretches himself,—with an air of a philosopher*)   I tell you, some white folks can't stand bein' po'. Guess, we don't feel it 'cause we've always been po'. Shoot his'self, —crazy, who ever heard of a cullud man shoot his'self, 'cause he's po'?

OFFICIAL (*to* FIFTH UNEMPLOYED)   Here is the card. See the address? Go there right away. Got no fare? Here take this nickel. (*exit* FIFTH UNEMPLOYED)

(FRANCIS TAYLOR *walks up to the gate*)

OFFICIAL   What can I do for you?

FRANCIS TAYLOR   I'd like to have a job, sir.

OFFICIAL   Have you registered here?

FRANCIS TAYLOR   No, sir.

OFFICIAL   Take a seat. What is your name?

FRANCIS TAYLOR   Francis Taylor.

OFFICIAL   Address?

FRANCIS TAYLOR   26 West 99th Street.

OFFICIAL   How old are you?

FRANCIS TAYLOR   Thirty-three years.

OFFICIAL   How many children?

FRANCIS TAYLOR   Eight.

OFFICIAL   Eight?—Did you get any work under the scheme of the Prosser Committee?

FRANCIS TAYLOR   Yes, I did. Fifteen dollars a week for three days work.

OFFICIAL   Were you able to live on $15 with a family of a wife and eight children?

FRANCIS TAYLOR   Well, we had to.

OFFICIAL (*reflecting*)   How old is your wife?

FRANCIS TAYLOR   Thirty years old.

OFFICIAL   Is she in good health?

FRANCIS TAYLOR   She has trouble with her heart, she goes to the hospital. I go there too, have lumbago pretty bad.

OFFICIAL   Have you ever heard of a Birth Control Clinic?

FRANCIS TAYLOR (*startled at turn of conversation, sulkily*)   Yes, the A. I. C. P. told me to go there with the wife.

OFFICIAL   Did you go?

FRANCIS TAYLOR   No, I don't believe in that.

OFFICIAL In what?

FRANCIS TAYLOR They say it's so you won't have no more babies.

OFFICIAL Do you want to have more?

FRANCIS TAYLOR No, we ain't going to have no more, but I don't believe in going to a hospital for that. Hospitals is for when you get sick.

OFFICIAL (*aroused*) So it's all-right when you are sick but you don't believe in preventing sickness. Who pays the hospital bills for you and your wife? Somebody does. If your children are underfed and become sick, charity must provide help. Somebody must pay. Why? Because you are obstinate and refuse to keep your wife in the best health possible. (SPEAKER OF WORKERS' LEAGUE *enters and distributes handbills*) Here is the address of the clinic, go there and find out what it is all about. Then act for yourself. (FRANCIS TAYLOR *reads the slip, rises slowly and disgruntled, joins the crowd.* OFFICIAL *notices tumult*) What's going on there. Here, lady, what are you doing? Do you hear me? (*gets up and advances towards her*) Stop giving out handbills. This is a public employment office.

SPEAKER Why don't you give these men work? By the way, who do you think I am?

OFFICIAL Why, you are the Communist speaker from the street corner.

SPEAKER I am speaking for the Workers' League, we are working for the emancipation of the working classes. . . .

OFFICIAL (*interrupting*) All right, make your speeches on the street. I cannot permit you to hold your meetings in here. This is a public employment office.

SPEAKER (*jeering*) Employment Office, yes, (*imitating*) sorry, I haven't anything men, come back tomorrow.

OFFICIAL Please, go now. (*takes her gently by the arm*)

SPEAKER Take your hand off my arm, you're forgetting yourself! I thought you were a gentleman. (OFFICIAL, *defeated, rushes to his desk, takes telephone in hand,—hesitates*) Here boys, take these handbills! (*to official, taunting*) I suppose you want to call the police. Tell'm you need protection from a little woman. They'll come and do their best to keep ideas out of the workers' head—with nightsticks. Ha, ha. . . . (*exit*)

OFFICIAL (*tense with excitement to student visitor*) Nothing would please her more than to have the police here, so she can get free publicity for her propaganda. (*to men talking and reading handbills*) That's all for this morning. We open again at one o'clock. (*a few leave, others rush suddenly to the window. Through right window, men can be seen running*) What's the matter now?

MEN AT WINDOW Another poor devil is being dispossessed. Putt'n out another family.

MECHANIC (*after having passed the windows enters excitedly*) My furniture is out on the street. I have been out all morning lookin' for work—just got home—found sheriffs putt'n out my furniture—wife and kids are on the street too—what can I do, Mr. Johnson?

OFFICIAL Be calm, just sit down. I will call up the Mayor's Emergency Committee. (*picks up the telephone*) Courtland 2340. Pardon me, Courtland 7-2340. Is this the Mayor's Emergency Committee on Unemployment? This is the Public Employment Office, Harlem. I have a very sad eviction case here, an eviction case. What? You do not handle any more eviction cases? Not since May 31st. Who is now taking care of . . . Nobody? What is going to happen to those poor families? Oh, you only take in children of broken homes and refer them to institutions. Call up the A.I.C.P.? The Association for the Improvement of the Conditions of the Poor is over-burdened with work. I know that. So, you can't do anything? All right, thank you. (*hangs up, dejected, troubled*)

STUDENT VISITOR Now, if we had Unemployment Insurance . . .

OFFICIAL Yes, but we haven't.

STUDENT VISITOR Isn't there a group of interested professional people to whom . . .

OFFICIAL (*interrupting*) The professional people have their problems. But they are not vitally interested in the problems of the laboring Negroes.

STUDENT VISITOR Maybe the political leaders . . .

OFFICIAL They are too busy with politics.

STUDENT VISITOR Isn't there a community organization . . .

OFFICIAL No, there is no civic organization representing the broad interests of the community. (*to himself*) No Prosser Committee now. A.I.C.P. over-burdened. No relief from the Red Cross, this is no Act of God. (*to* MECHANIC)

Listen, go to the police station, tell them about your troubles. Let's see what they will do. Come back here at once. I will do my best in the meantime to help you. (*shakes hands*)

(MECHANIC *leaves hurriedly, a group of unemployed, who had stood at the door, follow. Sad silence between* OFFICIAL *and* STUDENT VISITOR. *The voice of a newspaper boy can be heard behind the scene.*)

NEWSBOY The Harlem News—All about the Chicago Riot—Three dead in the Chicago Riot—the Harlem News.

OFFICIAL (*to* STUDENT VISITOR) Here is a nickel, please get me a paper.

(STUDENT VISITOR *runs out*)

OFFICIAL (*to himself*) I feel so helpless. Here is white society holding down the Negro to small jobs and small pay. Business becomes slack, the laborers are dumped on the street. But they must live! (*shakes head*) Real leadership is lacking. Oh, what is the way out of this misery?

STUDENT VISITOR (*returning with paper, reading*) Chicago Negroes stop eviction. Three Negroes killed. Court suspends all eviction orders.

OFFICIAL Blood, more blood. Force, the claws and fangs of the beast, is it the only way out of this brutal civilization?

(*Curtain.*)

Langston Hughes (1902–1967)

Don't You Want To Be Free?   1937

When Langston Hughes returned from his assignment in Spain as a war correspondent, he told Louise Patterson of his idea for establishing a people's theater. She suggested the hall of the International Workers Order (a leftist labor-cultural group) above Frank's Restaurant on 125th Street. This was the first home of the Harlem Suitcase Theater, in 1937.

Named for its arena staging and lack of scenic properties, Suitcase Theater was a people's theater composed of amateur actors. The audiences were 75 per cent black; admission was thirty-five cents. The program was usually two or three short pieces: *The Slave*, or *The Man Who Died at Twelve O'clock*, or several skits written by Mr. Hughes lampooning white caricatures of blacks: *Em-Fuehrer Jones*, *Limitations of Life* (in this volume), and *Little Eva's End*. The *pièce de résistance* was always *Don't You Want To Be Free?* It was the play written for this theater.

We had no play so the suggestion came up one evening as we were sitting there plotting the theater, that Langston should do a play and why not a play of music-drama of many of his folk poems? So that he went home that night after we had had that discussion and sat up all night writing it and came back the next night with *Don't You Want To Be Free?*
(from an interview with Louise Patterson
by Norma Markman, 1969)

Although the Suitcase Theater lasted only two years (it did not survive its transplant to the library basement on 135th Street) the idea of a Negro People's Theater spread to other cities. In March 1939, Mr. Hughes founded the New Negro Theater in Los Angeles.

The success of *Don't You Want To Be Free?*, which opened in February 1937 and ran for 135 performances, may be found in three factors: (1) the direct appeal to the problems of the audience (most businesses in Harlem were owned by whites and only one of every six employees of these businesses were black), (2) the simplicity and beauty of the poetry and songs, (3) the appeal to unite poor whites and blacks in a fight against exploitation by the rich. Was this last appeal ever a real possibility?

Don't You Want To Be Free?

From Slavery
Through the Blues
To Now—and then some!

With Singing, Music, and Dancing

CHARACTERS

A YOUNG MAN
A BOY
A GIRL
A WOMAN
A MAN
AN OLD WOMAN
AN OLD MAN
AN OVERSEER
A MULATTO GIRL
A WIFE
A HUSBAND
A LAUNDRY WORKER
A MEMBER OF THE AUDIENCE
TWO NEWSBOYS
VOICES
A CHORUS

(SETTING: *a bare stage, except for a lynch rope and an auction block. No scenery and very few props. No special lighting. Only actors needed— and an audience. There is no curtain, so a* YOUNG MAN *simply comes forward and begins to speak*)

YOUNG MAN Listen, folks! I'm one of the members of this group, and I want to tell you about our theater. This is it right here! We haven't got any scenery, or painted curtains, because we haven't got any money to buy them. But we've got something you can't buy with money, anyway. We've got faith in ourselves. And in you. So we're going to put on a show. Maybe you'll like it because it's about you, and about us. This show is for you. And you can act in it, too, if you want to. This is your show, as well as ours. Now I'll tell you what this show is about. It's about me, except that it's not just about me now standing here talking to you—but it's about me yesterday, and about me tomorrow. I'm colored! I guess you can see that. Well, this show is about what it means to be colored in America. Listen: (*crash of cymbals*)

I am a Negro:
  Black as the night is black,
  Black like the depths of my Africa.

I've been a slave:
  Caesar told me to keep his door-steps clean.
  I brushed the boots of Washington.

I've been a worker:
  Under my hand the pyramids arose.
  I made mortar for the Woolworth Building.

I've been a singer:
  All the way from Africa to Georgia
  I carried my sorrow songs.
  I made ragtime.

I've been a victim:
  The Belgians cut off my hands in the Congo.
  They lynch me now in Texas.

I am a Negro:
  Black as the night is black,
  Black like the depths of my Africa.

(*Tom-toms. From either side come an African* BOY, *left, and* GIRL, *right, dressed in clothes of bright colors. The* GIRL *begins to dance in the African manner, whirling slowly to the beating of the drums*)

BOY
  The low beating of the tom-toms,
  The slow beating of the tom-toms,
    Low . . . slow
    Slow . . . low—
    Stirs your blood.
      Dance!

A night-veiled girl
　Whirls softly into a
　Circle of light.
　Whirls softly . . . slowly,
Like a wisp of smoke around the fire—
　And the tom-toms beat,
　And the tom-toms beat,
　And the low beating of the tom-toms
　Stirs your blood.

(*Cool music like rippling water. Lifting her arms to the sun, the* GIRL *speaks*)

GIRL
　To fling my arms wide
　In some place of the sun,
　To whirl and to dance
　Till the white day is done.
　Then rest at cool evening
　Beneath a tall tree
　While night comes on gently,
　　Dark like me—

　That is my dream!

　To fling my arms wide
　In the face of the sun,
　Dance! whirl! whirl!
　Till the quick day is done.
　Rest at pale evening . . .
　A tall slim tree,
　Night coming tenderly
　　Dark like me.

(*The* BOY *has drawn near the* GIRL *and stands before her. She looks at him, takes his hands, and they gaze into each other's eyes*)

YOUNG MAN I guess I was like that boy a long time ago, when we lived in Africa, and the sun was our friend. I guess I was crazy about that girl that I met at night in the moonlight under the palm trees.

(*Roll of drums, like thunder! The* BOY *and* GIRL *run away, right. The* YOUNG MAN *speaks to the audience*)

　I was Africa then
　But the white men came.
　I was in my own land, then.
　But the white men came.

　They drove me out of the forest
　They took me away from the jungles.
　I lost my trees.
　I lost my silver moons.

　Now they've caged me
　In their circus of civilization.
　Now I'm in a cage
　In their circus of civilization.

In 1619 the first slaves came to Jamestown, brought in chains in sailing vessels to America.

(*Enter right four slaves;* GIRL, BOY, OLD MAN, *and* WIFE *chained by the wrists together. They walk in a straight line, moaning musically across the stage. The* YOUNG MAN *joins them. They are followed by an* OVERSEER *with a whip. All exit left except the* GIRL *and the* OVERSEER. *The* GIRL *mounts the slave-block, wild-eyed and frightened*)

OVERSEER Get along now! Get on! Step along there! (*approaching auction block*) Folks, look here what I got! A nice healthy black gal, folks. Wild! Ain't trained, but a little of this will break her in. (*holds up his whip*) Congo women can't be beat for working, and she's a Congo woman. Good for house or fields. Look at them legs, wiry and strong. (*feels her legs*) Look at them hands. Long fingers, just right for pickin' cotton. (*to the* GIRL) Open your mouth, gal! (*punches her with the whipstock*) Open your mouth. (GIRL *opens her mouth*) See! Healthy! Nice white teeth! (*with a leer*) This girl's all right for most anything. What am I offered for her, gentlemen? Speak up! Make your bids. What am I offered for her?

VOICE One hundred dollars.

OVERSEER Heh? One hundred dollars! What? That ain't a starter! What am I offered for this gal, gentlemen? I got a hundred.

VOICE One hundred fifty!

OVERSEER One hundred fifty! Hundred fifty! Good for cooking, washing, hoeing, anything you want.

VOICE Two hundred!

OVERSEER That's more like it! Two hundred! Two . . .

VOICE Two hundred ten.

VOICE Two hundred twenty.

VOICE Two hundred fifty.

OVERSEER Two hundred fifty! Two hundred fifty . . .

VOICE Three hundred!

OVERSEER Three hundred! Do I hear another? What? Three hundred dollars worth of black gal! Going! Going! Gone! (*strikes the floor with his whip. There is a loud scream from the*

GIRL) Gone for three hundred dollars! Here, take her. Make her work now. (*he pushes the* GIRL *off the block and she goes aside sobbing, right. Dark voices are heard chanting*)

   VOICES

      Cook them white folks dinner,
      Wash them white folks clothes,
      Be them white folks slave-gal,
      That is all she knows.
      Be them white folks slave-gal,
      That is all she knows.

(OLD MAN *enters left in the overalls and ragged shirt of a slave. He mounts the block*)

   OVERSEER Kinder old, folks, but still got plenty in him. Nothing like an old work-horse. He's well broke in. Something of a preacher, too. Helps keep the other slaves out o' mischief o' Sundays. What am I offered? Fifty?... Hundred?... Hundred fifty. Going, going, gone! For a hundred and fifty! Get off the block, you old ape! Get off the block, and lemme get somebody up here I can make money off of. (*he pushes the* OLD MAN *away. He goes aside, muttering*)

   VOICES

      Whip done broke his spirit,
      Plow done broke his back.
      All they wants a slave, that's all,
      When a man is black.
      Nothin' but a slave, that's all,
      If a man is black.

   OLD MAN No, no! No, no!

(*The* YOUNG MAN *enters left. The* OVERSEER's *face glows. He rubs his hands*)

   OVERSEER

      Ah! Here's a nice fine black buck!
      Strong's you'd want to see
      Boy, get up on that block
      And make some dough for me!

   YOUNG MAN

      No!

   OVERSEER

      What? No!
      Who're you talkin' to?

   YOUNG MAN

      YOU!

   OVERSEER

      You must've gone crazy
      Talking like that to me.
      Get up on that block!

   YOUNG MAN

      No! I want to be free! (*kicks block off stage*)

   OVERSEER

      Free?

   YOUNG MAN

      Yes, free!
      Not sold like a slave.
      Before I'll be sold again
      I'll go down to my grave.

(*The* OVERSEER *strikes him with his whip*)

   GIRL Oh!
   YOUNG MAN No! no! no! (*as he backs away and falls before the blows of the* OVERSEER's *whip*)
   OVERSEER I'll teach you to want to be free! To talk back to me! (*lashing him.* YOUNG MAN *falls*)
   GIRL Oh!... Oh!... Oh!
   OLD MAN (*begins to sing*)

      Go down, Moses,
      Way down in Egypt land,
      And tell ole Pharoah
         CHORUS

      To let my people go.

   OVERSEER (*turns to* OLD MAN *and strikes him with his whip*) Shut up, you dog!

(*As the* OLD MAN *falls, the* GIRL *takes up the song*)

   GIRL

      Go down, Moses,
      Way down in Egypt land,
      And tell ole Pharoah
         CHORUS

      To let my people go!

   OVERSEER (*in wild confusion, rushes to the* GIRL *and strikes her*) Shut up, you god-damned dogs! Shut up!

(*But then the* YOUNG MAN *rises and takes up the song*)

YOUNG MAN

    Go down, Moses,
    Way down in Egypt land,
    And tell ole Pharoah
    To let my people go.
        CHORUS

    And tell ole Pharoah
    To let my people go.

(*A great wave of revolt rises disguised as a song. The* OVERSEER *is powerless against it. He calls for troops, for arms. He pulls a gun*)

OVERSEER Send soldiers! Get out the militia! Shoot these dogs!

(*Shots are heard. The* OLD MAN *falls prone. The* GIRL *falls. An* OLD WOMAN *enters right and kneels over the dead*)

OVERSEER (*as he shoots*) Shut up! Shut up! Shut up! (*he exits left*)

Young Man (*coming forward toward the audience*) But we didn't shut up! We were never wholly quiet! Some of us always carried on our fight and kept alive the seeds of revolt. Nat Turner was one. Denmark Vesey was another who tried to lead the slaves to freedom. Harriet Tubman was another who sought roads to escape. Sojourner Truth another. Some they beat to death. Some they killed. But some of us always kept on, even though the way looked dark.

OLD WOMAN So dark! So dark! (*sings over the bodies of her dead*)

    Oh, nobody knows
    The trouble I've seen!
    Nobody knows but Jesus.
    Nobody knows
    The trouble I've seen.
    Glory, Hallelujah!

    Sometimes I'm up,
    Sometimes I'm down.
    Oh, yes, Lawd!
    Sometimes I'm almost
    To the ground.
    Oh, yes, Lawd!
        CHORUS

    Oh, nobody knows
    The trouble I've seen . . .

OLD WOMAN (*as the* CHORUS *hums*) Children scattered. Home gone. Sons and daughters sold away. I don't know where they are. (*rises*) But I look at the stars and they look at the stars. And somehow I feels better. And now I walks the world lookin' for truth. I'se a so-journer lookin' for truth.

YOUNG MAN Sojourner Truth!
OLD WOMAN Yes, son.
YOUNG MAN Is we ever gonna be free?
OLD WOMAN Son, we gonna be free. Ain't you heard them names?
YOUNG MAN What names?
OLD WOMAN Black names and white names in the air. Listen! (*flag rises*)
VOICES Douglass! Douglass! Frederick Douglass! William Lloyd Garrison! Emerson! . . . Whittier! . . . Lowell! . . . Douglass! John Brown! Lincoln! John Brown! Abraham Lincoln. (*roll of drums. Bugle calls*)
OLD WOMAN The Civil War! And freedom!
YOUNG MAN (*takes flag*) White soldiers and black soldiers fighting for our freedom.
OLD MAN (*rising*) Slaves rising from the dead for freedom.
GIRL (*rising*) Women lifting up their heads for freedom.

        CHORUS
    Glory! Glory! Hallelujah!
    Glory! Glory! Hallelujah!
    Glory! Glory! Hallelujah!

YOUNG MAN Everybody sing! (*he starts the verse*)
        CHORUS
    John Brown's body
    Lies a-mouldering in his grave . . .
    (Repeat Chorus)

(*As they sing, all exit, right. Enter the* MAN *and the* WOMAN *in old clothes, left, cross right. They begin to hoe in a field*)

WOMAN John, this ain't no freedom.
MAN Free, to work and get no pay. Lucy, how come we's

    Just a herd of Negroes
    Driven to the field,
    Plowing, planting, hoeing,
    To make the cotton yield.

    When the cotton's picked
    And the work is done
    Boss man takes the money
    And we get none.

    Leave us hungry, ragged
    As we were before.
    Year by year goes by
    And we are nothing more

Than a herd of Negroes
Driven to the field—
Plowing life away
To make the cotton yield.

WOMAN Yes, honey, all you say is true, 'cause

There stands the white man,
Boss of the fields—
Lord of the land
And all that it yields.

And here bend the black folks,
Hands to the soil—
Bosses of nothing,
Not even our toil.

MAN The South! Honey, the South's so pretty, magnolia trees and cotton, but sometimes it's bad, too. So evil and bad!

(*Enter* OVERSEER *bringing chair*)

WOMAN The white folks won't pay us nothing, that's the trouble. Besides the Jim Crow cars, and the Jim Crow schools, and the lynchings—when you work, they don't pay you nothing.

MAN That's what happened to Wilbur, to our boy! All over a little mite o' money.

WOMAN Yes, that's what happened to Wilbur. He went to ask the man for his money —and they killed him.

(*On the left, the* OVERSEER *sits in a chair tilted back, smoking a big cigar. Enter the* YOUNG MAN, *right, crosses left*)

YOUNG MAN Mr. Mallory, the crops all sold, ain't it? Can you gimme my part now?

OVERSEER Your part? What you mean, your part, George?

YOUNG MAN I mean my money that you owe me.

OVERSEER You better be careful how you use that word *owe*, boy. I don't owe you nothing.

YOUNG MAN (*trying to restrain himself*) But I raised nine bales, Mr. Mallory, And my contract calls . . .

OVERSEER Your contract? Hell! What about my bills? What about the commissary store? What about that sow belly and corn meal I been advancing you all the year for you and your lazy old woman, and them kids of yours that you thinks too good to work in the cotton fields. Trying to send pickaninnies to school! Huh! You're an uppity black boy, anyhow. Talkin' about what I owe you! Why even after the nine bales was sold, you owed me more'n a hundred dollars. Why, you ungrateful scoundrel. Get on back there in that field and start plowin' for next year's crop.

YOUNG MAN Mr. Mallory, I ain't goin'. Not till I see the figures.

OVERSEER You ain't going? What you mean, you ain't going? Don't talk back to me!

YOUNG MAN I ain't going. I'm tired o' workin' for nothing.

OVERSEER (*rising*) Are you trying to say I don't pay my field hands? Get out o' here. You impudent black cuss, you! Get out o' here!

YOUNG MAN No, sir, Mr. Mallory, not without my money.

OVERSEER You impudent dog! Get out o' here before I beat the hell out of you.

YOUNG MAN No!

(*The* OVERSEER *walks up to the* YOUNG MAN *and hits him in the mouth. The* YOUNG MAN *stands as if in a daze, then he suddenly deals the* OVERSEER *a blow that sends him reeling unconscious to the floor. There is a crash of cymbals. Whistles. The far-off cry of a mob. The* MOTHER *and* FATHER *are terror-stricken. The* YOUNG MAN *looks for a place to hide. There is no hiding place*)

MAN Hurry, son, hurry! They gonna kill you!

WOMAN Run, Wilbur! Oh, honey, run! Go the swamp way, so's the dogs can't smell no tracks. Run!

MAN Hurry! Hurry! Hurry! Son, hurry!

YOUNG MAN (*darting wildly about*) There ain't no place to run. I hit the white man. I done hit the boss! And there ain't no place to run. Nobody helps me. Nobody to protect me. (*he approaches the lynch rope that dangles from the sky and puts his head into the noose*) I know it! You got me! All you crackers got me. Dead! I'm dead!

(*His body slumps as if dead.* NEWSBOYS *enter selling papers*)

NEWSBOYS Negro lynched in Alabama! Big Lynching Near Selma! Read all about it! Read about the lynching! Negro accused of rape! Big lynching!

WOMAN (*standing before the hanging youth*) My boy is dead!

MAN (*bitterly*) Damn the ones what kilt him! Damn their souls to hell!

WOMAN John, my boy is dead, I'm all alone —and my boy is dead! (*begins to sing*)

> I couldn't hear nobody pray.
> Oh, Lawdy! Couldn't hear nobody pray.
> Way down yonder by myself,
> I couldn't hear nobody pray!

(*Enter a young* MULATTO GIRL, *who sits down beside the hanging body, center, and begins to recite*)

MULATTO GIRL

> Way down South in Dixie,
> (Break the heart of me!)
> They hung my dark young lover
> To a cross road's tree.
>
> Way down South in Dixie,
> (Bruised body high in air)
> I asked the white Lord Jesus
> What was the use of prayer.
>
> Way down South in Dixie
> (Break the heart of me)
> Love is a naked shadow
> On a gnarled and naked tree.

OVERSEER (*left—rising and shouting*)

> Pull at the rope! O!
> Pull it high!
> Let the white folks live
> And the black man die.

MAN

> Yes, pull it, then,
> With a bloody cry!
> Let the black boy swing
> But the *white folks* die.

OVERSEER

> The white folks die?
> What do you mean—
> The white folks die?

MAN

> That black boy's
> Still body says:

YONG MAN

> Not I!

MAN

> Not I!

VOICES

> Not I! NotI! Not I!

(*The* OVERSEER *sneaks away*)

YOUNG MAN They killed Christ, didn't they, when he tried to change the world?

WOMAN But did he die?

EVERYBODY *No!*

YOUNG MAN They killed John Brown, didn't they, when he tried to free the slaves?

WOMAN But did he die?

VOICES No!

YOUNG MAN What did Angelo Herndon say when they had him in prison for trying to help the poor? What did Herndon say?

VOICE Let them kill Herndon, if they will, but a million more will rise to take my place.

YOUNG MAN You can't kill the working class, he said. And when we rise ...

WOMAN (*begins to sing*)

> In that great gettin' up mornin'
> Fare you well! Fare you well!
> (*repeat*)

CHORUS

> There's a better day a-comin'!
> (*etc.*)

(*The old spiritual rises triumphally as the* YOUNG MAN *takes his head from lynch rope. He comes with tramp's bundle on stick and stands before the* MULATTO GIRL. *The* MAN *and* WOMAN *exit right as the singing dies down*)

YOUNG MAN So many things is wrong in this world, honey, but the wrongest thing of all is poverty. Being poor. You're the girl I loved once, now look at you! All painted and powdered, and wrong. But I know what happened. I don't blame you for it. You was young and beautiful once, and golden like the sunshine that warmed your body. But because you was colored, honey, this town had no place for you, nothing for you to do.

MULATTO GIRL So one day, sitting on old Mrs. Latham's back porch polishing the silver, working for two dollars a week, I asked myself two questions. They ran something like this:

Don't You Want To Be Free?

What can a colored girl do on the money from a white woman's kitchen?

VOICE   Two dollars a week.

MULATTO GIRL   And ain't there any joy in this town?

VOICE   Two dollars a week.

YOUNG MAN   Now the streets down by the river are your streets. (*turning away*) And the sinister shuttered houses of the bottoms hold a yellow girl seeking an answer to her questions.

VOICE (*softly*)   Two dollars a week.

MULATTO GIRL   The good church folks won't even mention my name any more.

YOUNG MAN   But the white men who visit those houses...

MULATTO GIRL (*triumphantly*)   Pay more money to me now than they ever did before when I worked in their kitchens. (*distant laughter*)

YOUNG MAN (*bitterly*)   I'm going away. I got to go away.

MULATTO GIRL   Goodbye, Wilbur.

YOUNG MAN (*without looking back*)   I'm going up North. (*as he walks left*) I'm going far away.

MULATTO GIRL   Goodbye, Wilbur! (*she powders her face and begins to recite*)

> My old man's a white old man!
> My old mother's black!
> But if ever I cursed my white old man
> I take my curses back.
>
> If ever I cursed my black old mother
> And wished she were in hell,
> I'm sorry for that evil wish
> And now I wish her well.
>
> My old man died in a fine big house.
> My ma died in a shack.
> I wonder where I'm gonna die,
> Being neither white nor black?

(*As she walks away, a piano begins to play the blues, the sad old Negro blues. She exits right. The* YOUNG MAN *sings as he picks up his pack and begins to trudge the road*)

YOUNG MAN

> Goin' down de road, Lawd,
> Goin' down de road,
> Down de road, Lawd,
> Way, way down de road.
> Got to find somebody
> To help me carry dis load.
>
> Sun's a-settin',
> This is what I'm gonna sing.
> Sun's a-settin'
> This is what I'm gonna sing:
> I feel de blues a-comin',
> Wonder what de blues 'll bring?
>
> Road, Road, Road, O!
> Road, road ... road ... road, road!
> Road, road, road, O!
> On de No'thern road.
> These Mississippi towns ain't
> Fit fer a hoppin' toad.

(*the* YOUNG MAN *sits down beside the road. Enter* WIFE, *right, and* BOY, *left*) Gee, but I got the blues. (*the piano sings with the sad weary notes of the blues*) Do you—all know what the blues is?

WIFE

> The blues ain't nothin'
> But the dog-goned heart's disease.
> I say, blues ain't nothin' but
> The dog-gone heart's disease.
> When you got the blues, you
> Sho can't find no ease.

(*sighs*) I got the blues. Reckon I'll run down the street a minute, see can I walk 'em off! (*she dresses and powders to exit later from her dreary flat. At left, undressing in a dark hall bedroom, the* BOY *answers, too*)

BOY   I got the blues. Guess I'll go to bed. Maybe I can sleep 'em off.

YOUNG MAN   The blues is songs folks make up when their heart hurts. That's what the blues is. Sad funny songs. Too sad to be funny, and too funny to be sad. (*exit* WOMAN) Colored folks made up the blues! Listen!

(*Loudly, the piano player beats out his blues*)

BOY

> I got the Weary Blues
> And I can't be satisfied.
> Got the Weary Blues
> And can't be satisfied—
> I ain't happy no mo'
> And I wish that I had died.

(*But the player keeps on playing softly in the night*)

YOUNG MAN   You see, that's the blues. (*at right, a* HUSBAND *comes home from work and throws his hat and dinner pail on the table*) Sometimes there's the family blues.

HUSBAND God-dog it!

> I works all day
> Wid a pick an' a shovel
> Comes home at night,—
> It ain't nothin' but a hovel.
>
> I calls for ma woman
> When I opens de door.
> She's out in de street,—
> Ain't no good no more.
>
> I does her swell
> An' I treats her fine,
> But she don't gimme no lovin'
> Cause she ain't de right kind.
>
> I'm a hard workin' man—
> But I sho pays double.
> I tries to be good but
> Gets nothin' but trouble.

(*he sits down at the table and begins to sing*)

Trouble, trouble, I has 'em all my days.
Trouble, trouble, has 'em all my days.
Seems like trouble's gonna drive me to my grave.

(*he snatches up his hat and leaves*) I'm gonna get drunk.

YOUNG MAN And sometimes there's the loveless blues—when all you got left is a picture of the one you care for.

(*At left, the* BOY *who has been looking at his girl's picture begins to sing.*)

BOY

> All I want is your picture,
> Must be in a frame.
> All I want is your picture,
> Must be in a frame—
> So when you're gone
> I can see you just the same!

(*he stops and begins to talk to the picture*)

> Cause you don't love me, baby,
> Is awful awful hard.
> Gypsy done showed me
> My bad luck card.
>
> There ain't no good left
> In this world for me.
> Gypsy done tole me,—
> Unlucky as can be.

(*throws down picture*)

> I don't know what
> Po' weary me can do.
> Gypsy says I'd kill ma self
> If I was you.

(*the* BOY *gets up, puts on his coat, and begins to sing*)

> I'm goin' down to the railroad
> And lay my head on the track,
> Goin' down to the railroad,
> Lay my head on the track,
> If I see the train a-comin,'
> I'm gonna jerk it back.

(*He exits, left. At right,* WOMAN *enters, looks around anxiously and begins to cry*)

YOUNG MAN And then there is them left-lonesome blues.

WIFE Oh, Lawd! Looks like Jackson done left me. And I wasn't gone nowhere but to put my numbers in. Jackson, you done broke my heart this evenin'.

> I ain't got no heart no mo'
> Next time a man comes near me
> Gonna shut and lock my door,
> Cause they treats me mean—
> The ones I love.
> They always treats me mean.

(*she begins to sing*)

> Oh, you mens treats women
> Just like a old pair o'shoes.
> You mens treats women
> Just like a old pair o'shoes.
> You kicks 'em round and
> Does 'em like you choose.

(*She goes and stands beside the piano on the opposite side from the* HUSBAND)

YOUNG MAN And then there is those morning after blues.

HUSBAND It's the next day now. (*begins to sing*)

> I was so sick last night I
> Didn't hardly know my mind.
> So sick last night I
> Didn't know my mind.
> I drunk some bad licker that
> Almost made me blind.
>
> Had a dream last night I
> Thought I was in hell.
> I drempt last night I
> Thought I was in hell.
> Woke up and looked around me—
> Babe, your mouth was open like a well.

I said, Baby, baby,
Please don't snore so loud.
Baby! Please don't snore so loud.
You jest a little bit o' woman but you
Sound like a great big crowd.

WIFE (*replies in song*)

Now, listen, Mr. Jackson,
Don't say that to me.
Listen, Mr. Jackson,
Don't say that to me,
Cause if you do,
We is bound to disagree.

HUSBAND   Baby, you ain't gonna leave me, is you? You's all I got.
WIFE   Yes, I'm gonna leave you. You all I got, too, but I sure can get along without you. So, goodbye!
ALL (*singing*)

Blues, blues, blues!
Blues, blues . . . blues, blues, blues!
Blues is what's the matter
When you loses all you got to lose.

(*Exit* HUSBAND *right*, WIFE *left*)

YOUNG MAN   Colored folks made the blues! Now everybody sings 'em. We made 'em out of being poor and lonely. And homes busted up, and desperate and broke. (*rises*) But me, I haven't got any blues! I got a little job, not much. (*leans against wall*) Got a little time to stand on the corner at night and watch the girls go by! Boy, these Harlem girls'ye sure got it! Looky yonder! (*enter, right, the* GIRL, *beautiful in a red dress. As she passes, he recites*)

Man alive! When Susanna Jones wears red
Her face is like an ancient cameo
Turned brown by the ages.

VOICE

Come with a blast of trumpets,
    Jesus!

YOUNG MAN

When Susanna Jones wears red
A queen from some time-dead Egyptian night
Walks once again.

VOICE

Blow trumpets, Jesus!

YOUNG MAN

And the beauty of Susanna Jones in red
Burns in my heart a love-fire sharp like pain.

VOICE

Sweet silver trumpets,
    Jesus!

(*The* GIRL *exits left and the* YOUNG MAN *takes off his coat and starts polishing a brass spitoon. As he works he talks to himself*)

YOUNG MAN   Gee, if I just had a little money, I think I'd get married. But I kinder hate to start out with nothing. Suppose we had a kid? Well, I'd want my kid to have a decent break, that's what. At least a chance to go to high school. I didn't even have that. Had to start to work soon as I was big enough. My folks never did get ahead. There ain't many decent jobs a colored boy can get nohow. Here I am polishing spitoons in a hotel. But I've travelled around plenty, been all over America mighty near. And most towns, there just ain't nothin' much for a colored boy to do. Lots of factories won't even hire colored men. Lots of places I can't join unions. Anyhow this old spitoon looks right good. (*he holds up the shining spitoon proudly*) When a thing's clean, it always looks better, no matter what. But, gee! Have *I* always got to do the cleaning? Always the dirty work? Me! Always? (*he recites as he polishes*)

Clean the spitoons, boy.
    Detroit,
    Chicago,
    Atlantic City,
    Palm Beach.
Clean the spitoons.
The steam in hotel kitchens,
And the smoke in hotel lobbies,
And the slime in hotel spitoons:
Part of my life.
    Hey, boy!
    A nickel,
    A dime,
    A dollar,
Two dollars a day.
    Hey, boy!
    A nickel,
    A dime,
    A dollar,
    Two dollars
Buy smokes, shoes,

A ticket to the movies.
House rent to pay,
Gin on Saturday,
Church on Sunday.
  My God!
Movies and church
and women and Sunday
all mixed up with dimes and
dollars and clean spitoons
and house rent to pay.
  Hey, boy!
A bright bowl of brass is beautiful to the Lord.
Bright polished brass like the cymbals
Of King David's dancers,
Like the wine cups of Solomon.
  Hey, boy!
A clean spitoon on the altar of the Lord.
A clean bright spitoon all newly polished,—
At least I can offer that.

(*The* BOSS *enters, left, crosses right*)

OVERSEER   Com'mere, Boy!
YOUNG MAN   Yes, sir.
OVERSEER   Listen, George.
YOUNG MAN   Wilbur's my name.
OVERSEER   Well, whatever your name is, listen. I'm the boss and I got to cut down expenses. You know, that bank crash—folks ain't spending money. I'm gonna let the bellboys do the house man's work from now on. You can get your check and go.
YOUNG MAN (*stunned*) Yes, sir, Mister Mallory, but . . .

(*The* OVERSEER *walks to the other side, and seats himself for a shine. He calls to the* OLD MAN *who enters, right*)

OVERSEER   Hey, George!
OLD MAN   Yes, sir! Yes, sir!
OVERSEER   Gimme a shine!

(*As he shines his shoes,* WOMAN *enters left and begins to dust*)

OLD MAN   Yes, sir! Yes, sir!

I must say yes, sir.
To *you* all the time.
Yes, sir! Yes, sir!
All my days
Climbing up a great big mountain
Of yes, sirs.

Rich old white man
Owns the world.

Gimme your shoes
To shine.
Yes, sir, boss,
Yes, sir!

YOUNG MAN (*pointing at the* OLD MAN) That was my grandfather. (*on the left, the* WOMAN *in a maid's apron is working*) And my mother, out working for the white folks. When I was a kid, never nobody home to take care of me. I don't want my kids to grow up that away. Look at my mother.

WOMAN

All day, subdued, polite—
Thoughtful to the faces that are white.

OLD MAN

Oh, tribal dance!
Oh, drums!
Oh, veldt at night!

YOUNG MAN

Forgotten watch-fires on a hill somewhere!

OLD MAN

Oh, songs that do not care!

WOMAN

At six o'clock, or seven, or eight, you're through
You've worked all day,
Then Harlem waits for you.
The el, the sub, a taxi through the park.

YOUNG MAN

Oh, drums of life in Harlem after dark.

WOMAN

Oh, dreams! Oh, songs!

OLD MAN

A little rest at night.

WOMAN

Oh, sweet relief from faces that are white!

(*takes off her apron, puts on her coat and hat, and goes home, crossing right, to her son, the* YOUNG MAN)

OVERSEER   Say, George! Be careful of my corns!

OLD MAN Yes, sir, Mr. Mallory, yes, sir!

OVERSEER And polish those shoes good now! I want to see my face in 'em when you get through. (*the* OLD MAN *bends over his task*)

WOMAN Good evening, son!

YOUNG MAN Mom, I lost my job!

WOMAN You lost your job?

YOUNG MAN Yes! They laid me off tonight.

WOMAN Well, honey, you'll find another one. Maybe.

YOUNG MAN I don't know, Mom. Things is so tight, I done lost heart! Look how long I been a man now, and ain't never had a job that amounted to nothing. I've been all over, and everywhere just the same. The dirty work for colored folks, the cheap work, underpaid work! I'm tired, Mom. Soon as I come here to be with you a while and we get this little flat, first thing I do is lose my job. And the landlord's just sent us a notice about raising the rent, too. Mom, I'm about ready to give up. I swear I am!

WOMAN Son, you ain't gonna give up no such a thing. Listen! You gonna keep right on just like I been keeping on. Did you ever stop to think about it, honey, about your mother, and all the rest of us colored women—what we been up against all through history, son. Sit down and lemme tell you, for (*piano music*)

I'm standing here today
Like a living story of that long dark way
That I had to climb, that I had to know
In order that our race might live and grow.
Look at my face, boy, dark as the night,
Yet shining like the sun with hope and light.
I'm the child they stole from the sand
Three hundred years ago in Africa's land.
I'm the dark girl who crossed the wide sea
Carrying in my body the seed of the Free.
I'm the woman who worked in the field,
Bringing the cotton and corn to yield.
I'm the one who labored as a slave,
Beaten and mistreated for the work that I gave—
Children sold away from me, husband sold, too.
No safety, no love, no respect was I due.
Three hundred years in the deepest South,
But love put a song and a prayer in my mouth.
Love put a dream like steel in my soul.
Now through my children, we're reaching the goal.
I couldn't read then. I couldn't write.
I had nothing back there in the night.
Sometimes the valley was filled with tears,
But I kept trudging on through the lonely years.
Sometimes the road was hot with sun.
But I had to keep on till my work was done.
I *had* to keep on! No stopping for me—
I was the seed of the coming Free.
I nourished our dream that nothing could smother
Deep in my breast—the Negro Mother.
I had only hope then, but now through you,
Dark child of today, my dreams must come true.
All you dark children in the world out there,
Remember my sweat, my pain, my despair.
Remember my years heavy with sorrow—
And make of those years a torch for tomorrow,
Make of my past a road to the light,
Out of the darkness, the ignorance, the night.
Lift high my banner out of the dust.
Stand like free men supporting my trust.
Believe in the right, let none push you back.
Remember the whip and the slaver's track.
Remember how the strong in struggle and strife
Still bar you the way, and deny you life—
But march ever forward, breaking down bars.
Look ever upward at the sun and the stars.
Oh, my dark children, may my dreams and my prayers
Impel you forever up the great stairs—
For I will be with you till no white brother
Dares keep down the children of the Negro Mother.

OVERSEER (*who is now a Landlord, coming to knock at their door, right*) Madam, did you get my notice about raising your rent, ten dollars a month more?

WOMAN Yes, sir, I got the notice, but I am tired of that. I ain't gonna pay no more. We're paying enough.

OVERSEER You'll pay it or move, and no smart talk about it, neither.

YOUNG MAN (*rising*) Say, listen here! Who're you to speak to my mother like that?

OVERSEER I'm the landlord. If you don't like it, get out of my place.

YOUNG MAN Lemme see you get instead!

OVERSEER What? This is my house!

YOUNG MAN Yes, but you don't live in it! We live here! (*he towers above the Landlord*) This is Harlem.

(*The* OVERSEER *backs away and puts on a waiter's apron.* WOMAN *begins to peel potatoes,* YOUNG MAN *to study. At the left a* BOY *holding a menu calls*)

BOY Say, waiter! Where is that waiter? ... Hey, waiter! Give me an order of spaghetti and a bottle of beer, please.

OVERSEER Sorry! We don't serve colored here.

BOY What? You mean on 125th Street, and don't serve colored?

OVERSEER Sure, this is a white place.

BOY (*rising*) And you don't serve colored people?

OVERSEER You heard me, big boy.

BOY I might of heard you, but this is Harlem speaking now. Get me that spaghetti. I'm tired of this stuff! Talking about you don't serve colored people. Ain't I an American?

(OVERSEER *backs away.* OLD WOMAN *enters left as a picket carrying a sign that reads*

DON'T BUY HERE!
THIS STORE DOES NOT
EMPLOY NEGRO CLERKS

Slowly she walks back and forth in front of a store bearing the sign: MEAT MARKET. *The* OVERSEER *rushes out in the white apron of a Butcher*)

OVERSEER What you doing in front of my store? What I done to you? What for you walking up and down with that sign, destructing my business? Long as you trade with me, what is this?

OLD WOMAN You know what it is, Mr. Schultz! You know how long I been trading with you, don't you?

OVERSEER More'n ten years, Mrs. Brown.

OLD WOMAN And all that time, I ain't never seen a colored clerk in this store, not one. My boy growed up and went through high school, and to college, and got more education than you ever had, but when one of your clerks died, and my boy come here to ask you for a job, you said: "No, you might give him a little janitor's job, but you got to have a *white* clerk." (*loudly*) That's why I'm picketing out here, Mr. Schultz. Harlem is tired! No work! No money! I tell you, Harlem's tired!

(OLD WOMAN *brandishes her sign and the* BUTCHER *flees, to take off his apron and put on a coat and a pair of pince-nez glasses with a flowing black ribbon. He is the editor of a daily paper and carries a handful of proofs. The* YOUNG MAN *enters.*)

YOUNG MAN You're the editor of the *Daily Scribe*?

OVERSEER I am.

YOUNG MAN I wrote a letter to your paper more'n two weeks ago about the hard times we colored folks've been having, and you didn't print it. I wish you'd tell me how come?

OVERSEER Ah yes! I remember that letter. I'll tell you, boy, why we didn't print it. That letter would stir up trouble. I know times are hard, but you colored people have always been good citizens, peaceful and nice. Why get excited now? Just wait. Times'll be better—the Republicans will be in again soon. Believe in God, boy, in the good old stars and stripes, and be loyal to your country.

YOUNG MAN

But, Mr. Editor,
I've been loyal to my country
A long time, don't you see?
Now how about my country
Being loyal to me?

I fought in 1812 and 1863,
San Juan Hill in Cuba,
And for Democracy—
And fighting's not the only thing
I've done for liberty:
I've worked and worked a plenty,
Slave and free.

So when I pledge allegiance
To our flag so fair,
I keep looking at the stars and stripes
A-waving there,
And I'm wishing every star
Would *really* be a star for me,
And not just half a star
Like Jim Crow Tennessee—
And no false convict's stripes such as
Scottsboro's put on me.

I want that red and white and blue,
Mr. Editor,
To mean the same thing to me
As it does to you—
For I've been just as loyal
To my country as you have,
Don't you see?

Now, how about my country
Being loyal to me?

OVERSEER Why—er—uh—you're a radical!

(*Enter a* WHITE WORKER)

WHITE WORKER I don't think so!

OVERSEER Who're you?

WHITE WORKER A white worker. You don't have to be colored to know what hard times are. Or to want a square deal. I can tell you that!

OVERSEER Well, what do you want?

WHITE WORKER A world where there won't be no hard times. And no color line—labor with a white skin'll never be free as long as labor with a black skin's enslaved.

OVERSEER By God, you're a radical, too!

(WHITE WORKER *and* YOUNG MAN *shake hands*)

YOUNG MAN Friend, you understand.
WHITE WORKER I understand!
OVERSEER Radicals! Radicals! Lock 'em up! Lock 'em up! Radicals! Lock 'em up! Radicals! Radicals! (*exits, yelling loudly*)
YOUNG MAN Quiet, please—'cause Harlem is tired!
WHITE WORKER (*as he leaves with* YOUNG MAN) We're all tired!

(WIFE *enters left, broom in hand*)

WIFE Yes, we're tired! Tired as we can be! (WIFE *sweeps.* OVERSEER *removes glasses, puts on dark hat, carries a brief case, and is now an insurance man: goes to* WIFE *and knocks.*) Yes?
OVERSEER (*cockily*) Insurance man! Got your book ready?
WIFE You want me to pay you?
OVERSEER Of course. It's due, isn't it?
WIFE Um-hum! You from the Cosmopolitan Company, ain't you?
OVERSEER I am.
WIFE And you don't hire no colored folks in your office, do you?
OVERSEER Not so far as I know. Why?
WIFE You won't give colored people certain kinds of policies you carries, neither, will you?
OVERSEER Well, you see, in some cases your people are bad risks.
WIFE But my money's *good* money, ain't it?
OVERSEER Of course, it is.
WIFE And you want my money, don't you?
OVERSEER Why, yes. Of course, I do.
WIFE Well, you ain't gonna get it! (*fiercely*) A company that won't hire none of my people, what won't half insure us, and then sends a man to Harlem to collect from me that keeps his hat on in the house! (OVERSEER, *frightened, snatches off his hat*) Well, you ain't gonna get nary a penny of mine! Get out of here. Go on back downtown to your Jim Crow office. Tell 'em Harlem is tired. (*she shoos him out*) I'm gonna join a colored insurance company myself.

(*The* OVERSEER *flees. Panting, he sits down in a chair right and is now a laundry boss. He begins to pay out money, while several girls pass before him*)

MULATTO GIRL Chile, you better wrap up good. It's kinder chilly out there.
LAUNDRY WORKER Catch your death o' pneumonia, working all day in this steaming oven.
GIRL You told that right.
MULATTO GIRL I sure am glad it's pay day. Let's get in line here and get our money.
OVERSEER Here, Dorothy Mae! Here's your wages. Now don't get drunk tonight! . . . Here, Miss Lizzie, something for your preacher tomorrow. Now, behave yourself in church! Here! (*as a good looking* LAUNDRY WORKER *approaches him for her wages*) Say, Toots, uh, listen . . .
LAUNDRY WORKER Toots, who?
OVERSEER Why, er . . .
LAUNDRY WORKER Is this six dollars all you're giving me for a whole week's work in your laundry?
OVERSEER That's all you earned, girlie.
LAUNDRY WORKER Sixty hours in this steaming hole, and that's all I've earned? You must be crazy. I've ironed six hundred shirts this week, at least.
OVERSEER Well, six dollars is your salary.
LAUNDRY WORKER Then you take that salary and stick it on back in your drawer, from now on, 'cause I am tired of working for nothing. Harlem is tired. You're living in a big house up in White Plains, and me slaving all day for nothing in your laundry. You making all your money off of colored folks, and taking every dollar of it out of Harlem to spend. I'm tired.
OVERSEER (*jumping up*) You must belong to the union. You move on before I call the police. You're an agitator!
LAUNDRY WORKER What police? Some of these days *you're* going to have to move on, because Harlem is tired. Fact is, I think you ought to move now.
WIFE Yes, you ought to move!
BOY Get going!

(OVERSEER *clutches his money and rushes away. But he is surrounded by people, threatening him and crying in anger. The Harlem riots of March 19, 1935 begin*)

WOMAN Gouging me for rent!
BOY You won't serve colored people!
YOUNG MAN Won't gimme a job!
LAUNDRY WORKER Working us like slaves!

OLD MAN   Living on Harlem!
WOMAN   Getting rich off of black people.
YOUNG MAN   Jim Crow landlord!
WOMAN   Won't rent us a house downtown.
OLD MAN   Starving my children!
LAUNDRY WORKER   Get out of Harlem!
WIFE   Yes, get out of Harlem!
OVERSEER   (*trying to escape*) Help! Help me! Help! What have I done? Help me! (*blows police whistle*) Help! Help! Help! Help!
NEWSBOYS   (*from all directions, enter* NEWSBOYS *shouting*) Riot in Harlem! Negroes running riot! Riot! Read all about it! Riot! Riot! Riot! MARCH 19th RIOT IN HARLEM! RIOT IN HARLEM. Read all about it. HARLEM IS TIRED! Harlem's tired!
WOMAN   (*as the siren dies down. Quietly*) Harlem is tired.
BOY   Yes, Harlem's tired.
LAUNDRY WORKER   Harlem is tired!
YOUNG MAN   You understand, folks? Harlem's tired.
MEMBER OF AUDIENCE   (*rising*) But say?
YOUNG MAN   Yes?
MEMBER OF AUDIENCE   Riots won't solve anything, will they, brother?
YOUNG MAN   No, riots won't solve anything.
MEMBER OF AUDIENCE   Then what must we do?
YOUNG MAN   Organize.
MEMBER OF AUDIENCE   With who?
YOUNG MAN   With the others who suffer like me and you.
LAUNDRY WORKER   Organize with the laundry workers, then.
WOMAN   Organize with the tenants' leagues.
BOY   Organize with the students' unions.
YOUNG MAN   Colored and white unions to lift us all up together.
MEMBER OF AUDIENCE   You mean organize with white folks, too?
YOUNG MAN   That's what I mean! We're all in the same boat! This is America, isn't it? It's not all colored. Not all white. It's both.
MEMBER OF AUDIENCE   You mean organize with that white waiter who won't serve you? Organize with him?
YOUNG MAN   Yes, I mean with that waiter, too. His problem's the same as ours—if he only knew it.
MEMBER OF AUDIENCE   Well, they ought to hurry up and find out then! Some of 'em won't even let us in their unions. Yet we're all workers! Let the white workers learn to stop discriminating against us, if they want us with 'em.
YOUNG MAN   Right! They've got to learn. And we must teach them. But when they do learn, and black and white really get together, what power in the world can stop us from getting what we want?
BOY   Nothing!
WOMAN   That's right!
WIFE   You tell 'em!
YOUNG MAN   Right! They've got to learn— but there are some who know already, and they've organized unions that are strong and growing.
MEMBER OF AUDIENCE   Who are they?
YOUNG MAN   The Auto Workers of Detroit. (*enter a Negro and a white,* AUTO WORKERS) The Sharecroppers of the South. (*enter a white and black,* SHARECROPPERS) The Miners of Birmingham. (*enter two* MINERS, *one white and one colored*) The Stevedores of the West Coast. (*enter a black* STEVEDORE *and a white* STEVEDORE) And others, too. I know—not yet enough, but they are learning. And when we do learn, and black and white really get together, what power in the world can stop us from getting what we want?
BOY   Nothing!
WOMAN   That's right!
WIFE   You tell 'em!
YOUNG MAN   Tomorrow belongs to the workers, and I'm a worker!
WOMAN   I am, too!
OLD MAN   And me!
LAUNDRY WORKER   Me, too!
MEMBER OF AUDIENCE   And me! I get your point. (*sits down*)
YOUNG MAN   Good! We're Negro workers! Listen! This is what we're going to say to all other workers, just this: I, a Negro, offer you my hand. I offer you my strength and power. Together, we can make America a land where all of us are free from poverty and oppression and where no man or woman need ever be hungry, cold, or kept down again. White worker, here is my hand. Today we're man to man.
MAN   White worker, here's my hand.
BOY   Here's my hand.
LAUNDRY WORKER   (*speaking*)

Who wants to come and join hands with me?
Who wants to make one great unity?
Who wants to say no more black or white?
Then let's get together, folks,
And fight, fight, fight!

ENTIRE CAST (*singing*)

Who wants to come and join hands with me?
Who wants to make one great unity?
Who wants to say no more black or white?
Then let's get together folks,
And fight, fight, fight!

Who wants to make America a land
Where opportunity is free to every man?
Who wants to test the power of the worker's might?
Then let's get together, folks,
And fight, fight, fight!

Who wants to make Harlem great and fine?
Make New York City a guiding light to shine?
Who wants, to lead the workers toward the light?
Then let's get together, folks,
And fight, fight, fight!

(*As they sing the audience joins with them, and various members of the audience, workers, doctors, nurses, professional men, teachers, white and black, come forward to link hands with the characters in the play until the players and the audience are one*)

Oh, who wants to come and join hands with me?
Who wants to make one great unity?
Who wants to say, no more black or white?
Then let's get together, folks,
And fight, fight, fight!

Theodore Ward (1902–)

Big White Fog
1938

America's second largest black community, in which a million black people live, is Chicago. Blacks make up one fourth of the population, concentrated on the South Side. They work in transportation, the stockyards, the meat-packing plants, the steel mills of Gary. In the city immortalized by Carl Sandburg as a brutal giant, in a city legendary for its police brutality and corruption, the strong survival spirit of the black family has been captured in three plays: *Big White Fog*, *Native Son*, and *Raisin in the Sun*.

Theodore Ward sets the climactic last half of *Big White Fog* in the depths of the Depression, the Chicago of 1932. In order to show how his characters made poor preparation for survival, he begins his play in the decade before, in 1922, at the height of Marcus Garvey's Universal Negro Improvement Association.

In the five years from 1916 (when Marcus Garvey arrived in America from Jamaica) to 1921, Garvey built the UNIA into the largest black organization America had ever seen—2 million dues-paying members and 6 million world-wide followers. He bought Liberty Hall in Harlem for his mass meetings. He established a weekly newspaper, the *Negro World*. He incorporated a steamship line and bought three vessels. A combination of reasons contributed to his success. First was the appeal of his four-point program:

1. to bring together the Negroes of the world into one solid and indissoluble body.
2. to relieve Africa of Anglo-Saxon oppression and domination.
3. to build Africa industrially and commercially, to establish schools and other educational institutions.
4. to promote and encourage agriculture so that Africa within the next few years may be the commercial and agricultural center of the world.

Coupled with this was the appeal of his own messianic personality and his genius for public relations. As Provisional President of Africa, Mr. Garvey created the Court of Ethiopia, in which he conferred titles (Count Strawder). He commissioned officers in uniform (Captain Mason). Women joined as Black Cross nurses. Classes were held for children in Negro history, etiquette, military tactics and race pride. Brown and black dolls were manufactured. Christ was declared the "Black Man of Sorrows," and the Virgin Mary a Black Woman. Only "100 per cent Negroid" people could hold office.

The UNIA appealed to the masses of blacks at the bottom of the economy as the Urban League, NAACP, and others never had. The returning veterans of World War I were disillusioned by what they had experienced in the service and by what they found at home. The large number of laborers migrating from the South to the northern industrial cities found increasing discrimination. In 1919, the "red summer," there were twenty-six racial rebellions in American cities. There was a need in the black populace to know that it was to inherit a homeland, that black was beautiful. Marcus Garvey offered hope and pride.

In addition to the general mood and times, Theodore Ward uses two specific incidents from the Garvey saga: The failure of the Black Star Steamship Line and the imprisonment of Marcus Garvey.

In 1921, Marcus Garvey wrote in the *Negro World*,

we are asking you again to support the great industrial enterprise of the Black Star Line Corporation, the desire of which is to float ships on the seven seas, to carry the commerce of the Negro from country to country and make him one of the great industrial captains of the age. You can support the Black Star Line by buying shares at $500 each.

The Line bought three used ships, all in poor condition. The Garvey group was taken by white agents, who exploited the fact that the

Line had no experience in marine purchase and maintenance. The first vessel, the *Yarmouth*—renamed the *Frederick Douglass*—was purchased for $165,000. Loaded with whiskey for Cuba, it broke down before it could leave the New York harbor.

In 1923 the federal government, pressured by a group of Negroes whose motivation may have ranged from jealousy of Mr. Garvey's success to a genuine concern that the black people were being bilked, indicted the President of the Black United States for using the mails to defraud. He was convicted and sentenced to five years. In 1925 he lost his appeal and was sent to Atlanta Federal Penitentiary. Two years later, he was pardoned and deported by President Coolidge, a man whose campaign Mr. Garvey had supported.

Theodore Ward uses the Garvey events as a vehicle to represent the success and the failure of black nationalism. Against nationalism he sets Dan, the brother-in-law, a black capitalist. Mr. Ward demonstrates that both philosophies fail the Negro in a crisis. A third approach—socialism/communism—is proposed as the correct path.

Big White Fog received its first production in 1938, by the Chicago unit of the Federal Theater, where it ran for ten weeks. In 1970 Mr. Ward in a letter to this editor, wrote:

There was considerable opposition to the play being produced because it seemed to advocate Communism, when despite my own political outlook at the time, in writing the play I had only sought to present the objective reality as an alternative to the situation and conditions of Victor Mason and his family. Happily, Mrs. Hallie Flanagan supported my aim for artistic integrity, so that the play was finally produced ... without adverse criticism from the press.

Incidentally, despite the fact that the Chicago production continued to show a large profit at the box office, the local officials of Federal Theater transferred the play to a local high school under the guise of making it more available to the Negro public, for four performances, after which it was closed. Thus, I take it that the play never had a chance on its merits.

In 1940 the Negro Playwrights Company was formed in Harlem. Its purpose was to reflect the realities of Negro life, and to provide a working theater for Negro artists. Langston Hughes, Powell Lindsay, Owen Dodson, Theodore Browne, George Norford, and Theodore Ward were active members of the Board of Directors. Associate members were Paul Robeson, Richard Wright, Edna Thomas, Max Yergan, Gwendolyn Bennett, Rev. John Robinson, Alain Locke, and George B. Murphy, Jr.

Big White Fog premiered on October 22, 1940 at the Lincoln Theater, on 135th Street and Lenox Avenue; it ran sixty-four performances. The cast included Canada Lee, Hilda Offley, Frank Silvera, and Lionel Monagas (who had played the lead in Garland Anderson's *Appearances* in 1925). Perry Watkins designed the setting. Powell Lindsay directed.

The major newspaper reviewers predictably praised the performers and the seriousness of the Negro Playwrights Company, but they condemned the play for its debate, its communism—in brief, its political nature. In his letter Mr. Ward stated:

The Negro Playwrights production in New York was condemned by the critics there, probably because the intellectual climate had changed following the Hitler–Stalin pact. In any case, the most truthful thing I remember is that the contrast was a bitter experience for me.

White critic Brooks Atkinson also found that color prejudice was "ugliest when it exists between members of the Negro race."

In 1940 it remained for black critic Ralph Ellison writing in *Sights and Sounds*, to see the value of the play:

In its three act attempt to probe the most vital problems of Negro experience, *Big White Fog* is like no other Negro play. The author takes a movement which has been passed off as a ludicrous effort by Negroes to ape British royalty and reveals in it that dignity of human groping which is characteristic of all oppressed peoples.

The playwrights have shown their willingness to accept the implications of Negro life and make them the stuff of their writings. How correct they are is witnessed by V. J. Jerome, who, in commenting on the play, stated that "Seldom in literature or on stage has the inner dignity of an oppressed people struggling to affirm its nationhood risen so indestructibly, so magnificently as in the Negro family portrayed in *Big White Fog*."

In 1938 Langston Hughes saw that the play was unusual. He wrote, "It is the greatest encompassing play on Negro life that has ever been written. If it isn't liked by people, it is because they are not ready for it, not because it isn't a great play."

The three ideologies in the play from which the black characters can choose are still alive today: nationalism (Muslims), socialism (Panthers), Negro business encouragement (U. S. Government's Black capitalism gestures). Have the issues changed?

Big White Fog

CHARACTERS

VICTOR MASON, *a Garveyite leader*
ELLA, *his wife*
LESTER ⎫
WANDA ⎬ *their children*
CAROLINE
PHILLIP ⎭
DANIEL ROGERS, *their brother-in-law*
JUANITA, *Ella's sister, his wife*
MARTHA BROOKS, *mother of Ella and Juanita*
PERCY MASON, *brother of Victor*
CLAUDINE, *friend of Wanda's*
NATHAN PISZER, *a Jewish student*
MARX, *a Jewish used-furniture man*
COUNT STRAWDER ⎫
COUNT COTTON ⎬ *Garveyites*
BROTHER HARPER ⎭
BLACK CROSS NURSES
BAILIFFS, POLICEMEN, WHITE AND NEGRO WORKERS, AMBULANCE ATTENDANTS

ACT ONE

Scene One

(*Living-room of the* MASONS, *in Dearborn Street, Chicago.*

TIME: *an afternoon in August, 1922.*

It is a large, congenial room, bearing the tell-marks of use polished by care, and indicating that people of means once lived there.

On the left, a large window with stained glass above and a window seat below. Beyond it, in the corner, is a hall-tree, and next to the latter, the front door with a transom of stained glass of the same pattern.

Against the rear wall, a flight of stairs leading to the upper floor. Downstage right, a door leads into the kitchen and dining room.

There is a couch in the center with an overstuffed chair to the left of it, and behind it is an oblong table, against the stairway. A typewriter is on the table with a small chair at the left end of it.

A Victrola is against the right wall. Downstage left is another easy-chair, and beyond it, near the window, is a rocking chair, commanding a view of Fifty-first Street as it intersects Dearborn Street.

A Postman's whistle sounds, and ELLA appears from the rear, going to the door where she retrieves a letter from the mail-box outside. As she reenters, she stands fingering the letter and immersed in thought—a buxom mulatto, aged about 38, and wearing a cool housedress which accentuates her general air of renunciation.)

JUANITA (*entering, unceremoniously behind her*) Hello, Ella.

ELLA (*startled*) Oh! Juanita—You liked to scared me to death—What storm blew you to Dearborn Street?

JUANITA (*a good looking mulatto, slender and smartly dressed—she has a decided verve of manner and vigor of speech*) Oh, I just thought I'd drop by to see how you all were—(*she turns to the mirror of the hall-tree in the corner behind her*) What's that you got there, a notice from your landlord?

ELLA (*tossing letter on table beneath stairway*) No. It's for Les. Must be the answer about his scholarship.

JUANITA (*coming down*) No! (*happily*) You know. I'd almost forgotten about him winning that scholarship!

ELLA (*going into rear*) Well, you wouldn've if you lived around here.

JUANITA (*sitting on arm of couch and looking off right*) I suppose not—But I hope it's good news.

ELLA (*returning with pan of green peas, which she takes to couch and begins to shell*) They've kept him in suspense long enough—Did you bring Mama's pattern?

JUANITA Lord, no! I knew there was something I was forgetting—Where is she?

ELLA Gone to the park. She took the children out for a breath of air.

JUANITA If you had any sense you'd make Vic take a flat near the park.

ELLA You know we can't afford the rent, Juanita.

JUANITA You could if you made Vic go into partnership with Dan.

ELLA (*wearily*) It's no use starting that talk again. Vic's made up his mind he's going to Africa, and there's nothing short of the voice of God likely to change him.

JUANITA (*sarcastically*) Ha! Ten years from today he'll still be in Chicago, carrying his hod.

ELLA They've got over four million paid-up members!

JUANITA (*searching for ash-tray*) That's a lot of bunk! Nothing but bunk to catch more suckers like Vic.

ELLA Vic's in the know, and he wouldn't lie to me. They've just made him a captain in the African Legionnaires.

JUANITA (*with an outburst of laughter*) Captain in the African Legionaires—That's a good one!

ELLA Stop your silly laughing. Vic's nobody's fool.

JUANITA No? He's being taken for a ride just like the rest.

ELLA That's all you know about it.

JUANITA (*pointedly*) You don't see any of our really big people falling for Marcus Garvey's jive, do you?

ELLA (*loyally*) They're too jealous of his power! They don't like it because the masses are with him.

JUANITA You mean they've got too much sense to let a monkey-chasing mountebank like him come over here and jive them out of their cold cash!

ELLA You make me sick—You can't see anything but money.

JUANITA No. You're quite right, my dear. But I don't make any pretense about it.

ELLA Is that an insinuation?

JUANITA Ella, you know damn well, if Vic was in the money, neither of you would give a damn about Africa.

ELLA I haven't lived with Vic nineteen years for nothing. He's interested in the race.

JUANITA Yeah. Then he ought to be trying to do something for it here—like going in with Dan and opening that Kitchenette—our people are crying for decent places to live, and they'll pay good money for the privilege.

ELLA Vic's planning to buy shares in the Black Star Line—

JUANITA (*laughing*) The Black Star Line—Why that's the biggest joke Marcus Garvey ever thought of—Where're they going to get men to run it?

ELLA From the West Indies—

JUANITA (*groaning*) Oh, my God... (*the door opens, and* CAROLINE, *seeing her aunt, dashes down*)

CAROLINE Aunt Juanita! I didn't know you was here!

JUANITA Was?

(PHILIP *enters—He is a little black boy of 10*)

CAROLINE Were—(*she is a child of 12, with long braids and copper-colored skin*)

JUANITA (*to* PHILLIP) Why haven't you been to see Aunt Juanita lately?

PHILLIP (*bouncing his ball*) We was over there last Wednesday, but you wasn't home—

JUANITA Aunt Juanita is a pretty busy woman, Honey—You should call me up and let me know when you're coming—(*Seeing her mother, as Phillip's ball gets away from him and he dashes behind couch to retrieve it*) Hello, Mama—

BROOKS (*coming down, brusquely*) Move, Caroline! Lemme get off these feet! (*a somewhat wizened mulatto, aged about 60, she is much spryer than she pretends*)

JUANITA (*as mother takes chair center*) How're you feeling?

BROOKS Them chillun jes 'bout wore me out, and what with the walk back from the park, I'm jes 'bout dead, I 'spect.

PHILLIP (*joining his mother on couch*) Grandma's been playing ball.

ELLA Playing ball?

PHILLIP Yes'm.—We had a lot of fun, didn't we, Grandma?

JUANITA Are you trying to kill yourself, Mama?

BROOKS Now you all jes let me 'lone—(*sharply*). And you get out of here, Phillip, with your big mouth.

ELLA You'll be laid up for a week—Why didn't you take the street car back, like I told you?

BROOKS (*to* JUANITA, *ignoring other*) Did you bring me mah pattern back?
JUANITA I forgot it, Mama. But I'll get Les to bring it tomorrow.
BROOKS Jes like I figgered. You so busy runnin' round with your bobbed-hair, and playin' cards, you can't remember nothin'. I told you I needed that pattern so I could make Wanda's waist 'fore school opens!
JUANITA Oh, calm yourself, Mama. You'll get it.
CAROLINE Mama, may I have a slice of bread and butter?
PHILLIP (*springing up*) Me, too, Mama?
ELLA It's pretty near time for your dinner. But I reckon so—(*as they run out rear*) And don't take but one apiece neither!
JUANITA (*playfully*) What's this, Mama, I hear about you planning to go to Africa?
BROOKS (*disgustedly*) Don't you mention no Africa to me, I'm sick o' hearin' it!
ELLA Yes, for God's sake, Juanita; don't get her started.
JUANITA Didn't you just tell me, Vic's made up his mind to go?
BROOKS (*vigorously*) And I reckon you think cause I'm poor and can't help myself I got to go, hanh? Well, don't fool yourself. I ain't no Affikan; I'm a Dupree! I was born in this country and I'm goin' die in it, Vic or no Vic!
ELLA (*exasperatedly*) Mama, nobody's trying to make you go anywhere!
BROOKS No, and they better not be. I done let that black crank root me up once with his fool talk 'bout we goin' find freedom up here in the North. But he ain't goin' 'suade me again. I'se too old for another transplantin'.
ELLA I guess you'd both rather be in Mississippi picking cotton—?
JUANITA Chicago's one thing but Africa's another.
BROOKS Yes, Lawd!
JUANITA Vic'd forget that stuff too, Mama—If it wasn't for her encouraging him, like a fool!
BROOKS (*sighing*) She ain't got mah blood in her veins—No Dupree would-er thought 'bout marryin' sich a *black* crank in the first place.
ELLA (*angrily*) You and your Dupree blood! You make me sick.—Furthermore, I've warned you. I'm sick of your flaunting Vic's color in my face—And especially when Phillip may hear you! And I'm not going to tell you again—
JUANITA (*seeing* LES *through window*) Drop it, Ella—Here comes Les.
ELLA Never mind. I mean what I say. If Vic's good enough to live on, you'll respect him—
LES (*entering, he sees his aunt as he tosses his baseball glove on table*) Hello, Aunt Juanita! (*he is light brown, about 20, in a white shirt and corduroy slacks*)
JUANITA Hi, Les!
ELLA (*excitedly*) Your letter's here!
LES My letter—Where? (*he dives for table*)
BROOKS What letter?
JUANITA From his scholarship.
LES (*nervously, fingering letter*) This is it! This is it, all right—Lawd, I wonder if the stuff is here . . .
JUANITA You'll never know, silly, unless you read it.
BROOKS No, he won't.
LES Jesus—You don't suppose—
ELLA Open it, Les.
LES All right. I'm going to—(*he opens letter*)
JUANITA What does it say?
ELLA Yes. Read it aloud so we all can hear—
LES (*dancing a gig*) Hot dog! Hot ziggedy damn! (*hugging his aunt*) Oh, boy, oh boy!
ELLA If you don't stop your foolishness and read that letter, Lester Mason, I'll pick up something and brain you!
LES Wait, Mama. Just listen to this: (*reading, excitedly*) "Jason Scholarship Fund . . . Copeland Technical Institute—"
ELLA (*impatiently*) Oh, skip all that!
LES (*going on*) "My dear Mr. Mason . . . I have just returned from abroad to find your application for appointment as a Jason Scholar of Chemistry in the Copeland Technical Institute, and likewise the letter of Principal Horace Judson, confirming your record and recommending you for the award—"
JUANITA Does that mean you get it?
LES He says it's up to the Board—But listen: (*reading*) "This, however, is of little consequence, since we shall be meeting again in a day or so, when considering the high quality of your performance in chemistry, I am convinced favorable action will be taken; so that you can be with us this Fall . . . Yours truly, Rothmore C. Galen, Chairman, The Jason Scholarship Fund."

JUANITA Well, that is something!
ELLA I'm so glad, Les. (*her eyes brim and she wipes away a tear of joy*)
BROOKS Don't seem to say a thing to me.
JUANITA It means he's certain to go to college, Mama.
BROOKS Seems like a mighty poor way of saying it.
LES (*hugging her*) That's just the way big men write, Grandma. (*she shakes him off*)
JUANITA And you say it's for four years, Les?
LES If my marks are good.
ELLA Your father will be tickled to death.
JUANITA Who wouldn't be. (*pointedly*) It should make him see this country in a better light.
LES Oh, Papa's all right. I won't be the first Negro to receive a scholarship—(*catching sight of* WANDA—*his very pretty mulatto sister—he joins her*) What d'you think, Wanda? I just got an answer from my application!
WANDA You mean about your scholarship?
LES Yah. Looks like I'm Copeland bound.
ELLA (*as* WANDA *goes to table to examine mail, her attitude belying the happiness of the others as well as the fact she's only seventeen*) Well, can't you say anything?
WANDA (*turning, embarrassed*) I was just thinking, Mama—(*quickly*) But I'm glad you got it, Les. I knew you would—When do you leave?
LES (*bringing her to chair*) I don't know yet. Everything's not really settled. Here—(*gives her letter*) Read it for yourself.
JUANITA (*as* WANDA *reads*) If it's for four years, Les—(*impishly*) your father'll have to leave you here, won't he?
LES (*puzzled*) What d' you mean, Aunt?
JUANITA (*laughing*) He's going to Africa, isn't he?
ELLA Oh, stop teasing him, Juanita—And, Les. It's time for you to be getting out on your route.
LES Lord, Mama. I had completely forgotten my papers! (*going*) See you all later. (*suddenly turning back to* WANDA) Give me that—(*to all*) And don't you all say anything to Papa, will you? I want to surprise him. (*exit running*)
ELLA All right. We won't.
BROOKS He sure is tickled pink.

JUANITA With a fine break like that, he'll be a big man someday.
BROOKS (*sourly*) Yeah. If he don't turn out like his Pa.
ELLA (*to* WANDA) Perhaps, you'll win one this year.
JUANITA There's no reason why she shouldn't with the brain she's got.
WANDA (*drily*) Thanks, Aunt. But I'm not interested in any scholarship.
ELLA What do you mean?
WANDA (*rising and going*) Oh, nothing.
ELLA (*arresting her*) Don't tell me. You did mean something?
JUANITA Yes, she did. (*to* WANDA) Surely, you aren't jealous of your own brother?
WANDA (*sarcastically*) Jealous! Don't kid me, Aunt Juanita. Les is perfectly welcome to the scholarship.
ELLA You don't act like it.
JUANITA She certainly doesn't. I've been watching her ever since she came in.
WANDA What am I supposed to do, shed tears over it?
JUANITA You ought to be proud to see him get such a break.
WANDA It's a fine break all right—Marvelous—Splendid! (*bitterly*) When he gets out of school, maybe they'll give him a job on the dining-car figuring out how many calories there are in the average bowl of soup!
ELLA Wanda!
JUANITA Well, did you ever!
WANDA You needn't pretend to be so astonished, either of you—
JUANITA (*sharply*) Why you're crazy. The field of chemistry is wide open to our people—Look at Doctor Carver!
WANDA Yeah, Doctor Carver! One out of a million! But what about Papa? Tuskeegee graduate, carrying a hod! And Uncle Dan, Butler's Black Pride, wearing a Kappa Key on a pullman car! I've heard him say himself, they must've given it to him to open the berths with!
ELLA (*feebly*) Your father was educated to be a farmer.
WANDA That's it. He's a farmer, but where's his farm?
JUANITA (*hesitantly*) But. But your Uncle Dan's working for a point.
WANDA They're both just kidding themselves. (*going*) But I'm not going to—(*turning to*

ELLA) And you might as well know it right now, Mama. I'm not going back to school!

ELLA (*indignantly*) Is that so? Since when did you get big enough to tell me to my face what you're not going to do?

BROOKS She needs slapping down!

WANDA I'm no longer a child, Grandma!

BROOKS You hear that, Ella! (*outraged*) Oh, if you was only mine. I'd take you down a button hole lower.

WANDA But I happen not to be yours, Grandma!

BROOKS Ella, are you goin' stand there and let her sassy me like this?

ELLA (*jerking* WANDA *around*) Stop your impudence and answer me!

WANDA (*belligerently*) Well, you had to know sooner or later. I'm sick of school, and there's no use in your trying to send me back.

ELLA (*nonplussed*) Well!

JUANITA But, Wanda. If you quit school, you won't even be able to make a decent marriage.

WANDA I'm not interested in marriage. I'm going to work.

JUANITA And what kind of job do you suppose you're going to find?

WANDA I've already got one.

ELLA Doing what?

WANDA Claudine's going to get me on with her... as soon as the other girl goes back to school.

ELLA (*incredulously*) In the drugstore?

WANDA Yes. The boss has already told me I'll do. I'm the type.

JUANITA (*contemptuously, in outrage*) Jerking soda! My own niece meeting every tramp who takes a notion to buy a bottle of pop!

BROOKS I warned you, Ella. I told you 'bout lettin' her run round with that fast Claudine!

JUANITA Can't you see if you go on, you could at least teach school?

WANDA Teach school! Aunt, you make me laugh!

ELLA What's wrong with that?

WANDA It's Jim Crow, that's what—even if you ever do get an appointment.

JUANITA But a drugstore?—Why, why it's ridiculous, positively ridiculous!

WANDA I don't care. I've as much right to nice things as anyone else. If I go to work I can get them.

ELLA So you think you've been neglected, hunh? I'd like to know who you think around here looks any better than you do?

BROOKS Nobody. There ain't a girl on this street looks any better.

WANDA Yeah. I'm right on Dearborn Street. But alongside the girls over East I look like mud.

JUANITA But I always try to help you, don't I?

WANDA Yes. And I thank you, Aunt Juanita. But I'm tired of wearing your castoff things.

JUANITA (*shocked*) Well...!

WANDA I meant no offense, Aunt. But in two months I'll be full grown woman, and I'm going to live!

BROOKS What do you mean you "goin' live?"

WANDA (*going*) Oh, you wouldn't understand, Grandma.

BROOKS (*cutting her off, boiling*) No. I'm too old, you little hussey. I ain't got sense enough to understand. But it might surprise you to know, you pigheaded little wench, I said them same words to mah Mammy fore yours was born!

WANDA (*going*) Then I don't see why you asked.

ELLA (*arresting her as she starts out*) Maybe Mother's just a back number, too, Darling. But she'd like to know?

WANDA (*animatedly*) Get some joy out of life, Mama! Have clothes and be able to go places and do things, like Uncle Percy!

BROOKS (*disgustedly*) The drunken bum. Your Uncle Percy's a disgrace to the family—Do you think just because he wears good clothes and sleeps in the cabarets, he's livin'?

WANDA At least he's not kidding himself like the rest of the family. He knows there's nothing for us in this country—And the white folks proved it, too; when they ripped his uniform off his back when he came home from France!

JUANITA You can't hold all the white people guilty for the act of a few hoodlums! And it's no excuse for his throwing himself away!

WANDA That's your idea. But Uncle Percy's living so when he gets old, he won't have anything to regret.

ELLA Nothing to regret, hunh?—You just wait till your father hears of this.

WANDA Let him. There's nothing in this country for a Negro girl to look forward to, and you know it as well as I. I'm going to make it for myself, and you and Papa might as well get used to the idea. Because whether you like it or not, I'm going to live my own life—(*she goes as* MASON *enters front door*) even if I have to leave here! (*she runs out*)

VIC (*a tall, very black man, dressed in an old suit, his hands stained with mortar—but his dignified bearing and keen eyes show him to be a man of considerable intelligence and character. He turns to* ELLA) What's the matter with her?

ELLA Nothing, Vic.

JUANITA (*grimly*) It's no use procrastinating, Ella. You might as well settle it right now.

VIC (*curious*) Wanda's not in trouble, is she?

BROOKS No. But if you don't watch out she's goin' be!

VIC Ella, what is this?

ELLA Wanda's going to quit school.

VIC Is that so?

ELLA Yes. She tried her best to lay me out. Says she's tired of wearing other people's castoff things, and is going to work so she can *live*!

VIC (*going to hall-tree to hang hat*) Well, I don't see anything to get excited about. Let her quit.

ELLA (*shocked*) Let her quit! You mean that?

VIC Sure. What difference does it make? They're only filling her head with a stack of white folks' lies anyway.

JUANITA White folks' lies!

VIC Yes, white folks' lies. There isn't a word of truth about the black man in all her books put together!

BROOKS If that don't prove you's cranky-headed, I donno what will.

ELLA (*to him*) Have you lost your reason?

VIC Ella, I see exactly what I'm talking about.

ELLA Oh, you do? (*seeing* CAROLINE *and* PHILLIP *entering*) Go get ready for your dinner—(*as the children ascend stairs, she continues bitterly*) Well, you just go right ahead. Let her quit. She's yours. Let her ruin herself. Let her slide down to hell!

JUANITA Now you're talking, Ella—Any father in his right mind—

VIC (*sharply*) Now, wait a minute, both of you. Give me a moment to explain—and I promise you—

ELLA (*furious*) I don't want to hear any explanations, or promises either—I've had enough of them.—"A stack of lies"—the whole world's a stack of lies! You brought me out of the South with one—You and your fine talk about freedom and giving the children a chance to be somebody!

VIC (*injuredly*) I'm sorry you feel that way about it, Ella. I know I haven't done all I promised. But you could at least give me credit for my effort—

ELLA I'll get a lot of comfort out of that!

VIC But, I'm still trying, Ella. What do you think I'm carrying a hod by day and wrestling in the movement all night for? Wanda's just reached the point where she sees what we're up against in this country. (*turning to the stairs*) Be patient a little longer. (*halting as he starts up*) We'll soon be out of this rut and on our way to Africa. I can see her now, like a mother weeping for her long lost children, calling to us, "come home." Soon, and it won't be long now. You're going to see the black man come out of the darkness of failure into the light of achievement with the cloak of human greatness about his shoulders... Yes, Lord! And our enemies shall tremble when he stretches forth his mighty hand to gather in his share of the God-given stars of glory! (*leaving them spellbound, he disappears with dignity above*)

ELLA (*helplessly*) What can you do with a man like that?

(*Curtain.*)

Scene Two

(TIME: *afternoon, a week later.*

LES *is observed seated in the window, reading a book. In a moment* PERCY *descends wearing a gaudy silk dressing gown*)

PERCY (*a handsome brown man, he stretches like a panther as he reaches the floor, and comes out of it with a grunt*) Phumph! Reading again, hunh?

LES Yep.

PERCY That's all you ever do... (*going out rear*) You're getting to be a regular sissy. (*returning shortly with glass of water*) Where's everybody?

LES Out, I guess—Except Wanda. Mama and Grandma went shopping.

PERCY (*takes pint of gin from pocket of robe and places it on end table of couch*) I gotta have some ginger ale.

LES Caroline and Phillip are out there playing.

PERCY (*crosses to window to call*) Phillip! . . . Come here a minute, will you? (*takes coin from pocket and sits on couch*)

PHILLIP (*entering*) Whatchu want, Uncle Percy?

PERCY (*giving him coin*) Here. Run get me a bottle of ginger ale. And hurry now—(PHILLIP *runs out*) Lawd, my head feels like a keg of nails. (*he pours drink then goes to table to search through papers*) Umph. No mail! (*goes back to couch to drink liquor and chase it with water*) What kind of a book did you say that was?

LES I didn't say.

PERCY (*sharply*) No! Well, what kind is it, then—love story?

LES No. It's a book Papa gave me.

PERCY Yeah—What's the name of it?

LES "Looking Backward" by Edward Bellamy.

PERCY Never heard of it.

LES No. It isn't likely.

PERCY Now just what did you mean by that crack?

LES Nothing, Uncle Percy—Only it's not exactly a novel.

PERCY (*rising and going to window*) Oh, What kind is it, then?

LES It's a book on Socialism.

PERCY What?

LES (*smiling*) Surprised?

PERCY (*disgustedly*) Socialism! You're going to keep on till your Daddy makes a nut out of you yet. (*going back to couch*) Have you heard anymore from the school?

LES Not yet. But I ought to get a letter any day now.

PERCY Do you think you'll get it?

LES You mean the letter or the scholarship?

PERCY The scholarship!

LES I don't see any reason why I shouldn't. I got an "A" out of the course.

PERCY (*pouring another drink*) I don't know what good it'll do you, from what I've seen of the rest of the educated bigshots in the family. But I guess you'll need clothes. You can have that pin-striped grey suit of mine and the brown you say you like so well.

LES (*unbelievingly*) Awh, you're kidding me, Uncle Percy!

PERCY You got to tog down if you want to go places—

LES Hot pajamas!

PERCY You got to make appearances—If I have any luck at the hotel this week, I'll set you up to a new one. With the three you ought to be sharp as a tack when you hit that campus.

LES (*overjoyed*) Lord, Lord, are you telling me!

(PHILLIP *enters with ginger ale*)

PERCY You sure took your time.

PHILLIP They was busy. (*he offers change*)

PERCY (*magnanimously waving change away*) That's all right.

PHILLIP (*gleefully, running out*) Thank you, Uncle Percy!

CLAUDINE (*entering, encountering boy*) Hey! Look out! (*exit* PHILLIP)

LES Oh, hello, Claudine!

CLAUDINE Hi! (*she is a very pretty mulatto of 18 wearing a summer frock*) Wanda home?

LES Yes—I'll call her. (*he runs upstairs, as she saunters in, suddenly determined to try her wiles on the older man*)

CLAUDINE What're you doing, Uncle Percy—having a ball all by yourself?

PERCY Just trying to give my aching head a break—Have a . . . er some ginger ale?

CLAUDINE (*laughing slyly*) Don't play me cheap, Big Boy. I've been around!

PERCY (*amused*) Oh, you have!

CLAUDINE I saw you in the Dreamland last week—and were you *high*!

PERCY (*surprised*) You, in the Dreamland—?

CLAUDINE Sure—Only—

PERCY Only what?

CLAUDINE Oh, the kids I run with only go for the noteriety—Three highballs and they pass out.

PERCY (*slyly probing*) Sure 'nough! Can't Wanda take it either?

CLAUDINE Wanda's too scared to go anywhere—but why don't you take me sometime?

PERCY Me take you cabereting?

CLAUDINE What's the matter—(*laughing petulantly*) Ain't I hot enough for you? (*suddenly whirling like a model*)

PERCY Oh, sure.

CLAUDINE You don't act like it.

PERCY You're too young for me, Kid. I'm a tough Papa.

CLAUDINE (*resting her knee on chair center*) I'm nineteen, almost—And don't think I can't take care of myself!

PERCY You're a keen little chick, all right. But you'd better give Les a break.

CLAUDINE I can't be bothered with the cradle—(*laughing as she sees* WANDA *descending*) Hi, kiddo! Are you ready?

(VIC *enters in his good suit.*)

WANDA Yes. (*greeting father*) Hello, Papa.

VIC Well, you're certainly looking cool, Claudine—How's your folks?

CLAUDINE Quite well, thank you.

WANDA Papa, Claudine and I are going to Thirty-fifth Street.

VIC Well, be sure you're back in time for dinner.

WANDA (*going*) OK, Papa.

CLAUDINE (*saucily*) Don't forget what I told you, Uncle Percy. (*exit with* WANDA)

WANDA (*as they disappear*) What's this between you and my Uncle?

VIC (*indicating gin*) At it again, hunh?

PERCY Take it easy, Captain—

(*Outside,* DAN *is heard exchanging greetings with girls*)

DAN (*appearing in front door*) Well, how's everybody?

VIC Just fine, Dan. And how're you?

DAN (*coming downstage, a stocky brown man aged about 37, immaculately groomed*) Never felt better nor had less in my life. (*seeing* LES *descending*) I hear you're fixing to leave us, Les.

LES Not for sure, Uncle Dan. I haven't received the final word yet.

DAN You'll get it. The thing for you to do now is get yourself in the right frame of mind to make the best of your chance.

PERCY You needn't worry about him—(*offering drink*) Have a little snort?

DAN (*taking chair*) No, thanks. I haven't time for that stuff these days. Furthermore, it's too hot.

PERCY You're getting to be as big a heel as Vic—How's the road?

DAN Things are picking up right along. I had eight sections all the way from Los Angeles—How's tricks on the bellstand?

PERCY They ain't walking no more.

DAN No?—And you, Vic?

VIC Still the same. My hod ain't getting no lighter. But the movement's swinging along.

DAN I hear you're planning a World Conference!

VIC How did you know?

DAN I picked up one of your Big Moguls in Denver, on his way to the Coast—(*laughing*) Called himself the Duke of the Niger!

VIC (*unamused*) Yeah.

DAN Yeah. And you talk about a spade. He sure was one for you. He kept the car in an uproar all the way to Los Angeles.

PERCY Clowing for the Pecks, hunh?

DAN (*emphatically*) And how!

PERCY (*acrimoniously*) I could drown one of that kind in a tub of carbolic acid!

VIC (*to* DAN) And you say he was a Garveyite?

DAN That's what he claimed.

LES What did he say, Uncle Dan?

DAN What didn't he say, the fool! "Jerusalem for the Jew!" he kept preaching, with the white folks egging him on; "Ireland for the Irish, and Africa for the Africans!"—It was disgusting. But I doubt if it ever occurred to him he was playing right into the white man's hands.

VIC How's that?

DAN (*warmly*) By telling them just what they want to hear, that's what—advocating segregation!

VIC (*defensively*) You don't understand the new spirit, Dan. We're out to wrest our heritage from the enemy.

DAN (*challengingly*) What *our*? My heritage is right here in America!

VIC (*quietly*) What? A lynchrope?

PERCY You said a mouthful, Captain.

DAN Like hell. If those chumps down South haven't got sense enough to get out from under Mr. George, they ought to be strung up.

VIC You talk like an imbecile, Dan—Have you forgotten East St. Louis, Tulsa, and Washington? And what about what they did to Percy there when he came back from France?

DAN (*irritatedly*) I haven't forgotten anything. But all this agitation doesn't mean a thing. You can't do anything for people who don't care anything about themselves. You only stir up strife. Let them alone, I say, and try to get something out of them for yourself. There's chance enough for anybody in this country if he's got get-up enough to take it.

PERCY   Yea. A chance to be door mats for the white folks' feet!

DAN   Doormats, my eye. Adjust yourself, I say. Outwit the white man. Get something in your pocket and stop expecting the millennium!

VIC (*grimly*) You know what, Dan. It just strikes me what's wrong with educated Negroes like you.

DAN   Oh, yeah! Give me the benefit of your great wisdom?

VIC   Your education is like a pair of knee pads, which enables you to crawl through the slime of white prejudice without the least sense of pain or dishonor!

DAN (*stung*)   If I didn't know you so well, I'd take that as an insult. But you're radical. You can't see that the only difference between your feelings and mine is simply a matter of control.

VIC   Of course, with the help of your education.

DAN   You bet. I've got too much sense to let prejudice blind me to the thing that counts in this world. Get your share of the *Mazuma*, I say, and all else will be added unto you!

VIC   We're all the same to the white man, rich or poor—But what I want is freedom here and now!

DAN   So do I. But I say first get the cash.

PERCY   By crawling on your belly?

DAN   Tommyrot! A man can do business with his own people—Take this proposition of mine now, Vic. Everywhere our folks are looking for a place to live—It's the chance of a lifetime—

VIC   You're still just thinking about yourself. But I'm not. If I was, I'd pack out of here for some foreign country before sunrise.

DAN (*earnestly*)   Even so, Man. You're not going to Africa tomorrow. And you can't deny you'll need money when you do go. Come in with me. To open this kitchenette will make us both public benefactors.

VIC   You mean private beneficiaries!

DAN   What?

LES   How's that, Papa?

VIC   Never mind.

PERCY   I don't know about that, Captain. As long as we've got to be bled by somebody, I'd rather it be a black man.

DAN   Now you're talking sense, Percy. If the race gave Negro business half a chance, we'd soon get somewhere.

VIC (*hotly*)   Bunk. Mixed up with the white man as we are, Africa is the only solution.

DAN   All right. But what about temporarily —just to help me get started—?

VIC   I'm backing the Garvey Movement, Dan. Right this minute I'm expecting the committee to bring me some stock—the shares I'm taking in the Black Star Line. I feel it's my duty to put what little money I can behind it.

DAN   Shucks, Vic. In six months we'll be sitting so pretty, you'll be able to purchase all the stock you want and then some.

VIC   Sure—So you say!

DAN   I've figured it all out, I tell you. We can lease a six-flat building for $400 a month. We'll cut it up into forty apartments that'll rent for twenty bucks apiece. That's an income of $800 a month—or $200 apiece after the rent is paid— Where're you going to beat that?

PERCY   That's a lot of dough.

BROOKS (*entering front door and heading for her favorite rocker*)   Make room you all and lemme git off these feet!

ELLA (*entering behind her, her arms full of parcels*)   Here, Les, make yourself useful.

LES (*joining her and taking parcels*)   Did you bring the paper?

ELLA (*tossing Negro Newspaper on table*) Yes—There it is.

(*Exit* LES *into rear*)

DAN   Looks like you're planning to open a grocery store.

ELLA (*following* LES *out back*)   We need one to feed this family. (*exit*)

DAN (*affably*)   You're sure looking well, Mama.

BROOKS (*pleased at being noticed*)   I'm doing pretty fair, thank you, Dan—though I'm tired out right now.

DAN   Juanita said "hello." (*turning back to* VIC) But as I was saying. If we put $1500 apiece in the business, we can furnish the building from top to bottom and soon be on easy street—

VIC   But $1500—

DAN We've got to avoid credit, and start off with a clean slate—
VIC But $1500. That's just about every single cent I own—!

(LES *reenters to pick up newspaper, crosses to window seat and begins reading*)

DAN What difference does it make? You'll have your principal back in eight months!
VIC (*going*) I'll have to think about it.
DAN Where're you going?
VIC I've got to get into my uniform before the committee comes. (*he ascends stairs*)
DAN It's the chance of a lifetime. Don't forget that, and you can always pull out anytime you say.
VIC So you say! (*exit above*)
PERCY (*to* DAN, *chuckling*) He's sure salty, ain't he?
DAN As a pickled herring.
LES (*springing up, excitedly*) For crying out loud! (*coming forward*) Listen to this—Where's Papa?
DAN Upstairs. What is it?
LES (*reading*) "Black Star Liner Halted at Pier!"
PERCY Halted? What for?
DAN No! (*joining* LES) Lemme see!
LES (*as other takes paper*) Lord, Lord—I wonder what Papa's going to say!
BROOKS (*anxiously*) What is it, Les?
LES They've stopped the *Republic* from sailing.
BROOKS To Affiki—How come?
PERCY Read it out, Dan.
DAN (*laughing*) This is a scream—(*he strides to foot of stairs to shout*) Vic! Oh, Vic! Come on down here! Wait till he gets an earful of this—Black Star Line, eh? If he ain't a lucky man, the Sante Fe's a bus line!
ELLA (*reentering*) What's going on here?
DAN They've stopped that piece of junk of Marcus Garvey's from sailing.
ELLA My God! Who stopped it?
DAN The government, that's who.
VIC (*appearing above*) What's the trouble?
DAN (*going up to foot of stairs*) Come on down here and take a look at this. (*as* VIC *descends, buttoning the jacket of his Garvey Uniform*) I told you a man'd be a fool to trust that Monkeychaser—(*handing him paper*) Read this—(*as* VIC *pauses to read, he himself rejoins others*) A hell of a movement. The only time they know what's going on is when they see it in the newspapers!
STRAWDER (*apparently having knocked, he appears in doorway, a heavyset black man of 40, with several others behind him—All dressed in the regalia of the Garvyites—black uniforms trimmed with red and white plummed helmets*) Good evening, Folks!
ELLA (*turning*) Oh, good evening, Mr. Strawder—Come in, won't you?
VIC (*oblivious of all*) It's a lie! A dirty rotten lie!
ELLA Vic!
VIC (*noticing guests*) Excuse me, Gentlemen. I didn't see you come in.
STRAWDER Is anything wrong, Captain Mason?
VIC (*leading* STRAWDER *down to couch*) Wait until you hear this—Here, Les, read this for me, Son—And you all sit down.
LES (*as Strawder gingerly eases himself into seat on couch, and others gather behind it*) "Black Star Liner Halted at Pier—"
COTTON What's that?
LES (*reading*) "New York—As the Black Star Line Steamship, *Republic*, prepared to sail on its maiden voyage today, passengers aboard and spectators upon the crowded Hudson River pier were thrown into panic, culminating in near riot, when Maritime Inspector Davis O'Rouke declared the boat unseaworthy and issued orders forbidding the Captain from clearing port—"
STRAWDER (*stunned*) Great God A'mighty!
VIC Sit down, Count Strawder. You haven't heard the worst yet—Read on, Les.
LES "Inspection of the *Republic* came as a result of widespread rumors which recently began circulating in Harlem to the effect that leaders of the co-operative enterprise, which sought to establish the line, had been buncoed, when they purchased the giant craft at a cost of approximately a million dollars, despite the fact that the antiquated ship had not been in commission since the World War—"
DAN (*laughing derisively*) Wouldn't that squeeze you! (*a glance from* VIC *quells him*)
LES (*continuing*) "It was reported that Marcus Garvey, Provisional President of the proposed Black Republic of Africa, and leader of the movement, had taken flight to Canada!"

COTTON (*with a cry of pain*) Oh, no!...
STRAWDER (*with an air of despair*) Well, suh!
HARPER What you make of it, Captain Mason?
VIC It's a lie, Brother Harper—a dirty trick!
DAN A trick—?
BROOKS (*derisively*) It's a trick all right. That Marcus Garvey's done tricked the folks out o' their money—Talkin' bout a *black* land for the *black* man! A *black* land for the *black* man!
VIC Hush, Mama! You don't understand.
BROOKS Don't tell me I don't understand. I told you he wasn't no good, and when I tell a pusson sometin' they can take it for granted. If I tell you a chicken dip snuff, jes look under her wing and you'll find the box! (DAN *explodes with irrepressible laughter*)
VIC (*angrily*) What do you think this is, a circus? This is no laughing matter. This is a dirty white frame-up on the whole race if ever there was one!
STRAWDER How you mean, Captain Mason?
VIC It's plain as the nose on your face, Count. They think if they discredit our leader, they'll bust up the movement!
DAN (*staggered*) Well, I'll be a—Are you crazy, Vic? That inspector was a Government man!
VIC That's just what I know.
COTTON (*incredulously*) And you think Uncle Sam had a hand in it?
VIC Open your eyes, Count. The big men run this country, don't they? Haven't they got everything to gain by destroying the confidence of our members?
DAN Tommyrot! Tommyrot! If it wasn't for the big white folks, they'd have kicked us out and imported enough Hunkies to take our place long ago.
STRAWDER There's something to that, Captain!
VIC (*bitterly*) The Negro's nothing to the white man but a good thing! As workers and consumers who can't get anywhere, we're sweeter than sugar cane!
STRAWDER I think I get what you mean, Captain. Now that I remember, I mentioned our movement to the boss, no longer'n a week ago, and he blew right up in the air about it. He say—

(*Sound of Postman's whistle*)

LES (*heading for door*) The mailman!... Lord, I hope it's for me! (*meeting* WANDA *entering with letter*) Who's it for?
WANDA (*handing him letter*) You.
LES (*going downstage left*) This is it! It's here, Papa!
PERCY From the scholarship, eh?
WANDA Yes.
ELLA I'm so glad, Les. (*she watches his countenance as he reads*)
VIC (*explanatorily to others*) My boy won a scholarship to college, and that's the letter about it.
ELLA (*seeing pain on boy's face*) What's the matter...? Is...?
LES (*biting his lip*) Well, I guess... It's all off!
VIC (*rising in consternation*) What?
ELLA Oh, God!
WANDA (*her eyes swimming*) Oh, Les... you don't mean... (*she joins him to take letter*)
LES (*crossing to chair*) I happen to be a little too black, I guess.
ELLA (*unbelievingly*) There must be some mistake—
DAN (*taking letter from* WANDA) Let me see! (PERCY *joins him as he takes step toward couch, to read aloud*) "My dear Mr. Mason. I have been instructed to inform you that on the basis of information received from one in your community, stating that you are a Negro..."
PERCY (*reading over his shoulder*) "the board has no other alternative than to deny your application, since under the provisions of the late Mr. Jason's will, the executors are expressly constrained from making any monies from the Fund available to members of your race—" The dirty bastards!
WANDA (*going to* LES) I'm so sorry, Les!
ELLA It isn't fair! God, you know it isn't fair!
PERCY (*going upstage left, angrily*) The only fair thing about a white man is the color of his skin!
VIC (*nodding his head slowly*) Nobody else could be guilty of such a cheap, petty piece of business—(*hoarsely to* LES) But it's all right, boy!
DAN (*darkly*) I wish I could put my hands on the one who told them he was colored!

BROOKS I bet it was somebody round here.
STRAWDER You can bet on it. Somebody did that out of jealousy.
COTTON (*woefully*) Yeah. One of our own people, too!
VIC They would've found out anyway, soon's he arrived—(*resolutely*) But this settles it! (*to* STRAWDER) Got your subscription list handy, Count?
ELLA What're you fixing to do?
VIC (*searching for his breastpocket, forgetful that he's wearing uniform*) Answer my son's letter—Are you with me?
ELLA (*with a tinge of dismay*) You know I am. But what're you—
VIC Wanda, run upstairs and get me my check book.
DAN (*as she runs up*) But, Vic!—
VIC Get your list out, Count!
DAN Ella! (*she is silent, and he turns back to* VIC, *sensing the futility of his action*) Oh, I know how you feel, Vic. But you can't afford to let this thing drive you to do anything so rash.
STRAWDER (*at end table, with pen and papers*) How many shares you going to take, Captain?
VIC (*firmly*) Fifteen hundred! (*the* GARVEYITES *crowd behind couch to watch the desperate transaction*)
DAN (*desperately*) But, Vic. It's worthless, Man!
VIC (*quietly*) To you, perhaps.
DAN This is madness!... Wait, Vic. Wait until you feel better. Let it go until tomorrow at least!
VIC (*exasperatedly*) You and your tomorrow. Will you never stop talking about tomorrow? What does it take to make you see there's none for us in the God forsaken country? (WANDA *returns to hand him check book*) Thanks. (*he makes out check*)
DAN (*to* ELLA) Are you going to be a fool, too? Can't you see what he's doing? Speak to him!
PERCY (*exploding, bitterly*) Speak to him! Speak to him! What do you want her to say? Tell him to drop everything and stay here and let these dirty, damn hypocrits tear the hearts out of the rest of the children? (*exit above*)
ELLA (*in tears*) I'd rather choke first!
DAN (*surrendering*) All right. All right. If you're going to let bitterness get the best of you, it's your funeral—But don't say I didn't

warn you. (*going*) With that damn steamship nothing but junk, that stock isn't worth the paper it's printed on! (*exit to street*)
VIC (*handing check to* STRAWDER) Here you are, Count.
STRAWDER (*rising*) I made out three certificates for $500 each.
BROOKS (*in despair*) Lawd! Lawd! Lawd!
VIC (*taking shares*) Thanks.
STRAWDER (*deeply moved, and extending his hand*) Don't thank me, Captain Mason. I don't deserve it. You're one out of a thousand. And I'm going to write to our leader and tell him how you're sticking by him in this hour of need.
VIC (*his eye on his star*) It's a mighty poor man that needs to be thanked for following the star of his people's destiny, Count. I'm looking East!
STRAWDER (*going, he dons his helmet*) Well—Gooday! (*he stalks with dignity toward door, as others offer their hands to Vic and follow him out*)
VIC (*as the last of the plumed figures disappear, and* ELLA *sinks onto couch in silent tears*) Don't cry, Ella! (*for a moment his hand rests upon her shoulder*)
LES (*bewildered, he stares upon the world with an inward eye*) Seems like the world ain't nothing but a big white fog, and we can't see no light nowhere!

(ELLA *sobs*)

VIC (*fervidly and with a sense of compassion for his wounded son*) Look to the East, Son, and keep on looking! Beyond the darkness and mist that surrounds us here, Africa the Sun of our hope is rising!

(*All is disconsolation, as the Curtain falls slowly*)

ACT TWO

Scene One

(TIME: *August, a year later.*

Everything is as we saw it last, except that now WANDA *is seated at the oblong table, typing as her father dictates from a batch of notes.*
MRS. BROOKS *occupies the rocker, watching the doings on the street through the window;* ELLA *is*

sewing, as she mends the jacket of VIC's *uniform.*

There is the steady rhythm of WANDA's *typing for a moment following the rise of the curtain, then she looks up at her father inquiringly.*

VIC (*dictating in response to her glance*) "Therefore, we must of necessity conclude that by relying upon the Nine tried and proven principles of the English Producers-and-Consumers-Cooperatives"—comma—"we shall eventually be able to build an agrarian cooperative economy—

WANDA How do you spell agrarian?

VIC A-g-r-a-r-i-a-n—Get it? (*she nods*) "cooperative economy of lasting benefit to the Republic"—Period. Paragraph.

ELLA (*preoccupiedly*) How long do you think the strike will last, Vic?

VIC (*casually*) A month or so, maybe— (*dictating*) Unfortunately—

ELLA (*anxiously*) That long—? What makes you think so?

VIC (*annoyed*) Never mind, Ella. Let the strike drop. I've got to get this paper done.

ELLA I was only thinking how Les is going to feel if you leave him behind.

WANDA That's right, Papa. He's bound to be disappointed after the way he's been boasting of going with you and seeing New York and Harlem!

VIC I can't help that. This is a general walkout—painters, bricklayers, plasterers and all—In fact, I wouldn't think of making the trip if I hadn't promised this paper— (*to* WANDA) Where were we?

WANDA "Unfortunately."

BROOKS (*looking out window*) Here's Les now.

VIC (*going on*) "Unfortunately, the hostile nature of the Negro's environment in the agricultural South does not permit of experimentation there." Period. "Otherwise—"

LES (*entering upstage left, excitedly*) You know what, Papa. Uncle Dan is just as dirty as he can be. He just put one of his tenants out this afternoon and she hasn't any place to stay!

VIC Is that so?

LES He set her right out on the sidewalk because her rent was three weeks overdue, and Mrs. Davis was a nice woman too.

ELLA Three weeks—? That all?

LES You don't know Uncle Dan, Mama. He's hard as they make 'em. Anybody get behind in their rent, he usually puts a plug in their doorlock the next day.

WANDA So he called himself giving her a break, huh?

LES Yeah. I guess so—Maybe because she has a baby and her husband ran off with another woman.

ELLA Poor thing!

VIC Dan has no more conscience than a bedbug.

LES For two cents I wouldn't go back to work for him—You ought to have seen her sitting on the sidewalk crying.

ELLA There ought to be a law against such things!—Poor soul, I wonder what she's going to do. . . . Was she a young woman?

LES About twenty-five I guess.

BROOKS (*emphatically*) I reckon she'll make it then.

VIC (*indignantly*) And he wanted me to be his partner!

WANDA Was Aunt Juanita there?

LES No. But it wouldn't've made any difference; the way she lays on everybody about their rent—

BROOKS (*strangely excited*) Here they come, now, driving a brand new car!

WANDA (*springing up from chair and crossing to join her*) A new car? (ELLA *follows suit*)

LES I forgot to tell you.

WANDA (*excitedly*) Come see, Papa.

ELLA (*Looking out*) My but it's beautiful! What kind of a car is it, Les?

LES A Cadillac.

BROOKS Lawd, a Cadillac!

VIC (*crossing to look*) Phumph! (*turning back, displeased*) A fortune on wheels!—But I guess it's no mystery how he got it.

JUANITA (*entering, breezily*) Well, are the travelers ready!

ELLA (*going back to seat*) Not quite. Come on in, you all.

DAN (*entering, proudly*) See my new boat, Vic?

VIC Yeah. And from the looks of it, you don't have to tell me your kitchenette's making money.

DAN (*grandly*) Just thought I'd make Juanita a little present. But it's costing me plenty. Thirty-eight hundred bucks is a lot of money, take it from Daniel.

BROOKS Thirty-eight hund'd dollars—Lawdy!

JUANITA (*laughing*) How do you like it, Mama?

BROOKS Lawd, chile; it's out of this world.

WANDA You must be tickled to death, Aunt.

JUANITA (*going to window seat*) Oh, I'm not shedding any tears, dear!

DAN (*sitting*) I reckon not.—But say, Vic. Aren't you making a mistake taking Les to New York? I really need him, and you know yourself he'll need every cent he can earn if he's going to enter the U this fall?

VIC (*with a tinge of bitterness*) Well, you can ease your mind on that score— (*As* LES *rises*) I'm sorry, Les. I was just going to tell you.... You see, they called a strike on the job—

DAN A strike!

VIC Yes. The contractors are defiant—! And you see, Les. Well, I don't know just how long I may be out of work—

LES (*crestfallen*) So you can't spare the money!

VIC I hope you don't feel too bad about it. I wouldn't go myself if I didn't have part on the program.

LES If you can't afford a thing, you can't.

DAN (*encouragingly*) At a boy, Les! In a few years you'll be able to take a trip around the world—Once you get your education.

ELLA Hadn't you better finish your paper, Vic.

VIC (*gratefully*) Yes, yes. Of course. (*to* JUANITA *and* DAN) Excuse me, will you—I've only got a paragraph or two more.

DAN Les was telling me about—What's the subject?

VIC The Outlook for Cooperative Farming in Africa.

DAN Sounds interesting.

VIC Read the last sentence back to me, Wanda.

WANDA (*at machine*) "Unfortunately, the hostile nature of the Negro's environment in the agricultural South does not permit of experimentation there. Otherwise—"

VIC (*dictating*) Oh, yeah. "Otherwise it would be distinctly advantageous to try out the plan here," comma, "as it might easily prove the solution of the race problem in this country." Period. "For should the Negro successfully wrest his economic independence from his white oppressors," comma, "their attitude of superiority would inevitably disappear, since it would then no longer possess any basis in reality." Period. Paragraph. "But this is, of course, merely to indulge in fortuitous wishing"; Semi-colon "so that in passing, I am constrained to give you: The Agrarian Co-operative Economy of the Provisional Republic of Africa, the hope and destined fulfillment of the Negro's dream. For just as the gigantic Pyramids of Egypt (*he is being moved by his own eloquence*) stand in eternal witness of the strength of our black forefather's hands, so shall the New Africa, which we shall have built through this means, stand before the generations of tomorrow in final testimony of the black man's wisdom." That's all.

LES Gee, Papa. That's good!

DAN (*admiringly*) It's too bad, Vic, you can't see anything but Garvey!

JUANITA I'll say so. You'll bring the house down.

VIC I'm glad you like it.—Get it together, Wanda—(*he joins her to lay aside his notes*) Where're the children, Ella?

ELLA (*going to door*) Outside, somewhere.

DAN There's only one thing, Vic—the doubtfullness of your ever establishing the Republic aside—especially since Garvey's conviction—There's only one thing I can see that's wrong with your conclusion.

ELLA (*in door, calling*) Caroline!

VIC (*to* DAN) Yeah—

ELLA (*to children*) Come, you and Phillip—Papa's going!

VIC (*to* DAN) What's that?

DAN You make the mistake of thinking the white man's idea of his superiority is something more than a delusion.

VIC I was speaking about the effect of him having everything in the palm of his hand.

DAN But that's temporary.

ELLA (*apprehensively*) Vic, you haven't got time to argue! (*she holds his jacket*)

VIC (*starting to don it, but only succeeding in getting in one arm*) All I'm saying is the white man's on top and he knows it, and as long as he stays on top all the books in the world won't change him.

DAN There's more ways than one to skin a cat—

VIC Yeah. Like what?
DAN Use the white man's method, that's what—the process of individual achievement.
ELLA (*desperately, still trying to get him into his jacket*) It's pretty near train time, Vic.
BROOKS They're goin' keep on till they'll be hot at each other again!
VIC Try offering your white man's method to the millions we got down South, (*shaking his finger*) living on corn bread and molasses and dying like flies from hook-worm and pellagra!
DAN (*sharply*) Let them come North!
JUANITA Oh, why don't you cut it out, Dan. Vic's got to—
DAN (*angrily*) You shut up! (*to* VIC) Why can't they come North, like we did—There's plenty of room up here for everybody!
VIC Bunk. But even if there was, I'd still be against it.
DAN (*acridly*) Of course. Because you know it would put you race saviors out of business!
VIC (*losing his temper*) Yeah—Well, there's one thing you can't deny: I'm against cutting my own brother's throat to get somewhere!
ELLA For God's sake, Vic, stop it!

(PHILLIP and CAROLINE *enter*)

DAN The weak and shiftless always find some idea to blame for not having anything!
VIC You're sitting pretty, ain't you?
DAN I don't have to want for anything!
VIC No you don't—living like a leach on the blood of your own people!
DAN That's a lie!
JUANITA Dan!
VIC If it's a lie, how is it in a year you've been able to pay $4,000 for that automobile out there?
DAN (*sneeringly*) What's the matter, getting jealous?
VIC (*blazing*) For two cents I'd tell you what to do with that car!
DAN Oh, yeah!
VIC You're damn right! (*to* LES) Go, call me a taxi! (LES *starts to obey, but is stopped by glance from* ELLA)
BROOKS I knowed it! I knowed it!
DAN (*angrily*) Suits me! (*going*) Come on, Juanita. To hell with him!
JUANITA (*arresting him*) No, Dan! This is all uncalled for.
DAN Like hell it is. Do you think I'm going to stand here and swallow his rotten insinuations?
ELLA You're both acting like children—Why don't you forget it—
VIC (*peremptorily to* LES) Didn't I tell you to call me a taxi!

(*Exit* LES, *running*)

JUANITA You ought to be ashamed of yourself, Victor Mason. Here you are two brother-in-*laws* arguing like cats and dogs. It's a shame!
VIC (*with finality*) You're wasting your breath!
JUANITA (*joining* DAN, *angrily*) Well, if that's the way you feel, *Goodbye!* (*exit, with* DAN)
BROOKS (*seeing* PHILLIP *with her work basket*) Phillip, you let that basket alone! (ELLA *dons hat at hall-tree*)
VIC (*to* PHILLIP) Can't you keep out of mischief, boy!
PHILLIP (*pouting*) Papa, I wasn't doing nothing with her old basket!
LES (*in door*) Here's your cab, Papa. (*he gets father's bags*)
VIC (*kissing* CAROLINE) Be a good girl, you hear. (*turning to* PHILLIP) Don't let your Ma have to give me any bad reports about you. (*patting his shoulder*) I'm going to try to bring you both something when I get back. (*to* WANDA) Did you get it together? (*she nods and hands him manuscript*) You've been a big help to me—(*kisses her forehead. Exit* LES) Take care of yourself. (*following* LES *out*) Goodbye, Mama! (ELLA *goes out behind him*)
CAROLINE (*following mother*) Mama, may I go to the station with you? (*exit* CAROLINE)
PHILLIP (*on her heels*) Me, too, Mama? (*exit* PHILLIP)

(BROOKS *turns to the window, as the Curtain falls*)

Scene Two

(TIME: *the following January.*

From the window the light of a dreary winter dusk shrouds the figure of MRS. BROOKS, *who stands there, gazing into the street.*

This atmosphere of bleakness, in fact, pervades the whole house and tends to emphasize the mood of the family which is one of apprehension and misgiving.

ELLA *enters from above, her descent slow, her aspect full of weariness and dejection*)

ELLA (*halting on stair*) Is it still snowing?

BROOKS (*immobile*) No. It's stopped.

ELLA (*strangely annoyed*) It would! (*she descends*)

BROOKS Some life—dependin' on the elements!

ELLA We have to be thankful, Mama; things aren't worse.

BROOKS (*turning, gruffly*) If you'd-er made Vic keep that money, he wouldn't have to be shovelin' no snow—How is she?

ELLA (*turning to table to inspect punch bowl and cups there*) About the same. She drank the tea, but she's complaining about a headache.

BROOKS (*apprehensively*) You better call the doctor, then. She may be comin' down with the flu!

ELLA (*wearily*) I just spent the last nickel I had for the stuff to make the eggnog.

BROOKS (*sharply*) Lawd, lawd! I don't know which one of you all is the worst, you or Vic—You know that chile's sick, and you ain't hardly got bread to eat, yet you spend your last cent for eggnog!

ELLA Oh, for heaven's sake, Mama! I can't have the leaders coming here to honor my own husband and not serve anything, can I?

BROOKS (*acridly*) If it was left to me, I'd serve em some water and give em a piece of my mind!

ELLA (*starting to kitchen*) If she isn't better by morning, I'll see Juanita—(*halting and turning*) Where's Phillip?

BROOKS Outside.

ELLA (*astounded*) Outside—! (*upbraidingly*) Why didn't you make him stay in here?

BROOKS (*coldly*) I told him. But he's jes like his Pappy!

ELLA (*crossing up to front door*) Lord, have mercy! (*opening door to call*) Phillip!... You Phillip!

PHILLIP (*in street*) Yes'm!

ELLA (*angrily*) You come in this house! (*shuts door and comes down*) I don't know what I'm going to do with that boy.

BROOKS Let him keep on runnin' round in the snow with them shoes he got on and he'll be up there with Caroline, if you don't have to bury him!

PHILLIP (*entering*) Yes'm—? (*he wipes his nose with the back of his sleeve*)

ELLA (*outdone*) Nose running! (*shaking him*) Didn't Mama tell you to stay in this house?

PHILLIP Mama, I wasn't doing nothin' but trying out Mac's new sled!

ELLA I should try your back-side! (*pushing him into chair*) Let me see those over-shoes? (*pulls off shoe and exhibits it*) Just look at that hole!

BROOKS I could-er told you their feet was on the ground a week ago. But I though I better hold my tongue.

ELLA (*to* PHILLIP) Go upstairs and get in bed—(*as he obeys*) And don't disturb Caroline ... I'll bring you some hot eggnog in a little while. (*on stairs the boy sneezes*)

BROOKS Phumph! You hear that? (ELLA *is silent, as she goes up to deposit shoes under hall-tree*) I don't blame you for not answerin'. You could-er took that money you spent for eggnog and bought em both a pair—'stid o' puttin' on the dog for that black crank you call your husband.

ELLA (*glancing out of window*) It's snowing again, Thank God! (BROOKS *grunts—and she, herself, crosses to switch on lights*) I reckon we'd better have a little light.

BROOKS (*seeing boy from window*) Here's Les, n' Wanda. (*turning to greet him, as he enters with sister, feeling his ears*) Gittin' colder, hunh?

(ELLA *turns anxiously toward* WANDA *and becomes hesitant*)

LES (*doffing overcoat, as* WANDA *removes over-shoes*) I don't think so, Grandma—(*seeing punch bowl*) Punch bowl out!

(ELLA *remains preoccupied*)

BROOKS (*feigning surprise*) Oh, ain't you all heard? We's havin' a lil celebration this evenin' —Your Pappy's goin' be decorated!

WANDA Decorated by whom? For what?

BROOKS Ask your Mammy—She know's all about it.

LES What is it, Mama?

ELLA I don't know myself—(*cheerfully*) Only, Mr. Strawder called up and said to keep your father home, as they were coming over to bestow some kind of honor on him.—But, Wanda—

LES (*admiringly, as he enters kitchen*) Good

Big White Fog

old Papa! He's sure forging right ahead! (*exit*)

BROOKS He's forgin' ahead all right—Right straight to the poor house!

WANDA (*turning to stairs*) Mama, when's it coming off?

ELLA I don't know. Mr. Strawder said they'd be here early.

WANDA (*going*) Well, I hope they come before I have to go.

ELLA (*intercepting her, hesitantly*) Wanda—

WANDA (*halting on stair*) Yes—

ELLA Have you—Could you spare me a little money—a few dollars?

WANDA (*exploding wildly*) Money! Money! Can't you find anything else to speak to me about except money? Where'd I get money from this time of week—I just gave you all I had payday!

ELLA (*hurt*) Well, you needn't shout at me.

WANDA I'm sorry, Mama. But you know I've no money.

ELLA I wouldn't've asked you. But you know your father's still on strike—and Caroline's sick—

LES (*re-entering*) Caroline!

WANDA What's the matter with her?

ELLA She got her feet wet and the teacher sent her home.

BROOKS (*volunteering*) For being ill-clad and needin' a doctor.

LES No! (*crossing to stairs*) Where is she—in bed?

ELLA Yes. (*as he runs up stairs*) I'm not worrying about the doctor so much. But she and Phillip both need overshoes.

BROOKS It's a shame 'fore Heaven.

WANDA I'm already in a hole, Mama. (*going*) But I'll see if I can get the boss to let me have a few dollars tonight.

ELLA Nevermind. Maybe your father'll get hold of a dollar or two today. (*exit* WANDA)

BROOKS (*warningly*) She goin' get tired of his money business pretty soon. You see how she flew off the handle, don't you?

ELLA Yes. But maybe it'll be a little easier for her after this. Vic said this morning he was going to ask Les to help.

BROOKS (*surprised*) Ask Les? (*sharply*) How in the world's Les goin' do anything, and him goin' to college?

ELLA (*going toward rear*) I reckon his father's going to make him drop out.

BROOKS Lawdy! It's goin' break his heart!

ELLA (*in door*) If he comes down, keep him here. Tell him Vic wants to see him.

BROOKS (*arresting her, as she hears stomping on porch*) I 'spect that's Vic now.

ELLA (*seeing* VIC *enter, she measures him for a moment in silence*) Well, what'd you do today?

VIC (*he sets shovel in corner and joins her, taking out change*) Made Six-bits!

ELLA (*takes change to weigh it in palm*) Phumph! Six-bits!—How long do you think we can keep this up?

VIC (*turning back to remove wraps*) I'm doing the best I can, Ella. (*she goes out rear in silence*)

BROOKS (*shortly, watching him*) Do you know Caroline and Phillip's sick!

VIC (*shocked*) What's the matter with them?

BROOKS They got the flu, I 'spect.

VIC (*crossing and calling*) Ella! What's this about the children being sick?

ELLA (*off-stage*) Take a look at their leaky shoes out there and you'll know for yourself.

VIC (*turning*) Their leaky shoes—?

LES (*descending and catching sight of him*) Hello, Papa—I hear you're going to be decorated tonight.

VIC What nonsense is this?

LES (*indicating table*) See the punch bowl!

VIC (*going up to table*) Now I wonder what this can mean!

LES (*getting coat*) I've got to go by the kitchenette. But if they come, hold everything for me.

VIC (*as he starts out*) Wait a minute, Son. There's something I wanted to ask you to do for me. (*regretfully*) I've been hoping to avoid asking you. But I reckon I needn't go into details. You see the hole I'm in—

LES Yes . . . But what is it?

VIC I guess there's no hope of my getting back to work before spring. So I thought I might ask you if you'd mind trying to help out with the house until times get better?

LES (*staggered*) But, Papa—How?

VIC Dan's paying you $10 a week, isn't he?

LES Yes. But I need every cent for school—(*suddenly understanding*) You don't mean you want me to drop out—?

VIC I hate mighty bad to ask it, son—.

LES (*regretfully*) I see.

VIC You'd only be out this Quarter—By spring I'm sure I'll be back on the job—?
LES (*going*) OK. Papa. I'll do it.
VIC (*gratefully*) Thank you, Son. You'll never regret it. (*exit* LES)
PERCY (*entering from street, as* LES *passes him hurriedly*) Well! What's the matter with him?
VIC Nothing.—How's things with you?
PERCY Oh, I guess I'm still kicking—How're you, Mrs. Brooks. (*he turns to hall-tree to doff wraps*)
BROOKS Pretty fair, I reckon.
VIC (*rejoining him*) Look, Percy. Do me a favor. It looks like Caroline's got the flu, and Phillip's trying to come down with it—Let me have a little money—About a hundred dollars.
PERCY (*staggered*) A hundred dollars! Captain, I ain't got the first quarter. Business at the hotel is shot to hell, and that Chippy I'm tied up with is bleeding me to death—(ELLA *enters and he nods to her*)
VIC (*sighing*) Well, I guess that settles that. (*pause*) I just thought I might be able to let Les stay in school.
PERCY Is it that bad?
VIC Couldn't be worse.
PERCY (*cynically*) I thought Wanda was doing all right!
ELLA (*catching note in his voice*) What do you mean?
PERCY (*darkly*) Where is she?
ELLA (*eying him*) In her room, I guess.
PERCY Where'd she get that fur coat?
ELLA What fur coat?
PERCY She's got a fur coat, hasn't she?
ELLA No. She's got a cloth coat.
PERCY Just like I thought.
VIC What do you mean, Percy?
PERCY I suppose you've got trouble enough. But for her sake, I guess I might as well tell you—
VIC Do you mean Wanda's been in some kind of trouble?
PERCY I don't know. But I saw her in the Dreamland with a *Nogooder*, wearing a sealskin coat.
BROOKS (*incredulously*) A sealskin coat...
PERCY Yep—
ELLA You can't mean it!
PERCY And if it didn't cost $500, it didn't cost a dime!
ELLA (*stunned*) Lord have mercy!
PERCY (*grimly*) I knew she was supposed to be taking care of the house. So...I figured it couldn't mean but one thing.
BROOKS (*outraged*) I been 'spectin' somethin' like this—(*to* ELLA) I told you! I warned you!
ELLA (*striding to foot of stairs, calling*) Wanda!
WANDA (*above, timorously*) Yes! What is it?
ELLA (*imperatively*) Come down here!
VIC (*hanging on to straw*) Maybe she borrowed it from somebody!
PERCY (*cynically*) Where're you going to find anybody dumb enough to take that kind of risk?
WANDA (*appearing above, a note of fear in her voice, sensing the impending storm*) What is it, Mama? (*slowly, she descends*)
ELLA (*abruptly, as she reaches floor*) Where's that sealskin coat you been wearing?
WANDA What sealskin coat?
PERCY (*coldly*) The one you had on last night, that's what!
WANDA (*speechless*) Last night? (*she glances desperately around, trapped*)
VIC You did have on one, didn't you?
ELLA And don't try to lie either, because Percy saw you!
WANDA (*cornered*) But, Mama—Uncle Percy doesn't know what he's talking about—I...I...
VIC (*sharply*) Answer my question! Didn't you have on such a coat?
WANDA (*after a moment*) Yes. I did.
ELLA Where'd you get it?
WANDA (*suddenly fighting*) I bought it.
ELLA You bought it? When? Where'd you get $500 to pay for it.
WANDA It isn't paid for...I just got it out Christmas.
VIC Well, where is it?
WANDA (*smoldering*) Claudine's.
BROOKS (*sharply*) Sounds mighty fishy to me!
ELLA What's it doing at Claudine's if you bought it?
WANDA I've been leaving it there because I knew you'd kick about my having it.
ELLA You're lying. You're lying as fast as you can open your mouth!
WANDA I'm not lying. It's the truth!

ELLA   And I suppose you're going to try to tell me you've got receipts to show for it?
WANDA   Yes, I have.
VIC   Get them!
WANDA   (*embarrassed*)   I can't right now. They're over at Claudine's.
BROOKS   (*grunting wisely*)   Ugh Phumn!
WANDA   (*desperately*)   Oh, I know what you're thinking. But it's true. I did buy that coat, and I've got the receipts to prove it!
ELLA   Well, you just get out of here and get them. And don't come back till you bring them, either. (WANDA *runs upstairs*)
BROOKS   (*coldly*)   Well, I reckon you'd better tell her goodbye, then!
VIC   (*loyally*)   I believe she's telling the truth.
BROOKS   (*angrily*)   If I was you, I wouldn't open mah mouth—You and Percy neither!
PERCY   (*angrily*)   Now what the hell did I have to do with it?
BROOKS   (*accusingly*)   She took after you, didn't she? If it hadn't been for you round here setting' her sich a bad example, she never would-er started this "goin' live" business—(*sharply*) And, Ella, if I was you, I'd bless him out, and Vic, too, right this minute—(*she pauses, as* WANDA *descends and goes out in silence, and a wave of loving regret flows over her and breaks in a note of sad prophecy*) That gal's goin' make your heartache one of these days, sure's you're born! (*silence*)
VIC   (*turning to stairs, after a moment*)   I'm going up and get into my uniform before the committee comes—(*seeing the door opening, he halts and* DAN *enters*)
DAN   (*pouncing upon him*)   Say, Vic. What do you mean by taking that boy out of school?
VIC   (*annoyed*)   Now hold your horses. Lester Mason happens to be my son!
DAN   So what? I'm responsible for him being in school.
VIC   I grant you that. But you can be civil about it—
DAN   You've got a nerve!
VIC   Nevermind. In the first place, it's only temporary. I just asked him to sacrifice going back this quarter.
DAN   What right've you got to demand such a sacrifice?
VIC   I'd rather not discuss that.
DAN   Oh, you wouldn't, eh? Well, let me tell you this: I'm not paying Les to support you. Not by a damn sight!
PERCY   I wouldn't take that attitude, Dan. Put yourself in his place. The children are upstairs sick in bed, and you know how far the little money goes Wanda's been making.
DAN   (*joining him, accusingly*)   Yeah. You can think of that now. But when I saw this coming and tried to warn him, you were the first to jump up and claim I was wrong.
PERCY   That's history now!
VIC   Nevermind, Percy. Let him go on. He's been waiting for a chance to try to rub it in.
DAN   (*surprised*)   I'm not trying to rub anything—
VIC   Actions speak louder than words. You know I'm up against it. You know I've been up against it for months. But you've got your first time to offer me a dime.
DAN   I'm not offering my money to anyone who's too proud to ask for it.
VIC   So you wanted me to come crawling to you, eh?
PERCY   Yeah, So he could Lord it over you!
DAN   Lord, hell! You're both just jealous of my success.—But just to show you there's nothing cheap about me, I tell you what I'll do. I'll let you have enough money to see you through—
PERCY   (*surprised*)   No!
DAN   That is, if you're willing to give up this foolish Garvey business and act like you've got some sense?
VIC   What exactly do you mean?
DAN   I'll let you have two or three hundred dollars, if you'll turn over that Black Star Line Stock.
ELLA   Dan, you don't mean it?
VIC   As collateral?
DAN   Collateral hell! What kind of a business man do you think I am?
VIC   You'd sell it, then?
DAN   What do you care, as long as I'm sucker enough to take it off your hands—
VIC   Phumph! Big hearted Dan—But forget it. I can't do it.
DAN   No. You'd rather frustrate the life of your son, while you hang on to your silly dream!
VIC   Call it what you like. At my age a man can't start looking forward to carrying a hod for the rest of his life.

DAN At your age a man should be thinking about the future of his children.

VIC That's just it. Things haven't changed for us in this country, have they? Aren't we still in the hands of the enemy, brow-beaten, stigmatized—(*wearily*) But what's the use—If you want to lend me a little money, all right. I'll appreciate it and pay you back, if it takes me till my dying day. But don't ask me to part with my stock.

(LES *enters*)

DAN Business is business—Ella, you see my point, don't you?

ELLA Yes, I do—Vic, give it to him. Take the money. It can't hurt Garvey. It will only be a matter of it changing hands—

VIC Ella, that stock's worth $1500, have you forgotten that?

ELLA It won't be worth a dime if Caroline needs a doctor!

PERCY (*supporting her*) A smart flea, Captain, knows when to hop!

VIC (*firmly*) I've had my say.

ELLA Yes, you have. But I haven't had mine. I'm getting sick to death of this scrimping and worrying and waiting from day to day for something that never comes—(*furiously*) Do you know the rent hasn't been paid? That we hardly got bread to eat in this house? And the children need shoes?

VIC It's no use getting hot, Ella. I know all that. But good sense should tell you; it's a mighty poor slave that'll give up trying to break his chains just because there's a nick in the hammer!

DAN (*going*) OK. Captain. If you're going to remain a fool, hang on to your stock. I'm not going to argue with you all night. I'm going. But get this through your head; you needn't expect a dime from me as long as you do. (*exit*)

ELLA Wait, Dan—(*desperately*) Call him back, Vic. Call him back!

VIC It's no use, Ella—(*going*) The stock is all we've got. (*he ascends stairs. Exit*)

LES What's it all about, Mama—(*she turns in silence, and crosses swiftly to go out back. to* PERCY) Is this because Papa's taking me out of school?

PERCY Not exactly—(*there is a knock at front door*)

BROOKS (*hearing it*) Answer the door, Les—Don't you hear somebody knocking?

LES (*opens door to admit* PISZER, *a young Jewish student, wearing a mackinaw and tam to match*) Piszer! This is a surprise! Come in!

PISZER (*warmly in response to the other's friendliness*) Hello, Mason. I was on my way downtown, and I just thought I'd drop by to see if you'd care to go along?

LES On a night like this! You're kidding. But come, I want you to meet my folks—

ELLA (*reentering*) Who is it, Les?

LES Mom, this is Nathan Piszer, my classmate—Piszer, my mother.

ELLA (*graciously*) I'm very pleased to welcome you into our home.

PISZER (*shaking hands*) You're very cordial, Mrs. Mason. Thank you.

LES My Grandmother, Mrs. Brooks—

BROOKS (*courtseying*) I'm pleased to meet you.

LES And my uncle, Mr. Mason.

PERCY (*shaking hands*) How do you do?

LES Give me your coat, and sit down.

ELLA Yes, do, Mr. Piszer. You're no stranger here. Les has talked so much about you, we all feel we know you.

PISZER Thank you, Mrs. Mason. But seriously, I can't stay. (*turning to* LES) I'm on my way down to Orchestra Hall, and I thought perhaps you might like to go along—Some Van Gorham is lecturing on Russia, and they say he's a pretty keen observer—?

LES Gee, I'd like to. But I'm afraid I can't tonight. You see, we're holding a little celebration for my Dad—and—

PISZER Is that so? Then I'm probably intruding—

LES No, no! Not at all. We'd like you to stay, wouldn't we, Mama?

ELLA Yes, you must, Mr. Piszer.

LES (*pressing him*) Then, I want you to meet my Dad—

PISZER (*intrigued*) I'd like to—

LES Good—Give me your coat—

PISZER (*doffing coat*) But why're you honoring him?

LES (*laughing*) You've got me there! But you see he's one of the local leaders of the Garvey Movement, and I guess it's a sort of surprise. (*he takes coat*)

PISZER (*following him*) You say the Garvey

Movement—? Gospell discussed it in class the other day—But I'd no idea your folks were connected with it.

LES (*joining him and going to couch*) What'd Gospell have to say?

ELLA (*going*) You must excuse me, Mr. Piszer. But I must get into the kitchen—Come, Mama, and fix Phillip's eggnog.

BROOKS (*all a-flutter*) I'm so sorry to leave you, Mr. Piszer. Your conversation is so interesting. (*exit with* ELLA)

LES (*offering Piszer chair*) Go on, Piszer. What'd Gospell have to say?

PISZER Well, frankly, he thought the movement visionary.

LES He did, hunh? But I guess he'd say the same about the Back-To-Palestine idea of your people. But there's nothing impractical about it. There's no hope for my race in this country, and any program that offers escape is all right with me—How about you, Uncle Percy?

PERCY Of course, Les. But you can't expect him to see it like we do.

PISZER I don't know, Mr. Mason. Gospell seemed to think neither of them would hold water—As he pointed out, there may be another solution.

LES Did he say what?

PISZER Yes. He thinks the only lasting solution for the problem of minority groups today is unity with the majority on a common ground.

LES (*laughing*) That's rich! Unity with the majority on a common ground!

PISZER You're skeptical—?

PERCY As a *Jew*, can *you* blame him?

PISZER In a way—yes.

LES (*convinced*) Nothing could be more visionary!

PISZER It may sound remote. But what's there to prevent all the underprivileged from getting together on problems in which they have a common interest?

LES You want me to tell you?

PISZER Sure—Go ahead.

LES (*bitterly*) The same thing that makes them call you "Sheeny" and me "Nigger!"

PISZER Oh, no doubt most of my people would say the same. But I'm beginning to wonder if it isn't a matter of simply being just distrustful.

LES We'd be fools not to be.

PERCY Right, Kid. All this inter-racial concilliation is nothing but a trap to catch the Negro in!

PISZER But what about Socialism?

LES (*laughing*) What?—Don't tell me you've gone Bolshevik?

PISZER Have you read Lenin?

LES (*subsiding*) No—Have you?

PISZER A fellow loaned me a copy of his "State and Revolution" yesterday, and it kept me awake all night.

LES (*glancing at* PERCY) Yeah—

PISZER Yeah. Perhaps, you'd like to see it—?

BROOKS (*crossing with eggnog*) 'Scuse passin, Les. I got to get upstairs to mah Sick.

(*There is a loud knocking and stomping out front*)

LES (*springing up, and going to door*) Sounds like a mob! (*admitting group*) Oh, hello, Mr. Strawder—Come on in, you all! (*calling*) Mama! Here's Mr. Strawder and them!

(STRAWDER *and the others pile in, doffing their overcoats to reveal the splendor of their regalia— The men, wearing colored sashes above their black, red-striped uniforms—the women, in white with black crosses on their sleeves, the insignia of the Black Cross Nurses of the Movement. All, in high spirits and good cheer*)

COTTON (*as they pile in, excitedly*) Where's Brother Mason—Where's the Captain what ain't no Captain no more!—(*one of the* NURSES *claps her hands across his mouth, and* STRAWDER *glares at him angrily*)

ELLA (*entering with pot of steaming eggnog*) I'm afraid we've only got standing room. But I've made some eggnog to warm you up!

HARPER (*leading cheering, as* BLACK CROSS NURSES *assist* ELLA *in serving*) Hurray, for Sister Mason!

COTTON Now that's right. It's just what we need on a night like this—(*seeing* VIC *descending with* MRS. BROOKS *behind him*) Make way for the Lord of Agriculture!—(*one of the* NURSES *snatches his arm, and he, recognizing his error, claps the palm of his hand across his mouth and creeps into corner, as* STRAWDER *glares at him angrily.* BROOKS *comes down to aid in serving*)

STRAWDER (*commandingly*) Silence! (*addressing* VIC, *as the latter halts on stairs*) Brother Mason, it is my great privelege and honor to greet you on this occasion, and to convey to you the sentiments of our great president. (*he pauses dramatically*) For your great paper on the Future of Cooperative Farming in Africa, what you read at the Negro World Conference, our great leader has commanded me to greet you with the title of Lord of Agriculture of the Provisional Republic of Africa—(*the crowd cheers*) Quiet, everybody. Let me finish before you start celebrating. (PHILLIP *and* CAROLINE *creep down on stairs to peep through bannister. To* VIC) Step down, my Lord—(*as* VIC *descends, he turns*) Sister Gabrella! (SISTER GABRELLA *and another* NURSE *step forward with long red sash, which they place on* VIC)

PISZER (*to* LES, *aside*) Lord of Agriculture? I don't get it!

LES (*aside*) It means head of the Department of Agriculture.

PISZER Why not "Secretary?"

LES It's more striking, I guess.

PISZER Yeah. But less democratic, eh?

STRAWDER (*as the* NURSES *step back from* VIC) And now, my Lord, I bestow upon you this emblem of your high and mighty rank! (*the group cheers, as he pins on medallion*)

PHILLIP Look at Papa!

ELLA Children—Get back to bed! (*they scamper off above*)

HARPER (*lifting glass*) I want to make a toast.... Friends and Brothers of the UNIA, let us drink to the man who has put us on the map and set our banner flying before the eyes of our black brothers all over the world, Victor Mason, Lord of Agriculture of the Republic of Africa, the glory of our local chapter today—

COTTON Speech! Speech!

VIC (*lifting his hand for silence, as others go on crying*) Brothers and Sisters, I thank you for this great display of affection. (*suddenly solemn*) But I cannot respond to your toast as something extended to me personally. I appreciate the great honor which our leader has conferred upon me. But I feel I ought to call your attention to the way I think about what I've done... I only prepared and read a paper... It may be good as some say. Yet it's only a paper, and none of the things it deals with have been accomplished. We're still in the hands of the enemy, with our children cut off from opportunity, and the lynch-rope and faggot lying ready for any black man who dares to raise his head. (*grievously*) We have yet, my friends, to acquire a single inch of the soil of Africa that we can call our own. And while we celebrate, our great leader stands within the shadow of the penitentiary, branded as a common criminal... These are dark and terrible truths, my friends, and as I face them, I feel—well, the only proper response I can make to your toast, is to ask you to drink a pledge with me. (*lifting cup, which is handed him*) Brothers and Sisters and members of my family, let us pledge our hearts and minds and the last ounce of our strength to carry on—to carry on without ceasing, until our cause is won, and the black man has achieved his place in the God-given sun: A free man, honored and respected in the eyes of the nations of the world!

(*The silence is eloquent, as they all drink*)

STRAWDER (*moved*) My Lord, that was a speech to be proud of! (*his tone is like a benediction, and* VIC *is seen aloof, his eye fixed on his dark star, as the curtain descends*)

Scene Three

(TIME: *early evening, a month later.*

The atmosphere remains the same, a dreariness hanging over all like a pall and seeming to penetrate through the window from the sooty snow-ladened street, as PHILLIP *sits there looking out.* CAROLINE *is lying on the couch beneath a quilt, with her grandmother beside her, whom she is watching as she dresses a black doll*)

CAROLINE (*petulantly, after a moment*) That's not right, Grandma!

BROOKS (*tossing the doll in the others lap with an impatient thrust, then rising*) Here, you take this black thing! I don't want no more to do with it! (PHILLIP *darts a glance at her, and simultaneously kicks the rocker in an automatic, vicious reflex*) Are you trying to break that chair? What's the matter with you? (*guiltily*) You act like you crazy. (PHILLIP *rises abruptly and crosses to Victrola, where he sulks, as she goes on, complainingly*) I never seen sich chillun—for gittin' on a person's nerves!

CAROLINE Awh, Grandma, I was just telling you, you got her skirt on backwards.

BROOKS (*annoyed at herself*) I reckon I ought to know which is the front, when I made it.

CAROLINE (*to her doll*) Poor lil black Judy. Grandma treats that honey-child like an orphan, don't she?

(*There is a sound of stomping on the porch*)

LES (*entering, as they all turn to look*) Phew! (*closing the door behind him, he blows his breath into his fists, then, flapping his armpits, goes on to* PHILLIP) You're lucky you didn't have to go to school today!

BROOKS How cold is it now?

LES (*hanging his coat up*) About 10 below, I guess. (*he goes up stairs*)

ELLA (*appearing from rear*) Was that Les?

CAROLINE Yes'm.

ELLA (*seeing* PHILLIP *in corner*) What're you doing sulking over there?

PHILLIP (*dully*) Nothing. (*she eyes him questioningly*)

BROOKS (*seeing* VIC *descending*) Dinner bout ready?

ELLA Just about.

VIC Anybody seen the paper?

ELLA (*turning to go*) There isn't any paper.

VIC (*annoyed, going to window*) There isn't?—I'm going to have to write in about that boy yet!

ELLA You'd do better paying his bill!

VIC (*turning in surprise*) You haven't paid him?

ELLA What was I going to pay him with?

VIC (*coming over*) But it ain't but fifteen cents a week! (*in huff*) I can't see why in God's world you can't manage that!

ELLA (*going, angrily*) Is that so? Well, hereafter you see that he gets it! (*exit rear*)

VIC (*sick*) Phumph! (*the entrance of* WANDA *from the street is like a shock to him, for she is in tears and shivering*) Now what's the matter with you? And where's your coat?

(LES *descends*)

WANDA (*sobbing*) They took it!

BROOKS Who took it?

LES (*excitedly*) Stickup men?

WANDA No . . . The Sheriff.

BROOKS (*excitedly*) The Sheriff! (*shouting*) Ella!

VIC (*amazed*) But how?

WANDA (*extending paper*) He just took it with this.

VIC (*joining her*) What is it—a lien?

ELLA (*entering*) What's the matter?

BROOKS (*dramatically*) The Sheriff's done had-er hold of Wanda. Done took that sealskin coat off her!

VIC (*to* WANDA) How many payments do you owe?

WANDA Only seven.

VIC Seven—That's $35—(*shaking his head, helplessly*) Lord, Lord!—But there's nothing I can do.

ELLA More good money burnt up! (WANDA *bursts into tears anew, and runs upstairs*)

LES But, Papa. She practically owns the coat!

VIC What does the law care!

BROOKS She had no business buyin' it!

(*There is silence, and* DAN, *swaddled in an expensive grey ulster, enters—a vulturous smirk on his lips*)

VIC What brings you here on a night like this?

DAN (*swaggering down*) Then you haven't heard—?

VIC Heard what?

DAN The news about Garvey.

VIC No. What about him?

DAN (*triumphantly*) They took him to Atlanta today, that's what!

LES Oh, no!

VIC (*staggered*) Are you sure?

DAN You bet! I told you that monkeychaser was no good!

VIC But the Supreme Court—?

DAN Denied his appeal, and they took him into custody this morning.

VIC (*sitting with an air of defeat*) Well, sir!

ELLA (*sympathetically*) Don't take it so hard, Vic. It's no more than you expected.

VIC I guess you're right, Ella. He never had a chance. But what makes it hard—the thing that really hurts so is the part our folks had in the whole frame up.

LES How do you mean, Papa?

VIC I'm talking about our so-called leaders, Son. They're the ones who sicced the white folks on him. In their jealousy and fear of his power they turned informers—The assassins! Assassins!

BROOKS Les, I thought you told me Marcus Garvey confessed 'bout that money?

LES (*hesitantly*) Well, he did, Grandma.

But not for stealing himself. It was the ones he trusted.

DAN Bah! They were all in cahoots together. It came out at the trial—(*turning to* VIC) But you can't stand the truth. Instead of admitting you were wrong, you've got to try to stigmatize your own people. I told you all along—

ELLA (*ominously*) Now just a minute, Dan. If you've come here to crow over us, you can get out!

DAN Hold on, Ella. Don't misunderstand me. I feel as bad over this thing as you do. But there's such a thing as reason—First he tried to put the blame on the white folks for wanting to break up the movement. Now it's our own leaders—What kind of sense is that?—Hell, the truth is the truth!

VIC (*rising*) Yeah. But if it was big as the Woolworth Building you wouldn't see it. (*goes to telephone*) Victory 11780.

ELLA Who're you calling?

VIC Strawder. (*as his call is answered*) That you, Count? This is Mason. Have you heard about Garvey? . . . (*after a moment*) Well, you needn't do that. We should call a meeting right away, in my judgment. Show the white folks we can't be fooled by their trickery. Explain to the members . . . How about Sunday? . . . Yes, yes, exactly. You get out the cards. What?—I'll see that you get the keys right away. Goodbye— (*hanging up*) We'll show them—Les, get your coat, and take these keys to the hall to Count Strawder.

LES (*taking keys*) Yes, Sir. (*he goes to get coat*)

DAN For Christ's sake, Vic. Why in the hell don't you wake up? Your movement's dead as a mackrel!

VIC (*angrily*) Why do you persist in meddling in my affairs?

DAN (*backing away*) OK, OK, Big shot. (*going. Prophetically*) But you mark my word: With Garvey in jail, your $1500 is burnt up, and from now on, your movement's going to peter out like a pail full of water with a hole in the bottom. (*exit*)

ELLA You'd better come and get your dinner, Vic. (*to* PHILLIP) Go set the table. (*exit* PHILLIP)

VIC No, Ella. You all go ahead. I'm going up and lie down for a while.

LES (*as father turns to go*) I'm sorry, Papa.

VIC It's a mighty blow, Son. But no man is indispensable to a good cause. We'll carry on.

ELLA (*arresting him*) If you don't mind, Vic. Take Caroline up to bed. She's been down here too long already—(*to* LES) And you'd better go get that dinner before you go out of here.

LES But the keys—?

ELLA They can wait. You need something in your stomach. (*to* CAROLINE, *as* VIC *bears her away*) I'll bring you some soup in a little while. (*exit* LES *to kitchen*)

VIC (*carrying* CAROLINE *above*) How do you feel?

CAROLINE All right. (*exit* VIC *and* CAROLINE)

ELLA (*seeing her mother trying to thread needle*) Give it to me, Mama.

BROOKS (*as* ELLA *threads it*) Well, Ella. It looks like Dan was right after all—

ELLA Mama, I'm in no mood to stand your criticism this evening!

BROOKS No. I reckon not. After the food we'll leave. (*she rummages through work basket*) Now, where's my sizzers? (*angrily*) Ain't nobody teched them sizzers but Phillip. (*rising to call*) Phillip!

PHILLIP (*in rear*) Yes'm!

BROOKS (*crossing*) Where's my sizzers?

PHILLIP (*in rear*) I don't know, Grandma. I ain't seen em!

BROOKS (*rushing out*) You ain't, hunh? . . . You stinkin' rascal! (*there is an outburst from* PHILLIP) Didn't I tell you not to bother my sizzers!

ELLA (*crossing, her voice rising above the shouts of the child*) Turn him loose, Mama! Turn him loose! (*the cries of the child subside, and* BROOKS *enters in a huff, out of breath*) Lord, Mama, I don't know what I'm going to do about you. I told you if you want any of the children whipped to call me or Vic to do it for you. You see how it wears you out. You can't be wrestling with that boy! The first thing you know you'll fall and knock your head against something! (PHILLIP *enters, meanwhile, sulking as he glares at* GRANDMOTHER)

BROOKS (*angrily*) You don't have to beat 'round the stump! (*shaking her finger at* PHILLIP) If you don't want me to put mah hands on that black scamp, why don't you say so?

ELLA (*angrily*) Mama, I've asked you not to call that boy black where he can hear you!

BROOKS Yes he's black. Black like his cranky Daddy!

ELLA Don't mind her, Phillip—Go upstairs and sit with Caroline till I call you. (PHILLIP *ascends stairs and slowly disappears*)

BROOKS But I know when my bread is brown. (*going out rear*) I'm goin' git my few rags and git out-er here. That's what I'm goin' do! (*exit rear*)

ELLA (*crossing to door there*) Oh, yeah? And where do you think you're going to find a place to stay—Juanita's?

BROOKS (*offstage*) Yes, Juanita's! She'll give me a place to lay mah weary head.

ELLA She will, hunh? You just wait. You'll see!

BROOKS (*entering with armful of clothing*) Don't you fool yourself. Don't you do it. Juanita's got Dupree blood in her veins! (*she dumps garments on couch*)

ELLA You and your Dupree blood!—But I know what's the matter with you. You want to get over to Dan's where you think you won't suffer—!

BROOKS That's a lie!

ELLA (*furiously*) For ten years this house has been good enough for you. But now you think we're in the bread line. So you want to save your own skin. You want to get over there where you think you'll be safe!

BROOKS That's another lie! Tain't no sich! (VIC *appears above, buttoning jacket. But she doesn't see him*) You's jes making that up out-er jealousy, like that evil, black, good-for-nothin' fool you call your husband!

VIC (*woundedly*) So!

ELLA (*glancing up, frightened*) Vic!

(BROOKS, *realizing she has committed the unpardonable sin in inner-racial relations, backs up*).

VIC (*coming down, his voice cold and hostile*) So I'm a evil, black, good-for-nothing nigger!

ELLA (*joining him, anxiously*) For God's sake, Vic. Overlook it!

VIC (*to* BROOKS, *as she stands at bay*) What've I ever done to make you say such a harsh thing about me?

ELLA (*soothingly*) Nothing, Vic. And she knows it.

BROOKS (*in belligerent fear*) Don't you put no words in mah mouth! I ain't scared of him and nobody like him.

ELLA (*striding toward her*) Will you shut up!

BROOKS Don't you tell me to shut up! Don't you do it!

ELLA (*turning to* VIC) Don't pay her no mind, Vic. She's just upset. Excited—because I got after her about whipping Phillip!

VIC You needn't try to cover up for her, Ella. I've stumbled into something and you know it!

ELLA But she's just imagining things—

VIC Like calling me the dirtiest thing she can think of, eh?

ELLA Don't get off on the wrong track, Vic. What she said she said out of anger with me. And if you hadn't come down here so quietly, you never would've heard her.

VIC (*angrily*) What am I supposed to do, blow a trumpet everytime I move in my own house?

ELLA No, Vic. Of course not. I only meant—

VIC (*to* BROOKS, *coldly*) I'm too black for your Dupree blood, isn't that it?

BROOKS (*venomously*) The cap must fit you or you wouldn't be wearing it!

ELLA (*pained*) Oh, Mama!

VIC You miserable old hypocrite.

BROOKS Well, there's one thing. I ain't never been no hypocrite with you!

ELLA Lord, Mama. You ought to be ashamed of yourself!

BROOKS Shame nothin'. I ain't got nothing to be shamed of!

VIC (*coldly*) No. But you let this sink into your twisted soul. You don't hate me. You envy me. You envy my black skin because in your heart, you know yours is nothing but a badge of shame!

ELLA (*hurt*) Oh, Vic!

BROOKS Ella, you goin' stand there and let him insult me like that?

ELLA (*to* VIC) Could she help it if she was born out of wedlock?

VIC (*sharply*) No. What I resent is her vicious attitude. She's got nothing against me, and she knows it. But she's like the rest of her kind, who let the color of their skin drive them to think black people are some kind of dirt beneath their feet, when nothing could be more idiotic than the pride they take in the blood of their raping ancestors!

BROOKS You hear that, Ella! (*crying in outrage, as she gathers clothing*) To think the day would ever come when anybody'd say sich things bout me! But I'll git you. I'll git even with you, you black viper, if it's the last thing I do! (*going to door and turning with parting shot*) You'll see if I don't! (*exit*)

ELLA (*stunned*) If anybody had told me you could be so petty, I'd've spit on them!

VIC (*quietly*) The truth always seem ugly when it's hard to look at. But a man can't stand everything.

ELLA (*preoccupiedly*) It serves me right. I should've listened years ago.

VIC Just what do you mean by that?

ELLA Don't ask me what I mean. Don't ask me anything.

VIC But, Ella—

ELLA (*venomously*) I despise you!

VIC Ella, for God's sake—

(LES *appears in door right*)

ELLA Yes, I despise you. You hear me. I despise you! And I think you're everything Mama said and then some. You ain't nothing but an evil, black fool!

LES (*plunging forward*) For Christ's sake, Mama! What're you saying?

ELLA Get back in that kitchen and finish your supper, and stay out of my business!

LES But, Mama—You can't mean what you said—Not you!

VIC Do as you're told, and get back in your place!

LES No, Papa. I heard everything, and it isn't fair!

VIC Shut up! Your Ma's just upset—though God knows I had no intention of hurting her feelings.—(*distraught*) I guess the news about Garvey, then this, just about floored me—(*to* ELLA) But you must know I meant no offense to you.

ELLA (*bitterly*) You can keep your apologies. I don't want them. For twenty years I've let you treat me like a doormat, and run things to suit yourself. (*furiously*) And now you've got the nerve to insult Mama right before my face. Who do you think you are, King Jesus!

VIC (*quietly*) I've always considered you, Ella.

ELLA You let Wanda quit school against my wishes! Who else but you and your fool ideas started her on the road to hell? And this Garvey business: Where's all the money I helped you save? (*in sudden tears*) Whose fault is it I can't stop a bread wagon to feed my children?

VIC (*shouting*) So you blame me for the world!

LES Oh, Please—! Both of you—calm yourselves—

ELLA (*ignoring him*) I've been a woman and a wife to you. But I'm through with you! (*she starts out*)

LES Oh, Mama, no! Wait a minute—

ELLA (*turning to shout*) You hear me. I'm through with you!

VIC (*joining her*) You can't mean that, Ella. You wouldn't leave me?

ELLA No. But I can make you wish I would! —If it wasn't for Caroline and the rest, I'd follow Mama out of this house and never put my feet back in it again!

VIC (*sadly*) I'll get out if you want me to.

ELLA (*going*) Suit yourself. Get out or stay! Or better still, go on to Africa. Maybe you'll find the company of your own kind in the jungle! (*exit above*)

VIC (*wounded grievously, and crying aloud, he staggers down to bang the back of the chair beside couch*) Prejudice! Prejudice! Everywhere you turn, nothing but prejudice! A black man can't even get away from it in his own house! (*overwhelmed by the irony, he emits a prolonged grunt*) Phummmmmnnnh! Phummmmmnnnh! Phummmmmnnnh! (*impelled by the onslaught of pain, as he recognizes the very essence of his oppression. his voice reverberates with agony*) And like a fool I dreamed of getting away from it in Africa! (*slowly, he sinks into the chair, and* LES *is seen drawing near to place his hand on his shoulder in sympathy and understanding, as the curtain falls*)

ACT THREE

Scene One

(TIME: *1932, or ten years later.*

The living-room is the same, except that now everywhere is manifest some sign of the family's desperate impoverishment, as it continues its struggle in the midsts of the general breakdown of the nation's economy, or the great depression.

Present are ELLA, *wearing a frayed apron and*

Big White Fog

the aspect of care; WANDA, *in a good skirt and sweater of light material—indicative of her continued capacity to earn a living; and* MARKS, *a Used-Furniture dealer, in a disreputable old suit and fedora*)

MARKS (*a man of fifty-odd years with eloquent gestures, seemingly at the end of his wits in the effort to strike a bargain*) Sell! Sell! Efery-body vants to sell. But nobody vants to buy.—Can I help it if effery-body vants to sell, Mrs. Mason, and nobody vants to buy?—Maybe you didn't hear there's a depression—?

ELLA (*stubbornly*) But, Mr. Marks, you can give me more than $3 for that couch. I paid $79 for it!

MARKS (*with a quick, snapping glance at couch*) You should pay $79 for such a couch—Oh, moi, oh, moi—$79 for such a couch!—Come, I'll make it $3.50.

WANDA (*outraged*) $3.50!

MARKS (*confidingly*) To anybody else I wouldn't pay half so much.

ELLA I wouldn't think of it.

MARKS (*appealingly*) Maybe I should keep it a whole year and couldn't sell it to nobody!

WANDA Oh, yeah!

ELLA (*indicating machine*) Well, what'll you give me for that Victrola?

MARKS (*throwing up his hands*) The Victrola you couldn't giff me!

WANDA Oh, no—?

MARKS (*annoyed by her sarcasm*) Listen, Lady. Buisness is bad—You know that? Nobody vants to buy a Victrola. Nobody wants to buy anything. (*to* ELLA) Vell, vat you say?

ELLA (*indicating chair center*) What about that chair—?

MARKS (*examining chair, slowly*) The chair—it isn't so good. But . . . maybe vit the chair and couch together I could giff you $5.

WANDA (*angrily*) Tell him to go to hell, Mama!

MARKS Vat's the matter vit you? I offer Mrs. Mason the top price, and you tell me to go to hell!—You think I ain't got no feelings?—I'm a man vit a family. You vant I should ruin myself?

WANDA Swell chance you've got to ruin yourself!

MARKS (*turning to* ELLA) Vell, vat you say? You vant to sell?

ELLA (*dejectedly*) No. Nevermind. I just thought I could raise a few dollars to help me get another place. But the little you offer won't do us any good.

MARKS (*sympathetically*) Times are bad, Mrs. Mason.—But you vant find anybody'll giff you more, even if you should search the city over.

ELLA (*bitterly*) I'd rather put them in the stove! (*she wipes her eyes*)

WANDA Don't, Mama.

MARKS Come, I'll giff you $6?

WANDA Big hearted Mr. Marks!

ELLA (*desperately*) Make it $10 and you can have them.

WANDA No, Mama. No!

MARKS I should make it $10? Vy I could buy a finer couch and chair for $5—(*he starts out*) You don't vant to do buisness, Mrs. Mason.

ELLA Take them for $8.

MARKS (*with finality*) I'll giff you $6.50 and no more!

ELLA (*breaking*) I'll chop them to pieces first!

WANDA (*furiously*) You get out of here—You—you—you're a disgrace to your race!

MARKS (*backing out*) All right! All right! Don't get sore!

CLAUDINE (*as he bumps into her as she enters*) Hey! Why don't you look where you're going—What're you a crab or something?

MARKS (*disappearing*) Escuse me— (*exit* MARKS)

WANDA (*half-heartedly greeting the newcomer—in a summer frock, quite chic*) Hello, Claudine.

CLAUDINE (*noticing* ELLA, *as she comes down*) What's the matter—?

WANDA (*embarrassed*) Don't cry, Mama. Everything's going to be all right. You go upstairs and lie down for a while and quiet your nerves.

CLAUDINE (*sympathetically*) Is there anything I can do for you, Mrs. Mason?

ELLA No. Claudine. I guess I'll just have to let them set us out, and make the best of it. (*she climbs stairs in tears*)

CLAUDINE (*sitting on arm of couch*) You all going to be evicted, too, hunh?

WANDA I guess so. Papa's gone to Court now.

CLAUDINE Well, that's too bad!

WANDA (*crossing to window seat*) Mama tried to raise a little money on the furniture. But I wish you could've seen how he tried to take advantage of her—

CLAUDINE Well, it's all your own fault!

WANDA Where do you get that stuff; it's my fault?

CLAUDINE If you had any sense you wouldn't be in this trouble.

WANDA Oh, yeah?

CLAUDINE · You're damn right! (*nervously, she lights cigarette*) I wish I could get a break with an old chump like Hogan. I'd show you something. I'd take his sugar so quick, he'd think I was a gangster!

WANDA I've told you, I don't go for *that*!

CLAUDINE No. You're too dumb.—Here you are with your Mama about to be set out in the street, and all you've got to do is ask that old sucker in order to save her.

WANDA I know. I know. But I just can't bring myself round to it.

CLAUDINE Balooney! Crazy as Hogan is about you, all you have to do is ask him for the dough.

WANDA I know. In fact, I already have.

CLAUDINE (*surprised*) You have?—Then you've got more sense than I gave you credit for!

WANDA I just thought I'd ask him last night to see what he'd say.

CLAUDINE Sweet patootie' And he shelled right out—

WANDA No. There's a catch in it. He wanted me to promise to be nice to him—I can't stomach that!

CLAUDINE Don't talk foolish, Wanda. There won't be nothing to it.—Hogan's not so bad. He's just old—Anyway ... (*going to table for ash tray*) you're no virgin, you know!

WANDA (*sharply*) No. But I'm no whore!

CLAUDINE (*snuffing cigarette*) You're a fool, if you ask me. But she's your mother, Kiddo. If you don't care whether she's set out in disgrace before all the neighbors, it's your lookout. But I'll tell you one thing: You'd never catch me turning my mother down for the sake of such a flimsy idea. (*going*) But I've got to get home. You'd better think it over like you got some sense. (*exit*)

WANDA (*contemplatively*) Think it over— (*she shudders*) God! (*she buries her face in the palm of her hands and is lost until she hears* ELLA *descending*) I thought you were going to liedown for a while?

ELLA My pillow's like a bag of rocks—Claudine gone?

WANDA Yes.

ELLA Isn't it time for you to be going to work?

WANDA What time is it?

ELLA My clock said 5:30. But I wouldn't trust it.

WANDA (*preoccupiedly, still sitting*) I guess I'd better get ready.

ELLA I guess you'd better.

DAN (*appearing, seedily dressed and bereft of his former cocksuredness—accompanied by* LES) Well, what'd they do? (*he sits*)

ELLA I don't know. Vic's still downtown.

LES (*in sweatshirt and trousers, he notices his mother's eyes*) You've been crying.

WANDA Marks upset her.

LES Marks? What Marks?

WANDA The used-furniture man—You should've heard what he offered her for that couch and chair—$6.50! (*she goes above*)

DAN Can you beat it?—But it's no more than you can expect from a Jew!

LES That's prejudice, Uncle Dan. (*he gets magazine from table*)

DAN Call it what you like. But I'm sick of them—They're all alike!

LES The white man says the same thing about us. But the Jews are no different from any other people. If *anything*, they've contributed a damn sight more.

DAN Oh, yeah—Another of your Communistic ideas, eh?

LES It didn't take the Communists to find that out. (*he sits*) The whole world's been aware of it ever since the coming of Christ—And look at Marx and Einstein, and Freud and Spinoza!

(CAROLINE *enters*)

ELLA (*coldly*) For God's sake, let the Jews rest! (*seeing* CAROLINE) I thought you went to Juanita's?

CAROLINE (*pretending to search for mail on table—A fine looking girl of twenty, neatly dressed*) I just left her.

ELLA (*suspiciously*) You didn't stay long.

CAROLINE (*glancing at* DAN, *who squirms*) I can't understand her anymore, Mama. She acts so funny.

ELLA What do you mean, she acts funny?

CAROLINE (*glancing at* LES, *who is smiling, apparently enjoying* DAN's *predicament*) Oh, I don't know, Mama—Did Papa get back?

ELLA (*persisting*) It's mighty strange you can't explain what you mean—

CAROLINE (*studiously avoiding* DAN, *who has inched toward the edge of his chair, she goes to couch*) I just don't know what to think, Mama. But everytime I go there lately, she watches me and Grandma like a hawk.

DAN (*uneasily*) That's just your imagination.

CAROLINE Maybe so. But she made me feel so much like I was in the way, I just told her goodbye and came home. (*she reads*)

DAN (*defensively*) Juanita's just worried like everybody else over these hard times.

ELLA (*after a moment*) I wish your father would come on!

LES The courts are packed, Mama. They're evicting right and left.

DAN (*relieved at turn of conversation*) They have to protect people's property.

LES Yeah. Protect the property and to hell with the people!

ELLA For fifteen years Cochran never missed a month getting his rent on this house.

DAN Sure. But what can you expect when nine out of ten tenants are nothing but dead beats.

LES That's a lot of hooey—Anyway, if the big dogs can't give us work, they've no right to expect any rent. Furthermore, a just Government would make them bear their part of the responsibility.

DAN (*bitterly*) Yeah. I bore my part and you see what it got me!

LES It serves you right for kidding yourself.

DAN Oh, yeah?

LES You doggone tooting! You've never been anything but a *Negro striver*, trying to go big. Now, even though you've been wiped out, you still can't see what hit you!

DAN (*angrily*) You rattle-brained, young snipe! If you weren't my own nephew—!

ELLA Dan, is that necessary?

LES Don't mind us, Mama.

ELLA We've all made mistakes—

DAN Mistake nothing. Suppose I'd-er kept my money in the bank, would I have it?

LES That's just another contradiction in the present rotten order. And you and Papa were both wrong—You for putting faith in it. Papa for thinking the Garvey Movement anything more than an impractical, chauvinistic dream.

DAN You wise punk! You're just like your Daddy: You think you see everything! Nobody can't—

ELLA (*exploding*) Oh, stop it! I'm sick of listening to nothing but talk, talk! For twenty years thats all we've had in this house—And ain't nobody done nothing yet!

DAN (*rising*) I guess you're right, Ella. (*joining* LES) Gimme a cigarette.

LES I can't afford them.

DAN (*going*) I guess not. But maybe you Reds'll include them in the rations when you get in power.

LES (*smiling*) At least, you can bet everybody'll be able to smoke them!

DAN (*ironically*) Oh, absolutely! (*turning to* ELLA) I'll be back, Ella. I'm just going to the corner. (*exit front door*)

ELLA (*going*) I guess I'll go put the little we got on the stove. (*exit into rear*)

CAROLINE I think you're foolish to argue with him, Les. You'll never recruit him in a thousand years. (WANDA *descends with purse*)

LES (*rising, his eyes on* WANDA) Yeah. I may not. But the times will.—(*to* WANDA) I've been waiting for a chance to see you.

WANDA (*going to front door*) Yeah. Well, you'll have to do it later.

LES (*intercepting her*) Oh, no you don't. I said I wanted to talk to you, and I don't mean tomorrow—(*to other*) Excuse us will you, Caroline.

CAROLINE (*going*) Of course . . . (*she starts above*)

WANDA But I tell you, I've got to get to the drugstore.

LES I can't help that—(*seeing* CAROLINE *has halted on stairs in curiosity, he casts a commanding glance on her, and she hurries out of sight*) Sit down.

WANDA I won't sit down. You can't bully me.

LES (*ominously*) Mama's in the kitchen. Perhaps, you'd rather I spoke to her?

WANDA (*frightened*) What do you mean?

LES You know what I mean.

WANDA You haven't got anything on me!

LES No? But let's not be melodramatic. Sit down and keep your voice low.

WANDA (*she hesitates, measuring him for a moment, then sits*) All right. (*he turns away in silence, and takes a stride or two apparently gathering his thoughts*) Well, why don't you say what you're going to say?

LES (*joining her*) I don't suppose you realize it, Wanda. But it's been pretty painful to Papa and me, sitting round here day after day, allowing you to bear the burden of the house—

WANDA When have you heard me complaining?

LES Never. But it's begun to look as if it's about to get you down, isn't that so?

WANDA (*rising—excited*) No. Who said it was?

LES Nobody. But the facts seem to indicate it.

WANDA (*rising*) Come to the point!

LES All right. I will. I saw you get out of that car around the corner last night.

WANDA (*flushing*) You what—

LES (*accusingly*) You're slipping!

WANDA (*desperately*) But it was nothing like that, Les. Honest. He was just an old drug salesman who always comes into the store.

LES Then why didn't you let him bring you to the door?

WANDA (*truthfully*) Because I knew you or some of the rest would misunderstand—that's why!

LES (*quietly*) Don't lie, Wanda. You're a grown woman, and you don't have to tell me anything. But you know damn well, (*his voice fills with bitter irony*) when a white man begins to take a "nigger girl" riding, it can't mean but one thing!

WANDA (*grieved*) But you're wrong!

LES (*with deadly conviction*) I'm not. You're trifling with him.—(*with a wave of moral indignation, he presses*) Aren't you?

WANDA (*cowering*) No! No!

LES (*twisting her wrist*) I say you are!

WANDA (*outraged, but surrendering*) All right. Have it your way.

LES You little bum!

WANDA (*hurt and angry*) You lie! Hogan never touched me!

LES Oh, no. And I suppose he didn't even try—That he had nothing but a wish to assist the poor little "nigger gal" home?

WANDA (*bitterly*) Am I responsible for what a man thinks?

LES That's a convenient little subterfuge!

WANDA I've got as much right to use it as any other woman.

LES (*sharply*) Oh, you have? Well, what was the purpose of it here, may I ask?

WANDA (*coldly*) You know as well as I do what we're up against!

LES (*darkly*) Umph phumn! Just as I thought. (*he turns away*)

WANDA (*following him, pleadingly*) We've got to have some place to stay, haven't we? Can't you see, Les? I only thought I might be able to borrow a few dollars from him!

LES (*whirling*) And you got them, I suppose?

WANDA (*suddenly resenting the implication*) That's my business!

LES You dirty little Chippy!

WANDA (*quailing*) Les!

LES (*furious*) You're not as good as a Chippy!—Any girl that'd stoop to such a thing and call herself decent—

WANDA (*growing hysterical*) That's right! Wipe your feet on me! Drag me in the dirt!

LES (*suddenly recalling their situation*) Sh! Mama'll hear!

WANDA (*wildly*) Let her. I don't care! I don't care about nothing! (*she starts for front door*)

LES (*catching her*) Hush, I tell you!

WANDA (*twisting away from him—ravingly*) I won't. You can tell the whole damn world for all I care. You think I'm nothing but a whore, why shouldn't she!

ELLA (*appearing from rear*) For God's sake, what's going on in here?

LES Nothing, Mama.

WANDA (*coming down*) Oh, yes there is. Come on in. You'll get the thrill of your life. Les's got a little story to tell you—(*turning to him, and going*) Go on, Les. Tell her. Tell it to Mama. Give her your spicy little tale—(*she runs into the street*)

ELLA What in the world is it?

LES Nothing, I tell you.

ELLA Don't lie to me. What is it?

LES She's just hysterical.

ELLA (*insistently*) Hysterical? Hysterical about what?

LES The house, I guess. She's worried about the notice.

ELLA (*shraply*) You're lying. Tell me the truth!

LES I am, Mama.—She's worried about getting money for another place.

ELLA (*sitting, partly satisfied*) Yes—Go on.

LES There isn't anything else to say.

ELLA Don't tell me.—What about this spicy tale business?

LES Nothing you'd be interested in.—(*suddenly seeing a way out*) She came up with a wild scheme to raise money to get a place.

ELLA What sort of wild scheme?

LES (*joining her—easily*) It's unimportant, Mama. I've already put my foot down. Anyway, I intended to tell you when I came in. I think we're going to get relief in another week or so.

ELLA (*puzzled*) What do you mean—"relief?"

LES Help, Mam—Food, rent, maybe even employment—We're moving in on Governor Emerson tomorrow.

ELLA Who's "we"?

LES Oh, just a bunch of folks like me, who're sick of waiting for "prosperity to turn the corner," while their folks starve and their sisters creep down into the gutter. (DAN *reenters*)

ELLA And you're going with them?

LES You bet!

DAN (*coming down*) Going where?

LES To Springfield—to see the Governor about conditions.

ELLA Have you said anything to your father?

LES No. Not yet.

DAN I guess not. (*suddenly sharp*) You haven't forgotten what the police did to that mob in Ohio the other day, have you?

LES I'm not worrying about that.

DAN No. You and that bunch of riff-raff I see you with don't give a damn about nothing—But I warn you, you're headed for trouble!

LES I'm already in trouble. And so's the rest of us. But you can't understand that.

DAN I can't, eh? Well, there's one thing I do understand, and so will you Reds before long!

LES (*laughing*) Yeah. What's that?

DAN (*pounding*) You can't beat the Government!

LES You and your blind pessimism—You make me sick!

DAN You'll learn when the rifles begin to talk!

LES Let them. The quicker the better.

ELLA Lester!

DAN The young fool!

LES (*immature and recklessly*) The disinherited will never come to power without bloodshed!

ELLA Les. don't say such things!

DAN Let him rave on. He'll wake up one of these days.

LES (*seriously*) It's you who're asleep, not me. Your world has crashed. But you're so full of capitalist dope, you don't even know we're building a new one. (*he starts upstairs*)

DAN (*angrily, seeming to pin him against the stairway*) You're building a wall to be put up against and shot!

LES (*going above*) I'd rather look forward to that than a pauper's grave! (*exit above*)

ELLA (*helplessly*) I don't know what in the world's come over him!

DAN (*darkly*) That's what you get for letting him raise himself!

ELLA Don't blame me. I've done the best I could by him.

DAN Like hell!—For ten years all you and Vic've done is sit around here like a pair of petrified mummies and let him go straight to the dogs!

PERCY (*on porch, singing, drunkenly*) "Is there anybody here want to buy a lil dog Buy a lil dog—(*appearing, he sways in doorway*) Is there anybody here want to buy a lil dog— I got one for to sell him . . . !" (LES *appears above*)

DAN (*gauging* PERCY, *disgustedly*) Just look at that!

LES (*descending quickly*) Lay off him, Uncle Dan. (*taking the drunk man*) Come on in, Uncle Percy, and sit down before you fall.

DAN A regular bum!

PERCY (*staggering, he pulls loose from* LES, *and halts swaying*) What you mean, I'm a bum? Whatcha mean?

DAN You'd better sit down and try to sober up!

PERCY (*fumbling in back pocket*) Sober up? Do I look like I'm drunk to you? Do I, hunh?

ELLA You'd better take him in the back, Les, and put him in Mama's room. He may get sick here.

LES Come on, Uncle Percy. I'll put you to bed.

(VIC *appears in doorway*)

DAN (*seeing* PERCY *pull flask, he joins them to try and take it away*) Gimme that!

PERCY (*hugging flask*) Oh, no you don't, Big Shot. No you don't. This is my *moon*.

DAN I say give it to me!

VIC Let him alone, Dan.

DAN (*angrily*) Can't you see he's drunk?

VIC (*coming in, his face grim with care—he is wearing his old Garvey uniform, which is now faded and beraggled*) What difference does it make! (PHILLIP *follows him in*)

PERCY (*Triumphantly*) That a boy, Vic, old man. Get him told!

VIC (*To* LES—*quietly*) Take him somewhere and put him to bed—Go on, now, Percy. Let him put you to bed.

PERCY (*obediently*) Awh right, Vic. Anything you say, old man. (*he allows* LES *to escort him across to door leading to rear, where he halts*) I know you wouldn't tell me nothing wrong—And if you say I'm drunk and ought to go to bed—Well, well, I'm drunk and ought to go to bed—(*going with* LES—*a ragged, broken, pathetic figure with one foot in the grave*) I know I must be drunk if you say so—(*exit*)

DAN He's going to keep on fighting that stuff until it kills him.

VIC (*gloomily*) Maybe he'll be better off dead.

DAN (*alertly*) I judge you didn't come out so well...?

VIC (*avoiding any direct contact with* ELLA, *with whom there has been no reconciliation and to whom he never speaks directly*) No. I didn't.

DAN (*sympathetically*) How much time did the judge give you?

LES (*reenters*)

VIC (*hollowly*) Twenty days.

ELLA (*gasping*) Twenty days!

DAN (*astounded*) That all—?

PHILLIP (*behind couch*) I guess Papa was lucky to get that—(*indicating fathers clothing*) after the Judge noticed that uniform.

VIC (*sharply*) Will you never learn to hold your tongue?

PHILLIP I didn't mean no harm, Papa—I just—

VIC Dry up! You never do.

DAN There's no use hiding anything, Vic. We're all in the family.

VIC I've nothing to hide. He just got tough when I admitted I used to be a Garveyite.

LES What did he say, Papa?

VIC (*quoting, bitterly*) "Oh, so you're one of the niggers who think this country isn't good enough for you, eh? Well, well, and you've got the nerve to appeal to this Court for leniency?"—As if that wasn't enough, he went on to rub it in by telling me how thankful we ought to be because his people brought us out of savagery—But I couldn't say anything.

DAN (*thoughtlessly*) You had no business wearing that uniform down there.

VIC (*sharply*) What was I going in, my ragged drawers?

DAN (*quietly*) I'm sorry, Vic. I wasn't thinking. (*after a moment, amid the general air of dejection*) Have you any idea what you're going to do?

VIC (*bitterly*) Move to Hooverville—I guess.

DAN Don't be sardonic, Vic.

VIC (*sharply*) If you think I don't mean it, find me a truck!

LES (*easily*) Forget it, Papa. We're not going anywhere.

VIC Eh?

LES I said we're not going to move a step!

VIC (*puzzled*) What're you talking about—(*he stiffens, hearing* MRS. BROOKS)

BROOKS (*on porch calling*) Les!... Where Les—

LES (*going to door—surprised*) It's Grandma! (*the others sit amazed*)

BROOKS (*entering in a huff with a bundle of clothing under her arm*) Les—Les, I want you to go yonder to Juanita's and bring me the rest of mah things. Cause I ain't fixin' to say there another blessed night! (*wearily, she drops into chair, center*)

ELLA For God's sake, Mama—What's happened?

BROOKS (*indignantly*) That hussey done come up here and forgot her raisin', that's what! But if she thinks I'm goin' live in sich dirt, she never was so wrong in her life! Mah garment's clean and spotless fore the Savior, and she and nobody else ain't goin' change it!

ELLA (*to* DAN) What in the world's she talking about?

DAN (*evasively*) You can search me. But it sounds like she's losing her mind.

BROOKS (*angrily*) Don't you try to call me crazy, you sneakin' blackguard! Don't you dare try it! If you don't want me to lay you out, don't you open your mouth!

DAN (*placatingly*) Awh, go on, Mama—Whatever it is forget it! (*cunningly*) Ella and Vic don't want to hear that stuff. They've got trouble enough of their own—Here they are about to be evicted, kicked out in the street—

ELLA (*suspicious of him*) Nevermind, Dan—There must be something wrong, or she wouldn't be here—Go on, Mama. What is it?

BROOKS You bet your bottom dollar there is! (*to* DAN) And you needn't think you can shut me up, neither! Cause—

DAN (*joining her, angrily*) Shut you up! Why should I want to shut you up? (*turning to others and quickly crossing to window*) If you all want to listen to her crazy tales, let her go ahead. It doesn't make a damn bit of difference to me what she says!

ELLA Go on, Mama. What happened?

BROOKS I got after her 'bout rentin' rooms and havin' all kinds of lowdown, good-for-nothin' tramps layin' up in her house—(*glancing around at* DAN) while some folks I ain't mentionin' keep duckin' in and out and makin' out they can't see what's goin' on—(*going on to others*) So she says: "Mama, do you know how you're livin? Do you know who's takin' care of you? Do you know nobody's givin me a dime to look after this house? Where you think I'm goin' git rent to keep a roof ovuh your head?" Like as if I never kept a roof ovuh bofe of you all's heads for twenty years without spottin mah garment—But ask me if I didn't bless her out? I bet you she'll remember what I told her to her dyin' day!—After that, I just got mah things together and come on to you, cause I know you'd give me a clean place to lay mah weary head, even if we did fall out bout the chillun and Vic and me had a word or two—Cause I know he ain't goin' hold no more malice against me for what I said 'bout him, than I hold against him for what he said 'bout me—(*turning to son-in-law*) Now ain't that right, Vic?

VIC (*smiling, admiring her shrewdness*) Of course, Mama—(*his smile fading*) though I'm sorry to say, things ain't like they used to be here. We're just about to be kicked into the street, and if something don't happen in the next twenty days, we will be. But you're welcome to stay if you want to.

BROOKS (*trapped*) Twenty days!

ELLA Twenty days!

BROOKS Lawd, lawd, Lawd! (*she catches sight of* DAN *smiling gloatingly*) But I'd heap rather sleep in the street with you all than spot mah garment in the wallow they got ovah there:

LES (*hugging her with smile*) Don't worry, Grandma. A lot of things can happen in twenty days!

(*Curtain*)

Scene Two

(TIME: *three weeks later.*

The light of a small lamp is burning, revealing the room in upheaval. There are packing cases and barrels about, showing that the family is preparing to vacate the premises, or to be evicted.

Though it is near 3:30 a.m., BROOKS, *in an old robe, is seen alone, peering out into the night from the window. In a moment, she turns toward door, expectantly*)

BROOKS (*as* LES *enters, her voice hushed but excited*) Les, has you seen anything of Wanda?

LES (*arrested*) Wanda?—No. Why do you ask?

BROOKS (*sotto voce*) Do you know she ain't come in this house yet—And it's after three o'clock?

LES (*placing batch of leaflets on table*) Wanda's a grown woman, Grandma.

BROOKS Grown or not grown, she's got no business out in the streets this time o'night—I'm worried about her.

LES You'd better go back to bed and try to get some sleep—(*laughing, as he turns to climb stairs*) You may not get another chance after tonight, you know!

BROOKS (*arresting him*) I ain't worried 'bout that. But somethin' must-er happened to Wanda!

LES (*joining her to give her a pat*) You're just imagining things, Grandma. Go on back to bed.

BROOKS (*tightening her robe*) I can't sleep—How Ella can, beats me. After the way she cried round here these last few days—'specially this afternoon 'fore Wanda come. Then she got calm as a picture of a Saint—(*probingly*) You reckon Wanda could-er told her somethin'?

LES Now, Grandma, what do you suppose she could've told her?

BROOKS I donno. Neither one of them don't talk to me like they used to—(*going back to window*) You'd think I was some stranger round here.

LES Oh, they're just worried—just as you are—(*going*) But I'm going to bed. Goodnight!

BROOKS (*peering out of window*) Wait, Les! (*waving to him, excitedly*) Come here a minute and see if that ain't Claudine yonder!

LES (*joining her*) Claudine!...(*he sees figure*) Now what do you know about that?—It's her all right—(*he goes to door to open it and call in a whispered voice*) Claudine! Come here!

BROOKS (*ominously*) I told you there was somethin' wrong. I knowed it. My mind don't fool me!

LES (*as girl approaches*) Claudine, what in the world are you doing out in the street this time of night?

CLAUDINE (*appearing, anxiously*) Wanda here? (*she is wearing a gown with a lace stole around her shoulders*)

LES (*closing door behind her*) No.

CLAUDINE She ain't come home?

LES No, not yet—Why? There isn't anything wrong, is there?

CLAUDINE (*nervously*) No. I just wanted to see her.

BROOKS It's mighty funny you got to be watchin' for her in the street, instid of coming to this house!

LES Yes, it is! Claudine, you're hiding something—

BROOKS (*seeing* CLAUDINE *signalling him to be silent*) Ugh hunh! So it is somethin!

CLAUDINE No, no, Mrs. Brooks—I was just feeling a little faint.

BROOKS You needn't tell that lie. You wouldn't be here this time o' night—You don't want me to hear!

CLAUDINE (*rapidly*) No, really, Mrs. Brooks—Wanda's all right—(*going*) You'll see if she isn't—I was just—

BROOKS (*intercepting her*) You hold on! You ain't goin' leave me like this—I'll call Ella first!

LES (*anxiously*) No, Grandma! For God's sake! Leave it to me.

BROOKS How come I can't be trusted?

LES (*helplessly*) It isn't that, Grandma—You wait here—(*he starts out with* CLAUDINE)

BROOKS (*striding to stairs*) Maybe she'll talk to Ella!

LES (*whirling to grab her*) No, Grandma! (*seeing* CLAUDINE *escaping*) Wait, Claudine! Wait! (*desperately*) She'll get away. I've got to catch her—But for God's sake, keep your mouth shut until I get back.

(*He runs out, leaving the door open, in his haste to catch the fleeing girl.* BROOKS *rushes to the window to remain there in her frustration, staring into the darkened street. Blackout.*)

Scene Three

(TIME: *the following morning.*

ELLA *is seen, packing blankets into a case*)

ELLA (*calling into kitchen*) Caroline, haven't you finished with those dishes yet?

CAROLINE (*off-stage, exasperatedly*) Oh, give me time, Mama. I'll be through in a minute!

ELLA You've been at them long enough to have them washed and packed—Lord, if I don't lose my mind this morning, I never will!

CAROLINE (*entering with armful of plates*) Well, it's not doing you any good to worry—Wanda and Les're both probably together somewhere. (*she goes to barrel where she begins packing dishes*)

ELLA It's mighty funny neither your Father nor Phillip's been able to find them.

CAROLINE You'd do better worrying about what we're going to do when the Bailiffs come.

ELLA We ain't going to do nothing but let them set us out. Then I'm going to thank them for doing us the favor.

CAROLINE (*struck by her unconcern*) You sound mighty calloused—like you've never seen the homeless in Washington Park.

ELLA (*turning with a smile*) I've got the money, Caroline, to get a place!

CAROLINE You have?

ELLA Yes. Wanda gave me $50 yesterday!

CAROLINE Mama, you're joking?

ELLA (*pulling roll of bills from her bosom and waving them triumphantly*) What do you call this?

CAROLINE (*incredulously*) But, Mama, where'd she get all that money?

ELLA (*laughing with joy*) Her boss. He loaned it to her.

VIC (*appearing in open door*) Well, did she get back?

CAROLINE No. Didn't you find her?

VIC (*coming in, wearily*) No. Nobody's seen hide nor hair of her. And she hasn't been near the drugstore since early last night.

CAROLINE What about Les—Was there no trace of him?

VIC (*shaking his head negatively*) I went to the Reds and saw Piszer. But he said Les left the park about 2:30 this morning—on his way here.

CAROLINE Well, he never showed up. His bed hasn't been slept in.

ELLA (*worried*) Lord, I wish that telephone wasn't disconnected!

VIC (*volunteering the remark for her benefit*) I called the police, and every hospital in town.

BROOKS (*entering with old suitcase, and seeing* VIC) Where's she?

VIC I've had no luck.

CAROLINE (*seeing* WANDA *and* LES *in door*) Here they are!

VIC (*whirling*) Thank God!

ELLA (*pouncing on* WANDA) Where've you been?

WANDA (*lying*) I'm sorry, Mama. But I was in an accident. Claudine and I went for a ride to Gary with some fellows last night, and the car broke down.

BROOKS (*sharply*) Of all the audacity!—Claudine and you! Then what was she doing here lookin' for you at three o'clock this mornin'?

ELLA (*surprised*) Three o'clock this morning!

LES (*covering for* WANDA) You don't understand, Grandma. The car Wanda was in broke down, and Claudine and them, not knowing, came on. But when they got here and the rest didn't show up, naturally, Claudine was afraid something might've happened to her.

BROOKS (*sighing*) Oh, then tell me somethin'.

WANDA (*relieved*) I thought several times we were going to have to walk back.

ELLA (*relieved, but mother-like*) It would've served you right! Worrying everybody to death!—I can't see to save my life why you haven't got more sense than to be going off in the rattle-trap of every Tom, Dick, and Harry you meet!

WANDA (*going*) I'm sorry, Mama. But it couldn't be helped. I'm going up and wash up. (*exit above*)

VIC Well, this sure is a relief—(*taking seat*) Now if only the Bailiffs weren't due, I'd feel like celebrating.

CAROLINE Shucks, Papa. Who cares about the Bailiffs?—They're welcome to set us out, aren't they, Mama?

ELLA (*proudly, as she continues packing*) I reckon they can come if they want to.

VIC (*to* CAROLINE) What're you talking about?

CAROLINE Oh, wake up, Papa. Mama's got the money to rent us a new place!

BROOKS (*surprised*) What's that?

CAROLINE (*happily*) Wanda borrowed it from her boss yesterday!

VIC God be praised!

LES (*darkly*) Forget it, Papa. This is no matter for rejoicing.

VIC Why not?—Do you think it's not a relief, knowing we don't have to sleep in Washington Park?

LES You can't afford to take this way out. (ELLA *whirls, puzzled, her heart skipping a beat*)

VIC (*dreading to question him*) I don't think I understand you, Les.

BROOKS Sounds like he's crazy.

LES (*ignoring her*) You've a duty to others, Papa.

VIC What duty?

PIZSER (*entering open door*) Good morning, Folks!

LES (*going on*) Your duty to yourself and the thousands who're facing eviction this morning —(*ironically*) with no daughter lucky enough to borrow from her boss!

VIC You mean refuse to get out?

LES It's the only way to stop the landlords, Papa. We've got to resist them.

VIC You're asking me to turn the family into guinea pigs, Son.

LES I am asking you to help us set an example for the rest, like any honest leader.

VIC Things can't go on this way, Les. I'd be a fool to jeopardize the family, knowing it.

LES I've always given you credit for seeing clean through this rotten society, Papa. But you talk like a blind man now. After preaching freedom and happiness all these years, you ought to know our only hope is in resistance— You saw what good it did us to try to appeal to the Governor, didn't you? Why didn't they even let us see him?

PISZER (*sophmorically, but earnest*) The State is only a reflection of the ruling class. It's impossible for it to be concerned about the poor, who have to struggle for every concession.

VIC (*impatiently*) I know all that, Son. But I can't blind myself to the facts. A poor Negro like me can only get it in the neck if he bucks the law—And anything may happen in another month.

LES (*desperate, knowing he cannot use the knowledge he possesses without disloyalty to* WANDA) In another month you'll be right back where you started from!—Suppose you take the money Mama's got and rent another place. Can Wanda keep up the rent, or do you think her boss is going to play the sweet Angel again?

PISZER You won't be alone, Mr. Mason. We set ten families back in their homes this week. We can do the same for you. Say the word and in ten minutes we'll have a thousand Comrades at your door—

JUANITA (*rushing in with* DAN *at her heels*) Has she come yet, Ella?

ELLA Yes. She's upstairs. She and Claudine drove off to Gary with some young men and the car broke down. But they got back all right.

JUANITA (*relieved*) Well, I'm sure glad to hear that. I was worried to death.

DAN Me too! (*jovially to* VIC) Well, old man, I see you're still here.

VIC (*gloomily*) Yeah. But my time ain't long.

DAN Well, don't let it worry you. You all can come over to my house, though I can't promise you how long it'll be before they kick us all out together.

VIC Thanks very much, Dan.—But (*he glances uneasily at* LES) we've got the money for a place.

JUANITA (*happily*) You have—?

CAROLINE Yes. Wanda borrowed it from her boss yester—(*she halts, hearing running footsteps on porch*)

PHILLIP (*bursting in to blurt*) Papa, you know what? (LES *tries to intervene*) Wanda's in jail!

VIC (*laughing*) In jail! Why you're crazy— (*The others join in the laughter, believing it's a good joke*)

PHILLIP (*defensively*) Well, Claudine said so!

BROOKS (*suddenly struck, and grunting as in a flash she suspects they'd been taken in*) Ugh phumn!

ELLA (*stunned*) She did?

PHILLIP Yes, she did! She told me—

LES (*nudges him, and interposes*) Awh, you don't know what you're talking about. Wanda and Claudine both spent the night in Gary— She's upstairs now!

PHILLIP She is?

LES Sure.

PHILLIP That's funny—(LES *nudges him again, but he's too carried away by his own feelings and embarrassment*) I wonder what Claudine wanted to go telling me that stuff for—?

ELLA (*still suspicious*) What did she say?

LES (*interposing, as he glares at* PHILLIP) Don't pay any attention to him, Mama. Claudine's just been pulling his leg.

PHILLIP (*heatedly*) Pulling nothing!—How you know she wasn't in jail? How you know she didn't just get out on bond, like Claudine said she was going to?

ELLA Claudine said that?

LES But, Mama, I tell you—

ELLA (*sharply*) You shut up! And let me hear the rest of this. Go on, Phillip, what did she say?

PHILLIP (*aware at last that something is wrong, but unable to restrain himself*) She said Wanda got caught in a raid last night—

JUANITA A raid?

PHILLIP (*going on*) with some white man named Hogan. But for us not to worry because the woman who runs the place was going to get her out on bond this morning. (*the family is stunned*)

BROOKS (*outraged—scandalized*) Caught in a raid with a white man! I knowed it! I knowed it!—I warned you, Ella. I told you—

LES Hush, Grandma, for God's sakes—

BROOKS Don't you tell me to hush— Claudine never would-er been hidin' out there three o'clock in the mornin' if there wasn't somethin' to this—

LES Awh, that's ridiculous, Grandma. If the

Big White Fog

police had caught them, don't you see Claudine couldn't've been here!

PHILLIP (*blurting*) Claudine said they would've caught her too, if she hadn't jumped out of the window!

ELLA (*striding to foot of stairs, and calling, imperiously*) Wanda! You come down here to me!

VIC (*loyally, though dreadingly*) I can't believe Wanda's mixed up in anything like this.

ELLA (*as* WANDA *appears above*) Come down here!

JUANITA (*as* WANDA *creeps down*) Give her a chance, Ella! (*in silence they watch as girl comes down*)

ELLA (*coldly*) Where were you last night?

WANDA (*frightened*) I—I just told you—Me and Claudine—

ELLA (*sharply*) I want the truth!

WANDA (*glancing around, like a cornered animal*) I'm telling you, Mama!

ELLA Didn't you just get out of jail?

WANDA (*desperately*) No, no—Who said that? (*to* LES, *accusingly*) Les, did you—(*she catches herself*)

ELLA (*shooting in the dark*) Oh, so you were!

WANDA (*striding to* LES, *she strikes him across the mouth*) Take that, Mr. Big-mouth! (LES *turns away and all are silent in their pain*)

JUANITA Lord, have mercy, Wanda. He didn't do it. It was Phillip.

WANDA Phillip?

JUANITA Yes.

WANDA (*quietly*) I'm sorry, Les.

LES Forget it.

ELLA (*woundedly*) Is it true, too, you were laying up with a white man?

WANDA (*on the verge of tears*) You had to have the money, Mama—(*pathetically, her eyes search their faces for a sign of understanding, and she utters with a sob*) What else could I do? (*unable to face their stony silence, she lingers for a moment, then runs above to hide her shame*)

BROOKS (*dumbfounded, as* ELLA *turns to the window with bowed head*) Lawd, Lawd, Lawd!

LES (*to* PHILLIP) I guess you're satisfied. (PHILLIP, *quailing, turns away*)

VIC (*rousing himself*) Well, I reckon this changes the face of everything.

LES How do you mean?

VIC (*ready at last to fight*) Suppose you can still get help?

LES All you want, Papa.

DAN (*excited*) Not the Reds?

VIC (*firmly*) Get them. The Bailiffs'll be along any minute.

LES (*going*) Come on, Piszer! (*they exit running*)

JUANITA (*gravely*) You're making an awful mistake, Vic!

VIC I've got to stand my ground!

DAN But there'll be trouble, Man!

VIC (*bitterly*) I got a taste for trouble now!

JUANITA Oh, Vic, why be a fool?

VIC (*angrily*) I suppose you think I should use that tainted money! (ELLA *whirls*)

JUANITA I thought she borrowed it!

VIC We were all fools enough to think so—the little tramp!

ELLA (*outraged, her old animosity surging up to condemn him, she extracts roll of money and hurls it into his face*) Here! You take this! It belongs to you!

DAN Ella!

JUANITA (*stepping between them, admonishingly*) Oh, Ella—For Heaven's sake!

ELLA (*as* VIC *stands bewildered*) Get out of my way, and don't tell me nothing!

CAROLINE Mama, Mama, please!

(PERCY *enters, half drunk and unshaven*)

ELLA (*raging*) Calling somebody a tramp! Who made her a tramp?

JUANITA Don't, Ella!

ELLA (*storming*) Who started her on the road to hell?—You! You!

DAN No, Ella. It was just fate!

ELLA (*seizing the idea*) It was fate all right. Fate from the day she was born—With something less than a black fool for a father she was booked for the gutter!

VIC (*bowed beneath the impact as one before a fatal blow*) Yeah!...

(PERCY *sobers*)

JUANITA (*catching his pain*) Oh, Ella. How can you say such a cruel thing?

ELLA You ask me how? I'll tell you how. Because I'm sick to death of him, that's how! I thought I had enough when he talked like he did about Mama. But now that I've lived to see my child ruined on account of his stupidity, there's nothing I'd like better than to see him dead!

PERCY (*angrily to* VIC) You going to stand there and let her talk to you like that?

VIC (*groaning*) That's all right, Ella. It's all right—

BAILIFF (*appearing in door with men behind him*) Does Victor Mason live here?

DAN Yes. What is it? (*he indicates* VIC)

BAILIFF (*entering, followed by his men*) I've a Court order to evict you. (*to his men*) Go on, Boys. Set them out! (*without ado, the men begin removing furnishings*)

VIC (*ominously*) You can save yourselves a lot of trouble, if you let that stuff alone!

BAILIFF (*as men pause*) What'd you mean?

VIC (*sharply*) I'm not going to stand no eviction!

BAILIFF Are you looking for trouble?

VIC (*angrily*) Call it what you like—(*he halts, hearing voices*)

VOICES (*singing as they approach in the distance*) "Mine eyes have seen the glory..."

PHILLIP (*at window, above the sound of the Battle Hymn*) It's Les and them. A whole army of them!

BAILIFF The Reds, eh? (*excitedly, to* VIC) Well, you'd better call them off! They won't get away with *this* case!

(*Police sirens roar in the distance, prophetically*)

DAN (*frightened*) Vic, my offer still stands!

VIC And what're you going to do when they set you out?

DAN There'll be time enough to think of that later.

(*The sirens cease, as brakes are heard screeching*)

BAILIFF (*to his men*) Go on, Boys. Set em out! (*as men carry out pieces, he turns to* VIC, *warningly*) You'd better be reasonable! The Cops have their orders! We're not going to stand for anymore of this Red interference!

VIC (*strides to door.* PHILLIP *attempts to follow him*) Go back!

BAILIFF (*following to door, as* VIC *disappears outside*) All right. You're asking for it!

BROOKS (*in terror*) Have mercy, Jesus!

(*The sound of the singing increases, then is suddenly drowned out by the screech of another siren, and silence reigns*)

VOICE (*commandingly, outside*) All right, Comrades. Let's go!

CAROLINE (*at window*) They're bringing the things back!

OFFICER (*ominously, outside*) Halt! In the name of the law I command you not to interfere!

VOICE (*raising song again*) "Glory, Glory, Hallelujah!

OFFICER Halt! Halt! I command you to halt!

BROOKS Help us, Sweet Jesus!

(VIC *is seen on porch at head-end of piece of furniture*)

CAROLINE (*screaming*) The police've got guns out, Mama. They've got guns out! (*suddenly screaming*) Look out, Papa! (*there is the sudden roar of gunfire, and* VIC *is seen clutching the door jam*)

VIC (*groaning*) Ahhhhhah! (*he clings to the door jam, where shortly he is caught by* LES. DAN *runs to join them*)

LES Help me get him on the couch— (CAROLINE *attempts to assist*) Move, Caroline!

WANDA (*appearing above, appalled by the sight of her father*) Oh, God! (*she runs below, as* LES *and* DAN *succeed in placing* VIC *on couch*)

PERCY (*suddenly enraged, he rushes to doorway to shake his fist in a futile gesture of defiance*) You God damn murdering bastards! You dirty killers! (DAN *runs up to grab him and pull him inside*) Turn me loose, Dan. Turn me aloose!

DAN (*wrestling him into chair*) No, Percy! No!

PERCY (*in tears, his stupor gone*) Them bastards shot my brother!

WANDA (*joining him*) You can't help him, Uncle Percy! (*he subsides in tears, and she joins* LES)

LES (*woundedly*) Shot in the back, like a dog!

LIEUTENANT (*appearing with* PATROLMAN, *he turns to cast over his shoulder*) Yeah. There's one in here! (*coming down*) Who told you to move that man?

PERCY (*springing up*) Get the hell out of here! (DAN *grabs him*) Don't hold me, Dan. Let em wash me! God damn em! Let em wash me!

WANDA (*joining them*) Please, Uncle Percy. There's no use getting yourself hurt. Calm down. You're disturbing Papa. (PERCY *subsides*)

LIEUTENANT (*to* LES) I asked you who gave you orders to move that man?

LES (*bitterly*)   What were we supposed to do, let him lie there like a dog?
LIEUTENANT (*looking around*)   You shouldn't 've moved him! (*he starts toward telephone*)
LES   That telephone is disconnected.
LIEUTENANT (*to* PATROLMAN)   Get an ambulance.
PATROLMAN   Mockleson's already sent in the call.
LES   How do you feel, Papa?
VIC   Just kind of numb! (LES *casts an appealing glance to his mother, but she turns to the window*)
LIEUTENANT (*noticing* BAILIFFS *re-entering, but that the doorways fills at once by grim-faced white and black men, acting in concert to prevent any further removal of furnishings*)   Get back! Clear out of here! (*the workers are immobile, and he pulls his gun*) I said clear out of here!
PISZER (*defiantly*)   Go on with your butchering. We're not budging an inch!
PATROLMAN (*after a moment*)   I think we'd better call in, Lieutenant. These bastards're crazy.
LIEUTENANT (*to* BAILIFFS)   You fellows had better drop this until we get further orders. (*going*) Let us by! (*the men in the doorway, accepting the victory, fall back, and the* OFFICERS *exit, the* BAILIFFS *following*)
VIC (*weakly*)   Where's Ella? (WANDA *draws behind couch*)
LES (*he glances toward her, but she doesn't turn, and he lies*)   She went in the back for a minute, Papa.
VIC   Don't lie, Son. (*shortly*) Lift my head up.
CAROLINE (*dropping beside him*)   Oh, Papa! (LES *raises pillow, and turns toward his mother*)
LES   Mama . . .! Won't you please—?
VIC   Don't make it hard for her, Son. I reckon she's got cause enough to hate me . . . beyond the grave. (*he pauses to gather his strength*) Anyway, It's no more than life's taught me a black man's got to expect. (*he caresses* CAROLINE's *hair*) I want you all to try to be true to yourselves and one another. I want you to stick by each other and never let nothing come between you—(*turning to* WANDA *above him*) And that goes for you, too, Wanda. (*she bows her head in silence*) I spoke a little hard about you . . . But I didn't mean it . . . because I understand. (*after a moment*) You'll all find it pretty hard . . . for like Les said . . . "This world ain't . . . nothing but . . . a big white fog, and nobody can't see . . . no light nowhere!"
LES (*quietly*)   I was mistaken, Papa.
VIC (*weakly, after a moment*)   You think so?
LES   I know I was, Papa. But you be quiet now, and don't tax your strength.
VIC   I've got to talk, Son. I'm done for.
WANDA (*turning away*)   Oh, God!
CAROLINE   No, Papa—
VIC   Hush, Caroline, If I've got to go, I've simply got to go, and your tears can't help me none—(*with difficulty*) But what did you mean, Les?
LES   Only, that I was looking in the wrong direction then, Papa.
VIC   Yes.
LES   There is a light.
VIC   What light?
LES (*he searches within for the means to express his truth. Then, turns to the door with its crowded faces*)   Look in the door, there, Papa.
VIC (*straining upward*)   What is it? . . . I can't seem to see.
LES (*swallowing*)   It's my Comrades, Papa.
VIC   Your Comrades—?
LES   Yes. You remember them, don't you?
VIC   Oh, yes. Of course—I owe them a much bigger thanks than—
LES   It's not that, Papa. I wanted you to see they're black and white.
VIC (*weakly*)   Tell them to come closer. (*the men draw near, and he feels for them with outstretched arms*) Where are they?
PISZER (*quietly*)   Here we are, Comrade Mason!
VIC   I guess my sight is gone. (*he sinks back*)
CAROLINE   Papa! Papa!
LES (*examining him*)   I guess he's gone! (*he turns away, broken—*ELLA, *hearing his verdict, turns from the window*)
ELLA (*relenting, she creeps toward the dead man, her voice filled with grief, though scarcely audible*)   Vic! . . . Vic!

(*In the distance an ambulance siren is heard, and slowly the Curtain descends*)

Owen Dodson (1914–)

Divine Comedy

1938

Divine Comedy is one of three verse plays published in this volume. It was originally written to fulfill the requirements for a Fine Arts degree at Yale University, where the play was presented by the drama department in February of 1938.

Set in the worse days of the Depression, the action centers on the appeal of the Apostle of Light for those who are hungry and tired. Although the character of the Apostle is generalized, as the title of the play suggests, the portrait was inspired by the amazing Father Divine. A contemporary account of Father Divine and other religionists of Harlem of the 1930's was assembled by the City Writers Project, a part of the Federal WPA program that ended in 1939. This research was published in *The Negro in New York*, edited by Roi Ottley and William Weatherby (copyright the New York Public Library; quoted by permission):

Religion in Harlem has many curious manifestations and strange facets, and these come to the fore in a number of cults. Closed picture houses, dance halls, empty stores, and lodge halls are converted into places of worship. Charlatans give a swing to their collars and overnight are "ministers." Harlem calls them "jackleg preachers." They are found in "churches" that appear and disappear almost overnight. A recent survey, made by the New York City Writers' project, showed nearly two hundred places operating as "spiritualist churches."

In the forty years of Harlem's existence as a Negro community, there has been a stream of cult leaders. Harlem has known Rev. Becton, of the "consecrated dime," who was murdered by kidnapping gangsters; the university-educated Prophet Costonie, who organized a boycott of public utilities and sold incense; Elder Martin Claybourne, the "Barefoot Prophet"; the "Bishop" Sufi Abdul Hamid; and Mother Horn and her "Pray For Me Church of the Air."

The most grandiloquent of the contemporary cults is that headed by Father Divine and known as the Righteous Government. It had its New York beginning in 1915. There have been, in recent years as in earlier periods of human history, persons whose followers claimed that they were the new Messiah. While Divine has never made any statement to this effect, his followers speak of him as "God." Well-informed individuals residing in Harlem place his actual local following as not exceeding four thousand persons, with little influence in the community. Divine's own claim is twenty thousand or more. His followers are drawn largely from the very wealthy and the very poor and illiterate.

Father Divine was born fifty or sixty years ago on a rice plantation on Hutchinson's Island in the Savannah River. In 1906, Divine, *né* George Baker, first turned up in the city of Baltimore; he was then a tiny underfed poverty-stricken man who maintained a measly existence mowing lawns, cutting hedges, and doing other odd jobs. A spark of ambition burned in his breast and in a short time he was teaching Sunday School. Gathering about him six men and six women, he made a southern tour and met with evangelistic success. The little band then set out for New York in 1915.

He took a place at Prince Street in Brooklyn and installed his "Communal System," and assumed the more dignified title of Major Morgan J. Divine. In 1919 he took his flock of a dozen souls to Sayville, Long Island, where he had purchased an eight-room house. There he obtained a license to conduct an employment agency to secure jobs for the domestic workers in the neighborhood.

His Sayville retreat soon became known for its sumptuous banquets, free of charge. The newspapers discovered him and blew him up into the proportions of a "mystic" who healed the sick and performed "miracles." Bus companies, with sound eyes for business, began running regular trips from Harlem to Sayville for a $1.50 round-trip, and advertising the blue-plate luncheons that Father Divine served. The publicity soon caused the townfolk to become alarmed as Divine's "angels" started to overrun the area. The property owners feared a sharp decline in real estate values. The fact that Negroes and whites mingled freely was also found irksome. In May 1932, Divine was convicted by the Nassau County Supreme Court for maintaining a public nuisance and was sentenced to one year in jail. Judge Lewis J. Smith, who sentenced him, spoke of him as a "menace to society." Father Divine said: "Pity the Judge, he can't live long now. He's offended Almighty God." The following month Judge Smith died suddenly, a victim of heart disease. Divine was heard to say from his cell: "I hated to do it."

He was released from jail. Thereupon he took his

followers to Harlem. Banquets were held at local dance halls and the movement swelled in numbers. His followers then began to assume other-worldly names like Beauty Smiles, Norah Endurance, Holy Shinelight, Pearly Gates, and Rose Memory. Divine bought a number of Peace Missions, known as "heavens," throughout the Harlem area and "Peace, it's truly wonderful!" became the password. In 1936 the Peace Mission Movement had expanded into the International Righteous Government with the platform: "One for all and all for one but not for one who is not for all."

Owen Dodson, the author of *Divine Comedy*, is a recognized poet who knows the theater and its language. Author of nearly fifteen plays, he was for twenty-five years Professor of Drama at Howard University where he, together with Anne Cook and James Butcher, built the department into a multimillion-dollar complex. Under his direction the Howard Players were the first college group to represent the State Department, touring Scandinavia and Germany in 1949. As a theater teacher and director he is as responsible as any man for the encouragement and training of a large number of talents. He has worked with Earle Hyman, Gordon Heath, Claire Lieba, Hilda Simms, James Baldwin, Norbert Davidson, Richard Wesley, Frank Silvera, Charles Sebree, Marilyn Berry, Ellis Haizlip, Frederick Lights, Ted Shine, Herb Davis, Vantile Whitfield, and Langston Hughes.

In an interview on July 20, 1973, Professor Dodson said, in part:

My belief in the theater is one that believes in total theater, that is, the use of poetry, dance, drama, and music. I have used these elements in *Divine Comedy*, a verse play in which I spoke of street people who inhabit bars as well as people of the middle class. I tried to show the frustrations of all people in the Depression of the 1930's.

In our time when there is so much talk of black power, and of black playwrights' throwing garbage in the faces of people, it should be the duty of black playwrights to show what theater can and should be. We should present all classes of people as human beings.

In addition to three published volumes of poetry (*Powerful Long Ladder*, *The Confession Stone*, and *The Morning Duke Ellington Praised the Lord and Seven Little Davids Tapdanced Unto*), his poems have appeared in over forty anthologies. In March 1973 he was invited to read his poetry before the Library of Congress. In reviewing his poetry, *Time* stated that his "work is peer to Frost and Sandburg."

Professor Dodson is now retired from Howard University. He lives in New York City where he lectures, directs, and writes.

Divine Comedy

CAST OF CHARACTERS

MRS. RACHAEL JACKSON (*later*, DIVINE ADORATION)
NORMA, *her daughter*
CYRIL, *her son*
MRS. CORA JENKINS (*later*, PRISCILLA PAUL), *her friend*
MOTHER *and* CHILD
MISTER STUFF
LIVER LIPS
NUMBERS
SHORT BOY
PINEAPPLE HEAD
WEASEL MOUTH
HAMMER HEAD
BARTENDER
PROSTITUTE
AGNA RAWLINS (*later*, GLORIOUS VISION)
JOHN STEWART
CARRIE PETERS (*later*, MOTHER HUMILITY)
BLIND BEGGAR
CHORUS
CHORUS LEADERS
PREACHER
PRIEST
APOSTLE OF LIGHT
HIS FOLLOWERS (CHORUS)
BEAUTIFUL LIGHT
HAPPY RELEASE, *a secretary*

(*The stage should be divided into five distinct areas: The stained-glass window place, the street, the Jackson home area, the church area, the Apostle's domain.*

Upstage center a stained-glass window extends from the stage level up as far into the proscenium as possible. In deep purple glass a cross with a halo in golden glass dominates. The cross shaft should be slanted: its head leaning to one side, one arm drooped, the other raised. It represents Christ's body. There is no figure. The rest of the window is deep red and blue. Stage left of the cross is the street area. This area is raised about nine feet above the stage level proper. Below the street area, on the stage proper, is the Apostle's domain. Steps connect the two. Stage right of the cross is the church area. It is raised about ten feet above the stage level proper. Steps lead from the street area down to a platform below the cross and up to the church area. Below the church level is the Jackson home place. Steps lead from the Jackson home place onto the platform before the cross and onto the church area.

Before the curtain rises the music of the CHORUS *is heard: slow, despairing, desolate, hollow music. Several of the* CHORUS *are on the stage as the curtain rises. A mother is sitting on a step rocking a baby; a bum is sprawled on the floor; a group is huddled on the church area. More ragged people come in from every entrance. They form the* CHORUS *of the poor: Negro and white.*

The choral speeches are for the most part compact. But sometimes they speak individually, sometimes in a mass, sometimes contrapuntally, sometimes they even chant. The director may break up the choral speeches almost any way he wishes. At the beginning, however, the choral speech should be broken up into individual speeches.

The sky is dimly lit at the beginning. It is gray purple. The cross is only faintly lighted. There should be enough light for the audience to see without difficulty.

The action of each act should be continuous)

ACT ONE

FIRST CHORUS Two Winters come in one this year:
The wind thrusts fingers through our fear,
Curves its palm into our walls,
And whistles and rumbles along the halls.

Where grass was feathers for our beds
The snow makes pillows for our heads:
We are Winter worn,
Wind torn,
Despair

Divine Comedy

               Leaps in the air,
               Falls down
               Like a clown
               We saw at a fair
               Long, long ago.
SECOND CHORUS Our bellies are large with the Wind in them;
               Our children are giddy for the taste of bread;
               Our tables and chairs are thrown on the street:
               And we walk with Winter shoes on our feet.
               We are Winter worn,
               Wind torn.
               Despair
               Leaps in the air'
BOTH CHORUSES "The Lord will provide" is only an echo
               Whispering in and out of these Winter branches.
               Where are the fertile days?
FIRST CHORUS Have the orchards gone to seed?
SECOND CHORUS Have the storehouses burned to ashes on the ground?
               How long shall our feet bleed?
FIRST CHORUS How long shall our feet bleed and change
               The color of the city snow?
SECOND CHORUS How long will our children cry out
               In the night with hunger awake on their bellies?
               Where is bread?
FIRST CHORUS Where is shelter?
BOTH CHORUSES Where is Christ?
FIRST CHORUS We are Winter worn.
               All doors are shut in our faces:
               The thud is a burning in our ears:
               We wander the streets like rats in a moldy Church.
BLIND MAN The blind in the haunted places
               Without fire to warm the hands they've never seen.
               What shall they do?
SECOND CHORUS Who shall lift a hand to help us?
               Who shall find bread for our children?
               Death comes blowing darkness into our hearts.
FIRST CHORUS He **is** a little man. Death is a little man.
               Who will grapple with him and win?
SECOND CHORUS Where is Christ?
FIRST CHORUS Death is a little man:
               A little, little man:
               A runt and an ugly dwarf.
               Who will grapple with him and win?
SECOND CHORUS Where is Christ?
               Where is Christ?

(*From behind the cross a* PRIEST *appears in full regalia. He makes the sign of the cross and swings incense. The* CHORUS *now is grouped about him on the steps. A tattered army of the poor*)

ONE We come asking for simple bread
      And fire to ease the coldness in our bodies.
      We have seen the blue flame of death lighting our streets,
      And we are afraid and alone.
      Where is our Master, Christ?
PRIEST (*unctiously but sincerely*) Christ is here and in your homes.
      Go home now and pray.
      Take the dusty hymnal down from the dusty shelf.
      Polish the silver rosaries again,
      Re-set the crooked cross,
      Re-clothe the naked Christ.
      Go back to your homes and light the flameless candle.
CHORUS The candle is guttered.
      Where is Christ?
      Our feet are cold,
      The skin is frozen on the bone:
      Two Winters come in one this year.
PRIEST The Lord's children are never alone or cold.
      Go home and pray. Prayer changes things.
CHORUS We *have* prayed in the bitter night.
      We *have* waited but still the hunger needles
      Press, press inward.
      We are too weak to pray:
      Too weak to lift our arms:
      Too desolate to hope.
      Give us bread,
      Give us shelter,
      Re-clothe our bodies!!
PRIEST Go home and pray!!
CHORUS We have no homes!!!
PRIEST Go home and pray!!! (*disappears after he has made the cross sign and swung incense*)
CHORUS We cannot go home when poverty leaks
      Down the gutters and cannot be drained.
      We cannot go home; we cannot go home!
      The fires are out,
      The children are crying,
      Death is eating our faith.
CHORUS-LEADER Incense swung by a bony hand,
      The sign of the cross traced in the air,
      The unctious chant of a faith-ridden Priest,
      Is not fire to offset the Winter in our flesh,
      Is not manna for our children or ourselves.
      Where shall we turn for a half-chewed crust of bread?
      Where shall we turn?
CHORUS-LEADER Call up the government on the telephone:
      Ask for Congress, tell them we're alone.

A MOTHER (*singing to infant in her arms*) Sleep darling sleep,
Sleep darling sleep,
There will be milk in the morning and bread;
There will be blankets to cover your bed.
Sleep darling sleep,
There will be toys to play with and keep.
Sleep darling sleep,
Sleep darling sleep. (MOTHER *hums tune during next lines*)

MOTHERS What shall we do with our children asleep
Dreaming the promise we never can keep.

LEADER Call up the government on the telephone:
Ask for Congress, tell them we're alone.

CHORUS We have called again and again
We get no answer from the silk-hat men.

SEMI-CHORUS At the bottom of the river
Salvation lies.
They have tossed away food
Right under our eyes.
We have called again and again:
We are the forgotten, the empty men.

MOTHER (*singing*) Sleep darling sleep,
Sleep darling sleep,
There will be milk in the morning and bread;
There will be blankets to cover your bed.
Sleep darling sleep,
There will be toys—(*screams as she realizes she has been rocking a dead child. Flatly*)
Burn the blanket:
The promise I said,
Let it be forgotten:
My baby is dead.

MOTHERS (*echoing. The background music emphasizes the words here*) Her baby is dead.
Dead.
The promise she said
Let it drift away,
Her baby is dead.
Husbands,
Sons,
Brothers,
Fathers,
Nephews,
Uncles,
Men who walk meekly in this Winter,
See what has come
To the golden-faced child.
And now it will go:
Be buried in snow.
When the sun shines hot
The baby will rot.

SEMI-CHORUS (*moaning*) Where is Christ?
Where is Christ?
He has not come in our sorest hour
Even to bring a faith-blooming flower.

(*Confusion but desolation. They go up the stairs, wander about. The background music continues— low and empty like wind in a hollow reed. The lights all dim out and then as the music fades on the crowd, a light comes up slowly in* MRS. RACHAEL JACKSON's *home area. The stage is now empty except for* RACHAEL. *She is dressing. The stained-glass window is bright. The sky is deep purple shading to gray.* MRS. CORA JENKINS *enters from the street place and goes slowly down the steps to* RACHAEL's *home. She stands outside the light and calls*)

CORA Rachael. Oh Rachael. Comin' to de meetin'?

RACHAEL Come right in Cora. I didn't' spect you so soon. (CORA *passes into the light and sits on a chair that has been placed there during the darkness*) Come in an' rest your rheumatism and your heart Whilst I finishes dressin'. How you tonight?

CORA Ma knees been kinda stiff dese last few months. Lawd only knows how much longer I kin stand dis scrubbin' floors and clothes for de white folks. It near kill me every time I gets near water. In fact everytime it rains ma knees twitches lak kingdom come. Its all tight in here (*hand on breast*). I gets tired so easy. Ma heart pound lak a hammer.

RACHAEL I can't complain none. Ma children takes care of me right well. Sometimes I feels bad, but its mostly that I gets lonely. Don't know what I'd do without you Cora. You'se a comfort.

CORA Thank you Rachael. (*breathing heavily all the while*)

RACHAEL Now that I don't work, the Church meetin's the only things I goes to. Ain't got no trouble so I only prays sunshine to the Lawd and waits for death. I'm jest wore out waitin' for something to happen. Folks don't come to Church much now. Church ain't got the old spirit.

CORA You shouldn't complain none. No ma'm you got de blessin's right here. I have to scratch 'bout for food and a place to lay dis head. Hit ain't no paradise I tells you. Hit sure ain't no paradise.

RACHAEL One way or the other it ain't no Eden. You'se right there. (*Pause*) Ought to see 'bout that heart.

CORA Hit come an' go.

RACHAEL Better see to it jest the same. (*pause*)

CORA Suppose you heard 'bout dat new man—calls himself de Apostle of Light. Some folks calls him Christ come back. Say he's healin' folks.

RACHAEL Lawd, Lawd what is we comin' to.

CORA He's givin' out food an' shelter sure 'nough. Yes Ma'm, dey say he's Christ come back, walkin' right here on earth, givin' out pieces of Heaven if you'll only believe in him.

RACHAEL Seems like I heard Sister Maria Lee talkin' 'bout him. But I don't set no store by these new-fangeled prophets. I puts ma trust in the Lawd. He's takin' care of me so far. I can trust him for the future.

CORA He's a-given me life dats all. I'se had to drag all de rest of de way alone.

RACHAEL The Lawd works in a mysterious way, his wonders to perform.

CORA He ain't worked no wonders on me. How you know dis Apostle ain't what dey say he is? T'would be a sorry thing if he really was Christ come back an' none of us knowed it. 'T would be a sorry thing, yes ma'm. An' they say he's givin' out food free, an' healin' the sick, yes my gracious. Healin' the sick an' givin' out food.

RACHAEL I puts ma trust in the Lawd that's all I got to say 'bout it. Guess we'd better be gettin' along.

CORA Guess we'd better. (*they get up and go out of the light. They pass up to the street level and talk as they go*)

CORA Did you hear 'bout Sister Ruby Howard's chile? Died. Undernourishment dey say.

RACHAEL Don't know what things a-comin' to. Folks dying all 'bout an' losin' jobs. Near time for the depression to be over an' some folks just feelin' it.

CORA Dat ole depression lak a black snake, you drive him away wid a stick an' he still come back.

(*A few of the* CHORUS *come in wearily and wander about on the stage level or just sit. They should not, however, detract from the two talking women. They are a background. As they come in the choral background music begins: hollow, despairing. When the* CHORUS *speaks their speech sounds far off: like an echo of their first lines*)

RACHAEL My children manages to keep their jobs; praise His name.

CORA Wish ma little ones hadn't died. Two inside one year. Tu-ber-cu-losis of the lung so de doctor say. Been a long time but I remembers well, yes m'am. An' since dat time I been knockin' from pillar to post, an' every pillar bin stone an' every post bin iron.

RACHAEL The Lawd will protect his own.

CORA ... Some in Park Avenue an' some in de slums of Harlem. De Lawd protects his own all right.

RACHAEL That's mighty bitter talk, Sister, for a church member.

CORA Yeh. You know I got to thinking. The church ain't doin' nothin' for me. It's me been doin' for de church.

RACHAEL If you would have your life, you must lose it first.

CORA I've done givin' ma life an' got nothin' 'sept rags an' poverty an' left overs from de white folks, an' those I work for ain't got much.

RACHAEL De Lawd works in a mysterious way his wond ...

CORA He ain't worked no wonders on me. I'se sick an' tired of hell on earth, an' kingdom after I'm cold and dust. I'se sick an' tired of prayin' an' gettin' only silence. I'se sick of de leftovers an' the cold-cellar nights, an' only rags for ma back, I'se tired, tired, I tells you, waitin' for the sky to rain manna. I wants heaven here. Here on dis earth. O Lawd, Lawd I wants to keep de faith but I'se tired of tryin' wid only dese two po' hands. I wants heaven now, an' I don't want to die to get it.

RACHAEL I knows. But you gotta have patience; you gotta keep the faith. Wait Cora, wait, I say, on the Lawd.

(*The music of the* CHORUS *has faded into the music of the* APOSTLE OF LIGHT. *It is way off but comes nearer.* CORA *and* RACHAEL *look at each other. The music becomes louder and* CORA *begins to walk toward it*)

CORA De music of de new Apostle. Listen. Listen! Ain't it sweet an' nice soundin'! (*she talks as if in her sleep*)

RACHAEL Come back, Cora, come back.

CORA Listen at that music. Listen! It's wonderful. It make me feel spry again. Ain't it blessed. Ain't it sweet. (*her voice takes on a new, happy quality*)

RACHAEL   Cora, come back. I knows whereof I speak. Don't go off to no man who calls himself Christ. Cora, Cora!

CORA   Oh, Rachael this music fills de lonely places. Yes Jesus ahm a-comin'. Yes Lawd ahm a-comin' to lay ma troubles at yo' breast an' take yo' song for mine. I'se waited so long in de cold an' de blackness not to come Lawd. Ahm comin' es fast es Ah kin. Ahm a-comin' Jesus. That music sure is blessed; that music sure is sweet. Hallelujah! Ahm so glad. (CORA *walks into the music and is lost in blackness and the music.* RACHAEL *stands with her hands stretched out to where* CORA *has gone*)

RACHAEL   Come back, Cora, come back. The Lawd sees. Give him a chance. Remember Job. Come back, Cora, come back. (*the music trails off and comes back with the* CHORUS *melody. The slow, empty music that swells while* RACHAEL *prays later on*)

CHORUS   We are Winter worn,
Wind torn,
Despair
Leaps in the air
Falls down
Like a clown,
We saw at a fair,
Long, long, ago.
Two Winters come in one year:
The wind thrusts fingers through our fear,
Curves its palm into our walls,
And whistles and rumbles along the walls.
Where is Christ?
Where is Christ?

(RACHAEL *walks down from the street level, through the* CHORUS *and into her lighted home area. As she prays the stained-glass window lights up. She kneels down by a chair and begins to pray*)

RACHAEL   It's a many times I come to you, Jesus, my hands stretched in pain and prayer, askin' for some of your sunshine.

CHORUS   Where is Christ?

RACHAEL   Many times I come askin' for shelter in thy cross.

CHORUS   Where is Christ?

RACHAEL   Beggin' that ma children might be raised up in thy light. Seekin' more faith to follow thy road.

CHORUS   Where is Christ?

RACHAEL   I come askin' in the dead of Winter when dere was no food, no coal for the fire.

CHORUS   Have the store-houses burned to ashes on the ground?

RACHAEL   An' you answered, Jesus, you answered this po' sinner's prayers.

CHORUS   How long will our children cry out
In the night with hunger awake in their bellies?

RACHAEL   Now I come, my ole knees creakin' an' sore, my ole heart full of gratitude for what you done for me an' mine, seekin' sunshine for another lost soul, Cora Jenkins.

CHORUS   Where is Christ?

RACHAEL   She's wandered away 'cause she's sick of waiting for thy mercy. She don't understand, Jesus. She don't know. Give her strength, Jesus. She don't understand thy ways an' thy power.

CHORUS   Where is Christ?

RACHAEL   Give her courage Lawd. Open her eyes and let her see thy light: let her feel thy tender mercy.

CHORUS   Where is Christ?

RACHAEL   For thy sweet blessin's and thy pain remembered, I ask that this my humble prayer be acceptable in thy sight, O my redeemer, Amen. (*the stained-glass window sends a glow down onto* RACHAEL. *The* CHORUS *is gone.* RACHAEL *is still on her knees*)

NORMA (*from the darkness and then appearing in the Jackson home area*) Mother, mother. Why mother what on earth are you doing on your knees?

RACHAEL   Praying.

NORMA   Will you help me fasten my gown? I've got to leave in a jiffy for the dance.

RACHAEL   On Sunday night!

NORMA   Yes, darling, on Sunday night.

RACHAEL   Well, I guess I'm too ole to say you nay.

NORMA   Old-fashioned, mother. Not really old.

RACHAEL   Ole. When you get so that you're left alone. You're gettin' old. There ain't no doubtin' that.

NORMA   Is it all right?

RACHAEL   I'm fine chile, 'cept . . .

NORMA   I know . . . my dress I mean. Is it straight?

RACHAEL   It's fine chile.

NORMA   I want to look my best tonight. Ralph is taking me out.

RACHAEL   Ralph? He's the man from

Chicago, ain't he?
NORMA   What?
RACHAEL   He comes from Chicago?
NORMA   Yes mother. Don't you like him?
RACHAEL   He jest live so far away. If you was to marry him you'd have to go to Chicago to live, wouldn't you?
NORMA   Who said anything about marriage? I hope he asks me just the same.
RACHAEL   He'll take you with him.
NORMA   Naturally. Don't be selfish, dear.
RACHAEL   Cora Jenkins say . . .
NORMA   Where's my purse? Have you seen my purse? The jewelled one . . .
RACHAEL   Miss' Jenkins say . . .
NORMA   Now where's that damned purse?
RACHAEL   Norma!
NORMA   I put it somewhere here.
RACHAEL   Norma!
NORMA   Yes mother I'm listening.
RACHAEL   Don't leave me alone again tonight.
NORMA   You're not afraid, are you, dear?
RACHAEL   Jest lonely—that's all—jest lonely.
NORMA   Here it is. Cyril will be home soon.
RACHAEL   I wants my girl here with me once in a while.
NORMA   I've *got* to go tonight.
RACHAEL   I can't be left alone tonight, chile. Stay with me.
NORMA   Why didn't you go to Church, dear?
RACHAEL   I fell to talkin' with Mis' Cora Jenkins. She was to go with me. It got late an' I come home.
NORMA   Why didn't she come with you?
RACHAEL   She went to the Apostle of Light.
NORMA   That one. (*laughing*) Not enough excitement at the Church of God and Saints of Christ?
RACHAEL   No that wasn't it. She were lonely and hungry.
NORMA   Poor dear.
RACHAEL   I'm lonely too. Don't go tonight, Norma.
NORMA   Oh mother please.
RACHAEL   You bin out every night this week.
NORMA   Cyril was around.
RACHAEL   Cyril's a man. I wants ma girl.
NORMA   (*suddenly realizing that she has been very brusque*)   Mother I'd stay if I could. And it's not only to-night but every night that you want. I'm not getting any younger. (*she says this with no bitterness but with heretofore undemonstrated tenderness*) I can't be here all the time Mother. You understand don't you? Try to understand. Try mother.
RACHAEL   Go on chile, don't bother 'bout me. I'll get along. I'll find something. Go 'long chile.
NORMA   Bye, dear. Pleasant dreams. (*she goes out. During the last few speeches the Apostle's music has begun and now begins to swell.* RACHAEL *stands up, is impelled toward the music. By a terrific grip of her will she does not go toward it. She goes back and sits. The music becomes more syncopated and she stands: goes a step or two and turns back, falls in her chair murmuring*)
RACHAEL   Help me Jesus, help me.

(*Blackout. The stage is dark for a few seconds except for a faint light behind the stained-glass window. Music of the* CHORUS *is heard and goes down and then out, as the lights slowly come up in the street area. The light comes from a street lamp. On a box a* BEGGAR *sits. He is blind and holds a tin cup. A* PROSTITUTE *walks across and puts a coin in the cup*)

BEGGAR   (*playing a harmonica*)   God bless you. God bless you.
PROSTITUTE   A fat chance. (*she laughs harshly and goes off. But she comes back again during the scene. All the people who pass during this scene have been or will be in the* CHORUS. *The street is never empty. Choral people pass and go out into darkness. It is Christmas Eve and very cold. Bells ring out a carol*)
CHILD   Mama what Sanny Clause gonna bring me for Xmas?
MOTHER   Santa Claus done died. How come you didn't know that?
CHILD (*whimpering*)   Why did he die Mama?
MOTHER   He starved to death!
CHILD   Is he gonna bring me a sled?
MOTHER   He's dead. Can't you understand, Santa Claus ain't for us Chile. He just ain't for us.
CHILD   Johnny's gonna get a sled. Is Sanny Clause gonna bring me one?
MOTHER   Shet your mouth before I slap all your teeth out.
CHILD (*tears coming*)   Mama ain't he coming any more. Ain't he ever gonna bring me . . .
MOTHER (*moans. They are out of the street and in semi-darkness*)   Lawd, teach him to under-

stand that it ain't my fault. If you can't send toys and food teach him that it ain't my fault. Make him understand, why I ain't got a thing to give him. Not even a rubber band. Teach him. Make him understand. (*she is crying and crying, her voice and body go into darkness*) Make him under . . .

(LIVER LIPS *turns up coat collar and walks across the street.* STUFF *comes across dressed like a "jelly-bean." They meet*)

LIVER LIPS How ya! Mister Stuff!

STUFF Great Gawd an' little fishes if it ain't ole Liver Lips. How ya' boy?

LIVER LIPS How ya' yourself an' see how ya' like it. (*both laugh*)

STUFF Where ya' been? Ain't seen ya' this winter?

LIVER LIPS Man, I been broke.

STUFF Don't try to jive me.

LIVER LIPS That's the truth, so help me Hannah.

STUFF How 'bout comin' down to the old place? They been askin' for ya'

LIVER Tell 'em I ain't got no money. No suh not even a dime for the numbers. I ain't played in three months.

STUFF I *know* you been flat broke then.

LIVER LIPS Flat as spit.

STUFF Come on down.

LIVER LIPS Man my pockets are so empty they leak.

STUFF It's on me then. Shake a leg.

LIVER LIPS You'se a pal. Liver this is your lucky day! (*their laughter goes out with them into the darkness*)

(*The Choral music comes up. The sky is deep blue and has stars. The stained-glass window is dim. The cross makes a shadow, on the stage. Most of the* CHORUS *is on as the lights come up. Others come in later*)

FIRST CHORUS We have heard from whisperings running on the wind,
From gossip belched out from reliable tongues,
From miracles performed without
The usual wand and basic contraptions,
From the fat look of hitherto skinny faces,
That a Prophet has come,
A protector,
A giver of food.

SECOND CHORUS What was whispered we have not heard,
For the wind only howls in our ear.
What miracles?
What gossip: The tongues we hear bring only hunger for a song;
And the looks we have seen have been skinny and haunted.
Where is this protector:
How can we find him,
Claim him,
Worship,
Have food,
And a light for guidance?

FIRST CHORUS It has been said that Christ has forsaken
The Angels, left them to their flutes and their wings,
And their heaven, pearly-gate songs.
He has raced down miles of time
To walk among us on earth.
He has brushed past stars,
His robe glitters with stars.

SECOND CHORUS Where is this man with a robe of stars?
Where is Christ?

OLD MAN Seeing our misery He has come to us.
He is walking right here on earth
Giving out pieces of Heaven if we'll only believe in Him,
And claim Him again.
He brings light,
He brings light!
He is the Apostle of Light!!

FIRST CHORUS He is here!
The Apostle of Light!!

SECOND CHORUS (*echoing*) The Apostle of Light!
Where shall we find him who comes again
As he said he would ages back,
When he ruled only half of the earth?
Where?
We are Winter worn,
We need him now on his birthday night.
Is there a new star to guide us to him?

BOTH CHORUSES For we have forgotten the look of the Bethlehem star
That shone in an easier world,
A warmer world,
A fig-tree,
Golden, Frankencense world.
Where is the new star?

LEADER Let us seek like Shepherds in modern rags.
Let us find the star.

BOTH Let us all seek.

(*Mother whose child died, has been sitting apart her back to the audience, down by the proscenium*)

MOTHER Seek, seek, all of you seek.
　　　　He comes too late by half a week.
　　　　Burn the blanket.
　　　　The promise: I lied,
　　　　Let it be forgotten,
　　　　My baby has died.

(*Some women comfort her*)

LEADER It is the living now.
　　　　The living.
　　　　Let the dead be warm in the earth,
　　　　Let the earth be warm on the dead!
　　　　We living, dying, seek shelter,
　　　　We want to be fed.
　　　　Re-consider your dead:
　　　　Consider them dead.

(*To the* CHORUS, *two stars seem to burn brighter than all the rest. One over the Church level, one over the Apostle area*)

CHORUS Which is the shelter star?
　　　　Which is his star?
　　　　We have waited long,
　　　　Wandered far,
　　　　Into misery looking for this star?
　　　　Now when it comes
　　　　We cannot choose.
BLIND MAN I have never seen a star.
　　　　I look up to darkness always;
　　　　Guide me to this shelter star.
LEADER Why do we wait?
　　　　Why do we hesitate?
　　　　Let us find the Apostle
　　　　Who sends this sign
　　　　For us to follow in the Wintertime.
ONE Come on
　　　　You who are left in the rain
　　　　With pain
　　　　In your bones.
ANOTHER You who feel death
　　　　Like a breath
　　　　On your hands.
　　　　Come on.
A MOTHER I have heard my children cry for food
　　　　In the night:
　　　　I will follow this light.
BLIND MAN Guide me to the shelter star.
　　　　I cannot find my way alone—
　　　　Don't leave the blind to wander where the wind is a wall!
LEADER Why do we wait?
　　　　Why do we hesitate?
PRIEST (*appearing again. Sign of Cross, Incense*)
　　　　The saints you pray to will hear
　　　　In spite of the long-coming answer.
　　　　And the dull Winter will turn back to Autumn again.
　　　　Return to prayer,
　　　　Return to the saints and their blessings!

SOME The church will hear the song of the forgotten;
　　　　We have not been deserted and we are not lost.
　　　　Wait and listen before you go to the earth-men for food;
　　　　Wait and listen before you plunge into falseness for faith.
CHORUS (*going up to* PRIEST *from all directions. Scornfully*) Do you know what hunger is?
　　　　Do you know what pain is?
LEADER Do you know the terrible slow crawling agony of living?
　　　　Have you seen the dead child without a coffin?
　　　　Have you watched the mother's eyes?
　　　　Don't trace the cross in the air:
　　　　Rip off your lace, rip it to thread,
　　　　Sell your images for us,
　　　　Mortgage the Church for us;
　　　　Let your brass constellations tarnish.
　　　　Go down.
　　　　You are not worthy.
　　　　Grow fat!
CHORUS Grow rich!
LEADER But go down.
CHORUS You are not worthy.
PRIEST Treason to God, to his Son and the order of earth.
　　　　Treason to yourselves!
　　　　How can I bring light if you thrust
　　　　His chalice from my hands?
　　　　You follow a false Prophet.
　　　　You stare at false miracles!
　　　　You desert the name and blow the candles out.
　　　　YOU are not worthy.

(CHORUS *begins to wander off, upstairs, on levels looking, looking, but the Priest and the Leader debate*)

LEADER As long as our bellies are empty
　　　　We will follow any god.
　　　　We would pawn the halo about the head of Christ,
　　　　Unhaunt the Ghost
　　　　Who knows the secret: the turning of stone to bread,
　　　　Of fishes to more fishes,
　　　　Of water to wine.
　　　　Our faces look downward for coins
　　　　On the pavement,
　　　　And our hands stretch downward
　　　　To soothe our rumbling bellies.

PRIEST You must wait; be tested.
LEADER This is not time for words from a crowded book.
PRIEST Wait; be tested; wait.

(*But the* LEADER *is gone and so is the* CHORUS. *Blackout. From the darkness a nickelodeon machine plays shrilly. The lights go up in the street area, that is now a gin mill. It is crowded.* STUFF *and* LIVER LIPS *are there, so is* NUMBERS. *Cigarette smoke and the men drinking from imaginary glasses give enough atmosphere*)

NUMBERS Man I had a dream last night; I was walking down Seventh Avenue with nothing to do but walk. Pretty soon a broad comes truckin' along. Dressed in yalla and green, man. Shook like jelly underneath. She crosses the street, the cars go "whiz," "whiz," but she keep on truckin', shakin' like jelly. I catches up to her and keeps my eyes peeled for hers. She say: 857—

STUFF 857 What?

NUMBERS That's my business. She say 857—That's all, see, Man. Then she says: Bring somethin' to eat.

STUFF Did ya' play the number!

NUMBERS Think I'm a fool! Sure, Man, I played it.

LIVER LIPS Did it come out?

NUMBERS I only had a dime but I put it smack on 857. Now I got enough to near buy this joint.

LIVER LIPS My buddy. (*laughs*)

NUMBERS (*to* BARTENDER) Gin 'em up. (*chimes begin to play "Come all ye faithful." The nickelodeon machine has ceased playing*)

STUFF Used to sing that in Church.

NUMBERS Turn that god-damned song off!

STUFF Can't turn it off. It's comin' from somewhere out there. Don't get hot and bothered.

NUMBERS Stop beatin' up your gums or I'll throw this gin in your eyes.

STUFF Listen at the Bank of the U. S. will ya!

NUMBERS Don't get me mad, man.

LIVER LIPS Com'on fellers Christmas time.

NUMBERS Christmas time! Nuts!

STUFF Why you gettin' mad with money enough to buy them chimes. (*laughs*)

NUMBERS I'll slap your teeth down your throat and not even look back.

STUFF Better button your lips.

NUMBERS Why you bastard, just because you're Mister Stuff you think that spells "tough guy!"

STUFF I'll ram this razor down your throat and cut your friggin' tongue out.

NUMBERS You an' what army.

LIVER LIPS He got you there Stuff. (*laughs*)

STUFF Lemme at him. (*as they are beginning to tussle, the mother and child seen on the street come in. She screams*)

NUMBERS What the hell do you want?

STUFF What do you want screamin' like a siren! ("*Come all ye faithful*" *is heard again but jazzed up*)

NUMBERS Damn that music!

LIVER LIPS It's a Christmas Carol. (*laughs*)

MOTHER Christmas! I ain't got hardly spit enough to say it, I'm so dry.

NUMBERS Sounds like a jump up song to me.

LIVER LIPS A Christmas Carol with gin. (*laughs*)

CHILD Is that Sanny Clause's bells mama?

MOTHER Shet your mouth or I'll tan your hide off.

LIVER LIPS That's the music of that new Apostle. I heard that that Apostle's givin' out food free.

FIRST MAN Chicken an' sweet potaters chillins an' duck an' everything. Got a pitcher of milk that never run dry.

MOTHER Who told you that?

SECOND MAN It's de truf. I bin there. You get much as you can eat an' a place to flop if you need it.

MOTHER How 'bout money.

SECOND MAN Ain't I told you' it's free. Just shout an' say "He's Jesus," an' "Ain't it grand" an' eat. Yes sir-re Bob.

MOTHER (*starting to leave child*) Maybe Santa Claus ain't died chile!

CHILD Is he gonna bring me a sled Mama?

MOTHER No child, food! (*they are gone*)

NUMBERS Gin'em up!

LIVER LIPS Gin—I've had gin a-plenty in fact that's all I've had. But food, that's another matter. I'm goin' down there an' get me some food and whatever else goes with it.

NUMBERS You can't be that hungry. Goin' to church!

LIVER LIPS I bin so hungry that ma' stomach belching like Fourth of July. Stop every once in a while to ask if ma mouth gone on a vacation. I bin so hungry, I woulda taken the cheese from a mouse trap. I'm on my way to that Apostle of

Light or whatever he is. I sure hope that light shines on some good victuals.

LIVER LIPS Com'on Stuff.

STUFF Will there be any broads there?

LIVER LIPS 'Spose so. I heard Pineapple Head say they're all sorts there. Masculine. Feminine. High yalla, low yalla, blue, black an' even white folks.

STUFF Sure 'nough.

LIVER LIPS Just 'bout everybody I guess. (*he goes out into the darkness.* SHORT BOY *and* PINEAPPLE HEAD *watch him go out*)

SHORT BOY Ya know I believe I'll go down there an' get me a good feed too. Com'on Pineapple Head.

PINEAPPLE HEAD You sure got de ticket!

SHORT BOY So long Numbers. See ya in Church.

NUMBERS (*watching them go off. Then he turns to* BARTENDER) Well I'll be goddamned! (*drinks his gin; smacks his lips loudly*) Maybe that Apostle got somethin'. Anything that Pineapple Head an' his Pal gets free is for Numbers too. Yes suh whatever they gets free is for Numbers too. See ya in Church. (*he goes out*)

BARTENDER (*taking off apron*) Hey Numbers, ya ole chiseler, wait for me. Wait for me—(*the gin mill is empty*)

(*The lights go up in the street revealing* CARRIE PETERS (*later* MOTHER HUMILITY). *She is seated on a step talking to herself. She is drunk. She has tuberculosis which makes her cough very often*)

CARRIE So I says to him I says: Judge I didn't so-li-c-it him like you says I done. I only asked him how he was feeling an' he struck up a bit of talk an' then it was then that old policeman taken me in. Well it don't matter. (*looking around and then pulling her rags about her*) God Almighty it's colder than heaven around these parts. (*thinking she sees a man on the street*) Just enough to buy a drink. That's all I want. (*then to herself*) Now you know Carrie Peters that that there was no man there. Youse cross-eyed that what the matter with you. Yes Sister Carrie your eyes they ain't right. (*puts a finger between her eyes to test them*) No you ain't nobodys cross-eyed. Youse drunk Mis' Peters, youse drunk what I mean. Yes Mis' Peters youse had much too much. Hallelujah! (*laughs*) Ain't so drunk Carrie that you forget your cough. Ain't too lit to remember that. (*a man crosses the street in time to hear her last sentence or two. He sees a cigarette butt near* CARRIE *and stoops to pick it up. But he has no light*)

OLD MAN (*to* CARRIE) Got a match?

CARRIE Now Carrie don't you look round 'cause there ain't nobody there 'cause you was just thinking fire with your hands so cold. Liquor don't even warm you up anymore.

OLD MAN (*amused*) There is someone here Carrie Peters.

CARRIE (*turning*) Name-a-God how did you know ma name? (*coughs*)

OLD MAN Youse sick.

CARRIE Ain't sick neither. (*to herself*) Yes you is, Carrie.

OLD MAN I'se heard of a man what could cure that.

CARRIE You ain't heard of any such thing. (*to herself*) Has he Carrie? No sir.

OLD MAN That's the truth. I was just goin'. Anybody can go. Don't you want to come.

CARRIE Ain't no truth in it. (*to herself*) No Carrie there ain't. Where a man like you say could work such a miracle.

OLD MAN I ain't seen him but I hear tell of him. I was just going.

CARRIE (*to herself*) You might go Carrie. You go Carrie. (*to man*) I don't believe but I'll go just the same. (*goes off muttering*) I don't believe it but I'll go to tell you to your teeth that youse just a plain low down liar. The whole world full of liars. Hallelujah! (*as they are going off* AGNA *and* JOHN *dressed in evening clothes enter*)

AGNA You know John that party was just too too dull.

JOHN That was because you wouldn't touch a thing. The cocktails were wonderful. Jane-Ann has the most wonderful recipe for what she calls a *Fizz-Manhattan-Sussie-Q*. Did you see Ellen and Fred tonight ... Perfectly wonderful ...

AGNA They've been going through that act for years. I know every cue, every line. Tedious. That's what it really is. Tedious.

JOHN Now you know it's fun ...

AGNA Was fun. I'm fed up. We go round and round like the music.

JOHN I didn't know you felt that way.

AGNA On and off for years.

JOHN You're perfectly wonderful Agna: always thinking of something new to shock people. Now that party you had last week was a riot.

AGNA   In a restrained way you must add.

JOHN   Riot all the same.

AGNA   It should have been. I spent two months planning it and five hundred in the execution. I'm fed up with this caviar-for-the-general life. The general being John and Ellen and Fred and Jane And Agna and Jane-Ann . . .

JOHN   Thanks for including me.

AGNA   The pleasure is all yours.

JOHN   I see you're on the serious side of the fence tonight.

AGNA   Not serious. Different.

JOHN   Jane-Ann's party was a stunt. A wonderful stunt in a night club. You must admit.

AGNA   Was stinking with boredom.

JOHN   Why, Agna!

AGNA   John, don't you hear music?

JOHN   Yes, I've heard it all along.

AGNA   Isn't it amazing? I feel like dancing or singing in the streets. It's very catching.

JOHN   Sort of a cross between Bach and Louis Armstrong.

AGNA   Very tempting. Let's go in.

JOHN   Where?

AGNA   To wherever it's coming from. Can't you see where it's coming from?

JOHN   Oh there's a sign. It says: *JOY SISTER AND BROTHER*.

AGNA   What?

JOHN   Oh just something absurd. A Baptist prayer meeting no doubt.

AGNA   I can't read it all from here. There is another phrase.

JOHN   Oh something.

AGNA   Well!

JOHN   This is too funny. *THE APOSTLE OF LIGHT IS GOD.*

AGNA   God!

JOHN   Yes don't you remember that man up there. Evidently he's come down.

AGNA   Let's go.

JOHN   Now Agna. I humor you too much!

AGNA   That's because you want to marry me. Let's go in. It'll be fun.

JOHN   I've had my fun.

AGNA   But I haven't had mine.

JOHN   All right. But only for a little while.

AGNA   *GOD IS HERE.* How absurd. I'm just dying to see what it's like. It will probably be amusing thank God and different. (*they are off*)

(*The stained-glass window becomes darker. The Apostle music begins softly and continues through this scene. The light comes on in the Jackson home area*)

CYRIL   Hello mom!

RACHAEL   Evening son.

CYRIL   Guess what.

RACHAEL   I'm guessing!

CYRIL   I'm going to teach English at Virginia State College. That's some Christmas present isn't it?

RACHAEL   What's the catch.

CYRIL   Catch?

RACHAEL   Whenever you get five dollars more son, look for a catch.

CYRIL   You've got a competent son that's what. Aren't you proud?

RACHEL   Yes son.

CYRIL   Mom you're sad. It's Christmas eve; no one is sad on Christmas eve. The only thing is . . .

RACHAEL   The only thing . . .

CYRIL   That I have to go away for a few months.

RACHAEL   You're goin' away.

CYRIL   Only for a little while.

RACHEL   You're leavin' me.

CYRIL   You know I hate to, Mom, but it's all part of the job.

RACHAEL   I know, son, I know. You're all right. I'm very happy for you. That's why I worked so hard to put you children through college. Mom's very proud. But you're goin' just the same.

CYRIL   Don't be glum. You'll have anything you want: dresses and a trip down home and all the money you want to put in the collection plate at church. Even if it's five dollars.

RACHAEL   (*from far off*) Cyril, . . . Cyril boy . . . the Church done closed, nobody goes no more.

CYRIL   Closed?

RACHAEL   The new Apostle of Light is really spreadin' his light.

CYRIL   I'm sorry Mom.

RACHAEL   An' as for the trip back home . . .

CYRIL   I knew you'd want that. I remember how you used to tell me about back home. The dogwood blooming and the wind in the cane and the funny houses in Charleston with beautiful white doorways. This house is beautiful too Mom, because you made it for us. You can go back and stay all summer if you like.

RACHAEL The're all dead, the folks I knew down there, the're all dead.

CYRIL What's the matter Mom? Have we done anything? You're so sad.

RACHAEL You been good children. No it ain't you but time Son, time strippin' my children from ma breast an' the church from ma heart an' all it's leavin' me is loneliness and death.

CYRIL Doesn't Mrs. Jenkins come around?

RACHAEL She's gone to the new prophet. A new Jesus, they say, made from the ole. So you won't be comin home now for a while. You got your life. I'm happy for you Son. Don't fret 'bout me. Wish I had you children but you got to push ahead. I knows that.

CYRIL I don't want you to be lonely.

RACHAEL I understand.

CYRIL ... An' Norma, she'll be here.

RACHAEL (*bitterly*) Yes Norma. She'll be here. When does your new job start?

CYRIL I've got to leave tonight.

RACHAEL On Christmas Eve!

CYRIL I've got to go downtown but I'll be back with your presents before I go.

RACHAEL I'll be right here.

CYRIL You sure you'll be all right. You promise not to be lonely?

RACHAEL I promise. I'll find something. I seem to have lost Jesus somewhere. Maybe somebody will be back in the church tonight to help me find him again.

CYRIL If you need me when I'm away Mom, I'll come.

RACHAEL If I need you when you're away you'll come. I'll remember that. Now go long an' come back before you leave for the country. You belong to the world now.

CYRIL How you talk.

RACHAEL Go 'long now.

CYRIL Sure you don't want to see the dogwood and hear the songs again.

RACHAEL The songs are in my heart. An' the dogwood—well I reckon it ain't bloomin' time for dogwood.

CYRIL (*starts to go. Comes back and looks at her*) Bye Mom.

RACHAEL Bye Son. (*he goes*)

(*She is alone now. The large light about her home space gets smaller and smaller. There is a pause.* RACHAEL *looks terribly alone. She gets up and starts to walk from her space to the church level singing*)

RACHEL "Sometimes I feel like a motherless child,
Sometimes I feel like a motherless child,
Sometimes I feel like a motherless child,
A long way from home,
A long way from home,
A long way from home."

(*The light in the Church area comes dimly on as she mounts the stairs. Several men and women on their knees, standing up and sitting on chairs, swaying: their shadows huge against the backdrop. They have taken up her song even before she gets there. Now* RACHAEL *kneeling makes another huge shadow. The cross has grown bright. Just below the street area on the stage proper a light comes on. This is the Apostle's space. Several people are sitting about but in contrast to the Church group, they seem happy, supremely content. They exchange such greetings as: "Ain't you glad," "He's come," "Joy, joy Sister," "Joy Brother," "Ain't He sweet," "Bless his name." They are also singing but with a softer tone than the other so that the spiritual music is predominant*)

FOLLOWERS He gave us all our tickets,
The train arrived on time,
O he gave us all our tickets,
The train arrived on time.
Now we are in heaven
An' didn't spend a dime.

(*louder*) He's come to us at last,
Now ain't you mighty glad.
O he's come to us at last,
Now ain't you mighty glad.
He's brung the warmin' sunshine
Forgivin' good and bad.

I think my heart will burst
With joy at seein' him
I think my heart will burst
With joy at seein' him.
He looked on me an' "pop"
My soul was free of sin.

(*to tune of "There Is Power"*)
He has come, come,
Oh yes he has come,

Bringin' light,
Bringin' light,
Bringin' light,
Bringin' light to all the earth.

(*Now some of the church people begin creeping down the steps to the Apostle's area. The cross light is dimming, the Church light is dimming. The* PREACHER *tries to keep them from going*)

PREACHER (*in Church area*) Comes death, the invader,
Pacing through the sky scatterin'
The planets and the lesser stars,
O my people.
When he comes,
When death the invader comes,
An' you have to stand before His great white throne,
What shall you say?
Shall you say you have deserted his Church?
O my people.
When the red hot tongs of death,
You know what tongs are.
Tongs handle fire.
When the tongs of retribution grasp you,
O my people,
What shall you say?
Come back, come back.
Death will ride over you,
One of these days!
Shall you be ready?
He'll scorch the sinners: singe the bone:
Tear the heart.
O my people,
Come back.
Repent.
Wait for the Lord.
Repent, come back.
Don't follow this false God!
Don't worship the golden calf.
God will smite you sure.
Pray, pray—

(*But they have all gone to the* APOSTLE OF LIGHT *except* RACHAEL. *The* PREACHER *goes to* RACHAEL *and lays a hand on her shoulder*)

PREACHER Sister, your faith is still strong. Don't let dat music an' dat dancin' turn you from yo' Christ. He still watchin' from above.

RACHAEL Dere all gone now. All those I loved have gone. Jesus has left me alone. Alone. Oh Christ I'm alone. I've gotta go. The church done closed, dere ain't no one here.

PREACHER This is de real test Sister. Christ never deserts his people.

RACHAEL Cora was right: I done given all for the church an' what happens. My son is gone, ma girl is gone, ma friend is gone. I wants some joy. Some little joy, not loneliness, not death.

PREACHER If you would have your life you must lose it first.

RACHAEL I said that once. It don't sound so good now.

(*The music becomes louder.* RACHAEL *stands deciding. She is swaying but the Apostle music impells her. As it swells up she begins to go down. Slowly not sure of her ground, but slowly she goes down. The* PREACHER *is the only one left and he kneels. His figure is a silhouette against the backdrop and finally the Church area light goes out and the light behind the stained-glass window goes out. Only the Apostle area is lighted. As more people enter this light it begins to spread*)

FOLLOWERS (*singing*) When we were lost in the forest of pain,
He came back to us bringing sunshine and rain.
All our pain was washed away,
All our sin is dried today.

Now shall we praise him,
The Apostle of Light,
Jesus come back
When even the night
Was starless.

Put ribbons in your hair,
Rejoice!
Cast off all despair,
Rejoice!
Be clothed all in white,
He came when our night
Was starless.

(*This ends with* "Ain't you glad," "Hallelujah," "It's wonderful," "Thank you, God Almighty," *etc. A voice comes over the* FOLLOWERS. *They are quiet as it speaks*)

VOICE My children, are you there?
FOLLOWERS Yes God Almighty.
VOICE Will you follow me?

FOLLOWERS Yes my Jesus!
Please your Grace!
All the way
Tell us what!
Yes my Savior!
Oh how sweet!

(*They sing hoarsely, blatantly*)
>He has come, come,
>Oh yes he has come,
>Bringin' light,
>Bringin' light,
>Bringin' light,
>Bringin' light to all the earth.

CORA I wuz starvin': Ma husband left me with two children but dey died of tu-ber-cu-losis of the lung, so the doctor say. Ma heart pounded lak a hammer. I strained it every time I walked upstairs. I kept on praisin' a Gawd I thought wuz beyond the sky. I emptied my pennies in a red plush plate. One evenin' I heard his music an' come an' wuz made well in mind an' body. There ain't no Gawd beyond the clouds. He's right here with us. Ain't you glad. Ma redeemer is right here. Praise his name. An' there ain't no death for me but only eternal life. It's so sweet. Thank you Apostle. Thank you GOD.

(*The usual "Amens," "Ain't it the truth," "Thank you, God Almighty," etc. Brief song. During* MOTHER HUMILITY'S *speech and as she begins, the* FOLLOWERS *accompany her*)

FOLLOWERS Listen at Mother Humility.
>Did he do dat sho 'nough?
>My, my ain't he de Savior dough.
>Tell us mo' Mother.
>Preach it Sister.
>Ain't it grand.
>Blessed Lover.
>Blessed Teacher.
>Blessed Father.
>Blessed Gawd.

(*As she finishes they say such phrases as*)

>Yes praise him.
>I knowed he could do all dat.

MOTHER HUMILITY I praised him. An' the more I praised him the more blessings he showered on me. He's a-givin' me new life. Two months ago I had only one lung an' the other was just a little piece. He cured that. I would sleep with any man who would pay me enough for liquor. He cured that. It's truly grand. I know he's GOD. He didn't only help me out he's raised the dead and cured the dying from cancer. He's the true an' livin' GOD. He don't need money to carry on His work, ain't he GOD. He don't need money.

FOLLOWERS (*singing*) My Lord's treasury never run dry,
>A-never run dry,
>My Lord's treasury never run dry,
>A-never run dry.
>It's everlastin' as the stars on high.
>A-never run dry,
>A-never run dry.
>My Lord's treasury like stars in the sky.
>He's given me a blank check,
>Ain't a-gonna die.
>He's given me a blank check,
>Ain't a-gonna die.
>I got the real faith that's a-why.
>Ain't a-gonna die,
>Ain't a-gonna die,
>He's given me a blank check an' that's a-why.

RACHAEL I can testify to His goodness tonight 'cause He's helped me. I wrestled with the Angel of our Lord here, seekin' to stay bound to earth. I struggled but one night I commenced to feel lifted up and that Angel spread out his wings an' carried me up here to Beulah Land. That Angel was robed all in white an' his wings were sparklin'. He was the Apostle. He was the *Apostle*. I was lonely but now I'm full; I saw Death comin' once but he been struck down an' I'm with my GOD. I was all alone but now I'm full. An' I'll never be lonely again. Never again. I have my Jesus.

(*Usual answers, exclamations, etc.*)

VOICE Are you there my children? I'm coming down.

(*Usual answers*)

CYRIL (*in Jackson home space with Christmas presents*) Mom, Mom! Mom!

(*Runs up to Church space*)

Mom!

(*Runs up and down, stairways*)

Mom! Mom!

(*But no one hears*)

Mom!

(*He goes dejectedly back to his home space. Sits. Lets the presents drop. The light fades on him. Where the* PRIEST *stood at the beginning of the act the* APOSTLE OF LIGHT *stands now. He is in ordinary business clothes. A light illumines him. As he speaks the* FOLLOWERS *bow down. The whole stage is full of kneeling people, as he speaks*)

APOSTLE   I come to earth because dust has blown into my people's eyes and blinded them: shut out my eternal light. O my people. I come because there's been iron resting on your hearts, with no one to lift the weight but me. I come because there's been a wall between my peoples an' I gotta hew it down: pick axe this wall of oppression and prejudice and hate. O my people. I come with my body before you but I've been with you. I'm with you always. I'm in your heart. Ain't you glad? O my people. I'm leading you into the promised land: heaven on earth. O my people ain't you glad? Are you with me? Will you follow me? I've come because too long my prophets have preached death and pain instead of joy and life. I come bringing a kingdom where you are. O my people. Ain't you glad? I come bringing light. Pray because prayer changes things. Don't have to pray out loud because I hear you when your mind talks. Ain't you glad? Pray in darkness, I see you. Pray with your mouth shut, I hear you. I see things you see and things you don't see. I hear the same. Ain't you glad? O my people, joy, joy, joy. The kingdom is here. Manna is here. Shelter, guidance is here. Ain't you glad? I come down because dust has blown into my peoples' eyes and blinded them. Joy, joy, joy.

(*His voice trails off, the light about him fades. He is gone. The* FOLLOWERS *begin to sing softly and then louder and louder; tambourines. Women prance up and down. Some of the men "truck" in time to the music. Some sway or move their shoulders rhythmically. A piano jazzes up the song, etc.*)

FOLLOWERS (*singing*)   He's hitched our wagon to a star;
Ain't you glad,
Ain't you glad.

He's hitched our wagon to a star;
Ain't you glad,
Ain't you glad.

He's made this earth a paradise;
Ain't you glad,
Ain't you glad.

He's made this earth a paradise;
Ain't you glad,
Ain't you glad.

(*The curtain slowly falls on a mass of ecstatic worshippers*)

ACT TWO

(*The choral music opens act two. The music has the same theme as in the first act, but now it has a syncopated strain running through it. The faces of the* CHORUS *seem brighter, happier. Their heads are held higher; their steps are jauntier*)

CHORUS   This is a dream without sleep.
A Lazarus miracle without tombs.

When hunger skimmed the unction from our flesh
We were less than men and walking in a mire,
We were less than men and crawling.

We will not think of the days way back:
Ancient, seedy days way back.
The Apostle has taught us to sing
As a robin teaches his child to fly.

Now that the garden reserved for Adam and Eve
Has been put out to hire and sold to the Apostle of Light,
Strange it is that we, the unworthy eat the corn,
Pull the lusty purple grape from the vine,
And call this Eden our own in spite of the old connotation.

Here is no serpent to coil a tempting sleek skin about us.
Here is no evil grinning inside a red apple.
Here is a yesterday caught up in a sunbeam
And shed on us as if it were the sun itself.

ONE   The mortgage that hung over my house like a knife, He has paid.
Now my house is a kingdom: a heaven,
Where once it was mortal ground for the peeling paint,
And the peeling wall-paper and the stamping of children,
And the bare and mouldy ice-box,
And the growling, desolate husband!
As I have given my house, so would I give my life,
Not through death,
For we cannot die: we are death-proof.

ANOTHER The nickles I doled out to the sly insurance shark
Are no longer sought,
For what use have I of money against a needed coffin
Or incense or a requiem mass or an inch of soil to rot in,
When I shall not die!

ANOTHER Now we are stripped and naked of our earth-trappings.
We have no tiny place to call a home place,
But a kingdom in exchange for a hovel,
A God in exchange for air beyond the stars,
Light instead of darkness.

BLIND MAN The ones without sight have more than darkness now.
I am guided by a voice and my hands are warm.

CHORUS We know the honey
Rolled on the curving tongue.
We know,
We know,
We know,
What laughter is,
What dancing is,
What praising is,
What hoping is.

This is a dream without sleep.
A Lazarus miracle without tombs.

(*They go off in darkness and their music goes off with them. As the light comes on in the Jackson home area* CYRIL *is pacing up and down. It is not an irritated pacing but slow and weary and downcast. He is saying not aloud but to himself and we see it through his pacing: what am I to do? Where is Mom? Where could she have gone? I should have stayed, I should have stayed*)

NORMA (*from offstage, happily*) Cyril, Mother, I'm married!

CYRIL (*goes to steps to greet her*) Norma! (NORMA *appears*) I'm glad you're married, Norma.

NORMA Oh I'm so happy. (*holding out her hand with the wedding ring*) Isn't it beautiful?

CYRIL (*hating to tell her*) Norma.

NORMA Yes, Cyril.

CYRIL Norma, Mom isn't here.

NORMA Where is she? I must tell her. I've so much to tell her.

CYRIL I don't know where she is?

NORMA Visiting, I expect. I'll pack till she comes. (*starts off*)

CYRIL Norma, she's not visiting. I can't imagine where she's gone.

NORMA What are you talking about? You sound as if she'd been swallowed up.

CYRIL I've been up all night waiting for her. She never stayed out all night.

NORMA She'll be back, don't worry.

CYRIL That's what I said last night. That's what I said this morning.

NORMA Cyril, you're upset.

CYRIL Norm, I went to the church, I even went to the police . . .

NORMA (*still thinking of her good fortune*) I'm sure she's alright. We'll just have to wait . . .

CYRIL (*continuing*) I went to Cora Jenkins . . .

NORMA Cora went to the Apostle's. Didn't you know?

CYRIL (*a new thought dawning upon him*) The Apostle's . . . I never thought of him. Norma, do you suppose that she has gone to him?

NORMA Of course not Cyril. She wouldn't do anything like that.

CYRIL But she might have. She was lonely. We've deserted her Norma.

NORMA No we haven't Cyril.

CYRIL Neither of us was here. And it was Christmas Eve.

NORMA Now you're making too much of this.

CYRIL We can't let her spend her last years on something false and cheap.

NORMA We won't Cyril.

CYRIL (*not hearing, too absorbed*) Do you know what he does to people? He takes their homes and their faith. That Apostle plays with people's souls. We couldn't let Mom lose her faith. We just mustn't let her.

NORMA Now Cyril you're tired and overwrought.

CYRIL I'm overwrought with good cause. I won't let Mom follow a fraud.

NORMA You're being ridiculous over this whole matter. I tell you mother's probably . . .

CYRIL You tell me. I tell you I know her. She was lonely. It's terrible to be lonely but what that Apostle would do to her would be more terrible still.

NORMA Cyril, Cyril be quiet. It's no use getting upset. I know Mom's all right.

CYRIL No—we don't know but I'll find out. (*starting to go*)

NORMA Where are you going?

CYRIL To bring my mother home.

NORMA Cyril . . . (*but before she can say*

anything he has gone. CYRIL *begins to walk up the steps. We hear* NORMA *humming.* CYRIL *is now in the street area; he walks down the steps into the Apostle's area. A light comes on. The singing of the* FOLLOWERS *offstage can be faintly heard. A girl is sitting at a desk*)

CYRIL I'd like to see my mother.
SECRETARY Joy, brother, peace.
CYRIL I'd like to see my mother.
SECRETARY Your mother?
CYRIL My mother. Mrs. Rachael Jackson!
SECRETARY We have no mortal names here; we have no mothers or children or fathers. There is only one father: The Apostle.
CYRIL My mother's mortal and she has a son and he's here and wants to see her.
SECRETARY Joy brother, peace, I don't know who you want.
CYRIL Rachael Jackson.
SECRETARY Peace.
CYRIL I'm going to find her!

(CORA JENKINS, *now* PRISCILLA PAUL, *enters. She is talking with another follower,* SISTER BEAUTIFUL LIGHT)

CORA So I says: "Lawd I'm still hungry." An' He says, beamin' down on me, He says: "Eat your fill, Sister Priscilla Paul. There is plenty an' to spare." "Yes ma JESUS," I says.
BEAUTIFUL LIGHT He's so sweet!
CORA He is dat, sho' 'nough. Dere ain't nothin' lak His grace and sweetness.
BEAUTIFUL LIGHT You said a mouthful Sister. A mouthful, please ma Savior.
CYRIL (*seeing* CORA) Mrs. Jenkins! (CORA *doesn't answer or even look his way.* CYRIL *asks* SECRETARY) What is her heavenly name?
SECRETARY Sister Priscilla Paul.
CYRIL Priscilla Paul!
CORA Joy brother, peace.
CYRIL Don't you remember me, Mrs. Jenkins?
CORA In de mortal condition I wuz Cora Jenkins, now I'm Sister Priscilla Paul. I likes de sound of hit: Priscilla Paul. Whut kin I do for you son?
CYRIL I'm looking for my mother.
CORA Sister Divine Adoration, you mean?
CYRIL (*with difficulty*) Sister Divine Adoration, I mean. Will you call her please?
CORA Joy Brother, 'cause I will. She inside gettin' her dress ready fo' de big meetin' tonight.

CYRIL Big meeting. What meeting?
CORA De meetin' whut goin' to' be tonight. Hits called: De Sheddin' of De Earth Meetin'.
CYRIL What does that mean?
CORA Dat's de meetin' we has once de month whare we brings in all we done earned durin' de time between de meetin' an' all else we kin bring.
CYRIL (*ironically but it is lost on* CORA) I thought the Apostle didn't need money to carry on his work. He's the Lord, isn't he.
BEAUTIFUL LIGHT Shall I call Divine Adoration for you.
CORA You do dat Beautiful Light. Tell her to come right away. She'll finnis dat dress fo de meetin' later.
BEAUTIFUL LIGHT I will sho' 'nough.
CORA (*to* CYRIL *again*) Yes ma Jesus, those meetin's is nothin' to compare. We brings all our earthly goods 'cause de Apostle say dat we should bring de goods 'cause in Heaven we shouldn't have no "material things," dat whut he say.
CYRIL Oh!
CORA He don't need de "material things," only he say dat dey will "co-corupt" us. Now yo former Ma say dat she goin' to give her house fo a kingdom.
CYRIL What's that?
CORA She probably will tell ya. Now ah gotta go fix ma dress fo tonight. Joy brother, peace. (CORA *goes out.* RACHAEL *enters and the Apostle music becomes louder*)
CORA (*to* RACHAEL) Joy!
RACHAEL (*to* CORA) Peace, Sister.
CYRIL Mom, oh, Mom!
RACHAEL Joy brother, peace.
CYRIL Don't you know me Mom?
RACHAEL You're Cyril Jackson.
CYRIL Your son.
RACHAEL I have no children. I have only a father which art here.
CYRIL Mom, come back home.
RACHAEL Ma home is here in heaven.
CYRIL Mom, I've come to take you home, home, your home.
RACHAEL Ma home is here.
CYRIL Your home is what you worked for all those years. Mom, don't forget the early places. Don't forget us, your children. Don't leave what must be nearest to you.
RACHAEL My father is nearest to me.

CYRIL   Remember Christ Mom, remember Christ.
RACHAEL   He's here.
CYRIL   Remember us, your home, your . . .
RACHAEL   I was alone 'till I found how sweet ma Savior is. Praise His Holy name.
CYRIL   Listen please. I'm alone now. Norma's left. I need you.
RACHAEL   Come here to his kingdom. No one is alone.
CYRIL   I can't.
RACHAEL   You won't believe. (*pause*) I want ma former dwellin' place to be a kingdom.
CYRIL   No . . . no, Mom, no!
RACHAEL   Peace, it's mine. Where's the deed to the house?
CYRIL   He can't have it.
RACHAEL   It's not for you to say. Where's the deed?
CYRIL   He can't have it.
RACHAEL   Peace brother, where's the deed?
CYRIL   It's home.
RACHAEL   I'll get it myself then.
CYRIL   It's yours. I'll get it out. Mom, won't you come home again? For me. For your only son, come back.
RACHAEL   His light is more to me than twenty sons. Praise His Holy name. I've found heaven and I shall not give it up.
CYRIL   Please, Mom . . .
RACHAEL   Have the deed ready tonight. I'm a-comin' for it. (RACHAEL *goes slowly out. The Apostle music swells into the tune of* Jacob's Ladder)
CYRIL   (*shouts*) This fraud, peace monger, joy monger, demon. Selfish grasping demi-god. Give my mother back. Give us all our people back again! (*with futility in his step,* CYRIL *walks sadly out. The* CHORUS *comes in from all directions singing. They form a compact body, march up steps and out the street way*)

CHORUS (*singing to the tune of "Jacob's Ladder"*)
We are climbing on His sunbeams,
We are climbing on His sunbeams,
We are climbing on His sunbeams,
Bringer of the light.
Every beam grows brighter, brighter,
Every beam grows brighter, brighter,
Every beam grows brighter, brighter,
Bringer of the light.

He came when our night was starless,
He came when our night was starless,
He came when our night was starless,
Bringer of the light.
We are stars and He is sunshine,
We are stars and He is sunshine,
We are stars and He is sunshine,
Bringer of the light.

Bow down now and worship, worship,
Bow down now and worship, worship,
Bow down now and worship, worship,
Bringer of the light.

(CYRIL *is in the* JACKSON *home space now.* RACHAEL *comes in from the Apostle's space, goes up the steps leading to the street level, crosses, and comes down the steps leading to her home. She is dressed in a white hoover apron: blue ribbons in her hair*)

RACHAEL   Peace, brother, joy!
CYRIL   You've come back?
RACHAEL   I've come for the deed.
CYRIL   Mom, look about you. This is yours, yours. Don't you want to keep it? Don't give it to him, don't.
RACHAEL   This will be a kingdom. He will cleanse it. It will be a kingdom. Give me the deed?
CYRIL   What has he done to you? You're so strange, you talk differently, you . . .
RACHAEL   He's filled my heart as he's filled hundreds of lonely hearts. He's a-givin' me peace. He's a-given me heaven. He's Jesus. What more could any po' sinner want. Joy, my soul.
CYRIL   What of me?
RACHAEL   Come to heaven. His breast is large and ready to receive you. Come.
CYRIL   No, I won't sell my soul for a song and a shout.
RACHAEL   You'll repent. It's joy my son.
CYRIL   Yes, your son.
RACHAEL   Where's the deed?
CYRIL   Here. (*gives her the deed*)
RACHEL   Thank you brother.
CYRIL   Son!
RACHAEL   Come to the meetin' tonight. You'll see His gracious bounty: His tenderness, His love.
CYRIL   When I look at you I can see his work.
RACHAEL   Thank you brother.
CYRIL   It's not a compliment, Mom.
RACHAEL   Thank you just the same, brother.
CYRIL   Son.

RACHAEL   Come to the meetin' tonight. Will you come?

CYRIL   If it will make you happy.

RACHAEL   Thank you brother. (*she goes up the steps humming an Apostle tune*)

CYRIL   Son, Mom. I'm your son. Don't you remember? What have I done? What has she ever done? Son, Mom, I'm your son. I'm Cyril, your only boy. SON, SON, SON. Son, Mom, Son.

(*he says this as if he were going mad. As he walks execitedly about he accidently touches his mother's rocking chair. He looks at it as it rocks*) Son, Mom. (*way off the "Jacob Ladder" tune is heard.* CYRIL *gets up and goes to the center of the stage level, his back to the audience. A halo of light comes on the Church area. The* PREACHER *stands in it. A halo of light comes on the platform before the cross. The* PRIEST *stands there*) I've come because the Apostle of Light has drawn my mother into his fold. She has given over our house to be a kingdom for him as thousands have already done. He has broken up our family and I am alone. It's no use going to the law, they cannot control faith and Gods or hearts. Now I come to the Church: asking: "What shall I do?"

PREACHER   Ma' son, there ain't nothing to do but pray. An' we've sent our anxious hands up an' prayed with heavy hearts. The Lord will bring wrath down on those who have deserted his Church. Pray because prayer changes things.

PRIEST   The Holy Church is doing everything in its power to bring those back who have strayed like lambs, away from the Shepherd.

CYRIL   What has the Holy Church done?

PRIEST   Sent special prayers, through his Saints, to the throne.

CYRIL   As long as people are hungry they will follow any God. Those who were not hungry for food were famished for spiritual guidance. Why should they have to turn from the Church for spiritual guidance? You have let your people down somewhere. That is why this false prophet has gotten a hearing. The Church has grown fat on the poor. It has followed an earth-dream and not a heavenly one. What are you going to do?

BOTH   We have done our best: we have prayed.

CYRIL   Then I must go alone.

PRIEST   If you cannot wait for God you must go alone without his sanction. We have done God's will.

PREACHER   We have tried to follow His way.

CYRIL   These people are being defrauded. They will be left with nothing one of these days. Form a union and petition God: demand, that this Apostle die: Strike on God. Do something to make him hear if you believe in His eternal power.

PREACHER   The Lord works in a mysterious way his wonder to perform.

CYRIL   Mysterious all right. Don't you see that this Apostle's cause is a mortal cause, doomed to failure, but not before it has wrecked a million lives or more.

PRIEST   My son we are not politicians, neither are we Communists. We are a spiritual guardian. And besides they don't contribute anything now.

CYRIL   Don't contribute. I see you want money. *Listen* they want money. I knew it. I felt it. The Church is a spider's web. The Church of jewels and incense and special saints and the church of white windows and bare walls are just the same. You are just chips off a rotten spiritual block. You clothe your fraud in Jesus, just as that Apostle has done. I wonder if God is angry. I bet he isn't. I bet he thinks it's a joke. So you want money do you! You betray the real Christ as Judas once betrayed him only you wouldn't take silver, only gold is good enough. Good-bye Spiders! (*music thunders up with* CYRIL's *last words, defiant syncopated Apostle music.* CYRIL *walks up the steps to the cross window*) So I must do it alone eh!

(*The Apostle music is a jazz song but more blatant even.* CYRIL *puts his hands over his ears and goes off from the Church level. The* FOLLOWERS *begin to come on from all entrances. They have on white hoover aprons and blue ribbons in their hair. The men are shabby but their one touch of finery is a blue ribbon in their button holes. Everyone seems happy. The children, of which there are only a few, when they remember go about with their wrists on their shoulder blades, their hands flapping like wings. This is the* big *meeting. They sing as they come in. Now the Apostle area which started in one small place has expanded into the Church area, into the Jackson home space. Only the street* is free of FOLLOWERS *after the meeting begins. The dancing that they do is sort of a jump up shimmy dance, an informal but none the less hot dance*)

FOLLOWERS (*singing*) When we were lost in a forest of pain,
He came back to us bringing sunshine and rain.
All our pain was washed away.
All our sin is dried today.
How shall we praise Him,
The Apostle of Light,
Jesus come back
Whenever our night
Was starless.
Put ribbons in your hair,
Rejoice:
Cast off all despair,
Rejoice:
Be clothed all in white,
He came when our night
Was starless.

(*Tambourines, dancing. The inevitable phrases: "Thank you Apostle," "Ain't it grand," "Bless His Holy Name," "Thank you Jesus," "Blessed Christ come back." Everyone seems to be enjoying himself.* RACHAEL *and* CORA *are together. They are near center stage. Now a white follower gets up and speaks in a cultured voice. The crowd accompany her with occasional "Amens," or "Hallelujah," "He did dat sho' 'nouth," or "Ain't He Sweet." As the* FOLLOWERS *enter they place on a table to the right of the cross what they have brought to the* SHEDDING OF THE EARTH MEETING. *They make much of going up to the table and placing their possessions on it. By the time the meeting begins in earnest the table is heaped up in a pyramid of possessions. When the* APOSTLE *appears for the first time in this scene he stands behind the table and holds his hands over the possessions as if blessing the materials. When the* APOSTLE *is shot his hands clutch the edge of this table and as he falls he pulls the table down and the possessions fall over him*)

GLORIOUS VISION I know of His goodness. He's helped me. Thank you God. Once I was in what people of the mortal condition call: "society." I had jewels with a fine bright shine and nothing I wanted was denied me if money would buy it. Every man I saw I desired if he was handsome. I spent my day on nothingness: bridge parties, cocktail parties. My nights I spent drinking and smoking imported cigarettes and sleeping with any man I wanted. I was empty inside, however. I had no faith, no love, no cause. My life was without any significance either to myself or the world. One night I heard His music as I was coming home from a night club. I decided to go in and see what it was like, just for the thrill. I was prepared to laugh and tell my friends about it over the next bridge game. Tell them how absurd it all was. But I felt His light that evening and I've been basking in it ever since. All I had I gave Him for the poor. He has given me new life, a faith, a love, His cause. I've forsaken the idle world for a sweet Heaven. I am with God. Thank you Almighty!

(*Usual answers, exclamations etc.*)

CORA (*to* RACHAEL) Joy Sister Divine Adoration. I see you enjoyed dat banquet right well. Hit sure was de best He ever gave. Dey's gettin' better an' better every day. You gettin' mighty high eatin' at His table. He asked me to do dat today but I told him I wuz one of de lesser angels an' unworthy.

RACHAEL You as worthy as anyone Priscilla Paul. He's made you well again. An' if He asks you to sit there again you accept.

CORA I sho' will. I'm so happy. Oh Divine Adoration, He's made me so happy. He's a-givin' me eternal life an' I shall never die.

RACHAEL That's right. I'm very happy for you, Priscilla Paul.

CORA Thank you Divine Adoration. I'm leanin' on His everlastin' arms, yes ma'm. I'm a-dwelling in Beulah Land. (*She begins to sing "Dwelling in Beulah Land." Others join in. As* CORA *sings she becomes more and more excited. She sways to the music that has a jazz strain: she jumps up and down, etc.*)

Far away the noise of strife upon my ear is falling.
Then I know the sins of earth beset on ev'ry hand,
Doubt and fear and things of earth in vain to me are calling,
None of these shall move me from Beaulah Land.

CHORUS

I'm living on the mountain, underneath a cloudless sky: Praise God!
I'm drinking at the fountain that never shall run dry:
Oh yes: I'm feasting on the manna from a bountiful supply
For I am dwelling in Beulah Land.

Let the stormy breezes blow, their cry cannot alarm me
I am safely sheltered here, protected by God's hand:
Here the sun is always shining, here there's naught can harm me,
I am safe forever in Beulah Land.

CHORUS

Viewing here the works of God, I sink in contemplation;
Hearing now His blessed voice I see the way he plann'd;
Dwelling in the Spirit here I learn of full salvation,
Gladly will I tarry in Beulah Land.

CHORUS

(CORA *is extremely excited now. In her testifying she shouts rather than talks. She works herself into a great pitch. She is breathing quite heavily*) I'm a-dwelling in Beulah Land, yes ma Gracious. He's forgiven ma sins, a-given me new life, cured ma ills. Glory to His precious name, yes ma Jesus Glory! When I wuz starvin' he fed me. Ma husband left me wid two little ones. Dey died. Ma heart pound, thump, thump, lak a hammer. I give up hope, but he helped me. Bless Jesus yes. There ain't no Gawd beyond de stars: He's here. Oh ain't ya glad dis evenin'. I can testify to His goodness 'cause he cured me in body and mind. Oh how sweet to dwell wid him. De fountain dat never run dry, de manna dat stays forever. Bless ma Gawd Almight. Bless His sweet name. Ma heart on fire wid love for him. Yes ma . . . Savior . . . ma heart . . . on . . . fire . . . fire Lawd . . . (*her voice falters, her body begins to sink beneath its load. Her heart has given way.* RACHAEL *rises from her seat to help* CORA *but* CORA's *body is lifeless on the floor.* RACHAEL *bends over it murmuring:* "Cora, Cora." *The* FOLLOWERS *are struck dumb. They have cleared the space about the body and there is silence. The humming has stopped, the tambourines are silent. All this while* CYRIL *has been watching from the street level*)

RACHAEL   Cora, you said everlasting life. Oh Cora come back. Cora you ain't dead. You can't be dead. He wouldn't let you die. Youse just tired from joy. Rest Cora, rest. You ain't dead, I know you ain't. He wouldn't let you. Cora, oh ma Cora. He wouldn't let you die!

(*The* FOLLOWERS *are still awe-struck, as if this were an omen. A light comes on in front of the cross and in it stands the* APOSTLE. *The* FOLLOWERS *one by one notice him and kneel.* CYRIL's *face becomes stern and determined as the* APOSTLE *speaks*)

APOSTLE   O my people when will you learn, when will you learn that there is no death unless you allow it. All pain is in your mind. There is only eternal life but you must believe it. If you allow pain, death will sneak upon you and you are no longer in the Kingdom. You must be death proof! Priscilla Paul has forsaken us. Her belief was not strong enough. She forsook eternal life because deep deep down she did not believe in it. She is no longer one of us. She has made herself mortal. I tell you there is no death. Do you believe?

FOLLOWERS   Yes Gawd. Yes Jesus Christ. Praise your name we believe.

APOSTLE   Will you follow me?

FOLLOWERS   (*amens*) Yes ma Jesus all the way.

APOSTLE   Go on with your singing, I am with you, go on with your dancing and praising: I am here. Follow me all the way. There is no death. He has no place with us.

FOLLOWERS (*singing*)   We will follow all the way,
Yes my Jesus, all the way;
Never from Thy path to stray,
We will follow all the way.

APOSTLE (*over the singing*)   Follow me and the earth is yours
Death may not enter. I am death-proof; you will be, but follow me.

FOLLOWERS   We will follow all the way,
Yes my Jesus all the way.
Never from Thy path to stray,
We will follow all the way.

APOSTLE   I am death-proof, you will . . .

CYRIL   You aren't. Evil, false Christ, you aren't!

APOSTLE   Who dares to blaspheme my name? Who dares to enter my Kingdom and call me false? Who dares to call death a living man when joy and faith can overcome him? Rid the earth of unbelievers, wipe its floors clean of the vermin, polish the marble floors of faith before you enter here!

CYRIL   I dare because I am mortal and can know death. I dare because your kingdom is mortal and you are mortal. Because my mother is no longer mine. Because these people should look to themselves for hope. Yes I dare and you shall answer now for these lost souls and this dead woman.

APOSTLE (*to* FOLLOWERS) Go on with your singing and your dancing. Some devil has come up to challenge your Lord.

CYRIL The devil is here all right.

APOSTLE (*to* CYRIL) This is a kingdom of peace and love. Even the devil cannot corrupt heaven.

CYRIL I once heard of a Christ of peace and love. The earth has forgotten him.

APOSTLE He has come back to make the earth remember. He has come back . . .

CYRIL Say it till your throat goes dry.

APOSTLE He has come back to give the earth back to his people . . . to give them shelter and food.

CYRIL Shelter and food perhaps—but only for a little while, only until the little they had is gone and too much of it salted away in a foreign bank . . . but not for them.

APOSTLE Choose your words . . .

CYRIL A little, little while. But their hearts and their faith . . . they are dying like common flowers.

APOSTLE Christ has come back. The Son and Father are here in one body.

CYRIL If Christ has come I should know him by his eyes, by his humility and not his arrogance. I would know him by his tenderness.

APOSTLE (*ignoring* CYRIL) My people are you there?

FOLLOWERS Yes Savior!
Yes ma Gawd!

APOSTLE Will you follow me?

FOLLOWERS Yes ma Jesus!
Praise your sweet Name!
We will follow all the way.

APOSTLE (*turns triumphantly to* CYRIL) He has come back.

CYRIL Not the Christ who knew the cross.

APOSTLE (*shouting*) Will you follow me?

FOLLOWERS (*singing*) We will follow all the way,
Yes ma' Savior all the way
Never from Thy path to stray,
We will follow all the way.

CYRIL (*to* FOLLOWERS) I have come to save you. He is false; he's not Christ or God but a mortal man leading you astray.

FOLLOWERS We are saved!!
He's Gawd!
He's Jesus!
Oh Praise the Savior!
We believe in Thy eternal power!

CYRIL It's wrong. He's false, I tell you. There is no eternal life in life. Look at Cora Jenkins. Look at her and learn. She's dead and Rachael . . . Rachael is mourning over her. (*at the sound of her name* RACHAEL *looks up, sees* CYRIL *as if for the first time*) Mom, Mom I'm here. I've come to save you.

RACHAEL But she ain't dead. Priscilla Paul ain't dead.

CYRIL She is dead Mom. I've come to save you before you go too. Eternal life is after the grave Mom, not before.

RACHAEL No. Eternal life is here. Jesus said that it's here on this earth, in this life.

CYRIL Can't you see. Can't you feel her death. Cora isn't moving, she is getting cold. Come home. (RACHAEL *takes a step toward her son: she has been moved, no doubt, by his tenderness*)

APOSTLE Divine Adoration, Divine Adoration (*his voice is soothing, hypnotic*), Divine Adoration listen to your Lord. Did I suffer that you should turn from me *before* my people; did I come back from my eternal peace for this? Priscilla Paul is not one of us any more. She let pain in. She died because she didn't believe.

FOLLOWERS Yes Jesus she didn't believe.
Priscilla Paul didn't believe.
She let pain in.

APOSTLE Divine Adoration you are in Heaven and it is sweet. Before all my people stay with us. You must not go the way Priscilla Paul went. (CYRIL *makes a convulsive movement as the* APOSTLE *says the last sentence*)

RACHAEL (*goes from her place near* CYRIL *toward the* APOSTLE) Jesus I believe. O Christ I believe.

CYRIL (*nearer the* APOSTLE) You've hypnotized her. Let her go. Mom, Mom it's Cyril your son. (*he goes to her and puts his arm about her, trying to get her to come with him*) You've got to come.

RACHAEL Leave me alone, leave me alone with ma Lord. (*she shakes him off roughly*) Leave me alone. (*she goes from him, turns and looks him straight in the eyes*) Leave me alone. I have no son!

CYRIL (*seeing futility, he turns to the other* FOLLOWERS. *Desperately*) Turn to yourselves, turn to the hope in yourselves. Don't let a false prophet wipe out your power and your real faith in the real Christ.

FOLLOWERS He is Christ. He is our Savior.

CYRIL Don't let him, don't let him.

APOSTLE (*breaks in*) Let there be more music, more . . .

CYRIL Let there be death for the wicked, let there be death for the fraud. (*he takes out his gun. The* APOSTLE *turns to go as* CYRIL *shoots him again and again. The* APOSTLE *totters and falls at the foot of the cross*)

CYRIL (*to the crowd*) Turn back to your real God now
 Turn to yourselves! (*he disappears*)

RACHAEL Oh my son, my son.

(*The crowd surges forth toward the* APOSTLE'S *fallen body but they dare not touch it. There is an utter silence. A level frightened pause. The crowd is huddled in frozen groups.* CYRIL *cries out from darkness*)

CYRIL The Apostle is dead!
 Turn to yourselves!!

(*There is confusion now. The crowd thrusts itself toward every exit, shouting, pushing. Some of them stay frozen near the* APOSTLE'*s body. During all the confusion they remain there fascinated*)

THE CROWD (*near the body, begins to moan*) He will come back.
 He said: "I will come back."

VOICES Jesus is dead,
 What shall we do?

OTHERS Run, run.
 God is dead.

VOICES Heaven is a tomb!

ECHO Is a tomb!
 Is a tomb!

ONE Get outta ma way.

ANOTHER Peace.

ANOTHER Peace hell!

ONE Someone has killed God.

ANOTHER Is a tomb!

BLIND MAN (*seen before on the street*) But what of the blind and those in the desolate places.

(*no one cares. He gets out as best he can*)

LIVER LIPS Man, lemme outta here. Get outta ma way.

CHILD Mamma, what's the matter?

MOTHER Shet your mouth an' com'on, com'on chile; don't stand there gapin'.

NEWSBOYS VOICES Extra, Extra, read all about it.
 Extra, Extra, the Apostle is dead.

SOME What shall we do:
 What? What?

ONE He's taken my home. Give it back!

ANOTHER He's taken my insurance!

ANOTHER He's taken my savings, what shall I do!

ONE Heaven is a tomb.

THOSE NEAR BODY He will come back. He is death-proof.
 This is only a test. He will come back.

NEWSBOYS Extra, Extra, read all about it.
 Read all about it. Extra, extra.
 God is dead.

VOICES (*rushing out*) What! What shall we do!!

SOME Run, run.

ONE Let me outta here.

ONE Heaven is a tomb!

(*The crowd is gone. The* APOSTLE'*s body at the foot of the cross lies in shadows. The* CHORUS *that was frozen about it is kneeling now. Some have gone out and come back with tall candles. Someone has put a deep purple covering over the body. On the stage level* CORA'*s body lies with* RACHAEL *mourning over it*)

NEWSBOYS Extra, extra, read all about it,
 The Apostle is dead.
 Read all about it, extra, extra,
 The Apostle's been shot.

RACHAEL (*back to audience. Hands stretched up to stained-glass window. The window lights up as she prays and sends a cross of light over her and the body of* CORA) Lawd, Lawd, she's dead. Gawd that I prayed to before listen to me now. Oh Jesus listen. I repent ma Jesus. How could I have strayed so far. Jesus forgive Cora; let ma humble prayer be sent up for Cora too Jesus. She only wanted to be happy. You said you'd forgive her strayin' Jesus. She's still one of your children. Forgive her now that she's dead.

An' forgive ma son. I come again in shadows askin' for ma chile again. He only wanted me to come back Lawd. He did it for me Jesus. I'm to blame. Not him. Not Cyril. Not ma boy. Forgive him for breakin' thy commandment. He did it for me. I'm to blame. Forgive us all our sins our Father which art in heaven, hallowed be thy name. Thy Kingdom come, Thy will be done in earth, as it is in heaven. Give us this day our daily bread and forgive us our debts as we forgive our debtors. And lead us not into temptation but deliver us from evil for thine is the kingdom and the power and the glory, forever. Amen. Amen. (*the lights dim on* RACHEL *and* CORA'*s body*)

NEWSBOYS Extra, extra, read all about it,
Read all about it, extra, extra.

(*The street lamp goes on revealing the gin mill. It is empty except for two men who are sitting at a table talking over a bottle of gin.*)

THIRD MAN Well them boys sure was taken in by that Apostle guy.

FOURTH MAN I looked into his joint long 'bout twelve o'clock midnight an' it was a killer. They was jumpin' up like fleas an' everything.

THIRD MAN Tonight's the night of one of them big sheddin' meetin's!

FOURTH MAN That guy done broken up our gang.

THIRD MAN Yeah. We's gangbusted. (*laughs at his attempted pun.* NEWSBOYS *are heard yelling the* Extras)

FOURTH MAN Say what them newsboys beatin' up their chops 'bout?

THIRD MAN Just another one of them extras.

FOURTH MAN Shhhh. Sound like more than that.

THIRD MAN Forget it. Here have another drink.

FOURTH MAN I'm goin out an' see what the excitement 'bout.

THIRD MAN Sit ya can down. Stuff and Numbers an' Liver will be back soon. They'll give us the lowdown.

FOURTH MAN Yer mean that Stuff an' Numbers will be in here gettin' mad with each other as usual.

THIRD MAN Ain't nothin' to their squabblin'.

FOURTH MAN Wat you know 'bout it. Them two is at each others throats all the time. Now Numbers there he made love to Stuff's broad. Stuff he swore to get even. One day Stuff sneaked up behind Numbers an' hit him plop over the head with a brick. Then he run down the street yellin': "Somebody done hit ma friend."

THIRD MAN Where'd that happen!

FOURTH MAN Right outside the Transfiguration Beauty Shoppe. (*noise of running feet is heard offstage.* STUFF, NUMBERS, LIVER LIPS, BARTENDER *and the* FIRST *and* SECOND MAN *come in breathless*) Say what goin on out there.

NUMBERS Man gimmie a drink. I hauled tail down here as soon as I could. That Apostle's dead. Dead as a door nail.

FOURTH MAN Yeah I heard them Newsboys beatin' up their chops. Tell me 'bout it.

NUMBERS Everythin' was going like usual. Them ole sisters shoutin' an' testifyin' like to beat de band. That music with gin stompin' to beat all hell. One ole sister she got up an' was sayin' as how she was dwellin' in Beulah land or Jerdon or somethin'. Man, she was shoutin' up a breeze an' singin'. Her voice goes out like a light an' she dies.

THIRD MAN I thought it was the Apostle that died.

NUMBERS Wait a minute man. Nobody moves see. An' then that Apostle he say, sing an' dance some more. Some ole crazy fool he yells out an' he an' that Apostle starts beefin'. That fool gets pretty mad, see, and he takes out a gun an' shoots. That was the end of that Apostle ladies an' gentlemen. It was like scrambled eggs in there so I hauls tail down here.

THIRD MAN I woulda given a quart of gin to have been there.

FIRST MAN Yeah an' then flames come out all over that Apostle.

LIVER LIPS I didn't see that.

FIRST MAN Yeah that's so. Flames an' a sound like flappin' wings.

LIVER LIPS It was somethin', boy.

NUMBERS Gin 'em up.

FIRST MAN I knowed somethin' was goin to happin 'cause I seen the handwritin' on the wall.

STUFF That was the gin workin' on ya. You ain't seen nothin'.

LIVER LIPS I tell you boys it was a killer. Even Stuff was singin' an' dancing. He was goin this way. (LIVER LIPS *begins to imitate*

STUFF *at the meeting. He sings*) We will follow all the way... (*changing the rhythm to blatant jazz. He trucks to his own time and the time of clapping hands*)

NUMBERS (*stands on a chair after* LIVER LIPS *finishes. He begins to preach like the* APOSTLE. *He lards his speech heavily with dialect*) Go on wid yo' singin' an' yo' dancin' an' have 'nother drink of gin. Dis is heaben folks an' de drinks neber runs dry.

MEN   Yeah man, do it boy, Skee da, Doo do won't be nothin' left when de worms get thru, Lay it Mister Numbers.

NUMBERS   Dat ole Pussy Poo she ain't one o' us enny mo'. She refused 't drink de sparkle wader o de Lawwd. Now ya knows es well as I does dat dat ole sister wuz a plain stick in de mud. Does yo' believe me!

LIVER LIPS (*shouts like a convert*) Yes yo great, worthy, grand, munificious, scrumptuous, hallelujah, hot stuff POTENTATE, we believes.

STUFF   You tell 'em Sister Liver I ain't got the heart.

NUMBERS   Does you believe?

MEN (*answering in jazz rhythm*)   Does ya think we don't.

NUMBERS   I say there folks: Does you believe!

MEN   Yes your Lordship we believes.

NUMBERS   Does you *believe*!!!!!!!!!

MEN   Ain't we told you we believe.
Hey, hey, hey, hey
Ain't we told you we believe. (*they all begin laughing.*)

LIVER LIPS   You sure can fool some of the people some of the time but you can't fool them all the time. That what I says.

NUMBERS   Let's have some gin. (*they get glasses*) What that you say Liver: You can't fool all the people all the time? Let's drink to that boys! (*the light fades on them as they lift their glasses*)

NEWSBOYS' VOICES   Extra, extra, extra...

(*Light goes up in Jackson home space.* RACHAEL *is sitting on a chair swaying*)

RACHAEL   Cyril, boy, Cyril. Has ya' left me sure' nough. Cyril, boy, come back. I'm sorry. Come back.

(*Light in Jackson home dims*)

NEWSBOY   Extra, extra.

BLIND MAN'S VOICE   But what of the blind and those in the wasted places.

CHORUS VOICES   We are winter worn,
Wind torn,
Two Winters come in one this year.
Despair,
Leaps
Through our fear,
Steeps
Us more firmly
In pain.
Despair
Leaps,
In the windy air.
There is no solace anywhere.
Where shall we turn for a half-chewed crust of bread
Now that he is dead.

(*the* CHORUS *comes on from all entrances. Those who have been guarding the body stay as they are*)

He will come back:
He said: "I will come back."

ANOTHER LEADER   What comet was ever a star again?
Look to your nights when one star burns
Brighter than all the rest,
Burns out of its place
And falls like a vertical fan of light.

ANOTHER LEADER   Shooting through the night
And into the earth.
The end of its burning is stone,
The end of its glory is stone,
The end is always stone.

CHORUS   He said he has no end...

LEADER   Wipe his awful memory from your lips,
Wipe the blunt horror from your eyes,
Thumb your ears against the swift bullet sound.
Remember he is dead and you are here.

(*Some will take his advice but others who will not wander over the stage and out, their formation exactly as it was in the beginning*)

CHORUS (*those who will always be desolate*) Two Winters come in one this year;
The wind thrusts fingers through our fear,
Curves its palm into our walls,
And whistles and rumbles along the halls.

BLIND MAN   The blind in the haunted places
Having heard destruction and death
Will go back to a year of two Winters
Without fire to warm the hands they never saw.

(The music which started as soon as the CHORUS *entered is the same now as it was at this passage in the beginning)*

CHORUS We are Winter worn,
Wind torn,
Despair
Leaps in the air,
Falls down
Like a clown
We saw at a fair
Long, long ago.

(They are off now. The Choral music fades into the Apostle music. It is less alive, less syncopated than before. Those about the body of the APOSTLE *begin to chant)*

CHORUS *(those about the* APOSTLE's *body)* He said He
   would not die.
This is the test
We must win as the years move by, lest
He look down from the sky on those he
   blest
To find them gone away.

Do not let your hair down,
Do not put the sackcloth on,
Now that he has gone.

Wrap the body in stone,
Lay it bone for bone
In the tomb.

He left it here for us to keep.
He left it here to guard our sleep,
To guard our faith,
So do not weep.
Galgotha, Galgotha
Death on a windy hill,
The winter wind is crying
Down the ages still.

Galgotha, Galgotha
Upon a windy slope,
Where Mary loosed her hair
Abandoning hope.

We feel your wind,
But our eyes are dry
Because we know
He cannot die.

He left this here for us to keep
He left this here to guard our sleep.
To guard our faith,
So do not weep.

Wrap the body in stone,
Lay it bone for bone,
In the tomb.

(They lift the body up. Some precede it with the candles, others follow after. They go off singing)

When we were lost in the forest of pain,
He came back to us bringing sunshine and
   rains
All our pain was washed away,
All our sin is dried today.
How shall we praise him,
The Apostle of Light,
Jesus come back,
When even the night
Was starless.

(Some of the THIRD CHORUS *seeing the procession go off follow behind. The last* CHORUS *led by the new* LEADER, *now form a compact group. They have been watching the service of the* APOSTLE *from this place and that on the stage)*

CYRIL'S VOICE Turn to yourselves!!
Turn to yourselves!
Turn to yourselves.
YOUNG MAN Turn to ourselves? We are empty
   and broken
Laden with grief that cannot be
   spoken.
OLD WOMAN Once were flying ...
YOUNG GIRL ... not high ...
OLD WOMAN ... but flying.
OLD MAN The birds have been shot and their
   wings have been closed.
YOUNG GIRL Oh it is bitter to lie in the Winter
   again,
Like grounded birds, like stricken
   men.

CHORUS OF NEGROES And still we thrive, lie close to
   earth,
Grounded birds, are healed and live again!
Anointed at our birth with dark water,
Bidden to crawl like worms: sliced or
   broken.
Still like worms we live with a dearth
Of stars and more soil than we can eat.

Can we repeat
The legends of three hundred years:
The fears,
The terrors,
The broken moons,
The fallen jungle stars?

Still we thrive, lying close to earth
With mirth
For a constellation,
And no elation
Save a zig-zag music

Shimming through our veins,
And after that the pains
Of a spirit ticking itself away,
And flesh rotting to clay
Rotting our day.

CHORUS OF WHITES And still we thrive, lie close to earth,
Grounded birds, are healed and live again.
Anointed at our birth with crystal water,
Bidden to part the earth communion bread among us.
We got the lesser part
From the start.
Yes we with a dove whiteness
Have been slighted.
We are the men underfoot too,
The same as you.
ALL What shall we do.
What shall we do!
LEADER This shall not be forever.
The black hand matching the black hand,
The white hand matching the black hand.
The hands that stab the machines to churning,
The hands that plant the corn,
The endless hands of yearning,
Hands that question:
These will have a tattered banner like a signal of faith
To flesh the bony army of the poor.
RACHAEL (*appearing in the church area*) "To flesh the bony army of the poor."

(*to* CHORUS)

He has given you the way of bread,
But ya needs the way of faith too—
The stir in your hearts that make the days,
Even the dark days, sweet to live.

(*walking nearer to* CHORUS)

I come to you an ole woman in this twelfth month of the year,
In the twelfth month of ma days—
I come lak any ole black woman who has had to carry
A weight like the world on her breast:
I has seen dark days with a wind an' a fire tearin' at ma house.
I has seen ma own girl leave me an' desert ma house,
I has seen ma boy kill for me an' ma best friend shout for joy an' die.
I knows. Lawd I knows the deep-well side of life.
Listen:
I has seen a golden calf turn to lead an' break.
O listen, you poor an' forgotten, an' you of little faith:
Pray to that cross, 'cause when you prays to it

You prays to the Christ in you that done stood against a great big hill of pain.
I can't pray now—I am unworthy to pray:
'cause ma son done killed to save ma soul,
'cause I'm ole an' it don't matter.
But you, you got the children an' yourselves,
The children that ain't yet born.
Lift your hands to the cross, lift them to yourselves an' your strength.

(*despair, Mournful. All hope, all lost happiness lies in her next line*)

I'm ashes an' you can't light ashes,
I'm ashes but you is great chunks of coal,
An' you can burn when the kindlin' is put to you.
CHRIST IS THE POWER IN YOU,

(*she says this with more emphasis than anything else in her speech*)

Christ is the power in you.

(*she begins walking off*)

The power an' the glory.

(*She goes past the* CHORUS *and up to the place before the cross. She pauses there a minute and begins singing the mournful "Nobody knows de troubles I've seen, nobody knows but Jesus." Her despair-song is heard for a second after she has left the view of the* CHORUS. *This song will contrast greatly with the triumphant choral music that is to come soon*)

CHORUS (*some turning to* LEADER) We feel no Christ, no power in His cross.
We feel our strength now, but not His strength and power.
Tell us leader:
Where is this Christ in us?
Where is this Christ in us in this new Winter.
The old woman spoke in riddles:
Spoke of her pain, and her death and her ashes.
Now is the time of our uniting, where is our Master, Christ?
The Lord we forsook for common bread,
The Saint who fled His Father's house to die for us?
Where is he?
LEADER He is the new strength you feel;
He has clasped the burning hand of Autumn and led the harvest into this Winter.

Divine Comedy

        He *was* the far-off dream of your uniting.
        He *is* the dream made real,
        The pain made courage,
        The hope made living.
        He is ourselves when you throw off the sackcloth of submission,
        When you wipe the begging eye of tears.
CHORUS He is ourselves when we throw off the sackcloth of submission,
        When we wipe the begging eye of tears.

(*triumphantly they continue*)

        Christ has clasped the burning hand of Autumn and brought a ripened harvest to our door.
        The earth is not barren this Winter,
        The Autumn burns through this Winter.
        The leaves are still red,
        The streams are still free,
        This harvest is harvest for every tree.
        We have fled back to Autumn,
        We have shed Winter for Autumn.
        The mystic hope in prophets has turned
        To a firmer hope in our hearts.
        The deserted places have burned
        And from them our Phoenix departs,
        Rises up and flies in our lands,
        Uniting our lands,
        Uniting our faith.

SEMI-CHORUS We need no prophets.
SEMI-CHORUS (*like an echo*) This Winter is Autumn.
SEMI-CHORUS We need no miracles.
SEMI-CHORUS We are the miracle.
ALL We *are* the miracle,
     We are the earth itself.

(*The cross sends a shadow over them: the whole* CHORUS *is kneeling to it; A triumphant Choral music rises up like a prayer, and the curtain decends like a benediction*)

6

Plays of Black History

Mary Miller   Theodore Browne   Willis Richardson

In 1935, Willis Richardson and May Miller edited *Negro History in Thirteen Plays*, a volume designed for black schools. Dr. Carter Woodson wrote in the preface: "The playwrights herein represented have the vision of the Negro in the new day.... The publication of this book must be considered another step of the Negro toward the emancipation of his mind from the slavery of the inferiority complex."

The "slavery of the inferiority complex" of which Dr. Woodson speaks was not only that imposed by the institution of slavery itself, but also that imposed in the American theater by the persistent images of stage types.

What then is the function of black authors in writing history plays? The major purpose is to liberate the black audience from an oppressive past, to present a history that provides continuity, hope, and glory. Such feelings and knowledge have positive survival value for the race.

The value of a black history play to a white audience is primarily informational. The fact that the drama critic on the *New York Times*, by his own admission, knew nothing about Frederick Douglass (see the introduction to *In Splendid Error*) is indicative of a general ignorance of black history.

History plays cannot be judged by how closely they follow historical fact. The author has dramatic license to create an aura of time and place. These plays should be judged by their verisimilitude to the black experience and by their art—keeping in mind how well the wedding of form and content has been celebrated. But celebrated for whom? Black students are weary of discussions of "artistic merit" which are really lengthy invidious comparisons of historical plays by black writers to Shakespeare's chronicle plays.

History plays are interpreted here as including myth (*Graven Images*), legend (*Natural Man*), and the reconstruction by fictional means of situations known to have existed (*The Flight of the Natives*). All the plays included here are costume dramas—that is, they are set in a past in which the authors never lived.

Graven Images   1929

Since ancient times the dark peoples of Africa have celebrated life and death in theater ritual. Much of this was oral drama, passed on by tradition but never written down. The Pyramid Texts of the ancient Egyptians were performed two thousand five hundred years before Western drama began with the Greeks.

Black people were spoken about in the Roman plays. An Ethiopian slave girl appears in *The Eunuch* by Terence. Moors abound in Spanish plays from the twelfth century onward. The black man makes his first entry onto the English stage in the Christmas liturgical plays; he enters as a king, one of the three Magi who come to offer gifts to the baby Jesus (who himself, of course, was a member of the darker peoples).

In an interview in March 1972, Mrs. May Miller (Sullivan) commented on the importance of Negro history plays and how she came to write them:

In many of the young leaders today I don't find an acknowledgment of the contributions of a man like Dr. Carter G. Woodson made when he aroused an interest in Negro history when very little interest was being paid. It was he who was responsible for the establishment of the Association for the Study of Negro History, and, in addition, he backed with his own funds the Associated Publishers for printing this material. In *Negro History in Thirteen Plays* Dr. Woodson furnished many of the books which Willis Richardson and I studied before we wrote those plays.

Another important influence was Randolph Edmonds of Morgan College who thought it idle to have children only read history; he believed that productions on stage of those great Negro characters would help the children understand. For a number of years at Morgan College they gave one-act plays, and we wrote plays for that occasion.

Then, under Dr. DuBois, the great Krigwa movement was sponsored by *Crisis* magazine, and they established all over the country little one-act play groups that performed in churches and schools, and all this was a forerunner to what we're doing now. We would have had no Lorraine Hansberry if there had not been behind her those people who were slowly leading up to her great productions (Hatch-Billops Oral Black Theatre History Collection, City College of New York).

Graven Images is a play for eighth grade children. It is inspired by an Old Testament verse: "And Miriam and Aaron spake against Moses because of the Ethiopian woman he had married" (Numbers 12:1). The play, written about 1929, may be the first in which the "snow white devil" is struck down through divine justice. Miriam's comeuppance is more than a *coup de théâtre*. It is a racial *coup de grâce*.

The purpose of *Graven Images* is to show how the black man is woven into the fabric of the universe. "We belong," this play exclaims; "we have always been, and we will always be."

May Miller (Sullivan) was born in Washington, D.C. and is a graduate of Howard University. For some years she was a teacher of speech and drama at Frederick Douglass High School in Baltimore. In addition to her work with Willis Richardson, writing and editing two volumes of Negro plays for school children, she has published two volumes of poems: *Into the Clearing* (1959) and *Poems* (1962).

Graven Images

"And Miriam and Aaron spake against Moses because of the Ethiopian woman he had married."

Numbers 12:1

PERSONS OF THE PLAY

MOSES
AARON, *the brother of Moses*
MIRIAM, *the sister of Moses*
ZIPPORAH, *the wife of Moses*
JETHRO, *the father-in-law of Moses*
ITHAMAR, *youngest son of Aaron*
ELIEZER, *the second son of Moses*
PLAYMATES OF ITHAMAR
ATTENDANTS AND MAIDENS BEARING INCENSE, OINTMENT, CANDLESTICKS AND THE HOLY VESSELS INTO THE TABERNACLE

TIME *1490* B.C.

PLACE *Hazeroth, Egypt*

(SCENE: *The arena before the tabernacle. Back stage a flight of steps leads to the tabernacle. On both sides of the steps the columns rise. At the base of the columns basins of incense are burning. To the left front stage an abandoned idol is half hidden by a tree. To the right a few trees are left standing and a stump shows plainly that the temple has been erected in a clearing. It is high noon. The scene is enveloped in a bright golden light.*

ITHAMAR, *a stout lad of twelve clad in a short tunic, runs hurriedly on the stage. He looks toward the tabernacle and then slowly around him. He spies the golden bull*)

ITHAMAR Oh! Oh! Uh-huh! Uh-huh! (*he smiles in satisfaction at having discovered the idol. He cautiously runs toward the tabernacle and up the steps. He peers in and listens. Nodding, he runs down the steps and to the side stage*) Lo, lads! Lo, lads! (*a troupe of boys of about* ITHAMAR'*s age run boisterously in*)

FIRST BOY What is it, Ithamar?

ITHAMAR They took it away and we knew not where they hid it, but I have found it. Here it is.

SECOND BOY (*in amazement*) The golden bull that our sires cast out of the tabernacle!

FIRST BOY The golden bull!

BOYS (*in chorus*) The golden bull!

FIRST BOY What fun!

SECOND BOY Now that we have found it, what shall we do?

FIRST BOY It shall be a target, of course, and we shall hurl stones. A prize to the one who hits the bull's eye!

BOYS (*in a chorus, as they rush to pick up stones*) The bull's eye! The bull's eye! (*amid much confusion they start hurling stones*)

ITHAMAR Stay! Stay! (*the noise subsides*) We shall try by turn.

SECOND BOY If our elders come, they will punish us by turn, too, for it is said they wish to keep the bull unscarred.

ITHAMAR But our elders will not come here. The tabernacle is empty.

SECOND BOY The noise might lead them here.

ITHAMAR Then we can't play target.

BOYS (*throwing down their stones*) Bah!

FIRST BOY Come, Ithamar, what can we play?

ITHAMAR We could play worship.

FIRST BOY Maybe, but it is not so pleasant as stoning.

ITHAMAR We can bow down before the bull even as our sires did before they built the tabernacle to God Jehovah.

SECOND BOY But our sires will punish us for that, too.

ITHAMAR We shall be quiet and our sires will not know.

SECOND BOY Some one might tell.

ITHAMAR You are the only some one I know, coward.

FIRST BOY Come, Ithamar, let the scared one alone. Let us start the worship.

ITHAMAR Who will begin?

FIRST BOY You, Ithamar, you shall start the worship. Every one will follow you in turn. Come, make high praise to the golden bull! (*the boys form a circle around the golden bull*)

BOYS (*in chorus*) Ithamar! Ithamar!

ITHAMAR (*stepping forward and kneeling before the bull*) O! most sacred bull, it is Ithamar, the son of Aaron, the first high priest of Israel, who kneels before you. He offers you this golden armlet worth two shekels of silver. Be kind to me and my playmates. (*he places the armlet on the bull's ears*)

BOYS (*clapping their hands and shouting lustily*) Well done, Ithamar! Well done! Next! Next!

ITHAMAR (*grasping the first boy*) You go next.

BOYS (*lustily*) Talba next! Talba!

FIRST BOY (*stepping forward and kneeling*) O! most sacred bull, I, Talba, am only a poor lad. My father is no high priest of Israel and I have no armlet to offer. This ragged girdle is all I have, but you may have it. (*he hangs the girdle from his tunic over the back of the bull*)

BOYS (*clapping and shouting lustily*) Next! Next!

ITHAMAR (*approaching the second boy*) Scared one, you shall make worship next, for then we shall know you will not tell.

SECOND BOY But I know not what to say and I have nothing to offer.

FIRST BOY I had nothing.

SECOND BOY I have not even a ragged girdle.

ITHAMAR Come, you cannot escape so easily.

BOYS (*pressing closer and pushing their frightened comrade forward*) No, come! Come!

SECOND BOY How shall I begin?

FIRST BOY Begin as I began—O most sacred bull!

BOYS (*echoing*) O most sacred bull!

SECOND BOY (*timidly kneeling before the idol*) O most sacred bull, I have nothing to give you —not even a girdle like Talba's. But, sacred bull, if you will promise not to hurt me, I shall let Ithamar chop off a curl and give it to you for your bald head.

FIRST BOY Bravo! come, Ithamar, chop off the curl.

ITHAMAR A golden curl for a golden bull! (ITHAMAR *picks up a sharp stone and the boys grasp the timid child and lay his head on a stump for* ITHAMAR *to chop off a curl. The child struggles*)

FIRST BOY Keep still; he does not want your head, fool.

SECOND BOY (*struggling*) Pray let me up. There's a curl at home I'd rather give, and it will not hurt so much.

BOYS No, no, a golden curl for a golden bull! (*while the boys have been busily engaged a group of little girls has entered*)

FIRST GIRL Pray, don't cut off his curl if it hurts so badly. Take one of mine; I have so many more.

FIRST BOY You are a girl, you would cry.

FIRST GIRL Indeed, I would not. (ITHAMAR, *looking up, stops the cutting of hair. The* SECOND BOY, *thus released, retreats to the edge of the crowd where he may escape readily*)

ITHAMAR Besides, the golden bull does not want a girl's curl.

BOYS (*in chorus*) A girl's curl! Bah!

SECOND GIRL If you will not take the curl, may we play?

ITHAMAR We are worshiping the golden bull and he does not like girl children.

SECOND GIRL Let him close his eyes; he will not know the difference.

ITHAMAR Oh, no, no, that would never do. We must not deceive when we worship.

FIRST GIRL Then you cannot let us play?

ITHAMAR Let me see, what are little girls good for? (*the boys look doubtfully at the girls*)

FIRST BOY Ithamar, I will tell you—let them dance their worship as the virgins of our sires.

ITHAMAR Maybe the golden bull would not mind that, but I am sure he does not want women to speak.

FIRST BOY All right, little girls, we may let you dance.

BOYS (*in chorus*) Yes, yes, a dance!

FIRST GIRL And will you, at the end of the dance, bow when we bow? Then we shall all worship together.

ITHAMAR But remember you must bow lower than we, for you are girls.

GIRLS (*eagerly*) All right.

ITHAMAR On with the dance, then.

FIRST BOY (*pushing the boys back*) The dance!

BOYS The dance! The dance!

(*The girls dance and at the end prostrate themselves before the golden bull. The boys follow their example, kneeling before the idol. While the dance has been going on a little brown boy of about ten years has quietly entered. Unobserved he has watched and as they bow he bursts into loud laughter*)

ELIEZER Ha! Ha! So in Hazeroth little boys and girls dance and worship idols while their parents worship Jehovah.

FIRST BOY Well, who are you to laugh and whence do you come?

ELIEZER I am Eliezer, but recently come from the household of Jethro, my grandsire, in the land of Midian.

ITHAMAR Oh, so you are my cousin of whom my sire, Father Aaron, spoke.

ELIEZER (*nodding anxiously*) Uh—huh.

ITHAMAR I am Ithamar, your cousin, son of Aaron, your uncle; and these, my friends and playmates. Welcome!

ELIEZER (*bowing*) I give thanks to you for the welcome.

FIRST BOY You may join us, if it pleases you.

ELEIZER But it pleases me not. In Midian we are never permitted to play with idols.

ITHAMAR You mean that you do not want to worship our idol.

FIRST GIRL Do not ask him again, Ithamar; we do not like foreign boys.

SECOND GIRL And I know not why, but the sight of him is strange.

FIRST GIRL He is Ithamar's cousin.

SECOND GIRL But they are so different.

ITHAMAR (*boastfully*) I am not a coward.

ELEIZER Neither am I.

ITHAMAR (*pushing* ELIEZER *toward second boy*) You two scared ones play together. Come, boys, back to our sport and leave them.

ELIEZER Yes, and when our elders come, they shall be punished for their sport.

SECOND BOY (*in fear*) Our elders are coming here?

ELIEZER Of course, our elders are coming. Moses is already gathering the worshipers that Jethro may carry back to Midian news of the great tabernacle.

FIRST BOY (*overhearing*) What do you know of our great Moses?

ELIEZER Your Moses, indeed! My Moses! Did you not know that I am the son of Moses and Zipporah?

FIRST BOY Bah! Bah! and who believes that?

SECOND BOY Are you truly the son of Moses?

BOYS Bah! Bah!

ELIEZER Tell them, Ithamar, am I not?

ITHAMAR Yes, he is; but my Aunt Miriam says that his mother is a black woman and that he and his brother, Gershom, are no true children of Israel.

SECOND GIRL I knew the sight of him was strange.

ELIEZER Yes, and I overheard my elders say that your two brothers, Nadab and Alihu, were struck dead for offering strange fire to God.

BOYS (*shrinking from* ITHAMAR) Oh! Oh!

ITHAMAR Yes, but they are dead and you are living and I shall not play with you. The others may do as they please.

FIRST BOY (*to* ELIEZER) Can you show any reason why we should play with you, son of a black woman?

SECOND BOY But he isn't black; he's only golden.

FIRST BOY And pray, what does he know that we should play with him?

SECOND BOY He knows more than Ithamar. He knew our sires were coming and Ithamar did not.

FIRST BOY (*to* ELIEZER) If we do play with you, what sport can you offer?

ELIEZER We can still play worship.

SECOND BOY How can we play worship without an idol?

ELIEZER I shall be your idol.

ITHAMAR Bah! such an idol!

ELIEZER Indeed, and why not? I shall make a far better idol than this (*he springs lightly to the platform in front of the idol*) Look, this idol is gold. (*he strips his tunic off to the waist*) Am I not gold? (*the boys press forward murmuring their assent*) Come feel your idol. It is cold but I am warm. Warm gold. (*the boys press closer*) And see! see! You worship this thing that does not so much as nod his thanks. It's still, but I move, I move.

SECOND BOY He might make a very good idol.

FIRST BOY We shall not listen to Ithamar. He is a better idol—warm, moving gold.

BOYS Aye! Aye!

SECOND BOY Well, let's begin playing before our sires come.

FIRST BOY   Come, boys! (*boys surround* ELIEZER, *crying their assent*)
FIRST GIRL   And you will let us play, too?
ELIEZER   Yes, you may worship me too.
SECOND BOY   When our sires come and ask, "What worship you?" ...
FIRST GIRL   We shall answer, "A little boy."
FIRST BOY   No, silly, we shall say, "Great sires, we worship a child whom God hath created in his own image." Then, our sires will be pleased and they will reply, "Verily, verily, peace be with ye," and pass into the tabernacle.
ITHAMAR (*going off stage*)   They will, indeed, eh? We shall see.
FIRST BOY   Pay no attention to him. Come, let's play.
ELIEZER   Let the girls dance again for me.

(*The girls have just formed a circle and are about to dance when a solemn chant is heard in the distance. The girls stop*)

FIRST BOY   Our sires are coming to the tabernacle.
SECOND BOY   I knew it; and now we can't play.

(*The strains of the chant grow louder as the procession files in. The prophets lead the line.* MOSES *and* JETHRO *are ahead of all others. As* MOSES *enters the children bow their heads*)

CHILDREN   Father Moses!
MOSES   Peace be with ye!

(*The worshipers enter the tabernacle and a long line of youths and maidens bearing incense, candlesticks and sacred vessels follows. When the last worshiper has entered, the chant dies away to an echo. The children who had joined the chant now return to their sport.* MIRIAM, *a plump handsome woman of forty, is led on the stage by* ITHAMAR)

ITHAMAR   Now, you see, Aunt Miriam, that which I told you is true. He makes himself an idol and the children worship him.
MIRIAM   No, no, this must not be. (*to the children*) What is this that you do, little ones? (*the children fall back in consternation*)
FIRST GIRL   We worship a child whom God hath created in his own image.
MIRIAM   In his own image, indeed! Pray did Father Moses tell you God was an Ethiop?
CHILDREN   No, no.

MIRIAM   This child is no image of God. Jehovah. He is black like his mother.
CHILDREN (*retreating from* ELIEZER)   Oh! Oh!
SECOND GIRL (*to first girl*)   I told you the sight of him was strange.
MIRIAM (*grasping* ELIEZER *and dragging him from platform*)   Black one, you had best hide your shame from the followers of your father and not place your complexion where all may see. (*to the children*) Now away with you! No more foolish sport of this kind; mind you.
SECOND BOY   I knew our elders would scold.
ITHAMAR (*to the children as they go off stage*) I told you not to listen to him, didn't I?

(ELIEZER *sobbing has retreated to the back of the platform behind the golden bull where he hides from dreaded blows from* MIRIAM. *A faint refrain of the chant is heard in the tabernacle.* MIRIAM *approaches and listens. She starts up the steps, then as if changing her mind, turns and starts off stage.* AARON *comes out of the tabernacle and stands at the top of the steps*)

AARON   Why do you delay? The worship has started and the maidens eagerly await you.
MIRIAM   Why do they await me? Surely the black Jethro has seen our great tabernacle 'ere this.
AARON   Yes, but they now patiently await the word of God concerning our going from Hazeroth. You must lead the worship of the maidens.
MIRIAM   I shall be with them. I delayed only to stop the children's foolish sport.
AARON   What sport?
MIRIAM   Eliezer, the young son of Moses, has been making of himself an idol.
AARON   And what matters that?
MIRIAM   Only it is not wise that the followers of Moses should be constantly reminded of his black wife and brown children.
AARON   And if they are, what?
MIRIAM   Surely they will say, "He is no true prophet of the God of Abraham, of Isaac and of Jacob, for he has married an Ethiop and his children are Ethiopian."—However, that may end happily, for the people may call for a new leader.
AARON   Sh! God will punish you for such talk.
MIRIAM   God may punish me, but the people will select a new leader.

AARON Who will that be?
MIRIAM You, of course. Are you not the first high priest of the children of Israel?
AARON Oh, no, that could not be!
MIRIAM Why not? Has the Lord spoken only to Moses? Has he not spoken to us also? Why should we, who are also the children of Amram, the Levite, follow that son who has forgotten so far as to marry an Ethiop?
AARON That which you speak is sinful. 'Tis God's will that Moses lead us and God Jehovah will punish you for speaking against him and me for listening.
MIRIAM Coward! What I have said is sweet to your ears, too. (*going up the tabernacle steps*) What you fear to say your sister, Miriam, dares!
AARON I fear only God.
MIRIAM Has God said that only Moses knows His will?
AARON So Moses has said.
MIRIAM Why should Moses not speak thus, as long as by so speaking he assures for himself the place of leader? And we cringe and follow.
AARON But who am I to lead Israel?
MIRIAM You are the first born of Amram and by far more ready of tongue than the brother you now follow.
AARON But that brother is the chosen leader of Israel.
MIRIAM He should lead Israel who is truly an Israelite, one uncontaminated by Ethiopian blood.
AARON O! to lead my people.
MIRIAM You can.
AARON (*as if dreaming*) And we should go out from Hazeroth and pitch tents in the wilderness and the people would cry out, "O! Father Aaron, where does Israel move now?" They would look to me for answer.
MIRIAM They would harken to your word and with one voice call, "Father Aaron! Father Aaron, the true leader of Israel! Moses is no more."
ELIEZER (*jumping hastily from the platform and coming forth to face* MIRIAM) You lie, you lie. My sire, Moses, lives. He is in the tabernacle praying for us.
MIRIAM (*grasping* ELIEZER) So you are eavesdropper, too, listening to words intended for other ears. (*she slaps his face*) Eavesdroppers are always thus rewarded for their pains.
AARON (*freeing the child from* MIRIAM'*s grasp*) He is only a child, Miriam.
MIRIAM Yes, child of an Ethiop!
AARON God shall surely punish you.
MIRIAM Indeed (*she turns and laughs, then starts toward the tabernacle*)
AARON (*grasping* MIRIAM'*s arm*) Hold! where do you go?
MIRIAM Into the tabernacle to speak against Moses, our brother. The evil is done. The child has heard; he will prate to his elders.
AARON Hold! Hold!
MIRIAM (*freeing her arm and grasping his*) Come, your sister, Miriam, dares.
AARON And may the God of our fathers have mercy upon us!

(MIRIAM *enters the tabernacle and* AARON *reluctantly follows. The second boy peeps slyly on the stage. Discovering* ELIEZER *hidden behind the idol, he approaches.*)

SECOND BOY Have our elders truly gone?
ELIEZER Yes, every one.
SECOND BOY And are you sure the wicked Miriam will not return?
ELIEZER She will not return soon. I heard Aaron, my uncle, tell Miriam that they were awaiting God's word of our going out from Hazeroth.
SECOND BOY Is Miriam really your aunt?
ELIEZER Yes, the sister of my father, Moses. Why?
SECOND BOY She doesn't like you much; does she?
ELIEZER I guess she does love Ithamar more; but you do not believe that which she said— do you?
SECOND BOY What—what did she say?
ELIEZER You remember well that she said I was not made in the image of God.
SECOND BOY Well, are you?
ELIEZER Of course, and God will punish anyone who says I am not.
SECOND BOY And how do you know that?
ELIEZER Aaron, the brother of my sire, said so. He told Miriam so, too.
SECOND BOY And what did she say?
ELIEZER She didn't believe it, for she laughed and went into the tabernacle.
SECOND BOY I laugh, too, for I don't believe that you are either.

(*As the children talk, a great uproar is heard in the*

tabernacle. The crowd surges to the door and down the steps with MIRIAM *running ahead. The children hide behind the idol*)

WORSHIPPERS Unclean! Unclean! (MIRIAM *runs down the steps and collapses at the foot.* AARON *starts to lift her but looks in her face and draws back in fear*) Unclean! Unclean!

AARON O! God of Abraham, of Issac and of Jacob, have mercy on her and forgive me, a sinner who spoke against thy servant.

(MOSES *stands in the doorway of the tabernacle; and* MIRIAM, *looking up, sees him*)

MIRIAM (*stretching her hands to* MOSES) Oh, my brother, Moses, I have sinned against God and you, but I beseech you to pray God to take away this leprosy. See, my arms are as white as snow. My flesh is half consumed. Let me not be as one dead.

WORSHIPPERS Unclean! Unclean!

(MOSES *lifts his arms in prayer and silence falls*)

MOSES God of my father, and of Abraham, Isaac and Jacob, heal her now, O God, I beseech thee!

MIRIAM (*looking hopefully to* MOSES *and at her arms*) Am I healed now?

MOSES (*shaking his head*) No, my sister.

MIRIAM Shall I be condemned to live on dead as I am?

MOSES For seven days thou shalt be ashamed and for seven days must thou be shut out from camp. 'Tis God's will.

WORSHIPPERS (*repeating in awe*) God's will.
(MIRIAM *rises and staggers off stage, the mob following at a distance shouting "Unclean"*)

MOSES (*stretching forth his hands*) Verily, verily, I say unto ye, my people, let not the camp be moved until she return to us after seven days. Then shall we journey and pitch camp in the wilderness of Param. Peace be with ye!

(*The psalm singers issue from the tabernacle and follow* MOSES, *chanting. When the last singer has gone, the boys come from behind the idol*)

ELIEZER So you laughed with Miriam, did you? Maybe you want to go with her into the wilderness.

SECOND BOY Oh! no, truly not. I will play worship again, truly I will, if you ask your God not to punish me.

ELIEZER Will you bring back your play-fellows?

SECOND BOY Yes, yes, and you shall be our idol.

ELIEZER And when our elders come, what will you say?

SECOND BOY When my elders come and ask, "What is this that you do, little one?" I shall answer....

ELIEZER (*impatiently*) Yes! Yes!

SECOND BOY I shall answer, "I worship a child."

ELIEZER (*prompting*) Whom God hath created....

SECOND BOY Yes, I know. Let me say all of it. "I worship a child whom God hath created in his own image." Now, will you ask your God to forgive me?

ELIEZER All right, but be gone and call your play-fellows.

SECOND BOY (*going off stage*) Lo, lads! Lo, lads!

(ELIEZER *springs to the platform and sits hugging his knees in delight in anticipation of the coming sport as the curtain falls*)

Theodore Browne (1910–   )

Natural Man
1937

Natural Man is based on the John Henry legends—unverifiable stories passed along by tradition. There probably was such a man as John Henry, although the ballad and legends may be a composite of several black steel-driving men.

One version has it that John Henry worked on the COR Railway in 1872, cutting rock for the Big Ben Tunnel, a one-and-one-half-mile shaft in Virginia. His contest with the steam drill lasted only thirty minutes. John Henry swung two twenty-pound hammers and beat the machine; he did not die until later during a cave-in.

Another story is that he was born in Tennessee, weighed 205 pounds, swung a thirty-pound hammer, was a full-blooded African, and died at the age of 34. His wife caused to be written on his tombstone, "Here lies a steel-driving man."

One scholar of the legend—either taken by the exotic notion of the black male or by a relentless Freudian bent—suggested that the story is an allegory of the railway drillers' fantasy regarding their sexual prowess. John Henry drives the steel into the mountain until the rock catches fire, goes the story. It is more enlightening to know that the southern railways were built with forced black convict labor, and that no wages were paid to the prisoners.

In any case, the decade of the 1930's saw a renewed interest in American folklore. Drama departments at the Universities of Carolina and Iowa encouraged plays on regional subjects; so did the Federal Theater Project.

The John Henry legends were popular. Herbert Kline wrote *John Henry* (1935); Frank Wells, *John Henry* (1936). Roark Bradford, co-author of *Green Pastures*, wrote a musical *John Henry*, which opened on Broadway in 1940; but even the singing of Paul Robeson did not save the bad script.

Theodore Browne's play about John Henry, *Natural Man*, premiered in Seattle, Washington, on January 28, 1937 with the Federal Theater Project. Its New York debut was four years later—May 7, 1941, at the American Negro Theater (ANT) in Harlem.

ANT, under the leadership of Abram Hill and Frederick O'Neal, was founded on June 5, 1940. "The American Negro Theater is working to develop a permanent cooperative acting company coordinating and perfecting the related arts of the theater. Each production of the group will endeavor to clarify and illumine some aspect, import, and meaning to our common life." ANT's first production, *On Striver's Row*, by Abram Hill, ran five months of weekend performances in the basement of the library on 135th Street. From this success, *Natural Man* was mounted.

The script was originally subtitled "A Negro Opera." The play was sparse and lyrical, very much like the later "folk operas," *Down in the Valley* and *The Lowland Sea*. It depended a great deal on music and staging.

The newspaper critics liked the production. Each saw his own interpretation, according to his own ideology. The *New York Times* critic said, "the *Natural Man* is in conflict with the forces of mechanization." The *Daily Worker* saw the struggle of the worker against the exploiter, and further the critic was disturbed:

Natural Man in its most dramatic scene in the prison cell where the other white prisoners taunt the Negro Giant—becomes a rallying cry for hatred of all white men and for Negro nationalism.
That it may possibly be subjectively interpreted as a rallying cry against all whites, including white workers and the poor exploited white agricultural laborers and sharecroppers of the South is a fault.

It was not the *Daily Worker* critic's misinterpretation that he saw the prison scene as black nationalist: it is. In the same scene John Henry declares, "I am a giant in a straightjacket".

Theodore Browne, the author, is a graduate of City College of New York. The year ANT produced *Natural Man* he won the Rockefeller Drama Award. In 1970, he had this to say about the black theater:

I've always felt strongly about a Negro Peoples' Theater that emphasizes the heroic aspects of the black experience in America—the Exemplars who triumphed over the odds. We still must draw upon their strengths to survive, to not go under, to overcome and to be uplifted. Black giants—the Harriet Tubmans, the Fred Douglasses, the John Henrys, the Booker T. Washingtons, the Bert Williamses, the George Washington Carvers and so on—have walked up and down this whole creation of a nation, helping it to evolve and to grow in consciousness and spirituality. Often they've stood alone and cried in the wilderness of Caucasian apathy until they were heard. As Afro-Americans, we've come a helluva long ways. It's high time we "entered the Silence"—become totally still and listen whilst this heroic record of our past strengths is played back to us frantic children. We need the balance of such an overview.

Natural Man

A Play in Eight Episodes based on the Legend of John Henry.

CAST OF CHARACTERS

JOHN HENRY, *a steel driving man*
CHARLEY, *a steel driver*
BIG'N ME, *a steel driver*
LUTHER, *a steel driver*
JIM, *a steel driver*
HARD TACK, *a steel driver*
BRITT, *a steel driver*
POLLY ANN, *John Henry's woman*
CAPTAIN TOMMY WALTERS, *white railway boss*
THE CREEPER, *a black troubadour*
SALESMAN OF STEAM DRILLS
SPECTATORS
WOMAN, *a street walker*
BARTENDER
SWEETMAN, *a pimp*
BUSTER, *a bouncer*
JESS, *a bouncer*
PICKPOCKET
WHITE POLICEMAN
WHITE JAILBIRDS
SHERIFF
FIVE CONVICTS
BOY
GUARD
CONGREGATION
PREACHER
OLD WOMAN
FOUR HOBOES

First Episode

(TIME: *noon. The early eighties, on the day preceding the great contest between John Henry and the steam drill.*

SETTING: *before the entrance to the Big Ben Tunnel in West Virginia. The setting is stylized. A framework of logs that form a crudely-shaped rectangle and supports the earth above the dugout. A raised landing, both ends of which slope down to the stage flooring. The entire action of the various episodes take place outside this entrance, except, at intervals, when we see the silhouette figure of* JOHN HENRY *wielding his hammer directly inside the tunnel.*

The whole stage is dark, except for a dullish spray of light falling upon the landing. From inside the tunnel comes the voice of JOHN HENRY, *singing a "Hammer Song," each line of which he underscores with a hammer beat. As he sings, a motley crew of negro steeldrivers issue, one after the other, from the blackness of the tunnel and into the shaft of the light on the landing. They sprawl about the landing and open up their dinner pails and commence to eat, silently, as* JOHN HENRY, *out of sight, sings and hammers*)

JOHN HENRY This old hammer—huh!
Rings like silver—huh!
This old hammer—huh!
Rings like silver—huh!
This old hammer—huh!
Rings like silver—huh!
Shines like gold, boys—huh!
Shines like gold—huh!

Ain't no hammer—huh!
In these mountains—huh!
Ain't no hammer—huh!
In these mountains—huh!
Rings like mine, boys—huh!
Rings like mine—huh!

CHARLEY Say, Big'n Me, what your old lady put in that pail?
BIG'N ME Never you mind what my old lady put in this pail!
LUTHER Tell by the way he's eating and sopping his lips, sure must taste good!
JIM Charley Boy's treening that there dinner pail just like some cat treening fishheads!
HARD TACK Won't do him a speck of good either! What you say, Big'n Me?
BIG'N ME Chirp it, Brother! My mouth's full and I can't talk!

JIM Why the name of God you don't get yourself an old lady, Charley Boy?

CHARLEY Too much the loser!

HARD TACK Know a certain old gal whose palms' just itching to handle your money!

BRITT Who? That little re-headed yaller gal from New Orleans?

HARD TACK She's soft as hell on Charley Boy, too!

CHARLEY She ain't no damn good! Got a hand full of gimmies and a mouth full of much-oblige.

BRITT Love'em and leave'em. That's my policy.

CHARLEY (*looks in* BIG'N ME's *pail*) Spare-ribs and sweet-potatoes! Lord, today!

BIG'N ME Tennessee you may see, *yet*, but not a damn rib of these here spare-ribs will you *get*!

CHARLEY Big'n Me's old lady sure must be powerful sweet on him!

BIG'N ME Don't you let my woman's sweetness worry you none!

HARD TACK May wake up one these mornings and find himself dead!

JIM Charley Boy, you can't make it off cheese and crackers!

LUTHER You need a mess of pork chops to drive that steel!

BIG'N ME Something to stick to your stomach. Something greasy!

VOICES OF MALE CHORUS (*off stage*) Never mind that fancy dish, Babe,
Never mind that silver knife and fork.
Just dump my vittles in a dinner-pail,
And, when I eat, don't talk!

Celery, lettuce—that's rabbit food.
Bring me some sow-belly and beans.
Them's what's going stick by you, Babe,
And help you blow up steam!

(*roars of belly-laughter from the Steeldrivers*)

CHARLEY Say, Hard Tack, where the hell was you last night?

HARD TACK I went in town to raise some righteous hell.

LUTHER There was hell-raising a-plenty right here in camp.

BRITT Tell him about that fancy city-slicker with them trained dice!

BIG'N ME Man, old Candy sure put his trade-mark on that Dude!

CHARLEY Never see such razor-slashing in all my born days!

HARD TACK Everywhere you go in town folks talking about the big contest tomorrow.

JIM John Henry and that steam drill! Like some world championship bout!

BRITT Who they saying'll win, Hard Tack?

CHARLEY They doing any betting? What's the odds?

HARD TACK Five to one on John Henry. White folks doing most the betting. Saw a white guy pull out a roll of yaller money, man, big enough to choke a mule, and he laid every God's bit of it on John Henry! Say he bet on John Henry any day when it comes to driving steel!

BIG'N ME White folks got to hand it to old John Henry! Boy, don't he make'em all sit up and take notice?

BRITT That fool sure can swing a wicked hammer!

LUTHER That's the living truth! All his brains is in his muscles!

CHARLEY Arms like steel and head like solid rock!

HARD TACK Any you-all ground-hogs like to bet? My five bucks says John Henry'll beat that old steel drill.

CHARLEY Five bucks? That wouldn't buy my gal a pair of shoes!

HARD TACK Hell you say! That slew-footed wench ain't never wore a pair of shoes cost that much!

LUTHER How's any meat-man going whip something run by steam?

HARD TACK All right, you put your money where your mouth is!

LUTHER White man smart. He sits up all night long figuring out a way to put us all right back in slavery.

BIG'N ME Steam may be all right, but she'll never take the place of a natural man. Nossir!

BRITT Them science guys so smart, though, they can invent most nigh anything.

HARD TACK You can take your brains and your deep books. I'll take mother-wit.

JIM Tell that fool something! Mother-wit! Now you talking!

CHARLEY Mother-wit and arms of steel! A solid, natural man!

HARD TACK (*as* POLLY ANN *appears*) Well, look who's here, boys! Polly Ann!

JIM Hot dog! I sure likes the way that gal walks!
BRITT Rears back her head and struts just like a maltese cat!
CHARLEY I'd dump my week's pay in her lap any day!
LUTHER Ah, do it, Pretty Mama, do it!

HARD TACK (*he clowns with her as the others watch approvingly*) Well, I ain't no lover,
No lover's son,
But, Baby, I can do your loving
Till your lover come!

LUTHER Look! She all dressed up in her Sunday-go-to-meeting!
CHARLEY Polly Ann sure do look like ready money and careless love!
HARD TACK New shoes! New dress! All she need now is a brand-new sugar-daddy!
POLLY ANN Don't get excited, Hot Papa! My shopping days is over!

HARD TACK (*cavorting*) Now, who bought you those pretty little shoes?
Who bought you the dress you wear so fine?
And who kissed your red rosy cheeks?
And who's going to be your man?
POLLY ANN John Henry bought these pretty little shoes.
John Henry bought the dress I wear so fine.
John Henry kissed my red rosy cheeks.
Doggone it! You know I don't need no man!
HARD TACK You know them pretty shoes she's dogging out?
Dress she wear so fine? Well I tell you:
Them shoes she got from a railroad man.
That dress she got from a driver in the mine!

(*The men all roar with laughter, as* POLLY ANN *rolls her eyes prettily*)

John Henry he had a little woman,
Just as pretty as she could be.
They's only one objection I has to her—

POLLY ANN What?—
HARD TACK She wants every man she see!
POLLY ANN That's a pop-eyed lie, and you knows it! John Henry never had a gal been truer to him.
CHARLEY If you weren't so true, I done had you for my woman long time ago. From the day I laid eyes on you!

POLLY ANN Say, tell me where is my steel-driving daddy?
BIG'N ME He never quit work yet.
JIM He claim he figuring out a new way how to swing that hammer tomorrow.
POLLY ANN Well, what's wrong with the way he been swinging it?
JIM That's what I'd like to know. Never could figure how he swing from both hips.
LUTHER (*suddenly*) Lord! Lord! Just listen to that man drive steel!
BRITT Listen to that hammer ring! Like a hollow-ground razor blade!

JOHN HENRY (*from inside, sings*) Come here, my pretty little mama—huh!
Come and sit on your daddy's knee—huh!
You have been the death of many a man—huh!
But you won't be the death of me!—huh!
POLLY ANN (*she sings back to him*) You might be bigger than me, Hot Papa—huh!
You might be the biggest man alive—huh!
But you try any two-timing with this gal—huh!
She'll cut you down to her size!

CHARLEY She sure talks like a natural woman!
POLLY ANN (*impatiently*) John Henry, you come on out here! Your somnteat's getting cold.
JOHN HENRY Just one more swing will get it! (*hammers, then he appears, smiling*)
BRITT Boy, you sure make that hammer talk!
POLLY ANN Way you swinging that hammer, won't be no rocks left for you to drill tomorrow!
JOHN HENRY Just thought I needed to sort of exercise a little more. Work up an appetite.
POLLY ANN I hopes you gets your fill of steel-driving!
JOHN HENRY Baby, a steel-driving champ's like a prizefighter. Always got to keep in condition.
POLLY ANN You ain't afraid you'll forget how to swing that hammer? (*rhapsodic*) Lord, when I come out the house, the earth rocked under my feet!
JOHN HENRY That was just my hammer falling down!
POLLY ANN And, when I get here to the tunnel, feel like the whole tunnel caving in!
JOHN HENRY Go way from here, gal! You only hear the echo of that hammer ring!

STEELDRIVERS She only hear the echo of that hammer ring!

JOHN HENRY There was once a mountain,
    And the mountain was so tall, that
    They sent word for me to come
    Blow that mountain small!
STEELDRIVERS Blow that mountain small, Boy!
    Blow that mountain small!

JOHN HENRY (*with boyish exuberance*) Man, I can hardly wait! Tomorrow seem so far-off like. Can hardly wait. Studying about how I'm going beat that old steam drill down, figuring out this kind of stroke, and figuring out some other, till my brains whirl like a spinning-top. All I can think of the whole week long: A brand-new ten-pound hammer and a brand-new drill, carved from solid steel. Buddy-boys, when I do commence to drive that steel, all of you going hear music such as you never hear before! Natural music. When you hears that hammer ring, it'll sound like the silver chimes in Glory and a band of snow-white angels singing! Sparks of fire will jump from them rocks like the Devil a-spitting thru his teeth. Ain't no hammer in this whole land going outring mine, Boys, going outring mine!

HARD TACK You tell'em, John Henry!
BIG'N ME You tell'em!
CHARLEY Boy, I ain't got the heart to tell'em!
JOHN HENRY Take all the rocks I done busted from here to Macon. Take all the spikes I done drove in railroad ties. The great large mountains I done hollow out, so to make a hole for trains to run through. Laying steel tracks for trains to fly over. Busting rocks to make smooth gravel roads. I done all that! Done the work of a natural man. Me and my hammer, Boy, building railroad tracks and gravel roads. Now, who comes first? Me or this man-made steam drill? Who fixed it so a locomotive engine can have a track to run on? Who? Well, it was me, that's who! I come first. Bring on your fancy, new-fangled steam drills, line'em up six in a row and start'em all drilling at the same time as me, and I'll bet you any kind of money that I beat every damn one of them put together!

(CAPTAIN TOMMY, *a middle-aged white man enters*)

CAPTAIN TOMMY What's this I hear you saying, John Henry?
STEELDRIVERS Captain Tommy! Howdy, Captain!
CAPTAIN TOMMY Howdy, Boys!
JOHN HENRY (*modestly*) Nothing much, Captain. Just letting these boys know how I feels about this steam drill.
CAPTAIN TOMMY Well, you think you man enough to beat that steam drill?
JOHN HENRY If I don't beat it, Captain, you can run me till I'm lean!
BIG'N ME He'll beat it sure, Captain.
BRITT Fastest steeldriver in the whole United States!
LUTHER Sure is! A steel-driving fool!
JIM A natural-born steeldriver!
BRITT That boy born with a hammer in his hand!
CHARLEY He drives steel out of this world!
HARD TACK He'll whip that old steam drill so, she'll moan and sigh!
CAPTAIN TOMMY All right! Tomorrow will tell the tale. May the best man win! Oh, yes—and speaking about tomorrow, I guess you boys may as well take the rest of the day off.
STEELDRIVERS Thank you, Captain Tommy! Thank you, Boss!
CAPTAIN TOMMY Sort of figured you boys would like to celebrate on the night before the great contest.
STEELDRIVERS Yessir, Captain, we sure do! Yessirree!
CAPTAIN TOMMY (*chuckles, then with affected sternness*) And see to it you behave yourselves. Don't get mixed up in no shooting or cutting scrapes. If you get in jail, might as well make up your mind to stay there until after the contest.
HARD TACK Boss, that jailhouse couldn't hold me whilst that contest was going on!
CHARLEY I'd carry on so that the jailer would throw me the key and let me unlock the cell door myself!
CAPTAIN TOMMY By the way, John Henry—I'm counting on you to win.
JOHN HENRY Well, you sure counting right, Captain Tommy!
CAPTAIN TOMMY Tomorrow, after the contest, I'll drive you and Polly Ann to town, and you can pick out the best suit of clothes in any tailor shop. I don't give a continental how much it costs either. The best! As good as anything

I wear myself. On top of that, I'm making you a present of fifty brand-new silver dollars.

BRITT Fifty brand-new silver cogwheels!

LUTHER Natural-made money!

JIM Money that rings like steel!

BIG'N ME Now, I knows he going win!

POLLY ANN You hear that, Honey Man? Fifty brand-new silver dollars to jingle in the pockets of your brand-new suit!

JOHN HENRY Thank you, Captain!—Say, you ain't now going to town?

CAPTAIN TOMMY I'm on my way there right now.

JOHN HENRY Well, bring me back a ten-pound hammer. I'm going drive that steel on down! (CAPTAIN TOMMY *exits*. JOHN HENRY *is exultant*)

> Tomorrow at sunrise,
> Like a natural man,
> Tomorrow at sunrise,
> Like a natural man,
> Going take that hammer, drive that
> Steel the fastest in the land!

STEELDRIVERS Going take that hammer, Drive that Steel the fastest in the land!

(*A small, nondescript Negro literally creeps into the scene. The steeldrivers and* POLLY ANN *are facing* JOHN HENRY *and do not see the stranger when he enters and stands in back of them. In his shirtsleeves and hatless,* THE CREEPER, *as he is called, is dressed in mismatched garish attire. A black troubadour, he carries a cheap-looking canvas-covered guitar case.* [*He is to be a one-man Chorus to underscore the legend-in-the-making charisma of* JOHN HENRY.] THE CREEPER *stands looking up at* JOHN HENRY, *grinning broadly.* JOHN HENRY *recognizes him instantly, a look of consternation comes into his face*)

JOHN HENRY Creeper! (*the others all turn around to behold the* CREEPER, *grinning like a spreading adder*)

CREEPER (*in a soft-spoken, "clabber-mouth" voice*) Nobody diffent! Yessuh, folks, I the old Creeper himself! Ain't nothing to me. John Henry knows me of old. (*to* JOHN HENRY) How is you, Boy?

JOHN HENRY (*vehemently*) Creeper, I've tried every which way I knows how to lose sight and sound of you, but somehow you always catch up with me. You and that tarnashun guitar-box. And you like a buzzard waiting 'round for something to heave its last breath!

STEELDRIVERS (*in unison*) Where this dude come from?
What th'hell you doing 'round here, Bo?
Let's we drive him to hell outta this camp!
He's a jinx!
Come on, you half-pint runt, travel!—

JOHN HENRY No, take your hands off him! Leave him 'lone. Leave him be. He ain't bother nobody. You-all don't know him like I do. He ain't the kind you shake off easy.—You hear me now, Creeper, I want you to git this straight, you hear me? I got myself a job to do. Biggest I ever yit tackle. I'm going beat that steam drill they bringing in here tomorrow, else lay down and die. Now, you and nothing you say going stop me!

CREEPER You knows I'm with you, John Henry. Yessuh, be with you to the end.

JOHN HENRY Come on, Polly Ann.

POLLY ANN John Henry, what is the meaning of this? (*as she follows him*) Who this Creeper dude, and why come he follow you like a bloodhound dog?—

BRITT Never seen John Henry worked up like this before.

HARD TACK Something's on his mind. Memories, I guess. This dude here bring up memories.

CHARLEY Say, Creeping Man, open her up and play something!

LUTHER Beat out some low-down blues on that guitar!

CREEPER (*grins, withdrawing*) I be round tomorrow. Play something for you. Something special. Song I make up bout John Henry. I has a heap of songs, and they's all bout John Henry, too. (*he ambles off*)

LUTHER I be a sonavagun!

HARD TACK Peoples!

CHARLEY Man, he walks like lice dropping off him!

BRITT Outta this world and in the next!

(*Fade out*)

Second Episode

(TIME: *sunrise, the following day.*

SETTING: *same as the first episode.*

CAPTAIN TOMMY WALTERS *and another white man, the* SALESMAN, *are discovered on the landing.*

They speak with rapid, stacatto precision, their voices hollow and metallic. They are like two competing auctioneers. They are heard above the murmur of the crowd of spectators below.)

SALESMAN All right, all right, if that's the way you want it.

CAPTAIN TOMMY My boy against your steam drill.

SALESMAN Right, sir!

CAPTAIN TOMMY Hell, it's a cinch my boy'll win!

SALESMAN I'm game enough to wager he hasn't got a chance.

CAPTAIN TOMMY We'll see about that. Fourteen-hour stretch. Let's see—*(he looks at his watch)* Pretty near to starting time. From four o'clock sharp to six in the evening.

SALESMAN You're putting him under an awful strain, Mister Walters.

CAPTAIN TOMMY I know what he can do.

SALESMAN Sunrise to sunset.

CAPTAIN TOMMY Yep, sunrise to sunset. You're going to see some genuine first-class steel-driving. Just wait. McCurdy, I've been in this business over twenty-five years. I reckon I know a good steeldriver when I see one. Most of my boys are hand-picked. I do the hiring and firing around here. I get most of them off the chain gang. Pay their fines, then give them a chance to work it off. Some of them boys were up for life. I buy their freedom and give them a new start.

SALESMAN That's downright charitable, Mister Walters.

CAPTAIN TOMMY Take that boy John Henry. Yep, John Henry. Most valuable hand I got. Wanted in Georgia for killing a white man. Was on the chain gang. He ups and kills one of the guards, then made a get-away. I could send him back today or tomorrow, but I'd be a damn fool if I did!

SALESMAN This steam drill's been tested. She's capable of doing the work of four men.

CAPTAIN TOMMY What th'hell do you Yankee carpetbaggers know about steel-driving? If this boy of mine don't beat your steam drill, I'll double that damn order!

SALESMAN Now, you're talking!

CAPTAIN TOMMY Two minutes to four. Better get your men ready to start that steam drill.

SPECTATORS *(cheering loudly, as they appear with* JOHN HENRY *and* POLLY ANN) John Henry, himself!
Steel-driving champ!
Here he is, folks!
John Henry! John Henry!
There's Polly Ann with him!
Gangway for the hammer-king!

CAPTAIN TOMMY *(to* SALESMAN) . . . and be ready to start the minute the gun fires! (SALESMAN *exits.* JOHN HENRY *mounts the landing)* Well, Boy, how do you feel?

JOHN HENRY Like the victory done in my hand!

CAPTAIN TOMMY That's the spirit!

POLLY ANN Sure is a heap of folks out there to see you beat that steam drill!

JOHN HENRY They expecting me to win, too.

CAPTAIN TOMMY That's right. You can't let them down.

JOHN HENRY Nossir, Captain, and I won't neither.

POLLY ANN Of course, you won't! I'm going be right by, shouting my lungs out for you to win. Look—a whole hamper basket full of fried chicken and clabber biscuits for your dinner!

CAPTAIN TOMMY *(over the cheering crowd)* All right, it's time to start!

POLLY ANN Go to it, Hot Papa! Show the whole wide world what a natural man can do!

CAPTAIN TOMMY *(to* JOHN HENRY) Be ready to start the minute the gun fires. *(as* JOHN HENRY *turns to enter the tunnel)* Oh, say—the warden of the Jasper County State Prison sent me your record the other day.

JOHN HENRY *(unnerved)* Jasper County? Is they going to take me back there?

CAPTAIN TOMMY *(cruelly, menacing)* You got a pretty bad record, John Henry. You're an escaped convict, don't forget.

JOHN HENRY I go back, it means a lifetime on that chain gang.

CAPTAIN TOMMY They won't be that easy on you.

JOHN HENRY What you mean by that, Captain Tommy?

CAPTAIN TOMMY You know damn, plague-take-it well what I mean! You killed a white man.

JOHN HENRY I wasn't aiming to, Captain. I done it in self-defense. He was going shoot my guts out over nothing. I never caused no trouble before. I always done the work of four men every day. I must have lost my head or something. I didn't aim to kill. I just couldn't stand there and—

CAPTAIN TOMMY Never mind, I know all about it. I'm a personal friend of the governor. Helped him get elected, in fact. Listen, Boy—I want you to win, do you understand? Do you hear me?

JOHN HENRY I'll win sure as my name is John Henry!

CAPTAIN TOMMY If you don't—well—I won't be needing you around here anymore.

JOHN HENRY (*grimly*) I understand, Boss... I'll win. I've got to now.

(*He goes inside the tunnel, as the crowd cheers. The lights dim out on the landing. During the loud cheering, the report of a revolver rents the air.* JOHN HENRY *starts hammering, the chugging noise of the steam drill is heard. We see only the silhouetted figure of* JOHN HENRY *inside the tunnel, wielding his hammer. He is assisted by a shaker who holds the steel drill in position*)

VOICES OF SPECTATORS (*in unison*) John Henry'll beat that steam drill down!
Look at that hammer fall!
No man-made steam drill will whip him!
He's making that hammer talk!
Lord, Lord! Glory be!
He's the best in the land!
That man's a mighty man!

(CAPTAIN TOMMY *and the* SALESMAN *are downstage at right*)

CAPTAIN TOMMY Cost more to run that machine than it does to pay a driller.

SALESMAN But she does the work of four men.

CAPTAIN TOMMY Well, I'm from Missouri. You got to show me!

SALESMAN You'll only need to hire about one-fourth of the men you have now.

CAPTAIN TOMMY I'm thinking about what will happen when this job closes up. Suppose I don't get another contract?

SALESMAN You don't have to worry about that.

CAPTAIN TOMMY The hell I don't!

SALESMAN Your excavation company is one of the biggest in the South.

CAPTAIN TOMMY Don't forget. I got plenty competition, too. Other companies cutting my throat, under-bidding me and using convict labor. I'll be in one devil of a fix with steam drills on my hand and nothing to drill. With hand labor you play safe. You work'em as long as you need them. Speed'em up when it's necessary. Hire as many as you like when times are good. When things get bad, you let as many go as you like, and nothing's lost. Play safe is my motto. I'll take cheap black labor any day!

(*A swell of cheering from the crowd. The stage is completely dark now. The cheering gives way to the mass chant of the spectators*)

VOICES OF SPECTATORS John Henry, if you don't win, well, I won't be needing you around here anymore. You are an escaped convict. You killed a white man. You know what they do with a black man who kills a white man? They burn him alive. They string him up and burn him alive!

POLLY ANN (*highlighted: she is hysterical*) Captain Tommy, you can't let them take my man from me! He's all I got in the world. He's all I want to have. I love him, and I been true to him. Don't take him away, please! They'll kill him, and that'll be the death of me. They kill him! They'll kill him!

(*The lights fade out on* POLLY ANN *and come up on* THE CREEPER. *He is downstage, extreme left, well outside the playing arena, which is now entirely blacked out and being readied for the sequence to follow.* THE CREEPER, *guitar in hand, strikes a detonating ominous chord, signal for the black-out on* POLLY ANN *and an instant shift to him, commanding the attention of the audience*)

CREEPER (*with authority*) No man born of woman can beat a steam drill down! (*plays and sings mournfully*)

> Say, a man's been round,
> Took John Henry's name.
> Say, a man's been round,
> Took John Henry's name.
> Say, "John Henry, your Maker calls you.
> Please, answer to your name."
>
> Polly Ann, your man's in trouble,
> Cain't ease his worried mind.
> Polly Ann, your man's in trouble,
> Cain't ease his worried mind.
> Win or lose with that steam drill,
> He still got his worried mind.

Natural Man

(*speaking*) Poor boy! Poor boy! You on trial for your life. Ol' Creeper knows what's going on inside that mind of yours whilst you down in that Big Ben Tunnel pounding, pounding your life away, oh, Lord, ha'mercy!—seeing it all pass in one big procession before you: Beale Street, the Jailhouse, Chain Gang, Hobo Jungle... Remember that Dive on Beale Street? Lord! Lord!—(*sings*)

> Let him go to Beale Street,
> Where life is gay.
> I say, let him go to Beale Street,
> Where life is gay.
> What he's looking for on Beale Street
> Wont drive his blues away!

(*Lights dim out on the* CREEPER *and come up on the Beale Street scene*)

Third Episode

(SETTING: *a dive on Beale Street in Memphis. Two opposing floods of lights, very soft, running diagonally left to right, leaving a semi-darkened area in between, form two lighted circles. One reveals a bar, the other a table and two chairs. A tall, thin man is attending bar. During the scene, men and women are discovered at intervals drinking there. At the table are seated* JOHN HENRY *and a street walker. Her make-up is exaggerated and her dress decorative, in keeping with her profession. The other patrons, all characters out of the Negro underworld, are seen in outline, shadowy, seated at other tables about the place.*

Throughout this episode, the speech, the action and everything have the slow, lethargic rhythm of the blues)

JOHN HENRY (*groggy from hard drinking*) One more drink, Baby, just one more drink...

WOMAN (*bored*) Your hand just glued to that bottle!

JOHN HENRY Likker never killed nobody. Say, come on have one with me. Ain't no fun drinking alone.

WOMAN Well, you'll drink this one alone, cause I ain't drinking, see.

JOHN HENRY What's the matter you ain't drinking? You my company, ain't you?

WOMAN I ain't drinking. Had enough.

JOHN HENRY Well, my likker's particular who drinks it!

WOMAN The undertaker won't have to mess burying you. Just pour you back in a bottle!

JOHN HENRY Having a little fun, Pretty Mama. Just out to enjoy life. (*he turns the bottle up to his head*)

WOMAN Say, that ain't no way to be drinking out in public! Use the glass. What you figger it was—a finger bowl?

JOHN HENRY I drinks like I suppose to drink. Like a natural man. That's way we drink where I come from. Likker never be my master, understand? Cause why? I ain't got no master! Shucks! Nobody make me take low. Never! Cause I'm natural born. President in the White House, Congress—nobody! All the same to me. I been everywhere. I seen everything. Makes no difference who they is, nor where they come from. Never take low, no time. That's me! President of the United States, Congress... Hell! Put a ten-pound hammer in his hand, wouldn't know what to do with it! Know that there road—the railroad what runs all the way from Atlanta to Shreeport? Well, I lay them rails, them pretty, sweet rails! That gravel road going into Macon? I built that road. Busted every damn rock of it!

WOMAN I listened to you say that once, I listened to you say it fifty times!

JOHN HENRY Lord, Lord, if there was no more rocks to bust, no more spikes to drive, I'd lay down and die! I went to Glory and I don't find none there, I'd up and leave and walk and walk till I find myself a brand new world, where there nothing but rocks and steel and ten-pound hammers!... Life! Hell, they ain't no life here. You call all this life? Well, you listen here to me, Babe. I tell you what life is, see. Life is a ten-pound hammer, a steel drill, and a great big solid rock! (*he rises, animated*) Where's my hammer? Steady that drill, Boy, cause here I come—Huh! Great day in the morning! Listen to that hammer ring—Huh!

WOMAN (*disgusted. She tries without success to yank him back down to his seat, but he brushes her aside*) You pike down! Where you think you is? (*sits back down*)

JOHN HENRY (*transfixed with joy*) Thirty miles to north of Macon! Throw some cool water on this hammer, Boy! She burning up. Every time this hammer falls, the ground just shakes under my feet. All I do is steady her, she hammers herself! Got to bust this rock all the way to Macon. Must make it there by dark. Sweet woman got fried chicken on the table waiting for me. Boy, steady that drill! This hammer sure means business. Crazy this hammer is, she liable to mistake your head for that drill! (*sings*)

> Steel-driving man—huh!
> Natural-born.
> Steel-driving man—huh!
> Natural-born.
> Got arms like steel, Babe,
> A heart like solid stone.

WOMAN Here, take it easy, Hot Papa! You ain't on nobody's rock pile!

JOHN HENRY I'm going find me some steel to drive.

WOMAN For the time being, you better sit down.

JOHN HENRY (*sits*) Say, I like you. Damn fi' don't! You talks way I likes to hear a woman talk. No fancy, high-English words. Natural, Baby, natural. How'd you like to be my woman? Travel and follow me every-which-a-where—all over this country—from coast to coast, Babe.

WOMAN What you offering me—a start in life? Listen, here, Brother Low-down—excuse me, Mister Steel-driving man—I left Yamicraw, Georgia for better or worse. So, I'll take the worse, and stay right here!

JOHN HENRY Here—buy some more likker.

WOMAN I thought you done spent out?

JOHN HENRY Here's the rest of it. Hell, money don't mean nothing to me. Today in my pocket, tomorrow in somebody else's. When this goes, I goes. Me and my old hammer, starting all over again!

WOMAN (*more friendly*) What kind this time will it be? Bourbon or rot-gut?

JOHN HENRY What kind I been drinking?

WOMAN Rot-gut.

JOHN HENRY All taste the same.

WOMAN Don't start that old wringing-and-twisting. I'm drinking Bourbon!

JOHN HENRY Bourbon? Name sounds too funny. I likes the sound of rot-gut.

WOMAN I still say I'm drinking Bourbon. (*snaps her fingers for the Bartender*) Say, Charleston, a drink of Bourbon and a shorty of rot-gut. (*to* JOHN HENRY) I don't see how a man can drink so much rot-gut whiskey and live!

JOHN HENRY Cain't nothing kill me. Not even a bolt of lightning. Not even a forty-five pistol. Only thing can kill me is a hammer—a ten-pound hammer and a steel drill. Got to bust me same as you bust a rock!

WOMAN (*as* BARTENDER *waits*) Ain't you going pay the man?

JOHN HENRY Won't this pay him? Take what you want, Buddy!

WOMAN (*to* BARTENDER) Oh, no, you don't! (*hands him a coin*) Here!

BARTENDER Double-crosser! I'll fix you!

WOMAN This is my trick, Skipper! (*to* JOHN HENRY) Come on, Big Daddy, drink up!

JOHN HENRY Gonna be long-gone, Brown Sugar, Long-gone from Memphis. Beale Street. Solid gone. These old bear claws of mine just itching for a grip-hold that hammer!

WOMAN (*laughing*) You the first man I see want to talk bout nothing but work!

JOHN HENRY That's all I know, Fair Brown. That's all I ever wonts to know! The rest don't count. Hammer. Steel. Rocks. Them's my friends. My bosom-friends. They's me! Don't even have to talk to them. Just sing, and they commence to sing right back at me. Like some echo from off the hills. Music. Great, natural music. Righteous music right out of Glory! . . . Memphis! Beale Street! Great mind to get my hammer and set fire to every blamed cobblestone! Despise this place! Ain't no good, nossir. Just ain't no good. And making a fool out'n me! Spending my hard-earned money—

WOMAN (*frightened*) Here, you need another. Steady yourself.

JOHN HENRY Rot-gut! (*raises bottle, breaking out in peals of bitter laughter*) You ain't no good, Rot-gut! Ruination of many a poor man! Creeping up on a man. Trying to make him forget . . . White folks . . . A man ain't nothing but a man!—(*he rises to his feet, decisively*) Can't stay here! Got to catch me a freight train, and ride! Ride over them steel rails I laid! Great day in the morning! Ride them rods! Travel! There still a heap of rocks in the world, and a heap of steel. I going out of here, gonna put my nose to the ground, scent steel and rocks like a bloodhound dog! (*he sings with abandon, determination*)

I'm a long-gone papa,
Ain't got no time to lose.
I'm a long-gone papa,
Ain't got no time to lose.
If I stay here, Pretty Mama,
'Fraid I'll get them low-down blues.
    (CHORUS)—them low-down blues.

Woke up late this morning,
Blue as a man can be.
Woke up late this morning,
Blue as a man can be.
Looked into the mirror,
Saw what Memphis done to me.
    —Memphis done to me.

Good Book tell you,
Man reap what he sow.
Good Book tell you,
Man reap what he sow.
Going where I can reap
The biggest rocks that grow.
    —biggest rocks that grow.

Long-gone from here, Fair Brown.
Don't you weep or sigh.
Long-gone from here, Fair Brown.
Don't you weep or sigh.
When you hear a freight train passing,
You know I'm passing by.
    —know I'm passing by.

CHORUS (*harsh and mocking*) Ha! Ha! Ha! Ha!

JOHN HENRY (*angrily*) What you-all Ha-hawing bout? Crazy?

CHORUS Ha! Ha! Ha! Ha!

(JOHN HENRY, *overcome by the whiskey, flops down in the chair, lays his head upon the table in a drunken sleep. A trio of sweetmen, loudly dressed and dandified, appear on the landing and "strut their stuff"*)

SWEETMEN   How he can hate Beale Street,
      I don't understand.
      How he can hate Beale Street,
      I don't understand.
      Rather be a lamp-post on Beale Street
      Than a pick-and-shovel man.
          —pick-and-shovel man.

      You know a man's a fool to work,
      When women are so free.
      You know a man's a fool to work,
      When women are so free.
      Gonna always have a sweet mama
      Doing my work for me.
          —doing my work for me.

(*The trio of sweetmen are blacked-out. The Chorus hums and moans the blues strains. The Woman, assuring herself that* JOHN HENRY *is now asleep, picks up the money from the table and starts out. On reaching the bar, she is waylaid by her lover or* SWEETMAN)

SWEETMAN   Come on, Sister, dig! Need some dough. Feel my gambling luck rising.

WOMAN   Didn't make but two dollars off that guy.

SWEETMAN   Stop lying! You wouldn't fool with him long as you did.

WOMAN   I'm telling the honest truth, Daddy.

SWEETMAN   Charleston put me wise to your tricks.

JOHN HENRY (*wakens, angry*) Beale Street. Damn it! Woman took my money and gone! Let her have it! Satisfied now. Broke. Somebody go bring me my hammer!

SWEETMAN   Come across, you lying—

WOMAN   Don't hit me, Sweet man!

SWEETMAN   Get on in there! (*he shoves her into the darkness, follows*)

(*Trio of streetwalkers appear on the landing. They are painted and gaudily garbed*)

STREETWALKERS   Love for sale on Beale Street.
      Man can pick and choose.
      Love for sale on Beale Street.
      Man can pick and choose.
      Woman take way all your money,
      Drink up all your booze.
          —all your rot-gut booze.

      If my style of love don't please you,
      Aint nothing I can do.
      If my style of love don't please you,
      Ain't nothing I can do.
      If you looking for the real thing,
      Beale Street's no place for you.
          —no place for you.

(*They are blacked-out.* JOHN HENRY *gets up, staggers over to the bar*)

JOHN HENRY   No place for me! No doggone place for me! (*to Bartender*) Say, Buddy, how bout one more rot-gut? On the house this time, Buddy. Ain't got no money left. Low-down strumpet run way with every penny to my name!

BARTENDER   Ain't giving way nothing but air, Brother, and that's hot!

JOHN HENRY I been a steady customer—
BARTENDER No free drinks. Get the hell outta here!
JOHN HENRY No man allowed to talk that way to me! Come from behind that counter. Come on out, you thieving hound! You messing with a man now—a natural-born man, hear me?
BARTENDER Hey, Buster! Jess! Throw this bum outta here!
BUSTER All right, Tickle Britches, let's travel!
JOHN HENRY I can walk out by myself.
JESS So you wonts to start a fight?
BARTENDER Bad for business, hanging round.
JOHN HENRY (*brushes bouncers aside*) 'Way from me! I didn't need no help coming in and I don't need no help going out!

(BUSTER *and* JESS *retreat. A pickpocket rushes in from the street, looks about nervously. One of the women in the place comes downstage and joins him*)

PICKPOCKET Here, Woman— (*grabs hold of her hand*) Get rid of this stuff. It's hot.
HOSTESS Police see you come in here?
PICKPOCKET Dunno, but they's after this ice.

(*A white policeman enters. The woman quits the pickpocket, goes up to* JOHN HENRY)

HOSTESS Big and handsome let's dance. (*she snuggles up to him, in full view of the audience she plants the jewelry on him*)
JOHN HENRY (*pushes her away*) Go way from me, Woman! Through being made a fool of. I'm using my head, see. Gonna be smart as the next one. Git it up, Bartender! How bout that drink? Do I git it, or must I destroy this place like a earthquake?
BARTENDER (*acquiesces*) Keep your shirt on. I hope it poisons you!
POLICEMAN (*to pickpocket*) Come on! What you do with it?
PICKPOCKET I swear, Officer!
POLICEMAN You'll hit the rock-pile for this!
HOSTESS Officer, he ain't took nothing. Yonder's the one.
POLICEMAN You sure? You better be!
HOSTESS You search him and see.
POLICEMAN (*crosses to* JOHN HENRY; *jabs him with billy*) All right, you—where is it?
JOHN HENRY Don't know what you talking bout, Policeman.
HOSTESS Feel in his left-hand pocket.
JOHN HENRY What you-all talking bout?
HOSTESS That's where he got it.
POLICEMAN Don't try anything.
JOHN HENRY (*feels his pocket, discovers*) How this get in my pocket? I don't understand . . .
POLICEMAN You gonna have all the time in the world, Big Boy, to figger that out! (*applies hand-cuffs*)
JOHN HENRY (*bitterly*) Memphis! Beale Street! I great mind to—
POLICEMAN Move on, move on!
CROWD Ha! Ha! Ha! Ha!

If you looking for the real thing,
Beale Street's no place for you!

(*as the lights dim out*)

Fourth Episode

(SETTING: *Jail.* JOHN HENRY *is visible in a soft blue light, seated on a stool before the iron bars of his cell. To one side of him crouches the dwarfed figure of the* CREEPER. *The off-stage voices throughout this scene are the voices of* WHITE JAILBIRDS)

A WHITE JAILBIRD Hey, Sambo?
JOHN HENRY My name ain't Sambo.
OTHER WHITE JAILBIRDS Say, what they nab you for, Colored Brother?
Yeah, how th'hell you get in here?
He asked the jailer for a night's lodging! (*laughter*)
What you do—get in a scrape?
JOHN HENRY No, I was minding my own business.
JAILBIRDS You hear that, Fellows? He was minding his own business! (*laughter*)
How deep did you cut that guy?
He didn't aim to cut him. His razor slipped!
CREEPER (*pacifying*) Now, cool down. Leave them smart guys talk. Say nothing, they shut up.
JAILBIRDS Did you leave your trade-mark on him, Bo?
What he do—Pull some loaded dice on you?

Natural Man

Maybe he caught him in bed with his gal! (*loud, side-splitting laughter*)

JOHN HENRY   Go ahead, Mister White Folks, laugh! Laugh all you wonts to. Laugh till your bellies ache! Go head, make fun of me! You got everything. Got the world in a jug and the stopper in your hand!

JAILBIRDS   Listen to that possum-eater! Say, Dark Boy, how bout a song? Yeah, sing that one about way down yonder in the corn field. "Who stole the lock on the chicken-house door?"

CREEPER (*restraining* JOHN HENRY)   Cain't you see they just trying to get your goat? Use your head!

JAILBIRD   Come on, Rufus-Rastus, be a good sport, and sing us a good old coon-song!

JOHN HENRY   I say I don't know no songs to sing.

JAILBIRD   Bet he just left the plantation, too!

CREEPER (*being a natural-born diplomat, obliges and plays his guitar and sings*)   My old Missy promise me
   —Raise rukus tonight!
When she die, she set me free
   —Raise rukus tonight!
Well, she live so long, her head got bald
   —Raise rukus tonight!
Thought I never get free at all
   —Raise rukus tonight!
CHORUS
   Oh, come along, Children, come along,
   Whilst the moon is shining bright,
   Get on board, down that river flow,
   Us gonna raise rukus tonight!

JOHN HENRY (*over the music*)   White man's country. White man's world. Big Mister Great-I-Am! Make all the high and mighty laws and rulings. Change everything to suit himself. Black man got to bow and scrape to him, like he was God Almighty Himself. Black man got to go to him with his hat in his hand and ask for the right to live and breathe, sleep and eat, sweat and slave! Got to go to Almighty White Boss for every little thing. Even down when it comes to thinking. Black man got to go to him for that, too. Nothing he say or do what the white man ain't got something to say bout it! (*the* CREEPER *has stopped playing*)

JAILBIRDS   What do you want, Black Boy—a seat in the White House? He wants a government of the blacks, for the blacks, and by the blacks! (*peals of mocking laughter*) Say, George Washington, what would you-all do they made you the President of the United States? He'd have white slaves to wait on the black aristocracy! Congress and the Senate full of greasy, pot-bellied Nigras! Eating hush-puppies, smoking big cheroots, feet propped on the desks! Sign outside the White House door read: "Check your knives and razors at the door!" Why, everybody in the army and the navy would be a general or an admiral! Wonder how it feels to be a nigger? A nigger? Never given it a thought. Who wants to be one anyway? Tell us, Sambo, how it feels to be like you?

JOHN HENRY (*stands before the bars, facing audience*)   You want to know how I feel?

JAILBIRD   Sure, tell us.

JOHN HENRY   Like a giant in a strait jacket!

JAILBIRD   Giant in a strait jacket? That must be a helluva feeling! (*the men all roar with laughter*)

JOHN HENRY   Like a natural man mongst a heap of muscle-bound sissies!

JAILBIRD   How do you get that way, you?

JOHN HENRY   Like a great king without a throne to sit on!

JAILBIRDS   Ha! Ha! Ha! Ha! King without a throne! Ha! Ha! Ha! Ha!

JOHN HENRY   You damned right, a king! Every inch, White Folks, every inch! That's me. King without a throne, but king right on. You may be sitting on the throne, but that don't make you king cause you sit there. Nossir! I built that throne. I built that stone palace you live in. Yes, even down built the roads so you could travel from place to place. And I ain't asking you-all to thank me for what I do. I ain't asking you to be my friend. Aint wishing to eat at the same table with you. Ain't wanting you to put yourself out of the way for me at all, understand? All I ask is that you let me *be*. You can have the swell palace and the golden throne, but don't mess up with my crown! I'm going strut the earth with that crown on my head, till Old Gabriel sounds his trumpet for me to go on up to Glory! And I'm going walk right smack into the Glory Kingdom with that crown still on my head!

JAILBIRDS   Give my regards to Saint Peter!

Boys, how about giving the black king a grand send-off?
Sure, why not? The old razzberries! For the king!—

(*The* JAILBIRDS *boo and hiss, until a Police Guard yells to them:* "*Hey, you mugs, pike down!*")

We're giving the black king a grand send-off! The king is croaked! Long live the king! (*more laughter, booing and hissing*)

JOHN HENRY (*towers above it all*) All right, you punks! Thanks for the send-off! But, that's where you wrong. The king ain't croaked yet. He's still walking the earth, and Old Death ain't laid his cold hands on him yet. He's still walking the earth like a natural man. When they do shove dirt in his face, his spirit's going rise up from the lonesome grave, and walk the earth for him. His spirit's going walk the earth like a natural man. Going walk and walk, till the whole earth is destroyed by fire, like the Good Book say it will on the Day of Judgment. And all your goddamned laws and man-made steam engines and gadgets'll be melted like wax! Then the spirit's going take on his natural flesh again, and wait till the earth cools off. The Almighty's going put a ten-pound hammer in his hand. Tell him, go on back to earth and see what he can do. Start all over again. Hammer out a new earthly kingdom, all his own. Yes, Lord, a solid, natural kingdom that'll last forever! And once more, the natural man's going take his rightful seat on the throne, and rule the earth like a mighty king!

(*Boos, hisses, bedlam. The* JAILER *comes on stage, followed by another white man, the* SHERIFF)

JAILER All right, all right! Damn it, quiet! Raised enough hell for one night! (*the bedlam gradually subsides*)
SHERIFF Open her up, and let's have a look at him.
JAILER O.K., Sheriff... (*unlocks cell. To* JOHN HENRY) Step out... I reckon he oughta do, Sheriff.
SHERIFF (*after a cursory appraisal*) Trouble-maker, ain't he? Uppity? Sassy? Got a heap of spirit?
JAILER I reckon you got a remedy for that, Sheriff.
SHERIFF Yeah. I reckon I has. I like spirit. Gimme something to work on!
JAILER Gonna take him back with you?
SHERIFF Uh, huh.
JAILER Oh, Phil—? (*voice answers*) One to go. Ball-and-chain!

(*the lights dim out*)

Fifth Episode

(SETTING: *a rock quarry. Five convicts are discovered just below the landing in a faint haze of light. Stripped to the waist, their torsos gleam with perspiration, as they go through the animated motion of pounding rocks with their hammers. The "hammer song" is led by a* LEADER *off-stage. The* CONVICTS *supply the "huh," striking the rocks at the same time*)

VOICE OF THE LEADER Swing that hammer—huh
Like a natural man.
Swing that hammer—huh
Like a natural man.
Guard behind you,
Rifle in his hand.

Ball and chain
Won't let me be.
Ball and chain
Won't let me be.
This chain gang, Babe,
Be the death of me.

Daybreak to sundown
My hammer ring.
Daybreak to sundown
My hammer ring.
Body so weary,
Can hardly sing.

If this hammer kill me,
And I dies,
If this hammer kill me,
And I dies,
I'll hant that white boss,
Scratch out his eyes.

White folks got no right
Treat me so cruel.
White folks got no right
Treat me so cruel.
Working me same like
They works a mule.

FIRST CONVICT Not so plague-take-it fast, John Henry!
SECOND The faster you swing that hammer, longer they going keep you here!

THIRD Way you work, warden throw that calendar way!
FIRST That old guard ain't watching nohow.
THIRD He over behind that bush.
FIRST I hope he strains himself!
SECOND I hope he sits on a diamond-back rattler!
THIRD Working a body to death, hot as it is!
FIRST Got nary a drop of human feeling in his veins!
JOHN HENRY Lordy! I didn't have this hammer, I go crazy thinking. Don't do for me to start thinking. Man, I fills up inside like I'm going bust wide open!—Larry, how you feels now, Boy? Is you feel any better?
BOY No, I sick. Right down sick. I feels worse now I ever was.
JOHN HENRY I wishes there was something I could do for you, Larry Boy. Gits my goat to stand by and see you in misery and nothing I can do to help.
BOY Hopes I be all right soon. I can only hold out. I was home, my ma'ud care for me.
SECOND They ought to get that boy to a hospital.
THIRD He ain't been right since they keep him in that sweat-box.
FIRST Three whole days, feed him only bread and water.
JOHN HENRY Rebbish bastards!
SECOND You mark my words. Some day God Almighty going send a cyclone throughout this land!
JOHN HENRY Will he spare us colored folks?
SECOND I ain't talking bout the colored folks.
JOHN HENRY Cain't wait for God!
FIRST I just wish I could organize a whole army!
THIRD White folks git through with you, wouldn't be a black man left!
FIRST Hell! I ain't got but one life nohow. A man ain't nothing but a man!
JOHN HENRY Buddy, you said something! That's my kind of preaching. A man ain't nothing but a man. Ain't they more of us put together then they is guards holding we-all here in slavery, flailing hell out of us when we don't move fast enough to suit them, feeding us swill even down a hog wouldn't want to eat, and driving we-all in the broiling sun, from daybreak to sundown, like we was some dumb ox? A handful of them holding us slaves!
THIRD They has guns and us ain't.
JOHN HENRY Is you afraid to die? Well, I ain't! I be blown to hell before I stays here the rest of my life. You going die anyhow, you stay here. And it won't be dying like a natural man suppose to die.
THIRD Better keep your trap shut, John Henry!
SECOND That old guard hear you, kill you sure!
FIRST Sure break your heart to die and not take a white man with you!
JOHN HENRY Brother, you looking at a man. Lord don't deal me out but one life to live. He give every man just one life. He didn't say or 'tend for you to be a slave. He didn't say for some to rule and the rest be slaves. He meant for every man to be a king. King in his own rights. I got my job to do. The white man got hisn' And I don't give a damn what the white man do. Long as he don't interfere with me, I'm satisfied.
FIRST Me and you both! Just let me be!
JOHN HENRY Black man's easy to get along with, long as folks treat him human. He do his work and never squawk. It's meddling with and mistreating what makes him mean. Cause he talk back and stand up for his rights, Mister Charlie don't like that. You a bad so-and-so when you ask for your rights. Work your fool head off to please him, try to be his friend, Mister Charlie ain't going let you. I'm this way: I ain't going be no door-mat for Mister Charlie to wipe his feet on. Nossir! I prize myself. I ask no favor. I does my work the best I knows how. All I ask is that he treat me honest. Don't cheat me. Don't mess up with my hard-earned money. Just pay me off and lemme go bout my business. Ain't that way you-all think?
FIRST That's what I think!
SECOND Nothing diffunt!
THIRD I don't ask to 'sociate with Mister Charlie.
SECOND Him and his business don't worry me none.
JOHN HENRY And you mean to tell me you willing to stay here and be treated like we is? Sweat blood? Only thanks you receive is a kick in the behind and a rawhide lash across your naked back!

FIRST Nossir, I ain't wishing to stay here!
SECOND Got a wife and youngun waiting for me.
THIRD Damn! I sure like to see old Beale Street!
FIRST Quick! Snap it up! Here come that guard!

VOICE OF LEADER Ball and chain—huh
    Won't let me be.
    Ball and chain—huh
    Won't let me be.
    This old chain-gang
    Be the death of me.

BOY (*delirious*) Oh, Lord! I can't! Lordy! Can't hammer no more!
GUARD (*off-stage. As* CONVICTS *pause*) Hey, up there! You-all git a move on! Swing them hammers!

VOICE OF LEADER Daybreak to sundown—huh
    My hammer ring.
    Daybreak to sundown—huh
    My hammer—

BOY (*gasping*) Mama! Lord, have mercy! Mama!—(*he falls in a dead faint*)
FIRST Oh, my Jesus!
SECOND What happen?
THIRD He fainted!
FIRST Boy ain't well nohow.
SECOND Ain't eat a mouthful in three days.
THIRD Food won't stay on his stomach.
FIRST He spit up blood.
SECOND He got the consumption.
JOHN HENRY (*ministering to the* BOY) Larry Boy—? Where at that water bucket? Wait a second ... No use now. His heart done stop beating ... He ain't breathing.
CONVICTS Dead as a door-knob!
Kicked the bucket!
Long gone from here!
JOHN HENRY Lord Jesus, have mercy on him!
GUARD (*from the landing*) What's wrong with him?
JOHN HENRY Boy took sick and died.
GUARD You're a damned liar! He's stalling. Come on, you there! Get on your feet!
JOHN HENRY I tells you the boy's dead.
GUARD See for myself how dead he is! (*he comes down with lash in one hand, his rifle in the other*)
JOHN HENRY You can't do that!
GUARD You tell me what I can't do?
JOHN HENRY You flog a man's what's dead?
GUARD Stand back!
JOHN HENRY It ain't human. I ain't going let you!
GUARD Stand back! Goddam you!
JOHN HENRY I respects the dead.
GUARD (*throws down his lash, raises his rifle*) So help me, I'll blow your soul to hell!

(JOHN HENRY *wrests the rifle from the* GUARD, *knocking him down, pounds his head with the butt. The lights dim, as he takes the keys from the* GUARD's *belt and frees himself of the ball and chain*)

CONVICTS You kill him!
Stone dead!
Split his head wide open!
Hurry, John Henry! Get way fast as you can!
Hurry! Them other guards is coming this way!
No time to waste. They catch you, they kill you sure!

(*Total darkness. The weird, prolonged blowing of a freight train whistle is heard and the chugging of the locomotive*)

FIRST Head straight for that freight train, Boy!
JOHN HENRY I'm long-gone from here!

(*Train noise mounts, a succession of rifle shots rent the air*)

Sixth Episode

(SETTING: *a camp-meeting. A small band of Negro worshippers are seated on benches facing a crude, make-shift pulpit, from which a portly preacher exhorts them to worship. There are two rows of benches with a narrow aisle between them. The meeting is well under way, as the lights come up, and there is a mood of unrestrained religious fervor as the Congregation, led by the* PREACHER, *sing "Shine On Me"*)

CONGREGATION "Shine on me, Lord, shine on me.
    I want the light from the lighthouse
    To shine on me...."

(*Incidental murmurs and cries of "Praise be the Lord!" "Have mercy, Lord!" "Blessed Savior!" etc., as the old hymn is being sung. Some of the members stand and sway to the rhythm, clapping their hands or patting their feet. As the Congregation relaxes softly into humming, the* PREACHER *speaks out over this, giving to his deliverance a sort of mournful, heart-felt quality*)

PREACHER Open up your troubled hearts to Jesus. Don't wait too long, Sisters and Brothers. Don't wait till you sick and afflicted on your dying-bed to call to Him. For we know not the hour, the time of day, and the night. We knoweth not when Old Death gwine snatch us way. Sometimes he creeps up on the sinner man, and the sinner man ain't expecting him. Overtakes the weary traveler a long ways from home. You working in the field. Whilst you sleep in your bed, lost in slumber. Old Death's a mighty reaper!

CONGREGATION Amen! Do, Jesus! Glory Halleluyuh!

PREACHER And he got no shame. Walks the troubled waters of the sea and the ocean. He visits with the rich and the poor alike. Stretches out his arms and spreads his pestilence and his destruction throughout the land! Amen!

CONGREGATION Amen! Yes, he do! Death's a mighty man!

PREACHER Onliest somebody is gonna hope you is Jesus! Praise His Name! I'm talking about Jesus! Through all your trials and tribulations, through the Valley of the Shadow of Death—

CONGREGATION Yes, Jesus! Walk with me! (*an* OLD WOMAN *rises and starts to sing, the whole Congregation joining in, swaying and intoning*)

> I want Jesus to walk with me.
> I want Jesus to walk with me.
> Whilst I'm on my pilgrim's journey,
> I want Jesus to walk with me.

PREACHER Don't you want Jesus to *talk* with you?

CONGREGATION Oh, do, Jesus! (*a young girl rises, filled with religious fervor, and shouts as she walks up and down the aisle, "Save my soul, Jesus! Don't let me sin no more!" She kneels before the pulpit, her face buried in her hands, and weeps*)

CONGREGATION I want Jesus to talk with me.
I want Jesus to talk with me.
Whilst I'm on my pilgrim's journey,
I want Jesus to talk with me.

PREACHER Don't you want Jesus to *comfort* you?

CONGREGATION I want Jesus to comfort me.
I want Jesus to comfort me.
Whilst I'm on my pilgrim's journey,
I want Jesus to comfort me.

OLD WOMAN (*her voice cracked and full of grief, she gives her "testimony"*) Jesus, have mercy on my boy, wherever he is tonight. I wants you to talk with him, Jesus. He left home, his heart troubled and hurt. Ain't there something you can do to hope him, Jesus? Thank you, Jesus. I'm a lone old woman, and all my days is numbered and short. I knows I wont be here long, Lord. May be I wont never see my boy's face again in this life, Lord, but, wherever he is tonight, wont you go to him and wont you tell him that his old mammy's praying for him? Tell him that his old mammy forgives all he's ever did. Take the grief out of his heart, Jesus. Tell him 'tain't right and Christian to gamble and drink and keep bad company. Tell him that the sinner life ain't the life his old mammy wonts him to lead. Thanks be to the Lord! (*she sits down, her head bowed*)

PREACHER (*over the humming of the Congregation*) Bless your heart, Sister Jones. Bless the hearts of mothers everywhere who got sons that strayed a long ways from home.

CONGREGATION Amen! Amen!

PREACHER That's fallen by the wayside.

CONGREGATION Wayside, Lord!

PREACHER Mothers whose boys is weary travelers long the dark and stormy highways, in the alleys, in the shameful houses of the red-light districts, and, and taking up with scarlet women of the evening!

CONGREGATION Ain't it so? Yea, yea!

PREACHER Bless them lonely sinners whose hearts may be racked with grief of sorrow. And guide them, O Heavenly Father, into the paths of righteousness!

(*Suddenly, there is a flash of lightning, followed by a terrifying clap of thunder. [The thunder and lightning will continue throughout the remainder of this scene, growing in intensity.] The* PREACHER, *to abate the fears of the group, immediately leads them in singing, "Amazing Grace, How Sweet The Sound." The ragged, mud-begrimed figure of* JOHN HENRY *appears at the rear. His appear-*

ance bespeaks of days of hardships encountered while hiding in the swamp, after his escape from the chain-gang. As he walks slowly, strangely up the aisle, the singing ceases abruptly and the faces of the worshippers are taut with dread and wonderment)

PREACHER (*bravely*) Come forward, Brother. Is your heart troubled?

JOHN HENRY Yes, Preacher, my heart is troubled, a heap troubled. I been standing outside listening to your sermon and to what the old lady here say bout her son. So, I made up my mind to come inside. I wasn't aiming to at first. I figgered, maybe, you-all church people wouldn't want me round.

PREACHER You in the house of the Lord, Brother. I don't know as whether I remembers seeing you round here before.

JOHN HENRY No, you ain't never seen me before.

PREACHER My name is Reverend D. K. Valley—Elder Valley, as most folks calls me. (*he shakes hands with* JOHN HENRY, *who carries in the other hand the gun he took from the guard*) ... Glad to have you, Brother— Sorry, you didn't tell me your name?

JOHN HENRY Just call me "Brother", cause who I is ain't nobody's business. (*he addresses his remarks partly to the* PREACHER *and partly to the Congregation*)—I ain't saying I'm a true Christian, and I ain't saying I'm no true sinner-man either. I only know that I'm natural born. I had a mother that birthed me, but, long time ago, fore I gits in trouble, my mother she was laid to rest in the lonesome graveyard, neath the oak trees and the sleeping willows. She's gone on up to Glory. And I been walking the earth all by myself ever since. Ain't no man living or dead I ever mistreated. But I gits in a mess of trouble and they shackled my feet with a ball and chain and took my rights away. But I done my work, till the white guard on the chain gang started messing up with me, and make me mad, then I—I killed him stone dead and upped and run way.

PREACHER (*recoils in terror*) You ain't oughta come here, Brother!

JOHN HENRY Where else could I come to?

PREACHER You liable to git us all in trouble.

CONGREGATION Us cain't help no convict! We's God-fearing people! We all be killed! They burn down our church!

JOHN HENRY Preacher, you understand? I had to come to somebody. I ain't got no friend in the world. Six weeks all by myself in the dismal swamp and not a living soul to talk to, nearbout drive me stracted! Cain't you tell me what to do? Cain't any you-all God-fearing Christians tell me what to do?

PREACHER (*regains his composure, benignly*) Hear me, Brother, hear me. They is two kinds of laws. They's the law of man, and they's the law of God. (*his remarks are punctuated by murmurs of "Amen" from the Congregation*)— Now, we mortal folks is jedged by both them laws. Go on back, I say, go long back to the chain gang and surrender yourself and be jedged by the law of man. Render unto Caesar! And after you done that, you render yourself unto God.

CONGREGATION Preacher right!

JOHN HENRY (*scornfully*) When Caesar git through with me, it be too late for God!

PREACHER The world, my Brother, ain't made for the natural man. God ain't round to protect you no more. God's turnt his back on this sinful world. Washed his hands clean of this abomination. I say, woe unto the natural man! Woe unto the proud and the high-and-mighty! For you is hemmed in by four walls of solid earth and, oh, my Brother, you cain't break through them! Harken unto the Word of the Lamb! Turn the other cheek! Yea! Yea! Praise God. Git humble. Pray. Git meek. Meek as the Lamb. For the Lord say, Blessed is the meek, for they shall inherit the earth and the Kingdom-Come! (*the* PREACHER *is now carried away by his own eloquence, as the Congregation shout "Amens"*)—Pray, Brother! Git down low ... low in the dirt ... Repent ye, saith the Lord!

(*Simultaneously, with a flash of lightning and the clap of thunder,* JOHN HENRY *drops to his knees, as if smitten by an unseen power. Confused, fear-ridden, he makes an effort to pray, shaking his head. The members have gathered round him, singing with great animation. Suddenly,* JOHN HENRY *rises to full height and cries out*)

JOHN HENRY You cain't move me! Let the lightning strike me dead! Oh, Lord, I ain't got nothing ginst your mighty laws and rulings, but I ain't going allow no man-made laws to rule over me!

A WORSHIPPER Man, you stay here, you bring trouble to all us colored folks!

JOHN HENRY I'm leaving.

OLD WOMAN Wait, Son. Where at is you aiming to go?

JOHN HENRY (*with bravado*) I cain't say. All I knows is I'm heading for the crossing and I'm catching the first freight train that comes along. She'll slow down at the crossing and I'll hop her. And I'm going where I can make some hard-earned money and spend it as I please. Enjoy life. That's what I'm going do. Have me some good times. Maybe, I run cross that son of yours where I'm going. I do, I tell him all you say—to pray and walk with Jesus. (*he laughs out loud, a hollow, denigrating laugh*) Why don't you just have me tell him that his old mammy loves the ground he walks on and she ain't caring what he do. Maybe, he ain't bad like way you think. Maybe he's just natural-born like me. Cain't live like you and the preacher want him to. Maybe he cain't bow his head and walk humble . . . You has to let him be. (*to the* PREACHER)—Well, Reverend, before I go, I want to leave you something for the church. This all I got—this here shot-gun. I won't be needing it no more.

(*Freight train whistle blows.* JOHN HENRY *gives the* PREACHER *and the Congregation a knowing look, departs. While the* PREACHER *contemplates the gun, suddenly, someone jumps to his feet, catalyzes the rest to join him in singing*)

CONGREGATION "This train is bound for Glory, this train!
This train is bound for Glory, this train! . . . etc."

(*Black-out*)

Seventh Episode

(SETTING: *a hoboes' camp near the railroad yard. It is close by a railroad siding.* JOHN HENRY *and several hoboes are discovered, gathered around a dying fire*)

FIRST HOBO Four days and we'll be blowing into Key West.

SECOND Going where that chilly wind don't blow!

THIRD That old Cannon Ball sure can fly!

FOURTH Awful cold at night through them mountains!

SECOND Hope we get one them empty banana cars that got a heap of straw inside.

FIRST Saw a great big flock of black birds this morning heading south.

FOURTH And here's one more going do the same!

FIRST South for me in winter. North won't see me till she thaws out.

THIRD Say, Partner—which way you heading?

JOHN HENRY Can't say yet. Don't know where I liable to go.

THIRD You better string along with we-all.

SECOND Go where there's summer whole year round!

JOHN HENRY I'm all twisted and turned round. Cain't seem to make up my mind which way to turn. I been on the move for six months, and still ain't got nowhere.

FIRST Them first six months always the hardest.

SECOND Yeah, you wait till you been at it eight long years!

THIRD This all I done since I left home.

FOURTH They say a freight train whistle scared my mammy whilst she carrying me!

JOHN HENRY All I done for the past six months or so, sleeping in box-cars, riding them rods. Onliest sound I hear is freight train whistle. Gimme the jim-jams listening to that lonesome whistle. Every time she blow, I feels like I ain't got a friend in the world!

FIRST That old whistle used to give me the lonesome blues too.

SECOND Now she sounds like pipe-organ music!

JOHN HENRY Listen, Buddy, your ears ain't heard no real, honest-to-God music, like when you hit the head of a piece of steel with a ten-pound hammer. Ain't no sound in the world carry so much sweetness!

THIRD I never hear tell of a hammer sounding like that!

SECOND Man, you crazy! Ain't never was no music in no hammer!

FIRST I tried steel-driving once—just once, and, boy, she near-bout ruint me!

THIRD I got a fair dose of it on the chain gang in South Carolina.

SECOND Hammer music, shucks! Freight train whistle sounds all right to me.

FOURTH Freight train any day! That what you say, Peg Leg?

THIRD Old Peg Leg here just a natural-born rambler!

SECOND Even down knows how to talk to a freight train!

FOURTH Come on, Peg Leg, show him way you talk to that Cannon Ball when she come round that mountain!

(*The men make the sound of a train engine puffing out steam, a slow chug, then increasing as the train gathers momentum.* PEG LEG *cups his hands to his mouth to produce the mournful wailing of the train whistle far away. He proceeds to make all sorts of variations upon train whistle sounds to the sheer admiration of the others, who break in with* "All aboard for Birmingham!" "We near that crossing just before to get to Atlanta!" "Blowing for that trestle outside Dallas!")

JOHN HENRY (*jittery, jumps to his feet*) Stop it, you guys! Cut it out, you hear me? What you trying to do, drive me stracted? Six months of hearing nothing but that damn noise. Hear them wheels rolling, them box-cars rattling, brakes a-squeaking so to make your flesh crawl. Hearing nothing but them mammy-less noises day and night. In my sleep even. I'm sick and tired of it!—(JOHN HENRY *has been withdrawing towards the tunnel entrance, backing away from the bewildered hoboes, until he is up on the landing*)—I can't stand it no longer! Goddam, I can't stand it!

(*Suddenly, the mouth of the tunnel begins to glow like an open furnace, coloring the entire background a fiery red, as though the mountain were ablaze; concurrently, the foreground darkens, the hoboes vanish.* JOHN HENRY *stalks into the tunnel and out of sight*)

Eighth Episode

(*The action is continuous. The Spectators mill excitedly about the entrance to the tunnel*)

FIRST SPECTATOR The mountain going burn to ashes!

CAPTAIN TOMMY (*addressing the Crowd from the landing*) Stand aside! Let'em through!

(*Several workmen, buckets hoisted above their heads, are pressing through the crowd*)

SECOND SPECTATOR John Henry done hammer till he set the rocks on fire!

CAPTAIN TOMMY Hurry, you-all, with them water buckets. Quick! Get in there!

MEN WITH BUCKETS Yassuh, we's hurrying! Lemme through here!
Gimme room!

SALESMAN (*wringing his hands*) What? This all you can do? Jumping Jehoshaphat! That steam drill cost me a fortune! My life's savings!

CAPTAIN TOMMY Go on, go on, you boys! Get in there and put that fire out! (*the men hurry into the glowing pit and out of sight*)

SALESMAN This contest was all your idea to begin with. Why th'hell you threaten him? He's a human being, same as you and me. And a mighty damn fine human specimen, you ask me!

CAPTAIN TOMMY Well, Dadblabbit, I ain't asking you! You blabbering carpetbagger!

SALESMAN God, what a man! You think you can break his spirit?

CAPTAIN TOMMY Think? I did break his spirit. He was cringing. He pleaded and begged. I twisted him round my little finger, because I'm his master. That's why he beat that steam drill! You've got to make them fear you!

POLLY ANN (*confronts* CAPTAIN TOMMY) Hate you! I hate you, Captain Tommy! I'm here to tell you, you the meanest man that ever live!

CAPTAIN TOMMY You dar talk to me—

POLLY ANN You sick that steam drill on John Henry, done drove him clear out his mind. You even down make him spite the Almighty. You turn him ginst the mountain. You done gone and make him so mad he hammer the rocks till he set them on fire, destroy himself and everything! (*she breaks down and weeps*)

SALESMAN Walters, you've got to get him out of there! I'm warning you, so help me God! If my machine is destroyed, I'll sue you for every damn cent it cost me!

CAPTAIN TOMMY Hard Tack, Britt, Charley, all you boys, get hell in that tunnel and bring John Henry out of there!

HARD TACK Cap'n, we cain't do a thing!

BRITT John Henry too powerful.

CHARLEY And he's angry. John Henry ain't no man to mess with when he's angry.

CAPTAIN TOMMY Talk back to me, you

onery rascals! Go in and get him—or I'll ship every rotten one of you back to the chain gang!

CHARLEY Lord, Cap'n, don't you know John Henry stronger than six of we-all put together?

HARD TACK He like that mountain, them rocks and the steel!

CAPTAIN TOMMY Stop him, do you hear? He's destroying my mountain, he's destroying your jobs, you swine!

(JOHN HENRY *emerges from the tunnel all by himself, worn, haggard, his hammer in his hand. He pauses on the landing, steadying himself, looking down upon the crowd of spectators*)

SPECTATORS Look—there he is!
John Henry!
There John Henry!

POLLY ANN (*she is downstage center*) John Henry—

JOHN HENRY I comes out peaceful.

POLLY ANN You hurt, Honey? Is you powerful hurt?

SALESMAN You boys give me a hand and we'll get him to a doctor. This man's hurt bad.

JOHN HENRY You cain't help me none. Too late. Too late now for me.

SALESMAN We want to help you, John Henry. It isn't too late. There is something we can do for you. Whatever it be, we want to do it. Believe me . . .

JOHN HENRY Brother, you just cain't help a dying man. I seen the handwriting on the wall. My whole life done passed before me in that tunnel. Then I knowed the cold hand of Death was upon me. I gits crying mad and I hammer till I sets them rocks afire. Then I comes to my senses. I gits still and quiet and very peaceful inside. I don't mind a thing, no, not a solitary thing in this world! (*his voice rising lyrical and eloquent*) I'm as free now as the Blueridge Mountain, the Mississippi River, the Tall Lonesome Pine! (*while he is speaking, the stage darkens, until there is only the solitary shaft of light upon the landing where* JOHN HENRY *stands. As he looks out over the heads of the audience, another light frames the face of the* CREEPER, *who is downstage, extreme right. The* CREEPER, *his back to* JOHN HENRY, *is also looking out over the heads of the audience*) They say they got mountains and rocks up there.

CREEPER It's all mountain and rock country.

JOHN HENRY And they building great tunnels right and left.

CREEPER Even under the river-beds!

JOHN HENRY And, say—If any the other boys should ask for me, just tell them the last thing you see of him was his coat-tail flapping in the wind! Tell'em, say, he long-gone from here to drive hell out of steel!

(*The* CREEPER *launches into his song, as* JOHN HENRY, *hammer across his shoulder, symbolically sets out for parts unknown*)

CREEPER (*alone*) O' come along, Boys, and line up the track,
A man ain't nothing but a man.
John Henry, Lord, ain't never coming back.
He died with his hammer in his hand.
He died with his hammer in his hand.
John Henry, Lord, ain't never coming back.
He died with his hammer in his hand!

(*Curtain*)

Willis Richardson (1889–)

The Flight of the Natives — 1927

The Flight of the Natives belongs to two genres: the folk play and the history play. The folk play vogue of the 1920's, which was a part of the Black Renaissance, had as its special interest the so-called "peasant" class of American Negro life. (*see introduction*, Black Folk Plays of the 1920's.) The history play is usually conceived as a specific fictional account based on a generalized historical condition (slavery) or an actual event (the assassination of Malcolm X).

From William Wells Brown to LeRoi Jones, black playwrights have used slavery as a dramatic theme: the passage and the auctions (*The Slave Ship*); the rebellions (*Nat Turner* and *Denmark Vesey*); the slave life and its escapes (*Frederick Douglass* and *The Drinking Gourd*); sometimes the entire slave history (*Liberty Deferred* and *Jerico-Jim-Crow*). Occasionally, slavery is even used satirically (*Plantation*). Three plays in this volume are set in ante-bellum slave days: *The Escape*, *The Drinking Gourd*, and *The Flight of the Natives*.

This play was first performed in Washington, D.C. in 1927 by the Krigwa Players, a group formed by W. E. B. DuBois to promote black plays by black people for black audiences.

Two features of Mr. Richardson's play may be noted: his attempt to exorcise the traditional image of the contented slave, and his use of the group protagonist. Given the severe institutional strictures of slavery, where rebellious individuals were closely watched and eliminated, the multiple protagonist that Mr. Richardson creates in this play may produce a more accurate picture than if he had presented one central hero.

The Flight of the Natives

CAST OF CHARACTERS

MOSE, *a slave*
PET, *his wife*
JUDE, *an informer*
TOM, *a slave*
SALLIE, *his wife*
LUKE, *another slave,—a mulatto, evidently an illegitimate son*
MONK, *a slave lasher*
JOHN, *the white slave owner*

SCENE   *A South Carolina slave cabin.*

TIME, *1860. A spring afternoon, towards sunset.*

(*We see the interior of a crude candlelighted hut. There is no floor save the bare ground and no ceiling save the rough boards, shingles and rafters of the roof itself. At the right is a door which leads outside and above this against the same wall are bunks such as are used by steerage passengers. In the rear wall are two windows below which are two rough benches. On the left side against the wall are bunks similar to those on the right. At the center of the rear wall exactly between the two windows hangs an old quilt on a cord. The cord leads forward and fastens to one of the rafters so that when the quilt is pulled forward on it the hut is temporarily divided into two compartments, the one on the right for men and the other for women. It is the early part of the night and on each window-sill is a lighted candle. The quilt is drawn partly forward on the cord.* JUDE, *a small, narrow-shouldered man of thirty-five, is seated on the end of the men's bench with his elbows on his knees and his head in his hands;* TOM, *another man, is lying in a bunk; while* LUKE *is standing by the wall with the quilt pulled slightly aside at the rear end so that he can look through the window.* PET, MOSE's *wife, is sitting on her bench sewing, and* SALLIE. TOM's *wife, is lying in a bunk*)

SALLIE (*looking at* LUKE)   What you watchin', Luke?
LUKE   Ah'm watchin' the river and wishin' y'awl wuz menfolks so's we could all make way from heah, same's Slim.
SALLIE   Ah hope to God Slim gets away, but Ah ain't thinkin' there's much chance.
PET   There ought to be much chance. He's gone.
SALLIE   Ah know he's gone, but dere's Marse an' his hound dawgs right on his heels.
PET   Slim went fo' daybreak—and lessen de Lawd's ag'in him, I reckon Marse John nevah ketch up wid him.
SALLIE   He mought have a chance, but ain't no man can outrun dogs and horses.
PET   Who knows they went the right way? Slim left in de dark and nobody ain't seen him go.
SALLIE (*knowingly*)   Yes, somebody did see him go. Ah seen him go. Ah know which a-way he went and Ah know somebody else that knows which a-way he went.
PET   Who den?
SALLIE   Somebody done told Marse John the way he went. Ah seen him. (*at this* JUDE *raises his head and listens*)
PET (*interested*)   Who told on Slim?
SALLIE   It wasn't nobody but Jude. Jude, that they lets come tuh the big house. Jude, that they lets eat the scraps off'n the table in the big house.
JUDE (*going quickly to the front end of the curtain*)   You talkin' about me, Sallie?
SALLIE   You the only one what's named Jude around here, ain't you? Ah reckon your mammy named you Jude 'cause she knowed you'd be a 'trayer.
JUDE   You stan' there an' tell me Ah told Marse John de way Slim went?
SALLIE   Yes, I say you tole him!
JUDE   Ah didn't!
SALLIE   You did! Ah heered you! An' Ah seen you with ma own eyes!

JUDE It ain't true!

TOM (*who has risen in his bunk*) 'Tis true! If Sallie says it's de truf, it's de truf!

JUDE (*more humbly*) Ah didn't tell him, Tom! Ah swear to de Lawd Ah didn't!

TOM Ain't no use o' swearin' to a lie! You tole it and if Mose finds out you tattled on Slim he's goin' to beat the life out o' you!

LUKE (*who has been staring at* JUDE *ever since* SALLIE *accused him*) He'll half kill you, niggah, and he ought to!

JUDE Mose ain't goin' to tech me! Marse John done said if Mose put his hands on me he'll sell him down the river.

PET (*indignantly*) So you been talkin' about Mose too, is you? You keep your mouth off Mose!

JUDE Ah ain't goin' to say nothin' about him if he don't do nothin' to me.

SALLIE If Slim gets away and dey don't catch him Ah won't say nothin'; but sho's you bawn if Slim gets caught Ah'm goin' to tell Mose on you!

TOM Slim an' Mose wuz bosom friends and Mose was moughty glad when Slim got away. Now, if Slim gets caught 'count o' you, Mose'll half kill yuh.

PET Don't you-all say nothin' to Mose, neither one of yuh. Ah don't want Mose to put his hands on Jude, 'cause they might sell Mose down the river sho 'nough, and if they done that Ah'd die. Ah 'clare to the Lawd, Ah'd die.

LUKE We mought not tel Mose and Mose mought not do nothin' to you; but Ah mought mahself. You can't tattle on none of us and get away with it.

SALLIE You can't beat him up half as much as Mose can, Luke; and Mose is the one Ah'm goin' to tell if Slim gets caught.

PET I done tole you, Sallie; don't you do it!

SALLIE You reckon we'd let that big-house Judas 'tray Slim, and do nothin' to him?

PET But Mose is ma husband! He ain't yo' husband, an' Ah don't want ma husband sold away from me, does I?

JUDE You-all don't like me! Ah know you don't; you just want to get me in trouble!

SALLIE You get yourself in trouble! If you had 'a' kept your tongue still in yo' mouth this never would 'a' happened. They never would 'a' found out the way Slim went!

JUDE Ah doan' care what you-all likes, but the one that lays his hands on me'll be sold down the river. Marse done said so.

LUKE Ah'd like to know what good that'll do you after you get busted to pieces.

JUDE It might not do me much good, you white-man's trash, but it'll do one of you-all a lot o' harm. (LUKE *sneers at him to hide his discomfort*)

SALLIE All Ah hope is they don't catch Slim.

PET Ah hope they don't neither.

TOM (*to* JUDE) All Ah've got to say,—ef you cares fo' yo' hide, you bettah pray dey don't ketch Slim. (*just then* MOSE, *a large, broad-shouldered man of thirty, enters.* PET *at once goes to him.* JUDE *slinks back to his seat*)

TOM (*after* MOSE *closes the door*) What's news, Mose?

MOSE Marse is back and back swearin'. Slim must 'a' made it.

PET Ah hope the Lord he's sho nuff gone lak de chillen ub Isreel.

MOSE Lawd a-mussy, Ah hopes so. (*he goes on* PET's *side and sits on the bench with her*)

TOM Haven't heerd de hound dawgs yet. Whah's dey at?

MOSE Ain't back yit. Dey's on de udder side wid Bark's men.

PET (*hopefully*) Slim ought to be miles and miles away from hyah by now, oughtn't he, Mose?

MOSE Yes, he ought to be out o' reach, way out o' reach. I reckon he's ketchin' his breath by now. Ah reckon there ain't nothin' in the whole world that's better'n bein' free.

PET Ah reckon not. Just like heaven.

LUKE (*going towards the door*) Must be a moughty fine thing to be out wha you kin stretch yo' ahms and laigs and breathe the air deep, and you know you ain't no mo' slave. Ah'm goin' out here and see how they're talkin'. (*he goes out*)

MOSE Ah'd give ten years o' ma life if Ah could live ten years a free man.

TOM Ah'm a common dog if Ah wouldn't give the rest o' ma life for five years free.

MOSE Sometimes Ah reckon Ah'd jus' like to break loose and make a dash for it. If it wasn't for Pet Ah'd 'a' done it long ago.

PET Ah'd be willin' to go with you, Mose. Ah'd be willin' to go with you to the end o' time.

MOSE Ah know you would, but the chances

The Flight of the Natives

is too big. You couldn't never swim the river in no kind o' time, and then you mought get shot.

PET When you talk like that Ah feel like Ah'm a millstone 'round yo' neck.

MOSE You mustn't think that. If it hadn't 'a' been for you Ah'd 'a' been dead long ago. Ah take a lot o' things every day Ah wouldn't take if it don't be fo' you.

SALLIE Mose, what you reckon ud happen if Slim got caught?

MOSE It ud be a mighty bad thing, Sallie. There ain't no tellin' what they wouldn't do to him.

TOM You think he's got a good chance, sho' nuff?

MOSE Bes' he's evah had. He's done gone over twelve hours and he's a powerful good swimmer and knows the woods like a fox. Ah'm thinkin' it won't be long before Slim'll be real free and out o' danger and brushin' elbows with men.

TOM Brushin' elbows with men—how Ah'd love dat. (*here* LUKE *enters hurriedly and speaks with great excitement*)

LUKE Mose! Mose! For God's sake!

MOSE (*leaping up*) What?

LUKE They done got Slim!

MOSE Got Slim! How you know?

LUKE That's what dey's sayin' out there! (JUDE *starts hastily towards the door but* LUKE *blocks him*)

LUKE No, you don't! You don't go nowhere, you dirty rat!

MOSE What's the matter 'tween you-all?

SALLIE He's the one that tole on Slim! He's done tole Marse John de way Slim went!

MOSE You-all mean to say he done that!

SALLIE Yes, he done it! Ah seen him! Ah heard him!

MOSE (*catching* JUDE *by the collar of his shirt*) You tole on Slim, did you?

JUDE (*frightened*) Ah didn't tattle on him! Ah didn't!

MOSE I reckon you did! Ah can see it in your lyin' eyes! Slim was mah friend and you done tole on him and now he's caught! Ah'll break your neck! (*as he draws back his fist to strike* JUDE, PET *runs to him*)

PET (*excitedly*) Don't hit him, Mose! Don't do it! He'll get you sent down the river! What'll become o' me if they sell you down the river? For God's sake, Mose, don't hit him! (MONK, *a short, ugly negro, enters with a whip in his hand*)

MONK Marse John wants Jude.

PET Let him go, Mose! Let him go! Oh, it's the best to let him go! (MOSE *finally relinquishes* JUDE, *who hurries out where there is a great commotion*)

MOSE (*sitting on the bench hopelessly*) They got him! They got Slim and Jude's the cause of it! Jude better look out for me when dis done blowed over!

PET Don't you put your big hands on Jude, Mose; he's moughty dangerous!

SALLIE Somebody ought to put de cat-er-nine-tails on him, dat's waht.

PET (*to* SALLIE) You doan' want Mose sold down the river, does you? Well den, take it quiet.

SALLIE The master wouldn't never sell Mose. He's too good a worker 'round here.

PET You don't know. Marse does mos' anything when he's in temper.

MOSE (*as the commotion outside continues*) Lemme see what's goin' on out here. (*he goes to the door and opens it just a little*) The dogs! They're tyin' him to a tree and Monk's goin' to lash him!

PET Sho bad 'nuff, lashes on your bare back, but it's better'n bein' sold down the river.

MOSE No real man'd let hisself be tied to a tree and beat till the blood runs out o' him! (*suddenly becomes infuriated*) Let me out o' yeah! (LUKE *and* TOM *hold him back. Then comes the sound of* SLIM *being lashed. The lashing is mingled with* SLIM's *moans; each time he is struck every person in the room shudders. Finally when the lashing is over there is a sigh of relief from everyone*)

SALLIE Lord, Ah'm glad it's over. Slim must be almost dead.

MOSE (*with determination*) And Jude'll be almost dead when Ah get ma hands on him!

PET Don't you lay your hands on Jude, Mose! They'll do you the same way they just done Slim!

MOSE Ain't no man goin' to whup me! (*just then the door is thrown open suddenly and* JOHN, *the slave owner, enters with the whip in his hand. He is followed by* MONK *and* JUDE)

JOHN (*to all save* MOSE *and* PET) You-all get out o' here! (*to* MOSE *after they have gone*) Mose, Ah hear you been sympathizin' with

Slim! And Ah hear you laid your hands on Jude for tellin' me the way Slim went!

MOSE   Slim was ma friend.

JOHN (*scornfully*)   Friend! What you doin' havin' a friend? You belong to me and Slim belongs to me and Jude belongs to me! All of you supposed to look out for what's mine and you ain't supposed to be glad when Ah lose it! You been a good worker, but for what you done tonight you goin' to be lashed just like Slim was!

MOSE (*in a determined tone*)   Ah ain't never been lashed! Ain't no man goin' to lash me!

JOHN   They ain't, ain't they? (*with a motion towards the door*) Come on out o' here!

MOSE (*not moving*)   Ain't nobody goin' to lash me!

JOHN (*handing the whip to* MONK)   If you won't come out you'll be lashed right here! Lash him, Monk! Give him the same you just gave Slim!

MONK (*afraid of the task*)   Ma arm's almost dead from lashin' Slim, Master John.

JOHN (*handing the whip to* JUDE)   You lash him, Jude! You the one to lash him anyhow! He laid his hands on you! After you get through with him maybe he won't be so anxious to lay his hands on you next time!

JUDE (*whiningly*)   Don't make me do it, Master John; Ah'm scared of him! He'd kill me soon as he got me by maself.

JOHN (*raging*)   All of you scared of him? Give me that whip, Ah'll lash him! (*taking the whip he starts towards* MOSE, *but at the same time* MOSE *starts towards him and he stops. He knows that a man as big and strong as* MOSE *is dangerous to strike under any circumstances*)

JOHN   You threaten me!

MOSE   Ain't no man ever whipped me! Ah always done ma work and took a lot o' things Ah didn't want to take, but ain't no man goin' to whip me!

JOHN   Ah'll do worse'n whip you! Slim's just been whipped and he's goin' to be sold down the river in the mornin'! You won't be whipped, but you'll be sold down the river in the mornin' along with Slim! And Pet'll stay here on the plantation! (MOSE *shows no emotion save a slight shudder, but* PET *flies past him and falls on her knees before* JOHN)

PET   Massa John! Massa John! For God's sake don't sell Mose away from me! He's good! He don't mean nobody no harm! Please don't sell him away from me!

JOHN   Mose'll be sold down the river in the mornin' and you'll stay here! (*with this he goes out followed by* MONK *and* JUDE)

MOSE (*lifting* PET *from the ground*)   That's all right, Pet; don't worry. De Lawd'll git us out o' dis somehow.

PET (*fearfully*)   But goin' down the river! Don't you know what dat'll mean? They'll kill you! They'll beat you to death!

MOSE (*taking her over to the bench*)   Ah ain't goin' down no river.

PET   What you goin' to do? They'll make you go! They'll tie you and take you!

MOSE   Ah might start out from here, but Ah ain't goin' down no river.

PET   What you goin' to do?

MOSE   After dey gets started good, Ah'm goin' to jump in the river and swim for it.

PET   But they'll shoot you! They'll shoot you like a dog!

MOSE   Ah'll take the chance. If they shoot me Ah'll be gone to Glory, but if they miss me Ah'll be gone north for freedom. Freedom is wuth it, ain't it?

PET   Ah reckon it is; but what'll 'come o' me? What'll 'come o' me without you?

MOSE—Ah hear they're talkin' about war in the north—talkin' about war and whisperin' about freedom. If the war comes and the freedom comes Ah'm comin' back and get you, Pet. And if freedom don't come Ah'm comin' back and get you anyhow. Ah'll have a taste o' freedom then and Ah'll take you somehow or 'nuther.

PET (*hopefully*)   Will you, Mose? Will you come back after me?

MOSE   Ah promise Ah will, Pet; Ah promise to God Ah will.

PET (*putting her arm around his neck*)   Ah'll wait for you, then; Ah'll wait for you till Ah die. (LUKE *enters followed by* TOM *and* SALLIE)

LUKE (*after* TOM *closes the door*)   What did they do, Mose? What did they say?

MOSE   They didn't do nothin' to me.

PET (*almost in tears*)   But Marse John said he was goin' to sell Mose and Slim down the river in the mornin'.

SALLIE (*hardly able to believe it*)   Sell Mose down the river?

PET (*angrily to* SALLIE)   Yes, they goin' to sell

him! Goin' to sell 'em both! Ah told you not to make Mose lay his hands on Jude!

TOM Is that what they goin' to sell Mose for?

MOSE No, it's cause Ah wouldn't stand up and let 'em whup me. Wouldn't Ah be a big ninny to stand up and let any man whup me? Ain't no man livin' goin' to whup me!

LUKE But they'll do worse 'n whup you down the river, Mose.

MOSE Ah ain't goin' down no river!

TOM What you goin' to do?

MOSE Goin' to make a break for it!

LUKE (*shaking his head doubtfully*) I dunno, Mose, as yuh could make it, but Gawd help yuh. (*in a sudden mood*) The Lawd help us all, fo' we needs deliv'rance.

PET Amen!—But what we gwine to do wid'out Mose?

LUKE We-all better go 'long wif Mose whichever way he's gwine; an' it don't much matteh. 'Sposin' we all made a breakaway! (*they stand aghast*) Yassuh, I mean it—ain't crazy, neither. (*they huddle round about him*) Ah got a plan, I has. (*he ponders and then whispers*)

TOM These women can't swim no river.

LUKE An' ain't goin' to—We's takin' the boat.

MOSE What! What yer sayin'?

LUKE I keep a' tellin' yuh, the boat.

MOSE D'yuh think we ought make it that a-way?

TOM We mought make it like a' that!

MOSE (*shaking his head and changing his tone at once*) No, we cain't make it nowhere like that. Fust thing, Jude'll be watchin' like a hawk to-night, an' we jes' cain't make it together.

TOM (*pressing his point*) Jes' wait a minute, Mose! Le's listen to Luke,—what he says 'bout it.

PET Ah'm willin' to try anything, ef it's being wif' Mose. Ah reckon Ah can swim de river—

SALLIE (*impatiently*) Let the men talk, Pet; let the men talk!

LUKE Jude's got to go ter the woodhouse shortly, ain't he? Well, he ain't comin' out to tell no tales on nobody. Mose kin sneak in behind him and fix him fo' sure. (*turning to* MOSE) An' be sho' an' lock de woodhouse door, Mose—de keys is allus in Jude's back pocket. You heah dat, Mose? Now that's ou'ah onliest chance!

MOSE (*elated*) Sho is—an Ah'm perticlar glad to go.

TOM (*detaining him*) No, Mose, you'd ruin it. Time Jude set his eyes on you he'd holler murder and everybody on the plantation ud be comin' round here. Let Luke do it.

LUKE Ain't likin' to go, mahself—but Mose sho' would spile it. (*after a minute*) Ah'm a-goin'. An'—(*hesitates*) Ah got a plan too. Dat's all right 'bout Mose bein' the stronges' man on the place, but—(*pointing to his forehead with his index finger*) folks, yo' jes' got ter use this sometimes.

MOSE (*grumpily*) Aw, go on den, an' hurry up.

TOM (*after cracking the door stealthily and peeping out*) Da' Jude now. Mought a' been list'nin'. No. Ah reckon he goin' to the woodhouse now. (*pause*) He be! (LUKE *goes out stealthily but with precision*)

TOM What we gwine do now?

MOSE (*rising to a sense of power*) Dat talkin', Luke! Ah got an ideah mahself! Got it clear as a whistle!

TOM What?

MOSE Luke an' me'll go steal out and hide fus', an' then you go tell Marse John we done run away—an' dat Sallie knows de way we went.

SALLIE (*surprised*) Me?

MOSE Yes, can you lie?

SALLIE Lie? Ah can do worse'n lie for a chance to get free!

MOSE When Marse John comes to you to tell him the way we went you put him off an' tell him wrong—yah hear?

SALLIE Ah won't never tell him!

MOSE Yuh got to tell him sumthin'. Tell him we took a boat and said we was goin' up the river and cross at Moseby's Landin' and goin' north from there.

SALLIE But you ain't goin' that a-way?

MOSE No, we all goin' together and we goin' a different way.

TOM Which-a-way.

MOSE When they take the dogs and the rowboats and go up the river lookin' for us on the other side, we'll take the flatboat and go south—(*proudly*) Now,—that Luke think he know so much!

TOM Go south!

MOSE Yes, we'll go down the river a mile or two and get out on this side and walk all around the plantation, then beat it north like the devil! That'll keep the dogs off our trail! We'll have the river between them and us.

TOM By daybreak we ought to be a long ways off, oughtn't we?

MOSE A long ways off.

TOM Ah wonder how Luke's makin' out.

SALLIE Ah hope to the Lord he makes out all right. (TOM *cracks the door and peeps out*)

PET If we can get away and get free it'll be just like goin' to heaven.

TOM (*suddenly*) Here he comes! Here comes Luke!

SALLIE Is he runnin'?

TOM No, and he don't want to be runnin'. Somebody mought notice him, moughtn't they?

PET What about Slim?

MOSE Po' Slim. We'll have tuh look after Slim! but he cain't travel none. (LUKE *enters and closes the door quickly*)

LUKE Ah got him! Got him good, gagged and tied! An' I found Slim in de woodhouse.

MOSE Sho' nuff! Po' Slim—we cain't hardly make it,—but Ah don't see how he can. (*pulling himself together quickly*) Now, you got to do your part, Sallie. Come on, Luke, we'll go hide! Ah'll tell you mo' 'bout it while we'se hidin'! Tom, you go and tell 'em we got away! (MOSE *and* LUKE *hurry out*.)

TOM (*earnestly*) Sallie, if you ever lied in your life, lie this time!

SALLIE Ah'll lie, all right. I 'clar I will.

TOM All right, Ah'm goin'. (*he hurries out*)

SALLIE Everything generally happens to a woman, Pet; but this is goin' to be somethin' that ain't never happened to us before in our life.

PET Ah know it ain't. They can say sickness is hard and bearin' children is hard; but ain't nothin' in the whole world as hard as livin' in slavery.

SALLIE 'Deed it ain't. If Ah can only lie right and make the master believe what Ah'm sayin' Ah reckon Ah'll be doin' ma part.

PET You will be doin' your part. Ah wish there was somethin' Ah could do.

SALLIE You can do somethin'. Get in the bunk and make believe you're 'sleep and Ah'll do the same thing; cause the master'll be here in a minute ravin' like a thunderstorm.

PET (*getting into the bunk*) If things work out all right it won't be long before we'll be able to stop sayin' "Marsa," sho' 'nuff.

SALLIE (*getting into another bunk*) I 'clar Ah'll be glad of it. (*they hear the noise of running feet*) Shet up. Here they come, Ah can hear 'em comin'! (*presently the door is thrown open suddenly and* JOHN *enters followed by* TOM)

JOHN (*to those outside*) You-all wait out there! Shut that door, Tom! (*looking around*) Where's Sallie?

TOM In the bunk, Ah reckon.

JOHN (*sharply*) Sallie!

SALLIE (*raising up*) Seh?

JOHN Come here! (SALLIE *gets out of the bunk and goes to him*) Where's Mose and Luke?

SALLIE (*in trembling tones*) Ah don't know, seh.

JOHN (*angrily*) Yes, you do know! Stop lyin'! You do know! Tom just told me you did!

SALLIE Ah don't know where they went, Marse John; 'deed Ah don't.

JOHN (*turning to* TOM) Tom, didn't you just tell me she knowed where they went?

TOM Yes, seh.

JOHN (*turning to* SALLIE *again*) Do you want to be sold down the river in the mornin'?

SALLIE (*pleading*) No, seh; for God's sake, Marse John, don't sell me down the river! Ah don't want to be sold down no river!

JOHN Which a-way did they go?

SALLIE Ah promised 'em not to tell.

JOHN Either you tell me the way they went or you'll be goin' down the river yo'self in the mornin'!

SALLIE They said— (*she hesitates*)

JOHN (*impatiently*) They said what? Hurry up!

SALLIE They said they was goin' to take a boat and go up the river and cross at Moseby's Landin', and goin' north from there.

JOHN If Ah gets ma hands on 'em they'll wish they wuz north, I'll tell ye! (*he hurries out*)

SALLIE (*to* TOM) Where's Mose? Where's Luke?

TOM (*going to the window*) Wait a minute, can't yah! Give 'em time to get out on the river! Mose and Luke's close by watchin' 'em, ain't dey?

SALLIE Is they goin'?

TOM Yes, dey's goin' down to the boats now.

SALLIE All of 'em?

TOM Yes, and takin' the dogs and guns. You-all better get some things together. But what we goin' tuh do 'bout po' Slim? (*the two women hustle about getting together the things they want to carry*)

TOM (*from the window*) Now, they're off! Mose and Luke ought to be runnin' in pretty soon!

SALLIE Tom, is you glad?

TOM Glad! You wait till Ah get away from here, Ah'll show you how glad Ah am!

SALLIE Pet, is you glad? Ah ain't heard you say a word in Ah don't know when!

PET Glad! Sallie, Ah'm jes' too scared ter talk! (*she cowers as* MOSE *enters*)

MOSE You folkses ready?

TOM Yes, Mose. Wha's Luke?

MOSE I knows wha' Slim is but I done los' Luke. He's a kind a' onedependable niggah, anyhow.

PET Now, Mose, don't you talk 'gainst Luke. He fixed Jude, didn't he?

MOSE Yas, Ah reckon so—but what's he doin' stayin' so long out dere? We got t' be gettin' away. Doubt's we get fuh anyway.

(*After several minutes of silent tension in the cabin, the door opens and a lank figure dressed in planter's costume, with a broad-brim hat well down over his eyes, enters. They all cower, but* SALLIE *shrieks. The man springs forward and stops her mouth with his palm, and discloses himself. It is* LUKE)

SALLIE Oh, Gawd, I thought you was Massa John or someone! What you doin'—

LUKE (*interrupting as they stand out in amazement*) Now folks, 'membah! You-alls my niggahs when we get away from heah. You understan'? (*they gradually come out of their stupefaction as the idea dawns on them*) An' you-all's—(*they begin to chorus "Yassuhs" in the intervals of his speech*) you-all's jes' been purchus', understand that?

ALL (*except* MOSE, *who turns sceptically*) Yassuh, Yassuh!

LUKE An' we-all had to turn off de road after Slim, 'cause he run away—an' yo' helpin' me back with him. (*grandiosely and making an effort to talk correctly*) You-all understand that?

SALLIE Yassuh! An', please yo', what shill we call yuh?

LUKE Marse John, of co'se! Ain't dese yeah Mars John's? (*pointing to the clothes*) I done took Jude's keys. (*drawing himself up proudly*) Ah told yo' I had plans. Does Ah look de part? (*they all draw close to scrutinize him.* MOSE *surveys him suspiciously and spreads* LUKE'*s tie to hide his lack of a shirt*)

SALLIE Lawd a' mussy, you sho' does look like quality!—I hopes we makes it.

MOSE Well, we'se got to try anyhow. (*to the women*) Don't you stan' there lookin' crazy like, come on! Come on, Ah tell yuh, ef you-all wants to be free. Ah'm not 'pendin' so much on Luke's foolin's, Ah'm goin' ta run. Ah am.

(LUKE *with a commanding gesture marshals them all out of the door and closes it. Curtain*)

7

Social Protest of the 1940's

**Richard Wright   Paul Green   Stanley Richards
Abram Hill**

In the early 1940's, the War Effort included such diverse elements as salvaging tin foil, conducting air raid drills, buying War Savings Stamps, working double shifts, rationing sugar, and practicing "racial tolerance".

"Racial tolerance," the government stressed, was necessary for the War Effort, for a strong America. On the other hand, Afro-Americans were expected to tolerate a segregated Armed Services, nonemployment in war industries, and continued discrimination in housing and education. Black leaders began to mobilize. A. Philip Randolph, president of the Brotherhood of Sleeping Car Porters, organized 50,000 people for a march on Washington scheduled for June 30, 1941, to protest directly to Congress and the President. On June 25, President Roosevelt, unable to call off the march, signed Executive Order 8802. This order set up the Fair Employment Practices Commission, aimed at ending discrimination in government employment and in industries with government contracts. But the failure to actually remedy the black grievances is evidenced in rebellions around the nation particularly in Harlem and Detroit, in 1943.

Poet Witter Bynner's verse perhaps caught the attitude:

> On a train in Texas German prisoners eat
> With white American soldiers, seat by seat,
> While black American soldiers sit apart—
> The White men eating meat, the black men Heart.

In the 1940's the motion picture industry rallied to the War Effort and released a steady flow of propaganda films depicting white heros defeating "yellow-bellied Japs" and "dirty Krauts." The black soldier, when not ignored, was used for comic relief or as a song and dance man to entertain the troops. Hollywood proved that it could mobilize the attitudes of a nation; yet it did nothing to better the lot of black soldiers or to improve race relations in general.

The theater did little better than the films. The socially relevant theater of the 1930's went, like Lucky Strike green, off to war. Actors entertained the troops; playwrights wrote patriotic scenarios and escape-fantasies. White writers continued to exploit Negro characters in *Carmen Jones* and *Cabin in the Sky*. Others substituted suffering Negroes for exotic Negroes in condescending plays like *Lost in the Stars*,

The Respectful Prostitute, and *South Pacific*. A few dramatists assayed changes of attitude. *Deep are the Roots* showed a black veteran returning home to the South, but not to his "place." *Finian's Rainbow* used satire to tickle the problem.

Afro-Americans sought ways to promote their own theatres. The American Negro Theater (see introduction to *Walk Hard*) and The Negro Playwrights Company (see introduction to *Big White Fog*) were formed. Only two plays by black playwrights were produced on Broadway in the 1940's: Theodore Ward's *Our Lan'* (1947) and Richard Wright's *Native Son* (1941). Paul Robeson opened on Broadway in *Othello* (1943); his performance, heralded as brilliant, set a record of 296 performances. Yet a few years later the same Paul Robeson and his concert audience were assaulted with rocks and bottles by a racist crowd at Peekskill, New York, while State Police stood by and watched.

By the end of the decade, the slogan "racial tolerance" had been dropped. With President Truman's order to end segregation in the armed services, "integration" became the key word. *Native Son* was written before the war; *District of Columbia* was written during the war; *Walk Hard* was written after the war—but all three take an attitude that is pre-integration.

Richard Wright (1908–1960) and Paul Green (1894–   )

Native Son   1941

Native Son is at once contemporary and pertinent, and frozen in 1940. The injustices that sent Bigger Thomas to the electric chair are the same ones that murdered Fred Hampton in 1969. Racism in Chicago remains, but the black response to it has changed.

In *Native Son*, the white defense lawyer, Mr. Max, points to the painting of Thomas Jefferson behind the judge and says: "There, under that flag, is the likeness of one of our forefathers—one of the men who came to these strange shores hundreds of years ago in search of freedom." Compare this oratorical device with Bobby Seale's statement to Judge Hoffman in Federal Court, Chicago, 1969: "You have George Washington and Benjamin Franklin in a picture behind you, and they were slave owners. They owned slaves. You are acting in the same manner, denying me my constitutional rights."

Bobby Seale speaks out directly. He does not buy the myth of American forefathers landing on Plymouth Rock with freedom and justice for all. Bigger Thomas does not speak for himself; he is a tongueless creature. Part of his crime is being inarticulate. He cannot express political consciousness. Bigger's lawyer traces the young man's flight from Mississippi (much like Richard Wright's) to the North. It is an old story, told in many plays—in *Rachel*, in *Don't You Want To Be Free?* in *'Cruiter*. The migrant arrives to find that he has escaped nothing—in *Job Hunters*, in *Big White Fog*.

The story is continued in the next generation. The Thomas family becomes the Younger family of *Raisin in the Sun*. They still live on Chicago's South Side. Walter, like Bigger, is unemployed; he cannot be head of the house. His mother, like Bigger's, is in charge. Walter, like Bigger, is sometimes a chauffeur to a rich white. The difference lies in a generation—1939 and 1959. In 1959 Walter Younger *may* "join" America. (Lorraine Hansberry questioned the value of integrating into a house that is burning down.) Bigger Thomas is another generation—integration was never a question for him.

America gave birth to Bigger, her native son, in the late nineteenth century. The Brute Negro, as Sterling Brown points out in his famous essay, "Negro Characters as Seen by White Authors," (*Journal of Negro Education*, 1933), was a white man's fictional creation, a black beast given to rape, pillage, and murder. The prime characteristic of this white man's monster was hatred—hatred for whites, for his community, even for himself. No good could come from him. No matter how many police were fielded against him, he would appear on the lawns, in the schools, in the banks, and in the bedrooms of white America to confront his creator. The genius of Richard Wright was to take this monster and present him for what he was—a creation of the white world.

The novel, *Native Son*, appeared in 1940. Paul Green, a white dramatist, was contacted to work on a stage adaptation. He and Richard Wright spent one month together in Chapel Hill writing the play. Aside from the inevitable pruning to condense the story to two hours for the stage, the character of Bigger was softened and made more sympathetic.

Native Son opened twice on Broadway, the first time on March 24, 1941. This Mercury Theater production directed by Orson Welles and starring Canada Lee ran ninety-seven performances. After touring major U. S. cities, *Native Son* returned to open again, October 23, 1942—this time to run eighty-four performances. Canada Lee in the role of Bigger Thomas was unanimously praised. Nearly everything else in the production was controversial. Was the play as powerful as the novel? Was the script merely a vehicle for Communist propaganda? Had Orson Welles gimmicked the production and sensationalized the story? Was the audience let off the hook or accused of complicity in the murder of Bigger Thomas?

In 1969, Mr. Green revised *Native Son*, bringing the story into a 1960's black power context. The version published here is the original.

Native Son

CAST OF CHARACTERS

BIGGER THOMAS, *Negro youth about twenty or twenty-one years old*
HANNAH THOMAS, *his mother, fifty-five*
VERA THOMAS, *his sister, sixteen*
BUDDY THOMAS, *his brother, twelve*
CLARA MEARS, *his sweetheart, twenty*
JACK HENSON
"G. H." RANKIN   } *cronies of* BIGGER *and about his age*
GUS MITCHELL
ERNIE JONES, *a cafe and night club owner*
HENRY G. DALTON, *a capitalist, about fifty-five*
ELLEN DALTON, *his wife, about fifty*
MARY DALTON, *their daughter, twenty-two or three*
PEGGY MACAULIFE, *the* DALTON *cook and maid, forty*
JAN ERLONE, *a labor leader, twenty-eight*
JEFF BRITTEN, *a private detective and local politician, forty-five*
DAVID A. BUCKLEY, *state's attorney, forty*
EDWARD MAX, *an elderly lawyer*
MISS EMMET, *a social worker*
A NEWSPAPERMAN
OTHER NEWSPAPERMEN, NEIGHBORS, GUARDS, A JUDGE, AND OTHERS

TIME   *The present*
PLACE   *The Black Belt of Chicago*

Scene One

(*The* THOMAS *bedroom, an early mid-winter morning. In the darkness of the theater, a strident alarm clock begins ringing. It continues a while and then dies out as the curtain rises upon a small poverty-stricken apartment house in the crowded Black Belt of Chicago's South Side. A door at the right leads into the hallway, and at the right center is a pallet of quilts upon which two of the* THOMAS *family,* BIGGER *and* BUDDY, *sleep. Farther back and at the right is a rusty iron bed upon which* VERA *and* HANNAH *sleep, and at the center rear is a small dresser with a dull and splotched mirror. At the left rear, screened from view by a cheap chintz curtain is a corner nook with a gas stove, a sink, and shelves for groceries. A drop-leaf table, covered with an oil-cloth, is against the wall at the left front. There are a couple of chairs, a box and a chest about the room. The plastered walls are cracked and show the lathing here and there. A few crayon likenesses of dead relatives are on the wall—*BIGGER's *father, his grandfather and grandmother. And in clear dominance above the one bed at the right rear is a large colored lithograph of Jesus Christ hanging on the Cross, with the motto—"I am the Resurrection and the Life." A flower pot on the sill of the window at the left center with a single red geranium is the room's one pretense to beauty. As the curtain rises, the family is busy getting dressed and preparing breakfast. The muffled form of* BIGGER THOMAS *lies bundled under a quilt on the pallet. Far away in the distance, the chimes of a great clock are heard ringing*)

HANNAH (*the middle-aged careworn mother who is busy at the stove, and still wearing her flannel nightgown*). You children hurry up. That old clock done struck the half-past. Hear me, Vera?

VERA   Yes, Ma. (VERA *is a slender brown-skinned girl of sixteen, dressed in a pink cotton nightgown*)

HANNAH   And you too, Buddy. I got a big washing on my hands today. (BUDDY, *a dark sober little fellow of twelve, is standing by the stove buttoning his shirt with one hand and warming the other at the gas flame. He is shivering from the morning chill*)

BUDDY   Yessum.

HANNAH   And, Vera, you got to git to that sewing class. (BUDDY *sneezes*) Yes, look at that boy, caught cold again sleeping on that old floor. Told you better sleep with me and Vera at the bed foot. (HANNAH *is now fastening her* skirt which she has pulled on over her nightgown) Turn your head, son, so we can get our clothes on. (silently BUDDY turns and looks toward the pallet where BIGGER lies, buttoning his shirt the while. The sleeping BIGGER turns over, muttering under his quilt and stuffs a pillow against his head)

VERA Ma wants you to get up too, Bigger. Somebody'll stumble on you lying there. (she pulls her dress over her head and slips her cotton nightgown off underneath it. HANNAH looks toward the pallet and sighs)

HANNAH Get the milk from the hall, Buddy.

BUDDY Yessum. (he quickly pulls on his little old coat, his lips blubbering from the cold. HANNAH pushes the table out from the wall and begins setting a few dishes on it. BUDDY goes out as HANNAH calls after him)

HANNAH Take the empty bottle. Every time I got to tell you. (he turns back, picks up a bottle by the door and disappears) And, Vera, spread up the bed. (she begins singing her shrill morning song as she works)

> Jordan River, chilly and col'
> Chill the body but not the soul—
> Every time I feel the spirit
> Moving in my heart I will pray.

BIGGER (muttering from his pallet) How the hell can a man sleep with all this racket?

VERA (a little testily) Who'd want to sleep when the rest of us have to work so hard?

BIGGER (growling) Yeah, start right in soon's I git my eyes open! (he covers his head with the quilt again)

HANNAH Let him alone, Vera.

VERA It's the truth, Ma. He ought to be up looking for a job.

HANNAH Well, he's got his application in down at the relief station.

VERA But he ought to get out—hunt for work—Maybe ask that truck man to take him back, and we'd have something for Christmas!

BIGGER (sitting suddenly up) And him sassing at me? (BIGGER is a dark muscular young fellow of some twenty or twenty-one with deep-set eyes and sensitive heavy face. He is dressed in rumpled trousers, shirt and socks)

VERA Thought it was you sassing at him?

BIGGER You go to—(muttering darkly) The white boys got all the good runs—They don't want no niggers driving trucks down to Florida—

HANNAH Maybe you'd better get up, son.

BIGGER Might as well—all the tongues clanging like fire bells. (HANNAH goes out. BIGGER rises and stands over his shoes, kicks one into place with his foot, and then rams his left foot down halfway into it. He stomps against the side of the wall to get the shoe on. A pot clatters to the floor behind the curtain, bang-a-lang-lang) These old shoes wet from that snow four days ago. I was looking for a job then.

VERA (who is now putting things on the table) Well, knocking the house down won't dry 'em. (BIGGER stomps his right foot against the wall to get his other shoe on. BUDDY enters at the right with a bottle of milk)

BUDDY (coming up to the table and helping VERA) Goody, peaches to go with them cornflakes.

VERA And we better go slow on 'em, too. That relief box got to last till Saturday. (BUDDY ducks into the alcove and out again with a couple of glasses and pours the milk. BIGGER stands smoking and staring before him. HANNAH returns, still singing her song.)

HANNAH By thy bleeding breast and side,
By the awful death he died—
Every time I feel the spirit
Moving in my heart I will pray.

(She hands her towel to VERA, who takes it and goes out at the right. BUDDY strains at the can of peaches with a large pocket knife. HANNAH starts working busily at the breakfast) Gimme that knife—And get away from this table until you done washed yourself—Go on. Vera's got the towel. (BUDDY shies away and goes out. HANNAH appraises the knife an instant in her hand) Why any human being wants to carry around a knife as big as this, I don't see. Why you give it to him, Bigger?

BIGGER (mumbling) He wanted to tote it a little bit. (HANNAH opens the can. BIGGER now sits bent over in a chair smoking and idly turning the pages of a movie magazine spread on the floor before him. She looks over at him)

HANNAH Bigger, try for one time to roll that pallet up. No telling when Miss Emmet might come by.

BIGGER (still lazily reading) That old case worker ain't studying 'bout us.

HANNAH She got us on relief—and kept us from starving. (VERA comes in again. BIGGER rises *and rushes out at the right, bumping into somebody in the hall. A flooding high-pitched woman's voice fills the air with a whorl of words)*

VOICE Heigh—you! Yeh, look at you, just look at you—a-tromping and a scrouging. I'm ahead of you and you knows it! Git back in there and wait your turn, boy. (BIGGER *turns back and stands sheepishly in the door)*

VERA (*with a biting little laugh*) Reckon Sister Temple told him his manners.

BIGGER (*wrathfully*) All right now, and what's so funny about that old woman with the toilet trots? (BUDDY *enters*)

BUDDY Here's yo' towel, Bigger. (BIGGER *grabs the towel, balls it up and hurls it across the room, then goes over to the chest, sits down and resumes his magazine.* VERA *and* BUDDY *help their mother at the table, passing in and out of the alcove with a few dishes and food)*

VERA (*coming from the stove*) And that's another thing he ain't got—no respect.

HANNAH Sister Temple lives with her Lord.

BIGGER And her Epsom Salts! Eats it like oatmeal. Jack says so.

VERA Yeh, and that Jack's breaking his grandma's heart like you're breaking Ma's.

BIGGER I wish you'd stop being a little snot, dirting up where you don't belong.

HANNAH (*opening a box of cornflakes*) That's no way to speak to your own sister, son, and she getting to be a young lady now. (BIGGER *flaps his magazine over irritatedly)*

VERA If you was the kind of man Ma always hoped you'd be, you'd not have to wait for your turn to go to the bathroom. You'd be up early and get there first. But no—you'd rather hang around Ernie's place with Jack and that lowlife gang and let us live on relief.

HANNAH Hush, Vera.

BIGGER Yeh, hush—always hush. (*muttering*) Relief didn't say more'n forty people got to use the same toilet every morning—lining up like women to see Clark Gable. (*with sudden viciousness as he flings his arm around*) It's the way the white folks built these old buildings!

VERA Now don't start cussing the white folks again . . .

HANNAH They what keep us alive right this minute. (*he gets up and strides into the hall.* HANNAH *wags her head dolefully*) Now here we go again. Said to myself last night, we was gonna quit fussing at him. Don't do no good.

VERA How can we help it and seem like some strange devil growing in him all the time. (*her voice filled with angry earnestness*) He gets more like a stranger to us every day. He ain't never got a smile for anybody. And there's that Clara woman he runs with. Here I try to make myself respectable and be somebody, and he—

HANNAH Oh, Lord, I don't know. (*calling contritely*) Come on back, son. Le's try to eat in peace, Vera.

BUDDY (*piping up*) Bigger says we ain't got nothing to smile about, says that's what wrong with the niggers—always smiling, and nothing to smile about. (*he leans over, smells the peaches, and wrinkles his nose in delight)*

HANNAH Shut yo' mouth, boy.

BUDDY That's what he say—

HANNAH Yeh, he say a lot he hadn't ought to. If the white folks ever hear him—

VERA And some these days they're gonna hear him—

HANNAH Bigger needs God in him, that's what. I've prayed, and Sister Temple's prayed, and Reverend Hammond's put up special prayers for him. Yeh, God's what he needs, po' boy.

BIGGER (*who has reappeared in the door*) God! (*flinging out a gesture, his voice rising mockingly*) Yeh, you got him hanging on the wall there—the white folk's God!

VERA Yeh, every morning he gets up like something mad at the world.

HANNAH (*with a touch of piteousness as she looks fervently at the picture on the wall, her lips moving audibly, quoting*) "I am the Resurrection and the Life." Your pa knowed that, son, your pa lived by it.

BIGGER And he died by it. (*half chanting, mockingly*) "They hung his head on the thorny cross, the red blood trickled down."

HANNAH Bigger, stop that!

VERA (*quickly*) Come on, le's eat breakfast.

HANNAH This ain't the way to start the day off.

BIGGER Way you start every day—when I'm around.

BUDDY (*uncertainly*) Yeh, let's eat! (*they sit to the table.* HANNAH *lifts the family Bible from the top of the chest and opens it. Suddenly there comes a thin, dry rattling sound in the wall at the rear. They all sit listening an instant.* BUDDY *calls out*) Listen!

BIGGER Yeah, that's old man Dalton, all right. (*hacking a hunk of bread off from the loaf and buttering it*) If that old rat stick his head out this time, I'm gonna scrush it for him.

HANNAH (*reading*) "I have trodden the winepress alone; and of people there was none with me; for I will tread them in mine anger, and trample them in my fury; and their blood shall be sprinkled upon my garments, and I will stain—" (*the noise in the wall is heard again*) "—all my raiment. For the day of vengeance is in my heart, and the year of my redeemer is come—And I will tread down the people in mine anger, and make them drunk in my fury, and I will bring down their strength to the earth." Blessed be the name of the Lord. (*the noise in the wall is heard still again*)

BUDDY (*whispering*) That's him, aw right.

HANNAH (*closing the Bible*) Bow your heads. (BUDDY *and* VERA *bow their heads.* BIGGER *sits munching his bread and staring moodily before him.* HANNAH's *words rise in deep humility*) Lord our Father in Heaven, we thank Thee for the food You have prepared for the nourishment of our humble bodies. We thank Thee for the many blessings of thy loving grace and mercy. Guide our poor feet in the path of righteousness for your sake. Bless this home, this food, these children You gave me. Help me to raise them up for a pride and witness to their Lawd. And thine be the power and the glory forever and ever—Amen. (*they all begin eating as* HANNAH *lifts her gaze again to Jesus on the wall. Suddenly* BIGGER *springs out of his chair with a shout*)

BIGGER There he go! (*he lunges across the room, flings himself over the bed and begins jabbing in the corner with his foot. Then, springing back, he seizes an old baseball bat from the floor.* BUDDY *grabs the bread knife and hops up*)

BUDDY (*as* VERA *and* HANNAH *jump to their feet*) Where is he? Where is he?

BIGGER He's our meat this time. We got his hole stopped up.

HANNAH (*shakily*) There he goes.

VERA (*with a squeal*) Where, Ma, where?

BIGGER (*creeping toward the trunk*) The sonofabitch, I see his shiny eye. (*there is a knock on the door, but no one heeds it.* BIGGER *lunges behind the trunk and strikes a shattering blow against the floor. There is a scramble as* BUDDY *rushes across the room and peers under the bed.* BIGGER *creeps forward, his whole body tensely alive*)

BUDDY (*pointing*) Yonder—yonder—

BIGGER (*bending down*) Jesus, look at them teeth! (*he grabs the end of the bed with one hand and swings it around the room*) He's behind that box now. (*his voice is charged with a harsh intensity. Again there is a knock at the door*)

VERA (*half-weeping*) Let him go, Bigger. Let him go.

HANNAH (*piteously*) Unstop the hole, let him out.

BIGGER Gimme that skillet, quick! (BUDDY *rushes over to the alcove and hands him the skillet.* BIGGER *takes aim, and hurls it into the corner*)

BUDDY (*excitedly*) You hit him, you hit him! (*the door opens silently and a smallish young white woman, carrying a black portfolio in her hands stands in the doorway. She looks inquiringly and then half-frightenedly at the scene before her. Now* BIGGER *creeps toward the kitchen nook.* HANNAH *and* VERA *have their arms about each other, watching him breathlessly.* BIGGER *stands waiting, poised, his hand raised*)

BIGGER (*his feet weaving to the right and left*) Yeah, there you sit on your hind legs and gnashing them tushes at me—I'm gonna beat your brains out—Wheeooh! (*with a yell he jumps forward and strikes with flailing, lightning blows along the curtain edge on the floor*)

HANNAH Bigger, Bigger!

BIGGER (*lifting the rat up and holding it by the tail, a murmuring chant running from his lips*) I got you, old man Dalton, got you that time! I put out your light, mashed you into a mushy, bloody pudding. You dead now—dead, dead, dead, dead—

VERA Stop him, Ma! (*the woman in the door now stands shaken and weakly leaning against the lintel*) Look, Ma!

HANNAH (*moaning*) Mercy sake, Bigger. Here's Miss Emmet.

BIGGER Try to run now—try to bite me—just try it, you black, fat, slimy, ratty, greasy— (*his words gradually die out as he looks up and sees* MISS EMMET. *She comes on into the room*)

HANNAH Miss Emmet!—Bigger, take that thing out of here right now!

MISS EMMET I came a little early—before you got to work. (*she is a kindly young woman, serious-faced and tired*)

BUDDY We just killed a rat. Yessum. (*with a*

touch of boyish pride) Bigger done it. Ain't he a big one?

BIGGER (*softly*) That scutter could cut your throat—the biggest one we ever killed. (*holding him up*) See him, Miss Emmet?

MISS EMMET Yes, I see it. (*drawing back*) Better throw it away.

BIGGER (*feeling him*) See how fat he is—feeding on garbage. They get more to eat than we do. Yeh, old Dalton, you're going to the incinerator and there ain't no coming back. (*he shakes the rat at* VERA *and she squeals*)

MISS EMMET (*quietly*) Why do you call it Dalton, Bigger?

BIGGER Just call 'em that.

BUDDY Yessum. Last week us killed another rat in here—we calls 'em "Old Man Dalton"—the big man what owns all the houses round here—

HANNAH I said to him, "Anyhow, Bigger, you might leastwise say 'Mr. Dalton.'" (*a small meek smile passes around* MISS EMMET's *lips*) Sit down, Ma'am.

MISS EMMET Yes, considering Mr. Dalton's kindness to the people of your race. (*she sits down and opens her portfolio*)

BIGGER (*softly*) Kind—(*flaring up*) I wish old Dalton'd show up around here sometime—I'd fix 'im up—Like I did that rat—

VERA Hush, Bigger!

HANNAH (*soothingly*) He don't mean nothing by it, Miss Emmet—

BUDDY Gimme heah, Bigger.

BIGGER (*now beginning to grow silent again, the excitement dying in him*) Okay. (*he hands the rat to* BUDDY *who takes it proudly and goes out.* BIGGER *sits down on the chest, finishing a hunk of buttered bread*)

HANNAH (*watching Miss Emmet eagerly, holding her cup of coffee in her hand*) I pray the Lord you got some good news for us, ma'am.

MISS EMMET I hope so.

HANNAH Bless you, ma'am. I knowed you'd help us.

MISS EMMET Just a final question or two, Bigger, about your application. As head of the house—(*she takes out a double-leaved form sheet and unstops her fountain pen.* VERA *leaves the table and goes over to the mirror*)

BIGGER (*with a little laugh*) We ain't got nothin' but this one room, and there ain't no head to it.

MISS EMMET But as soon as we place you in a job, Bigger, you'll feel differently.

BIGGER (*fumbling with the movie magazine*) What kind of job I going to get?

MISS EMMET Mr. Dalton is interested in placing his jobless tenants.

BIGGER (*with the faintest touch of a snicker*) Yessum.

HANNAH (*happily*) Hear that, Bigger? (*she sets her coffee cup down and wipes her hands on her apron.* BUDDY *reappears and goes back to his bowl of cornflakes*)

MISS EMMET (*as she looks at her wrist watch*) There's an opening with Mr. Dalton's family itself—the job of chauffeur. You might get that place. According to the record here, you're a first-rate driver.

BUDDY He sure can drive. (*snapping his fingers*) She's gone from here. Hot dog!

MISS EMMET But we must supply Mr. Dalton with all the facts. Here under previous history you failed to mention that matter of the reform school, Bigger.

BIGGER Yeh, yeh—I knowed they was gonna find that out. Jesus! You white folks know everythin'.

MISS EMMET When did it happen? We must have the facts.

VERA Go ahead, Bigger. Tell the lady.

BIGGER You tell her, Ma. I done forgot them things.

HANNAH It was a year ago last June, ma'am. That old no 'count Gus Mitchell fellow told on him. (*eagerly*) But please, Miss Emmet—

MISS EMMET (*writing*) Three months term, ending June 15th, 1939. Metropolitan Home for the Detention of Juvenile Delinquents—Theft—Taking of three automobile tires from a colored garage—Is that right?

BIGGER (*with a faint touch of mockery*) Yessum, that must be about right.

MISS EMMET And you haven't had any other trouble since, Bigger?

BIGGER No'm—

MISS EMMET (*holds out her fountain pen*) Now please sign there.

BIGGER (*with apparent reluctance as he takes the pen*) I done signed that paper once.

MISS EMMET Yes, but this is added material and we must follow the Washington rules.

BIGGER Sure if the big man in Washington

say so. He the boss. (*with a flourish in the air, he writes his name*)

MISS EMMET (*taking the blank, breathing on it, and then giving it a little drying wave in the air*) I'll send Mr. Dalton a confidential report recommending you, Bigger. In fact, I'll take it down to his office this morning.

HANNAH (*joy breaking over her face*) God bless you, ma'am. I been praying to hear something, and now to know that Bigger gonna have a good job—(*touching her hands together evangelically*) Bless the Lord, bless the Lord. Bigger will make a new start—From now on he will, ma'am. Won't you, son?

BUDDY (*with fervent admiration*) You gonna drive Mr. Dalton's big car, Bigger. (*suddenly putting his hands up on the steering wheel of an imaginary car and driving it around the room*) Swoos-s-hh, look out, everybody—old twelve-cylinders coming round the curve. (*he bumps into* MISS EMMET *who stands up with a little gentle laugh*)

HANNAH Look out, boy, you 'bout to run over the lady!

BIGGER (*flinging up his hand and grinning as he adopts the attitude of a traffic cop, at the same time blowing a sharp whistle through his teeth*) Hey, what you mean running through that red light? Pull up heah and lemme see your license, boy. (*he scuffs* BUDDY's *hair a bit in spontaneous friendliness; then his face grows heavy again*) But, pshaw, I ain't gonna get that job.

MISS EMMET Now good-by, Mrs. Thomas. Good-by, Bigger. You'll hear as soon as I contact Mr. Dalton. Keep your head up—(*she smiles wanly at them and goes out*)

HANNAH (*following her to the door*) Bless you, ma'am, bless you—whole soul and body—(*she closes the door and turns happily about the room*) And my prayers are answered. I knowed they'd be. (*she begins piling the household wash rapidly into a sheet*)

VERA (*coming by* BIGGER *and stopping with deep earnestness*) Maybe this is the real break. We are all so glad, Bigger. And we can quit living in one room like pigs.

BIGGER Aw, cut it out.

VERA Good-by, Ma. (*she goes by her mother, gives her a little pecking kiss, and then turning gives* BIGGER's *arm an affectionate squeeze*) And you'll help me pay for my domestic science, won't you?

HANNAH Sure he will.

VERA Yes. Come on, Buddy, time you was out selling your papers.

HANNAH (*jubilantly*) Ain't it the truth? And let's all hustle. (BIGGER *is now sitting at the table idly marking across the movie magazine with a pencil*)

BUDDY (*putting on his overcoat and cap*) 'Bye, Ma. (*standing in front of* BIGGER) You lemme ride in that old Dusenberg sometime?

BIGGER (*spreading out an imaginary document in front of him and beginning to write gravely*) Have to examine the archives of the Commitment Home first. How the hell I know what you been doing on the sly?

BUDDY (*his face crinkling into a smile*) Bigger you sure a case. Look, Ma, Bigger's smiling.

BIGGER Hell, I ain't smiling none. (BUDDY *scampers out after* VERA)

HANNAH (*laying a coin on the table by him*) Here, son, take this fifty cents. Run down there to the corner and get me two bars of that hard soap, a bottle of bluing, and a box of starch, and a can of Red Devil lye, and make a bee-line back to the basement. Sister Temple and me will be needing it for the work. (BIGGER *continues to scrawl with his pencil*) Hear me?

BIGGER Yeh.

HANNAH (*turning to him, her voice affectionate and serious*) Bigger, that good white lady is right. From now on, you're the real head of the house. She gonna get you that job. I ain't gonna be with you always, trying to make a home for you children. And Vera and Buddy has got to have protection. Hear me, son? (*she lifts the bundled sheet of clothes over her shoulder*)

BIGGER Uhm—

HANNAH I'll be too old to work soon. (*laying a hand gently on his shoulder*) And some day yet you'll believe like me—my boy—(*she bends over, touches him lightly on the hair with her lips and goes silently and suddenly out. For an instant he sits stock still. His hand goes up into the air, as if to feel the top of his head, and then comes down on the table in a clenched fist. He looks upward at the picture of Christ on the wall. He begins to study it closely, and gradually a wry twisting smile slides around his lips*)

BIGGER (*reading*) "I am the Resurrection and the Life"—Uhm—(*he gets sharply up and puts on his old leather coat and cap. The chimes begin to ring again. He stands listening*) They ringing your bells, Lawd—(*as if irritated by some inner thought, he slaps the coin down on the table*) Heads I do, tails I don't. (*disgustedly*) Heads. (*he gives a little laugh, shakes his shoulders and spits angrily at the stove. A signal whistle comes up from outside the window at the left. It is repeated. He stands in indecision a moment and then goes over and looks out. Finally he raises his hand in a sort of fascist salute and waves it across the pane*) Okay, be right with you, Jack! (*he turns back toward the bed, pulls forth a wooden packing box and unlocks it. He takes out a pistol, and looks at it and then back at the picture*) Here's what you didn't have—but I got it! (*hurriedly he crams it into his blouse.* HANNAH *comes in still carrying the sheet of clothes slung over her shoulder*)

HANNAH (*to herself*) Seem like my mind failing away. Forgot my washboard again. (*queryingly*) What you up to, boy? (*without answering* BIGGER *kicks the box back under the bed and goes quickly out. Something in his actions disturbs* HANNAH. *She gazes worriedly after him and then hurries to the door and calls*) Bigger! (*more loudly*) Bigger! (*but there is no answer. Slowly and heavily she turns into the room again. Dropping the bundle of clothes, she hurries into the hall, calling*) Come back here, boy!

(*The chimes continue to ring. Fadeout*)

Scene Two

(*A street, that afternoon. The chimes die away as the scene opens again on a street and sidewalk in front of Ernie's Kitchen Shack, somewhere on Indiana Avenue near 47th Street. At the right front the gullet of a narrow alleyway leads back into the shadows. And at the mouth of the alleyway sits a garbage can, looking like a squat molar in its maw, across which is a staring label saying "Keep Our City Clean." The entrance to Ernie's place of business is through a door in the center with windows on either side. Adjoining the "shack" is an empty building with a boarded-up window on which are posters announcing the candidacy of two men for the office of state's attorney for Cook County. One of the men depicted is middle-aged, of imposing bearing, and declared to be "The Party's Choice." The other is somewhat elderly, less commanding, and announced to be "The People's Choice." Their names written in large letters respectively are David A. Buckley and Edward Max. At the left front is a hydrant and near it a steel lamp-post topped above with the usual globular glass. The sounds of a busy thoroughfare are heard off at the left—a streetcar clanging, automobile horns, now and then a tremulous roar of a heavy truck, and once or twice the siren of a squad or ambulance car—a great wash of droning sound.*

When the curtain rises, BIGGER *and sporty* JACK HENSON, *one of his buddies, are seen leaning against the wall near the left rear. Their caps are pulled down and coat collars turned up to warm them in the splotch of winter sun that shines upon them and the wall. Now and then they look up and down the street with watchful, roving eyes*)

BIGGER (*spitting and looking at his watch*) Time G. H. was here.

JACK They'll be here. Everything's jake. (*softly*) Passed old Blum's while ago—setting back in there like a crab.

BIGGER (*looking carefully about him*) Yeh, I seen him. Back to the door—bent over by the cash register working in his books. How much you think we get?

JACK Hundred-fifty bucks anyhow. It's a cinch.

BIGGER Cinch—and a white man. Don't seem right.

JACK Getting up into big time, boy. (*he laughs*)

BIGGER Uhm—twenty minutes till. Gimme another cigarette, Jack.

JACK (*peering at him*) Twenty minutes till—(*narrowly*)—and ain't no gun in it. (*he pulls out out a package of cigarettes*) This is our second pack already.

BIGGER (*taking a cigarette*) Who said a gun?

JACK Nobody. Somebody get killed—then the hot seat. (*whistling*) Jesus! (BIGGER *stares at him*)

BIGGER That Gus Mitchell—old tongue wags at both ends. He keep mo' out of trouble just wagging one end. (*he lights up his cigarette and holds the match for* JACK)

JACK Gus got mighty sharp eyes, though. (*after a few draws*) Gosh, you shake like an old woman. And what your hands doing sweating so?

BIGGER (*throwing down the match*) Hell. light it yourself. (JACK *lights up.* CLARA MEARS, *an attractive, kindly young Negro girl, comes in at the right, carrying a package under one arm. She smiles brightly over at* BIGGER *and stops*)

CLARA Hy, Bigger.
JACK Hy, Clara.
BIGGER (*nonchalantly*) Hy, Clara.
CLARA Thought I'd find you here.
BIGGER Smart girl—
CLARA Missed you last night, honey.
BIGGER I was busy. (*she puts out a hand and touches him affectionately on the arm*)
CLARA Gonna see you tonight?
BIGGER Maybe.
JACK (*laughs*) Maybe.
CLARA (*with a slap in the air at* JACK) The Burtons got a house full of company for Christmas—but I'll get off. Maybe we'll go to a picture? (*looking at her wrist watch and then up at the sun*) Gee, I got to hurry. (*giving* BIGGER'*s arm a farewell squeeze*) It's a date.
BIGGER (*still nonchalantly*) Okay. (*she gazes deep into his face and then hurries out at the left*)
JACK Shucks, that gal loves the very ground you walk on.
BIGGER It don't matter.
JACK Uh?
BIGGER Love 'em and leave 'em.
JACK Not Clara.
BIGGER Huh?
JACK Nothing. (*they puff in silence a moment and then stare off before them.* BIGGER *runs his fingers around inside his collar and twists his head*) Kinder warm today—for December.
BIGGER Almost like summer . . . (*sharply*) Summer or winter—all the same. (*he pulls out his dollar watch again*)
JACK Yeh, all the same. Quit looking at that old watch—time never pass. (*he chuckles*)
BIGGER Now what? (*he spits*)
JACK Gus say he don't want you in on the job neither—too nervous, he say.
BIGGER Lousy runt!
JACK Say you too hair-trigger. Now keep your shirt on and quit that spitting. There he come. (JACK *straightens up and stares off as* GUS *comes briskly into the scene from the left. He is a small-sized Negro about Bigger's age and wears his cap turned round like a baseball catcher. As he enters he cups his right hand to his mouth as though holding an imaginary telephone transmitter and his left hand to his ear with a receiver. He grins as he bows*)

GUS Hello-hello.
JACK (*responding quickly and pantomiming*) Hello—Yes—uhm—old Gus boy—
GUS Who's speaking?
JACK Why—er—this is the president of the United States of America.
GUS Oh, yes suh, Mr. President. What's on your mind?
JACK I'm calling a cabinet meeting this afternoon at three o'clock—as secretary of state you must be there!
BIGGER (*satirically*) Hah-hah.
GUS Well, now, Mr. President, I'm pretty busy. Bombs falling all over Europe. I'm thinking of sending that old Hitler another note.
JACK And them Japs—they . . .
BIGGER (*pantomiming like the others*) Hello, Mr. President. I just cut in from the sidelines and heard what you said. Better wait about that war business. The niggers is raising sand all over the country! You better put them down first.
JACK Oh, if it's about the niggers, Mr. Willkie, we'll wait on the war!
BIGGER Yes, suh. At a time like this, we Republicans and Democrats got to pull together!
GUS Reckon we can do without you, Mr. Wilkie. (*they bow about in sudden and rich physical laughter, slapping their thighs, their knees easy and bent*)
JACK Lawd, Lawd, Lawd—
BIGGER I bet that's just how they talk.
JACK Sho, it is—(ERNIE *comes to the rear door, and stands looking out. He is a stoutish phlegmatic Negro of fifty or more*)
ERNIE 'Bout time to open up here, and how you speck me to have any customers and you all wallowing all over the pavement?
BIGGER Aw, go suck something.
ERNIE (*angrily*) I don't want none of your back-talk, Bigger Thomas.
BIGGER Three o'clock our zero hour—ten minutes and we go.
ERNIE Ten minutes then, 'fore I call a cop. (*he turns back into the shadow*) You're up to devilment, I know you. (*he disappears*)
BIGGER (*muttering*) Sonofabitch. (*turning toward* GUS *and staring at him with hard bright eyes*) So you don't want Mr. Willkie in on the deal—huh—meaning me?
GUS Aw, I was just joking, Bigger.

BIGGER You wanter live and keep doing well—... drop the joking. (*he pauses a moment*) But, hell, I ain't against no war. I'd just soon fight as to stand here waiting all day.

JACK Fight who?

BIGGER Hell, anybody. I'd just soon take a gun and pop off a few of these white folks—old Blum too. Eight minutes to three... Goddamit! I feel old Blum gnawing round my liver here.

JACK (*softly*) Yeh, and in your lungs and throat too—like fire. We gonna spit him out in a few minutes now.

BIGGER Sometime you can hardly breathe. You know what—sometime—(*with sudden anger*) Where's G.H.? Goddammit. I'm ready for old Blum!

JACK Christ, don't talk so loud. Ernie'll hear you. We got five minutes yet. (*they are silent for a moment.* BIGGER *tilts back his face and the sun shines full upon it.* JACK *stares up at the sky and sneezes twice*)

GUS That's sign o' bad luck!

BIGGER (*yelling*) Go to hell! Superstition—you niggers—signs, wonders—Look up there—the white man's sign.

JACK What?

BIGGER (*dramatically*) That airplane—writing on the sky—like a little finger—(*they all three look up*) So high up, looks like a little bird. (*waving his hands*) Sailing and looping and zooming—And that white smoke coming out of his tail—(*he walks restlessly about*)

JACK (*reading—afar off*) "Use Speed Gasoline"—

BIGGER (*exultantly*) Speed! That's what them white boys got!

GUS (*whispering*) Daredevils—

BIGGER Go on, boys, fly them planes, fly 'em to the end of the world, fly 'em smack into the sun! I'm with you. Goddam! (*he stares up, the sunlight on his face*)

GUS (*unable to let well enough alone, doffing his cap in a mock bow to* BIGGER) Yessuh! If you wasn't *black* and if you had some *money* and if they'd let you go to that *aviation* school, you might could be with 'em.

BIGGER(*fiercely*) Yeh, keep on, keep on now!

JACK (*flexing his hands as though holding onto controls, he makes the sound of an airplane motor*) Thrr—hu-hu-hu-hu—

GUS Wish I could fly now!

(BIGGER *joins* JACK *in the roar of the plane, primping his lips.* GUS *also joins in, and for a moment the sound of the motor goes on uninterruptedly.* G.H., *a darkish heavy-set young Negro comes in at the left. He lifts one hand in a mocking "Heil Hitler" salute, holding his nose with the other.* BIGGER *sees him and barks out an order*)

BIGGER You pilot!

G.H. (*falling in with the game*) Yessuh!

BIGGER Give her the stick and pull right over! (*he bends over, squinting, as if peering down through glasses from a great height*) Machine gunner, give that crowd down there on Michigan Boulevard some hot lead.

JACK Yessuh! (*making the rat-tat-tat of a machine gun*) Rat-tat-tat-tat-tat-tat, rat-tat-tat-tat-tat—

BIGGER Looks at the white folks fall—(*he speaks in a half singsong as he turns with growing excitement about him—exultantly*) Now we gonna dive-bomb that Tribune Tower. (*he leads off with the zooming roar of an airplane throttle opened at full speed. The others join in.* BIGGER *cries out wildly*) Turn 'em loose! (*he makes a kicking motion downward with his foot, and then in a high whine depicts the passage of the bombs earthward. They all make the "boom" of the explosion together*)

GUS (*bent over, staring down*) Lawd, look at the smoke.

BIGGER A direct hit, sergeant. (*loudly*) Look at the fires—things flying through air—houses—people—streetcars—hunks of sidewalk and pavements. Goddam! Whoom—Tracer bullets. (*yelling*) Look out! There come the fighter planes! (*frantically pulling his pistol*) Cold steel! Watch the turn—Put it through the navel. (*the three boys look at him and then spring back in fear, their playful spirit suddenly gone*)

G.H. That crazy fool!

GUS (*pointing*) Look he's got a gun. I knowed it. (BIGGER *continues to aim about him. The others mumble in half fear*)

BIGGER (*hunching out his shoulder and running at* JACK *who dodges him*) Crash him! Crash him!

GUS (*throwing out his hands in fear*) Put up that gun, fool!

BIGGER (*whirling and leveling the gun at* GUS) Ride into 'em or I'll shoot your lights out. (*he gives a high wild laugh*)

G.H. Bigger, for Christ's sake! Somebody'll see you!

GUS I told you he's crazy! Now just look at him!—

BIGGER (*advancing upon* GUS *with gun leveled*) You sonofabitch, don't you call me crazy—

GUS (*backing away toward the other two boys, who stare at him silently*) He's yellow. He's scared to rob a white man, that how come he brung that gun. (*he moves behind* JACK) I told you to leave him out of it. (BIGGER *puts up his gun and suddenly darts out his hand, seizes* GUS *by the collar, and bangs his head against the wall*)

BIGGER (*his face working in violent rage, as he pulls his knife again*) I don't need no gun. Yellow, huh? (*pushing the knife against* GUS's *stomach*) Take it back.

JACK That ain't no way to play, Bigger.

BIGGER Who the hell said I was playing?

GUS Please, Bigger. I was just joking.

BIGGER (*his lips snarled back over his teeth*) Want me to cut your belly button out?

G.H. Aw, leave him alone, Bigger.

BIGGER Put your hands up. Way up! (GUS *swallows and stretches his hands high along the wall. He stares out with wide frightened eyes, and sweat begins to trickle down his temples. His lips hang open and loose*) Shut them liver lips.

GUS (*in a tense whisper*) Bigger!

BIGGER (*pressing the point of the knife deeper against his belly*) Take it back. Say "I'm a lying sonofabitch."

GUS (*with a moan*) Quit!

BIGGER Say it, say it.

G.H. (*staring horrified at him*) For Christ's sake, Bigger!

BIGGER Take it back. Say it. (GUS *begins to slump down along the wall.* BIGGER *jabs him slightly. He straightens up quickly with a howl*) Say, "I'm a lying sonofabitch."

GUS I'm—I'm a lying sonofabitch. (*his arm falls down and his head slumps forward.* BIGGER *releases him*)

BIGGER Next time you whimper on me I'm gonna kill you. Now scat. (*hissing*) You ain't gonna be in on this. I'll take your share of the haul. (*he starts at* GUS *again, who gazes wildly around him a moment and then flies out of the scene at the right. For a while they are all silent. The noise of the city rolls in across the scene*) Goddamit, somebody say something!

JACK (*watching him*) Don't cuss at us.

BIGGER I am cussing at you. Come on, will you?

G.H. (*angrily*) Aw, lay off! (*somewhere from a tower a clock booms three times. They listen, stock still*)

BIGGER All right, zero hour.

G.H. I ain't going nowhere—now.

BIGGER Hundred fifty bucks waiting in that cash drawer. (*they eye him in cold silence*) Goddamit, you scared!

JACK Yeh, we was gonna walk in quiet—"Hand over your money," we say, and then back out. Now, you bring along a gun and a knife—maybe kill somebody and put us in the 'lectric chair. (*laughing harshly*) who's scared? (*he pulls a sort of wooden peg from his pocket and throws it into the alley*)

BIGGER Just one more word out of you. (*laughing hysterically*) So you all turn against me—huh? I knowed you bastards was scared! I'll do it by myself—Just watch. And when I do, don't nobody even speak to me, don't ask me for time to die, you hear? (ERNIE *comes to the door*)

ERNIE Bigger, get away from here.

BIGGER (*whirling on him and jerking out his knife*) Make me!

ERNIE I'll fix you this time—(*he turns around and reaches up as if to lift a hidden weapon down from above the door. But* BIGGER *springs forward, grabs him and jerks him out to the sidewalk. With a swipe of his knife he cuts off a piece of* ERNIE's *coat and holds it up, yelling*)

BIGGER This is a sample of the cloth. Wanta see a sample of the meat?

ERNIE (*gasping*) I'll get my gun—I'll shoot you—

G.H. Let's go, Come on. (BUDDY *comes running to the scene carrying a bundle of papers under his arm and an envelope in his hand. He stops for an instant and looks at the scene, and then hurries forward*)

BUDDY Bigger—that lady come by the house —sent a message for you. (BIGGER *stares at* ERNIE *and chuckles, at the same time reaches out and takes the letter from* BUDDY. BUDDY *looks off, then springs away out at the left, calling*) Paper, mister, paper!

BIGGER You all keep quiet while I read my mail. (*he backs off a few steps and opens the letter with a rip of his knife*) Good Gordon gin! (*the others watch him*) Old Man Dalton wants to see me at my convenience—immediately if not sooner. (*shouting out at them*) Damn all of you now—you can all go to hell. I'm gonna be driving for a millionaire, and don't you speak to me no more, none of you. Hear me? (*he laughs and spits*) I spit in your slimy faces—a bunch of yellow cowards.

JACK (*placatingly, as he edges forward*) Is it a job for real, Bigger?

BIGGER And when I go riding by, tip your hats—you'd better—yeh, you had—(ERNIE *has been edging back into the door*) Yeh, get your gun, Ernie. I ain't afraid of it—I'm finished with all you cheesy little punks—I'm on my way now—(*he makes an upward gesture, then feeling in his coat pocket, pulls out a coin and scornfully throws it at them*) Here, take this fifty cents and buy you some hash. (*he turns and goes quickly out at the left*)

ERNIE On his way now—(*mopping his forehead*) Somebody gonna kill that fool yet.

JACK Or he's gonna kill somebody. Takes more'n a job to cure what ails him!

G.H. (*picking up the piece of money from the pavement*) Come on, let's get something to drink, Jack.

JACK And a nickel for some canned music.

G.H. Old boogie-woogie take the pressure off.

ERNIE (*still staring in the direction* BIGGER *has gone*) Yeh, come on in. What'll you have? (*the boys start into the cafe. The automatic phonograph immediately begins playing a drum-beaten blues song, and continues. Fadeout*)

Scene Three

(*The following morning. As the blues music dies away, the curtain rises on the sun-filled, spotless* DALTON *breakfast room. To the left is a door which opens into the dining room, and to the right another door leading into the kitchen and back hall. In the center room is a wide triple window, giving a view beyond of the* DALTON *private grounds. The table in the center room is decorated with a vase of hothouse poinsettia, and by the window is a canary's cage.*

When the curtain rises, MR. *and* MRS. DALTON *are seated at the table and* PEGGY *is making toast on an electric toaster at the right. A portable tea wagon, with plates and hot dishes, is just behind her.* PEGGY *is the Irish cook and maid. She is about forty years old and wears a blue dress with white apron, collar and cap—the typical maid's uniform.* MR. DALTON *is holding an application form in one hand and a coffee cup in the other. He is about fifty-five or sixty and wears a pair of pince-nez be-ribboned glasses on the bridge of his nose.* MRS. DALTON *is middle-aged, thin, almost ascetic, and dressed in flowing white, with a knitted shawl draped loosely about her shoulders. She holds a white pet cat in the crook of her arm, and one pallid hand fumbles at the food in front of her. Her eyes are staring and blinkless.* BIGGER, *dressed as usual in his old black leathr jacket, is standing before them with his cap in his hand*)

DALTON (*reading in a hurried slurring tone*) Twenty years of age—grammar school education—poor student but learns quickly when he applies himself—(*he glances at* BIGGER) Counted as head of the house—color complex—father killed in a race riot in Jackson, Mississippi, August 15th, 1930. (*he looks up again, clearing his throat*) Quite a lot of background factors, Ellen.

MRS. DALTON (*quietly*) Yes.

BIGGER (*mumbling uncertainly*) Yessuh, they told me to bring it.

(PEGGY *sets a glass of milk by* MRS. DALTON *and re-fills* MR. DALTON'S *coffee cup*)

DALTON (*as* DALTON *goes on,* BIGGER *now and then lifts his slumbrous eyes and gives* MRS. DALTON'S *sightless face a somewhat awed and inquiring look*) Knows how to obey orders but is of unstable equilibrium as to disposition. (*chuckling*) Never mind all these words, Bigger —part of the new social philosophy. Uh, what kind of car did you drive last?

BIGGER A truck, sir.

DALTON Got your license?

BIGGER (*showing it*) Yessuh, I can drive most any kind. I can handle a Dusenberg right off.

DALTON I have a Buick.

BIGGER Yessuh.

DALTON Now, Bigger, about this reform school business. Just forget it. I was a boy myself once, and God knows I got into plenty of jams.

MRS. DALTON (*softly*) But he's colored, Henry.

DALTON I know, I know, Ellen. (*looking at his watch and rising*) I've got to be getting on down to the office. They're threatening a rent strike over on Prairie Avenue... Old man Max's labor speeches... Peggy, suppose you show Bigger around. Let him try his hand at the furnace. (*to* MRS. DALTON) He suits me all right, Ellen. Bigger, I always leave the final decision in these matters to Mrs. Dalton.

BIGGER Yessuh. (*a buzzer on the back wall sounds a sudden thur-rrh.* PEGGY *turns quickly*)

DALTON No you don't. Mary will have her breakfast here.

PEGGY Yes, sir.

DALTON No more of this breakfast in bed business.

MRS. DALTON (*always in her gentle unhurried manner*) She was out late last night—at the university—

DALTON She can get up just the same—(*he comes over and kisses* MRS. DALTON *on the forehead*) What about those flowers you wanted me to take down to be entered?

MRS. DALTON I'll show you. (*she rises and goes out with him.* BIGGER *watches them go, and* PEGGY *starts clearing the table. The buzzer begins ringing again, and* BIGGER *glances at it*)

PEGGY (*shaking her head*) I know—in my soft heart I want to answer it. But Mr. Dalton's right—We've got to—Want one of my hot rolls?

BIGGER No'm—no'm—I ain't hungry.

PEGGY (*deftly buttering a roll and sticking it out to him*) Take it. (*he takes it with a slow hand and bites into it*) Good?

BIGGER Yessum—Sure mighty good. (*the sound of an automatic furnace turning itself on in a great windy draught comes up from below.* BIGGER *stands listening to it*)

PEGGY That's the furnace. It works by machinery. One of your jobs will be looking after it... keeping it stoked and the ashes cleaned out.

BIGGER Yessum. I learn machinery easy.

PEGGY I hope you're going to like it here.

BIGGER Yessum.

PEGGY (*still working at her duties*) Before I forget it, Miss Mary's going to Detroit tomorrow. You'll have to come early in the morning and drive her to the La Salle Street Station.

BIGGER Yessum.

PEGGY That'll be one of your jobs—looking after Miss Mary.

BIGGER Yessum.

PEGGY She's not a bit like her folks. Drives her father crazy! Runs around with a wild bunch of radicals. But she's good-hearted—she'll learn better. She'll marry and settle down one of these days.

BIGGER Yessum.

PEGGY Now Mrs. Dalton—you'll like her. She's wonderful.

BIGGER She—she can't see, can she?

PEGGY (*pouring herself a cup of coffee and drinking from it*) She's blind. Went blind years ago when her second child was born. It died, and she's been blind ever since. Never talks much, but she loves people and tries to help them. Loves that cat and her piano and her flowers. (*she sets her cup down and wipes her hands on her apron.* MRS. DALTON *comes feeling her way in from the left dressed as before and still carrying the white cat.* BIGGER *rises abruptly, clattering the dishes on the table*)

MRS. DALTON Have you told the young man his duties, Peggy?

PEGGY Part of 'em, ma'am. I haven't spoke about the flowers yet.

MRS. DALTON Yes, Bigger. You are to water the flowers every morning.

BIGGER Yessum.

PEGGY I'll start the cleaning, Ma'am. (MRS. DALTON *makes her way along the table and sits down.* PEGGY *goes out at the right.* MRS. DALTON *takes one of the blossoms from the vase on the table and strokes it against her cheek*)

MRS. DALTON (*detached*) Flowers are wonderful creatures, Bigger. Each with a personality of its own. You'll learn to love them while you are here.

BIGGER (*in almost mumbling incoherence*) Yessum. (*he looks about him and nervously lifts a glass of water from the little table. He drinks and watches Mrs. Dalton over the rim*)

MRS. DALTON Bigger, we've decided to engage you. This is your new start.

BIGGER Yessum....

MRS. DALTON Now you are one of us—a member of the family—We'll do all in our power to help you find your way in this new life.

BIGGER (*spasmodically*) Yessum. Thank you, ma'am.

MRS. DALTON (*her face tilted up, as if drinking in the sunlight that pours through the window. Reminiscently*) Bigger, I used to teach school, and I once had a colored boy in one of my classes who was so distrustful that he carried a knife and a gun.

BIGGER Huh? (*the glass of water drops from his hand and crashes to the floor* Oh—(*he bends down in a scramble to pick up the glass, but his eyes remain on her face. His hands feel blindly among the splinters, gathering them. He stands up again, his knees bent a little*) I'm sorry, ma'am. I broke one of your glasses.

MRS. DALTON (*quietly*) That's all right—accidents will happen. (*rising*) That is all, Bigger. You have the job. Your pay will be twenty dollars a week, which will go to your mother. There will be five dollars more for yourself. You will have every second Sunday off. Is that clear?

BIGGER (*still in a whisper*) Yessum.

MRS. DALTON (*turning*) And if you're ever bothered about anything, come to me and we'll talk it over. We have a lot of books in the library. You can read any you like.

BIGGER No'm. Yessum.

MRS. DALTON You don't have to read them. Peggy'll show you the rest of the routine. (*she turns and moves slowly out at the left.* BIGGER *stares after her as the door closes. Then he begins to look about him; goes over to the table, picks up a silver knife and weighs it in his hand*)

BIGGER Uhm—(*he puts down the knife, glancing apprehensively at the door. Then he goes over to the sideboard and quickly opens two of the drawers and peers into them. He hears someone coming and quickly closes the drawers.* MARY DALTON *enters from the left, dressed in a flowing red robe, opened at the bosom. It blows and trails behind her. Her hair is bunchy and tousled, and she is puffing a cigarette.* MARY *is a slender, pale-faced girl of some twenty-two or three, with wide, restless dark eyes. Her lips are rouged heavily, and her fingernails done to a deep vermilion. Her whole appearance denotes a sense of boredom and weary child-like disillusionment. She comes on over to the table, then stops and glances at* BIGGER. *He takes a back step*) Yessum.

MARY (*quenching her cigarette in a coffee cup*) I'm not going to hurt you—(BIGGER *stands with downcast eyes, saying nothing.* MARY *pours herself a cup of coffee, pulls a little tin box from her pocket and puts a couple of aspirin tablets into her mouth. She gazes over at* BIGGER *as she gulps from her cup*) What's your name?

BIGGER Bigger—Bigger Thomas, ma'am.

MARY Funny name—Where'd you get it?

BIGGER (*without looking up*) They just give it to me, ma'am.

MARY (*sitting down and picking idly at a roll*) Our new chauffeur?

BIGGER Yessum.

MARY Do you belong to a union?

BIGGER No'm—No'm, I ain't never fooled with them folks, ma'am.

MARY Better join a union or Father'll exploit your shirt off. My name's Mary Dalton. And I've got the most God-awful hangover in the world. Did you ever get drunk, Bigger?

BIGGER (*uncertainly*) No'm.

MARY Has Mother hired you?

BIGGER Yessum.

MARY Well, don't take the job. (*now* BIGGER *looks at her*) I mean it. You'd better keep away from us—from Mother. She'll try to give you a serious, ambitious soul—make you want to be something in the world. And you've got no chance to be anything. None of you colored people have—Where do you live?

BIGGER Over on Indiana Avenue.

MARY You know, some time I'd like to meet some colored people—You know, Bigger, sometimes I drive down South Park way, and I look at all those brick buildings crowded with black people, and I wonder what's going on inside of them. Just think, I live ten blocks from you, and I know nothing about you. I've been all over the world, and I don't know how people live ten blocks from me.

BIGGER (*swallowing*) Yessum.

MARY (*mockingly*) "Yessum, yessum"—Don't you work in this house. Do you hear me? They made a law-abiding punk out of Green. I'll have you meet Jan Erlone and Max and some of our friends. We're having a celebration down at Ernie's tonight. D'you know where it is?

BIGGER Yessum.

MARY You'll drive me down there—

BIGGER Got to—got to stick to my job.

MARY That's your job—to take me where I want to go. (BIGGER *blinks helplessly at her*) Have you got a girl, Bigger? (BIGGER *stares at her*) Bigger, how do you colored people feel about the way you have to live? Do you ever get real mad? Why don't you talk? Oh, maybe I'm not saying the right things, but what are the right things to say? I don't know. Bigger—say something.... How is it that two human beings can stand a foot from each other and not speak the same language? Bigger, what are you thinking about? What are you feeling? (BIGGER *doesn't answer*) D'you think I'm crazy?

BIGGER   No... No, ma'am!

MARY   And you won't be like Green, will you, with your hat in your hand? Who knows, you might be a leader among your own people. And I'd have a part in it. Mother's little spoiled darling'd have a part it... Tonight, Bigger, you're going to meet Max, a man who can tell you things...

BIGGER   Yessum.

MARY   And I appoint you a committee of one to look after me—get me home. If I should happen to drink too much—Hell, I always drink too much.

BIGGER   Got to stick to my job.

MARY   Your job is to do what I tell you! (PEGGY *comes in at the left*)

PEGGY (*sighing*)   Is your head better?

MARY   No.

PEGGY   I'll get you an aspirin.

MARY   I've had one...

PEGGY   I wanted to bring your breakfast up, darlin', but your father—

MARY   Go away and leave me alone!

PEGGY (*after a moment, quietly*)   Come with me, Bigger, and I'll show you about the furnace.

BIGGER   Yessum. (*in the distance, in a room upstairs, a piano begins to play a sentimental piece.* MARY *shudders*)

PEGGY   And the flowers.

BIGGER   Yessum. (*he follows her abjectly out. The piano continues to play.* MARY *lights a cigarette and stands smoking, gazing before her*)

MARY (*quietly*)   Yassum... yassum...

(*The piano continues to play. Fadeout*)

Scene Four

(*The bedroom of* MARY DALTON, *before dawn, a day later. When the curtain rises, the piano stops playing. At the left front is a door opening into the hall, and to the left, and set at an angle from the audience, is* MARY's *bed draped in ghostly white and raised like a dais or bier. At the center rear is a filmy curtained window, and to the right of that a huge oblong mirror, so tilted that its depths are discernible, but only a vague blur of images is reflected in it. In front of the mirror is a delicately-patterned chaise longue and stool. An entrance to the dressing-room is at the right front. The walls of the bedroom are cold and dead, and the whole scene is bathed in the snowy city's pallid light which glimmers through the window.*)

BIGGER'S VOICE (*in hushed anxiety*)   Please, Miss Dalton. Please, stand up and walk. Is this your room? (*her voice, stiff-lipped and almost mechanical, is heard in the hall at the left, drunkenly*)

MARY'S VOICE   A great celebration, Bigger. God, I'm drunk!

BIGGER'S VOICE (*tense and in a hushed pleading*) Sh-sh—(MARY *appears in the door, her hat awry, her hair hanging down, her eyes set in a frozen stare and her face mask-like and dead. She grasps the lintel with her right hand. She has some pamphlets in her hand*)

MARY   And you're drunk, too, Bigger. (*jerking with her left hand*) It's a victory, Bigger. Hooray for the rent strike. Hooray for our side!

BIGGER   For Christ sake! (*still unseen, his voice a sort of moan*) This ain't my job, Miss Dalton.

MARY   It is your job—to see me home—safe home. (*she pulls* BIGGER *on into the room. His head is lowered, his face somewhat averted from her. On his left arm he carries* MARY's *red handbag, hung by its handle. He is dressed in his chauffeur's uniform, his cap off*) The people are strong, Bigger—you and me—thousands like us—Poor Father—Gimme a drink. Why don't you give me a drink? (*she reaches for the handbag*)

BIGGER   No'm.

MARY (*rocking her head from right to left, mockingly*) Yessum—yessum—My father—a landlord that walks like a man—And we had a big celebration, didn't we? Here, Bigger, I want you to read these—The road to freedom—

BIGGER (*moaning again*)   Lemme go, Miss Dalton. (*suddenly his head snaps about him as if he hears an enemy in the dark*) I got to go—ain't my job—got to get out of here.

MARY (*stuffing pamphlets into* BIGGER's *pocket*) Here, take those! Put them in your pocket! (BIGGER *pulls away*) What are you scared of? You don't frighten me, Bigger. I frighten you, now—See, it's all turned around. Crazy world, isn't it?

BIGGER This your room, Miss Dalton? They kill me—kill me—they find me in here—

MARY (*insistently*) Know what I am?

BIGGER (*peeping furtively out from beneath his brows*) I dunno—No'm—I dunno.

MARY I'm what the Russians call "the penitent rich"—I feed the poor—(*her hands go out as if scattering largesse to a begging world, and she strews the pamphlets about the room*) And I'm drunk—and I'm dead—drunk and dead—inside I am—(*giggling, as though at herself*) I'm just a girl falling to pieces—(*shaking her head*) I want to talk—Trouble with the world, Bigger—Nobody to talk to—Mother and Father—they—talk up to God in the sky—I talk down—way, way down to you at the bottom—(*with wild, emotional impulsiveness*) Oh, I wish I was black—Honest, I do—Black like you—down there with you—to start all over again—a new life—(*she puts out her hand toward him. He shivers and stands helplessly paralyzed. She touches his hair*) Your hair is hard. Like little black wires—I know—It has to be hard—tough—to stand it—(*she touches his cheek*)

BIGGER (*in a whispering scream*) Naw—Naw. (*the air of his lungs hisses through his lips and dies, as it were, in an echoing supplication. His face glistens more brightly with the sweat that drenches it. He spits emptily*)

MARY (*looking at her hand*) See, not shoe polish—it don't come off. (*now touching her own cheek and gazing at her crooked, spread-out fingers and wagging her head hopelessly*) There's a difference, and there's not a difference—(*his eyes are lifted, gazing blindly at her*) Bigger, what are you thinking—what are you feeling? (*she begins to weep noiselessly*)

BIGGER (*moaning, twisting his shoulders as if in the grip of some overpowering, aching pain. Gasping*) Lemme go.

MARY Yes, that's what I want—to break through and find you—

BIGGER (*as he speaks, MARY falls, and he lifts her suddenly into his arms*) Ain't my job—ain't my job—

MARY Your arms—hard—hurt—make me feel safe—and hurt—I want to suffer—begin all over again—home—take me home (*singing*) "Swing low, sweet chariot, coming for to carry me home—" That's Mother's favorite song . . . (*with a cry*) Mother! (*her eyes blare wide with fear*) Let me go! Let me—(*but still his arms, as if against his will, hold to her.* MARY *is now staring at him coldly*) Who are you? (*lifting a weak hand, she strikes him blindly in the face*) Stop—(*shrieking*) Stop it! (*wiggling like a rubber thing, queerly alive, the breath goes out of her. Her head falls back and she lies still and limp in his arms. For a moment* BIGGER *does not move. Fascinatedly, he gazes at her face, his lips open and breathless*)

BIGGER (*he jerks his face away from hers, and lowers her feet to the floor; but the upper part of her body hangs over his arm. He looks frantically about him, then eases and half-drags her to the bed. A sob rises into his throat*) Miss Mary—Mary—Mary—Miss Dalton—(*with his head still bowed, his hands go up and onto her reclining figure. Whispering, as his head flies up*) Gotta get away—get away quick. (*now, as if from some interminable distance deep in the house, comes the sound of* MRS. DALTON's *gentle voice*)

MRS. DALTON'S VOICE Mary!—Is that you, Mary?

(BIGGER *springs up terrified. The door at the left swings open and the blur of* MRS. DALTON's *tall form stands there in its white dressing gown. And now, as if the calling voice had penetrated into* MARY's *deep unconsciousness, the bed heaves and a murmur rises from it.* BIGGER's *whole body grows taut, caught in a flooding horror of fear. He stares at* MRS. DALTON *with wide eyes, and as she moves farther into the room he backs noiselessly around the bed from her, the palms of his hands outstretched as if in piteous supplication before her unseeing vision, and his lips making a gasping, soundless cry. For an instant the scene is silent.* MRS. DALTON *clasps her long fingers in front of her and stands listening at the bed*)

MRS. DALTON (*in her normal voice*) Mary? Where are you? (BIGGER *remains across the bed from* MRS. DALTON, *his face tilted and his eyes glued in awe upon the white figure. One of his hands is half-raised, the fingers weakly open as if an object he had been holding had just dropped from them.* MRS. DALTON *calls again*) Mary, are are you asleep? (*there is no answer from the bed. The white figure turns slowly and seems to look about the room.* BIGGER *shrinks back into the shadows as if unable to face the blinding condemnation of that sightless face.* MRS. DALTON *feels toward the bed, and then, as if touching* MARY *through the air itself, suddenly draws back*) You've been drinking. You reek of liquor. (BIGGER *carries his right hand to his mouth as if about to scream. The white figure now sits brokenly down on the edge of the bed. Her hand goes out and rests lovingly on* MARY'S *brow*) My poor child—why do I fail you? Sleep—sleep then. (*rising, she fumbles for the coverlet, spreads it over* MARY'S *feet and turns back toward the door. A low sigh of relief passes through* BIGGER'S *lips.* MRS. DALTON *wheels about*) What is it? (*the sleeping figure lifts a hand and mumbles as if waking up. Quick as a flash and with an instinctive action,* BIGGER *picks up a pillow and pushes it down against* MARY'S *face. Her hands flash in the gloom, clawing helplessly at his arms. But he holds the pillow against her, heedless of her struggle, his face turned watchfully toward* MRS. DALTON. *She takes a step back toward the bed, then stops—in alarm*) Mary—are you ill? (MARY'S *form on the bed moves, and there is a sound of a heavy breath. A quick, muscular taughtness in Bigger's entire body indicates the enormous strength with which he is holding the pillow. The white hands continue to clutch futilely at his wrists.* MRS. DALTON'S *voice calls out sharply*) What is it, Mary? (*pause*) Mary! (*listening. A long pause. The white hands have fallen limp by the pillow now*) Good night, Mary. I'll call you early for your train.

(*She moves silently from the room. There is a loud sound as the door closes behind her. For a moment there is no sound or movement; then with a deep, short gasp of relieved tension,* BIGGER *falls to the floor, catching the weight of his body upon his hands and knees. His chest heaves in and out as though he had just completed a hard foot-race. Gradually, his breathing subsides, and he stands slowly up, looking at the door. His body is relaxed now, the burden of fear gone from him. Then he looks toward the bed, his whole attitude changing, his body becoming taut again. He takes a step forward, then stops uncertainly. He stares at the white form, his face now devoid of that former hard concentration. With a quick movement, he springs to the bed, bends, and stares down at* MARY'S *face. Slowly his hand goes up into the air, the fingers sensitively poised, until again he assumes the same position in which he was standing and looking when the white blur of* MRS. DALTON *first roused him. He stares anxiously at* MARY'S *face, as though a dreadful knowledge were on the threshold of his consciousness. His right hand moves timidly toward* MARY *and touches her, then is jerked quickly away. He touches her head, gently rolls it from side to side, then puts his hands behind him as if they had suffered some strange and sudden hurt*)

BIGGER (*in a whisper*) Naw—naw—(*for a moment he stands looking at the still form, as though it had in some manner deeply offended him. Once more he places his hand upon* MARY'S *head. This time it remains there and his body does not move. He mumbles frenziedly*) Naw—naw—naw—(*he is silent for an instant, then whispers*) I didn't do it—(*he takes a quick step back*) I didn't, I tell you, I didn't. Wake up, wake up, Miss Dalton. (*his voice takes on a note of pleading*) Miss Dalton, Miss Mary—(*for a second he stands, then straightens up suddenly. He turns, walks swiftly to the door, opens it, and looks out into the darkness. All is quiet. He walks back to the center of the room and stands looking at the bed. He mumbles piteously*) Naw—naw—naw—I didn't do it—I didn't go to do it—(*in a clear, sober, deep voice, as if all his faculties were suddenly alive*) They'll say I done it—I'm black and they'll say I done it—(*again he bends over the bed*) I didn't go to do it. You know I didn't. I'm just working here. I didn't want to come here to work. You know I didn't. I was scared—I didn't want to come to your room—you made me come—(*his voice dies out of him in a sob, and he is silent. Far away a clock booms the hour. Slowly his body straightens with intent and purpose. Looking back over his shoulder, at the door, he slides his hands under* MARY'S *body and lifts her in his arms. He turns undecidedly about and sees himself in a mirror on the dressing-table*) Don't you look at me—don't say I done it—I didn't, I tell you—(*for a moment the image in the mirror holds him fascinated. He clasps* MARY *tightly to him as if to protect her and himself. Then suddenly, vehemently, to the image in the mirror, as the hum of the furnace switching itself on is heard below*) Naw—ain't nothin' happened —(*he listens to the furnace draft. He jerks his head up as if struck by a smashing thought. He goes through the door with the body of* MARY *in his arms, and the sound of the furnace draft continues. Fadeout*)

Scene Five

(*The sound of the furnace draft dissolves gradually into the metallic tingling of a telephone. The curtain rises on the* DALTON *study. Afternoon of the same day. At the right of the room are bookshelves, and at the left a fireplace in which some logs are burning. There is a large flat-topped desk in the rear center and across the back a glass partition looking into the fairy-land of flowers and plants of the conservatory. The conservatory is bathed in golden artificial sunlight. On a table near the partition, in which there is a glass door on the right, is a large bouquet of flowers spilling luxuriously over.*
DALTON *is standing by the desk using the telephone.* MRS. DALTON *is sitting in a chair, bolt upright, listening*)

DALTON No, she's not here. (*he pauses, then hangs up the receiver and turns to* MRS. DALTON) Well, that's final. She didn't go to Detroit, Ellen.

MRS. DALTON (*with a tremor in her voice*) Mary had been drinking again last night, Henry. When I came into her room—

DALTON Yes, yes—maybe that Erlone fellow knows something. She was out with him last night.

MRS. DALTON He was down at the station waiting to see her off. He called up—

DALTON Well, Britten ought to be back any minute. (PEGGY *comes in with a tray at the right front. Her face shows signs of recent weeping*)

PEGGY Here's your tea, Mrs. Dalton—

MRS. DALTON (*with a gesture*) No thank you, Peggy.

PEGGY But you must eat and drink, Mrs. Dalton.

MRS. DALTON No, thank you.

PEGGY Mr. Jan Erlone just phoned again—said he was coming right over. He seems worried too. (*she turns and hurriedly goes out, meeting* BRITTEN *in the doorway. She stops.* BRITTEN *comes on in. He is a little man of forty or forty-five, with a thin florid face, and given to a flashy watch chain and ring. He goes over to the fireplace and shakes a bit of snow from his hat and coat*)

BRITTEN Snow's pouring down, all right—regular blizzard for old Santa Claus. Well, Mr. Dalton, looks like Buckley better get busy. That labor crowd's talking up this fellow Edward Max.

DALTON I know, I know—What did you find out at the station, Britten?

BRITTEN Nothing. Absolutely nothing. (*a sob breaks from* PEGGY. *She goes out*) Mmm—I don't understand that car sitting out there, the window open—must have been there for hours—snow four inches deep on the top—I measured it. Your chauffeur says he brought Miss Dalton home about two-thirty.

MRS. DALTON About two-thirty this morning. I heard the clock strike. Later I went to her room.

BRITTEN Ahm—By the way, that colored boy—is he all right?

DALTON He seems all right.

BRITTEN Yeh, he does—dumb-like—Seems to know his place.

DALTON We have his complete record. I talked to him. I'm sure he's all right.

(PEGGY *comes in and listens. While they are talking,* BIGGER *slowly enters the conservatory at the rear. He has a watering can in his hand and goes about quietly and methodically watering the flowers. But even in his nonchalant and detached manner, we sense that he is straining every sense and nerve to hear the words of the group in the study*)

BRITTEN (*to* PEGGY) And what do you think of this colored boy?

PEGGY He's just like all colored boys to me.

BRITTEN Is he polite? Does he pull off his cap when he comes into the house?

PEGGY Yes, sir.

BRITTEN Does he seem to be acting at any time? I mean, does he appear like he's more ignorant than he really is?

PEGGY I don't know, Mr. Britten.

BRITTEN I'd like to talk to that boy again.

PEGGY (*gesturing toward the rear glass door of the conservatory*) He's out there.

BRITTEN (*in a loud voice*) Come in here, boy! (BIGGER *turns, opens the glass door and comes slowly through, still carrying the watering can in his hand.* BRITTEN *turns to him and shouts*) I want to ask you some more questions!

BIGGER (*blinking and starting back*) Yessuh.

BRITTEN What time do you say you took Miss Dalton from here last night?

BIGGER About eight-thirty, suh.

BRITTEN You drove her to her night class at the University? (BIGGER *hangs his head and makes no answer*) Open your mouth and talk, boy. (*he puts out a placating hand to the* DALTONS. *They wait*)

BIGGER Well, Mister, you see—I'm just working here.

BRITTEN You told me that before. You drove her to school, didn't you? (BIGGER *still makes no answer*) I asked you a question, boy!

BIGGER (*his face strangely alert and yet impassive*) No, suh. I didn't drive her to school.

BRITTEN Where did you drive her?

BIGGER Well, suh, she told me after I got as far as the Park to turn around and take her to the loop.

DALTON (*his lips parted in surprise*) She didn't go to school?

BIGGER No, suh.

BRITTEN Huh?

DALTON Why didn't you tell me this before, Bigger?

BIGGER (*quietly*) She told me not to.

BRITTEN Where did you take her, then?

BIGGER To the Loop, suh.

BRITTEN Whereabouts in the Loop?

BIGGER To Lake Street.

BRITTEN Do you remember the number?

BIGGER Sixteen, I think, suh.

BRITTEN (*rubbing his chin*) That's a good boy—Uhm—Sixteen Lake Street, then?

BIGGER Yessuh.

BRITTEN (*kindly*) Say, boy, your water is pouring out on the floor.

BIGGER Thank you, suh. Yessuh! (*he jerks the watering can up and hugs it in front of him*)

BRITTEN How long was she in this place—Number Sixteen?

BIGGER 'Bout half an hour, I reckon, suh.

BRITTEN Then what happened?

BIGGER (*quietly*) Then they came out.

BRITTEN They?

BIGGER Her and this—this Mr. Jan.

BRITTEN Jan Erlone.

DALTON Jan Erlone—that's a friend of hers—

BRITTEN (*he looks triumphantly around him*) And then you drove 'em to—?

BIGGER He wanted to drive and she told me to let him.

BRITTEN And where did they go?

BIGGER To the speaking—to hear that man —Mr. Max—

BRITTEN Ah-hah—Erlone's one of his crowd—Hear that, Mr. Dalton?—And then where did you go?

BIGGER Mr. Jan drove to Ernie's Kitchen Shack.

BRITTEN And how long did they stay there?

BIGGER Well, we must have stayed—

BRITTEN We? Didn't you wait outside in the car?

BIGGER Naw, suh. You see, Mister, I did what they told me. I was only working for 'em.

BRITTEN And then what did you do?

BIGGER They made me eat with 'em. I didn't want to, Mister, I swear I didn't want to. They kept worrying me until I went in and had a drink with 'em.

BRITTEN (*with a placating gesture toward* MRS. DALTON) A drink, eh? So they were drinking—

BIGGER Farewell party and Christmas and all—

BRITTEN And then you brought them home here?

BIGGER Yessuh.

MRS. DALTON (*in sad, but firm graciousness*) How intoxicated was Miss Dalton, Bigger?

BIGGER (*not looking at her*) She—she couldn't hardly stand up—up—ma'am.

BRITTEN And he—this Erlone—he helped her to her room? Huh? (PEGGY *bows her head in her apron*)

DALTON That's all right, Bigger. Go ahead and tell us.

BIGGER Yessuh.

BRITTEN She had passed out, huh?

BIGGER Well, yes, suh. I 'spect you'd call it that.

BRITTEN (*conclusively*) And they told you to leave the car outside, huh?

BIGGER Yes, suh, he told me to leave the car. And I could go on home, get my things, and come back this morning.

BRITTEN How was this Erlone acting? Drunk, eh?

BIGGER Yes, suh, I guess he was drunk. (*suddenly* BRITTEN *takes from his pocket a small batch of pamphlets and holds them under* BIGGER'*s nose*)

BRITTEN Where did you get these?

BIGGER I ain't never seen them things before.

BRITTEN Oh, yeah? I got 'em out of your overcoat pocket—in the basement. Is that your coat?

BIGGER Yessuh.

BRITTEN   Is that the coat you were wearing last night?
BIGGER   Yessuh.
BRITTEN   Then where did you get them?
BIGGER   Miss Dalton, she gave 'em to me, but I didn't read 'em—
BRITTEN   What unit are you in?
BIGGER (*backing away*)   Suh?
BRITTEN (*savagely*)   Come on, Comrade. Tell me what unit you are in? (BIGGER *stares at him in speechless amazement*) Who's your organizer?
BIGGER   I don't know what you mean, suh!
DALTON   Britten, he doesn't know anything about that.
BRITTEN   Didn't you know this Erlone before you came to work here?
BIGGER   Naw, suh, naw, suh—You got me wrong, sir. I ain't never fooled around with them folks. The ones at the meeting last night was the first ones I ever met, so help me God.

(*Now* BRITTEN *comes pushing nearer to* BIGGER *till he has forced him back against the wall at the right. He looks him squarely in the eye, then grabs him by the collar and rams his head against the wall*)

BRITTEN   Come on, gimme the facts. Tell me about Miss Dalton and that Erlone. What did he do to her?
BIGGER   Naw, suh, I ain't—I don't know—Naw, suh.
DALTON (*sternly*)   That's enough, Britten.
BRITTEN   Okay. I guess he's all right. (*smiling kindly at* BIGGER) Just playing a little, son. (BIGGER *gulps and stares at him*) If you say he's okey, then he's okey with me, Mr. Dalton. (*to* BIGGER) You say Erlone told you to leave the car in the drive and then he helped Miss Dalton up to the steps.
BIGGER   Yes, suh.
BRITTEN   And did he go away?
BIGGER   He helped her up the steps, suh, and—uh, she was just about passed out.
BRITTEN   And he went with her into the house?
BIGGER   Yes, suh—(*he suddenly stops and stares toward the door at the right front.* JAN ERLONE *enters. His manner is nervous and agitated, and his face is pale*)
JAN   What are you telling these people, Bigger Thomas?

BRITTEN   Oh, so you walked right in?
JAN (*ignoring him*)   What's all this about? Have you heard anything from Mary—Miss Dalton?
BRITTEN (*savagely*)   You're just in time to tell us. (JAN *stares at* BIGGER, *who straightens up and gazes fearlessly before him.* JAN *looks around*)
JAN   What's happened? Tell me.
BRITTEN   Take it easy. You got plenty of time. I know your kind—you like to rush in and have things your way. (*he turns to* BIGGER) Bigger, is this the man that came home with Miss Dalton last night? (JAN's *lips part. He stares at* BRITTEN, *then at* BIGGER)
BIGGER (*without flinching*)   Yes, suh. (JAN *stares at* BIGGER *with wide incredulous eyes*)
JAN   You didn't bring me here, Bigger. Why do you tell them that? (*crossing to* MRS. DALTON) Mrs. Dalton, I'm worried too. That's why I'm here. What is this? (*to* BRITTEN) What are you making this boy lie for?
BRITTEN   Where is Miss Dalton, Erlone?
JAN   She was supposed to go to Detroit this morning, to see her grandmother.
BRITTEN   We know that. But she didn't go. Did you see Miss Dalton last night?
JAN (*hesitating*)   No.
BRITTEN   But you were with her and with this Negro boy—at Ernie's Kitchen Shack.
JAN   All right then, I saw her. So what?
BRITTEN (*sarcastically*)   So you saw her. Where is she now?
JAN   If she's not in Detroit, I don't know where she is.
BRITTEN   You and Miss Dalton were drunk last night.
JAN   Oh, come on! We weren't drunk. We just had a little to drink.
BRITTEN   You brought her home about two in the morning.
JAN (*after a pause*)   No. (BIGGER *is seen to take a quick step backward and his hand takes hold of the knob on the glass door*)
DALTON   Mr. Erlone, we know my daughter was drunk last night when you brought her here. She was too drunk to leave here by herself. We know that. Now do you know where she is?
JAN (*stammering*)   I—I didn't come here last night.
BRITTEN   But you were with her and she was drunk. Do you mean you left her in that condition?

JAN (*hesitating and swallowing*) Well, I came as far as the door with her. I had to go to a meeting. I took the trolley. Had to hurry. (JAN *turns to* BIGGER) Bigger, what are you telling these people? (BIGGER *makes no answer*)

MRS. DALTON (*in an agitated voice*) I'll see you in my room, Henry—please. (PEGGY *comes over to her, helps her up and assists her from the room. Just before she leaves,* MRS. DALTON *turns and gazes toward* JAN *with her sightless eyes. Then lowering her head, she goes away with* PEGGY)

JAN (*beseechingly around him*) Bigger, didn't you get Miss Dalton home safely? What's happened to her? (BIGGER *gazes stonily at him and does not answer.* JAN *seems to read a strange and ultimate antagonism in* BIGGER's *face, for he gradually lowers his head and stares at the floor*)

BRITTEN (*chuckling*) So Bigger brought her home and you didn't?

JAN Yes.

BRITTEN You're a liar, Erlone. First you say you didn't see her, then you did. Then you didn't bring her home, then you did. Then again you didn't—Come on, what's your game?

JAN (*in a low desolate voice as he stares about him*) I was trying to protect her.

BRITTEN You're trying to protect yourself, and making a damn poor job of it.

JAN I didn't come here, I tell you.

BRITTEN You got Miss Dalton drunk, Erlone—you brought her here early this morning. You told the boy to leave the car out in the driveway. You went inside and went upstairs with her, and now she's disappeared. Where is she? (JAN *looks at him with staring, bewildered eyes*)

JAN Listen, I told you all I know.

DALTON (*stepping forward*) Erlone, you and I don't agree on certain things. Let's forget that. I want to know where my daughter is.

JAN I tell you I don't know, Mr. Dalton. (DALTON *throws up his hands in futile, desperate anger*)

DALTON We'll see you upstairs later, Britten. (*he goes out*)

BRITTEN (*blocking the way to the door and glaring at* JAN *as he yells*) Get over there! (JAN *backs away from his menacing look*) Now listen to me, you goddam red—

JAN I tell you I don't know where she is!

BRITTEN All right. You don't know now—eh? But you will know, and you'll know damn soon. We've a way of handling your kind— (*he turns to go as* PEGGY *appears in the door*)

PEGGY Mr. Dalton said please come up. And you better look after the furnace, Bigger. It needs tending—

BRITTEN Okay. That's all I got to say now, Erlone. (*he follows* PEGGY *out. For a moment,* JAN *stares at the floor.* BIGGER *watches him with steady, smoldering eyes. In the street outside, a chorus begins singing a Christmas carol. Slowly* BIGGER's *hand goes up and slides into his coat and rests there. Presently* JAN *looks up*)

JAN Bigger.

BIGGER (*in a low humming voice*) Go on away from here, Mr. Jan. Go on way.

JAN What's all this about, Bigger? Why did you tell those lies?

BIGGER You heard me.

JAN I haven't done anything to you, have I? Where's Mary?

BIGGER (*mumbling*) I don't want to talk to you.

JAN (*desperately*) But what have I done to you?

BIGGER I don't want to talk to you. (*with a sharp cry*) Get out!

JAN Listen, Bigger. If these people are bothering you, just tell me. Don't be scared. We are used to this sort of persecution. Mr. Max will help you in your rights. He knows their crooked law. Listen, now. Tell me about it. Come on, we'll go out and get a cup of coffee and talk it over. (JAN *comes toward him.* BIGGER *suddenly whips out his gun, and* JAN *stops with white face*) For God's sake, man, what are you doing?

BIGGER I don't need you—that Mr. Max neither—(*hoarsely*) Get out!

JAN I haven't bothered you. Don't—

BIGGER (*his voice tense and hysterical*) Leave me alone.

JAN (*backing away from him*) For Christ's sake, man!

BIGGER (*his voice rising almost to a scream*) Get away from here! Now! Now!

(JAN *backs farther away, then turns and goes rapidly out at the right front, looking back over his shoulder with hurt and helpless eyes. For a moment Bigger stands still, then slowly his hand replaces the pistol in his coat. In the basement below the windy draft of the furnace begins blow-*

ing. BIGGER *jerks his head up with a shudder, listening. Gradually a low moaning sound rises from his lips. For a moment he remains so, then wheeling quickly, he goes into the conservatory and passes out of sight through the flowers at the right rear, leaving the watering can sitting on the floor. The music of the carol singers comes in more strongly from the street and continues. Fadeout*)

Scene Six

(*The music of the carol singers melts into the evangelical fervor of a Negro song service in a church across the street. The curtain rises upon* CLARA MEARS' *one-room kitchenette apartment. A bed is at the left rear, a window by it, and a dresser at the right front next to the door. In the right rear are a sink and little table. It is night, a few hours later.* CLARA *is standing in front of her mirror arranging her hair. She is partly dressed.* BIGGER *is sitting on the edge of the bed dressed in trousers and undershirt. His shoulders are hunched over. The Negro song service continues intermittently throughout the scene*)

CLARA (*glancing over at* BIGGER'S *coat hanging on the chair at the left*) Look, puddles of water dripped all over the floor from your coat. (*she moves the chair and coat over near the radiator, then goes back to the mirror*)

BIGGER (*muttering musingly*) Yeh, like a little brown doll talking about a wet coat and puddles on the floor—rain and snow, they don't matter. (*he flings out a clenched fist and bangs the railing of the bed. Clara turns toward him questioningly*)

CLARA Bigger, what's wrong with you?

BIGGER (*musingly*) She asks me what's wrong—yeh, what's wrong?

CLARA You don't seem like yourself—You ain't yourself—

BIGGER All right, I ain't. I'm different, then.

CLARA (*tripping swiftly over and dropping on her knees by him*) Bigger, honey, don't be like that. Don't stay away from me. You stay away from me for two days—then when you show up—

BIGGER Aw, can it.

CLARA All the time I loved you in my arms there, seemed like you full of something different.

BIGGER You done had all you want from me now, and I better go.

CLARA (*impulsively grabbing his hand and kissing it*) Please, Bigger, I don't mean to make you mad. I want to make you happy—that's all I want. You know that. I know your folks tries to turn you against me—say I ain't no good.

BIGGER (*growling, he turns and seizes her roughly by the shoulders, his voice a mixture of anguish and cruelty and bitter love*) Goddam it, you know why I come here—'Cause I can't help it. I wish I could help it—Now I wish I could—(*springing up*)

CLARA Bigger, what's the matter? Don't you love me no more?

BIGGER Sometimes I do love you—Then I feel you holding me down—pulling at me—

CLARA (*half weeping*) I don't—I don't—

BIGGER And it's your little soft baby-talk again—fumbling around my heart—and then we get some liquor—and end up by kissing and going to bed. You all around me—Like a swamp sucking me under—Can't see—Can't think—Goddam, I hate it! I hate it! Wish it was different. Now I do.

CLARA (*echoing*) Now! How come you keep saying "now" all the time? (BIGGER *stares unseeingly.* CLARA'S *inquiring, begging eyes are fastened on his face. He breaks into hoarse, raucous laughter and pounds his knees with his fists.* CLARA *whispering*) How come you laughing like that? (*she shudders*)

BIGGER Yeh, I'm laughing—laughing at everybody—everybody in the whole damn world. Laughing at you.

CLARA (*piteously*) Please, Bigger. (*frantically*) Bigger, you talk wild, drunk-like—

BIGGER (*gesturing*) That little old bottle of whisky? Hunh, didn't even feel it.

CLARA Why don't you try to sleep some? I'll fix you supper. You tired. Your po' face all tight, and yo' eyes full of blood. (*she rises and stands by his side*)

BIGGER (*his arm clutching around her as though suddenly doubting everything*) You love me, Clara?

CLARA You know that. (*she bends down and kisses him on the forehead*) And it ain't things you give me and all that money don't matter. (*indicating the dresser*) It don't matter at all. (*her arm is tight along his side. Suddenly she draws it away with an exclamation*) Something hard in your pocket, Bigger. You got a gun—(*gasping*) Is that why you got all that money? Rob somebody?

BIGGER   I ain't, I tell you. (*snickering*) Maybe they give me something in advance on my job.

CLARA   Who? (*looking at him sharply*) Old white gal I seen you eating with, down at Ernie's last night?

BIGGER   Maybe.

CLARA (*in fierce jealousy*)   She's crazy. Her face say she's crazy.

BIGGER (*sharply*)   Aw, don't worry 'bout her.

CLARA (*anxiously*)   Leave her alone, honey. She'll get you in trouble.

BIGGER   Nunh-unh.

CLARA   Say, Bigger, where is this you working—the Dalton place?

BIGGER (*sharply*)   How come you want to know that?

CLARA   I just like to know, honey! How come you don't want to talk none?

BIGGER   Over there on Drexel...

CLARA   That's where them rich folks live... That's where they had that kidnaping last year.

BIGGER   Huh?

CLARA   Kidnap that girl—and tried to get money from her folks?

BIGGER (*staring off*)   Tried to get money. Yeh, yeh, I remember. (*springing up*) Money! Goddamit. Everybody talking about it—papers with headlines, telephones ringing. Yeh, let 'em ring—ringing all over America, asking, asking about Bigger. The bells ringing; they'll sound the sirens and the ambulances beat their gongs.

CLARA   Bigger! Bigger! (*in sharp and unbelieving reproof*) There's something wrong, make you talk like that.

BIGGER (*turning to her and speaking almost kindly, as he touches her face affectionately*) Yeh, Clara, plenty wrong. I tell you now, and you stay with me?

CLARA   What is it, Bigger?

BIGGER (*shouting*)   You stay with me, I say?

CLARA   Yes, anything, Bigger. I stay with you.

BIGGER   Sit down (*she sinks obediently to the bed*) Listen, now. I'm a fool to tell you, but I got to tell you. (*queerly*) Got to tell somebody. I don't know what's gonna happen, Clara. (*suddenly matter-of-factly*) Maybe I got to get out of town soon.

CLARA   What you done?

BIGGER   Right now, it come to me, you help me, you and me together—nobody won't know—we be safe then, money make us safe.

CLARA (*her eyes wide and still*)   What you talking about?

BIGGER (*turning and beginning to pace the floor*) Listen. This gal where I work—this Dalton gal—she crazy. Crazier'n hell, see? Father's a rich man—millionaire—(*pauses*) Millionaire—(*shooting his words out again*) And she's done run off—Always hanging around with them reds—maybe done run off with one of 'em.

CLARA   I told you.

BIGGER   Nobody don't know where she's gone. So last night I—maybe she give me money to hush my mouth. See? They throw money around everywhere. They don't care none. Just pay in advance maybe.

CLARA   I don't care none, Bigger. It ain't the money.

BIGGER (*shouting*)   Shut your damn mouth. (*pulling the back of his hand nervously across his lips*) They don't know where she is—so, they sit worrying. All day they been worrying. The old man pacing the floor like me now. (*a harsh laugh breaking from him*) But I'm walking different. See? Different. And that blind woman—holding them white flower hands together and crying out, "Where's my daughter?" And that detective tromping about, mashing things down. "Where is she?" they saying. They don't know. I know.

CLARA (*crying out*)   Bigger, what you talking about? What you done?

BIGGER   I tell you. They think she's kidnaped. Yeh, them reds got her. I heard 'em say so. Gonna ask for money, see? Plenty.

CLARA (*pleadingly*)   Maybe she'll show up, Bigger. She'll come back.

BIGGER (*waving his hand excitedly*)   Don't worry about that. Yeh, money. They got plenty of dough. They won't miss it. And we get some of it. How come? Then you and me—we's free. Goddamit, free! You hear me? Free like them. (*suddenly sitting down and turning excitedly and close to her*) One of them old empty buildings over there—Yeh, 36 Place and Michigan—door open all the time. I'll write 'em a letter, and we'll wait for 'em there.

CLARA (*weeping*)   But you can't do that, Bigger. They'll catch you. They'll never stop looking. The white folks never stop looking—

BIGGER Yeh, but looking for the wrong folks.

CLARA But you know where the girl is. She'll show up.

BIGGER She won't.

CLARA How you know?

BIGGER She just won't.

CLARA Bigger, you ain't done nothing to that girl, has you?

BIGGER (*throwing back his hand*) Say that again and I'll slap you through the floor. Yeh, I'll get the pencil and paper—(*springing up and moving toward the dresser*) Write them a letter—print it. Think they sharp, huh? We see. We see. (*he rummages in the dresser.* CLARA *gazes helplessly at him, words beginning to break through her dying sobs*)

CLARA Bigger, what you doing? What you doing to me?

BIGGER (*unheedingly*) Here she is. (*he gets the paper and pencil. Looking about him for a place to write, he drops down on the floor and spreads the sheet out, biting the pencil ruminatively the while*)

CLARA All you ever caused me was trouble—just plain black trouble. I been a fool—just a blind, dumb, black, drunk fool; and I'll go on being a fool 'cause I love you—love you clean down to hell—ain't never had nobody but you—nobody in my arms but you, close against me but you—(*she moves unsteadily over and stands behind him. Falling down on her knees, she lays her face against the back of his neck, her arms around him*)

BIGGER Shut up, now. I got to write. No. I'll print it—with my left hand. Yeh, I'll sign the note "Red." They're all scared of Reds. You see it in the newspapers—(*exultantly*) Won't ever think we done it. Think we too scared. (*excitedly*) We ain't scared, is we, Clara? Ain't scared to do anything. (*writing*) "Dear Sir." Ha! Ha! Naw, just "Sir." (*cocking his head*) Look at that word. A few more of them and the whole world turn upside-down, and we done it. Big headlines in the papers, police running around like chickens with their heads cut off—and all the time we stay back watching, waiting to pick up the dough where they put it. (*his voice rising to a croon which mockingly apes the rhythm of the distant singing*) Twenty years, up and down the dark alleys, like a rat. Nobody hear us—(CLARA *slides further down on the floor beside him, her face buried protectively and protectedly against him*)—nobody hear you, nobody pay any attention to you, and the white folks walking high and mighty don't even know we're alive. Now they cut the pigeon wing the way we say—

CLARA (*moaning*) Bigger, Bigger! (*she falls sobbing on the floor*)

BIGGER (*his head raised, staring off, his face alight with his vision*) Like bars falling away—like doors swinging open, and walls falling down. And all the big cars and all the big buildings, and the finery and the marching up and down, and the big churches and the bells ringing and the millionaires walking in and out bowing low before their God—Hunh-huh. It ain't God now, it's Bigger. Bigger, that's my name! (CLARA's *sobs break hopelessly through the room.* BIGGER *bends his head and begins to write*) "Sir:—We got your daughter—say nothing—the ransom is—"

(*The song service comes more loudly into the room. Fadeout*)

Scene Seven

(*The song service dies away, and the curtain comes up on the basement of the Dalton home, the next night. The walls of the scene are painted a solid, glistening gray; the ceiling is high, and crossed by the tubes of many white asbestos-covered pipes. To the left rear is a squat iron furnace, with dull baleful eye of the fire showing through its isinglass door and reflecting on the wall. Behind it is the jutting angle of the coal bin. At the center rear are steps leading up to the kitchen pantry. At the center right is a door leading to the outside. To the left, near the stairs, are trunks, boxes, and piles of old newspapers, and on the opposite side of the stairs, clothes are hanging to dry.*

When the curtain rises, BIGGER *is seen standing by the furnace, motionless and looking intently before him. He starts in terror as the door at the upper center rear opens and* BRITTEN *stands looking down into the reddish gloom*)

BRITTEN That you, Bigger?

BIGGER Oh—(*he whirls and backs quickly to the wall, his hands groping for the ax that hangs within reach. He comes to himself quickly)* Yessuh. Yessuh.

BRITTEN *(descending the stairs)* Fixing the furnace?

BIGGER *(still gripping the ax in his right hand)* Yessuh.

BRITTEN *(with a little laugh)* What? With the ax?

BIGGER *(in confusion)* No suh—no, suh—Huh—I—*(he breaks off, hangs the ax back on the wall and picks up the shovel)*

BRITTEN You sure jumped like the devil was after you. *(coming over to the furnace)* Yeh, I reckon you are a little on edge. Dogonne it, I'm nervous as a cat myself with all this "Who shot John" around here. *(BIGGER still stands with the shovel in his hand, watching his movements. BRITTEN opens the furnace and stoops to gaze inside. BIGGER quickly gets behind him with the shovel and slowly raises it. BRITTEN clangs the door shut and straightens up)* No wonder the house is freezing upstairs—a ton of ashes banked up in there.

BIGGER *(lowering the shovel and backing away, his eyes fastened intently upon BRITTEN's face)* Yessuh, I'm gonna fix it right away.

BRITTEN *(as a pounding begins on the door at the right)* What's that? Just listen to 'em. Goddam newspapermen. *(the pounding continues)* Say, Bigger, did you lock that gate to the driveway? *(before BIGGER can answer, the door at the right opens and several newspapermen crowd their way in, some of them with cameras. BRITTEN tries to stop them)* You can't come in. Get out and stay out.

VOICE We're in, Mr. Britten.

(One of them is a lean, lynx-eyed, horse-trader type of man with an old dark felt hat set back on his head. BIGGER backs slowly away to the wall at the left and stands alert in the shadow. As the scene progresses, the NEWSPAPERMAN begins to watch BIGGER)

BRITTEN Now, listen here, boys. This is Mr. Dalton's home. And Mr. Dalton's got no statement to make.

VOICES What's the dope? Come on. What's going on?

BRITTEN Nothing! *(the FIRST NEWSPAPERMAN pushes forward, a cigarette in his mouth and snow on his old hat and coat. He wanders aimlessly around the scene)*

VOICE How about that red you picked up?
SECOND VOICE Jan Erlone?
THIRD VOICE Was she sleeping with him?
VOICE He says he didn't even come here that night. Says he's got witnesses. Says you had him arrested because he's a Communist.
BRITTEN *(shouting)* I don't know a thing—not a goddam thing.

(The reporters have their pads and pencils out. They crowd around BRITTEN, shooting questions at him)

VOICES When was she seen last?
Can we get a picture of her room?
Is the girl really missing?
Or is that a publicity stunt, Britten?

(A flash bulb goes off in BRITTEN's face. He blinks and backs away)

BRITTEN Hey, steady, boys.
VOICE What's the matter?
BRITTEN I only work here. For Christ's sake, give me a break. *(another flash bulb explodes in his face)*
VOICE Then talk.
ANOTHER VOICE Maybe this boy'll talk.
BRITTEN He don't know a damn thing.
VOICE Say, Mike, what do you think?
BIGGER *(in a hard, cold voice)* My name ain't Mike.
VOICE That's the Thomas boy. Bigger Thomas.
VOICE I'd like to ask you a few questions, Mr. Thomas. *(BIGGER makes no reply)*
BRITTEN He's dumb. He don't know nothing. *(a bulb goes off in BIGGER's face. BIGGER dodges, throwing his hands before his eyes)*
BRITTEN *(helplessly)* Cut it out, will you? Listen, boys—they're worried about the girl—Mrs. Dalton's ill. The whole house is upset—*(a newspaperman walks over to BIGGER and slips something into his hand)*
VOICE Come on, boy. Give us a break.
BRITTEN *(hurrying forward)* No, none of that. *(he snatches the money from BIGGER's fingers and returns it to the newspaperman)* Take your damn money back. *(BIGGER inches away from them, his head lowered. All fall abruptly silent as the door at the upper center opens and MR. DALTON—old, weary, and shaken—stands framed in the light, the red shadows flickering across his wan features. He holds a white piece of paper trembl-

ingly in his hand. The photographers begin hastily loading their cameras)

DALTON Gentlemen—(*they all watch him, waiting, as he descends the steps.* BRITTEN *moves to his side with the protection of the law. Several flash bulbs now blind the scene as* DALTON *lifts his hand, emphasizing his words*) Please, gentlemen—just a moment. (*pause*) I am ready to make a statement now. (*his voice fails, then goes on*) I want you to listen carefully—(*pause*) The way you gentlemen handle this will mean life or death to someone—someone very dear to me. (*the bulbs flash again, making* DALTON *blink and lose the train of his thought. Pencils are already flying over their pads.* MRS. DALTON, *dressed in white, holding the white cat in her arms, appears in the doorway and descends the stairs and stops. One photographer is on his knees, pointing his camera upwards.* PEGGY's *face also comes timidly into the doorway, looking down.* BIGGER *remains silent by the wall, his right hand going now and then to his lips in a nervous gesture*) Gentlemen, I have just phoned the police and requested that Mr. Erlone be released immediately. I want it known and understood publicly that I have no charges to prefer against him. It is of the utmost importance that this be understood. I hope your papers will carry the story. Further, I want to announce publicly that I apologize for his arrest and inconvenience. Gentlemen, our daughter, Mary Dalton—(*his voice fails*)—has been kidnaped. (*there is a commotion in the basement.* BRITTEN *confirms the news with a sage nod of his head as if he knew it all the time*)

VOICE How do you know, Mr. Dalton?

VOICE When did it happen?

DALTON (*recovering himself*) We think it happened early Sunday morning.

VOICE How much are they asking?

DALTON Ten thousand dollars.

VOICE Have you any idea who they are?

DALTON We know nothing.

VOICE Have you received any word from her, Mr. Dalton?

DALTON No, not directly, but we *have* heard from the kidnapers.

VOICE Is that the letter there?

DALTON Yes, this is it.

VOICE Did it come through the mail? How did you get it?

DALTON Someone left it under the door.

VOICE When?

DALTON An hour ago.

VOICE Can we see it?

DALTON The instructions for the delivery of the money are here, and I have been cautioned not to make them public. But you can say in your papers that these instructions will be followed, and I shall pay the ransom.

VOICE How is the note signed? (*there is silence*)

DALTON It's signed "Red."

VOICES Red! Do you know who it is? What does that mean?

DALTON No.

VOICE Do you think some Communist did it, Mr. Dalton?

DALTON I don't know. I am not positively blaming anybody. If my daughter is returned, I'll ask no questions of anyone. Now that's all, gentlemen—all—(*with a final wave of his hand, he turns and follows* MRS. DALTON *up the steps. There is a babble of noise among the newspapermen*)

VOICES (*swirling around the confused* BRITTEN) Get a shot of her room. Climb a tree if you have to. And play up the blind mother and the cat. (*the newspapermen begin rushing out of the basement at the right.* BRITTEN *stands guarding the entrance up the stairs at the rear*) Hell, this is bigger than the Loeb-Leopold case. Do you believe it? What do you think?

BRITTEN (*half-forcing, half-following them out*) Come on, fellows, have a heart. Give the old man a break.

(*And now the newspapermen have all scrambled out except the* FIRST NEWSPAPERMAN, *who stands gazing with apparent idleness at* BIGGER's *form in the shadow. He turns and strolls over toward the door at the right, whistling aimlessly, through his teeth.* BRITTEN *mops his forehead and goes hurriedly up the stairs and out at the rear.* BIGGER *comes tremblingly forward and stands in front of the furnace, gazing at the red, gleaming light. And now we see that the* FIRST NEWSPAPERMAN *has stopped in the shadow at the right and is looking back at* BIGGER. PEGGY *comes swiftly down the steps*)

PEGGY Bigger!

BIGGER Huh? (*whirling again*)

PEGGY For goodness sake, get the fire going.

BIGGER Yessum.

PEGGY Now! Mrs. Dalton's had to wear her shawl all day to keep warm. (*she picks up the shovel and hands it to him*) Go ahead. It won't bite you—(*at the tone of her voice the* FIRST NEWSPAPERMAN *looks around*) I'll have your supper ready soon.

BIGGER (*taking the shovel mechanically*) Yessum.

(*She goes hurriedly up the stairs.* BIGGER *stands holding the shovel in his hand. He bends down, reaches out to open the door, then takes his hand away and backs off. The lean figure of the* FIRST NEWSPAPERMAN *comes strolling back out of the shadows at the right*)

FIRST NEWSPAPERMAN What's the trouble, boy? (BIGGER *springs around, the shovel flying instinctively up in the air as if about to strike something*)

BIGGER (*dropping the shovel swiftly down, its edge hitting the top of his foot*) Nothing, suh—Nothing, suh. (*his foot, as though a separate and painful part of him, lifts itself up from the floor and wiggles in its shoe, then grows still again*)

FIRST NEWSPAPERMAN Awful nervous, huh?

BIGGER Naw, suh. Naw, suh, I ain't nervous.

FIRST NEWSPAPERMAN Have a cigarette.

BIGGER Nawsuh, nawsuh.

FIRST NEWSPAPERMAN (*pulling one out and lighting it, then holding the package out to* BIGGER) Don't smoke?

BIGGER Yessuh. (*he takes one of the cigarettes, his hand trembling in spite of itself*)

FIRST NEWSPAPERMAN Here, let me light it for you. (*he strikes a match, and holds it for* BIGGER, *staring keenly at his face*) Sort of warm, ain't you?

BIGGER Naw, suh.

FIRST NEWSPAPERMAN You're sweating a lot. And I'm freezing. You're supposed to tend the furnace, ain't you?

BIGGER Yessuh.

FIRST NEWSPAPERMAN (*staring at him*) Then why don't you do it?

BIGGER (*without moving*) Yessuh.

FIRST NEWSPAPERMAN Sit down, son. I want to talk with you a little. (*he pulls a couple of chairs out from the rear, sits in one, and motions* BIGGER *to the other.* BIGGER *sinks quietly down, breathing heavily. He sucks the smoke of the cigarette deep into his lungs, and as if through that action gaining control of himself, he lifts his face and looks directly at his questioner*)

BIGGER (*in a clear hard voice*) How come you want to talk to me?

FIRST NEWSPAPERMAN Just a few questions. You know anything connected with this story is news. Say, what do you think of private property?

BIGGER Suh? Naw, suh, I don't own no property.

FIRST NEWSPAPERMAN (*soothingly*) Sure, sure. (*puffing on his cigarette, his eyes crinkling into a gentle smile*) Tell me, what do *you* think of Miss Dalton? I've heard she was sort of wild.

BIGGER (*quickly*) Nawsuh, nawsuh. She was a mighty fine lady.

FIRST NEWSPAPERMAN (*coolly, blowing a ring of smoke*) Why do you say she *was*?

BIGGER I—uh—I mean she was fine to me.

FIRST NEWSPAPERMAN Yes, the Daltons are mighty fine folks. (*as though veering off from the subject*) What did old Max talk about at that meeting last night?

BIGGER Suh?

FIRST NEWSPAPERMAN Some of his radical ideas? What did he say to you—well, about the rich and the poor?

BIGGER Well, suh, he told me that some day there'd be no more rich folks and no more poor folks, if folks could get together . . .

FIRST NEWSPAPERMAN Here's hoping, son—especially about the poor.

BIGGER And he said that a black man could have a chance to get a good job like anybody else—and stand up high and equal.

FIRST NEWSPAPERMAN And there wouldn't be any more lynchings?

BIGGER Yessuh, no more lynchings.

FIRST NEWSPAPERMAN And what did the girl, Miss Dalton, say?

BIGGER She said so too.

FIRST NEWSPAPERMAN And what did he say to you about white women?

BIGGER Nothing, suh, nothing.

FIRST NEWSPAPERMAN (*sighing*) Too bad! You know, Bigger, such things as this ought to be a warning to this country. Here was a happy family, living in peace, loving their neighbor, with one daughter—a beautiful daughter—You agree with that, don't you, Bigger?

BIGGER Yessuh.

FIRST NEWSPAPERMAN Yes, it's a warning to

us. You might say she was a martyr, died to help us to see the error of our ways. We've got to learn to treat people better in this country—raise up the oppressed, give them a chance. From what I've heard, Mary Dalton thought like that, too. (BIGGER *now and then gives him a queer, questioning, baffled look*) What do you think has happened to her?

BIGGER   I don't know, suh.

FIRST NEWSPAPERMAN   Look, that cigarette's burning your fingers. (BIGGER *drops it like a hot coal. The* FIRST NEWSPAPERMAN *offers him another. Bigger shakes his head*) They must have killed her, don't you think?

BIGGER (*spasmodically*)   They must've done it, sir.

FIRST NEWSPAPERMAN   Who?

BIGGER   Them reds, sir.

FIRST NEWSPAPERMAN   And then write a note signing their name to it. You don't think you'd do that, do you, Bigger? (*his voice is low and cool and insinuating*)

BIGGER   Nawsuh, nawsuh.

FIRST NEWSPAPERMAN (*hunching his chair confidentially up toward* BIGGER)   Just suppose you had killed her, Bigger—

BIGGER (*wildly*)   Nawsuh, I didn't do it. I didn't do it!

FIRST NEWSPAPERMAN   Aw, take it easy. Just suppose I had killed her. Now that we both agree she's dead. Well, what would *I* do? (*he rises slowly out of his chair, pushes his hands into his pockets, and begins walking slowly back and forth in a weaving semicircle around* BIGGER, *his hat tilted back on his head*) Let me see. Yes, I need money. I'd write a ransom note, collect that before they found out she'd been murdered. Wouldn't you do it that way, Bigger?

BIGGER   Nawsuh.

FIRST NEWSPAPERMAN   What would you do?

BIGGER   I didn't do it.

FIRST NEWSPAPERMAN   I'm just imagining. Where were we? Oh, she's murdered. So now, we've got to dispose of the body—no traces—nobody ever to know. Well, what about a trunk —ship it off somewhere? Nunh-unh, that wouldn't do. What about weights—sink her to the bottom of the lake? Nunh-unh, they always rise to the surface. Bury her? No, that's too difficult. Somebody see you. What is it that wipes away all traces, Bigger?

BIGGER   Dunno, sir.

FIRST NEWSPAPERMAN   I'll tell you—fire. (*whirling and snapping his fingers*) Yeh, that's what I'd do—I'd burn the body up. Wouldn't you, Bigger? (*with sudden loudness*) Go ahead and shake the ashes down, like the woman said. (BIGGER'*s head sinks lower still, his shoulders shaking. With a click the thermostat turns the furnace fan on. There is a deep, blowing draft of sound.* BIGGER *springs out of his chair. The* FIRST NEWSPAPERMAN *looks at him wonderingly*) Come on, now. Shake 'em down. (*flipping a coin in his hand*) Bet you two bits you won't. (BIGGER *bends puppet-like down and reaches for the shovel. The* FIRST NEWSPAPERMAN *steps briskly over and lifts down the ax, and weighs it idly in his hand.* BIGGER *turns slowly around. The* FIRST NEWSPAPERMAN *smiles at him*) This is a good ax, Bigger. Old Kelly. I used to chop with one like this when I was a kid, back on the farm. And I was good at trapping in the winter—used to catch a lot. (*and now in desperation,* BIGGER *turns fiercely back to the furnace, flings open the door and plunges the shovel into the blinding bank of glowing, red-hot ashes. A puff of dust sails out and settles about the room. Then flinging the shovel down, he hysterically seizes the upright grate handle and shakes it with a great clatter*) Hell of a lot of ashes in there, boy.

BIGGER (*breathing deeply*)   It's all fixed now. Draws fine—everything be warmed up now. (*yelling at the ceiling above him*) Miss Peggy, the furnace okay now! Listen at her sing! (*making a puffing noise with his lips*) She's putting on the steam now! Going to town. Goddam, Goddam. (*he begins whistling cheerily*)

FIRST NEWSPAPERMAN (*hanging the ax behind him and strolling over again*)   Sing on, boy, sounds mighty good.

BIGGER (*joy breaking in his voice*)   Yessuh, and I can do the boogie-woogie if I'm pushed. Listen to that old coal roll on down! The old valve creeping up—soon be popping off. Hear them drivers roll. (BRITTEN *comes hurriedly down the steps at the rear*)

BRITTEN   What's going on here? Hell of a time to be singing. (*the* NEWSPAPERMAN *is now standing by the pile of ashes idly stirring them with the toe of his shoe*)

FIRST NEWSPAPERMAN   He's a croon-baby. Come on, baby, sing us some more.

BIGGER   Got to clean up now. (*he grabs a broom from behind the furnace and goes to work.*

The NEWSPAPERMAN *bends down and picks something out of the ashes)*

BRITTEN So you're still here, huh?

FIRST NEWSPAPERMAN Yeh, just poking around—looking for my story.

BRITTEN (*sarcastically*) Ain't found it, I reckon.

FIRST NEWSPAPERMAN Maybe—according to deduction—

BRITTEN Hell of a note. We just called up the jail and that Erlone fellow won't leave. He's raising hell—

FIRST NEWSPAPERMAN Says this Bigger boy's been lying, don't he? (*he stares at a tiny object he holds between his fingers.* BIGGER *stops stockstill, staring at the* NEWSPAPERMAN, *caught again suddenly in the grip of his fear*)

BRITTEN How'd you know? That's just what he said.

FIRST NEWSPAPERMAN (*holding his hand out toward* BRITTEN) Here's an earring, Britten. It might interest you. (BIGGER's *mouth flies open and a horrified gasp breaks from him.* BRITTEN *takes the earring and looks at it inquiringly*)

BRITTEN Where'd you get it?

FIRST NEWSPAPERMAN Just picked it up. Tell him where I got it, Bigger.

BIGGER (*screaming*) Let me out of here! Let me out! (*he staggers as if about to fall, then stumbles drunkenly across the room and flies through the door yelling as he goes*) I didn't do it! I didn't do it!

BRITTEN (*pushing back his hat*) Holy smoke! What's the matter with him—having a fit or something?

FIRST NEWSPAPERMAN You'd better catch him. He killed Mary Dalton and burned her in that furnace.

(BRITTEN *stares at him, dumbfounded, then pulling a whistle from his pocket begins blowing it wildly as he rushes toward the door at the right. In the distance other whistles begin to sound continuously. Fadeout*)

Scene Eight

(*The sounds of commotion and pursuit die away, as the curtain rises. It is the next night—an empty room on the top floor of an abandoned house. The rear wall of the room has collapsed and gives a view of a ruined balcony at the back, with frozen roof-tops, chimneys, and a stretch of night sky beyond. Remaining in the extreme left of this rear wall is a jagged section, on which is hanging a once ornate and gilded picture frame, now cankered and dark from the beatings of the weather. The frame contains a semblance of a family portrait. Part of the wall at the right rear leans forward, and in, to form a sort of shelter. In the shadow at the right front is the distorted shape of a doorframe. The color of the scene runs from thick black shadow at the right to a diffused yellowish glare in the center and back. The wind moans intermittently. From the deep canyon below, comes the muffled drone of the great city, punctuated by an auto horn, a snatch of radio music, and vague wandering noises—all hushed and muted down by the thick snow enveloping the world. The room is lit up at intervals by the changing colors of what is evidently a large electric sign on a neighboring roof. Less noticeable at first, is the faint light from a revolving beacon far away.*

When the curtain rises, BIGGER *is seen standing half-crouched in the shadow of the wall at the right rear. An old piece of rotted blanket is pulled protectingly around his shoulders, and his feet are tied up in pieces of wrapped tow-sacking. He is peering out toward the rear and listening, as if some sound had just disturbed him and he is trying to discover what it is. The glint of his pistol barrel shows from beneath the blanket where he holds it in his hand. Presently he turns and begins to pace up and down, beating himself with his arms to keep from freezing. A mumble of words rises from his lips*)

BIGGER Pshaw, nothing but that old piece of tin banging. They ain't found me yet! From the first jump I out-figure 'em. (*stopping*) Uhm—everything sleepy and 'way off—(*with sudden loudness*) I ain't scared, naw. They all scared, feeling me in the night, feel me walking behind 'em. . . . And everywhere, the bulls is searching them old nigger houses—Indiana, Calumet, Prairie, Wabash! Ha! But I ain't 'mong the niggers. (*calling softly*) Clara! (*he listens at the door at the right*) Why don't she come on here? (*he sinks down on an old box and pulls his blanket shiveringly about him. The flopping tin bangs off at the left. He springs instinctively and nervously up, then sits down again*) Ain't nothing—that old tin banging again, hanging loose and ready to fall. Fall on down, old tin, but I ain't gonna fall. They ain't gonna get me. (*gazing back over his shoulder at the night sky. Chuckling with low and bitter irony*) They smart, them white folks! Yeh, they get the niggers. But maybe not too smart—(*he spits in the air. He beats his arms about him and stares out into the night*) That's right! Flash away, old sign! "Sun-kissed oranges." Ha! I'll be in them orange-groves soon . . . with the sun on my back! (*he raises his head more and sees far away, above him, the revolving beam of the beacon in the sky*) Uhmm—an' look at that old Lindbergh beacon, shining there 'way out through the darkness—(*musingly*) Old Lindbergh—he knowed the way. Boiling icy water below him, the thunder and the lightning, the freezing and the hail around him. Keep on driving—riding through. (*imitating the sound of an airplane propeller with his numbed lips*) V–r–r–rh–h–h–h! V–r–r–ruh–uh–uh! Yes, he made it, got there. And all the people running and shouting, and the headlights switching and sweeping the sky! Old Lindbergh—he made it—got home, safe home. He not scared! (*snapping his head up, his hollow eyes burning through the shadows before him*) Aw, I ain't scared neither! (*he laughs*) An' when I light, ain't goin' to be no lot of people running to *me* with flowers! Hell, no! When I come, they run! Run like Hell! (*laughs. And now from the depths of the great city below comes the sound of a siren. He springs around, the piece of rotted blanket falling from his shoulders. He grips his gun tightly in his hand and crouching down, moves swiftly to the window at the left. Inching his head up against the sill, he peers over. The sound dies away. He turns from the window*) Sure, nothing but a' ambulance! Another fool white man done broke his neck somewhere. (*he moves back toward the box, flapping his arms like a bird to restore the circulation of his blood. A soft sound of fumbling footsteps is heard at the right. Holding his pistol, he backs away, keeping his eyes fastened on the door. The footsteps come nearer, then stop. He calls out softly*) That you, Clara?

CLARA'S VOICE (*outside*) Open the door. (*he springs over, unbars the door, and lets* CLARA *in. Ramming the bar of plank back in place, he grabs a package from her*)

BIGGER Okay?

CLARA (*in a low dull voice*) Eat something, Bigger. (*with shaking, eager hands, he opens the bag of food and begins devouring the sandwiches she has brought*)

BIGGER Thought you was never coming back. And me sitting here freezing to death. Things going 'round in my head! How everything look?

CLARA Go ahead and eat—

BIGGER (*his mouth full of food*) Anybody notice you?

CLARA Went to a new delicatessen—Thirty-ninth and Indiana.

BIGGER And you come back under the El like I told you?

CLARA I come back that way.

BIGGER Get the papers?

CLARA Here's some liquor—you 'bout froze. (*she pulls a bottle from her pocket. He grabs it, unstops it and drinks half of it swiftly down, then lays the bottle on the floor. She stands with her hands shoved by each other into her coat sleeves, looking at him*)

BIGGER Where the papers? I ask you.

CLARA Didn't get 'em, Bigger.

BIGGER Damn it, told you to—See what they say?

CLARA They got your picture.

BIGGER On the front page?

CLARA On the front page.

BIGGER Reckon they have. And big headlines—huh?

CLARA Big headlines, black—(*her mouth twists with pain*)

BIGGER Humm. Where they think I hid?

CLARA Section down by Ernie's all surrounded.

BIGGER Hah—knowed it. Dumb nuts. If them cops' brains was dynamite, wouldn't have enough to make 'em sneeze! (*angrily*) Why'n hell didn't you bring me that paper? (*she stares at him with dull, dead eyes, saying nothing*) What's the matter? What time is it?

CLARA Forgot to wind my watch.

BIGGER What the big clock down there say?

CLARA Ten till one, it say.

BIGGER Ten more minutes and I'm gone from here. Ten more minutes and that big old sign out there goes off, and I make it 'cross that old stairway over there in the dark to the next building and down that long alley.

CLARA (*piteously*) Then what, Bigger?

BIGGER I find somebody with a car—(*with the gun, he indicates a jab in the side*) He drive me till I say stop. Then I catch a train to the west—Still got that money?

CLARA   I got it.

BIGGER   How much?

CLARA   'Bout ninety dollars.

BIGGER   Gimme. (*she pulls it out of her pocket and hands it to him*)

CLARA   Bigger, you can't make it that way—You can't.

BIGGER   Goddamit, what do you think? Set here and freeze stiff as a poolstick and wait for 'em to come and pick me up? I got everything figured to the minute. (*now from the city below comes the sound of the siren again. It continues longer than before. He jerks his head around*) Don't like the sound of that. Jesus, won't that sign hurry and go off?

CLARA   Bigger, you can't do it.

BIGGER   (*with a shout*)   Cut that out!

CLARA   They offer ten thousand dollars reward—paper say.

BIGGER   (*after an instant of silence*)   Uhm—they want me bad. Well, they ain't gonna get me. (*thoughtfully*) Ten thousand—same we put in that kidnap note—

CLARA   It say you killed her, Bigger.

BIGGER   All right, then, I killed her. I didn't mean to. (*angrily*) But hell, we got no time to talk about that. Got to keep my mind clear, my feet free. (*he bends down and begins unwrapping the sacking from around his feet*)

CLARA   You told me you wasn't never gonna kill nobody, Bigger. (*she chokes down the sob that keeps rising up in her throat*)

BIGGER   I tell you, I wasn't trying to kill her. It was an accident—

CLARA   Accident—

BIGGER   She was drunk—passed out cold—She was so drunk she didn't even know where she was—And her ma might hear her bumbling about.

CLARA   And what she do?

BIGGER   Nothing—I just put her on the bed and her blind ma come in—(*shuddering*) Blind. She came in and I got scared. (*his voice quickening*) Yeh, her ma come into the room—had her hands stretched out like. So I just pushed the pillow hard over the gal's mouth to keep her from talking. (*there is a pause. His voice drops to a low note of helpless confession*) Then when she left I looked at that gal and she was dead—that's all—it happened just like that—(*he looks at* CLARA *as though imploring her belief*) She was dead!

CLARA   You—you smothered her.

BIGGER   Yeh, I reckon I did—I reckon I did—but I didn't mean to—I swear to God I didn't. (*in a hopeless tone*) But what difference do it make? Nobody'll believe me. I'm black and they'll say—(*flinging a rag savagely away*)

CLARA   The paper say—

BIGGER   Yeah, I know what they say. They say rape. But I didn't . . . I never touch that girl. (*pause*) And then when I see she dead, I, oh . . . Clara, I didn't know what to do—I took her to the basement and put her in the furnace—burnt her up. (CLARA *stares at him, her fist stuffed against her mouth as if to keep herself from screaming*) Jesus, I couldn't help it! (*he stands up suddenly*) It don't seem like I really done it now—really it don't seem like I done it. (*he looks off, his face hard and tense*) Maybe I didn't do it. Maybe I just think I did. Maybe somebody else did all that—(*his body relaxes and his shoulders slump*) But I did, Yeh . . . (*he goes on unwinding the rags. She gazes at him, her eyes filled with their dull nameless look of horror and despair*)

CLARA   (*as if with stiffened tongue*)   You—you said you was never going to kill—you said—

BIGGER   What the hell difference do it make now? I got to scram! (*he looks anxiously off at rear*) Damn snow quit falling hours ago—Roads be cleared up now. Jesus, that blizzard—like it stopped all the traffic to keep me shut up here. (*he picks up the bottle and takes another drink*)

CLARA   (*monotonously*)   You can't get away. You got to walk down—meet 'em—tell 'em how it happened—

BIGGER   (*with a wild laugh*)   And they believe me, huh? Goddamit, I stick my head out that door, my life ain't worth a snowflake in hell. They shoot me down like a dog. Jesus, that tin keeps banging. (*and now a strange light flares into the scene an instant and then is gone.* BIGGER *leaps to his feet with a cry*) What the hell was that! (*across the dark blue sky at the rear, a tall, slender cone of penciled light begins weaving back and forth. It continues its slow and monotonous sweep a moment like a gigantic metronome finger silently ticking out the minutes of* BIGGER*'s life, and then is gone. He turns and stares at it*) Look at that light moving. (*he tilts the bottle again,* *finishes it, then throws it away into the darkness)* But I ain't scared! *(his voice beginning to grow vacant and dreamy)* I'd begun to see something. Aw, Christ, it's gone again. I'm all mixed up, but I ain't scared now.

CLARA   Maybe you ought to be scared—Scared maybe 'cause you ain't scared.

BIGGER   Huh? Aw, to hell with it.

CLARA   What you gonna do?

BIGGER *(with sudden rage)* Gonna scram, I tell you. Goddamit! *(with rough brutality)* And I don't need you now.

CLARA   I know—all last night and today. Don't do no good now—nothing do any good. Your eyes so cold, your face so hard—like you want to kill me. And my heart's all heavy like a lump of lead—and dead.

BIGGER   Yeh. Anything get in my way now, I kill it. *(another siren sounds in the streets below, and now, faintly comes the sound of a mumbling multitude.* BIGGER *darts back into the shadow and stops)* Listen there! *(again as if from an unseen brilliant eye, the ruined room is illuminated in a white light reflected in a million diamond facets from the icicles, snow and ice.* BIGGER *draws his gun)* Goddamn, they got a spotlight somewhere. They found me. *(whirling on* CLARA *and seizing her by the throat)* They seen you coming back. *(hissing)* I ought to kill you. You tell 'em.

CLARA   Naw! Naw! Bigger! Bigger!

BIGGER *(his lips snarled back, his eyes cold as a snake's)* Yeh, weak, blind—couldn't do without you. Tell 'em where I am. *(he shakes her like a rag-doll. He hurls her from him against the ruined wall at the right. She lies still in the darkness, shivering and gasping. A low, dog-like whimper rises from her. He rushes over and kicks her)* Goddamit, stop that whining. *(she crawls toward him)* Don't you come toward me. I'll kill you. *(the noise in the streets below has increased in volume)*

CLARA *(now clinging to his feet)* Go ahead. Shoot me. Kill us both—and then, no more worry ... no more pain—Do it, Bigger.

(He jerks his foot loose from her. She falls forward on her face and lies still. The brilliant light floods into the scene again from the faraway hidden spot, and BIGGER *stands, naked and alone, outlined in it. He whirls around him as if trying to beat it from him. He runs to the window and looks out. Suddenly the electric-sign falters in its cycle of going on and off—then goes out entirely—A clock is heard striking one. In a convulsive gesture, his hand rises to his lips, then drops to his side)*

BIGGER   Yeh, you done it. They coming along that roof over there with their saw-off guns. *(he rushes to the right, starts to unbar the door when a heavy pounding sets up below. He springs back)* They coming up there, too. *(he runs over and jerks* CLARA *violently from the floor, an ooze of blood is seeping from her mouth)* You set 'em on me, you bitch! *(her head sways weakly from side to side, saying "no." He throws her from him. She stands tottering and about to fall. He runs out on the balcony at the rear. The powerful light remains on him. He starts back with an oath, then runs wildly along the balcony toward the left. The sound of the mob rises more loudly)*

CLARA   They kill you! Kill you! *(she moves blindly toward the rear. A shot rings out.* BIGGER *ducks back into the room behind the piece of ruined wall. Another shot barks, and the sound of breaking glass is heard)*

BIGGER *(yelling)*   Shoot! Shoot! *(the pounding at the right increases and shouts are heard near at hand off at the left. He grabs* CLARA *and holds her in front of him, moving swiftly over to the right rear)*

VOICES *(at the left)*   There he is! Let him have it! We got him!

*(*BIGGER *whirls now, holding* CLARA *protectingly in front of him with one hand. Her arms go up and about him in an impulsive gesture of love. Another shot rings out and she sags down in his arms. He looks at her, then lets her slide out of his arm onto the floor)*

BIGGER   Yeh. In front of me, and they shot you—All right, goddamit, I killed you. *(wagging his head)* Yeh. I said I would. I said so.

A VOICE *(beyond the door at the right)*   Come on out of there, nigger!

*(*BIGGER *fires at the door, and now the air is permeated with voices, as if an invisible ring of persons were squeezing the scene in a tightening circle. A voice at the left calls out)*

VOICE   Come on out if you're alive!

SECOND VOICE   You're going to wish you was dead! *(the sound of horns, sirens, and voices from the distance have grown to a roaring volume. Above the tumult,* BIGGER's *voice lashes out, high and clear)*

BIGGER Yeh, white boys! Come on and get me! You ain't scared of me, is you? Ain't nobody but Bigger in here—(*he shoots at the door*) Bigger! Bigger! Bigger standing against the lot of you! Against your thousand ... two thousand ... three thousand ...

(*He fires again and a volley of shots answers him. He is hit, tumbled completely over by the impact of the bullet. His gun flies from his hands and he falls back against the wall. Mouthing and snarling, he crawls toward the pistol, then collapses over* CLARA's *body. The door at the right is kicked in, and a policeman steps swiftly out of the shadow, his gun drawn. A second policeman runs in along the balcony fom the left rear, his gun also drawn. Through the open door, two plainclothesmen enter behind the policemen*)

FIRST MAN (*bending over* CLARA's *dead body*) Uhm, bullet went clean through her.

FIRST POLICEMAN The sonofabitch—killed her too. Just let that mob get at him!

SECOND POLICEMAN Come on, get him downstairs. They'll fix 'im! (*he seizes* BIGGER's *heels and lifts them up. Walking into the scene at the right comes an elderly man in an enveloping overcoat. An old plug hat is pulled low over his forehead hiding the ringlets of his gray hair. He stops and stares down at* BIGGER)

FIRST POLICEMAN (*looking around*) Hum—better be law and order, boys—Here's old Max.

SECOND POLICEMAN (*hurriedly*) Try the back way, fellows. (*the sound of the sirens rises and continues. Fadeout*)

Scene Nine

(*The sound of the mob dies away and the curtain goes up on the court room, two weeks later.*

Behind the desk, on an imposing dais at the rear, sits the JUDGE, *draped in a long black gown, and with a gray and heavy juridical face. Hanging directly above him, and behind, is the picture of an eighteenth century statesman resembling the likeness of Thomas Jefferson and surmounted by the graceful folds of the Stars and Stripes. Down in front of the* JUDGE's *desk is an oblong table. Between the desk and the table sit the Sheriff, the Clerk and the Court stenographer. To the right and left rear, somewhat framing the scene, stand two Militiamen at stiff attention, their bayoneted rifles held straight by their sides. At the right front sit* HANNAH THOMAS, VERA *and* BUDDY. BUDDY *is holding tightly to his mother's hand. In the same positions at the left sit the* DALTONS *and* PEGGY. *The two women wear veils and are in deep mourning.* BUCKLEY, *the Prosecuting Attorney, is sitting to the right of* DALTON. *At the table, with his back to the audience is* BIGGER. *He seems to pay no attention to what is going on around him. The scene is in darkness as the curtain rises, and out of this darkness comes the deep tumult of many voices, and then other voices raised in argument. As if in rhythm to the banging of the* JUDGE's *gavel the light comes swiftly up on the scene, showing* EDWARD MAX *and* BUCKLEY, *both on their feet, in front of the* JUDGE's *stand.*

MAX, *now that we see him in the light, is a big, flabby, kindly-faced man, with something sad and tragic in the pallid whiteness of his skin and the melancholy depths of his eyes. His hair is silvery white. There is a general air of poverty and yet of deep abiding peace about him.* BUCKLEY *is a suave, well-built man of about 40, with the florid, commanding face of the American business executive. He wears a carnation in the lapel of his morning coat*)

BUCKLEY (*shouting*) Your Honor!

MAX (*quietly*) I am not out of order, your Honor.

BUCKLEY The counsel for the defense cannot plead this boy both guilty and insane!

MAX I have made no such plea.

BUCKLEY If you plead him insane, the State will demand a jury trial.

JUDGE Go on, Mr. Max.

MAX Your Honor, I am trying to make the Court understand the true nature of this case—I want the mind of the Court to be free and clear—And then if the Court says death, let it mean death. And if the Court says life, let it mean that too. But whatever the Court says, let it know upon what ground its verdict is being rendered. (*glancing at his notes*) Night after night I have lain without sleep trying to think of a way to picture to you, and to the world, the causes, the reasons, why this Negro boy sits here today—a self-confessed murderer—and why this great city is boiling with a fever of excitement and hate. And yet how can I, I ask myself, make the picture of what has happened to this boy show plain and powerful upon a screen of sober reason, when a thousand newspaper and magazine artists have already drawn it in lurid ink upon a million sheets of public print? I have pled the cause of other criminal youths in this court as his Honor well knows. And when I took this case I thought at first it was the same old story of a boy run afoul of the law. But it is more terrible than that—with meaning more far-reaching. Where is the responsibility? Where is the guilt? For there is guilt in the rage that demands that this man's life be stamped out! There is guilt and responsibility in the hate that inflames that mob gathered in the streets below these windows! What is the atmosphere that surrounds this trial? Are the citizens intent upon seeing that the majesty of the Law is upheld? That retribution be dealt out in measure with the facts? That the guilty, and only the guilty, be caught and punished? No!

BUCKLEY   I object, your Honor!

MAX   (*continuing*) The hunt for Bigger Thomas has served as a political excuse, not only to terrorize the entire Negro population of this city, but also to arrest hundreds of members of suspect organizations, to raid labor union headquarters and workers' gatherings!

BUCKLEY   Objection!

JUDGE   Objection sustained! Strike all that from the record. You will confine your remarks to the evidence in the case.

MAX   Your Honor, for the sake of this boy, I wish I could bring to you evidence of a morally worthier nature. I wish I could say that love, or ambition, or jealousy, or the quest for adventure, or any of the more romantic emotions were back of this case. But I cannot. I have no choice in the matter. Life has cut this cloth, not I. Fear and hate and guilt are the keynotes of this drama. You see, your Honor, I am not afraid to assign the blame, for thus I can the more honestly plead for mercy! I say that this boy is the victim of a wrong that has grown, like a cancer, into the very blood and bone of our social structure. Bigger Thomas sits here today as a symbol of that wrong. And the judgment that you will deliver upon him is a judgment delivered upon ourselves, and upon our whole civilization. The Court can pronounce the sentence of death and that will end the defendant's life—but it will not end this wrong!

BUCKLEY   Your Honor, I object—

JUDGE   The Court is still waiting for you to produce mitigating evidence, Mr. Max!

MAX   Very well. Let us look back into this boy's childhood. On a certain day, he stood and saw his own father shot down by a Southern mob—while trying to protect one of his own kind from violence and hate—the very violence and hate represented in the mob gathered around this court-house today. With his mother and sister and little brother, Bigger Thomas fled North to this great city, hoping to find here a freer life for himself and those he loved. And what did he find here? Poverty, idleness, economic injustice, race discrimination and all the squeezing and oppression of a ruthless world—our world, your Honor—yours and mine! Here again he found the violence and the degradation from which he had fled. Here again he found the same frustrated way of life intensified by the cruelty of a blind and enslaving industrial mechanism. It is that way of life that stands on trial today, your Honor, in the person of Bigger Thomas! Like his forefathers, he is a slave. But unlike his forefathers there is something in him that refuses to accept this slavery. And why does he refuse to accept it? Because through the very teachings of our schools and educational system he was led to believe that in this land of liberty men are free. With one part of his mind, he believed what we had taught him—that he was a free man! With the other he found himself denied the right to accept that truth. In theory he was stimulated by every token around him to aspire to be a free individual. And in practice by every method of our social system, he was frustrated in that aspiration. Out of this confusion, fear was born. And fear breeds hate, and hate breeds guilt, and guilt in turn breeds the urge to destroy—to kill. (*the* JUDGE *is now listening intently to* MAX)

BUCKLEY   (*shouting out*) I object! All this is merely an attempt to prove the prisoner insane—

JUDGE   (*rapping with his gavel*) Objection over-ruled.

MAX   (*turning toward* MR. *and* MRS. DALTON) Consider these witnesses for the State, Mr. and Mrs. Dalton. I have only sympathy for these poor grieving parents. You have heard their testimony and you have heard them plead for leniency toward this boy. (*pause*) Well may they plead for leniency for perhaps they are as guilty of this crime as he is!

BUCKLEY Your Honor—

MAX Unconsciously, and against their will, they are partners in this drama of guilt and blood. They intended no evil—yet they produced evil.

BUCKLEY (*furiously*) I object. He is impugning the character of my witnesses.

MAX (*quietly*) I am not. I have only sympathy for them. But I am trying to state the facts, and these are the facts. This man rents his vast real estate holdings to many thousands of Negroes, and among these thousands is the family of this boy, Bigger Thomas. The rents in those tenements are proportionately the highest, and the living conditions the worst of any in this city. Yet this man is held in high esteem. Why? Because out of the profits he makes from those rents, he turns around and gives back to the Negroes a small part as charity. For this he is lauded in the press and held up as an example of fine citizenship. But where do the Negroes come in? Nowhere. What do they have to say about how they live? Nothing. Around the whole vicious circle they move and act at this man's behest, and must accept the crumbs of their own charity as Mr. Dalton wills, or wills not. It is a form of futile bribery that continues, and will continue, until we see the truth and stop it. For corpses cannot be bribed—And such living corpses as Bigger Thomas here, are warnings to us to stop it, and stop it now before it is too late—

BUCKLEY Your Honor! (*the* JUDGE *waves him down, and* MAX *goes on*)

MAX One more word, your Honor, and I am done. (*pointing towards the portrait on the wall at the rear*) There, under that flag, is the likeness of one of our forefathers—one of the men who came to these strange shores hundreds of years ago in search of freedom. Those men, and we who followed them, built here a nation mighty and powerful, the most powerful nation on earth! Yet to those who, as much as any others, helped us build this nation, we have said, and we continue to say, "This is a white man's country!" Night and day, millions of souls, the souls of our black people, are crying out, "This is our country too. We helped build it—helped defend it. Give us a part in it, a part free and hopeful and wide as the everlasting horizon." And in this fear-crazed, guilt-ridden body of Bigger Thomas that vast multitude cries out to you now in a mighty voice, saying, "Give us our freedom, our chance, and our hope to be men." Can we ignore this cry? Can we continue to boast through every medium of public utterance—through literature, newspapers, radio, the pulpit—that this is a land of freedom and opportunity, of liberty and justice for all—and in our behavior deny all these precepts of charity and enlightenment? Bigger Thomas is a symbol of that double-dealing, an organism which our political and economic hypocrisy has bred. Kill him, burn the life out of him, and still the symbol of his living death remains. And you cannot kill Bigger Thomas, for he is already dead. He was born dead—born dead among the wild forests of our cities, amid the rank and choking vegetation of our slums—in the Jim Crow corners of our busses and trains—in the dark closets and corridors and rest rooms marked off by the finger of a blind and prejudiced law as Black against White. And who created that law? We did. And while it lasts we stand condemned before mankind—Your Honor, I beg you, not in the name of Bigger Thomas but in the name of ourselves, spare this boy's life! (*he turns to his seat at the table beside* BIGGER. *Immediately the roar of the crowd outside swells in upon the scene. The* JUDGE *bangs with his gavel again and the lights dim down. For a moment the noise continues and then dies away as the lights come up again.* BUCKLEY *is now addressing the* JUDGE. *His manner is earnest, kindly and confident*)

BUCKLEY The counsel for the defense may criticize the American nation and its methods of government. But that government is not on trial today. Only one person, the defendant, Bigger Thomas, is on trial. He pleads guilty to the charges of the indictment. The rest is simple and brief. Punishment must follow—punishment laid down by the sacred laws of this Commonwealth—laws created to protect that society and that social system of which we are a part! A criminal is one who goes against those laws. He attacks the laws. Therefore the laws must destroy him. If thine eye offend thee, pluck it out; and if the branch of a tree withers and dies, it must be cut off lest it contaminate the rest of the tree. Such a tree is the State through whose flourishing and good health we ourselves exist and carry on our lives. The ruined, the rotten and degraded must be cut out, cleansed away so that the body politic itself may keep its health. I sympathize with the counsel for the defense. I understand his point of view, his persuasive argument. But the simple truth is, your Honor, he is deluded. His thinking, his arguments, run contrary to the true course of man's sound development. Yes, if the Defense wishes, let us speak not in terms of crime, but in terms of disease. I pity this diseased and ruined defendant. But as a true surgeon, looking to the welfare of the organic body of our people, I repeat that it is necessary this diseased member be cut off—cut out and obliterated—lest it infect us all unto death. Your Honor, I regret that the Defense has raised the viperous issue of race and class hatred in this trial. Justice should, and must be, dispensed fairly and equally, in accordance with the facts, and not with theories—and justice is all I ask. And what are the facts? That this Bigger Thomas is sane and is responsible for his crimes—And all the eloquent tongues of angels or men cannot convince this honorable court that it and I and others gathered here are the guilty ones. Bigger Thomas is guilty and in his sould he knows it. Your Honor, in the name of the people of this city, in the name of truth and Almighty God, I demand that this Bigger Thomas justly die for the brutal murder of Mary Dalton!

(*Through the whole scene, the spectators have remained motionless, and even* BUDDY *has sat like a little black statue, his eyes fastened straight on the bowed figure of his brother. As* BUCKLEY *takes his seat, the lights begin to dim on the scene, and once again the sound of the great mob outside permeates the room in a heavy, undulating drone. The scene seems to recede from us, and now, out of the thickening gloom, comes the voice of the* JUDGE)

JUDGE'S VOICE   Bigger Thomas, stand up.

(*The murmur of the mob continues. Blackout*)

Scene Ten

(*The sound of the mob dies away and the curtain goes up on the death cell. It is a few weeks later.*

Directly across and separated by only a few feet of corridor is the death chamber, its heavy iron door closed. There is a barred door in the left wall of the cell, and on the wall at the right a porcelain wash basin is fastened, sticking out like a frozen lip. Along the wall at the right rear is an iron cot covered with a white morgue-like sheet. The atmosphere is one of scientific anaesthesia and deathly cleanliness.

Seen through the slanting bars at the left rear are two uniformed guards seated at a little table playing rummy. One is an elderly man, the other much younger. The cell is lighted by a single electric bulb on the ceiling, and the streaking shadows of the bars cut across the figures of the two guards behind.

When the curtain rises, BIGGER *is standing against the wall by the door, looking out to the front, with his body half turned towards the rear. He is dressed in a white short-sleeved shirt open at the throat, and dark gray flannel trousers, one leg of which is slit open from the knee down. His head is shaved, and he is staring out after the retreating forms of his mother, sister and brother. Sobbing, the mother tries to go back to* BIGGER, *but is restrained by the younger guard who rises to meet her*)

HANNAH   My boy, my poor boy—

BUDDY   Ma, don't do that! Ma—(HANNAH *is led away and her sobs die out.* BIGGER *continues to stare after her without a sound*)

FIRST GUARD (*in a quiet voice laying down a card*)   That old woman takes it hard.

SECOND GUARD (*coming back*)   It's her son.

FIRST GUARD (*jerking his head towards* BIGGER)   He don't seem to care though.

SECOND GUARD   Since that time he cried all night long, he don't say much.

FIRST GUARD   And how he cried—But reckon that old water hose stopped him—(*there is a rush at the left and* BUDDY *runs up to the cell bars and grips them in an agony of grief*)

BUDDY   Ma says don't you worry—we gonna take care of you—later.

SECOND GUARD   Go on, sonny.

BUDDY   And it gonna be at Reverend Hammond's church, Bigger. And plenty of flowers—and folks, Bigger. (*at a gesture from the first guard, the second guard leads* BUDDY *off.* BIGGER *has stood motionless.* BUDDY *goes away, straining his eyes on* BIGGER *to the last*)

BIGGER (*calling quietly*)   Tell Vera good-by.

BUDDY'S VOICE (*brokenly*)   Yeh, yeh. Good-by—ee—(*his voice dies away*)

FIRST GUARD (*with meaningless comfort calling*

toward BIGGER) I know—Time passes slow. Ten more minutes, boy, that's all.

SECOND GUARD (*returning*) Then eight seconds after that you won't worry. Just take a deep breath—eight seconds! Go ahead and talk, son. Make it easier, maybe. (*but* BIGGER *remains silent*)

FIRST GUARD Your lawyer's here—(BIGGER *shakes his head*)

SECOND GUARD He'll wanta walk with you in case—

BIGGER Don't need nobody—

SECOND GUARD (*admiringly*) Got iron in his blood, all right, I'll say that. (*he seats himself at the table again*) Damn, he's tough! (*they resume their card playing. A third guard comes up to the door out of the darkness, followed by* MAX. *He goes back the way he came. The second guard lets* MAX *into the cell and then reseats himself, his face still caught in its look of hurt and nauseous pain.* MAX *stands mopping his brow, his face flabby and old*)

MAX No word yet, son. I'm sorry.

BIGGER (*in a muffled voice*) That's okay, Mr. Max.

MAX We're doing all we can. Mrs. Dalton's with the Governor now. There's maybe still a chance—

BIGGER (*with an odd touch of shame as he suddenly indicates his shaved head*) They changed my looks.

MAX Mr. Dalton too. He's got power. I'm still hoping—

BIGGER I'm all right, Mr. Max. You ain't to blame for what's happened to me. (*his voice drops to a low, resigned and melancholy note*) I reckon—uh—I—uh—I just reckon I had it coming. (*he stands with his lips moving, shaking his head, but no words come*)

MAX (*leaning forward*) What is it, Bigger?

BIGGER (*in a heavy expiring breath*) Naw.

MAX Talk to me, Bigger. You can trust me, you know that.

BIGGER Trust or don't trust, all the same. Ain't nobody can help me now. (*he sits down, his lips moving inaudibly again*)

MAX (*quietly*) What are you trying to say, Bigger?

BIGGER (*after a moment, shouting*) I—I just want to say maybe I'm glad I got to know you before I go!

MAX I—I'm glad I got to know you too, Bigger. I'll soon be going, son. I'm old. But others will carry on our fight—

BIGGER What I got to do with it?

MAX And because of you—whether you live or die, Bigger, we will be nearer the victory—justice and freedom for men. I want you to know that.

BIGGER (*his voice dropping down*) Ain't nobody ever talked to me like you before. (*he breaks off and turns distractedly about him*) How come you do it—and you being a white man? (*with wild impulsiveness*) You oughta left me alone. How come you want to help me in the first place, and me black and a murderer maybe ten times over?

MAX (*placing his hand on* BIGGER's *shoulder as he pulls away*) Bigger, in my work—and the work the world has ahead—there are no whites and blacks—only men. And you make me feel, Bigger, and others feel it—how badly men want to live in this world—to say here is where I once was. This was me, big and strong ... till the years quit falling down. You feel like that, don't you, Bigger? You felt like that?

BIGGER Sometimes I wish you wouldn't ask me all them questions, Mr. Max. Goddamit, I wish you wouldn't. (*he chokes on his words in regret and impotent despair, and then regains his voice*) I was all set to die maybe. I was all right. Then you come and start talking, digging into me, opening up my guts.

MAX I want to understand you, get near to you, Bigger.

BIGGER (*almost whispering*) Understand me. She said that—understand me—(*his voice dies out. The guards now sit muffled and motionless in the gloom*)

MAX And she was trying to help you, wasn't she? (*pause*) Don't you know she was trying to help you?

BIGGER She made me feel like a dog! Yeah, that's the way all of 'em made me feel. In their big house I was all trembling and afraid. (*his voice trails off again*)

MAX (*suddenly*) Didn't you ever love anybody, Bigger?

BIGGER Maybe I loved my daddy. Long time ago. They killed him. (*suddenly shouting as he springs up and begins to pace the cell*) Goddamn it, there you start again. You mix me all up! (*with a wild moan*) You make me feel something could happen—something good maybe—

(*frenziedly*) You creep in on me, crowd me to the wall, smother me and I want my breath, right up till that lightning hits me. Go away, Mr. Max.

MAX That day I said we had made you what you were, a killer—maybe I was wrong—I want to know I was wrong—(*he gazes at* BIGGER *with white pained face*)

BIGGER (*softly, half to himself*) His po' face like the face of Jesus hanging on that wall—like her face too.

MAX You killed Clara. Why? She loved you, she was good. You say you killed her.

BIGGER (*stopping his pacing*) Yeh, I killed her—

MAX You're not crazy, and there's not that kind of crazy logic in this world. I ask you and all the time you say, "I just did." That's not it, not it.

BIGGER Then I didn't kill her. They said I shot her. I didn't. Wasn't no use talking 'bout it. She didn't count. I just let 'em say it.

MAX (*an uncertain joy in his voice*) You didn't shoot her?

BIGGER One their bullets went clean through her. I had her in my arms, I let her fall down—

MAX (*with a shout*) We could have proved it. It might have—Thank God. (*he sinks down on the cot, staring at* BIGGER)

BIGGER But I killed her just the same. All the time I'd been killing her the way I'd been killing myself. She'd suffered for me, followed me, and I didn't want it—wanted to be free to walk wild and free with steps a mile long—over the houses, over the rivers, and straddling the mountains and on—something in me—

MAX And you didn't want to be hindered—you'd kill anything that got in your way—

BIGGER Reckon so. But I wasn't thinking of that then.

MAX (*watching him*) And would you kill again, Bigger, if you could?

BIGGER (*quieting down*) I dunno—Naw—Yessuh, I dunno. Sometimes I feel like it. Maybe you're wrong now and I am bad and rotten the way you thought at the trial—made bad, and like that other man said. I dunno what I am—got no way to prove it. (*wetting his lips*) All the time I lie here thinking, beating my head against a wall, trying to see through, over it, but can't. Maybe 'cause I'm gonna die makes me want to see—know what I am maybe. How can I die like that, Mr. Max?

MAX If we knew how to live, Bigger, we'd know how to die.

BIGGER Yeh, people can live together but a man got to die by himself. That don't make sense—He needs something to die by more than to live by. (*as* MAX *is silent*) I ain't trying to dodge what's coming. But, Mr. Max, maybe I ain't never wanted to hurt nobody—for real I ain't, maybe. (*his eyes are wide as he stares ahead, straining to feel and think his way through the darkness*)

MAX Go on, Bigger.

BIGGER Seem like with you here try to help me—you so good and kind—I begin to think better. (*shaking his head again*) Uh, but why the folks who sent me here hate me so? That mob—I can hear 'em still—'Cause I'm black?

MAX (*with gentle, yearning comfort*) No, that's not it. Bigger. Your being black just makes it easier to be singled out in a white man's world. That's all. What they wanted to do to you they do to each other every day. They don't hate you and they don't hate each other. They are men like you, like me, and they feel like you. They want the things of life just as you do, their own chance. But as long as these are denied them—just so long will those millions keep groping around frightened and lost—angry and full of hate—the way you were, Bigger. (*he pauses*) Bigger, the day these millions—these millions of poor men—workers, make up their minds—begin to believe in themselves—

BIGGER Yeh, reckon the workers believe in themselves all right. Try to get into one them labor unions. Naw, Mr. Max. Everywhere you turn they shut the door in your face, keep you homeless as a dog. Never no chance to be your own man. That's what I always wanted to be—my own man—(*staring at* MAX) Honest to God, Mr. Max, I never felt like my own man till right after that happened—till after I killed her.

MAX (*fiercely*) No, Bigger.

BIGGER Yeh—and all the peoples and all the killings and the hangings and the burnings inside me, kept me pushing me on—up and on to do something big—have money like that kidnap note—power—something great—to keep my head up—to put my name on the hot wires of the world—big—And, yeh, and all the bad I done, it seemed was right—and after they caught me I kept saying it was right and I was gonna stand on it, hold it—walk that long road down to that old chair—look at it, say, "Do your worst! Burn me. Shoot your juice, and I can take it. You can kill me but can't hurt me—can't hurt me—It's the truth, Mr. Max, after I killed that white girl, I wasn't scared no more—for a little while. (*his voice rises with feverish intensity*) I was my own man then, I was free. Maybe it was 'cause they was after my life then. They made me wake up. That made me feel high and powerful—free! (*with growing vehemence*) That day and night after I done killed her—when all of them was looking for me—hunting me—that day and night for the first time I felt like a man. (*shouting*) I was a man!

MAX (*loudly*) You don't believe that, Bigger.

BIGGER Yeah, yeah, I felt like a man—when I was doing what I never thought I'd do—something I never wanted to do. And it was crazy—wrong and crazy. (*with a piteous childlike cry*) Why, Mr. Max? Why!

MAX That's the answer men must find, Bigger.

BIGGER (*lowering his head*) I'm all right now, Mr. Max—I'm all right. Don't be scared of me. I'm all right. You go on. I don't feel that way now. It didn't last.

MAX It never lasts, Bigger.

(*The dynamo in the death chamber at the left begins to hum, and the light in the ceiling of* BIGGER's *cell dims down and then regains its brilliance. The humming dies away*)

BIGGER They 'bout ready now. (*whispering queerly*) And that midnight mail is flying late.

MAX Hold onto yourself, son. There's still a chance—

BIGGER They ready but I can't see it clear yet. (*licking his lips*) But I be all right, Mr. Max. Just go and tell Ma I was all right and not to worry none—see? Tell her I was all right and not crying none.

MAX (*his words almost inaudible now*) Yes, Bigger.

BIGGER Yeh, I'm going now and ain't done it, ain't done it yet.

MAX What, Bigger?

BIGGER (*panting and beating his fists together*) Nothing really right yet—like what I wanted to do. Living or dead, they don't give me no chance—I didn't give myself no chance. (*the two guards rise from the table. They look off and up at the left rear*)

FIRST GUARD Well—

SECOND GUARD Yeh.

(*A low mournful harmony, hardly heard at first, begins among the prisoners in the cells stretching away to the rear. The third guard comes swiftly up out of the darkness. He hands a telegram to* MAX *who seizes it.* BIGGER *begins gazing up at the ceiling of his cell, as if listening for a sound afar off*)

MAX (*in a low voice*) Bigger. (*he opens the telegram—For an instant he looks at it and then his shoulders sag slowly down. He murmurs*) Want to read it, son—(*but* BIGGER *does not answer.* MAX *sticks out his hand in farewell, his face old and broken, then lets it fall*)

FIRST GUARD One minute past midnight.

SECOND GUARD All right, son. (*they start moving toward the cell.* BIGGER *still stands with his face lifted and set in its tense concentration*)

BIGGER (*in a fierce convulsive whisper*) There she comes—Yeh, I hear you. (*far above in the night the murmuring throb of an airplane motor is audible.* BIGGER's *voice bursts from him in a wild frenzied call*) Fly them planes, boys—fly 'em!—Riding through—riding through. I'll be with you! I'll—

FIRST GUARD Come on, he's going nuts! (*he quickly unlocks the cell and they enter*)

BIGGER (*yelling, his head wagging in desperation*) Keep on driving!—To the end of the world—smack into the face of the sun! (*gasping*) Fly 'em for me—for Bigger— (*the sound of the airplane fades away and now the death chant of the prisoners comes more loudly into the scene. In the dim corridor at the rear the white surplice of a priest is discerned*)

SECOND GUARD (*touching* BIGGER *on the arm*) This way, son.

(*They start leading him from the cell. As if of its own volition the door to the little death house opens and a flood of light pours out.* BIGGER, *with his eyes set and his shoulders straight, moves toward its sunny radiance like a man walking into a deep current of water. The guards quietly follow him, their heads bent down*)

MAX (*staring after him, his big white face wet with tears*) Good-by, Bigger. (BIGGER *enters the door*)

PRIEST'S VOICE (*intoning from the shadows*) I am the resurrection and the life.

(*The death chant of the prisoners grows louder. The door to the death house closes, cutting off the light. The end*)

Stanley Richards (1918–)

District of Columbia 1945

Stanley Richards dedicates his play to Canada Lee,

a very close and dear friend who also was one of the nation's first and foremost great Negro dramatic stars. The play is far from fictional for it deals in the main with an actual occurrence that happened to Canada and myself, starting in Hollywood when he was there making *Lifeboat* for Twentieth-Century-Fox and I was a contract writer for Universal Pictures. Of course, "fiction" and "drama" need that embellishment and so I transferred the actual locale of the incident to Washington, D.C. where Canada also visited me while I was doing radio and documentary films for the government. It was, as far as I know, the first of the short plays that dealt with the subject.

District of Columbia is the only play in this collection that is not written by a black playwright. It is included because its subject matter bridges an important gap between pre- and post-World War II attitudes in this country. Blacks were drafted into the armed services in World War II and gave their lives with the belief that when they returned conditions would be better. This illusion was short lived. Race riots involving black and white servicemen, as well as civilians, were common in southern towns near army training camps. (The 1943 Harlem uprising began when a white policeman shot a black soldier in the lobby of a West Side hotel.) President Truman finally ordered an end to segregated services in 1948.

The incident that Mr. Richards depicts in *District of Columbia* has occurred hundreds of times in this country and often in foreign lands where American armed forces are stationed. Charles Sebree recounts a similar experience when he and several other black sailors were rejected from a Chicago bar because their policy was not to serve "colored." They left, but not until the bar had literally been destroyed.

The attitude in the play of the black soldier toward his treatment in the nation's capital is mild by present-day standards, and some readers may want to label him an Uncle Tom or to dismiss the play as another example of a white writer not allowing a black character to express his manhood. This is not the author's intent. Edwards, the black serviceman, although retaining faith in his country, has not been disillusioned by the system or the fantasy that drastic changes will occur without a struggle immediately following the war. He knows white America. The white soldiers, O'Hara and Munn, do not. They believe in the illusion and when reality confronts them *they* are angered. Edwards knows that he is back home and that black life is just as dispensable in Washington, D.C. as it was in Roanoke, Virginia; or Jackson, Mississippi; or Guam. He intends to survive, placing his faith in the future when "all this fightin' and shoutin' about liberty and equality ain't just idle talk."

Stanley Richards is author of some twenty-five plays. He has edited a number of drama anthologies, including *The Best Short Plays* series. *District of Columbia* was first published in *Opportunity* magazine in 1945.

The play presents the Black American in uniform. It is interesting to speculate on why so few Afro-American playwrights have portrayed the black soldier on stage.

District of Columbia

CAST OF CHARACTERS

(in the order in which they speak)

CORPORAL MUNN
SERGEANT O'HARA
A GENTLEMAN
CORPORAL EDWARDS
PROPRIETOR
MANAGER

Episode One

(SETTING *Union Station, Washington, D.C.*

The setting is a suggestion of the station. The tracks and platforms are presumably out in the auditorium of the theater—therefore, the players face the audience while awaiting the train's arrival. A gate stands in center stage. The gate is open, guarded by a uniformed station attendant. A small staircase connects the stage with the auditorium. The lighting is dim and those portions of the stage which aren't being used during each individual episode, should be blacked out so that they may be set for succeeding episodes. The over-all effect should be one of a busy railroad terminal during a great war.

TIME *the present.*

AT THE RISE *Through the open gate, we glimpse the various types waiting for the train's arrival. They are the people one is apt to encounter at a busy terminal. There's the mother of a returning serviceman, the wife of a sailor, friends, sweethearts, government workers, officials, service-men, civilians—in short, the people. They all seem to be part of a huge tableaux—standing motionless and silently in groups and singly, coming alive only when the train pulls into the station.*

In the center of them all, and directly forward, a GENTLEMAN, *of about fifty or so, stands reading his evening newspaper. Two soldiers suddenly appear and take their places next to the* GENTLE-MAN. *The two soldiers are* CORPORAL MUNN *and* SERGEANT O'HARA *of the U.S. Army. Both are rather good looking American types. However, of the two,* O'HARA *seems the more rugged. Both have been wounded in action and* MUNN's *arm is wrapped in a sling.* O'HARA's *injury is not a visible one*)

MUNN Better make sure this is it, O'Hara.
O'HARA (*to* GENTLEMAN) S'cuse me, major. The five from Roanoke come in on this track?
GENTLEMAN That's right, soldier. Due on schedule.
O'HARA Thanks.
O'HARA (*turning to* MUNN) Okay, Munn—five more minutes and prohibition ends for us!
GENTLEMAN (*dropping his newspaper*) Prohibition? Why, I thought that belonged to history?
O'HARA Sure. But this one's self-imposed. Tell him how we spell that, Munn.
MUNN (*with a little laugh*) Don't let O'Hara frighten you, sir. It's just a pact we made. You see, this here friend we're waiting for—on the five—well, sir—he saved both our lives on Munda. He picked us up in the jungles after we been hit. Took care of us 'til the medics arrived. He's with the Engineers, sir.
GENTLEMAN Damn good outfit, I hear. But that's getting away from your pact. Go on.
MUNN—Well, sir—when things looked toughest, we made this agreement. We decided that if we all came out of it alive—none of us would take a drink until the three of us could meet in the States and have a first drink together. This is our first chance, sir. O'Hara and me got this week-end pass from Walter Reed General—
O'HARA Yeah. You can imagine how dry my throat must be!
GENTLEMAN (*winking slyly*) None of you been unfaithful?
O'HARA Not us, major. Most guys when they hit civilization, rush to gin-mills like flies

to a garbage wagon. But with us, a pact's a pact.

MUNN   And since none of us have ever seen Washington before—well—we kinda thought it appropriate—

GENTLEMAN   What better place is there, for drowning loyalty in a glass of bourbon, eh?

(*A Voice comes over the station's amplification system*)

A VOICE   Paging Mr. Frank Wall—paging Mr. Frank Wall—report to station master's office—(*the* GENTLEMAN *listens attentively. From his manner, we gather that he is* MR. WALL)

GENTLEMAN   Excuse me.

(*He goes. We hear the sound of the train pulling into the station. The people on stage suddenly come alive. Their faces light up in anticipation of seeing their loved ones. Some come forward. Others crane their necks anxiously as they watch the imaginary train puffing its way into the station. None speak, except* O'HARA *and* MUNN)

O'HARA   Lookit! Five. Right on the button!

MUNN   We waited for this a long time, O'Hara. I gotta keep pinching myself to believe it!

O'HARA   It's real all right. You can get down and kiss the station!

MUNN   I told him to look for us at the gate. He can't miss us here.

(*The* GENTLEMAN *returns*)

GENTLEMAN (*eagerly*)   Say! I just got word that my wife has taken a later train. Means I won't be tied up for a while and I thought—well—perhaps you fellows would let *me* buy you that first drink?

MUNN   It's nice of you to suggest it, sir—but we're so damn religious about that first one.

GENTLEMAN   Well, *I* could buy it for you—couldn't I? There's nothing I enjoy better than drinking with servicemen, 'specially heroes.

MUNN   What do you say, O'Hara?

O'HARA   Well—if the major gets a kick out of it, Munn, what the hell, let him splurge!

GENTLEMAN (*patting him gently on shoulder*)   Sure. That's it. We'll find a nice, cheerful spot —soon as your friend arrives.

(*The train has finally pulled into the station and only occasional blasts of steam from the locomotive can be heard. The passengers come pouring down the aisles of the theater, and up onto the stage. A sailor dashes to his wife. A soldier to his mother, etc. They embrace, then go off.* O'HARA *and* MUNN *wait impatiently, looking forward anxiously*)

O'HARA   See him?

MUNN   Not yet—

(*By now, all the others have disappeared. Only* O'HARA *and* MUNN *and the* GENTLEMAN *remain in the dim light*)

GENTLEMAN   Are you *sure* your buddy's on the train?

MUNN   Wait, sir. There's more—down at the end of the platform—there's more—

O'HARA (*to* GENTLEMAN)   Now look, major—he wouldn't give us a stand-up. See! Not if he lost a leg getting here!

(*Slowly and silently down the aisle, comes Corporal Edwards, of the U.S. Army. He's a tall good-looking, sensitive Negro youth. He is supported by crutches and has been decorated with the Purple Heart*)

MUNN (*shouting*)   Edwards!

O'HARA   Why you old beaver, we thought you wasn't coming!

GENTLEMAN (*stunned*)   He—your friend?

O'HARA   Sure.

(MUNN *and* O'HARA *help* EDWARDS *up to the stage, excitedly greeting him. The* GENTLEMAN, *however, moves back mechanically*)

EDWARDS   Gosh, it's good to see you both again. How you been?

MUNN (*indicating his leg*)   You—you never said a word—in your letters—

EDWARDS   Oh, this? Heck. She ain't nothing. Happened after you left. But y'oughta see the Jap! Well, whatta you say about that drink? I come a long way. Roanoke's sure a long way.

O'HARA (*with broad and exaggerated gestures*)   Corporal Edwards—meet our esteemed benefactor—or, put short an' sweet, the guy who's offered to get stuck, with the tab—(*he turns to* GENTLEMAN, *bowing low*)

EDWARDS (*to* GENTLEMAN—*pleasantly*)   How do, sir.

GENTLEMAN (*flustered*)   I just remembered—there's a—a little chore I've got to do—for my wife—probably take me a couple of hours—so, maybe some other time, huh? (*he goes off quickly*)

O'HARA (*angrily, starting after him*) Why, the son-of-a—

EDWARDS (*stopping him*) No. Don't O'Hara. He ain't the last one. We're in Washington now. Not in the Islands.

MUNN (*taking a small sheet of paper from his pocket*) Sure. To hell with him! Here. We got a whole list of places. The fellows in the ward know this town like a love song. There's a little bar on "F" Street—right off Pennsylvania Avenue....

(*they start off, as the lights fade*)

Episode Two

(*The stage relights on another part. Now we see the entrance to a small bar. The Proprietor stands arguing with* O'HARA *in the doorway—as* EDWARDS *and* MUNN *stand silently a few feet away.* MUNN *clutches the list in his hand. The rest of the stage remains dark*)

O'HARA Now look, mister, he's wearin' the Purple Heart and he's got a bum leg and he didn't get neither because he's white nor black, but because he's a human being and he's interested in decency!

PROPRIETOR (*defiantly*) I don't care. I told you once no.

O'HARA (*equally defiant*) He's wearing the Purple Heart. Where's your respect goddammit?

PROPRIETOR The Purple Heart don't whitewash his face none! (*he goes off angrily into the bar.* O'HARA *pauses a moment, then joins* EDWARDS *and* MUNN)

O'HARA C'mon, I don't like the stink around here.

EDWARDS This is Washington, O'Hara. Y'ain't gonna get nothin' much different.

O'HARA (*hotly*) I don't give a damn! Do y'hear? I ain't givin' up! What's the matter with you? Goin' chicken on us? (*pause*) Sorry, Edwards. Didn't mean to blow my top.

EDWARDS (*quietly*) That's all right, O'Hara. Let's go to that bar on Third Street like the taxi driver said—it's for colored people—and I'm sure you'll be welcome there—and—

MUNN We still got a couple of more on the list, Edwards. May as well continue—I guess—like O'Hara says—

(*The lights fade*)

Episode Three

(*The stage relights on another part, and now we see the outside of a little cafe. From inside, comes the melee of juke box music and the laughter of gay crowds. The* MANAGER, *a middle-aged, good-natured Italian, talks to* MUNN. O'HARA *and* EDWARDS *quietly wait on the side*)

MUNN (*to* MANAGER) So, Mickey Santini, being a regular patron, suggested this place. And since you got two of your own sons in the service, we thought—

MANAGER I wish I could, believe me, I wish I could.

MUNN Why don't you then?

MANAGER Rules. I only run the place. If the owner he ever discover this—he drown me in the Potomac.

MUNN He wouldn't care. He's got a heart, ain't he?

MANAGER Many people with hearts—they don't open 'em, boy. If I let you in—I have to put you in corner, maybe behind door. Then you no be comfortable, I no be comfortable, my patrons, they no be comfortable. Sorry—(*he turns and goes.* MUNN *returns to the others*)

MUNN Well—last joint on the list. (*as he crumples it and tosses it away*) There goes nothing.

O'HARA (*to* EDWARDS) Great, isn't it? Great welcome to your Capital! Soak it in, fella, then ask yourself what you're fighting for.

EDWARDS (*sadly*) I'm sorry about you and Munn, O'Hara. If I knew I'd spoil your fun—gosh, sometimes I—I almost wish I were back on the island.

MUNN Forget it, Edwards. You're not spoiling anyone's fun. Not you.

O'HARA (*impulsively*) Wait! I got it! We ain't givin' up so easy, Edwards! We came through on the island, didn't we? Well, we're gonna come through here, too. We'll drink goddammit! And I promise you, there'll be no objections!

EDWARDS Why not call it a night, O'Hara? I don't really care about a drink. Just seein' you and Munn's all I cared about. I can go on and leave you two—

MUNN Nothing doing, Edwards. We made a pact. We're going to stick to it.

O'HARA Sure! If you think the Marines finish things, boy, they never heard about the Army! Look—it's almost ten. Remember that package store we passed down the street?

MUNN What've you got in mind, O'Hara?

O'HARA We want that drink don't we?

MUNN Yeah—

O'HARA Well, there's one guy I know in this town who won't object. C'mon!

(*They start off once again as the lights fade*)

Episode Four

(*The lights rise on stage center disclosing the huge white steps of the Lincoln Memorial. At the landing, leading into the Memorial, there might be a suggestion of several huge Greek Ionic columns. And, if possible, a suggestion or shadow of the Lincoln statue.*

O'HARA *stands in the center, his back to the audience, flanked on each side by* MUNN *and* EDWARDS, *both several steps below him*)

O'HARA (*quietly*) "Four score and seven years ago, our fathers brought forth on this continent a new nation conceived in liberty and dedicated to the proposition that all men are created equal...." (*pause. He turns, revealing a bottle of gin clutched in his hand*) Not a bad memory for a guy who flunked history twice, huh?

EDWARDS (*pause*) Funny. Drinking here.

O'HARA No, Edwards, it's good drinkin' here. It's clean drinkin' here. 'Cause he didn't care whether a man was white or black, if they wanted to drink together, it was okay by him! No, Edwards—you're wrong. It's *good* drinkin' here.

MUNN (*gazing into the audience*) Look out there. You can almost see the world—

O'HARA Yeah. Look out there, Edwards—look out at the world. And drink to it, Edwards. Drink to it, 'til your belly's full and your head is light and your heart lets you forget! Yeah, drink to it. Drink to a strange new world!... And if you ever get out there again—I mean, if that limb ever heals up and they stick you up as a target again—ask yourself, is it worth it?

EDWARDS (*quietly*) I like to think—maybe someday it will be, O'Hara. Maybe what we been goin' through ain't all for nothin'—maybe all this fightin' and shoutin' about liberty and equality ain't just idle talk. Anyway, I like to think so, O'Hara—I really like to think so—

(O'HARA *passes the bottle to* EDWARDS *as the lights fade*)

Abram Hill (1911–)

Walk Hard   1944

What white America demands in her black champions is a brilliant powerful body and a dull bestial mind. . . .

Essentially, every black champion until Muhammed Ali has been a puppet, manipulated by whites in his private life to control his public image. . . . For every white man, feeling himself superior to every black man, it was a serious blow to his self-image. (Eldridge Cleaver, *Soul on Ice*)

The hunt is a traditional emblem of male prowess. The drive to multiply and expand the self through wealth and procreation has woven elaborate systems of power from the once simple animal kill. The hunt has become abstracted into a nine-to-five job or a corporation merger; conquest has compromised with marital bondage—but the felt need for one male to physically demonstrate his superiority to other males has not lessened in proportion to the lessening of opportunity. The solution to a vanished frontier was to create an artificial contest (shooting clay pigeons for sport). The pinnacle of this ritual struggle is the modern warrior's sport—the prize fight. Here the single gladiator attains a hero's stature in the perfect symbol: The Heavyweight Championship of the World. Here maximum brute force and cunning smashes maximum brute force and cunning in a sharply focused contest that team efforts such as football cannot match.

Some early white boxers—John L. Sullivan and Jack Dempsey—refused to fight black challengers, but the implicit question remained: was the black man a superior animal? White America wanted it both ways: the black man must be more animal than the white man, but he must not be a superior animal. To demonstrate this paradox the white man had to submit to black competition, but he did it on his own terms. There was money to be made.

The black man placed his pride and hope for vindication on black champions. Joe Louis' victory over James Braddock brought 100,000 celebrants into the streets of Harlem, greeting every white they saw with "Howdy, Mr. Braddock." An apocryphal story tells of a black man about to be executed in prison, praying for deliverance to Joe Louis.

The dramatic nature of the prize fight has not been lost on the theater. The cinema has been better able to show the actual match; the theater has placed the fighting offstage and shifted the focus to related themes: racial conflict (*The Great White Hope*); sensitivity conflict (*Golden Boy*); racial and gangster exploitation of the fighter (*Walk Hard*).

Set in 1939 (first performed in 1944), *Walk Hard* reflects the "walk hard, talk loud, tough guy" character of the gangster genre that the movies perfected with James Cagney, Humphrey Bogart, and Edward G. Robinson. Concomitant with the tough male, the woman is shown as a lesser object. *Walk Hard* presents the male chauvinism of the boxers who treat women as objects. The hero is a human exception. The dialogue is unique in black drama because it captures the almost-conscious use of 1940's slang—"Nertz to you!" "Outa my way, drip!" and "the noive of this lug askin' me to hotfoot it to New York." The play was adapted from Len Zinberg's novel.

"As a director and a playwright," Mr. Hill wrote, "I have tried to bring a balance in the Negro theater. Most big-time commercial productions on race themes have dealt with only about 10 per cent of the Negro people—as a rule the exotic lower depths. All I'm trying to do is introduce a few of the other types who run the gamut from the professionals, middle class, and everyday Dicks, Toms, and Harrys."

Toward this end Mr. Hill, in collaboration with Frederick O'Neal and others, established the American Negro Theater (ANT) in 1940. Their first production, *On Striver's Row* ran 101 performances in the basement of a Harlem library (*see introduction to Natural Man*). ANT's greatest commercial success was an adaptation of white writer Philip Yordan's

Anna Lucasta, which was later moved to Broadway.

Walk Hard opened on December 19, 1944, to favorable reviews. Ruby Dee played the hero's sweetheart. In March, 1946, *Walk Hard* was moved downtown by producer Gustav Bloom to the Chanin Auditorium on Forty-fifth Street. Most reviewers found Mickey Walker, the one time welterweight and middleweight champion, a successful actor in the pug role of Larry Batchelo. But the critics were less enthusiastic about the play and its anti-Jim Crow message. Ward Morehouse of the *New York Sun* wrote that *Walk Hard* "is about a race-concious negro and the problems he creates for himself...."

In 1967, undefeated heavyweight champion Muhammad Ali "created problems for himself"; he refused induction into the Army on the grounds that he was a Muslim minister. Within an hour, the New York State Athletic Commission withdrew its recognition and suspended his license. This was done without a hearing, although that same commission during the decade had licensed nearly 100 convicted felons, including rapists, murderers, child molesters, arsonists, and sodomists—including at least three who had been awarded undesirable or dishonorable discharges from the armed services.

The language of *Walk Hard* is 1940. The situation is twentieth-century boxing.

Walk Hard

CAST OF CHARACTERS

BOBBY
MACK JEFFRIS (JEFFERSON)
MR. BERRY
LOU FOSTER
HAPPY
MICKEY
LARRY BATCHELO
BECKY
CHARLIE
SUSIE
RUTH LAWSON
A BARTENDER
SADIE
DOROTHY
GEORGE, *the bellhop*
HOTEL CLERK
LADY FRIEND
A REFORMER

TIME *Spring, 1939*

ACT ONE

Scene One

(*The forefinger of twilight is just beginning to smudge the clearcut lines of a corner building located in the West Forties of downtown New York. To the left of the building and facing its sharp angle is a subway kiosk. Light from the street corner lamp post and from the subway entrance filters the scene. Whereas the background is in semi-darkness, as the buildings rise and merge upward with the sky, the eye is lost in pyramidic shadows. Sufficient though is the light to reveal a certain hardness and implacable quality that seems to grow out of the buildings. The face that is one side of the building is decorated with a huge billboard displaying a heavyweight boxer.*

Just before the curtain rises, the whizzing traffic of midtown New York dwindles as clipped indistinct Yankee chatter swells and fades. This is followed by the quick snap of a shine cloth rhythmically polishing shoes. As the lights dim in BOBBY, *a white shoeshine boy—a regular New York toughie as hard as the background building, is polishing the shoes of* MACK JEFFERSON, *a stout smiling face man who chews rapidly on his cigar. The cigar darts from one end of* MACK'*s mouth to the other and when he speaks, his words have to dodge past the cigar to get out. He listens smirkingly as* BOBBY *gabs away*)

BOBBY I'm goin' into the bizness . . . see? I'm goin' into the bizness on me own hooks. I tell my old man. His face draws up into a knot. You'll end up fishing for lost nickels in subway air holes, you dope. Says him. You gotta brain the size of a lima bean. I'm still goin' into the bizness. So here I am.

MACK So your old man's in *business*, too?

BOBBY Yeah—he's got a cellar fullah ice, coal, ashes and rats.

MACK The ice and coal rake off ain't bad.

BOBBY Are you kidding?

MACK Sure the profit's good.

BOBBY Drop dead. Drop dead, willyu. Twenty years in the bizness and the most dough my old man ever spent on me old lady is for a pair of false teeth. Even then just because he knocked her real ones out. All she done was snitch two bits out of his pocket and he scatters her poils . . . (*indicating his teeth*) all over the floor. Took him three years to pay for 'em. You think I wanna go into that kinda racket. Three years to buy some teeth! Nix!

MACK I followed in my old man's footsteps.

BOBBY (*tapping* MACK'*s foot having finished*) Shift, buddy, shift.

MACK (*placing his other foot on the stand*) My old man was a bookie.

BOBBY Where's he now—in jail?

MACK Naw—passed out. Passed out because for once the nag he had a stack of dough on came in first. His ticker stopped beating. On his deathbed, he says, Mackie, my boy, I never knew anything so full of hay could be so hard to beat. Lay off the nags.

BOBBY I thought you say you followed in his footsteps?

MACK Up to a point. Now I handle human horses—the kind that wear gloves.

BOBBY (*after a pause*) Sure, do what you like, says me. This is a free country, ain't it? A man can do what he wants and nobody to stop him.

MACK Except the cops.

BOBBY Yeah—they stop you and take the swag you pick up and keep it for themselves. Now on this block, there's a lousy flatfoot that—(*sniffing*) Hey, mister, where do you hang out with them human horses, in a stable?

MACK Stable?

BOBBY Dese lousy shoes got crap on 'em! (*rising*)

MACK G'wan, finish the job, you're nearly through anyway. (*rising*)

BOBBY It'll cost you twenty cents instead of a dime.

MACK In your old man's cellar it does! Your sign says "shoe shine a nickel"—not a dime.

BOBBY (*removes cloth covering the bottom of his shine box, revealing sign which reads*: "*Shoe shine a Nickel apiece*") You got two feet, ain'cha? That's a dime. And the extra fertilizer'll cost you anudder dime.

MACK A wise guy huh? Okay, I'll toss you double or nothing. I'll flip a coin. Heads, I pay you twenty cents. Tails, you get nothing. Okay?

BOBBY (*reluctantly*) Lemme see both sides of the coin. (*he does*) Okay, okay, cheap bas—

MACK Careful with your lingo or you might find yourself with a pair of false teeth.

BOBBY For Chris' sake! Even Shakespeare uses bastard.

MACK Then you better stop hanging out with Shakespeare. (BOBBY *steps back aghast as* MACK *flips the coin then reveals the results which is satisfactory to him*) You lose, kid. Sorry, now finish knocking off my shoes.

BOBBY In your hat, fat slob! Do 'em yourself! (MACK *takes* BOBBY's *brush and strokes his shoe*)

MACK It ain't healthy to be a bad loser.

BOBBY Whyn't the hell you don't shine your own in the foist place?

MACK Tell you the truth, once I did. Then some wise ape started manufacturing shoe polish in collapsible tubes. I got up one morning drunk and made a mistake. Polished my teeth with black shoe polish instead of toothpaste! Imagine that!

(ANDY WHITMAN, *a full-shouldered Negro boy of 19, enters carrying his shine box and stool. He has a narrow waist, tight lips, hard and sensitive face with a nose that tends to spread. Not seeing* BOBBY, *he goes immediately up to* MACK)

ANDY Shine, mister, shine?

MACK Sure, kid, just put the gloss on 'em. (ANDY *sets up his box and begins polishing before* BOBBY *can realize he has taken his customer*)

BOBBY (*flabbergasted*) Some noive! Some noive! (*to* ANDY) Git da hell outa here befaw I bust you one! Scram! (MACK *laughs as* ANDY *ignores* BOBBY) A zillion blocks in dis burgh and he drifts in on my spot. Hey, bud, you can't shine shoes here!

ANDY You better go ahead, buddy.

MACK (*chuckles with contempt*) Go on—you little bum.

BOBBY Da hell wid you and your beer barrel belly. If you was my old man, I'd give you poison. (*to* ANDY) Clear outa heah, you—

ANDY You make me move.

BOBBY (*towering over* ANDY) You lousy dinge, I'll bust you—(*slugs at* ANDY, *who as he swiftly straightens up, sends a wild left punch into* BOBBY *who hits the street half dazed*. ANDY *is up and set for another blow*)

MACK Jesus, the kid's out! That was a damn good left hook! Fast!

ANDY You got enough? Get up!

BOBBY (*sits up rubbing his chin*) Don't tell me when to get up.

ANDY Don't hand me that line I can't run my shine box in this neighborhood. Come on. Get up!

BOBBY Take your time. I like to sit here if I want to.

ANDY Okay, sit there then.

BOBBY I will.

MACK (*laughing*) Hahahahahahahah. Get up you crazy jerk!

BOBBY I can still sit here and not take up as much space as you do when you're walking.

MACK (*to* ANDY) Gee, kid, if you throw a

punch like that from your knees, I guess if you had been standing when that gorilla jumped you, you would have knocked him into the middle of next week. What a slaughterhouse mit you got.

BOBBY (*rising*)   Nertz! I stumbled.

MACK   Yeah—well never hit a man while he's down—he may get up—sucker.

BOBBY (*gathering his paraphernalia*)   In any lingo, you stink. Yeah, you both stink! (ANDY *steps up threateningly as* MACK *steps in front of him. Tossing* BOBBY *a quarter*) Here's two bits. it's worth that to see you get slugged. Now run along and buy yourself a gown. As a matter of fact you would look swell in something flowing—like the Hudson River.

BOBBY (*exiting*)   Sonvabitch ... sonvabitch ...

ANDY   Okay, mister, I'll finish your shoes now.

MACK   Forget 'em. (*pays him*)

ANDY   Thanks. (MACK *stands grinning at him.* ANDY *sits shining his own shoes ... finally growing tense at* MACK'*s grinning face*) What's the matter with you?

MACK   You're wild as a drunken chorus girl. How old are you?

ANDY   Whatta you care?

MACK   I see I started something. Look, I'm Mack Jeffris. Ain't you heard of me? What a crappy rope! This one must have been made in Havana—by a dog. Look, I want to talk to you.

ANDY (*rises—crosses downstage evasively*) You are? But don't crowd my box. Them dime a dozen ropes don't draw me no trade.

MACK (*crossing to* ANDY *with a rolled dollar bill which he fingers under his nose*)   Here's a buck. Take it, kid. This ain't no circus confetti. Never turn down dough. (ANDY *takes it suspiciously*) Atta boy. Play smart. Never turn down dough. You know, when I was a kid, a guy gimmie a dime to beat up a toughie. Being smart, I hired another mug who did it for me. Besides the six cents I paid my stooge, he got a bloody nose and his old man decorated his mouth with a missing tooth ... hah—hah—hah —(*slapping* ANDY'*s shoulder*) I got four cents and had a damn good laugh.

ANDY   Whatta you want to talk about?

MACK   It's my dough so let me do the talking. Now how old are you?

ANDY   Nineteen.

MACK   That ain't bad. How much do you weigh?

ANDY   About a hundred and forty-five.

MACK (*examining him like a trader buying a horse*)   The mob yells louder for bigger beef. You're sorter lanky.

ANDY   Maybe you'd like a picture of me in a bathing suit. I got a figure.

MACK   Muscles hard. Legs long and ropey. Full of fight, ain'tcha?

ANDY   Stop feeling me up!

MACK   Chest hard as a washboard.

ANDY (*forefingering his lips*)   Get all the big white teeth.

MACK   Be still. Ain't you got no sense of humor? You ain't gonna get killed.

ANDY   I ain't got no rhythm in my eyes. And I don't sing hi-di-ho.

MACK   That's the way it is, if you can back it up.

ANDY (*a woman pedestrian passes*)   I think I can. (*to woman*) Shine, lady, shine? (*crossing as* MACK *wheels drawing him back by the hand*)

MACK   Shut up, for Christ sake! My buck ain't up yet! These bum ropes! I'm a sucker for every cigar that comes out. Look, you want to make five bucks, tomorrow?

ANDY (*backing away*)   Huh?

MACK   For the love of God! I don't wear any lavendar drawers!!! I'm *Mack Jeffris*. I manage fighters. You mean you ain't never heard of me! (*goes to Billboard*) See that poster? That's Larry Batchelo. He's a screwball with uncorned feet and a yen for women you can smell.

ANDY   He looks like a drip to me.

MACK   That's because he sweats too much—in bed. I own a piece of that pug. That drip as you call him has saved himself 20 grand. (ANDY *stares at the billboarded* BATCHELO *and unconsciously rests his eyes on his own hands*) With those mits, kid, you can stop living on stale crumbs. You heard of Lou Foster, the big shot? Well, he owns him and makes a bale of dough on him. Now I would like to manage you. We could clean up plenty.

ANDY   My fist—in gloves—and 20,000 dollars!

MACK   Think of it! Money, the sweetest word in the book. Now listen, meet me at 10:30 sharp tomorrow morning at, the Bleecker

Gym. I'll give you a tryout and a nice new five spot.

ANDY Couldn't you make it a dirty old ten spot?

MACK Hey, don't try to squeeze me before we get signed up. Now you better lam it before that stinking flatfoot on this beat comes along. He's down on the next block looking like he would knock the rear axel from underneath his own mother.

ANDY (*crossing*) I'll stay here for a while yet.

MACK Even the Governor would run from that flatfoot.

ANDY (*looking down the street*) I'm sticking. Here comes that guy who's still going to try to make me clear off this corner.

MACK Forget him. Don't waste your sap on riff-raff.

ANDY Calling me a dinge! My name's Andy Whitman!

MACK Okay, Andy. We'll broadcast that over NBC. He called my belly a barrel. Has my wife complained? No! Don't fight dopes. Get up on the roof and throw bricks and bedpans down on 'em.

ANDY You go ahead. I'll see you tomorrow.

MACK (*giving up*) All in one piece—I hope. I want to try out a fighter and not a corpse. So long. See you tomorrow. (*exits into subway.* BOBBY *returns very chummy*)

BOBBY Hey—

ANDY (*tensing*) I told you I'm sticking here long as ah damn please.

BOBBY Look, you beat me, so I don't give a damn whether you shine shoes here or in Flatbush. But the cop on this block will crack your konk.

ANDY I ain't scared of no flatfoot.

BOBBY But he don't like no—dark guys.

ANDY Cops ain't the only ones. You're sorter that way yourself.

BOBBY Naw, t'aint because you're black. I don't want no muscling in. I chase all shine guys no matter what they are. Listen, once there was a colored guy—just walking down the street. He was just a little pie-eyed . . .

ANDY So what?

BOBBY I seen this cop run down the street like he had been called for dinner and give this guy a crack on the head that damn near busted his stick.

ANDY Thanks for the tip, but I'm staying.

BOBBY It'll go bad with you.

ANDY It's worse if I go away.

BOBBY But why?

ANDY I don't know! I mean . . . I'd feel bad.

BOBBY Yeah?—any worse than a knot on the rump?

ANDY Weeks later it would come back to me that I ran away and I'd feel bad.

BOBBY You sound nertz!

(*The voice of a singing drunk trails in from down the street*)

MR. BERRY (*offstage*) . . . I hate to see that evening sun go down . . .

ANDY Mebbe, see, he's chasing me . . . because I'm black . . . and . . . well, you know how you feel after you'd done something yellow . . .

BOBBY Anyway, it was a good fight. Shake? (*offering his hand which* ANDY *at first suspiciously then fraternally shakes*)

MR. BERRY (*closer by*) . . . I hate to see that evening sun go down . . .

BOBBY You are nertz, though.

MR. BERRY (*staggers in dressed in the casual manner of an intellectual. He is a Negro obviously drunk, but underneath there is an inner spirit most recently crushed. He perks up at the two bootblacks*) How you all? Are you all right? You all—I all—He, she, it all? Why, put her there man. Put it right there and truck on down.

BOBBY He's lit up like a Christmas tree. Let's rook 'im.

ANDY What the heck you think I am?

MR. BERRY Well—look aheah—another black boy. Black like me . . . No, darker. So with you it's harder. Howya, gate. Whatsa matter? I'm that tap dancing fool. All colored boys are tap dancing fools. All I know is what I read in the papers.

ANDY For Christ sake! Cut it out, will you! What the hell you going around assing before the ofays for?

MR. BERRY Mammy! 'Fraid of living, and scared of dying. That's why darkies were born. That's digging us deep. Ain't it, Sambo?

BOBY Hahahahahahah—he's crazy, I swear!

MR. BERRY Ain't I a mess?

ANDY (*thoroughly embarrassed*) Shut up!!!

MR. BERRY (*seriously*) That's me. The big black clown. The joker to the bricks. This old world is anaemic. So they invented me, the black clown.

ANDY Man—why don't you go on about your business?

MR. BERRY (*shouting*) You know that Haaaaaallllllemmmmmmmmm jive! Come on, be yourself nigger—(*struck to the quick,* ANDY'S *fist shoots out like a quick stab of lightning, punching* BERRY *in the stomach. He doubles over in pain*) Wah——o—o—h! Oh, Lord!

BOBBY (*after a frightful silence*) De whole police force'll be here in a minute. You've killed 'im.

MR. BERRY (*staggering to stool*) My stomach is wide open.

ANDY Whyn't you shut up?

MR. BERRY Who are you to tell me to shut up? (*sitting*)

ANDY You got no right to go round making a fool of the race. All loud and wrong and clowning up a breeze, just like white folks say we do.

BOBBY Hey, you some kinda of jack-of-good-will out to keep your folks in a straight jacket?

ANDY How do you feel when you see some white drunk making you feel shame before people?

BOBBY If people ain't looking, I try to see how much dough he's got in his pocket.

ANDY (*whimsically*) Well, if you white, you're right—and if you're black you're wrong—in anything you do. Anyway, I'm sorry, Mister.

MR. BERRY (*rallying*) Sorry, Mr. Berry, but we had no idea you were a Negro . . . damage the morale of our employees. Why don't you find out before you're so free with your fist?

ANDY You mean—you—lost—your—job?

MR. BERRY I didn't even get it. I was turned down and I had been preparing for it for six years.

ANDY (*painfully*) I'm sorry.

MR. BERRY That's what they said, "sorry," *Mister* Berry. I'm surprised they called me mister. You know what I am. An architect . . . finished Cooper Union. Don't be nothing, boy, not a Gawd damn thing and you'll be happy.

ANDY (*rising from bewilderment to the emphatic*) A few minutes ago a fight manager just offered me a big chance in the ring. Boxing! The dough will pour like rain. Becky, my granny and Charlie, my old man, will crow like a couple roosters.

MR. BERRY Your granny and—(*second thought*) What will I tell my wife? My application rejected for that draftsman's job. I got to go on living on cabbage and fish! (*rising by the impact of his own thoughts, he crosses downstage bitterly*)

ANDY I'll help you home, Mr. Berry.

MR. BERRY (*breaking from him*) Help me, nowhere. I'm going back to pressing pants with an A.B. Always black . . . always broke. I found the same old pot at the end of my rainbow—and so will you. You're going to be a boxer. (*to* BOBBY) Tell him, white boy. Tell him quick he can't win! (*guffaws hysterically as* ANDY *fidgets at Berry's scorching denunciation*)

BOBBY (*to* ANDY) Geez, you're shaking like an American flag in the breeze!

ANDY America! This block, this city, this country—they're yours! (*gathers his things*) It stinks!

MR. BERRY Laugh, boy, laugh! I'm going back to pressing pants on an A.B. Always broke and always black. You got to make them laugh . . . You can't win . . . hahahahah . . . you can't win . . . hahaha.

(*As his voice trails off,* ANDY, *overwhelmed by his predictions, flees into the subway.* BERRY *follows staggering, while* BOBBY *sits, hunches his shoulders askance. The lights dim out*)

Scene Two

(LOU FOSTER's *office, the next morning.* LOU FOSTER's *office is located on an upper landing of the Bleecker Gym. Dominant in the back wall is a door marked* "LOU FOSTER—PRIVATE." *In the right wall is the door to the gym and the street, beyond this door is a small window overlooking the gym proper. At extreme left is a door leading to the shower. The walls are decorated with pugs and pin-up gals. The furnishings include couch with one end raised, chairs, desk with a telephone. Downstage left is a punching bag. At the rise of the curtain, the dull thuds of explosive blows trail in from the gym.* MACK, *chewing violently on his cigar, rushes in from the gym. He heads for* LOU's *office.*)

MACK Lou . . . Lou . . . the kid hits like a

powerhouse . . . (*a sudden surge of noise from the gym, he turns instead to the window, yelling*) Hey—hold that heel up! I want Lou to see Andy hit him again. Hold 'im up, I said! (*turning*) Lou, look at this! That boy musta worked in a butcher shop! (*tries* LOU's *door. It is locked. Back to window*) He did it! He did it! And his nose is as clean as a baby's face. (*rushing out into gym*) I've just given birth—birth to a fighter . . . mine!

(LOU FOSTER, *drawn by the excitement out in the gym, emerges from his private office. He is a narrow-chested man with sloping shoulders and a thin face with eyes like burnt embers; dressed in clothes that yell out high price. His attitude is one of complete nonchalance as he stares through the window. After a pause, he returns to his office just before* HAPPY, *a bald-headed Negro second with a natural smiling face, enters making way for* ANDY, *who follows him wearing a worn robe over his boxing togs. He is sweating and his whole body is alive and throbbing*)

HAPPY Great Gawd! Your right has that old sleep! And that left—why man, it's educated! (*massaging* ANDY *who is perched on the desk*)

MACK (*offstage warning the reporters*) No, boys, no. Not until I get him signed up. No pictures now.

HAPPY Man, you shore followed my instructions XYZ. Sidestep faster. Have your left ready in case you miss with your right. Come in close. If you miss, fall into a clinch. (MACK *enters and closes the door on the hub-bub from the gym crowd*) Yeah man, down went the other guy—kissing the floor!

MACK Quiet, Happy! Now put in a new needle.

ANDY (*strutting*) I look like a fighter. Damned if I don't. One time they was about-a burn a guy in the chair. He said, "Joe Louis save me!"

HAPPY (*seconding*) Andy Whitman save me! (*clicks his tongue*) You too skinny to be a Joe Louis but—

MACK Gone are the days of the big beef, Happy. Those guys were made when meat was cheap. As long as Andy's got a place for meat, we'll feed him till he gains weight like an old chorus girl. (*to* ANDY) What you keep slugging in that first round for? Didn't you hear me say stop?

ANDY I didn't hurt 'im much, did I?

HAPPY (*at window*) That Mickey is still out there counting sheep.

ANDY (*to* MACK) But you said Mickey McGown once beat the lightweight champion.

MACK Yeah—at poker.

HAPPY Serves him right because he's got a china jaw mounted on a ton of muscle. But when somebody taps you on the kisser your muscle fold up like a flat tire. Andy's jaw's made of pig iron.

MACK Quiet, Happy. So is your head. Okay, Andy, it will take about six months to train you right. Happy will teach you. I may even take you to Pompton Lakes. Larry Batchelo trains out there.

ANDY How do I eat while this is going on?

MACK I'll take care of that.

ANDY You ain't took care of this yet.

MACK (*gives him the money*) Sure thing. Here, five smackers like I promised you. Ain'tcha gonna say thank you?

ANDY You got your money's worth, didn't you?

MACK Every time I talk with you, I end up in a debate. Wash up and cool off, while I get your contract ready for you to sign. You can write, can't you?

ANDY Sure. Can you? (*exit* ANDY *and* HAPPY)

MACK Sure . . . sure . . . (LOU *enters*) Lou, you should have seen that kid when he—

LOU I saw him.

MACK (*calmly*) We been pals a long time, ain't we, Lou?

LOU Yeah, Mack, why?

MACK Even as a kid, I took all the black-eyes for you.

LOU But you was the biggest.

MACK And you was the toughest—with a brick or an ice pick.

LOU What are you driving at?

MACK Somehow another you always come out on top. You find the best fighters and sign them up. The mugs have made you rich, Lou. If my old lady hadn't died and left me her insurance dough, I'd be a bum.

LOU I always give you a percentage of anything I get.

MACK Yeah—enough to keep my belly from caving in on my spine.

LOU Now, why all the ceremony?

MACK My day has come. I've found the best hunk of flesh that will ever step into the ring. *I* found him, Lou! For me, this is the best day the damn sun ever set on. My shyster has drawn up the contract that will make me manager of the most perfect fighting machine ever built. (*rambles in desk drawer*) Where's that contract?

LOU In my pocket, Mack.

MACK (*dumbfounded*) But how—

LOU You know you can't do anything without my knowing, Mack.

MACK (*mild desperation*) Gimmie my contract. It's mine. I found him . . . I—

LOU (*nonchalantly gives it to him*) Here's your papers, Mack.

MACK (*shamefully*) I—I won't try to squeeze you out, Lou. I'm selling you ten per cent of him, now. Yeah, you can sign up for it right now. See—I'm giving you the same break you give me.

LOU Your boy is sorta skinny, ain't he?

MACK He'll grow up like corn. By the time he is 22, if he ain't a heavyweight, I'll eat your brown underwear. Here—sign for your ten per cent. (*gives him contract*)

LOU How old is he now?

MACK Nineteen.

LOU (*studying contract*) If you don't die from ignorance, Mack, you'll never croak.

MACK Whatcha mean?

LOU That boy is under age. This contract don't have a minor clause in it. Furthermore—his folks will have to sign it, too.

MACK Christ! When they dished out dumbness, I musta been on the front of the line. (*calling* ANDY *in shower*) Hey, Kid—is your old man alive?

ANDY (*appearing in doorway—half dressed*) Sure—is yours? (HAPPY *also appears*)

MACK Sure—sure . . . (ANDY *exits*) We have to get him to sign this contract, too. I'm running next door to get my shyster to insert the minor clause. Look, Happy, don't let any managers get near that kid. Those guys would steal the the nipple out of a baby's mouth.

HAPPY I got 'im covered, boss.

MACK Anyway—you can sign up, Lou, even without the clause.

LOU I never buy till I see what makes a fighter tick.

MACK (*puzzled*) Tick? Why that kid—

MICKEY (*a groggy white fighter in togs and robe, enters trying to wad off his defeat lightly*) Three knockouts in ten minutes ain't no rest cure. That's the first time I been knocked kicking in years.

HAPPY Sorry you got done in so, Mickey.

MICKEY What the heck, I'm paid for it. (MACK *pays him without looking at him*) Thanks, Mack. Where's the kid?

HAPPY Dressing.

MICKEY You got something there, Mack. Reminds me when I first had my tryout—remember? Only it was another guy getting the five bucks and me the contract.

MACK (*a little pained*) Well, kid—every dog has his day—and his night, too. (*exiting*) I got to see my lawyer. See you, kid. (*exits through gym door*)

ANDY (*entering dressed in trousers and sweater*) You know, Happy, my old man wants me to go to college and he may stall on signing—(*seeing* MICKEY)

MICKEY I went to college.

HAPPY Yeah, this Mickey, he was a big college boy, big football star and all that. Now look at him, washed up, taking a licking for five bucks.

MICKEY Huh—huh—S'all right, Happy. I'm going to the coast. Take a job with a big Syndicate. Not fighting, though. Of course it ain't a bad calling, but you can't grow old at it. It's like whoring, you can't grow old at that either. The rich don't go in for boxing or whoring. That is, *professionally*. (*he shrugs casually and exits into shower room*)

ANDY What does a guy wanna be a fighter for, Happy?

HAPPY Whatta you think? A empty belly is fighter's best second.

ANDY My belly is pinching me now. Let's go eat.

HAPPY Not till Mack gets the contract all fixed up, brother. No going nowhere for you. No manager's snatching you. Mack is smart.

ANDY Okay—okay—Look, you think I'll ever fight in South America or Europe?

HAPPY Mebbe if Lou Foster buys a piece of you. He's the kingpin in this racket and got connections everywhere. That's *Lou Foster*, pal!

ANDY You mean he could take me outa this country?

HAPPY (*snaps his finger*) Just like that—(*curiously*) But why so anxious for outside USA?

ANDY (*after a searching pause*) Nothing—Boy, this is my racket! This is it!

HAPPY (*very chummy*) You know, we colored folks must hang together.

ANDY (*angrily*) Who wants to hang?

HAPPY (*stung*) That ain't no way to take things, man.

ANDY Don't man me! And don't hand me no sales talk about hanging together. You chumps always bowing low, so you'll get a better whack in the tail.

HAPPY All the boys like me, Andy.

ANDY The boys tell me you ran through ten thousand dollars. And three dames ran through you.

HAPPY You'll get on top, kid. Just don't ride the hog so high—you'll get humpbacked ... There's always, I mean ain't there no room in your life for—

ANDY For what?

HAPPY A pal?

ANDY Don't windbag me! I travel alone. I want no stooge chisling my dough and spreeing off with some dizzy dames!

(LOU *enters inquisitively*)

LOU (*after* HAPPY, *scorned and hurt, sinks into a chair*) What's all the gassin' about?

HAPPY (*rises and strives to come out of it*) Oh, Mr. Foster—I was just telling the kid—

LOU (*to* ANDY) So, you're the new fighting Sambo?

ANDY (*instinctively*) My name ain't Sambo! It's Andy Whitman!

(*A sudden inner fury rages for an instant between the two—a tension that slices the air.* LOU *simply stares at* ANDY *as he breaks a pencil he's holding in his hands. Then* HAPPY *tries desperately to break the tension—gasping trying to speak, but can't*)

LOU I want to talk to you, Happy, inside. (ANDY, *driven by his resentment, makes for the gym door*)

HAPPY Andy! Mack says for you to stay here!

ANDY (*stops*) But he said for you not to let nobody in.

HAPPY But this is *Mister Lou Foster*!

LOU I want to talk with you, Happy, inside! (*exits into office.* HAPPY *follows.* ANDY *reluctantly forces himself into chair next to desk.*

Then the deep and happy voice of LARRY BATCHELO *is heard out in the gym*)

LARRY (*offstage*) Boy, that's a sweet kid with plenty of meat in the right places. (*enters. He is a big faced heavyweight with a faint scar over his eyebrow and a somewhat flattened nose*) Nothing like laying in bed getting mellow on good wine and listening to a good hot band. (LARRY, *chewing on a straw, makes overtures to* ANDY) Ayah, Kid, you like jazz? Naw, you ain't the sort. So you're Mack's new find. (*feeling his arm*) Nice frogs in your arm, kid.

ANDY Stop feeling me up.

LARRY Hah—hah—hah—hah! You're all right. Cocky, smart, alert. Pack up your bag, kid and kiss your jane goodbye. We train at Pompton Lakes—Okay, so you don't like me. Be a cold guy then. Right, kid, never trust a stranger. And never trust a dame after she's two years old. They make you feel stinko. I know. I been tail chasing up and down Broadway for five years. I found out one thing. Lay off the broads and the high priced mud-kickers. I wise up and quit the sucker list. They slow down your timing. Why marry a cow when milk is so cheap ... hahahahahahahah ... (*failing to stir* ANDY *with his own joke,* LARRY's *face drops*) You got a goil, Kid?

ANDY I know some girls. I mean, I got a nice girl.

LARRY You're damn right, she's nice.

ANDY I mean better looking than chorus girls.

LARRY Hell, them pots. Some of them have figures—(*relaxes on couch*) But most of them is just skinny body holding up a big pair of balloons. Is your dame a virgin?

ANDY What—what difference does it make?

LARRY Stop lying. Any dummy shouldn't marry a tomato.

ANDY I'm kinda dumb that way. Tell me, what the hell difference does it make? (*rising, being drawn by* LARRY's *fraternalism*)

LARRY Nix, kid, never pluck tomatoes that's been shot to pieces. (LOU *enters again and is unseen by* LARRY. HAPPY *follows him*)

ANDY No kidding—I always thought a chick was—(*sees* LOU)

LARRY (*sensing something*) S'matter, kid?

LOU Larry?

LARRY (*rising*) Now, listen, boss. A dame only stopped me to tell me she saw a pair of stockings she thought *I'd* like. That's why I'm late.

LOU   I want to talk to you, Larry, inside.

LARRY   Sure, boss—you know this kid's all right.

HAPPY   Mister Foster is in a hurry, Larry.

LARRY   Sure, for me to lay off skirts (*to* LOU, *playfully*) Look at Lou, so businesslike. You know, he really likes me. I'm such a big chunk of beef, and he's such a little shrunk. Don't you sweetheart? Can I help it because all the dames stop me on the street and just pass you up? That dame I just left—What you sore about, boss?

LOU   (*faking a sickly smile*)   Am I sore? (*exits into office.* LARRY *follows, gesturing innocently*)

HAPPY   (*in a screaming whisper*)   Andy Whitman, for the Lord sake, watch your step. That's Lou Foster.

ANDY   Who does he think he is, looking at me like I was nothing.

HAPPY   Shut up!

ANDY   That frig looked at me like I stunk.

HAPPY   Shut up! If he heard you cuss him, you'd be dead by tonight. That ain't no baloney. He don't *think* he is, he is! That guy run this corner of the world. The real big shot. A fighter can't get to first base in this racket, if Lou don't get a piece—if he wants it.

ANDY   He don't have to buy no part of me.

HAPPY   You say you want to fight abroad. Well, he's your passport. Mack can start you on the road. But Lou puts your name up in lights—(MICKEY, *dressed in worn street clothes, enters from shower and crosses toward gym door*) Mickey—tell him who Lou is. Tell him—

MICKEY   (*stopping*)   Him? He's the heel that took the word sport out of the boxing game. Fight racket is the name now. Yessir, he rose up from the gutter and got on top. But now, he don't want nobody else to rise up. You're looking pretty heated up. Well, don't let it throw you before you get started. Look at me, twenty-five years old, and only five bucks to get to California. I'm going to try to get in with a big sport syndicate out on the coast. (*slaps* ANDY's *shoulder and faces* LOU's *door, then heads for gym door*) There's many names for him, but I call him but one name only, and that's sonofabitch! (*exits and slams the door*)

ANDY   And that goes double for me. (*exits huffing and slams the door doubly hard, the impact of which draws* LOU *out of his office, who stares at the door as* LARRY *follows, talking.* HAPPY *is too flabbergasted to speak*)

LARRY   Okay, sweetheart, no more matinees with the janes. Though I'm stale from training. I can't even work up a good sweat. I need a vacation, Lou. Even you need a vacation. You who ain't never hit a lick of work.

LOU   (*still gazing at the door*)   Open that door, Happy, and—

HAPPY   (*frightened*)   Naw—boss, naw! Whatcha mean—?

LARRY   Jesus, Happy—

LOU   Open that door—and close it *properly.* (HAPPY *obeys*) What did you mean by "what I mean?"

HAPPY   I don't know, boss... Excuse me, I ain't feeling good. (*exits into shower room*)

LARRY   (*as* LOU *takes out a cigarette*)   Aw, he's been around here so long, he's getting gym batty. But honest, boss, I'm getting stale.

LOU   Come on, lug. You got a big fight coming up three months from now. I'm betting eight grand on you.

LARRY   Yeah—and you'll bet 20 thousand on the mug I fight. You're a smart man, Boss. I'd be funny as hell if I'd win one time instead of losing.

LOU   (*lighting up*)   Stop imagining miracles. And lay off dames till we start training.

LARRY   All right, boss. We go to Jersey where tomatoes hang from every bush. Me and the kid. You know I bet he's got more imagination than Joe Louis. Him and me is going to get stewed to the ears... boiled to the hair.

LOU   (*smoke fogging his face; lights dimming slowly*)   That's an awful fresh kid—Larry—

LARRY   Yeah—boss—plenty hard—(*second thought*) Yeah—yeah—you once said that about —Mickey—(*quits brushing his nails on his sleeve, uneasily*)

LOU   Awful fresh—an awfully fresh—nigger!

(*Lights black out as* LOU *clinches his cigarette into the tray*)

Scene Three

(*The* WHITMAN *Home the same evening.*

The front room of a typical railroad flat, located in deep Harlem. The furnishing, including a sofa, table, chairs, cloak-rack and pictures are all old, but clean and neat. The room is divided from the remaining part of the flat by a pair of heavy portiers. Center of the back wall is a mantle over which holy pictures and a GOD BLESS OUR HOME tapestry hang. Prominent on the wall is the picture of a stern open-mouthed brown woman. Downstage right is a window overlooking the countless harlem roofs. Upstage right is the door to hall bearing several locks. At curtain rise, BECKY, ANDY's *granny, fiery old woman in her sixties but whose energy might rate her in her forties, sits comfortably near the table with a large sewing kit on the floor near her.* CHARLIE, ANDY's *father, rallies from a nap and reads the newspaper.* BECKY, *having just finished sewing a garment, lays it aside and picks up a pair of union suit underwear. Holding them up, she reveals a big hole in the seat of the suit*)

BECKY (*in disgust*) It would be bye-bye Charlie Whitman, if a good draft ever caught you in these things.

CHARLIE Aw—put them things away.

BECKY (*flinging them back into basket*) I have, for good. I've darned them, I've patched them —now if you want 'em upholstered, you'll do it yourself. (*taking sock from basket*) The way holes can get between the world and your— skin!—Which end of this sock do you want me to darn—now? (*rams her arm through a sock which has the entire toe missing*)

CHARLIE You know in my business, I'm on my feet all day. (BECKY *quickly picks up the underwear and looks at him askance.* CHARLIE *then apologetically*) Well, I have to set down between train trips, don't I?

BECKY Umph!

CHARLIE Aw—just throw 'em out. I'll be able to buy new ones now. The depression is breaking. Travelers tip me quarters now instead of dimes.

BECKY Not two whole bits!

CHARLIE Two bits! You didn't get that kinda talk from nobody but Andy. By the way, with me making more, why together we oughta have enough soon to send him off to college.

BECKY Yeah—I suppose so in about 1970.

CHARLIE Hannah wanted him to go to the big college in Washington. I don't want him to go there though. I heard that the boys and girls there use the same curriculums! (*relaxes on sofa*)

BECKY (*staring up at stern brown photo of* HANNAH) Good old Hannah. I never understood why she had that picture taken with her mouth wide open.

CHARLIE The photographer told her to look natchel, didn't he? (*suddenly surprised at something he sees in the newspaper. Whirls his feet to the floor, sitting straight up*) Great day in the morning! Becky, here's my boy's picture in the newspaper!

BECKY (*rushes to see it*) What in the world is he doing in the paper? (*taking paper*) It shore is!

CHARLIE Lemme read what it says.

BECKY Wait ... wait ... It says: "Andy Whitman, Harlem bootblack, showed sensational promise today when he fought—"

CHARLIE And went to jail! Is that boy in trouble? I knew it!

BECKY (*walking about reading as* CHARLIE *trails her* Stop giving birth to trouble. Some man name Mack Jeffris is making a boxer out of—my grandson! It says he's good, and done out tried him.

CHARLIE Gimme—(*reads and then*) You mean tried him out.

BECKY (*goes to window calling*) Ruth ... Ruth ...

CHARLIE Why you have to tell her?

BECKY (*winking*) Charlie, I wish I had know you when you was alive. (*back to window*) Ruth ...

RUTH (*next door*) Yes?

BECKY Guess what, honey. Andy's picture is in the evening paper! Come on over, child ... What?

RUTH I'd love to see it, but my aunt from Pennsylvania is here visiting me now.

BECKY Bring her with you. You must see the picture.

RUTH All right.

BECKY (*returning*) She'll be thrilled to death. (*second thought*) I never knew that child had any folks. (*takes paper from* CHARLIE *who is lost in thought at that moment*) I'm going to put it in a frame and hang it on the wall. Where's my scissors? (*searches for scissors, finds them and clips picture*) His picture will look right nice up there next to his high school diploma.

CHARLIE You ought to be hanging his college degree up there.

BECKY Just like I'm cutting out this picture,

some folks just ain't cut out for college. And from a bootblack to a B.A. may not be as good as from a bootblack to a boxer.

CHARLIE Them fighters always end up either blind or bums.

BECKY All the grocer man's son was able to do after he finished college was to teach his Pa how to open a bottle of whiskey with a half a dollar. (*takes stool and mounts getting frame*)

CHARLIE It's sacrilege for you to mess with them holy pictures.

BECKY Honest, your religion spills all over into my soup. (*screaming as she knocks something from her bosom*) Ee-e-e-e-ek! Get him off me! Get him off!

CHARLIE (*to her aid*) What the devil you doing?

BECKY Them redbacked no good be—

CHARLIE Becky!

BECKY Roaches!

CHARLIE You seen roaches before.

BECKY Yeah—but not crawling out of God's bosom and from 'neath Setting Bull. No wonder that Indian looked so uncomfortable setting on that hoss!

CHARLIE That bug nearly set you back on your fanny. That's the Lord's way of punishing you for offending him.

BECKY He may work in the mysterious way, but that sure ain't one of them. (*spanks herself with a sweeping gesture*) Go in the kitchen and get me my spray.

CHARLIE (*exiting*) Such ugly talk for a grandma.

BECKY It's gonna be too damn hot for me and thee to stay here.

CHARLIE (*offstage*) Will you stop that kind of talk.

BECKY Aw go 'long and may the Lord like you.

CHARLIE (*entering*) I'm plenty filled up at the way you been grouching at me. You sound more like Andy every day. How so much of you jumped clear of me and into him is a thing I sure would like to know.

BECKY (*snatching spray*) Gimme that spray! (*spraying*) It has been truly written that ye roaches shall not rule the earth.

CHARLIE (*exasperated*) Now you joke the good book. How old are you anyway, Becky?

BECKY Charlie, you ought to know that any woman that will tell her age, will tell anything.

CHARLIE You talk like you in your second childhood.

BECKY (*finishing with her foot stamping the insects*) Well, if I am, I'm having a lot better time than I did in the first one.

CHARLIE (*sitting*) Ten to one, you bossed that boy into turning boxer.

BECKY I did nothing of the kind. (*mounting picture*) Big things happening, while you're asleep. Look how your head's growing through your hair. And ever since 1918 when the boat brought you back, you went down to Pennsylvania Station, put on a redcap, fell asleep and ain't never woke up... You know, Charlie, there's lots of people die at 20 and are buried at 50.

CHARLIE What—did you say?

BECKY (*hanging* ANDY's *photo*) Nothing—I didn't hear myself. (*rap at door*) Come in— (MACK *enters beaming, contract in his hand* BECKY *doesn't look around*) Ruth child, ain't this the sweetest—

MACK It sure is.

CHARLIE (*perplexed*) Carry your bag, sir— I mean, who do you want to see?

BECKY (*seeing* MACK) Omigod! I thought you was the child from next door. What do you want?

MACK I'm in the right place, all right. Where's my wonder boy?

CHARLIE Andy hasn't come home yet, if that's who you mean. (BECKY *has dismounted and stands puzzled*)

MACK Must be out celebrating with his g.f. Let him take it easy, because boxing and broads don't mix well.

BECKY His girl, Ruth, is coming up here in a few minutes. And he ain't with her. But what is this all about?

MACK Let's sit down and talk turkey. (*they sit at the table*) You're his granny, I guess and you're his dad. Well, dad, I just want you to sign his contract. I'm Mack Jeffris, his manager. See he's still under age and you have to stick your John Hancock right on the dotted line. You know what it means, granny, money enough to send you to heaven in a golden chariot.

BECKY Heaven can wait. I'd much rather have a Buick here on earth. Tell me, how much can that boy make for us now?

MACK Thousands! Maybe more... what

did you raise him on, gunpowder? All I need is for pops to sign right here.

CHARLIE (*rising*) Then that newspaper story ain't altogether right. Andy ain't really in the business till I sign that paper?

MACK Yeah—some newshound stole a march on me.

CHARLIE I can't sign that paper—Mister—

BECKY Lord, as I live and breathe!

MACK (*choking*) Listen Charlie—it's like throwing a million dollars right out of a window.

BECKY With me tied to it.

CHARLIE Andy is a funny boy. He's got a strong streak of bitter, flaming pride that burns inside him like a red hot poker. Always sore and can get as raving mad as a nest of wild tigers. That's my son mister, and a helluva thing to turn loose in a ring.

MACK Feeling through a pair of boxing gloves will change all that.

BECKY I don't know nothing on God's green earth that a dollar won't cure. And I don't see—

CHARLIE How can you see? Him, you and Hannah, his ma, are too much of the same blood.

MACK (*sprightly*) Maybe his mother will sign. Where's she?

BECKY Up in heaven talking everybody to death, the same as she did here on earth.

MACK Well—he's made out all right this far in life. The future is rosy with dough.

CHARLIE So far because God has sheltered him—kept his insides from bursting through his outsides.

BECKY And out there in the ring, God will be with him, too.

MACK As a matter of fact, Andy's first fight will be with a Mexican named Jesus Perez.

BECKY Hear that, Charlie?

CHARLIE You see if you put too much heat under a jug with a stopple in it, the stopple will pop off.

BECKY The thing to do is plug up the hole.

CHARLIE If what comes out don't kill you first. Put that boy out there in the ring, raw, unmasked with the hinges off his mind, and the Lord only knows what may happen. I got a feeling—though—an awful feeling . . .

MACK (*perturbed*) Well what do you want the kid to do?

CHARLIE Go to college.

BECKY Charlie spent about fifteen minutes at Tuskegee and got a hangover for learning that he ain't never done nothing about.

MACK Look, your boy will make out allright if he stays out of street fights and cat houses.

CHARLIE I can't sign, Mr. Jeffris.

BECKY Well, I will.

CHARLIE I'm his father.

BECKY I'm his grandmother.

MACK And I'll be damned!

BECKY (*after an awkward pause*) Charlie— if you don't sign that contract, I swear I'll make Andy run away on one of them freight boats like he's always wanted to do. Yessir, I'll even go with him—even if it's to Africa! I swear on this Bible. (*raising book*)

CHARLIE (*resignedly*) All he needs is encouragement from you. Give me your pen, Mr. Jeffris.

MACK (*enthusiastically accommodates* CHARLIE, *who sits and hesitatingly begins to sign slowly*) Just jot down your John Hancock. And we'll soon ride down Broadway—*the* Broadway, the diamond stickpin on the shirtfront of America —in a Rolls Royce!

(CHARLIE *is still signing as* RUTH *an attractive Negro girl about 18 and obviously vivacious, romantic with a sparkling personality underneath which a deep seated streak of wisdom occasionally flashes through*)

RUTH Hello—the door was open—so I—

BECKY (*warding off any distraction for* CHARLIE) Ss-s-s-s-sh! Close it.

RUTH But Aunt Susie is—

BECKY SS-s-s-s-s-!

SUSIE (*entering breathlessly.* AUNT SUSIE *is self-centered, airish and impetuous. Attracting no attention and sensing the quietude*) After four flights of steps, is it all right if I breathe?

MACK (*hurrying after getting the signed contract from* CHARLIE) Atta fella. Now you keep a copy for yourself. Thank you, Granny. You and your Bible did it. (*kisses "bible," then discovers*) Hey— this is a cook book! (*winks at* BECKY *and then exits, beaming joyously.* CHARLIE *reads as he wanders towards the next room without noticing the guest*)

CHARLIE I hope I don't regret signing these papers. (*exits in deep study*)

BECKY Ruth, ain't you tickled? Andy's going to be a boxer.

RUTH A boxer?

BECKY Just like Joe Louis!
RUTH But Andy's so different from Joe Lewis. That's why the pict—
SUSIE (*to* RUTH) And where does that put you?
BECKY (*realizing her indecorum*) Do sit down, Miss—
RUTH This is granny Becky and this—
SUSIE (*sharply*) Madame, I'm Susie Smith, Ruth's aunt on her mother's side. My niece is that way about your grandson and—
BECKY (*shocked*) Naw—she can't be!
RUTH I can take care of my own affairs. I told you.
SUSIE So independent! That's what becomes of a young girl living in New York alone.
RUTH You came up here alone.
SUSIE That was different. What it took to take care of me, I had plenty of.
BECKY (*chokingly*) Ugggggh!!!!! What in the devil is this all about?
SUSIE Your family may be the swellest one in the world. Andy could be the nicest guy in New York, as Ruth says, but—
RUTH Aunt Susie pops up from nowhere and wants me to come live with her.
BECKY (*suspiciously*) What is this *that way*?
SUSIE Ruth is in love with your grandson.
BECKY (*relieved*) Aunt Susie, I could drown you. Don't you know I know how them two kids feel about one another? Could she come in and out of my house every day for the past year? Could she be living right next door with her window closer to my flat than this room is from the kitchen? Could she know—without me knowing?
SUSIE Then you're aware of the fact that I can offer my niece a home, companionship and love instead of New York hard knocks? If you are the good granny to her she says you are, then why not tell her she belongs with her only relative?
BECKY I never knew she even had you till just now. Besides, Ruth's a full grown woman and she can decide things for herself. What do you say, Honey?
RUTH Well—my mind was all made up to stay in New York when I came in just now. But now with Andy as a fighter I'm not so sure.
SUSIE These fighters keep enough women to burn... Ah—ah—my glove! (SUSIE *bends down to retrieve her dropped glove.* RUTH *glances at* BECKY. *Meanwhile* CHARLIE *entering the room almost stumbles over* SUSIE *whom he hadn't noticed. Then stepping back, recognizes her back*)
CHARLIE Ain't that the hula-hula dancer? Yeah, the one who used to stand perfectly still and twiddle her tom tom. It is. It sure is! Snake hips Susie Smith! Last time I saw you was at the Red Cap Inn on 59th Street. Why Becky, with one foot, Susie could kick the back of her head.
BECKY That explains *everything*!
SUSIE I beg your pardon. I didn't get the name.
RUTH Aunt Susie, that's Mr. Whitman—Charlie Whitman.
SUSIE (*evasively*) Pleased to know you.
CHARLIE Know me! Why, your face may slip some folks, but I'd recognize you from behind anywhere. Turn around again. (*half circles her*) Yeah—that coco cola bottle figure has sorter spread into a milk bottle, but that's you all in one piece.
RUTH Aunt Susie, you never told me you were a hula-hula dancer.
SUSIE Well—well, there'er lots of things you don't know.
BECKY Ruth, I want to talk to you alone, if your aunt don't mind. Come with me. I never knew you had an aunt.
RUTH I didn't either. She started writing me just before they let me out of the home. Maybe she's right. I shouldn't live here alone.
BECKY That's what I want to speak to you about. (*eyeing* SUSIE) You can hardly boast of the *same protection* she had then. (RUTH *and* BECKY *exit*)
SUSIE (*very chummy*) Lord, Charlie, where have you been?
CHARLIE Same old station and the same old hangouts.
SUSIE It's good seeing you. You look the same. Your hair is thinner.
CHARLIE Age, honey, age. If you don't thin out in one place, you get thick in another. Now take you—
SUSIE Remember the time I was dancing with you—when I started running across the floor—you thought I was doing some new kind of step? Hahahahahah... you didn't know the joint was being raided.
CHARLIE Yeah... the good old days. One raid right behind another.

SUSIE I got tired of the prohibition squad. I quit and joined TOBA the vaudeville circuit ... With my joints getting stiff and my feet always hurting I quit the bumping and grinding and just posed behind a fan.

CHARLIE Hahahahahah, how could all of you get behind a fan!

SUSIE That's fun in it ...

CHARLIE You was one hip slinging mama. I never will forget the time when Eddie made a pile of dough at the track and celebrated at the club. Trying to get his eye, you nearly wrenched your back twirling.

SUSIE You telling me! 'Twasn't in vain. I finally married Eddie.

CHARLIE Naw—where is he?

SUSIE Dead.

CHARLIE Oh—too bad. Guess he left you plenty dough.

SUSIE To me and four other wives. When he died, five of us showed up claiming his estate. He was one grand rascal. We're still battling in court. Doggone judge got so confused at us five loudmouth huzzies, he's holding the big chunk in escrow for further investigation.

CHARLIE Whatta you know? But who's escrow?

SUSIE You're still as dumb as they come. Anyway, I saved enough on my own to buy a chicken farm down in Pennsylvania.

CHARLIE That's good. That's good. You always did use your—head.

SUSIE Now—this is where you can help me. It's awfully lonesome down there on the farm.

CHARLIE Look here now. I'm too old to be keeping you the type of company you'll be needing.

SUSIE Put that talk down and let it walk. You—pshaw! I want you to get your boy to talk Ruth into leaving New York and come live with me.

CHARLIE Oh—that—

SUSIE He could do it. You could help him.

CHARLIE I got plans of my own for that boy.

SUSIE Do they include Ruth marrying him?

CHARLIE Who thought that up?

SUSIE Well, she is good enough for him.

CHARLIE No marriage and neither this fight business is my plan. He's got to get more schooling.

SUSIE Good! Then you'll do what you can. May take a little time, but it's worth it, right?

CHARLIE Yeah—yeah—sure—I guess so.

SUSIE I could kiss you, you old rascal.

CHARLIE Careful now. Don't start nothing your health can't stand.

SUSIE Bye, bye, sugar pie. (*calling*) Ruthie—are you ready to go? I am.

RUTH (*entering with* BECKY) Just a minute, Aunt Susie.

SUSIE Let's go, child. The whole thing is practically settled.

RUTH I'm 18 now and this is a helluva time for you to start giving me orders.

SUSIE Well—I'd better sit down before you knock me down with that kind of language. (*sits*)

RUTH Before you go, Becky has something to say. Remember what she says means as much to me as if she was my own mother.

SUSIE Well—*mother*?

BECKY When Ruth's mother died and her father disappeared, whyn't you take care of this child instead of the city putting her in a home?

SUSIE Where was I going to keep her, in my trunk? I was touring the TOBA vaudeville circuit. TOBA, that means tough on black actors. If you don't think that's the roughest, toughest experience for anybody, ask any old vaudeviller. A child there, is ridiculous!

BECKY You think this milk and honey you're offering her is better than making her own way here? I can't see how anything you can do will fill up all those empty years of childhood.

SUSIE But you obviously can see her life get tangled up with Andy. Any justification you may have had has fizzled. He's a boxer now. Don't tell me about those guys! They skip between rounds from one gal to another. The steady love of an aunt is damn strong by comparison.

CHARLIE Look here now—

BECKY But not strong enough for you to quit touring and take a job doing something home, and give Ruth a home when she was a baby.

SUSIE I couldn't give up my career!

BECKY I am afraid you were a little selfish ... still is if you ask me. But then, you're her aunt and I guess you have the legal right to guide her.

SUSIE (*rising*) Is that all?

BECKY Yes ma'am, I enjoyed your visit.

RUTH I'm sorry you left yourself neutral, Becky. You've been all but a mother to me. Still I guess if you had decided for me, I would be playing right into Aunt Susie's hands. Showing that I can't do my own deciding and making my own way.

SUSIE Are we going, now?

RUTH Just a minute, Aunt Susie. You've had a life of sunshine. Glamour on the road and in the big cities. A career, money, clothes and all the trimmings. You must have beamed like a sunflower in your heyday. You've faded now. All that life is gone. You want to settle down now. Home, security and a real friend.

SUSIE (*obviously hit hard*) Well, that is—well?

RUTH You've loved nobody but yourself. And that's becoming less and less comforting. I'm sorry I can't go. I think I have something you probably never had—love! Until I met Andy, I had an empty spot in my life. He has filled it. So completely, I have no vacant room in my heart for you. I *am* sorry.

SUSIE (*submissively*) Maybe you'll just come visit me sometime.

RUTH Perhaps we all will some day.

SUSIE (*primping fastidiously to conceal her emptiness*) Well—as the saying goes, when your friends are all gone, and you turn to a relative, the relative may turn on you. (*exits*)

RUTH (*regretfully crossing to stop* SUSIE) But she does need me.

BECKY (*stopping her*) The old gal's got enough stuff left in her to hook another husband.

RUTH And here I am sticking around here like Andy would be ready to marry me tomorrow. Even when I approach the subject . . .

BECKY Honey, don't ever *mention* marriage to a man! You got to ease up on him and ooze him along . . . till you get 'fore a preacher.

RUTH Even after we're married, what's to keep him from going away? He's always talking about it.

BECKY You got a education, ain't you? Then read a book on how to keep your husband home.

RUTH Is that what you did?

BECKY I didn't have to. His trouble was other women. I soon put that to an end. I caught him once in the wrong company with his britches down. I came down on him with a red hot poker. Honey, he wasn't born with a birthmark, but he sure died with one.

ANDY (*enters*) Hiya, Becky! (*embracing* RUTH) Why Ruth, hiya doin'?

RUTH The same as I've been doing. But take it easy. *I'm* not a boxer.

ANDY Boxer—how do you know?

BECKY Why, it's all over town, (*showing him photo*) And Mr. Jeffris that was here tonight says we're all going to be rich.

ANDY Was he here?

BECKY Of course he was and Charlie signed the contract for him to manage you.

RUTH (*seeing* ANDY's *disappointment*) Andy—what's wrong?

CHARLIE (*entering reading contract*) Why Becky, you know this paper says—(*seeing* ANDY) Son—is your nose going to sleep on your face? Or did the other guy flatten it in your tryout?—

ANDY You shouldn't have signed it. I hadn't fully made up my mind.

RUTH But isn't this the big opportunity that—

BECKY Done hit him so hard across the head till he's still dizzy.

ANDY Yeah—opportunity today knocked me clear out of America's backyard onto the front porch.

BECKY That's better than down the alley.

ANDY It's crazy! That's what it is—crazy! This guy Mack Jeffris puts the whole world in the palm of my hands. When I boxed Mickey today, I felt the world behind a pair of boxing gloves. It was great. It was like someone had reached down my throat and untied my guts!!!

RUTH You always say you felt tied up in a knot. Boxing must be what you always wanted—and didn't know it.

ANDY But there's a catch. Signing with Mack is okay. But there's a kingpin over him. You can't make big time—big money, not *really* get up there unless this guy buys in on the contract, too.

BECKY What's wrong with that?

ANDY His eyes looks at me like they could spit on me. I don't like him and I think he hates me. That's why I hadn't decided to sign up.

CHARLIE I'll just tear the thing up! (*tries to,* BECKY *leaps for it*)

BECKY Charlie, you fool! Gimme that thing.

(*retrieving it*) That man's eyes are just probably gin shot.

CHARLIE   I knew I shouldn't have signed that thing.

ANDY   I guess it'll be all right. It's got to be now. Anyway, I'll make plenty dough.

BECKY   I'm going to put this paper where Charlie can't find it. (*exits*)

CHARLIE   You know you're still going to college, regardless.

ANDY   You still think if a guy passes through college, he can pass through life with a smile. You should have seen a drunk I met yesterday. Howling and mad as hell because after studying for six years, he found the same old pot at the end of his rainbow.

CHARLIE   Just the same, you *got* to go.

ANDY   But why?—

CHARLIE   Listen—(*pausing—at* RUTH) Daughter, will you excuse yourself a minute? (RUTH *exits*) Sit down, son. (*reluctantly obeys*) That's it, Andy, you got a strong head and a strong body. Both of them are wild. Now learning has a way of taming you down. Making you able to get along better with the world.

ANDY   Okay, Charlie, I'll go to college and get a Ph.D. Yeah, six of them. Then get one job as a redcap—(*leaps up from chair*)

CHARLIE (*stung, then after a pause*)   Sit down, son. Let's change the topic. (ANDY *sits*—CHARLIE, *too*) Don't this bring back the days when we used to sit here, you, me, and your mother? Don't you feel her spirit in this room?

ANDY   I don't feel nothing but a draft . . . a few more bouts and we'll dump this joint.

CHARLIE   It's done for all these years. Besides, they don't allow much living for us outside of Harlem.

ANDY   You get the dough and they'll allow room for you in heaven. (*rising*)

CHARLIE   You sure got your mother's spirit in you.

ANDY   I wish she was here. I could spend some of my dough on her.

CHARLIE   She is here. Watching and looking down on us from above.

ANDY   You mean through that crack in the plaster. That ceiling is going to fall and kill us one of these days.

CHARLIE   I wonder if she could bear seeing you in the ring.

ANDY   I wonder. There's always a queer feeling travelling with me. Sometimes I think I duck it, then it creeps up on me again. And I don't like it.

CHARLIE   But you said out there fighting today you felt different . . .

ANDY   Till I saw that Lou Foster.

CHARLIE (*rising*)   Look here, just stay outa that man's way!

ANDY   Let him stay out of mine!

CHARLIE   I tell you you gotta understand things!!!!

ANDY   Understand what?

BECKY (*calling offstage*)   Charlie! Come help me lift this pot!

CHARLIE (*caught in his fervor, he pauses then starts towards* BECKY *halts and grabs his hat, exiting*)   Lift it yourself. I'm going out.

BECKY (*enters mischievously, followed by* RUTH) Where'd he go?

ANDY   Out to get some air, I guess.

BECKY   Good—may the Lord watch between him and the first gin mill he reaches. (*exits*)

RUTH   Well—big shot, it looks like you've got plenty trouble on your hands.

ANDY   Oh, him—his mind'll change soon as he gets used to hundred dollar bills instead of dimes.

RUTH   I don't mean him. I mean me.

ANDY   Oh you—I'll be yelling out of my window across the court into yours. Let's go for some fun. Real fun with plenty of money to keep us company. No more two bit dates . . . ice cream sodas and bus rides. That's for suckers.

RUTH   I enjoyed them, though.

ANDY   Now it'll be redhot times in this old town. Me and you sitting on a cushion of money—riding on a wave of happiness. Yeah—grabbing some of the fun from the jerks who've been hogging it . . . from us.

RUTH   All that right here.

ANDY   And why not?

RUTH   You've lost that look. That stare like somebody stepped in your face, Andy.

ANDY   Punching that guy today, I felt great —like somebody had reached down my throat and untied my guts.

RUTH   You look so definite now, so sure, so solid. All that vague dreamy gleam in your eyes are gone. This boxing chance is just what you needed. For the first time, I feel the real you and not a shadow. I feel great, too. Let's get married, Andy!

ANDY Huh?

RUTH You heard me.

ANDY Take it easy! I'm just getting out from under Charlie's hammer and loose from Becky's apron strings. I want some fresh air before I hook up. Gosh, I never had a girl as anxious as you before. Why all the rush?

RUTH I should have tagged along to Aunt Susie's farm.

ANDY That's the long lost relative you used to talk about. Where's she cropping up from?

RUTH She popped in from Pensylvania today with the sins of middle age and lonesomeness weighing her down.

ANDY A helluva time to be offering you milk and honey mixed with plenty of fresh country air. You ain't sticking to me in vain.

RUTH She offers me security. All you want is fun.

ANDY I can't marry you now. Why, we ain't—why, we don't even know each other.

RUTH You know the reason why.

ANDY But you're stacked up so fine from head to foot. Your eyes are so soft and cool—not like a cow's.

RUTH You have a fine body, too.

ANDY Why can't we spend the week-end together somewhere? (*embracing her*)

RUTH (*resisting*) Don't touch me! Please! Holding onto you is like being latched to a shooting star that's dashing off into space. A week-end of fun for you! What happens to me?

ANDY Gosh—we've always sorter melted in each other's arms.

RUTH Things were different. As of now, I don't want you holding me a minute if you aren't holding me for life.

ANDY Just because I'm putting on a pair of pig skins!

RUTH That's all, is it? You'll be bouncing on your knee a different pair of glamour gals every night.

ANDY You sure can read a whole lot into nothing.

RUTH You and I are headed in two different directions—with me holding a bag of washed out hopes.

ANDY For heaven sake, quit hoping and believe in me.

RUTH For a whole year I have. Not only the times I'm with you, but the hours alone in my two-by-four room over there—every day on my job at the CIO headquarters. My thoughts full of you. Will Andy ever marry me and settle down? A few minutes ago you said we'd paint this town red. Was that hot air or are you still going to leave America?

ANDY Twenty thousand dollars and it's goodbye America forever. (*a hurting pause*) I've told you, Ruth. I always feel there's something over my shoulder. Now my stomach is hard as a damn rock. But this feeling creeps up on me and makes it jerky and sweaty. I tell you I'm hemmed in and bottled up.

RUTH And hemming us off from each other —from life.

ANDY Believe me. I'll find a place where this black boy and his g.f. can live without being pushed around.

RUTH But as a boxer you—

ANDY And still black. Name me the colored man that don't feel miserable as hell in this country.

RUTH What about Joe Louis?

ANDY Why—he's—different.

RUTH *He* has brains. Brains enough to make the world stand up and cheer him.

ANDY Aw—he's a superman. Yeah—a superman. That's what you gotta be to stick to the soil of the USA and be respected. Too bad I'm not.

RUTH Call him what you like—you admire him, don't you?

ANDY Joe's okay by me.

RUTH Would he be if he gobbled up all the money he could and ran out of the country to some hole in the wall?

ANDY Well—I—

RUTH The answer is no.

ANDY I don't want to be no tin hero—I want—

RUTH To be a coward.

ANDY Me!!!

RUTH Call it by any name you wish, but you're too big a coward to stand by and slug it out with Jim Crow. You rather run off and hide. I tell you you're scared stiff! You're trembling now.

ANDY That's because I want you so bad.

RUTH (*going to him*) Don't you see me and your trouble is rooted in hate? A hate that comes from greed. That means take all from the little guy and—

ANDY But what have I got that *anybody* wants?

RUTH What does this Lou Foster you spoke of want from you?

ANDY I dunno—I—you give me the shudders...

RUTH (*embracing him strongly*) For pete sake, Andy! There's been ten feet of backyard between your room and mine. Now your attitude makes it seem like there's a whole world between us. Shove it aside, honey.

ANDY (*in gross distress*) Will—that—mean our week-end away?

RUTH It could mean a lifetime of week-ends.

ANDY I'll try to see it your way, Ruth. I'll try, I swear! (*lightly*) I'll knock the world off its axis if that's what's between me and thee and our week-end.

(CHARLIE, *loaded with evening newspapers, enters.* RUTH *and* ANDY *break and stare at him as he sits, unfolds the papers and begins tearing out* ANDY's *photos. Looking up, smiling, satisfactorily, he speaks proudly*)

CHARLIE Tell Becky to get me the address book of all our relatives.

(*Curtain*)

ACT TWO

Scene One

(*A Jersey tavern, an evening ten months later.*

The tavern is an American version of the famous French sidewalk cafe. The downstage interior is divided from the upstage exterior by a double screened door. Flanking both sides of the door is green shrubbery, attractively mounted on sills running off on both sides. Above this is an awning which adds a bit of swankiness to the setting. The interior is in semi-darkness, while the exterior is revealed by the blue moon. Barely visible inside are a couple of tables, chairs and the edge of a bar. Nearby is a telephone booth. Faint jazz music segues as the blue moonlight brightens up the exterior. Then ANDY *and* LARRY *come trotting down the road.* ANDY's *success has given him more self-assurance and the sprinting gait of the fighter. Through association, he has also acquired some of* LARRY's *relaxation and casualness.* LARRY *is a bit breathy and boisterous*)

LARRY The hell with chasing the moon to New York.

ANDY It's only half a mile to the bus station.

LARRY We've hiked eighteen miles from camp. Even if we got to the big city, what good would broads be? Let's down our tonsils in here and forget them.

ANDY I ain't seen my broad in three weeks!

LARRY Keep them waiting. Then when she sees you, she'll do anything you say. It'll be double or nothing.

ANDY It will be plenty of nothing, if I don't go.

LARRY But this is Jersey. The heart of the tomato crop. Look at that one coming down the road. Mighty Liquor Rose, how are you?... She's running. Hahahahahahahah—What's the matter, Mary?

ANDY What's the joke? A friend of yours?

LARRY Naw—but she looked like a Polock. And all Polock girls are named either Helen or Mary. That's a fact. I'd like to put a little salt and pepper on that.

ANDY Okay—you go for your sport. And I'll hotfoot it on to New York.

LARRY Nertz! I know what to do over here —and I'll make it for two.

ANDY Are you kidding?

LARRY Look at that coming down the road! Hello, Helen.

ANDY Polish?

LARRY Naw—half scotch and half soda. Wow! Hahahah ahah. I got a pip of a right tonight. A great thing to have. It's like packing a gun. (*slugging playfully into the tavern.* ANDY *follows*) Hey, barkeep—how about some light? (*lights come up accenting two tables, leaving tavern still in semi-darkness*)

BARKEEP (*big, beefy and babyface enters*) Is there some point in burning lights when no customer's around? (*seeing* ANDY, *he freezes*)

LARRY (*posing*) Look at me in that glass. Larry Batchelo, you're pretty strong slug. Good build and plenty hard muscle. Yet, the weakest scissorblade in the world. Yeah, even a lizzard thin as Lou can lay your 200 pounds out. It's odd, eh? (*crosses and sits at table*)

ANDY Larry—does Lou pack a gun?

LARRY A regular forty-five calibre gent.

(*seeing* BARKEEP *staring*) Hey—a couple ryes, doubled. Make it snappy. (BARKEEP *exits, reluctantly*) Double that order, slow drag. I don't like that slob. I could reach from here and knock him colder than last year's girl friend.

ANDY Is last year's girl friend very cold?

LARRY They all are after the first ten minutes. You can't get married in this game.

ANDY I'm getting hitched some day.

LARRY Broads and boxing don't mix in this racket.

ANDY I'll have to give it up, because I got it bad.

LARRY Love is like a rose with a bee in it. My gal is always putting the bee on me. One night I opened a beer and it squirts all over her dress. She laughs, kisses my hand and calls me a big cluck. A minute later she socks a bill on me for a hundred bucks. Crazy! A hundred bucks for a lousy dress! (*meanwhile the* BARKEEP *has set up drinks*) Drink up, kid. Here's to women. May we fall into their arms without falling into their hands.

ANDY I could do a lot of harm in my broad's arms.

LARRY I *bet* you have.

ANDY Never yet. You see—

LARRY (*notices tarrying* BARKEEP) If you ain't a case of the walking dead! Blow! (BARKEEP *exits*) Fill them again. Bring the damn bottle, dribble puss! (*to* ANDY) Look, kid, everything you got goes into the ring. Chicks know this. So all they want is dough.

ANDY But Ruth's shooting at me with a double-barrel shotgun. Dough means dooley squart to her—nothing. Get a load of this. All she wants is me to stay in this damn country. And I want to go to Asia or maybe Europe.

LARRY (BARKEEP *returns with bottle, marking it*) What gives with you and Europe?

ANDY I can live in any house or eat in any shop.

LARRY Boy, you're crazy. Going to Europe to eat in a coffee pot. I got an uncle over there. He's taxed on everything from the cat to the lousy outdoor johnny.

ANDY A rat-hole in Europe is better than a penthouse here. Shadows always over shoulder, hemming you in—

LARRY Shadows where?

ANDY You can't see them because you got milk in your face and mine's full of ink.

LARRY Milk and ink! You've had too much sweetwater and getting heavy under the eye. Brace up! (*tickles* ANDY *under the arm*)

ANDY (*jumping up, shouting*) Hahahahahahahah—Cut it out, will you? (BARKEEP *enters staring*)

LARRY Boy—you're goosey. Just like a big slap-happy dope I used to ship with. Whatta card!

ANDY You ship long?

LARRY Did I? I was with the N.M.U. for ten years. What a life! A swell bunch of guys from every damn place in the world.

ANDY Africa, too?

LARRY And even Brooklyn. This guy was a big ticklish wop. Like a steam engine, I'd suck some air through my teeth—UHU—HUGH—HUGH—This joker would go into spasms—fall and bite the floor. Zip—(*gesturing downward at* BARKEEP *who steps quick and exits*)

ANDY I feel great.

LARRY Me, too. I feel like I'm walking behind myself. (*drinks*)

ANDY I wonder what Ruth's doing now.

LARRY Hunting another guy, I bet.

ANDY Naw—not her.

LARRY Okay—so this angel is somewhere praying instead of exercising her passion. (*drinks*)

ANDY Listen to me good, will you? Just because I don't want to live in this country, she won't even go to bed with me.

LARRY (*gulps*) Hey—I don't want to puke in here.

ANDY Uh huh!

LARRY One of you ought to be studied under a microscope.

ANDY I ain't against marriage. I'm against living in the backyard of the U.S.A.

LARRY Kid her till you—

ANDY Naw—not like that.

LARRY Marry her then and become known as Mister Louse—that is in the ring.

ANDY (*restlessly*) Goddammit! She so pretty, popular and passionate! I'm up a tree! Her room is just across the court from mine. I see her dabbling around with little things-a-ma-bobs, making her room look nice. See—brought up in a home, she never had anything of her own. I'm hers. She's mine, but that damn courtyard between us ain't just ten feet, but the world! I'm a miserable little wart on the earth's behind.

LARRY You've caught that fancy disease called success. That means do-re-mi. With that, not only will broads drop a notch, but the whole world nods to you.

ANDY Even Jim Crow?

LARRY Everything. Why, my old man used to say even God loves money people.

ANDY If there is a God, I don't think he likes me very much.

LARRY Come out of it, will you! You and your broad.

ANDY Ain't I proving I'm right? I've had sixteen fights and ain't lost a one. Week after next down in Scranton, I'm going to knock this big Swede into the ice box. Then I'll have a chance at the belt.

LARRY This champ glory is a lot of hot air!

ANDY The heck with glory. I'm thinking of dough. If I win Saturday after next, it means pay off in four figures.

LARRY Aw, nertz. I'm in the mood for—If I had my car. Dammit! (*rises and crosses*) If Lou hadn't took my keys, I could punch the clock at my jane's house and be back in an hour. (*going to booth*) Maybe she'll come out here. I'll phone her.

ANDY Lou would blow up.

LARRY So he would, that sonovabitch!

ANDY He sure is.

LARRY (*rousing, drowsily*) Who is?

ANDY Lou is.

LARRY Sure he is. But don't let him hear you say that. He's so mean, he has to beat his gal, Lady Friend, before h—(*whispers*)

ANDY That snake!

LARRY Whether you like snakes or not, don't play rough with them. They always bite.

ANDY Even you're scared of him.

LARRY He ain't no ordinary guy. He's like a king or something. He's got so much pull, he carries it around in a trailer.

ANDY He makes me feel—

LARRY ME feel twenty thousand bucks in the palm of my hand.

ANDY But he won't even buy a piece of me.

LARRY Win your next fight and ten to one he will. With the dynamite you got in your fist, you can double 20 G's and live like a prince.

ANDY Not here.

LARRY Why not?

ANDY You're—you're all right, Larry.

LARRY Just take low around Lou, Kid. Squart if you have to. Remember, she squarted to conquer. And you'll have the world in a jug with the stopper in your hands.

ANDY Buttonhole the globe, eh?

LARRY It ain't where you are. It's what you got.

ANDY Europe, nertz! There must be plenty guys like you. Why ain't it? This old place ain't so bad.

LARRY Yeah—get off the edge of suspense. Kick your ambition in the pants and live.

ANDY I been acting like a lost donkey in a blizzard. (*rises and crosses*)

LARRY What now?

ANDY I'm phoning my gal, Larry. I'm telling her that a few ryes and a flatnose guy opened my eyes. *Everything* is jake. (*exits into booth*)

LARRY (*drools as he drinks*) Whew! The end of round one. Round two will come up with twins. Barkeep, why don't you wrap this hot weather up and ship it away?

(*Two glamour girls enter. Their vivid conversation prevents them from seeing* LARRY. *They are* DOROTHY *and* SADIE)

DOROTHY But Sadie, what was so unusual about him?

SADIE His technique, Dorothy. He should have it copyrighted and sold to the cheap drips.

DOROTHY Didn't I tell you you'd need a slot machine to get a quarter out of him?

SADIE He didn't have one cockeyed penny. I told him, I didn't mind dancing with him till my feet burn, but when a gentleman takes me for a drive, I expect him to spend something. I searched him and started to leave. Like a brawling brat, he burst out crying. So I let him hug me.

DOROTHY You don't say. Is that all?

SADIE Whatta you expect for nothing? (*both enter.* DOROTHY *goes to juke box*)

DOROTHY What's this, a morgue? How about some life in this joint? (*plays juke box and dances*)

SADIE (*seeing* LARRY *rally*) Larry Batchelo!

LARRY Ayah, Toots! Who's your second?

SADIE Dorothy, meet Larry. The guy who could have beaten Braddock.

DOROTHY Before you spend any time, you

better see if he's got anything to spend. Search him.

SADIE Can it! Larry is saving all his dough for a rainy day.

DOROTHY The paper says it's raining tomorrow and I saw the cutest little celophane umbrella this morning—

LARRY Hey—where's your jackass and pick, blondie?

SADIE You ain't calling me a gold-digger, are you?

LARRY Ah, sit down and rest your mind.

SADIE But my mind ain't tired. I wanna dance. (*both sit*)

LARRY Then it's empty. Let's fill it with booze.

SADIE Hahahahahahah—you're funny.

DOROTHY Larry pays five bucks just to someone to listen to his jokes.

SADIE Gee—tell another one, quick.

LARRY Hey—barkeep, another bottle of that block and fall.

SADIE Block and fall?

LARRY Yeah—you walk a block and fall one.

SADIE Hahahahahah—you're a scream. Say, does your bent nose ever get in the way of your kissing a girl?

LARRY Does your mouth stay closed long enough to get kissed?

DOROTHY Larry, you should have been a farmer the way you sprout corn out of your mouth.

LARRY Corny, eh? Get this one. An old maid rang the fire alarm and twenty firemen showed up—

LARRY *and* DOROTHY (*simultaneously*) So she said, there ain't no fire, so nineteen of you go back. (LARRY *is embarrassed*)

SADIE Hahahahahahah—

LARRY (*nobly pays* SADIE *five dollars*) You hit the jackpot, blondie. Five laughs in a row. Take it.

SADIE (*faking*) But I don't take money from men, mister (*she grabs it quickly*)

DOROTHY It pays to be silly, doesn't it?

SADIE Gee—it's hard for me to sit still when I hear good music. Can't you do something besides tell jokes?

LARRY What's the matter with your b.f.? Don't he give a damn no more?

SADIE He's all work and no pay—I mean play. I like excitement and—

ANDY (*exiting from booth and with glowing satisfaction*) Larry—everything is jake—(*pause*)

LARRY Girls, meet my shadow, Andy, the best little fighting machine since Kid Chocolate. This is Dorothy and that's Sadie.

SADIE Get a load of that smile! Negroes have the whitest smiles.

DOROTHY Sit down and join us in some corny jokes.

ANDY (*sits*) This day was made to order for me.

LARRY Did I ever tell you the one—

DOROTHY Sign off, Larry! Not even for five bucks can I stand another one.

ANDY Larry, I got a new lease on life. My mind's been wandering and I just caught up with it.

LARRY Aw—he's in love.

DOROTHY I was in love once, and it gave me the stomach ache. (*looks significantly at* LARRY)

SADIE I have a hotel heart—always a room for one more.

DOROTHY Not this guy. He's got the one woman look reeking all over him. Who is this Juliet?

ANDY The finest little package of brown—

LARRY That he ain't never touched—if you get what I mean.

SADIE *and* DOROTHY What!

LARRY It's a fact!

SADIE She's colored, isn't she? Then it can't be. I always heard that niggers were free lovers and—(DOROTHY *delivers a swift kick to* SADIE, *but it is too late.* ANDY *instinctively rises, drawn up by his super-sensitive racial attitude, he struggles for self-control which his tortured body cannot conceal*) What happened? (DOROTHY *stares embarrassingly*)

LARRY Yeah—what'sa matter? (BARKEEP *enters*)

BARKEEP Hey—this is a respectable cafe. You all will have to leave. None of that stuff in here.

LARRY You ain't even an old pug. Just a little boy who grew up and thinks he's a bouncer. The bus stopped with a jerk—and you got off. Whatta you mean by none of that stuff?

DOROTHY (*painfully*) Pay him, Larry, and let's go. (*rising, and* SADIE *also*)

SADIE Let's go, but what did I say? What did I do?

LARRY (*flinging money at* BARKEEP) I oughta slug you... (*draws back, the* BARKEEP *recoils*) Come on, kid. I don't know what's wrong though.

SADIE He looks mad enough to arouse the dead. What did—

DOROTHY Come on, *Miss Rankin.*

ANDY (*as they are all about to exit, he has brought his emotions under control and stares at* SADIE, *then with complete mastery and instead of leaving, returns*) Let's all have a drink! (*they look at him understandingly. To the* BARKEEP's *amazement, they return congenially. Curtain*)

Scene Two

(*A hotel lobby, two weeks later.*

As the curtain rises, a young CLERK, *very neat looking as if he belonged behind the desk with the rest of the furniture, is fumbling a racing sheet. A door in back of him is distinctly marked* MANAGER. *The* CLERK's *attention is divided between the racing sheet and the door. A second passes. The Manager's door opens and a fat pink hand reaches out. The finger snaps. The* CLERK *drops the sheet nervously and exits behind the door.*

MACK *enters with* ANDY *and both are escorted by a* BELLHOP *who carries their luggage. The* BELLHOP *stops in front of the desk and bangs the bell, then moves to the side.* MACK *removed his cigar and sends a line of tobacco juice past the big cuspidor with a perfect miss*)

MACK Doggonit, I missed it!

ANDY You ought to spit through a spray. You could cover more ground.

MACK Okay, a year from now and you'll be pointing at this dump as the place where you got your real big start. (*the* CLERK *enters, smiling at first, his face drops on seeing* ANDY) I'm Mack Jeffris from New York, and this is Andy Whitman who's fighting here tonight. Where's Larry's room and where do we sink for tonight?

CLERK (*eyeing* ANDY) How many rooms do you want?

MACK I made reservations for two connecting rooms. Didn't you reserve them? I telephoned.

CLERK (*observing register*) Why—er—I don't seem to have any reservations for you. The hotel is all full. The fight brings people to town—you know.

MACK You're fuller hay! Do I look like a horse? Do you see my puss in that racing sheet? Lou ought to hear about this. What's his room number? I'll phone him. (*picking up telephone*)

CLERK (*looking about helplessly at* MACK *and then* ANDY, *who appears quite calm. The pink hand reaches and snaps. The* CLERK, *relieved, tries to escort* MACK *into Manager's office*) Would you like to speak to the Manager?

MACK Gimme Lou's number.

CLERK (*hustling* MACK *out*) The Manager may know something about your reservation. Right this way, please.

MACK What the hell! I want Lou. (*both exit*)

ANDY (*giving the lobby the once over, turns to the* BELLHOP *who has a sly twinkle in his eye*) I'm going to sleep here if I got to sleep in this damn lobby. You hope I'll get a room or do you think I'm one of those wise black boys from the big city?

BELLHOP You can bunk with me at my house, if you wanna, buddy.

ANDY Sorry to disappoint you, buddy! (*the* BELLHOP *shrugs his shoulders*)

MACK (*returns hurriedly—pauses—then with a purpose*) Listen here, kid. There's only one room left. I'd better take it. I gotta be near Lou. But this bellhop is nuts about fighters. He's just crazy to have you stay with him—and it won't cost you a dime... (*self-consciously*) You're the big city boxer—a real big shot.

ANDY No, Mack.

MACK No?

ANDY NO!

MACK Why, I thought you'd like being the hero all your boys—

ANDY Cut it out! You don't play the liar—unless you're lying to yourself. (CLERK *enters*)

MACK (*an appealing gesture to* CLERK *gives him no aid, to* ANDY) Now, Kid—

ANDY Don't hand me that. This State has a Civil Rights Bill. I'll slap a suit on them if they don't get me a room. You know damn well those rooms were res—

CLERK (*strongly, but politely*) There are no rooms.

ANDY Shut up! Why don't you let us call up Lou?

CLERK Now—young man, why don't you do what your manager tells you? You know how things are.

ANDY (*going to desk*) Don't hand me that line of jive!

CLERK Then I'm sorry. All our rooms are taken.

ANDY You just said there was one room. Okay—I'll take that. (*to* MACK) Mack, you can bunk with the bellhop. How about it?

MACK (*stung*) Well—sure—kid—sure— (*going to* CLERK, *explosively*) Listen, here, I'm tired of this run-around. You got to win bingo to get a room in this joint? We get rooms or Larry and his gang will move out and say the food damn near killed them. That would make swell advertisement, won't it? And I don't believe this outhouse was ever full.

CLERK Be reasonable, Mr. Jeffris.

ANDY Reasonable? Mack, you know a good lawyer in this town? I'll show these hicks. They ain't got a leg to stand on. (*again, the finger emerges from behind the door and snaps. The* CLERK *sees the thumb pointing upward*)

CLERK Very well! (*snatches two cigars from* MACK's *lapel pocket*) I believe we have a vacancy now.

MACK Take it easy. The manager gimme them ropes . . . (ANDY *catches a guilty look on his face, he scowls*)

CLERK Sign here. Rooms 312 and 313. (*they sign as* CLERK *throws key to* BELLHOP) Show them up, George! (*exits*)

BELLHOP This way, please. (*exits*—ANDY *starts to follow*)

MACK Hey, kid, you acted like a regular damn shyster. That Civil Rights stuff—where'd you get it?

ANDY (*halting*) I took a correspondence course.

MACK That's a hot one. You didn't get excited. That shows you've become a real pro. I guess your g.f. Ruth has been wising you up, eh?

ANDY She tells me I can knock this thing in the pants and still stay within the law. (*starts again*)

MACK (*crossing*) Better take a course from her on how to get yourself straightened out. This racket's got an awful grapevine. One that gets you all tangled up—if you go against the grain.

ANDY (*coming to him fullface*) Come to the point, Mack.

MACK Well now, you take Larry. He'd blame his own Ma for his being born with big feet. I'll never forget the time he comes around with his arm in a sling. Said he'd been hit by a car. Later, I found out that he'd fallen out of a box—at a burlesque.

ANDY (*turning to go*) I'll make a note of that and goose myself later.

MACK *Of course* when word got around about you and that trouble in that Jersey joint two weeks ago, Larry never said you was to blame . . . Lou is slated to buy ten percent of you after your fight tonight. How will he, with you acting like that?

ANDY Speak plain to me, Mack.

MACK You're the oddest punk I ever had. Got everything to make a champ. But some sort of jinx wrapped up inside all that muscle—

ANDY (*searching himself in anguish*) Up until the time you picked me up, I hadn't been trained for nothing. I did what you told me. I've knocked off the bums as fast as you've dug them up. Spit my blood in the pit, like a horse. The rake-off, well, you're getting yours.

MACK Hey, you ain't thinking of running out on me. I'm on the nut for plenty of dough spent on your training. They've raised the ante on this fight fifty bucks more. It ain't legal for you to quit!

ANDY Who said anything about quitting? You'll get your dough back.

MACK Take your time. I ain't no shark—if that's what's bothering you.

ANDY It ain't that. It's something you didn't tell me.

MACK Come out of it. Now, what didn't I tell you?

ANDY You didn't hep me to the mob. They drag me with dinge, black bastard—coon! All that in the ring. The kids in the street follow me like I was champion of the world. They make me feel big. Then all of a sudden, I feel something queer. The kids are gone. I'm alone. My knees shaking—

MACK Aw—forget them stupid suckers. They pay for blood. We're going up like a balloon and taking all the dough with us.

ANDY This hotel stuff pulled on me—

MACK Hell, I'm helping you get what you want. I didn't promise to put the whole world inside the ring for you to slug at. Money sweetens anything. To get it, you got to play the game.

ANDY Yeah, how—

MACK Don't pay no attention to them names. Maybe we can fix that up.

ANDY How?

MACK By putting cotton in your ears.

ANDY (*painfully*) Well, whatta you want, Mack? Or don't you know, either?

MACK A helluva lot, but right now it wouldn't be a bad idea if you bunked with the bellhop.

ANDY Well—I'll—be—damned!

MACK (*in a deeply injured tone*) Why, kid, you and me have been like father and son.

ANDY Can the soft soap!!!!

MACK (*driven by an inner explosion, he expostulates back and forth*) So I pulled a fast one!! Okay, worry about that big Swede, kid, you got to fight tonight. You better knock this egg kicking or we don't win.

ANDY Why not! Don't decisions count in this town?

MACK Things ain't according to Hoyle in this racket. Don't forget that I'm on the nut for plenty of jack. Suppose you break a leg or drop dead? Suppose you turn out to be a bum? What if you grew punch shy? Who'd be holding the bag? Me! Who'd be holding me? The one guy who's got us both wrapped in the palm of his hand, Lou Foster! Decisions count? Hell, nothing counts with him!

ANDY What would God do if He had Lou's drag?

MACK Yeah—well just hope God gives you enough punch to knock out this egg tonight. Otherwise there'll have to be a decision. With you staying in this country outhouse called a hotel, you may get a bum decision. The first fight you will have lost.

ANDY Nearly a whole year has turned the corner before you turned heel on me... telling me to stay in my place.

MACK So I'm a heel! We both can be rich heels if you win and Lou buys part of you. Suppose you scram now and bunk somewhere's else?

ANDY (*indecisively*) What—have—I got—to lose! (*starts to leave the hotel*) The odds are stacked too high. I'll go. This is what you want. This is what everybody wants. Okay—sleep well, *pal*.

MACK Atta boy!

ANDY (*near exit—pause—turns*) I can't do it! I can't!

MACK Kid—please don't rouse the whole town against you.

ANDY If the world falls off its axis, I can't. You're asking me to go the way of all tramps.

MACK (*angrily*) It's the only way we're sure of beating—

ANDY I'll win this fight or die trying. I'll win, I tell you.

MACK You got two strikes against you. The other guy is a hometown favorite and he's *white*!

ANDY Keep still before the Chamber of Commerce skins you alive.

MACK Cut the clowning! Wise crack! Wise crack! Wise crack! You got to knock him out to win. You're right at the point of jumping off into big time. Dammit, if you lose, it won't be because of what happened in the ring, but what happens outside. This hotel stuff is just a sample. You can't lose, you hear or—

ANDY Like Uncle Tom, I'll be sold down the river.

(MACK *gulps, trying to restrain himself from growing limp. Overcome by his physical weakness, he drags himself to lobby chair and sits. There is a moment of silence, then* MICKEY *enters. He is well-dressed and carefree*)

MICKEY (*not seeing* MACK) Andy—glad to see you, kid!

ANDY Whatchu know, Mickey?

MICKEY Nothing much. (*sensing the situation*) What's the matter, Mack? Your mother-in-law put you out? (*smacking* MACK's *jaw*)

MACK (*nervously*) Naw—naw—you look like a million.

MICKEY Just flew in from the coast to see the fight. I ain't got the million, but I'm right next door to them. (*shows him a ring*)

MACK That's great.

MICKEY (*crossing to* ANDY) I been keeping up with you in the papers, kid. I want to have a spiel with you. (*going to desk*)

ANDY What about?

MICKEY Wait until after your fight tonight.

BELLHOP (*entering with bags*) Reservations for Mister Lou Foster.

(LOU *enters with* LADY FRIEND *proudly laughing and hanging onto his arm. He stops at the sight of* ANDY. *The tension mounts with only* LADY FRIEND'*s giggles heard. Then she grows conscious of* MICKEY'*s presence, who speaks with a saving grace*)

MICKEY   You're certainly being brought along, kid.

ANDY   Thanks, Mickey, I've just been sold down the river for a couple nickel cigars. I'm going up. See you later. (*exits*)

LOU   Where's he going?

MICKEY   To his room. Where do you think?

LOU   His room?

MICKEY (*starts signing up*) After all, you don't own the joint.

CLERK (*entering*) You see, Mister Foster, it was like this—

LOU   Quiet! (*to* MICKEY) What are you signing in for, Lug? I've reserved every room in this dump.

LADY FRIEND   Quit your kidding, Louie. You ain't still sore at Mickey—

LOU   You're still weak on this ape?

LADY FRIEND   What if I was, Louie? You just keep me going around in circles. Now, they're wound up around my eyes. What's the black boy done to you—(LOU *smacks her severely*) Why you dirty—

LOU   Shut up. Sign up and take it upstairs.

(*The pink hand emerges and the fingers snap.* LOU *exits into the manager's office*)

LADY FRIEND   If ever you need a second-hand dame, Mickey, look me up. (*signing in*)

MICKEY   Thanks, I'll remember that.

CLERK (*observing register*) Make that *Mrs.* Lou Foster. This is Pennsylvania.

LADY FRIEND   I gave him the best years of my life and look what I get for a receipt. (*rubs her face*) Look at me talking about me after the break you got under Lou. You got out from under the hammer, Mickey. Be a good egg and take me with you.

MICKEY   Sorry, it's just like it's always been —I travel alone—

LADY FRIEND   I tell you, I'm sick of that guy and—

LOU (*returns from the Manager's office, his* face having lost all its agitation. He goes to MACK *still draped over the chair, limp*) Your dark hope has stuck his neck out, Mack. (MACK *remains blank and* LOU *goes to* LADY FRIEND) Take it up suite 217, Mrs. Foster. (LADY FRIEND *throws him a quick glance and exits as* BELLHOP *follows*) Why Mickey, didn't you sign up yet?

MICKEY   Are you kidding?

LOU   Sure—whatta you think? I wasn't trying to squeeze you out of a room. Go on, sign in. There ain't another flop house in this town. Go on.

MICKEY (*signing in*) You're doing me no favors. I could easily bunk with Andy. What made you change your mind?

LOU   All right you got an in on something. Spill it.

MICKEY   I have, and when I spill it, there's going to be a certain kingpin in this racket who is going to get drowned.

LOU   You sound like a prize jerk. But come into the office. We're going to have a little poker game.

MICKEY   No thanks. I want to look up some of your feeble-minded stumble bums. The ones you washed out of the ring and threw on the slag pile! (*exits defiantly*)

LOU   What do you think he fell into? Or do you think it's all a front? Damn college boy— think's he's smart! I shut him out once. I can keep him out—rat!

MACK (*lifelessly*) Because he had high class ideas about the racket—wanted it to be on the level. So decent till Lady Friend wanted to leave you for him . . . We're a couple of skunks, Lou.

LOU   Why Mack, you must have woke up this morning with a grouch. I never knew you slept with one.

MACK   There're bigger guys than you moving in, Lou. They're shooting straight. Making the mob respect this racket again. (*rising*) I've done all I could to keep that kid out of here—

LOU (*turning*) Come on, Mack. There's a game inside . . . So you won't. Well, tell Larry I'm inside when he comes in. Got to stop to see every dame in town. I don't want him messing up in this burg. Eight grand bet on him ain't no play money. I don't know why I take so much off that wop. (*exiting*)

MACK (*crossing to desk*) Yeah, you bet $8,000 on him, then double that amount on the other guy.

LOU (*stopping*) And I don't know why I take anything off you.

MACK Goddammit, Lou—

LOU (*face to face*) Well—

MACK This is the only kid I ever brought along that had the makings of a champ.

LOU That's what the papers say.

MACK You always gimme sure shots—

LOU Good investments . . . fighters . . . horses . . . baseball pools . . .

MACK But none of the real rakings.

LOU You're got a piece of Larry Batchelo.

MACK So has five other managers, none of us trusting each other. All trusting you—because we gotta.

LOU (*annoyed at* MACK's *puffing cigar*) Your cigar stinks, Mack. (*yanks it out of his mouth and crushes it under his heel*)

MACK This is the first real fighter I ever had.

LOU (*grabbing* MACK *by lapel*) That's the second time!!! (*shoves him off balance*)

MACK (*cowering*) I'm fed up on taking crumbs off the edge of your plate. This is the last chance I'll ever have to get in on big time. Make them give him a fair chance tonight . . . (LOU *stuffs* MACK's *mouth with a fresh cigar*) B-B—B—buy a piece of him now—please, Lou—

LOU (*after a terrible tension—*LOU *strikes a match to light his cigarette*) I could make a lot of money with that—black boy—big money. (MACK's *face brightens*) He made his decision to stay in this hotel. Now he'll have to back it up by a knockout, or the judges will make a decision. The manager is one of the judges. You know how they are. The trouble with that boy is he just won't stay in his place.

(*Having lighted his cigarette, he drops the burning match into* MACK's *lap and heads for the Manager's office.* MACK, *knocking the burning match from his lap, rises and goes to the desk, grabs the phone, swings it back and readies to smash* LOU *in the back of his head. At* MACK's *highest emotional pitch,* LOU *turns furiously, then as* MACK's *fighting instinct fails,* LOU *allows a calm but threatening look settle on his face.* MACK *drops the phone limply—and recedes.* LOU *exits. Dim out*)

Scene Three

(*At the ringside, that evening.*

KONG—KONG—KONG—KONG—KONG—KONG—KONG—KONG—KONG—KONG—*The slow surf sound of the bell, each mighty stroke announces the passing of a round in the darkness of the theater. Then there is silence—suddenly interrupted by* WHACK—WHACK—H-U-G-H!! *The smack of leather cracking flesh with the dull roar of fans—swelling—exploding—softening—muttering and shounting*)

FANS Use ya left!
Follow 'im up, ya bum!
In la panza!
In the belly. Black boy can't take it in the belly.
Do youse guys want to be alone?
Break it up!
Wot's dis a waltz?
Hey, ref—break it up!
Atta boy—cut 'im to pieces.
You're in the blood pit. Let if fly.
Come on hommy—knock 'im back to the jungles!
YeeeeeeeeEEEEEeeeeeeooooooooooooooooo!

(*A flicker light dimly reveals* ANDY *and* KIN *bobbing—weaving—slugging in the ring at which time only a corner of the ring can be seen.* MACK, *chewing frenziedly on a cigar;* LOU, *quiet, calmly watching;* LADY FRIEND, *whacking away at a wad of chewing gum and* HAPPY *twisting and tearing a towel are barely visible in the semi-darkness*)

THE ANNOUNCER (*meanwhile*) This is the tenth and last round of one of the greatest slug fests I've seen in years. The crowd's goin' wild. They're strong for that very clever newcomer, Andy Whitman who is givin' the local boy, Kin Reynolds, an awful shellackin' and not a scratch on him. We're goin' to hear lots from this colored boy. He's got the stuff, a boxer, a puncher and knows how to keep out of trouble. Andy's got him up against the ropes now and pummelin' him plenty. Andy socks one to Kin's jaw. Wow—what a haymaker. What's holding Kin up? It'll be a miracle if he lasts the round. They're in the center again. Kin is swingin' wild. They should stop this. It's murder. Kin's eye is closed. Ouch—I felt that one myself. Andy landed a straight jab to Kin's nose. That sock did it folks. He's wobbling. Andy's coming in for the kill...

MACK (*rises to his feet, screaming*) Twist that mitt! Twist that mitt! He's staggering. He's dizzy! He's—one more, Andy! One more—YOU'VE GOT TO KNOCK HIM OUT!!!!!

(*The gong sounds*)

ANNOUNCER Saved by the bell. Boy, that was a fast three minutes. (*pandemonium swells as* MACK, *as if paralyzed, grabs the rope to support himself, his spirit completely broken.* HAPPY *covers* ANDY *with a robe as the latter breathlessly, beams hopefully*) The referee is collecting the two slips from the judges and we'll have the decision in a few seconds.

ANDY I won every round—except the first.

(*The gong rings*)

MACK Did you watch this—

ANNOUNCER Commissioner Louis Gordon gives Andy Whitman two rounds, one even and seven to Kin Reynolds. (*howls and catcalls*) Col. James Saunders, the other judge, gives Andy Whitman six rounds, one even and three to Kin. (*cheers!!!*) And Bill Daniels, the referee, gives four to Andy and six to Kin. The winner and still leading contender, *Kin Reynolds*.

(MACK *snaps his fingers significantly and* ANDY *cracks up, bitterly and befuddled. Boos and catcalls crescendo as the scene blacks out. Curtain*)

ACT THREE

Scene One

(*A Room in the hotel, later that night.*

In the dimly lighted Foster-Batchelo suite of rooms, LARRY's *victory party is nearly over. Noticeably in the room is an improvised bar behind which the* BELLHOP *is preparing drinks. Music and chatter is heard emanating from the surrounding rooms. The door in the left wall leads to* LOU's *private room, while the door in the right wall leads to the hall.*

A drunk reporter sprawls in a chair downstage left facing a couch on the other side of the room. In the back wall is a window overlooking the street.

At curtain rise, the BELLHOP *exits with a tray of drinks.* LARRY *and* ANDY *enter.* ANDY *looks very downcast while* LARRY *lights a match giving the* REPORTER *"the hot foot." The* REPORTER *jumps up astonished and then relaxes again—giving* LARRY *a good laugh which fades when he sees* ANDY *sitting unhappily on the sofa*)

LARRY Come on, kid, brace up! You got one decision against you. So what!

ANDY It ain't that. I don't give a damn about the fight.

LARRY They nailed you with a bum decision. So you go out walking the streets of this burgh at midnight—alone. Don't you know a mule or something might kick you in the dark?

ANDY I was too dumbfounded to sit still. There was nothing else to do but walk and let off steam.

LARRY So my party ain't good enough for you. With all the newsboys and local tail lapping up my liquor. Take a drink. It'll brace you up.

ANDY (*rises and crosses*) Naw—you smell like you had too many already.

LARRY What you come to my party for?—to pray? (*drinks*)

ANDY I don't want no jane. I don't want no drink. I came because you pulled me up here and—

LARRY (*goes to bar*) You're letting defeat get you down.

ANDY They robbed me, I tell you.

LARRY I've had the same thing happen to me. Maybe even tonight if I hadn't kayoed that joker in the third round. I walloped the hell outa him and he fell to the canvas stiff as a frozen mackerel.

ANDY Look, Larry—what's wrong with me?

LARRY Aw—they robbed you because they wanted the other egg to win.

ANDY It wasn't even close. I was winning all the way.

LARRY Aw—cut it, will you.

ANDY I know one thing. You have the right dope. I don't care if the record book remembers me twenty years from now or not. I don't want glory. I want *money* . . .

LARRY (*as the* BELLHOP *returns with a tray from which a woman's stocking hangs*) Sure, kid, get wise. This is a racket, not a boy-scout camp fire meet—(BELLHOP *offering him hose*) Where is the leg that came in this stocking?

(BELLHOP *winks and whispers to him and* LARRY *exits with a purpose*)

BELLHOP (*goes to bar*) Hey, how about a drink of scotch, buddy? Sorry—out of scotch—Got some mighty fine rye though.

(ANDY, *sitting downstage right, ignores* BELLHOP, *meanwhile* LADY FRIEND, *quite high, staggers in from* LOU's *room and falls into the reporter's lap*)

LADY FRIEND Quick—give me a drink, I'm starving!

REPORTER (*rallying*) Take off your make-up and scare me to death.

LADY FRIEND Buy me a drink.

REPORTER Beat it, pot! I ain't your stove. I live in this town. (*avoiding—gets up and goes to bar*)

LADY FRIEND You see a man half shabby, with eyes a gin shot blue, with dandruff on his collar—knowing more than J. P. Morgan and Shakespeare put together.—If you ain't a reporter, I'm no lady... Hahahahahahahahah. Buy me a drink, Winchell.

REPORTER You're getting absent-minded. The drinks are free.

LADY FRIEND Well—blow me down. (*to the bar*) I'll take the scotch and you take the chaser...

BELLHOP Sorry, Miss—we're out of scotch. Got some rye, though.

LADY FRIEND (*impatiently*) Oh, any old drink will do... hurry—hurry—(*takes drink and empties it quickly tossing back her head—and sees* ANDY *and draws herself toward him*) Hey—you're the fighter—I bet you make lots of money.

REPORTER (*stepping in between* LADY FRIEND *and* ANDY) Yeah—and sends it home to his wifie and ten kids—

LADY FRIEND Hahahahahah... ten kids... oh my—(*coyly*) Have you any kids? Hahahahahahah—

REPORTER Please stop laughing—my nose is tired.

LADY FRIEND Hahahahahahah—(*going toward* LOU's *room—pauses—realizing the insult—then—as* REPORTER *is removing his hat, revealing a bald spot*) I've seen better heads on beer! (*exits, slamming the door*)

REPORTER That's the kind of a dame whose make-up needs an editor. (*to* ANDY) Well, fellow, they gave you a rough deal. But the local boy is the only drawing card they got around here. He makes good copy for us sports reporters... (*seeing his bottle empty*) Mr. Batchelo—Mr. Batchelo...

LARRY (*offstage*) Yeah—what is it?

REPORTER We're outa scotch.

LARRY (*offstage*) Sure, kid, I'll tell the boss.

REPORTER (*to* ANDY) I can't say in my story that you were chiseled—just something about it being very close.

LARRY (*enters and crosses to* LOU's *door*) Put on a veil, Lou—I'm coming in.

LOU Who's that?

LARRY Me—Larry.

LOU Whatta you want?

LARRY We're outa scotch... (LOU *enters, shaking off his drunken stupor*) And I ain't giving this shindig.

LOU Sure—I'm paying for it. I always do—when you win—Tell the barkeep—(ANDY *exiting catches* LOU's *eye. A sudden valve releases in* LOU—*a valve for too long wanting to explode*) What the hell—how did he get in here? (ANDY *stops*)

LARRY What—who—oh! I told him to come up. How about the scotch?

LOU (*shoving* LARRY *aside*) You told him to come! Who in the hell are you? (BELLHOP *is glued to the wall with fear.* REPORTER *is out on couch.* LOU *breaks forward*)

LARRY Wait—Lou—wait—

LOU (*launching at this enigma who firmly stands before him*) I don't want no *niggers* at my party—

(W-H-A-M!!!!!!!!!! *With a hard right,* ANDY *cracks* LOU's *chin which sends him crumbling to the floor. The tension is terrific with everyone frightened and speechless except* ANDY, *whose whole body is alive, throbbing, defiantly, relentlessly, but says calmly*)

ANDY I don't like for nobody to call me that—

LARRY You don't know who you've hit.

ANDY (*with a growing consciousness of his act and with unbelievable reproof, raucous, bitter and triumphant*) Gawd damn! Look at it. Look at him! That's it! Them's the eyes always over my shoulder. Everywhere I go! Everything I do! His eyes cutting me like a dagger... cutting me—sending a chill up and down my spine. Look at you all—scared. I feel great!

For once I got that face laying on the floor. Get up, Jim Crow! Meet me man to man. Get up, Lou! Come out punching!

(*The hushed silence is broken by* MACK *who breaks through the hall door with such a force behind his body that he stumbles within a foot of the outstretched* LOU. *Seeing him, he turns his ashen face towards* ANDY)

MACK Jesus Christ! I've been training a corpse! (*Lou rises and suddenly whips out a revolver*) Don't Lou! There's a thousand front pages listening in.

LOU Shut up!

MACK Use your dome! You can't kill a whole race!

LOU (*smacking* MACK *backward*) Out of my way!

MACK (*stepping back in between*) Nobody ain't never seen you kill a guy—but me.

LOU (*pause*) Why you sonova—(*realizing the full meaning of* MACK's *statement and implication*) How much you got invested in that—dinge?

MACK About a thousand bucks—mebbe more.

LOU (*flinging a roll of bills to the floor*) Here's two hundred. I just bought his contract. Pick it up.

MACK (*desperately*) No, Lou! You might as well kill the kid—and me, too!

LOU (*slapping him to his knees*) Pick it up! (MACK *gathers the money trembling, then rises—giving* LOU *the contract*) You're both lucky. (*backing away*) Keep him and all his kind out of my sight, before I change my mind. (*exits into his room, slamming the door as* MACK *shrinks into nothingness and sits downstage right*)

LARRY (*finally able to speak*) Come on, kid, Lou's got his punks all over this place. The safest thing for me to do is to have you pinched.

ANDY Until death do us part, I ain't leaving. Maybe you think I'm just a bad black boy. Okay, I am, as far as you know. (LADY FRIEND *lets out a bold hearty laugh offstage*) You ain't never had Jim Crow tangle you all up. I hit back and the whole world's trembling. (LADY FRIEND *laughs again, then a sharp slap is heard*)

LOU (*offstage*) Get out of here! (*ejecting* LADY FRIEND *through the door and throwing her bag behind her. As she flings on her coat, a triumphant sense of release comes over her*)

LADY FRIEND He had it coming to him. And am I glad! I'm checking out of this joint and on him, too. You put him to sleep and woke me up. Love him, pshaw! I hate him! Yes, I was hating him all along. Giving in because I was scared. But no more! I wish he was dead! (*ponders a bit, gathers herself independently and exits*) My bag, George. (*exits as* BELLHOP *picks up bag*)

BELLHOP (*to* ANDY) Buddy, tomorrow is my last day. The Manager fired me because you made them give you a room. That's all right with me, though. So long. (*exits*)

LARRY See—you hit back and tied your hands into a knot.—You tied up lots of others, too. You're wrongside out, kid.

ANDY I'm fully out and I know it. Didn't I try to sidestep trouble? Just to get money, I took it. Well, money ain't everything. Nothing if I got to duck and bow to get it—nothing!

LARRY (*coming to him*) Look, I'm a wop. But out there on the sea, we were just guys. I get you now. I didn't though at first.

MACK (*verging on ironic laughter*) It's okay. (*raising the dough*) Everything is okay. I don't know what keeps you alive.

LARRY Yeah.

MACK The thin thread that keeps you in this sweet misery of life are the boys with the typewriters—the reporters. What did you have to start something for?

ANDY Me? He come shooting off his gums—

MACK But that was Lou Foster.

ANDY I'd slug him again.

MACK (*rising*) You're the luckiest punk I ever saw. What a break! You'd better leave town before Lou starts using his nasty temper instead of his dome.

ANDY I ain't running from that crumb.

MACK I ain't your manager no more.

ANDY (*feeling empty and clammy*) Maybe—I don't want—to fight for nobody else.

LARRY Will Lou sell Andy or give him the freeze?

MACK Whatta you think?

ANDY I won't fight for Lou Foster!

MACK You won't!

ANDY Don't—won't—what the hell is this?

MACK When he took your contract, he took your life. As far as the ring is concerned, you're dead!

LARRY You been dumped, kid.

ANDY So I'm tied up like a million other suckers. That's the air.

MACK Even if Lou didn't have the drag to keep you out of the ring, he has the legal right. As your manager, he will see that you never fight again, nowhere.

ANDY (*anguishly*) If I don't fight, I'm through.

MACK As a fighter—yes.

ANDY As a fighter—what else can I do?

LARRY This is a lousy racket, anyway. Nertz! Is being a janitor any better! (*explodes and moves upstage*)

ANDY Don't I get just one more chance?

MACK Be smart. Staying around here won't help you to live to ripe old age.

ANDY Aw—I'm sick of this town anyway.

MACK (*paying* ANDY *off*) I picked you up out of the street telling you to run. Run now. Count this, it's your share—a hundred...

ANDY Thanks, Mack.

MACK And here's another fifty for fare.

ANDY The fare ain't fifty.

MACK Take it!!! Grab the first thing leaving town—bus—plane—horse, or anything. Here, take another twenty-five.

ANDY A hundred and seventy-five bucks outa two hundred!

MACK Sure, this twenty-five is enough for me to pay up my insurance. I've always wanted to see Lou get his, but not you taking the lumping.

LARRY That's a fact.

ANDY Stop it. When do I see you in New York?

MACK You were telling me about taking a week off—go ahead.

ANDY Sure. But after that, where?—at the gym?

MACK I'll mail you your share of the gate by check.

ANDY I ain't talking about the money. When will I see you?

MACK You don't.

ANDY I don't? What do you mean?

MACK Only chance you got is if Lou dies—and that ain't likely soon.

ANDY (*tortured—in finality*) Okay, Mack—I'm through—I'm licked.

MACK (*nervously*) For Chris' sake, with his pull, he could make Shirley Temple champion. Grab yourself a cab. Scram, kid, scram. When I signed you up, I must have signed up a whole race. I don't go in for this sucker stuff. Whatever that thing inside you that makes you fight, keep it ticking. It's good for you, but it's a jinx for me. Here I am, fifty and white. If I had it, I'd be free, too. Like a million other suckers, we're all fighting to be free. (*striving for control*) I'm going back to handling horses. People, hell, there's too much wrong with them. So long, kid. (*shakes* ANDY's *hand, avoiding his grief, goes to bar—drinks*)

ANDY Here goes a dead man. (*exits as* LARRY *looks significantly and with self-condemnation*)

LARRY Ain't we all! (*after a glance at* MACK, *he exits hotly*)

(*curtain*)

Scene Two

(*The Whitman home. Dawn, the next day.*

The dawn of the morning cracks through the window, splicing the semi-dark room which shows evidence of a modest prosperity. The light strikes the wall where ANDY's *photo hangs, proudly. Over the photo is a hand embroidered tapestry. It reads:* OUR ANDY—THE NEXT CHAMP. *All is quiet.*

As ANDY *quietly tiptoes into the room with his travelling bag, a fog of catastrophe befalls the room. Downcast and remorseful, his recent escapade has left him crushed and a beaten man with all his high hopes exploding. He sets his bag down and stares into space fearing the household will suddenly realize his return and he will have to face the ordeal of telling them...*

There is a mild ripple of noise. He turns suddenly. No one appears. His thoughts travel back to himself. Then as he surveys the room, his eyes are caught on the champ sign. Drawn to it, he touches it tenderly, then with an inner explosion of terror, he snatches it from the wall, grips it, crushes it and flings it aside and exits into his room.

BECKY *peeps in from behind the portiers. She enters. The fiery* BECKY *seems to have caught* ANDY's *anguish; she strives to regain her own strength and readies to face* ANDY. *But as her eyes fall on the ruffled champ sign, she picks it up—studies it—grips it—nods her head hopelessly and exits just as* ANDY *returns with an armful of clothes and another bag. He begins packing his things.*

BECKY *steps again from the portiers, bolsters herself. Then softly goes to window and raises shade offering more light.* ANDY *halts and is unable to look at her.*

BECKY Your shoulders look like the wings of a broken bat. I don't like the way you drop your head. Straighten up! (ANDY *self-consciously obeys*) That's it. Can't you pack? Want me to help you?

ANDY (*words burning his throat*) I can do it.

BECKY You at least could take this scarf with you. It took me six weeks to knit it. (*flings him scarf*)

ANDY (*attempting lightness*) Happy and me is planning to—

HAPPY (*followed by* CHARLIE *steps from behind the portiers*) To what?

ANDY (*at first puzzled, looks from one face to the other, then realizing they all know, he, for an instant strives to escape, but finally in submission*) So you told them?

HAPPY I told them about a ghost. That's what you are, a plain stinking ghost. No man could be living that socked Lou Foster. Here was me all set for the slag pile. Bunking on the Bowery. Just outside the door to the old folks home. All ready for a twenty-five buck casket in the potter's field. You come along. I latched on to a ghost.

ANDY We're still pals, Happy.

HAPPY Pal—what's this you planning including me?

ANDY It's—(*looking wishfully at* BECKY *who wisely saves his face*)

BECKY Charlie—help me get the boys' things together. (*both exit after* BECKY *pauses with great pain*)

ANDY (*quickly*) How would you like to take a chance on me?

HAPPY What kind of chance?

ANDY I could go to the coast. Enter the Golden Gloves under a different name. In a couple of months, I could make a name as an amateur then turn pro with you as my manager.

HAPPY Maybe Lou's got reasons for not knocking you off. But he ain't got no reasons for letting me live—if I cross him.

ANDY Three thousand miles away and I'd change my boxing style.

HAPPY Handling you is like handling a coffin. Changing your style won't change the color of my casket.

ANDY So we colored folks must hang together.

HAPPY People—are just about the funniest things I know.

ANDY Thanks, pal.

HAPPY If Lou dies, I'll be looking you up. Gee—just to mention his name, makes me feel like I'm breathing backwards. (*exits*)

ANDY (*unable to restrain himself any longer, his bitterness explodes in a violent attack on his luggage which he shoves scornfully to the floor*) Why didn't he kill me? I wish I was dead! (BECKY *and* CHARLIE *enter.* CHARLIE *is alarmed, but* BECKY *folding clothes remains outwardly calm*) I was so near my goal of getting away. He busted me flat!

CHARLIE You should have just stayed out of that man's way.

ANDY A man? I tell you his eyes are like daggers that stick me all the time. I don't believe he is a man.

CHARLIE More learning will help you understand such people.

BECKY Is more schooling a life insurance for what he's fighting for?

CHARLIE And my God, what's that?

BECKY Freedom, Charlie, freedom of spirit.

CHARLIE A free spirit. Well, books enlighten the mind. Ain't that freedom and will help him adjust—

ANDY Myself to being called nigger! (CHARLIE *stares stupefied*) Naw, Charlie the book ain't been written that can explain why I can't eat any place I want or stay in any hotel I want —long as I have the money. It's all wrong or maybe I'm crazy.

BECKY No, son, you were born with a nature that soaked up all the resentment of your race against suffering. I understand. I'm that way myself. So was your Ma. But we didn't pack our bags and leave it.

CHARLIE What else you expect him to do?

BECKY Charlie, don't encourage him to leave.

CHARLIE For the first time I understand him. Yet, I don't know how to advise him. What does the black father tell his son in cases like this? I got to get ready to go to work. (*exits*)

ANDY You look shaky.

BECKY You got me all tangled up. If I tell

you to go, it's like saying I mis-raised you. And telling you to stay without telling you how you can stay here and get along is wrong. (*as she makes an effort to fortify herself, footsteps are heard on the roof*) That's Ruth coming. (ANDY *lowers his head, seeking a way out rather than face* RUTH)

ANDY I don't want to see her.

BECKY Don't drop your face like the jaws of a hound dog. You ain't killed nobody. You ain't robbed nobody. If you're shamed for hitting back for your rights, then you're shamed of being a Negro. If you're shamed of that, then I'd rather see you deader than a doorknob.

RUTH (*entering briskly*) I heard everything through my window. I came as soon as I could get my clothes on . . .

ANDY Please—don't give me no more pep talk.

BECKY (*so absorbed in her thoughts she ignores* RUTH *and her strength is recaptured*) Soon you'll be twenty-one and will have to figure things out for yourself. I just want you to know that I raised you to be tough because the world is hard and tough. Walk out of here wheresoever you will. Which way you walk, I don't know. But till hell freezes over and the devil walks on ice, you got to walk hard and talk loud to live in it.

RUTH Not as a braggard alone, but together with the little people and me. (BECKY *touches her consolingly and exits*) Two weeks ago, you telephoned me you were sticking.

ANDY I was drunk—like fifteen million other suckers—I was drunk. Then I hadn't hit—

RUTH You didn't hit Lou Foster. You hit a whole system.

ANDY Yeah—Jim Crow.

RUTH More than that. It's greed and hate where the mean guys keep their feet on the little guy's neck. It takes a long time and a lot of people to tear down a world built on hate.

ANDY I'm living in a world I have nothing to do with its making. Aw, shucks! I love you, Ruth. Let's forget the whole thing and get out of here.

RUTH I can't—I—

ANDY Okay! Every goddamn thing I've been through pointed exit and I am—alone . . . (*a knock at the door*) Come in, everybody, and say goodbye! (MICKEY *enters*)

MICKEY Boy—am I glad to see you. What's the idea of ducking me last night? Anyway, you're in on big time.

ANDY Yeah—with the has-beens.

MICKEY Has-been my foot! Loosen that leash around your neck. You ain't Lou's dog no more. The Western Sport Syndicate, the outfit I'm scouting for, wants to buy your contract from Mack.

ANDY Didn't you hear what happened?

MICKEY Sure—you got a bum decision. Blew up at Larry's party and clipped Lou.

ANDY And Lou took the papers that will make me a pauper.

MICKEY That sonovabitch!!!! He'll freeze you out of the business. Lou would die before he'd let you out. And I've been laying for the day I could get that guy!

ANDY Whyn't you tell me before I—

MICKEY I had to see you in action. I wired the Syndicate . . . the way you beat this yokel. They wired back to sign you up. (*shows him wire and then throws it away*)

ANDY (*to* RUTH) See what I mean about staying here?

RUTH As Becky says, you'll soon be twenty-one and you'll do your own deciding.

MICKEY A lotta good that'll—Hey—I was eighteen when I signed up with Lou. But I had to resign when I hit twenty-one. Don't you see your contract with Lou will be null and void . . . Ain't worth the paper it's written on.

ANDY But Charlie signed that contract, too.

MICKEY Still no good. Ask any mouthpiece. A minor must resign his contract when he hits the manhood mark. Boy, you'll have a swell birthday party. We've licked Lou Foster!

RUTH You mean he can fight again?

MICKEY All he wants.

ANDY Well—I swear.

MICKEY You wouldn't pass up this chance—or am I screwy?

ANDY I'll think it over.

MICKEY I got to know now. I'm going back to the coast. Are you signing or not?

ANDY No.

MICKEY You can't mean that. He kicked me around, too—just because his dame fell for me. Ain't I getting on top? Signing you up is my next step.

ANDY You're offering me a chance on a

silver platter. It's—it's too easy. Ruth says he's a system and it takes a lot of guys to knock him off his pedestal.

MICKEY Sure—me and you and others. She's right.

ANDY Not this way, Mickey. I can't sign up with you. Thanks.

MICKEY You'll change your mind. I'll be around again in four months.

ANDY Don't waste your time.

MICKEY It'll be worth it. I'll keep a light in my window for you. (*shakes hands*) So long. (*exits as the door closes behind him.* RUTH *is glowing with ecstacy and goes to* ANDY *reverently*)

RUTH I'm proud of you! Oh, I'm so proud!! You shut the fight game out cold. Boxing doesn't matter to you any more. Why did you do it, Andy?

ANDY Because I got enough money to skip this country—at least by freighter.

RUTH No—you see the racket for what it is, mean, vicious and raw. Get rich quick by hook or crook. Tear the muscles of your body up by the roots for the almighty dollar. Box to the tune of the big shots or be kicked out.

ANDY The racket is all right, except—

RUTH It's the same as life. Only the pitfalls are more subtle. In life, it would take you a longer time to know what Lou means. In the game, you, always tense, raw and keyed up, was exposed and he was, too. You learned a great lesson. More than you know. You admitted it just now. You told Mickey, Lou is a system we all have to beat. That fierce and terrible strength is beginning to show in your head instead of your fist. That's where it belongs and along with all the little people—the common people. That's struggle of all men.

ANDY All men? White people don't have no Jim Crow.

RUTH Since working at Union headquarters, I've learned that everything from slapping a baby's face to murder can be traced to whether a guy is or isn't making a decent living. Call it Jim Crow or any other name, but didn't Lou push white guys around, too?

ANDY Mickey—Larry—Lady Friend. Yes, he did. Sure he did.

RUTH You'll find them in all walks of life and right here, Andy. All we got to do is find them. If you must go, go on. As long as you walk hard and talk loud with the right spirit in the right company, I can give you up, as much as I love you.

ANDY You can be happy with just that?

RUTH Freedom is greater than love. It is, to me.

ANDY (*holding her embracingly*) Gosh—if you can do that, I can go you one better. I'm staying.

RUTH (*warmly*) Thank you, Andy—thank you.

ANDY And thanks to the little guys in our corner. (*they embrace*)

(*Curtain*)

8

Black Family Life

Thomas Pawley   James Baldwin   Louis Peterson

It is no accident that these three family plays are also autobiographical. Of what family can a man most truly write if not his own? Perhaps every good playwright at some time writes the story of himself and his family or lack of family. Loften Mitchell's *Phonograph* tells of his boyhood in Harlem. *To Be Young, Gifted, and Black* contains much of Lorraine Hansberry's life.

In a play of family life, the writer is potentially able to reach his largest audience. No matter how disparate the economic and social position, the experience of mother, father, brothers, and sisters is nearly a universal one. This is not to argue that a black family's life is identical to a white family's—not in America.

Raisin in the Sun enjoyed enormous success with both white and black audiences. But when white critics lauded *Raisin* with "why, after all that Younger family was just like us," a black critic like Harold Cruse was moved to write,

> the Negro made theater history with the most cleverly written piece of glorified soap opera I, personally, have ever seen on a stage.
> ...the Younger family was carefully tidied up for its on-stage presentation as good, hardworking, upright, decent, moral, psychologically uncomplicated ghetto folk; poor but honorable, they kept their head above water and had not sunk down into the human dregs. There were no numbers-runners in sight, no bumptiously slick, young "cats" from downstairs sniffling after Mama Younger's pretty daughter on the corner, no shyster preachers hustling Mama into the fold, no fallen women, etc.
> ...it is a foregone conclusion that Negro writers who are middle-class from birth will pass from Negro plays (which are not Negro plays) to writing plays which are universally human, before they will ever write a play that would have to portray some unpleasant truths about their own class.

The argument, then, is that if a white audience can fully identify with the characters to the point of saying that the family could have been white, the play is not about the black experience. Professor Floyd Gaffney zeros in on the problem:

> This fixation about *universality* is often an unconscious assessment by some whites to mean literally "has this black writer translated his experiences into a language that reaches me mentally and emotionally?"... [Whites] have, in essence, insisted that black writers create black-white men who reflect the white world of experience. This is idiocy!

Both Mr. Cruse and Mr. Gaffney are insisting that the subject matter of the theater be broadened to include black life not previously presented, and that this new life not be condemned because it does not conform to old standards of how white people think black people should act.

The three families presented in this section are from varied backgrounds: the poor storefront church of *The Amen Corner*; the poor but educated family of the southern school teacher in *The Tumult and the Shouting*; and the northern, middle-class urban dweller in *Take a Giant Step*. The families and the characters are diverse. How well do they represent the black experience? How much can a white audience empathize with the families? Is there a universality of experience in the family situation for both whites and blacks?

Thomas Pawley (1917–)

The Tumult and the Shouting 1969

Since the time of Moliere, the stage has subjected the white middle class to laughter. The bourgeois who lives beyond his means, who pretends to "culture," who apes poor taste, has been the happy theme of comedy. Sociologist Franklin Frazier observed the black bourgeoisie, and he did not spare them his ridicule.

Dr. Thomas Pawley observed something else: the tragedy of a college teacher who dedicates his life to "lifting the veil of ignorance" from the children and grandchildren of slaves, only to find himself rejected by the system to which he sacrificed his life.

David Sheldon, Sr., the black school teacher of the play, is not a black Willie Loman (who perhaps deserved the fate of his poor material dream). David Sheldon, Sr. believes in a good dream—young people taught to read and write so that they can provide for themselves in a difficult America. Through this dream he seeks an honored place in the community, he seeks security for his family, he seeks to avoid the ugliness of a racism. Dr. Pawley shows very clearly that those who wish to lead respectful and respected lives may perish if they are at the bottom of a capitalist ladder that has made no room for them in white America.

The Tumult and the Shouting is a new play. This is its first printing. Its first production was at the Institute of Dramatic Arts, Lincoln University, in 1969. But *Tumult* is new in another way. It is the first play to show the life of a southern black college teacher in the generation between the wars. The author has dedicated the play to his father.

Dr. Pawley is himself a teacher. After his graduation with distinction from Virginia State College, he taught English and drama in several Negro Universities. He received his Ph.D. in theater arts, his "meal ticket," from the University of Iowa. He is presently chairman of the Department of Humanities and Fine Arts at Lincoln University in Jefferson, Missouri. He is author of a number of articles, essays, poetry, and plays, including a full length script on Crispus Attucks.

The Tumult and the Shouting will please a large audience of people who, while applauding the black theater of the 1960's, ask for a widening of its subject matter. Many professionals whose parents and grandparents lived and worked in the South between the two Great Wars will find themselves here.

The Tumult and the Shouting

CAST OF CHARACTERS

DAVID SHELDON
DAVID SHELDON, SR., *his father*
WILLA SHELDON, *his mother*
BILLY SHELDON } *his brothers*
JULIAN SHELDON }
HARRIET SHELDON, *his sister*
JOHN CRENSHAW, *a farmer*
MR. BLANKENSHIP, *a grocer*
EMMA, *a young white woman*
MAMIE TOWNES, *the college librarian*
LAWYER CLARK
DR. BOWEN, *a physician*
DR. WALKER, *president of the college*
MISS JACKSON, *a secretary*
A VOICE
TAXI DRIVER
STUDENTS

ACT ONE

Scene One   Processional

SCENE: *The façade of a two-story brick house cut away to reveal the interior: a living room, kitchen, dining room on the first floor and two bedrooms upstairs. The house remains on stage always in the background throughout the play.*

TIME: *1918–1948. The action is continuous.*

PLACE: *A Negro college in the town of Warwick, Virginia.*

(*The musical overture fades into the Recessional theme as* DAVID *enters*)

DAVID Recognize that tune? They used to play it quite a lot at college commencements when I was a kid around here. It's called "The Recessional." Students used to march out to it after getting their diplomas. Nowadays there's little or no music. They just walk in very casually and walk out. You've probably guessed that this is a college play. Actually it's the story of a college teacher—a man who gives thirty years of his life to a single institution of higher learning as they say in the jargon and then suddenly finds himself retired—a condition for which he is totally unprepared. I know. You see, this man, this teacher was my father. I hope this does not confuse you because I am both a character in this play and yet I stand outside of it, watching the events as they move irresistibly toward a climax. This gives me an advantage over you. I know what's coming. I saw it happen. My father was an amazing person—an orphan at two, raised by his older sisters, educated in the North, he returned to his native South to Mississippi at thirty-five, just before the great war broke out, with his brand new Bachelor of Arts degree. When most men his age were becoming established he was just getting started. He intended to remain "down home" only long enough to earn money for divinity school, but he never made it. He remained a teacher all of his life. Why? That's what this play is all about.

(*The lights fade. In the darkness a newsboy is heard shouting*)

NEWSBOY Allies start big push! Extra! Marines go over the top! Extra! Extra!

(*The lights come up on a spot set: a piano and a divan on the forestage.* DAVID SHELDON *and his young wife* WILLA *are playing a duet. She plays the piano and sings. He accompanies her on the violin. The song is "O Promise Me." Suddenly* SHELDON *stops*)

WILLA What's the matter, Mister?
SHELDON Thought I heard the mailman.
WILLA At this time of day? It's only your imagination.
SHELDON No. I'm sure I heard something on the porch.
WILLA The evening paper. Come on. Let's start again. (*she resumes playing*)

SHELDON It's no use, Willa. I can't keep my mind on it.
WILLA If that college is going to hire you it'll hire you.
SHELDON But there's so little time left. I can't hold off signing my contract much longer.
WILLA Then sign it. You can resign later if the offer comes.
SHELDON I can't do that. Once I sign it I'll have to stay on for another year.
WILLA You and your scruples.
SHELDON After you've been at a place five years you owe something to the people. And when I leave—*if* I leave—I want to leave on good terms with everybody, especially President Adams.
WILLA I don't see how anybody could become attached to these rundown buildings on fifty dollars a month. (*closing the piano*) Well, I guess that ends the music for today.
SHELDON Sorry, Willa.
WILLA That's all right. (*she kisses him*) It's time to start dinner anyway. And I've got to heat the baby's bottle.
SHELDON (*putting the violin in the case*) Why don't we run up to Yazoo City this weekend?
WILLA What'll we use for train fare?
SHELDON Then let's take in the concert tomorrow night. It's free.
WILLA One of those student recitals. No, thank you. We've already been to three.
SHELDON It'd be something to do.
WILLA Mister, if you are really serious about doing something we can ask some people over for five hundred.
SHELDON But you just said we're broke.
WILLA It won't cost anything. I've got some Jell-O and I can make some cookies and punch.
SHELDON Oh, I don't know.
WILLA Why not? Don't tell me you've lost interest in cards?
SHELDON Not exactly.
WILLA What's the matter then?
SHELDON It's the people we play with.
WILLA What's wrong with them? They're all faculty members and their wives.
SHELDON It's the way they gossip.
WILLA But harmless gossip.
SHELDON And when they're not gossiping, it's nonsense, trivialities.
WILLA Serious conversation and five hundred don't mix. It's not relaxing.

SHELDON Well, I can't relax around them.
WILLA But they're our friends. We've got nobody else to associate with. And they're good people even if they're not intellectuals.
SHELDON Let's not argue, Willa.
WILLA But you've become so grouchy the last few weeks—ever since you wrote to that college in Virginia.
SHELDON It'll be better for us up there, Willa. Better salary, better schools, better white people and better—
WILLA Negroes? They're the same everywhere.
SHELDON I was going to say race relations. (*he starts toward an imaginary door*)
WILLA Where are you going?
SHELDON To get the paper.
WILLA Before you get settled, I want you to go to the store. I'm out of corn meal.
SHELDON (*pulls out his empty pockets*) I'll have to charge it.
WILLA Our credit's good.
SHELDON I don't know for how long. Mr. Blankenship's been very patient. If he takes a notion to cut us off—
WILLA We'll take our business elsewhere. (*she hands him his hat and jacket*) And please don't let him start a conversation.
SHELDON That's how I keep our credit going. I'm about the only one from the institute who'll listen to the old geezer. (*he goes out*)

(*The light fades on the living room and comes up on the store—a counter with shelves of groceries behind.* MR. BLANKENSHIP, *the proprietor, is a kindly looking and loquacious white man. He is waiting on a customer.* SHELDON *enters*)

BLANKENSHIP And what else'll it be, John?
JOHN How much this come to?
BLANKENSHIP (*figuring*) Sixty-five cents.
JOHN That'll leave me twenty-five out of a dollar, won't it?
BLANKENSHIP Thirty-five.
JOHN Slice me up thirty-five cents of bacon.
BLANKENSHIP Sure thing, John.
JOHN How much that gon weigh?
BLANKENSHIP Bout a pound and a half. (BLANKENSHIP *takes down a slab of bacon and puts it on the machine*)
JOHN Don't make 'em too thick, Mr. Blankenship.

BLANKENSHIP Bout medium?
JOHN Yes, sir.
BLANKENSHIP (*noticing* SHELDON) Oh, hello, Professor. Be with you in just a minute.
JOHN Howdy, Professor.
SHELDON (*nodding*) Mr. Crenshaw. How's your boy?
JOHN Doing just fine, Professor. We hear from him regular. Says he got awful sick on the boat going over but he likes it fine there in France.
SHELDON Glad to hear it.
BLANKENSHIP Well, he can have it. I'm going to stay as far away from the shooting as I can.
JOHN Oh, he ain't in the front lines. At least he ain't doing no shootin. He's in one of them labor batallions.
BLANKENSHIP He's lucky. He'll come back in one piece.
JOHN Well, I don't know, Mr. Blankenship. He might not never come home. Says he might stay over there after the war.
BLANKENSHIP Oh—?
JOHN Yessir. (*there is an awkward pause*)
BLANKENSHIP Well, that'll be exactly one dollar, John. (*he wraps the bacon and ties it.* JOHN *pulls out an old change purse and extracts a wrinkled dollar bill and hands it to* BLANKENSHIP)
JOHN Thank you, Mr. Blankenship. (*he starts out*)
BLANKENSHIP Oh, John—(JOHN *stops*)
JOHN Yes, sir.
BLANKENSHIP When you write to Lon tell him I'm holding his delivery job for him.
JOHN I'll do that, sir. (*he goes*)
BLANKENSHIP Now then, Professor, what's for you?
SHELDON I need half-pound of corn meal, Mr. Blankenship.
BLANKENSHIP Charge or cash?
SHELDON Charge.
BLANKENSHIP (*opens a gray ledger and consults it*) That'll bring your account to just over eighteen dollars. Twenty dollars the limit on credit, you know.
SHELDON (*swallowing hard*) Yes, sir.
BLANKENSHIP Which reminds me. Something ought to be done about the salaries they pay you teachers at the institute. You doing a fine job with our boys and girls around here.
SHELDON Thank you, Mr. Blankenship.

BLANKENSHIP Yes, sir. I've heard my father say how years ago folks was dead set against setting up an institute for colored in this town. But it's done a world a good. I'm all for it.
SHELDON (*resigned to a long discourse*) Yes, sir.
BLANKENSHIP Now you take John Crenshaw. Known his family for years. Didn't get past the fourth grade but he's getting to educate all his children. (*he starts for the corn meal bin*) Why you spose Lon don't want to come home? He owes something to his daddy, don't you reckon?
SHELDON (*trying to avoid conversation*) Yes, sir.
BLANKENSHIP Then why you spose he ain't coming back?
SHELDON It's probably his being away from home for the first time and seeing how different things can be.
BLANKENSHIP Hum—I spose. But he could do a lot of good around here for his folks—the colored people, I mean.
SHELDON That's true. (*he sees that* BLANKENSHIP *has forgotten about the corn meal*)
BLANKENSHIP Now take you for instance. You're from South Carolina, ain't you?
SHELDON Yes.
BLANKENSHIP How come you come back to the South?
SHELDON This was the only place I could find a job teaching in college.
BLANKENSHIP That's what I mean. Folks was afraid you wouldn't fit. Said as much to Principal Adams. You know, you being educated up East. But he said they ought to give you a chance, by George, he was dead right. Folks like you Sheldon. You might even be the head some day.
SHELDON Thank you.
BLANKENSHIP But you can't keep good people if you don't pay 'em. And I'm going to say as much to Professor Adams the next time he's in here. Now what was it you wanted?
SHELDON Corn meal, Mr. Blankenship.
BLANKENSHIP Right away. (*at this moment a young white woman enters the store*) Excuse me a moment.
SHELDON Yes, sir. (*he steps to one side*)
BLANKENSHIP Afternoon, Miss Emma. What can I do for you?
EMMA (*noticing* SHELDON) I can wait.
BLANKENSHIP Oh, he don't mind waiting, do you, professor?

SHELDON Well, I am in a hurry, Mr. Blankenship.
BLANKENSHIP It'll only take a minute. Miss Emma?
EMMA Mamma says to send her two quarts of your best snap beans, Mr. Henry.
BLANKENSHIP All right, little lady. (*he proceeds to ladle out huge handfuls of stringbeans.* EMMA *turns to* SHELDON)
EMMA You from the normal school?
SHELDON Yes, ma'm.
EMMA I thought so—how you dress an all. You all sure do ave a wonderful choir.
SHELDON Yes, ma'm. (*pause*)
EMMA Are you in the choir?
SHELDON No, ma'm. I don't sing.
EMMA Well, what do you do?
SHELDON I'm an English teacher.
EMMA Oh, how nice. But I'm sprised to hear you don't sing.
SHELDON I play the violin occasionally.
EMMA Oh, a fiddler! How wonderful. Do you play for parties?
BLANKENSHIP Here you are, Miss Emma. He ain't got time to play for no parties. He's a teacher.
EMMA Well, that's a shame. I know he could pick up right smart on the side if he'd a mind to. Charge this, will you, Mr. Blankenship.
BLANKENSHIP Right now, Miss Emma. (*she leaves*) Better write this down before I forget it. (*he licks the end of the pencil and writes laboriously.* SHELDON *fidgets*) All right, now let's see. Corn meal wasn't it, Professor?
SHELDON (*brusquely*) Yes. (BLANKENSHIP *looks at him sharply*)
BLANKENSHIP (*ladling out the corn meal into a sack on the scales*) One half-pound of corn meal. Good measure. Never short change my customers. There you are. (*he folds and wraps the sack tying it with a piece of string*) Charge, wasn't it? (SHELDON *nods.* BLANKENSHIP *writes after wetting the pencil*) Corn meal, twenty cents. D. Sheldon. All right, Professor, here you are. (SHELDON *starts out*) Oh, Professor.
SHELDON Yes. (*he stops. At the same time a middle-aged white woman enters.* SHELDON *does not see her. She pauses in the door*)
BLANKENSHIP Sorry you had to wait. (*pause*) But you know how it is.
SHELDON Yes. I know how it is. (SHELDON *turns, almost bumps into the woman*)
WOMAN Here, boy, why don't you look where you're going?
SHELDON (*stiffly*) Pardon me, madam.
WOMAN You almost bumped into me.
SHELDON I'm sorry.
WOMAN That all you got to say? (SHELDON *starts to reply but leaves abruptly*) What's the matter with that boy? He better mind his manners.
BLANKENSHIP He apologized, Sally.
WOMAN Funny way of apologizing. He speaks awful proper. Can't be from round here.
BLANKENSHIP South Carolina.
WOMAN He don't talk like it.
BLANKENSHIP He teaches at the Institute.
WOMAN Well, now that explains it. His airs and all . . .
BLANKENSHIP Oh, come on, Sally. He didn't touch you.
WOMAN Well, I just can't stand an uppity nigger. (*the light fades on the store*)

(SHELDON *enters the living room*)
WILLA What took you so long?
SHELDON He made me wait while he served some white woman.
WILLA Well, I forgive you then. Beggars can't be choosers.
SHELDON (*angrily*) I'm no beggar. I pay my bills like anyone else.
WILLA Don't shout at me—I didn't make you wait. Tell him.
SHELDON But I can't tell him. I don't dare tell him. As decent as he has been, he'd say I was forgetting my place and cut off our credit.
WILLA Why are you getting so upset? This isn't the first time this has happened.
SHELDON I'm fed up. I've got to get away from this town. It's hard to keep your self-respect on fifty dollars a month and always having to remember your place. That's why I've got to get that job in Virginia. Down here I'm just an underpaid nigger teacher.
WILLA And up there you'll still be underpaid and you'll still be a nigger teacher.
SHELDON But they even got a law against lynching up there. And that college is an oasis. Everything's right there on the campus. We won't even have to come in contact with white people.
WILLA I wouldn't be too hopeful.

(*The lights fade and the music rises*)

Scene Two

DAVID That's how we came to this house. I don't remember anything about it since I was barely a year old. But the salary was seventy-five dollars a month and Virginia *was* an improvement over Mississippi. This is quite a big house as houses go. It's got four bedrooms, a living room, dining room, kitchen and a room my mother called the pantry where she kept the food, the icebox, and her dishes. Just the kind of house for raising a family like ours. And the rent was only twenty-five dollars a month, including utilities. You didn't even have to pay for gas unless you exceeded the maximum. Imagine. Twenty-five dollars a month for a house like this. And never once did they raise the rent in thirty years. Right on campus too. Just a short distance from Old Main. You see, the college used this as inducement to get teachers. They couldn't afford to pay much in salaries directly, so this kind of made up for it. Trouble with this was it made you accustomed to good living and it didn't encourage you to own your own home. And then it kind of left people at the mercy of the administration, which was beholden only to the white folks in Richmond. (*pause*) By 1923 I had a brother and another was on his way. Coming to Virginia had isolated the family from the race problem but hadn't solved the financial one. Dad was under pressure to get his Master's degree so he had to go to school every summer. This only increased the financial strain and it didn't help the marriage—tensions began to develop. Of course there had been a couple of small salary raises. But after ten years of teaching he was making less than a hundred dollars a month.

(*The lights fade on the forestage and rise on the interior of the house*)

WILLA David, you stay out of Mr. Townes' toolshed. (*she is on the porch*)
DAVID (*off*) Yes'm.
WILLA Come on around this side where I can watch you.
DAVID (*off*) Oh, mama.
WILLA Right now. Do you hear?
DAVID (*off*) Yes'm.

(MAMIE TOWNES, *a tall spare woman with a pleasant disposition, comes up on the porch and knocks on the front door*)

MAMIE Willa, it's me. Mamie.
WILLA Come on in, Mamie. I'm in the kitchen. (MAMIE *enters*) You're home early.
MAMIE We've started closing at five for supper. Nobody uses the library then anyhow.
WILLA I know you can use the rest. I don't see how you can stand on your feet all day.
MAMIE It's an occupational hazard. Show me a librarian and I'll show you a case of varicose veins.
WILLA Why do you do it, Mamie? You don't need to work. Your husband's perfectly able to take care of you.
MAMIE True. But I don't know of anybody around here who's got too much money. Besides, I'd go stark, raving mad if I had to sit in that house all day while Jim's at school. Now if I had children like you—
WILLA You'd be looking forward to the day when they were grown. And I'm looking forward to their being old enough for me to get a job. The president's promised me work. God knows we need the money.
MAMIE Can't you get someone to take care of the children? So you could work now, I mean?
WILLA Mister wouldn't hear of it.
MAMIE Old fashioned, eh?
WILLA I guess. But you know he was raised by his sisters and he says even that is not like being raised by your mother and father.
MAMIE Obviously you agree with him.
WILLA I suppose I do.
MAMIE Well, I've only got a minute. What I stopped by to ask is what are you wearing to the faculty social Friday evening?
WILLA Social?
MAMIE Yes. The invitation said semi-formal. For the life of me I never know what to wear when I get that kind of invitation. I wish they'd just say formal and get it over with.
WILLA Well, I don't know.
MAMIE You mean you haven't even thought about it?
WILLA Well, I've been so busy with the house and children—
MAMIE But you're going, aren't you?
WILLA I don't know—we haven't decided.
MAMIE Haven't decided? But Jim said those that were going had to respond by last Friday.
WILLA Oh?—
MAMIE (*suddenly*) Willa, didn't you know

about the dance? Didn't Sheldon tell you?
WILLA   It must have slipped his mind.
MAMIE   Like fun it did.
WILLA   Oh, you don't know him. He gets so absorbed in his work he hardly knows the time of day. He's teaching five courses this quarter plus the debating team. He's dead tired when he gets home evenings. Yes, I'm sure it just slipped his mind.
MAMIE   Then all you have to do is ask him.
WILLA   But isn't it too late now? You just said—
MAMIE   Oh, come on. They always expect somebody to change his mind at the last minute. That's no problem.
WILLA   It'll mean buying a new dress.
MAMIE   No, it won't. I'll lend you one of mine.
WILLA   (*laughing*)   I'd never get in it.
MAMIE   (*laughing*)   Then borrow one from Susie Parker. You and she are an exact match.
WILLA   Oh, no, Mamie.
MAMIE   Why not? Susie won't mind.
WILLA   It's like accepting charity and I know Mister won't like it.
MAMIE   You're crazy. Why everybody borrows from everybody else on this campus. You know that.
WILLA   I get tired of borrowing from people, Mamie. And Mister would be furious if I did it again.
MAMIE   Tell a lie then. Say you made it or your sister sent it to you.
WILLA   That's the last thing on earth I'd say. He doesn't like them sending me things either.
MAMIE   Poor but proud, huh?—But you need to get out together, you two. When you first came you were going all the time. But now—people will soon get the notion you've gone high hat and stop inviting you out.
WILLA   I guess so.
MAMIE   Don't you really want to go?
WILLA   I'd love to.
MAMIE   Then tell him.
WILLA   I'll mention it to him after supper.

(SHELDON *enters, crosses to the porch and opens the door*)

MAMIE   Good. I've got to run now and heat up the leftovers. I'm due back at six-thirty.
SHELDON   (*entering and going to the hall tree*) Willa, I'm home.

MAMIE   Seems to me there was something else I wanted to ask—oh, well, it couldn't have been important. (*she goes into the hall*) Hello, Professor.
SHELDON   Oh, hello, Mamie.
MAMIE   I'm afraid I've kept Willa from finishing your supper.
SHELDON   Oh, that's all right. She likes to talk to you.
MAMIE   Well, I've got to run. (*she goes out of the front door*)
SHELDON   (*proceeding to the kitchen*)   Mamie quit her job?
WILLA   Un-unh. Library's closing for meals. Started today.
SHELDON   (*shaking his head*)   A shame. (WILLA *starts to protest*) I know—not many students use the library between meals but then that's the only time some can.
WILLA   Librarians need a break too. It's a long day for them.
SHELDON   Yes. They're pretty much overworked like the rest of us. And I'm afraid there's not much can be done about it till those people in Richmond have a change of heart. I'm going upstairs and catch a few winks before supper. Prudential committee meets tonight.
WILLA   All right, dear. Any mail?
SHELDON   On the hall table. Nothing much except bills.

(*He ascends the stairs to the bedroom.* WILLA *waits until she hears the door close then she goes into the hall and thumbs through the mail on the table. Finding nothing, she pulls out the drawer and rummages through the letters there. Not finding what she's looking for she goes to the hall tree and searches the pockets of* SHELDON'*s overcoat. She finally gives up and returns to the kitchen where she sits deep in thought. After a moment she lifts her head as if staring through the ceiling. She rises and goes up the stairs to the bedroom and pauses at the door*)

WILLA   Mister, are you still awake? (*receiving no answer she enters softly.* SHELDON *is asleep, fully clothed. She goes to the bureau and thumbs through the letters there. Seeing* SHELDON'*s coat on the back of a chair, she crosses to it and searches the pockets carefully. Then she replaces the coat and crosses to the door. She is about to leave when she turns and faces the bed. She pauses and coughs gently.* SHELDON *stirs*)

SHELDON That you, Willa? What time is it?

WILLA Mister, can I talk to you for a minute?

SHELDON (*sitting up*) What's the matter? Something wrong? Don't you feel well?

WILLA I'm all right.

SHELDON You sure?

WILLA I'm sure.

SHELDON I thought maybe the baby was acting up again.

WILLA (*placing her hand on her stomach*) No. He's behaving himself.

SHELDON *He?* But it's going to be a girl.

WILLA It's too early to tell. I'll let you know when I'm about six months.

SHELDON (*laughing*) How'll you know?

WILLA By the way it kicks.

SHELDON You mean you can tell the difference between a football player and a ballet dancer? (*he is laughing*)

WILLA I can.

SHELDON (*lying back*) I'm glad you're all right, Willa. (*pause*)

WILLA Mister?

SHELDON Yes?

WILLA Are we going to the dance?

SHELDON What?

WILLA Are we going to the dance—Did we get an invitation to the faculty social?

SHELDON Oh, that?

WILLA Well, did we?

SHELDON Yes.

WILLA Where is it? Why haven't you told me about it?

SHELDON I left it at the office.

WILLA Why didn't you bring it home?

SHELDON I didn't want you to get excited about going.

WILLA (*not understanding*) What?

SHELDON You know—in your condition—

WILLA My condition? Being pregnant doesn't mean I'm dead. (*she is angry*) Besides the doctor hasn't said I shouldn't go out.

SHELDON That's not what I mean.

WILLA I don't understand.

SHELDON I don't think expectant mothers should go to dances.

WILLA Who's going to know I'm pregnant? The baby won't come for another seven months. I'm not showing at all.

SHELDON I guess I'm old fashioned.

WILLA Women don't go into seclusion any more because they're pregnant.

SHELDON Well, my mother did. And I'm sure your mother did.

WILLA I don't know about your mother but my mother did not. She went right ahead doing exactly what she did before and that's exactly what I intend to do.

SHELDON (*falling back on the bed*) All right, Willa.

WILLA Then we're going?

SHELDON I don't know.

WILLA But why don't you know? You've had the invitation for over a week.

SHELDON It'll mean new clothes, for you at least.

WILLA If I can arrange to get a dress, will you go?

SHELDON You mean borrow one? I don't think we should advertise our poverty.

WILLA Mamie will help me find one.

SHELDON So that's what Mamie was doing doing here. I wish she'd keep her mouth shut.

WILLA I'd have heard about it sooner or later, you know that. Besides she came over to ask what I was wearing. She assumed I already knew.

SHELDON Well, she needn't go around offering you dresses. I've got some pride, you know.

WILLA I'm the one who'll be wearing the dress.

SHELDON And I'm the one who couldn't afford to buy you one.

WILLA Have I ever complained?

SHELDON No, you haven't. You've been wonderful.

WILLA If I had known soon enough, I could have made a dress.

SHELDON (*abruptly*) What about the boys? Who'll stay with them?

WILLA I can get one of the girls out of the dormitory.

SHELDON Who?

WILLA I'll ask Miss Lillian to recommend someone. It won't be a problem. Girls like to have an excuse to get out of the dormitory to eat some home-cooked food.

SHELDON She'd stay overnight?

WILLA Why not?

SHELDON Oh, I don't know. We've got a case before the Prudential tonight. Some girl slipped out of the dormitory to meet her boyfriend.

WILLA   Don't be ridiculous. She wouldn't meet him here. (*pause*)

SHELDON   How much do they charge?

WILLA   They usually leave it up to you.

SHELDON   You have to be careful whom you leave with young children.

WILLA (*exasperated*)   One night, Mister.

SHELDON   Willa, would you go to the party without me?

WILLA   You mean go by myself?

SHELDON   Well, with Jim and Mamie.

WILLA   No, I wouldn't. Besides that's the whole point, for us to go out together.

SHELDON   I really don't want to go, Willa. I'm just not in a dancing mood.

WILLA   And you haven't been for some time now.

SHELDON   No, I haven't.

WILLA   You're beginning to show your age.

SHELDON   Willa, please—let's not argue.

WILLA   It's what my friends warned me about before we got married, your being so much older than me.

SHELDON   And you believed them?

WILLA   Would I have married you if, I had believed them? (*pause*) You used to be so gay, so debonair—wearing the latest styles and all. All the boys at the Institute tried to dress like you. I would never have believed you'd go into retirement so soon.

SHELDON   It's this damned poverty.

WILLA   But we don't have to give up everything. We're not that poor.

SHELDON   Once we pay our bills there's nothing left for parties.

WILLA   Your salary's the same as the others around here. And they manage to do things.

SHELDON   But their wives are working.

WILLA   Well, I could work too if you weren't so squeamish about the boys. So afraid someone is going to poison their little minds. It's your attitude that's keeping us back, not your salary.

SHELDON   I don't think a husband should have to rely on his wife to make ends meet. And I won't have to after I get my degree.

WILLA   What's that got to do with our going out this weekend?

SHELDON   Everything. We'll be able to go out on weekends.

WILLA   What about *this* weekend?

SHELDON (*wearily*)   Willa, I'm tired. I'd like to get a little rest before debate practice. Please.

WILLA   Then you won't go?

SHELDON   No, Willa.

(WILLA *rushes out of the room slamming the door. She pauses at the head of the stairs and cries. Composing herself she descends to the kitchen where she begins setting the table. After a moment she slumps into a chair and buries her head on the table and sobs uncontrollably. There is a knock at the kitchen door which she does not hear. A second knock and she raises her head and wipes her eyes on her apron*)

WILLA   Who is it?

MAMIE (*off, rear*)   It's me. Mamie.

WILLA   Just a minute. (*she wipes her eyes again, arranges her hair then moves to the back door*)

MAMIE   What took you so long? (*looking around*) You and Sheldon down here smooching? I'm out of butter. Can you lend me some until I can get to the grocery?

WILLA   Sure. How much do you need? (*goes to ice box*)

MAMIE   One stick will do.

WILLA   Oh.

MAMIE   What's the matter? You out too?

WILLA   No, but (*removing butter dish*) we buy it this way. (*she reveals a solid block of butter*) It's cheaper. You'll have to slice it.

MAMIE   What's the difference? It all comes from the same cows.

WILLA (*laughing and relieved*)   Take as much as you want. There's a knife in the drawer. I'll get something for you to wrap it in. (*she goes to the cabinet and removes wax paper, while* MAMIE *slices away*)

MAMIE   I meant to borrow some on my way home just now but I clean forgot until we were ready to sit down to the table.

WILLA   It's no trouble. We hadn't started. Mister's resting.

MAMIE   Have you asked him about the social?

WILLA   Yes—but nothing's definite—yet.

MAMIE (*staring at her*)   Have you been crying?

WILLA (*surprised*)   What?

MAMIE   I heard you through the door.

WILLA   Oh.

MAMIE   You've had an argument.

WILLA (*reluctantly*) Yes.
MAMIE And he's refused to go. (WILLA *does not answer*) Well, it's none of my business but if it were me I'd go anyhow.

(SHELDON *sits up on the bed upstairs, rises, stretches, and crosses to the stairs. He pauses when he reaches the bottom*)

WILLA I won't go by myself.
MAMIE Then come with Jim and me. (WILLA *shakes her head*) Why not? And you don't need to worry about being a wallflower. I'll see to it that all the husbands dance with you.
WILLA Mister already suggested that.
MAMIE Then what's stopping you?
WILLA I don't want to get started going out by myself.
MAMIE Suit yourself. But look at it this way. You're young for only a little while. When you get older like Sheldon naturally you won't want to go as much.

(SHELDON *enters the kitchen*)

SHELDON Mamie, your butter's getting warm.
MAMIE What? Oh, yes. Excuse me. (*she heads quickly for the back door*)
SHELDON And Mamie—why don't you mind your own business? (MAMIE *exits*)
WILLA You've got no right to talk to her like that.
SHELDON I've got every right when she starts meddling in my affairs.
WILLA She invited me to go along with Jim and her. Is there anything wrong with that?
SHELDON No. But when she begins to discuss the differences in our ages, she's meddling.
WILLA (*defensively*) Well, she's my friend. One of the few people I ever see and I won't have you talking to her like that.
SHELDON Won't "have" me?
WILLA Don't threaten me.
SHELDON I'm not threatening you. (*he starts out*)
WILLA You are. And just for that I am going to that social! (SHELDON *stops*) And what's more I'm going to all the other socials from now on. You stay here and dry rot if you want to but not me! (SHELDON *goes out quietly*. WILLA *follows to the entry door, pauses then leans against the door jamb and weeps softly. The lights fade and the music swells*)
DAVID But she didn't go to the dance. She never really meant to. She was a faithful and dutiful wife with the highest of scruples.—But to get on. The baby was born—another boy, Billy—a sickly little fellow from the instant of his birth. Soon there would be a girl and the family, my family, will be complete. It's 1928 now and time for me to join the story.

Scene Three

(WILLA *is in the upstairs bedroom sitting in a rocker. She is in labor. Every once in a while as the pains strike she moans softly. Outside the house* JULIAN *and* DAVID *are playing catch with a tennis ball. In the living room the younger boy,* BILLY, *is lying on the floor reading.* SHELDON *sits nearby grading papers. He continues for a moment, finishes a paper and enters a grade in his rollbook. Then he gathers all the papers and puts a rubber band around them. He rises and puts on his coat*)

SHELDON (*glancing at his pocket watch*) Nearly four. I'd better hurry or I'll be late for class. (*as he passes* BILLY) What're you reading, Billy?
BILLY Nothing.
SHELDON Aren't those the comics?
BILLY Yep. But I've finished them. I'm thinking.
SHELDON Oh. (*pause*) Why don't you go outside and play?
BILLY I don't want to. It tires me out. Can I go with you?
SHELDON *May* I go with you.
BILLY Well, may I?
SHELDON I'm going to class.
BILLY At four o'clock? Why?
SHELDON Because it's my job.
BILLY Why is it so late? David and Julian are home from school.
SHELDON College is different. You go to school all day.
BILLY Oh (*pause*) Daddy—
SHELDON Yes.
BILLY I don't want to go to college.
SHELDON (*smiling*) All right. I'm going up to look in on your mother. I'll be back in a minute.

The Tumult and the Shouting

BILLY Okay. (*as* SHELDON *ascends the stairs* BILLY *crosses to the porch*)
JULIAN Hey, Billy, want to catch?
BILLY No, thank you.
DAVID Oh, come on.
BILLY Nope.
JULIAN Why not?
BILLY I'd rather watch.

(SHELDON *enters the room upstairs*)

SHELDON How's it going?
WILLA They're about a half hour apart now.
SHELDON That's getting close. I'll send David for Dr. Bowen.
WILLA It's still an hour or so away.
SHELDON Maybe. You sure you don't want to go to the hospital?
WILLA No. It'd mean another doctor since Dr. Bowen isn't allowed to practice there. I'll be all right. Everything's ready. I've even got water on the stove ready to heat. (*she winces*) That was a sharp one.
SHELDON I'll dismiss my class and come right back. I hate to leave you alone.
WILLA No, don't do that. The boys will be here. I'm sure you'll get back before anything happens. I'll send for you if I need you.
SHELDON Promise?
WILLA Promise.
SHELDON (*reluctantly*) All right. (*he kisses her on the forehead and descends the stairs.* BILLY *hears him and moves to the front*)
BILLY You going to class now?
SHELDON Yes.
BILLY Why? It's past four o'clock.
SHELDON Yes. I'm late.
BILLY Won't your students be gone?
SHELDON (*patting him on the head*) I wouldn't be surprised. (*he goes out on the porch.* BILLY *follows*)
SHELDON David, you and Julian come here. (*the boys stop playing and come up on the porch*)
SHELDON I'm going to class now. I want you to stay close by and do whatever your mother tells you.
BILLY What's the matter with mama?
JULIAN Nothing. She's having a baby.
DAVID How do you know?
SHELDON (*interrupting*) All right, all right. David, I want you to go to the infirmary the moment she tells you. And then come to my class and get me.
DAVID Where is your class?
SHELDON Old Main, second floor. Room 212. Okay?
DAVID Okay.
SHELDON Be good now and look after your little brother.
JULIAN He don't need to look after me.
SHELDON I'm talking about Billy.

(*As* SHELDON *leaves the porch*, WILLA *is struck by another sharp pain. She arches backward stifling an outcry. The lights dim up on the classroom*)

RUSSELL I tell you, man, he ain't coming.
CANDY He never misses.
SNEAD Well, it's five minutes after.
CANDY The rule says you got to wait ten minutes.
VIVIAN I sure hope he misses today.
RUSSELL Let's go.

(WILLA *is suddenly convulsed with pain and screams aloud. The boys hear her and stop playing.* DAVID *rushes inside.* BILLY *starts after him but is held back by* JULIAN. DAVID *enters the bedroom.* WILLA *indicates he should go get the doctor. The scene in the classroom continues*)

SNEAD I hear his old lady is expecting again.
SHIELDS Then that's what's keeping him.
RUSSELL I don't care what's keeping him. But being as how I got a report to make and I ain't ready, I move we cut.
CANDY You better be glad he didn't hear you say that. He'd flunk your behind sure.
NELLIE What are we going to name the new baby?
SHIELDS Well, now let's see. The oldest boy is Noun, the brother is Pronoun and the baby is Participle. I move we name the new one Conjunction.
HELEN Shame!
NELLIE We don't mean any harm.
GRIFFIN Here he comes!
RUSSELL Nine minutes past four. Made it with a minute to spare, Goddammit.
CANDY What did I tell you?

(*There is a general scrambling around for seats*)

RUSSELL What the hell are you so happy about?
CANDY (*grinning*) I'm anxious to hear your report, daddio. (SHELDON *enters in a hurry. He crosses to his desk*)

SHELDON   I must apologize for being late and I want to thank you for waiting. This shows that you are really interested in getting an education. I realize we've lost nearly ten minutes but perhaps you won't mind staying a little longer and making it up. (*there is a groan*) I beg your pardon. Did someone say something? (*silence*) As you know, Mrs. Sheldon is—uh—not feeling well. (*someone snickers*) And I may have to leave suddenly. (*the class brightens perceptibly*) Meanwhile let us turn to the lesson for today which is (*consulting his notes*) the subjunctive mode. Oh, yes, we're to be favored by a report on the subject from Mr. Russell. Mr. Russell? (*silence*) Is Mr. Russell present?

RUSSELL   Yes, sir.

SHELDON (*sitting*)   You may come forward, Mr. Russell, and proceed.

RUSSELL (*rising wearily*)   Professor, I don't have my report. I'm not prepared.

SHELDON   Eh, what's that?

RUSSELL   I said I'm not prepared.

SHELDON   Why not?

RUSSELL   I—I didn't understand the assignment.

SHELDON   Why didn't you come in and see me about it then?

RUSSELL   See you?

SHELDON   Yes. You know where my office is, don't you?

RUSSELL   Oh, yes, sir.

SHELDON   Well?

RUSSELL   I don't know, Professor, I just can't seem to get interested in grammar.

SHELDON   Earlier in the year you told me English is your favorite subject.

RUSSELL   Oh, yes, sir. English is my favorite subject but not grammar English.

SHELDON (*after the laughter subsides*)   Hum. (*pause*) You don't really like it, do you?

RUSSELL   Oh, yes, sir. I like stories and stuff like that. (*someone laughs*)

SHELDON   Don't laugh. He's simply saying what most of you feel. (*loud protests*) I know, I know. There are one or two exceptions but most of you would rather you didn't have to be bothered.

RUSSELL   I'm sorry, Professor Sheldon.

SHELDON (*closing his book and putting up his notes*)   Let's forget today's lesson for the moment. Anyone have any ideas why we're studying grammar?

HELEN   It's a requirement. (*laughter*)

SHELDON   Yes, Miss Quander, it is. But why is it?

SPENCER   Because we need to be able to speak and write correctly.

SHELDON   All right. That's one reason. College graduates need to know how to write and speak correctly. Any others?

HAZEL (*lisping*)   Well, I don'th know, thir. But it theems to me that no matter what we want to be we've goth to be able to communicate.

SHELDON (*smiling*)   Very good. Someone else? (*silence*) Can't anyone think of a special reason why *we* need to study English?

SNEAD   By *we*, do you mean colored people?

SHELDON   Exactly.

A VOICE   So we can talk like white people.

SHELDON   Right church, wrong pew. (*there is a buzz*)

CANDY   Is that the reason? Is he right, Professor?

SHELDON   Have you ever been to a minstrel show? (*murmurs of affirmation including:* "Florida Blossoms, Georgia Peaches, Silas Green from New Orleans")

SHELDON   What's it like?

SNEAD   A lot of Negroes in blackface running around singing plantation songs and telling darky jokes.

SHELDON   Yes, and using a dialect so thick you could cut it with a knife. You and I know we don't talk like that but that's the stereotype the average white person has of us. They're shocked and surprised when they're confronted with someone who doesn't say, "Here, ah is." But that's the stereotype we've helped to build for ourselves. And that's why "Amos and Andy" has made millionaires out of Freeman and Gosden. The whole thing's a burlesque, a caricature. But it's also true that after fifty years of education many of us are still illiterate, unable to read and write or spell our own name. And we rationalize it and say it's not important and go on perpetuating illiteracy. And it's being constantly used as an argument against a college education. "They can't learn English," they say. "Listen at the way they talk." Now I don't give a tinker's damn about sounding like white people or being accepted by them. But I do want to be able to communicate with them and with my own people. And there are limitations to what I can do with the language that's used on Old Street.

RUSSELL (*protesting*) But grammar, Professor.

SHELDON I know. It seems so pointless. But let's think of it as a tool, Russell, as a means to an end so that you can say what you want to say. Take tense for example. We'd all be pretty confused if we didn't have past, present, and future to indicate when something happened.

RUSSELL You got a point, Professor. But since so many of us don't talk the way they do, wouldn't it be easier for us to make our own grammar? How about them learning to talk like us?

SHELDON That's a very interesting point. But I'm willing to bet my meager salary that if the federal government decreed that our speech—the so called Negro dialect—would become the official language and we started teaching it in the schools and requiring it to be used, most of you would start complaining it was too difficult.

SHIELDS But how could that be?

SHELDON As an experiment I want each of you to write a short essay using jive language There is only one requirement. You must communicate an idea.

RUSSELL But how can we? Professor, you don't know jive talk.

SHELDON Try me, (*he pauses*) "Jack." (*the class howls*) Mr. Russell, I know what the problem is, really I do. But we can lick this thing—I know we can. The trouble is formal English is so far removed from our experience—that is, for most of us. That's why I'm writing a new grammar based upon our needs, upon the language as it is used today. It will be quite practical. In fact I call it Practical English Grammar. It will stress the kinds of errors which our students make.

SPENCER When is it going to be published?

(*The lights come up on the bedroom. The doctor and nurse are there. The baby has been delivered. The doctor comes downstairs and calls* DAVID. *He talks to him for a moment after which* DAVID *runs off*)

SHELDON I don't have a publisher yet.

SNEAD Do you think you can get one? You a Negro college professor?

SHELDON Of course.

RUSSELL Professor, you know, I might really start studying if I had a book like that. And I ain't jiving.

(*David appears in the doorway and attempts to signal his father*)

SHELDON That's an encouraging sign.

HELEN Professor?

SHELDON Yes? (HELEN *indicates* DAVID *who is standing nervously at the door*) All right son. (*as he begins to gather his books and papers together*) I've got to go. My wife's having a baby. Class dismissed. (*he stops at the doorway*) Mr. Russell?

RUSSELL Yes, sir.

SHELDON I'll expect your report next time.

RUSSELL Oh, yes, sir. I'll be ready, sir.

SHELDON Hum (*he goes*)

A VOICE Hey, Russell, I know what we can name the baby.

RUSSELL What?

VOICE Subjunctive mode!

(*The lights fade*)

Scene Four

DAVID It happened in October, 1929—black Tuesday, or was it Thursday? By the fall of the next year the breadlines stretched from New York to California. On the campus we didn't see the breadlines but we knew they were there. Fewer students were coming to college and those that came were begging for jobs. At the opening faculty meeting the President announced that the college had suffered a ten per cent cut—ten per cent from their already meager resources. This would mean cutting salaries for everybody. It was hoped that by the end of the year things would be better so that the salaries could be restored. Families like our neighbors with both husband and wife working didn't feel the pinch so badly. But in ours it was another story.

(*As the lights rise* SHELDON *is seated in the living room reading the Richmond* News Leader. WILLA *is in the kitchen mixing oleomargarine. A pause. Then shouts from outside the house and the three boys enter the kitchen from the rear door*)

JULIAN How long before supper?

WILLA Soon.

BILLY   What are you doing?
WILLA   Mixing oleo.
BILLY   Can I help?
WILLA   No. I want all three of you to get your hands washed.
DAVID   Last one up is a dirty dog. (*they race for the stairs with loud shouts.* BILLY *is knocked down in the scuffle but gets up and runs manfully after his older brothers. As they reach the stairs,* SHELDON *puts down his paper*)
SHELDON   Boys! (*they stop*) Walk up the stairs. You'll wake the baby.
DAVID   Yes, sir. (*they resume the ascent, walking but with* JULIAN *trying to get by* DAVID. *As they reach the second floor the race is resumed.* SHELDON *puts down his paper in disgust. Shouts from upstairs mark the battle for position around the washbowl. Suddenly the door is closed with a loud slam. Silence.* SHELDON *resumes his reading as* WILLA *begins to set the supper table in the dining room. She places a cereal bowl, a knife, spoon, and glass beside each plate. Then she gets a box of shredded wheat biscuits, breaks them in half and places a half in each bowl. Suddenly the door to the bathroom swings open. A water fight is in progress*)
BILLY   Mama, David and Julian throwin water on me.
WILLA   Mister, see after them, won't you?
SHELDON (*crossing to the bottom of the stairs*) David! (*the fighting stops*)
DAVID (*off*) Yes, sir.
SHELDON   If I have to come upstairs, I'm bringing my razor strap. Understand?
DAVID (*off*) Yes, sir.
BILLY   Daddy, Julian's shaking his fist at me.
SHELDON   David, you come down here and wash your hands in the kitchen.
DAVID   I've finished, daddy.
SHELDON   Come on down anyway. (*pause*) Did you hear me?
DAVID   Yes, sir. I'm coming. (DAVID *appears at the head of the staircase*)
SHELDON   And don't sulk.
DAVID   I'm not sulking.
SHELDON   You go sit at the table. And I don't want to hear another peep out of you.
DAVID   Yes, sir. (DAVID *enters the kitchen.* SHELDON *resumes his seat.* WILLA *is now removing a can of evaporated milk from the cabinet. She punches holes in both ends with a can opener then pours the contents into a glass pitcher*)
WILLA   David, get me the ice water.

(DAVID *goes into the pantry, opens the icebox and removes a green water bottle which he gives to* WILLA)

DAVID   Don't put too much water in it mama. I don't like it when it's watery.
WILLA   All right. (*she pours the water and stirs it*)
DAVID   When we going to start using bottle milk again?
WILLA   Soon I hope. (*she now removes a loaf of whole wheat bread and begins to slice it*) Go call the others. I'm just about ready.
DAVID   Yes'm. (*he crosses to the foot of the stairs and shouts*) Supper's ready! (*to* SHELDON) Supper's ready, Daddy.
SHELDON   You all go ahead. I'll eat later.
DAVID   Yes, sir. (*he returns to the kitchen*) Daddy says he'll eat later. (WILLA *comes into the living room*)
WILLA   Mister, what's the matter? You haven't eaten with us all week.
SHELDON   I'm not hungry.
WILLA   Then come and sit with us. Are you angry with me about something?
SHELDON   No.
WILLA   There's something troubling you, I know. Whenever you start acting like a hermit. Won't you tell me what it is?
SHELDON   Later. (WILLA *shrugs her shoulders and turns to the stairs*)
WILLA   Julian, you and Billy, come on. (*she goes into the kitchen. The bathroom door swings open and another race begins.* BILLY *and* JULIAN *are met at the foot of the stairs by* SHELDON)
SHELDON   This ripping and tearing about the house has got to stop!

(DAVID *hearing the lecture appears in the door behind* SHELDON *grinning and poking fun at his helpless brothers*)

SHELDON   You act more like wild savages than the sons of a college professor. Cultured and refined people do not yell and shout all over the house. Do you understand?
JULIAN   Yes, sir.
BILLY (*blameless but manfully imitating his brother*) Yes, sir.
SHELDON   Now go and get your supper. (DAVID *ducks out of sight.* JULIAN *and* BILLY *walk meekly to the table.* SHELDON *shakes his head, resumes his seat and picks up the paper*)

The Tumult and the Shouting

WILLA   Whose turn is it to say grace?
JULIAN   It ain't mine.
BILLY   Isn't.
JULIAN   Well, it ain't.
BILLY   It's David's.
DAVID   I said it this morning.
WILLA   All right. We'll all say it together. Let's bow our heads. (*they do so.* WILLA *leads off with the Grace. The others chime in*) "Thank thee, Lord, for all these blessings. Amen."
DAVID   I don't like our grace. It's too short.
JULIAN   Well, why don't you find another one?
DAVID   I already know one.
JULIAN   Aw, you don't.
DAVID   I do. Can I say it, Mama?
WILLA   If you wish.
BILLY   But we already said one. I'm hungry!
DAVID   Let us bow our heads. "Lord make us truly thankful for these and all other blessings. Amen." There!
JULIAN   (*counting*) It's only four words longer.
BILLY   Pass the bread, please.
WILLA   (*pouring milk in each bowl of cereal*) Eat your cereal first.
JULIAN   I want mine with my cereal so I can dunk it.
WILLA   All right. (JULIAN *reaches for the bread and margarine simultaneously*) Ask for things to be passed.
JULIAN   Pass the bread and butter, please. (*after receiving them he proceeds to apply the margarine liberally*)
BILLY   May I have a glass of milk, please? (WILLA *pours milk for him*) It tastes funny. (WILLA *pats his head and puts a tiny bit of sugar into the glass*)
WILLA   Try it now.
BILLY   (*grinning*) Fine.
JULIAN   Butter dish is almost empty. (WILLA *takes the butter dish and begins to refill it with margarine*)
DAVID   It's not butter. It's margarine.
JULIAN   Same thing.
DAVID   No, it isn't. Butter's made from milk and oleo's made from vegetables, ain't it, mama?
WILLA   Yes.
JULIAN   Well, they look alike. You can't tell the difference.
DAVID   I can.
BILLY   Mama, why does butter from cows and butter from vegetables both come out yellow?
WILLA   They aren't. Margarine's white. I mix it with coloring so it'll look yellow.
BILLY   Why are we eating vegetable butter instead of real butter?
WILLA   It's cheaper.
DAVID   Don't you know there's a depression on?
JULIAN   Mama, can I go to the movies tomorrow?
WILLA   I don't know.
JULIAN   Please, mama. There's a cowboy picture and a serial.
WILLA   You'll have to ask your father for the money.
JULIAN   It'll only cost me five cents.
WILLA   I thought it was ten.
JULIAN   Well, it is. But I can get in for five.
WILLA   How?
JULIAN   I saw a boy do it. He had only five cents and he asked Mr. Goldstein to let him in. So Mr. Goldstein asked him about the other five cents and the boy said he'd pay him later. Mr. Goldstein said, "I don't allow credit. You'll have to pay me now. Come here." So he took the boy by the nose and whacked him on his head and said, "Okay, you can go in."
WILLA   He didn't?
DAVID   We do it all the time.
JULIAN   (*brightly*) Yeah. We Jew him down.
WILLA   (*sharply*) Where did you hear that?
JULIAN   Hear what?
WILLA   That expression. What you just said.
JULIAN   All the kids say it.
WILLA   Well, I don't want you saying it. It isn't nice.
JULIAN   But—
WILLA   Mr. Goldstein can't help it because he's a Jew.
JULIAN   I didn't mean any harm.
DAVID   What's wrong with it, Mama?
WILLA   Just don't let me hear you say it again—ever. Why aren't you eating, David?
BILLY   It's those candy bars. (DAVID *signals him to be quiet*)
WILLA   What candy bars?
BILLY   The candy he was eating outside.
WILLA   David, where did you get money for candy bars?
DAVID   Working—
WILLA   For whom?

DAVID For Miss Fannie in the bookstore.
WILLA And she paid you in candy bars?
BILLY She gave him a whole box.
WILLA I don't believe it. David, tell me the truth. Where did you get that candy? (*silence*) David? (*he does not answer*) Julian, do you know where he got them? (*silence*) Well, I guess I'll have to tell your father.
DAVID (*blurting it out*) I took 'em.
WILLA Where?
DAVID At school.
WILLA You took candy at school? How? Why?
DAVID We're supposed to sell it to raise money for our trip.
WILLA Yes?
DAVID One day last week after school we were playing football behind the school when one boy got the idea to go inside. He found the supply closet unlocked and all the candy in it. Then he called us and gave each of us a box.
WILLA Oh, David.
BILLY I'm going to tell Daddy.
WILLA (*grabbing him*) Sit down, Billy. David, why did you do this? Why? Don't you know that's stealing?
DAVID Well, it wasn't really stealing, Mama—
WILLA It is and you know it. Why, David? Why did you do it? Haven't we taught you right from wrong?
DAVID (*breaking down*) I'm sorry, Mama. I'm sorry. I won't do it again. I promise.
WILLA But why did you do it, David?
DAVID I overheard you and Daddy talking one night about his salary cut—I knew you were having a hard time so I didn't want to ask you for the money for the show and stuff like that—so I thought I could sell the candy.
WILLA But stealing, David—
DAVID (*breaking down again*) I'm sorry, Mama. I'm sorry. Please don't tell Daddy, please.
WILLA That money will have to be repaid. And we'll have to tell Miss Butler.
DAVID She'll put me out of school.
WILLA We'll have to take that chance. I don't want any of you to say a word of this to anyone. Is that clear? Billy?
BILLY Yes, Mama.
JULIAN Yes'm.
WILLA (*sternly*) Finish your supper and then go upstairs. And I don't want a peep out of any of you. I'll have to tell your father about this.
DAVID Mama, please—
WILLA No, David. He'll have to know.
DAVID He'll whip me.
WILLA I wouldn't be at all surprised.
(WILLA *rises, closes the door, and enters the living room. The lights dim on the kitchen*)
WILLA Mister, you said that after supper you'd tell me what's the matter.
SHELDON (*putting down his paper*) Where are the boys?
WILLA Still eating. What is it?
SHELDON There's going to be a second salary cut.
WILLA Oh, no.
SHELDON (*nodding*) Starting the first of January. Another ten per cent.
WILLA But what are we going to do?
SHELDON I don't know. I honestly don't know.
WILLA Mister, I'll have to go to work.
SHELDON Now let's not start that.
WILLA But we can't live on your salary after another cut.
SHELDON I know.
WILLA Then what are we going to do?
SHELDON The book'll be published soon. That'll make up the difference.
WILLA But how can you be sure?
SHELDON Both Hampton and Virginia Union are going to adopt it.
WILLA But twelve hundred copies have to be sold before your royalties start.
SHELDON Yes, I know.
WILLA And God knows how long that'll take. Mister, you've got to let me go to work.
SHELDON (*wearily*) There may not be any work now, Willa.
WILLA The President's told me any time I want to—
SHELDON That was *before*.
WILLA Before—
SHELDON They're eliminating some jobs, consolidating others. Business manager and cashier are going to have the same secretary.
WILLA What?
SHELDON So you see even if I say yes your chances are slim.
WILLA Then I'll try the city. I'm a good practical nurse.

SHELDON   No. It'll mean leaving the children all day.
WILLA   It's the children I'm thinking about.
SHELDON   You mean the money?
WILLA   Of course I mean the money. They all need new shoes and Billy ought to have his tonsils removed. You know the doctor's warned that if they don't come out soon, it might lead to serious trouble. We had to take him out of school for the last two winters.
SHELDON   All the more reason for you to be at home.
WILLA   (*abruptly*)   There's another reason.
SHELDON   What?
WILLA   David took a box of candy from the school.
SHELDON   Took? You mean he stole it?
WILLA   Yes.
SHELDON   (*rising*)   I'll give him the whipping of his life.
WILLA   I think you'd better listen to me first.
SHELDON   I'm not raising any thieves.
WILLA   That's exactly what you *are* doing.
SHELDON   You're crazy. What're you talking about?
WILLA   Will you please listen to me? (SHELDON *sits down startled*) David has overheard us talking. He knows we've been having a hard time.
SHELDON   So he decided to steal?
WILLA   He didn't want to bother us about money.
SHELDON   Couldn't he do without? He's almost fourteen. I did without when I was his age and I didn't steal either. And I didn't have a father or mother to guide me.
WILLA   This constant talk of money. Children are impressionable.
SHELDON   I'm sorry but I don't agree. He knows right from wrong. And if he doesn't I'm going to teach him.
WILLA   We are to blame. Telling him that he had to set an example for the other children by doing without things.
SHELDON   What kind of example has he set by stealing?
WILLA   He's sorry—he's genuinely sorry. He broke down and cried just now telling me about it. I don't know when I've seen him do that.
SHELDON   David cried?
WILLA   He's tried to be a man because we asked him to. But after all he's only a child.
SHELDON   Yes, he is a child. And that's why you must stay home with him and the others. If he's done this with you here there's no telling what notions he might develop with both of us gone all day.
WILLA   They'll be at school. Mrs. Givens can take care of the baby. I'll be home at five. Mrs. Givens is a good woman. Raised six children. She won't let them go astray.
SHELDON   My job is to earn the money to keep the family going. Yours is to make a home for them.
WILLA   You'll never change, will you? I'll bet that if we were actually starving and living in a hovel, you'd say my place was by the hearth.
SHELDON   I can't help being what I am.
WILLA   (*quietly*)   And I can't help being what I am. Mister, I'm going to work if I can find a job.
SHELDON   Even if I say no?
WILLA   Yes.
SHELDON   Then there's nothing more I can say. I'll have my supper now. (*he turns and enters the kitchen as the lights fade and the music swells*)

Scene Five

DAVID   She tried but there were no jobs. And the breadlines in the cities grew longer. Soon the black masses would abandon the Grand Old Party for the man in the wheelchair—the great white father who would assuage their hunger. But the W.P.A. and P.W.A. were still letters in the alphabet. Grand Central Station was overflowing with black M.A.'s and Ph.D.'s moonlighting to make ends meet. And with increasing frequency white faces began to appear beneath the red cap. The first of the year came and with it the second salary cut. As winter closed in on the campus Billy began having asthmatic attacks and had to be taken out of school for the third straight year. He was slowly falling behind in school, a fact which later on made him want to quit. As the attacks grew worse he was put to bed.

(*The lights come up on the bedroom.* BILLY *is in bed sleeping.* SHELDON *sits nearby reading. He has on his eye shade. Occasionally he glances toward* the bed. BILLY *begins to toss fitfully.* SHELDON *puts the book aside and goes to the bed. He takes* BILLY's *hands then feels his forehead. His face shows alarm. He crosses quickly to the door and calls)*

SHELDON   Willa. *(no answer)* Willa.
WILLA   Yes.
SHELDON   Come quickly. *(he turns to the bed)*
WILLA *(entering)*   What is it?
SHELDON   The fever seems to be getting worse. Feel his head.
WILLA *(after doing so)*   Yes, he's burning up.
SHELDON   Stay here. I'm going to call the doctor.
WILLA   Try the infirmary. He's usually there this time of evening.
SHELDON   I'll be back as quickly as I can. *(He grabs his coat on the run and dashes out of the house)*
BILLY   Mama.
WILLA   Yes, baby.
BILLY   I'm hot. Can I have some water?
WILLA   All right. *(she pours out a glass)* Here you are. (BILLY *sits up.* WILLA *holds the glass to his mouth and puts her arm around his back.* BILLY *drains the glass)*
BILLY   More!
WILLA   No. That's enough. Lie back and go to sleep.
BILLY   I can't—it's too hot. *(he throws off the bedcover)* Can't you open a window?
WILLA *(covering him)*   No. I'd create a draft. Lie back now and try to sleep till the doctor comes. He'll give you something that'll make you feel better.
BILLY   I'll try. *(he lies back.* WILLA *straightens the cover.* DAVID *and* JULIAN *stick their heads in the door)*
JULIAN   How's Billy?
WILLA   Ssh—*(she motions them to keep quiet and go into the hall. She follows. In the hallway)* His temperature's up.
DAVID   Much?
WILLA   A whole lot.
DAVID   What you going to do?
WILLA   Your father's gone for Dr. Bowen.
JULIAN   Is Billy ever going to get well? Seems like he gets sick every winter.
DAVID   Well, at least he gets to miss school.
JULIAN   What's he got, mama?
WILLA   Asthma and his tonsils are bad.

JULIAN   Can't they cure it?
WILLA   Sometimes. But mostly people have to grow out of it.
DAVID   I wish we could do something for him.
WILLA   You can—pray. (JULIAN *and* DAVID *look at each other)*
DAVID   Yes'm.
WILLA   It's time you were doing your homework. Go into your room and no fighting tonight, please.
JULIAN   Okay.

(They go into their room across the hall. The light comes on. We see them going about the routine of getting school books, notes, etc. and settling down at their desk. WILLA *goes back into the sick room and settles into a rocker. For a moment all is quiet, broken only by the soft squeak of the rocker.* WILLA *closes her eyes and hums softly to herself)*

JULIAN   David—you going to pray for Billy?
DAVID   I spose. You?
JULIAN *(nods)*   What you going to say?
DAVID   I don't know.
JULIAN   It's kind of hard, ain't it.
DAVID   Isn't it.
JULIAN *(starts to argue but remembers his promise)*   Isn't it? To pray I mean?
DAVID   Awfully hard.
JULIAN *(after a pause)*   You spose it'll really help?
DAVID   Mama thinks it will—but I don't know. Seems like that's all our folks do—is pray.
JULIAN   I don't guess it'd do no harm. *(pause)* Would the Lord's prayer do?
DAVID   We say that every night.
JULIAN *(helplessly)*   Yeah—*(pause)*
DAVID   But I spose it's better'n nothing. At the end you could add a couple of lines like "an please help our little brother to get well."
JULIAN *(repeating)*   "an please help our little brother get well"—Thanks, David.
DAVID   That's okay. *(they resume their studies.* BILLY *has begun to toss fitfully. Suddenly he starts to scream)*
BILLY   Mama, mama.
WILLA *(putting her arms around him)*   Here I am, baby. I'm right here with you.
BILLY   Mama, mama—
WILLA   I'm here, Billy, here. (BILLY *tries to force his way out of bed, screaming and waving his arms.* DAVID *and* JULIAN *are on their feet)*

The Tumult and the Shouting

BILLY Save them! Save them! They're drowning!

WILLA No one's drowning, baby. You're here with mama.

BILLY Save David—save Julian. They're in the river. Don't let them drown.

WILLA They're in their room, Billy. They're here with us.

BILLY No. They've gone swimming again. Down in the river. Down in the Appomatox.

WILLA David, Julian, come here! (DAVID and JULIAN *enter the room*)

WILLA Here they are, Billy. Here they are. See they're safe. They're right here.

BILLY (*suddenly sobbing*) Ohhhh—Ohhhh—they're gone.

WILLA No, baby, they're here. Can't you see them?

BILLY (*moaning*) They're gone—they're gone.

WILLA Oh, my god.

DAVID He's out of his head, mama. He's delirious from the fever.

JULIAN (*becoming frightened*) He's gonna die. He's gonna die!

WILLA (*sharply*) Don't talk like that.

BILLY Miss Phillips—Miss Phillips!

JULIAN He's calling his teacher.

BILLY Miss Phillips—Miss Phillips.

DAVID Mama, what are we going to do?

WILLA (*struggling to contain* BILLY) Julian, run to the infirmary. Get your father. Hurry! (JULIAN *hurries out of the room*) Help me, David. Help me to hold him. (DAVID *goes to the bed*)

BILLY David, David! Save Miss Phillips. Save Miss Phillips.

DAVID (*starting to cry*) I'll save her, Billy—I'll save her.

BILLY Ohhhh—ohhhh—

WILLA Go to the bathroom. Bring me a wet cloth. (DAVID *runs down the hall and returns almost immediately*) Put it on his forehead. (*he does so.* BILLY *continues to sob. Below,* SHELDON, *the* DOCTOR, *and* JULIAN *enter*)

SHELDON Upstairs, doctor. (*the three of them ascend the stairs to the bedroom*)

WILLA (*as they enter*) He's delirious, doctor.

(*The doctor makes a quick examination feeling* BILLY'*s hands and forehead*)

SHELDON David, you and Julian wait outside. (DAVID *and* JULIAN *leave, go down the hall and enter their room*)

DOCTOR Hand me my bag, Mrs. Sheldon. (WILLA *hands him the bag. The* DOCTOR *removes a hypodermic needle*) I'm going to give him a sedative. (*he holds the syringe up to the light, squeezes it, then places it on the table in a piece of cotton. He then removes a bottle of alcohol and a swab of cotton and begins to clean* BILLY'*s arm. He then makes the injection.* BILLY *flinches slightly*) Now he'll sleep. (*he puts the cotton, alcohol, and hypodermic needle back into the bag*)

WILLA Doctor, what's wrong with him?

DOCTOR Tonsillitis and he's got a very high fever, Mrs. Sheldon. His tonsils are badly infected as I told you. They'll have to come out soon or his heart may be damaged. I just hope we haven't put it off too long.

SHELDON Will that stop the asthma too?

DOCTOR That I can't say. But it certainly won't make it any worse. I'm going to give you a prescription for the fever and something to reduce the inflammation. Where can I write?

SHELDON Downstairs in the living room, doctor. (JULIAN *and* DAVID *appear in the hallway. The* DOCTOR *goes down*)

DAVID Daddy?

SHELDON Yes, David.

DAVID Can we go in?

SHELDON No. You'd better not. (*he starts down*)

JULIAN Daddy?

SHELDON Yes (*a bit impatient*)

JULIAN How is he?

SHELDON Don't bother me now, boys. I'm busy.

DAVID (*calling after him*) Is he going to be all right? (SHELDON *does not answer.* JULIAN *and* DAVID *turn and go back down the hall.* SHELDON *enters the living room*)

DOCTOR He'll be all right now, Professor. (*hands him the prescription*) Here you are. Have this filled right away. I think he'll be all right now but if you need me, don't hesitate to call. (*glancing around*) You have a telephone, don't you?

SHELDON There's a pay phone in Old Main. I can get the night watchman to let me in.

DOCTOR Fine. (*he shakes hands with* SHELDON *and leaves.* SHELDON *accompanies him to the front door*) Uh, professor.

SHELDON Yes, doctor.

DOCTOR I mean it.

SHELDON What will an operation cost?
DOCTOR Let's not talk about that now. The main thing is Billy's health.
SHELDON Thank you, doctor.
DOCTOR Well, good night. (*he goes.* SHELDON *stands there examining the two prescriptions as* WILLA *comes down the stairs*)
WILLA He's asleep.
SHELDON (*showing her the prescriptions*) I'm going to get these filled.
WILLA Mister—
SHELDON Yes?
WILLA What about the operation?
SHELDON I don't know—
WILLA (*exasperated*) You don't know what?
SHELDON I don't know where the money's coming from—that's all.

(*He puts on his hat and coat and goes out the front door as the lights fade*)

Scene Six   End of the Processional

DAVID Somehow Billy survived and somehow money was found for the operation. I didn't know it at the time but they cashed in an insurance policy. Things didn't get better. They got worse. By my senior year in high school the biggest bank in the city had closed and the teachers had received still another salary cut. Things were at rock bottom. I knew my dream of going away to college was impossible. I would have to remain at home. In March the Squire of Hyde Park moved into the White House and the fireside chats began. Abroad rumblings and flashes of lightning along the Rhine.
JULIAN (*off*) Hey, David!
DAVID And now it's time for me to become an active part of the story.

(*The lights dim.* JULIAN *continues to call in the darkness*)

JULIAN Hey, David. David!
DAVID Yeah!
JULIAN Where are you?
DAVID Upstairs.

(*The lights dim up and* JULIAN *is seen bounding up the stairs, two at a time*)

DAVID (*as* JULIAN *enters the bedroom*) What's up?
JULIAN Mutt Johnson's recruiting guys for summer work.
DAVID Virginia Beach?
JULIAN Yeah.
DAVID How much?
JULIAN Fifteen dollars a month, room and board.
DAVID What the hell—that ain't no money.
JULIAN Waiting table or hoppin bells—He says you'll pick up a hundred a month in tips.
DAVID I'm still for going to Atlantic City or Asbury Park.
JULIAN Man, you sure are on that up north kick. Why?
DAVID You can make more.
JULIAN Says who?
DAVID Pretty Boy Jones.
JULIAN You believe him? He's the biggest damn liar in school.
DAVID And then there's more to do when you're off work. The Beach hasn't got more'n a couple places where colored can go and they're dumps.
JULIAN That's true.
DAVID And in upstate Jersey you can tell a paddy to go to hell. On the beach, those peckerwoods will climb up side your head in a minute.
JULIAN But what'll the old man say? It's pretty far from home.
DAVID He won't like the idea.
JULIAN I'm for going anyhow.
DAVID You mean just up and leave?
JULIAN Sure. He'll get over it.
DAVID Man, there ain't nothin to do around this place in the summer. No decent jobs *or* chicks. Nothin. I sure am fed up with staying here year around.
JULIAN Me, too. (*pause*) Well, what we going to do?
DAVID Let's talk it over with Mama. Maybe she'll talk to Daddy.
JULIAN What the hell makes you think she'll approve?
DAVID She's more realistic. Always was.
JULIAN And if she says no?
DAVID Don't count your chickens—
JULIAN Well, I can tell you what I'm going to do—I'm going someplace upstate or downstate—I ain't spending the summer here.
DAVID (*uncertainly*) Aunt Mamie has promised me a job in the library.
JULIAN How much can you draw out?

DAVID   Nothing til next year's tuition is paid.
JULIAN   How you going to get any new togs?
DAVID   Daddy will have to buy 'em.
JULIAN   With what?
DAVID   Damn if I know.
JULIAN   Well then?
DAVID   Okay, you win.
JULIAN   Where's Mama?
DAVID   In the kitchen.
JULIAN   Okay, let's go. (*they descend the stairs in silence and enter the kitchen*)
WILLA   Too soon for dinner, boys.
JULIAN   Mama, can we talk to you?
WILLA   Something wrong?
JULIAN   No, ma'm. We just want to talk.
DAVID   Sit down, Mama. You look tired.
WILLA   What are you two up to?
DAVID   Go ahead, Julian.
JULIAN   Huh?
DAVID   Go ahead. Tell her.
JULIAN   I thought you were going to do the talking.
WILLA   Look. Your father will be coming home soon. (*starts to rise*) I've got to finish supper.
DAVID   Wait, Mama. It'll only take a minute.
WILLA (*resuming her seat*)   Well—
DAVID   Mama, Julian and I want to go off this summer.
WILLA   Off? Where?
DAVID   Some place to work.
WILLA   But you've already got a job. (*silence*) Where do you want to go?
JULIAN   To the beach.
WILLA   I see. (*pause*) You'll have to ask your father.
JULIAN   That's just it, Mama. We want you to ask him.
WILLA   What makes you think *I* approve of you going? (*silence*) Why do you want to go?
DAVID   To make some real dough. I need clothes when I enter college next fall.
JULIAN   And I need clothes period.
WILLA   I see—
JULIAN   Will you do it, Mama?
WILLA   I'll have to think about it.—You're both so young.
DAVID   Oh, Mama, don't start that. That's why we've got to get away. People around here treat us like children. Little David and Little Julian. We'll never grow up if we stay here.
JULIAN   Yeah, I can't even walk a girl home from school before some old bat is over here tattling to you.
DAVID   And then you and Daddy are always telling us to remember that we are a college professor's sons. We can never relax.
JULIAN   And then look at it this way, Mama. With me and David gone you won't have to have as many mouths to feed for a couple of months.
WILLA (*smiling*)   Well—
DAVID   Please, Mama—
WILLA (*sighing*)   All right. (*the boys are elated*) It's hard for me to realize you're growing up. And three months isn't such a long time. I'll speak to him as soon as he comes home.
JULIAN   Thanks, Mama.
DAVID   Thanks, Mama.
WILLA   You'd better hold your thanks until after.
DAVID   Thanks anyhow.
WILLA   Now I've got to finish dinner. (*she goes back into the kitchen*)
JULIAN   That was easy.
DAVID   What'd I tell you?
JULIAN   Solid, Jack, solid. (*they shake hands*)
DAVID   And she'll handle daddy, too.
JULIAN (*as they go upstairs*)   Boardwalk here I come!

(*They disappear down the hall chattering. A pause.* SHELDON *enters the front door. He looks old and tired. He carries a brief case bulging with papers. He removes his hat and coat and hangs them on the hall tree*)

SHELDON   Willa, I'm home.
WILLA   Supper'll be ready soon.
SHELDON   There's no hurry. I'm not going out tonight.
WILLA   There's a telegram on the table. Came about three o'clock.
SHELDON   I suspect it's from my publisher. (*he opens the telegram, reads it several times, then slumps on the divan*)
WILLA (*entering*)   Bad news?
SHELDON (*nodding*)   From the publisher. They're going out of business. The company which bought them out has declined to handle my book so they're shipping me the balance of the printing. Eight hundred and fifty copies.
WILLA   Too bad.
SHELDON (*wearily*)   I've been expecting it. Oh, well—at least the college will continue to

use it. Maybe I can find another publisher before the supply is exhausted.

WILLA Do you really think you can?

SHELDON I don't know, Willa. I don't know.

WILLA Well, at least I've got some good news.

SHELDON What's that?

WILLA I've got a job.

SHELDON Where?

WILLA Here on the campus as assistant house director of Craig Hall.

SHELDON You're going to be a dormitory matron?

WILLA Yes. At seventy dollars a month. They couldn't find a replacement for Mrs. Billings so—

SHELDON Mrs. Billings—you're going to be a night matron.

WILLA From four until closing time.

SHELDON That's hard work, Willa, hard work, running up and down those steps, answering calls, keeping the girls quiet.

WILLA We need the money. And it may lead to something better.

SHELDON Yes, we need the money and it'll be a long time before I get my salary back, not to speak of a raise.

WILLA Mrs. Givens will come in each afternoon at three-thirty.

SHELDON (*wearily*) All right. (*silence*)

WILLA Mister, what do you think of the boys going off to work this summer?

SHELDON Going off?

WILLA Yes.

SHELDON David's got a job in the library and Julian doesn't need to work. He'll have to go to summer school if he's to graduate with his class next year.

WILLA They're set on doing it.

SHELDON Why? Why are they so anxious to leave home?

WILLA They're at that stage.

SHELDON But they're too young. And they've lived on the campus all their lives. They don't know anything about the outside world.

WILLA Maybe it's time for them to find out.

SHELDON They'll find out soon enough. (*silence*) Where do they want to go?

WILLA The Beach.

SHELDON Which beach?

WILLA I don't know. You'll have to ask them.

SHELDON I will not ask them. They should have come to me directly anyhow instead of bothering you.

WILLA To tell you the truth, Mister, I think they're afraid of you.

SHELDON Afraid of me? Why? Haven't I been a good father—a good provider?

WILLA (*nodding*) Of course you have. But you haven't spent much time with them in recent years.

SHELDON I haven't had much time to spend.

WILLA When you come home you go directly to your room. And after dinner you go back to the office.

SHELDON But I've always been here when they really needed me.

WILLA That's just it. Their problems are not really big problems, but it's awfully important to be able to talk to someone. That's why they always come to me first. (*pause*) What shall I tell them?

SHELDON Tell them—No. I'll tell them. (*he crosses to the stairs*)

WILLA Don't lose your temper. (*she goes into the kitchen.* SHELDON *ascends the stairs and enters the boys' bedroom*)

SHELDON (*entering*) May I come in?

DAVID Hello, Daddy. Sure.

SHELDON May I sit down? I've been on my feet all day.

JULIAN Sure. Sit here. (*he dumps clothes from a chair*)

SHELDON You really should hang them up.

JULIAN (*picking up clothes*) Yes, sir.

SHELDON Your mother tells me you want to leave us this summer. That right?

DAVID We want to work—yes, sir.

SHELDON What's the matter? Don't you like your home? Getting tired of us?

DAVID Oh, no, sir.

SHELDON Why then?

DAVID We need clothes, Daddy.

SHELDON What's the matter with the clothes you have?

DAVID They're out of style, everybody's wearing English togs now.

SHELDON That why you want to go off, Julian?

JULIAN Yes, sir. And this campus is a pretty dead place in summer after you've been here all the year round. It's not like living in Richmond or Norfolk.

SHELDON This is your home.

JULIAN Yes, sir. But we never get to go any place. We stay here year in and year out—we don't even take vacations.

SHELDON I can't afford them.

JULIAN I'm not blaming you. We know you're doing the best you can.

SHELDON What do you know about working? Have you ever waited table? Worked in a hotel?

DAVID We can learn quickly enough. There's nothing complicated about it. And there'll be enough guys from the college around to show us the ropes.

SHELDON It's not the kind of life for sixteen and seventeen-year-old boys.

JULIAN I don't mind hard work.

DAVID Neither do I.

JULIAN If you stood it when you were our age, we can too.

SHELDON It's not a decent life either. All kinds of immoral things go on at those beach hotels, bootlegging, prostitution, gambling—

JULIAN You saw them didn't you?

SHELDON Yes.

JULIAN Well, it didn't make you immoral.

SHELDON I was older, much older. And I had to do it. There were my sisters and brothers who relied on me.

DAVID You've always said that nothing could overcome good home training. Why are you so afraid that we'll go astray?

SHELDON I didn't say that.

DAVID But you implied it.

SHELDON I'm only trying to suggest that it's not so glamorous as you've been made to believe.

JULIAN I'm not going for glamour. I'm going for money.

SHELDON Watch your tone, young man.

JULIAN (*defensively*) Well, I mean it.

SHELDON Now, I've had about enough of this. I'm trying to reason with you but if you won't listen to reason so be it. You're not going to the beach or any place else to work next summer. You, David, are going to work in the library. And you, Julian, are going to summer school to remove those deficiencies you've been piling up for the last three years.

JULIAN Oh, no I'm not.

SHELDON What did you say?

JULIAN Tell him, David.

SHELDON David?

DAVID We want to help, Daddy, in our own way.

SHELDON You mean you're going without my approval?

DAVID I'm sorry, Daddy, but that's the way we see it.

SHELDON You go and you're gone for good.

JULIAN That's all right with me.

DAVID Shut up, Julian!

SHELDON That's the way you feel, is it?

DAVID I just don't see why we've got to argue about it. That's all.

SHELDON (*strangely calm*) Arguing? I'm not arguing. I'm still your father and as long as you're in this house, I expect you to obey. When the day comes that you can't, you're welcome to leave.

DAVID (*after looking at* JULIAN) We're still going, Daddy.

(SHELDON *looks at them for a moment, starts to speak but suppresses the impulse. He goes out quietly, slowly pausing at the door to look at them once more. He descends the stairs slowly, thoughtfully.* WILLA *is waiting*)

WILLA Supper is ready. (SHELDON *passes without speaking and enters the living room*) Mister, supper is ready. (SHELDON *does not respond*) What happened?

SHELDON My own sons are defying me.

WILLA Oh.

SHELDON They can go if they like, I'm through with them, for good.

WILLA You don't mean that.

SHELDON I do mean it. And as long as I'm supporting them they'll do as I say, When they don't, they go.

WILLA You can't dictate their lives.

SHELDON Am I wrong in wanting them here at home?

WILLA I didn't say that. But you've got to begin to treat them as men. They'll be leaving us for good in a few years anyhow. I'm just trying to face reality.

SHELDON And what is the reality?

WILLA That they're men—that they're grown up right under your nose without you realizing it. I tried to warn you. I begged you to spend more time with them.

SHELDON So what am I to do? Go back up there? Beg their pardon? Tell them I didn't mean what I said?

WILLA Tell them the truth.
SHELDON What truth?
WILLA That you want them here at home with you. That you want them to continue to lean on you. That you don't want them to grow up.
SHELDON But I do.
WILLA Do you? I don't. I dread the day they'll leave this house for good. But I know it's coming. So I want them here with me as long as possible.
SHELDON Must I eat crow?
WILLA You'll lose them for good if you don't.
(*After a long pause* SHELDON *walks slowly to the staircase*)
SHELDON Willa, there are times when I feel as if I've never known you.
WILLA Mister, there are times when I think you never have.

(*The lights fade and the curtain closes*)

ACT TWO

Scene One   The Recessional

(*Music rises with the curtain and continues until* DAVID *appears*)

DAVID The war came. Julian and I were drafted. Billy tried to join up but was rejected. He stayed home, finished college, and got a job as a mail carrier. Lots of college grads did that. It beat teaching and there wasn't much else a black man could do in those days. Somehow my mother and father had stuck it out. He is now seventy, still vigorous but seventy. Mother, fifteen years his junior, is a beautiful middle-aged woman. There is a great serenity about their lives. Having grown tired of fighting, they take each other for granted. There are still occasional flareups but they don't mean anything. But now, two years after the war they are going to face the greatest crisis of their lives.

(*The lights come up on the house.* WILLA *is busy preparing the evening meal. The* PROFESSOR *enters slowly, stopping in the hallway to remove his coat and hat*)

WILLA That you, Mister?
SHELDON Yes.
WILLA Supper'll be ready in a little while. I just got in.
SHELDON Something the matter?
WILLA No. Relief was late coming on. Any mail for me?
SHELDON Yes, one. I'll leave it on the table. (*he drops the letter on the hall table and continues upstairs, carrying his briefcase and other mail. He sits down in the rocking chair and begins thumbing through the letters. One catches his attention. He holds it up to the light, carefully tears it open and reads it slowly. Shock, dismay, and disbelief creep into his face. Finally, he rises in anger*) Willa!
WILLA (*downstairs*) What is it?
SHELDON Come here, please. (WILLA *wipes her hand on her apron, leaves the kitchen and ascends the stairs*)
WILLA (*entering the bedroom*) Something wrong?
SHELDON (*handing her the letter*) Read this. (*he crosses to the front window and stares out*)
WILLA (*glancing at the signature*) From the President? (SHELDON *does not answer.* WILLA *reads*)
WILLA (*as she finishes*) It's come.
SHELDON You were expecting this? (WILLA *nods*)
WILLA Mrs. Willis received her retirement notice this morning. It upset her so she couldn't come to work. Notices went out yesterday following the Board meeting. You didn't pick up your mail this morning?
SHELDON No.
WILLA It's been there all day—(*silence*)
SHELDON What am I to do?
WILLA Do?
SHELDON Yes. I can't retire now. I've nothing to retire on.
WILLA You'll have your pension.
SHELDON Eighty-five dollars a month. We can't live on that. I've got no savings.
WILLA I'll still be working.
SHELDON (*slowly*) That's right. They're not firing you, are they?
WILLA (*trying to be pleasant*) I've a little while longer.
SHELDON Fifteen years. A whole lifetime. (*pause*) So now you're going to take care of me.
WILLA I wish you wouldn't look at it that way.

SHELDON How should I look at it?
WILLA We should both be grateful that I can still work.
SHELDON So can I work—I'm not an invalid.
WILLA I didn't mean it that way. (*pause*) They want the house in August.
SHELDON Yes. The job and the house, just like that.
WILLA We've known it was coming—ever since the college joined the Retirement System.
SHELDON Somehow I couldn't believe it. Somehow I just couldn't believe they'd retire me—after all these years of not caring what went on over here—just as they do at the other state colleges. Time was you could teach here until you dropped.
WILLA You thought they'd let you go on teaching past seventy?
SHELDON Why not? The least I expected was the same treatment as Dr. Stanley. He's still living on campus and has an office in the library.
WILLA But after all, he was the president for more than thirty years.
SHELDON Don't we count? We teachers?
WILLA You know the answer to that.
SHELDON No, I don't. They buy us for a dime a dozen. Then when they're through with us they kick us out no matter how much service we've given—or how unprepared we are for it.
WILLA (*after a pause*) Well, we'd better start looking.
SHELDON For what?
WILLA A house. It'll take some doing to find one. A decent one.
SHELDON You mean accept this? (*pointing to the letter*)
WILLA What else can you do? You *are* seventy.
SHELDON I'm not so sure.
WILLA But the law is specific, optional retirement at sixty-five, compulsory at seventy.
SHELDON I'm talking about *my* age.
WILLA (*perplexed*) What?
SHELDON You remember I've always had some doubt about how old I actually am.
WILLA (*nodding*) Yes.
SHELDON And I indicated as much at the time I filled out the retirement forms?
WILLA I don't remember.

SHELDON That'll give me a fighting chance —perhaps as much as two more years.
WILLA I doubt it.
SHELDON At least it's worth a try. They owe me that much after thirty years.
WILLA Mister, those white people on the Board don't care about you.
SHELDON Perhaps not. But they'll listen to the President. They'll do anything he says—or almost anything.
WILLA I don't know—
SHELDON Why else would they have made him President—an ignorant, unknown, itinerant teacher-trainer, elevated to the presidency of a college?
WILLA That's why.
SHELDON What?
WILLA He follows orders.
SHELDON But he knows how to get what he wants. If he'd been a general during the war the Germans wouldn't have had a chance. He may be an Uncle Tom but he's a shrewd one.
WILLA You mean you would go to him? Ask his help?
SHELDON Yes.
WILLA A man you despise?
SHELDON Yes.
WILLA I can't believe it. He'll make you crawl. He knows what you think of him.
SHELDON Yes.
WILLA What makes you think he'd want to fight for you?
SHELDON I don't. I think he'll be flattered I've come to him at all. I never have before.
WILLA (*slowly*) He'll make you lick his boots.
SHELDON (*desperately*) I know it. But I can't retire now. I simply can't afford to retire now.
WILLA And I simply can't believe it. I simply can't believe it. A man whose pride made him leave Mississippi. (*pause*) If it's money you're worried about, Julian and David will help.
SHELDON They've got their own families— and I've always promised myself that I would never be a burden to them.
WILLA Billy will help.
SHELDON What's he got? A monthly paycheck which he spends on liquor and women.
WILLA But we don't need much. My salary and your pension will take care of us.
SHELDON For how long? Will it buy us a house?

WILLA (*quietly*) Does teaching mean so much to you?

SHELDON It means a great deal.

WILLA Then apply to one of the private colleges. I'm sure you could get on at one of them.

SHELDON I don't want to get on at one of them. I'm needed here.

WILLA All right, Mister, do what you want to do. I just don't think it'll do much good.

SHELDON Thanks for encouraging me.

WILLA (*starts to answer then changes her mind*) I've got to finish supper.

(*She goes out and down the stairs.* SHELDON *goes to his bureau and opens the bottom drawer. He removes a small black strong box which he places on the bed. Opening the box with a key on his chain, he hurriedly rifles through the contents. Finally he discovers what he is looking for and his face lights up. He moves quickly to his desk and proceeds to write a letter. The lights fade on him and come up on the kitchen below as* HARRIET *enters*)

HARRIET Mama, guess what?

WILLA What?

HARRIET Guess?

WILLA I've no idea.

HARRIET I've been invited to Roanoke for a party.

WILLA That's nice. By whom?

HARRIET Bobby's mother and father. I'm dying to go. Can I?

WILLA Ask your father.

HARRIET Right away. (*she starts out*)

WILLA Harriet, I don't think right now is a good time.

HARRIET Why?

WILLA Your father's being retired.

HARRIET Oh?

WILLA He's awfully upset.

HARRIET Doesn't he want to retire? He's worked so hard all his life.

WILLA No.

HARRIET Why? Isn't he seventy?

WILLA Yes and no.

HARRIET (*puzzled*) What?

WILLA He's never really known his age. Birth records of colored people weren't kept in South Carolina when he was born.

HARRIET What about Aunt Thelma? Wouldn't she know?

WILLA Yes but then it would be hard to prove. All the old records, the family Bible and papers were lost—burned in a fire years ago. It'd be guesswork.

HARRIET That's too bad.

WILLA We've never been able to save much on the little he's made—never even bought a home. We couldn't. I tried to warn him several times we should get ready but he wouldn't listen to me. And now it's come. We've got to give up the house by August. I just don't know what we're going to do.

HARRIET Don't you think after the shock's worn off he'll be all right?

WILLA No. He's going to appeal.

HARRIET But that'll only postpone it for a year or so even if he wins.

WILLA I know. (*pause*) So you see, I don't think you'd better ask him about Roanoke right now. Maybe tomorrow or the next day—

HARRIET (*disappointed*) I'll tell Bobby I can't go.

WILLA No, don't do that. When's it to be?

HARRIET A week from next Friday.

WILLA How soon must he know?

HARRIET He didn't say.

WILLA Then let's wait a day or two. If you must, explain to Bobby why you have to wait.

HARRIET Okay.

WILLA Set the table for me, will you baby, while I get your father.

HARRIET Will Billy be home?

WILLA I don't know. Haven't seen him all day. But you might as well set a place for him although I suspect he's at Mary Kay's.

HARRIET Lord, what he sees in that girl I don't know.

WILLA Now, baby—

HARRIET She's nothing but a tramp.

WILLA (*gently*) Go ahead and set the table.

(WILLA *leaves the kitchen and ascends the stairs.* HARRIET *proceeds to set the table. The lights come on in the bedroom.* WILLA *enters*)

SHELDON (*looking*) Oh, Willa, I was just getting ready to call you.

WILLA Supper's ready.

SHELDON Listen to this. It'll only take a minute. (WILLA *sits on the bed*) "Dear *Doctor* (*clearing his throat contemptuously*) hunh—Walker: I am writing to ask reconsideration of the action taken on yesterday by the Board of Visitors, placing me on permanent retirement as of August 1 of this year. Five years ago at the time of our joining the State Retirement System I indicated that I was uncertain of the exact year of my birth. The age which I listed on the membership application was a guess. Therefore, in view of the uncertainty concerning my age, I respectfully request that any action regarding my retirement be delayed until I can appear before the Board. Please consider this letter a formal request for a hearing on the matter. (*he swallows*) Knowing that you will be sympathetic to my position, I will greatly appreciate anything you can do to assist me. Very respectfully yours, David Sheldon, Senior."

WILLA All right—I suppose—
SHELDON Well, is it or isn't it?
WILLA It must have hurt you to write the last line, didn't it?
SHELDON It doesn't hurt to be courteous.
WILLA I remember when you would call it something else.
SHELDON What's the matter? You sound as if you want me to be retired?
WILLA No, I'd like to see you go on for as long as you want. But I hate to see you beat your head against a stone wall. Come on, supper's ready.
SHELDON Go ahead. I want to address the envelope. (WILLA *starts out but stops in the doorway*)
WILLA Oh, by the way—
SHELDON Yes? (*he's writing*)
WILLA Harriet has an invitation to spend next weekend in Roanoke with the Nelsons. (SHELDON *nods*) What do you think? (*he doesn't answer*) Mister?
SHELDON Yes—what?
WILLA What do you think?
SHELDON About what?—Oh, the invitation. Do what you think best.
WILLA You really mean that?
SHELDON (*looking up*) Why shouldn't I mean it?
WILLA Why, no reason at all. (*She leaves the room, pauses at the head of the stairs and looks back. The lights come up in the kitchen.* HARRIET *is seated at the table reading.* WILLA *descends the stairs thoughtfully and enters the kitchen.* HARRIET *puts the books aside*)
HARRIET Where's Daddy? Isn't he going to eat?
WILLA Yes.

HARRIET What's the matter, Mama, don't you feel well?
WILLA I'm all right. (*pause*) You can go.
HARRIET Hunh?
WILLA You can go—to Roanoke.
HARRIET (*delighted*) You mean *you* asked him? (WILLA *nods*) And he said yes?
WILLA *I* said yes. He left it up to me. He actually left it up to me.
HARRIET (*overjoyed*) Wonderful.
WILLA He's worried—that man's worried.
HARRIET Then maybe I oughtn't to go.
WILLA His whole nature's changing—giving up his pride and his parental authority—
HARRIET Maybe I shouldn't—
WILLA Don't you want to go?
HARRIET Yes, but it'll cost. And we don't have money to throw around.
WILLA Going to Roanoke is throwing money around?
HARRIET Well—(*pause. Then suddenly*)—I know, I'll get the money from Billy.
WILLA I wouldn't count on it. He's always broke.
HARRIET But he gets paid next week. I'll be right there when he cashes his check.
WILLA I wish Billy would pull himself together—go back to school or get married. He just doesn't seem to have any ambition. When he was little even though he was sickly he was the one who showed more promise than the others. But now—(*she gestures hopelessly*) I wonder what's keeping your father?

(*The lights come up on the staircase.* SHELDON *is descending the stairs the letter in his hand. As he passes the hall table he drops the letter on it. He stands there for a moment then picks the letter up reopens it and reads. When he finishes he slowly tears it to pieces and drops it on the table. He enters the kitchen*)

WILLA (*after he sits*) Will you say the grace, Mister?
SHELDON I tore it up.
WILLA You what?
SHELDON The letter. I tore it up.
WILLA You've decided not to appeal.
SHELDON No, not at all. It's just easier to deny a written request. I'm going in to see Walker in person. I'm going in with my hat in my hand and my pride in my hip pocket. But I'm going.

HARRIET Daddy—
WILLA Mister—
SHELDON Let us bow our heads. Gracious Lord . . .

(*The lights fade*)

Scene Two

DAVID He begged and won a year's reprieve. I can only imagine what must have occurred. A man who had never begged for anything. How he was able to humble himself and contain that fierce pride is something I'll never understand. Originally I had planned to describe what happened but since it happens again I've decided against it. You see, my father blindly believed that he was right and he was prepared to reenact the scene as often as necessary. Six months later he had done absolutely nothing about his retirement. In spite of the entreaties of Willa and inflated by his temporary victory, he ignored the omens and portents around him.

(*As the lights rise* WILLA *and* BILLY *are in the kitchen.* WILLA *is putting a meat loaf in the oven.* BILLY *is "high."*)

WILLA But why must you stay out all night, Billy?
BILLY I don't mean to, Mama, the time just flies. (*he gestures like a bird flying*)
WILLA (*sitting*) Where do you go? What do you do?
BILLY (*smiling*) I visit—people—and places—
WILLA (*insistently*) But there's no place to visit in Warwick. (BILLY *gestures vaguely*) Don't you know what people are saying, baby?
BILLY What people?
WILLA People on the campus.
BILLY I thought so. Well, I don't give a damn what they're saying—snoopin, prying busybodies.
WILLA They're saying all sorts of nasty things.
BILLY Like what?
WILLA That you stay drunk most of the time—that you're even drunk on the job.
BILLY It's true. They're threatening to fire me.
WILLA And that you're spending your nights at Mary Kay's—
BILLY How would they know that? What are they doing in that part of town—slumming?
WILLA Is it true, Billy? About Mary Kay, I mean?
BILLY (*nodding*) Yes.
WILLA Oh, my god.
BILLY I'm sorry, Mama. I can't help myself.
WILLA Why don't you marry the girl since you're sleeping with her?
BILLY Is that all there is to marriage, Mama?
WILLA Answer me.
BILLY She wants me to.
WILLA Then why don't you?
BILLY I don't know—I wouldn't make a good husband—for Mary Kay or anybody for that matter.
WILLA Why not?
BILLY Look at me. I'm an alcoholic—I've got chronic asthma—and I've got a father to worry about.
WILLA He's not your responsibility.
BILLY Honor thy father and mother—that's what you taught us.
WILLA If you want to honor your father, you'd think about yourself. Do you think your carousing and whoring is making it any easier for him during his last year?
BILLY No, I don't suppose it is.
WILLA Well then?
BILLY But then we've heard that all of our lives, haven't we? Think about your father, remember his position. Well, I have thought about it. I acted like a little gentleman—we all did. And what good's it done him. Here he is old, an old, old, man and nothing to show for it. No home, no savings, no nothing.
WILLA Think about your sister.
BILLY What about her?
WILLA What kind of example are you setting for her?
BILLY (*musing*) Dear, sweet little Harriet. Pretty innocent little Harriet.
WILLA She knows what's going on, Billy.
BILLY Only on the outside—not what's here. (*he touches his heart*) None of you do.
WILLA We all love you, Billy. Your life is your life. But living here we do worry about you.
BILLY Maybe I ought to move.
WILLA You still need someone to look after you, to fix your meals, to wash your clothes.

You know you've got to be careful, very careful. (*pause*) When have you seen the doctor?
BILLY   I—I can't remember.
WILLA   There you are. And with your constitution. Oh, Billy, I'm so worried about you.
BILLY   And I'm worried about you. What's going to happen to you when Dad—What's going to happen to Dad when he's no longer working? And what's going to happen to Harriet?
WILLA   Baby, baby—you're not to think about us. You must begin to think about yourself.

(HARRIET *enters from the outside carrying a load of school books*)

HARRIET (*in the hall*)   Anybody home?
WILLA (*calling*)   Back here.

(HARRIET *drops her books in the living room and enters the kitchen*)

HARRIET   The closer I get to finishing, the more I wonder if it's worth it.
WILLA   What's the matter?
HARRIET   Another term paper. Durn it—that makes four. I think all my teachers have gone stark, raving mad. I might as well move into the library.
BILLY   Want me to do a couple for you?
HARRIET   Aw, cut it out, Billy. It's not funny.
BILLY   I'm not kidding. I'll just dust off a couple of my old ones and give them to you.
HARRIET   I'll have you know I do my own work.
BILLY   My idealistic little sister.
WILLA   Children, children. (*she rises*) I've got to get dressed. Go on duty soon. Don't let the meat loaf burn. (*she leaves the kitchen and goes upstairs*)
BILLY   Hey, little sister, want a drink? (*he reaches inside his jacket*)
HARRIET   No, thank you.
BILLY (*after taking a swig*)   Harriet, are you still a virgin?
HARRIET (*shocked*)   Billy!
BILLY   Well, are you?
HARRIET   What business is it of yours?
BILLY (*harshly*)   Are you?
HARRIET (*startled*)   Yes.
BILLY   I don't believe you.
HARRIET   What you believe is your business.
BILLY   You don't drink you don't smoke, and you don't screw. Beautiful.
HARRIET   You're drunk.
BILLY (*nodding*)   I am.
HARRIET   Do you have to get that way in front of Mama?
BILLY   Nooo—I don't have to—in fact, I didn't intend to. It just happened.
HARRIET   Oh, Billy, Mama and Daddy are worried to death about you.
BILLY   And I'm worried to death about you, little sister.
HARRIET   I can take care of myself.
BILLY   Crap.
HARRIET   Well, I can.
BILLY   You're so idealistic. You've grown up so protected more so than we were—the wolves will eat you up alive.
HARRIET   I know a thing or two.
BILLY   I'll bet. Book learning and Mama's lectures. Some of these cats on the outside make a specialty of your type—pigmeat.
HARRIET   What do you want me to do? Become a sybarite so that I can be "hep?"
BILLY   That's an idea, but you'd never make it.
HARRIET   Well, what are you talking about?
BILLY   About life, little sister, about life. You're going to graduate next year and you'll be on your own. No mother and father to look after you. No profligate brother to embarrass you.
HARRIET   Billy, I—
BILLY   Don't be afraid of life, Harriet. Get away from this place. Don't stay here.
HARRIET   I intend to help Mama all I can.
BILLY   Do so but do so away from here—from this campus—from these—these niggers! They'll destroy you if you stay around here. This place is insidious—evil—it gets inside of you—turns you into the very devil and it'll destroy you—like it's destroying me.
HARRIET   Billy, what on earth are you talking about?
BILLY   About us—about our lives, we campus brats. David and Julian got away but I didn't. I couldn't. Innocent little kids, growing up in a fairyland—away from reality—protected from dirt and filth—living in a dream world where we don't even realize that we are black and despised. I was unprepared for the outside—the great beyond. It's mean and ugly.

And it's full of lustful men *and* women waiting to sap up little lambs like you and me.

HARRIET   I feel sorry for you, Billy.

BILLY   Don't, little sister. Don't feel sorry for me—just get away—leave.

HARRIET   Just like that.

BILLY   As soon as you can.

HARRIET   And the family?

BILLY   We'll survive and if we don't—who cares?

HARRIET   You've got me all confused. (*pause*) I want to leave when I finish, but when I think of Mama and Daddy and the struggle they've had—

BILLY   They'll go on struggling—

HARRIET   It just doesn't seem right. A lifetime of giving—and they don't even have a home to go to in their old age. What's it all about, Billy? What's it all mean? I've been protected as you say and I don't understand things like that.

BILLY   It means life's miserable, rotten rat race. Some make it, some don't. It means those that *can*, look out for number one and they survive. It means you can't give everything to everybody and keep nothing for yourself. Only God can do that and even he was crucified.

HARRIET   So what am I to do?

BILLY   Marry and be happy. Try to be happy. I wish I could love somebody enough to get married but sick as I am it wouldn't be fair to the girl. I'm practically a walking corpse. I'm no good to anybody—

HARRIET   But there are things you could do —there are people who could help you.

BILLY   But first I must admit I need help, right?

HARRIET   Yes.

BILLY   If I thought it was worth it, I'd go up to Burkeville this minute. If I thought it could help the folks I'd do it. But what's the use? They prop me up—rehabilitate me—and I'd still be Billy Sheldon, A.B., mail carrier.

HARRIET   Is being a mail carrier that bad?

BILLY   When you've dreamed of reaching the stars and your feet are mired in clay? All those years I had to stay home, you know, each winter when I had those attacks and they'd take me out of school? How I dreamed of becoming a great artist—a painter. I built another fairyland within the one in which we were living. Shimmering crystal palaces where all of us would live—Mama, Daddy, David, Julian, you, and me. Then the coughing would begin and the palaces would crumble, year after year until I was four years behind my class.

HARRIET   I remember.

BILLY   So many times I thought how nice it must be in heaven—I figured that I'd surely go there since I hadn't done anything wrong— and Mama was constantly praying over me. Many times as I crossed the Campbell Street bridge I'd stand looking at the water remembering Langston Hughes' poem: "The cool, calm face of the river, asked me for a kiss."

HARRIET   No, Billy, don't ever do that.

BILLY   But then when I'd look down expecting to see my reflection, I'd see that the waters were dirty and muddy and I'd remember all the filth and sewage that comes into the river below the bridge and I couldn't do it. I'm a coward, little sister. Along with everything else, your brother is a coward.

HARRIET   Oh, my brother, how I wish I could help you.

BILLY   Just move away from here, little sister. Don't let yourself get trapped the way I am.

(*The professor trudges wearily on from the direction of the campus. At the same time the lights come on in the upstairs bedroom.* WILLA *has finished dressing*)

SHELDON   (*as he enters*)   Willa? Willa, where are you?

WILLA   I'm upstairs, Mister.

(HARRIET *crosses to* BILLY, *stands behind him with a hand on his shoulder. He takes the hand without looking up. The lights fade on the kitchen. The* PROFESSOR *enters the bedroom*)

SHELDON   Here, read this.

WILLA   What is it?

SHELDON   Another notice that I'll have to vacate the house—that the one year extension of my contract will not be renewed.

WILLA   Then we'd better start looking.

SHELDON   What?

WILLA   I said we'd better start looking for a house.

SHELDON   I'm going to see a lawyer.

WILLA   There's nothing for you to see a lawyer about.

SHELDON   It's entirely possible that I can

establish a legal age which will allow me to continue to work.

WILLA Oh, Mister, we went through that before. That's why the Board gave you another year.

SHELDON But it's not fair.

WILLA I think they've been very fair.

SHELDON I'm not talking about my age. I'm talking about what they've done for Stanley.

WILLA He was the President.

SHELDON That's what I mean. Why should an exception be made for him?

WILLA (*shrugging*) Because he was the President.

SHELDON I don't begrudge him the house. Stanley is a grand old man, a real educator. But they have an obligation to me too. I've given just as much as he has.

WILLA Apparently they don't see it that way. Apparently that's not the way it's going to be.

SHELDON It's not right, I tell you, tossing a man aside like an old hat just because he's seventy. What's age got to do with how good a teacher you are? Some teachers ought to be retired when they're thirty.

WILLA But the system doesn't work that way.

SHELDON I don't feel seventy. Do I look seventy? My mind's clear, my heart's good. And I've got offers from several of the private schools.

WILLA Then take one.

SHELDON But don't you see, if I'm good enough to teach elsewhere then I'm good enough to teach here. Why should I move to Harper's Ferry or Lawrenceville when they need me here?

WILLA But it's no use protesting any more, Mister, believe me. We'd do better to get ready to move.

SHELDON You give in too easily, Willa.

WILLA Lawyers cost money—and you still have to pay even when you lose. (*she starts to leave*)

SHELDON I haven't finished. Where are you going?

WILLA Time to go on duty.

SHELDON Oh. Yes. How late will you be tonight?

WILLA Usual time, I hope. Dormitory closes at eleven. Don't wait up for me.

SHELDON I've got some papers to grade.

WILLA The meat loaf should be ready now. Harriet will serve you when you're ready.

SHELDON (*almost timidly*) Can—can't you eat with us?

WILLA No, I'm late. Don't want to keep the day hostess waiting.

SHELDON All right. (*he turns away*)

WILLA Goodnight. (*pause*)

SHELDON Goodnight, Willa.

(*The lights fade and the music rises*)

Scene Three

(*A few days later. A storm is threatening. Heavy masses of dark storm clouds have blotted out the sun. A steady wind is blowing. There is the sound of an automobile. It stops. A car door slams.* LAWYER CLARK *appears from the rear of the house and crosses to the front door. He rings the bell.* WILLA *appears from the kitchen*)

WILLA Oh, Lawyer Clark, come in. You needn't have come out with a storm threatening. And it's likely to be a cloudburst. The radio says we may get a little hail.

CLARK Well, I didn't want to keep the Professor waiting. (*he stamps his feet and enters the house*)

WILLA (*taking his coat and hat and putting them on the hall tree*) Go on in, Lawyer Clark, and have a seat. I'll get Mister.

(CLARK *enters the living room and sits.* WILLA *goes half way up the stairs and calls*)

WILLA Lawyer Clark is here.

SHELDON I'll be right down.

(WILLA *returns to the living room*)

WILLA Well, how is your family?

CLARK Fine, Miz Sheldon. They're all going just fine.

WILLA Let's see, the oldest boy finishes high school this year, doesn't he?

CLARK Yes, ma'm, he does.

WILLA How nice. And is he going to be a lawyer too?

CLARK I hope not, Miz Sheldon. I hope not. I'd rather he become a doctor or a dentist. Our people will get sick and call the doctor and if their teeth hurt they'll go to a dentist. But most of 'em don't know what a lawyer's for.

WILLA Well, I declare.

CLARK Yes, ma'm. Most of my work is in buying and selling real estate now. I don't get many cases to speak of.

(SHELDON *enters from above*)

SHELDON (*profusely*) Lawyer! Good to see you. (CLARK *rises*) Sit down. Can I get you something? Coffee? Tea?

CLARK No, thank you, Professor. It's started to rain and it may hail too. So I'd like to get off the streets since my tires—well, the treads are kinda thin.

SHELDON Of course.

CLARK I finally got an answer from the city clerk in Georgetown. Here it is.

SHELDON I don't have my glasses. What does it say?

CLARK Well, in brief, they have no record of your birth—no record of your family either.

SHELDON What about property—deeds, etc.

CLARK Nothing there either.

SHELDON But my parents and grandparents did own property. I know that.

CLARK Someone would have to go through the records. That'd mean employing a local lawyer. I couldn't go down there myself. It would be quite expensive and time consuming.

SHELDON I suppose it would.

CLARK The clerk suggests that most of the old families in South Carolina kept pretty careful records of births and deaths in the family Bible.

SHELDON Ours was lost in all the moving about and the church we attended was destroyed in a fire.

CLARK Sometimes the plantation owners kept records of their people.

SHELDON I wouldn't know where to begin.

CLARK That's too bad. Without any supporting evidence, Professor, I would advise against going to court. Without the records of someone we don't have much chance of establishing a younger age for you.

SHELDON But we do have a chance.

CLARK Is there anyone down there who knew your family—who knew you?

SHELDON (*shaking his head*) They're either dead or moved away long ago.

CLARK Then our chances are practically nil.

SHELDON So what am I to do?

CLARK Professor Sheldon, you still have a good many years left and you're a good teacher—I ought to know—you taught me.

(BILLY *comes to the front door, realizes that there are people in the living room and goes around to the back of the house*)

SHELDON Thank you.

CLARK I understand you've got some offers to teach. Why don't you take one?

SHELDON It would mean moving away, separating from my family.

CLARK You could commute to Richmond if you got on there.

SHELDON No.

CLARK Why not?

SHELDON At my age driving the round trip every day over the turnpike would leave me a nervous wreck. That highway traffic terrifies me. And I'd have to leave at daybreak to make an eight o'clock class.

CLARK Why?

SHELDON Thirty miles an hour is my speed limit.

CLARK (*laughing*) I see what you mean.

(BILLY *enters the kitchen, sits and listens*)

CLARK You'll need a house, won't you?

SHELDON If they make me give up this one. Yes.

CLARK How many rooms?

SHELDON Well, there's four of us—about the size of this one. We're accustomed to space.

CLARK As houses go this is a pretty big house. It'd be quite expensive even if you rent.

SHELDON But I can't afford to buy.

CLARK On the other hand you won't be getting any equity if you rent. It would be better in the long run to buy, Professor, and a small cottage.

SHELDON No, I'll need a big house so we won't get in each other's way.

CLARK The kids will all move away eventually—they always do. I was telling my wife the other day—

SHELDON Not Billy. He isn't well, as you know. (BILLY *reacts to this*) And what about the boys when they come to visit with their families? Where'll we put them?

CLARK You can always double up for a couple of weeks. I would strongly suggest that you buy a small house for you and Miz Sheldon. If you like I'll try to find one for you and we'll forget about my commission. I owe you that much.

SHELDON I'm very grateful to you, Lawyer Clark, and I'm very proud to have been your teacher. But I can't accept charity. (*he goes upstairs*)

CLARK Miz Sheldon, did I say something wrong? Wouldn't hurt the Professor's feelings for anything in the world. If I did I'll apologize.

WILLA He's naturally disappointed and a little sensitive right now. You were his last hope. But he'll get over it. No need to apologize—he's very fond of you.

CLARK I wish I could help him but—(*he gestures hopelessly*)

WILLA Don't blame yourself. He knows you've done everything you could.

CLARK Why won't he accept one of those teaching offers, Miz Sheldon?

WILLA He just can't believe that the college can get along without him after nearly thirty years. He wants to stay here where he can watch over things, be available should they ever need him.

CLARK It's an admirable thought—self sacrificial and all that—not many of the old teachers left like the Professor. But he's going to have to face up to it. They can and they will get along without him.

WILLA It's something that we've all got to face some day—isn't it?

CLARK Yes, ma'm. (*pause*) Well, I've got to go. (*he starts for the hall*) Shall I try to find a cottage?

WILLA Yes. I'll talk to Mister. I'm sure he'll appreciate what you're trying to do. (*she helps him with his overcoat*)

CLARK I'll get started on it right away. (SHELDON *reappears*)

WILLA And thank you for coming out. Be careful, now, driving home.

CLARK Yes, ma'm. Goodnight. (*he goes*)

SHELDON What's he going to get started on?

WILLA A cottage.

SHELDON You told him to go ahead?

WILLA Yes.

SHELDON Well, you just tell him you've changed your mind—I'm not leaving here. They'll have to carry me out. And I'll get another lawyer if need be. (*he disappears slamming the bedroom door*)

WILLA Oh, Mister. (*she shakes her head and wearily ascends the stairs to the bedroom. She pauses then enters the room*)

WILLA Mister, why won't you be reasonable? (*the door closes and the lights fade, shutting off the argument*)

(HARRIET *enters the front door. She goes immediately to the hall tree, removes her overcoat and hat. Entering the kitchen she sees* BILLY *sitting at the table staring into space*)

HARRIET Hi, Billy boy. (*he does not answer*) You passing? (*pause*) Billy, you all right? (*she crosses to him*)

BILLY What?

HARRIET Are you all right?

BILLY Yeah, I'm okay—just hungry. (*he shivers*) Is there a door open somewhere? It's chilly in here. I think there's a draft.

SHELDON I'm not blaming Clark. I'm sure he's done his best.

WILLA Then why?

SHELDON Because I'm not ready to give up.

HARRIET Billy, are you sure you're okay? (*he nods vaguely*)

BILLY I'll be all right when I get some food in me. I haven't eaten all day. (*he shivers*)

HARRIET No wonder. (*feeling his forehead*) Hey, you've got a fever.

BILLY You're crazy.

HARRIET Yes, you have. And you're probably coming down with something.

BILLY (*a little irritated*) I'm all right, I tell you.

WILLA You're just being stubborn—obstinate.

SHELDON I have other reasons.

WILLA What, for example?

HARRIET Why don't you go lie down on the sofa? I'll call you when supper's ready.

BILLY All right. (*he rises, staggers slightly*)

HARRIET I'm going to call the doctor.

BILLY No, no don't. Just let me lie down.

(*He moves slowly into the living room and eases on to the sofa.* HARRIET *watches at the door for a moment then returns to the kitchen. A pause, then the bedroom door opens and* WILLA *comes out into the hallway*)

WILLA I can't understand this sudden concern over Billy. (BILLY *sits up*)

SHELDON It's not so sudden.

WILLA He's a grown man.

SHELDON He's a sick man.
WILLA But he'll have to face the fact that we won't always be around to look after him.

(BILLY *sobs, rises, almost falls, and stumbles out the front door. He staggers off the* PORCH *and collapses in front of the house*)

SHELDON But where will he live?
WILLA I don't know—I just don't know. (*she descends the stairs into the hallway*) That's funny—I'm sure I closed that door. (*she closes the door and enters the kitchen*) Hello, baby, when did you come?
HARRIET Just now.
WILLA What're you doing?
HARRIET Fixing dinner for Billy.
WILLA Oh, will he be home tonight?
HARRRIET He's in the living room.
WILLA Oh, then he must have left the front door open.
HARRIET What?
WILLA The front door was open just now. I closed it.
HARRIET No—he was here when I got home.
WILLA Well, I declare—
HARRIET I wonder? (*She hurries into the living room followed by* WILLA)
WILLA What's the matter?
HARRIET (*in the living room*) He's gone.
WILLA And without closing the door—that boy.
HARRIET He's sick, Mama—he's got a fever.
WILLA And he went outside in this snow? What do you suppose?—(*they go out on the porch. As they reach the front steps* BILLY *groans.* WILLA *screams*) There he is. He's fallen. (*the two women rush to* BILLY. SHELDON *appears at the upstairs window*)
SHELDON What's going on out there?
HARRIET It's Billy, Daddy, he's collapsed.
SHELDON I'll be right down. (*he disappears from the window. The two women pick* BILLY *up laboriously between them and half carry, half drag him toward the porch*)
BILLY (*screaming*) No, no—leave me here. I want to die. I want to die.

(*Blackout*)

Scene Four

DAVID They took Billy to the hospital. He had come down with double pneumonia. Afterwards they took him to Burkeville when it was discovered that he had a spot on his lungs. (*musing*) Burkeville Sanatarium—the State Hospital for colored T.B. patients. Like Billy said, once you stepped off the campus you discovered you were black. In the spring I got an urgent letter from Mama asking me to come home—Daddy was deteriorating rapidly she said—had begun to drink. It made me miserable but I couldn't go. I promised I'd spend the month of August with them before going on my leave of absence from Douglass U. I had decided it was time to start on my Ph.D. What happened during the ensuing months I'll never know. When I arrived in August things were in a bad way—Mama looked twenty years older. My father had written to the Board over the President's objection. Of course they turned him down. The President was so incensed he threatened to take Mama's job but later he recanted when she assured him there would be no repetition of the incident. Daddy's occasional drinking had increased and he was no longer rational about his inevitable retirement although he was perfectly lucid about other things. When I arrived he insisted that I go in to see the President with him. Somehow he had gotten the notion that I could work a miracle. He was sadly mistaken. Against my better judgment I consented. I wish now I hadn't.

(*The lights fade. In the darkness* SHELDON'S *voice is heard*)

SHELDON David, David.
DAVID I'm on the porch, Dad.
SHELDON (*entering*) It's awfully hot, isn't it?
DAVID Yes.
SHELDON And those fans inside don't seem to help at all.
DAVID No. August is always fierce.
SHELDON They tell me that some people are beginning to use air conditioning in their homes.
DAVID Yes.
SHELDON How the world has changed—is changing—I almost feel lost. (*pause*) Would you like a little something before we go?
DAVID Something to drink you mean?
SHELDON No thanks. (*pause*) Well, shall we plan our strategy?
DAVID What?

SHELDON Our strategy.
DAVID What strategy?
SHELDON Well, I didn't exactly mean that. But if you're going to change his mind—
DAVID Change whose mind, Dad? About what?
SHELDON The President, Dr. Walker. About my retirement, about giving me another year.
DAVID Dad, I only agreed to see him because you insisted.
SHELDON I know—I know. But the President has great respect for you. He might just possibly ask the Board to give me another year if you were to ask him to.
DAVID Please don't ask me to do that.
SHELDON (*angrily*) Why do you think I wanted you to go? To pay a social call?
DAVID You said you wanted me to hear the President's explanation.
SHELDON Yes, and show him that he's wrong.
DAVID No, I won't. And if you insist I won't go at all.
SHELDON All right, all right. No need to get angry. (*pause*) I'll go upstairs and change my shirt and tie, then I'll be ready. (*he goes inside*)
WILLA (*after a pause, entering from the house*) It's warm.
DAVID It's hot.
WILLA Yes. (*pause*)
DAVID I dread this interview.
WILLA I know.
DAVID It won't do a bit of good.
WILLA Do it to please him, David. If you don't he'll spend the rest of his life blaming you.
DAVID That doesn't make sense. When we were little he was too busy to talk to us and now he's relying on me. I don't understand him. I guess I never will.
WILLA He loves you, David. You're the apple of his eye. He believes you can do anything.
DAVID That's crazy.
WILLA Try to control your temper and don't become upset.
DAVID Oh, I'll play it cool. (*glancing at his wrist watch*) What's keeping him?
WILLA Probably bolstering his courage.
DAVID With whiskey you mean?
WILLA Vodka. You can't smell it. But don't let on. He's been very careful with his drinking since you've been here. He'd be mortified if he thought you knew.
DAVID Why, mama? Why'd he *start* drinking?
WILLA Why do any of us do what we do? I don't know, David. I suppose it's partly an escape, partly the result of the insecurity he feels now that he's to be retired.
DAVID He could write all those books he's wanted to.
WILLA (*shaking her head*) It's not enough. When you've been as active as he has, when you've been in the thick of things and suddenly you're put out to pasture like an old stud horse, it's not enough even to graze knee-deep in clover. And when there is no clover—(*she gestures hopelessly*)
DAVID But we all love him.
WILLA But we don't have to depend on him any more. He'll be dependent on us.
DAVID What the hell are we going to do, Mama?
WILLA I just don't know.

(SHELDON *enters holding his coat*)

SHELDON I'll carry this. I'll put it on when we get there. (DAVID *rises*)
WILLA Well, good luck, you two.
SHELDON (*jovially*) Oh, don't worry, Mama. Everything's going to be all right. (*they go out.* HARRIET *comes out on the porch*)
HARRIET Daddy seemed very happy.
WILLA He always is when David's home.
HARRIET What do you think?
WILLA I think you and I'd better get inside and start dinner. (*she crosses to the front door*)
HARRIET (*following*) But the kitchen's like an oven.
WILLA We'll make a tuna salad and some iced tea so we won't have to light the stove.

(*They enter the house as the lights fade on the porch and rise on the office.* DR. WALKER, *a genial looking gentleman who looks like the man in the whiskey ads, is dictating to his secretary*)

DR. WALKER The Honorable Garland Claytor, Holly Tree Lane Farms, Sussex County, Virginia. Dear Mr. Claytor (*pause*) We are extremely gratified that our esteemed governor has selected you to serve on our Board of Visitors. I know of no one in the state who is better qualified for this appointment than you. Your keen interest in our *little* college (*pause*) over the years (*pause*) and the generous contributions you have made through the Claytor Scholarships (*pause*) have established you as one who is deeply interested in the higher education of Negroes. I am especially pleased because of our *long, personal* friendship which has transcended the barriers of race and because I know that this augurs well for the continued progress of this institution. Welcome to the college family. Very respectfully yours, H. Sam Walker. How's that, Miss Jackson?

SECRETARY   A bit thick, isn't it?

DR. WALKER   He'll love it.

SECRETARY   (*as* SHELDON *and* DAVID *enter*) That's probably Professor Sheldon. Can you see him now?

DR. WALKER   Send him in. (*the* SECRETARY *crosses to the outer office*)

SECRETARY   Go right in, gentlemen. (*she pretends to hold open a door and closes it after they enter*)

DR. WALKER   (*rising*) Come right in, gentlemen. (*he approaches* SHELDON, *extending his hand*) How are you, Professor?

SHELDON   Oh, I'm bearing up, thank you.

DR. WALKER   David, it's good to see you.

DAVID   (*shaking hands*) It's good to see you, Dr. Walker.

DR. WALKER   How's your family?

DAVID   They're fine. They stopped off in Roanoke with Julian and his family.

DR. WALKER   And how are things at Douglass?

DAVID   We're managing to survive.

DR. WALKER   And my friend Dr. Carroll?

DAVID   Oh, the President's doing very well. He asked to be remembered to you.

DR. WALKER   Fine man—fine man. He's president of our land grant college association, you know.

DAVID   Yes, sir. (*there is a pause.* SHELDON *fidgets*)

DR. WALKER   And Professor, how are your plans coming along?

SHELDON   We're still looking around, Mr. President.

DR. WALKER   Oh?

SHELDON   I had no idea how difficult finding a house would be.

DR. WALKER   I see.

SHELDON   I guess I've been blessed living all these years in a campus home.

DR. WALKER   Does Douglass provide faculty housing, David?

DAVID   No, sir. Only the President lives on campus.

DR. WALKER   Faculty all own their homes?

DAVID   Some. But mostly they rent. It's pretty tough to find what you want. Good property for our people's scarce.

DR. WALKER   Yes, I suppose that's true everywhere. That's been one of our big problems—housing and salaries. We've been fortunate here in Warwick in being able to provide homes for our staff as a part of their salary. But then that has limitations as well as advantages. Take a man like your father. When it comes time to retire, he's got to start from scratch.

SHELDON   I'm glad you understand, Mister President.

DR. WALKER   Oh, yes, I understand. That's why when you requested a delay I was only too glad to go before the Board. But it wasn't easy, I tell you. Those white people in Richmond believe in the letter of the law. The days when we could do just about as we pleased are over, Professor.

SHELDON   Times are changing—I was just saying so to David.

DR. WALKER   Yes, indeed.

SHELDON   But the Board was also kind to Dr. Stanton—

DR. WALKER   That's what they call good public relations—

SHELDON   Pardon—?

DR. WALKER   A man who'd been president for more than thirty years and a teacher for fifteen before that—but he didn't have a dime. If he'd been turned out there'd been hollering from all over the state from both white and colored. Oh, these white people are smart all right.

SHELDON   But haven't they set a precedent? Won't that permit them to do the same things for others?

DR. WALKER   For you, you mean.

SHELDON   I don't have a dime either.

DR. WALKER   (*sadly*) I'm afraid not, Professor.

SHELDON   Why not?

DR. WALKER (*impatiently*)   Oh, now, Sheldon, let's stop playing games. You know how the system operates.

The Tumult and the Shouting

SHELDON No—I'm afraid I don't. I'm a department head or *was*, it's true. But I have very little contact with the Board. They were just so many names to me. What little information I got came from the Dean. And he didn't know much either. We were all in the dark about what the Board did or thought about the college.

DR. WALKER Then I'll tell you. There's one person whom they all respect and that's the President—sometimes it's the fiscal officer. It doesn't matter—whoever's in charge gets their respect. So now I'm the one they look up to. What about Missouri, David?

DAVID Same thing. From what I've observed it's true in every Negro college—in every community.

DR. WALKER Yes, the black overseer or as they say on the street, H.N.I.C.

SHELDON I beg your pardon.

DR. WALKER Head nigger in charge.

DAVID It's funny but they don't know anybody but him. Take Dr. Young—he's always the Negro representative on any civic committee. They even call him up if we try to make a loan or buy a suit of clothes.

SHELDON Are you trying to tell me—

DR. WALKER Stanley *was* the H.N.I.C. He rendered faithful service for years. He didn't make too many demands, made do with what he had. And for that he was rewarded.

SHELDON And so you, too, will be rewarded?

DR. WALKER No—times are changing. NAACP is giving 'em hell in the courts. I don't think the Gaines decision will hold up much longer. Time will come when we'll have to desegregate. When that happens, goodbye H.N.I.C.

SHELDON You're not even willing to try?

DR. WALKER No. Because I had to play the Uncle Tom to get you the one year postponement. I explained your thirty years of devoted service, teaching five and six classes a quarter, coaching debate, directing plays, and raising a family of four. You should have seen me. I put on quite a show for you. I had 'em sniffling and the women actually weeping. But I can't do it again.

SHELDON I've got no place to go.

DR. WALKER Even if I were inclined to help I couldn't.

SHELDON Why not?

DR. WALKER The house, you see. It's already been promised to your replacement.

SHELDON (*after a pause*) My replacement?

DR. WALKER Yes. And we promised him to have it renovated, you know, repainted, floors done, etc. And that'll take a little while.

SHELDON (*shocked*) Who is my replacement?

DR. WALKER A young fellow just got his Ph.D. from Wisconsin. Comes highly recommended. He'll carry on the Sheldon tradition of excellence.

SHELDON (*emotionally*) But what am I going to do? What am I going to do?

DR. WALKER Perhaps David can help.

SHELDON No, he's on his way to school—to start on his degree.

DR. WALKER Then I don't know.

SHELDON That's all you've got to say?

DR. WALKER What do you want from me, Sheldon, blood?

SHELDON I'd die of anemia. (WALKER *is stung*) I'll tell you what I want. I want thirty-five years of my life back. I want the dignity and respect of my beloved teachers at Amherst and Harvard when *they* retired. I want you—I want *somebody* to assure me that it's all been worth it —spending a lifetime trying to help the children and grandchildren of slaves 'lift the veil of ignorance." Because I've begun to wonder. I'm not so sure any more. I think somebody sold me a bill of goods. Education may not be the answer. Whoever said, "You shall know the truth and the truth shall make you free" told a *god damn lie*!

DR. WALKER Professor, this is doing no good. I think you'd better go.

SHELDON You'll have to put me out of the house.

DR. WALKER Oh, now, Sheldon, that's ridiculous.

SHELDON I mean it. You'll have to carry me out.

DAVID Dad, stop it.

SHELDON Don't you yell at me.

DAVID (*approaching*) Dad, I think we'd better go. (*he reaches out for him*)

SHELDON Keep your hands off me. I can walk. I'm not an invalid. (*he breaks down and sobs violently*)

SECRETARY (*entering in a hurry*) Dr. Walker, is there anything wrong?

DR. WALKER Everything's all right, Miss

Jackson. Professor Sheldon's been overcome by the heat. I'd appreciate you bringing him a glass of water.

SECRETARY Yes, sir. (*she goes quickly to the water fountain in the outer office, fills a paper cup and returns.* SHELDON *has begun to control himself*)

SECRETARY (*handing him the cup*) Professor Sheldon—

SHELDON Thank you. (*he sips*)

SECRETARY Dr. Walker, we'll just have to do something about cooling this office. It's just like an oven. You can't expect elderly people to bear up under it like you do.

DR. WALKER Yes, Miss Jackson, we'll look into it. (*she leaves*) Let's see, it's the middle of August now. If a two week extension will help you, you can have it. Don't know how I'll explain the delay to the new Ph.D. but I'll do it. We'll put 'em in the guest house. (*pause*)

DAVID Thank you, Dr. Walker, and goodbye. (*he crosses to his father and speaks gently*) Dad?

(SHELDON *looks up as if in a coma, sees* DAVID'S *extended hand which he rejects and rises slowly*)

SHELDON (*stiffly*) I'm all right, thank you. (*he moves toward the door*)

DR. WALKER Goodbye, Professor.

SHELDON Goodbye, Mister President. (*he goes out, followed by* DAVID. HARRIET *comes out on the porch*)

WILLA (*inside*) Can you see them?

HARRIET (*looking off*) No. Yes, they're just coming out of Old Main.

WILLA (*entering*) Does he seem pleased?

HARRIET They don't seem to be talking.

WILLA They never did talk much to each other, those two.

HARRIET I guess I'd better go inside.

WILLA Yes—no. You stay here. Whatever is said I want you to hear it. (SHELDON *and* DAVID *appear. They cross the stage in silence*) How did it go? (SHELDON *says nothing. He trudges wearily into the house and upstairs to the bedroom. After watching* SHELDON *disappear*) David?

DAVID It was awful—whimpering and begging the president to intercede for him. It was awful. I felt so ashamed.

WILLA It was that bad—you felt ashamed of your father?

DAVID Yes. And all he got for it was a two week reprieve.

WILLA He's not himself any more, David. He hasn't been for a long time now.

DAVID But where is his pride?

WILLA I don't know. I just don't know.

DAVID What do we do now?

WILLA We start packing and looking for a room for your father.

DAVID Room? Aren't you going with him?

WILLA No—I've got to live in the dormitory if I want to keep my job. New regulation. Besides we can't find a cottage that quickly.

DAVID What about Harriet?

WILLA She'll live in the senior dorm next year. That'll give me a whole year to find a place for Billy when he comes home from the sanatarium.

DAVID He'll be by himself.

WILLA It can't be helped.

DAVID Alone.

WILLA We'll be close by. I'll visit him every day.

DAVID My god. What a comedown.

(*The lights fade and music is heard*)

Scene Five End of the Processional

(*The lights rise. Two men, professional movers, come out of the house carrying a divan. Another enters as they disappear around the house.* DAVID *comes out dressed for travel. He puts his luggage on the porch and saunters back and forth gazing at the house. The movers continue to come back and forth*)

DAVID It's all over now. Movers are here and the house is all but empty. Just a few pieces left. Some Mama will take with her to the dormitory to fix up her room and make it homey. Dad rejected the two week extension. Said *he'd* decide the time of his departure. He's upstairs now in the bedroom. Won't come down he says till we're all gone—like the captain of a sinking ship. Up there with his rocking chair and his Bible. He's taking the chair with him. That's all he'll have to remind him of this house. In a few minutes now I'll be on my way. I'm to meet my family in Roanoke and from there we'll take the Norfolk and Western and head back into the midwest for the great

University of Iowa. I'm off to school again—going to start on my meal ticket—my Ph.D. Kids joke about the letters. Say it stands for phenomenally dumb. But I've got to get it if I'm going to make it in this racket—that's the only way you can beat the system. And that's what they're paying for nowadays—looks good in the catalogue. Nobody cares very much about teaching. It's the degree that counts. (*pause*) Dad's got a room in a boarding house just across from the campus. He'll take his meals there, too. It's not so bad—small but comfortable. (*pause*) No, that's a goddam lie. It's tiny, cramped and no place for a man who's lived in a big roomy house with children romping about. (*the last of the movers come out*) Well, that should do it. It's bare and empty—a house that's seen so much of joy and sorrow, happiness, sickness, and death. Oh yes, I didn't tell you about that—but there was another birth—a stillborn. They might have saved it in the hospital. But Mom wouldn't go—didn't trust 'em she said where our people were concerned. (*pause*) I hate to go back in there but I've got to say goodbye. (*he enters the house. The lights come up in the bedroom.* SHELDON *sits alone reading. He looks up as he hears* DAVID's *footsteps echoing on the stairs.* DAVID *enters. For a moment neither speaks*)

SHELDON I didn't hear the taxi.

DAVID It hasn't come. But they said ten minutes so I thought I'd better come up now.

SHELDON Well, you've a few minutes. Here, take my chair.

DAVID No thanks, Dad. I won't have time.

SHELDON Well, keep in touch. And come see us whenever you can.

DAVID Okay.

SHELDON (*almost too confidently*) I'll be buying a place soon. And don't worry about your mother and Harriet. We'll make out. Got several teaching offers, you know.

DAVID (*softly*) That's fine, Dad. (WILLA *and* HARRIET *appear from around the rear of the house*)

SHELDON Now you go ahead and get that degree and don't stop until you've finished. Don't make the mistake I did of assuming that a Master of Arts represented security. And if you get in a jam financially let me know. My credit's good.

DAVID All right. (*a long pause, then a taxi horn*)

HARRIET (*downstairs*) David, taxi's here.

DAVID I'll be right down. (*to* SHELDON) Got to go now, Dad. (*He holds out his hand.* SHELDON *grasps it firmly rising as he does so.* DAVID *leaves and* SHELDON *goes to the window. Downstairs* DAVID *embraces* HARRIET *and then* WILLA)

WILLA Take care of yourself. Write often and give our love to Connie.

DAVID Sure, Mom. (*He embraces her again, picks up his bags and hurries to the left. He is met by the taxi driver who takes his bags*)

DRIVER Got to hurry, sir. We're a little late and train's on time.

DAVID Right. (*he turns, waves to* WILLA *and* HARRIET *on the porch and* SHELDON *at the upstairs window. The lights fade as the music of the Recessional rises. When the lights are completely down except for a spot on* DAVID, *he turns and faces the audience*)

DAVID (*listening*) They're getting ready for the summer commencement exercises. It'll be as hot as hell in the auditorium. (*listening*) "The tumult and the shouting die, the captains and the kings depart, still *stands* our ancient sacrifice"—(*he turns, back to the audience and stares at the dim outline of the house*) We're done. The story's finished. And now, my story begins. (*he jams his hands into his pockets and strolls into the darkness. The music swells*)

(*The Recessional ends*)

James Baldwin (1924–   )

The Amen Corner   1954

James Baldwin had just published his first novel, *Go Tell it on the Mountain* (1953), when he turned to writing his first play, *The Amen Corner*. "I was armed", he wrote, "I knew, in attempting to write the play, by the fact that I was born in the church. I know that out of the ritual of church, historically speaking, comes the act of the theater, the *communion* which is theater."

The play's first production was at Howard University, under the direction of Owen Dodson. In an interview in 1971, Professor Dodson recalled the experience:

One of the things we tried to do at Howard University at the end of the 1940's and through the 50's and 60's was to produce new plays by vital young playwrights. In 1954 I decided to direct a play, *The Amen Corner*, by a then little-known writer, James Baldwin.

After I had first read this script, I thought, "Here is a wonderful voice that doesn't need to scream to make itself heard . . . here is a play that has so many depths, so many eddies and plumbings into human relations. The depth of this play goes beyond the relations of man and woman who just spit at each other, who just love and hate at the same time. All through the play there is a flexible sense of humanity amid the terror of the heart: a son that loses his father, and a mother who loses her lover, people who love each other but find each other's company impossible."

And I knew the church that James Baldwin was writing about and so did the actors at Howard. We knew about the store front churches and their songs, the songs of our own childhood. And the crammed audience on opening night must have known them too, for there was applause, like a rock and roll applause. And they kept it up until we finally pushed Jimmy up on the stage.

(Hatch-Billops Oral Black Theatre Collection, City College of New York)

The script then languished for several years until producer-director-actor Frank Silvera founded his Theater of Being in the early 1960's in Los Angeles. The purpose of his theater was "to bring the truth of black experience to the stage in a way that would exist beyond the mere words of the play."

In Mr. Silvera's production, *The Amen Corner* was almost an instant public success. After beginning in the small, eighty-seat Robertson Playhouse, *The Amen Corner* moved to the larger Coronet Theater where it played eight performances a week for over a year. The audiences were mostly black; many were church groups.

In April 1965 *The Amen Corner* came to Broadway. It lasted twelve weeks. The critics were unanimous in their condemnation of the play's turgidity; they were unanimous in their praise of the lead, Beah Richards. All the critics noted the third act moment when Miss Richards, as Sister Margaret, recognizes what her existence has meant. It is enlightening to compare what four white newspaper critics saw at that moment with what a black person saw. First, Walker Kerr of the *Herald Tribune*:

I do not normally care much for actresses who actually cry on stage and I was offering the moment some resistance because Miss Richards was actually crying. But that is when she fooled me, on the double. Suddenly, as though a meat-axe had cut straight through all of the inhibitions binding her, she turned her tears into a whoop of laughter, slapped the table hard with an open palm, and let her left leg slide into an abandoned 18-year-old limpness.

She was that girl, after all, released by a bolt of lightning. The moment is a remarkable one, swiftly intelligible in spite of all that has gone to contradict it beforehand.

Next, Howard Taubman of the *New York Times*:

The tears are streaming down Miss Richard's face. Suddenly she sees the ludicrous side of her predicament. Her speech shades from a preoccupation with her suffering to a wry joke. She laughs at herself through her tears, and you laugh with her. She remarks on something else that is funny. She laughs and you laugh. Through her and your laughter there emerges the perception of a woman for whom at long last you can muster up a deep fellow feeling.

And Richard Watts of the New York *Post*:

When, with her world collapsed about her, one of her troubles suddenly strikes her as funny, and she bursts into laughter that is not hysterical but a genuine appreciation of the absurdity of such an accumulation of woes, she captures a moment of unforgettable acting.

Finally, John McClain of the *Journal American*:

With tears making rivulets down her cheeks she is able suddenly to turn to laughter at the thought that, after all this, the Frigidaire still isn't paid for.

Everything these men report is perceptive and true. Mr. Kerr saw Margaret, the 18-year-old girl. Mr. Taubman saw a woman laughing at herself. Mr. Watts saw her appreciate the absurdity of her woes. Mr. McClain saw the recognition that the Frigidaire was not paid for. Here is what Miss Josie Dotson, a black actress in the Broadway cast, saw:

If you read the literature about blacks up to not long ago, that within it you could never see how could these people survive for so long. What was it they had? If you just look at the literature, we were a bunch of singin', finger poppin'... nothing. There was nothing.

Now in that scene where Beah broke into laughter, one of the most marvelous laughs in the world, in that scene, I understood how we, a people, could be the kinda people who could take it. I knew that Beah knew that black people had got something. We don't get wiped out. We don't. Particular individuals get wiped out, but the people do not. No! No! What is that something that keeps us doing it?

In that moment of Beah Richards' laughter, I knew what it was. She showed me that, forever. It was one of the greatest moments the theater has ever seen. I knew that Beah knew what she was talking about and she wasn't just living the lines, she was really talking about it.

Miss Dotson did not see quite the same play as the white critics. It is this difference in perception that led in the late 1960's to the demand for black drama critics to judge the validity of the black experience, an experience that rests not only in the script and its theatrical production, but also in the eye, ear, and life of the beholder.

One final first should be noted about *The Amen Corner*'s New York run. The entire production—set, lights, costumes—were designed by a black man, Mr. Vantile Whitfield. Although Mr. Whitfield was not the first to design on Broadway (Perry Watkins did the set for *Mamba's Daughters* in 1939), he may have been the first to do an entire production design for a black show on the Great White Way. The Scenic Designers Guild never invited Mr. Whitfield to become a member. It may be that Mr. Whitfield holds the second distinction of being the first production designer on Broadway who was not first required to join the union.

The Amen Corner

CAST OF CHARACTERS

MARGARET ALEXANDER, *pastor of the church*
ODESSA, MARGARET's *older sister*
IDA JACKSON, *a young woman*
SISTER MOORE ⎫
SISTER BOXER ⎬ *elders of the church*
BROTHER BOXER ⎭
DAVID, MARGARET's *18-year-old son*
LUKE, *her husband*
SISTER SALLY   ⎫
SISTER DOUGLASS   ⎪
SISTER RICE   ⎬ *members of the congregation*
BROTHER DAVIS   ⎪
BROTHER WASHINGTON ⎭
WOMAN
OTHER MEMBERS OF CONGREGATION

ACT ONE

(*We are facing the scrim wall of the tenement which holds the home and church of* SISTER MARGARET ALEXANDER.

It is a very bright Sunday morning.

Before the curtain rises, we hear street sounds, laughter, cursing, snatches of someone's radio; and under everything, the piano, which DAVID *is playing in the church.*

When the scrim rises we see, stage right, the church, which is dominated by the pulpit, on a platform, upstage. On the platform, a thronelike chair. On the pulpit, an immense open Bible.

To the right of the pulpit, the piano, the top of which is cluttered with hymnbooks and tambourines.

Just below the pulpit, a table, flanked by two plain chairs. On the table two collection plates, one brass, one straw, two Bibles, perhaps a vase of artificial flowers. Facing the pulpit, and running the length of the church, the camp chairs for the congregation.

To the right, downstage, the door leading to the street.

The church is on a level above the apartment and should give the impression of dominating the family's living quarters.

The apartment is stage left. Upstage, the door leading to the church; perhaps a glimpse of the staircase. Downstage, the kitchen, cluttered: a new Frigidaire, prominently placed, kitchen table with dishes on it, suitcase open on a chair.

Downstage, left, LUKE's *bedroom. A small, dark room with a bed, a couple of chairs, a hassock, odds and ends thrown about in it as though it has long been used as a storage room. The room ends in a small door which leads to the rest of the house.*

Members of the congregation almost always enter the church by way of the street door, stage right. Members of the family almost always enter church by way of the inside staircase. The apartment door is stage left of the kitchen.

At rise, there is a kind of subdued roar and humming, out of which is heard the music prologue, "The Blues Is Man," which segues into a steady rollicking beat, and we see the congregation singing)

ALL   One day I walked the lonesome road
     The spirit spoke unto me
     And filled my heart with love—
     Yes, he filled my heart with love,
     Yes, he filled my heart with love,
     And he wrote my name above,
     And that's why I thank God I'm in His care.
   CHORUS

     Let me tell you now
     Whilst I'm in His care,
     I'm in my Saviour's care,
     Jesus got His arms wrapped around me,
     No evil thoughts can harm me
     'Cause I'm so glad I'm in His care.

CONTRALTO   I opened my Bible and began to read
     About all the things He's done for me;
     Read on down about Chapter One
     How He made the earth then He made the sun.
     Read on down about Chapter Two
     How He died for me and He died for you.
     Read on down about Chapter Three
     How He made the blind, the blind to see.
     Read on down about Chapter Four

How He healed the sick and blessed the poor.
Read on down about Chapter Five
How it rained forty days and Noah survived.
Six, Seven, about the same
Just keep praising my Jesus' name.
Read on down about Chapter Eight,
The golden streets and the pearly gates.
Read on down about Chapter Nine
We all get to heaven in due time.
Read on down about Chapter Ten
My God's got the key and He'll let me in.
When I finish reading the rest
I'll go to judgment to stand my test.
He'll say come a little higher, come a little higher,
He'll say come a little higher and take your seat.

ALL   Let me tell you now
Whilst I'm in His care,
I'm in my Saviour's care,
Jesus got His arms wrapped around me,
No evil thoughts can harm me
'Cause I'm so glad I'm in His care.

MARGARET   Amen! Let the church say amen!

ALL   Amen! Hallelujah! Amen!

MARGARET   And let us say amen again!

ALL   Amen! Amen!

MARGARET   Because the Lord God Almighty—the King of *Kings*, amen!—had sent out the word, "Set thine house in order, for thou shalt die and not live." And King Hezekiah turned his face to the wall.

ODESSA   Amen!

SISTER MOORE   Preach it, daughter! Preach it this morning!

MARGARET   Now, when the king got the message, amen, he didn't do like some of us do today. He didn't go running to no spiritualists, no, he didn't. He didn't spend a lot of money on no fancy doctors, he didn't break his neck trying to commit himself to Bellevue Hospital. He sent for the prophet, Isaiah. Amen. He sent for a saint of God.

SISTER BOXER   Well, amen!

MARGARET   Now, children, you know this king had a mighty kingdom. There were many souls in that kingdom. He had rich and poor, high and low, amen! And I believe he had a lot of preachers around, puffed up and riding around in chariots—just like they is today, bless God—and stealing from the poor.

ALL   Amen!

MARGARET   But the king didn't call on none of them. No. He called on Isaiah. He called on Isaiah, children, because Isaiah lived a holy life. He wasn't one of them always running in and out of the king's palace. When the king gave a party, I doubt that he even thought of inviting him. You know how people do, amen: Well, let's not have him. Let's not have her. They too sanctified. They too holy. Amen! They don't drink, they don't smoke, they don't go to the movies, they don't curse, they don't play cards, they don't covet their neighbor's husband or their neighbor's wife—well, amen! They just holy. If we invite that sanctified fool they just going to make everybody else feel uncomfortable!

ALL   Well, bless the Lord! Amen!

MARGARET   But let the trouble come. Oh, let the trouble come. They don't go to none of them they sees all the time, amen. No, they don't go running to the people they was playing cards with all night long. When the trouble comes, look like they just can't stand none of their former ways—and they go a-digging back in their minds, in their memories, looking for a saint of God. Oh, yes! I've seen it happen time and time again and I know some of you out there this morning, you've seen it happen too. Sometimes, bless the Lord, you be in the woman's kitchen, washing up her cocktail glasses, amen, and maybe singing praises to the Lord. And pretty soon, here she come, this woman who maybe ain't said two words to you all the time you been working there. She draw up a chair and she say, "Can I talk to you, sister?" She got a houseful of people but she ain't gone to them. She in the kitchen, amen, talking to a saint of God. Because the world is watching you, children, even when you think the whole world's asleep!

ALL   Amen! Amen!

MARGARET   But, dearly beloved, she can't come to you—the world can't come to you—if you don't live holy. This way of holiness is a hard way. I know some of you think Sister Margaret's too hard on you. She don't want you to do this and she won't let you do that. Some of you say, "Ain't no harm in reading the funny papers." But children, *yes*, there's harm in it. While you reading them funny papers, your mind ain't on the Lord. And if your mind ain't stayed on Him, every hour of the day, Satan's going to cause you to fall. Amen! Some of you say, "Ain't no harm in me working for a liquor company. I ain't going to be drinking the liquor, I'm just going to be driving the *truck*!" But a saint of God ain't got no business delivering liquor to folks all day—how you going to spend all day helping folks into hell and then think you going to come here in the evening and help folks into heaven? It can't be done. The Word tells me, No man can serve two masters!

ALL Well, the Word *do* say it! Bless the Lord!

MARGARET Let us think about the Word this morning, children. Let it take root in your hearts: "Set thine house in order, for thou shalt die and not live." (MARGARET *begins to sing and instantly* DAVID *strikes up another "shout" song and the congregation sings—loud, violent, clapping of hands, tambourines, etc.* MARGARET *rises and sits*)

MARGARET I got the holy spirit
To help me run this race.
I got the holy spirit,
It appointed my soul a place.
My faith looks up to heaven,
I know up there I'll see
The Father, the Son, the Holy Spirit
Watching over me.

BARITONE Once I was a sinner
Treading a sinful path;
Never thought about Jesus
Or the fate of His wrath.
Then I met the Saviour
And ever since that day
I been walking my faith,
Praying with love,
Looking up above.
With His arms around me,
I'm just leaning on Him.
For there is no other
On Him I can depend.
When my life is ended
And I lay these burdens down
I'm gonna walk with faith,
Pray with love,
Looking from above.

ALL I got the holy spirit
To help me run this race.
I got the holy spirit,
It appointed my soul a place.
My faith looks up to heaven,
I know up there I'll see
The Father, the Son, the Holy Spirit
Watching over me.

(SISTER MOORE *comes forward. The excitement begins to subside*)

SISTER MOORE Well, I know our souls is praising God this morning!

ALL Amen!

SISTER MOORE It ain't every flock blessed to have a shepherd like Sister Margaret. Let's praise God for her!

ALL Amen! Amen!

SISTER MOORE Now, I ain't here to take up a lot of your time, amen. Sister Margaret's got to go off from us this afternoon to visit our sister church in Philadelphia. There's many sick up there, amen! Old Mother Phillips is sick in the body and some of her congregation is sick in the soul. And our pastor done give her word that she'd go up there and try to strengthen the feeble knees. Bless God! (*music begins and underlines her speech*) Before we close out this order of service, I'd like to say, I praise the Lord for being here, I thank Him for my life, health and strength. I want to thank Him for the way He's worked with me these many long years and I want to thank Him for keeping me *humble*! I want to thank Him for keeping me pure and set apart from the lusts of the flesh, for protecting me—hallelujah!—from all carnal temptation. When I come before my Maker, I'm going to come before Him *pure*. I'm going to say "Bless your name, Jesus, no man has ever touched me!" Hallelujah! (*Congregation begins to sing*)

ALL Come to Jesus, come to Jesus,
Come to Jesus, just now.
Come to Jesus, come to Jesus just now.
He will save you, He will save you,
He will save you, just now.
He will save you, He will save you just now.

SISTER MOORE Now before we raise the sacrifice offering, the Lord has led *me*, amen, to ask if there's a soul in this congregation who wants to ask the Lord's especial attention to them this morning? Any sinners, amen, any backsliders? Don't you be ashamed, you just come right on up here to the altar. (*tentative music on the piano*) Don't hold back, dear ones. Is there any sick in the building? The Lord's hand is outstretched. (*silence*) Come, dear hearts, don't hold back. (*toward the back of the church, a young woman, not dressed in white,, rises. She holds a baby in her arms*) Yes, honey come on up here. Don't be ashamed. (*the congregation turns to look at the young woman. She hesitates.* MARGARET *rises and steps forward*)

MARGARET Come on, daughter! (*the young woman comes up the aisle. Approving murmurs come from the congregation.* SISTER MOORE *steps a little aside*) That's right, daughter. The Word say, If you make one step, He'll make two. Just step out on the promise. What's your name, daughter?

YOUNG WOMAN Jackson. Mrs. Ida Jackson.

SISTER MOORE (*to the congregation*) Sister Ida Jackson. Bless the Lord!

ALL Bless her!

MARGARET And what's the name of that little one?

MRS. JACKSON His name is Daniel. He been sick. I want you to pray for him. (*she begins to weep*)

MARGARET Dear heart, don't you weep this morning. I know what that emptiness feel like. What's been ailing this baby?

MRS. JACKSON I don't know. Done took him to the doctor and the doctor, he don't know. He can't keep nothing on his little stomach and he cry all night, every night, and he done got real puny. Sister, I done lost one child already, please pray the Lord to make this baby well!

MARGARET (*steps down and touches* MRS. JACKSON) Don't fret, little sister. Don't you fret this morning. The Lord is mighty to save. This here's a Holy Ghost station. (*to the congregation*) Ain't that so, dear ones?

ALL Amen!

MARGARET He a right fine little boy. Why ain't your husband here with you this morning?

MRS. JACKSON I guess he at the house. He done got so evil and bitter, looks like he don't never want to hear me mention the Lord's name. He don't know I'm here this morning. (*sympathetic murmurs from the congregation.* MARGARET *watches* MRS. JACKSON)

MARGARET You poor little thing. You ain't much more than a baby yourself, is you? Sister, is you ever confessed the Lord as your personal Saviour? Is you trying to lead a life that's pleasing to Him?

MRS. JACKSON Yes, ma'am. I'm trying every day.

MARGARET Is your husband trying as hard as you?

MRS. JACKSON I ain't got no fault to find with him.

MARGARET Maybe the Lord wants you to leave that man.

MRS. JACKSON No! He don't want that! (*smothered giggles among the women*)

MARGARET No, children, don't you be laughing this morning. This is serious business. The Lord, He got a road for each and every one of us to travel and we is got to be saying amen to Him, no matter what sorrow He cause us to bear. (*to* MRS. JACKSON) Don't let the Lord have to take another baby from you before you ready to do His will. Hand that child to me. (*takes the child from* MRS. JACKSON'*s arms*)

SISTER MOORE Kneel down, daughter. Kneel down there in front of the altar. (MRS. JACKSON *kneels*)

MARGARET I want every soul under the sound of my voice to bow his head and pray silently with me as I pray. (*they bow their heads.* MARGARET *stands, the child in her arms, head uplifted, and congregation begins to hum "Deep River"*) Dear Lord, we come before you this morning to ask you to look down and bless this woman and her baby. Touch his little body, Lord, and heal him and drive out them tormenting demons. Raise him up, Lord, and make him a good man and a comfort to his mother. Yes, we know you can do it, Lord. You told us if we'd just call, trusting in your promise, you'd be sure to answer. And all these blessings we ask in the name of the Father—

ALL In the name of the Father—

MARGARET And in the name of the Son—

ALL And in the name of the Son—

MARGARET And in the name of the blessed Holy Ghost—

ALL And in the name of the blessed Holy Ghost—

MARGARET Amen.

ALL Amen.

MARGARET (*returning the child*) God bless you, daughter. You go your way and trust the Lord. That child's going to be all right.

MRS. JACKSON Thank you, sister. I can't tell you how much I thank you.

MARGARET You ain't got me to thank. You come by here and let us know that child's all right, that's what'll please the Lord.

MRS. JACKSON Yes. I sure will do that.

MARGARET And bring your husband with you. You bring your *husband* with you.

MRS. JACKSON Yes, sister. I'll bring him.

MARGARET Amen!

(MRS. JACKSON *returns to her seat.* MARGARET *looks at her watch, motions to* ODESSA, *who rises and leaves. In a moment, we see her in the apartment. She exits through* LUKE's *room, returns a moment later without her robe, puts coffee on the stove, begins working.* SISTER MOORE *comes forward*)

SISTER MOORE Well now, children, without no more ado, we's going to raise the sacrifice offering. And when I say sacrifice, I *mean* sacrifice. Boxer, hand me that basket. (BROTHER BOXER *does so.* SISTER MOORE *holds a dollar up before the congregation and drops it in the plate*) I know you don't intend to see our pastor walk to Philadelphia. I want every soul in this congregation to drop just as much money in the plate as I just dropped, or *more*, to help with the cost of this trip. Go on, Brother Boxer, they going to give it to you, I know they is.

(*The congregation, which has been humming throughout all this, begins singing slightly more strongly as* BROTHER BOXER *passes around the plate, beginning at the back of the church*)

ALL Glory, glory, hallelujah, since I laid my burdens down,
Glory, glory, hallelujah, since I laid my burdens down,
I feel better, so much better, since I laid my burdens down,
I feel better, so much better, since I laid my burdens down,
Glory, glory, hallelujah, since I laid my burdens down.

MARGARET *leaves the pulpit and comes downstairs. The lights dim in the church; the music continues, but lower, and the offering is raised in pantomime*)

ODESSA Well! My sister sure walked around Zion this morning! (MARGARET *sits at the table.* ODESSA *pours coffee, begins preparing something for* MARGARET *to eat*)
MARGARET It ain't me, sister, it's the Holy Ghost. Odessa—? I been thinking I might take David with me to Philadelphia.
ODESSA What you want to take him up there for? Who's going to play for the service down here?
MARGARET Well, old Sister Price, she can sort of stand by—
ODESSA She *been* standing by—but she sure can't play no piano, not for me she can't. She just ain't got no *juices*, somehow. When that woman is on the piano, the service just gets so dead you'd think you was in a Baptist church.
MARGARET I'd like Mother Phillips to see what a fine, saved young man he turned out to be. It'll make her feel good. She told me I was going to have a hard time raising him—by myself. (*service is over, people are standing about chatting and slowly drifting out of the church*)
ODESSA Well, if he want to go—
MARGARET David's got his first time to disobey me. The Word say, Bring up a child in the way he should go, and when he is old he will not depart from it. Now. That's the Word. (*at the suitcase*) Oh Lord, I sure don't feel like wasting no more time on Brother Boxer. He's a right sorry figure of a man, you know that?
ODESSA I hope the Lord will forgive me, but, declare, I just can't help wondering sometimes who's on top in that holy marriage bed.
MARGARET (*laughs*) Odessa!
ODESSA Don't waste no time on him. He knows he ain't got no right to be driving a liquor truck.
MARGARET Now, what do you suppose is happened to David? He should be here.
ODESSA He's probably been cornered by some of the sisters. They's always pulling on him.
MARGARET I praise my Redeemer that I got him raised right—even though I didn't have no man—you think David missed Luke? (DAVID *enters the apartment*) Ah, there you are.
DAVID Morning, Aunt Odessa. Morning, Mama. My! You two look—almost like two young girls this morning.
ODESSA That's just exactly the way he comes on with the sisters. I reckon you know what you doing, take him to Philadelphia.
DAVID No, I mean it—just for a minute there. You both looked—different. Somehow—what about Philadelphia?
MARGARET I was just asking your Aunt Odessa if she'd mind me taking you with me.
DAVID Mama, I don't want to go to Philadelphia. Anyway—who's going to play for the service down here?
ODESSA Sister Price can play for us.
DAVID That woman can't play no piano.
MARGARET Be careful how you speak about the saints, honey. God don't love us to speak no evil.
DAVID Well, I'm sure she's sanctified and

all that, but she *still* can't play piano. Not for *me*, she can't. She just makes me want to get up and leave the service.

MARGARET Mother Phillips would just love to see you—

DAVID I don't hardly remember Mother Phillips at all.

MARGARET You don't remember Mother Phillips? The way you used to follow her around? Why, she used to spoil you something awful—you was always up in that woman's face—when we—when we first come north—when Odessa was still working down home and we was living in Mother Phillips' house in Philadelphia. Don't you remember?

DAVID Yeah. Sort of. But, Mama, I don't want to take a week off from music school.

MARGARET Is the world going to fall down because you don't go to music school for a week?

DAVID Well, Mama, music is just like everything else, you got to keep at it.

MARGARET Well, you keeping at it. You playing in service all the time. I don't know what they can teach you in that school. You got a *natural* gift for music, David—(*a pause. They stare at each other*)—the Lord give it to you, you didn't learn it in no school.

DAVID The Lord give me eyes, too, Mama, but I still had to go to school to learn how to read.

MARGARET I don't know what's got into you lately, David.

DAVID Well, Mama, I'm getting older. I'm not a little boy anymore.

MARGARET I know you is getting older. But I hope you still got a mind stayed on the Lord.

DAVID Sure. Sure, I have.

MARGARET Where was you last night? You wasn't out to tarry service and don't nobody know what time you come in.

DAVID I had to go—downtown. We—having exams next week in music school and—I was studying with some guys I go to school with.

MARGARET Till way late in the morning?

DAVID Well—it's a pretty tough school.

MARGARET I don't know why you couldn't have had them boys come up here to *your* house to study. Your friends is always welcome, David, you know that.

DAVID Well, this guy's got a piano in his house—it was more convenient.

(BROTHER *and* SISTER BOXER *and* SISTER MOORE *leave the church and start downstairs. The church dims out*)

MARGARET And what's wrong with that piano upstairs?

DAVID Mama, I can't practice on that piano—

MARGARET You can use that piano anytime you want to—

DAVID Well, I couldn't have used it last night! (*the* BOXERS *and* SISTER MOORE *enter.* DAVID *turns away*)

SISTER MOORE I come down here to tell Sister Margaret myself how she blessed my soul this morning! Praise the Lord, Brother David. How you feel this morning?

DAVID Praise the Lord.

SISTER BOXER Your mother sure preached a sermon this morning.

BROTHER BOXER Did my heart good, amen. Did my heart *good*. Sister Odessa, what you got cool to drink in that fine new Frigidaire? (*opens the Frigidaire*) You got any Kool-aid?

SISTER BOXER You know you ain't supposed to be rummaging around in folks' iceboxes, Joel.

BROTHER BOXER This ain't no icebox, this is a *Frigidaire*. Westinghouse. Amen! You don't mind my making myself at home, do you, Sister Odessa?

MARGARET Just make yourself at home, Brother Boxer. I got to get ready to go. David, you better start packing—don't you make me late. He got any clean shirts, Odessa?

ODESSA I believe so—I ironed a couple last night—he uses them up so fast.

SISTER MOORE Why, is you going to Philadelphia with your mother, son? Why, that's just lovely!

DAVID Mama—I got something else to do—this week—

MARGARET You better hurry. (DAVID *goes into* LUKE'*s bedroom, pulls a suitcase from under the bed*)

BROTHER BOXER I believe David's sweet on one of them young sisters in Philadelphia, that's why he's so anxious to go. (DAVID *re-enters the kitchen*) How about it, boy? You got your eye on one of them Philadelphia saints? One of them young ones?

MARGARET David's just coming up with me

because I asked him to come and help me.

SISTER MOORE   Praise the Lord. That's sweet. The Lord's going to bless you, you hear me, David?

BROTHER BOXER   Ain't many young men in the Lord like David. I got to hand it to you, boy. I been keeping my eye on you and you is—all right! (*he claps* DAVID *on the shoulder*)

SISTER BOXER   How long you figure on being gone, Sister Margaret?

MARGARET   I ain't going to be gone no longer than I have to—this is a mighty sad journey. I don't believe poor Mother Phillips is long for this world. And the way her congregation's behaving—it's just enough to make you weep.

ODESSA   I don't know what's got into them folks up there, cutting up like they is, and talking about the Lord's anointed. I guess I *do* know what's got into them, too—ain't nothing but the Devil. You know, we is really got to watch and pray.

SISTER MOORE   They got more nerve than I got. You ain't never going to hear me say nothing against them the Lord is set above me. No sir. That's just asking for the wrath.

ODESSA   It'll fall *on* you, too. You all is seen the way the Lord is worked with Sister Margaret right here in this little tabernacle. You remember all those people tried to set themselves up against her—? Where is they now? The Lord is just let every one of them be dispersed.

SISTER BOXER   Even poor little Elder King is in his grave.

BROTHER BOXER   I sort of liked old Elder King. The Lord moved him right out just the same.

SISTER MOORE   He'd done got too *high*. He was too set in his ways. All that talk about not wanting women to preach. He didn't want women to do nothing but just sit quiet.

MARGARET   But I remember, Sister Moore, you wasn't so much on women preachers, neither, when I first come around.

SISTER MOORE   The Lord opened my eyes, honey. He opened my eyes the first time I heard you preach. Of course, I ain't saying that Elder King couldn't preach a sermon when the power was on him. And it *was* under Elder King that I come into the church.

BROTHER BOXER   You weren't sweet on Elder King, were you, Sister Moore?

SISTER MOORE   I ain't never been sweet on no man but the Lord Jesus Christ.

SISTER BOXER   You remember Elder King, son? You weren't nothing but a little bundle in them days.

DAVID   I was reading and writing already. I was even playing the piano already. It was him had this church then and we was living down the block.

BROTHER BOXER   I reckon you must have missed your daddy sometimes, didn't you, son?

SISTER MOORE   If he'd stayed around his daddy, I guarantee you David wouldn't be the fine, saved young man he is today, playing piano in church, would you, boy?

DAVID   No'm, I reckon I wouldn't. Mama, if I'm going to be gone a whole week, there is something I've got to—

BROTHER BOXER   He better off without the kind of daddy who'd just run off and leave his wife and kid to get along the best they could. That ain't right. I believe in a man doing *right*, amen!

MARGARET   You hear him, don't you? *He* know—miss his daddy? The Lord, He give me strength to be mother and daddy both. Odessa, you want to help me with my hair? (*they start out*)

DAVID   Mama—!

MARGARET   What is it, son?

DAVID   There is something I got to get down the block. I got to run down the block for a minute.

MARGARET   Can't it wait till you come back?

DAVID   No. I want to—borrow a music score from somebody. I can study it while I'm away.

MARGARET   Well, you hurry. We ain't got much time. You put something on. You act like you catching cold. (ODESSA *and* MARGARET *exit through* LUKE's *room*)

BROTHER BOXER   You got to say goodbye to some little girl down the block?

DAVID   I'll be right back. (*he rushes into the street, vanishes in the alley*)

BROTHER BOXER   Hmmph! I wonder what kind of business he got down the block. I guarantee you one thing—it ain't sanctified business.

SISTER BOXER   The Word say we ain't supposed to think no evil, Joel.

BROTHER BOXER   I got news for you folks. You know what I heard last night?

SISTER BOXER Don't you come on with no more foolishness, Joel. I'm too upset. I can't stand it this morning.

SISTER MOORE Don't you be upset, sugar. Everything's going to turn out all right—what did you hear, Brother Boxer?

BROTHER BOXER That boy's daddy is back in New York. He's working in a jazz club downtown.

SISTER MOORE A *jazz* club?

SISTER BOXER How come you know all this?

BROTHER BOXER Heard it on the job, honey. God don't want us to be ignorant. He wants us to know what's going on around us.

SISTER MOORE Do Sister Margaret know this?

BROTHER BOXER I bet you David, *he* know it—he been keeping bad company. Some young white boy, didn't have nothing better to do, went down yonder and drug his daddy up to New York—for a comeback. Last time anybody heard about him, he was real sick with TB. Everybody thought he was dead.

SISTER MOORE Poor Sister Margaret! A jazz club!

SISTER BOXER Poor Sister Margaret! She ain't as poor as I am.

BROTHER BOXER You ain't poor, sugar. You got me. And I ain't going to stay poor forever.

SISTER MOORE I'm going to talk to her about that job business now. She reasonable. She'll listen.

SISTER BOXER She ain't going to listen.

SISTER MOORE Of course she's going to listen. Folks is got a right to make a living.

BROTHER BOXER Uh-huh. Folks like us ain't got nothing and ain't never supposed to have nothing. We's supposed to live on the joy of the Lord.

SISTER MOORE It ain't like Brother Boxer was going to become a drunkard or something like that—he won't even *see* the liquor—

SISTER BOXER He won't even be selling it.

SISTER MOORE He just going to be driving a truck around the city, doing hard work. I declare, I don't see nothing wrong with that.

SISTER BOXER Sister Moore, you know that woman I work for, sometime she give a party and I got to serve them people cocktails. I *got* to. Now, I don't believe the Lord's going to punish me just because I'm working by the sweat of my brow the only way I *can*. He say, "Be in the world but not of it." But you got to be *in* it, don't care how holy you get, you got to *eat*.

BROTHER BOXER I'm glad Sister Boxer mentioned it to you, Sister Moore. I wasn't going to mention it to you myself because I was sure you'd just take Sister Margaret's side against us.

SISTER MOORE Ain't no taking of sides in the Lord, Brother Boxer. I'm on the Lord's side. We is all sinners, saved by grace. Hallelujah! (MARGARET *and* ODESSA *re-enter. The* BOXERS *and* SISTER MOORE *begin to sing*)

SISTER MOORE What a mighty God we serve!
SISTER *and* BROTHER BOXER What a mighty God we serve!
TOGETHER Angels around the throne,
'Round the throne of God,
Crying, what a mighty God we serve!

MARGARET Bless your hearts, children, that sure done my spirit good. You all ain't like them wayward children up in Philadelphia. It sure is nice to be here with my real faithful children. (DAVID *enters the alley, slowly, looking back; enters the apartment*)

BROTHER BOXER Oh, we's faithful, Sister Margaret. (*jazz version of "Luke's Theme" begins*)

SISTER MOORE Yes, I'm mighty glad you said that, Sister Margaret. I'm mighty glad you *knows* that. Because the Lord's done laid something on my heart to say to you, right here and now, and you going to take it in the proper spirit, I know you is. I know you know I ain't trying to find fault. Old Sister Moore don't mean no wrong.

MARGARET What is it, Sister Moore?

DAVID Mama, can I see you for a minute?

MARGARET In a minute, son.

SISTER MOORE Why, Brother and Sister Boxer here, they just happened to mention to me something about this job you don't think Brother Boxer ought to take. I don't mean no wrong, Sister Margaret, and I know you the pastor and is set above me, but I'm an older woman than you are and, I declare, I don't see no harm in it.

MARGARET You don't see no harm in it, Sister Moore, because the Lord ain't placed you where he's placed me. Ain't no age in the Lord, Sister Moore—older or younger ain't got a thing to do with it. You just remember that I'm your pastor.

SISTER MOORE But, Sister Margaret, can't be no harm in a man trying to do his best for his family.

MARGARET The Lord comes before all things, Sister Moore. All things. Brother Boxer's supposed to do his best for the Lord.

SISTER MOORE But, Sister Margaret—

MARGARET I don't want to hear no more about it.

(SISTERS MOORE *and* BOXER *exchange a bitter look and they begin singing a church tune.* ODESSA *closes* MARGARET's *suitcase and puts it on the floor.* LUKE *appears in the alley, walking very slowly.*)

SISTERS MOORE AND BOXER 'Bye and 'bye when the morning comes
All the saints of God are gathering home,
We will tell the story how we overcome,
And we'll understand it better 'bye and 'bye

(LUKE *climbs the stairs into the church, walks through it slowly; finally enters the apartment as they finish the song*)

LUKE Good morning, folks. (*silence. Everyone stares, first at* LUKE, *then at* MARGARET. MARGARET *stands perfectly still*) Maggie, you ain't hardly changed a bit. You *still* the prettiest woman I ever laid eyes on.

MARGARET Luke.

LUKE Don't look at me like that. I changed that much? Well, sure, I might of lost a little weight. But you gained some. You ever notice how men, they tend to lose weight in later life, while the women, they gain? You look good, Maggie. It's good to see you.

MARGARET Luke—

LUKE (*to* ODESSA) Hey, you look good too. It's mighty good to see you again. You didn't think I'd come to New York and not find you? Ain't you going to say nothing, neither?

ODESSA Ah. You bad boy.

LUKE I bet my son is in this room somewhere. He's got to be in this room somewhere—(*to* BROTHER BOXER)—but I reckon it can't be you. I know it ain't been that long. (*to* DAVID) You come downtown last night to hear me play, didn't you?

DAVID Yes. Yes, sir. I did.

LUKE Why didn't you come up and say hello? I saw you, sitting way in the back, way at the end of the bar. I knew right away it was you. And, time I was finished, you was gone. (*a pause*) Cat got your tongue, Maggie? (*to* DAVID) I never knowed that to happen to your mama before.

MARGARET I never knowed my son to lie to me, neither. God don't like liars.

DAVID I was going to tell you.

MARGARET Luke, how'd you find us?

LUKE I had to find you. I didn't come to cause you no trouble. I just come by to say hello.

ODESSA Luke, sit down! I can't get over seeing you, right here in this room. I can't get over it. I didn't reckon on never seeing you no more—

LUKE In life. I didn't neither. But here I am—

ODESSA With your big, black, no-count self. You hungry?

LUKE Odessa, you ain't never going to change. Everytime you see a man, you think you got to go digging for some pork chops. No, I ain't hungry. I'm tired, though. I believe I'll sit down. (*he sits.* ODESSA *and* DAVID *glance at each other quickly*)

MARGARET How long you going to be in New York, Luke? When did you get here? Nobody told me—(*she looks at* DAVID)—nobody told me—you was here—

LUKE A couple of weeks is all. I figured I'd find you somewhere near a church. And you a pastor now? Well, I guess it suits you. She a good pastor?

SISTER MOORE Amen!

LUKE What do you think, David? (DAVID *is silent*) Well, she sure used to keep on at me about my soul. Didn't you, Maggie? Of course, that was only toward the end, when things got to be so rough. In the beginning—well, it's always different in the beginning.

MARGARET You ain't changed, have you? You still got the same carnal grin, that same carnal mind—you ain't changed a bit.

LUKE People don't change much, Maggie—

MARGARET Not unless the Lord changes their hearts—

LUKE You ain't changed much, neither—you dress a little different.

MARGARET Why did you come here? You ain't never brought me nothing but trouble, you come to bring me more trouble? Luke—I'm glad to see you and all but—I got to be going away this afternoon. I stay busy all the time around this church. David, he stays busy too—and he's coming with me this afternoon.

LUKE Well, honey, I'm used to your going. I done had ten years to get used to it. But, David—David, you can find a couple of minutes for your old man, can't you? Maybe you'd like to come out with me sometime—we could try to get acquainted—

DAVID You ain't wanted to get acquainted all this time—

LUKE Yes, I did. It ain't my fault—at least it ain't *all* my fault—that we ain't acquainted.

ODESSA Luke!

DAVID You run off and left us.

LUKE Boy, your daddy's done a lot of things he's ashamed of, but I wouldn't never of run off and left you and your mother. Your mama knows that. (*a pause*) You tell him, Maggie. Who left? Did I leave you or did you leave me?

MARGARET It don't make no difference now.

LUKE Who left? Tell him.

MARGARET When we was living with you, I didn't know half the time if I had a husband or not, this boy didn't know if he had a father!

LUKE That's a goddam lie. *You* knew you had a husband—this boy knew he had a father. Who left the house—who left?

MARGARET You was always on the road with them no-count jazz players—

LUKE But who *left*?

MARGARET I ain't going to stand here arguing with you—I got to go—David—

LUKE Who left?

MARGARET *I* did! *I* left! To get away from the stink of whisky—to save my baby—to find the Lord!

LUKE I wouldn't never of left you, son. Never. Never in this world.

MARGARET Leave us alone, Luke. Go away and leave us alone. I'm doing the Lord's work now—

DAVID Mama—you just said—God don't like liars.

MARGARET Your daddy weren't hardly ever home. I was going to explain it all to you—when you got big.

LUKE I done spent ten years wishing you'd leave the Lord's work to the Lord. (*he rises slowly*) You know where I'm working, boy. Come on down and see me. Please come on down and see me.

MARGARET Luke, he ain't going down there. You want to see him, you come on up here.

LUKE He's big enough to find his way downtown.

MARGARET I don't want him hanging around downtown.

LUKE It ain't no worse down there than it is up here.

MARGARET I ain't going to fight with you—not now—in front of the whole congregation. Brother Boxer, call me a taxi. David, close that suitcase and get yourself a coat. We got to go. (BROTHER BOXER *hesitates, rises, leaves*)

ODESSA Maggie, he's sick. (LUKE *sways, falls against the table.* SISTER BOXER *screams.* DAVID *and* ODESSA *struggle to raise him*)

SISTER MOORE Try to get him back here in this little room. Back here, in this bed, in this little room. (DAVID *and the women struggle with* LUKE *and get him to the bed.* DAVID *loosens his father's collar and takes off his shoes*)

LUKE (*moans*) Maggie.

SISTER BOXER We better send that man to a hospital.

MARGARET This here's a Holy Ghost station. The Lord don't do nothing without a purpose. Maybe the Lord wants to save his soul.

SISTER MOORE Well, amen.

MARGARET And Luke, if he want to keep on being hardhearted against the Lord, his blood can't be required at our hands. I got to go.

DAVID Mama, I'm going to stay here. (*a pause*) Mama, couldn't you write or telephone or something and let them folks know you can't get up there right now?

SISTER BOXER Yes, Sister Margaret, couldn't you do that? I don't believe that man is long for this world.

SISTER MOORE Yes, Sister Margaret, everybody understands that when you got trouble in the home, the home comes first. Send a deputy up there. I'll go for you.

MARGARET In this home, Sister Moore, the Lord comes first. The Lord made me leave that man in there a long time ago because he was a sinner. And the Lord ain't told me to stop doing my work just because he's come the way all sinners come.

DAVID But, Mama, he's been calling you, he going to keep on calling you! What we going to do if he start calling for you again?

MARGARET Tell him to call on the Lord! It

ain't me can save him, ain't nothing but the Lord can save him!

ODESSA But you might be able to help him, Maggie—if you was here.

DAVID Mama, you don't know. You don't know if he be living, time you get back. (*the taxi horn is heard*) But I reckon you don't care, do you?

MARGARET Don't talk to your mother that way, son. I don't want to go. I got to go.

SISTER BOXER When a woman make a vow to God, she got to keep it.

MARGARET You folks do what you can for him, pray and hold onto God for him. (*to* ODESSA) You send me a telegram if—if anything happens. (*to the others*) You folks got a evening service to get through. Don't you reckon you better run, get a bite to eat, so you can get back here on time?

BROTHER BOXER (*off stage*) Sister Margaret!

MARGARET Go, do like I tell you. David, see if you can find a doctor. You ain't going to do no good, standing there like that. Praise the Lord.

ODESSA Praise the Lord.

MARGARET (*to the others, dangerously*) Praise the Lord, I say.

SISTERS MOORE *and* BOXER (*dry*): Praise the Lord. (MARGARET *goes through the church into the street*)

LUKE Maggie. Maggie. Oh, Maggie.

ODESSA Children, let us pray.

(*Slowly, all, except* DAVID, *go to their knees. They begin singing*)

ALL If Jesus had to pray, what about me?
If Jesus had to pray, what about me?
He had to fall down on His knees,
Crying Father, help me if you please,
If Jesus had to pray, what about me?

In the garden Jesus prayed
While night was falling fast.
He said Father, if you will,
Let this bitter cup be past
But if not I am content,
Let my will be lost in Thine.
If Jesus had to pray, what about me?

(*Curtain*)

ACT TWO

(*Late afternoon the following Saturday. The sun is bright-red, the street is noisy. Cries of children playing, blaring radios and jukeboxes, etc.*

LUKE'*s room is dark, the shades drawn. He is still.*

ODESSA, SISTER BOXER *and* SISTER MOORE *are in the kitchen*)

SISTER MOORE (*to* ODESSA) We all loves Sister Margaret, sugar, just as much as you do. But we's supposed to bear witness, amen, to the truth. Don't care *who* it cuts.

SISTER BOXER She been going around all these years acting so *pure*.

SISTER MOORE Sister Margaret ain't nothing but flesh and blood, like all the rest of us. And she is got to watch and pray—like all the rest of us.

ODESSA Lord, honey, Sister Margaret, *she* know that.

SISTER BOXER She don't act like she know it. She act like she way above all human trouble. She always up there on that mountain, don't you know, just a-chewing the fat with the Lord.

SISTER MOORE That poor man!

ODESSA Sister Moore, you ain't never had no use for men all your life long. Now, how come you sitting up here this afternoon, talking about that *poor* man and talking against your pastor?

SISTER MOORE Don't you try to put words in my mouth, Sister Odessa, don't you do it! I ain't talking against my pastor, no, I ain't. I ain't doing a thing but talking like a Christian.

SISTER BOXER Last Sunday she acted like she didn't think that man was good enough to touch the hem of that white robe of her'n. And, you know, that ain't no way to treat a man who knowed one *time* what you was like with no robe on.

SISTER MOORE Sister Boxer!

SISTER BOXER Well, it's the truth. I'm bearing witness to the truth. I reckon I always thought of Sister Margaret like she'd been born holy. Like she hadn't never been a young girl or nothing and hadn't never had no real temptations. (BROTHER BOXER *enters*)

ODESSA I don't know how you could of thought that when everybody knowed she's been married—and she had a son.

BROTHER BOXER Praise the Lord, holy sisters, can a man come in?

ODESSA Come on in the house, Brother Boxer. (*to the others*) You be careful how you talk about your sister. The Lord ain't *yet* taken away His protecting arm.

BROTHER BOXER   Look like it might rain this evening.

ODESSA   Yes. The sky is getting mighty low.

SISTER BOXER   Oh, sure, I knowed she'd been married and she had this boy. But, I declare, I thought that that was just a mistake and she couldn't wait to get away from her husband. There's women like that, you know, ain't got much nature to them somehow.

SISTER MOORE   Now, you be careful, Sister Boxer, you know I ain't never been married, nor (*proudly*) I ain't never knowed no man.

SISTER BOXER   Well, it's different with you, Sister Moore. You give your life to the Lord right quick and you ain't got nothing like that to remember. But, you take me now, I'm a married woman and the Lord done blessed me with a real womanly nature and, I tell you, honey, you been married once, it ain't so easy to get along single. 'Course, I know the Holy Ghost is mighty and *will* keep—but, I declare, I wouldn't like to try it. No *wonder* that woman make so much noise when she get up in the pulpit.

BROTHER BOXER   She done gone too far, she done rose too *high*. She done forgot it ain't the woman supposed to lead, it's the man.

ODESSA   Is you done forgot your salvation? Don't you know if she'd followed that man, he might have led her straight on down to hell?

SISTER BOXER   That ain't by no means certain. If she'd done her duty like a wife, she might have been able to lead that man right straight to the throne of grace. I led *my* man there.

BROTHER BOXER   Well, you's a woman, sugar, and, quite natural, you want your man to come to heaven. But I believe in Sister Margaret's heaven, ain't going to be no men allowed. When that young woman come to the altar last Sunday morning, wanted the saints to pray for her baby, the first words out of Sister Margaret's mouth was "You better leave your husband."

SISTER BOXER   Amen! The *first* words.

ODESSA   Children, you better be careful what you say about a woman ain't been doing nothing but trying to serve the Lord.

SISTER MOORE   Is she been trying to serve the Lord? Or is she just wanted to put herself up over everybody else?

BROTHER BOXER   Now, that's what I'm talking about. The Word say, "You going to know a tree by its fruit." And we ain't been seeing such good fruit from Sister Margaret. I want to know, how come she think she can rule a church when she can't rule her own house? That husband of hers is in there, dying in his sins, and that half-grown, hypocrite son of hers is just running all roads to hell.

ODESSA   Little David's just been a little upset. He ain't thinking about going back into the world, he see what sin done for his daddy.

BROTHER BOXER   I got news for you, Sister Odessa. Little David ain't so little no more. I stood right in this very room last Sunday when we found out that boy had been lying to his mother. That's *right*. He been going out to *bars*. And just this very evening, not *five* minutes ago, I seen him down on 125th Street with some white horn player—the one he say he go to *school* with—and two other boys and three girls. Yes sir. They was just getting into a car.

ODESSA   It's just natural for David to be seeing folks his own age every now and then. And they just might be fixing to drop him at this very doorstep, you don't know. He might be here in time for tarry service.

BROTHER BOXER   I don't hear no cars drawing up in front of this door—no, I don't. And I bet you prayer meeting ain't what David had on his mind. That boy had a cigarette between his lips and had his hand on one of them girls, a real common-looking, black little thing, he had his hand on her—well, like he knowed her pretty *well* and wasn't expecting her to send him off to no prayer meeting.

SISTER MOORE   The Lord sure has been causing the scales to fall from the eyes of His servant this week. Thank you, Jesus!

ODESSA   You ought to be ashamed of yourselves! You ought to be ashamed of your black, deceitful hearts. You's liars, every one of you, and the truth's not in you! (*a pause*) Brother Boxer, Sister Boxer, Sister Moore. Let's go upstairs and pray.

SISTER MOORE   Yes, we *better* go upstairs and pray. The Lord's been working in the hearts of some other folks in this church and they's going to be along presently, asking the elders of this church to give them an accounting—amen!—of their spiritual leader.

ODESSA   What kind of accounting, Sister Moore?

SISTER MOORE Well, I just happened to be talking to some of the saints the other day and while we was talking some of them got to wondering just how much it cost to get to Philadelphia. Well, I said I didn't know because the Lord, He keep *me* close to home. But I said it couldn't cost but *so* much, ain't like she was going on a great long trip. Well—we got to talking about other things and then we just decided we'd come to church this evening and put our minds together. Amen. And let everybody say his piece and see how the Lord, *He* wanted us to move.

ODESSA Was you there, too, Brother Boxer

BROTHER BOXER Naturally I was there too. I'm one of the elders of the church.

ODESSA I'm one of the elders, too. But *I* wasn't there—wherever it was.

SISTER MOORE We wasn't planning to shut you out, Sister Odessa. Some folks just happened to drop by the house and we got to talking. That's all.

ODESSA Is folks thinking that Margaret's stealing their money?

SISTER BOXER That ain't no way to talk, Sister Odessa. Before God, ain't nobody said a word about stealing.

SISTER MOORE Ain't nobody accusing Margaret of *nothing*. Don't you let the Devil put that idea in your mind. Sister Margaret's been blessed with a real faithful congregation. Folks just loves Sister Margaret. Just the other day one of the saints—was it you, Sister Boxer?—one of the saints was saying to me how much trouble she have with her old refrigerator and she say it sure done her heart good to know her pastor had a nice, new frigidaire. Amen. She said it done her heart good.

(*They exit into the church. The lights go up slightly as they enter and sit. The church blacks out.*

For a moment the stage is empty. Then DAVID *appears, enters the house. He is very tired and nervous. He wanders about the kitchen; goes to* LUKE's *room, looks in. He is about to turn away when* LUKE *speaks*)

LUKE Hello, there.
DAVID I thought you was asleep.
LUKE I ain't sleepy. Is it night-time yet?
DAVID No, not yet.
LUKE Look like it's always night-time in this room. You want to come in, pull up the shade for me? (DAVID *does so. A faint sound of singing is heard from the church upstairs*)

LUKE Ain't you going to play piano for them tonight?

DAVID I don't much feel like playing piano right now. (*he is flustered; reaches in his pocket, takes out a pack of cigarettes, realizes his mistake too late*)

LUKE Didn't know you was smoking already. Let's have a cigarette.

DAVID You ain't suppose to be smoking. The doctor don't want you smoking.

LUKE The doctor ain't here now. (DAVID *gives* LUKE *a cigarette, lights it, after a moment lights one for himself*)

DAVID Look like you'd of had enough of smoking by now.

LUKE Sit down. We got a minute. (DAVID *sits on the hassock at the foot of* LUKE's *bed*)

LUKE Didn't I hear you playing piano one night this week?

DAVID No.

LUKE Boy, I'm sure I heard you playing *one* night—at the beginning of the service?

DAVID Oh. Yes, I guess so. I didn't stay. How did you know it was me?

LUKE You play piano like I dreamed you would.

DAVID I been finding out lately you was pretty good. Mama never let us keep a phonograph. I just didn't never hear any of your records—until here lately. You was right up there with the best, Jellyroll Morton and Louis Armstrong and cats like that.

LUKE You fixing to be a musician?

DAVID No.

LUKE Well, it ain't much of a profession for making money, that's the truth.

DAVID There were guys who did.

LUKE There were guys who didn't.

DAVID You never come to look for us. Why?

LUKE I started to. I wanted to. I thought of it lots of times.

DAVID Why didn't you never do it? Did you think it was good riddance we was gone?

LUKE I was hoping you wouldn't never think that, never.

DAVID I wonder what you expected me to think. I remembered you, but couldn't never talk about you. I used to hear about you sometime, but I couldn't never say, That's my daddy. I was too ashamed. I remembered how you used to play for me sometimes. That was why I started playing the piano. I used to go to sleep dreaming about the way we'd play together one day, me with my piano and you with your trombone.

LUKE David. David.

DAVID You never come. You never come when you could do us some good. You come now, now when you can't do nobody any good. Every time I think about it, think about *you*, I want to break down and cry like a baby. You make me—ah! You make me feel so bad.

LUKE Son—don't try to get away from the things that hurt you. The things that hurt you—sometimes that's all you got. You got to learn to live with those things—and—use them. I've seen people—put themselves through terrible torture—and die—because they was afraid of getting hurt. (*he wants to get rid of his cigarette.* DAVID *takes it from him. They stare at each other for a moment*) I used to hold you on my knee when you weren't nothing but a little—you didn't have no teeth then. Now I reckon you's already started to lose them. I reckon I thought we was a-going to bring down the moon, you and me, soon as you got a little bigger. I planned all kinds of things for you—they never come to pass.

DAVID You ain't never been saved, like Mama. Have you?

LUKE Nope.

DAVID How come Mama, she got saved?

LUKE I reckon she thought she better had—being married to me. I don't know. Your mama's kind of proud, you know, proud and silent. We had us a little trouble. And she wouldn't come to me. That's when she found the Lord.

DAVID I remember. I remember—that was when the baby was born dead. And Mama was in the hospital—and you was drunk, going to that hospital all the time—and I used to hear you crying, late at night. *Did* she find the Lord?

LUKE Can't nobody know but your mama, son.

DAVID A few months ago some guys come in the church and they heard me playing piano and they kept coming back all the time. Mama said it was the Holy Ghost drawing them in. But it wasn't.

LUKE It was your piano.

DAVID Yes. And I didn't draw them in. They drew me out. They setting up a combo and they want me to come in with them. That's when I stopped praying. I really began to think about it hard. And, Daddy—things started happening inside me which hadn't ever happened before. It was terrible. It was wonderful. I started looking around this house, around this church—like I was seeing it for the first time. Daddy—that's when I stopped believing—it just went away. I got so I just hated going upstairs to that church. I hated coming home. I hated lying to Mama all the time—and—I knew I had to do something—and that's how—I was scared, I didn't know what to do. I didn't know how to stay here and I didn't know how to go—and—there wasn't anybody I could talk to—I couldn't do—nothing! Every time I—even when I tried to make it with a girl—something kept saying, Maybe this is a sin. I hated it! (*he is weeping*) I made Mama let me go to music school and I started studying. I got me a little part-time job. I been studying for three months now. It gets better all the time—you know? I don't mean *me*—I got a long way to go—but *it* gets better. And I was trying to find some way of preparing Mama's mind—

LUKE When you seen me. And you got to wondering all over again if you wanted to be like your daddy and end up like your daddy. Ain't that right?

DAVID Yeah, I guess that's right.

LUKE Well, son, tell you one thing. Wasn't music put me here. The most terrible time in a man's life, David, is when he's done lost everything that held him together—it's just gone and he can't find it. The whole world just get to be a great big empty basin. And it just as hollow as a basin when you strike it with your fist. Then that man start going down. If don't no hand reach out to help him, that man goes under. You know, David, it don't take much to hold a man together. A man can lose a whole lot, might look to everybody else that he done lost so much that he ought to want to be dead, but he can keep on—he can even die with his head up, hell, as long as he got that one thing. That one thing is *him*, David, who he is inside—and, son, I don't believe no man ever got to that without somebody loved him. Somebody *looked* at him, looked *way* down in him and spied him way down there and showed him to himself—and then started pulling, a-pulling of him up—so he could live. (*exhausted*) Hold your head up, David. You'll have a life. Tell me there's all kinds of ways for ruined men to keep on living. You hears about guys sometimes who got a bullet in their guts and keeps on running —running—spilling blood every inch, keeps running a long time—before they fall. I don't know what keeps them going. Faith—or something—something—something I never had. (*a pause*) So don't you think you got to end up like your daddy just because you want to join a band.

DAVID Daddy—weren't the music enough?

LUKE The music. The music. Music is a moment. But life's a long time. In that moment, when it's good, when you really swinging—then you joined to everything, to everybody, to skies and stars and every living thing. But music ain't kissing. Kissing's what you want to do. Music's what you *got* to do, *if* you got to do it. Question is how long you can keep up with the music when you ain't got nobody to kiss. You know, the music don't come out of the air, baby. It comes out of the man who's blowing it.

DAVID You must have had a time.

LUKE I had me a time all right.

DAVID Didn't you never call on God?

LUKE No. I figured it was just as much His fault as mine.

DAVID Didn't you never get scared?

LUKE Oh yes.

DAVID But you're not scared now?

LUKE Oh yes.

(DAVID *goes off, stage left. The lights come up in the church, dim down in the apartment.* SISTER MOORE, SISTER BOXER, BROTHER BOXER, *along with some members of the congregation seen in the first act, are grouped together in camp chairs.* ODESSA *sits a little away from them.* SISTER RICE, *fortyish*, SISTER SALLY, *extremely young and voluptuous*, SISTER DOUGLASS, *quite old and slow and black*)

SISTER SALLY Why, a couple of months ago, just after we got married? Why, Herman and I, we had to go to Philadelphia *several* times and it don't cost no forty some odd dollars to get there. Why, it don't cost *that* much round trip.

SISTER DOUGLAS It ain't but up the road a ways, is it? I used to go up there to see my nephew, he stay too busy to be able to get to New York much. It didn't seem to me it took so long. 'Course, I don't remember how much it cost.

ODESSA I don't know why you folks don't just call up Pennsylvania Station and just *ask* how much it costs to get to Philadelphia.

BROTHER BOXER Most folks don't go to Philadelphia by train, Sister Odessa. They takes the bus because the bus is cheaper.

SISTER MOORE Now, of course ain't nothing these days what you might call really *cheap*. Brother Boxer, you remember when Sister Boxer had to go down home to bury her sister? You was going up to Philadelphia quite regular there for a while. You remember how much it cost?

SISTER BOXER You ain't never mentioned you knew anybody in Philadelphia.

SISTER SALLY Men don't never tell women nothing. Look like you always finding out something new.

BROTHER BOXER Man better not tell a woman everything he know, not if he got good sense. (*to* SISTER MOORE) It didn't cost no more'n about three or four dollars.

SISTER BOXER That round trip or one way?

SISTER DOUGLASS How much you folks say you raised on the offering last Sunday?

SISTER MOORE Brother Boxer and me, we counted it, and put it in the envelope. It come to—what did it come to altogether, Brother Boxer? Give us the *exact* figure, amen.

BROTHER BOXER It come to forty-one dollars and eighty-seven cents.

SISTER RICE Don't seem to me we ought to be sitting here like this, worrying about the few pennies we give our pastor last Sunday. We been doing it Sunday after Sunday and ain't nobody never had nothing to say against Sister Margaret. She's our pastor, we ain't supposed to be thinking no evil about her.

SISTER MOORE That's what I say, amen. Sister Margaret our pastor and the few pennies we scrapes together by the sweat of our brow to give her she got a right to do with as she see *fit*, amen! And I think we ought to stop discussing it right here and now and just realize that we's blessed to have a woman like Sister Margaret for our shepherd.

ODESSA You folks sound like a church don't have to pay no rent, and don't never pay no bills and nothing in a church don't never wear out.

Them chairs you got your behinds on right now, they have to keep on being replaced—you folks is always breaking them during the service, when you gets happy. Those of you what wears glasses, though, I notice you don't never break them. You holds yourself together somehow until somebody comes and takes them off'n you. Rugs on the floor cost money, robes cost money —and you people is just murder on hymn books, tambourines and Bibles. Now, Margaret don't use hardly none of that money on herself— ain't enough money *in* this church for nobody to be able to live off it.

BROTHER BOXER You folks got a new Frigidaire, though. I ain't saying nothing, but—

ODESSA That Frigidaire is in *my* name, Brother Boxer—it's the first new thing I bought for that house in I don't know how many years —with money *I* made from scrubbing white folks' floors. Ain't a one of you put a penny in it. Now. You satisfied?

SISTER MOORE How's your mother getting along, Sister Rice? I hope she feeling better. We ain't seen her for a long time.

SISTER RICE We's holding onto God for her. But she been doing poorly, poor thing. She say she sure do miss not being able to come out to service.

SISTER MOORE But Sister Margaret's been there, praying for her, ain't she?

SISTER RICE No, Sister Margaret ain't got there yet. She say she was going to make it last Sunday, but then she had to go to Philadelphia—

SISTER MOORE Poor Sister Margaret. She sure has had her hands full.

SISTER BOXER She got her hands full right down there in her own house. Reckon she couldn't get over to pray for your mother, Sister Rice, she couldn't stay here to pray for her own husband.

SISTER DOUGLAS The Word say we ain't supposed to think no evil, Sister Boxer. Sister Margaret have to go the way the Lord leads her.

SISTER BOXER I ain't thinking no evil. But the World *do* say, if you don't love your brother who you can see, how you going to love God, who you ain't seen?

SISTER SALLY That is a *true* saying, bless the Lord.

SISTER DOUGLASS How is that poor, sin-sick soul?

SISTER BOXER He ain't long for this world. He lying down there, just rotten with sin. He dying in his sins.

SISTER MOORE He real pitiful. I declare, when you see what sin can do it make you stop and think.

SISTER RICE Do David spend much time with him, Sister Odessa? I reckon it must make him feel real bad to see his father lying there like that.

ODESSA Luke so sick he do a lot of sleeping, so David can't really be with him so much.

SISTER DOUGLASS Oh. We ain't seen David hardly at all this week and I just figured he was downstairs with his father.

BROTHER BOXER Little David—I'm mighty afraid little David got other fish to fry. The Lord has allowed me to see, with my *own* eyes, how David's done started straying from the Word. I ain't going to say no more. But the brother needs prayer. Amen. Sister Moore, do you recollect how much it cost us to get that there window painted?

SISTER MOORE Why, no, Brother Boxer, I don't. Seem to me it cost about fifty dollars.

SISTER BOXER It cost fifty-three dollars. I remember because Sister Margaret weren't here when the work was finished and I give the man the money myself.

SISTER DOUGLASS It a mighty pretty window. Look like it make you love Jesus even more, seeing Him there all in the light like that.

BROTHER BOXER You remember who she got to do it?

SISTER BOXER Why, she got one of them folks from Philadelphia to do it. That was before we was even affiliated with that church.

BROTHER BOXER I believe we could of got it done for less, right down here among our own.

SISTER RICE I don't know, Brother Boxer, that's fine work. You got to have *training* for that. People think you can just get up and draw a picture, but it ain't so.

SISTER DOUGLASS That's the truth, Sister Rice. My nephew, he draws, and he all the time telling me how hard it is. I have to help him out all the time, you know, 'cause it ain't easy to make a living that way—

SISTER BOXER I don't know why your nephew couldn't of drew it for us. I bet you he wouldn't of charged no fifty-three dollars, either.

SISTER SALLY   My mother, she go to Bishop William's church up there on 145th Street, you know, and she was saying to me just the other day she don't see why, after all these years, Sister Margaret couldn't move her congregation to a better building.

SISTER MOORE   Sister Margaret ain't worried about these buildings down here on earth, daughter. Sister Margaret's working on another building, hallelujah, in the *heavens*, not made with hands!

SISTER SALLY   Why, that's what my mother's doing, too, Sister Moore. But she say she don't see why you got to be in dirt all the time just because you a Christian.

ODESSA   If anybody in this church is in dirt, it ain't the dirt of this church they's in. I know this ain't no palace but it's the best we can do right now. Sister Margaret's been doing her best for every one of us and it ain't right for us to sit up here this evening, back-biting against her.

SISTER MOORE   Sister Odessa, I told you downstairs it ain't nothing but the Devil putting them thoughts in your head. Ain't nobody back-biting against your sister. We's just discussing things, the Lord, He give us eyes to see and understanding to understand.

SISTER BOXER   Amen!

SISTER MOORE   I got yet to say my first word against your sister. I know the Lord is seen fit, for reasons *I* ain't trying to discover, to burden your sister with a heavy burden. I ain't sitting in judgment. I ain't questioning the ways of the Lord. I don't know what that half-grown son of hers done seen to cause him to backslide this-a-way. *I* don't know why that man of hers is down there, dying in his sins—just rotting away, amen, before her eyes. I ain't asking no questions. I'm just waiting on the Lord because He say He'll reveal all things. In His own good time.

SISTER BOXER   Amen! And I believe He's going to use us to help him reveal.

(SISTER MOORE *begins singing*)

ODESSA   Sister Moore!

SISTER MOORE   You can run on for a long time,
You can run on for a long time,
You can run on for a long time,
I tell you the great God Almighty
gonna cut you down.

CONTRALTO   Some people go to church just to signify
Trying to make a date with their neighbor's wife.
Brother, let me tell you just as sure as you're born
You better leave that woman, leave her alone.
One of these days, just mark my word,
You'll think your neighbor has gone to work,
You'll walk right up and knock on the door—
That's all, brother, you'll knock no more.
Go tell that long-tongued liar, go tell that midnight rider,
Go tell the gambler, rambler, backslider,
Tell him God Almighty's gonna cut you down.

(*During the last line of song* MARGARET *enters*)

MARGARET   Praise the Lord, children. I'm happy to see you's holding the fort for Jesus.

SISTER MOORE   Praise the *Lord*, Sister Margaret! We was just wondering if you was *ever* coming back here!

SISTER BOXER   Praise the Lord, Sister Margaret, we sure is glad you's back. Did you have a good trip?

MARGARET   Praise the Lord, children. It sure is good to be back here. The Lord, He give us the victory in Philadelphia, amen! He just worked and uncovered sin and put them children on their knees!

ALL   What a wonder, what a marvel,
And I'm glad that I can tell
That the Lord saved me and He set me free,
He endowered me with power,
And gave me the victory.

What a wonder, what a marvel,
And I'm glad that I can tell
That the Lord saved me and He set me free,
He endowered me with power,
And gave me the victory.

What a wonder, what a marvel,
And I'm glad that I can tell
That the Lord saved me and He set me free,
He endowered me with power,
And gave me the victory.

SISTER MOORE   When it come time for the Lord to uncover, He sure do a mighty uncovering!

MARGARET (*to* ODESSA)   Has everything been all right, sugar?

ODESSA   Yes, Maggie. Everything's been fine.

SISTER BOXER   How did you come down, Sister Margaret? Did you take the train or the bus?

MARGARET   Honey, one of the Philadelphia saints drove me down.

SISTER BOXER *Drove* you down! I reckon you *did* get the victory. (*laughter*)

SISTER MOORE Well, bless the Lord, that's real nice. I reckon they was trying to help you cut down on expenses.

MARGARET Children, tomorrow is going to be a mighty big Sunday. The Philadelphia church is coming down here, all of them, for the evening service. Even Mother Phillips might be coming, she say she's feeling so much better. You know, this church is going to be packed. (*to* BROTHER BOXER) Brother Boxer, you going to have to clear a little space around that piano because they bringing their drums down here. (*to the others*) They got drums up there, children, and it help the service a whole lot, I wouldn't have believed it. (*the merest pause*) They even got a man up there making a joyful noise to the Lord on a trumpet!

BROTHER BOXER He coming down here, too?

MARGARET Oh, yes, he'll be here. Children, I want you all to turn out in full force tomorrow and show them Philadelphia saints how to praise the Lord.

SISTER DOUGLAS Look like they going to be able to teach us something, they got them drums and trumpets and all—

SISTER MOORE That don't make no difference. We been praising the Lord without that all this time, we ain't going to let them show us up.

MARGARET You better *not* let them show you up. You supposed to be an example to the *Philadelphia* church.

SISTER RICE But, Sister Margaret, you think it's right to let them come down here with all that—with drums and trumpets? Don't that seem kind of worldly?

MARGARET Well, the evil ain't in the drum, Sister Rice, nor yet in the trumpet. The evil is in what folks do with it and what it leads them to. Ain't no harm in praising the Lord with anything you get in your hands.

BROTHER BOXER It'll bring Brother David out to church again, I guarantee you that. That boy loves music.

MARGARET I hope you don't mean he loves music more than he loves the Lord.

BROTHER BOXER Oh, we all know how much he loves the Lord. But he got trumpets or *some* kind of horn in his *blood*.

ODESSA I reckon you going to have to speak to David, Maggie. He upset about his daddy and he ain't been out to service much this week.

SISTER MOORE When you upset, that's the time to come to the Lord. If you believe He loves you, you got to trust His love.

MARGARET Poor David. He don't talk much, but he feel a whole lot.

SISTER BOXER How is his daddy, Sister Margaret? You been downstairs to look at him yet?

ODESSA We ain't allowed to break his rest.

MARGARET I pray the Lord will save his soul.

SISTER MOORE Amen. And, church, we got to pray that the Lord will draw our David back to Him, so he won't end up like his daddy. Our pastor, she got a lot to bear.

MARGARET David ain't foolish, Sister Moore, and he done been well raised. He ain't going back into the world.

SISTER MOORE I hope and pray you's right, from the bottom of my soul I do. But every living soul needs prayer, Sister Margaret, every living soul. And we's just trying to hold up your hand in this time of trouble.

SISTER BOXER Sister Margaret, I ain't trying to dig up things what buried. But you told Joel and me he couldn't take that job driving that truck. And now you bringing down drums and trumpets from Philadelphia because you say the evil ain't in the thing, it's in what you do with the thing. Well, ain't that truck a *thing*? And if it's all right to blow a trumpet in church, why ain't it all right for Joel to drive that truck, so he can contribute a little more to the house of God? This church is *poor*, Sister Margaret, we ain't got no cars to ride you around in, like them folks in Philadelphia. But do that mean we got to *stay* poor?

MARGARET Sister Boxer, you know as well as me that there's many a piano out in them night clubs. But that ain't stopped us from using a piano in this church. And there's all the difference in the world between a saint of God playing music in a church and helping to draw people in and a saint of God spending the whole day driving a liquor truck around. Now I know you got good sense and I know you see that, and I done already told you I don't want to talk no more about it.

SISTER BOXER It don't seem to me you's being fair, Sister Margaret.

MARGARET When is I ain't been fair? I been

doing my best, as the Lord led me, for all of you, for all these years. How come you to say I ain't been fair? You sound like you done forget your salvation, Sister Boxer.

(DAVID *reappears, carrying a phonograph and a record. He enters* LUKE's *bedroom.* LUKE's *eyes are closed. He goes to the bed and touches him lightly and* LUKE *opens his eyes*)

LUKE What you got there?

DAVID You going to recognize it. Be quiet, listen. (*he plugs in the phonograph*)

SISTER MOORE Now the Word say Blessed is the peacemaker, so let me make peace. This ain't no way to be behaving.

MARGARET Sister Moore, I'm the pastor of this church and I don't appreciate you acting as though we was both in the wrong.

SISTER MOORE Ain't nobody infallible, Sister Margaret. Ain't a soul been born infallible.

ODESSA We better all fall on our knees and pray.

MARGARET Amen.

(DAVID *has turned on the record, watching* LUKE. *The sound of* LUKE's *trombone fills the air*)

SISTER MOORE Where's that music coming from?

ODESSA It must be coming from down the street.

MARGARET (*recognition*) Oh, my God.

SISTER MOORE It coming from your house, Sister Margaret.

MARGARET Kneel down. (*they watch her*) Kneel *down*, I say!

(LUKE *takes his mouthpiece from his pajama pocket and pantomimes a phrase, then stops, his mouthpiece in his hand, staring at his son. In the church, slowly, they kneel*)

MARGARET Pray. Every single one of you. Pray that God will give you a clean heart and a clean mind and teach you to obey. (*she turns and leaves the pulpit. Upstairs, they turn and look at each other and slowly rise from their knees. The church dims out.* MARGARET *stands for a moment in the door of* LUKE's *bedroom*)

MARGARET David!

DAVID Mama—I didn't hear you come in!

MARGARET I reckon you didn't hear me come in. The way that box is going, you wouldn't of hear the Holy *Ghost* come in. Turn it Off! Turn it off! (DAVID *does so*)

MARGARET You ain't supposed to let your daddy come here and lead you away from the Word. You's supposed to lead your daddy to the Lord. (*to* LUKE) It seems to me by this time the very sound of a horn would make you to weep or pray.

DAVID It's one of Daddy's old records. That you never let me play.

MARGARET Where'd that box come from? What's it doing in this house?

DAVID I borrowed it.

MARGARET Where'd you get that record?

DAVID It's mine.

LUKE That's right. It's his—now. (*a pause*)

MARGARET I ain't trying to be hard on you, son. But we's got to watch and pray. We's got to watch and pray.

DAVID Yes, Mama. Mama, I got to go now.

MARGARET Where you going, son?

LUKE Maggie, he ain't five years old, he's eighteen. Let him alone.

MARGARET You be quiet. You ain't got nothing to say in all this.

LUKE That's a lie. I got a lot to say in all this. That's my son. Go on, boy. You remember what I told you.

DAVID I'm taking the record player back where I got it. (*at the door*) So long—Daddy—

LUKE Go on, boy. You all right?

MARGARET David—

DAVID I'm all right, Daddy. (DAVID *goes*)

LUKE So long, son.

MARGARET Luke, ain't you never going to learn to do right? Ain't you learned nothing out all these years, all this trouble?

LUKE I done learned a few things. They might not be the same things you wanted me to learn. Hell, I don't know if they are the same things *I* wanted me to learn.

MARGARET I ain't never wanted you to learn but one thing, the love of Jesus.

LUKE You done changed your tune a whole lot. That ain't what we was trying to learn in the beginning.

MARGARET The beginning is a long time ago. And weren't nothing but foolishness. Ain't nothing but the love of God can save your soul.

LUKE Maggie, don't fight with me. I don't want to fight no more. We didn't get married because we loved God. We loved each other. Ain't that right?

MARGARET   I sure can't save your soul, Luke.

LUKE   There was a time when I believed you could.

MARGARET   Luke. That's all past. (*she sits on the edge of the bed*) Luke, it been a long time we ain't seen each other, ten long years. Look how the Lord done let you fall. Ain't you ready to give up to Him and ask Him to save you from your sins and bring peace to your soul?

LUKE   Is you got peace in your soul, Maggie?

MARGARET   Yes! He done calmed the waters, He done beat back the powers of darkness, He done made me a new woman!

LUKE   Then that other woman—that funny, fast-talking, fiery little thing I used to hold in my arms—He done done away with her?

MARGARET   (*rises*) All that's—been burned out of me by the power of the Holy Ghost.

LUKE   Maggie, I remember you when you didn't hardly know if the Holy Ghost was something to drink or something to put on your hair. I know we can't go back, Maggie. But you mean that whole time we was together, even with all our trouble, you mean it don't mean nothing to you now? You mean—you don't remember? I was your *man*, Maggie, we was everything to each other, like that Bible of yours say, we was one flesh—we used to get on each other's nerves something *awful*—you mean that's all dead and gone?

MARGARET   You is still got that old, sinful Adam in you. You's thinking with Adam's mind. You don't understand that when the Lord changes you He makes you a new person and He gives you a new mind.

LUKE   Don't talk at me like I was a congregation. I ain't no congregation. I'm your husband, even if I ain't much good to you no more.

MARGARET   Well, if it's all dead and gone—you killed it! Don't you lay there and try to make me feel accused. If it's all dead and gone, you did it, you did it!

LUKE   Ah. Now we coming. At least it wasn't the Holy Ghost. Just how did I do it, Maggie? How did I kill it?

MARGARET   I never knew why you couldn't be like other men.

LUKE   I was the man you married, Maggie. I weren't supposed to be like other men. When we didn't have nothing, I made it my business to find something, didn't I? Little David always had shoes to his feet when I was there and you wasn't never dressed in rags. And anyway—you want me to repent so you can get me into heaven, or you want me to repent so you can keep David home?

MARGARET   Is David been talking about leaving home?

LUKE   Don't you reckon he going to be leaving home one day?

MARGARET   David going to work with me in these here churches and he going to be a pastor when he get old enough.

LUKE   He got the call?

MARGARET   He'll *get* the call.

LUKE   You sure got a lot of influence with the Holy Ghost.

MARGARET   I didn't come in here to listen to you blaspheme. I just come in here to try to get you to think about your soul.

LUKE   Margaret, once you told me you loved me and then you jumped up and ran off from me like you couldn't stand the smell of me. What you think *that* done to my soul?

MARGARET   I had to go. The Lord told me to go. We'd been living like—like two animals, like two children, never thought of nothing but their own pleasure. In my heart, I always knew we couldn't go on like that—we was too happy—

LUKE   Ah!

MARGARET   And that winter—them was terrible days, Luke. When I'd almost done gone under, I heard a voice. The voice said, Maggie, you got to find you a hiding place. I I knowed weren't no hiding place to be found in you—not in no man. And you—you cared more about that trombone than you ever cared about me!

LUKE   You ought to of tried me, Maggie. If you had trusted me till then, you ought to have trusted me a little further.

MARGARET   When they laid my baby in the churchyard, that poor little baby girl what hadn't never drawn breath, I knowed if we kept on a-going the way we'd been going, He weren't going to have no mercy on neither one of us. And that's when I swore to my God I was going to change my way of living.

LUKE   Then that God you found—He just curse the poor? But He don't bother nobody else? Them big boys, them with all the money and all the manners, what let you drop dead in the streets, watch your blood run all over the gutters, just so they can make a lousy dime—He get along fine with them? What the hell had we done to be cursed, Maggie?

MARGARET We hadn't never thought of nothing but ourself. We hadn't never thought on God!

LUKE All we'd done to be cursed was to be *poor*, that's all. That's why little Margaret was laid in the churchyard. It was just because you hadn't never in your whole life had enough to eat and you was sick that winter and you didn't have no strength. Don't you come on with me about no judgment, Maggie. That was my baby, too.

MARGARET *Your* baby, yours! I was the one who carried it in my belly, *I* was the one who felt it starving to death inside me. *I* was the one who had it, in the cold and dark alone! You wasn't nowhere to be found, you was out drunk.

LUKE I was *there*. I was *there*. Yes, I was drunk, but I was sitting at your bedside every day. Every time you come to yourself you looked at me and started screaming about how I'd killed our baby. Like I'd taken little Margaret and strangled her with my own two hands. *Yes*, I was drunk but I was waiting for you to call me. You never did. You never did.

MARGARET I reckon the Lord was working with me, even then.

LUKE I reckon so.

MARGARET Luke. Luke, it don't do to question God.

LUKE No, it don't. It sure as hell don't.

MARGARET Don't let your heart be bitter. You'd come way down, Luke, bitterness ain't going to help you now. Let Him break your heart, let the tears come, ask Him to forgive you for your sins, call on Him, call on Him!

LUKE Call on Him for what, Maggie?

MARGARET To save your soul. To keep you from the fires of hell. So we can be together in glory.

LUKE I want to be together with you now.

MARGARET Luke. You ain't fighting with men no more. You's fighting with God. You got to humble yourself, you got to bow your head.

LUKE It ain't going to be like that, Maggie. I ain't going to come crawling to the Lord now, making out like I'd do better if I had it all to do over. I ain't going to go out, screaming against hell-fire. It would make *you* right. It would prove to David you was right. It would make me nothing but a dirty, drunk old man didn't do nothing but blow music and chase the women all his life. I ain't going to let it be like that. That ain't all there was to it. You know that ain't all there was to it.

MARGARET Stubborn, stubborn, stubborn Luke! You like a little boy. You think this is a game? You think it don't hurt me to my heart to see you the way you is now? You think my heart ain't black with sorrow to see your soul go under?

LUKE Stop talking about my soul. It's me, Maggie—*me*! Don't you remember *me*? Don't you care nothing about *me*? You ain't never stopped loving me. Have you, Maggie? Can't you tell me the truth?

MARGARET Luke—we ain't young no more. It don't matter no more about us. But what about our boy? You want him to live the life you've lived? You want him to end up—old and empty-handed?

LUKE I don't care what kind of life he lives —as long as it's *his* life—not mine, not his mama's, but his own. I ain't going to let you make him safe.

MARGARET I can't do no more. Before God, I done my best. Your blood can't be required at my hands.

LUKE I guess I could have told you—it weren't *my* soul we been trying to save. (*low, syncopated singing from the church begins*)

MARGARET Luke. You's going to die. I hope the Lord have mercy on you.

LUKE I ain't asking for no goddam mercy. (*he turns his face to the wall*) Go away.

MARGARET You's going to die, Luke. (*she moves slowly from the bedroom into the kitchen.* ODESSA *enters from the church, goes to* MARGARET)

ODESSA Honey—they's going to have a business meeting upstairs. You hear me? You know what that means? If you want to hold onto this church, Maggie—if you do—you better get on upstairs. (MARGARET *is silent*) Where's David? He ought to be here when you need him.

MARGARET I don't know.

ODESSA I'll go and see if I can find him. You all right?

MARGARET It looks like rain out there. Put something on. (*after a moment,* ODESSA *goes.*

MARGARET *walks up and down the kitchen. Her tears begin*) Lord, help us to stand. Help us to stand. Lord, give me strength! Give me strength!

(*Curtain*)

ACT THREE

(*Music is heard offstage, a slow, quiet sound.*
Early the following morning. A bright quiet day. Except for LUKE, *the stage is empty. His room is dark. He is sleeping.*
The light comes up very slowly in the church. After a moment, MRS. JACKSON *enters. She is wearing a house dress and slippers. She puts her hands to her face, moaning slightly, then falls heavily before the altar.*
MARGARET *enters through* LUKE's *bedroom. She pauses a moment at the foot of* LUKE's *bed, then enters the kitchen, then slowly mounts to the church.*
As she enters, MRS. JACKSON *stirs. They stare at each other for a moment.*
MRS. JACKSON *is weeping*)

MRS. JACKSON Sister Margaret, you's a woman of the Lord—you say you in communion with the Lord. Why He take my baby from me? Tell me why He do it? Why He make my baby suffer so? Tell me why He do it!

MARGARET Sister—we got to trust God—somehow. We got to bow our heads.

MRS. JACKSON My head is bowed. My head been bowed since I been born. His daddy's head is bowed. The Lord ain't got no right to make a baby suffer so, just to make me bow my head!

MARGARET Be careful what you say, daughter. Be careful what you say. We can't penetrate the mysteries of the Lord's will.

MRS. JACKSON (*moves away*) Why I got to be careful what I say? You think the Lord going to do me something else? I ain't got to be careful what I say no more. I sit on the bench in the hospital all night long, me and my husband, and we waited and we prayed and we wept. I said, Lord, if you spare my baby, I won't never take another drink, I won't do nothing, nothing to displease you, if you only give me back my baby, safe and well. He was such a nice baby and just like his daddy, he liked to laugh already. But I ain't going to have no more. Such a nice baby, I don't see why he had to get all twisted and curled up with pain and scream his little head off. And couldn't nobody help him. He hadn't never done nothing to nobody. Ain't nobody never done nothing bad enough to suffer like that baby suffered.

MARGARET Daughter, pray with me. Come, pray with me.

MRS. JACKSON I been trying to pray. Everytime I kneel down, I see my baby again—and—I can't pray. I can't get it out of my head, it ain't right, even if He's God, it ain't right.

MARGARET Sister—once I lost a baby, too. I know what that emptiness feel like, I declare to my Saviour I do. That was when I come to the Lord. I wouldn't come before. Maybe the Lord is working with you now. Open your heart and listen. Maybe, out of all this sorrow, He's calling you to do His work.

MRS. JACKSON I ain't like you, Sister Margaret. I don't want all this, all these people looking to me. I'm just a young woman, I just want my man and my home and my children.

MARGARET But that's all I wanted. That's what I wanted! Sometimes—what we want—and what we ought to have—ain't the same. Sometime, the Lord, He take away what we want and give us what we need.

MRS. JACKSON And do I need—that man sitting home with a busted heart? Do I need—two children in the graveyard?

MARGARET I don't know, I ain't the Lord, I don't know what you need. You need to pray.

MRS. JACKSON No, I'm going home to my husband. He be getting worried. He don't know where I am. (*she starts out*)

MARGARET Sister Jackson! (MRS. JACKSON *turns*) Why did you say you ain't going to have no more babies? You still a very young woman.

MRS. JACKSON I'm scared to go through it again. I can't go through it again.

MARGARET That ain't right. That ain't right. You ought to have another baby. You ought to have another baby right away. (*pause*) Honey—is there anything you want me to do for you now, in your time of trouble?

MRS. JACKSON No, Sister Margaret, ain't nothing you can do. (*she goes.* MARGARET *stands alone in the church*)

MARGARET Get on home to your husband. Go on home, to your man.

(*Downstairs,* ODESSA *enters through* LUKE's *room; pauses briefly at* LUKE's *bed, enters the kitchen. She goes to the stove, puts a match under the coffeepot.* MARGARET *stares at the altar; starts downstairs*)

ODESSA (*sings, under her breath*)
Some say the rose of Sharon, some say the prince of Peace.
But I call Jesus my Rock! (MARGARET *enters*)
How long you been up, Maggie?

MARGARET I don't know. Look like I couldn't sleep.

ODESSA You got a heavy day ahead of you.

MARGARET I know it. David ain't come in yet?

ODESSA No, but don't you fret. He's all right. He'll be along. It's just natural for young boys to go a little wild every now and again. Soon this'll all be over, Maggie, and when you look back on it it won't be nothing more than like you had a bad dream.

MARGARET A bad dream!

ODESSA They ain't going to turn you out, Maggie. They ain't crazy. They know it take a *long* time before they going to find another pastor of this church like you.

MARGARET It won't take them so long if Sister Moore have her way. She going to be the next pastor of this church. Lord, you sure can't tell what's going on in a person's heart.

ODESSA The Bible say the heart is deceitful above all things. And desperately wicked.

MARGARET Who can know it? I guess whoever wrote that wasn't just thinking about the hearts of other people.

ODESSA Maggie you better go on in the front and lie down awhile. You got time. Sunday school ain't even started yet. I'll call you in time for you to get dressed for service.

MARGARET I reckon I better. (*she starts out, stops*) They talk about me letting my own house perish in sin. The Word say if you put father or mother or brother or sister or husband—or *anybody*—ahead of Him, He ain't going to have nothing to do with you on the last day.

ODESSA Yes. The Word do say so.

MARGARET I married that man when I weren't hardly nothing but a girl. I used to know that man, look like, just inside *out*, sometime I knowed what he was going to do before he knowed it himself. Sometime I could just look up, look up at that face, and just—*know*. Ain't no man never made me laugh the way Luke could. No, nor cry neither. I ain't never held no man until I felt his pain coming into me like little drops of acid. Odessa, I bore that man his only son. Now, you know there's still something left in my heart for that man.

ODESSA Don't think on it, honey. Don't think on it so. Go on in front and lie down.

MARGARET Yes. (*she starts out, stops*) Odessa—you know what amen means?

ODESSA Amen means—*amen*.

MARGARET Amen means Thy will be done. Amen means So be it. I been up all morning, praying—and—I couldn't say amen. (*she goes*)

ODESSA Lord, have mercy. Have mercy, Lord, this morning. (*sings, under her breath*) Some say the Rose of Sharon, some say the Prince of Peace. But I call Jesus my rock! (*she goes to the door of* LUKE's *room.* BROTHER *and* SISTER BOXER *and* SISTER MOORE *enter the church. The two women are all in white*) Yes, Lord. Everytime a woman don't know if she coming or going, every*time* her heart get all swelled up with grief, there's a man sleeping somewhere close by. (SISTER BOXER *crosses the church and comes down the stairs*)

SISTER BOXER Praise the Lord, Sister Odessa. You all alone this morning?

ODESSA I didn't know you folks was upstairs. How long you been there?

SISTER BOXER We just this minute come in.

ODESSA You all mighty early, seems to me.

SISTER BOXER Well, Sister Moore, she thought if we got here early we might be able to see Sister Margaret before anybody else come in.

ODESSA Sister Margaret ain't ready to see nobody yet.

SISTER BOXER It almost time for Sunday school.

ODESSA Sister Boxer, you know right well that Sister Margaret don't hardly never come to Sunday school. She got to save her strength for the morning service. You know that.

SISTER BOXER Well, Sister Moore thought —maybe *this* morning—

ODESSA Sister Boxer—don't you think enough harm's been done with all them terrible things was said last night?

SISTER BOXER Ain't nobody said nothing last night that wasn't the gospel truth.

ODESSA I done heard enough truth thesen

last couple of days to last me the rest of my life.

SISTER BOXER The truth is a two-edged sword, Sister Odessa.

ODESSA It ain't never going to cut you down. You ain't never going to come that close to it.

SISTER BOXER Well—do Jesus! Soon as something happens to that sister of yours you forgets all about your salvation, don't you? You better ask the Lord to watch your tongue. The tongue is a *unruly* member.

ODESSA It ain't as unruly as it's going to get. (*a pause*) Sister Boxer, this ain't no way for us to be talking. We used to be *friends*. We used to have right *good* times together. How come we got all this bad feeling all of a sudden? Look like it come out of nowhere, overnight.

SISTER BOXER I ain't got no bad feeling toward *you*, Sister Odessa. (*after a moment,* SISTER BOXER *turns and mounts to the church.* ODESSA *follows*)

SISTER MOORE Praise the Lord, Sister Odessa. How you this Lord's day morning?

ODESSA I'm leaning on the Lord, Sister Moore. How you feeling?

BROTHER BOXER Praise the Lord, Sister Odessa. I'm mighty glad to hear you say that. We needs the Lord this morning. We needs to hear Him speak peace to our souls.

ODESSA How come you folks want to see Sister Margaret so early in the morning?

SISTER BOXER Well, we ain't really got to see Sister Margaret, not now that you're here, Sister Odessa. You is still one of the elders of this church.

SISTER MOORE We want to do everything we got to do in front, amen. Don't want nobody saying we went around and done it in the dark.

ODESSA You's doing it in front, all right. You's supposed to do it in front of the whole congregation this afternoon.

BROTHER BOXER Well, the Lord's done led us to do a little different from the way we was going to do last night.

ODESSA How's that, Brother Boxer? (*a pause*) Well, now, the way I understood it last *night*—you folks say that Margaret ain't got no right to call herself a spiritual leader. *You* folks say that Margaret done let her own household perish in sin and—you folks say—that all these things is a sign from the Lord that He ain't pleased with Margaret and you was going to put all that in front of this church and the church from Philadelphia and see what *they* thought. Ain't that right?

SISTER BOXER We done already spoken to the members of this church. Margaret's as good as read out of this church already, ain't hardly no need for her to come to service.

SISTER MOORE I spoke to them myself. I been up since early this morning, bless the Lord, just ringing doorbells and stirring up the people against sin.

ODESSA You must of got up mighty early.

SISTER MOORE When the Lord's work is to be done, I gets up out of my bed. God don't love the slothful. And, look like the more I do, the more He gives me strength to do.

BROTHER BOXER We thought it might be easier on Sister Margaret if we done it this way. Ain't no need for folks to know all of Sister Margaret's personal business. So we ain't said nothing about Brother Luke. Folks is bound to try and put two and two together—but *we* ain't said nothing. We ain't said nothing about Brother David. We is just told the congregation that the Lord's done revealed to the elders of this church that Sister Margaret ain't been leading the life of a holy woman, especially a holy woman in *her* position, is supposed to lead. That's all. And we said we weren't sitting in *judgment* on Sister Margaret. We was leaving it up to her conscience, amen, and the Lord.

SISTER BOXER But we did say—since we're the elders of the church and we got a responsibility to the congregation, too—that the Lord ain't pleased at Margaret sitting in the seat of authority.

SISTER MOORE It's time for her to come down.

ODESSA And how did folks take it when you told them all this?

BROTHER BOXER Well, folks ain't in this church to worship Sister Margaret. They's here to worship the Lord.

ODESSA Folks thought Margaret was good enough to be their pastor all these years, they ain't going to stop wanting her for pastor overnight.

BROTHER BOXER She rose overnight. She can fall overnight.

SISTER BOXER I tell you, Sister Odessa, like the song says: "You may run on a great, long time but great God Almighty going to cut you down." Yes, indeed, He going to let the truth be known one *day*. And on that day, it's just too bad *for* you. Sister Margaret done had a lot of people fooled a long time, but now, bless God forever, the truth is out.

ODESSA What truth? What is that woman done to make you hate her so? Weren't but only yesterday you was all saying how wonderful she was, and how blessed we was to have her. And now you can't find nothing bad enough to say about her. Don't give me that stuff about her letting her household perish in sin. Ain't a one of you but ain't got a brother or a sister or somebody on the road to hell right now. I want to know what is she *done*? What is she done to you, Sister Moore?

SISTER BOXER *I* ain't got no brothers or sisters on the road to hell. Only sister I *had* is waiting for me in glory. And every *soul* I come in contact with is saved—except of course for them people I work for. And I got no trombone-playing husband dying in my house and I ain't got no half-grown son out fornicating in the wilderness.

SISTER MOORE Don't you come up here and act like you thought we was just acting out of spite and meanness. Your sister ain't done nothing to me; she *can't* do nothing to me because the Lord holds me in His hands. All we's trying to do is the Lord's will—you ought to be trying to do it, too. If we want to reign with him in glory, we ain't supposed to put nobody before Him. Amen! We ain't supposed to have no other love but Him.

SISTER BOXER I looked at that man and I says to myself, How in the *world* did Sister Margaret ever get herself mixed up with a man like that?

ODESSA Ain't no mystery how a woman gets mixed up with a man, Sister Boxer, and you sure ought to know that, even if poor Sister Moore here *don't*.

SISTER MOORE Don't you poor-Sister-Moore *me*. That man put a demon inside your sister and that demon's walking up and down inside her still. You can see it in her eyes, they done got all sleepy with lust.

ODESSA Sister Moore, I sure would like to know just how come *you* know so much about it.

SISTER BOXER Sister Odessa, ain't no sense to you trying to put everybody in the wrong because Sister Margaret is falling. That ain't going to raise her back up. It's the Lord's *will* she should come down.

ODESSA I don't understand how you can take her part against my sister. *You* ought to know how much Sister Margaret's suffered all these years by herself. *You* know it ain't no easy thing for a woman to go it alone. She done spent more'n ten years to build this up for herself and her little boy. How you going to throw her out now? What's she going to do, where's she going to go?

BROTHER BOXER She didn't worry about Elder King when she took over this church from him.

SISTER MOORE I think you think I hates your sister because she been married. And I ain't never been married. I ain't questioning the Lord's ways. He done kept me pure to Himself for a purpose, and that purpose is working itself out right here in this room this morning—right here in this room, this upper room. It make your sister look double-minded, I do declare it do, if she done tried, one time, to bring peace to one man, and failed, and then she jump up and think she going to bring peace to a whole lot of people.

ODESSA Sister Margaret done give good service all those years. She ain't been acting like she was double-minded.

BROTHER BOXER But I bet you—she is double-minded *now*.

(DAVID *enters the apartment. He is suffering from a hangover, is still a little drunk. He goes to the sink and splashes cold water on his face. He moves with both bravado and fear and there is a kind of heart-breaking humor in his actions*)

SISTER BOXER Odessa, a church can't have no woman for pastor who done been married once and then decided it didn't suit her and then jump up and run off from her husband and take a seat in the pulpit and act like she ain't no woman no more. That ain't no kind of example to the young. The Word say the marriage bed is holy.

ODESSA I can't believe—I can't *believe* you really going to do it. We been friends so long.

(DAVID *dries his face. He goes to the door of* LUKE'S *room, stands for a moment looking at his father. He turns back into the kitchen. At this moment,* MARGARET *enters, dressed in white. She and* DAVID *stare at each other*)

SISTER BOXER You the one I'm sorry for, Sister Odessa. You done spent your life, look

The Amen Corner

like, protecting that sister of yours. And now you can't protect her no more.

ODESSA It ain't been me protecting Sister Margaret. It been the Lord. And He ain't yet withdrawed His hand. He ain't never left none of His children alone. (*she starts for the rear door of the church*)

SISTER BOXER How come you ain't never been married, Sister Odessa?

ODESSA Suppose we just say, Sister Boxer, that I never had the time.

SISTER BOXER It might have been better for you if you'd taken the time.

ODESSA I ain't got no regrets. No, I ain't. I ain't claiming I'm pure, like Sister Moore here. I ain't claiming that the Lord had such special plans for me that I couldn't have nothing to do with men. Brothers and sisters, if you knew just a little bit about folks' lives, what folks go through, and the low, black places they finds their feet—you *would* have a meeting here this afternoon. Maybe I don't know the Lord like you do, but I know something else. I know how men and women can come together and change each other and make each other suffer, and make each other glad. If you putting my sister out of this church, you putting me out, too. (*she goes out through the street door. The church dims out*)

MARGARET Where you been until this time in the morning, son?

DAVID I was out visiting some people I know. And it got to be later than I realized and I stayed there overnight.

MARGARET How come it got to be so late before you realized it?

DAVID I don't know. We just got to talking.

MARGARET Talking? (*she moves closer to him*) What was you talking about, son? You stink of whiskey! (*she slaps him.* DAVID *sits at the table*)

DAVID That ain't going to do no good, Ma. (*she slaps him again.* DAVID *slumps on the table, his head in his arms*)

MARGARET Is that what I been slaving for all these long, hard years? Is I carried slops and scrubbed floors and ate leftovers and swallowed bitterness by the gallon jugful—for this? So you could walk in here this Lord's-day morning stinking from whiskey and some no-count, dirty, black girl's sweat? Declare, I wish you'd died in my belly, too, if I been slaving all these years for this!

DAVID Mama. Mama. Please.

MARGARET Sit up and look at me. Is you too drunk to hold up your head? Or is you too ashamed? Lord knows you ought to be ashamed.

DAVID Mama, I wouldn't of had this to happen this way for nothing in the world.

MARGARET Was they holding a pistol to your head last evening? Or did they tie you down and pour the whiskey down your throat?

DAVID No. No. Didn't nobody have no pistol. Didn't nobody have no rope. Some fellows said, Let's pick up some whiskey. And I said, Sure. And we all put in some money and I went down to the liquor store and bought it. And then we drank it. (MARGARET *turns away*)

MARGARET David, I ain't so old. I know the world is wicked. I know young people have terrible temptations. Did you do it because you was afraid them boys would make fun of you?

DAVID No.

MARGARET Was it on account of some girl?

DAVID No.

MARGARET Was it—your daddy put you up to it? Was it your daddy made you think it was manly to get drunk?

DAVID Daddy—I don't think you can blame it on Daddy, Mama.

MARGARET Why'd you do it. David? When I done tried so hard to raise you right? Why'd you want to hurt me this way?

DAVID I didn't want to hurt you, Mama. But this day has been coming a long time. Mama, I can't play piano in church no more.

MARGARET Is it on account of your daddy? Is it your daddy put all this foolishness in your head?

DAVID Daddy ain't been around for a long time, Mama. I ain't talked to him but one time since he been here.

MARGARET And that one time—he told you all about the wonderful time he had all them years, blowing out his guts on that trombone.

DAVID No. That ain't exactly what he said. That ain't exactly what we talked about.

MARGARET What *did* you talk about?

(*A sound of children singing "Jesus Loves Me" comes from the church*)

DAVID Well—he must have been talking about you. About how he missed you, and all.

MARGARET Sunday school done started.

David, why don't you go upstairs and play for them, just this one last morning?

DAVID Mama, I told you. I can't play piano in church no more.

MARGARET David, why don't you feel it no more, what you felt once? Where's it gone? Where's the Holy Ghost gone?

DAVID I don't know, Mama. It's empty. (*He indicates his chest*) It's empty here.

MARGARET Can't you pray? Why don't you pray? If you pray, pray hard, He'll come back. The Holy Ghost will come back. He'll come down on heavenly wings, David, and (*she touches his chest*) fill that empty space, He'll start your heart to singing—singing again. He'll fill you, David, with a mighty burning fire and burn *out* (*she takes his head roughly between her palms*) all that foolishness, all them foolish dreams you carries around up there. Oh, David, David, pray that the Holy Ghost will come back, that the gift of God will come back!

DAVID Mama, if a person don't feel it, he just don't feel it.

MARGARET David, I'm older than you. I done been down the line. I know ain't no safety nowhere in this world if you don't stay close to God. What you think the world's got out there for you but a broken heart?

(ODESSA, *unnoticed, enters*)

ODESSA You better listen to her, David.

MARGARET I remember boys like you down home, David, many years ago—fine young men, proud as horses, and I seen what happened to them. I seen them go down, David, until they was among the lowest of the low. There's boys like you down there, today, breaking rock and building roads, they ain't never going to hold up their heads up on this earth no more. There's boys like you all over this city, filling up the gin mills and standing on the corners, running down alleys, tearing themselves to pieces with knives and whiskey and dope and sin! You think I done lived this long and I don't know what's happening? Fine young men and they're lost—they don't know what's happened to their life. Fine young men, and some of them dead and some of them dead while they living. You think I want to see this happen to you? You think I want you one day lying where your daddy lies today?

ODESSA You better listen to her David. You better listen.

MARGARET No. He ain't going to listen. Young folks don't never listen. They just go on, headlong, and they think ain't nothing ever going to be too big for them. And, time they find out, it's too late then.

DAVID And if I listened—what would happen? What do you think would happen if I listened? You want me to stay here, getting older, getting sicker—hating you? You think I want to hate you, Mama? You think it don't tear me to pieces to have to lie to you all the time. Yes, because I been lying to you, Mama, for a long time now! I don't want to tell no more lies. I don't want to keep on feeling so bad inside that I have to go running down them alleys you was talking about—that alley right outside this door!—to find something to help me hide—to hide—from what I'm feeling. Mama, I want to be a man. It's time you let me be a man. You got to let me go. (*a pause*) If I stayed here—I'd end up worse than Daddy—because I wouldn't be doing what I know I got to do—I *got* to do! I've seen your life—and now I see Daddy—and I love you, I love you both!—but I've got my work to do, something's happening in the world out there, I got to go! I know you think I don't know what's happening, but I'm beginning to see—something. Every time I play, every time I listen, I see Daddy's face and yours, and so many faces—who's going to speak for all that, Mama? Who's going to speak for all of us? I can't stay home. Maybe I can say something—one day—maybe I can say something in music that's never been said before. Mama—*you* knew this day was coming.

MARGARET I reckon I thought I was Joshua and could make the sun stand still.

DAVID Mama, I'm leaving this house tonight. I'm going on the road with some other guys. I got a lot of things to do today and I ain't going to be hanging around the house. I'll see you before I go. (*he starts for the door*)

MARGARET David—?

DAVID Yes, Mama?

MARGARET Don't you want to eat something?

DAVID No, Mama. I ain't hungry now. (*he goes*)

MARGARET Well. There he go. Who'd ever want to love a man and raise a child! Odessa—you think I'm a hard woman?

ODESSA No. I don't think you a hard woman. But I think you's in a hard place.

MARGARET I done something, somewhere, wrong.

ODESSA Remember this morning. You got a awful thing ahead of you this morning. You got to go upstairs and win them folks back to you this morning.

MARGARET My man is in there, dying, and my baby's in the world—how'm I going to preach, Odessa? How'm I going to preach when I can't even pray?

ODESSA You got to face them. You got to think. You got to pray.

MARGARET Sister, I can't. I can't. I can't.

ODESSA Maggie. It was you had the vision. It weren't me. You got to think back to the vision. If the vision was for anything, it was for just this day.

MARGARET The vision. Ah, it weren't yesterday, that vision. I was in a cold, dark place and I thought it was the grave. And I listened to hear my little baby cry and didn't no cry come. I heard a voice say, Maggie. Maggie. You got to find you a hiding place. I wanted Luke. (*she begins to weep*) Oh, sister, I don't remember no vision. I just remember that it was dark and I was scared and my baby was dead and I wanted Luke, I wanted Luke, I wanted Luke!

ODESSA Oh, honey. Oh, my honey. What we going to do with you this morning? (MARGARET *cannot stop weeping*) Come on, honey, come on. You got them folks to face.

MARGARET All these years I prayed as hard as I knowed how. I tried to put my treasure in heaven where couldn't nothing get at it and take it away from me and leave me alone. I asked the Lord to hold my hand. I didn't expect that none of this would ever rise to hurt me no more. And all these years it just been waiting for me, waiting for me to turn a corner. And there it stand, my whole life, just like I hadn't never gone nowhere. It's a awful thing to think about, the way love never dies!

ODESSA You's got to pull yourself together and think how you can *win*. You always been the winner. Ain't no time to be a woman *now*. You can't let them throw you out of this church. What we going to do then? I'm getting old, I can't help you. And you ain't young no more, neither.

MARGARET Maybe we could go—someplace else.

ODESSA We ain't got no money to go no place. We ain't paid the rent for this month. We ain't even finished paying for this Frigidaire.

MARGARET I remember in the old days whenever Luke wanted to spend some money on foolishness, that is exactly what I would have to say to him: "Man, ain't you got good sense? Do you know we ain't even paid the rent for this month?"

ODESSA Margaret. You got to think.

MARGARET Odessa, you remember when we was little there was a old blind woman lived down the road from us. She used to live in this house all by herself and you used to take me by the hand when we walked past her house because I was scared of her. I can see her, just as plain somehow, sitting on the porch, rocking in that chair, just looking out over them roads like she could see something. And she used to hear us coming, I guess, and she'd shout out, "How you this Lord's-day morning?" Don't care what day it was, or what time of day it was, it was always the Lord's-day morning for her. Daddy used to joke about her, he used to say, "Ain't no man in that house. It's a mighty sad house." I reckon this going to be a mighty sad house before long.

ODESSA Margaret. You got to think.

MARGARET I'm thinking. I'm thinking. I'm thinking how I throwed away my life.

ODESSA You can't think about it like that. You got to remember—you gave your life to the Lord.

MARGARET I'm thinking now—maybe Luke needed it more. Maybe David could of used it better. I know. I got to go upstairs and face them people. Ain't nothing else left for me to do. I'd like to talk to Luke.

ODESSA I'll go on up there.

MARGARET The only thing my mother should have told me is that being a woman ain't nothing but one long fight with men. And even the Lord, look like, ain't nothing but the most impossible kind of man there is. Go on upstairs, sister. Be there—when I get there.

(*After a moment,* ODESSA *goes. Again, we hear the sound of singing:* "*God be with you till we meet again.*" MARGARET *walks into* LUKE's *bedroom, stands there a moment, watching him.* BROTHER

BOXER *enters the kitchen, goes to the Frigidaire, pours himself a Kool-aid*)

MARGARET (*turns*) What are you doing down here, Brother Boxer? Why ain't you upstairs in the service?

BROTHER BOXER Why ain't *you* upstairs in the service, Sister Margaret? We's waiting for you upstairs.

MARGARET I'm coming upstairs! Can't you go on back up there now and ask them folks to be—a little quiet? He's sick, Brother Boxer. He's sick!

BROTHER BOXER You just finding that out? He *been* sick, Sister Margaret. How come it ain't never upset you until now? And how you expect me to go upstairs and ask them folks to be quiet when you been telling us all these years to praise the Lord with fervor? Listen! They got fervor. Where's all your fervor done gone to, Sister Margaret?

MARGARET Brother Boxer, even if you don't want me for your pastor no more, please remember I'm a woman. Don't talk to me this way.

BROTHER BOXER A woman? Is *that* where all your fervor done gone to? You trying to get back into that man's arms, Sister Margaret? What you want him to do for you—you want him to take off that long white robe?

MARGARET Be careful, Brother Boxer. It ain't over yet. It ain't over yet.

BROTHER BOXER Oh, yes it is, Sister Margaret. It's over. You just don't know it's over. Come on upstairs. Maybe you can make those folks keep quiet. (*the music has stopped*) They's quiet now. They's waiting for you.

MARGARET You hate me. How long have you hated me? What have I ever done to make you hate me?

BROTHER BOXER All these years you been talking about how the Lord done called you. Well, you sure come running but I ain't so sure you was called. I seen you in there, staring at that man. You ain't no better than the rest of them. You done sweated and cried in the nighttime, too, and you'd like to be doing it again. You had me fooled with that long white robe but you ain't no better. You ain't as good. You been sashaying around here acting like weren't nobody good enough to touch the hem of your garment. You was always so pure, Sister Margaret, you made the rest of us feel like dirt.

MARGARET I was trying to please the Lord.

BROTHER BOXER And you reckon you did? Declare, I never thought I'd see you so quiet. All these years I been running errands for you, saying, Praise the Lord, Sister Margaret. That's *right*, Sister Margaret! Amen, Sister Margaret! I didn't know if you even knew what a man was. I never thought I'd live long enough to find out that Sister Margaret weren't nothing but a woman who run off from her husband and then started ruling other people's lives because she didn't have no man to control her. I sure hope you make it into heaven, girl. You's too late to catch any other train.

MARGARET It's not over yet. It's not over.

BROTHER BOXER You coming upstairs?

MARGARET I'm coming.

BROTHER BOXER Well. We be waiting. (*he goes.* MARGARET *stands alone in the kitchen. As* BROTHER BOXER *enters, the lights in the church go up. The church is packed. Far in the back* SISTER ODESSA *sits.* SISTER MOORE *is in the pulpit, and baritone soloist is singing*)

BARITONE Soon I'll be done with the troubles of the world,
Troubles of the world, troubles of the world,
Soon I'll be done with the troubles of the world,
Going home to live with my Lord.

Soon I'll be done with the troubles of the world,
Troubles of the world, troubles of the world,
Soon I'll be done with the troubles of the world,
Going home to live with my Lord.

Soon I'll be done with the troubles of the world,
Troubles of the world, troubles of the world,
Soon I'll be done with the troubles of the world,
Going home to live with my Lord.

SISTER MOORE (*reads*) For if after they have escaped the pollution of the world through the knowledge of the Lord and Saviour Jesus Christ they are again entangled therein and overcome, the latter end is worse with them than the beginning.

ALL Amen!

SISTER MOORE (*reads*) For it had been better for them not to have known the way of righteousness than after they had known it to turn away from the holy commandment delivered unto them. Amen! Sister Boxer, would you read the last verse for us? Bless our God!

SISTER BOXER (*reads*) But it is happened unto them according to the true proverb, the dog is turned to his own vomit again and the sow that was washed to her wallowing in the mire.

(*the church dims out.* MARGARET *walks into the bedroom*)

MARGARET   Luke?

LUKE   Maggie. Where's my son?

MARGARET   He's gone, Luke. I couldn't hold him. He's gone off into the world.

LUKE   He's gone?

MARGARET   He's gone.

LUKE   He's gone into the world. He's into the world!

MARGARET   Luke, you won't never see your son no more.

LUKE   But I seen him one last time. He's in the world, he's living.

MARGARET   He's gone. Away from you and away from me.

LUKE   He's living. He's living. Is you got to see your God to know he's living.

MARGARET   Everything—is dark this morning.

LUKE   You all in white. Like you was the day we got married. You mighty pretty.

MARGARET   It were a sunny day. Like today.

LUKE   Yeah. They used to say, "Happy is the bride the sun shines on."

MARGARET   Yes. That's what they used to say.

LUKE   Was you happy that day, Maggie?

MARGARET   Yes.

LUKE   I loved you, Maggie.

MARGARET   I know you did.

LUKE   I love you still.

MARGARET   I know you do. (*they embrace and singing is heard from the darkened church: "The Old Ship of Zion"*) Maybe it's not possible to stop loving anybody you ever really loved. I never stopped loving you, Luke. I tried. But I never stopped loving you.

LUKE   I'm glad you's come back to me, Maggie. When your arms was around me I was always safe and happy.

MARGARET   Oh, Luke! If we could only start again! (*his mouthpiece falls from his hand to the floor*) Luke? (*he does not answer*) My baby. You done joined hands with the darkness. (*she rises, moving to the foot of the bed, her eyes on* LUKE. *She sees the mouthpiece, picks it up, looks at it*) My Lord! If I could only start again! If I could only start again! (*the light comes up in the church. All, except* ODESSA, *are singing, "I'm Gonna Sit at the Welcome Table," clapping, etc.* SISTER MOORE *leads the service from the pulpit. Still holding* LUKE's *mouthpiece clenched against her breast,* MARGARET *mounts into the church. As she enters, the music dies*) Praise the Lord!

SISTER MOORE   You be careful, Sister Margaret. Be careful what you say. You been uncovered.

MARGARET   I come up here to put you children on your knees! Don't you know the Lord is displeased with every one of you? Have every one of you forgot your salvation? Don't you know that it is *forbidden*—amen!—to talk against the Lord's anointed? Ain't a soul under the sound of my voice—bless God!—who has the right to sit in judgment on my life! Sister Margaret, this woman you see before you, has given her life to the Lord—and you say the Lord is displeased with me because ain't a one of you willing to endure what I've endured. Ain't a one of you willing to go—the road I've walked. This way of holiness ain't no joke. You can't love the Lord and flirt with the Devil. The Word of God is right and the Word of God is plain—and you can't love God unless you's willing to give up everything for Him. Everything. I want you folks to pray. I want every one of you to go down on your knees. We going to have a tarry service here tonight. Oh, yes! David, you play something on that piano—(*she stops, stares at the piano, where one of the saints from Philadelphia is sitting*) David—David—(*she looks down at her fist*) Oh, my God.

SISTER BOXER   Look at her! *Look* at her! The gift of God has left her!

MARGARET   Children. I'm just now finding out what it means to love the Lord. It ain't all in the singing and the shouting. It ain't all in the reading of the Bible. (*she unclenches her fist a little*) It ain't even—it ain't even—in running all over everybody trying to get to heaven. To love the Lord is to love all His children—all of them, everyone!—and suffer with them and rejoice with them and never count the cost! (*silence. She turns and leaves the pulpit*)

SISTER MOORE   Bless our God! He give us the

victory! I'm gonna feast on milk and honey. (*she is joined by the entire congregation in this final song of jubilation*)

(MARGARET *comes down the stairs. She stands in the kitchen.* ODESSA *comes downstairs. Without a word to* MARGARET, *she goes through* LUKE's *room, taking off her robe as she goes. The lights dim down in the church, dim up on* MARGARET, *as* MARGARET *starts toward the bedroom, and falls beside* LUKE's *bed. The scrim comes down. One or two people pass in the street. Curtain*)

Louis Peterson (1922–)

Take a Giant Step
1953

The Metropolitan Museum, in its retrospective show "Harlem on My Mind," characterized the decade of the fifties as "Frustration and Ambivalence" for the blacks of Harlem. The second great war to save the world for democracy had been fought. Approximately 920,000 Negroes served in the U. S. Armed Forces, twice over the number in World War I. Segregation and discrimination in jobs, housing, and schools were still frustrating. But there was ambivalence. In 1954, the Supreme Court declared that separate schools were inherently unequal (see Loften Mitchell's play, *Land beyond the River*). The Interstate Commerce Commission banned segregation in interstate travel. In 1957, Congress passed the first Civil Rights Act since 1875. Maybe ... maybe ... the breakthrough was coming.

While Senator McCarthy hunted for Communists and homosexuals in the American government, the United States entered an undeclared war in Korea.

A headline in the *Amsterdam News* read: "Harlem left out of A-bomb shelter plans!" Broadway theater programs notified each patron that "in the event of an air raid alarm, remain in your seats and obey instruction of the management."

Frustration and ambivalence. Some good plays by blacks were produced—*Mrs. Patterson*, *In Splendid Error*, *Trouble in Mind*, *Land beyond the River*, *Simply Heavenly*, *Take a Giant Step*—but they did not draw large audiences. There were not many jobs for blacks in the theater. For the role of Spencer Scott (a role which Louis Gossett, then a high school senior, captured) there were 446 applicants. Louis Peterson, the 31-year-old author of *Take a Giant Step*, admitted that the play was partially autobiographical. He was born in Hartford, Connecticut; his father and mother worked in a bank to send their children to college. Mr. Peterson studied piano and went to Morehouse College. Finding drama his first interest, he came to New York City and his first role in a Blackfriars production, *A Young American*. The part was that of a talented young black musician. His first professional role was in Theodore Ward's *Our Lan'*.

"*Take a Giant Step*," Mr. Peterson told the *New York Times*, is not about "the real Negro problem, such as might exist in the South today." Walter Kerr, critic for the *Herald Tribune*, concurred: "Mr. Peterson's point [is] that Negro adolescence is, in essence, not very different from any other kind of adolescence." Mr. Kerr might have added "in middle-class America," for the family in the play is middle class. Mr. Robert Browne, director of New York Black Economic Research Center, has suggested the term "middle-class" connotes three distinguishing characteristics: first, level of income; second, values held; and third, life style. The Scott family of the play can be examined in these terms. In 1950 a black family averaged $3,125 per year, $2,000 less than white families. Given only this one statistic, was black adolescence the same as white? Second, the Scott family's values are those of the puritan ethic: cleanliness, industry, and education lead to achievement and success. Finally, what is the Scott family life style? In his *Black Bourgeoisie*, Professor E. Franklin Frazier satirized the black middle class of the 1950's for its "status without substance." Frazier lashed the class that denied its black roots in favor of emulating the life style of the white middle class. To an extent, the Scott family has done this; Louis Peterson is examining the results.

There is much written about the black experience, as though it were a monolithic maze through which every black person in America must pass. Some arbitrators of the black experience go so far as to insist that a middle-class experience is not black. Spencer Scott knows that his experience is not white. If it is not white, what is it? Who is he? This is the question that makes the play.

A week after the play opened (in September 1953), the producers ran an advertisement in the *New York Times*: "To the New York Theatregoer: We've got a hit!—where are you? The reviewers say it is 'fresh, moving drama! real and touching! Important! Hilarious! Immense warmth! Irresistible!'" The theatergoers did resist; *Take a Giant Step* closed after eight weeks.

The play was revived three years later in an off-Broadway house with Bill Gunn, Beah Richards, and Godfrey Cambridge in the cast. It ran for 264 performances. A film was made but was dismissed as "a Negro Andy Hardy film." But Andy Hardy films were great successes. What did the critic mean?

At the time of the original production, Louis Peterson, who went on to Hollywood and television writing, commented, "I believe you have to show hope for the Negro in terms of what you know." Frustration and ambivalence. Mr. Peterson knows that black families have survived every terror and disgrace the world provides. He writes of the family he knew. He presents hope.

Take a Giant Step

CAST OF CHARACTERS

SPENCER SCOTT
GRANDMOTHER
TONY
IGGIE
FRANK
MAN
VIOLET
POPPY
ROSE
CAROL
LEM SCOTT
MAY SCOTT
CHRISTINE
GUSSIE
JOHNNY REYNOLDS
BOBBY REYNOLDS

ACT ONE

Scene One

(*If you walked down a rather shady, middle class street in a New England town, you would probably find a house very similar to the one in which the Scotts live. It was a rather ordinary house when it was built and it is a rather ordinary house now, but it has been well cared for, devotedly watched and cared for, and it gives off an aura of good health and happiness if houses can ever know such things. The house has been cut away to expose to view to the audience the back entrance hall, a kitchen up left, a dining room left, a living room and a hall right in which there is a front door and a staircase leading to the upstairs. At the very top of the stairs, there is a little chair almost like a child's chair. If the house has any character at all it should resemble a fat old lady who has all the necessary equipment of living about her person.*

If you walked down a rather shady, middle class street in a New England town you would probably hear the same sounds that you are hearing when the curtain rises. The sounds of boys playing baseball in the lot across the street. SPENCER SCOTT *enters from right into his own yard. He is a Negro boy of seventeen years. He has a croquet stake in one hand that he has pulled up out of the ground, and books in his other hand. He is hitting the side of his leg with the stake. The time is the present—Fall—late October. It is a fine day—a golden warm day which is typical of New England at this time of year. After a moment* SPENCE, *still carrying the stake, walks into the hall. He slams the front door. On the door slam off-stage noises stop.* GRANDMA *immediately calls offstage*)

GRANDMA (*in bedroom upstairs*) Spence. Spence. Is that you?

SPENCE Yes, it's me, Gram. Who the hell does she think it is—Moses? (*jacket and books on sofa*)

GRANDMA Where have you been?

SPENCE No place.

GRANDMA Well, why are you so late coming home?

SPENCE No reason in particular, Gram. I just took my time. You know how that is—don't you, Gram—when you just want to take your time coming home? (*sits on sofa. Takes off shoes*)

GRANDMA Just a minute—I can't hear you. I'll be right down.

SPENCE If you do—I'll tell Mom that you've been horsing around again today.

GRANDMA Just you be quiet and come up and help me.

SPENCE (*gets up, goes upstairs*) You know you haven't got any business coming downstairs. Mom told you to stay up. Not only am I going to tell Mom, but when the doctor comes, I'm going to tell him too.

GRANDMA (*appears at door*) Tell him. You think I care. Now come up and help me.

SPENCE (*goes all the way upstairs and helps her*) Just lean on me, and hold tight to the railing, and I think we'll make it.

GRANDMA (*comes downstairs*) I don't know why I can't come downstairs if I want to. (*pauses as she labors down the stairs*) And you keep your mouth shut about it, too.

SPENCE (*coming downstairs*) I've already told you what I'm going to do. I'm going to spill the beans all over the house.

GRANDMA You do and I'll tell your mother you were late coming home from school and that you haven't practiced yet.

SPENCE You'd better put all your concentration on getting down the steps, Gram, or you're gonna fall and break your behind.

GRANDMA Now you stop that kind of talk—you hear me?

SPENCE Now be careful, Gram—and don't get excited.

GRANDMA Well then—you stop it—you hear me?

SPENCE All right, Gram. All right. Just stop hopping around like a sparrow.

GRANDMA I never thought I'd live to see the day when my own daughter's child was cursing like a trooper.

SPENCE Haven't said anything yet, Gram. All I said was if you weren't careful you'd fall down and break your behind. And you will, too.

GRANDMA Take your hands off me. I can do the rest myself. (*crosses down stage toward kitchen. She notices the stake*) What are you doing with that dirty thing in the house?

SPENCE I wanted it. Something to bang around.

GRANDMA You're banging dirt all over the rug. (*she is going into the kitchen.* SPENCE *is going toward the living room*) Where are you going?

SPENCE I'm going in and practice. (*crosses to piano*)

GRANDMA Wouldn't you like something to eat first?

SPENCE No, I wouldn't. You think you can trick me—don't you? (*crosses down center to* GRANDMA. *Crosses to piano*) I'm going in and practice and then you won't have a thing to tell Mom when she gets home.

GRANDMA Suit yourself. (*she sits on sofa. He sits down and begins practicing scales. There is a pause*) Spencer, would you get me a glass of water? I'm so out of breath.

SPENCE (*still practicing*) You mooched down all those stairs without batting an eye. You can get your own water. (*piano starts*)

GRANDMA You're a mean little beggar.

SPENCE I know it.

GRANDMA Well, come out and talk to me. I won't tell her.

SPENCE You're sure?

GRANDMA You don't take my word?

SPENCE I took your word the day before yesterday, and as a result I had to practice two hours in the morning.

GRANDMA Well go get it and stop that racket.

SPENCE (*gets up, crosses to bookcase for book*) You know, sometimes Gram, I think that you're uncultured and have no respect for art. (*crosses to sofa with book*) Put your right hand on this. Now repeat after me.

GRANDMA I'll do no such thing.

SPENCE (*taking the book*) O.K. then—don't. (*moves right*)

GRANDMA What do you want me to say?

SPENCE (*coming back, sits on sofa*) I swear and promise that—no matter what happens—I will not tell anybody that Spencer Scott did not practice this afternoon—and if asked I will lie and say that he did.

GRANDMA I swear and promise that—no matter what happens—I will not tell anybody that Spencer Scott did not practice this afternoon—and if asked I will lie and say that he did.

SPENCE Telling also includes writing notes to said parties.

GRANDMA Telling also includes writing notes to said parties.

SPENCE I swear and promise under fear of death.

GRANDMA I swear and promise under fear of death.

SPENCE Amen.

GRANDMA (*starts to answer, changes her mind*) No—I'm not—(*he puts her hand on book*) Amen.

SPENCE Kiss the book.

GRANDMA I'll do no such thing. It's dirty.

SPENCE Just one more time, Gram. Kiss the book.

GRANDMA (*she kisses and notices*) This isn't the Bible.

SPENCE (*gets up. Puts the book on TV*) It's "Crime and Punishment." Don't try welching. (*crosses toward kitchen*) What do you want to eat?

GRANDMA Anything will do.

SPENCE We'll have some crackers and

cheese. (*gets cheese out of refrigerator*) Gram—now there's just one more thing. I won't tell Mom about your coming downstairs if you'll—

GRANDMA (*crossing for shoes at window right*) No—I'm not going to do it. I'll be a party to no such thing.

SPENCE O.K., Gram. It's your funeral. You don't even know what kind of a bargain I was going to strike up with you.

GRANDMA Yes, I do. You want a bottle of your father's beer.

SPENCE (*closes refrigerator*) All right, Gram. Fine. When you're taking twice as many of those ugly, nasty tasting pills—don't say I didn't try to be a good sport.

GRANDMA (*gets shoes at window*) One glass.

SPENCE (*opens refrigerator*) It's a deal. One glass. (*to kitchen*) What shall I do with the rest of the bottle? (GRANDMA *crosses left*) If he sees half a bottle he'll know right away.

GRANDMA Pour it down the sink (*crosses to right of table*)

SPENCE Good idea. (*he opens the bottle and pours a glass*)

GRANDMA (*as he starts to pour the rest out*) How much is left?

SPENCE Not much.

GRANDMA Well bring it here. Shame to let it go to waste.

SPENCE (*as he brings another glass over to the table*) You know, Gram. You ought to be in politics. You sure strike a hard bargain. (*sits left of table*)

GRANDMA (*sits right of table*) If I didn't you'd walk all over me. (*pouring beer*) This is nice—isn't it?

SPENCE Sure is. (*he picks up the stake again and starts hitting his leg*)

GRANDMA Put that dirty thing down. Stop hitting yourself with it. Where have you been?

SPENCE (*still hitting himself*) Well I suppose I might as well tell you. Mom's probably going to hear it coming up the street.

GRANDMA Well—what is it?

SPENCE What could you possibly imagine as being just about the worst thing that could happen to me?

GRANDMA You haven't gotten any little girls in trouble—have you?

SPENCE Nothing like that, Gram. Worse.

GRANDMA What have you done? Will you stop hitting yourself with that thing.

SPENCE Well, Gram, I just went and got my ass kicked out of school today.

GRANDMA Spencer Scott! What were you doing?

SPENCE Nothing much. Just smoking in the john.

GRANDMA Smoking! Where?

SPENCE In the john—the can, Gram. The Men's Room.

GRANDMA Well that's a pretty nasty place to be smoking if you ask me. What were you smoking?

SPENCE A cigar.

GRANDMA A cigar. Cigarettes are not dirty enough, I suppose. You have to start smoking cigars.

SPENCE What are you getting so excited for? I took one of Pop's.

GRANDMA Well you ought to be ashamed of yourself. Disgracing yourself in school.

SPENCE (*gets up, crossing right*) Well I sure loused myself up proper this time.

GRANDMA Where are you going?

SPENCE To see if there's any mail. (*at piano. Takes mail*)

GRANDMA There's none for you.

SPENCE Well you don't mind my looking anyhow, do you? (*he goes through the mail*)

GRANDMA You come right back here. I want to know more about this.

SPENCE Just a second, Gram. Be patient—will you? (*pause*) I sure think that's a crummy way to behave. (*crosses down*) I've written him three letters now—the least he could do is answer one of them. (*puts letters on TV*)

GRANDMA Who are you talking about now?

SPENCE Mack—I'm talking about Mack.

GRANDMA Your brother's probably busy with his lessons. You know what college is like.

SPENCE No, I don't know what college is like. He's probably busy with the broads. The last letter I wrote him was about some damn important problems I got. He'll answer soon enough when he finds out they've shoved me into some loony bin. (*crosses back to left of table, hitting himself with stake*)

GRANDMA What's the matter with you, Spence?

SPENCE Aw! I don't know, Gram.

GRANDMA Stop hitting yourself with that thing.

SPENCE Will you leave me alone? Don't you understand that when a guy's upset he's got to hit himself with something? You gotta do something like that.

GRANDMA (*softly*) What's the matter, Spence?

SPENCE Aw, Gram. Cut out the sympathy please. Go on and finish your beer and get back upstairs before Mom catches you.

GRANDMA Tell me about it, Spence?

SPENCE (*pause*) There's nothing to tell. What's there to it. (*pause*) If you're gonna sit there and look at me that way I'm gonna start feeling sorry for myself and then I'm gonna start bawling—and then you'll start bawling and we won't get anywhere.

GRANDMA What do you want me to do?

SPENCE Keep eating.

GRANDMA All right. I'm eating.

SPENCE (*pause*) Well—from the very beginning of school I could've told you that that Miss Crowley and I weren't going to see eye to eye.

GRANDMA Who's Miss Crowley?

SPENCE The history teacher, Gram. The one that thinks she's cute. She's always giving the guys a preview of the latest fashions in underwear.

GRANDMA Nasty little hussy.

SPENCE That's the one. Well, today they started talking about the Civil War and one of the smart little skirts at the back of the room wanted to know why the Negroes in the South didn't rebel against slavery. Why did they wait for the Northerners to come down and help them? And this Miss Crowley went on to explain how they were stupid and didn't have sense enough to help themselves. (*crosses chair left of table; sits*) Well, anyway, Gram, when she got through talking they sounded like the worst morons that ever lived and I began to wonder how they'd managed to live a few thousand years all by themselves in Africa with nobody's help. I would have let it pass—see—except that the whole class was whispering and giggling and turning around and looking at me—so I got up and just stood next to my desk looking at her. She looked at me for a couple of minutes and asked me if perhaps I had something to say in the discussion. I said I might have a lot of things to say if I didn't have to say them in the company of such dumb jerks. Then I asked her frankly what college she went to.

GRANDMA What did she say?

SPENCE She told me I was being impudent. I told her it was not my intention to be impudent but I would honestly like to know. So she puts one hand on her hip—kinda throwing the other hip out of joint at the same time—and like she wants to spit on me she says "Scoville." Then I says, "And they didn't teach you nothing about the *uprising* of the slaves during the Civil War—or Frederick Douglass?" She says, "No—they didn't." "In that case," I said, "I don't want to be in your crummy history class." And I walk out of the room. When I get out in the hall, Gram, I'm shaking, I'm so mad—and I had this cigar I was going to sell for a sundae. I knew I couldn't eat a sundae now 'cause it would just make me sick so—I just had to do something so I went into the Men's Room and smoked the cigar. I just had about two drags on the thing when in comes the janitor and hauls me down to old Hasbrook's office—and when I get down there—there's Miss Crowley and old Hasbrook talking me over in low tones—and in five short minutes he'd thrown me out of school.

GRANDMA I should've thought he would've given you another chance.

SPENCE He's given me many other chances, Gram. I guess I'm just a chronic offender.

GRANDMA How long are you out for?

SPENCE It would've been one week, but since we have a week's vacation next week, he made it two weeks. Then I'm supposed to come back dragging Pop behind me like a tail. Is he going to be burned! (*pause*) Do you suppose Mom will go for the story, Gram?

GRANDMA I'm not sure.

SPENCE You mean she's not going to go for it at all.

GRANDMA I'm afraid that you're going to get what you rightfully deserve.

SPENCE That's a nasty thing to say—considering the fact that I was justified.

GRANDMA There are ways and ways of being justified.

SPENCE You mean that I shouldn't have gotten sassy with the fruit cake.

GRANDMA Spencer, I'm not going to say one more word to you if you don't stop using language like that—and put that stick down.

SPENCE (*gets up, throwing the stake on the*

floor) God—you're getting to be a crumb—just like the rest of the whole crummy world.

GRANDMA Where are you going?

SPENCE No place. Where in hell is there to go?

GRANDMA You ought to be thrashed with a stick for using that kind of language to me.

SPENCE Listen—are you my friend or not? (*crosses back to* GRANDMA)

GRANDMA No—I'm not—not when you talk like that.

SPENCE (*closer to* GRANDMA) Well—thanks for that. Thanks. You're a real good Joe. You're a psalm singer—just like the rest of them, Gram. Love me when I'm good—hate me when I'm bad. Thanks. (*crosses right*)

GRANDMA Don't mention it.

SPENCE You're welcome. (*sits in armchair right*)

GRANDMA The pleasure was all mine.

SPENCE For an old lady—you can sure be plenty sarcastic when you want to be. (*pause*)

GRANDMA These will be exactly the last words I will say to you today, Master Scott.

(*From outside a voice begins calling* SPENCE. *Softly at first, and then more loudly*)

TONY Spence.

GRANDMA Who's that calling you?

SPENCE Tony.

TONY Hey—Spence!

GRANDMA Well—what does he want?

SPENCE I don't know, Gram. I haven't asked him yet.

TONY Spencer!

GRANDMA Well, why don't you answer him?

SPENCE Let him wait—let him wait—it won't hurt him. He likes to holler like that anyway—he has to use his voice some place. No one could ever accuse him of speaking up while he's in school. (*rises*)

TONY Spencer!

GRANDMA (*gets up*) Spencer Scott—if you don't answer him—I will.

SPENCE All right, all right. (*he starts for the door and opens it*) What're you doing there? (TONY *bounces in. He is a young Italian boy*) Rehearsing for the Metropolitan or something? Come on in. (*crosses to* GRANDMA *left*)

TONY (*crosses to center*) Hi, Spence. Hello, Mrs. Scott.

GRANDMA Tony—since the first day you could talk—(*sits*) I've told you that I'm not Mrs. Scott. I'm Mrs. Martin. How long are you going to keep doing that?

TONY I forget, Mrs. Martin (*front of sofa*)

SPENCE You forget lots of things—don't you, pal. (*pause. Back of chair*) Well—you got a week's vacation so it certainly can't be because you want me to help you with your algebra—besides I won't be doing algebra for a while. I got the heave-ho as you well know.

TONY Thrown out?

SPENCE Yep.

TONY For how long? (*crosses to right*)

SPENCE Not counting vacation—for a week.

TONY Gee!

SPENCE You can say that again. (*crosses to below table left*)

TONY Gee!

SPENCE Well—you said it. Thanks, pal. (*pause. Sits Left of table.*) Well, Tony—what little favor can I do you?

TONY Gee, Spence. I'm sure sorry. All the guys were talking about it on the way home from school.

SPENCE Yeh! Yeh! I know. I caught their sympathy when Miss Crowley was bitching me out.

GRANDMA I'm going to tell your mother.

SPENCE (*looking at* GRANDMA) Gram.

TONY That's not the way it was at all. (*pause*) What could we say?

SPENCE Exactly what you did. It was fine. What'd I call you when you came in—a pal? That's what you all were. (GRANDMA *goes into kitchen*) Two hundred carat, solid gold plate pals. (*to piano. Sits*)

TONY (*crosses right*) Geez—Spence—I'm sorry you feel that way about it.

SPENCE (*gets up*) Ah! You're scratching my back with a rake, Tony. Remember the time the cop had you for stealing apples down at Markman's?

TONY Sure I remember.

SPENCE Did I or did I not shoot him with my slingshot? Remember the time Mrs. Donahue comes out of her house and calls you a dirty wop?

TONY Well, hell, this was in school. (GRANDMA *crosses to sink with glass*)

SPENCE Did I stand there and let her get away with it? I did not. That night, as nice as you please, I throw a nest of caterpillars through her window.

TONY (*to center*) Yeah! And when she found out who did it—I cut your telephone wires for three nights running so she couldn't get to your mother.

GRANDMA (*enters room*) I think I should warn you both now—that everything you're saying is going to be used against you—because I'm going to tell all of it.

SPENCE (*crossing to* GRANDMA) Oh! No, you won't. If you so much as open your craw, Gram, I'll spill everything—and I'll really spill. I'm desperate. (*crosses to* TONY) So there's a big difference about whether it's in school or not. Has that ever made any difference to me?

TONY Naw!

SPENCE Naw! Is that all you've got to say?

TONY No—it isn't.

SPENCE You're a crumb, Tony—just like the rest of them. (*crosses to right*) And another thing—I dunno—maybe I'm getting deaf and need a hearing aid or something, but I don't hear you guys calling me for school any more in the morning.

TONY (*crosses to* SPENCE) Ah, Spence—how many times do I have to tell you. I'm taking Marguerite to school in the morning.

SPENCE And where are you taking her at night when you mozey past the house with her curled around your arm like a snake?

TONY We're doing our home work together.

SPENCE It's a little dark up in the park for home work.

TONY Spence—cut it out—your grandmother.

SPENCE My grandmother knows what the score is. She's been knowing it an awful long time now. She's going on eighty-three years old. You can talk freely in front of her.

TONY Lay off—will you?

SPENCE I'll lay off, Tony. I'll lay off plenty. You and that Marguerite Wandalowski. Two crumbs together. That don't even make a damn saltine.

TONY (*close to* SPENCE) It's not her fault. I told you before. (SPENCE *crosses to center*) She likes you. She thinks you're a nice kid. (*crosses; sits on ottoman*) It's her father—he—well he just doesn't like colored people. I'm sorry, Mrs. Martin. But that's the damn truth. Spence—he just doesn't like them. (SPENCE *goes to piano*)

GRANDMA Well, I don't like Polish people either. Never have—never will. They come over here—haven't been over, mind you, long enough to know "and" from "but"—and that's the first thing they learn. Sometimes I think Hitler was right—

SPENCE (*down two steps*) You're talking off the top of your head, Gram. You know he wasn't right. What've you got to say that for?

GRANDMA I don't care—I don't like them. Never have—never will.

SPENCE (*crosses to* GRANDMA) You say "them" as though it was some kind of bug or something. *Will* you do me a favor like a real pal, Gram? Quit trying to mix in things that you don't understand. (*to* TONY) O.K., Friend —you've said your piece—what did you come over for? (*crosses down to* TONY)

TONY Nothing—I didn't want nothing.

SPENCE Aw—cut the bull, Tony. You must've come over here for something. You just don't come here for nothing any more. What do you *want*? (TONY *crosses to TV set*. SPENCE *crosses to above chair right*) You feel uncultured—you want to hear a little Bach or something? You want to see a little television— borrow a book? I just read a good one—all about the causes and preventions of syphilis.

GRANDMA Spencer Scott!

SPENCE (*turns to* GRANDMA) That's what the book said, Gram. Bring it out in the open—so I'm bringing it out.

GRANDMA I'm going to tell your mother about that.

SPENCE (*crosses left*) I'll betcha I'll tell her about it before you do. (*to* TONY) So what'd you come over for? (*no answer*) Maybe I can guess. You're playing baseball over in the lot. You haven't got enough equipment. You thought maybe I'd be willing to lend some of mine. Right, Tony?

TONY The guys asked me. I didn't want to.

SPENCE Aw!—why didn't you want to? You're my friend, aren't you? Just because I'm sore at you? Damn sore at you?

TONY Cut it out now, Spence. I did the best I could.

SPENCE There's no doubt—and I'm a bum to be mad at you—(*crosses to kitchen*) So I'll tell you what I'm going to do. (*he goes out into the back hall off kitchen and comes back with a baseball glove*) Who's the pitcher?

TONY Gussie.

SPENCE (*back to* TONY. *Throws glove*) Give this to Gussie with my regards. (*crosses to kitchen*)

TONY Give it to him?

SPENCE (*crossing back to living room with mask and mitts*) As a gift—you know what I mean—like Christmas—give it to him. And here's a catcher's mitt and mask for you. (*crosses to kitchen*)

GRANDMA What on earth are you doing? Are you drunk, Spencer?

SPENCE They're mine—aren't they—well, I don't want them any more. (*crosses to* TONY) And here's a bat I'm contributing to the game. I think that's just about everything.

TONY (*picks up stuff*) You're sure you won't be wanting these back?

SPENCE Geez—the things you can't understand. I'm giving them to you because you've been such good friends to me—one and all.

TONY (*starts to pick up equipment. Starting to go*) Well thanks, Spence—thanks.

SPENCE Think nothing of it. But there's just one more thing I want you to know. If I couldn't do any better than Maguerite Wandalowski and her old man I'd cram my head into a bucket of horse manure.

GRANDMA Now see here—

TONY (*crosses to* SPENCE) See—that's the way you are. You can't do one nice thing without a dirty dig at the end. I ought to throw these things in your puss—

SPENCE You won't though—will you?

GRANDMA (*gets up*) Take 'em back, Spence. Take them right back.

TONY Somebody—some day is going to take a poke at you.

GRANDMA (*takes swing*) If he hits you, Spence—hit him right back.

SPENCE (*crosses up*) He's not going to hit anyone, Gram. He's just talking to be sure he hasn't lost his mouth some damned place. (*throws* TONY *to door*) Now scram the hell out of my house before I beat you and your whole team over the head. Get out! (TONY *exits quickly*) Well, I sure went and milked myself in public that time. (*sits on chair right*)

GRANDMA What are you talking about now?

SPENCE Aw, Gram—I just went and did it again. You think I wanted that crumb to know how he hurt me?

GRANDMA (*crosses to* SPENCE) Come on, Spence, let's you and I go watch television.

SPENCE Sometimes, Gram—you get the most disgusting ideas.

GRANDMA Well, then I'm going back upstairs. I don't understand what's wrong with you. You're just no fun to be with any more—cussing and ripping and tearing. Won't even watch a little television with me.

SPENCE (*gets up, crosses to ottoman*) Go on in and watch it by yourself then—go on. Spend the rest of life with your head stuck in front of an old light bulb. (*sits*)

GRANDMA What on earth is wrong with you, Spencer?

SPENCE (*rises*) Gram—you've been sitting down here listening all afternoon. Don't you see that I'm an outcast? (*sits ottoman*)

GRANDMA How?

SPENCE They don't want me around any more, Gram. I cramp their style with the broads.

GRANDMA Why?

SPENCE Why! That's a stupid question. Because I'm black—that's why.

GRANDMA Well, it's a good thing if they don't want you around. (*turns right to window*) I told your mother years and years ago, "May—stay out of the South End, cause mark my words there's nothing down there, nothing— (SPENCE *crosses to kitchen*) but Wops and Germans and Lord knows what else they'll get in the future." And what did they get—more Wops and Germans and a few Polacks thrown in for good measure and not one self-respecting colored family in the whole lot.

SPENCE (*crosses to sofa*) Cut out that kind of talk. Sometimes, Gram—you're no help at all. I tell you my troubles and you tell me how we shouldn't have moved here in the first place. (*sits sofa*) But we're here, Gram—right here—and I was born here—and they're all the friends I've got—and it makes me damned unhappy, Gram.

GRANDMA (*crosses close to* SPENCE) Now—now—don't cry. Don't cry, Spencer. Everything's going to be all right.

SPENCE I had it all planned how I was going to make Tony feel like two cents the next time I saw him—and I had to go and get mad.

GRANDMA Your father is going to get you a new bicycle.

SPENCE Shove the bicycle.
GRANDMA Now why would you want to do that? The best thing to do, I should think, would be to get on it and ride it. (*crosses to ottoman with pillow*) Go and get the hair brush, Spencer. Your hair's a mess.
SPENCE I don't want you messing around with my hair. That's sissy.
GRANDMA Suit yourself. (*sits ottoman*)
SPENCE (*rises, crosses to kitchen*) If I get the hair brush you've got to promise to help me.
GRANDMA All right. (*he exits left in kitchen for the hairbrush*) Spence, you don't suppose you could go back up to school and tell them you were eating one of those chocolate cigars, could you?
SPENCE (*returns; sits down at* GRANDMA's *feet; gives her brush*) I got a feeling that those things don't light too well, Gram. (*pause*) What am I going to do, Gram?
GRANDMA (*brushing his hair*) Well, now—I'm not sure—but one thing I am sure of. I don't know why you gave that boy all of your things. I think that's silly—damn silly if I might say so.
SPENCE Do you suppose this happens to everyone, Gram?
GRANDMA I suppose so. (*pause*) We haven't done this in a long time—have we?
SPENCE What?
GRANDMA Don't you remember when you were a little boy I used to do this every day. You'd stand—you were much shorter than you are now—and I'd brush and comb your hair. I used to do that for all my boys. They'd sit and tell me all their troubles while I combed and brushed their hair.
SPENCE One dumb crummy girl at school the other day asked me if we had to comb and brush our hair.
GRANDMA What did you tell her?
SPENCE I told her we very seldom bothered until the bugs got so fierce they started falling into food and things like that—then it was an absolute necessity.
GRANDMA Spencer—you didn't?
SPENCE I would've if I'd thought of it in time. (*pause*) Gram—if you take the bus down at the corner and stay on it when it gets to Main Street—it will take you right out to the colored section, won't it?
GRANDMA Well, it used to. I don't know if it still does or not. Why?
SPENCE I was just wondering. It's getting late, Gram. Mom will be home in about a half hour. You'd better get back upstairs
GRANDMA (*putting down the brush*) Yes—hurry—come on and help me. (*gets up, crosses to stairs*)
SPENCE (*stays seated*) Gram—I don't suppose you could lend me five dollars, could you?
GRANDMA (*at foot of stairs*) What on earth do you need that much money for?
SPENCE Well, Gram—you and I know that an hour from now I'm going to be about the smallest thing crawling on two legs. The Old Lady is sure going to give me hell.
GRANDMA You shouldn't talk about your mother that way.
SPENCE (*rises, crosses to stairs*) I know, Gram—I know. It's easy for you to say—but it's true. And then I'm going to get cussed out. Pop is going to say that I'm no good and I'm no son of his. In short—he's going to call me a bastard.
GRANDMA That isn't what he means.
SPENCE (*helping* GRANDMA *upstairs*) It's sure the hell what it sounds like. In other words, Gram—if you'd lend me five dollars—I could go out and get some flowers for Mom and some cigars for Pop and begin by telling them how sorry I am, and it might take the edge off what is going to be at best a hell of an evening. (GRANDMA *on landing*) What do you say, Gram?
GRANDMA Well—all right. You go back downstairs and I'll get it for you.

(SPENCE *helps her off. Pause. Then he runs to kitchen, gets suitcase and clothes. Doorbell rings*)

SPENCE Dear, dear God—if that's my mother, just kill me as I open the door. (*crosses to door. He hides suitcase left of piano. Opens door*) Hi! Iggie—did you give me a scare!
IGGIE Hiya, Spence.
SPENCE I'm in a terrible hurry, Iggie. What do you want?
IGGIE I just came over to see if you have any stamps to trade.
SPENCE (*crosses left, gets shoes*) I haven't got much time. Come on in—but you can't stay long. I've got to go somewhere.
IGGIE (*comes in*) Where are you going?
SPENCE No place. (*pause*) You sure you came over to trade stamps?
IGGIE (*at sofa*) Sure—that's what I came

over for. I finished my home work early—and so I thought I might—

SPENCE (*sits in chair left of table*) You know, Iggie—you're going to be out of school for a week. You didn't have to get your home work done so soon. That's the most disgusting thing I ever heard.

IGGIE (*crosses to table*) Now look, if I want to get my home work done—that's my business. I don't tell you it's disgusting when you don't get yours done at all, do I?

SPENCE (*crosses back to sofa*) O.K.—O.K., Iggie. I only thought you came over because you heard I got kicked out of school.

IGGIE No, Spence—I hadn't heard.

SPENCE You're sure?

IGGIE I told you I hadn't heard, didn't I? (*sits right of table*)

SPENCE (*crosses right to close door*) That kind of news has a way of getting around. (*looking at him*) Well, what are you thinking about? (*crosses back to sofa*)

IGGIE Nothing. I was just thinking that if I got kicked out of school, I guess I'd just as soon I dropped dead right there on the floor in the principal's office.

SPENCE O.K., Iggie. You don't need to rub it in. I get the picture. (*looks upstairs*)

IGGIE I'm sorry, Spence. Is there anything I can do?

SPENCE Now, Iggie—pardon me for being so damn polite—but what in the hell could you do about it?

IGGIE I only want to help, Spence.

SPENCE (*crosses left to below table*) Well, you can't—so let's drop it, shall we?

IGGIE I didn't mean that business about dropping dead. I probably wouldn't drop dead anyway. There's nothing wrong with my heart.

SPENCE (*sits sofa*) Iggie—will you please cut it out.

IGGIE Anything you say. I didn't mean to offend you.

SPENCE You didn't offend me, Iggie. You just talk too much—that's all.

IGGIE I'll try to do better in the future.

SPENCE Look, Iggie—I've gone and hurt your feelings—haven't I? Hell—I'm sorry. I've always liked you, Iggie. You're a good kid. I'm apologizing, Iggie.

IGGIE It's O.K., Spence. I know you're upset.

SPENCE (*crosses down left*) I know how sensitive you are and all that and I just mow into you like crazy. I wish someone would tell me to shut my mouth. (*he walks to the stairs*) Gram—hurry up with that dough, will you. Iggie—look—I'll tell you what I'm going to do for you. (*he goes over to the piano and comes back with his stamp album*) Here—Iggie—it's yours. I want you to have it—because you're my friend.

IGGIE Your album! But don't you want it, Spence?

SPENCE No, Iggie. I don't want it.

IGGIE But why? I think you must be crazy. (*stands*)

SPENCE Hell, Iggie—because I'm growing up. I'm becoming a man, Iggie. And since I'm going out in just a few minutes with my girl friend—you know it's time for me to quit fooling around with stuff like that.

IGGIE Have you got a girl friend?

SPENCE Yeh! Yes—I have—as a matter of fact I might get married soon. Forget all about school and all.

IGGIE Really. Who is the girl, Spence?

SPENCE Just a girl—that's all. And if everything works out O.K., I won't be coming back. You know, I'll have to get a job and stuff like that. Now you've got to go, Iggie, cause I've got to finish packing and get dressed. (*leads* IGGIE *center*)

IGGIE Where are you going, Spence?

SPENCE I can't tell you, Iggie.

IGGIE Are you sure you're feeling all right?

SPENCE Yes, Iggie, I'm feeling all right.

IGGIE (*crossing to door*) Thank you for the gift. I appreciate it.

SPENCE Forget it.

IGGIE It's a beautiful album.

SPENCE It certainly is.

IGGIE (*crosses to center*) Hey, I was just thinking—maybe I could go up and talk to old Hasbrook. It might do some good.

SPENCE (*crosses to door*) I don't care about that any more, Iggie. I'm pretty sure I won't be coming back to school.

IGGIE Are you sure you want me to have this, Spence?

SPENCE Yes, Iggie, I want you to have it.

IGGIE (*crossing to door*) Well—I hope I'll see you soon. (*he is opening the door*)

SPENCE (*at door*) Hey, Iggie! You won't

mind if just once in a while—I come over and see how you're doing with it?

IGGIE I hope you will. Goodbye. (*exits*)

SPENCE Geez—I don't know what's wrong with me. I think maybe my brains are molding or something. (*gets suitcase, shoves clothes inside and runs upstairs*) Hey, Gram—will you hurry up with that five bucks so I can get the hell out of here before I really do something desperate!

(*Curtain*)

Scene Two

(*The Curtain rises on a bar and restaurant. It is a very small bar with very few bottles. The bottles that are there are mostly of blended whiskey and rum. A woman stands at the telephone which is on the right wall. There is one table and a booth at left; a table and chairs down center, table up center; juke box left. The bartender,* FRANK, *stands behind the bar, getting it ready for the evening.* ROSE *and* POPPY *are seated at the center table, and* CAROL *sits at the table in the left corner. Violet, the woman at the telephone, is speaking.* FRANK *and a man are arguing loudly at the bar.*)

VIOLET (*at phone*) Hello. Hello. Is Lonny there? What's that you say? Hey, Frank, I can't hear a god damned thing.

FRANK Aw, shut up.

VIOLET What's that you said to me?

FRANK I said "Aw, shut up." Now shut up.

VIOLET Listen, Frank, don't you be jumping salty with me.

POPPY (*at center table*) Hey Violet—cut the crap, will you, and get back on the phone.

FRANK Comes in here, spends the whole damn afternoon, and buys two bottles of ginger ale. Cheap—(*he smothers the last word under his breath*)

ROSE (*gets up*) What's that you called us?

FRANK You didn't hear it, did you?

ROSE It's just as well I didn't—cause if I'd heard it—(*sits*)

VIOLET Hey! All of you—shut up. I can't hear a word. (*returns to the phone*) I said is Lonny there? He's not. Well, Sugar, could you tell me when you expect him? What? Would you mind telling me for how long? What in hell did he do? Lonny did that? Well, ain't that something. Well, if you happen to see him on visiting days—just tell him Violet called. Violet—roses are red—you know. That's right—thank you. (*hangs up*) Well, Poppy, you can scratch Lonny's name out of the book. (*sits stool, faces right*)

POPPY Hell, Violet—by the time we're through today—you're going to have more scratched-out names than anything else in this book. What happened to him?

VIOLET (*faces center*) You remember reading in the paper about that girl—in the three paper bags at the railroad station—in the locker?

POPPY (*nods*) Yeh.

VIOLET Lonny!

ROSE Girl—are you kidding?

VIOLET (*crosses to table, sits back of it*) Frank, bring us another bottle of ginger ale.

FRANK What do you want in it?

VIOLET We still have whiskey of our own—thank you.

FRANK Then it'll be fifteen cents a bottle.

(*Man crosses to right of juke box.* SPENCE *enters down right. He is carrying some books. He stands by the door looking left at* CAROL *at the corner table*)

ROSE Fifteen cents?

FRANK Either put your money where your mouth is or shut up.

VIOLET Well—give us the bottle and some ice.

FRANK The ice will cost you a dime. (*crosses to* CAROL *with drink*)

POPPY Damn—let's get the hell out of here before he begins charging for sitting down.

VIOLET It's all right, Poppy. Pay the man.

POPPY (*to* FRANK) Well, bring it on over—you chinchy skunk.

FRANK Call me names like that—you can come over and get it yourselves. (FRANK *notices* SPENCE *at bar*) Can I help you, pal? (SPENCE *doesn't hear at first. Everyone turns around*) Hey! You—over there.

SPENCE You talking to me?

FRANK Yeh. What do you want?

SPENCE Nothing. It's kind of warm outside—and I kind of came in here to get cool.

FRANK Out.

SPENCE (*with great discomfort*) I'm cool now. So—I'll be going. (*looks at* CAROL. *He hovers about door back of bar and finally exits.*)

FRANK *crosses back to bar*)

POPPY (*after a pause*) Well—do we get our stuff or don't we?

FRANK I told you—get it yourselves.

ROSE (*rising*) Let's get the hell out of this dump.

VIOLET It's all right—I'll get it. (*goes to bar and picks up the bottle of ginger ale and the ice*) And here's a quarter tip for you, Frank, for being so gracious.

POPPY All right, Violet—don't be going crazy over there now. Every little bit helps, and if we don't raise the money for the rent, we'll be out in the street tomorrow.

VIOLET (*ignoring her*) Thank you, Frank. You're a real gentleman. I'm going to tell all my friends to come over and trade with you. (*crosses to table with glasses and ice*)

FRANK You can tell those whores that I don't want them in my place.

POPPY Aw man—shut up.—Who else is left in that book of yours, Violet?

VIOLET I don't know—let me see. Well, there's Sidney. We haven't called Sidney.

POPPY What's his number? (*gets up*)

VIOLET Two—eight nine two seven. Whose turn is it?

POPPY (*crosses to phone*) Mine. Why in hell you think I'm getting up?

FRANK And don't be coming in here with food. This ain't no lousy picnic grove.

VIOLET Well, it's lousy.

POPPY Shh.

FRANK (*throws rag at her*) You heard what I said. Just be sure you clean up that mess before you leave.

VIOLET (*throws rag back*) I ain't no janitor.

POPPY (*on phone*) Hello, Sidney. This is Poppy. One and the same. Haven't seen you lately. Well that's too bad. (*pause*) Sugar, we're in a bad spot 'cause tomorrow the rent man is coming around, an—(VIOLET *crosses to phone*) Well now, Sugar, Violet is sitting right here and she's upset about the rent too. Do you remember the time you took Violet down to New York and registered in that hotel as Mr. and Mrs.? (ROSE *crosses to bar above* POPPY) Well now—Honey—to get down to New York, you had to cross a state line. Now have you ever heard of the Mann Act? Well, Violet has. Well—I don't know all the details of it, but it seems you can get into about ten or fifteen years worth of trouble for carrying girls over state lines for the kind of purposes you had in mind. (*man crosses to bar*) Now all Violet is asking for is about ten dollars—that roughly comes out to seventy-five cents a year, and she wants it tonight—at Carter's drug store—or else the F.B.I. Now have you got all that, Sugar? Fine—we'll be looking for you, hear? (*she hangs up, crosses back to her chair*) Well, Sidney suddenly decided he had ten loose dollars around some place. We're supposed to meet him in Carter's in fifteen minutes. (*sits in her chair.* VIOLET *follows, sits above table*)

ROSE (*crosses back to her chair, sits*) Girl! I ain't never seen anything like you in my whole life.

POPPY How much more we got to raise, Violet?

VIOLET Let's see—that's Sidney—ten dollars! (*gets up, crosses up to rear table*) All we need is fifteen more.

FRANK —Coming in here—blackmailing people on my telephone.

POPPY We ain't blackmailing anybody. We're just keeping ourselves available. There's no telling—next week sometime—one of those boys might be glad that we're still here.

MAN (*at the bar*) I can't see why.

ROSE Why don't you shut up?

MAN This is a place of business. Man comes in here to have a quiet drink. If it ain't a bunch of whores, it's a television set.

POPPY Mister—don't you be calling us whores, hear—or I'm liable to come over there and knock you breathless.

ROSE Come on, Poppy. Don't pay no attention to him.

VIOLET Coming in here for a quiet drink—he calls it. I seen you lamping the little girl over in the corner. You ought to be ashamed of yourself. (*crosses to* CAROL) Baby, if he bothers you—just come over and tell me and I'll knock his brains out. Hear? (CAROL *says nothing.* VIOLET *returns to center table.* SPENCE *appears down right, outside door; carries books*)

ROSE Violet—come on and get your book out. We ain't got all night.

POPPY I don't know why in hell we ain't got all night. We haven't got anything else to do. (*they look at her*) Well—have we?

VIOLET No—we haven't, stupid. (SPENCE

enters, sits stool below bar, puts books on bar) But you don't have to say it in here—do you? Hell—you have to keep up some pretenses, Poppy. (*crosses up stage; sits in chair*)

SPENCE (*knocking on the bar*) How about a little service here—sport? (ROSE *crosses to* VIOLET)

FRANK (*eyeing him*) What do you want now?

SPENCE A glass of beer. (FRANK *laughs, still eyes him*) I said a glass of beer.

FRANK How old are you?

SPENCE (*pointing at the man*) Did you ask him how old he was?

FRANK No—I didn't.

SPENCE Then why in hell are you asking me?

FRANK I know him. He comes in here all all the time. (*man crosses left to juke box*)

SPENCE Well, my name is Spencer Scott—so now you know me. Give me a glass of beer.

FRANK What're you—just coming from school with all those books? The teacher didn't keep you after school all this time, did she? (*he laughs. He reaches for a book*) What's this? (*reading the title*) The Interpretation of Dreams by Sigmund—(SPENCE *gets up, grabs book*) You don't believe in that stuff, do you?

SPENCE Hey—do you run a quiz show or something? You know there are other joints on this street that probably got colder beer than you got anyway. (*pause*) I've been to the library, see. And inside this book is my library card. They have pink cards for children and yellow cards for adults. This is a yellow card. Now as to more personal things—I've been walking a hell of a long way and I've got a headache—now will you please give me a glass of beer. I've got money for it—see—I can pay for it. I'm not drunk already. What do you say?

FRANK How old are you?

SPENCE Twenty-one.

FRANK When were you born?

SPENCE (*without batting an eye*) January 20, 1932.

FRANK (*getting a piece of paper*) Let's see. Yep. (*figuring it out*) That makes you—twenty-one.

SPENCE That's what I said.

FRANK You look mighty young to be twenty-one.

SPENCE Beer—Hah? A nice tall one.

FRANK We got a special on whiskey today.

SPENCE You know—hot shot—you got remarkable powers of persuasion there. But I asked you for a beer.

POPPY That's right, Sugar—don't drink none of that man's whiskey. He ferments it himself.

VIOLET You sure are right, Frank—that whiskey is special. Specially awful. (THREE FLOWERS *laugh uproariously*)

FRANK Quiet over there. I'm minding my business.

POPPY Say, Sugar—did I hear you say something about a dream book?

SPENCE Yeh—I found it in the library. (*man blows smoke at* CAROL) It's supposed to be pretty sexy.

VIOLET Come on over and sit down with us.

SPENCE Sure. (*crosses to center table*)

POPPY Does that book say anything about umbrellas? I keep having the damndest dreams with umbrellas in them.

SPENCE I don't know. I've just glanced through it. (*sits left chair*)

POPPY Do you mind if I take a look? (ROSE *crosses down, sits center*)

SPENCE Help yourself. (*looks at* CAROL) You girls hang around here a lot?

ROSE No, this isn't one of our usual hangouts. We come here about once a month to take care of a financial transaction. Do you live around here?

SPENCE. Yeh—around here. (*pause*) Say—do any of you know the girl over in the corner? (*man crosses to bar*)

ROSE No—we don't know her at all. Mousey little thing—ain't she?

SPENCE No, I don't think she's mousey at all.

POPPY Hell, I can't find a thing about umbrellas in this book. This is the damndest dream book I ever saw.

SPENCE Give it to me—Here I'll find it for you. (*he takes the book*)

VIOLET (*gets up, crosses to* ROSE. *Looking at her book*) Whose turn is it next?

ROSE Mine. (*gets up, starts for phone*)

VIOLET You call Homer. The number is two—five eight seven six.

ROSE Two—five eight—

VIOLET Seven six—and here's the dime. (*both cross to phone.* ROSE *dials.* VIOLET *at bar*)

SPENCE Did you say a cane or an umbrella?

POPPY An umbrella, Sugar. (*moves to center chair*) Hell—there ain't much difference between canes and umbrellas, is there? What does it say about canes? (VIOLET *turns to center*)

SPENCE It doesn't say much. It just says that a woman dreams about a man carrying a cane. It must mean you're plenty batty because they got her whole case history written up here.

POPPY Well, I didn't say I dreamed of canes, did I? Don't be trying to push her dreams off on me. Look for umbrellas—and don't be looking in those crazy people's dreams either. Look for some nice person that dreams of umbrellas.

ROSE Nobody answers.

VIOLET Well, keep ringing—his mother is always home.

ROSE Well, what will I say if his mother answers?

VIOLET Just ask for Homer, stupid.

ROSE (*in phone*) Hello, Homer? This is Rose. Well, I know an awful lot of Homers, too, and I know which one you are. Rose Thompson. How you been? Haven't seen you in a month of Sundays.

SPENCE Wouldn't that be a hell of a thing—a month with only Sundays in it? You'd spend your whole life in church.

VIOLET Ssh.

POPPY Shut up.

ROSE (*in phone*) Well, Sugar, I was calling you because we are kind of in a jam. Violet—Poppy and me. That's right—the three flowers. We need money for the rent. I don't know—I guess everyone is trying to save money what with Christmas coming and all and they must be cutting down on the little luxuries. Oh! Homer—you say the most terrible things. (*putting her hand over the mouthpiece*) The son of a bitch. (*she takes her hand off*) Well, how about it? Well, I guess we'll just have to talk to your wife, Sugar. No, I don't think I want to talk to her tonight. You'd never. Well just thanks for nothing, Homer. The same to you quartetted. (*hangs up and sits on stool*) Can you beat that? He said he didn't give a damn whether his wife knew or not. There's something terrible immoral about that.

POPPY You're damn right. It's getting to the point where no one has any respect for marriage these days. I just wish somebody would ask me to marry them. I'd split their heads wide open.

SPENCE (*putting down the book*) Hey! Pardon me, are you girls prostitutes or something? (ALL *turn to him*)

POPPY Honey—we try to be.

SPENCE You know—I've never met any real prostitutes before. You wouldn't mind if I asked you a couple of questions—would you?

VIOLET Well, Honey—right now we're in a little hot water—and we also got to go out and pick up a little something down at Carter's drug store. (*at table down center*) But as soon as we come back we'll answer all your questions. Why don't you go over and talk to the little girl over there until we come back? (*crosses back to table up center*)

SPENCE Are you sure she wouldn't mind my bargin' over there like that?

POPPY What if she does? You can sit anywhere you want in this place. Go over there and sit down. (*gets up*)

VIOLET (*crossing down to table*) Let's go, girls.

ROSE I don't see why all of us have to go to get a little ten dollars from Sidney.

POPPY Because in union there is strength. (*crosses to* ROSE) Now get the hell off that stool and let's go. I assume that none of us have any more names in our books? (*exits up right*)

VIOLET Your assumption is absolutely correct. (VIOLET *and* ROSE *exit up right.* FRANK *crosses table center, gets bottles, cleans table, returns to bar*)

SPENCE (*who has been going over to the left table very slowly—has just arrived—and is standing undecided right of booth*) Do you mind if I sit down? (CAROL *shakes her head.* SPENCE *sits down. He sits looking at her for a time*) You're sure I'm not bothering you or anything, 'cause if I am, I can get the hell up and go someplace else.

CAROL These tables aren't reserved. You can sit anywhere you please. If you bother me I can get up and get the hell out of here, that's all.

SPENCE (*rises, crosses right*) I'm sorry.

CAROL Where are you going?

SPENCE I guess—

CAROL Sit down, kid. I didn't mean to scare you away.

SPENCE (*looks at man*) I suppose a nice girl does have to be careful about who she talks to in a joint like this. (*crosses back to booth*) You don't need to be afraid of me, though.

CAROL What makes you think that I'm such a nice girl?

SPENCE (*sits right in booth*) You can just tell—that's all.

CAROL What makes you think that I'm not like Violet, Rose, and Poppy?

SPENCE Aw! Quit your kidding.

CAROL Well, thanks for thinking that I'm different from Violet, Rose, and Poppy.

SPENCE Well, you are—aren't you?

CAROL Yeh—in one or two respects I guess I am.

SPENCE (*relieved*) I thought you were. (*pause. Gets closer—hand out*) My name's Spencer Scott. Everybody calls me Spence.

CAROL (*takes hand*) I know. I heard you when you came in.

SPENCE Yeh. That's because I've got such a damn big mouth. I've got a theory as to why I talk so loud. I think it's because of my youth. I guess as I get older like Mack maybe—I won't talk so loud. (*pause*) Mack is my brother. (*pause*) He used to talk loud when he was a kid.

CAROL You're not really twenty-one, are you?

SPENCE I was lying then. See, I've got to lie about my age until I get to be twenty-one. Since I lie about that, as you can guess, I lie about other things too. But as soon as I get to be twenty-one not another goddamn lie is going to pass my lips.

CAROL That's very sweet.

SPENCE I really honestly mean it.

CAROL I really honestly believe you. (*she takes a sip of her drink and then nervously bangs the drink down on the table. Looks at man*) Damn it. Who in the hell does he think he's looking at?

SPENCE Who?

CAROL That guy over there. He keeps staring at me.

SPENCE You want me to go over and speak to him?

CAROL (*restraining him*) No! No! Don't bother. (*pause. Man sits at chair up stage, reads paper.* FRANK *has fallen asleep, his head on the bar*)

SPENCE Well, now that we know each other—would you mind telling me your name?

CAROL My name's Carol—Carol Pearson.

SPENCE Is that Carol spelt with an "e" or with the "e" left off?

CAROL That's Carol with the "e" left off.

SPENCE I never knew a Carol with the "e" left off before except in a book I used to read as a kid. It was called "The Birds' Christmas Carol." Did you ever read it?

CAROL No, I don't think I ever did.

SPENCE I know you'd never believe it to look at me—but I read that book around ninety times I guess. That book used to make me cry like a baby. It was about a little girl named Carol who was doomed to die—and finally at the end, she dies—on the same day she was born—Christmas Day. Well, the last time I read that book I expected to cry again. I grabbed the old box of Kleenex and opened the book, and as I was reading, it was like me and the author had a big fight. She was trying to make me cry and I was damned if I was going to do her the favor. The whole book, believe it or not, was set up to make you cry. I gave the book to Iggie the next day.

CAROL (*after a pause*) So—what about it?

SPENCE Iggie's a friend of mine. He's kind of hard to talk to because he's real shy. You know what I mean? But he knows I like him and I think he's getting a lot better. I got a theory about that. Would you like to hear it?

CAROL I can hardly wait.

SPENCE Well—it's this. My theory is that everybody needs somebody else. What do you think about that?

CAROL I think you've got something.

SPENCE I kind of thought that you'd think so. (*pause*) I need somebody too, I guess. I know you wouldn't believe it to look at me but you're looking at one of the most friendless persons in the whole United States.

CAROL Aw! Come on—

SPENCE Well, I guess that that wasn't exactly the truth—because you see there's my Gram. She's the only pal I got left—I guess.

CAROL (*pulling out a cigarette*) Have you got a match, kid? (SPENCE *pulls out matches.* CAROL *takes them*) Thanks. So your Mom and Pop don't trust you, is that it?

SPENCE They'd like to—but I sure as hell think they're not so sure that I'm not going to turn out the family skeleton.

CAROL So what makes you think that you're so friendless? (*crosses to juke box*)

SPENCE Well, that's a story and a half. You see I live—I mean used to live down at the South End. (*turns right*) There aren't many colored families down there; in fact; there are about two. So Mack and I grew up with the white kids who lived on our street. We had lots of good times together—and it wasn't until the kids started getting interested in sex that my troubles began.

CAROL   How do you mean?

SPENCE   Well, actually it started happening last summer. For weeks they wouldn't call me. To be frank with you—I thought it was because my personality wasn't so hot maybe. You see—I'm a real guy. (CAROL *has put a nickel in juke box which doesn't work. She gives up and returns to booth. Sits*) I play the piano—but not enough for the guys to think I'm a sissy. I'm a little thin but I got a build that would knock you out to be perfectly honest with you—but I still thought that something was wrong with me—

CAROL   That's an old, old story, kid.

SPENCE   What do you mean?

CAROL   I can finish it for you. You're pretty fed up with the whole business, aren't you? You don't know what the hell to do because you're lonely. It's a hell of a feeling. So you start smoking, drinking beer. You want to be a real grown up guy before your time. The only thing you know is that this kid stuff is for the birds—so you're going to run away from it—get to be an adult because maybe being an adult will bring a couple of things with it. Happiness —a nice girl—maybe—

SPENCE   Yes, I guess that's it. But all the kids my age are interested in the broads now. So I was passing by here—saw you in the window—and decided to give it a whirl.

CAROL   (*laughs*) Thanks—for seeing me in the window.

SPENCE   I know you think it sounds pretty silly because I know how girls are about going around with boys that are younger than they are—but have you ever gotten a really good look at the Kinsey report?

CAROL   No, I'm afraid I don't read much.

SPENCE   Well—I'm honestly not one to boast—but it says in that book that boys my age are usually pretty sexy. In fact, they're sexier at my age than they ever will be again in their whole goddamn lives. And what with my other qualifications that I told you about, I should be a pretty good boy friend to have.

CAROL   You know—I'd almost bet that that was the truth.

SPENCE   Well, what do you say? I know I started off all wrong. I should have started off by shooting you the old bull about how lovely you are and all that stuff, but I figured that if I asked you to be my girl friend you'd know that I thought you were pretty and all that because I really couldn't be interested in a lemon. I also want you to know that if everything goes right between me and you and we decide that we love each other, I'm perfectly willing to get married. (CAROL *moves down stage on bench*) My father wants me to go to college but I'd be perfectly willing to forego that if everything works out okay. How about it?

CAROL   Spence, you're a sweet kid and that was about the sweetest proposal I've ever had. (*she watches* SPENCE *who has pressed glass to forehead*) Is there something wrong?

SPENCE   Naw—just a headache. Too much beer, I guess.

CAROL   (*taking glass from him*) You know what you ought to do? Go on home and let your grandmother give you a great big kiss and tuck you in.

SPENCE   Don't you understand? I won't be going home. I've got to look for a job. What do you say?

CAROL   I've already told you what I say. Go on home. I don't want to hear any more of your troubles. I've got troubles of my own. You talk about getting a job. What in hell could you do? You couldn't do any better than my husband.

SPENCE   Your husband?

CAROL   Yes. He works all day and he works all night and we've still got nothing. He's what is commonly known as unskilled labor. I guess you know what that means. (*pause*) I'm sorry, kid.

SPENCE   You should have told me you were married in the first place. I feel like a great big can of garbage. (*turns away*)

CAROL   You didn't hear a word I said, did you, kid? (*gathers her purse. Man crosses bar*) I've got to go now.

SPENCE   Where are you going?

CAROL   You see that guy in the corner of the bar? Well, he's been staring at me all night. I hope he has some money. I hope he has a car—a nice car with a top that goes down. I can go for a drive in the country and for maybe two hours I can have some fun.

SPENCE   I think that's terrible.

CAROL   So do I—so there's two of us. (*finishes drink*) And if my husband ever finds out, he'd kill me, so I guess there's three of us.

But I'm going anyway because I've got to. I can't go home to that lousy one-room flat and wait all night. It's too quiet there. There's nobody to talk to. It's just no fun—that's all.

SPENCE (*pause*) If you're going—why don't you go?

CAROL It's funny how when you're young you can be so selfish about your feelings, isn't it? Thank you for the proposal. (*rises, crosses right of table*) Please don't be sore. I tried to help you, Spence. There's a nursery rhyme I used to know. It goes,

Merry have we met, and merry have we been,
Merry let us part, and merry meet again.

Let's not part angrily. (*he doesn't answer*) Spence! (*she walks over and kisses him squarely on the mouth*) Good luck, kid. (*she walks over to the man at the bar. He pays for her, and they leave together up right. The* THREE FLOWERS *reenter up right.* VIOLET *enters first*)

VIOLET (*offstage*) I don't care what you say, it's a stinking way to behave. (*sees money man has left on bar, picks it up, crosses to center table, sits*) Standing us up like that.

POPPY Every little bit helps.

ROSE (*crosses to juke box, puts nickel in*) And then not answering the phone is the rudest thing I ever heard of.

POPPY (*crosses to right of table, sits*) I told you to stop worrying about it. Tomorrow morning, on his way to work, I'll get him. And he'll either cough up that ten bucks or I'll snatch him baldheaded. That ten-spot is as good as got—so stop worrying about it. (*juke box starts playing*)

VIOLET Hey! Spence. We're through with our business. You can come over now if you want to (SPENCE *doesn't move*)

ROSE (*crossing to center table, sits left*) Well as far as I can see we might just as well be dead. We might just as well amble on over to the graveyard and lie down.

(SPENCE *sits for one more moment, with his head hidden from them, and then he rises, crosses in*)

SPENCE Hey! Violet—is there any lipstick on my mouth to speak of?

VIOLET There sure is, Honey.

POPPY What're you doing smearing lipstick all over your mouth like that? You queer or something?

SPENCE Cut the comedy. Did you see that girl over there in the corner?

ROSE You mean she kissed you?

SPENCE Yeh. I guess I'm what you call a pretty fast worker, huh?

VIOLET How would you like to come with me? (*gets up*)

SPENCE Where are we going?

VIOLET You said you wanted to talk to me, didn't you? I just thought we could go some place where we could be alone—a quieter place.

SPENCE Sure—that's okay with me.

VIOLET Let's go, Sugar—I know just the place. (SPENCE *leans against booth*) What's the matter, Honey?

SPENCE Nothing. Been drinking too much, I guess.

VIOLET Well, come on, Sugar—You got enough money to buy me a sandwich or something?

SPENCE (*as he exits up right,* VIOLET *following*) Sure—I got two dollars and thirty-nine cents.

VIOLET (*coming back to table down center*) That sounds like the price of something in a fire sale—doesn't it? Well, Hell—(*exits up right*)

(*Curtain*)

Scene Three

(VIOLET's *room.* VIOLET *is turning the key in the lock as the curtain rises.* SPENCE *is behind her. When they enter there is the distinct sound of muffled voices*)

SPENCE What's that?

VIOLET (*sits chair right, takes off shoes*) The two men next door. Don't worry about them—they're deaf.

SPENCE (*standing center*) It sounded like they were in the next room.

VIOLET They are. The walls here are very thin.

SPENCE Thin is hardly the word. You might say they were put together with spitballs. You been away or something?

VIOLET (*crossing left to drapes*) No, why?

SPENCE Nothing except that it looks like you've put everything to bed for the night.

VIOLET (*crosses to bed, takes off cover, folds it, puts it behind curtain*) Oh, Those are my covers. It keeps things neat and clean.

SPENCE Say, I thought you wanted to go to another restaurant where we could talk?

VIOLET It's much more comfy to talk here. We can have something sent in if we want it. Don't you want to take your jacket off? It's pretty warm in here. (*turns on light above bureau*)

SPENCE (*crossing chair right*) Thanks—I guess I will. You wouldn't happen to have something to eat hanging around, would you? (VIOLET *crosses behind drapes*) I'm feeling pretty groggy. I think perhaps it's because I haven't had any supper.

VIOLET There's some crackers up there. (*she points to the bureau. Crosses to bureau—then behind drapes*)

SPENCE Thanks. (*crosses to bureau, gets crackers and starts eating them*) What kind of radio is this?

VIOLET It's a short wave radio. It gets the police calls. (*takes clothes off line, crosses behind drapes*)

SPENCE Why would anyone want the crummy police calls?

VIOLET For a number of reasons.

SPENCE What ever happens in this crumby town that should interest anybody?

VIOLET (*crossing to him*) Sugar—that radio is like a husband to me. Now why don't you stop worrying about the radio and take off your tie and get comfortable so we can talk.

SPENCE (*at bureau*) I can talk with my tie on. That's never been one of my difficulties.

VIOLET Would you like to hear a little music?

SPENCE That would be nice.

VIOLET (*turns on the radio. Crosses back of drapes*) You wouldn't mind if I changed into something a little more comfortable, would you?

SPENCE Not at all.

VIOLET I won't be a minute.

SPENCE You wouldn't have a little cheese to go with these crackers, would you? (*radio plays Chopin Sonata in B flat minor. Opus 35. Funeral March*)

VIOLET Look around and see.

SPENCE Any place in particular? (*looks in sink*)

VIOLET Just look around. I seem to remember seeing some cheese around here a couple of days ago. What's that they're playing?

SPENCE It's Chopin.

VIOLET Is he playing or being played?

SPENCE He's being played. Chopin's dead.

VIOLET Recently?

SPENCE (*crossing right*) Not too recently. Over a hundred years ago.

VIOLET Isn't that sad?

SPENCE (*looking on bed table and under bed*) I guess it was when it happened. Well—I don't seem to find any cheese around here at all.

VIOLET I guess Poppy must've taken it for the trap. (*re-enters*) Now—how do I look? (*she has emerged in a bronze satin negligee with maribou around the collar and down the front*)

SPENCE Do you honestly feel more comfortable in that?

VIOLET Oh! Much much more. (*she moves over to the bed, sits*) Now come on and let's sit down over here so we can talk.

SPENCE (*sits in chair right*) I should think that it would tickle the back of your neck something awful. What shall we talk about?

VIOLET Why I thought you wanted to talk to me. (*pause*) Do you have to listen to that?

SPENCE Not necessarily. (*rises and switches radio off*) These crackers don't seem to be doing a damn bit of good.

VIOLET Come on back.

SPENCE Sure. (*he sits back down on the chair right*)

VIOLET Come on closer.

SPENCE What for? I can hear you from here.

VIOLET (*crawling over bed*) Aw! Come on, Sugar. Stop being so bashful.

SPENCE I'm not being bashful. (*she pulls* SPENCE *by the hand*) All right, I'll come. You don't have to pull me. (*he sits on bed*)

VIOLET (*puts her arms around his neck*) Now tell Violet all about it.

SPENCE All about what?

VIOLET What's troubling you.

SPENCE Nothing's troubling me.

VIOLOT Supposing you give Violet a little kiss. That might make you feel better.

SPENCE I honestly don't see how a kiss is going to do anything for my hunger.

VIOLET Well, try it, baby, and see. (SPENCE *gives her an experimental peck on the cheek*) Oh! Come on, Sugar. You can do better than that. (*she grabs* SPENCE, *pulls him back on the bed and kisses him*)

SPENCE (*after some time breaks away, crosses right*) God damn it.

VIOLET What's the matter?
SPENCE (*gets jacket from chair and starts to put it on*) I left my books over in the bar.
VIOLET Well—what about it?
SPENCE They're library books. If they were my books I wouldn't care.
VIOLET (*gets up, stands left of bed*) Say—what's the matter with you anyway?
SPENCE I told you. My books are over there.
VIOLET So let them stay there. No one's going to run away with them.
SPENCE How can you be so sure of that?
VIOLET Listen, Sugar—no one that ever goes in Frank's ever reads nothing. Take my word for it.
SPENCE I'd better go.
VIOLET (*jumps onto bed, runs over it, and holds door*) Hey! Are you trying to run out on me?
SPENCE Why would I do a thing like that?
VIOLET (*still standing on bed*) Well that's sure as hell what it looks like. (*pause*) What happened to all those questions you had to ask me? What happened to all that big talk you were throwing around in the bar?
SPENCE Nothing happened to it. I got a headache and I'm hungry—at least I think I'm hungry.
VIOLET I think you're just plain scared.
SPENCE Scared of who?
VIOLET Scared of me—that's who. (*a thought dawning on her, gets down from bed*) Hey! How old are you anyway?
SPENCE I told you—twenty-one.
VIOLET (*sits on bed*) If you're twenty-one, I'm sweet sixteen. Come over here. (SPENCE *sits in chair*) You've never been in a place like this before—have you? You're kind of scared, aren't you?
SPENCE Well—to be perfectly honest with you, I guess I am kind of scared. I guess I just want to go and get my books—if you don't mind. (*crosses to door*)
VIOLET (*crossing to door*) Look, kid—I most certainly do mind. (SPENCE *sits chair*) Let me tell you how this mess works. You've taken me out of circulation for roughly fifteen minutes now—fifteen minutes in which anything could happen—and if you think that you're just going to put your coat on and walk out of here—you've got another thought coming. I want my two dollars and thirty-nine cents.
SPENCE But that's all the money I have.
VIOLET I know it's all the money you have. You think if you had more I'd be asking for two dollars and thirty-nine cents? What do you take me for anyway? It ain't that I don't understand, Sugar, it's just that business is business.
SPENCE (*reaching into his pocket*) Is it all right if I keep a half a dollar for supper?
VIOLET You can take the crackers as you leave. I want my two thirty-nine. (*taking it, crossing to bureau, puts money away*) Thank you. And another thing—if you ever tell anybody that all you paid me was two thirty-nine I'll have your head on a platter. You hear me? (*sits on bed, leans back*)
SPENCE I understand. Is it all right if I go now?
VIOLET Suit yourself. (*puts key on bed table.* SPENCE *starts to go, then stops*) What's the matter—did you lose something?
SPENCE I was just thinking.
VIOLET Thinking what?
SPENCE Well—if I go back to that bar—Poppy and Rose are still there—aren't they?
VIOLET They'd better be.
SPENCE Well—I was just thinking—if I go back over there in such a short time they'll know that—
VIOLET You was a bust? They sure will,
SPENCE I was just wondering—if you'd mind terribly if I stayed about fifteen minutes more.
VIOLET Help yourself.
SPENCE (*goes over and sits stiffly in down right chair*) You wouldn't tell them—would you?
VIOLET Tell them what?
SPENCE That I was such a—bust?
VIOLET If you can keep my secret I can keep yours. (*they sit in silence for some time*) You know—if you're going to sit there—I'm afraid that you're going to have to say something. If there's one thing I can't stand it's silence.
SPENCE What do you want me to say?
VIOLET I don't want you to say anything that you don't want to say. Just talk. (*gets pillows and doll from behind drapes*)
SPENCE What time is it?
VIOLET The fifteen minutes ain't passed yet. You know the old saying about a watched pot never boiling. (*sits back on bed, arranges doll's dress*)

SPENCE Would you like me to read to you for a while?
VIOLET Do I look like an old lady to you?
SPENCE No.
VIOLET Well I can see to read to myself, thank you very much.
SPENCE I'm sorry. I'm—
VIOLET Forget it. Just forget it.
SPENCE I wonder—if you'd do me a favor?
VIOLET As long as there's no money involved—yes.
SPENCE Well—there is. I was wondering if you'd loan me a dime for bus fare. I want to go home.
VIOLET Well, can't you walk?
SPENCE It's down at the South End.
VIOLET Well that's what I get for playing around with kids. Just reach in and take a dime—and only a dime. (SPENCE *walks over to the bureau and opens it and takes a dime.* VIOLET *watches carefully, lying on her stomach, head down stage. He closes it and then stops and leans on it*) What's the matter with you, anyway?
SPENCE Nothing—I just don't feel good. (*starts for the door*) Thanks for the dime.
VIOLET Don't bother thanking me. It hurts me to give it to you.
SPENCE (*at door*) Well—thanks anyway. But there's one thing I want you to know.
VIOLET What's that?
SPENCE I think that's one of the ugliest bath robes I've ever seen in my life! (*he walks out the door as—*)

(*Curtain*)

ACT TWO

Scene One

(*As the curtain rises on* SPENCE'*s home—there is one light on—the light over* LEM SCOTT'*s chair. He is in it. He is asleep with a newspaper in his lap. The rest of the house is quiet—superficially at least. It is later the same evening. Someone passes in the street outside,—they are whistling. It wakes* LEM)

LEM (*half-asleep*) May—we got to—(*rises, crosses to center below stairs*) Well, I'll be damned. May! May!

MAY (*upstairs*) What do you want?
LEM What time is it?
MAY Five minutes have passed since you asked me that the last time. It's ten minutes after ten.
LEM (*yawns*) Well—where the hell is he?
MAY Daddy—I don't know. I've told you that over and over again. I haven't got one idea left.
LEM Well, how can you be up there asleep—when for all you know he could be dead some place? (*crosses down right*)
MAY If he's dead, Daddy—there's nothing we can do about it until we know. I'm not asleep.
LEM Is that mother of yours asleep?
MAY I don't see how she could be.
LEM (*picks up more newspapers*) I think she knows more than she's letting on.
MAY Well, there's a five hundred watt light downstairs in the pantry. Why don't you bring it up along with your rubber hose and give her the third degree?
LEM Why don't you cut out being so smart. That's the trouble with your whole family—they think they're smart. (*kicks stool*)
MAY (*appears at head of stairs*) Why don't you just go back to your paper, Daddy—or watch the television for a while?
LEM When I get my hands on that little bastard I'll break every bone in his body.
MAY (*coming down the stairs to left side of sofa, sits*) Now that's no way to talk, Daddy.
GRANDMA (*offstage*) It most certainly is not. It's disgraceful.
MAY Mama—will you please keep out of it? (*turns on lamp by sofa*)
GRANDMA The truth is the truth and should be spoken at all times.
MAY Mother, please!
GRANDMA (*enters, sits landing*) Don't please Mother me. The truth is the truth. It's disgraceful. If there are any bastards around—it's you who've sired them. My May is a good girl.
LEM Would you please tell her to stay out of it?
MAY Mother, please.
GRANDMA Well, speak up to him. Don't let him get away with talk like that. Just speak up.
MAY I'd speak up, Mama, if you'd give me half a chance.
GRANDMA Calling your husband "Daddy"

all the time. If that isn't the silliest thing I ever heard.

MAY Mother, if you don't keep out of this, I'll come upstairs and give you a pill and shut your door.

GRANDMA And I'll spit out the pill and open the door. So there.

LEM (*gets up—crosses to foot of stairs*) Will you two stop that bickering and let's get down to the point at hand. (*calling up to* GRANDMA) Do you know where he is? (*no answer*) Hey! Old lady—I'm talking to you.

GRANDMA If you're talking to me—my name is Mrs. Martin, and I'd thank you to remember that. No—I don't know where he is, and if I did I wouldn't tell you. (LEM *turns away*)

MAY Would you tell me, Mama?

GRANDMA Tell you?—after your telling me to shut up? I wouldn't tell you a thing.

MAY I didn't tell you to shut up, Mama.

GRANDMA Well, you said "Mother please," which is the same thing.

LEM There's no use talking to her. (*sits in his chair, takes up paper*)

GRANDMA Calling your son a bastard—the very idea. No wonder he uses such terrible language. No wonder he's in trouble down there at— (*she stops*)

LEM Where is he in trouble? (*no answer*)

MAY Mama—what trouble is Spence in?

GRANDMA (*rising*) I'm a little tired. If you don't mind I think I'll go to bed now. (*from arch*) Good night.

LEM (*rises, crosses to stairs. On stairs*) I'm gonna—

MAY It's no use, Lem. She won't tell you. She's as stubborn as an old mule.

GRANDMA I heard that—and I'll remember it.

LEM (*from stairs*) What are we going to do?

MAY We'll sit here and wait for him—that's all. (LEM *crosses right to chair*) I'm a little worried now, Lem.

LEM It's about time.

MAY Oh, don't be silly. I was worried before. You don't suppose we should call the police, Lem?

LEM What for? We haven't done anything—have we?

MAY They'd help us find him.

LEM There'll be no police in this house—ever—for any reason.

MAY Now you're being silly.

LEM You heard what I said. I don't want any police in this.

MAY (*rises; crosses right to window*) Ssh! He's coming up the steps—and he's carrying a bag, Lem.

LEM (*crosses to center*) A bag? Well, I'll be damned!

MAY Now don't holler at him until we find out what's wrong.

LEM Don't worry. I'll handle this. You just stay out of it. (SPENCE *enters right.* LEM *lights cigar*)

GRANDMA (*as* SPENCE *shuts door*) Spence—is that you?

SPENCE (*takes off coat; crosses to foot of stairs*) Yes, it's me, Gram.

GRANDMA Would you come right upstairs, please. I've dropped my glasses and can't seem to find them.

SPENCE I'll be right up, Gram.

LEM You'll come in this house and sit down, young man. I want to talk to you.

SPENCE It'll just take a second, Pop.

LEM A second too long. Sit down now. The traitor upstairs can wait for her glasses. She can't read in the dark, anyhow. (SPENCE *sits on stool*)

MAY (*crosses to left of* SPENCE) Spence—you don't look well. Where have you been?

SPENCE To the library.

GRANDMA Spence—I haven't told them a thing. If they say I have they're lying.

LEM (*crossing down to* SPENCE) Will you shut her up?

MAY (*to center*) Mother, please.

GRANDMA Oh! Shut up, yourself. Mother please—Mother please. Why don't you tell me to shut up and be done with it?

LEM (*over* GRANDMA's *last sentence*) I can't even think with her carrying on up there. So—you were at the library and you brought a suitcase to carry home a couple of books. (MAY *crosses to* SPENCE)

SPENCE Well—I had a tough time finding the books.

LEM I get it. You knew you were going to have a tough time finding the books so you just packed an overnight bag in case you had to spend the night.

MAY Have you had anything to eat, Spence?

SPENCE As a matter of fact I haven't.

LEM Will you please stop interrupting?
MAY I'll go and heat up something. (*goes into the kitchen, turns on kitchen light*)
LEM Do you think I'm crazy, Spence?
SPENCE I honestly don't think you're crazy, Pop.
LEM Well, you must think something like that. Don't you think I know what time the library closes?
SPENCE What time does the library close, Pop?
LEM (*a pause*) May! (*crosses to arch up left center*)
MAY Yes?
LEM You'd better come in here and talk to this little bastard before I break his neck.
GRANDMA There he goes again. It's disgraceful. (MAY *comes in with saucepan and ladle.* LEM *crosses up right*)
MAY (*to* GRANDMA) All right now. Spence, where have you been?
SPENCE I told you—to the library. I got the books to prove it.
MAY I think it's been pretty well settled, Spence—that you did go to the library. The point is, where did you go after that? (*he doesn't answer*) It isn't like you Spense, not to answer. (*they wait.* MAY *puts pan on dining table, crosses to* SPENCE) Very well, Spence. When you came in I smelled beer on your breath. Have you been drinking beer?
SPENCE Yes.
LEM Well, I'll be damned.
MAY Daddy—please.
GRANDMA Don't be calling that man "Daddy." He's no husband of mine.
MAY Who have you been drinking beer with, Spence?
SPENCE I'd rather not say.
MAY Why not, Spence?
SPENCE (*gets up, crosses to TV*) Well, Mom, to be frank with you, I don't honestly think that you'd know any of them.
MAY I'd still like to know.
SPENCE Mom, I'm trying to be honest with you. If you keep asking me I'm going to lie about it—and I'd rather not lie about it, Mom.
MAY (*crosses to* SPENCE) Very well, Spence—we'll let that pass for now. A few minutes ago your Grandmother said that you were in some kind of trouble.
GRANDMA I didn't quite hear that. What's that you said I said?
MAY Are you in trouble, Spence?
SPENCE I sure am.
MAY What happened?
SPENCE I—got kicked out of school.
LEM (*crosses to left*) Well, I'll be good and goddamned.
MAY Do you know what you did that was wrong?
LEM (*crossing to right*) The little genius gets kicked out of school.
SPENCE I don't think that I honestly did anything that was wrong.
LEM That cinches it. He gets kicked out of school for doing nothing.
SPENCE I didn't mean that, Pop. I didn't mean that I didn't do anything. I just felt that I was justified.
MAY What happened, Spence?
SPENCE Look, Mom—I don't want to go through all that again. I don't feel like it. (*crosses to ottoman down stage of* MAY) The teacher, Miss Crowley, that is, said something about Negroes. I was sitting there. I told her she was wrong. She got mad—I got mad. I walked out of her room and went into the Men's Room. I was mad so I smoked a cigar. (*sits on ottoman*) They caught me and brought me down to the principal. They threw me out of school for a week. That's all there was to it.
LEM (*moves to* SPENCE) What are you talking about—that's all there was to it? We got a genius on our hands, May. He knows more than the teacher. What do you think of that? (*turning on* SPENCE) Where did you get that cigar?
SPENCE Out of your box.
LEM (*to* MAY) There you are!
MAY In other words you stole cigars from your father?
SPENCE I wouldn't exactly call it that.
LEM Well, that's damn well what I'd call it. (*crosses to above chair right*)
MAY You and I will go back to school Monday, Spence, and you will apologize to Miss Crowley and be reinstated in school.
SPENCE There's a week's vacation.
MAY Then we will go up on the following Monday.
SPENCE I don't think I can see my way clear to doing that, Mom.
MAY (*crosses sofa table for knitting*) There

will be no more discussion about it, Spence. A week from Monday—and it's settled.

SPENCE I'm not going up to school with you, Mom. I'm going to stay out for the week. I won't go back to school and apologize to anyone.

MAY You want to disobey both your father and me?

SPENCE I don't want to disobey either of you. I kind of felt that you'd be on my side.

LEM You'll do what you're told. (*comes down stage*)

SPENCE I suppose you can make me go up there with you—but I won't apologize to anyone.

LEM Stop talking back to your mother.

SPENCE I'm not talking back to her. I just want her to understand how I feel. (MAY *is above* SPENCE)

LEM (*crossing to* SPENCE) We don't care how you feel. Now, what do you think of that? You talk about what you'll do and what you won't do. We do things we don't like to do every day of our lives. I hear those crumbs at the bank talking about niggers and making jokes about niggers every day—and I stay on—because I need the job—so that you can have the things that you need. And what do you do? You get your silly little behind kicked out of school. And now you're too proud to go back. (*crosses up right*)

GRANDMA Will you listen to him running his big mouth.

MAY (*crossing down*) Mama. We've given you boys everything that you could possibly want. You've never been deprived of anything, Spence. I don't need to tell you how hard we both work, and the fact that I'm in pain now doesn't seem to make any difference to you. I have arthritis in my wrist now, so badly that I can barely stand it, and it certainly doesn't help it any to hear you talk like this.

SPENCE I'm sorry your wrist hurts, Mom. (LEM *is at piano*)

MAY (*crosses right*) You're not sorry at all. If you were, you'd do something about it. We've bent every effort to see that you were raised in a decent neighborhood and wouldn't have to live in slums because we always wanted the best for you. But now I'm not so sure we haven't made a terrible mistake—because you seem not to realize what you are. You're a little colored boy—that's what you are—and you have no business talking back to white women, no matter what they say or what they do. If you were in the South you could be lynched for that and your father and I couldn't do anything about it. So from now on my advice to you is to try and remember your place.

SPENCE You'll pardon me for saying so—but that's the biggest hunk of bull I've ever heard in my whole life.

LEM (*crossing down to him*) What's that you said?

SPENCE (*rises*) You both ought to be ashamed to talk to me that way.

LEM (*walks over and slaps him full across the face*) Now go upstairs and don't come down until you can apologize to both of us. Go on.

SPENCE (*crosses to foot of stairs, stops second step.* MAY *crosses down right*) I'll go upstairs, Pop, because you're my father and I still have to do what you tell me. But I'm still ashamed of you and I want you both to know it. (*he is walking upstairs*)

LEM (*crossing to foot of stairs*) That smart mouth of yours is going to get you into more trouble if you don't watch out. (SPENCE *has disappeared.* LEM *crosses down right*) It's those damn books you've been reading—that's the trouble with you.

MAY I don't think you should have slapped him, Lem.

LEM What was I supposed to do? Let the little skunk stand there and cuss us both out? (*going over to the stairs*) And be sure you go straight upstairs. Don't be stopping in the traitor's room.

GRANDMA He can stop in my room if he wants to. Who's to stop him, I'd like to know?

LEM (*starts upstairs, holding paper*) I will.

GRANDMA If you come into my room with your nasty mouth I'll bat you on the head with my cane.

LEM (*returns to room, waves paper*) It's a fine thing when a man can't get a little respect in his own house.

GRANDMA What have either of you done to get respect, I'd like to know? Nothing but bully the boy.

MAY All right, Mother—now you keep out of it.

GRANDMA (*on stairs*) I'll not keep out of it. When I've got something to say, I say it, and you know it, so don't try to hush me up.

MAY (*crossing to foot of stairs*) Mother, if you come down those stairs I'm going to tell the doctor.

GRANDMA (*comes downstairs.* MAY *crosses to piano*) Oh! Tell him, smell him, knock him down and sell him. What you think I care? All this slapping and going on.

LEM Where did Spence go? (*sits on his chair*)

GRANDMA (*at banister, crossing to sofa*) He went to his room. Where do you suppose he would go? He still does what you tell him, though why I'll never know.

MAY Mother—please.

LEM Oh! Let her go ahead and run herself down. It won't take long.

GRANDMA That's where you're wrong. I have no intention of running down. I've got a few things to say and I'm going to say them. (*picks papers off sofa, throws them at* LEM)

LEM Well, hurry up and say them and let's get it over with.

GRANDMA I will. Don't you worry your head about that. I'm going to sit down first. (GRANDMA *sits sofa.* MAY *crosses to piano*) Now, in the first place—that nasty little hussy that's teaching history in that school deserves exactly what she got—and the only thing that I think is that Spence didn't tell her enough.

MAY He can't go around talking to people like that.

GRANDMA That's a lot of twaddle and you know it. (MAY *crosses left to kitchen arch*) Now, in the second place—when you moved down here, did you ever stop to take into consideration that something like this was bound to happen sooner or later, and that the most important thing might be just having your love and company? You did not. You kept right on working—and instead of your company, they got a book or a bicycle or an electric train. Mercy—the stuff that came in this house was ridiculous.

LEM (*gets up, crosses to piano*) That's none of your—

GRANDMA Will you let me finish? Well, I don't agree with that kind of raising one bit—and allow me to be the first to tell you both. You got away with it with Mack because Mack had Spence. But do you know that that boy is absolutely alone? He hasn't a friend in the world. You didn't know, did you, that all his little pals around here have taken to the girls and the little girls' mothers don't want their little daughters going around with a colored boy. Did you know that there was a dance up at school last week and Spence couldn't go because he didn't have anybody to take? Well, whether you know it or not, he's alone. And now you want to desert him completely by not backing him up. You moved him out of a slum and taught him to think of himself as something to be respected—and now you get mad when he does the things that you made it possible for him to do. That bull—as he called it about staying in his place. I'm ashamed of you both and I want you to know it. I've said what I came down here to say—now help me out of this sofa. Well, don't just stand there like a dumb ox—help me up. (LEM *moves over, helps her*)

MAY You hadn't ought to come downstairs, Mother. You know that.

GRANDMA I'll come downstairs when I want to. Now—what do you think of that? (*shoves* LEM *away*) The trouble with you two is that you're too careful. I'm an old lady and I haven't got much longer to live one way or the other. I'll come downstairs when I want to. (*crosses to stairs*)

MAY Did Spence tell you all this? (*crosses right*)

GRANDMA Well, I certainly didn't find it out by talking to the neighbors.

LEM (*crosses to sofa, sits*) Well—why in hell didn't he say so when we were talking to him?

GRANDMA How could he? You attacked him like a rattlesnake the minute he came in the door.

LEM I did not.

GRANDMA You laid in wait and attacked him just like a rattlesnake. I heard you. (*she is staring up the stairs*) I'm going to send him downstairs. (*she is slowly mounting the stairs*) Talk to him. Be nice to him. (*on landing*) Don't be crumbs all your lives. (*she disappears*)

MAY (*starting to go to kitchen*) I'd better go and put the food on again.

LEM (*gets up, follows her*) You'll stay right here.

MAY He's hungry, Lem.

LEM You can do all of that when we're through. You're not going to leave me here by myself. What will I say to him?

MAY I don't know.

LEM Why didn't you tell me all this was going on anyway?

MAY Because I didn't know, Daddy.

LEM It's a mother's place to know what's happening to her son—isn't it?

MAY (*crossing to* LEM) You know—I didn't know how it was going to take place, but somehow I knew it would turn out to be my fault.

LEM (*moves right*) I didn't say—

MAY Oh! Shut up.

LEM (*turns to her*) What did you say to me?

MAY (*moves right*) I said "Shut up." I told you not to hop on him the minute he came into the house. Maybe if you'd asked him questions instead of calling him names you would've found all this out and you wouldn't have to stand here looking so foolish now.

LEM You were just as bad as I was.

MAY I'm going out in the kitchen. You can talk to him by yourself. (*she starts to exit as* SPENCE *starts down the stairs*)

LEM (*sotto voce*) You stay in here.

MAY I will not. So there. (*she exits into kitchen*)

LEM (*his back to stairway, pretends not to notice* SPENCE; *gets up his nerve and then*) Come on down, Spence. (SPENCE *starts down again.* LEM *crosses right*) We're going to have a little talk. (SPENCE *comes into the room*) Sit down—Son.

SPENCE (*walking over to the chair right*) Thanks, Pop. (*sits on stool*)

LEM Are you comfortable?

SPENCE Yes, Pop.

LEM (*at right of* SPENCE) How do you feel?

SPENCE I feel all right, Pop. I'm a little groggy, but I guess that's from the—(*he pauses*) stuff I've been drinking.

LEM (*moves close to* SPENCE) Serves you right. Now you gotta stop going around doing things like that. You hear? And another thing— You've got to stop talking back to me. If there's one thing that makes me good and damned mad it's talking back. I can't stand it and I won't stand it. (*crossing left*) It don't show the proper respect. You got that?

SPENCE Yes, Pop.

LEM (*after a glance into the kitchen*) You heard from Mack lately?

SPENCE No, I haven't, Pop.

LEM (*crossing right*) Well, I guess he's busy. You know how it is when you go to college.

SPENCE Yes, I guess he is busy.

LEM And that's what you've got to start thinking about—because you'll be busy, too, when you get to college. And you're going to college—you know that, don't you?

SPENCE Yes, Pop—I do.

LEM Well—just be sure. Now you go on and forget these little bastards around here. Don't pay any attention to them. (*crosses chair right*) You've got bigger things to think about—and if they won't play with you—you just tell them to go to hell—because you're better than any ten of them put together. All right. Now—you got your books and you've got your music—and if there's anything you want—you just tell me about it and I'll get it for you. Understand? (LEM *sits*)

SPENCE Yes, Pop.

LEM (*rises, crosses up*) And don't mind what those lousy teachers say either. The big thing is for you to graduate and get the hell out of that lousy school. And if they say anything you don't like—just forget it—'cause you're going to college—and you can't afford to get your butt thrown out of school too often. You understand?

SPENCE Yes, Pop.

LEM All right then (*crosses to chair, sits*) It's all settled. Now just forget the whole business. And if anything else happens—you just come to us and we'll take care of it. Understand?

SPENCE Yes, Pop.

LEM All right then. (LEM *returns to paper. Pause*) Your mother's fixing you something to eat. You'd better go out and get it.

SPENCE If you don't mind, Pop, I don't feel like eating. I think I'll just go to bed now.

LEM Now—that's what I'm talking about. It's silly to go around moping.

SPENCE (*rises, crosses to stairs*) I know it's silly, Pop. I know that. I'm going to try to do what you told me, but I want to go to bed now —that's all. (*he is on the stairs*) Goodnight, Pop. (*he turns*) And thanks for helping me, Pop. (*starts up*)

LEM It's all right. (*he is sitting down with the paper. From upstairs a voice—muffled and rather terrified, cries*)

GRANDMA Spence! Spence! (SPENCE *pauses for a moment and then rushes upstairs*)

LEM (*jumping from the chair and running upstairs*) May! Come up here.

MAY (*from the kitchen*) What? What's the matter? (*she comes out*) Where are you?

LEM   Up here—come up here quickly. (MAY *runs up the stairs. There is the sound of* LEM's *voice*) Now that's right—up here on the bed. There. Go down and call the doctor; tell him to get here as soon as he can. The number is on the pad.

MAY   Mama! Mama!

LEM   Get out of the way, May.

SPENCE (*rushes downstairs, goes to the telephone and dials the number. He waits*) Hello! Is Doctor Sloane there? This is Dr. Sloane? This is Spencer Scott. You've got to come over as soon as you can. It's my Grandmother. I don't know what's the matter with her. You've got to come—

MAY (*enters from the top of the stairs*) Spence! (SPENCE *puts his hand over the mouthpiece and waits*) Tell him he doesn't have to hurry. She's dead. (SPENCE *hangs up the phone without telling him.* MAY *keeps coming down the stairs and down right; sits in chair*) She didn't have to suffer, Spence, and she died quickly. We can thank God for that. (SPENCE *starts for the stairs as* LEM *starts down. He meets his father, who holds him*)

LEM   Where are you going?

SPENCE   Let me go—Pop, I said let me go. Damn it, Pop—take your hands off me.

MAY (*rising*)   Let him go, Lem.

(LEM *releases him.* SPENCE *goes off as* LEM *comes down the stairs.* MAY *sits down and* LEM *stands silent, above her.* SPENCE *comes down the stairs again and goes into the kitchen. He doesn't notice his father or mother and goes quickly to get his coat, off left in kitchen*)

LEM   Where are you going, Spence?

SPENCE (*putting on coat*)   Out—outside for a while.

LEM (*crosses to center*)   I think you'd better stay here with your mother, Spence. She needs you.

SPENCE   I can't. She's got you anyway.

LEM   I don't think you'd better go out now.

SPENCE   Leave me alone! Will you?

LEM   How can you be so selfish? Your mother needs you. (*he starts right.* LEM *holds him*) What's the matter with you anyway? You've got a fever. You'd better go to bed.

SPENCE   I'm not going to bed. I want to go out for a few minutes. That's all. I want to be by myself for a few minutes.

MAY   You don't have to go outside to cry, Spence. You don't have to be ashamed before us. (SPENCE *begins to sob incoherently, his head on* LEM's *shoulder; breaks away from his father and runs out of the house.* LEM *starts after him*) Let him go, Lem.

LEM (*stopping at front door*)   But he's got a fever. He can't—

MAY   Let him alone, Lem.

LEM (*crosses down right to her*)   I'll call the doctor. You go and rest. He can have a look at Spence while he's here.

MAY   You'd better call Mack too, Lem. He's so far away. I don't think he'll be able to come home.

LEM   I'll call him.

MAY   What's Spence doing, Lem?

LEM   He's standing over in the lot—that's all.

(*Curtain*)

Scene Two

(*At the curtain's rise,* SPENCE's *room is in semi-darkness because the shades are drawn. The door is shut. On the chair by* SPENCE's *bed stands a tray of food. On the bureau is a decanter of water, a bottle of pills and medicine.* SPENCE *is in bed—asleep to all obvious intents. A woman appears climbing the stairs outside of the room and enters. She is carrying a clean pillow slip, which she places on the chair right. She glances over at the bed and then begins to pull the shades. Sun springs into the room as she does so. She is a woman perhaps in her late twenties, good-looking and trim. It is two weeks later—early afternoon*)

CHRISTINE   You know, I've met many a mulish critter in my day, but you're the worst mule I've ever met. Now you ain't asleep because I heard you tipping around up here not ten minutes ago. Now open your eyes and eat your lunch.

SPENCE   I don't want it.

CHRISTINE (*crosses with tray to bureau*)   You know you don't have to eat it? You know that, don't you? But don't blame anyone but yourself when your bones are rattling around inside of your skin like two castanets hit together—you understand? I suppose you don't want your medicine either. (*crosses up of bed*) Boy, you sure do beat all. You're the stubbornest cus I ever met. I'll ask you one more time. Are you going to take this medicine or aren't you? Speak up, cause I don't have all day.

SPENCE No.

CHRISTINE I didn't quite catch that. Don't be mumbling at me, boy. Was it "Yes" or "No" that you said?

SPENCE I said "No."

CHRISTINE Boy, you know you're going to make some girl a pretty miserable husband one of these days. Course, you know, I don't believe you're not eating. (*crosses to bureau*) I think you sneak downstairs after I leave and eat everything in sight. (*pause*) Did you hear me? (*no answer. Crosses to bed*) Spence, won't you please sit up and eat something? Anything? Crust of bread? You know it kills me when folks don't eat. (*no answer*) I never knew anybody who could pick out just the right way to worry somebody. Won't you eat just a little bit?

SPENCE (*head up in bed*) I said "No."

CHRISTINE (*crosses to chair for pillowslip, returns*) Well, I guess that settles it—don't it? Then you can get out of bed so I can make it.

SPENCE You don't need to make it today.

CHRISTINE The devil you say. I've taken enough from you today already. Now just get out of that bed before I pick you up and throw you out of it. You're not supposed to stay in bed all day anyway. The doctor said to get up and walk around and to get some air if you felt like it.

SPENCE Don't you get sick of repeating yourself?

CHRISTINE (*crosses to bureau, returns with decanter*) You've got 'til I count three. One—two—three—(*throws water*)

SPENCE (*throwing the covers off and laughing in spite of himself*) All right—all right. I'm getting up now. (*he goes right and sits in chair*) You make me sick.

CHRISTINE The feeling is oh so mutual. (*she begins to make the bed—stands above it*) I've seen a mess of mourning in my day, but if the mourning you do don't beat anything I've ever seen yet, I don't want a nickel. But at the rate you're going you're not going to have much longer to mourn. You're going to be joining them that you're mournin' for if you don't watch your step.

SPENCE What do you say to my making a little bargain with you?

CHRISTINE What is it?

SPENCE I'll eat that slop that you brought up here if as soon as that bed is made you get the hell out of here and leave me alone.

CHRISTINE (*takes food tray from chair to bureau*) There ain't no call to be rude and nasty. All I'm saying is that you look like a bag of bones and you do.

SPENCE I've always been skinny.

CHRISTINE (*pours medicine in soup*) It's humanly impossible for somebody to be as skinny as you are and live. Consumption is chasing you in one direction and pneumonia is chasing you in the other—and when they meet with you in the middle, it's sure going to be a mess.

SPENCE Why don't you shut up?

CHRISTINE (*moves to above bed, continues making it*) Why don't you eat your lunch instead of sitting up there looking like death warmed over?

SPENCE (*gets out of the chair and viciously picks up the tray from the bureau; brings it back, sits down with it and begins to eat*) Now will you let me alone?

CHRISTINE (*crosses to bureau, gets out socks*) Who's bothering you?

SPENCE You are.

CHRISTINE (*crosses to him, puts wrapper around shoulders*) Aw! Go on, boy. You know you love it.

SPENCE (*tasting the soup*) What kind of soup is this?

CHRISTINE (*putting on left sock*) What'd you say?

SPENCE I said, "What kind of soup is this?"

CHRISTINE Chicken.

SPENCE Well, it tastes damn peculiar. (*tasting it again*) What's in it?

CHRISTINE Nothing.

SPENCE What's in this soup? (*pause*) You put the medicine in the soup.

CHRISTINE Does it taste awful?

SPENCE It tastes just like hell. You sure are a lousy cook. No wonder you can't keep a husband.

CHRISTINE I'll have you know that I've only had one husband—and he died.

SPENCE I'm not surprised.

CHRISTINE (*throws socks down, rises, crosses to

Take a Giant Step

bed, works on sheet) I'm not speaking to you again today. And that's final.

SPENCE You're not really mad, are you, Christine? (*pause*) Christine, I was just kidding. (*pause*) Aw! Come on, Christine. You know I don't really think that you killed your husband.

CHRISTINE (*laughing. Crosses to* SPENCE) Boy, you sure are a mess. (*they look at one another*) You feel better now—don't you?

SPENCE I guess so.

CHRISTINE (*puts on right sock*) You're getting some color in your cheeks.

SPENCE Don't you think that you're hurrying things a little, Christine? I haven't finished eating yet.

CHRISTINE If there's one thing I can't stand it's skinny men around me. Never could stand skinny men since I can first remember. You wouldn't be a bad-looking boy if you just weren't so skinny.

SPENCE Thanks, Christine. Thanks. You're a real tin pitcher full of complaints today. You're as generous with the old complaints as Gram. (*he stops eating*)

CHRISTINE (*rises, stands over* SPENCE *left of him*) Now what's the matter? What've you stopped eating for?

SPENCE You know what's the matter.

CHRISTINE (*fixes something on tray*) Now there isn't any point in thinking about that now.

SPENCE I know there isn't, but I can't help it.

CHRISTINE Just don't think about it.

SPENCE That's a very stupid thing to say. You can't just stop thinking about someone because they're dead, can you?

CHRISTINE Yes, yes you can if you want to. You just don't open the door and let yourself in, that's all.

SPENCE What are you talking about?

CHRISTINE Nothing. Now eat your lunch. (*to above bed*)

SPENCE (*begins eating again*) You know, it's funny. I got expelled from school—Gram died—and I got sick—and so I couldn't go to school anyway—even if they hadn't kicked me out. Funny the way things turn out.

CHRISTINE Yes, it is—isn't it? (*she stops work, listens*)

SPENCE You know, Christine, I was just thinking. Course last week was the funeral and I figure maybe the guys didn't want to come and see me then. But I've been home all this week. (CHRISTINE *crosses to him, gets tray*) Wouldn't you have thought that one of them would have come over to see me by now?

CHRISTINE (*putting tray on bureau*) Nothing surprises me any more.

SPENCE What do you mean by that?

CHRISTINE Nothing. (*feels his head*) I don't think you have any more fever. You want to take your temperature?

SPENCE Naw! (*pause*) Your hands are very warm, Christine.

CHRISTINE Warm hands—warm heart.

SPENCE That would be fine except that that's not the way it goes.

CHRISTINE (*crossing to bed*) It goes that way for me and that's what matters.

SPENCE (*rises, crosses to right of bureau*) Were you born here, Christine?

CHRISTINE No. I was born in Alabama. Birmingham, Alabama, in Ensley, near the steel mills.

SPENCE I'll bet you didn't like it much down there, did you?

CHRISTINE No, I didn't like it much down there.

SPENCE Is your family still there?

CHRISTINE (*crosses down to front of bed. Changes pillow slip*) My father was killed in the mills when I was a little girl. My Ma died a couple of years ago. I had two brothers and two sisters. I don't know where they are now.

SPENCE (*crosses to bed, sits*) What made you come way the hell up here by yourself?

CHRISTINE (*laughing*) I wanted something better, I guess. I decided I was coming up North to try my luck. I worked for a whole year before I'd saved the money, and the day I had what I thought was enough, I went down to the railroad station. (*stops work*) Boy was that some day! The sun was shining and I felt real good like you feel maybe once or twice in your whole life. When I got to the ticket window, the man had a calendar, and it had an advertisement for a big insurance company on it. So I looked at the name of the town and then I told him that that's where I wanted my ticket to take me. Then I went home and packed my mama's cardboard suitcase, and that same night I caught the train. And that's the last I ever saw of my mother and my brothers and sisters and Rusty.

SPENCE Who the hell was Rusty?

CHRISTINE (*sits at head of bed.* SPENCE *sits in middle*) Rusty was my dog. Well, I didn't go to work for the insurance company. I went into service for a while and then I got married. And that's what I meant when I was telling you about the doors. See, my husband died about two years after that and about two months after he died, I had a baby and he was born dead.

SPENCE Christine!

CHRISTINE Well, I tell you for a while I felt like all I wanted to do was die myself. Then I realized that you just can't go on like that. It's like your mind is divided into little rooms and each time you go back into one of those rooms your heart likes to break in two. So all you do is shut the doors—and lock them—to those little rooms in your mind and never let yourself in them again. So I've got two little locked rooms in my mind. One for Bert, my husband, and one for my baby that never had a name. Do you want some more to eat?

SPENCE No, Christine, I don't think so. You sure do make me feel crumby, Christine.

CHRISTINE Why?

SPENCE Well, I've been giving you a pretty hard time about what's been happening to me. (*pause*) I'm sorry, Christine.

CHRISTINE That's all right, boy. You're just unhappy—that's all. But you'll get used to that. Pretty soon you'll be able to laugh a little bit and make jokes, even while you're unhappy. It won't be this bad forever. (*rises*) Well, the bed's made, the house is clean, and you've had your lunch. So—

SPENCE Don't go, Christine. Stay with me.

CHRISTINE (*crossing to bureau for tray*) I've got another cleaning job, Boy.

SPENCE Just for a little while longer. (*pause*) If you have to go, well then I guess you have to, but if you could stay just a little while longer it would mean a lot to me. It isn't that I'm afraid of anything, but I get to thinking about all the things I've got to do.

CHRISTINE What have you got to do?

SPENCE Well, I've got to really get well—first of all. I'll take the medicine and I'll take a hell of a lot of vitamins and I figure that'll fix me up all right.

CHRISTINE (*crossing to him with pills*) There's no time like the present to begin.

SPENCE Honest, Christine.

CHRISTINE A little water? (*she gets water glass from the tray*)

SPENCE (*takes the pill*) I know what you're going to say. "You're beginning to look fatter already." (*she laughs merrily and hugs him*) You're going to make me spill the water.

CHRISTINE (*releases him. Takes glass and puts it on tray*) What else?

SPENCE Well, I'm going to cut out the damn smoking and drinking and that ought to fix up the old body. (*rises, crosses right*) Then I've got to go up to school and make peace with old Hasbrook and Crowley. But the other things are going to be a hell of a lot harder to do.

CHRISTINE What are they?

SPENCE (*sits chair right*) I've got to do something about the guys and my Gram, Christine. I'm going to be honest with you about Gram—it's going to be hard. I miss her a hell of a lot. But she's dead, Christine. She's dead—and you can tell yourself that and you can accept it, and maybe I'm a little selfish about it, but you know that no other living soul is talking with her or having fun with her. She didn't ditch you. She died. But the guys are different, Christine. They're not dead. They're over in the lot playing baseball. They're still horsing around up in the park. I don't suppose they can really help what's happened because that's the way it is. I've said some pretty lousy things to them, Christine, and I don't want it to be that way. (*he pauses. He is near tears*) God damn it—I hate being black, Christine. I hate it. I hate it. I hate the hell out of it.

CHRISTINE (*crosses to him, holds him*) Ssh!

SPENCE I'm sorry I said that, Christine.

CHRISTINE It's all right, Spence. You don't have to explain to me. (*she releases him, but still holds his hand*)

SPENCE And I've got to cut out this goddamn crying. Everything makes me cry. I don't understand it. I was watching television the other day—a damn soap opera—and started crying like a baby. That's damn peculiar.

CHRISTINE It's not so peculiar as you think.

SPENCE There's just one more thing, Christine.

CHRISTINE What is it?

SPENCE I don't know whether I should tell you or not.

CHRISTINE Sure you can tell me.

SPENCE How are you so sure? You don't even know what it is yet.
CHRISTINE I'll take the risk.
SPENCE You promise you won't say anything about it to anybody?
CHRISTINE I won't mention it to a soul.
SPENCE No matter what it is?
CHRISTINE I've already said I won't tell it, haven't I?
SPENCE Well. I want to sleep with a girl, Christine. (CHRISTINE *turns away laughing*) What's the matter with you?
CHRISTINE Nothing. I just swallowed wrong.
SPENCE Yeh!
CHRISTINE (*turns to him*) Yeh! And many more of them right back at you. Who's the lucky girl?
SPENCE Aw! Christine. You know I haven't got any girl in mind. I think about it quite often, but I can't think of anybody. I suppose you think that sounds pretty horny to be thinking of it all the time?
CHRISTINE (*turns away*) No, I wouldn't say that.
SPENCE You wouldn't?
CHRISTINE No, I wouldn't.
SPENCE You know, Christine. You're a funny Joe. To look at you no one would think that somebody could talk to you like this.
CHRISTINE (*quite dryly, turns to him*) Thanks.
SPENCE Have you had much experience, Christine?
CHRISTINE Enough.
SPENCE Off hand—how much experience would you say you've had?
CHRISTINE Now that's the kind of question it's every woman's right to leave unanswered.
SPENCE You think that's a pretty nosey question?
CHRISTINE I not only think it's a nosey question. I know it is.
SPENCE O.K. (*rises. Crosses to below bed.* CHRISTINE *sits chair right. Pause*) Would you say, off hand, that I was trying to rush things, Christine?
CHRISTINE How do you mean?
SPENCE (*crossing down right*) You'd just as soon we talked about something else, wouldn't you?
CHRISTINE I just didn't understand what you meant, that's all.
SPENCE (*crossing to center*) Well, I mean about my age and all. Do you realize that I'm going on eighteen and have never slept with a girl?
CHRISTINE That's terrible—isn't it? (*turns away*)
SPENCE It sure as hell is. Hell. I'm practically a virgin. And you know I was thinking when I was sick, supposing I died. Supposing I just passed out now and died. (*indicates imaginary body on floor*) Why, I'd regret that I hadn't slept with anybody for the rest of my life practically.
CHRISTINE I guess that would be pretty terrible—wouldn't it?
SPENCE I think that you're having a hell of a good time laughing at me.
CHRISTINE I most certainly am not.
SPENCE You sure as hell are. You've got a sneaky laugh line around your whole mouth.
CHRISTINE (*turns to him*) Spence—I'm not laughing. I wouldn't laugh at you when you're telling me things like this. If I'm doing anything I'm remembering, and I might be just smiling a little bit at the memory, but I'm not laughing at you.
SPENCE You really honestly don't think that it's peculiar or anything?
CHRISTINE How could anything so natural be peculiar?
SPENCE That's a funny thing for you to say.
CHRISTINE Why is it so funny, might I ask?
SPENCE (*sits on foot of bed*) Well, I'm pretty sure, although I've never asked her, that Mom would give me a swat for my pains if—
CHRISTINE (*rises, crosses to him*) And what makes you think that your mother and I should have the same ideas?
SPENCE Well—you're both older than I am.
CHRISTINE Well, I'm not anywhere near as old as your mother. I might be a widow, but I'm a young widow, and I'm not through yet by a long shot.
SPENCE I didn't mean—
CHRISTINE I know exactly what you meant. Just remember you're no Tiny Tim yourself.
SPENCE I didn't mean what you thought I meant at all. I just meant that you seem to understand a lot of things. Aw! Hell—I don't mean that. I mean you seem to understand me—and I'm grateful. That's all.
CHRISTINE (*crosses to chair left. After a pause*)

Well, we've done enough talking for one afternoon. I've got to go.

SPENCE Christine!

CHRISTINE (*turning around*) What is it now?

SPENCE (*pause*) Nothing.

CHRISTINE (*crossing to center*) Nothing is what you ask for, nothing is what you'll get.

SPENCE (*rises*) Christine!—(*she stops*) I'd appreciate it if you didn't turn around.

CHRISTINE Why?

SPENCE (*standing behind her*) Because I'm going to ask you something and if you're going to laugh at me I'd just as soon you weren't laughing in my face.

CHRISTINE I won't laugh.

SPENCE Well, would you mind not turning around just the same?

CHRISTINE All right.

SPENCE Well—I don't know quite how to say it. (*pause*) Do you like me, Christine?

CHRISTINE I certainly do.

SPENCE No kidding?

CHRISTINE No kidding.

SPENCE I was sure hoping you weren't. Because I like you too, Christine.

CHRISTINE Thank you.

SPENCE Well, I know that liking doesn't mean loving—but I kind of thought—that since—well—you're lonely, aren't you, Christine?

CHRISTINE I've been lonely for a long time now, Boy.

SPENCE Well—in case you didn't know, I'm lonely too, Christine—and I know that you're older than I am and I know it makes a lot of difference.

CHRISTINE I have to go, Spence.

SPENCE But what I'm lacking in age, Christine, I sure make up for in loneliness, and so we do have that much in common. Don't we, Christine?

CHRISTINE Yes.

SPENCE So maybe—if you stayed, Christine —since things are like I said they were—we might find a little happiness together. I don't mean for forever or anything like that—but could you call and say that you couldn't make it?

CHRISTINE You know you're very young, Spence, and you could be very foolish too. You know that—don't you?

SPENCE Yes, Christine. I know.

CHRISTINE And I could be very foolish to listen to you.

SPENCE I know, Christine.

CHRISTINE (*turns to him*) It's funny. I have to look at you, because I can't believe that you said what you just said. You said, that since we were both lonely maybe—just for an afternoon—we could find happiness together. You know that so soon?

SPENCE Yes, Christine.

CHRISTINE You see, I didn't laugh. I ain't laughing at all. I'll try to come back. I'll try. (*she gets the tray from the bureau and goes to the door*)

SPENCE You know where the phone is. If you can't come back, Christine, you don't need to come up and tell me. Just go. But if you can, there's a bell downstairs on the table that Mother uses to call us to meals. Would you ring it—if you can?

CHRISTINE I'll try. (*she exits*)

SPENCE (*crossing down right, then to door; listens*) Why in hell is she taking so long? (*Sound of hand bell off right.* SPENCE *crosses slowly to window, pulls shade down as lights fade. Curtain*)

Scene Three

(*The scene is the same as scene one. As the curtain rises,* MAY *is coming out of the kitchen. She walks over to the piano and rings the bell. It is the following afternoon—Saturday*)

MAY Spence! Spence! Are you asleep?

SPENCE (*upstairs*) No.

MAY Well, suppose you come downstairs and get lunch. Hurry up now. I have a lot of work to do, and you're holding me up.

SPENCE What's the big hurry?

MAY (*crosses to dining room, gets fruit salad and milk from refrigerator*) Never mind. Just come downstairs and don't ask so many silly questions.

SPENCE (*appears at head of stairs*) O.K. So I'm coming. You sure do get yourself upset about nothing at all. Why don't you take it easy? (*makes basketball throw with sweater from stairs onto armchair right*)

MAY Have you gotten your clothes together yet?

SPENCE (*coming downstairs, crossing to dining table*) What clothes?

MAY (*counting groceries on shelf*) Your school clothes. I told you to get them ready and I'd have them pressed this afternoon.

SPENCE (*sits right of table, starts eating*) They're all right.

MAY I'm not going to have you going to school looking like a tramp.

SPENCE You sure got peculiar notions of what a tramp looks like.

MAY Never mind the sass. Did you get them ready?

SPENCE They're hanging up in the closet—just waiting to be taken off the hangers and brought down to the tailor's. How much more ready could they be?

MAY I told you to bring them down. You know you could cooperate a little bit more. Now I suppose I'm going to have to climb upstairs and bring them down. I told you my knee—

SPENCE All right. All right. I'll get them—(*gets up, crosses to stairs*)

MAY You're hollering at me, Spencer. (*pause*) You can't get them now. Just sit down and eat your lunch.

SPENCE (*crosses back to chair*) You know, Mom, I got to give it to you. You sure do know how to fix a guy's stomach for this lunch. (*pause as he sits again*) You know, I could wear my Sunday suit to school Monday and Chris could take these clothes. I don't want you to strain your knee any more than you have to. Or I could take them down myself?

MAY (*turns to shelf*) Chris? Christine won't be back Monday or any other day.

SPENCE (*pushes chair back*) What are you talking about?

MAY Christine will not be back. You're no longer ill. There's no need for Christine any longer.

SPENCE (*rises, crosses to* MAY) But I thought you said—

MAY I changed my mind. I called her and told her this morning.

SPENCE What did you tell her?

MAY I told her that her services were no longer needed by me. I decided that there was no need to spend that money since I could do the things myself. I've been doing them myself anyway.

SPENCE But you said you were too tired when you got home.

MAY Well, I've changed my mind. Why all this interest in Christine?

SPENCE (*crossing back to table*) Nothing. I just thought—

MAY I know what you just thought, young man, and don't think I don't.

SPENCE Now what are you talking about?

MAY You know my eyes weren't put on—

SPENCE The way they were put on for nothing. I know.

MAY All that pampering and coddling she did with you makes me sick to my stomach.

SPENCE (*crossing to her*) Will you please explain what you mean by that?

MAY I don't know. What should I mean by that? Maybe you can tell me. Well, I've heard those stories about maids being left alone in houses with boys before. I'm not saying it's gone that far yet. But an ounce of prevention is worth a pound of anybody's cure.

SPENCE (*crossing down*) You know, you sure have got a dirty mind.

MAY Don't be so sure that it's I that have a dirty mind. And if you say that to me again you'll get a good slap for your pains.

SPENCE How in hell—

MAY Don't use that kind of language before me.

SPENCE All I did was come down to eat lunch and then you start on me about a suit of clothes. (*crosses right*) I'll take the suit down to the tailor myself. I wouldn't have you strain yourself. As far as Christine is concerned, if she pampered and coddled me—then I'm grateful to her. And you promised her a job after I was sick and I think you're damned dirty—

MAY Spencer!

SPENCE (*crossing to table*) Yes, I think you're damned dirty to get rid of her. Now—that's all I've got to say and you can take this food away now because I can't eat it. (*crosses right*)

MAY (*taking glass away*) Suit yourself. No one is going to beg you to eat, young man.

SPENCE Mom—no one had to beg me to eat. All I wanted was a little peace to eat. I was perfectly willing to eat (*crosses to stairs*)

MAY Where are you going?

SPENCE (*climbing stairs*) To the tailor. Where did you think I was going?

MAY You haven't got time.

SPENCE What do you mean I haven't got time? All in hell—

MAY (*crosses to living room*) Be careful.

SPENCE All in hell I got left in the world is time—time for everything. If there's any little thing you want done from now on—just let me know.

MAY (*crosses to table, takes plate away*) You haven't got time to go to the tailor's now.

SPENCE (*on landing*) Why not?

MAY Because I asked some of your friends over this afternoon.

SPENCE You did what?

MAY (*turning to shelf*) I asked some of your friends over for ice cream and cake this afternoon.

SPENCE (*coming downstairs*) Are you kidding?

MAY I'm perfectly serious.

SPENCE (*in center*) Why didn't you make a little pink punch to go with it?

MAY I did.

SPENCE Well, you can call them the hell back up and tell them to stay home.

MAY (*turns, crosses to him*) Spence—don't you dare.

SPENCE You heard what I said. You can call them up and tell them to stay home. (MAY *crosses left.* SPENCE *follows her*) What right did you have to do that? It's none of your business. It's my business and you stay out of it. I'm not bribing those kids with ice cream, cake or pink punch. I'm never going to bribe anyone to be my friend.

MAY You'll do what you're told and you'll stop being so fresh. Do you understand that? (SPENCE *crosses to below table*) And I don't want to hear another word out of you about what you'll do and what you won't do. When you start talking like that it's about time you went out and got a job of your own and bought a house of your own—(SPENCE *tucks in shirt-tails*) but as long as you're under this roof, you will do what you're told. (SPENCE *turns to go to front door*) Where are you going?

SPENCE I'm going to get the hell out of here. That's where I'm going.

MAY (*following him*) Go ahead—and see how far you get acting the way you act. (*both at front door*) Your father's right about you. You're too proud. You think you can go through life being proud, don't you? Well, you're wrong. You're a little black boy—and you don't seem to understand it. But that's what you are. You think this is bad; well, it'll be worse. You'll serve them pink punch and ice cream—and you'll do a lot worse. You'll smile when you feel like crying. (*she begins to cry*) You'll laugh at them when you could put knives right into their backs without giving it a second thought—and you'll never do what you've done and let them know that they've hurt you. They never forgive you for that. So go on out and learn the lesson. Now get out of here. Get out of here and don't ever come back. (MAY *crosses to sofa, sits. Pause*) You think it's easy for me to tell my son to crawl when I know he can walk and walk well? I'm sorry I ever had children. I'm sorry you didn't die when you were a baby. Do you hear that? I'm sorry you didn't die. (*she is completely overcome*)

SPENCE (*crossing down*) Don't cry, Mom. I'm sorry. I'm sorry I've made it so difficult. I didn't mean to hurt you, Mom. (*pause*) What time did you tell them to be here?

MAY Around one.

SPENCE Well, they'll be here any minute. Is everything ready?

MAY It's in the pantry. The ice cream is in the refrigerator. (TONY *and* GUSSIE *enter outside the door*)

SPENCE Don't cry, Mom. I'm sorry. It seems to me that for the past two weeks all I've done is apologize to people. I seem to be apologizing for trying to be a human being. (*the bell rings*) That must be some of them now.

MAY Do you want me to stay?

SPENCE No. You can go out if you want to.

MAY (*crosses to stairs, starts up*) I have some shopping to do. (*stops on landing, turns*) Spence, don't be rude to them. (SPENCE *opens the door*)

GUSSIE Hi, Spence!

SPENCE Hi, Gussie! Hi, Tony! (TONY *and* GUSSIE *enter.* GUSSIE *first. He crosses to right of sofa*) What's the matter, Tony? You're not speaking or something?

TONY Hi, Spence! I'm sorry about your grandmother. (*crosses to below armchair right*)

SPENCE Thanks. Where are the rest of the guys?

GUSSIE They'll be around. (*pause*) You going back to school Monday?

SPENCE Yeh! I'm going back Monday. It's kind of creepy having a party for no reason—isn't it? See—I've been sick—you probably didn't know—my Mom thought it would be a big surprise if the gang came in today. That's all. Sit down.

TONY (*sits on stool*) We didn't see you around. We wondered what was wrong.

GUSSIE (*sits right arm of sofa*) You're better now—ain't you?

SPENCE Yeh! I'm better now. (*pause*) What you guys been doing?

GUSSIE Knocking around. That's all. (*pause*)

SPENCE You been playing baseball lately?

TONY Not much—No. We've had too much homework lately.

SPENCE (*crosses left*) Oh! I thought I heard you guys a couple of times but it was probably somebody else.

GUSSIE Yeh! It must have been somebody else.

SPENCE Would you like some ice cream or anything? (MAY *appears at head of stairs. They rise*)

MAY (*coming downstairs*) Don't get up. It's nice seeing all of you again.

TONY and GUSSIE How do you do, Mrs. Scott!

MAY Just stay where you are. I'm going down to the grocer's. Haven't seen you in a long time, Tony.

TONY I've been pretty busy lately.

MAY Well, don't be such a stranger. We miss you.

SPENCE (*crosses to kitchen*) I'll get the ice cream.

GUSSIE Yeah. We've been pretty busy.

(IGGIE *enters right, crosses to door, followed by* JOHNNY *and* BOBBY REYNOLDS)

MAY Well, any time you want to come over and watch television—come. Spence will be very glad to see you. (*bell rings*) I'll get it.

SPENCE (*puts ice cream, plates and spoons on table as* MAY *opens door*) Well, here you are. Help yourselves.

(TONY *crosses to table, sits left of it.* GUSSIE *crosses to left of table*)

MAY Hello, boys. Come on in.

IGGIE Hello, Mrs. Scott. (*crosses left*)

JOHNNY Hello, Mrs. Scott. (MAY *is at door.* IGGIE *crosses left to table.* JOHNNY *is right of* BOBBY) My brother and I were very sad to hear of your recent—

BOBBY —death in your family.

MAY Thank you, boys. I have to go now. Spence will entertain you. I'll be back in a little while. (*exits.* BOBBY *and* JOHNNY *cross left*)

SPENCE (*crosses to them*) Well, if it isn't the Reynolds boys. Come on in.

IGGIE (*above table, his rear in* TONY'S *ice cream*) Hey, Spence. I didn't come to see you, because I thought maybe you wouldn't want any visitors, but I kept asking your mother about you.

SPENCE (*crossing to* IGGIE) Well—thanks, Iggie. Thanks.

TONY Hey, Iggie, will you get your ass out of my ice cream?

IGGIE I'm sorry. (*crosses to ottoman, sits.* SPENCE *is just about to tell* TONY *off*)

TONY Nothing to be sorry about. Just get out of it is all.

GUSSIE (*interupting impending fight between* TONY *and* SPENCE, *crosses in. Nervously*) This is fun—ain't it, Spence?

SPENCE Yeah! (*crosses* REYNOLDS BOYS *in living room*) Come on, you guys. Get yours while the getting is good. (BOBBY *and* JOHNNY *cross to table.* GUSSIE *crosses right*)

GUSSIE Hey! Spence. This is fun. We ain't had so much fun since we made that party that time—stealing off Mr. Markman. Remember that? (IGGIE *rises, crosses to dining room shelf for cake*)

SPENCE I sure do. I was responsible for getting dill pickles. What did you have to get?

GUSSIE The ice cream. I had to get the ice cream.

JOHNNY (*crosses to ottoman, sits*) How did you do it?

GUSSIE (*to center*) Gee, you guys are new around here. Well, Tony here—was the onliest one of us that had any money. He had a lousy dime—a lousy dime—so we all goes into Sam Markman's store big as you please and tells him we want a ten-cent guinea grinder. (*puts ice cream on sofa*) Can you imagine—that fat Jew bastard—with a damn Jew store making guinea grinders.

TONY (*crosses right to* GUSSIE, *then to stool, sits*) For Christ sake. Will you cut it out? Iggie's here.

GUSSIE (*turns left*) Who? Oh! Iggie—I didn't even see you, Iggie. Geez—I'm sorry. No offense meant, Iggie.

IGGIE (*by refrigerator*) It's all right.

GUSSIE (*with rising intensity*) Yeh! Well,

there we all were. So while he's cutting the damn bread in two, I'm practically falling into his ice cream freezer. I'm pulling the pints of ice cream out as fast as a son-of-a-bitch and throwing them out the door. Tony is behind the candy counter stuffing his pocket with chocolate bars. (IGGIE *crosses to center*) And old Spence is in the barrel with the pickles. They're way down at the bottom, see, and he can't reach them—so there he is practically swimming in the pickle juice when Old Markman turns around and sees him. So he pulls his arm out, and he's got a pickle in his hand, and he says without blinking an eyelash, "Looks like you'd better be ordering some more pickles, Mr. Markman. They're getting pretty damn hard to reach." Remember that, Spence? (*sits right end of sofa*)

SPENCE   Sure—I remember. You want some more cake, Iggie?

IGGIE   No thanks, Spencer. (*sits left end of sofa*)

SPENCE   Well, if you want more just reach for it. (*sits piano chair*)

BOBBY   What happened after that, Gussie?

GUSSIE   (*rises, crosses down*) What do you mean what happened? We goes up to the park with a guinea grinder, six quarts of ice cream, twelve chocolate bars, and a big loaf of cake that Spence finally got under his sweater. Geez —did he look funny. He looked like he had eight babies in there. (*sits sofa*) Boy, did we have fun. (JOHNNY *crosses to table*) Got any more of the cake, Spence? Goddamit your mother sure does make good cake.

SPENCE   Sure! (*he takes the plate. Crosses to shelf for cake*)

GUSSIE   Gee, I don't know why we been staying away from here so long. I've been missing that good stuff your Mom dishes out. (*pause*)

SPENCE   (*at shelf*) That was the day Tony broke his arm, remember?

GUSSIE   (*taking the cake*) Geez, that's right.

JOHNNY   (*crosses to ottoman, sits*) How did that happen?

GUSSIE   Geez, you guys are new around here, ain't you? (*rises, crosses to* JOHNNY) Well, after we'd stuffed with all that food, we decided to play Tarzan. So, you know that big oak tree over near the golf course? We decides to play in that. We're all leaping for the branches and making the ape call—(*he imitates it*) then it gets to be Tony's turn—so Tony makes with the ape call and jumps for the branch, and the next thing you know he's falling right through the goddamn tree, hitting his head on one branch, his can on the next, and finally *VOOM* he hits the ground with the damndest noise I've ever heard. I'm convinced that he's dead. We're both honestly convinced that he's dead, he's so still. We're both scared to go near him so we keep calling from a distance—(*calling to* TONY *who sits on stool right*) "Tony! Tony!" Finally we notice his stomach moving, so we goes over, and son of a bitch if there ain't a big piece of bone sticking right through his damn shirt. What the hell did they call that, Tony?

TONY   A compound fracture.

GUSSIE   Yeh! That's right. We sure did have fun that summer. (*sits sofa*) Remember, Spence? (TONY *crosses to table, sits*)

SPENCE   Yeh! I remember.

GUSSIE   Those sure were the good old days. (*pause*) Hey! As a matter of fact we're going up to the park tonight. We're going on a hay ride. You're all better, ain't you Spence?

SPENCE   Yes.

GUSSIE   Well, why in hell don't you come along?

TONY   (*puts down his plate sharply on the table, rises. Everybody reacts to the slip*) You did say you were coming back to school Monday, didn't you, Spence?

SPENCE   Yes, Tony. Monday I'm coming back to school.

TONY   (*crosses to living room*) Well, I guess we gotta be going. (BOBBY *rises*) Why don't we call you for school on Monday?

SPENCE   (*rises*) Well, as a matter of fact my father is going to be driving me up to school on Monday. He's got to come with me—so we'll go up together.

TONY   Yeh! Well, Gus and me gotta be going. (GUSSIE *rises*)

SPENCE   (*crosses down right*) As a matter of fact, you know, I said when you first came in there was no damn reason for this party. Well, actually there is.

TONY   (*crosses down right to* SPENCE) Yeh! What? It ain't your birthday. I know when your birthday is.

SPENCE   Well, you know, I've been doing a hell of a lot of fooling around and I've been neglecting my lessons, not practicing, and all manner of things like that. And if you're going to college you got to be a little more serious about things than I've been. So from now on I've got to buckle down to the old books and concentrate on things of the mind.

GUSSIE   Yeh! I guess you're right.

SPENCE   So I've got a little schedule made out for myself. In the morning before school I've got to practice. And in the afternoon after school I've got my homework to do. So you see I'm going to be pretty busy.

GUSSIE   Geez, Spence. You sure do play the piano damn good. You know that? Are you going to be a musician or something?

SPENCE   I don't know. Maybe. I haven't given it too much thought. So I had all you guys over to kind of say goodbye and all 'cause I don't think I'm going to have much time for playing around. 'Course, it's going to be a little hard at first 'cause I'm not used to it, so all you guys could help me if you just kind of let me alone and let me get my work done.

TONY   Sure, we'll do that, Spence.

GUSSIE   Sure. Sure, Spence. (GUSSIE *crosses to left of piano*)

SPENCE   Thanks—you're real pals.

TONY   Thanks for the ice cream. (*he exits front door*)

SPENCE   It's O.K. It was fun.

JOHNNY (*on exit*) Sure. Geeze, you guys sound like you must've been pretty crazy in those days. See you, Spence. (IGGIE *rises also*)

SPENCE   Stay a second, Iggie. I want to talk to you.

BOBBY (*on exit*) Thanks for the party, Spence.

GUSSIE (*crosses down to* SPENCE) Hey, Spence! Geez, I can't get over that summer. We really did have a hell of a lot of fun, didn't we?

SPENCE (*with a hand on* GUSSIE's *shoulder*) Yeh! We sure did. It was the best summer I ever had.

GUSSIE   Goodbye, Spence. (*they shake hands. General ad libs from* BOYS *off right*)

SPENCE (*crosses left to* IGGIE) Hey! Iggie, I'm sorry for what happened—I mean Gussie's talking that way. He's just dumb and he needs a good paste in the jaw for his pains, but I couldn't do it. I'm sorry, Iggie.

IGGIE   I understand.

SPENCE   Then O.K., Iggie. That's all I wanted to talk to you about. Thanks for coming to my party. (*crosses to ottoman, sits*)

IGGIE   Sure. (*starts to go, stops*) Did you really mean it, Spencer, about going to college?

SPENCE   Yeh! Yeh, I did. That is something, isn't it? (*live ad libs blend into recorded baseball game*)

IGGIE   You don't know which one?

SPENCE   No, no, not yet.

IGGIE   Well (*pause*) I'd better be going. (*he starts for the door*)

SPENCE   Iggie! (IGGIE *turns*) Look, I know you're busy and all that but would you mind if I came over and looked at the old stamp collection?

IGGIE   Do you want it back, Spencer?

SPENCE   No, I don't want it back. I'd just like to see what you've added to it—that's all.

IGGIE   Come over any time.

SPENCE   Thanks, Iggie. Thanks.

IGGIE (*on exit*) Goodbye, Spence. (*pause.* IGGIE *has exited, leaving front door open*)

SPENCE   Goodbye, Iggie. (SPENCE *rises, crosses to table to get plates as* MAY *enters up left, crosses to kitchen door and enters. She carries a full shopping bag*)

MAY   Where is everyone?

SPENCE   Gone.

MAY   They didn't stay long.

SPENCE   No, they didn't.

MAY (*puts bag on dining table*) What happened?

SPENCE (*center. Stopping*) Nothing—nothing. I just told them that I didn't want to see them anymore. That's all. I just said it to them before they said it to me.

MAY   You'll never learn, will you?

SPENCE   Mom, you've just got to believe that I'm trying to learn. I'm trying as hard as I know how. I might be wrong, but if I am, I think I'd like to find that out for myself.

MAY   What are you going to do?

SPENCE   I don't know, Mom. I don't know.

MAY (*crosses in*) Spence, look at me—You're not running away, are you?

SPENCE   No, Mom, I'm not running away—and if you don't mind, Mom, let's not talk about it any more—I did the right thing. So let's just both try to forget it happened and go on to something else. Okay? (*he walks to piano, starts to sit, then walks to front door and closes it, shutting out the baseball sounds. He sits at piano and starts to play "Praeludium,"*)

MAY (*after a few bars*) Spence.—I love you very much. (MAY *picks up bag, crosses to kitchen.* SPENCER *watches her, surprised, then turns back to the piano. As he resumes playing,* MAY *crosses to dining table and starts collecting dishes*)

(*Slow curtain*)

9

Biography

William Branch   Loften Mitchell

Black playwrights have written about Crispus Attucks, Ira Aldridge, Nat Turner, Denmark Vesey, Frederick Douglass, Harriet Tubman, Sojourner Truth, George Washington Carver, Booker T. Washington, Florence Mills, Bert Williams, Marcus Garvey, Mary McLeod Bethune, Martin Luther King, Jr., Malcolm X, and others.

The two plays in this section, *In Splendid Error* (about Frederick Douglass) and *Star of the Morning* (about Bert Williams) both focus on a central character's divided mind. The question is how best to proceed to advance a cause without compromise to principle. Both are costume dramas. Both are based in historical fact.

Playwrights are seldom patient with detailed research; they grasp at crises that stimulate the imagination and write stage pieces that make historians shake their heads. The general purpose is inspirational: to provide the audience with an image of a black man who struggled to overcome great obstacles. Some of the plays place an emphasis on the human struggle, others on the racial conflict. *In Splendid Error* and *Star of the Morning* do both.

William Branch (1927–)

In Splendid Error
1954

The premiere of *In Splendid Error* took place in the Greenwich Mews, an off-Broadway theater, on October 27, 1954. The play ran seven weeks, closed, and then reopened in January 1955. William Marshall portrayed Frederick Douglass, the black abolitionist; Clarice Taylor played Douglass' wife; Alfred Sander played John Brown.

In Splendid Error is a play about revolution, but not everyone saw that in 1954. The drama critic on the New York *Herald Tribune* saw John Brown's raid on Harper's Ferry as "some of the insanity that plagued the Brown family."

The issue of John Brown's sanity is an old one, an issue more political than medical. Frederick Douglass, when he heard charges that Mr. Brown was insane, published in his *Monthly* an editorial entitled, "Captain John Brown Not Insane." He went on to say, "Heaven help us when our loftiest types of patriotism, our sublimest historic ideal of philanthropy, come to be treated as evidence of moon-struck madness."

Modern black revolutionaries have declared John Brown an example of what most white men are not. When Malcolm X was asked if whites could join his organization, he replied, "If John Brown were alive, maybe him."

The parallels between the 1850's and the 1950's, the frustrations that lead to thoughts of revolution, led William Branch to research and write his play. This is his own account.

As a young actor in New York in the early 1950's, fresh from Northwestern University, I swiftly became disillusioned by the patronizing, Uncle Tom nature of the few roles written for Blacks in plays by white playwrights (and in some plays by black playwrights, as well). Challenged by fellow actors to write something for them which would "tell it like it is," I wrote my first play, *A Medal for Willie*, about the ironies of a Black soldier fighting and dying abroad for freedoms for others that he was openly denied here at home. Drafted into the Army the morning after the play opened (despite all conjectures, a matter of pure coincidence!), I spent weekend passes in New York delving into historical references as background for my next play.

I wanted to write about a Black hero. I felt the strong need for black people—and white people as well—to know of the wealth of great and positive images in our heritage, images which somehow rarely showed up in works by white writers.

(As an example, a telephone conversation with Brooks Atkinson, learned and greatly respected drama critic of the *New York Times*—who missed covering the opening of *In Splendid Error* due to his annual stint at jury duty—revealed that he had never heard of Frederick Douglass. Nor had a number of other reviewers, some of whom questioned whether the playwright wasn't over-romanticizing in "creating" such a figure. In another instance the neglect of black historical personages occurred in a personal conversation with noted Civil War historian Bruce Catton. Although he had heard and read something of Douglass in his research, he had never bothered to read Douglass' immensely valuable autobiography or any of Douglass' other writings, such as his famous journal, *The North Star*. Thus, Douglass is barely mentioned in Catton's best selling books on the Civil War period.)

As I delved into the little-known story of the relationship between Frederick Douglass and John Brown, I sensed something much deeper than a mere historical self-pride builder. Here was a theme worthy of the grandest Greek tragedy: an essentially moral protagonist faced with an agonizing practical choice between two ways of fighting for a worthy cause. Further, in Douglass' dilemma I saw uncanny parallels between the pre-Civil War racial-political struggles of the 1850's and the post-World War II racial-political climate of the 1950's. Thus in subsequent drafts, the play became more and more of a personal statement as to the differing roles people could play in a revolutionary movement.

Much later, in 1967, after seeing a production of the play at Spelman College in Atlanta, Ga., the Rev. Andrew Young, then executive Secretary of Dr. Martin Luther King's Southern Christian Leadership Conference, told me he and King had sat through many a stormy SCLC session in which the same fundamental points were hotly debated.

Some recent productions, to stress today's relevance, have had Douglass stride off at the end of the play with the musket, rather than the flag.

In Splendid Error

CAST OF CHARACTERS

(In Order of Appearance)

THE REVEREND LOGUEN
JOSHUA
ANNA DOUGLASS
LEWIS DOUGLASS
GEORGE CHATHAM
THEODORE TILTON
FREDERICK DOUGLASS
JOHN BROWN
ANNIE DOUGLASS
SHEILDS GREEN
COLONEL HUGH FORBES
SANBORN

ACT ONE

(SCENE the parlor of Frederick Douglass's house in Rochester, New York.

TIME: *a late afternoon in the spring of 1859, two years before the Civil War.*

The parlor is a large, "company" room on the first floor of the Douglasses' modest residence. Furnished in a manner far from lavish—or even necessarily stylish for the period—it nevertheless suffices as a comfortable sitting room for the Douglass family and an orderly, dignified reception room for their guests.

In the center of the left wall is the customary fireplace. Up left, at an angle, are large French doors leading into the dining-room, and through the curtained glass may be seen the end of the dining table, a few chairs, sideboard, etc. A low settee squats against the wall up center, to the right of which is a large archway opening onto the front hall. The "front door" of the house is off right of the hallway, while a flight of stairs can be plainly seen rising to the left. There is a window in the hallway wall, and down right is a door opening onto a small library or study.

Left center is a horsehair sofa. To right and left of the sofa are partly upholstered parlor chairs. At far left is another, next to a small table.

At rise, the REVEREND LOGUEN *and* JOSHUA *are discovered. The* REVEREND, *who sits at the table far right, is dressed soberly in dark suit with clerical collar. He is a Negro, slight of frame and advanced in years. Yet there is perennial youth about him in his sharp, distinct speech and quick, virile mind. His hat is on the table beside him, and with spectacles on he is making entries in a small notebook as he questions* JOSHUA, *who sits to his left.*

JOSHUA *is a young Negro dressed in ill-fitting but clean clothes. He is obviously a little out of place in these surroundings, but endeavors to respond with dignity to* LOGUEN's *queries*)

LOGUEN (*writing*) Haynes . . . Point, . . . Maryland . . . Tell me, where is that near?

JOSHUA Uh, it's near Washington Town, suh. 'Bout five mile down the 'Tomac River on the east'n sho'.

LOGUEN I see. And are all three of you from there?

JOSHUA Uh, yes suh. We all belongs to d' same massuh.

LOGUEN (*chiding gently*) That's true, very true, Joshua, but a different master than you refer to. Now that you've made your escape you must realize that you never belonged to the man who held you in bondage. Regardless of what they taught you to think, we are all the children of God the father, and equal in His sight. Now . . . You and your companions escaped from Haynes Point, and hiding by day, picked your way to New York where you contacted our agents, is that right?

JOSHUA Uh, yes suh. Ol' Miz Ossning, white lady who talk real funny, she giv' us dese clothes and gits us a ride on a big ol' furniture wagon comin' up dis way, an' she tell d' man to put us off in Rochester. Den we s'pose to ax 'round fo' a man name a Douglass. Frederick Douglass.

In Splendid Error

LOGUEN I see. And when did you arrive?

JOSHUA Jus' now, suh. Little befo' you come.

(ANNA DOUGLASS *enters from the dining-room. She is a Negro woman of forty, of medium height and build, and though not handsome, she nevertheless radiates the beauty of warmth of heart. Overshadowed outwardly by her husband's fame, she concentrates on being a good wife and mother and manages the household and occasional business with assurance and dispatch.* ANNA *has an apron on over her print dress and holds a cooking spoon in her hand*)

ANNA My goodness, Rev'n Loguen, you two still in here talkin'? Let the poor man eat—the other two's nearly finished and the food's gettin' cold!

LOGUEN Eh? Oh, I've about got it all now, it's all right, Mrs. Douglass. Uh—one thing, Joshua, before you join the others. Joshua, from now on, no matter what happens, you are never to reveal to anyone again the names of the people who helped you get away. I want you to explain that to the others, do you understand?

JOSHUA Uh, yes suh, I unnerstan'. I tell 'em.

LOGUEN All right. Now there's a man standing by over at the blacksmith's shop with a rig, ready to take you on to where you'll catch a boat for Canada. You'll be safe there. You'll be among friends, men and women like yourselves who've made their way to freedom, following the northern star. I congratulate you, Joshua, and welcome you to the fraternity of free men.

JOSHUA (*nodding*) Yes suh. Thank you, suh.

LOGUEN (*starting again*) And when you get to the settlement in Canada, Joshua, I want you to—

ANNA (*impatiently*) Rev'n Loguen, if you don't shut your mouth and let this poor man come on in here an' get his supper, you better!

LOGUEN Oh—I'm sorry, Anna. It was just that—

ANNA Come on, Joshua. Your plate's all ready for you. If you need anything, you jus' call me, now, hear?

JOSHUA Yes ma'am. Thank you, ma'am. (*he goes out left*)

ANNA (*turns to* LOGUEN) I declare, Rev'n Loguen, I don't know what in the world I'm gonna do with you. You know them poor boys is got to get to the boat landin' by six o'clock. Fred's gone down there hisself to make the arrangements and he says have 'em there on time, 'cause the boat don't wait!

LOGUEN I know, I know, Anna. (*proudly*) Do you know how many we've taken care of already this year, Anna? Thirty-three! Thirty-three free souls passing through our little station on the Underground Railroad.

ANNA Yes, but if you keep on holdin' 'em up to pass the time of day, there's gonna be somebody up here lookin' for 'em 'fore they *gets* their souls free. (JOSHUA *reappears at the door up left*) Why, Joshua. You want me for something?

JOSHUA (*somewhat sheepish*) Uh, no ma'am. It's jus' dat I—I forgit somethin'.

LOGUEN Yes? What is it, son?

JOSHUA Well... Dis Miz Oss—I mean, dis ol' white lady, she... she gimme what y' call a message. I'se s'pose to tell Mr. Douglass, but I... I forgit.

ANNA Well, that's not so terrible, Joshua, you can tell us. It'll be all right.

JOSHUA (*considers, then*) Yes, ma'am. Thank you, ma'am. Well, ... dis lady, she say for to tell Mr. Douglass dat dere's a new shipment comin' through mos' any day now. One what's wuth a lots a money. She say for to be on the lookout for it, an' to han'le with care. Dat's it. Dem's d' words she spoke to me, tol' me to use 'em too. "A new shipment... han'le with care."

LOGUEN (*echoes*) Handle with care...

JOSHUA An' now—now kin I go an' eat, ma'am? I feels a whole lots better, now dat I 'members!

ANNA Yes, Joshua, you go right ahead. You did a fine job.

JOSHUA (*grins*) Thank you, ma'am. Thank you. (*he exits*)

ANNA (*soberly*) What you make of it, Rev'n?

LOGUEN I don't know... I don't know.

ANNA Sounds to me like somebody awful important. Somebody we have to be extra careful to keep secret about.

LOGUEN Yes, that's logical. But who?

ANNA I may be wrong, but seems to me, couldn't be nobody else... but him! (*her eyes shine strangely*)

LOGUEN Who? (*looks at her, then comprehends*) But—it's too dangerous! He'll never make it. Why, they'd pick him off in an instant—you know what a price there is on his head!

ANNA I know, I know. But he'll get through. Don't know how he does it, but he'll get through.

LOGUEN God help him...! Well, I suppose I'd better go back and get those boys started if they're going to make that boat. (*starts for the dining-room*)

ANNA (*heading him off*) Hmmph! *Now* you're hurryin', jus' when Joshua's sittin' down to eat. I declare, Rev'n, sometimes I think if you wasn't a man of the cloth—

LOGUEN (*laughs*) Now, now, Anna. Give me another sixty years and I promise you, I'll reform! Well, I'll go down to the corner and signal Jim to bring up the rig so we won't lose any time. As soon as Joshua's finished, have them come right out and join me.

ANNA All right, Rev'n. I'll do that.

(REVEREND LOGUEN *goes up to the hallway as* ANNA *sighs, smoothes her apron and starts for the kitchen. As* LOGUEN *passes the window he halts, glances out and whirls around*)

LOGUEN Quick! Anna! Tell them out the back way!

ANNA What is it, Rev'n—?

LOGUEN Somebody's coming up the walk! Lewis and two white men—quickly, now! We've got to get them out. Here, Joshua—! (*he and* ANNA *hurry off left*)

ANNA (*off*) Wait, I'll get that door for you...! (*from off left comes the sound of the front door opening and closing. Then* LEWIS *is heard calling*)

LEWIS (*off*) Mother! Oh, Mother! (LEWIS *enters, a tall, pleasant-faced Negro youth, ushering in two distinguished-looking white gentlemen*: GEORGE CHATHAM *and* THEODORE TILTON)

LEWIS Come right in, please. Let me take your hats. (*he does so and places them upon the clothes tree as the gentlemen stand poised in the archway, glancing over the room.* CHATHAM *is the larger and older of the two. With balding head and large, greying sideburns, his stout form suggests a successful, comfortable businessman just past middle age.* TILTON *is small, wiry, with sharp quick eyes behind his spectacles, and is perhaps in his middle forties. Both are well-dressed and obviously men of importance in their fields*) Won't you both be seated? I hope it will not be long before my father arrives.

CHATHAM Thank you, thank you very much, Lewis. We'll be quite comfortable, I'm sure.

LEWIS (*bows and goes out through the dining-room, calling*) Mother! Oh, Mother! I've brought guests...

CHATHAM (*sitting*) Well-mannered lad, isn't he?

TILTON (*has been absorbed in gazing around*) What? Oh—oh, yes. Very.

CHATHAM Cigar?

TILTON Well, if you think it...

CHATHAM Of course, of course. I've been here many times before, the lady of the house won't mind in the least. Here, try this if you will. Havana. Delux. Imported, mind you, none of these home-grown imitations.

TILTON Why, thank you.

CHATHAM (*smiling*) Of course, it is still probably not so fancy as those you're accustomed to in your editorial board sessions in New York, but... (*he breaks off with a little light laughter*)

TILTON Oh, come now, come now, Mr. Chatham. Despite the fact that you practically dragged me here by the scuff of my neck, you don't have to flatter me.

CHATHAM (*smiling, as he extends a match*) And if I had to I would have gotten ten strong men to help me, too! Ah—here.

TILTON Thank you. (*he draws upon the cigar, considering*) Ah... excellent. I must be sure to recommend these to my editors. (CHATHAM *nods in deference.* TILTON *again appraises his surroundings*) So this is his house... I've never been in the home of a... (*choosing his words carefully*) ... of a man of color before. I must say I'm impressed.

CHATHAM (*nods*) And a warmer and more friendly household you'll not find in all of Rochester.

TILTON Yes, I gather you're all rather proud of him here.

CHATHAM But of course! Any city would do well to have a man of such prominence as Frederick Douglass choose to live within its bounds. And to think of it, Mr. Tilton. A scant twenty years ago this man was a slave—a chattel, a "thing." A piece of property forced with lash and chain to grovel under the tyranny of his "masters"! Oh, it just goes to show you, sir, that—

TILTON (*smiling*) I take it also, Mr. Chatham, that you are an abolitionist.

CHATHAM (*emphatically*) That I am, sir, and proud of it!

TILTON (*calmly*) Well spoken, sir. I like a man who speaks the courage of his convictions. It makes it so much easier to classify him, then.

CHATHAM (*alert*) Why, sir, what do you mean by that?

TILTON (*urbanely*) Oh, don't misunderstand me, my dear Chatham, I have nothing against the abolitionists. Quite the contrary, I am opposed to slavery, in principle. What I mean is that in New York, a man who declares himself an abolitionist *per se* is sure not to be a very popular figure.

CHATHAM Popular?

TILTON Why, yes. There have been cases where men have been stoned in the streets if they so much as spoke a disparaging word over a glass of beer in the corner saloon against the slave system. Why I believe William Lloyd Garrison himself, the "High Priest of Abolition" as it were, has sometimes been forced to close his meetings and flee for his very life before the onslaught of armed ruffians.

CHATHAM Yes, that is true. I have heard many such accounts, of *New York* and other places.

TILTON Well, practically each time your own Douglass speaks, outside of a few chosen localities that know him well, he does so at constant risk of personal assault.

CHATHAM That cannot be denied. It is one of the reasons we admire him so. He has been shot at, stabbed and bludgeoned half to death, but he goes on.

TILTON Well, you can hardly blame one then, can you, for being rather wary of...

CHATHAM (*frowns*) Mr. Tilton, since when have we become so debased, so unmanly that we allow fear of a little retribution to abridge our sacred right of free speech and conviction?

TILTON Well, now, I—

CHATHAM And especially, sir, if you will permit me, in terms of the press, with its responsibility for fearless...

TILTON (*hastily*) Yes, yes—let me hasten to apologize, my dear Mr. Chatham, if I have offended through the slightest reflection upon the abolitionists. It merely seems to me at this time rather more *wise* to devote oneself a little less obtrusively to one's ideals. After all, you must admit there are great numbers of good people who intensely hate slavery who are not numbered among the ranks of the abolitionists *per se*.

CHATHAM True, still—

TILTON Well, in any event, it should be interesting after all to meet the celebrated Frederick Douglass: escaped slave, abolitionist orator, and self-made genius. (*this last with a trace of amused scorn*)

CHATHAM (*retaliates*) Yes, it should be. It isn't every day I'd go out of my way to bring even the noted editor of one of New York's most influential newspapers to meet a man like Douglass.

TILTON (*smiles icily*) Again, you do me more than honor.

CHATHAM It's a pity you must rush on so. On Friday nights, you see, we have a series of public lectures in Corinthian Hall. Douglass is a frequent figure on that rostrum and he is scheduled again for tomorrow. Couldn't you possibly—?

TILTON You tempt me, my dear Chatham, really you do. But I have pressing appointments in the City, and by the way, what time is it getting to be? (*he reaches for his watch*)

CHATHAM Oh, never fear, Mr. Tilton, there is ample time, ample. (*starts for the window*) I'm sure if Mr. Douglass knew we were coming he... (*he breaks off as* ANNA *enters from the dining-room*) Well, Mrs. Douglass!

ANNA How d' do, Mr. Chatham! It's so nice to see you again. (*she curtsies*)

CHATHAM (*with a little bow*) The pleasure is all mine. Mrs. Douglass, I have the honor to present Mr. Theodore Tilton of New York City, editor and publisher of the *New York Independent*. Mr. Tilton, Mrs. Douglass.

TILTON It is my very great pleasure. (*he bows stiffly in reply to her curtsey*)

ANNA We're happy to have you, Mr. Tilton. Are you enjoyin' our little city?

TILTON Oh, very much, very much indeed! It's always a pleasure to visit Rochester. And this time I told my friend Mr. Chatham here I should never forgive him if he didn't bring me around to meet your husband.

ANNA That's very kind of you. Gentlemen . . . ? (*she motions and they sit, after her*) I understand you went by the office?

CHATHAM Yes. Young Lewis told us Mr. Douglass had gone to the Post Office. I should have remembered that Thursday is publication day . . .

ANNA Oh, that's all right. I guess you supply paper to so many big publications you just couldn't expect to remember 'bout all the little ones like us.

CHATHAM Oh, quite the contrary, Mrs. Douglass. I have no client I think more highly of than "The North Star."

ANNA Now, just for that you'll have to stop and have supper with us. Both of you. (TILTON *looks distressed*)

CHATHAM Thank you so much, Mrs. Douglass, but I'm afraid my Ellen has already prepared. Else we surely would take you up on your generosity. (*to* TILTON) Mrs. Douglass has the reputation of spreading one of the finest tables in Rochester.

TILTON (*weakly*) Yes, I'm sure.

ANNA (*flattered*) Well, at least let me get you a cup of tea while you're waitin'. No, now you just make yourself t' home.

CHATHAM All right, Mrs. Douglass. I know there's no use trying to get around you.

(*From off in the hallway a door opens and closes.* ANNA, *who has started for the kitchen, stops and turns*)

ANNA Why, I b'lieve that's Mr. Douglass now. (*calls*) Fred? That you, Fred?

DOUGLASS (*off*) Yes, Anna.

ANNA (*coming to the archway*) You got company.

DOUGLASS Well, now. (FREDERICK DOUGLASS *enters, a bundle of papers under his arm. He is a tall, broad, compelling figure of a man, forty-two years of age. His face, of magnificent bone structure, would be a sculptor's delight with the high cheekbones, the strong broad nose, the proud flare of the nostrils. His eyes, brown, deep-set, peer intently from beneath the ridge of his prominent brow, and the straight grim line of the mouth seems on the verge at any moment of an awsome pronouncement. A long mane of crinkly black hair sweeps back from his stern forehead, and, to-gether with heavy moustache and beard, lends a strikingly distinguished, leonine air. His large frame, bolt erect, is dressed conservatively in a suit of black broadcloth, with embroidered waistcoat and gold watch fob. His is an impression of challenge, achievement, dignity, together with strength, quiet but omnipresent.* DOUGLASS *pauses in the archway, then depositing his bundle on the small table nearby, he strides forward to* CHATHAM, *hand extended*) George Chatham! Well, this is quite an unexpected pleasure.

CHATHAM (*beaming*) So it is, so it is!

DOUGLASS (*his voice is sonorous; he speaks with cultured ease*) And is this a business visit? Am I more than two years behind in my account.

CHATHAM Well, if that were so, I should hardly have come myself. I should rather have had my creditors, to collect *my* debts from *you*! (*they both laugh heartily*) Frederick—Frederick, I wish to present Mr. Theodore Tilton of New York City. Mr. Tilton is the editor and publisher of the *New York Independent*, and I wanted him to make your aquaintance while he is in the city. Mr. Tilton, Mr. Douglass.

TILTON (*again bowing stiffly*) It is my very great pleasure . . .

DOUGLASS Not at all, the honor is mine, Mr. Tilton. (*he goes to* TILTON *hand extended.* TILTON *shakes hands uncomfortably*) Will you be long in Rochester?

TILTON No, I'm afraid I must return to the City tonight.

DOUGLASS That's too bad. Anna, have you asked our guests to stay for supper?

CHATHAM Yes, she has, Frederick, but I'm afraid Mrs. Chatham has already prepared.

ANNA I was just goin' to make some tea—

TILTON Pray don't, Mrs. Douglass. You see, we really don't have much more time to stay, I'm afraid.

DOUGLASS Oh? Well, another time perhaps. Meantime, please be seated again. I refuse to let you leave at once.

ANNA Oh, uh—Fred . . . ? 'Scuse me, but did you get them letters off in the mail while you was out? Three letters, goin' to Canada . . . ? (*she looks at him with meaning*)

DOUGLASS Oh . . . ! Yes, my dear. They're safely in the mail and on the way.

ANNA (*smiles*) I'm glad. 'Scuse me. (*she gives a little curtsey and goes out via the dining room*)

DOUGLASS (*turns back to his guests*) Now, then...

CHATHAM Oh, er—will you have a cigar, Frederick? I have some special—

DOUGLASS No thank you, George. I've never been able to develop the habit personally, but by all means... (*indicates for them to continue. They settle themselves. After a pause*) Tell me, Mr. Tilton. What is the talk in New York these days?

TILTON Oh, the same as here, I would suppose. Stocks and bonds... the railroads... migration west... Kansas... the Indians...

DOUGLASS Ah, Kansas! So they speak of Kansas, do they?

TILTON Oh, yes. It is much in the conversation round about.

DOUGLASS And what do they say of Kansas, Mr. Tilton?

TILTON Well, they discuss its impending admission into the Union. It seems certain by now that it comes as a free state, though there is much bitterness on both sides. And there's a great deal of pro and con about this fellow Brown...

CHATHAM You mean Captain John Brown?

TILTON Yes, yes, I do believe he calls himself by some military title or other. Personally, I will be very happy to see Kansas enter *our* fold, so to speak, instead of the South's. But I can't very well agree with the way in which it was won.

DOUGLASS Oh? And why?

TILTON Well, I'm thoroughly against slavery, *per se*, you understand—you'll find our paper has stood out staunchly on that matter. But I think old Brown has done more to hinder the cause of the slaves, with his self-appointed crusade to keep Kansas free, than all the splendid work of the past several decades by persons like yourself to advance things.

DOUGLASS Has he now?

TILTON Why, of course! Good God, for him and his lawless band to call men out from their cabins in the dead of night, and without note or warning, judge or jury run them through with sabres! Why, it's ghastly even to contemplate.

CHATHAM But, sir, you overlook that it was the partisans of slavery that first made war in Kansas, burning farmhouses and towns, assassinating and driving out those who dared voice opinion that Kansas should be kept free. It was these murderers—known to all—that Captain Brown avenged himself upon.

TILTON Yes, but—

CHATHAM And then, when the slave state of Missouri sent an armed militia across the border into Kansas, who but old Ossawatomie Brown with a comparative handful of men—

TILTON Oh, there is no doubt as to their bravery—or even foolhardiness, if you will allow—but to seize the lawful prerogative of the federal government, whose authority it is to protect these territories, is a very dangerous and outlandish course of action!

DOUGLASS (*has picked up a copy of his paper, reads*) "... still today, and with no help from the federal government, Kansas stands at the gateway to statehood as a free territory. Is there any denying it would not have been so except for old John Brown?"

TILTON Then you give your endorsement to such guerilla tactics?

DOUGLASS I have never particularly enjoyed the prospect of human beings wantonly killing one another. But from what I have gathered, there was left no choice in Kansas. It was either be driven out at gunpoint, or face those guns and fight. And that I think John Brown has done most admirably.

TILTON (*frowns—considering*) Hmm... Well, actually, Mr. Douglass, the conflict in Kansas has proved little point with respect to abolishing slavery. Rather, keeping the system from spreading—Free Soil, as they call it—was the actual issue there. For all his reckless bravado, old Brown liberated not a single slave.

CHATHAM Ah, but to prevent the spread of the system across a single mile of border is a noble service indeed!

DOUGLASS Quite so, George, but more than that: Free Soil and freedom for slaves must be regarded as coats of the same cloth. The one will never be secure without the other.

TILTON Why, how do you mean?

DOUGLASS (*smiles—pointedly*) I mean, sir, that those who seek only to exclude slavery from the territories—for their own political or business interests—without concerning themselves about abolishing the system altogether, are merely evading the ultimate issue. Slavery is like a spawning cancer; unless it is cured at its core, then despite all precaution it will eventually infect the whole organism. It must be stamped out entirely, not merely prevented from reaching other parts of the body.

TILTON Ah—but we are dealing here with semi-sovereign States, not hospital patients. Unlike a physician, we have no license to delve into the internal affairs of the South.

DOUGLASS Human slavery cannot be considered a purely internal affair of the South, Mr. Tilton. Especially when it seeks with guns and powder to extend the system further.

TILTON I feel quite confident the federal government is capable of preserving law and order in any such eventuality.

CHATHAM The government! A government rife from top to bottom with Southerners?

TILTON (*protests*) President Buchanon is not a Southerner—

CHATHAM Buchanon—hah! A northern man with Southern principles who bends over backwards to concede every fantastic demand of the hot-heads from Dixie! Or take Congress—frightened into hasty compromise every time the "Gentleman" from Carolina or Georgia or Mississippi bellows threats and abuse at his Northern colleagues! Or must I even mention the Supreme Court, its blasphemous Dred Scott decision still fresh upon the page? And you speak to me of the government, sir! Why, if I had my way, I'd line 'em all up at my sawmill, start up that blade and hold a Bastille Day such as the French never dreamed of . . . !

DOUGLASS (*amused*) Careful, now, George. You'll have poor Mr. Tilton thinking Rochester's a nest of fiery revolutionists.

TILTON Well, at least there's an election next year. You may then express your opinions of your government under the protective mantle of party politics—without being liable to arrest for sedition.

CHATHAM Hah—if I did adequately express my opinions I should still be arrested. For use in public of profane and obscene language!

TILTON (*wryly*) A great loss to the cause of abolition that would be. (*turning to* DOUGLASS) Seriously, though, I do believe the continued existence of slavery is fast becoming the prime political issue of the day.

DOUGLASS Quite so, quite so! Why, take even last year's Senatorial campaign, the widespread debates out in Illinois between Senator Stephen Douglass and this other fellow, Lincoln—

CHATHAM (*interrupts*) But Lincoln was defeated!—a paltry, small-town, hay-seed lawyer with more audacity than ability. Think no more of him. He's politically, uh—*passé*.

DOUGLASS Nonetheless, George, the issue there was plain: the enslavement of human beings and all the evils it gives rise to must either be sanctioned nationally, or it must be abolished. Try as it may, the nation cannot much longer avoid decision on the matter. I believe the outcome of the election *will* depend upon this one burning issue.

TILTON (*craftily*) And perhaps the outcome of the nation too, eh? However, I can only reiterate that drastic measures—such as old Brown's—can at best only aggravate the situation.

CHATHAM (*protesting*) But slavery, sir, is an outrageously drastic condition. And when other means have failed, drastic conditions call for drastic measures!

TILTON (*tolerantly*) Now, my dear Chatham, I have heard of many instances where masters are voluntarily freeing their Negroes. And of others who provide in their wills for manumission upon their deaths.

CHATHAM Whose deaths? The master's?—or the slave's! Ha!

DOUGLASS (*calmly*) May I point out to you, sir, that my own freedom was not given to me: I had to take it. And if you were a slave, Mr. Tilton, knowing full well that you of right ought to be free, would you be content to wait until your master died to walk on your own two feet?

CHATHAM Ha! I for one would help him along a little.

TILTON (*ignoring this—to* DOUGLASS) But can you not see that to press for all-out abolition at a time like this can but only further alienate the South? Why already they have threatened an ultimatum in the elections next year: unless a man friendly to them and their policies continues to sit in the White House they may bolt the Union! And you know we can never permit such a split.

CHATHAM Quite so, but—

TILTON (*exasperated*) Well, think of it, man! It would mean war, actual all-out fighting, one section of the citizenry against another, with muskets and sabres and cannon. Why it would be disastrous, catastrophic!

CHATHAM Certainly—disastrous to the slaveholders, catastrophic to slavery!

TILTON (*turning to* DOUGLASS) Surely, Mr. Douglass—notwithstanding the great multitude of wrongs committed against your enslaved people, the cardinal crime of bondage itself—still, surely you must see that if war comes between the States, not only will your people not benefit, but the nation as a whole stands in imminent peril of perishing!

DOUGLASS (*quietly*) Mr. Tilton, if I spoke to you as a slave, I would say: "No matter, let it perish." As a being denied of all human dignity, reduced to the level of the beasts of the field, it would be of no consequence to me whether this ethereal idea known as a government survived or disintegrated. I would have nothing to lose, quite possibly everything to gain. If I spoke to you as a free man and a citizen. I would say: "War is destructive, cruel, barbaric. It must be avoided—if possible." But wrongs will have their righting, debts will have their due. And if in the last resort it should come to war, then we must make intelligent use of it, once involved to destroy the malignant growths, to set right the festering wrongs, and to eliminate for all time this present grounds for complaint.

CHATHAM Hear, hear! (*he thumps the arm of his chair vigorously*)

TILTON (*with a smile*) I see you drive a hard bargain.

DOUGLASS No more than the slaveholders, sir.

TILTON (*slowly*) Mr. Douglass . . . though I cannot say that I altogether agree with you, nonetheless I can recognize a forceful sincerity when I see one. Will you permit me, sir, to make a note or two of this for publication? (*he takes out pad and pencil*)

DOUGLASS (*spreading his hands*) If my humble words—

TILTON Oh no, no modesty here. I am sure our readers will be as interested as I in giving your arguments careful thought. (*he busies himself with making notes.* CHATHAM *flashes a congratulatory smile at* DOUGLASS *and is about to speak when from off in the hallway the front door knocker is heard*)

DOUGLASS (*starting for the door*) Will you excuse me . . .

LEWIS (*appears, coming from the rear of the house*) I'll get it!

DOUGLASS All right, Lewis.

CHATHAM I've tried to interest Mr. Tilton in hearing you speak sometime, Frederick. But unfortunately, he's a rather busy man, and . . .

TILTON (*looks up*) I mean to correct that fault, Mr. Chatham, as soon as possible. When will you be in our city again, Mr. Douglass?

DOUGLASS New York? Oh, I couldn't say. I've been trying to confine myself as much as possible to the paper lately, and I—

TILTON (*reaching inside his coat*) If you will permit me, here is my card. Please do me the honor of stopping with me when next you're in the City.

DOUGLASS (*taking the card*) Why, that's kind of you, Mr. Tilton. (LEWIS *appears at the archway*)

LEWIS Excuse me, father. There's a Mr. Nelson Hawkins here to see you.

DOUGLASS (*puzzled*) Hawkins? Nelson Hawkins?

LEWIS Yes sir—he . . . Well, I mean—(*he seems to be suppressing some excitement*)—he just got in from out of town, and he—Shall I ask him to wait in your study?

CHATHAM (*rising*) Oh, by no means, Frederick, please don't neglect your guest on our account. We have to be going now, anyway. That is, if Mr. Tilton—

TILTON (*still writing*) Yes, yes. I'm nearly ready. Just one minute . . .

DOUGLASS (*to* LEWIS) Ask him to step into the study for a moment, Lewis. I'll be right with him.

LEWIS Yes sir! (*he goes off*)

CHATHAM Well, Frederick, it's been much too long since I've seen you.

DOUGLASS Yes, it has. You must have dinner with us again very soon, George. We've missed you.

CHATHAM I mean to take you up on that. In the meantime, the wife and I will be at the lecture tomorrow night, as usual.

DOUGLASS Good. I'll be looking for you. (*to* TILTON, *who has put away his notebook and risen*) And so you're leaving us tonight, Mr. Tilton?

TILTON Yes, I must. Though I'd very much

like to be at the Hall tomorrow. What is your subject?

DOUGLASS I'm speaking on "The Philosophy of Reforms."

TILTON Oh, I would very mightily like to hear that!

DOUGLASS Then perhaps you would care to take along a copy of "The North Star" to glance at in your free time. (*he secures a copy*) My remarks will be merely an expansion of this week's editorial.

TILTON (*accepting it*) Thank you, sir, you are most kind. Our office subscribes to your paper, but it is not every week that I get to read it first hand.

DOUGLASS Well, I shall have to remedy that by placing you personally on our subscription lists.

TILTON Excellent! But you must bill me for it.

DOUGLASS (*nods in deference*) You may send us your check if you wish.

CHATHAM And now, we really must be going, or my Ellen will be furious.

(*They go out via the hallway, ad libbing amenities, the murmur of their voices continuing in the background. After a pause, the door down right opens and* LEWIS *appears. Making sure the others are out of sight, he turns smiling and holds open the door*)

LEWIS Please step in here now, Mr. Hawkins. Oh, let me get your bag. (HAWKINS *enters. He is a lean sinewy man of over fifty. His flowing hair and ragged beard are streaked with grey, and his steel-grey eyes bore with deep, lively penetration. Dressed in plain woolen, cowhide boots, and carrying a well-worn leather strap bag, he presents a figure of indomitable energy and determination*)

HAWKINS (*crossing to a chair*) Oh, no thank you, Lewis. I can manage all right for an old man, don't you think? (*he grins at* LEWIS *with a twinkle in his eye and lays down his bag by the chair*) Well, Lewis, you've grown—haven't you—since I was here last. Getting to be quite a young man. How old are you now?

LEWIS Seventeen, sir.

HAWKINS Seventeen! Why, that's hard to believe. (*his eyes twinkle*) And I suppose you cut quite a figure with the young ladies now, do you?

LEWIS (*blushes*) Why, no sir, I—

HAWKINS Oh, come now! I'll wager you've already picked out your young lady-fair.

LEWIS Well, not exactly, sir.

HAWKINS Not exactly? Ha, then *she* has picked *you* out!

LEWIS Well—I do like a certain girl, but . . . It's just that—well, girls can act pretty silly sometimes. You just don't know what they're thinking or what they're going to do next. Sometimes they say no when they mean yes and yes when they mean no. I can't understand them at all!

HAWKINS Well, well. This sounds pretty serious, Lewis. Tell me. Is she pretty?

LEWIS Oh, yes! She's very pretty, I think. (*pause*) She . . . she's the minister's daughter.

HAWKINS I see. And is she religious?

LEWIS Well, rather, I suppose. (*an afterthought*) She's the minister's *daughter*, you understand.

HAWKINS Ah, yes! That does make a difference.

LEWIS I walked home with her from church last Sunday. I couldn't think of anything much to say, so we started out talking about the weather. And when we got to her house we were still talking about the weather. Six blocks about the weather!

HAWKINS My, that certainly is a lot of weather!

LEWIS (*miserably*) I just don't understand them, that's all.

HAWKINS Well, Lewis, if you ever arrive at the point where you think you do, come and tell me, will you? I've had two wives and eleven children, and if God has ever seen fit to distribute understanding of women, then I must have been behind the barn door when He passed it out!

LEWIS (*grins*) Yes sir. (DOUGLASS *re-enters from the front, glancing hastily at his watch*)

DOUGLASS And now, Mr. Hawkins . . . (*pause.* HAWKINS *turns toward him expectantly, but does not speak*) Mr. Hawkins? . . . (*he stares questioningly at* HAWKINS *while* LEWIS *watches eagerly*)

HAWKINS (*an amused twinkle in his eye*) Hello, Frederick Douglass!

DOUGLASS (*slowly recognition—and joy—come into* DOUGLASS' *face*) Why . . . bless my soul, it's Captain Brown! (*he rushes to him*) John!

John! (BROWN *laughs and they embrace in delight and exits towards the kitchen*) But that beard!—you were always clean-shaven. And these clothes! Why, if it hadn't been for your voice I never would have—!

BROWN (*laughs loudly*) You're looking well, Frederick!

DOUGLASS Why, so are you, only—Well, come and sit down, John. How did you ever manage to get through? Why, there's an alarm out for you in seven states!

BROWN (*laughs*) Oh, I have means, Frederick. I have means.

DOUGLASS Oh, I must tell Anna. (*calls*) Anna! Anna, guess who's here! (ANNA *rushes in from the kitchen followed by* LEWIS)

ANNA Lewis just told me! Welcome, Captain Brown! Welcome!

BROWN Thank you, thank you, Anna. My, but you're the picture of health and brightness! You've got a wonderful wife here, Frederick. A fine woman!

ANNA Oh, go on with that kind of foolishness, John Brown!

BROWN Oh, yes, yes! God has been bountiful to you both. How are all the children?

ANNA They're all very well, thank you.

BROWN Good, good.

DOUGLASS And how's your family, John?

BROWN (*his smile fading*) Oh . . . well. Well. For the most part, that is. These past few years have been hard on us, Frederick. Kansas . . . the price was very dear.

DOUGLASS (*concerned*) Sit down, John. Tell us about it.

BROWN (*sitting*) Thank you. I am a little tired.

ANNA And you must be hungry too, poor man. Supper's nearly ready, but now that you're here I'll have to get up somethin' special for dessert. A pie, maybe. Sweet potato still your favorite?

BROWN It certainly is!

ANNA All right. Now you just make yourself t' home. Lewis! Come on and set the table for me, son.

LEWIS (*reluctantly*) Aw . . . (*glances at his father, then rises quickly and follows* ANNA *out*)

DOUGLASS John, we've had no word of you for months. We didn't know if you were alive or dead.

BROWN (*smiling*) Oh, I'm still above ground, Douglass. It will take more than a few cowardly ruffians in the Territories to put John Brown in his grave. And a lot more to keep him there! (*sobers*) They did get one of my sons, though. My Frederick.

DOUGLASS Oh, no . . . !

BROWN Yes. They shot him down one night, not far from Ossawatomie. Owen, too—the big one. But Owen still lives. Back on the farm at North Elba, Mary's nursing him back to health. He's . . . paralyzed. The waist down.

DOUGLASS (*softly*) My God! And you, John are you well?

BROWN Oh, yes. I've been a little tired, but I'm gathering strength to go on with the work.

DOUGLASS To go on? But John, Kansas is won! Surely now you can rest. You've done what no other man has been able to do: you've stopped the slave power dead in its tracks!

BROWN Not quite, Douglass, not quite. Try as we might, the Free Soil constitution adopted in Kansas says nothing about the emancipation of slaves. It offers sanctuary to not a blessed black soul. I must get back to my true work: to free enslaved black folk, and not further waste my energies and resources on political patridges like Kansas. That is why I am here.

DOUGLASS Yes?

BROWN I shall want you to put me up for a time, Frederick. Several weeks, a month perhaps.

DOUGLASS You know, John, that my house is always yours.

BROWN Good. I know I could count on you. I will pay for my accommodation. Oh, no—no, I insist! I will not stay with you unless I can contribute my fair share to the household expenses. What shall it be?

DOUGLASS Now, now, John—

BROWN Come, come, Douglass! We must be practical.

DOUGLASS Well, all right. Shall we say—three dollars a week for room and board. No, not a penny more! You are my guest.

BROWN All right, settled then. (*he withdraws a purse and hands to* DOUGLASS *three dollars in silver coin*) For the first week.

DOUGLASS You are now a member of the Douglass household, in good financial standing.

BROWN   Fine! And one other thing, Frederick. While I am here I wish to be known in public only as "Nelson Hawkins." I want John Brown to be thought still in the Territories. Though Kansas is won, still there's a price on my head some enterprising young scamp might be ambitious to collect.

DOUGLASS   Ha! I shall turn you in at once! (*they laugh*) As you wish, John. I shall inform the entire household at supper.

(*The outside door opens and a child's voice cries, "Momma! Momma! We're back!"* DOUGLASS *smiles and looks up expectantly. In runs* ANNIE DOUGLASS, *a vivacious little six-year-old, followed by* SHEILDS GREEN, *a stockily-built Negro with a bundle of papers under his arm*)

ANNIE   (*sees her father and runs to him*)   Oh, Poppa! Guess what I've been doing! Me and Sheilds. I helped Sheilds take out the papers!

DOUGLASS   (*lifts her in his arms*)   You did? Well now, aren't you Poppa's big, big girl!

ANNIE   Yes, I am! (*she gives him a hug, then giggles*) Oh, Poppa, your whiskers. They tickle! (*she squirms around in his arms and for the first time sees* BROWN *across from them. She abruptly stops her laughter and her eyes grow big with wonder*)

DOUGLASS   (*setting her down*)   John, this is the light of my life, my little Annie.

BROWN   Well, she's quite a young lady now, isn't she!

DOUGLASS   Annie, this is Mr.—Mr. Hawkins. Say how-do-you-do like Poppa's big girl.

ANNIE   (*steps forward timidly and gives a little curtsey*)   How de do? (*then rushes back into her father's arms*)

BROWN   And how-do-you-do to you, little lady!

DOUGLASS   Mr. Hawkins is going to stay with us for a while, Annie. Is that all right with you?

ANNIE   (*considers—suspiciously*)   Doesn't he have a house of his own?

BROWN   Yes, I have, Annie. But it's a long way off.

ANNIE   (*bolder now*)   Do you have a little girl?

BROWN   Why, yes—in fact one of my girls has the same name as you. Annie. Only she's a big girl now.

ANNIE   Bigger than me?

BROWN   (*smiles*)   Yes, a little. But you'll soon be grown up and married too. You just wait and see!

DOUGLASS   Hold on there! Don't go marrying off my baby so soon.

ANNIE   (*her timidness dispelling, she leaves her father's arms and moves toward the stranger*)   You got whiskers, just like my Poppa. Do they tickle too? (DOUGLASS *laughs and winks at* SHEILDS, *who stands in the background, watching the proceedings with a wide grin*)

BROWN   Well, I don't know. Do they? (*he bends down and juts out his chin.* ANNIE *reaches out and tugs gently at his beard*) Uh-uh, careful! (*they laugh as* ANNIE *jumps back, startled*)

DOUGLASS   Well, how about it, Annie? Has he passed the test? May he stay, or shall we turn him out!

ANNIE   (*considers this idea for a moment—then joyously*)   No, no! He can stay! He can stay!

DOUGLASS   Good! It's all settled.

BROWN   (*with a little bow*)   Much obliged to you, ma'am! (ANNA *enters from off left*)

ANNA   I thought I heard another woman in here!

ANNIE   (*running to her*)   Oh, Momma, Momma! I helped Sheilds with the papers! I helped with the papers!

ANNA   You did, sweetie? Well, that's nice. And did you meet our guest?

ANNIE   Oh, yes! He's got a little girl too, with the same name as me, and his whiskers tickle just like Poppa's.

DOUGLASS   A dubious compliment!

ANNA   All right, dear. Suppose you run on upstairs now and get yourself ready for supper. Make sure you hang up your coat.

ANNIE   All right, Momma. (*she curtsies to* BROWN) 'Scuse me, please. I have to go now. (*she runs over to* SHEILDS) Can I help you again sometime, Sheilds?

SHEILDS   Yes, honey. Anytime you want.

ANNIE   (*as she runs off and up the stairs*)   Gee, Momma, I'm so hungry I could eat a whole hippopotamus!

DOUGLASS   (*to* BROWN)   Now you see where all our money goes. To buy her hippopottami! (BROWN *laughs.* ANNA *returns to her kitchen, and* SHEILDS GREEN *starts to follow*)

DOUGLASS   Oh, Sheilds! Come, I want you to meet our guest, er—Nelson Hawkins. (*to* BROWN) This is Sheilds Green, sometimes known as "the Emperor."

BROWN (*extending his hand*) The Emperor? Am I in the presence of royalty here? Glad to know you, Mr. Green. (*he shakes hands vigorously*)

SHEILDS Glad to know you, suh.

DOUGLASS Royalty in a sense. Because of his great strength, Sheilds' master nicknamed him "The Emperor"—used to point him out to his guests, laugh and make fun of him. Now it's Sheilds' turn to laugh. Not agreeing to be whipped one day, he left his master with a wrenched arm, three loose teeth and a dislocated collar bone.

BROWN Well, well! Now that's an odd going-away present. And you reside here in Rochester now, I take it?

SHEILDS Yes suh.

DOUGLASS Sheilds has made his home with us since his escape.

BROWN Good! We'll be seeing a lot of each other then, Mr. Green. I have an idea you may fit into our scheme quite handily, too, if you've a mind to. I shall need a number of men like you—strong, courageous, unafraid.

DOUGLASS Tell us, what is this scheme of yours? (*he motions them toward seats*)

BROWN All right. Now is as good a time as any. (*he reaches for his bag, and withdraws a large rolled parchment*) All the while I was in Kansas, Douglass, I have been thinking, planning, praying over this thing. Kansas was but an interlude, an opening skirmish. It has given me a hard core of trusted men, baptized in fire and blood, who will follow me anywhere. And now ... now the time has come to carry the war into Africa itself, into the very heart of the Southland. (*unrolling the parchment, he lays it over the table down right*) Here. Will you be so good as to hold one edge for me, Mr. Green?

SHEILDS Yes suh. I got it, suh.

BROWN Now. If you will look carefully, Douglass—and you too, Mr. Green—here we have a map of the States from New Hampshire to Florida, and Maryland to Missouri. Now: here are the Allegheny Mountains sweeping from the North clear through to Alabama. Do they portend anything to you, eh?

DOUGLASS I don't quite know what you mean. They form more or less a natural chain from North to South, but—

BROWN Exactly! These mountains are the basis of my plan, Douglass. I believe these ranges to be God-given, placed there from the beginning of time by some divine pre-arrangement for but a single purpose... the emancipation of the slaves. (*he pauses, eyes shining*)

DOUGLASS Go on. Explain.

BROWN Look here, at the Blue Ridge Mountains of Virginia. These ranges are full of natural forts, where one man for defense would be the equal to a hundred for attack. Now, I know these mountains well. My plan, then, is to take a force of men into the Virginia hills. There I will post them in squads of fives along a line of twenty-five miles. Now, when these are properly schooled and drilled in the arts of mountain warfare, it will then be possible to steal down to the plantations and run off slaves in large numbers. Think of it, Douglass! Think of the consternation among the Virginia slavemasters when they see their slaves disappearing into the hills!

DOUGLASS (*weighing it all*) Yes ... yes, I can imagine.

BROWN Not only for the good of delivering these people from their bondage, you understand—though that is of course the paramount end. But the prospect of valuable property which is disappearing in the middle of the night—ah! Here Douglass, we attack the slave system at its core, and that is its pocketbook! (*springing up*) Oh, Douglass, you and I know that eloquent appeals to men's emotions, their reasons, their sense of justness and fair play have little effect if the evil you would have them discard is the means of their bread and syrup. They may turn a deaf ear to God himself, but once you remove the monetary profit their vices, take away the means by which they gain their filthy dollars, they will desert it as if in fear of plague and seek other means more economically secure to furnish their tables.

DOUGLASS (*has been listening carefully*) Yes ... yes, there is much truth in what you say. But—suppose you succeed in running off a few slaves. What is to prevent them from merely selling their slaves further South?

BROWN Ah! That in itself would be a show of weakness. Besides, we would follow them up. Virginia would be only the beginning.

DOUGLASS But they would employ bloodhounds to hunt you out in the mountains.

BROWN That they might attempt, but we would whip them—and when we have whipped the squad, they would be careful how they pursued again.

DOUGLASS   And the slaves themselves? What would become of them once you had liberated them from their bonds?

BROWN   We would retain the brave and the strong in the mountains, and send the rest north into Canada by way of the Underground Railroad. You're a part of that operation, Douglass, and I'm counting on you for suggestions along that line.

DOUGLASS   I see. But won't it take years to free any appreciable number of slaves this way?

BROWN   Indeed not! Each month our line of fortresses will extend further South—Tennessee, Georgia, Alabama, Mississippi... To the Delta itself. (*he points them out on the map, which* SHEILDS *now holds, gazing in wonder*) The slaves will free themselves!

DOUGLASS   And those you retain in the mountains. How do you propose to support this growing band of troops?

BROWN   We shall subsist upon the enemy, of course! Slavery is a state of war, Douglass, and I believe the slave has a right to anything necessary to obtain his freedom.

DOUGLASS   (*thoughtfully*) Now, if you were surrounded, cut off... If it's war, then you must not underestimate the enemy.

BROWN   True, that's true, but I doubt that we could ever be surprised in the mountains so that we would not be able to cut our way out.

DOUGLASS   Perhaps... Still, if the worst were to come?

BROWN   (*impatiently*)   Then let it come! At least we will have been doing something. Action... action is the basis of reform, and long ago, Douglass, I promised my God I had no better use for the means, the energies and the life He gave me than to lay them down in the cause of the slaves. (*turns to* SHEILDS) Mr. Green You've been silent. Let us hear from you.

SHEILDS   (*admiration in his voice*)   You're Cap'n John Brown, ain't you?

BROWN   (*with an amused glance at* DOUGLASS) Why, yes—yes I am, Mr. Green.

SHEILDS   Jus' call me Sheilds.

BROWN   All right. Sheilds.

SHEILDS   I'm not a what-you-call eddicated man, suh. Mr. Douglass here's jus' now learnin' me readin' and writin'. I ain't much to offer, I knows, but when you gits ready to sen' them mens into the mountains, please let me know. I'd powerful like to be one of 'em, Cap'n Brown.

BROWN   And so you shall, Sheilds, so you shall! (*he strides to* SHEILDS *and shakes hands vigorously. To* DOUGLASS) There, you see? My first recruit! I'll have to write Forbes about this. Oh, I haven't told you about Forbes, have I.

DOUGLASS   Forbes?

BROWN   Yes. Colonel Hugh Forbes. By an extraordinary stroke of good fortune, Douglass, I've met a certain Englishman, a military man who has engaged in several of the revolutionary movements of Europe. I've verified that he fought with old Garibaldi himself. I've engaged this man as drillmaster for my troops.

DOUGLASS   Drillmaster?

BROWN   Yes. I have induced Colonel Forbes to join me and supervise the proper training of a fighting force. I consider it very fortunate that I could persuade him.

DOUGLASS   Where is he now?

BROWN   In New York, writing a Military Manual for the use of our troops.

DOUGLASS   Why, it all sounds so incredible! An English drillmaster and a military manual...! I know your accomplishments, John. You were successful in Kansas by personally leading a small band of men. But now all this talk of a drillmaster and a special manual—

BROWN   But you fail to realize the scope of the mission, Douglass! This is to be no minor skirmish, this is war and war demands extensive preparation, you can see how important it is to make allowances now for whatever might arise in the future. Douglass... (*intensely*), Douglass, I've spent years perfecting this plan in detail. I've tested my methods under fire. Believe me I know whereof I speak!

DOUGLASS   (*slowly*)   Yes, in the past you've proved that beyond all question, John.

BROWN   Oh, Douglass! Douglass! (*he grasps* DOUGLASS *by the shoulders*) I knew I could count on you! It's coming... I can feel that it's coming! As Moses led the children of Israel from Egyptian bondage to the land of Canaan, so shall we lead the children of Africa from Southern bondage to the land of Canada. It is God's will! Together—together we will free the slaves!

(*He stands with arms outstretched toward* DOUGLASS *and* SHEILDS *as the curtain falls*)

ACT TWO

Scene One

(TIME *Several months later. Noon.*

At rise, ANNA DOUGLASS *is discovered tidying up in the hallway. She comes down into the parlor for a quick look around, then starts to leave, when she spies a hat resting on a chair. She picks it up and examines it; it is of curious military design. She glances ominously toward the closed study door then drops the hat back onto the chair in disgust.*

Off right the front door opens and LEWIS *enters, whistling gaily*)

LEWIS Hello, Mother.
ANNA Oh, that you, son? You're home early. I ain't fixed dinner yet.
LEWIS Oh, that's all right. There was nothing going on at the office anyway. Where's Dad?
ANNA (*indicates the study*) In there. That man is here again.
LEWIS What man?
ANNA That soldier man. You know, Captain Brown's friend. Colonel somebody.
LEWIS Oh, you mean Colonel Forbes.
ANNA That's the one. He's in there with Fred.
LEWIS What's he want this time?
ANNA I don't know, but I'll bet it's money. Fred's keepin' the old man's funds for him and he has to handle his business when he's gone.
LEWIS But Captain Brown's not ready to move yet. He's still out raising funds. Doesn't seem right to be paying Colonel Forbes for doing nothing.
ANNA That's what I been tellin' Fred! But he says the old man insists. Says he'll need Forbes and he'll be ready pretty soon now.
LEWIS I hope he knows what he's doing.
ANNA So do I, Lewis. Every time Fred talks to him he just says, "God'll take care of everything." 'S if God ain't got enough to do already. (*the front door slams and* ANNIE *runs in, shrieking*)
ANNIE Momma! Momma!
ANNA My gracious! What's the matter, baby?
ANNIE Quick, Momma, I have to hide!
ANNA Hide from what, Annie?
ANNIE From Bobby and Henry. They're after me!
ANNA Bobby and Henry? What are they after you about?
ANNIE We was playin' slavery, an' I'm the slave. Only I ran away! (LEWIS *grins and shakes his head, exiting towards the kitchen*)
ANNA Oh... Well, you better get away quick then, 'fore you get caught. That'd be just terrible, wouldn't it?
ANNIE No, it won't be so bad. Jackie's playin' Mr. Hawkins and he always helps me get free again.
ANNA Oh, I see. Well, your poppa's got company in the liberry and I hate to turn you out. But you better go back outside and play. (*she guides Annie toward the hallway*)
ANNIE All right, Momma. But if they catch me, they're gonna sell me off to the highest bidder!
ANNA Oh? Well, if that happens, I'll come out an' see if I can't buy you back with some gingerbread and cookies. Run on, now. (ANNIE *starts out but then, glancing out the hallway window, she squeals and comes running back*)
ANNIE Momma, Momma! They saw me! I have to get away! I have to get away! (*she dashes off towards the kitchen*)
ANNA (*following*) Lawd-a-mussy! I don't know what I'm gonna do with you... (*as they leave the study door opens and* DOUGLASS *enters, followed by* COLONEL HUGH FORBES. FORBES *is a tall, once-handsome man in his thirties with a harried, hungry look about his eyes*)
DOUGLASS (*is frowning*) ... I'm very sorry, Mr. Forbes, but that is the state of affairs and I don't see that there's anything more to say. Now, if you'll excuse me, I have quite a bit of work to do.
FORBES Now, just a minute, just a minute here! Am I to understand, then, that you refuse to discharge these obligations?
DOUGLASS (*displeased*) I am under no obligation to you whatsoever, sir.
FORBES Well, perhaps not you personally, Mr. Douglass, but you *are* acting for Brown. And I tell you that he is behind on my salary. Again! Now really, old chap, just how much do

you fellows expect me to put up with? I have tried to be patient, man, but even my endurance has its obvious limitations. Why, so far I think I have been rather agreeable about this whole thing, and—

DOUGLASS (*smouldering*) Oh, you have, have you? And I suppose you were just being agreeable when you wrote this letter to George Chatham demanding by return mail a check for fifty dollars! Mr. Chatham is not responsible for your salary, Mr. Forbes. Nor am I. From here on you will have to make your arrangements personally through Captain Brown, or not at all. Now again, I am asking that you excuse me. I have more important matters to attend to. (LEWIS *appears at the dining-room door and stands listening*)

FORBES Important matters! What is more important than my salary? Really, Mr. Douglass, I am amazed at your apparent lack of understanding. Can you possibly fail to appreciate that I am in a rather unique position here? That a word from me in the proper ears could spell the end of this whole scheme? The end of Brown and you and all the rest?

DOUGLASS So now it's out! At last!

FORBES (*daring*) Yes, at last, if you couldn't get it before! Where do you think you'd be, any of you, if it weren't for me? Why, this whole thing constitutes in essence a conspiracy—a conspiracy against the peace of Virginia and a plot against the government. All I'd have to do would be go to Washington and seek the proper authorities, and it would be a bad day for you, sir!

DOUGLASS (*flaring*) Bad day for me indeed! Mr. Forbes, if you think you're going to blackmail me—or John Brown either, for that matter —you've got quite a surprise coming. I'll not give you another cent of his money. You may go where you like and tell whom you please, but you'll not intimidate me one whit! Now, I'll thank you to leave my house.

FORBES (*placatingly*) Now, now—there's no need for haste. You needn't upset yourself so, Mr. Douglass. I—

DOUGLASS We will speak no more about it, sir!

FORBES Take until tomorrow to think it over. After all, only two hundred dollars.

DOUGLASS Take your hat and get out. Before I feel compelled to assist you!

FORBES (*indignant*) Now, really, I—! (*he draws himself up with arrogant dignity*) Very well. You force me to take action. I have tried to reason with you, but I should have known that that is impossible. And I am not in the habit of being insulted by . . . By . . . (DOUGLASS *removes his spectacles, calmly.* FORBES *turns and beats a hasty exit*)

LEWIS (*steps into the room*) We can stop him! I'll catch him before he gets around the corner—!

DOUGLASS No, Lewis, let him go! I must reach the old man at once—I want you to go to the telegraph office and get off a message. Here, take this down. (*he looks around for paper and pencil, but* LEWIS *withdraws his own*) To Nelson Hawkins, Esquire. Care of Gerrit Smith, 17 East Locust Street, Peterboro, New York . . .

LEWIS I've got it. Go on.

DOUGLASS "Return at once. A wolf has upset the pail."

(*Curtain*)

Scene Two

(*A few nights later.*

Gathered in the room are DOUGLASS, BROWN, CHATHAM, LOGUEN, SHIELDS, *and another gentleman to be identified as* SANBORN. *They appear to have been having a conference, but now they have paused and are finishing up refreshments of cake and coffee.* LEWIS *is circulating with a plate of cake slices, but everyone seems to have had enough.* ANNA *has the coffee service and pours another cup for one or two of the guests. Several light up cigars or pipes, and the room begins to take on the air of a political caucus. At length,* SANBORN *puts down his cup and calls the meeting to order. He is a mild, cultured gentleman with a Boston accent*)

SANBORN Gentlemen. Gentlemen. It's getting very late. Shall we get on with our business? (*there are ad libs of* "*Yes. Quite so. By all means*") All right. (*he turns to* BROWN *who sits near the fireplace facing the others, as if in a witness chair*) Captain Brown, we have all listened earnestly to your arguments in favor of continuing with your plan. I think I can speak for all of us here when I say that we greatly admire your spirit and have implicit faith in your capabilities. We have supported you before, and are most anxious to do so again, in order to advance the day of freedom for our enslaved brethren. However—and here I speak not only for myself but also the committee I represent—however, we cannot afford to ignore this new and most distressing development. A trust *was* misplaced. The man *has* gone to the authorities—Senator Seward himself telegraphed me in Boston and asked me to get to you right away. He is trying to keep it quiet, but still for all we know, right now we may be under the watchful eye of federal agents merely awaiting the opportune moment to pounce! Under these circumstances it seems that your plan is doomed to failure if you insist upon pursuing it now. You have convinced us in the past that you are worth supporting. We have subscribed funds and promised supplies and arms and ammunition. We do not withdraw them now! All we ask is what is to prevent you from postponing this venture until there can be more certainty of success? (*there are ad libs of disagreement from the others*)

BROWN Mr. Sanborn, I do not concede that now is a less favorable time than in some distant future. We can do it still! We must not be made timid by the first dark shadow that falls across our path. A swift blow, a swift blow now, gentlemen, before they get a chance to believe the scoundrel—! (SANBORN *frowns and shakes his head firmly*)

CHATHAM But why not, Sanborn, why not? If we could get things rolling now, catch them off their guard—!

SANBORN You mean let them catch us off our guard! And remember—they've got Forbes with them, now. He knows the whole plan in detail.

BROWN If you will only leave that matter to me—I have those who can be put on his trail. Forbes will get what traitors deserve! (*there is a disapproving murmur*)

SANBORN That is simply impossible, Brown. In the face of what has happened, it's sheer madness!

LOGUEN Careful... Careful, Captain.

CHATHAM Well, John, I'm not so sure that that's at all advisable...

SANBORN You should never have taken the man into your confidence.

DOUGLASS Well, I think we've *all* been fools not to have seen through his game from the very first. But still, Frank, it seems so... tragic to have to postpone the entire operation now.

CHATHAM Of course! What's the matter with Gerrit and Higginson and the others on the committee, Sanborn? Are they getting cold feet because of a handful of stupid men in Washington, or have they been this timid from the very first—

SANBORN Now, now, Chatham, there's no need to go too far over the matter. From the first we've had to consider that we could all be prosecuted for conspiring to violate the Fugitive Slave Law and a score of other such measures. But we all take our chances in this work and regard it as our Christian duty, and I'm sure none of us regrets a single action or dollar spent up to now.

CHATHAM Well, good. Who was it said: "We must all hang together, or most assuredly we shall all hang separately." (*there is a little light laughter*)

LOGUEN (*with a frown*) Well, gentlemen, it is all very well to joke about it, but I for one am behind Captain Brown one hundred percent. I protest against any postponement. If the thing is postponed now, it is postponed forever —because Forbes can do as much evil next year as this. I believe we have gone too far to turn back now!

BROWN (*encouraged*) Aye, Reverend Loguen! And I tell you, sirs, that I can do it. I have the means and I will not lose a single day now. I tell you we can be freeing slaves a week from tonight in Virginia.

CHATHAM What? So soon?

BROWN Absolutely, sir! (*rises*) There is no need for delay. I would have been in Virginia now were not Harriet Tubman lying ill in Canada. But she can send me others who know the "Railroad's" route as well as she. I and my men will free the slaves, and her's will lead them out.

CHATHAM But with so small a band? I thought you needed scores—

BROWN General Tubman will dispatch a good-sized force to me as soon as I have need of them. And when the first blow is struck the slaves will rise throughout the countryside. Men from the free states will come down and join. An army will form, consolidate and march Southward. Oh, I tell you, sir, it can be done and I can do it now! (*he pauses, trembling with the emotion of it, and all eyes turn toward* SANBORN. SANBORN *meets* BROWN's *gaze gravely, then slowly and firmly shakes his head. There is a pause as the others register their disappointment*) But my men will fall away ... Everything that I have been building in my lifetime will come down to nothing, nothing ... (*he sinks to his chair*) You don't know what you're doing ... You just don't know ...

SANBORN   We know how disappointed you are, Captain Brown, and we regret it exceedingly believe me. But we cannot listen further. Our hearts are still with you, but I believe it is pretty well decided. (*turns toward* DOUGLASS) Frederick ... ?

DOUGLASS   I ... No. No, Frank, I have nothing further to add to what I've already said.

SANBORN   All right. Captain Brown, this is what you must do. You must stay low, let time pass. The alarm will die down, the suspicions. Then you will return and strike, and we shall be behind you. In the meantime, tell us no more of your plans. We still trust you with our money, but we can aid you no further for now. Go back to Kansas and wait. Time must pass. (*there is silence.* BROWN's *eyes are smouldering but he does not speak.* SANBORN *rises, signifying that the conference is at an end, and the others follow suit.* SANBORN *turns to* DOUGLASS) We must thank you, Frederick, for receiving us so graciously on such short notice.

DOUGLASS   That's quite all right, Frank. I'm only sorry that I can't put you all up for the night.

CHATHAM   Oh, we have plenty of room at our place. I'll take good care of him.

SANBORN   That's very kind of you, George.

DOUGLASS (*one last try*)   Stop by tomorrow, unless you have to hurry back.

SANBORN (*smiles and shakes his head*)   I'm afraid I'm catching the early Boston train. So I'll say goodbye now. Until the next time. (*he grasps* DOUGLASS' *hand, then turns to leave. He stops, seeing* BROWN *still sitting brooding by the fireplace, but* BROWN *abruptly turns away, refusing to say goodbye, and* SANBORN *continues out via the hallway.* CHATHAM *follows.* LOGUEN *puts a sympathetic hand on* BROWN's *shoulder before passing on.* DOUGLASS *accompanies them all to the door as* SHEILDS *stands looking after, flashing hostile eyes at the departing guests.* ANNA *and* LEWIS *reappear and gather up the cups and saucers. They exit.* SHEILDS *seats himself dejectedly by the table and gazes with sympathy at* BROWN, *who continues to sit in defeated silence, solemnly regarding the fire. Presently* DOUGLASS *returns. He pauses near the archway, then comes slowly down and sits, drawing his chair nearer the fire. For a moment he does not speak*)

DOUGLASS (*quietly*)   I'm sorry, John.

BROWN (*stirs and smiles weakly*)   It's all right, Frederick. You told me how it would be.

DOUGLASS   Perhaps it *is* better to wait.

BROWN (*sighs*)

There is a tide in the affairs of men,
Which, taken at the flood, leads on ...

I am at my tide, Frederick. Despite what they say, I cannot turn back now.

DOUGLASS   You don't mean that. Another year, a few months perhaps—

BROWN (*shakes his head*)   I cannot delay further.

DOUGLASS   Surely you can't mean that you're going on with it now.

BROWN   It will be now or never.

DOUGLASS (*alarmed*)   Has all this tonight meant nothing to you?

BROWN   Oh yes, yes. It has meant a great deal. They have failed me at the first small sign of difficulty. I cannot afford to leave them that opportunity again—I will proceed without them. It means altering my plans somewhat, but I have already prepared for that. You see, Frederick, I leave nothing to chance.

DOUGLASS (*sympathetically*)   You're tired, disappointed ...

BROWN   For twenty years this plan to free slaves has held me like a passion. It will be desperate, perhaps, but it will be holy. For I was created to be the deliverer of slaves, and the time is now.

DOUGLASS (*goes to him*)   Come up to bed, and we will speak more of it tomorrow.

BROWN   No, my friend. There is no time to waste in sleeping now.

DOUGLASS   Now, really, John, you're taking this too far. After a good night's rest things will look different in the morning.

BROWN   Morning must find me on my way.

I am leaving tonight. (SHEILDS, *sitting silently on the other side of the room, sits up at this, and listens intently*)

DOUGLASS   Leaving? But what can you do now, alone?

BROWN   I still have my band, Frederick. I must get them word immediately—listen to this: (*he takes out a telegraph sheet and reads*) "The coal banks are open. Old miners will come at once." Ha! They'll know what I mean. And where.

DOUGLASS   But what about arms, supplies—?

BROWN   I already have enough cached away in a warehouse in Pennsylvania with which to begin. Once we reach Virginia, we'll live off the land. As for arms, there will be all we can use just waiting for us at Harper's Ferry. Once there, we can begin our operations without want of—

DOUGLASS   Just a minute! Did you say . . . Harper's Ferry?

BROWN   Yes.

DOUGLASS   There is a United States Government Arsenal at Harper's Ferry.

BROWN   Of course! That is what I mean. We shall seize it first. With its store of weapons and supplies we can arm our forces as they expand, equip Harriet Tubman's men as they come, supply the slaves for miles around.

DOUGLASS   Brown! What are you thinking of?

BROWN   (*speaking fervently now*) Can't you see it, Frederick? The word traveling from lip to lip . . . the slaves rallying to the call . . . the mountain passes sealed with bullets . . . liberty spreading southward like a trail of fire! . . .

DOUGLASS   John!

BROWN   The nation roused—

DOUGLASS   Do you know what you're saying?

BROWN   The chains dropping—

DOUGLASS   It's mad. It's madness, I tell you!

BROWN   Free men rising from the muck of enslavement!—

DOUGLASS (*shouts*)   John!! Listen to me. You cannot do it!

BROWN   (*slowly realizing what* DOUGLASS *is saying*) What? . . .

DOUGLASS   It is impossible, insane! You must not even think of it.

BROWN   You're . . . going to fail me, then? You too, Douglass? I'm counting on you to help me, Frederick, are you going back on me too?

DOUGLASS (*taking him by the arm*)   Sit down. Sit down, John. (*they sit*) Do you believe I'm your friend? That I want to do what's right?

BROWN   I believe you, Frederick.

DOUGLASS   Then listen to me. I have helped you as much as I could. I intend to help you further, when the right time comes, in your great slave-freeing raids. But what you are saying now is wholly different.

BROWN   Wherein is it different? This is greater, that's all, greater. We shall free more slaves and free them faster.

DOUGLASS   But don't you realize what you'd be doing? You can't attack Harper's Ferry. You'd be attacking the United States Government. It would be treason!

BROWN (*eyes flashing*)   Treason! Government! Laws! Blast them all to hell! I answer you back, Douglass. I answer you back with humans and right! I answer you back there is a higher law than all!

DOUGLASS   John, you're living on earth—you're dealing with men.

BROWN (*defiantly*)   I deal with God!

DOUGLASS   Oh, I see! You deal with God. And is it God who counsels you to rash, inopportune action? Is it God who calls you to dash away your talents and your usefulness in a single ill-considered stroke? And what of the slaves themselves—you want to help them, you say. Why then do you think of doing the very thing that will harm them most? Why bring the nation's anger on them? *You* may defy the federal government, but they cannot.

BROWN   But we will rouse the nation behind them! It needs rousing. It's cursed. It's dying. It needs to be startled into action.

DOUGLASS   Oh, can't you see, John? By running off slaves from Southern plantations, you attack the slave system without endangering retaliation by the whole nation. Aye! There will be many who will approve and come rallying to your support. But if you start by attacking Harper's Ferry your blow is not at slavery itself. Your blow is against the whole nation, and will bring down on your head—and the slaves—the panic and condemnation of thousands whose sentiment would otherwise be with you.

BROWN   I cannot concern myself with public

opinion just now. Action! Action is the only means to reform. You know that, Douglass... you've said it yourself.

DOUGLASS Yes, John, yes—but must we have action, any action, at so great a price? Tell me. Tell me, John: is there ever any justification for such unprovoked violence, even in pursuit of a righteous cause?

BROWN Yes! Yes, by God, I believe there is. If we cannot persuade the nation with words to purge itself of this curse, then we must do so with weapons. This is war, I tell you, and in war there must often be sacrifices made to expediency.

DOUGLASS Be careful, John! Think now of what you say. Some day *you* may be sacrificed to *their* expedience.

BROWN I am thinking. And I am unafraid. In God's good time, as we sweep Southward those of good faith will see their trust was not misplaced.

DOUGLASS You'll never get South, John! Not if you insist upon starting at Harper's Ferry. I know the area—it's like a steel trap. Once in you'll never get out alive. They'll surround you, hem you in!

BROWN (*defiantly*) They surrounded me in Kansas! They never took me there!

DOUGLASS They'll hurl all their military might against you!

BROWN We'll cut our way through! We'll take prisoners and hold them as hostages.

DOUGLASS Virginia will blow you and your hostages to hell rather than let you hold the arsenal for an hour!

BROWN I'm not afraid of death! Is that why it's insane, Frederick? Because we may spill a little blood?

DOUGLASS We're talking about freeing slaves, John! Not throwing lives away in a hopeless insurrection!—

BROWN But this is the way to free slaves—all of them, not just a few! (*intensely, with great passion*) It must be by blood! The moral suasion of Moses and Aaron was in vain, even with the abetment of the locusts and the boils. Not till the shedding of the blood of the first born of Egypt was there release for Israel. Through blood out of bondage, Douglass! Without the shedding of blood there is no remission of sins—

DOUGLASS John! Do you think you are God?

BROWN (*stops, momentarily stunned*) God? ... God is different things to different men, Frederick. To some He is a separate entity, dispensing wrath or reward from philanthropic heights. To some He is watchdog conscience, gnawing at the marrow. To me... God is simply the perception and the performance of right. And so I am a little bit of God. Or trying to be.

DOUGLASS (*starts to speak, then sighs*) I cannot argue with you further, John Brown. I see I cannot hope to change your mind.

BROWN Then you're coming with me, Frederick?

DOUGLASS I cannot.

SHEILDS (*interrupting from the background*) Wait for me, Cap'n Brown! I'm goin' up to get a few things.

DOUGLASS (*turning*) What? Sheilds...?

SHEILDS Yes, Mistuh Douglass. I believe I'll go wid de ole man. (*he turns and goes upstairs*)

BROWN Come with us, Frederick. I need you.

DOUGLASS I cannot.

BROWN Douglass! I will defend you with my life.

DOUGLASS John—

BROWN I want you for a special purpose. When I strike the bees will begin to swarm and I shall need you to help me hive them.

DOUGLASS You have changed your plan. I cannot go with you now.

BROWN Will you fail me then? Will you fail your people? (*suddenly smoldering*) Or are you so far removed from slavery that you no longer care!

DOUGLASS (*taken by surprise*) What—?

BROWN (*tauntingly*) Have you carried the scars upon your back into high places so long that you have forgotten the sting of the whip and the lash?

DOUGLASS John, that's not being fair! Don't—

BROWN (*like a whip*) Or are you afraid to face a gun? (DOUGLASS *gasps as if struck. Then, catching himself, he grasps the back of a chair for support*)

DOUGLASS (*slowly*) I have never really questioned it before, John. If it would do good ... if it would do good, this moment I would die, I swear it, John! But I cannot cast away that which I know I can do for that which I know I cannot do. I have no right to do that. I should rather fail you, John, than feel within myself that I have failed my people. For them ... I believe it is my duty to live, and to fight in ways that I know can succeed. (BROWN *stares at* DOUGLASS *for a moment, then turns and starts for the stairway. Reaching it, he pauses and turns to* DOUGLASS)

BROWN I shall miss you, Frederick.

(*Curtain*)

Scene Three

(*A few weeks later. Early morning.*

Except for a faint glow from the fireplace, the room is in darkness. Breaking the stillness rudely is the sound of someone knocking at the door, excitedly. There is a pause, and the knocking resumes, louder than before. A pause, then again. This time a light appears from the top of the stairway, and ANNA's *voice is heard calling:* "Yes, just a minute! Just a minute!" *Then* LEWIS *is heard saying,* "I'll go down, Mother, you stay up here."

LEWIS *appears descending the stairway with a candle, a pair of trousers pulled on hastily over the bottom of his nightshirt. He goes off to the door*)

LEWIS (*as he unbolts the door*) All right, just a minute. (*the door opens*) Yes?

VOICE (*off*) Are you Lewis Douglass?

LEWIS Yes.

VOICE Fred Douglass's boy?

LEWIS Yes, I am.

VOICE Then this here telegram must be for you.

LEWIS Telegram? For me? (ANNA *appears on the stairway with a light. She descends halfway, peering toward the door. She is in nightgown with a shawl thrown over her shoulders and her hair hangs down in a braid.*)

VOICE That's right. Telegraph operator asked me to drop it by to you right away. Urgent.

LEWIS Why, thanks. Thanks very much, Mister—?

VOICE Oh, that's all right. You don't need to know my name, it's better that way. You just get to what that wire says.

LEWIS Hey, wait! Wait a minute, mister.

VOICE (*farther away*) Good night!

ANNA Lewis! What is it, son?

LEWIS (*closes the door and returns*) It's a wire, Mother. It's addressed to "B. F. Blackall, Esq."

ANNA That's Mister Blackall, the telegraph operator.

LEWIS (*opens it hastily and reads*) "Tell Lewis, my oldest son, to secure all important papers in my high desk at once." That's all it says. Not even signed.

ANNA It don't have to be, you know it's from Fred.

LEWIS Gee, Mother, do you think he's in trouble?

ANNA I don't know, son. But I been on pins and needles for the past two days now. The high desk, did he say?

LEWIS Yes, Mother.

ANNA Then he must mean those letters and papers he been keepin' for Captain Brown. Come on, son. (*she heads for the study*)

LEWIS Oh!—but the high desk is locked. And Poppa always keeps the key with him.

ANNA (*turning*) Then look in the kitchen and get a knife or something. Lewis, hurry!

LEWIS All right. (*he goes*)

(*From the stairway comes a small voice crying,* "Mom-ma...?" ANNA *looks up and sees little* ANNIE's *face peering from between the banisters*)

ANNA Annie! What you doin' out of bed?

ANNIE (*affecting baby talk*) Big noise wake me up. Peoples talkin' and bangin' on doors.

ANNA Now you know you ain't supposed to be gettin' up out of your bed in the middle of the night, even if the Walls of Jericho is tumblin' down! And you with such a cold.

ANNIE But I'm scared, Mom-ma...

ANNA Not half as scared as you're gonna be if you don't put your little behin' back in that bed! (ANNIE *begins to cry.* ANNA *goes to her*) Now, now there, baby. That's no way to do. There ain't nothin' to be afraid of. (*takes her in her arms*) Hush, now, everything's gonna be all right.

LEWIS (*re-enters with a chisel*) This ought to get it open, Mother!

ANNA All right, Lewis. You go ahead. You know what to take out?

LEWIS Yes. Yes, I know. (*he goes into the study*)

ANNIE Mom-ma, where's Poppa?

ANNA Poppa's in Pennsylvania, honey, tendin' to some business.

ANNIE When's he comin' home? I miss him.

ANNA I know you do, darlin'. So do I. He'll be home soon, though. Maybe tomorrow or the next day.

ANNIE Is Sheilds comin' back with him?

ANNA (*quietly*) I don't know, honey.

ANNIE Mister Hawkins?

ANNA No...No, I don't think so, baby. You come on here, now, 'n let me tuck you back in like a nice little lady, 'fore you catch your death of—(ANNIE *sneezes*) There! You see? (*she rises and starts upstairs with* ANNIE *in her arms*) Now you just come on and go right back to sleep. There's nothin' for you to be afraid of, an' nobody's gonna wake you up again... (*her voice trails off as they move from sight*)

(*Knocking begins at the door again.* LEWIS *comes out of the study, startled, a bunch of papers in his hands. The knocking repeats. After a hasty look around,* LEWIS *stuffs the papers into his waist, arranges his nightshirt over them, and starts for the hallway. Remembering the library door, he dashes back to close it, then on to the front*)

LEWIS (*breathlessly*) Who is it?

CHATHAM (*off*) It's George Chatham, Lewis.

LEWIS (*relieved*) Oh! (*he opens the door*) Come in, Mr. Chatham, you gave me quite a start.

CHATHAM (*enters, removing his hat*) Thank you, my boy. Now, where's Frederick?

LEWIS Oh, he's not here. He's away on a trip to Pennsylvania.

CHATHAM I know, Lewis, but he's due back tonight, isn't he? Have you had no word from him?

LEWIS Well, yes. But he didn't say when he was coming. Just told me to take care of a little business for him, that's all.

CHATHAM But I just left Reverend Loguen. He said he was looking for Frederick tonight. I even went down to meet the train, but he wasn't on it.

LEWIS Well, I'm sorry, sir. Is something the matter?

CHATHAM Yes, by God, there's a great deal the matter! This attack on Harper's Ferry has stirred up a regular hornet's nest. I've got to see your father to find out what's going on.

ANNA (*appears at the head of the stairs*) Lewis? Who is it?

CHATHAM (*turns*) It's George Chatham, Mrs. Douglass.

ANNA (*descending quickly*) Oh, Mr. Chatham. What is it!

CHATHAM Oh no, don't become unduly alarmed. I bear no bad tidings. I just came here looking for Frederick.

ANNA He's on his way home?

CHATHAM Why, yes, didn't you know? Loguen had a telegram from Philadelphia. He should have arrived on the twelve-forty. Perhaps he'll be in on the three-oh-two.

ANNA Oh, Well, I'm so glad. I been near 'bout worried to death, wonderin' where he was and what's goin' on.

CHATHAM You're not the only one, Mrs. Douglass. This thing has set everybody back on their heels.

LEWIS Uh—'scuse me. (*he heads for the study*)

ANNA Go 'head, son... Well, what do you think, Mr. Chatham. Have they got much of a chance?

CHATHAM I'm afraid it looks bad, pretty bad right now, Mrs. Douglass. So far the Captain's still managed to hold the Arsenal with his little band. But Buchanon's ordered in government troops, you know.

ANNA Aw-aww...!

CHATHAM They've got the place surrounded. It'll take a miracle to get them out now. (*shakes his head in grudging admiration*) Oh, that Brown, that Captain Brown! Even if he fails, you've got to give it to him. We told him no, but he went right ahead anyhow. And the sheer nerve of it all—Harper's Ferry! Well, God help him. (LEWIS *returns from the library with a sheaf of letters and papers*)

LEWIS Here, Mother. What shall I... (*conscious of* CHATHAM's *presence*)

ANNA (*distressed*) Oh, I don't know, Lewis, I—Out in the woodshed! Hide them under the eaves!

LEWIS Good! (*he dashes out*)

ANNA (*impatient for something to do*) I... I think I'll go on back and fix up a little somethin' to eat. I know Fred'll be near 'bout starved when he gets off the train. Sit down, Mr. Chatham, and make yourself 't home.

CHATHAM No, thank you, Mrs. Douglass.

I'm going to run on back to the telegraph office to catch the latest news. Then I'll meet the train and look for Frederick.

ANNA All right, but at least you ought to stop and take a cup of tea. It's gettin pretty chilly out, and you know you're gettin' too old to be chasin' aroun' in the middle of the night like some young buck.

CHATHAM Thank you, Mrs. Douglass. But if I were a young buck I'd be out chasing around for different reasons than I am now! (*from off right the front door is heard to open.* CHATHAM *and* ANNA *move to the archway*)

ANNA Fred! (DOUGLASS *enters, carrying a traveling bag. He removes his hat as* ANNA *runs to greet him*)

DOUGLASS (*surprised*) Anna, my dear. What are you doing up so late? And George!

CHATHAM Hello, Frederick, I'm so glad you're back. What happened?—I met the train, you weren't on it.

DOUGLASS No, I got off in the freight yard and walked home, as I often do.

CHATHAM No matter, as long as you're here. Frederick—this Harper's Ferry business. Did you know about this?

DOUGLASS Yes, Yes, I knew.

CHATHAM But Frederick! This wasn't the plan. And even if it were, I thought we'd decided—

DOUGLASS You're perfectly right, George. I tried to talk him out of it, but to no avail. I even went down to Pennsylvania, caught up with John in an abandoned stone quarry near Chambersburg. We argued on and on. But the old man was like steel . . . !

CHATHAM So you couldn't stop him, eh? Oh, that's just like him—stubborn as an old mule. A magnificent old mule! Tell me, Frederick. How much longer do you think he can hold out?

DOUGLASS (*looks at them both quickly—they haven't heard*) The arsenal fell an hour ago. It's all over now.

CHATHAM What!

DOUGLASS Yes. The Army troops, under a Colonel Robert E. Lee, they stormed the place. John and his men fought bravely, but it fell.

CHATHAM Frederick! And the Captain?

DOUGLASS They took John alive, though they say he's badly wounded. One or two escaped but the others are all killed or captured.

ANNA Have mercy . . . ! And Sheilds? How 'bout Sheilds, did you hear—?

DOUGLASS Yes, Anna, they have him too. According to reports, Sheilds was on the outside when they surrounded the place. He could have gotten away! Instead he slipped back in, said he had to go back to the old man.

ANNA (*turns away*) Poor Sheilds . . .

CHATHAM Well, that's that. So it's all over.

ANNA Oh, Fred—what will they do with them now?

DOUGLASS It doesn't take much to imagine. If they're lucky, they'll get a trial first. And that's where you can help, George, if you will.

CHATHAM (*eagerly*) Yes?

DOUGLASS We may have a slight chance of saving them if we act right away.

CHATHAM All right, Frederick. You just point the way.

DOUGLASS Good. Now first we have to contact Sanborn and Gerrit Smith and Higginson and the others. We'll have to hire a lawyer, the most brilliant legal mind we can obtain.

CHATHAM (*beginning to make notes*) All right. Just give me a list and I'll get off wires at once. (*from off in the hallway comes a banging at the door and a voice crying: "Douglass! Douglass!"*)

DOUGLASS (*looking up*) What's that? (ANNA *scurries to the door and opens it*)

ANNA (*off*) Why, Rev'n Loguen!

DOUGLASS (*as* LOGUEN *enters*) Loguen! What's all the excitement?

LOGUEN (*breathing heavily*) I've . . . I've just heard—

DOUGLASS About John and the arsenal? Yes. We're just mapping plans for their defense. In the next few days we have to rally support from all quarters, perhaps even go to Virginia ourselves, and—

LOGUEN Virginia! In the next few days *you'll* be as far away from Virginia *or* Rochester as the fastest ship can sail!

ANNA What!

DOUGLASS What does this mean?

LOGUEN It means you've got to get away, Douglass. At once! They're after you.

DOUGLASS Who?

LOGUEN Federal agents!

CHATHAM But what for?

LOGUEN They found papers in Brown's knapsack, some of them letters from Douglass. They've issued a warrant for his arrest!

CHATHAM But Frederick wasn't there! They can't—

LOGUEN They *have* I tell you. Listen, Douglass. I've just come from Selden's house. the Lieutenant Governor of the state.

DOUGLASS Yes?

LOGUEN Selden summoned me half an hour ago to tell me the Governor's office had just received requisition from the Governor of Virginia for "the deliverance up of one Frederick Douglass," charging him with "murder, robbery, and inciting servile insurrection." *And* two United States Marshals—with no less than President Buchanon's authorization—have been secretly dispatched from Buffalo and should arrive here before dawn.

ANNA Tonight!!

LOGUEN That's right!

DOUGLASS Well, I expected they might send someone here. But so soon! (*to* ANNA) Did you get my message? Did you see to the papers?

ANNA Lewis is takin' care of them right now.

DOUGLASS Good. Well, let them come. (*he turns back to* CHATHAM *and his notebook*)

ANNA (*goes to him*) Fred. Fred, listen. If they're after you you've got to get away!

LOGUEN Don't you understand, Douglass? You can't stay here.

DOUGLASS (*smiles*) But I wasn't *at* Harper's Ferry. And now that my papers are secure—

LOGUEN And you actually think they'll stop to consider that? Listen—Selden has instructions from Albany. He will have to surrender you if they find you here.

DOUGLASS But we must help John and Sheilds and the others—

LOGUEN Right now you have to help yourself! Or you'll be in the same jailhouse they're in.

CHATHAM But Frederick wasn't involved in this thing, Loguen. Why should he—

LOGUEN (*exasperated*) That's not the point, George! Just once let them get their hands on him. Just once let them get him down to Virginia—

CHATHAM (*to* DOUGLASS) But you can prove, can't you, that—

LOGUEN What do you think he can prove at the end of a rope! (CHATHAM *halts*) Listen, now. I have Jim Mason standing by down at the smithy's shop with his team and rig. With a little luck he can get you over the border by sunrise. You'll be safe in Canada for a few days, and by then we can arrange for your passage to England.

DOUGLASS To England!

LOGUEN Yes, Douglass, yes! Once they find out you're in Canada, don't think for one minute they won't try to bring you back.

DOUGLASS You're right, of course, Loguen. But... (*he looks with concern towards* ANNA)

ANNA You go 'head, Fred, don't you worry none about us.

CHATHAM I'll look out for them, Frederick. They'll be safe, believe me.

(LEWIS *has returned quietly and stands in the background, his joy at seeing his father back giving way to bewilderment as he catches on to what is being said*)

DOUGLASS (*with a wry smile*) And so this time you've come for me, eh Loguen?... And Jim, Jim Mason's standing by again with his rig, for me... Well, I've been a fugitive before... hunted, running like a beast... pursued by human hounds.

LOGUEN (*nods*) I know the feeling well, Douglass. Now—(*indicates that it is time to go*)

DOUGLASS (*shrugging him off—bitterly*) Then tell me, Loguen—how long this night? How long this dark, dark night when no man walks in freedom, without fear, in this cradle of democracy, no man who's black? How will it happen, what will we have to do? Nat Turner tried it with guns, and he failed. Dred Scott went to the high courts, and they hurled him back into slavery. Old John said it must be by blood, and tonight he lies wounded in a Virginia prison. When will it end, Loguen—how long this night?

LOGUEN (*slowly*) Douglass, this I believe as surely as God gives me breath to speak it: no man lives in safety so long as his brother is in fear. Once arouse consciousness of that, and there will be those living and those dead, there will be guns and blood and the high courts too. But it will come. I may not be here to see it, Douglass, but it will come.

DOUGLASS How often do I wonder. (*he turns to go, sees* LEWIS)

LEWIS Poppa!

DOUGLASS (*reaching toward him*) Hello, son.

LEWIS You're going away?
DOUGLASS You'll have to take care of the family for me, Lewis. You're the man of the house, now.
LEWIS (*choking up*) Poppa, I—!
DOUGLASS Now, now, son. In front of your mother?
LOGUEN I hate to rush you, Douglass, but— (*from the stairway comes* ANNIE's *voice, asking,* "*Poppa?*")
DOUGLASS (*looking up*) Yes, Annie, darling! (ANNIE *races down the stairs and leaps into* DOUGLASS' *arms*)
ANNIE Oh, Poppa! You're back, you're back.
ANNA (*aware of the time*) All right, now, baby. It's back to bed for you, before you catch any more cold.
DOUGLASS (*concerned*) What? Has she been sick?
ANNA Only a little cold, Fred. Here, Annie. Let's go back upstairs.
ANNIE (*hugging* DOUGLASS *more tightly*) I don't wanna! I wanna see Poppa some more!
ANNA Now, Annie. That's no way for a little lady to act. You'll see Poppa again—(*she stops*) Again . . . Come on, honey. Kiss Poppa goodnight.
ANNIE (*kissing him*) Goodnight, Poppa. See you in the morning.
DOUGLASS Yes . . . Yes, dear. In the morning. (*he lets her down*)
LEWIS (*sensing the situation*) Here, Mother, I'll take her up.
ANNA Thank you, Lewis. (ANNIE *sneezes*) Be sure and tuck her in tight, now.
LEWIS I will. (*he turns to his father*) Poppa, I—(DOUGLASS *indicates for him not to say more in front of* ANNIE. LEWIS *turns and goes upstairs with* ANNIE)
ANNIE (*as she goes off*) Goodnight, Poppa. Goodnight, Momma.
DOUGLASS (*watching her*) Goodnight, dear . . . !
ANNA (*goes to him*) Fred!—
DOUGLASS Now I'll be all right, Anna. Take care of yourself.
ANNA (*her arms around him*) Oh, Fred! Be careful!
DOUGLASS I'll send you word as soon as I can. Maybe I won't have to go very far or stay very long. Maybe—

LOGUEN (*he and* CHATHAM *are in the hallway*) Douglass—! Time grows short.
DOUGLASS Yes, Loguen, I'm ready. (*he starts for the door.* ANNA *runs to him again and they embrace. He breaks away quickly and goes out, giving a last glance up the stairway.* CHATHAM *preceeds him, carrying* DOUGLASS' *bag*)
LOGUEN (*to* ANNA *as he follows*) If anyone comes . . .
ANNA (*nods her head*) I know. I know what to say. (*he exits, and the door is heard to close.* ANNA *stands at the window for a moment, fighting back the tears. Then she comes slowly back into the room. She goes quickly to the lamps and blows them out, leaving herself just a candle. Then she pauses, looking into the fireplace. Taking up a poker, she stirs the dying embers and sings softly to herself*)

>Didn't it rain, children . . .
>Rain, oh my Lord . . .
>Didn't it . . . ?
>Didn't it . . . ?
>Didn't it—
>Oh, my Lord, didn't it rain . . .

(*There is a sharp rap at the door.* ANNA *looks up, frightened The knock sounds again, crisply.* ANNA *goes to the archway and looks toward the front door. The knocking sounds again, louder and more insistent.* ANNA *lifts her head, draws her shawl about her shoulders, and strides bravely towards the door with her candle, as the curtain falls*)

ACT THREE

(TIME Six months later. Early evening.
LEWIS *is seated at the table at right, going over a ledger book with pen and ink. There is a stack of* "*North Stars*" *on a chair nearby. From off right, at the front door,* ANNA *is heard talking with a caller*)

ANNA (*off*) All right. Thank you, thank you very much. I hope you enjoy it. Goodbye . . . (*the door closes and* ANNA *enters. She sighs happily*) Well, that's another one. Here Lewis, put this with the rest. (*she gives him a bill and some change*)
LEWIS Fine! Say, we could use you at the office. You're getting to be our star salesman.

ANNA (*smiles*) My, the word certainly got around in a hurry. I don't know how many times today I've answered that door to folks wantin' their copy.

LEWIS Same way at the office. Guess they really missed it while Pa was gone.

ANNA That's what everybody says. But there's a lot of people comin' by who never took it before. (*proudly*) I sold nine new subscriptions today.

LEWIS That's fine! Well, I'm certainly glad we're back in business again. Though I still can't get over them calling off that investigation all of a sudden.

ANNA Well, what with the election campaign comin' up, there wasn't much else they could do. By the way, them folks out in Chicago. Them Republicans. Have they nominated anybody yet?

LEWIS Last I heard this afternoon, Senator Seward of Massachusetts was still leading on the second ballot. But Abraham Lincoln of Illinois was coming up strong.

ANNA (*frowns*) Poor Mr. Seward certainly has worked hard for it. Well, soon's you find out you better go in there and tell your father. That's all he's been studyin' 'bout all day.

LEWIS But isn't that newspaper man still in there?

ANNA Mr. Tilton? Yes, son. Seems he came all the way up here from New York to get Fred to write some articles for his paper.

LEWIS Oh?

ANNA Yes, and then—(*she breaks off as the study door opens and* DOUGLASS *enters, frowning*)

DOUGLASS (*searching about among papers, books, etc.*) Anna, what did you do with that little book I use for keeping names and addresses in? I can't find it anywhere.

ANNA Well, I don't know, Fred. I haven't bothered it. Lewis, you know what he's talkin' about?

LEWIS Why, no. No, Pa, I haven't seen it.

DOUGLASS (*annoyed*) Well, somebody must have moved it! I always keep it in the lower right hand drawer of my high desk, and now it's not there. Anna, are you sure . . . ?

ANNA (*calmly*) Now, Fred, you don't have to holler like that at me! . . .

DOUGLASS What? Oh—oh, I'm sorry, I . . .

ANNA When did you have it last, do you remember? Have you looked in all the drawers?

Try all your pockets? How 'bout upstairs? Here, let me go see—(*she starts for the stairway, but halts as* DOUGLASS *feels his pockets and withdraws a small book*)

DOUGLASS (*slowly raising his eyes*) I'm . . . sorry, Anna.

ANNA That's all right, Fred. (*pause*) Now don't stay 'way from your guest.

DOUGLASS Huh? Oh, yes. Yes . . . (*he goes back into the study, closing the door*)

ANNA (*shakes her head*) Lawd-a-mussy!

LEWIS Mother, what's wrong? Do you think he's sick?

ANNA Well, Fred ain't really sick, not like you usually think of somebody being sick.

LEWIS Then what is it?

ANNA I don't know just how to explain it, son. But there's somethin' pressin' on his mind. Somethin' heavy. Yes, I guess Fred is sick, Lewis. Sick somewhere in his soul. He's not the same since he's been back.

LEWIS Mother, do you think maybe it's because . . . because of Annie?

ANNA (*softly*) That may be part of it, son. Fred loved that child more than anything else in the world, and when she died—especially with him away in Europe—I . . . I guess a part of him died, too. I know it's the same way with me.

LEWIS (*comfortingly*) Mother . . . Do you think maybe if *I* talked to him . . .

ANNA No, Lewis. Leave him alone. When he's ready to talk about it, he will. (*the door knocker sounds*) Lord-a-mussy! I been answerin' that door all day.

LEWIS You sit right down now, I'll get it. Probably another one of those subscribers. (*he goes to the door*)

ANNA All right, Lewis. If you need me I'll be back in the kitchen. (*she straightens up the newspapers and goes out left. The study door opens and* DOUGLASS *appears, ushering out* THEODORE TILTON)

DOUGLASS . . . and believe me, Mr. Tilton, it is with great reluctance that I must turn you down.

TILTON (*somewhat in annoyance*) Yes, and it is with great reluctance that I must leave without getting what I came for. (*stops and turns*) You know, Douglass, the first time we met I was impressed, greatly impressed. Completely aside from considerations of race, I thought: "Here is a man of whom the whole nation should be proud!" And now I find you here, twiddling your thumbs, as it were, sulking in the wake of your exile because of this Harper's Ferry business—

DOUGLASS   Mr. Tilton, it is well known that I was not present at Harper's Ferry. Perhaps I should have been, but the fact of it is I had no part in the matter.

TILTON   But do you deny you had dealings with John Brown? I was at the trial, I saw the letters and documents, I—

DOUGLASS   (*electrified*) You were at the trial?!!

TILTON   Why, yes. I covered the sessions personally for my paper...

DOUGLASS   Then you saw John Brown before—before...

TILTON   Yes, Mr. Douglass. I was there.

DOUGLASS   Tell me... Tell me, Mr. Tilton. I... (*he indicates a chair.* TILTON *sits*)

TILTON   (*solemnly*) The old man was quite a brave soul. His conduct and deportment during the trial were commendable—even the prosecution had the greatest respect for him, you could tell... Of course, they did rush things a bit. Brown's wounds hadn't healed before they dragged him into court... But his mind was clear and his tongue quite sharp. When the counsel they appointed to him tried to introduce a plea of insanity, he rejected it himself, told the court in booming tones that he considered it a "miserable artifice and pretext," and he viewed such a motion with contempt... And then, after the verdict, when they asked him if he had anything to say... he rose erect, though it must have pained him terribly to do so... and he said—

DOUGLASS   (*staring into space*) "... had I so interfered in behalf of the rich, the powerful, the so-called great... every man in this Court would have deemed it an act worthy of reward. To have interfered in behalf of His despised poor, I did no wrong, but right."

TILTON   (*nods his head*) It was... well, little short of magnificent.

DOUGLASS (*whispers*) John!...

TILTON   I tried to get to see him afterwards. But they kept him under heavy guard, barred all visitors except his wife....

DOUGLASS   Mary... Poor Mary.

TILTON   President Buchanon ordered a detachment of federal troops in to guard the town, three hundred strong, under Colonel Robert E. Lee—he's quite famous now, you know, they say he'll be made a general for sure. All Charlestown became an armed camp... the army troops, State Militia with cannon, volunteers, even fresh-faced cadets from Virginia Military Institute. Ha!—every so often some young fool would cry out, shoot at a branch in the dark, and the whole lot of them would scurry around in the night like terrified idiots!

DOUGLASS   And... then?

TILTON   (*starts to speak, then rises, shaking his head*) I cannot talk about it. I'd never seen a hanging before, and I hope to God I shall never see one again. (*turns*) But you, Douglass...

DOUGLASS   Don't... don't. (*to himself*) I know the old man was wrong, but I should have gone with him anyway... Sheilds! Did you see Sheilds Green? The Negro they called the Emperor?

TILTON   No. I did not stay for the other trials. But, of course, you know...

DOUGLASS   (*turns away*) Yes, I know.

TILTON   When I learned you were back from England, it excited me! Here is a man so brave, that even with the shadow of a congressional investigation stalking him, he comes home to continue the fight—I must have articles, a whole series of writings from this man for my paper, I said! And then your letter, turning me down...

DOUGLASS   You give me more credit than I am due, Mr. Tilton. I came home at this time only because of death in the family.

TILTON   Oh, I'm sorry to hear that. But still, why not back to the struggle?

DOUGLASS   (*evasively*) I... need time to think, I—If I could have brought my family to England I might have stayed there.... Slavery ... this whole situation, Mr. Tilton... Frankly, I'm beginning to think it's... hopeless.

TILTON   (*stunned*) Hopeless...? Hopeless...? (*begins with sadness and builds toward anger*) So... The great Frederick Douglass creeps home, tail between his legs? The man who argued so bravely that the philosophy of reforms lies in earnest struggle is tired of struggling himself. "If there is no struggle, there is no progress," he says. "Those who profess to favor freedom, and yet depreciate agitation, are men who want crops without plowing up the ground. They want rain without thunder and lightning... the ocean without the roar of its many waters." And now this sterling writer, this august philosopher declares the situation hopeless. He writes words of fiery revolution to others, and after he persuades them *he* sinks to the ground, exhausted and faint!

DOUGLASS (*stiffly*) So... you read my paper?

TILTON Every issue you sent me! And I must say I was taken in like a perfect fool. Even started echoing your sentiments on the editorial pages of my own paper, causing me to lose circulation by the thousand and forcing me into debt to raise funds for its continued existence. Hah! And now I find my inspiration, my dauntless messiah has lost his faith. Behold...! He heals the blind, and when they see enough to follow him, lo! the man is blind himself!

DOUGLASS (*calling a halt*) Mr. Tilton! (*turns away*)

TILTON (*emotion subsiding*) No matter, no matter!... The newly enlightened will carry aloft the brazier even if it does burn the hands a bit. As a matter of fact, I shall be surprised when I reach New York if my plant is still standing.

DOUGLASS Why so?

TILTON (*smiles*) Oh, I'm quite the radical abolitionist these days, you should see! I've passionately eulogized John Brown, attacked the federal government as a pro-slavery bunch of horse-thieves, and called President Buchanon a pig-headed ass in inch-high headlines on the front page! Oh, you should see the stack of law-suits filed against me.

DOUGLASS You are either very brave or very foolish.

TILTON Who cares—I've been having fun! (*impishly*) And besides, I'm right. Why, have you ever taken a close look at a picture of Buchanon's face?... But I see you are in no mood for jest. Well, can't say I haven't tried. No harsh feelings, I hope?

DOUGLASS No. No, of course not. (*there is a knock at the door. Presently* ANNA *appears going to answer it*)

TILTON I'll be going now. Got to get back down and start beating the drums for the election campaign. If you should change your mind, and decide to help me make a little music, don't hesitate to join the band, eh?

DOUGLASS If I should, I'll let you know—

TILTON No—no, no promises now one way or the other. If you come to the point where you must, you will. (ANNA *comes on with* GEORGE CHATHAM) Well... Chatham!

CHATHAM (*carries an odd-shaped bundle which he leaves in the hallway*) Mr. Tilton! Why, I didn't know you were in town. Hello, Frederick.

DOUGLASS Hello, George.

TILTON I didn't expect to be, but I ran up on a little editorial business. How's Ellen and the girls?

CHATHAM Oh, fine, just fine. You're not leaving, are you? I just—

TILTON Yes, I'm afraid I must. My mission was fruitless and I must go on back. What's the latest on the convention, have you heard?

CHATHAM Yes, they've just finished the second ballot and are getting ready for a third. Our man Seward's still leading. Perhaps he'll take it on the next ballot.

ANNA And how about Lincoln? I thought he was pressin' pretty hard.

CHATHAM Oh, I wouldn't give him a second thought. He's gained a few votes, true, but they'd never be so stupid as to nominate such an idiot!

TILTON Well, Lincoln might not be as bad as we expect. He has already distinguished himself in debate with Stephen Douglas, and as for the "rump" candidate, Breckinridge, I don't think we'll have to worry much about him. So pluck up, George!

CHATHAM Well, if they do nominate Lincoln, I shall have the greatest difficulty in resigning myself to the necessity of supporting him, hayseeds and all. Why the man's simply impossible! "Honest Abe" they call him. Sounds like a used carriage dealer.

TILTON Now, now, George. Just because the man is not of solid New England Abolitionist stock is no reason to give him up for lost. He may prove his worth, in time.

CHATHAM (*hands together*) Let us pray...

TILTON (*laughs*) On that, I'll take my leave! Goodbye, Chatham. (*bows*) Mrs. Douglass. (*to* DOUGLASS, *who starts to see him out*) No, that's all right, I can find my way to the door. And Douglass!... (*extends his hand—sincerely*) I'm leaving my first drummer's chair open. Just in case... (*with a wave of the hand he is off, escorted to the door by* ANNA)

CHATHAM (*smiling*) What's all this, Frederick? Are you going in for musicianship these days?

DOUGLASS No... No, George. I'm afraid I'd play out of tune. Now, what have you come to see me about?

CHATHAM Well, two things, really. The first I think you already have some idea of.

DOUGLASS (*turning away*) Yes. Yes, I know.

CHATHAM Then what is it, Frederick? Yesterday at your office I asked you to join with us in our rally tonight at Corinthian Hall. But tonight I hear you have tendered your regrets. Is this true, Frederick?

DOUGLASS Yes. It's true.

CHATHAM But Frederick! Why are you refusing us now, when we need you most? We haven't had so good a chance in years to upset the slave-holders' stranglehold on the Presidency. We have to stir up all the support we can get.

DOUGLASS I know all that, George, you don't have to—

CHATHAM Then you'll do it, Frederick? The whole town will be so glad to see you. You know, you've become quite a celebrity since you've been gone.

DOUGLASS Oh. And why?

CHATHAM Why? Why, you ask! Why, because l'affaire John Brown has captured the hearts and imaginations of the whole North! It's fired the flame of liberty and turned many a pussyfooting ne'er-do-well into an ardent Abolitionist! John Brown's gallows has become a cross. And all Rochester is proud to know that you helped him, that you believed in him when other less hardy souls failed him. That you had to flee the screaming, anguished wrath of the Virginia slavers because of your part in the undertaking.

DOUGLASS (*stricken*) Is that what people think?!!

CHATHAM Why, you're a hero, man! Rochester's own representative in John Brown's great venture.

DOUGLASS George... ! George... (*suddenly*) I cannot speak for you tonight. That's all.

CHATHAM But Frederick. I told the Rally Committee I'd come here personally, and—

DOUGLASS (*curtly*) You should have consulted me before making any such promise.

CHATHAM (*at first, taken aback. Then, challenging*) Frederick... what's wrong.

DOUGLASS Wrong? Why—I'm tired... I haven't been feeling too well, lately. Yes, I've been ill.

CHATHAM Frederick... we've been friends for a long time. Ever since you first came to Rochester and started your paper.

DOUGLASS Please! Please, George, I'd be the first to admit that I owe you a great deal, but don't try to use that to force me to do something I am not agreed to doing.

CHATHAM That's not it at all, Frederick! I meant that I had come to believe the two of us could sit down and talk openly and fairly with each other. But it is hardly honorable of you, is it, to hide behind such a paltry excuse? You, who have braved storms and mobs and defied death itself in bringing your message to the people?

DOUGLASS (*turns to him*) George, I cannot speak for you. I can no longer stand upon a platform and address an audience as I have in the past.

CHATHAM Why, Douglass, you're one of the ablest public speakers I've ever known.

DOUGLASS Able or not, I am not worthy.

CHATHAM Not worthy? Why, who—if not you, of all people—who can lay claim to greater right?

DOUGLASS I have forfeited my right! I have failed to live up to the confidence placed in me.

CHATHAM Douglass!... You're talking in riddles!

(DOUGLASS *turns despairingly, and starts into his study. His hand freezes on the doorknob, then, resignedly, he closes the door and turns again to face* CHATHAM)

DOUGLASS George... you mentioned that the people of Rochester think of me as a hero, their own representative in John's great venture. You know as well as I do that it isn't true.

CHATHAM Frederick, I have always known you to be a man of the highest dedication to the cause of liberty, and—

DOUGLASS We're not talking about past reputation, George, and we cannot base supposed fact upon such schoolboy idealism as dedication to a cause! The question is: was I or was I not an accomplice of John Brown in his raid on Harper's Ferry on October 16, 1859?

CHATHAM Listen, Frederick, I—

DOUGLASS Why, you have me sailing under false colors, cloaked by the public imagination in a role of glory that is as false to me as if I played Romeo upon the stage. (*turns*) Shall I tell you the truth of the matter? Shall I—

CHATHAM But Frederick, I don't see—

DOUGLASS Well, I'll tell you whether you want to hear it or not! (*he wheels about and paces, the Prosecuting Attorney, his own conscience on trial*) George, that night after you and Sanborn and the others left, John told me he was going on with it, that he was going to start at Harper's Ferry. I argued against it, but in vain. When he implored me to go with him, I told him I thought it was more important for me to speak and to write, to stay alive for my people, than to take the chance of dying with him at Harper's Ferry. And so I let him go, alone—except for Sheilds Green ... But George ... I have discovered that it is possible for a man to make a right decision, and then be tormented in spirit the rest of his life because he did not make the wrong one. There are times when the soul's need to unite with men in splendid error tangles agonizingly with cold wisdom and judgement ... Then in London, when the news came ... how brave the old man was ... how steadfastly he refused to name or implicate anyone ... how he died upon the gallows, it came to me in a rush that John, in his way, had succeeded! In splendid error he had startled the sleeping conscience of the nation and struck a blow for freedom that proves stronger every hour. And now you come to me and ask me to play the hero. To accept the plaudits of the crowd for my "gallant alliance" with a man who was wrong in life, but in death has scored a victory—a victory you propose me to take the bows for.

CHATHAM Frederick, you must hear me—

DOUGLASS Don't you see, George, that I cannot do it! John believed in his mission and however wrong he was he gave his life for it. But what have I done, except talk about it—I who have *been* a slave!

CHATHAM (*rising*) Frederick, you're torturing yourself! Don't—

DOUGLASS I will not go on masquerading as a crusader, a leader of my people, a brave warrior for human rights!

CHATHAM Will you stop a moment and listen!

DOUGLASS You are in the presence of a fraud! I resumed publishing my paper because I must feed my family, but do not believe that I can stand on a platform and look an audience in the eyes with this burning inside me: "*Are you afraid to face a gun?!!*"

CHATHAM (*takes* DOUGLASS *forcibly by the arm—shouts*) Frederick, I demand that you be quiet! (DOUGLASS *grasps the back of a chair, his energy spent.* CHATHAM *speaks gently*) That's it. Listen. There is a second reason I came to see you tonight, Frederick. It is to fulfill a request.

DOUGLASS (*wearily, as in delerium*) Request ... request ... what kind of request?

CHATHAM (*as he secures his package from the hallway*) Early this winter I made a trip to North Elba. There, by a great boulder in which he himself once carved the letters "J. B." is where they buried Captain Brown. I talked to his widow, Mary, a proud, fierce-eyed woman whose composure made me half ashamed of my tears. When she learned I was from Rochester, she gave me something to give to you, Frederick. (*he takes the package to the sofa*) I told her you were in England, but she smiled and said you would be back. You had a job to do, she said, and she knew you would be back to finish it. (*he undoes the canvas and withdraws a tarnished old musket and a torn, bespattered American flag*) She asked me to give these to you personally, Frederick. That John wanted you to have them. (*he carries the musket to* DOUGLASS, *who slowly reaches out for it, then suddenly cringes, folding his hands*)

DOUGLASS His ... musket?

CHATHAM Yes ... (*he takes the musket back to the sofa and lays it down, carefully. Then picks up the flag and drapes it over the musket*) And the flag he carried with him to Harper's Ferry ... (*fumbles in his waistcoat*) He gave her a message for you, there in the prison, while he was waiting. (*withdraws a folded piece of paper*) Here.

DOUGLASS (*takes it slowly, and reads; barely audible*) "Tell Douglass I know I have not failed because he lives. Follow your own star, and someday unfurl my flag in the land of the free." (*he bows his head, his shoulders shaking silently. Then slowly, haltingly, he makes his way toward the sofa. Dimly, from a distance, comes the sound of the booming of a drum.* CHATHAM *goes to the hallway window and looks out. He turns and watches* DOUGLASS, *who, having reached the sofa, bends over to touch the flag and musket*)

CHATHAM (*softly*) It's nearly time for the rally, Frederick. They are marching from the square. (*comes to him*) Come, Frederick. Will you join us?

DOUGLASS (*quiet now. When he speaks his voice is steady*) You go on ahead, George. I'll be along in a moment.

CHATHAM (*understandingly*) All right. All right.

DOUGLASS But... I must tell them the truth. I did not go with John.

CHATHAM (*nods admiringly*) You tell them, Frederick. You tell them what you must. (*he goes to the hallway just as* LEWIS *comes rushing in from outside, where there is excitement in the air. The drum-beats are nearer and there are voices*)

LEWIS (*joyously*) They're coming! They're coming! It's a torchlight parade!

CHATHAM Well, let's see it, son! Let's see it!

LEWIS And the convention's decided. The candidate is chosen!

CHATHAM (*stops*) What! Who is it, Lewis?

LEWIS Lincoln!

CHATHAM (*astonished—roars like a wounded bull*) Lincoln?!! We cry out for a leader, a savior, a knight in shining armor! And who do they offer us? Barrabas! (ANNA *comes quickly down the stairs*)

ANNA Lord-a-mussy! What's goin' on out here!

CHATHAM It's a torch-light parade, Mrs. Douglass. Come! (*he guides* ANNA *and* LEWIS *out, then stops and turns for a moment, puffing his cheeks indignantly*) Lincoln!... (*he stomps out*)

(DOUGLASS *stands gazing down at the flag and musket. Outside the excitement has increased, and now a bright flicker of orange and yellow light dances in from the street, bathing the hallway with bobbing shafts of light. The booming drum is very near now, and amid the accompanying babble a voice cries,* "There's Fred Douglass's house!" *Another takes it up:* "Yeah, where is he?" *And another:* "We want Douglass!" *And now the others join in, shouting:* "We want Douglass! We want Douglass!" DOUGLASS *stirs and turns his head to listen.* ANNA *rushes back into the room excitedly*)

ANNA Fred! Where are you, Fred! They callin' for you! For you, Fred! (*she pauses upstage, arm extended*) Well, come on! They callin' for you!

DOUGLASS (*lifts his hand*) I'm coming, Anna. (ANNA *goes back off. A fife and drum corps has approached and now swings into* "Battle Hymn of the Republic," *and the voices take it up, singing:* "John Brown's body lies a-mould'ring in the grave..." DOUGLASS *picks up the flag. He folds it. He holds it against his breast for a moment. Then laying it over his arm, he draws himself to full height and strides manfully off to the door, as the curtain falls*)

Loften Mitchell (1919–)

Star of the Morning   1964

Loften Mitchell has chosen to dramatize twelve years in the life of the actor Bert Williams—1895 to 1907. These years are the ones in which the comedian met his partner George Walker, learned his trade, and established his talent in the American theater.

In 1895, black actors were emerging from fifty years of minstrel shows—whites in blackface and blacks in blackface. Rising prices, worn-out material, the development of the motion pictures, and the introduction of girls into revues all hurried the collapse of the minstrel show, but not before a number of black musicians and comics had learned their trade.

When Bert Williams met George Walker in San Francisco in 1895 the black musical commercial theater was entering a new form—a loose revue structure, with enough book not to be vaudeville, but with lots of music, particularly the new infectious ragtime.

The so-called Gay Nineties, a decade of lynchings, saw the Supreme Court make Jim Crow the law of the land with the *Plessy v. Ferguson* decision. In 1906, the Reverend Thomas Dixon adapted his novel *The Clansman* to the stage. The same ten years encompassed a series of shows written, acted, and often produced by blacks: Sam Jack's *Creole Show* (1890); Nat Salesbury's *Black America* (1895); S. H. Dudley's *Smart Set* (1896); A. J. Field's *Darkest America* (1897); J. A. Shipp's *Senegamian Carnival* (1898); Cook and Dunbar's *Clorindy; or, The Origin of the Cake Walk* (1898); Cole and Johnson's *A Trip to Coon Town* (1898); Walker and Williams' *Sons of Ham* (1899). In 1896 John Isham's *Oriental America* featured the first Negro troupe to play in a commercial Broadway theater *sans* hog fat and burnt cork—heretofore the black man's passport if he wished to appear in minstrelsy.

These shows and the ones that followed (until World War I) were transitional revues—between the darkey minstrels of the nineteenth century and the musicals of the 1920's. They demonstrated to audiences that the black man could present himself with or without dialect; could create new ethnic and nonethnic material, and could write America's only original music —ragtime and jazz. Without this fountainhead American musicals might still sound more like *The Merry Widow* and *Desert Song* than they now do. The fact that the black musicals of the *fin de siècle* were commonly called "Coon Shows" should not bring the reader to think that they were merely "Tom Shows" in ragtime.

Bert Williams was a well-educated West Indian who repeatedly spoke his mind to individuals and to the press. "This is the only civilization in all the world where a man's color makes a social difference, other matters being regarded as equal. . . in the United States, which fought four years for a certain principle, I am often treated with an air of personal and social condescension by the gentleman who sweeps out my dressing room." Some students may be puzzled about why this courageous man insisted on wearing blackface on stage until his death in 1922. *Star of the Morning* offers an explanation in terms of where America and the theater were in 1900. In recalling his first stage experience at the age of eighteen, Mr. Williams stated: "I wouldn't do blackface. Nothing could have induced me to. So I worked straight and made $8 a week for a whole year. I awoke to the fact that $8 wasn't conducive to clean linen so I went to work using black cork. I got $50 a week then." It is also possible that blackface was to Bert Williams what whiteface makeup was to Perriot the clown: a badge of his trade, a disguise from which to work, and a positive reminder to his audience that he was a black man. Many a critic wrote, like Heywood Broun, that Williams' comic art was raceless. Some insisted that his skin was nearly light enough to pass.

Bert Williams dreamed of a black theater in

1909 that was not possible. "The day is not far off when the traveling Negro dramatic company will come to town as often as the Negro musical company. The Negro actor will then take rank with the Negro teacher in the Negro school. . . .

With the development of the Negro actor will come the Negro playwright. . . . When we picture the Negro on stage we think of him singing, laughing, and cutting up. That seems his nature. But has it ever occurred to you that under this mask of smiles and this cloak of capers there is hidden dire tragedy?"

Beginning with *Sons of Ham*, Williams and Walker achieved wide recognition in 1902 with *In Dahomey*. They pyramided their success with *In Abyssinia* (1906) and *Bandana Land* (1908). Then George Walker became ill. Bert Williams was invited to join the Ziegfeld Follies; the entire Follies company went on strike. Finally they agreed that the black man could do a solo number. He did. He became the star of the Follies. He rarely received a bad review. A special postman was required to deliver his mail. His salary had jumped from $14 a week to $2,500. An admirer of Mr. Williams, Eddie Cantor recounts how Williams ordered a drink in a white New York bar. The bartender did not want to serve him. He said to Williams, " 'It will cost you $50 for one drink.'

Williams very quietly took out his billfold and laid a $500 bill on the bar. Then he said, 'Give me ten.' "

Some of the comic routines in *Star of the Morning* are taken from Bert Williams' own. However, the music and lyrics were written by musician Louis Mitchell and artist Romare Bearden. Loften Mitchell has kept the book close to the facts and the characters of history.

Mr. Mitchell has written a number of other history plays: the story of Afro-American theater (*Tell Pharaoh*), the theater life of Florence Mills (*Ballad of a Blackbird*), the history of the first blacks in New Amsterdam (*The Walls Came Tumbling Down*), and the story of the Reverend Joseph DeLaine's fight to end school segregation (*Land Beyond the River*). Professor Mitchell's *Black Drama, The Story of the American Negro in the Theatre* is a standard reference work.

Few plays are meant to be read; musicals least of all. Yet if the reader can find an old recording of "Come After Breakfast, Bring Your Own Lunch, and Leave Before Suppertime," and maybe locate a photo of Bert Williams costumed as a blackbird with tail feathers and top hat, he may grasp what Mr. Mitchell has intended for the production. *Star of the Morning* is a tribute to a great artist.

Star of the Morning

CAST OF CHARACTERS

BERT WILLIAMS
OLIVER JACKSON
JACK RIDGE
GEORGE WALKER
THEATER MANAGER
LOTTIE THOMPSON
JESSE SHIPP
ADA
HATTIE
MR. DUDLEY
CHARLIE
ABRAHAM ERLANGER
BELLE BLAZER
MEMBERS OF THE ENSEMBLE

The play is written to be performed on a ramped stage with the use of lights to assure fluidity of movement and continuity. At the rear of the stage is a large cyclorama that, depending upon the scene, is lighted accordingly. Four major parts make up the total setting: One large piece extends from extreme right and another from extreme left. These may meet in center and form a playing area above the lower stage level. These pieces may also be used separately for individual scenes. There should be a pair of steps leading to the upper level. Chairs and table placed as needed make up the fourth group of objects.

The on-stage action described in the play takes place in center. The wing-areas are at extreme right and extreme left.

The entire action of the play takes place during the latter part of the nineteenth century and the early part of the twentieth century.

ACT ONE

Scene One

(The scene is a San Francisco honky-tonk. The time is late one night in the year 1895.

The lights fade in slowly on this dark, smoke-filled, dimly-lit, crowded place. At the extreme right is a small room with a table and chair. The honky-tonk literally splashes across the remainder of the playing area. The entrance from the street is upstage, left.

A crowd of white patrons sit at the tables, drinking noisily. Loud voices, laughter and beer-spilling predominate. JACK RIDGE, *the proprietor, a short, plump, middle-aged, pleasant, white man, stands upstage near the door.*

BERT WILLIAMS *enters, walks through the small room out into the center of the honky-tonk. He has a banjo under his arm.* BERT *is nineteen years old, but he seems much older than his years. He is tall, well developed, quiet, reserved, somewhat reticent and a trifle supercilious, but not without humor. He is what is known as fair-skinned and wavy-haired, neatly dressed in a dark suit.*

BERT *plucks the banjo. There is a moment of silence from the crowd. He then plays a few bars of a sugary, sentimental Calypso-like melody. The crowd becomes restless)*

A MAN What the hell is this?
A WOMAN Come on, boy. Get hot! Get hot!
A MAN Get something, damn it!

(The others echo these remarks. BERT *freezes, bites his lips, sticks his banjo under his arm, turns and walks into the small room. He puts banjo on the table and sits, silently.* OLIVER JACKSON, *a tall, stocky, elderly Negro, well over sixty-five, steps into the back room. Despite his age, he is an agile man with movements much like those of a dancer. He goes directly to* BERT)

OLIVER What's wrong, Bert?
BERT They—want something I can't give them.
OLIVER I been saying it like a parrot: If you ain't got no beat, you liable to get beat.
BERT When life is full of cloud and rain,
And I am filled with naught but pain—

(OLIVER *starts to say something, stops.* RIDGE, *in the meantime, has stepped into centerstage. He holds up his hands to the noisy crowd*)

RIDGE Folks! Folks! Oliver Jackson says this boy's gonna be great! You got to give him a chance—

A MAN Gimmie a drink! I don't wants hear from you or him!

(*A roar of agreement from the crowd. Their voices drown out* RIDGE. GEORGE WALKER *steps inside the doorway. He is a small, thin, ragged black man, just about twenty years old. He is an active, quick-thinking young man with little formal training but with keen native intelligence. He goes directly to* RIDGE)

GEORGE Mister, I'm hungry. I need a job and—(*more noise*) Mister, I can stop 'em.

RIDGE Who the hell are you?

GEORGE Nash Walker. George Nash Walker. I sing and dance some. (*he cuts a few steps*)

RIDGE Well, start! (*calling out*) Williams!

OLIVER Ridge's calling you. You get out there and ring that banjo!

RIDGE (*as* OLIVER *practically pushes* BERT *forward*) Play for this boy—George Walker.

(BERT *confers with* GEORGE. *Now* GEORGE *steps into center-stage, smiles. The crowd looks at him, then sits, silently as* BERT *accompanies him on the Banjo. He sings*)

GEORGE And when it rains, the rain is a refrain
Right on that beat from Golden Gate to Maine—
Who can explain it?
It's vain to disdain it,
So hear me while I explain it:

Follow the beat whenever you hear it!
Follow the beat—listen and get with it.
I repeat: Folks, always follow the beat!
Follow the beat whenever you feel it—
Follow the beat—no one can conceal it.
I repeat: Folks, neatly follow the beat!
Da Da Da Dee Dum—one, two, three, four! Once more!
Da Da Da Dee Dum—you have felt it before!
Follow the beat—listen and get with it—
I repeat: Be discreet, lift your feet,
Life's complete!
Folks, always follow the beat!

(*By the end of the song, the crowd is applauding*)

MAN Yeah! Dance, black boy! (BERT *slaps the banjo, angrily, with open palm, then glares at the man.* OLIVER *rushes to* BERT)

OLIVER Now, don't go getting all touch-us.

GEORGE No. 'Cause I'm hungry.

(BERT *controls himself then pours his anger into his playing. The music becomes furious and driving.* GEORGE *dances until he becomes weak and tired.* OLIVER *steps forward and joins him. They perform a number of intricate steps as* BERT *accompanies them. Now,* OLIVER *takes* GEORGE *by the arm and they dance off into the small room.* BERT *follows them. The crowd is applauding, wildly.* BERT *takes* GEORGE's *arm, leads him back into the honky-tonk. He bows as does* GEORGE, *then they return to the small room.* GEORGE *slumps into chair.* OLIVER *pats* GEORGE *on the back, then goes offstage*)

BERT Excellent! Excellent!

GEORGE Thanks.

(*In the meantime the crowd is beginning to leave the place.* RIDGE *is at the doorway, bidding people Goodnight.* OLIVER *steps back into the small room with a tray of food. He places this before* GEORGE. *There are four cups of coffee on this tray*)

OLIVER Look what the cook left. (GEORGE *begins to eat, savagely.* OLIVER *gives* BERT *a cup of coffee, takes one for himself and gives one to* RIDGE *as the last of the crowd leaves*)

RIDGE You got a job, Walker! Three dollars a week. Start tomorrow night.

GEORGE Thanks, Mister. Thanks—

RIDGE (*with coffee*) That the only clothes you got?

GEORGE Yes, sir. They was good, but riding the rails ain't no good for a suit or the body that's in one . . .

RIDGE You got to show up looking decent. (GEORGE *continues eating.* RIDGE *smiles*) Be careful you don't eat the plate.

GEORGE I won't. This sure is good of you.

OLIVER Oh, Mr. Ridge is good. Long as I been working here, I never was scared of fire, 'cause I knowed if my place burned down, he'd let me sleep in his stable. (BERT *laughs.* RIDGE *looks at him, turns to* OLIVER)

RIDGE Oliver, I'll bet your Master was glad when slavery ended.

OLIVER He sure was, 'cause that lye I was putting in his coffee was eating his insides out. (RIDGE *nearly spits coffee on himself.* OLIVER *asks,*

innocently) Something wrong, Mr. Ridge?
RIDGE No. Nothing. I just remembered—I've got to close up the rest of the place. (*and he rushes out*)
GEORGE Nice man.
OLIVER Yeah, but sometimes you got to straighten him. First night I walk in here, he says to me, says: "Boy, you mighty old for night work." I says: "I ain't too old to muzzle you, puppy dog!"
BERT You told him—that???
OLIVER Well—it's what I woulda told him if I'd a got a chance. Play with a puppy and he'll mistake you for a pole. (*then*) Time to move on.
BERT Thanks for everything, Mr. Jackson. And good luck to you and the Touring Minstrels.
GEORGE (*impressed*) You going with *them*?
OLIVER They sent for me. Train tickets and all. (*holds up tickets*)
GEORGE That what train tickets look like?
OLIVER Yeah. They call it success when you can ride in style. Right now I'm rich with the smell of success.
GEORGE (*looks at his clothing*) I ain't sure that's success you smelling right now.
BERT Mr. Jackson, if they need anyone else—
OLIVER Not you.
BERT But, you told me—
OLIVER That you got talent. I sure did. But, you got something else, too. You think you a man in a house where they and some of us think we boys.
GEORGE That's what I been called all my days.
OLIVER Ain't no successs in going with Minstrels nohow. Back there when I was a slave, it was, though. You know what Minstrels was, boy? We did 'em on the plantation to poke fun at Old Master. We got that house Negro to stand up and say: "Gentlemen, be seated!" Then we'd line up with Tams and Bones as the end men.
BERT Tams and Bones?
OLIVER That was the instruments they played. You think we could afford pianos? (*remembering and reenacting*) We used to take off on that house Negro 'cause he was the Master up and down. (*imitating Tams*) Tams would say: "Mistah Stafford, do darkies go to heaven?" (*moves over, imitates Bones*) Old Bones would say: "Yes, suh, Mistah Stafford, do us darkies go to heaven?" (*moves back, imitates the house Negro*) House Negro would say: "Now, why would you darkies be going to heaven? That's for white folks!" (*imitates Tams*) Tams would say: "We just wanted to know who opens them Pearly Gates for white folks to get inside!" (BERT *and* GEORGE *roar with laughter at his antics.* OLIVER *stops now and becomes serious*) That's how it *was*. Then white folks come from up north and copied what we was doing. They made me a fool and now I got to go out here and make money laughing at me!
BERT Mr. Jackson—
OLIVER Ain't no success no kinda way. You all ever see greens growin'?
BERT Greens?
OLIVER Collard greens. They come up, bunched together. Some get tall and you got to pull up the small ones. Night-times we slaves used to sit on the cabin floor, rubbing our backs 'caused they ached from pulling up small greens. One real old slave, a preaching man, always talked about how much smarter it'd be if we planted different so all the greens could grow tall. I didn't know what he meant so one night he took me outdoors and pointed up to the stars, the bright stars, and showed me how they could all shine together 'cause the Good Lord had planted them right. (*then*) That's what success is, boys: Planting right. (OLIVER *turns, quickly, goes out*)
GEORGE Lord Jesus! Colored folks ain't even happy when they oughta be!
BERT No one is happy in America, but everyone pretends he is.
GEORGE Watch that stuff! I'm an American.
BERT Yes. I know. You get enough to eat?
GEORGE I ain't never got enough to eat or wear in all my life. (*quickly*) What I had's all right for now, thanks.
BERT I don't mean to be forward. I have an old suit. My mother can cut it down for you.
GEORGE Sa-ay, thanks. We gonna be friends after all.
BERT Why shouldn't we?
GEORGE I thought you was real proper. Where you from?
BERT Antigua. British West Indies.
GEORGE An—what??? That sounds further'n Kansas.
BERT It is.

GEORGE Hope it ain't no worse.
BERT It was nice—till my father took sick. We moved here for his health.
GEORGE You could say I come here for mine, too. And I aim to stay.
BERT I don't. Someday I'll return and buy our old house. Then I'll sit there on that mountainside and figure out why I'm here.
GEORGE (*curiously*) You don't know why you here? I'm here 'cause this man's gonna pay me three dollars a week!
BERT For that matter I'm here because I couldn't afford Leland Stanford University. Without formal training there are only menial jobs for us.
GEORGE You doing something high-class 'round here now?
BERT No. I'm singing, mimicking, playing the banjo. Temporarily. (*then, animated*) But, when I speak of being here, I mean *really* being here. On this earth. John Stuart Mill said man's in an early stage of development. He hoped for the day we could ease our burdens and pursue intellectual things—
GEORGE Say—you not only talk funny, but what you say is funny.
BERT (*stops, suddenly, picks up banjo*) I live 15 Chestnut. You may come by in the morning for the suit.
GEORGE Wait a minute! I hurt your feelings. (BERT *shakes his head*) I did, too. Don't be mad.
BERT Why must you Americans insult a man then tell him how to react to it?
GEORGE I'm sorry. I oughtn't a done that. But, you treated me like I'm real dumb and—
BERT I did not say you are dumb. You have good basic intelligence—
GEORGE You signifying on me, man? I know what base means.
BERT I am not going to stay here and argue with you.
GEORGE Please don't go! (*he is subdued.* BERT *looks at him*) Oh, I am dumb! Real dumb to be 'way out here, hungry. (*walks away, sits*) It wasn't supposed to be like this. Told Mama I was gonna make us rich—that I was gonna buy me a new suit of clothes for every day I went raggedy—which is a heep of days. Never gonna do if off'n three dollars a week.
BERT (*goes to him, awkwardly, trying to console him*) Now, look—this is temporary. An early stage of development. Later—the train ride. (GEORGE *stares at him*) You think I'm—silly?
GEORGE I think you smart as hell! (*suddenly, on his feet*) We oughta team up! We can do big things! You be my straight man and—(*stops*) Only, you look funnier'n me.
BERT What's funny about me?
GEORGE That awkward way of yourn. We'll put some burnt cork on you and—
BERT No, sir.
GEORGE And we'll take you to a Baptist Church where you can learn to talk right.
BERT I'm an Anglican.
GEORGE What the hell is that?
BERT The Church of England. They call it the Episcopal Church here.
GEORGE Never mind all that. Do they shout?
BERT Hardly.
GEORGE Don't say "hardly." Say "No, suh, indeed."
BERT "No, suh, indeed."
GEORGE Quit interrupting! (*paces, excitedly*) We gonna stay here a while and get known. I'm gonna pester every booking agent 'round here till they know Williams and Walker is hotter'n fire. We gonna get booked into theaters so fancy that folks will have to wear their Sunday clothes to get inside to see us! (BERT *toys with banjo*) You ain't even listening!
BERT I am. I play the banjo when I'm thinking.
GEORGE Where was I?
BERT We just played to folks in their Sunday clothes.
GEORGE And we're getting ten dollars a week. (*taps, emphatically.* BERT *hits banjo*) Then, fifteen! (*taps again. Another note*) Twenty-five! (*another tap. Another note*) Fifty dollars a week—a piece! (GEORGE *taps, then sails into the air.* BERT *looks at him, tucks banjo under his arm*) Folks gonna know us in Chicago, New York, England—*and* Europe.
BERT We travel quickly.
GEORGE We gonna make so much money we won't have time to spend it.
BERT (*ringing the banjo*) Talk on! We'll find a way! (*they shake hands, smiling.* RIDGE *steps back into the room*)
RIDGE Well, boys—time to call it a night.
BERT You know, if you studied the human anatomy, you'd discover a remarkable difference between a boy and a man. (RIDGE *looks at*

him. GEORGE *grabs* BERT's *arm, cautioning him. Slowly, a grin appears on* BERT's *face—an all-too-patient, understanding grin. He lapses into a sing-song, rhythmic pattern)* Yas, suh, boss. Ah didn't mean to be cross—
Lawd, shut my mouf 'bout dis sad nation
So Ah can be shut off from dis trial and tribulation!

(GEORGE *and* BERT *lock arms and start out, almost strutting.* RIDGE *looks after them, puzzled. He shrugs his shoulders, turns and blows out the lamp. The lights fade as the music rises)*

Scene Two

(*A Milwaukee theater. One month later.*
The lights fade in on a scrim. On it we see a theater marquee. It reads: "Milwaukee Theater: Four Big Acts: Belle Blazer. The Strutting Jugglers. Dandy and Candy, dance stylists. Williams and Walker Comedy Team."
LOTTIE THOMPSON *and* JESSE SHIPP *enter and look at the marquee.* LOTTIE *is a pleasant, attractive, well-groomed young lady with an air that is decidedly nontheatrical. She is honest, straightforward, utterly lacking in grand gestures and poses.*
JESSE *is a tall, thin, intelligent young Negro, smartly dressed in the style of the period.* LOTTIE *points to the marquee)*

LOTTIE   Here they are, Jesse. Williams and Walker.
JESSE   Oliver Jackson said catch their act. He didn't say what we'd have to go through to catch them. Talent hunting is damned expensive!
LOTTIE   If these are our men, it'll all be worthwhile. Let's go—

(*They move into the shadows. The lights come up in centerstage. Framing this center area we find two vaudeville cards: "Milwaukee Theater: Williams and Walker Comedy Team."*
The THEATER MANAGER, *a tall white man, stands in what represents the theater wings beside an old trunk.* GEORGE *and* BERT *march into the center area. Both have rolls of bills and they count)*

GEORGE   Ten. Twenty. Thirty. Forty. Fifty. One hundred! Count yours.
BERT (*counting*)   One—
GEORGE   One what??? (*snatches bill from* BERT) Where the hell did you get that one dollar bill? (*rips it to shreds*) Man, as long as you know me, don't you ever be caught with no damn one dollar bill!
BERT (*picking up pieces*)   You shouldn't a done that. (*singing*)

When all my luck has turned out bad
And I am weary, blue and sad,
The only friend I's ever had
Was my last dollar!
Now, I ain't never been low-down—
I's been the honest man in town,
But when I'm broke I never frown
At my last dollar!
But what you ain't got, you can't get.
I ain't paid nothin' on no debt
'Cause all I gets is sympathy
From all the folks who asks 'bout me.
When I'm feelin' down and out
And I am just about give out,
There ain't no one to fight my bout
But my last dollar!

(*He has picked up the pieces of the torn dollar. Now he counts out his other money, sticks this in his pocket, tips his hat to* GEORGE *and shuffles from the stage.* GEORGE *follows him out into the wing area. The* THEATER MANAGER's *face registers his disapproval.* GEORGE *bends, picks up one end of the trunk.* BERT *picks up the other end. The* MANAGER *places a bill in* GEORGE's *hand.* BERT *and* GEORGE *leave with the trunk. The* MANAGER *looks after them, shakes his head. The vaudeville cards flip. They now read: "Belle Blazer, Song Stylist." An attractive white woman appears in center stage and we hear applause from the audience. She sings:)*

BELLE (*singing*)

They call it love and from birth until we die,
I'll love him so and I know that I know why.
Though love's a game for fools they claim,
Played by none who have won.
They call it love, no other word will do.
I'll love him so and I know he loves me, too.
The world's a stage for clown and sage,
And love's the play to be done.
When he smiles, my heart leaps
Though I tell it to be still.
All the while my soul keeps measuring my every thrill.
They call it love, no other word will do—
I'll love him so, though our days of joy are few—
It's all the same in any game,
They'll always call it love!

Star of the Morning

(*As the song ends, the lights fade* LOTTIE *and* JESSE *are in the wing area. They approach the* THEATER MANAGER)

JESSE We're looking for Williams and Walker.

MANAGER They've gone. I sent them away to keep them from going to jail.

LOTTIE To jail. For what?

MANAGER For robbing people of their damn money, their damn time and their God damned patience! (*the lights fade out quickly*)

Scene Three

(*The scene is a freight car. Late night of that same day.*

This scene is played on the lower level. The train's sliding door is in the ramp. It is partially open and occasional light from the countryside homes slips through the doorway opening. BERT *is sitting, trying to read a book by the slivers of light.* GEORGE *is on the floor nearby, trying to sleep.*

The train whistle blows. Light streams into the freight car and into GEORGE's *eyes. He jumps up, goes to the door and slams it shut*)

GEORGE How can you be reading at a time like this?

BERT I can't now. You blocked out the light. (*the train sweeps around a curve.* GEORGE *is thrown half-way across the car.* BERT *reaches up and grabs him, preventing his falling*)

GEORGE Good Lord!

BERT We turned a curve. Are you all right?

GEORGE Yeah. Thanks. (*he sits*)

BERT In the West Indies they speak of America's luxurious train service. Apparently not enough West Indians have ridden trains here.

GEORGE Not this kind in this way. What was that man's name? Oliver Jackson?

BERT Yes.

GEORGE He said, walk together and we gonna find some train tickets. We been walking together, all right—from one job to the next!

BERT We didn't walk in Omaha.

GEORGE No. Them white folks run hell outa us.

BERT I didn't think we were any worse than the other performers.

GEORGE The audience did.

BERT (*as* GEORGE *stretches out again*) George—I've been thinking: There may be something wrong with our act. We've worked exactly two weeks in the last two months.

GEORGE I can count.

BERT I didn't say you couldn't.

GEORGE You mighta been thinking it. (*then*) Our act ain't funny, that's what's wrong. Them folks got notions 'bout what's funny and when you get out there, acting all proper like, we end up not eating proper—and riding freight cars!

BERT George—our people's faces are black, beautiful. I will not ridicule them by wearing burnt cork.

GEORGE Others do it. And they work regularly.

BERT My father's plantation workers worked regularly, too. And no one knew their names. My father depended upon me to remember each worker. He didn't want to pay the same man twice. (*he laughs.* GEORGE *gives a mocking laugh*)

GEORGE I could laugh, too, if I wasn't weak from not eating.

BERT Listen—Man gets smaller each year. When he came out of darkness, he saw a ray of light and thought he was the center of things. Along came Galileo, Newton, Copernicus. Man found this earth's a tiny part of a large universe—and he's a speck of dust.

GEORGE This speck here is so hungry his stomach is playing tag with his backbone.

BERT A man has only his identity. He's a fool to lose it behind a false face. (*then*) Art must represent truth. I've been reading of Ahmed Baba and the learned men of Timbucktu, of Pietro who captained one of Columbus' ships, of Crispus Attucks and Salem Poor and Toussaint and Douglass and Banneker.

GEORGE Who the hell are they?

BERT Great black men whose lives we should portray on the stage. That's why we should be in the theater—to tell their truths, not lies about their ancestors!

GEORGE Will we eat if we do?

BERT (*exasperated*) Avarice will be the death of you Americans!

GEORGE I wish I had the energy to pronounce words like that.

BERT Avarice—

GEORGE Does that mean eating?

BERT Listen—we'll eat when we get to Chicago.

GEORGE With what??

BERT I don't know. Something will turn up. Meantime, we should give serious consideration to putting on stage the truthful history of the black man in this hemisphere—

GEORGE (*annoyed*) Ohhhh!

BERT What's wrong, George?

GEORGE There's nothing wrong! Nothing! (*angrily*) What you think? We been fired in Los Angeles and Omaha and Milwaukee—and you ask me what's wrong?... It don't bother you, does it? No—'cause you can read a book or fly off into the clouds. Well, man, I can't do it 'cause I got to make something and fast! You hear me? I got to get so big in this business that that there theater in Lawrence, Kansas will beg me, beg me to come home and play there. I got to be so big I'll be able to tell them: No! No, *Mister* George Walker ain't playing there 'cause when I was shining shoes outside your door, you wouldn't let me in! I got to tell 'em: You made my mother cry—made her cry 'cause I asked her to take me to that theater and she had to tell me: "Son, we can't go in them places!" (*then*) Oh, what'm I wasting words on you for? Read your book!

BERT George—don't talk like that. Don't get discouraged. Remember: This is the early stage of development. Later—the real train ride. (*the whistle blows. He goes, opens the sliding door and light seeps in*) That's Chicago, George. A big city! Look out there at the dawn breaking over the lake. The waves are rolling into the city, but the city's standing there, rising up like a mighty mountain, not moving. It looks like we're riding in on the lake waves and the dawn. And nothing's going to stop us—not even that mountain of a city! We're going to make it here, George! We're going to make it! (*he stands there, swerving just a little as the train whistle shrieks, loudly. His feet are planted firmly now. The music rises and the lights fade out*)

Scene Four

(*The Chicago Theater. Two days later.*

The lights fade in on a marquee which shows the theater name and headliners. Included we find "*Ada and Hattie: Dance Team*" *and* "*Williams and Walker Comedy Team.*"

LOTTIE THOMPSON *and* JESSE SHIPP *appear beneath the marquee.* LOTTIE *takes some money from her pocketbook*)

LOTTIE I'll pay this time, Jesse.

JESSE Wait. Don't pay. Let's wait in the alley and meet them as they're being bounced.

LOTTIE Don't be silly. They're going to hit it big someday, Jesse.

JESSE I hope it's soon. I'm going broke following them around.

(*They move off into the darkness. Now the lights come up and we see* ADA *and* HATTIE, *two attractive black women, performing a dance routine in center stage. They are framed by vaudeville cards which identify them by name. At the extreme right we see the wing area where* MR. DUDLEY, *manager, stands, watching* ADA *and* HATTIE. *This large, fat, middle-aged white man chews on his cigar, approvingly as the dancers conclude their number and move off into the wing area.*

GEORGE *steps into the wing area, preparing to go on stage. He meets* ADA *and* HATTIE *as they dance off.* GEORGE *looks at* ADA)

GEORGE Yum-yum-yum! You can play the same bill with me any day!

HATTIE Lord! Who hired you? You know the Man ain't letting more than two of us work one place at the same time!

DUDLEY Hey, you, Walker! You hired to do a show back here or out there?

GEORGE Oh! Yes, sir! (*and he rushes towards the onstage area.* ADA *looks after him, draws a deep breath*)

ADA He's cute!

HATTIE (*grabs her arm*) Come on, starry eyes! He's after your job, not your loving!

(*She pulls* ADA *completely off stage. The music has now become low and mournful. The vaudeville cards flip and we see:* "*Chicago Theater: Williams and Walker Comedy Team.*" BERT *enters from stage right, neatly dressed, banjo in hand.* GEORGE *enters from stage, left. In center stage they pass without seeing each other. This action is obviously designed to create laughter by suggesting that both men are so dark-complexioned that they cannot be seen. It fails because* BERT *is without blackface.*

Both men leave the stage, then return with lamps. They meet in center stage, hold up the lamps to each other's faces, then there is recognition)

GEORGE Hey, man!

BERT Hey yourself! I didn't know that was you. I sure am glad to see you. I wanted to ask you: Who was that lady I saw you with last night?

GEORGE That wasn't no lady. That was my mother-in-law! (*both men laugh.* DUDLEY *bites his cigar in disgust*)

BERT Boy, you is a mess!

GEORGE Listen, I got a deal for you. The only reason I'm letting you in on this is 'cause we is friends, see—?

BERT I done seen so many deals that I closes my eyes when one comes along. This house I just bought is right by a cemetery. Coming home the other night, I saw a ghost. Ummm—I run so fast my feet never touched the ground. About a mile away, I set down to rest some. I looked around and the ghost was right beside me. The ghost says: "That was some purty running. Purtiest piece of running I ever saw." I says: "Yeah? Well, you wait till I catch my breath and you gonna see some more!" (*the drum "punctuates" this remark.* DUDLEY *groans and nearly swallows his cigar*)

GEORGE But, listen—this deal of mine means money!

BERT (*playing banjo and singing*)
    Money is the root of all evil
    No matter where you happen to go.

GEORGE (*singing*)
    But nobody pays any objection
    To the root—now, ain't that so?

BERT You know how it is with money—
    How it makes you feel at ease—
    The world puts on a big, broad smile

GEORGE And your friends am thick as bees!

BERT But, oh, when your money is running low,
    And you clinging to a solitary dime—
    Your creditors are num'rous and your friends are few—

GEORGE Oh! That's the awful time!

BOTH That am the time—oh, that am the time
    When it's all going out and nothing's coming in!
    That's the time when the troubles begin:
    Money getting low, people say: I told you so!
    And you can't borrow a penny from any of your kin,
    And it's all going out and nothing's coming in!

BERT Had my share of this world's trials—
    Nobody knows how hard I has tried
    To keep my little boat from sinking
    And to battle with the tide!

GEORGE You know when you've got money
    You can easy keep afloat—
    The stream is smooth and all your friends
    Tries to help you to row your boat.

BERT But, oh, when your money is running low,
    And the stream gets rough,
    And things look mighty blue,
    You look around for help and find

GEORGE Each of your friends is paddling his own canoe!

BERT That am the time! Oh, that am the time!

BOTH When it's all going out and nothing's coming in!
    That am the time when the troubles begin—
    Money getting low, people say: I told you so!
    And you can't borrow a penny from any of your kin,
    And it's all going out and nothing's coming in!

(*They face each other and dance the Cakewalk. They move off into the wing area.* DUDLEY *is obviously annoyed. He gives* GEORGE *a bill*)

DUDLEY That's your carfare. Get outa here before the audience catches you!

BERT What's wrong?

DUDLEY What's wrong??? Damn it, I coulda hired *any* two comedians to do *that*.

GEORGE Come on, Bert.

BERT Wait. We were hired and—

DUDLEY Now you're fired.

BERT You have to give us our pay.

DUDLEY I'll give you hell! Get your black asses outa my theater!

BERT Why, you parasitic paranoid—!

GEORGE (*rushing between them, pushing* BERT *offstage*) Man, come on! You wanta start a riot???

(DUDLEY *puzzles a moment and he is about to start after them when* ADA *and* HATTIE *reappear. He turns to them*)

DUDLEY   Ada—Hattie. What the hell does parasitic para-something mean? (*the girls look at each other, then shrug*) I think that son-of-a-bitch might've insulted me! After all I did for him! (*he bites on cigar. The lights fade*)

Scene Five

(*The scene is a small room in a Chicago boarding house. An hour later.*

The room is small and cluttered. There is a closet door, center, rear, the suggestion of a window opening onto a balcony at extreme left, a balcony rail. In the room there are chairs, a table, an armchair and the old trunk.

A knock is heard offstage as the lights fade in, then)

A WOMAN'S VOICE   Mr. Williams! Mr. Walker! (*no answer*) They ain't in, folks.

(*Footsteps are heard, moving away. A moment later the closet door is opened.* BERT *is in the closet on hands and knees.* GEORGE *is on* BERT's *back.* GEORGE *jumps off and into the room.* BERT *follows, stretching his limbs*)

GEORGE   She got the law after us! Over a coupla days rent! Come on! Let's get outa here. (*he takes one end of the trunk and* BERT *takes the other. They start for the door, then stop*) Wait! We can't go out that way! (*they drop the trunk with a thud*) Shhh! Fool!

BERT (*sitting on trunk*)   Someday I hope we'll be able to pay a landlady and not have to slip this thing out.

GEORGE   Yeah... You said things would be better in Chicago.

BERT   "A dark man shall see dark days." Who said that?

GEORGE   Probably you. (*sits on the other end of trunk*) This trunk gets heavier and heavier. What you got in there?

BERT   Your stuff's in there, too.

GEORGE   A few suits wouldn't make that much difference.

BERT   The price of those suits would've paid our rent.

GEORGE   You spent as much on books as I did on clothes.

BERT   A book is something you can keep forever.

GEORGE   Yeah? Well, you let your behind get cold and see which does you the most good, a book or a suit.

BERT   At times your utilitarianism is misdirected.

GEORGE   You got words like that in them books? No wonder they so big! (*suddenly*) What you do with them books? (BERT *avoids his look. Realization strikes* GEORGE *who closes his eyes, points to trunk*) No! Don't tell me! (BERT *shrugs*) Now, listen—(*and he jumps up, stops, then*) Wait! I got an idea! We can go out the window—

BERT   With the trunk?

GEORGE   No. With just the books. We can take 'em, sell 'em and pay our rent.

BERT   No, indeed!

GEORGE   You got any better ideas?

BERT   Yes. Let's pawn your clothes.

GEORGE   Man, you gone grazy? You put my clothes in the pawn shop and you gonna put me in there, too! (*then*) These clothes is new! Some of them books is old as hell. You said yourself one was wrote three thousand years ago—the one by Harry Bottle.

BERT (*corrects him, sharply*)   Aristotle!

GEORGE   Whatever his name was! Anyway, everybody's read a book that old.

BERT   You haven't!

GEORGE   Stop changing the subject! What the hell good are them books?

BERT   They keep me in harmony. (GEORGE *looks at him*) Especially after trying days among people.

GEORGE   You stuck-up, stubborn West Indian fool! No wonder we can't get no place! You keep holding us back!

BERT   I???

GEORGE   Yes, you! You won't wear burnt cork! You won't do nothing but act hincty! That manager in Omaha told me I ain't gonna get no place 'cause of you. You think you something!

BERT   Don't echo the attitude of your arrogant whites.

GEORGE   *My* arrogant whites? I didn't invent them, you know. (*then*) Yours any better? And don't tell me Yes, either! Your Pa went and built up that fine rum-exporting business, then his white relatives come in to help him out. And they helped him right outa his business! (*angrily*) I get sick and tired of folks complaining about this country!

BERT   It's the people, not the country.

GEORGE   What's the difference between my white folks and yourn?

BERT   The British knife with subtlety. (*then*) What are we arguing about?

GEORGE   I don't know. You started it.

BERT   I did not. American whites started it.

GEORGE   I ain't talking about them. To hell with them!

BERT   That's wrong, too.

GEORGE   Then, to hell with you *and* them! I mean it, too! Just try seeing how far you can get without me! Go ahead! (BERT *rises, reaches into trunk to remove his books*) Never mind! I'll get *my* things out. Your folks brung this trunk here from the island and I sure don't want it! (*getting his things*) Looks like Noah brought it here on his Ark! (*he pulls out his suit, shoes, socks, shirts, stacks these in his arms. A shirt drops to the floor.* BERT *reaches for it.* GEORGE *shouts*) Leave it alone! That's my good shirt! (*he starts to pick it up and as he does, he spills the other things.* BERT *again starts to help him and* GEORGE *snaps*) I don't need your help! (GEORGE *finally gets all the pieces in his arms, then stands there.* BERT *reaches into the trunk, gets out a pair of shoes, holds them out to* GEORGE. GEORGE *reaches for the shoes and as he does, he drops the whole stack of clothing.* BERT *laughs.* GEORGE *is furious. He starts to pick up things and this time* BERT *gets down and helps him. Now, they stand there, both with their arms full. They look at each other and* GEORGE *smiles, feebly*)

BERT   Put this damn stuff back in the trunk! (*they are both smiling. They put the stuff back into the trunk.* BERT *shuts the lid, tries to lock it and snags his finger*) Owww! (*he sticks his finger in his mouth.* GEORGE *takes handkerchief, goes to him*)

GEORGE   Lemme see it.

BERT   (*as* GEORGE *wraps finger*) That's your lace handkerchief.

GEORGE   The devil with it!

BERT   Thanks. (*they sit back down on the trunk.* BERT *turns, looks at* GEORGE. *They both smile.* BERT *places an arm around* GEORGE's *shoulder*)

GEORGE   We got to get that lock fixed!

BERT   Yeah. (*suddenly* GEORGE *jumps up*) You have another idea.

GEORGE   Yes! One of us oughta go down and try sweet-talking the landlady while the other one slips the trunk outa the window. Then we can meet outside. (*charitably*) I'll move the trunk.

BERT   It's pretty heavy. Besides, you talk faster than I do.

GEORGE   Well—if you insist. Meet you outside in five minutes.

BERT   How will I get outside?

GEORGE   Jump (*and he goes out.* BERT *now begins to move the trunk towards the window. It is heavy. He pulls it to window, reaches for one end, starts lifting it so he can get behind the other end and push it out the window. He has it in the right position when we hear* GEORGE's *voice*) Bert! Bert! Wait—

BERT   (*as* GEORGE *dashes in*) Man, you're supposed to be outside!

GEORGE   No! We're staying here!

BERT   George, did you promise the landlady you'd marry her?

GEORGE   No. Of course not.

BERT   Then you must've promised her I'd marry her. (*and he starts trying to push the trunk.* GEORGE *grabs his arm*)

GEORGE   Man, will you wait? She called us 'cause Jesse Shipp and Lottie Thompson was here to see us. (BERT *looks at him*) You heard me. I said Lottie Thompson, the concert pianist. And Jesse Shipp, the producer-director-writer-singer and everything else—the man who knows folks so big they use five dollar bills to light their cigars with.

BERT   Someone's playing a joke on us. Help me with this trunk.

GEORGE   Will you listen? We're on her good side now.

BERT   Wait'll she finds out this was a fake.

GEORGE   (*struggles with* BERT *who struggles with trunk*) Will you stop a minute? Here's Jesse Shipp's card—saying that they'll be stopping back this way soon.

BERT   They can't come here and find the place like this! (*they look around, then launch into the furious business of cleaning the room. In rapid-fire tempo the trunk is put back into its place, the chairs are properly placed and* BERT *has swept the floor.* GEORGE *holds up the armchair and* BERT *sweeps the trash under it. The men now flop into chairs and try to catch their breaths*)

BERT We should be reading when they arrive.

GEORGE They'll think we're putting on airs. Let's play Smut.

BERT They'll think we're gamblers.

GEORGE Not the way we play! (*they sit at table.* BERT *deals cards.* GEORGE *promptly beats him.* BERT *reaches for the lamp as* GEORGE *laughs. We hear a woman's voice*)

WOMAN Mr. Walker! Mr. Williams! (GEORGE *goes, admits* JESSE SHIPP *and* LOTTIE THOMPSON)

JESSE Good evening. I'm—

GEORGE Jesse Shipp. And this is Miss Thompson.

LOTTIE Yes. Good evening.

GEORGE Come in, please. I'm George Walker. And this is Bert Williams.

LOTTIE Are we interrupting?

BERT No. We were just playing Smut—

GEORGE That's poker without money. The loser puts lamp soot on his face. You just saved him. (BERT *has moved armchair for* LOTTIE *to sit in.* GEORGE *reaches over, pulls his coat, gestures towards trash they have swept under it.* BERT *puts chair back, quickly*) We—we don't think that's chair's comfortable enough for you.

LOTTIE Oh, I'm sure it's all right. (*and she crosses and sits in chair*)

JESSE Oliver Jackson told us—

BERT Mr. Jackson!

JESSE Yes. He told us to be sure and catch your act. We did today.

BERT Yes. (*looking at* LOTTIE) You sat in the first row balcony. Right side.

LOTTIE Ye-es.

BERT I glanced that way. You also saw us in Milwaukee.

GEORGE (*to* BERT) Keep your mind on your work and we might keep a job.

JESSE We're here on business. Lottie—

LOTTIE Yes. In this growing country every town and hamlet will have a theater by the year 1900.

GEORGE Yeah, but will we play in them?

LOTTIE *How* will we play in them is the question. The Irish will be the drunks, the Jews the moneylenders, the Italians the fools. You know what that means for us: (*in dialect*) "Poor black me is just old Black Joe— The white man is boss, the whole show!"

BERT Say, you have a wonderful ear! Of course, your subject matter—

JESSE That's why we're here. To bring truth to the theater—

BERT (*to* LOTTIE) I love mimicry! Back home I used to study the birds and—

JESSE Miss Thompson and I have been attacking this obliquely—doing ragtime and classics.

BERT (*continues, to* LOTTIE) I would copy their gestures and—

JESSE Mr. Williams!

BERT Oh! Yes?

JESSE We're attacking minstrels head on. I'm producing an all-colored show on Broadway, then in England. I want you two to star in it.

GEORGE (*as he and* BERT *exchange looks*) Slap me. I wanta see if I'm awake. (BERT *raises his hand*) No. Never mind!

JESSE Interested?

GEORGE Well—we ain't talked about money yet.

JESSE That'll be your decision. You'll be producers, too.

GEORGE Bert, maybe you better slap me after all. (*then*) Now, wait a minute. This is all fine and we appreciate the compliment, but we can't produce our rent, let alone a show.

JESSE No one's asking you for a dime.

LOTTIE This is no quick decision. We scouted a hundred people before deciding on you two.

JESSE We book you into Koster and Bial's in New York, along with Oliver. We'll team you with Ada and Hattie.

GEORGE Forget Hattie. I'll team with Ada.

JESSE Please let me finish! You do a long sketch there. In a week's time the script's worked out, the money's raised—and you're paid and headlined!

BERT Sounds good!

GEORGE Too good! What's the catch?

JESSE There may be one: Williams must wear burnt cork.

BERT Why?

JESSE Everything else is going for you: Voice. Gestures. In Lottie's words: You have the hands of an artist.

BERT Why burnt cork?

LOTTIE Because—because you're not like we're expected to be.
GEORGE Told you to forget that Anglican stuff in a Baptist world!
BERT I thought you were breaking with minstrels.
JESSE We will.
BERT Slowly, I suppose. (GEORGE *nudges him*) Stop elbowing me!
JESSE Mr. Williams, theater is *business*.
BERT I happen to know that.
JESSE Sentiment is for audiences. And they're not going to finance your personal revolutions. In fact, you're naive if you think we *want* a revolution. We're struggling for the right to be mediocre.
BERT So far you're a blazing success.
JESSE You could be, too. A success, I mean.
BERT Yes. In the parade of indistinguishable comedians.
JESSE The cork washes off, you know.
LOTTIE Jesse!
BERT (*facing him*) Maybe it does, Mr. Jesse Shipp. But can it be washed out of my mind, out of the minds of people who'll say: That's what he is, what they all are! (*then*) No, thank you. I'll starve first. (*he turns, goes out onto the balcony. An annoyed* LOTTIE *faces* JESSE)
LOTTIE Jesse, for God's sake! If our future depends upon your tact, we'll die young deaths in the poorhouse.
JESSE I swear to God, when I leave here I'm going to the zoo and stick my head in the lion's cage. And I'll bet he'll be gentler with me than you folks.
LOTTIE Take some bicarbonate of soda along for the lion! (*she goes out towards the balcony area.* GEORGE *starts to follow, stops, faces* JESSE)
GEORGE Mr. Shipp, I'm sorry. Look—my parner doesn't handle business matters. Let's you and me talk.
JESSE Yeah. Let's go down to the corner bar.
GEORGE Well, I—er—don't drink after five o'clock. Not good for me.
JESSE Oh. I was going to buy you a couple.
GEORGE Well, in that case—rather than disappoint you, I'll forget my health. Let's go. (*they start out.* JESSE *stops, makes a gesture towards* LOTTIE *who is on the balcony with* BERT. *The lights fade in this area*)

Scene Six

(*The balcony area, just outside the window of the room. Immediately following the previous scene.*

As the lights come up in this area we see BERT *standing alone, leaning against the building. He toys with his banjo, then sings. During the course of the song* LOTTIE *appears behind him on the balcony*)

BERT (*singing*)

I left my home on an island shore
Where sailfish played all day long.
I came a-knocking at the stranger's door
With my funny smile and my brand new song.

I left my home on a tropic isle
Where sky and sea kissed the sand—
Though through my tears I am compelled to smile,
There's a sadness I cannot understand!

Dreams haven't always come true!
I suppose I've always understood
That the sun hasn't shone as it should!
If it could!
Dreams haven't always come true!

I left my home with a dream to try
To climb the mountains and sky,
And now I find there's a tear in my eye
For my memories cannot ever die!

LOTTIE Beautiful. You wrote that?
BERT Once. In the wild dream it could be used in a show about us. Not one *he'd* produce.
LOTTIE Jesse's excitable—but nice. He'll love your song. And use it someday.
BERT I'll be dead by then.
LOTTIE I don't believe you believe that.
BERT

Full many a flower is born to blush unseen
And waste its sweetness on the desert air.

LOTTIE Gray's *Elegy*. Poetic masochism.
BERT Eh-eh!
LOTTIE "A city on a hill must be seen." I like that better. It was my father's favorite sermon.
BERT He was a minister?
LOTTIE A great one!
BERT I didn't say he wasn't.
LOTTIE Forgive me. I'm defensive about our men. They're shoved into the shadows of that city.

BERT (*impulsively*) I like you! You're brilliant and beautiful!

LOTTIE Thank you. I like you, too. (*he starts to reach for her hand, stops, turns away*)

BERT I forgot: You're working on me.

LOTTIE I'm what?

BERT (*imitating the gesture* JESSE *made to her*) I don't miss anything, Miss Thompson. The flight of a bird. A wisp of smoke. A gesture to a lady. I might use them someday.

LOTTIE To make that someday a reality. That's what interests me.

BERT Enough to ask a man to wear a false face.

LOTTIE Face? Is that all you see, Mr. Williams? Can't you talk from the inside—or are you afraid to show what's really there?

(*She moves away from him, annoyed, steps to the balcony rail. He smiles at her outburst. Suddenly, she whirls around, dizzily, then tries to move from the rail. Her hand flies up to her head as she starts to collapse. He rushes to her side, grabs hold of her*)

BERT Miss Thompson! Miss Thompson! (*he stands there, holding her. Now he leads her back into the room as the lights come up in that area*)

Scene Seven

(*Inside the room.* BERT *assists* LOTTIE *into the room, takes her to a seat and he sits beside her*)

BERT Miss Thompson—can I get you something?

LOTTIE No. I'll—be—all right.

BERT I'll get you some water.

LOTTIE Please. Just let me sit like this a minute.

BERT (*his arm around her*) You sit like this as long as you want to... (*her head is on his shoulder*) Feel better?

LOTTIE (*disengaging herself*) Yes. Thank you.

BERT You certainly have marvelous recuperative powers! (*tries to embrace her again*) Are you sure you're all right?

LOTTIE (*avoiding his embrace*) Positive.

BERT I looked around and you were—

LOTTIE I know. I know. I feel silly.

BERT You people here punish yourselves for being different.

LOTTIE Don't people everywhere?

BERT I like to think they don't back home. What happened?

LOTTIE Nothing.

BERT Something *did* happen. Suddenly the direct business woman became very feminine. (*insistently*) Miss Thompson, why does height make you dizzy?

LOTTIE You'll laugh at me.

BERT I won't. I hate people who laugh at others. (*he takes her hand. She looks at him, then seemingly beyond him*)

LOTTIE We had an apple tree in our backyard. Tall, almost touching the sky. When I was a girl I thought it's peak was the top of the world. Sometimes in my dreams I'd climb the tree, then reach up and touch the tip of a star—and it would lift me out over the town and people would point at me and say: "There she is! She stands for something!"... When I was ten I decided to climb the tree. At the top I reached for that star. I crashed to the ground. I was near death for two months.

BERT Good Lord!

LOTTIE After that a flight of stairs frightened me. Papa said it was a warning: Beware of the top of the world. He was right. When I overstep myself, it always happens.

BERT No. It happens to others. I've had that same dream—of the highest Antigua mountain, of climbing it, but never reaching the top—because I was always alone. (*then*) I wish we were there together.

LOTTIE We will be someday. (*he holds her hand*) We've brought you a way back to your island.

BERT You're working on me. I know it. But, I love it! (*singing, impulsively*)

> I'm glad I'm gone from that island shore
> Where sky and sea kissed the sand—
> Now through my tears I am compelled to smile—
> There's a gladness I cannot understand!

LOTTIE (*as music carries under*) Mr. Williams, don't wallow in tears. No one gets to a mountain top climbing alone. (*he walks away in thought, sits at card table, lights cigarette, toys with the cards*)

BERT America is one place where everything is done in excess—and quickly. (*he plays cards, somewhat mechanically. He spreads out a dummy hand, takes a card from the dummy, then plays a winning card from his own hand. He reaches into the dummy and carefully, deliberately, chooses the wrong card.* LOTTIE *now stands over him. She reaches and takes the wrong card that he has played. She puts it back in the dummy hand, then she selects the right and winning card. He looks up at her. She smiles, takes the lamp, pushes it towards him*)

LOTTIE You have your first citizenship papers. (BERT *smiles, ruefully, takes the lamp and starts to apply lamp soot to his face. A smile appears on her lips. The music rises and the lights fade out*)

Scene Eight

(*The scene is Koster and Bial's, New York City. A month later.*

When the lights fade in we see JESSE *and* OLIVER *in the wing-area with* LOTTIE. *They are watching* GEORGE, ADA *and* HATTIE *in the on-stage area. Vaudeville cards frame them, reading: "Williams and Walker Company."* GEORGE *talks over music*)

GEORGE

I'm a summer breeze on a cold, cold night—
I'm a girdle holding a figure tight—
I'm the key to a winekeeper's cellar,
I'd have been the Queen of Sheba's feller!
I'm the scent to a skunk,
I'm the dough lent a drunk,
And if you want to know what's next:

(*Lively music. He sings*)

I'm absolutely, positively, I'm most acutely unperplexed
'Cause I'm the key to sex!

The critics doubt that I'm good,
It's understood their heads are wood,
For they don't rate me as they should,
For positively I'm the most!
I'm real sure of all that I've got.
I have much more than I have not—
My lot is Johnny-on-the-Spot,
For positively I'm the most!
I hold the upper hand in each situation,
Have the answer to all aggravation,
Nature will allow just one like me per nation!
I own the key to Paree—
Its women are my cup of tea!
In fact, the world's in love with me,
For positively I'm the most—
For positively I'm the most!

(GEORGE *and the girls perform a dance routine.* GEORGE *then breaks into his famous strutting routine and the girls join him. As the routine continues* LOTTIE *steps into the wing-area, carrying a telegram*)

LOTTIE Telegram, Jesse.
JESSE (*opens it, reads*) Look, Lottie! Look! (*she reads it. They embrace, happily*)
OLIVER Jesse, you gone crazy? You better unhand that girl 'fore Bert sees you!
JESSE Here it is! Here it is!
OLIVER Jesse—you lost your mind?
JESSE Listen! Our agent—(*trying to read*) "You open—you—"
LOTTIE (*reads for him as his voice trembles*) "You open Majestic Theater Broadway in six weeks, then England. Can you do it?"
OLIVER Can we do it? (*jumping up and down*) We made it! We made it! We had to go through Third Avenue burlesque houses and outhouses, but we made it! (*starts towards onstage area*) George! George!
JESSE (*recovers, grabs him*) Where the hell you going?
OLIVER Out there to give George something to strut about!
JESSE Fool! Come back here! (*he practically tackles* OLIVER *as the lights fade out quickly*)

Scene Nine

(*The Majestic Theater. Six weeks later. The lights fade in on the playing area.* GEORGE, ADA, *and* HATTIE *continue their strutting routine from the previous scene.* OLIVER *has joined them.* LOTTIE *and* JESSE *remain in the wing area, watching.*

BERT *wanders into the playing area, in black-face. He attempts to join the dance routine. He is ridiculously awkward and both feet slide out from under him. He lands on his backside in vaudeville fashion.* GEORGE, ADA, HATTIE *and* OLIVER *dance off. The music becomes low and mournful*)

BERT (*singing*) I'm a Jonah man, I'm a Jonah man
　　　　　　And no matter how much right I do
　　　　　　It always comes out wrong.
　　　　　　I sing the bluest song.
　　　　　　I'm a Jonah man.

I'm a Jonah man, I'm a Jonah man
Who's 'bout left the belly of the whale,
When almost gettin' out
I falls back in and shout:
I'm a Jonah man.

I tries a little bit of this,
I tries a little bit of that.
There ain't a thing that I has missed.
I give my underwear and hat.
I reach a helping hand to all,
The more I reach, the lower I fall.

I'm a Jonah man, I'm a Jonah man
Who's lost about all a man can lose,
The blues I'd never choose
But caught the Jonah blues.
I'm a Jonah man.

(*He sits there.* GEORGE, ADA, HATTIE *and* OLIVER *strut by him, ignoring him. Now* BERT *pulls out a roll of bills from his pocket. The four stop, abruptly, and their stops are accentuated by drumbeats.* BERT *pulls out another roll.* GEORGE *dances forward, offers* BERT *his hand.* OLIVER *dances forward, offers* BERT *his hand.* ADA *whirls around, suggestively, beckoning to* BERT. HATTIE *dances a few more suggestive steps.* BERT *shakes his head, starts putting the money back into his pocket. Singing*)

You're in the right church but you're going to the wrong pew—
You're on the right street but you don't know what to do.
You're in the Lord's house but you don't know 'bout the right score.
You're in the right church, still you don't know what to do.
If you plays with fate,
You'll be dealt with straight.
You can't expect to win
If you play with sin.

You're in the right church but you're going to the wrong pew—
That's all.
That's all!

(*He places all the money back into his pockets, turns, tips his hat, then walks off. The lights fade in that area and they come up in the wings.* LOTTIE *embraces* BERT)

LOTTIE Honey! You remembered all the words to the song this time!
BERT Couldn't miss. I had the lyrics written on my gloves. (*holds up his white gloves She laughs, then hugs him, impulsively*) Look out! You'll get this cork on you.
LOTTIE I don't care, I don't care.
BERT I do. I'll remove it during intermission and propose to you in style.
LOTTIE I'll take you any way I can get you.
BERT You deserve me at my best, not in this stuff. It eats into my skin.
LOTTIE You eat into my heart!
BERT (*kissing her*) Lottie—Lottie—(*they remain in an embrace as the music rises. The lights fade out completely*)

Scene Ten

(*Buckingham Palace. London, England. A few years later.*

Across the backdrop, etched in lights, we see the Tower of London. The lights now fade in on the wing area where ADA, HATTIE, GEORGE, JESSE, BERT *and* LOTTIE *stand, watching* OLIVER *perform a soft-shoe tap routine in the onstage area.* JESSE *holds a script in his hand. The others are in costume, waiting to go on*)

LOTTIE That man gets younger ever year.
BERT Oliver? Yes!
JESSE You climax sixty years of knocking around with a Command Performance and you'll find the Fountain of Youth, too!
ADA I still can't believe it! Me! Playing before the King of England. And all *these* English *men*! They look at a woman and undress her at the same time.
GEORGE They better not look at *you*.
ADA I'm not letting England go to my head, dear.
HATTIE It wouldn't be going any place if it did.
ADA Hattie, shut up!
HATTIE Don't you—
JESSE Both of you shut up! Every day for two straight years I've had to listen to your mouths! Stop for tonight. (*then, as* OLIVER *completes his number*) Cue 112—(*a spotlight is on* OLIVER *in the onstage area. We hear a blues number as he sings*)

OLIVER (*singing*) We have a young man who's in a low-down jam!
We have a young man who's in a low-down jam!
He's stole a vase. His fate's not worth a damn!

(*Now another light comes up on* BERT *who is*

Star of the Morning

sitting behind bars. GEORGE *stands on the other side of the bars, talking to* BERT. *The light on* OLIVER *is down*)

GEORGE Now, you went and done it! I brought all the way here to Abyssinia and you got to wind up in jail! For stealing a vase! Man, I done took you outa the country, but I sure can't take the country outa you!

BERT I sure wish you could take me outa this country fast!

GEORGE Oh, keep still! You know the punishment for what you done? They gonna cut off your hand! What you gonna look like with one hand and a nub?

BERT (*finally*) Oh, I'll put a hook on it!

GEORGE Lord, how much can a man stand? I brung you over here where you can get some culture and refinement and you go walking through all this culture, looking like some *vulture*! I even take you swimming, half-hoping you gonna drown, but the water takes one look at you and it begins to frown! And it backs up to your knees! You just one great big worriation to me. Like a bad penny, always turning up when you oughta be turning down! (*music. He sings*)

> You like a bad, bad ole penny—
> It's time for me to toss you away,
> But when I do, you'll just roll back one day!
> You like a bad, bad ole penny—
> I can't see how you're worth one cent,
> And don't tell me you're going to repent!
> Bad, bad ole penny—
> Bad, bad ole penny!
> You do disgrace poor Mr. Lincoln's face!
> Yes, you're a bad, bad ole penny—
> You're counterfeit and who wants you,
> And when you fall you can't seem to ring true!
> You good-for-nothing ole penny,
> Now since I can't give you away,
> Must I be stuck with you each weary day?
> Bad, bad ole penny!
> Bad, bad ole penny!
> You do disgrace poor Mr. Lincoln's face!

BERT (*singing*) Now, listen, George Walker, don't say that to me!
> Now, listen, George Walker, don't say that to me!
> 'Cause if you do, we is bound to disagree!
> My friends treat me like a old pair of shoes.
> You kicks me 'round and does me like you choose!

GEORGE (*singing*) Bad, bad ole penny—
> Bad, bad ole penny!
> You do disgrace poor Mr. Lincoln's face!

(*The music carries under.* CHARLIE, *a young Negro actor, steps into the scene, dressed as the Emperor. He goes to throne that has appeared in center stage. Two guards remove* BERT *from behind the bars and bring him before the Emperor.* GEORGE *gets out of there.* BERT *kneels before the Emperor.* OLIVER *steps forward as the music continues*)

OLIVER Say, listen, young man, you're in a low-down mess!
> Say, listen, young man, you're in a low-down mess!
> You stole a vase—you ain't 'bout to be blessed!
> You've done a few things since you've been in our midst.
> You've done a few things since you've been in our midst,
> So we've compiled and we've a lil' old list!

(*He produces the list. The little old list turns out to be fifteen feet long. Music carries under*)

BERT Your Honor—I mean, Your Majesty—I know you got the sentence all writ, but ain't no sense giving it to me 'cause I can't read it. (*he laughs, nervously. No one joins him. He stifles his laugh, then*) I can't read 'cause when I was a young'un old schoolhouse was six miles away. I couldn't walk that fur 'cause I didn't have no shoes to walk in. Besides, I hadda work in the fields and raise crops for my Ma and six brothers... Your Majesty, I just don't unnerstand the ways of the folks back home, let alone over here. And I done the wrong thing. But, I ain't never seen a vase as purty as that one. (*looks at his hand*) Don't know how I'm gonna eat with one hand and a nub. 'Course, I ain't always had something to eat so I reckon it won't matter much if I ain't got nothing to eat with... When I was borned hard luck was flying 'round my head and it lit smack on me, and there it's stayed. But, I ain't never meant to do no wrong. I ain't never done nothing to nobody no time—(*music. He sings*)

> I ain't never done nothing to nobody—
> I ain't never got nothing from nobody no time,
> And until I get something from sombody some time,
> I don't intend to do nothing to nobody no time!

> When life is full of cloud and rain
> And I am filled with naught but pain,
> Who soothes my aching, bumping brain,
> Umm—nobody—no time.

I had a steak some time ago,
With sauce I sprinkled it over—
Who said that was tobasco sauce?
Nobody—umm—Nobody!

When I was in that recent railroad wreck
And I thought I cashed in my last check,
Who pulled that engine from 'round my neck?
Who? Umm—Nobody!

I ain't never done nothing to nobody no time,
I ain't never got nothing from nobody no time
And until I get something from somebody some time,
I don't intend to do nothing for nobody no time!

CHARLIE (*as the music breaks*) You'll be told the judgment by the ringing of our great bell. If it rings four times, you'll be pardoned. If it rings only three times, you'll have your right hand cut off—up to here! (*he indicates the shoulder, then gets up and leaves the stage.* BERT *stands there*)

BERT I ain't never done nothing to nobody—

(*The bell rings*)

I ain't never got nothing from nobody no time—

(*The bell rings again*)

And until I get something from somebody some time,
I don't intend to do nothing for nobody no time!

(*The bell rings a third time.* BERT *opens his mouth, but the words will not come. He gasps through the song, his hand in midair. He tries to move it, but he cannot. He sinks to his knees. Suddenly, the bell rings a fourth time. He becomes hysterically joyful, but he is unable to speak or sing. He simply gestures, wildly. The music breaks. He stands, speechless, as the lights fade*)

Scene Eleven

(*The backstage area. Immediately following the previous scene.* LOTTIE, ADA, *and company stand there, revelling in the applause we hear from the previous scene.* BERT *and* GEORGE *step into the wing area.* LOTTIE *rushes into* BERT's *arms.* ADA *hugs* GEORGE)

GEORGE I tuned 'em up for you, Ada, baby!
ADA You make beautiful music.
GEORGE Wait'll after the show when I get my whole orchestra to swinging for you!
ADA I'll dance to your music any day. (*she kisses him.* LOTTIE *gives* BERT *a towel*)
LOTTIE After two years I know. The cork eats into your skin.
BERT Thanks, honey. (*he wipes his face. The others, with the exception of* GEORGE *and* ADA, *leave*)
GEORGE Ada, with this behind us we're going places. Even gonna do Shakespeare, with me playing Bologna.
BERT Polonius!
GEORGE Yeah. That's the man! He talks for pages and pages—and dies right on stage. (*stops*) Say, what act does he die in? I seem to remember a whole lot of talking *after* he dies. What act do you die in?
BERT The last one.
GEORGE We'll get Alex Rogers and Jesse to do a little rewriting.
LOTTIE On Shakespeare?
GEORGE He won't say anything about it.
BERT Man, that's like rewriting the Bible!
GEORGE I've seen some preachers do just that! (BERT *laughs, waves at him, then turns back, embraces* LOTTIE, *who is also laughing*) Ada—look! They married all this time and still honeymooning!
ADA I don't want to ask you when we're going to start—
GEORGE Hey, when y'all gonna start collecting diapers instead of books? (*as* LOTTIE *practically freezes*) What's wrong, Lottie?
LOTTIE Nothing. Nothing at all. (*she turns, starts off*)
GEORGE Lottie—
BERT (*steps in front of him*) The only reason I don't stick my fist in your big mouth is fear of hydrophobia.
GEORGE What did I do wrong?
BERT It would take me all year to tell you! (*and he follows* LOTTIE *off*)
ADA Honey—even I know that you don't ask married women when they're having children. Or—for that matter—single women, either. (*she goes.* GEORGE *stands there, puzzled. Then, suddenly he realizes that* LOTTIE *cannot have children. He kicks himself on the shin as* JESSE *appears*)
GEORGE Jesse, what in the hell is wrong with me?
JESSE Ask me when I'm on a ten year vacation! Where's Bert? (GEORGE *points*) Abraham

Erlanger sure wants him. He left him this note.

GEORGE   He ain't left nothing for me.

JESSE   He didn't get to be a smart producer by accident. (*they start moving across the stage together, both laughing. Suddenly,* GEORGE *stops, catches his chest*) George—what is it?

GEORGE (*draws a deep breath, then*)   Nothing. This damn indigestion.

JESSE   You've complained all week. I think we'd better get back to the States so we can all vacation a while. (*the lights have come up in the dressing room where* LOTTIE *sits beside* BERT)

LOTTIE   I'm all right, Bert. It was just that I was soaring and—the crash of reality hurt.

BERT   Having children isn't the only thing in life.

LOTTIE   It isn't if you're not a woman.

BERT   Honey, we'll have millions of children. Audiences, audiences and more audiences. (*he holds her close.* GEORGE *and* JESSE *step into the scene*)

GEORGE   Excuse us—for a lot of things.

JESSE   Here. (*and he gives* BERT *a note*)

BERT   Thanks . . . Erlanger wants to see me tonight. (*then*) In Antigua a rich man left his estate to a barefoot orphan. Everybody on the island suddenly wanted to adopt the boy, but the boy kept right on, walking around, barefoot.

GEORGE   Why?

BERT   So he could stick out his foot and tell folks to kiss it. (GEORGE *and* BERT *laugh*)

JESSE   Man, don't you tell Erlanger to kiss your foot. His Syndicate controls theater.

BERT   It doesn't control the Williams and Walker Company.

GEORGE   Right! And if he comes in here I'll tell him: "Don't you send us no more notes without fancy paper and envelopes."

BERT   And he'll tell you—(*imitates the way he believes* ERLANGER *would speak*) "Mister George Walker, we don't even send notes to whee-eet dolka on fancy paper."

GEORGE   Oh, sorry, Boss! I shoulda sanded. I got special shoes for sanding so's I can be called "Mister." (*freezes*) Damn it! (*holds up suspenders*) I been sanding so much I busted my ten cents suspenders!

(BERT *and* JESSE *are laughing at* GEORGE's *antics. A knock is heard.* LOTTIE *crosses, admits* ABRAHAM ERLANGER, *a medium sized, pleasant-faced white man of middle years.* GEORGE *does not see him and continues speaking directly to* BERT)

GEORGE   Look here, Mr. Erlanger: Sanding is expensive!

LOTTIE   Yes?

ERLANGER   I'm Abraham Erlanger.

GEORGE (*to* BERT)   I know who you are, so don't be interrupting me. It's got so a colored man can't even get a sentence finished.

LOTTIE   George, this is Abraham Erlanger. (*her words reach* GEORGE's *ears. He freezes, one hand in the air, then he brings it down slowly, pretending he was flexing a muscle.* JESSE *and* BERT *also become aware of the visitor*)

GEORGE   Oh, How do you, do, Mr. Erlanger?

BERT   Mr. Erlanger. I'm Bert Williams. Mrs. Williams. Mr. Walker. Mr. Shipp.

ERLANGER   How do you do? I'm interrupting a—a rehearsal?

LOTTIE   No.

GEORGE (*quickly*)   Yes! . . . For a new skit. We call it "How to Sand, Man, Without Holding the Bag."

ERLANGER   What's that?

BERT (*he glares at* GEORGE, *then*)   A family joke. You don't do a Command Performance every day and it's made us giddy. I light two cigarettes at one time. Mr. Walker gets delirious and Mr. Shipp irascible.

ERLANGER   Success has a way of going to the head.

BERT   We started off this morning with Mr. Shipp setting up the stage. A short man in a red vest kept coming around, asking how things were going. The third time he appeared, Mr. Shipp exploded and told him in direct American terms what is wrong with England, its people and its customs. The man smiled and walked away. Tonight when the Band played "God Save the King," Mr. Shipp peeped out through the curtains and he saw the red-vested man. "My God!" he yelled. "Is that the King? I was expecting the King to look like a King!" (ERLANGER *laughs*) I'm just glad it happened to a liberal head of state, not, say to the governor of Alabama or Georgia.

ERLANGER   It's happened to me. My first hit and I'm in the box office. A lady demands four front row seats. She tells me: "I'm a personal friend of Abraham Erlanger, America's greatest producer." I give her four tickets and tell her: "This is on me." It's during intermission that I realize: I never saw the women before in my life. (*then*) I'd like a word with you, Mr. Williams.

BERT Please speak freely. We're all one family here. (*but* LOTTIE, JESSE *and* GEORGE *leave.* BERT *gestures for them to remain*)

ERLANGER I'll be brief: I'm a man with a mission.

BERT A mission?

ERLANGER Yes. There's no Bible under my arm, but the spirit's in my heart. The spirit of theater, of projecting images through art.

BERT We're not at odds.

ERLANGER We will be in a minute. Theater in America is fairy tales. Unreal.

BERT You produce theater there.

ERLANGER As a means to an end. The Wright brothers took up an airplane over North Carolina. Flew twenty-four and a half miles in little over half an hour. Soon you can fly from New York to Philadelphia, from New York to Jackson, Mississippi.

BERT Who wants to fly to Mississippi?

ERLANGER You missed the point. In a shrinking world, organization rules. Railroad, coal, steel, oil. Organized! My Syndicate's bringing that to theater.

BERT For whose sake?

ERLANGER The theater's. Because I love it, want it to mean more than Cinderella tales, want it to speak directly to human beings. I intend to put it back on the right track. I told you I have a mission.

BERT Napoleon Bonaparte wanted a United States of Europe.

ERLANGER I resent that!

BERT The shoe pinches. West Indians say: Beware of those helping others for in the end they help themselves.

ERLANGER You're in the West Indies and I'm in America, even now, standing on British soil. Later for polemics. I want you in my company—to become the first featured Negro performer in an all-white company.

BERT Why?

ERLANGER Because artistically, financially and theatrically it's worthwhile.

BERT And my company?

ERLANGER I won't believe you're so naive. Companies like this will evaporate like water vapor over a desert.

BERT Man, you've got nerve!

ERLANGER Just sense. Know something? Every Jewish section in New York had a theater company like yours, saying what should be said. In fifty years you can count on one hand the Jewish theatres left.

BERT Hell, if you think that of Jews—

ERLANGER You *are* naive! In fifty years someone's going to assume Jews—and maybe Negroes—are humans—and even forget to persecute them. Then—how many Jews will speak Yiddish? How many Negroes will have dialects?

BERT I don't have to wait fifty years to be human. I'm doing a Command Performance.

ERLANGER On the shore. I want to put you in the mainstream.

BERT There's muck in the mainstream.

ERLANGER We'll pump life from these small companies into it and clean it out. You'll need me as I need you.

BERT What're you telling me? That I can be the greatest violinist in the world, but I'm second fiddle until you recognize me?

ERLANGER You're doing a show now about Emperor Menelik of Abyssinia. Three people in the audience may know his name—

BERT He's part of our history.

ERLANGER Four people in the audience, then. If five people know, then you're in trouble. When western society lets a people keep their identity, those people are in trouble. Ask the Jews! The star of David was on every ghetto lock. (*then*) Enough polemics. I'm offering you real recognition. Meantime you live. In first-rate hotels. Fine theaters. Audiences in mink applauding you. I'm giving you the chance to fly upwards among the stars, the bright stars—

BERT (*intrigued, but slowly shakes head*) No. I'd be riding freight elevators in those hotels—with the applause still ringing in my ears.

ERLANGER Think of the opportunity—

BERT Excuse me, Mr. Erlanger.

ERLANGER Mr. Williams—

BERT I said: Excuse me!

ERLANGER (*looks at him, then*) Good evening, Mr. Williams. (*he goes out.* BERT *stands there as* LOTTIE, JESSE *and* GEORGE *reenter*)

JESSE Man! That was Abraham Erlanger!

BERT If I had some island foo-foo dust, I'd sprinkle it after him!

JESSE You might need him someday.
BERT For what? To fly to Mississippi?
GEORGE Come on, Jesse. Let's check on the company.
BERT What the hell's wrong with you two?
LOTTIE They're trying to tell you you bungled. I think so, too.
BERT I thought you'd understand. With him I'm chained to burnt cork the rest of my days. Here—there's a way out.
LOTTIE If we live. He wasn't optimistic.
BERT Talk straight! First it was wear cork for a while. Now, it's listen to him—
LOTTIE The cork got you close to the mountainside.
BERT And we're near the top. Just a few more steps—

(OLIVER *bursts into the room.* HATTIE, ADA *and* CHARLIE *follow him*)

OLIVER Bert! I've got to talk to you!
HATTIE We've got to talk to you. Right now, too!
ADA Folks say you're joining Erlanger.
BERT No, no, no—
HATTIE Damn it, soon as we get a table, they come and take our bread and butter!
ADA And break up our family. That's what this is—a family. And I've got to leave home all over again. A good home this time.
CHARLIE After all of this glory I've got to go back to running elevators and hoping for a part here and there—
BERT Wait a minute—
HATTIE Honey, in this business all you got is Hope and you sure God can't take that in a store and buy a thing with it!
BERT Will you wait a minute??? (*then*) I am not joining Erlanger. This is my company.
HATTIE For how long?
BERT Forever! We're going on from tonight—to do real theater, not the typical colored show they expect from us.
OLIVER So—ain't we still colored?
CHARLIE Oliver, this is important. Don't interrupt.
OLIVER Boy, don't you tell me what to do and what not to do.
CHARLIE When you're interferring with my career, I will.
OLIVER Your career? Manure!
CHARLIE What??? ... Now, look, Bert, George, Jesse. Ideals kept me with this company. I'm not really a musical type. (*to* OLIVER) I don't want to tell you what type you are!
OLIVER One sure thing: You ain't big enough to erase my type! (*to* BERT) Bert, these folks looking for theirselves. I'm looking out for you 'cause I know you. You and me—we colored and we like it. We come from something and I don't wanta see it wasted away. And that's what's gonna happen if you get up with Erlanger.
CHARLIE Exactly what are you talking about?
OLIVER Lord, these young Negroes don't know what I mean. How can I expect white folks to know? (*he turns and walks out*)
ADA Uh-uh! Can't colored folks do nothing without arguing?
HATTIE Let 'em argue. What you want 'em to do? Pass?
ADA Who's trying to pass?
HATTIE I didn't say *you* was!
ADA You better not!
GEORGE Good Lord! What'd you all have for supper? Ground-up razor blades with acid for appetizers? We got enough headaches without adding ulcers to them! (*the others become silent, then suddenly* LOTTIE *breaks into tears*)
HATTIE Oh, Lord!
ADA George, what's happening to us? We ain't this kind of company.
BERT (*goes to her*) Lottie, honey, what is it? (*they are standing now, apart from the others who are in the shadows*)
LOTTIE I'm sorry. I can't stand any more arguments.
BERT Don't, honey. That damn Erlanger's upset everybody.
LOTTIE It's not really—him. It's something more. Maybe me. (*quietly*) Ever since I told you about my fall—about not having children—you've acted strange.
BERT Nonsense!
LOTTIE No! I feel it, you hear me—feel it in every part of my body, in my very soul. You hold me close and our heartbeats thump in broken rhythms. The rhythm of yours keeps saying: "She robbed me! She robbed me!"
BERT I won't listen to any more of this!
LOTTIE You will listen! Listen to my heartbeat for once. It's telling you that what I have

tried to bring you is love—love to inspire you towards greatness. And all my love has done is send us both to hell!

BERT   Lottie, stop it!

LOTTIE   You don't want to see it, but I have to! I'm not able to leave you anything but theater to carry your name through the years. You'll always want a company like this so you can play Papa to it. Or you'll need books, or audiences or parties and people to hide you from the reality of our lonely lives. And things will get worse. When you're not working, you'll be reading, or dreaming, and you'll have less and less to say to me. Then—one day there'll be another woman.

BERT   To hell with this damn foolishness!

LOTTIE   I'm looking directly at rows of lonely nights, of pillows rainsoaked with tears—

BERT   Lottie, I love you—but this is no time to be acting like a woman. I have a show on my hands!

LOTTIE   I am a woman! I can't hide behind makeup and stage techniques. (*he reaches to touch her. She trembles, afraid, hurt. His shoulders sag. He draws a deep breath.* OLIVER *reenters*)

BERT   What the hell do you all want from me? Everybody wants me to be something else! (*angrily*) Jesus, God! Something powerful and evil is in every sound and sight, in theater lights and in people's eyes! I wish to God I didn't have a heart and mind!

OLIVER (*steps forward*) Easy, boy, Easy. You going on—in another minute.

BERT   What for? What the hell for?

OLIVER   'Cause you got to, that's all. Now, get ready.

GEORGE   Yeah. Get ready.

(BERT *whirls around, angrily, begins dabbing his face with burnt cork. The music rises. The company lines up, somewhat mechanically.* BERT *now joins them and they start out, singing, half-heartedly*)

COMPANY   Ohhh—keep your eye on a star
And you'll find your way
Where your troubles are few
If only you
Don't let your dreams go astray!

(*They file out towards stage area as the lights fade*)

Scene Twelve

(*The scene is on stage. Immediately following. The lights come up as the company moves into the area*)

GEORGE (*singing*)   I rode the rails to Kansas City
Without a dime or a word of pity,
My soul was sagging,
My body dragging,
But I kept looking for the Golden City!

COMPANY   Ohhh—keep your eye on a star
And you'll find your way
Where your troubles are few
If only you
Don't let your dreams go astray!

JESSE   I had a song I knew folks would sing,
I kicked around doing any old thing—
But I kept in mind that wonderful day
When I'd wind up on the Great White Way!

COMPANY   Ohhh—keep your eye on a star
And you'll find your way
To that glorious state
That chance of fate
No matter what comes your way!

LOTTIE   My life has had its ups and downs
With hasty meals in nameless towns,
But on the stage my life has its appeal,
It burns with quite a different kind of zeal!

COMPANY   You can't go wrong when there's a song—
You can't deny
With head held high
You'll follow one star
And find that there are
Wonders still to try!

BERT   I've been a minstrel all my life
And just one thing through all this strife
Has filled my heart where all the meanings are—
I've kept my eye on a star!

COMPANY   Ohhh—keep your eye on a star
No matter what they say,
And so hopefully dream,
You will seem
To turn the night into day!
So, keep your eye on a star!

(GEORGE *moves into center now and he begins to lead the group*)

GEORGE   Ohhh—keep your eye on a star
And you'll find your way—
Where—where—where—

(*His voice begins to drone and he becomes thick-lipped, struggling and shaking as he sings. The company looks at him, not knowing whether or not he is clowning.* GEORGE *begins to tremble, violently, then starts for the off-stage area. He barely reaches the wings when he sinks to the floor.* BERT *rushes to him as the others crowd around*)

LOTTIE (*over* GEORGE) Get a doctor—quick!
ADA Is he—?
LOTTIE No. Call for a doctor! (CHARLIE *rushes out.* JESSE *points to onstage area, indicating* ADA *and* HATTIE *should go. They do so, reluctantly*)
BERT George! George!
LOTTIE He's going to be all right. I'm sure of it.
BERT He's got to be! (*then*) George, you can't get sick now! You can't die! We're making it, partner. We're making it! (GEORGE *is still.* BERT *looks up at* LOTTIE. *She is crying and so are the others. He throws up both arms and shouts*) Almighty God! What do you want from us? What? All we want to do is our work? Is there something wrong with that? Answer me, God. Is there something wrong with that?? ... (LOTTIE *reaches for him, holds him close. The music rises and the lights fade out. Curtain*)

ACT TWO

Scene One

(*A New York theater. 1909.*
A light fades in gradually on LOTTIE. *She stands in the wing area of the theater, her face turned upwards*)

LOTTIE Oh, God! I sometimes think that devastating natural forces make mockery of the petty ills of man. Don't let George Walker's stroke cripple him and our company! Stop this nightmarish hurricane from roaring into the calm of our dream ... Forgive us for not understanding the earlier warnings—the Jim Crow laws being passed, the race riots, the assaults upon us by press and public. We felt the rain, but we had to believe the sun would come out! .·. And this night—let there be light, for too many hopes and dreams of others are here with us. Let us not write their epitaphs here tonight. Let us fly forward, their banners flying, soaring above the night and setting the darkness on fire!

(*The lights now slowly fade in around her and we see a section of the wings of a New York theater.* JESSE *is standing looking off towards the action that is out of view.* OLIVER *stands beside him. We hear the sound of dancing feet.* LOTTIE *remains, standing alone, apart from the others.* OLIVER *calls to her*)

OLIVER Lottie ... (*she does not move*) Lottie—
LOTTIE Oh! Yes?
OLIVER Jesse said stand by. Two minutes. (HATTIE *charges in from the onstage area. Faint applause is heard*)
HATTIE Damn it! I have to keep looking out there to make sure somebody is in the house! Told you to put this show off till George got well!
JESSE We couldn't afford to. It's that simple.
HATTIE Go out there and find out what the word bad means. And, Lord, just a few years ago I was walking 'round England with my neck hurting from holding my head up so high!
LOTTIE Don't be discouraged. You're an old pro, Hattie.
HATTIE I ain't that old.
LOTTIE I didn't mean in age.
HATTIE When I die of old age, you make sure your insurance is paid up. (*then*) Blame your husband for this jam! They sure letting him know who owns the fruit and the jars!
LOTTIE My husband has made no jam.
HATTIE Now I'll tell you something you're old enough to know: You can't fly up in Abraham Erlanger's face and get away with it. You got to make deals with folks like that and then you get financing and big audiences—
LOTTIE But you said before—
HATTIE I don't care what I said! What I'm telling you now is: We are in hot water and we ain't taking baths!
OLIVER All right, Hattie! Cut, Lottie—
ADA (*entering from onstage area*) Good luck, Lottie. You're going to need it. (ADA *and* HATTIE *go off.* LOTTIE *goes in the opposite direction. Now we hear the music and a sugary, sentimental ballad*)
OLIVER Ten laughs all night. I counted 'em.
JESSE Stop counting and start praying.

(BERT *steps into the area, unseen by them. He stands apart*)

BERT This one moment must redeem all the rest. There was a star burning a hole in the night. We reached for it, and the world turned over and crippled us. We've got to keep reaching, reaching—

LOTTIE (*in the playing area, singing*)

When shadows darken your day
No need to give you dreams away,
The shadows will go and you'll learn to know
That laughter follows after tears.
Sometimes a song is the way
To see you through a troubled day—
With heart on your sleeve, you'll learn to believe
That laughter follows after tears.
We'll go along as the old Pied Piper went
And sing his song to the smiling innocence of
  merriment!
We'll take the world by the hand
And find our promised wonderland
Where fear disappears and love fills the years
Where laughter follows after tears!
Where laughter follows after tears!

(*The lights fade out as she concludes the song*)

Scene Two

(*The scene is the theater. The next morning. The set is being struck.* OLIVER *and* JESSE *are unhooking flats and moving them off.* GEORGE *is sitting on the old trunk in centerstage, reading over stacks of morning newspapers.* GEORGE *has a cane near him which he uses for support:*)

GEORGE Damn! (*puts down paper, takes another, scans it*) Another damn! (*puts this down, picks up another, then*) Gawd-damn! (*reading*) "The Negro musical comedy plot is running thin."

JESSE We read the reviews. I hope you don't think we're striking this set so we can play games.

GEORGE They got a smash hit down the block and its two inches thinner than wet tissue paper.

OLIVER That ain't *our* show. We liable to need this flat, Jesse.

JESSE I told you, Oliver: There's no next show.

OLIVER You all are the giving-up-est folks I ever saw! If you'd been slaves, you never woulda got free! You'da given up walking the Underground Railroad 'cause you didn't have the proper shoes to wear!

JESSE You put up the money and we'll produce another.

OLIVER Me? Boy, you gone crazy? I ain't gonna enterprise you *and* advise you. (*he takes the flat and starts out.* ERLANGER *enters*)

ERLANGER Good morning, Mr. Walker. Mr. Shipp.

JESSE Good morning.

GEORGE I hope yours is good.

ERLANGER It's not. I read the reviews. I'm sorry.

GEORGE For years I been wondering what they use to make printer's ink. Now I know: Blood. *My* blood.

ERLANGER I'm looking for Mr. Williams.

GEORGE He ain't around.

JESSE Mrs. Williams is upstairs packing. I'll get her. (*and he leaves*)

ERLANGER Actors look for me. I don't look for them.

GEORGE The man you looking for ain't just an actor.

ERLANGER I know. That's why I'm here. Where is he?

GEORGE Walking. Which he does when he's hurt. After these reviews, he's liable to be trying to walk New York Bay.

LOTTIE (*enters*) Yes, Mr. Erlanger?

ERLANGER Mrs. Williams, I'm very sorry. I came to help. The news is out that your husband lost six weeks of summer bookings with the reviews. I'm here to offer him work.

LOTTIE I'll tell him.

ERLANGER I had a role written into my new Follies for him the moment I heard Mr. Walker was sick.

LOTTIE You were that certain?

ERLANGER Of only one thing: Your husband is a compulsive artist who must work. And I'm the key to his working.

LOTTIE You needn't gloat. We know your syndicate and the price of not cooperating with it. You forced Mrs. Fiske to play in second-rate theaters and the great Sarah Bernhardt to appear in a tent. And we know where that leaves us: Outside.

ERLANGER It does. I'm not proud of the record.

LOTTIE You helped write it.

ERLANGER I had to help write it!

GEORGE Why?

ERLANGER (*angrily*) Who the hell are you to question *me*? (*then*) I can read the contempt in your eyes. You think my life is luxury next to yours. Maybe. Maybe not. People don't just look for a pound of my flesh but for my neck. I'm made into a businessman when I want to create beauty and a good life. I have to wander when I want to stay home. (*bitterly*) I don't give a God damn about the syndicate, but I've got to have it to be in theater. (*then*) I—I talk too much. I don't have to apologize to you for being human.

LOTTIE No. You don't.

ERLANGER I hope you mean it. I'm talking to you because I think you're like me. American. Practical. Ready to ride the tide but feeling the undercurrents to change the stream. Will you tell your husband that on that basis he has a job in my new show.

LOTTIE I'll tell him.

ERLANGER Thank you. Thank you so much. (*he goes out*)

GEORGE Lord! To sell Bert on that one you're gonna need God, Buddha, Allah and a few voodoo tricks at the same time.

LOTTIE I talked him into the burnt cork. Reality's going to have to help out. I'll finish packing. (*she goes.* GEORGE *sits there on the trunk.* JESSE *enters, starts to remove other pieces of scenery.* GEORGE *rises to help.* BERT *enters*)

BERT Who said: "Death is an empty theater?"

JESSE I don't know. He had a point.

GEORGE You got all your things?

BERT All that I want.

GEORGE (*as* BERT *sits on trunk, lights cigarette*) You'll get other jobs, Bert. You're a star.

BERT At night. This is the morning and stars don't shine then.

GEORGE Some do. (HATTIE *enters with her bag. She is followed by* ADA, CHARLIE, *then* LOTTIE. OLIVER, *in the meantime, has joined* JESSE *in helping to remove things*)

HATTIE The key, Jesse—

JESSE Put them on the table out there.

HATTIE Somebody said maybe you'll re-write the script. We'll get Erlanger and the syndicate to book it on the road. (*before anyone can say a word*) It's a great idea. Know what else I think? My part needs a bit more—er—uh—development. Needs to be doing *something*. I thought that before, but I didn't want to second guess you.

JESSE That was considerate.

HATTIE You know me. When you're ready for the road, just get in touch—

CHARLIE Same here. Especially if you have a part for a good elevator boy.

ADA I'll be available, too, although I'll be doing some vaudeville gigs in the meantime. I just got a brand new four room apartment in Harlem and the rent's thirty-four dollars a month. So—you know I've got to work! (*she turns, abruptly, goes out before she breaks into tears*)

GEORGE (*following her*) Ada—Ada—

(CHARLIE *and* HATTIE *leave.* BERT *crushes cigarette*)

BERT Jesse—

JESSE No. It takes three things to do a show: Money, money and more money. Those kids will hear the alarm clock soon. Not every star shines in the morning. I'll finish my work.

BERT Jesse. Where'll you go?

JESSE Uptown. A hundred thousand Negroes in New York now. Lots of them moving to Harlem. I'll go there. Maybe they'll be needing a theater. (*smiling*) There's no airplane linking Broadway to Harlem yet.

BERT Erlanger said there'll soon be one to Philadelphia.

JESSE It's a longer distance from Harlem to Broadway than it is from Philadelphia to New York. (*then*) Those days, those dreams. Burned out. Gone.

BERT No. They're here now in this empty theater and I can almost touch them!

JESSE Only the truth is here: The organized control the theater, the audience, the backers. If we could afford to do a show, we'd have no place to put it. Either we go off to a place they haven't reached—or some of us may join them.

BERT What do you mean?

JESSE I mean, you have responsibilities and no dream of yours can change them. (*he goes.* BERT *sits on trunk.* LOTTIE *has been standing, listening. She moves down, sits beside him*)

LOTTIE Jesse's excitable. Ignore him. (*then*) I found the bills you hid in Aristotle's *Poetics*.

BERT I thought the old boy might have bright ideas of how to pay them.

LOTTIE Don't make jokes.

BERT   It's time to laugh or cry a river full of tears.

LOTTIE   Abraham Erlanger was here—to offer you a part in his new show. (GEORGE *enters, stands, listening*)

BERT   I can't go begging to that man.

GEORGE   What else you gonna do? Hang around an empty theater? Look, man, you got no job now.

BERT   I know that.

GEORGE   I just wanted to make sure you did. Call him.

BERT   We'll go into that tomorrow.

GEORGE   What's wrong with today? Hell, I'll call him—(*starts out*)

BERT   Will you wait?

GEORGE   Man, look at what's happening! Swallow your pride or go back to the honky-tonks! I wanta see the hopes from Kansas City and San Francisco live on. I wanta see just a little bit of the millenium 'fore I die.

LOTTIE   George, leave him alone. It's not his fault, it's mine—mine for not being able to support him when he needs me.

BERT   Lottie, stop trying to make me over.

GEORGE   Damn it, don't bark at her 'cause you scared of me!

BERT   I'm only afraid of myself. God, I don't understand life here under this heel where you're a coward if you run and a brave man if you turn the other cheek!

LOTTIE   It's time you tried.

BERT   I have tried. From the seventh grade on. Their insults ripped my ears. Their stones bruised me. Then, I almost caught their leader—caught him and beat him half to death. That's when I decided to stay away from them—because I don't want to be a murderer! (*then*) And you—you're pushing me back to that class. Well, I can't stand being alone out there with them, holding my breath every minute, waiting—waiting for their insults. I can't stand walking into places, waiting for a silence full of slurs!

LOTTIE   Are you suggesting that I like it? Are you?

BERT   Shut up a minute!

LOTTIE   Not when you're rattling like an idiot!

BERT   Shut the hell up, I said! You damn American Negroes spout streams of stagnant words. You've talked yourselves into buying a bill of goods that says anything all-black is wrong, inferior. You've got to get white approval to take a deep breath—even when that approval is cutting your insides, killing you! (*then*) And, oh, Lord, if I sign with Erlanger there'll be oceans of words. You'll call me a deserter. You'll swear I'm doing things for Erlanger that I argued against doing in our shows. You'll want to picket the place every night I play. When I sign and go to the barber-shop, they won't keep me there for hours telling them stories. I'll get fast service! (*then*) Damn it, I won't take this. I'm going back to Antigua.

LOTTIE   (*her voice becomes low, threatening, with a strange undercurrent*)   Do you remember Antigua? Really remember it?

BERT   Of course I do.

LOTTIE   I mean the Antigua your mother told me about... What happened to your father when he lost his business? He went to work, unloading ships, didn't he?

BERT   Yes.

LOTTIE   Then there was the sun—gentle in the morning, slashing at high noon, lashing his body like a whip. What happened to him when your mother lit the lamp at night?

BERT   Nothing. Nothing.

LOTTIE   Something did happen!

BERT   He thought it was the sun!

LOTTIE   (*moving in now suddenly, for the kill*) Yes! And he cried for her to put it out. He shouted: "God, never let my son know this place exists!" (*then*) It's a false dream. There is no Antigua and no mountain top. There's no hiding place now. Here and everywhere. There are only streets, modern streets, and we're trying to crawl from their gutters. That's the way it's been written for us and I can't play it any other way!

BERT   (*flops on trunk*)   What's wanted from me in this life? All I ever wanted was to do my work, to please troubled people, then go home and read my books. (*then*) There was an Antigua once. I was six years old and my granny lay on her death bed. I used to climb the stairs to her dark room. Light seeped in through the curtains and you could see the pain gnawing at her face. I hated pain, especially for what it did to her! Then—I had an idea. I began imitating the birds she could no longer see, the crawfish, the clouds. And a smile broke out on her sick face. The day of her death she told me: "You don't know how much joy you brought me." (*slowly*) That's why I went into this business—to bring joy, not pain to myself nor to others. Well, I picked the wrong damn business!

GEORGE   I—I'll go—take Ada home. (*and he goes out.* BERT *remains sitting on the trunk.* LOTTIE *goes to him*)

LOTTIE   Forgive me, Bert. (*he looks up at her*) For trying to make you over. The moment I saw you, I knew you were the answer to our prayers for leaders. I saw something pushing you towards greatness, telling you to say: "I have not coveted. I have been coveted. I have not killed. I have been killed. I cannot destroy because I've been sent to redeem."

BERT   You thought that of me?
LOTTIE   Yes.
BERT   Why?
LOTTIE   Because I loved you—love you now.
BERT   I love you, too, Lottie. (*they embrace*) Lottie—
LOTTIE   Yes, Bert?
BERT   You're shuddering.
LOTTIE   I'm cold.
BERT   (*holding her close*)   That better?
LOTTIE   Yes. (*then*) I feel—lik—our wedding night. When I was undressed.
BERT   I remember. You were embarrassed.
LOTTIE   At first. Then, suddenly I was free of weights bogging me down. I pulled a feather from the pillow and flung it into the air. It floated and I floated with it.
BERT   I remember, Lottie. I remember. And suddenly—I can fly again, fly upwards and nothing is big enough to stop me. (*they are sitting there on the trunk.* JESSE *and* OLIVER *enter*)
JESSE   That flat, Oliver—(OLIVER *removes flat*) This is goodbye, folks.
LOTTIE   Goodbye, Jesse. (*she embraces him*)
JESSE   (*as* OLIVER *reenters*) See Erlanger, Bert. You'll do him good. I'll be rooting for you.
BERT   Thanks, Jesse. Goodbye, Mr. Jackson.
OLIVER   Bert, I'll be praying for you.
BERT   Thank you. That's good to know.
OLIVER   Praying you don't feel what I felt one time. After the war we settled on some land where nothing growed. Me and a bunch of young'uns got up and left. Years later when I was doing pretty well, I passed through the old place. The folks I'd left behind asked me if we wouldn't a all been better off if we who left had stayed on. They made me cry.
BERT   I don't feel too good right now.
LOTTIE   Well, we're not farming now. Come on, Bert. (*she has him by the arm and she starts leading him off.* JESSE *turns to* OLIVER)
JESSE   We'll move that trunk now. (OLIVER's *shoulder sag. He turns, pulls the trunk offstage. It is the only thing left on stage.* JESSE *takes one last look at the empty stage, draws a deep breath, then goes out as the lights fade*)

Scene Three

(*A New York theater. Later that week. The lights fade in on a bare stage.* ERLANGER *sits in a chair, watching* ADA *and* HATTIE *singing and dancing to a lively period tune*)

ADA AND HATTIE (*singing*)   I see laughter in the distance,
He's holding both his sides
And then the chances are
He's cried a tear besides—
Oh, isn't it exciting, delighting and inviting
If you pretend!
I could suggest the best of Old Broadway—
I could propose repose in San Jose—
Oh, isn't it exciting, delighting and inviting
If you pretend!

(*They go into a dance routine as* BERT *enters. He stands, watching them. When the dance ends,* BERT *and* ERLANGER *applaud*)

BERT   Excellent!
ERLANGER   Beyond excellent!
ADA   Thank you.
ERLANGER   No. Thank *you*! I'll get in touch with you shortly.
HATTIE   Thank you very much, Mr. Erlanger. And, Bert.
ADA   Yes, thanks again. And 'bye now. (*the girls go out.* ERLANGER *calls a "Goodbye" after them, then turns to* BERT)
ERLANGER   It was good of you to recommend them. They're talented. Spirited. Full of freshness! (*dancing sprightly*) Isn't it exciting, delighting and inviting—(*steps*) They take the grey out of your hair. (*again, imitating their steps*) If you pretend!
BERT   You like them!
ERLANGER   Oh, yes!
BERT   You plan to use them?

ERLANGER (*stops dancing*) Er—uh. Sit down a minute, Mr. Williams. (BERT *sits*) You and I—we understand things so well that sometimes we don't understand. It never dawned on me before that I can only hire one Negro.

BERT I hired many.

ERLANGER Don't sound holier-than-thou. How many times did I read where you complained because the public wouldn't accept love scenes in your shows? (*then*) I can't hire them. I can only hire you. Even that caused problems. I had a role written into this show for you. The cast threatened to strike.

BERT It's no sin to be colored, but it sure is an inconvenience.

ERLANGER I started to fire them all, but some of my backers threatened me, too. It was negotiate or lose out. I never lose.

BERT What're you talking about?

ERLANGER This: I told the cast you'd do a set of monologues in this show. On stage. Alone. They agreed to that.

BERT As long as I'm not mixing with them, it's all right. (ERLANGER *nods*) You know, that's exactly what I wanted, too. Only now it's not—simply because it's what they want.

ERLANGER This really wasn't directed at you. They're afraid. It would've been the same if I'd hired any star. With you—a little more so. (*then*) The whole thing's temporary, anyway. The most inconsistent thing in existence is emotion in the theater.

BERT I'm glad you're able to take a long view.

ERLANGER I've had to. What do you say?

BERT What can I say? It's been said for me.

ERLANGER That means???

BERT When I was captured in our show, *Abyssinia*, there was a way out—

ERLANGER What does that mean?

BERT I wish I were back in *Abyssinia* again . . . (*he stands there, fighting back the tears as he realizes he is about to be forever trapped. He turns, abruptly, goes out, leaving* ERLANGER *alone. Music rises as the lights fade out*)

Scene Four

(*The scene is Harlem. Later, that night.*

The lights come up on a scrim and suggested here is a Harlem street. At the extreme right we see a store front. Painted across the window is "Ralph's Rib-House." *Next to this, center, is a marquee over a door. The marquee reads:* "Al's Alley." *Next to this, stage left, is an apartment building.*

BERT *walks along the street, obviously under the influence of alcohol. He stops in front of Al's Alley.*

Music is heard, loud, brassy. The lights behind the scrim come up and we see the inside of Al's Alley. It is a dimly-lit place with brass railings circling an elevated dance floor. Couples move off the dance floor to the tables at ringside. OLIVER JACKSON *stands at ringside. He waves to* BERT.

The drummer goes into a fast break, then OLIVER *races into the center of the floor*)

OLIVER Yes, indeedy, folks! Yes, indeedy! I am pleased to meet and greet you here tonight in good old Harlemtown where things are done up a solid brown . . . But, before we start spinning our propellers and taking off, I wanta tell you the great Bert Williams just walked in the door. Stand up, Bert, and take a bow! Bert! (BERT *stands. There is applause*) Man! Come on up here and share a stage with me! (BERT *starts for the stage*) You all don't know it, but Bert's going to work for Abraham Erlanger on Broadway!

BERT (*on stage by now*) Thank you, Oliver Jackson. Thank you, folks! I'm like the old preacher who wandered into the whiskey still. He said: "I know I ain't supposed to be here, but I sure am glad I am here!" (*noisy laughter*) Seriously, folks—I had to come home tonight, not just because my friends are here, but because this is one place where insults don't bounce off your ears all day long.

OLIVER Tell us a story, Bert!

AUDIENCE Yeah! Come on, man!

BERT Are we all Negroes here? (OLIVER *tries to signal that there are whites in the house, but the audience is laughing now and* BERT *continues*) Maybe you all heard about my Uncle Ben. He was a big, black preacher and he was always going off to preach folks sermons. One night he's walking down the road and it come-est to storm something terrible. Uncle Ben stopped off at a farmhouse and asked the owner to let him stay overnight. The man said: "Rev, I ain't got no room, but that whole house up yonder on the hill is empty. You can stay there all night. But, I'm gonna tell you something: That house is haunted!" Uncle Ben said: "Ain't no haunts gon' bother me whilst I'm reading my Scripture Book here!" (*stops*) Wait a minute now! (*to the band*) Let's here some spooky music back there, boys! (*the band plays a couple of eerie notes.* BERT *holds up his hands*) That's enough! I just wanted to make sure somebody was listening! (*noisy laughter from crowd*) Well, Uncle Ben went on up the road and into the house and he made hisself a big fire. He set in the rocking chair, reading and rocking, rocking and reading. The wind howled and the rain beat down on the rooftop. A little white cat come down the chimney, washed his paws in the ashes, then sat down beside of Uncle Ben's left leg. Uncle Ben rocked and he read out loud: "In the Sixth Chapter in the Seventh Verse—" And another cat, the size of a bulldog, come down the chimney. This was a Angora cat and he washed his face right in the fire, then he set down side of Uncle Ben's right leg. Angora cat licked his lip and he says to the first cat, says: "When we gwyne begin on him?" The first cat says: "We can't do nothing till Martin gets here." Uncle Ben read his Scripture Book: "In the Fifth Chapter, in the Sixth Verse—" And another white cat come down the chimney. This one was the size of a Newfoundland dog. He washed his face and paws in the fire, chawed on some live coals, then spat out blazes. He licked his lips and said: "Shall we commence on him now or shall we wait till Martin gets here?" The other two cats shook their heads and said: "We can't do nothing till Martin comes." Uncle Ben closed his Scripture Book and started running out, shouting: "When Martin comes, you tell him I was here, but I done gone!"

(*The drummer punctuates the ending of this story with a crash of cymbals. The crowd applauds.* BERT *returns to his table, shaking hands around, then grabs a glass and gulps its contents.* OLIVER *steps back into spotlight*)

OLIVER   I'll betcha Uncle Ben run right to Harlem. That's what lots of us did. (*he turns now, signals to band. It plays a number with a blues, calypso, work-song base—a three part number that describes the people who settled in Harlem and their aspirations. The refrain to that number of theirs is a smashing up-tempo number, sung feverishly, in exultation over the founding of a new community*)

I had the blues downtown and I had to move uptown—
I had the blues downtown and I had to move uptown—
It was so hard down there that my world went 'round and 'round!
I said: "Listen here, world, don't you treat me that-a-way."
I said: "Listen here, world, don't you treat me that-a-way."
World said: "Son, you better go someplace where you can stay!"

Harlem, Harlem—that's the place for me!
Harlem, Harlem—where a man is free!
Harlem, Harlem—way, way, way uptown!
Harlem, Harlem—home for black and brown!
Nobody making you walk a chalk line,
Nobody telling you you ain't fine as wine,
From late Saturday evening to Monday morn
You find out exactly how you oughta been born!
Harlem, Harlem—that's the place for me!
Harlem, Harlem—where I've got to be.
Harlem, Harlem—show the world the way
Harlem, Harlem—how it oughta stay!

HATTIE (*appears. The blues again*)   I tilled the soil in the old, old romantic South.
I tilled the soil in the old, old romantic South,
But I couldn't get a piece of bread to stick in my mouth!
I told my Mama: "I got to leave this land of bliss!"
I told my Mama: "I got to leave this land of bliss!"
I'm headin' north, Mama, to face that snowman's kiss!"

HATTIE AND OLIVER   Harlem, Harlem—that's the place for me!
Harlem, Harlem—where I've got to be!
Harlem, Harlem—you're the world on a stage,
Harlem, Harlem—let them make you its sage!

ADA (*appears. A calypso note*)   They got blue skies and deep brown eyes
All over the Caribbean—
They got lots of cries and plenty signs
For it's no real millenium!
You cut that cane and you know pain,
And at you the boss man hollers,
But he keeps those Yankee dollars!

HATTIE, ADA AND OLIVER   Harlem, Harlem—a world for all to see—
Harlem, Harlem—where folks are truly free!

(*They continue with a rousing, special vocal arrangement, then they break into a series of torrid dance steps. The music is loud and furious.* BERT *continues drinking, wildly, and pounding the table, rhythmically. The crowd joins in the singing and dancing.* BERT *turns and staggers out as the number continues to a rousing climax. The lights fade out*)

Scene Five

(*The scene is the Williams home. Later, that same night.*

GEORGE *is sitting in a chair. He rises, starts to pace, then stops as he hears* BERT'*s voice.* LOTTIE *enters*)

BERT'S VOICE Harlem—Harlem—that's the place for me.
Harlem—Harlem—where a man is free!

(*He enters, sees them, stops, tries to get his bearing*)

LOTTIE Honey—
GEORGE Man! We been waiting for you!
BERT I made a stop.
GEORGE So I smell.
LOTTIE How did it go?
BERT It went. Tell you about it—tomorrow.
GEORGE Don't play in the low-key, man. We ain't British. We get excited.
LOTTIE The doctor said no excitement, George.
GEORGE The doctor's best friend ain't making history! This could pull a man back from the graveyard. We got a foot in the door now and we gonna all walk through it. Told Ada today I'm marrying her and supporting her by managing you.
BERT Will you two stop it? (*steadying himself*) What would you say if I told you—there's no contract—that the actors wanted me to work by myself. That I walked out—
GEORGE (*clutches cane as his lips form the word, "No." He shakes his head*) I—I wouldn't believe it. I'd believe you—joking. (*fumbles for watch*) getting late. I got to go. Near morning time—and I ain't got time for jokes. (*he turns, goes, quickly.* LOTTIE *draws a breath, then speaks in low, hushed tones*)
LOTTIE I don't believe it, either. I have a husband. Bert Williams.
BERT I am your husband. Bert Williams.
LOTTIE He is man's dignity. Gentle. Sometimes moody. Always understanding.
BERT I am understanding.
LOTTIE My husband angers quickly. His heart's big. Injustices hurt him. But, he's brilliant. If something like this happened, he'd stay on and show them Bert Williams is more important than any of them. He'd never get in the dirt with them.
BERT Lottie, I am he—your husband, Bert Williams.
LOTTIE (*crying out*) Liar! You're not! You're not! You've killed him! You're a murderer and you killed my husband!
BERT Lottie—
LOTTIE (*as he reaches for her*) Don't put your hands on me! I'm a minister's daughter, raised in the church, to love one man till death. Death has robbed me of Bert Williams.
BERT It hasn't!
LOTTIE I believe in the Resurrection and the Life. Will he come back?
BERT Lottie, are you out of your mind?
LOTTIE I wish I were. The lost mind knows no pain. And I know pain, do you hear me? I know pain—
BERT Lottie! (*she starts out. He tries to follow, stumbles, drunkenly, falls to the floor*)
LOTTIE Stay away from me, Stranger. My husband—he's dead.
BERT He's not dead!
LOTTIE He's not here, not here! I won't believe he's here! (*she goes. He sits on the floor, shaking his head, trying to sober himself*)
BERT I am Bert Williams. Yes. Comedian. Tragedian. Star-gazer. Trail-blazer. Wisdom's tool. And complete fool! That's who the hell I am! Nobody! (*then*) Man, what're you doing talking to yourself? (*bitterly*) You've got to talk to yourself! You've driven your wife out of her mind. You're in the trap you've always tried to avoid. You've got no place to go. (*angrily*) You need somebody, Bert Williams. A lot of somebodies. You need your own private union! (*rises, paces floor*) Well, organize your own! Isn't that what you always said? (*he goes to cabinet, gets a bottle and drinks from it. Now he lines up four chairs in a row*) The Bert Williams Union is now officially organized! (*bangs table*) The union will now come to order. The question on the floor is: Should Bert Williams strike and stay out of Erlanger's show? I recognize Member Number One. (*goes, sits in first chair and speaks as first member*) Mr. Chairman, Mr. Chairman! Why is there a Bert Williams Union? Can't he belong to one with others? Everyone belongs to something! (*suddenly*) Yes! Yes! I belong to my wife—(*then*) It's your job to make people know, to

show them you belong. (*goes to second chair, speaks as second member*) Belonging to something didn't make the other actors want to work with you. They had no other choice—(*then*) Now, look, gentlemen; Don't send this man along a blocked road towards a mountain top. For—there are no mountain tops here nor in Antigua. They've been shorn, made into shifting plateaus. Let this man stay in the back alleys with yesterday's laughter. (*moves to third chair, as third member*) Mr. Chairman, I've listened patiently to these other two members and I submit that these gentlemen are—to put it euphemistically negativistic... I submit a third approach—a gradual one. (*raises his hand*) Please! Let me finish! (*then*) In the eighteenth century Edmund Burke said: "Public calamity is a mighty leveller".... And Williams faces a calamity. But to what will he be levelled? What is the middle ground in this levelling process? (*quickly*) It is not Williams'! It is theirs who say: "What is European is civilized. What is not is uncivilized"... Gentlemen, I state categorically that neither the Bert Williams Union nor its allies can bring a readjustment. Let's accept this bone and thank God for it! (*moves to fourth chair, as fourth member*) Now, I been listening to you all and I don't know what you wants from this here boy. Bert, son, you got to put your trust in the Lord, then you got to give Him a little bit of help yourself. He didn't mean for you to listen to no Uncle Toms, no matter how fancy they talks. He give us a job to do and you carrying His banner. It's mighty heavy, too. It'd be a heap easier for you to put it down. The Lord don't want no scared chickens carrying it. Ain't many folks fit and if you gonna stop and worry about it being heavy, you ain't fit, either! (*returns to chairman's seat*) It has been stated in effect that Bert Williams does not now belong to anything—and that he can't belong! (*suddenly, bangs table with his fists*) But, I do! I do! And I always will! (*angrily he knocks over chairs, one by one*) You lie, damn you! You all lie! I do belong! I belong to the world and the world will know it! Shut up! Shut up! I won't listen to you! (*he has knocked over all the chairs by now and he stands there, panting. Slowly now, he straightens up and he calls*) Lottie—(*then*) Lottie Thompson Williams!

LOTTIE (*in doorway*) You called me.

BERT I have found your husband. (*then*) Lottie, I'm going to shove everything down their throats. I'm going to make them sorry for what they tried to do! (*calling out*) You out there in the night and in the stars, listen to me! I'm going to walk here on this earth and breathe like other men! You're going to hear my footsteps thundering through the darkness you've tried to wrap around me! Do you hear me out there in the darkness? Do you hear me? (LOTTIE *has rushed into his arms. They cling together as the lights fade and the music rises*)

Scene Six

(*The lights fade in on a theater marquee which indicates it is opening night of the Follies. A white girl and boy are singing and dancing*)

GIRL (*singing*) There's a reason you and I are here—
Why of all the flowers you can see
You should pick a lonely rose like me,
Love ain't nobody's fool!

There's a reason you and I are here,
Why the apple tempted even Eve,
Why I need a man I can believe,
Love ain't nobody's fool!

Although every child begins to feel
All kinds of things when he's in school,
It's only life that can reveal:
Love ain't no one's fool!

There's a reason you and I are here,
Why the moon could never leave the sky,
And it's love that knows the reason why,
Love ain't nobody's fool!

BOY There's a reason you and I are here—
Why Delilah cut off Samson's hair,
Why old Jezebel was not a square—
Love ain't nobody's fool!

GIRL There's a reason you and I are here—
Why a young man's fancy turns in spring,
Why the nightingale finds songs to sing:
Love ain't nobody's fool!

BOY Old Sol, it is said, found him a wife
Who taught him 'bout love's golden rule—

GIRL Which only shows that all through life

BOTH Love ain't no one's fool!

(*As the number concludes, they dance off. Now*

there is a single spotlight on the curtain. BERT's *gloved hand slips through it. Now, he steps into center stage*)

BERT Welcome to opening night of the Follies, folks. In case you all wondering what I'm doing here, they didn't have no place for me backstage so they sent me out here whilst the girls are changing their costumes. (*he turns, steps back between the curtains. Suddenly, he comes charging out, falling down in vaudeville style. We hear a crash of cymbals. He leans on his elbow as he speaks to the audience*) The girls ain't finished dressing yet. (*rises*) My luck is running about like Bill Johnson's. Y'all know who Bill Johnson was—? (*music. He sings*)

Bill Johnson was a dud—
He joined the Darktown Poker Club
And cursed the day they tell him he could join—
When he held Queens, they held Kings
And each night he would contribute all his coin—
So he said: "I'm gonna play 'em tight tonight,
No bob-tail flesh gonna make me bite,
And when I go in my hand will be a peach!
You see this brand new pistol?
I had it polished just today—
I want you to follow these rules
Hereafter when you play:
Keep your hands above the table when you dealing, please—
And I don't want to see no cards between your knees.
And stop dealing from the bottom 'cause it looks too rough:
When you playing poker five cards is enough!
We ain't gonna play this game according to Hoyle.
We gonna play this came according to *me*!"

(*The music carries under. He sits in a chair and performs his Poker Game Pantomime. He deals imaginary cards. Five times around he deals, then puts down the imaginary deck. The drum punctuates these gestures. He picks up his cards and glances at his imaginary companions. Now he puts down his hand and deals the extra cards. He is pleased to give out three cards, curious when a player draws two, and filled with misgiving when someone draws one. In the end he draws two for himself and we can see that these are just the cards he needs. Some lively betting starts. He becomes so confident that soon his whole stack of chips is in the pot. Now comes the moment for the call. He prepares to rake in his winnings. But, there is a turn of events! He cranes his neck nad looks. He has lost! His face and body become*

that of the saddest man in the world. He gets up, starts away, sadly, his shoulders slumped. The music rises as he walks from the stage.

Applause is heard over. He returns with a towel, bows to audience, then begins to wipe the burnt cork from his face)

Thank you. And now—a song I wrote. One that's a little different from those you associate with my work. (*music. He sings*)

Excuse me, but there's something in my eye,
Yet somehow I see things clearly today—
The dreams that I dreamed beneath that tropic sky
Have come true in life's tragic way as poets say.
The way has been long—my life's been a troubled brew.
I've learned that the song that's saddest is sweetest, too.
Excuse me, but there's something in my eye,
And somehow I've known this feeling before—
Our laughter it seems is closest to a cry,
And through years and tears I've found love's forever more—
Excuse me, but there's something in my eye!

(*He walks from stage into* LOTTIE's *arms as lights fade*)

Scene Seven

(*The lights are up in* BERT's *dressing room.* LOTTIE *and* BERT *step into the dressing room as* GEORGE, ADA, JESSE *and* OLIVER *burst into the place. The stage literally explodes with energy and enthusiasm—with the exception of* OLIVER *who stands off to one side in silence*)

JESSE Congratulations!
GEORGE Yeah, man!
ADA You were nearly as good as you were in our shows!
GEORGE (*nudging* ADA) Man, tomorrow's reviews are gonna look like Erlanger's press agent wrote them. They'll call you an overnight success. Nobody knows how many nights a man stays up to become an overnight success. (*then*) I'm so happy I'm gonna let you beat me at Smut!
BERT I've done nothing. What're they saying uptown? I expected them to picket the show.
ADA They were scared to.
BERT Because it had the stamp of white approval.
LOTTIE Honey, don't be caustic.
BERT I may be naive, but I'm not stupid.

OLIVER That old slave, Bert, who pointed up to the stars and showed how the Lord had planted them right—he said: "Even the little ones—they different from the big collards that grow while the little ones die. The big collards get holes eaten in 'em by worms." Seemed like he was talking silly then, but that's what he said. (*then*) You a big collard, Bert, not a star. (OLIVER *turns and goes out. The others stand, looking after him*)

GEORGE Well, damn!

LOTTIE Forget him, Bert. Time's passed him by and now he's trying to play philosopher. A fancy way of showing envy.

BERT I wish it were that, Lottie. (ERLANGER *rushes into the room, bubbling with enthusiasm*)

ERLANGER Mr. Williams! Mr. Williams,—the cast just met with me! They asked me to put back into the show the scenes between you and the others! (*laughing*) What did I tell you about the inconsistency of emotions in the theater?

BERT The worms are biting.

ERLANGER What's that?

BERT They were so sure I'd jump at the opportunity! What the hell do they think I am?

ERLANGER Truthfully—they don't know what to think. One called you: The funniest man I ever saw, the saddest man I ever knew.

BERT Tell them all to go to hell!

LOTTIE Bert, please don't!

BERT I will! I will!

LOTTIE Not now. Not now.

BERT How long, then? Even a dog bites back when he's kicked!

LOTTIE Don't—(*her hand flies to her head. She reels a bit.* BERT *starts towards her, then stops, suddenly, stands firmly*)

BERT Step on over and fall, honey. I'm not picking you up this time.

GEORGE Lottie—(*and he is at her side, attempting to support her. He looks at* BERT) Man!!!

LOTTIE (*suddenly moves out of* GEORGE's *arms, resolutely determined. To* BERT) The time's run out for overstepping. When you do, you need someone strong enough to support you.

BERT I don't like that!

LOTTIE That's too damn bad!

ERLANGER Excuse me. I have to go—

LOTTIE You have to go nowhere. Just stay and listen! (*to* BERT) You've cried an ocean, but you don't know what in hell it's all about! You came here with something! You knew your parents and your grandparents. Some of us were lucky to know *one* parent! (*angrily*) It was no accident, either! It was planned from the day a bunch of sniveling, starving European rogues raped African royalty and enslaved it. They placed rogues and thieves and serfs over a people that they wouldn't have been allowed to speak to in another land. These rogues and thieves and serfs had no status and they had to achieve it by denying status to black people. The Europeans were not men and they had to prove they were men by killing, looting, stealing and raping! (*then*) What do you think George Washington's great-grandfather was? A sailor! And Washington himself would have been poor white trash if he hadn't inherited thirty slaves from his father! And God knows the number of slaves Washington himself fathered! What do you think Patrick Henry was when he cried: "Give me liberty or give me death?" He was the owner of twenty-three slaves!

BERT Lottie, wait—

LOTTIE You wait! And shut up a minute! I've read a few books myself and I've had some thoughts you haven't had! (*then*) The one thing these Europeans knew was that to destroy a people they had to destroy men. They learned it over sixteen centuries from the kings your Shakespeare idolized! They knew it when they reached Plymouth Rock and made love to animals while killing off the Indians! They knew it when they sold black men away from their families. And they knew it after slavery time when black men had to wander off from home to earn a pittance. They know it, still, for they kill black men who are men! (*fiercely*) Well, who in the hell was left to keep the family together? Black women! We had to work in the fields with our babies at our sides. We had to wash and cook and clean for ourselves and for white folks. And who was beside us late at night when we wanted a gentle touch, a kind word? Who was there to protect us from the night noises and the night riders? Nobody! We *had* to overstep our bounds, to be more than women—to be maneuverers. It wasn't our fault, but you weren't around. You American Negroes were going off someplace and you West Indians were standing around, criticizing! (*annoyed*) This white man—he will give you nothing! Oh, he'll smile and give you a few dollars to fly up in his face, to pout and rave and rant at him. He'll give you a few dollars for that and he won't feel guilty worth a damn because he'll have cleansed his soul. And he'll go out and kill and make millions and keep on doing that while you're letting off steam!... Do you think I like pushing you down the road to heartache, trying to get a little bit of something in a land of nothing? Do you think I like holding out hope in the midst of hopelessness? Well, I don't like it, but what else can I do? (*sinks into chair, annoyed. Tears stream down her cheeks.* BERT *goes to her*) We didn't want to be the poor cousins begging for a corner in a land we built! We didn't want to be reduced to that...

BERT   Lottie, Lottie—I'm glad you told me. Glad because now I know what I have to do. (*he holds her close. She stops crying. Now, he releases her, gently, then stands, facing* ERLANGER) Mr. Erlanger, I was going to send the cast a message—something subtle—about waiting till Martin came. I couldn't wait because you've always made me run from Martin. I was going to leave your show and it would've had to close because I, Bert Williams, made your show. And that would've been my revenge—putting them out of work. (*suddenly*) Only I'm not going to do it! I'm not because now I know what they are! They're lost children here on this shifting plateau called America. This plateau has cut down the mountains all across the sea and its sickness is imposed on foreign lands. I know now that no mountain can be built here. But, I'm an artist and I intend to kick up so much dirt that maybe a small hill might appear. Yes, I'm an artist and I can't resist standing here, trying to be remembered as Somebody not Nobody—of trying to be remembered beyond the walls of time. You tell the mountain's bulldozers I'll kick and I'll kick and I'll build my own mountain for the world to see! (*then*) And tell them not to cry for me. Cry for the children—the lost children. They'll look at me and see two-thirds of the world as clowns. When they have to face those people they call darkies and chinks and brown beasts, they won't know how to deal with them. Every laugh at me and every abuse is a nail in white America's coffin! (BERT *stands there with just a trace of a smile on his face*)

ERLANGER   Yes. Yes, I'll tell them. Time for me to go back—(*and he goes out, quickly*)

GEORGE   (*to* BERT) You stuck-up, stubborn West Indian fool! You still being Anglican in a Baptist world! And damn if I ain't hoping you'll convert even me! (*he goes out, followed by* JESSE *and* ADA. BERT *and* LOTTIE *stand alone. He moves down to her*)

BERT   No tears, Lottie. Never.

LOTTIE   Never.

BERT   Even after death.

LOTTIE   Even then.

BERT   For there's one consolation for that star shining over the big collards, seeing it eaten by worms. The consolation is the star will be there, morning and night, long after the collards have been eaten by worms and people. (*then*) Let's go home and have a drink to that.

LOTTIE   Let's just go home and have a drink. (*he puts his arm around her and they start out together as the lights fade out. The music rises through the darkness. Curtain*)

10

Comedy as Protest

**Langston Hughes   Charles Sebree   C. Bernard Jackson
James V. Hatch   and   Douglas Turner Ward**

The Emperor cannot be laughed at. All allusions to his new clothes must be suppressed. The forbidden subject is driven underground. "This story will kill you!" says one. "I thought I would die laughing," says another. By means of jokes the people circumvent the Emperor; they find subtle ways to speak the unmentionable. The fear and hatred of the Emperor is now expressed in laughter.

As political jokes are popular in a fascist state, so jokes about race and sex have been a part of the American folklore: the subjects evoke emotions too deep and too unsettling to be revealed openly. In the 1950's and 1960's, stand-up comics like Shelly Berman, Lenny Bruce, Moms Mabley, and Dick Gregory brought race and sex out of the toilets and into the nightclubs, onto records, and finally onto speakers' stands and television. To hear the forbidden spoken aloud in public audience was very funny. The Freudians were smiling too.

Henri Bergson's theory of laughter does not contradict Freud's. According to Mr. Bergson, laughter is the society's way of keeping the individual alert, awake, and within the norm of the group. Laughter is healthy, and corrective for the overly-serious, the vain, the pompous, the ugly, the eccentric, even the vicious and the mean. It is a force of control. Mr. Bergson saw the *élan vital*, the life force, as being in constant motion and change. If individuals are to survive, they must be alert and adaptive. Laughter keeps them this way. Freud explains the process inside the mind; Henri Bergson explains why that process is there.

The use of laughter in the commercial theater as a weapon against racial injustice is a recent device. Although there were works, like *Finian's Rainbow* (1947), that used laughter to ridicule white superiority, black playwrights did not make wide use of the device until the 1960's. The first example on Broadway was *Purlie Victorious*, followed by *Fly Blackbird*, *Jerico-Jim-Crow*, *Day of Absence*, *Plantation*, *The Reckoning*, and others.

Why was the flood of comedy, satire, burlesque, and farce so long in coming? Blacks had developed over many years an elaborate vocabulary of race jokes. The oft-heard remark by whites that the Negroes were happy because they were always laughing is testimony to laughter's ethnic existence as well as its necessity. Why did this life-sustaining humor wait until the 1960's to come to the legitimate stage?

The answer perhaps lies in the Supreme Court decision on segregation, the Birmingham bus strike, the Greensboro sit-ins, the success of *Raisin in the Sun*, Dick Gregory, Martin Luther King, Malcolm X—everything that raised black consciousness in the 1950's, liberating humor until blacks could dare come on the commercial stage and demand that the white audience pay to laugh at itself. Racial oppression in America had lifted to the point where humor could come off the streets, out of the pool halls, bars, beauty salons, up from the kitchen, and into the theater as a business.

By the last half of the 1960's a large black audience was beginning to attend the theater and pay for the pleasure of publicly laughing at the absurdity of the system and the Negroes who had developed unproductive ways of dealing with that system.

Fly Blackbird (1960) and *Day of Absence* (1965) seem to be written for black and white audiences. The laughter is aimed at the absurdity of segregation; the theme is integration. The main thrust of *Limitations of Life* (1938) is to delight black audiences. *The Dry August* (1949) is a fantasy intended to evoke soft smiles in any audience.

Langston Hughes (1902–1967)

Limitations of Life   1938

The American motion picture industry since its inception has perpetuated the idea of the superiority of white Anglo-Saxons. All other races have been subjected to ridicule, caricature, mockery. Stereotypes of Italian, Jewish, Spanish, Irish, Oriental, Indian, and black Americans have emerged, but the black stereotype has remained the longest. The country's economic system has stabilized the black man's "place" in society; since blacks generally cannot visually lose themselves in the melting pot, they continue to be portrayed as primitive, childish, lazy, lewd, good-for-nothing buffoons, and faithful servants.

The 1934 film *Imitation of Life*, adapted for the screen by Fanny Hurst from her novel, may have been "novel in Hollywood," as Sterling Brown points out in his review (*Opportunity*, March, 1935), but "the old stereotype Mammy, and the tragic mulatto, and the ancient ideas about the mixture of the races" still existed. Miss Hurst was quick to defend her work:

> The important social value of the picture is that it practically inaugurates into the important medium of the motion picture, a consideration of the Negro as part of the social pattern of American life.
> (*Opportunity*, April, 1935).

Mr. Brown and other blacks viewed this social pattern as romantic rather than realistic—a pattern that the motion picture industry helped mold and shape, and which was firmly embedded in the consciousness of an extremely large portion of American whites as absolute truth.

Langston Hughes obviously sides with Brown in his views of the film, and through the satiric *Limitations of Life* makes his point. The ridiculousness of the situation is pointed up by reversing the roles of the characters as they appear in the movie. No white viewer can identify with Audette Aubert and her motives in the play—anymore than a black could identify with Delilah in the film.

Although *Limitations of Life* satirizes *Imitation of Life*, it is not necessary to have seen the film to get the point of the play.

Mr. Hughes' satiric skit is no less applicable to the 1959 remake of the film, even though there was an attempt in the later film to add dignity to the roles of the blacks by eliminating the dialect and placing more emphasis on the mulatto problem. Still, the movie remains a romantic concept based on white attitudes about what black Americans ought to think, feel, and be, rather than a realism relevant to the times.

Companion skits by Langston Hughes, *Little Eva*, a satire on *Uncle Tom's Cabin*, and *Em-Fuehrer Jones*, a caricature of Eugene O'Neill's *Emperor Jones*, were presented on the same bill at the Harlem Suitcase Theatre in 1938 (see introduction to *Don't You Want To Be Free?*).

Limitations of Life

CAST OF CHARACTERS

MAMMY WEAVERS
AUDETTE AUBERT
ED STARKS

PLACE *Harlem.*

TIME *Right now.*

SCENE *A luxurious living room. Swell couch and footstool. At right, electric stove, griddle, pancake turner, box of pancake flour (only Aunt Jemima's picture is white), and a pile of paper plates. Also a loaf of white bread.*

(AUDETTE AUBERT, *pretty blond maid, is busy making pancakes on the stove. Enter* MAMMY WEAVERS, *a colored lady, in trailing evening gown, with tiara and large Metropolitan Opera program, speaking perfect English with Oxford accent*)

AUDETTE (*taking* MAMMY'*s ermine*) Mammy Weavers, ah been waitin' up for you-all. Ah thought you might like some nice hot pancakes before you-all went to bed.
MAMMY You shouldn't have waited up for me, my dear.
AUDETTE Aw, chile!
MAMMY Besides, I don't want any pancakes, Audette. I've just had lobster à la Newburg at the Mimo Club.
AUDETTE Well, now! How did you-all like the opera, Mammy Weavers?
MAMMY Flagstad was divine tonight, but Melchior was a wee bit hoarse.
AUDETTE Oh, ah'ms so sorry, Mammy Weavers! Maybe Melchior ought to use Vicks like Nelson Eddy.
MAMMY (*sighing*) I'm just a little tired, Audette.
AUDETTE Oh, Mammy Weavers, set right down and rest your feet. I'll run fetch your slippers, honey.
MAMMY I don't know what I'd do without you, Audette.
AUDETTE I'll never leave you, Mammy Weavers. (*runs and gets slippers*) Just lemme put your carpet slippers on. (*kneels*) I'll rub your feet a little first.
MAMMY (*relaxing*) Oh, that feels so good!
AUDETTE (*looking up like a faithful dog*) Do it, Mammy Weavers?
MAMMY Tell me, Audette, where is your little Riola tonight?
AUDETTE Lawd, Mammy Weavers, ma little daughter's tryin' so hard to be colored. She just loves Harlem. She's lyin' out in de backyard in de sun all day long tannin' herself, ever day, tryin' so hard to be colored.
MAMMY What a shame, the darling's so fair and blue-eyed! Even though her father was an Eskimo, you'd never know it. Never.
AUDETTE He wooed me on a dog sled when I were on that Re-Settlement Project in Alaska. How romantic it were! But he melted away after Riola was born. Then I started workin' for you, Mammy Weavers.

(*Enter* ED STARKS, *a sleek-headed jigaboo in evening clothes*)

ED Delilah, here's your car keys, my dear. (*to the maid*) Audette, why don't you go to bed?
AUDETTE I can't sleep till Mammy Weavers gets home.
MAMMY Darling Audette! I want to do something nice for you, my sweet. Try to think of something you want more than anything else in the world.
AUDETTE All I wants, Mammy Weavers, is a grand funeral when I die.
MAMMY Darling! But don't you want a nice home of your own?
AUDETTE No, Mammy Weavers, that little room down in your basement's all right for me! (*jumping up*) I gwine make Mr. Ed Starks some nice pancakes right now. Don't you want some, Mr. Ed?

Limitations of Life

ED You know I like your pancakes, Audette. But if it's all the same with you tonight, give me some of that fine white bread.

MAMMY No, Ed! No! Pancakes will do! I got a patent on that flour so we get it free. Bread's too high.

ED O.K.

AUDETTE (*turning pancakes*) Does you want butter, 'lasses, or honey on your pancakes, Mr. Ed?

ED I want jelly on mine!

AUDETTE Then I'll run downstairs to the pantry and get you some, Mr. Ed.

MAMMY Oh, Audette, you shouldn't do so much for us.

AUDETTE I never gets tired doin' for you and Mr. Ed, Mammy Weavers. I like colored folks!

MAMMY I like white folks, too, my dear. (*musing*) I was raised by the sweetest old white mammy! When I remember all my dear old New England mammy did for me, I want to do something for you, Audette. Something you'll never forget. (*with great generosity*) Darling, maybe you'd like a day off?

AUDETTE (*flipping a pancake*) Not even a day off, Mammy Weavers! Ah wouldn't know what to do with it. (*exits, head down*)

ED (*throwing up his hands*) Once a pancake, always a pancake! (*picks up Jemima box with white auntie on it, and shakes his head*)

(*Curtain*)

Charles Sebree (1914–)

The Dry August
1949

The version of *The Dry August* printed here is a shortened version of the full-length script written by Mr. Sebree in 1949. It is from this original script that Mr. Sebree and Greer Johnson adapted the Broadway musical, *Mrs. Patterson*, in 1954.

The Dry August is a dream play—not because it has a dream sequence, but because it is a reflection of a childhood in the distant past; a childhood filled with suppressed desires that could only be realized or fulfilled through *dreams*.

The Dry August is a play about the agonies of black youth. Some critics have compared it to Carson McCullers' *The Member of the Wedding*, but Mr. Sebree's young girl, Teddy, is a complete contrast to Miss McCullers' character, Frankie. Frankie's world is secure; when she realizes this she matures and can absorb herself completely into it. Teddy's world is one of poverty and insecurity; when she does mature, the world that she must confront is one filled with prejudices and restrictions. She is the pathetic, lonely symbol of black frustration. A bright girl, filled with hope and ambition, she is aware of her inferior education and will rise above her environment only through self-determination. This is the story of a young mind warped by the white values that have been instilled in it, white goals that can never be realized—values and goals that Martie Charles warns us against in her play, *Job Security*.

Teddy's education is limited and useless. If she is fortunate enough to get to college she "might" become a teacher or maybe a nurse, or she "might" make a career for herself as a beautician. At the end of the play, when Aunt Matt and Anna question her about the future, her response is humorous, shocking, and a pathetic comment on society: "I want to be a rich white woman." The statement is not to be taken literally. Innately Teddy hates Mrs. Patterson, the rich white woman, who is to some degree directly responsible for the girl's position. At the same time, Teddy has been groomed by her society to desire material things, to dream the American dream—which, in her limited world, is a reflection of Mrs. Patterson. It is easy to comprehend Teddy's feelings during this particular phase of black history, and for a number of years to follow. To be black was to be labeled "inferior," and "inferior" lives were snuffed out at the slightest whim. To be black was to live in mortal fear, but fearlessness, one of the splendors of youth, is what Teddy possesses. She is determined to escape her immediate environment because she knows—as we see it in the dream sequence—that she is being cheated.

Mr. D. has confined Bessie Bolt to a tree because she "cheats," and when Mrs. Patterson is discovered cheating, Teddy realizes that the woman is no better than either Bessie or Mr. D. The illusion is destroyed, and she must face reality—not only the reality of herself, but of the world in which she lives. Her world is corrupt—preaching one philosophy, adhering to another. The corruption is evident in blacks (Aunt Matt is a thief, yet she professes to be a Christian, and by contemporary standards she is); the corruption in whites is finally evident to Teddy. When the play ends, however, Teddy does not yet see how the corruption of one leads to the corruption of the other.

Charles Sebree is a poet of mood and character for the theater. He has directed and designed sets and costumes for the American Negro Theater. Mr. Sebree was a member of the first Katherine Dunham Dance Company, working both as a designer and as a dancer. Above all he is an artist, a painter of a private world that is occult, yet familiar.

The Dry August

CAST OF CHARACTERS

THEODORA (TEDDY) HICKS
MILK PEDDLING GIRL
WILLIE (B.) BRAYBOY
ANNA HICKS
AUNT MATT CROSSY
MR. D.
BESSIE BOLT
MRS. PATTERSON
JUNE EVANS
ROSE EVANS
FERN EVANS

(*The scene is the house and yard of* ANNA HICKS, *in Halls' Bottom, on the edge of some town in Kentucky.* ANNA'*s house is a two-room dilapidated shack with a small crumbling porch in front. On the porch there is a rough table and a few cane chairs. A pail of drinking water. The front wall of the two rooms is cut away to show the small kitchen and the larger warming room. The kitchen is furnished with a small rusty iron stove, a box of firewood and a scuttle of coal beside the stove, a begrimed kitchen cabinet with broken doors, a carryall for kitchen implements: china, eating tools, etc., and a few battered cane chairs. The warming room is a little larger than the kitchen. Across the back wall is a tarnished brass bed covered with a patchwork quilt of many-colored silks. Two gaudy fringed souvenir pillows stand erect at the bed's head and a bare window is over the center of the bed. On the wall at the side of the window is a fly-specked calendar, and on the other a faded charcoal portrait of* ANNA'*s mother reminiscent of the '80's. Jammed in one corner is a dresser bedecked with cheap glass objects, a pin cushion, a heart shaped red satin candy box, etc. On the other side of the room is an old fashion tray trunk, and the fireplace is a begrimed white washed brick. The mantle is covered with a scarf of newspapers cut out in designs. On top are a silly cupid doll, paper flowers, and a Mason fruit jar of money, hidden behind a picture on the mantle. The red clay yard is barren except for a few patches of tough weeds. Near its edge there is a large Magnolia tree with low-hanging branches, a large greyish rock jaunting from the ground directly to the side of the tree. The yard is surrounded by a makeshift fence. A worn path leads from the steps of the house through the yard, and back to the road. To the left there is a break in the fence that leads off stage to the water well. When the curtain goes up,* TEDDY *is sitting on the rock dressed in a woman's long skirt, a hat and a crêpe de chîne blouse. She pretends to be a grown woman. She fans herself*)

TEDDY (*talking to herself, she goes over to the gate*) Why is that you, Mrs. Patterson. Is that you, surely? I'm so proud to see you! The sight of you is good for sore eyes. If I had known you was coming, I would have gotten something delish—(*together they move back to the rock*) But I guess it's the welcome that puts the good taste in the mouth, huh? Now let me get you a great big bowl of sherbert. It will cool you off some. (*the jay birds hacking call interrupts her*) Damn it! Why don't you shut your big mouth. How can I play with you making all that racket! (*she returns to pretending*) I see on the Society page of the *Southern Journal* that the fall season's going to be something—with the fox hunt in Bowling Green—and the all blue dance at the country club—my, I don't see how I will ever get myself together for so much activity—(*she goes into the house, gets a book and comes back into the yard, and begins to read*) Paris is the playground of the world, and the queen city, with a population... (*jay bird interrupts again*) Shut up! I say. Shut up! (*she throws the book aside*) Damn bird! (*a thin underfed white girl appears at the gate with a basket of eggs and a pail of milk*)

GIRL Teddy, you all want any milk today?

TEDDY No, we get plenty milk.
GIRL Eggs?
TEDDY We got eggs too.
GIRL Butter?
TEDDY We got so much butter now its getting rancid.
GIRL (*laughing*) You niggers ain't got a pot to—
TEDDY I would be obliged if you would call me by my name.
GIRL Darkey! (*she exits*)
TEDDY (*after her*) Sticks and stones will break my bones but never words—honey.

(WILLIE B. *enters. He is a spare, loosely built boy of sixteen. He is given to telling tall tales and his eyes twinkle cunningly when his tall tales reach a climax and he has the habit of rolling his tongue in his cheek and smiling to himself. Like* TEDDY, *he too is given to dreaming of escape. He is dressed in a vivid green shirt and faded overalls. His battered felt hat is cut out in designs for ventilation and fits him becomingly*)

WILLIE B. Hi there, Teddy! What you been up to today?
TEDDY (*walking to the rock and sitting*) I been thinking. Kinda' taling to myself.
WILLIE B. You always thinking. Thinking makes you grow old too quick, girl.
TEDDY I wish I was older. I wish I was a grown lady so I could get out of this place.
WILLIE B. Grown people have to think from night to day. What you want to be grown for?
TEDDY So I can go off to some big city on my own. I get so tired doing nothing, seeing nothing. All I like about this place is to hear the passenger train and the B & O freighter whistles blow at night.
WILLIE B. Aw, you be grown before you know it. Besides school will be openin' in a month, and you won't be so bored. (*the jay bird hollers*)
TEDDY Well don't be looking at me like that, Boy, ever since you went to Chicago to visit your uncle, you've had a real dreamy look.
WILLIE B. Maybe I ain't woke up yet.
TEDDY Come on, let's play a little Black Jack—Naw, I'd better get these greens on. (TEDDY *goes into the kitchen and gets a pan of greens, and comes back to the porch*) Come on help me pick these greens, I should of had them on, but it don't take long for them to cook.

Colored people cook they greens too long, anyway. (TEDDY *and* WILLIE B. *move to the rock and begin picking the greens*) If I see any more greens, I'll turn into them.
WILLIE B. I like 'em.
TEDDY Wouldn't it be nice if we had a whole acre of corn and tomatoes.
WILLIE B. Not to say nothing of all the okra and radishes and young scallions.
TEDDY Be nice to have a fruit orchard too.
WILLIE B. I wonder what a orange tree looks like?
TEDDY Must be pretty. Now here, let me get these greens on. (*she goes into the house and puts the greens in a pot and onto the stove*)
WILLIE B. What else you having?
TEDDY Just greens and cornbread, same old thing. Wouldn't it be nice if we had a lot of money and could take a trip to Chi and, see all . . . (*the jay bird's fierce call interrupts her*) There goes that blasted jay bird! He's been making so much noise all day I can't hardly think, or do nothing! (*she picks up a rock and throws it at him*) I almost hit him. I scared him anyway . . . fool thing! (TEDDY *starts to get wood for the stove*)
WILLIE B. You better not hit the devil's friend, girl. They the most wicked birds on earth.
TEDDY I wonder why they make so much racket. They're worse than an old woman.
WILLIE B. They tormented that's what. Every Friday all the jay birds visit hell to take a grain of sand to the devil to burn the dead with. And every grain is a ransom for the souls in hell who can't get free until all the sand on the surface of the word's been carried below.
TEDDY (*laughing*) Boy, you try to know so much. Sometimes I get to listening to you, I get carried away by all your talk. (*the jay bird hollers*) If you the devil's friend why you hang around here so much? (*the jay bird hollers again*) Besides ain't no such thing as the devil, mama says. The devil's a kind of spirit that gets into people.
WILLIE B. (*with tongue in cheek*) He gets into people all right, one way or the other. I've heard tell of people who would sell their souls to the devil for as little as a gold watch. (*jay bird hollers*)
TEDDY (*laughing*) Shute, Willie B., you ought to be ashamed of yourself. If there was

any truth in that you'd have an automobile right now. (*slightly interested*) You know so much, how do you go about selling yourself to the devil?

WILLIE B.   I hear tell if you cross one hand over the other while there's a full moon, and raise them above your head and spit seven times to the east and west; the devil will appear to give you anything you want or any kind of power.

TEDDY   Shute, boy, that ain't nothing but talk. You'd lie at the drop of a hat. (*laughing*) If there was anything to that I'd sell myself to him, (*more seriously*) and go to one of Mrs. Patterson's teas. Might even sell myself to him for a string of peal beads or a bottle of toilet water.

WILLIE B.   I'd just as soon sell myself for an automobile. Get out of this place, go to Chicago.

TEDDY   You and me both.

(*There is a moment of silence as* TEDDY *and* WILLIE B. *look at each other. In each of their looks there is a hope and recognition of each of their desire to escape the monotony of Hall's Bottom. A piano is heard off stage*)

WILLIE B.   Old Blind Lemon can really whip that piano.

TEDDY   Can't be though. Why're you looking at me like that?

WILLIE B.   Oh, I was just thinking.

TEDDY   Go on, tell me ... I like to hear. Tell me some more about your Chicago trip.

WILLIE B.   I've told you just about everything I know about it.

TEDDY   I could hear about Chicago forever, and never get tired of it, even if it ain't all true.

WILLIE B. (*sitting on the rock besides* TEDDY) Well, you take that time that I was down on State Street. It was lit up like day, but it was night. The music was coming from every place. People balling the jack and eagle rocking to beat the band ... and the women were dressed like everything, in spangles, silk shoes and furs. That was some night girl! It was just like a million stars had come down to throw their light all around. And the theaters, you ought to have seen them. I went to one theater called the Grand—

TEDDY (*in wonderment*)   The Grand Theater.

WILLIE B.   I went there to see Bessie Bolt— She was the Queen of the blues; when she came onto the stage it was like looking to the east with four suns sitting at once her dress shone so—and pretty, she was just as pretty as a red bird in a white blooming tree—

(ANNA *comes in during* WILLIE B.'*s talk and stands at the gate listening. She is a woman of 30, who has been coarsened by work. She is kind, but resolute, and a little uneasy about* TEDDY'*s tall imagination and desires. Being resigned to her way of living, there is a note of haunting sadness in her voice and laughter. She is wearing a simple cotton dress, a weartherbeaten white straw hat. She is carrying a few bundles. At the moment she is trying to be angry*)

TEDDY   Colored people carry on up North, huh?

ANNA (*enters the yard and interrupts their reverie*)   Teddy, ain't I told you to stay out of that trunk a 100 times? First thing I know you'll ruin that silk dress on playing woman. You've ruined my crêpe de chîne blouse and got a run in my silk stockings.

TEDDY   They had holes in them when Mrs. Patterson give them to you.

ANNA   Don't talk back. And stop standing back in your legs.

TEDDY   Yes, mama.

ANNA   I don't know what's wrong with you, all them books got you crazy!

TEDDY   Yes, mama.

ANNA   Now just let me catch you dousing yourself in my toilet water, and using my face powder, you hear me! All you can do is sit around and play Black Jack with Willie B. Didn't I tell you to stop standing back in your legs?

TEDDY   Yes, mama.

WILLIE B.   I guess I'll be going. (*gets up to go. There's a moment's silence*)

ANNA   Don't snatch yourself off, Willie B., I ain't mad.

WILLIE B.   May be this heat rouses you. (*he sits*).

ANNA (*she decides to let the matter of the dress drop. She turns to* TEDDY *who is about to get out of her costume*)   Here's fifty cents more to add to your high school money. (TEDDY *instead takes the money into the house and puts it into the Mason fruit jar and returns to the porch*)

TEDDY   Pretty soon that jar will be running over.

ANNA How much we got saved now?

TEDDY Over twenty dollars, mama, you want me to put the rest of your money in the trunk?

ANNA That fifty cents is all I got. I broke some of Mrs. Patterson's sherbert dishes and she took it out my pay.

WILLIE B. I'll be damned—

TEDDY How did Mrs. Patterson's tea turn out, mama?

ANNA Right nice. (*she sits on the edge of the porch*)

TEDDY Who was there?

ANNA (*takes her hat off and fans herself*) Just them rich Evans girls.

TEDDY I was reading about them in the paper the other day. They're southern belles, real aristocrats.

ANNA They all must have been born in the summer time.

TEDDY How's that?

ANNA Well, they're named June, Fern, and Rose. They right cute little old things, and real nice. They made a pretty picture sitting on the lawn sipping their tea.

TEDDY What did they have on?

ANNA Thin organdy.

TEDDY I bet I can guess the colors.

ANNA What colors?

TEDDY Yellow, pink and green.

ANNA I believe you're right.

TEDDY I bet Mrs. Patterson was dressed fine—like me. What did they talk about?

ANNA Aw, about their travels and who they know. Just small talk.

TEDDY Didn't they play cards or nothing? Just talked?

ANNA Just talked. Didn't say nothing, either. Mrs. Patterson sent you some cookies. (TEDDY *takes the bag and starts eating a cookie. She gives* WILLIE B. *one*)

WILLIE B. Ain't they good.

TEDDY Delicious.

ANNA (*goes into the kitchen, puts the cornbread in the stove*) They ought to be good, they cost three-fifty a pound, more than I get a week.

TEDDY I wonder why she gave them to me? Taste like they got whiskey in them.

ANNA They're rum cookies.

TEDDY (*gets a cookie and gives one to* WILLIE B.) It was nice of her to send them.

ANNA Don't eat them all now, save some until after supper.

TEDDY Someday, I going to have me a tea and . . . (*jay bird hollers*) Shut up! Mama, did Mrs. Patterson use the Havlin or the Spode?

WILLIE B. I was to a tea, up in Chi once.

TEDDY Who gave it?

WILLIE B. Colored people. It was a tea, girl, but they didn't have no tea. They had gallons and gallons of red punch served out of a cut glass bowl, pretty near as big (*pointing*) as that tub hanging on the house, and it was spiked with pure bourbon.

TEDDY Aw . . . boy . . .

WILLIE B. I tell you, colored people carry on up North. When they have a tea, it's a tea!

ANNA Willie B., a liar's tongue is long enough to cut his own throat. Colored people don't carry on nowhere, and ain't got nothing nowhere.

TEDDY The people that live in India are colored, the geography books says they live in marble houses; and dress in silk and gold.

ANNA Reach for the moon and get a cinder.

WILLIE B. Aw . . . we can get places if we're smart.

AUNT MATT (*off stage and down the road a piece*) The damned will burn forever in hell's fire. The devil is up with night. Hell's children are on the march. All you sinners repent now. Keep they tounge from evil and they lips from speaking gall. (*the jay bird hollers*)

ANNA Here comes that Aunt Matt Crossy with all that wild talk about the devil and hell again. Teddy, go to the well and get me some water.

TEDDY Aunt Matt's always preaching. She's nothing but an old thief.

ANNA You don't know that—that's just hearsay—

WILLIE B. Hearsay my eye, she would steal the wax right out of your ear. (TEDDY *gets the pail in the kitchen and goes off to the well*) You know that brooch she wears.

ANNA Why yes.

WILLIE B. Stole it right of Mrs. Ethel Jones dead body and her praying as big as day at the wake.

ANNA When you're her age you might be stealing too. When you're alone and old you get queer, Willie B.

WILLIE B. She don't have to steal. She gets state aid—

ANNA Shhhhh, here she is.

AUNT MATT (*by now she has reached the break in the fence and enters the yard. She is a wiry, rather gaunt and ancient woman. She is a religious fanatic. Her face is like a dried prune and her small black eyes shine and have a piercing look. She carries herself with the upper part of her body slightly forward and her walk and gestures are reminiscent of the prophets of old. Her voice is husky and dark and she has a habit of scratching her thighs. She is dressed in black faded calico with small green flowers. The cut of her dress hints of the nineteenth century*) The devil is up with night and He's after all the sinners in this land. Have you been saved? Have you been bathed in the holy fire? Have you been saved from Hell's fire? (*to* ANNA *in a conversational tone*) Good evening, Anna, How're you?

ANNA Pretty well. Had a hard day today. Mrs. Patterson had another tea. I had to clean that big old house from top to bottom.

AUNT MATT (*with disgust*) Yeah, the rich and the poor they all alike. Sinning all over the place. All these teas. (*prophetically*) Well, hell's fire made for the rich as well as the poor and for the white as well as the black. (*pause*) I was just down the road apiece trying to save that Joe David boy. (AUNT MATT *sits down on the edge of the porch*) That crap-shooting, card playing colt! I prayed with him 'bout an hour. He couldn't see nothing ... couldn't hear nothing ... he don't want to get saved. Chasing scarlet women and cussing. He's hell's own child. Besides all that he lies! And I ain't got no piece with a liar. (*she throws an accusing glance at* WILLIE B. *and then says to him*) How you Willie Bray boy?

WILLIE B. All right I guess.

TEDDY (*off stage*) Willie B., come here and help me pull this pail up. The rope stuck. (WILLIE B. *goes off in the direction of the well*)

AUNT MATT I just stopped in for a spell to see how you was. I'm on my way down to Minnie's before dark. She's real sick ... too much snuff dippin'. Doctor told her to lay off the stuff. Can't seem to give it up. It's the devil keeping her on it.

ANNA I guess we all get tempted now and then—Aunt Matt, I'm worried about Teddy. Seems like the older she gets the worse she gets. Sometimes when she's talking her eyes have a haunted look.

AUNT MATT Don't see why you let Willie B. take up so much time with Teddy. He's just filled with lies about Chicago and all the things he's seen. The tongue deviseth trouble like a sharp razor. (*the jay bird hollers*) Youngun's that age draw lightening. First thing you know she and Willie B.'ll be getting in with the devil.

ANNA (*laughing*) Ain't no such thing as getting in with the devil. I don't think the devil's real but more kind of a spirit. (*sarcastically*) I know you ain't never seen him.

AUNT MATT Of course I ain't never seen him walking around. (*in earnest and with a great deal of mystery*) But I seen his tracks. It was back in the year when they had that big frost in late August. That was some frost, even killed the grasshoppers. (*jay bird hollers frantically and* TEDDY *and* WILLIE B. *enter.* WILLIE B. *places the water pail on the edge of the porch*)

ANNA (*sarcastically*) That must have been something.

WILLIE B. Miss Anna, those greens smell so good....

TEDDY Willie B., why don't you stay for supper. The greens 'most done. We got plenty ... ain't we mama?

WILLIE B. If you sure you got enough, I'll be glad to join you. At home we're havin' sideback and dried beans again. Third day now. We had all kinds of beans since mama passed.

ANNA Willie, B., there's plenty. Aunt Matt, why don't you stay for a bite?

AUNT MATT No, I gotta get on down to Minnie's. I don't...

ANNA Come on and stay, Aunt Matt. I'll walk down to Minnie's with you after we eat. (*they enter the house and sit*)

AUNT MATT Well, I guess I will stay for a bite or so. I ain't so hungry, but I just love mustards.

ANNA Then you offer the blessing.

AUNT MATT (*moment of silence*) Dear Lord bless this humble food that we are about to partake to nourish our bodies, we thank thee O Lord from our hearts—Amen.

TEDDY I tasted steak once. Mama brought me a piece from Mrs. Patterson's anniversary party. (*they all begin to eat*)

AUNT MATT I heard that Mrs. Patterson wouldn't let you bring a string off the place. Wouldn't even give you a pinch of salt. Is it true, Anna, that you don't take your meals there?

ANNA   I always like to eat with Teddy. It's so lonesome eating by yourself, you know.

AUNT MATT   The truth is, Mrs. Patterson's too stingy to feed you, huh! The devil himself would feed you better.

WILLIE B.   I seen the devil once.

AUNT MATT   Now here we go with—

WILLIE B (*interrupting* AUNT MATT)   You don't believe me but I did.

TEDDY (*laughing*)   Oh, Willie B.

AUNT MATT   I ain't got no time to listen—

WILLIE B. (*interrupting* AUNT MATT *again*)   I swear. (*raising his hand*) I hope to die, I seen the devil.

TEDDY (*doubtfully*)   And when did you see the devil and where?

WILLIE B.   Well, it was quite a little piece from the Bottoms more near Vinegar Hill. I was on my way to Cox's store one Saturday night. The moon was bright as day. When I pass the gulley, I noticed a man sitting on a rock. I didn't pay no attention to him until I got closer. Then I heard some of the prettiest singing ever. It sounded like it was coming from across water—like cow bells in the evening. When I got closer, I noticed some sparks flying from all around him. And lo, and behold when I got right up on him, the singing wasn't coming out of his mouth, he wasn't moving his lips.

AUNT MATT (*sarcastically*)   Yeah, go on.

WILLIE B.   Well, I said to myself, this must be the devil. By this time I was getting a little scared so when I passed him I said, "Good Evening, Mr. D. Pretty night, ain't it." He just nodded his head yeah. Then I began to run a little. Just before I got to the hill, I looked back, you know what he was doing when I looked back?

TEDDY (*laughing*)   No, what?

WILLIE B. (*intensely*)   He was throwing little pieces of lightning out of a sack he was carrying. Then, all at once, he started cutting his toe nails with gold scissors. And he smiled and waved at me. (AUNT MATT *gives a disgusted gesture with her hand*) He looked just as kind and full of fun.

TEDDY (*laughing*)   He don't sound bad at all. I wish I could' meet him.

ANNA (*getting up from the table and laughing*)   Willie B. you're a good tale teller. Old Satan sounds like real fun.

AUNT MATT (*nibbling on a rum cookie*)   Sounds like that old road peddler that use to go by here.

WILLIE B.   Aunt Matt, you been eating them rum cookies.

AUNT MATT (*spitting them out*)   That's what I get for listening to that lie you just told. (*looking around, getting up, and walking slowly towards the road*) Lord, it almost night. And Minnies' more an' a piece from here. But my works calling me. (*turning to* ANNA) Come on Anna.

ANNA (*turning to* TEDDY)   Teddy, now don't you sit around and talk all evening. (*pointing to the table*) Get them dishes washed by the time I'm back. And get this yard sprinkled down, the dust is blowing everywhere. And get out of those clothes. (ANNA *goes off down the road with* AUNT MATT. *Both talking as they go off. The jay bird hollers frantically*)

TEDDY (*laughing*)   Did you really see the devil?

WILLIE B.   Cross my heart and hope to die.

TEDDY (*laughing*)   Aw, shute.

(WILLIE B.'*s father can be heard calling him home*)

WILLIE B. (*laughing*)   Well, Teddy, poppa's calling.

TEDDY (*holding her hand to* WILLIE B., *across the table*)   Good night.

(*again* WILLIE B.'*s father can be heard calling in the distance:* "*Willie B.! Willie B.!*")

WILLIE B.   I sure enjoyed those mustards. They was as tender as the night that coming. (*looking up at the sky*) Looks like it going to be a rider moon tonight.

TEDDY   Wish I could have more of your company. I feel kinda' queer listening to all that devil talk.

WILLIE B.   Aw . . . shute, go long girl, I'll see you tomorrow. (WILLIE B. *exits and his father can be heard calling again*) I'm coming poppa! (*as he goes down the road he falls to singing* "*Back Train Back*")

(TEDDY *sits at the table a moment thinking. Dusk grows into darkness. She goes into the kitchen gets the kerosene lamp and takes it to the table in the yard. In the distance the whistle of the Big Dixie is heard, a long and mournful sound.*

The Dry August

Teddy is caught in the web of its sound and begins to dream. Going to the gate she says)

TEDDY   The Big Dixie! There it goes. Someday I'll be on it. When I'm a lady I'm going to be so fine. I'll have more 'an Mrs. Patterson and I'm going to Chicago, Paris, Detroit, and London, and in style. Who knows, maybe I'll go to China or India. Ain't no telling where I'll go. (TEDDY *goes into the kitchen, gets water from the stove, pours it into the dish pan and carries it to the table in the yard and begins washing the dishes. The last faint whistle of the Big Dixie is heard. The night sounds increases. The moon comes out*) There is someday I'm going to have a tea to outdo Mrs. Patterson. It'll be on the society page in the *Southern Journal*. Nothing, I don't ever get to see nothin', do nothin', I wish, I wish . . . (*she places her hands above her head and spits seven times to the east and west. At this point a cloud passes over the moon leaving the stage in darkness except for the dim light of the lantern on the table. When the cloud pass by the moon, a man is seen sitting on the rock under the tree cutting his toe nails with a small pair of gold scissors. He is a puckish man of fifty or so, dressed in an ancient black frock tail coat covered with campaign buttons. Beside him on the rock is a large sack, and an old pair of shoes decidedly turned up at the toes, covered with red clay mud. He is dirty and begrimed as if he has worked among fires and forges. At first*, TEDDY *engaged in drying dishes, doesn't see him, then, sensing his presence, is still for a moment. She turns suddenly and upon seeing him is frightened and drops the dish she is drying*) Wooooooo . . . weeeeeee. Who you? (*the music stops and the man laughs a rich mellow laugh*)

MR. D.   I'm Mr. D. and you?

TEDDY   My name is Teddy.

MR. D.   Pleased to know you Teddy. (*he makes a sweeping gesture with his hat reminiscent of the medicine man of the South, and puts his shoes on and stands up*) Could I sell you anything Ma'am? I sell for nothing and I got most everything you ever heard of. (*reaches into his sack*) Silks from China. (*throws up several pieces of brightly colored silk. The silk shimmers and floats to his feet*) Playing cards. (*ruffling out a pack of trick cards and places them back in the sack*) Magic lightning sticks from India. (*holds up lightning stick from which comes green and purple lights*) Toilet water. (*sprinkles some on her and pulls out articles in rapid succession as he mentions them.* TEDDY *is pleased by the toilet water and whiffs in the aroma*) I got song books, hand mirrors, pocket combs, hair ribbons, face powders, stockings of silk, smelling bottles, ear drops, colored beads, broaches and bracelets, and gold and silver trinkets and mouth organs. Can I please you ma'm with any notions?

TEDDY   I'm mighty tempted to select something. But I don't know whether or not I'd be getting in league with you. What you say your name was?

MR. D. (*with a great deal of mystery*)   Mr. D. (*changing the subject*) Where you'd get that awful ribbon?

TEDDY (*touching the tattered ribbon*)   It's the best hair ribbon you can get. Mrs. Patterson gave it to me for Christmas. Came all the way from New York.

MR. D.   I got a better hair ribbon right here. (*he shows her a ribbon*, TEDDY *reaches for it but* MR. D. *hurriedly places it back in the bag*) That ribbon come all the way from Biglow.

TEDDY   Biglow, is that a big city?

MR. D.   Yep, the biggest.

TEDDY   I've heard of Chicago, Paris, Detroit, and New York and London, but Biglow, tell me some more about this Biglow.

MR. D.   Biglow is a city that ain't nowhere in particular. It's big and down . . . down . . . down.

TEDDY (*laughing*)   That sounds like a funny place. It could be maybe like hell?

MR. D. (*scratching his ribs*)   No Biglow ain't hell. Ain't no more hell than any old place, Teddy.

TEDDY   Yeah, Mama said hell was where you made it, even on earth. Aunt Matt said it was an evil place with everlasting fire to burn the wicked.

MR. D.   All nonsense. (*changing subject*) Why are you dressed up?

TEDDY (*sarcastically*)   Oh, for some occasion

MR. D.   Like what, may I ask?

TEDDY   Well, I might have a little tea this evening.

MR. D.   Yeah.

TEDDY   Uh-huh, if I live and nothing happens.

MR. D.   Aw, .. now, plenty can happen about this time of evening.

TEDDY I got to get out of this dress before mama comes.

MR. D. You'd better stay dressed, Teddy, I got a feeling ... (*he points towards the audience*) What do you see out there? (*the lights dim*)

TEDDY I see the stars popping out as big as dollars.

MR. D. Well, light the wish in your heart. (MR. D. *comes and sits beside her*) Light the wish in your heart and dream, dream, dream in the mind's eye.

TEDDY I am, I am. (*the lights fade to pinkish evening*)

MR. D. Teddy, your mind's eye is working. Now dream, dream ...

TEDDY Mr. D., they're coming here! My dream's comin' real! What must I do?

MR. D. Just be cool, I will handle things. (*by this time* MRS. PATTERSON *appears at the gate followed by the three* EVANS' *girls,* JUNE, FERN *and* ROSE. MRS. PATTERSON *is overdressed in lavender organdy, with black draw strings at the neck. Many buttons run down the back of the dress. The dress is caught up to one side with a huge black velvet bow. She wears white kid shoes, and carries a crochet bag. The white and yellow daisies on her white straw hat are larger than usual. She carries a frilly parasol. Altogether her appearance is that of a large summer butterfly. The* EVANS *girls are dressed similar except for the colors:* JUNE *in yellow,* FERN *in green, and* ROSE *in pink. Their hats are bedecked with the usual: summer flowers, etc. They talk in unison and very Southern. They enter the yard and lower their parasols*)

TEDDY Why good evening, Mrs. Patterson, I'm so glad you were able to come.

MRS. PATTERSON Good evening, Teddy, I'm sorry I'm late, but its so trying driving on these dirt roads. (*the jay bird hollers*)

TEDDY Yes, I know what a problem it is.

MRS. PATTERSON You must excuse my appearance (*turning around*), it's so hot, I dressed down consciously. (*while* MRS. PATTERSON's *back is turned,* TEDDY *starts counting the buttons down the back of her dress.* MR. D. *cuts across stage and whispers to* TEDDY)

MR. D. Don't cut no hog girl. (*he goes into the house and puts the tea-kettle on the stove*)

TEDDY Yes, its been awful all day.

MRS. PATTERSON Allow me the pleasure of introducing you to the Evans girls: June, Fern and Rose Evans, Miss Teddy Hicks.

GIRLS (*in unison*) It's a delight to meet you, honey.

TEDDY It's nice meeting you too. I've heard so much about you, why just this morning I was reading in the *Southern Journal* about you all being home for the summer, and about the fine school you attend in Virginia. All the social activities must keep you on the go.

MRS. PATTERSON The social whirl is awful for them. (*in unison, the girls giggle at* MRS. PATTERSON)

TEDDY Won't you ladies have some tea? (*they all sit*)

GIRLS Yes, thank you, honey.

(MR. D. *brings the cups from the kitchen*)

MRS. PATTERSON Not just now, I just want to sit here and relax for a minute, it's so tiring to be light-hearted and gay in this heat.

TEDDY Ain't it though. Maybe you ladies would like iced tea instead of hot.

FERN No, we never take it iced. It's just not done you know.

JUNE Spoils the true flavor.

TEDDY Good that you like it hot, I was just dying to show off my Havlin.

ROSE (*picking up one of the cups*) I was just admiring it. Such a fine pattern. Thin as paper.

MRS. PATTERSON I use Spode mostly in the summer, not as heavy as Havlin.

(MR. D. *brings out the steaming black tea kettle and places it on the table*)

JUNE What a fine silver pot.

TEDDY I like it. (*the jay bird hollers*)

MRS. PATTERSON My silver pot is over a hundred years old. It was handed down by the Flucks side of the family.

MR. D. Pardon me, but this pot has been around awhile, came from Miss Teddy's father's side of the family. The Washington's no less. If I ain't mistaken it came on the Mayflower, right Miss Teddy?

TEDDY Uh-huh, that's why we don't use it much, I'm afraid it'll get dented.

(*At this point* MR. D. *knocks a cup on the group*)

MR. D. Sorry, Miss Teddy.

TEDDY That's all right.

MRS. PATTERSON Servants are so careless these days. Why just two days ago, Anna broke two of my best sherbert dishes. (TEDDY *coughs*)

I don't see how I will ever replace them. I'll just take it out of her pay, that's all!

FERN Oh, I don't see how you can do that, Mrs. Patterson.

MRS. PATTERSON And why?

ROSE Colored people have such a time making out.

JUNE Why they work for a song.

FERN I think its a shame to pay them so little, more than likely—

ROSE —That's why they are all going up North.

MRS. PATTERSON Teddy, how much do you pay your man?

TEDDY I don't know exactly, but I do know it's over eight dollars a week.

MRS. PATTERSON Eight dollars? My goodness!

TEDDY We don't believe in working our help for nothing. I know people right around here that pay as little as two-fifty a week, counting the week's washing to boot.

MRS. PATTERSON (*coughs*) I think it's enough. We have to keep colored people in their place you know.

TEDDY Everybody is entitled to a place, and things. Mr. D.'s worth his weight in gold.

MRS. PATTERSON You call him Mister?

TEDDY Indeed I do.

GIRLS Honey you talk like a Yankee. Mama would just about die if we called Mammy Myrtle Mrs.

TEDDY Well, you see I'm changing with the times.

MRS. PATTERSON Well, I guess I will have that cup of tea now.

FERN What did you mean, you're changing, Teddy? (*the jay hollers*)

TEDDY Can't you feel things changing?

GIRLS Like what?

TEDDY Well, you can even feel it in the air. Just this morning when I got up the leaves were dancing in the wind (TEDDY *looks up at the tree*), and flashing diamonds of dew, seemed like the whole world was bright and happy as a king. (*she moves center stage, down front*) Seemed like there was plenty to eat in the whole world, and not a sick person nowhere and everybody had clothes and a fine house to live in, even old colored people. (*turning back to* MRS. PATTERSON *and the girls*) And when you get a feeling like that—things are changing.

MRS. PATTERSON Well let's change the subject. We ought to be thankful to be Southern ladies.

FERN This heat! Thank God for organdy!

MR. D. Why don't you all engage yourself in a nice card game? Now you all ain't got nothing to do. You all could have yourselves a ball this evening.

GIRLS How would we ball?

MR. D. (*whispering*) You ever heard of Black Jack?

(*A cloud passes over the moon and a woman's wild hysterical laughter is heard. With a light roll of thunder the moon comes up and* BESSIE *is sitting on one of the branches with her legs crossed powdering her face with a huge puff.* BESSIE BOLT *is a pretty woman of about twenty-five. Her face is almost always a widespread smile of complacency. She is a woman of the world and she has a habit of giggling and singing to herself like she was a little insane. She is dressed in scarlet with gold spangles and on her head is a man's stetson hat adorned with owls' eyes and eagles' feathers that glow in the dark*)

TEDDY (*looking up at* BESSIE) Well, I'll be . . .

BESSIE Did I hear somebody mention Black Jack?

MRS. PATTERSON Lands sakes what you doing up there?

GIRLS Did you ever?

MRS. PATTERSON (*looking up at* BESSIE) Who in the world are you?

MR. D. Aw, don't pay her no mind, the word Black Jack makes her tremble. She's an old Black Jack expert.

BESSIE The best that ever played it! Bessie Bolt is my name. I used to could count to 1044; but now I can't count to but three. What's your name?

TEDDY My name's Teddy.

BESSIE (*laughing and giggling as she sings*)

Wish I was a bumble bee
I'd fly right out a' this tree.
I use to could count to 1044
Now I can only count to three.
Doomed to this old Magnolia tree;
Look what a stack of gold dollars done to me.
Stack 'em high; stack 'em low;
Can't roam this earth no more.

MRS. PATTERSON Well I'll be . . .

MR. D. Come on, let's get on with the game.

(*he begins to clean the table*) There's going to be some sport here tonight. Yes Sirreee.

BESSIE BOLT Wish I was a bumble bee
Fly right out this old tree
Lord, look what a stack of gold dollars done to me.

(*While all are engaged watching* BESSIE BOLT, MR. D. *spikes the kettle of tea with a bottle of whiskey from his pocket*)

1,2,3-1,2,3—can't roam this earth no more.

MR. D. (*taking the trick cards out of his pocket, ruffles them*) You ladies all sit. (*he places the cards on the table*) Cut for the deal.

MRS. PATTERSON I really ought not to play. (*she draws a card*) Well, as long as nobody hears bout it—

(JUNE, FERN *and* ROSE *draw and then* TEDDY. BESSIE BOLT *throws down some dollars to* TEDDY, *she picks them up and takes a seat at the table*)

MR. D. What's your cards ladies?
MRS. PATTERSON Ace.

(*The* EVANS *girls are busy taking dollars from the crochet bag*)

FERN Jack.
JUNE Queen.
ROSE King.
TEDDY Deuce. (MR. D. *stands aside picking his teeth*)
MR. D. Your deal, Mrs. Patterson.
MRS. PATTERSON (*dealing around*) What interests me is that woman in the tree...
TEDDY Aw... that's Miss Bolt. Miss Bessie Bolt, Mrs. Patterson, and Miss June, Fern and Rose Evans.
BESSIE BOLT Why, I declare to goodness gracious, I'm so proud to meet you ladies.
MRS. PATTERSON How do you do? (*by this time she has finished dealing*)
GIRLS How do you do?
MRS. PATTERSON (*turning her cards up*) Black Jack!
BESSIE BOLT Damn! (*all look up at* BESSIE BOLT, *except* MRS. PATTERSON, *who puts an ace in the bow on her hat*)
MR. D. Two Black Jacks in a row.
MRS. PATTERSON Un-huh. Just like picking money up in the streets. (*she racks in the money*) Here we go girls, all bets down (*they all place their bets.* MRS. PATTERSON *takes the ace out of her hat and puts it with her high card and eases the low card to the floor with her elbow*) Black Jack!
TEDDY *and the* GIRLS Did you ever in your life?
BESSIE BOLT Never.
MR. D. Your deal again, Mrs. Patterson, directly you'll be worn out from dealing.
MRS. PATTERSON You said it! (*ruffling cards*) Now tell me some more about this Bessie Bolt.
TEDDY Ask her she's of age.
MRS. PATTERSON Well, Mrs. Bolt, how come you're up in that tree?
BESSIE BOLT It's a free country, if you ain't careful you'll be sitting right up here with me.
MRS. PATTERSON How's that? (MR. D. *throws* BESSIE BOLT *a glance*)
BESSIE BOLT I ain't talking.
MRS. PATTERSON You must find it trying to live up there.
BESSIE BOLT People have died on trees, why can't I live in one? Wish I was a bumble... bee, etc.
MRS. PATTERSON (*by this time she has dealt around and repeated her cheating act of placing ace in her hat etc.*) Black Jack!
GIRLS You a real expert, honey.
MRS. PATTERSON Yes, I am kind of handy with cards. Now, Mrs. Bolt, did I hear you say that you made that tree your home? (*she begins to ruffle the cards slowly*)
BESSIE BOLT Didn't say, but, indeed, it is my home.
MRS. PATTERSON Now how's that?
BESSIE BOLT I was put up here for cheatin' at cards!
MRS. PATTERSON You don't say. (*ruffling cards slowly*) You don't say. By the way, where did you get that outfit you're wearing?
BESSIE BOLT Don't talk about my duds now, I might have to slip you in the dozens.
GIRLS What's the dozens?
BESSIE BOLT Well it's...
TEDDY (*interrupting*) Miss Bolt don't spoil my tea with cuss words.
MR. D. Yes, shut up Bessie.
BESSIE BOLT You go to—
MR. D. Shut up I said!
MRS. PATTERSON (*staring at* MR. D.) You know this man D., here looks familiar. I could swear I've seen... ain't you the same old road peddler that was selling for nothing some years back? (MR. D. *laughs*)

The Dry August

BESSIE BOLT Born in the year three. He's been around, honey.

MR. D. Shut up you Bessie!

MRS. PATTERSON Well, girls, place your bets.

BESSIE BOLT Hey, Mrs. Patterson, was that dress cut to order?

MRS. PATTERSON Yes, why?

BESSIE BOLT Well I'm sorry they ever invented the color you wearing.

TEDDY *and the* GIRLS Goodness sakes.

MRS. PATTERSON I like it!

BESSIE BOLT Aw... the color's all right but I thought monkey backs was out of style...

MRS. PATTERSON Are you trying to upset me?

BESSIE BOLT Upset you? No, you're too cool. The way you cheating them girls, you'd have to be cool.

MRS. PATTERSON Let's get on with the game.

BESSIE BOLT Hey, Mrs. Patterson, can I hold that ace for you?

MRS. PATTERSON What ace?

BESSIE BOLT That ace you just put in the bow on your hat.

MRS. PATTERSON (*ignoring* BESSIE) Bets down, girls.

BESSIE BOLT Hey, Mrs. Patterson.

MRS. PATTERSON What in the world do you want?

BESSIE BOLT It appears to me that ace you just put in that bow on your hat is awful heavy for a slim young woman like you to carry. It would be a burning shame if the weight of it made your head more lop-sided than it is.

MR. D. More tea, ladies? (*he pours, they all sip*)

GIRLS Thank you. Mrs. Patterson don't tell us you've been cheating.

MRS. PATTERSON Indeed not.

FERN (*she reaches and gets the ace from* MRS. PATTERSON's *hat*) What's this ace here?

MRS. PATTERSON Aw... that, it got there accidently like. (*she sips the tea*)

GIRLS You don't say, honey. (*they all take a sip of tea*)

FERN Now, Mrs. Patterson you've got a right smart brains.

ROSE To let them be going to seed in your head.

FERN We're not blind, you were cheating honey. (*sips tea*)

MRS. PATTERSON Indeed, I wasn't!

TEDDY *and the* GIRLS Well, in any case, we'd like our money back.

(BESSIE BOLT *begins to hum 1, 2, 3 etc. The girls reach for* MRS. PATTERSON's *pile of money*)

MRS. PATTERSON (*protecting her money*) Over my dead body!

FERN Well, I'm going to get mine or some of them flowers off your hat. (*she reaches for* MRS. PATTERSON's *hat*. MRS. PATTERSON *gathers the money into her bag and runs to stage left or right*. JUNE *and* ROSE *hold* FERN)

JUNE *and* ROSE Let's go Fern.

FERN (*squirming*) Turn me loose!

MR. D. Here, ladies, now now, now, and all about a little ol' black jack game—it was all in fun, ladies.

MRS. PATTERSON Calling me a cheater, why I am a real aristocrat! The idea!

TEDDY *and the* GIRLS She's an aristocrat, Lawdy—(JUNE *and* ROSE *let* FERN *go*)

FERN I'm not leaving until I get my money back, honey. (*she walks towards* MRS. PATTERSON) Mrs. Patterson, I'm asking you politely, will you give me back my money that you just had the gumption to cheat me out of.

MRS. PATTERSON No.

FERN Well all right. (*she tears into* MRS. PATTERSON. MRS. PATTERSON *runs to the other side of the stage and gets her umbrella*. MR. D. *grabs* FERN *by the arm*. MRS. PATTERSON *raises the umbrella to strike* FERN) Turn me loose, I'm going to get my money!

MRS. PATTERSON (*holding umbrella, ready to strike* FERN) Turn her loose! She appears kinda weak.

JUNE *and* ROSE Come let's go Fern. If she needs the money that bad let her keep it. It's no credit to give her the good lickin! she deserves, honey—the poor trash!

MRS. PATTERSON Poor trash nothing! I'm from Old Virginia, and my names Mrs. Bridget Patterson, and I'm telling you because I ain't ashamed where I'm from or the family I belong too! We've got heaps of plunder and lots of money to burn!

BESSIE BOLT You got so much plunder and money to burn, you ain't got no manners.

MRS. PATTERSON What do you know about manners?

BESSIE BOLT Nothing at all from what I see before me.

GIRLS Ain't it the truth.

MR. D. Here, you fine ladies ought not carry on so what you want to do. Get mad enough to burst and spatter the place up now. Shake hands and be ladies. Be the aristocrats that you are.

FERN You're so right, the aristocrats that we are.

TEDDY Mrs. Patterson, if you give us back our money we will all be aristocrats again.

MRS. PATTERSON All right, honey. Here's your money, girls. (*she gives the girls their money back*)

MR. D. Now if you ladies can get in good enough spirits again, this evening will turn out to be real grand, I'll tell you—real grand!

MRS. PATTERSON And how . . . (*in the distance Blind Lemon's piano starts up slowly*)

MR. D. You ever do any dancing, Mrs. Patterson?

MRS. PATTERSON Un-hun.

MR. D. What kind?

MRS. PATTERSON A little Fox Trotting.

MR. D. That ain't no kind of dancing. You ever hear of Balling the Jack?

MRS. PATTERSON Yes I have, but ain't that kinda of a common dance?

MR. D. No, I should say not! (*the piano grows louder*)

GIRLS We would love to learn Balling the Jack.

MR. D. (*half singing, when piano grows louder*) Well now, does everybody want to learn?

ALL Yes.

MR. D. (*half singing*) Well everybody line up. (*now they all line up with* MR. D. *in front of them*) Now everybody follow me. First you put your left foot out, then bring it back. Then you put your right foot out and bring it back. That's what you call Balling the Jack. You spread your loving arm way out into space . . . (*Etc. the dancing and singing and the music grows then fades as the voices of* ANNA *and* AUNT MATT CROSS *are heard at first faintly and then more and more distinctly, as they come up the road. A cloud passes over the moon. When the moon appears again,* MR. D. *and the ladies, have all disappeared and* TEDDY *is sitting alone—dreaming.* AUNT MATT *enters the yard slowly, holding a potted plant. She walks to porch.*)

AUNT MATT Can I come in with you a minute, Anna?

ANNA Come on in, Aunt Matt.

ANNA (*looking around*) Teddy! (TEDDY *is still dreaming*). Teddy! My goodness, were you asleep? Come on now, get yourself out of that dress and get ready for bed. I'll do the dishes.

TEDDY I'll do them.

AUNT MATT Well, I don't think Minnie's going to make it. When she dies, I don't know how they going put her away. Her husband's pocket is just as empty as the left hand corner of the mammoth cage.

ANNA Poor little Selma Mae. Her mother, now Minnie's going.

AUNT MATT That Joe David done took to drank, honey, beside all his other vices of sin. Oh he's the drinkin'est man I ever seen, can't make out which eye is the other. Drink, drink, drink, from sun up to sun down. Now Lena's done left him. All his fodder done rotted in the fields.

ANNA Aunt Matt why do you talk so much?

AUNT MATT It's so quiet in here. And I thought I would just break the quiet—well, I guess I'm getting old. The old just talks someday. Here of late my eyes are so bad, I think its night. Yea, I'm old. (*silence for a few seconds*) Teddy, you going to be mighty pretty when you grow up and fill out some.

ANNA I think she will too.

AUNT MATT What you want to be when you grow up, one of them uppity teachers, I guess. (*train whistle blows*) And maybe if you don't want to be one of the uppity teachers, you might like to be one of them trained nurses.

TEDDY (TEDDY *turns to* AUNT MATT) No, I don't want to be no uppity teacher, and I don't want to be no trained nurse.

ANNA Well, Teddy, what do you want to be when you grow up? Last year you wanted to be a beauty operator.

TEDDY I don't want to be no beauty operator.

AUNT MATT What in God's name is there left to be, beside a houseworker.

TEDDY If I told you what I wanted to be when I grow up, it would throw you both into a fit.

AUNT MATT I hope it ain't one of them blues singers!

TEDDY When I grow up I want to be a rich white woman. (AUNT MATT *sits back in the chair and rocks.* ANNA *drops her hands and stares at* TEDDY. *The train whistle fades out. Slow curtain*)

C. Bernard Jackson (1927–) and James V. Hatch (1928–)

Fly Blackbird   1960

Fly Blackbird was born of the sit-in movement, which began in February 1960, at the five and dime lunch counter in Greensboro, North Carolina. The musical began its Los Angeles career as a one-act play in the Shoebox Theater that same autumn. Supported by neither the press nor the theater-party audiences, *Fly Blackbird* found its encouragement among the young and the political who believed that theater should be pertinent to social reality.

The authors expanded the musical into a full-length script, and opened at the Metro Theater in Los Angeles on February 10, 1961—the first anniversary of the original sit-ins.

The performers were mostly students; the names of the characters in the play are often those of the actor-student who created the parts. Some went on to professional theater and film careers—George Takei, Micki Grant, Irene Nicholi, Thelma Oliver, Jack Crowder, Gloria Calomee, Ron Reardon, Gail Zifferstein, Palmer Whitted, Bart Patton, Mary Dingham, Carl Gipson, Josie Dotson, Camille Billops, Lee Korf, Janice Johnson. The issues of the play—violence/nonviolence, now/wait, confront/conform, new/old, integration/segregation—were issues with which students wrestled. In the early 1960's it was not naive to ask, "Should one risk a police record by Freedom Riding to Jackson, Mississippi?" Many of the youths who sat-in, who worked in SNCC voter registration drives, who offered themselves to the dogs and clubs of Bull O'Connor, have since grown disillusioned with the Movement's means and ends.

The original version of the play is printed here. The considerably revised version, which played in New York City in 1962, where it won an Obie award, is printed in the *The Black Teacher and the Dramatic Arts*, William Reardon and Thomas Pawley, eds. (Westport, Conn: Negro Universities Press, 1970).

C. Bernard Jackson, composer and co-author is, at this writing, Executive Director of the Inner City Cultural Center in Los Angeles, a group he founded for the purposes of training third world artists, and for encouraging the third world community to express its own cultures. In 1970, Mr. Jackson had this to say about the musical:

NOTES ON *Fly Blackbird*
A "MUSICAL WITH A CONSCIENCE"

Fly Blackbird does not properly belong in a black theater anthology. Although many of the play's central characters are black, although one of the authors is black, although it can be said the work grew directly out of the mid-twentieth-century struggles of blacks and their allies to make the concept of equal treatment under the Law apply to all citizens, *Fly Blackbird* is not really about the confrontation between black and white or even black and black. *Fly Blackbird* is really about the young and foolish—the immature—who, because they have no vested interests (or are at least not yet aware of them), can dare to demand instantaneous correction of evil—"Freedom Now." *Fly Blackbird* is about the "mature," "wise," "reasonable" elements in society who "understand" the need for "caution, patience, restraint, and due process"; who "understand" that there is a "right" and "wrong" way to go about things and that it is sometimes, in their opinion, better to not go about some things at all. *Fly Blackbird* is about *certainty*—the certitude—of a crop of almost-grown-up war babies who in the early '60's knew that victory was close at hand because America is "basically good" and once its mistakes are pointed out, the nation will move quickly to correct them. *Fly Blackbird* is about the equal and opposite certainty of their elders that the naive, idealistic rantings of American youth will disappear and things will "get back to normal, by God!" *Fly Blackbird* is about unity—about black, white, red, yellow, and brown together overcoming "non-violently" through reason and with love all obstacles to progress. *Fly Blackbird* is about bringing new audiences into a theatre which before it, was primarily the domain of the well-to-do, the cultured elite, the intellectual snob. *Fly Blackbird*, a musical about integration not just of ethnic groups but of all elements of American society—young, old, men, women—into a cohesive, homogeneous force capable of forging a bright "new day," a "new time," seems somehow irrelevant at this moment in history ... or does it? What a pity America did not "*wake up*" in time ... or will it?

Fly Blackbird

CAST OF CHARACTERS

GIRL, *less than 15*
LIBRARIAN, *white and matronly*
BOY, *black and 14*
HECKLERS, *white and 16, 17*
CARL, *leader of the Blackbirds, about 19 or 20*
JOSIE, *daughter of Sweet William Piper, about 18*
CLARRY, *a black picket*
BETTY, *sometimes loud and wrong, but alive*
TAG, *Betty's little sister*
GEORGE, *a Japanese-American*
SWEET WILLIAM PIPER, *an old movie star of the '30's.*
OFFICER BROWN, *a black cop*
CAMILLE, *a black picket*
GLORIA, *a black picket*
ERNIE, *a white picket*
LOU, *a white picket*
RON, *a white picket*
IRENE, *a white picket*
PALMER, *a black picket*
PAT, *a white girl picket*
GAIL, *a white picket*
JUDGE CROCKER, *an older white liberal*

ACT ONE

(SCENE *A Street. A 5 & 10¢ store is seen stage right. A little* GIRL *enters singing a children's song as she dances between the cracks on the sidewalk*)

GIRL (*singing*) Step in a hole, break your mother's sugar bowl. (*shouting is heard off stage left. She looks at the noise which stops and goes on with her song*) Step on a crack, you'll break your mother's back. (*more shouting. Again it stops when she looks*) Step off the trail, you land in jail. (*this time the shouting is less muffled and she runs into the library where the lights come up revealing the middle-aged* LIBRARIAN, MISS BROWN)

GIRL Miss Brown! Miss Brown! Do you know what I saw on the street?

LIBRARIAN Hello dear. What'd you see on the street?
GIRL People with signs! Some of them were fighting!
LIBRARIAN And did you see any lions or bears?
GIRL There are people fighting! Come and look!
LIBRARIAN Now don't run away. It's nearly Story Hour time. I bet you can't guess what our program's about today?
GIRL Fairies and elves.
LIBRARIAN Not today. Our program's on Brotherhood. Will you get me the sign over there.

(*A black* BOY, *chased by two white* HECKLERS *runs into the library for safety*)

HECKLER Chicken liver.
BOY Cracker heads.
HECKLER Coward. (*the* HECKLERS, *unable to get him, wait outside*)
LIBRARIAN (*as boy enters*) Oh hello. You can help make our little circle. Would your friends like to come in?
BOY They don't like books.
LIBRARIAN Would you like to help me hold this sign?
BOY Yes ma'am.
LIBRARIAN That's a good boy. The title of our program is: The Negro and You. (*she hands the boy a sign which reads: "THE NEGRO AND YOU"*)
BOY (*looks at it and scratches his head*) And who?
LIBRARIAN And you . . . (*laughs*) . . . and me. Do you know the motto of Brotherhood Week? Boy?
BOY Yes ma'am. It's Brotherhood Week so take a spook to lunch.
LIBRARIAN (*taps bell*) Oh, I'm afraid not! The motto is "Be kind to your colored friends."
BOY Amen. (*as the* LIBRARIAN *proceeds with her little program the* BOY *watches the* HECKLERS

Fly Blackbird

outside walk away. The LIBRARIAN's *words are backed with a dissonant version of "Old Black Joe"*)

LIBRARIAN (*she assumes her dramatic voice*) Down through the ages the Negro has endeared himself to us all as an entertainer and musician. His simple childlike nature, his sweet gentle disposition . . . (*the* HECKLERS *leave*) What seems to be the trouble out there, boy?

BOY No trouble now. Everything's fine. (*the* BOY *takes the stick from the* LIBRARIAN's *sign and, using it as a club, exits*)

LIBRARIAN Boy! Where are you going?

BOY Later Ma'am.

LIBRARIAN (*to* GIRL) Now where are you going?

GIRL To see what's happening. (*exits*)

LIBRARIAN Don't go. I have such a nice story about Uncle Remus.

(*Blackout Library. The street scene lights pop on revealing the stage filled with pickets with sit-in and civil rights signs. They are students—Negro and White. They sing "Now"*)

NOW
Sung by: TAG, CAMILLE, CARL, PALMER, PAUL, GEORGE, *and* GROUP

NOW! Not another hour
NOW! Not another day
NOW! Not a minute longer
But now. Right now. Right now!

We've waited two hundred years or more
But the time is drawing near
When we will stand up and say
Today is the day. The time is here.

NOW! Not another hour
NOW! Not another day
NOW! Not a minute longer
But now. Right now. Right now!

We've got to do something
To let people know how we feel
Right! As long as we
Keep our mouths shut
Things'll stay just as they are
See no evil. Hear no evil.
Think no evil. Know no evil.

We've waited two hundred years
But the time is drawing near
When we will stand up and say
Today is the day. The time is here.

NOW! Not another hour
NOW! Not another day
NOW! Not a minute longer
But now. Right away!

(*When the song is finished, they begin a quiet picketing of the 5 & 10¢ store. Enter three hecklers playing catch. They see* PICKETS *and mimic them*)

FIRST HECKLER Hey look at this.
SECOND HECKLER What are they doing?
THIRD HECKLER This a parade?
FIRST HECKLER Who wound them up?
SECOND HECKLER Come on. Don't get us in trouble.
FIRST HECKLER Good pickets don't cause trouble. (*they mimic the* PICKETS *and tease them . . . they see* JOSIE, *a pretty negro girl who tries to cross the picket line and enter the 5 & 10. They whistle*)

CARL (*leader of the group, a black of 19 or 20 . . . smitten by sight of* JOSIE *and vice-versa*) Hey! Where you going?

JOSIE In the store. All I want is stuff for my brother's birthday party! (*she exits into store*)

CLARRY (*a tall negro boy*) Hey, where's that All-American IQ Carl? Why didn't you stop her?

CARL Dumb woman. Can't tell them anything.

FIRST HECKLER Your I.Q. All-American, Carl?

CLARRY They're just trying to bug you.

HECKLER Why don't you go back to Africa, Carl? Live with your relatives, Carl.

CARL Get to your kennel before I tie a can to your tail.

(*Enter* BETTY *in a dance—big and bold*)

BETTY Yeah. We'll tie a can to your tail. (*general greetings and rallying to her*) Stand back, people eaters, this is Big Betty. (BIG BETTY *song*), "*loud and wrong*")

LOUD AND WRONG
Sung by: BETTY

This is Big Betty. Loud and wrong.
This is Big Betty, Loud and wrong.
So stand back. Look out. Get outa' the way
'Cause this is Big Betty's song.

I don't do the waltz. I can't stand the shag.
Never cared for the minuet and you can bet
I'm not about to do no Fox Trot.

But I can Rock and Roll from pole to pole
'Cause I've got cinnamon in my soul.
So when I start to move. If you don't approve
Just stand back!

'Cause this is Big Betty. This is Big Betty.
This is Big Betty. Loud and wrong.
This is Big Betty. Loud and wrong.

BETTY   Look out.

HECKLER   Stand back.

BETTY   Get outa' the way.

CLARRY   (*intervening*)   All right. Let's get the line moving. Betty, this is a picket line.

BETTY   You're kidding me.

CLARRY   Look, if you're gonna make trouble, we don't want you around.

BETTY   I wasn't making trouble. (*to group*) Was I making trouble?

CARL   Let it go, Clarry.

CLARRY   We can't have this kind of nonsense. Why, in the South, this behavior would . . .

BETTY   In the South. This is not the South.

CLARRY   Every day I'm here, I become more aware of that. (*walks away*)

BETTY   Oh Clarry!

CARL   (*to* BETTY)   Betty, where's the coffee? It's one-thirty.

BETTY   It's one o'clock.

CARL   It's one-thirty.

BETTY   That's one o'clock C. P. Time, right, George?

GEORGE   (*a Japanese-American*)   C. P. Time?

BETTY   Colored People's Time, plum pit.

CARL   Yeah. Just a little bit behind everybody else. (*general laughter by the* PICKETS)

CLARRY   Betty, where's our coffee?

BETTY   Oh, my raggedy sister's got it. Tag! Taaag! Move, child! (*enter* TAG, *a very young black girl, with thermos, cups, etc. She drops some cups*) Bring it over here. (HECKLERS *needle* TAG *as she tries to pick up cups etc.*)

GEORGE   Hi Tag—here, let me help you. (*he goes over to help*)

HECKLER   My God! What will they think of next. A Chinaman and a coon! Harry—hey, Harry, come take a look at *this*!

GEORGE   I'm a Japanese-American.

HECKLER   Well, one gook's the same as another to me—

BETTY   (*rushing over*)   Why, you big—

CLARRY   (*taking hold of her*)   Betty!

HECKLER   Come on . . . come on!

CARL   (*unable to restrain himself, and stepping in*)   O.K. White boy, you asked for it! (*fight almost breaks out between* CARL *and* HECKLERS)

PIPER   (*an older Negro man, nattily dressed, apparently* "SOMEONE")   Hold it, son! You kids beat it. (*the* HECKLERS *retreat after several taunting remarks*) . . . Go on,—Hoodlums! A bad element . . . (*to* CARL) Aren't you Carl Eldridge? Of course . . . I've heard you sing at your father's church. A fine talent. (*shakes his hand—*PICKETS *look on with interest*)

CARL   Thank you, sir.

PIPER   Does the Rev. Eldridge approve of his son picketing? (CARL *withdraws his hand, shrugs*) Well, I'm sure he wouldn't approve of your engaging in street brawls.

CARL   But Sir—

PIPER   Look, Mr. Eldridge, no one is more anxious than I to do something for those southern students, but what does picketing accomplish? You know, it's so important that we do things the right way.

BETTY   The right way?

PIPER   (*sings:* "*The Right Way*"; *throughout the rest of the scene, the melodic line can be heard. He is generally rejected by the* PICKETS. *to* TAG) What a pretty little girl . . . And what does your sign say? Hummm—"Support the Sit-Ins." Does this store refuse to serve Negroes?

TAG   (*confused*)   Well, no . . . but—

CARL   No, but it does in Atlanta!

PIPER   But not *here*.

GEORGE   "The rights of anyone are the concern of everyone." That's from Thomas Paine . . . Thomas Paine? (*he is embarrassed as the other* PICKETS *laugh at his erudition*)

PIPER   Look, Thomas Paine, in the South I can understand this, but here in Los Angeles? Maybe we shouldn't offend those people who may already be sympathetic. (*sings*)

> When I was just a little tyke,
> Upon my mother's knee
> She told me what the world was like
> And this is what she said to me:—
> There's a right way and a wrong.
> You can catch more flies with honey
> Than with vinegar.

BETTY   Who are you?

PIPER   William Piper's my name.

TAG   Oh, Betty, I know! That's "Sweet William" Piper!

PIPER   You've been reading your *Ebony*. (*to* CARL) Mr. Eldridge, the race needs people like you. Why with talent like yours, you could go right to the top. No promises, mind you, but there *are* ways—when you know the right people. (*gives him card*) Think it over . . . give

me a call. (*as he exits,* CLARRY *blocks his way with sign which reads:* "*NOW!*")
BETTY   Who's that guy anyway?
CARL (*reading*)   Sweet William Piper.
BETTY   So what's the big deal?
CARL   That guy's worth a million bucks. He was a big movie star a few years back.
CLARRY   Yeah, big star. He's played more "Tom" roles than any other black man in the country.
CARL   Yeah ... but he's still a big man.
BETTY   Well, so are we!
CLARRY   Come on. Let's get this line going again. (JOSIE *comes out of the store with a package*)
A PICKET   Here she comes. Give her the sign. (*one of the* PICKETS *holds a sign over her head that reads:* "*Down With Uncle Tom!*" JOSIE *tries to walk on but the* HECKLERS *block her path*)
HECKLER   Oooeee! Look what crossed the line!
HECKLERS   Miss Dark Meat of 1961. Hey, how about a little integration?
HECKLER   Whatcha got in the sack dearie. (*he reaches for it.* JOSIE *pulls away and the* HECKLERS *grab it*)
HECKLER   Bet it's brownies. (*the* HECKLERS *play keep away with her package.* CLARRY *attempts to keep the picket line moving without violence, but* CARL, *unable to restrain himself, hits one of the* HECKLERS *teasing her*)
CARL   Bounce, rubber ball! (*he hits one and grabs the other. A general free for all breaks out. Police whistle and siren. The* LIBRARIAN *light comes up. The Fight scene freezes.* BOY *runs into the library, out of breath, with his club still in his hand*)
LIBRARIAN   Oh, Boy? Did you find out the trouble?
BOY   Oh, yes ma'am. It's some kind of celebration ... of ... of ... brotherhood week.
LIBRARIAN   I see. Why don't you sit right down here and read a nice book. Here's "Little Black Sambo and the Tigers." (*he's not enthusiastic*) And here's one on the Great Emancipator.
BOY   Who?
LIBRARIAN   President Lincoln. He set the Negro free and made him an equal citizen nearly a hundred years ago.
BOY   You don't say.
LIBRARIAN   Yes—see, here's his picture. Now what would you do if you were President today?

BOY   Me President?—of what country??
(*Blackout. The street unfreezes. The* PICKETS *and* HECKLERS *run as a police whistle is heard.* CARL *carries* JOSIE *off to avoid arrest.* GEORGE *is arrested*)
GEORGE   You can't arrest us for picketing, Officer. (*the stage empties*)
COP   Not for picketing; for street fighting. (*blackout as he hauls* GEORGE *away*)
VOICE ON AMPLIFIER (*in blackout*)   This is the police. We are the duly constituted law enforcement authorities. (*spot directly overhead lights a black uniformed cop with helmet, gloves and dark glasses. He is grim and impersonal. He stands legs apart, arms akimbo, unmoving*) ... We arrest people without discrimination. We make no distinction between Mexicans and Negroes. The high proportion of arrests of minority groups indicates that minority groups commit more crimes. That minority groups commit more crimes is proved by the fact that they have a higher percentage of arrests. Crimes are proved by arrests! Arrest proves crime! (*lights dim*)
COP   Hey, wait! (*runs in front of curtain as it closes ... we see he is a Negro*)
VOICE   What is it, Patrolman Brown?
BROWN (*wiping his face*)   I'd like to request a transfer, Sir.
VOICE   Where's your district?
BROWN   Thirty-six, Sir.
VOICE   Transfer to where?
BROWN   Sir, I'd like to transfer to Glendale* ... (*silence*) ... or Brentwood?*
VOICE   Promotion and transfer are based on examination.
BROWN   I study all the time, Sir.
VOICE   That's commendable. But study your family history.
(*Lights down and up on library.* BOY *is reading* "*Little Black Sambo*")
BOY   "... and Black Mumbo ate 36 pancakes, and Black Jumbo ate 64 pancakes, but Little Black Sambo ate 167 because he was so hungry."
LIBRARIAN   Beautiful, wasn't it? It's a classic. Do you know who wrote that book?
BOY   Aunt Jemima? (*enter* OFFICER BROWN)
BROWN   Pardon me.

* Exclusive white suburbs near Los Angeles.

LIBRARIAN Oh hello, Officer. Has there been some trouble on our block?
BROWN Yes ma'am. But we cleared it up. (*looking at* BOY) How long you been here?
BOY (*pretends to read*) ... and Little Black Sambo, he said to the tiger ...
BROWN I said how long you been here?
BOY All afternoon, Sir. But now I have to go home so I can go to church. (*exits after by-play of* BROWN *taking club away from* BOY)
LIBRARIAN My, did you see the admiration he had for you.
BROWN Yeah. You got a book on family histories?
LIBRARIAN A genealogy?
BROWN Yeah. I'm bucking for a promotion to get off that crazy beat.
LIBRARIAN We've recently received a new addition. It includes 634 families in alphabetical order. See. Here's Abbott and Addington, and there's Brown. That was my name.
BROWN That's my name too.
LIBRARIAN Oh. Really? Well, there are lots of Browns, aren't there? Pages and pages. Pages and pages and pages. (*blackout*)
JOSIE (*sirens up again.* CARL *enters carrying* JOSIE *forcibly into an old theater. A remains of an old setting are covered with dust*) Put me down! Hear me! Put me down. Now!
CARL Everything comes to those who wait for it.
JOSIE Put me down! NOW!
CARL All in good time! (*she hits him. He drops her*) What do you think you're doing? Hey, where are you going? You go back out on the street you'll get arrested.
JOSIE Let go of me.
CARL Be quiet, I tell you.
JOSIE I'll have you arrested. Help! Help!
CARL (*gags her mouth with his hand*) Damn it, woman! Now sit down there. I said sit down! (*she does*) You're the one who started that fight on the street. That's better. Ever been here before? This is the old El Gato Theater. It doesn't operate anymore so we use it for a meeting place—a base for the picketline. Nice, huh? See, we got our own tree. It's a lilac tree. Here. (*hands her an imaginary flower*) Take it. It's a lilac—a symbol of love. And if you use your imagination—swish! (*sings*) "See the green tree standing on the hill with its arms outstretched to the summertime breezes ... "
JOSIE (*pained*) Oh boy, magic.
CARL Well, we have our own ever-ready coffee-pot. How about some coffee? (*she nods*)
JOSIE When may I leave?
CARL Soon as the cops are gone.
JOSIE You got a big ego thing going, but far as I can see, you're no better than anyone else.
CARL (*pulls up chair*) Oh? Honey, three years ago I was elected track and field All-American. That means I'm probably stronger, quicker, more agile than 98 per cent of the population—Negro and white. Know what my brain can do? My IQ? It's over 172. That was on a bad day. 172 puts me in the top 5 per cent of the nation and that's white man's IQ, Baby—measured by his own yardstick, his own culture, his language, his words. My Negro IQ is over 200. So when you say I'm no better than anyone else, you're wrong.
JOSIE Well, don't-you-love-you, you pretty thing!
CARL Somebody has to.
JOSIE Brer Rabbit!
CARL Brer Rabbit?
JOSIE Once upon a time there was a rabbit named Brer Rabbit. One day Brer Fox heard Brer Rabbit sitting inde briar patch saying, "Ise de best rabbit in de world!" "Does you know everything?" "I does" say Brer Rabbit. "I bet," say Brer Fox, "you don't know how to get me into your briar patch home without gettin' me stuck on the thorns." Brer Rabbit say, "Oh, dat's easy. Ise All-American rabbit. And he carry Brer Fox right into his own house. Den when dey's in, Brer Fox eats up Brer Rabbit. Den he licks his chops and say, "Brer Rabbit was right—he was de best rabbit in de world."
CARL Is there a moral to this story, Uncle Remus?
JOSIE Uh huh, but my name's not Uncle Remus.
CARL Brer Fox?
JOSIE Nope. Josie Piper.
CARL All right. Is there a moral, Josie Piper? ... Josie Piper! Are you Sweet William's ... ?
JOSIE I'm *Mr.* Piper's daughter.
CARL Well, I guess that makes me Brer Fox's lunch. (*he hands her* PIPER's *card*) Your father's card.
JOSIE Where'd you get that?

CARL He told me to look him up if I ever wanted a gig.
JOSIE A what?
CARL A job. I'm a singer. Aren't all our people?
JOSIE That wasn't necessary.
CARL I sing loud.
JOSIE My father has a lot of contacts.
CARL He doesn't agree with my picketing.
JOSIE It is kind of adolescent.
CARL Adolescent?!
JOSIE Parading up and down with those crazy signs—everywhere I looked "Now!" "Now!"
CARL And we mean "Now!"
JOSIE Look. (*sings*) "Everything comes to those who wait for it." (*they sing in competition. He growls, she laughs*)
CARL You're great. Maybe we could make a team.
JOSIE "Piper and Picket."
CARL Or, "Brer Fox and Rabbit." I sing ballads mostly.
JOSIE Like..."
CARL (*sings first two lines from "Lilac Song"*) How's it sound?
JOSIE I like it.
CARL Aren't you going to ask me to go on?
JOSIE Please. (*they conclude song*)

THE LILAC TREE

Sung by: CARL *and* JOSIE

See the green tree standing on the hill
with its arms outstretched to
the summertime breezes.

Oh bumblebees sting the gentle lilac
but oh—honey is sweet.
There's a blackbird hidden in the tree
with a sharp pointed beak and a broken wing.

Oh—honey is sweet.

There's a young man underneath the tree
standing arm to arm with a willowy maiden.
Here them sing.
Oh—oh—how they sing.
Oh—oh—see the blackbird rise into the air.

Oh—bumblebees sting the gentle lilac.
Oh—see the green tree standing on the hill.
Oh.

CARL We don't do too badly.
JOSIE Why don't you see my father. (*he hesitates*) He'll be home tonight.
CARL I can't make it...
JOSIE Tomorrow...
CARL No... I'd rather not. (*explains*) I've got a broken wing... like the bird.
JOSIE Huh?
CARL This may sound funny, but I don't want to get into the business where I'll be typed.
JOSIE You don't even have a job and you're worried about being typed?
CARL I gotta think about not playing "Uncle Tom" roles...
JOSIE Who says you have to. My father, he doesn't... (CARL *knows he does*)... He doesn't "Tom!"
CARL I didn't say he did.
JOSIE No actor can have good parts all the time.
CARL I know it.
JOSIE Negroes are valets and porters, and chauffeurs—why shouldn't he play them?
CARL No reason if we ever get to play any other roles.
JOSIE There's *Raisin in the Sun*, and... *Carmen Jones*... and *Porgy and Bess*... *Showboat*...
CARL Sure.
JOSIE Well, if he didn't play them, somebody else would. How do you get to be so superior. You haven't done anything. No job at all. You're a nobody.
CARL I don't want to fight about it.
JOSIE My father's a fine actor and a good man.
CARL Sure he is.
JOSIE (*near tears*) He's gone out of his way to help you, and you put him down for it.
CARL I just said I didn't want to "Tom," never...
JOSIE You implied it! (*she's trying very hard not to cry*) Damn it!
CARL Josie...
JOSIE Leave me alone. I hate cry babies. And I hate people who haven't done anything, or struggled when the going was really hard, mocking those who have. (*to herself and her tears*) Stop it! Stop it! (*she turns away from him. Helpless,* CARL *turns to the tree and breaks off a stem. There's an instrumental reprise of "The Lilac Tree." He sings a line to her, then another. He pecks at her neck with the twig. She cannot remain angry; she smiles*) Oh honey, smoney!

(GLORIA *and* CAMILLE *enter*)

    GLORIA Carl! Carl!
    CARL What is it?
    CAMILLE The police—they're chasing us.

(*Lights fade. Library scene up.* BROWN *is reading a big book*)

    BROWN Oh no! Granddaddy Brown!
    LIBRARIAN Who?
    BROWN My great-great grandfather Charlie Brown.
    LIBRARIAN Charlie Brown. That was the name of my great... Let me see that book. (*reads*) Oh no! This is terrible!
    BROWN This is awful.
    LIBRARIAN Did you read...
    BROWN What I read...
    LIBRARIAN That was my great-grandfather... your grandfather Charlie Brown.
    BROWN A mister Charlie Brown. Yes, Mister Sneaky Charlie Brown.
    LIBRARIAN Sneaky, Sneaky Charlie Brown.
    BROWN Was he Caucasian?
    LIBRARIAN I cannot see this through.
    BROWN Oh, my God, that means...

    LIBRARIAN O Sneaky Charlie Brown
        If this book is right.
        If your granddad was white,
        I'll never live it down,
        Cause it means... I'm brown.

    BROWN Say it is not true.
        Whatever will I do?
        For if you are right.
        That means I am white!

(*Blackout. Theater scene lights up. The pickets come in quickly and hushed*)

    CARL What's happening? Will somebody tell me what's happening.
    PALMER Is the door closed?
    LOU Yes.
    PALMER Did we shake the police?
    LOU They went right on by.
    CARL What's happening?
    IRENE We wasted the hecklers.
    ERNIE We sure did. And this is the man. Mr. Carl Blackbird! (CARL *is lifted up*)
    CLARRY (*bitter*) Yeah, that's the man. Mr. Carl Blackbird, the famous fighter and rabble rouser. (*general boos from group*)

    BETTY Oh Clarry. Come on gang, I want to fly. (*she is picked up*)
    CLARRY What have you got to shout about? A street brawl?
    BETTY Clarry, why are you so down on anybody who wants a good time? You're not living in the South anymore. (CLARRY *turns away and sits down*) Hey Carl Blackbird!
    CARL Hey Betty Blackbird! What's happening?
    BETTY How you like flying?
    CARL Crazy, look down there.
    BETTY I see four and twenty Blackbirds.
    CARL Yeah.
    BETTY Couldn't get off the ground.
    CARL Amen!
    LOU Up jumped one and said this ain't no fun. I'm tired of being held down.

("*Fly Blackbird*" *dance and verses—sung by* PALMER, BETTY, CARL *and group.* JOSIE *watches and is gradually included by* CARL)

FLY BLACKBIRD

Four and twenty Blackbirds couldn't get off the ground.
Up jumped one, said, "This ain't no fun!
I'm sick and tired of bein' held down."

Four and twenty Blackbirds couldn't get off the ground!
Then up jumped Joe, said, "Come on! Let's go!
Look out! We're skyward bound!

Fly Blackbird. Fly Blackbird. Fly Blackbird.
Rise into the air!

Four and twenty Blackbirds sittin' in a pie.
Some sang low. Some sang low.
Some sang high. Some sang high.
Some sang "Re-bop..."
Some sang "Re-bop... Oop Shoop!
Oop Shoop! Razz ma tazz! Razz ma tazz!"
And all that jazz. And all that jazz.

Fly Blackbird. Fly Blackbird. Fly Blackbird.
Rise into the air!

Four and twenty Blackbirds said
"We do believe the Pharaoh's walls are crackin' up!"
And it ain't gonna grieve me.
Ain't gonna grieve me.
Sally don't cha leave me!
Don't leave!
We're gonna
Fly Blackbird. Fly Blackbird. Fly Blackbird.
Rise into the air!

Now, flap your wings.
Flap your wings.
Stand and shout.
Stand and shout.
Wiggle your toes.
Wiggle your toes.
We're movin' out.
We're moving' out.
Now gimme some skin.
Now gimme some skin.
Well, come on in.
Well, come on in.
When I give the word . . .
Give the word!
We'll take another chorus of *Fly Blackbird*.
Hold it! Now!
Fly Blackbird. Fly Blackbird. Fly Blackbird.
Rise into the air!

(*Dance Sequence*)

The bumblebee's stinger is ten feet long.
The bumblebee's stinger is ten feet long.
The Blackbird has a beak.
The Blackbird has a beak.
Mister Charlie got pecked by a little Blackbird.
Mister Charlie got pecked by a little Blackbird.
And he couldn't sit down for a week! Ow!

Fly Blackbird. Fly Blackbird. Fly Blackbird.
Rise into the air!
Fly Blackbird. Fly Blackbird. Fly Blackbird.

See the Blackbird.
See the Blackbird.
See the Blackbird.
Fly! Fly! Fly! Fly!
Rise into the air!

(*Enter* TAG *running into the scene at the dance's end*)

TAG Hey, they got George. (*she has his cane*) They got George. They've arrested George. (*the dance stops. Consternation. What are we going to do?*)
CLARRY Ask Carl Blackbird, the famous fighter and rabble rouser.
CARL Where they have him?
TAG In the city jail!
CLARRY Charge down to the station house and drag him out.
CARL Clarry, lay off me.
BETTY Okay, but who's gonna get George out?
JOE I'd go, but they might recognize me.
PAT Same with me—and any of us.
CARL So? Let's all go.
PAT Huh?

CARL Sure. Make them arrest us all as the book says. (*agreement*)
CLARRY You're outa your mind.
CARL The papers would pick it up and people'd find out what we're trying to do.
CLARRY Yeah. I can see the headlines. "Hoodlums jailed for starting street riot." When you started swinging your fist we lost every bit of purpose and dignity we ever had. (*vocal agreement from group*)
CARL Clarry, would you have stood around and let those hoods hurt her? (*indicates* JOSIE)
CLARRY Where'd she come from?
CARL Blackbirds, this is Josie Piper, daughter of Mr. William Piper. (*recognition whistles*) How about it, Clarry?
CLARRY No one's worth losing the whole scene for.
CARL We haven't lost it, Man!
CLARRY Yeah? You think the police are going to let us picket that place anymore? Or any place in this city? We're finished.
CARL Mr. Piper'll help us.
BETTY Sweet William Piper?
CARL Yes.
BETTY That's all, brother. So long, babies.
CARL Where you going?
BETTY See you in jail. (*snaps her fingers*)
TAG Yeah, in jail. (*snaps in a weak imitation of Betty and exits*)
CLARRY Listen, Carl. In Atlanta, Georgia, I saw a boy, 17, sit-in at a lunch counter. A heckler took a lighted cigarette and ground it into the kid's neck. He never moved. Never made a sound. He wasn't sitting in there for himself—he wasn't sitting in for the Negro—he was a white boy—but he was sitting there for something more important than one girl, or the personal spleen of Carl Eldridge.
CARL Why the hell you riding me? You think I get paid for picketing? I could be making good money singing in clubs. You know that? All those who are coming down to the station with me, let's go. (*they hesitate*) Come on. I said let's go. Josie, tell them your father understands.
JOSIE I . . . yes, but he doesn't like Negroes to get bad publicity.
CLARRY She's right. Going to jail for peaceful picketing. I'm for that, but to be jailed for a street fight—I'm against it. We'll get George a lawyer.

LOU We fought for the wrong thing.
PAT At the wrong time. Carl, I think Clarry's right.
CARL (*regards them a moment*) Okay, I'll tell George what a loyal bunch you all are. (*to* JOSIE) You coming?
JOSIE My father ... he wouldn't like ...
CARL Somebody see she gets home. (*exits*)
JOSIE Carl.
CLARRY (*minor key*) Four and twenty blackbirds couldn't get off the ground.

(*The lights fade. From the other side of the stage, in front of the curtain, comes* JUDGE CROCKER *and* SWEET WILLIAM PIPER, *both dressed in the parade regalia of the fraternal order of Caribou. They sing.* CROCKER *is white and walks with a cane. They are good fellows out on the town, singing*)

JUDGE (*singing*) Oh Sweet William.
PIPER (*singing*) Yes Judge Crocker.
JUDGE Oh Sweet William.
PIPER Yes Judge Crocker.
BOTH When we walk down the street, all the people we meet say, "Hello Sweet William, Good Morning Judge Crocker"; we're living in the promised land. (*they laugh at this bad harmony*)
JUDGE The parade has been a joy, Brother Piper.
PIPER Brother—your honor—Crocker.
JUDGE May I say, before leaving, that I find your Fraternal Order or Negro Caribou one of the finest organizations in this city.
PIPER We try to fit properly into the community.
JUDGE You do, Mr. Piper. Now I must return to my chambers. Crime and the Law do not stop for parades and brotherhood.
PIPER Have you a ride, Sir?
JUDGE Yes, that's my black Cadillac parked over there.
PIPER Ah, beautiful car. 1960 isn't it?
JUDGE Can I drop you somewhere?
PIPER No thank you, your honor, that's my Lincoln Continental parked beside yours.
JUDGE The white one?
PIPER Yes. The 1961.
JUDGE Side by side. (*a siren is heard*) There they go again. Let me call on my car phone to see what's happening. Sam! Sam! My phone. (*a brown chauffeur's hand extends the phone to him from behind curtain*) This is Judge Crocker. Why all the sirens in District 36 today? That so? I see. I'll return at once. (*hangs up*) Those Negro pickets down in front of the chain store starting a street riot. Now, Brother Piper, it's things like this that make it hard on the good Negroes like yourself. Why don't you come along to the station with me? They might be more inclined to listen to one of their own kind. Care to ride with me?
PIPER Why not ride with me?
JUDGE We'll both drive. Separate but equal. (*laughs*)
PIPER But mine's a 1961. (*exits. Blackout. Jail. An officer escorts* GEORGE *into set and leaves him*)
COP Prisoner Nishida, wait here until otherwise instructed.
GEORGE Yessir. (*to audience*) I'm sorry you see me like this. I have been in prison three hours. I should have run, but I had done nothing wrong. To do nothing wrong, it seems, is sometimes a mistake.

(*Area to side. Same cop and two colored washerwomen*)

COP Where you going there?
BETTY (*in red bandana and carrying bucket ... thick Negro dialect*) You talkin' to me, Sir?
COP Yes, you, that room's closed.
BETTY Oh, we knows dat, but Judge Crocker, he say—go clean dat room, Bertie—don't he?
TAG (*also in thick Negro dialect*) Dat's right. He say clean dat room good. He say make dat room shine like a policeman's boots. Yes sir, he say you gonna clean up dat room for me til it gleam, he say.
BETTY Yeah, dat's what he say.
COP All right—go on in. (*they enter in with* GEORGE)
BETTY Prisoner George Nishida?
GEORGE I confess to everything.
BETTY Be cool, man.
GEORGE Betty.
TAG Hello, Georgie.
GEORGE Tag, you shouldn't be here.
TAG Did they beat you?
BETTY Down, girl! George, baby, you're good as sprung.
GEORGE What?
BETTY We'll get you out. (*pulls out suit coat*) Here, put this on.
GEORGE Why?

Fly Blackbird

TAG Hold your arms out.
GEORGE What!
BETTY Now this!
TAG And this!
BETTY And this!
TAG And these!
BETTY Good baby! Now smile. Smile! Crazy! Okay, go out that way.
GEORGE Out? Are you insane? I can't go out.
BETTY *sure you can.* (*turns him around so audience can see his disguise*) You now famous Oriental detective—like Charlie Chan.
GEORGE Oh no.
BETTY Oh yes. (BETTY *and* TAG *sing and dance "The Gong"*)

THE GONG

Sung by BETTY, TAG, *and* GEORGE

BETTY and TAG The Oriental Detective is always
accompanied by a gong
and temple blocks
and a melody built on a Pentatonic scale.
Nyn nyn nyn nyn nyn nyn nyn nyn nyn nyn nyn
nyn nyn nyn nynh!

Have you ever been to a Hollywood moving picture?
Then you know what I mean. You know what I mean.

That's the way it always is on
the Hollywood Movie Screen.
The Oriental Detective is always
accompanied by a gong.
Do you remember Charlie Chan?
That famous policeman.
From the Orient
the mysterious East!

Then there was Fu Manchu.
When he blinked those eyes at you . . .
The chills began to trickle down your spine.

Terry and the Pirates and the Dragon Lady . . .
She was kinda' shady.
Not like Rosie O'Grady, the "girl next door."
"The girl next door." To who? Not you!
And then we had "The World of Susie Wong."

And once again we had the GONG!

The Oriental Detective is always
accompanied by a gong.

GEORGE Why must it always be a gong?
Why can't it ever by the Samisen or the Sho?
BETTY What's a Samisen, man?
GEORGE Well, it's like a . . . guitar . . . Or the koto?
TAG What's a koto, Mr. Moto?
GEORGE Ah . . . the Koto is a long, narrow, stringed instrument which is plucked . . . and the most amazing thing about it is that it can be retuned during performance!

BETTY and TAG Wow!

GEORGE Or how about the Hichiriki, which is like an oboe,
or the Kokyu or the Shakuhachi . . .
ALL But . . . why does it always have to be a gong?

How come an Oriental Detective is
always accompanied by a gong
and temple blocks
and a melody built on a Pentatonic scale
Nyn nyn nyn nyn nyn nyn nyn nyn
nyn nyn nyn nyn nyn nyn nyn
NYAÁAAAAAH!

BETTY Oh, I dig you—you cool thing. But later for it. Bug out, man. (GEORGE *pulls off beard*) What are you doing?
GEORGE I have to stay.
BETTY Are you crazy?
GEORGE (*returning glasses and hat*) Thank you very much.
BETTY George, you don't know what it's like in jail.
GEORGE Yes I do. When I was seven, I was in prison for three years.
TAG For what?
GEORGE For being Nisei—Japanese-American. During the war our whole family was moved from our home to a relocation center.
BETTY What's that got to do with now?
GEORGE We did nothing wrong then. I did nothing wrong now. See what I mean. It was nice of you to think of me. (*gives* TAG *last of disguise*)
COP (*entering*) You, prisoner, the judge is coming to see you. (*to* BETTY) You done in here?
BETTY Yas sir, Mr. Policeman. We is done. Everything here is done. (*to* GEORGE) Goodbye Mr. Ignorant. (*to* TAG) Come on, Gal. (*exits with cop*)
TAG George.
GEORGE Yes?
BETTY Come on, Tag—Lawsie Officer, dat room sure was dirty . . . (*exits*) (JUDGE *and* PIPER *enter from other side*)

JUDGE Mr. Piper, what these young people want is to be sent to jail. They fight to be martyrs.
PIPER That's what I'm thinking in my mind.
COP He's in here, Judge.
JUDGE Thank you, Officer. If he's white, I'll talk to him. If he's Negro...
PIPER I'll straighten my boys out. (JUDGE and PIPER enter)
JUDGE Let's have a look at the prisoner. Prisoner, on your feet. (*they're both confused. Both wait for the other to speak*)
PIPER Don't look at me. He's not mine.
JUDGE What the hell are you Chinese doing in the picket line? Well, what have you to say for yourself?
GEORGE I pledge allegiance to the flag and to the country for which it stands, etc. (*he completely shames the men. blackout. Library.* BROWN *on chair reaching down a book under the* LIBRARIAN'*s direction*)
LIBRARIAN The one clear on top. Careful you don't fall.
BROWN This the one you want?
LIBRARIAN What's the title?
BROWN "How to Identify a Negro."
LIBRARIAN That's the one.
BROWN (*still standing on chair and looking into book*) "Who's a Negro legally..."
LIBRARIAN What does it say? What's it say?
BROWN In Kentucky you are Negro if you have 25 per cent Negro blood. In Mississippi, and North Dakota, you're colored if you have 12.5 per cent Negro blood. In Alabama, it's one drop.
LIBRARIAN One drop? But which drop?

(*Blackout. The Chambers.* CARL *seated.* CROCKER *and* PIPER *standing behind him in examination*)

CARL Where's George Nishida?
JUDGE He's been released. (*reaction*) We have no desire to punish idealism.
PIPER Only to help.
CARL Then why'd you arrest him?
PIPER I warned you that you'd get into trouble. But the idea behind this boy's work is good, Judge.
JUDGE But the means are bad.
PIPER True. True.
JUDGE He's immature.
PIPER He's young.
JUDGE He's headstrong.

PIPER Over-anxious. I'd like to help you, son. I'm sure Judge Crocker would.
CARL Yeah? How?
PIPER Wisdom.
JUDGE Guidance.
PIPER Maturity.
JUDGE Patience.
CARL I've waited long enough.
PIPER Young man, I've waited all my life.
JUDGE But now the Supreme Court has made equal opportunity the law of the land...
CARL That was six years ago.
PIPER But it has been decided.
JUDGE You're whipping a dead horse. The issue's been settled.
CARL Not in Mississippi.
JUDGE That's 2,000 miles away.
CARL Can I buy property in... Glendale?
JUDGE Yes, I read in the papers where a family has just moved in.
CARL Why'd it have to be in the papers?
PIPER Hasty, hasty. Give people time to accept the law.
CARL They've had 200 years.
JUDGE Mr. Piper tells me you're interested in becoming a singer, Mr. Eldridge, and that you have the talent for it.
CARL The first part's true.
JUDGE Then why throw your chance away?
PIPER No one wants to hire a troublemaker. Look what happened to that fine career of Paul Robeson.
JUDGE But as a successful entertainer...
PIPER You'll be an inspiration to all our people.
JUDGE You'll be an example to the white community of the good Negro.
PIPER You'll have influence.
JUDGE You'll have financial power.
PIPER If you're patient.
JUDGE If you wait.
PIPER Think it over.
JUDGE I'm on your side, young man. I am. I don't have a prejudiced bone in my body. Bill here knows that.
PIPER Yes sir.
JUDGE Why, when I look at Bill, I don't see a Negro. He doesn't even act like a Negro. I don't care if your black, brown, or red, white and green—as long as you're white inside.
CARL I'm black inside.
JUDGE Now don't twist what I say. I've

Fly Blackbird

never done you Negroes any harm, and I won't be slapped in the face.
PIPER Well now, we mustn't become excited. That certainly won't help, will it? Perhaps we should go out to dinner and have a cooling off period.
JUDGE If there's anything I can't stand, it's the pushing Professional Negro, with a capital "P," capital "N."
CARL Then why do you bother with them?
JUDGE I'm trying to help you. You see, young man, I know what bitterness is; the feeling of being outside. See this? (*shows cane*) When other boys ran to play ball, I learned patience.
CARL Were you ever refused service in a barbershop, or a restaurant because of that?
JUDGE Young man, I've tried to talk with you as a friend, as a father would. Now I must speak to you as the law. If there is any more sidewalk picketing, any more of this rowdiness whatsoever, you'll be arrested, fined, and sent to prison. You and everyone connected with you. Think that over!!

THINK IT OVER

Think it over
Consider well
Don't jeopardize a fine young career

Are you a radical? a revolutionary?
Don't let your bitterness
Lead you along a path you may regret.

Think it over!
Think it over!
Think it over!

(*Curtain*)

ACT TWO

(*Street. Night. It has been raining. Thunder.* BETTY, GEORGE *and* TAG *are heard offstage singing* "*Fly Blackbird*"—*they enter singing*)

TAG Hey, wait! (*they stop*) I have to tie my shoe. (*she does*) Gee, George, I thought they would never let you out of that jail.
BETTY The kids'll sure be glad to see you.
GEORGE I'll be glad to see them... Hey, look—there's the sign I dropped this morning.
BETTY (*starting off*) Aw leave it, George. Let's get back to the theater.
GEORGE We don't want to be accused of being litterbugs, do we? (*picks up sign*) Let's go!
THREE (*form a mock picket line*) Now! Right Now! Right Now! Right—(*enter cop*)
COP Ah hah! Picketing again! You've all been warned—now line up! (*there is a mad scramble*, BETTY *and* TAG *escape, but* GEORGE *is caught again*)
GEORGE (*loud wail*) But Officer, I just got out of jail. (*he is dragged off. Enter* JOSIE *who sees sign* GEORGE *dropped. She crosses and picks it up, cradles it and tries picketing a few steps. She stops and begins a soft reprise of the song "The Lilac Tree".* CARL *appears upstage and joins her. She stops. They gaze at one another. Thunder*)
CARL That was close. It's going to rain.
JOSIE Where's your coat?
CARL I haven't had time to go home yet.
JOSIE (*taking hers off*) Here.
CARL Don't do that. I don't need it.
JOSIE There's room for both of us. Here.
CARL (*holding the coat like a tent over their heads*) We could stand over there in the doorway... but I think I like this better.
JOSIE You think I'm chasing you.
CARL I hope you are.
JOSIE I never chase boys. Never... before.
CARL Josie, ever since I saw you this morning I've wanted to... to shout... (*thunder.* JOSIE *holds her hand out*)
JOSIE It's not raining.
CARL Too bad. (*puts coat down. Thunder*)
JOSIE Sounds like the sea... waves...
CARL Do you like the ocean?
JOSIE Mmmmmmm.
CARL Someday, I'd like to have a home on the beach.
JOSIE So would I.
CARL Maybe we could work something out together.
JOSIE Good way to keep the rent down.
CARL Josie, I've got a problem... I'm falling in love.
JOSIE You do have a problem.
CARL Darn right. We don't agree on anything. There's Judge Crocker and your father...
JOSIE And your picketing. (*more thunder...* JOSIE *begins song:* "*Couldn't We*")

COULDN'T WE?

Sung by: JOSIE *and* CARL

We could settle down in a
little green cottage by the sea.
Couldn't we?
Couldn't we?

A little green cottage
with a welcome mat by the door.
And windows that let the sun come through,
waves pounding on the shore.

Hear them roll
Hear them roar

We'd run down to the beach
and welcome the morning tide.
Wouldn't we?
Wouldn't we?

We'd fly down the sand like
seagulls on the wing.

When night falls, we'll see the mirror
of the moon glist'ning on the water
and the stars twinkling in the sky.

We could settle down in a
little green cottage by the sea.
Couldn't we?
Couldn't we?

(*They kiss. Enter* PIPER)

PIPER Josie!—Rather late to be standing on the street, isn't it?

JOSIE (*nervously*) You've met Carl Eldridge, father.

PIPER Indeed I have, but I didn't realize you two were such good friends.

CARL We just met.

PIPER OH really.

JOSIE This afternoon.

PIPER Mr. Eldridge, I don't intend to have my daughter mixed up in any of this nonsense.

CARL Sir, I'd like to apologize for the way I spoke to you this afternoon. I've been thinking about what you and Judge Crocker said.

PIPER Well! I'm very glad to hear that, Carl. You're entirely too intelligent and talented to be mixed up in such emotionalism. When you've been around as long as I have, you'll come to realize that Rome wasn't built in a day. (CARL *nods*) Tomorrow morning I'm planning to visit one of the studios. Why don't you come with me?

CARL Thank you. I'd like that very much.

PIPER Good. Come, Josie! (*she lingers with* CARL) . . . Drop over about nine o'clock in the morning, Carl. (*they exit*)

CARL I will . . . I will! (*runs off singing*) "We'd run down to the beach and welcome the tide . . ."

(*The Library.* BROWN *and* LIBRARIAN *are dead tired. The scene is covered with the litter of their books from their search*)

LIBRARIAN Did you find something?

BROWN Not yet.

LIBRARIAN We may as well give up and go home.

BROWN What am I going to tell my wife? "Honey, for eight years you've been married to a white man?"

LIBRARIAN You've been passing as a Negro —simply keep on.

TWILIGHT ZONE

Sung by: LIBRARIAN *and* BROWN

What are we gonna do?
I can't believe it's true.
Oh, I could sit right down and cry.

Where do we go from here?
How I'd like to disappear from view.

We're all alone in the TWILIGHT ZONE.

Oh, I used to walk along the street,
smile at folks that I'd meet.
Life was just a bowl of cherries.

I'm quite beyond recovery
since I made the discovery
that cherries have a pit.
I'm it!

Oh, what a mockery,
Fate, what have you done to me?
Life has dealt a crushing blow.
Sadness and misery.
The Heavens high have laid me low.

There's nothing more worth living for
when you find you're neither nor
I can see the surprise in everybody's eyes,
when they discover that I'm
Nature's little compromise.

We're all alone
in the TWILIGHT ZONE!

LIBRARIAN Oh, Lawd, what is I gonna do???

Fly Blackbird

(*Blackout. The group sits around the stage, completely depressed.* BETTY *surveys the situation and stands up with the intention of getting something going. She attempts to tickle and tease a few of the kids, who give her a dirty look and move away*)

BETTY Well, this sure is a cheery bunch. Come on, Ernie, get your face off the floor and flap your wings! Say that's it!—Flap your wings! Stand and shout! Wiggle—

PALMER Ah, Betty, knock it off, will ya'?

BETTY Look, it isn't our fault George got arrested. He coulda' run if he wasn't so square.

PALMER Maybe he was too honest.

BETTY Same thing. Well, if I have to, I'll get him out myself. (*sings*) "Cause this is Big Betty—This is Big Betty. And I can rock 'n' roll from pole to pole, 'cause I've got cinnamon in my soul . . ." (*messes* CAMILLE'S *hair*)

CAMILLE Betty! Why don't you go home!

BETTY What?

CAMILLE Or else stop being so loud and raunchy.

BETTY (*angry and hurt*) Your mama! (*she senses the group agrees with* CAMILLE)—"Cause this is Big Betty . . ." (*she walks over to another group and they also reject her*) . . . Well, what do I have to have anyway? A college degree to walk your picket line? And I suppose you think my parents didn't go to college—well they did! (*they didn't*) My folks . . . my folks . . . (*near tears*) sat on the back of the bus just as long as yours. (*she starts to leave*)

TAG Betty . . . wait!

BETTY (*she's crying*) Why do you have to follow me everywhere I go? Get lost, will you? (*she exits.* JANICE *and* BEN *enter*)

BEN (*to* TAG) What's the matter with her? (TAG, *hurt, starts to walk away*)

CAMILLE (*to* TAG) Tag, you don't have to take that from Betty. She treats you like dirt.

TAG What do you know about how Betty treats me.

CAMILLE Well, anyone can see it—she's never quiet and ladylike. (*general agreement*)

PALMER Amen. We got enough trouble as it is.

BRENDA She gives a bad picture of the Negro. People point to her and say—"See, that's what the Negro is like."

TAG (*angry*) Well, that's how Betty is; that's what she's really like! You make me sick, Brenda! In fact you all make me sick! Well, I don't care what you say about Betty, I don't care—'cause I wish I were just like her!

GAIL (*on* TAG'S *side*) So do I! (*she happens to look down at her arm and sees the color of her skin, and realizes what she has just said—she and* TAG *look at each other and laugh*)

TAG Oh you—you've been around us so long that you're just like one of us.

GAIL So I'm a spook already.

CLARRY "Four and twenty blackbirds, couldn't get off the ground." (*he laughs gently*) Big Betty's right—there's no reason for us all to be down, when so many important things are happening—little things. And you never know which one's going to be important.

RIVERS TO THE SOUTH

Sung by: CLARRY, PALMER, *and* GROUP

Oh there are mighty rivers to the South.
Rivers deep and long.
I have listened to the rivers of the South,
heard them singing:

New day! New day!
New time! New way!
Comin' soon.

I have followed the rivers of the South,
rushing down to the sea.
I have followed the rivers of the South,
come follow me!
To a new day, new day!
A new time and a new way comin' soon.

Stood on the banks of the Mississippi,
New day! New day!
Heard the waters of the Bayou,
dark and cold.
New day! New day!
Crossed the wide Missouri,
Listened to the Chippewa ages old.

New day! New day!
New time! New way!
New way! New way! New way comin' soon.

Little drops of rain fall from the branches
Form a pool at the bottom of the tree.
The pool flows into the babbling brook,
the brook flows into the stream.

Then the stream plunges down the side
of the mountain into the river, filling the river.
I have seen the mighty rivers of the South,
filled to the brim by a driving rain.
New day! New day!

When the dam breaks
The cup runneth over
New day!
The river will rise and flood the shore.
New day! New day!

River foam. River roar.
River rage! River thunder!
Aaaaaah.

Oh there are mighty rivers to the south,
rivers deep and long.
Listen to the rivers of the South.
Hear them sing.

Coming soon. Coming soon.

(*After song, their spirits are up again, and* GAIL *starts toward door*)

GAIL I'm going to see how Betty is—anybody coming with me?

BEN Yeah—I'll go with you. (*others agree to go with* GAIL *and* BEN *and exit*)

TAG You know what? I think we ought to all go down to that jail and sit there until they either let George out, or put us in!

CLARRY I've got a better idea. Why don't we get the line moving in front of the store tomorrow morning? (*general agreement*) ... say about 9 o'clock ... bright and early. (*they move off enthusiastically, talking about tomorrow's picket line.* TAG *lingers*)

CLARRY What's the matter, Tag?

TAG Clarry—will you see about George?

CLARRY Sure. After I take you home. First thing I gotta do is find out what happened to Carl.

(*Enter* CARL *boisterous and a little drunk*)

CARL Carl died and went to heaven, man.

TAG Carl!

CLARRY (*good humor*) Where the hell have you been?

CARL Celebrating.

CLARRY Celebrating?

CARL I'm in love. Tag—I'm in love.

TAG With me?

CARL (*dancing with her*) "We'd run down to the beach and welcome the morning tide ..."

CLARRY Hey man, knock it off and tell us what happened at the station.

CARL Clarry, I am in love with the most beautiful female in the whole human race. Josie Piper—she's gorgeous!

CLARRY Yeah, I've seen her.

CARL She's got the softest, brownest, most tender hands. When I touched her—ZAP! I was paralyzed! (*he swoons to floor*)

TAG Carl! Are you all right—Carl! (*she reaches for his bottle, and he quickly comes to life again*)

CARL Yep!—All I need is another shot of love elixir.

CLARRY You've had enough love elixir.

TAG Carl, we've decided that we're gonna picket that store again tomorrow, cops or no cops.

CARL See you in jail.

CLARRY What happened at the station, Carl?

CARL You're lookin' pretty sour these days, Clarry—here! (*offers bottle*) "It'll take away your troubles, leave you floating on a bubble ..."

CLARRY (*getting irritated*) What happened, Carl?

CARL Awright ... I went chargin' down to that jail, big and bad as you please—right?

TAG Right.

CARL Well, they let me talk to this guy Crocker, Judge Crocker ... And you'll never guess who was there with him.

CLARRY Amos n' Andy.

CARL Mr. William Piper—the father of the girl I'm gonna marry—father of the most beautiful girl in ...

ALL THREE The Whole Human Race!

CARL I know you're down on Piper, but he's not a bad guy. If it hadn't been for actors like him, there wouldn't be Poitiers or Belafontes today. Crocker listens to him. He's the one who got George out.

TAG But they got George again.

CARL You're kidding.

TAG Really.

CARL Oh man. Maybe Crocker and Piper are right.

CLARRY What do you mean?

CARL Here we are messing up our lives and causing nothing but trouble. Maybe we ought to try working with Crocker instead of against him.

CLARRY We've tried working with Crockers.

CARL He just feels that you oughta try to be a little more subtle.

CLARRY Subtle?—What the hell's so "subtle" about Alabama?

CARL Don't shout, Clarry. I got an interview at one of the studios tomorrow. I might get a part in the movies.

CLARRY What kind of a part? Playing "Mr. Bones?" See you later, *Uncle*. Come on, Tag. (*she reluctantly follows*)

CARL (*shouting after them*) You're jealous. That's what's the matter with Negroes—never like to see another Negro get ahead . . . Oh, my head . . . Why should I turn down a break like this? Piper's a big man . . . wonder if he can really get me into the movies . . . then I'll marry the most beautiful girl in the entire . . . (*he falls asleep. Lights out . . . thunder . . . music. Electric colored sign in dark says* "MEDICINE SHOW." CROCKER'*s voice is heard as the lights come up on* CARL'*s dream.* CROCKER *and* PIPER *are dressed in medicine show costumes*)

DOC Sweet William—have enough Elixir for tonight's show?

PIPER Yes, Doctor Crocker—300 gallons.

DOC Good. And make sure the stage has been swept. What's this? (*discovers* CARL) Young man, wake up. (CARL *is groggy*) Wake up, I say. Sweet William, is this one of your boys?

PIPER Son, what are you doing here in Dr. Crocker's theater. Oh!—It's you. This is young Eldridge . . . the boy I mentioned might be interested in joining . . . our happy troupe.

CARL Judge Crocker . . . what . . . ?

DOC *Dr.* Crocker. Owner of the world's oldest traveling medicine show—purveyor of the best in "pure" entertainment.

CARL Medicine show? This theater's not used any more.

DOC Not . . . Not used anymore. Why my troupe and I perform here every night. (*indicates audience*)

CARL Where'd they come from . . . this theater's not used . . .

DOC Sweet William. My Troupe. (SWEET WILLIAM *snaps his fingers. The troupe enters singing "The Love Elixir Song"*)

THE LOVE ELIXIR SONG

Sung by : THE CROCKER BOYS *and* GIRLS

CROCKER BOYS   Doctor Crocker's Love Elixir is the most successful trouble fixer, known to mortal man.

PIPER   Have you got troubles? Do you have headaches? Do you have pains?

CROCKER BOYS   It will take away your troubles, leave you floating on a bubble of champagne!

PIPER   You'll feel good again!

CROCKER GIRLS   We're lovely, we're charming,

CAMILLE   Doctor Crocker's Love Elixir has done this for me.

CROCKER GIRLS   We're done this for me. Ooo.

CAMILLE   I used to be dissatisfied and unhappy.
Nothing seemed right to me . . .
I was mad at the world.
Then, I discovered Crocker's Love Elixir.
"Why, there's nothing wrong with the world!" I said. "The trouble is inside me
. . . Why, it's been me all along!"
But now . . . now I've found . . . peace . . . and love.

CROCKER BOYS   Doctor Crocker's Love Elixir has done this for me.

PIPER   So I ask you friend and neighbor . . .

PAUL   Why not do yourself a favor?

LOU   You'll love it!

GEORGE   It'll do you good.

ROGER   It'll knock you out.

PIPER   You'll be a new man!

ALL   We ask you not to hesitate.
A minute more may be too late.
It's going fast!
It's a blast! Doo wah!

DOC What do you think now, young man?

CARL (*after the Troupe has finished*) Ev? Pat? Clarry! What have you done to them?

DOC They've been legitimately hired as members of my Troupe. Non-Equity, of course. Sweet William has told me that you are highly talented as a singer. (CARL'*s modest*) I would like to offer you a position in our show. Of course, I must start you at the bottom, but as time goes by, as you drink the love elixir . . .

CARL What's that?

PIPER Our sponsor's product. It cures all pains, mental, physical, spiritual.

DOC Here, drink, courtesy of the house.

CARL I don't think I better. I... I've already had quite a bit to drink.
DOC But this will make you feel better.
CARL No... I'd rather not.
DOC I insist.
PIPER Do as Dr. Crocker tells you, Boy. It's for your own good.
CARL No! I don't want any. (CROCKER *snaps his fingers. The crocker boys come forward and seize* CARL)
PIPER Don't make a fool of me. You drink! Drink! (*he's about to force* CARL *when* JOSIE *enters*)
JOSIE (*sings operatic style*) Hold! Harm not a hair on his nappy head. Stand aside. I have the power of a woman in love.
PIPER Josie, he hasn't drunk the Love Elixir. (*to* CARL) Drink!
CARL No. Josie!
JOSIE (*advancing*) I warn you.
DOC Let him go. Let him go. (*they do*) There, my dear, we meant him no harm. He merely became frightened before he had an opportunity to adjust to the idea.
JOSIE (*to* PIPER) You cannot be trusted. (*to* CARL) He promised that he wouldn't harm you. But I've saved you. I'm yours. Carl, I'm yours.
CARL But you've changed.
JOSIE Yes, I'm like you are—strong, virile, intelligent.
CARL But I liked you weak, feminine, and stupid.
JOSIE Then you can save yourself! (*exit* JOSIE *with* CARL *after her*)
CARL Josie, I didn't mean that. Josie...
DOC Ah, there they go. A young couple filled with pain. Sweet William. (*snaps his fingers and Crocker Troupe goes to places*)
PIPER He's a little skittish, but Josie'll bring him around. She was just a little upset with the way we were handling him.
DOC She doesn't realize the peace and harmony that can be his. My friends. Here in this little bottle is the famous power potion, the Doctor Crocker Love Elixir. In this cup is the secret remedy to the white man's problems and the colored man's pains. My friends, if you have bitterness in your job, trouble with your neighbors...
BOY (*from the audience in real theater*) Mister, I do.
DOC Ah, my colored friend, do you have trouble with your white neighbors?
BOY Yeah, mister. The trouble is, I don't have any.
DOC What's your name, boy?
BOY Boy.
DOC All right, boy, if you'll come...
BOY That's Mr. Boy.
DOC Mr. Boy. Mr. Boy, if you'll come up here, I will give you a free sample of my Love Elixir so you can testify to the power of this sweet remedy. Come, Mr. Boy, come right over here and up on the stage. Don't hesitate. Some of my best friends are colored people.
BOY All my best friends are colored people.
DOC The elixir will change all that. Come, Mr. Boy. How do you do. (*they shake hands.* CROCKER *wipes his hand on his coat, so does* MR. BOY) My friends, you're about to witness the God-given power of this medicine. (*Chorus: Doo-ah*) Watch the change that envelops Mr. Boy as he drinks the Elixir. (*Chorus: Doo-ah*) Drink, Mr. Boy.
BOY What's in it?
DOC Spirits of Christianity.
BOY Will this make you and me brothers?
DOC Yes it will.
BOY Then I don't want any.
DOC Wait a moment. Don't you want to be friends with all men and women?
BOY Maybe women.
DOC This Elixir'll fill your life with peace and harmony. Here, drink it.
BOY (*takes elixir and drinks*) Ooooooooo.
DOC Drink some more.
BOY Ooooooooo (*he goes into transformation of complete darkey*) I feels fine. I feels fine. Thankya Doctor Crocker.
DOC Filled with peace.
BOY Yes sir, peace and harmony.
DOC Good boy, good boy. Is that a speck of dust on my shoe?
BOY Sho is, sir. I'll dust it off for you.
DOC Wait, wait! Here. (*gives* BOY *handkerchief*)
BOY Thank you sir. (BOY *gets down on his knees and shines shoes*)
DOC Thank you, boy. There we are, folks. The white race and the colored race living side by side in love and friendship. (MR. BOY *hiccoughs*) What's that? (*hiccoughs again*) It goes down easier with some than others but it does

go down. And peace and God walk upon the earth. (*Mr. Boy song*)

MR. BOY

Sung by: MR. BOY *and* DOCTOR CROCKER

CROCKER When I go walkin' with Mister Boy,
I wear a smile on my face
because there's nothin' better
in the whole wide world
than a colored man in his place.
O Mister Boy!

BOY Yas Doctor Crocker?

CROCKER O Mister Boy!

BOY Yas Doctor Crocker?

CROCKER When we walk down the street
all the people we meet
say "How ya' doin' Boy?
Good mornin' Doctor Crocker!"
We're living' in the promised land

When we walk down the street
all the people we meet say:
"How ya' doin' Boy?
Good mornin' Doctor Crocker!"
We're livin' in the promised land.

They got a whole lotta trouble in Africa
They got trouble in Tennessee
Because the color'd man is gettin' out of hand
My friends you better listen to me.

He's got to be pacified.
He's got to be dominated.
He's got to be willin' to do
what I tell him to 'cause this is
the order that God created.

He's got to be pacified
He's got to be dominated
He's got to be willin' to do
what I tell him to 'cause this is
the order that God created.

CHORUS MEMBER Now just a minute, Doctor Crocker,
there's one thing wrong
and other folks think so too
from what I can see you won't listen to me
How come I got to listen to you?

CROCKER Give that boy a shot of the love elixir!

He's got to be pacified
Convinc'd he's satisfied.
He's got to be willin' to do
what I tell him to 'cause this is
the law that God implied.

Now I realize that the colored man
hasn't always been treated right.
But I can guarantee equality
If we separate black from white.

He's got to be separated
and kept dis-integrated.

As long as he's willin' to do
what I tell him to
he'll find himself well situated.

When I go walkin' with Mister Boy
I wear a smile on my face
Because there's nothin' better in the
whole wide world than a
color'd man in his place
O Mister Boy!

BOY Yas Doctor Crocker?

CROCKER O Mister Boy

BOY Yas Doctor Crocker?

CROCKER When we walk down the street
all the people we meet say:
"how ya doin' Boy?"
Good mornin' Doctor Crocker"
We're livin' in the promised land.
We're livin' in the promised land.

DOC You have seen it, Ladies and Gentlemen, you have witnessed it.

CARL Come on.

JOSIE Just go right up to him, Carl.

DOC Oh, it's you?

CARL Yeah, it's me. I want to know what you've done to my pickets. Okay, Blackbirds, we're movin' out. (CROCKER *motions them to sit down. They do*) I said let's go. Betty! Let's move. (*she offers him the tray*) Betty?

DOC No need to be upset, Carl.

CARL I don't know what you've done to them, but you'll let them go if you know what's good for you.

DOC Young man, violence is no solution. (*signals boys*)

CARL If you don't want violence . . .

JOSIE (*ready to fight*) Stand back, people eaters. This is Big Josie.

CARL No! Violence is not the answer. (CARL *takes a chair from the side of the stage*) Grab a chair, Josie.

JOSIE What are you doing?

CARL Sitting. Over here, Josie.

JOSIE   On the stage?
CARL   You scared, Blackbird?
JOSIE   I'da broken their heads.
DOC   Are you going to just sit?
CARL   Just sit.
DOC   May I suggest you move your chairs to the side so we can go on?
CARL   No.
DOC   Boy, if you just want to sit . . .
CARL   Sit-in.
DOC   Then why don't you do as everyone else does, sit in the audience.
CARL   Sitting out there is like . . . sitting still. But sitting-in is like moving.
DOC   What, young man, are you driving at?
CARL   I'm driving to that promised land. You with me, Blackbird?
JOSIE   All the way.
CARL   Off we go. (CARL *pretends to be driving a car.* JOSIE *is his passenger.* CROCKER *is confused*)
DOC   (*to chorus*) You understand them? (*to audience*) You understand them? (*horn*) Only thing I can deduce is that they're pushing themselves into my show. (*intimately*) Give those colored people an inch and they take a mile. (CARL *slams on the brakes*) Boys like you are the reason the Negro isn't loved anymore.
CARL   Was he ever?
DOC   He most certainly was. People wrote songs about the colored folks. Songs that spoke with love and affection. *Swannee River* and *Old Black Joe*. Now there's a wonderful song.
CARL   To me it isn't so wonderful.
DOC   Stephen Foster loved the Negro.
CARL   Well, maybe he did. But while Old Massa' Foster was sitting in the house writing songs about how much he loved the Negro, the Negro was out in the fields singing songs like "O Freedom" and "Steal Away!"—Ever hear of those?
DOC   If you don't love Stephen Foster, you're a very bitter man.
CARL   Well, why didn't he write a song called: "Old White Tom"?—He should have! (*sings*)

> This is the song of Old White Tom
> And it's never been sung before
> Some say he was a friend to the colored man
> But it's never been proven for sure.

(*Troupe chuckles*)

> When there was work to be done in
>   the cotton fields,
> He was nowhere to be seen
> You could find him in the shade
>   of an old apple tree
> Just pickin' his fingernails clean.

DOC (*lights dim on* DOC, *who begins to play role of "Old White Tom"*) Let the slaves do the dirty work, no job for a white man . . . Boy! Another speck of dust on my shoes. (BOY *scampers over and dusts* CROCKER's *shoes*) After all, dirt don't show up so much on them.
CARL (*sings*)

> Old White Tom, he went along through life
> Thinkin' he was better than the black man,
> red man, yellow man—Hot Damn!
> This is the song of Old White Tom,
> Who just didn't realize his time had come!

(*Troupe sits up and takes notice upon seeing* CROCKER *attacked*)

DOC   That's not bad! Not bad at all. (*to audience*) You know, there's nothing I enjoy more than hearing colored folks sing. (*to* CARL) But take it from an old showman, you'd sound a whole lot better if you'd thicken your speech a bit, accentuate the cultural differences, you know, smile and roll your eyes. Why, with a little training, you could be one of the top entertainers in the nation. Oh, I can see it now —Mr. Carl Blackbird, the famous recording artist, the television star, the Movie Star!! (*the Troupe rallies round* CARL, *picks him up on their shoulders*) You'd be loved by everybody—what do you say, Carl?
CARL   I am not interested!!
DOC   Then you're nobody!! (*they drop* CARL)
VOICE   Who's Carl Blackbird, anyway?
SECOND VOICE   Nobody!
ALL (*moving offstage in stylized exit*)   NOBODY! NOBODY! NOBODY!
JOSIE (*appears upstage as from a dream. Sings*)

> We could settle down in a little cottage
>   by the sea
> Couldn't we?

CARL (*joining her*)   Couldn't we?
PIPER (*appears*)   Come on, Josie! You can't marry a nobody!
JOSIE (*sings*)

> A little green cottage with
>   a welcome mat by the door . . .

(PIPER *leads her off*)

Fly Blackbird

CHORUS (*offstage*) Nobody!... Nobody!... Nobody!... Nobody!!—

DOC Carl! You'd be loved by everybody. Think it over!

CARL I'll do it!

DOC Betty, the Elixir! Here, Mr. Blackbird—drink! Go on, drink! Sweet William, get him into his costume. (*they lead* CARL *off*) Ladies and gentlemen, a career has been launched, a star has been born... Crocker Productions presents Mr. Carl Blackbird in his first starring role.

(*the stage blacks out. The follow spot comes up on a sign that reads "SAFARI." Enter the white hunter and his wife. Chorus is making jungle sounds*)

AGATHA Charles, this infernal heat is driving me mad.

CHARLES The jungle is no place for a white woman, Agatha.

AGATHA I'm simply dying for a cigarette.

CHARLES (*snaps his fingers*) Boy, give Mrs. Harrington an "Alpine." (*enter* CARL *loaded with gear and dressed in minimum clothes. He struggles to light the cigarette. Offstage is heard a lion's roar*)

AGATHA Charles, what was that?

CARL Oogawawa hugoowaootee ya!!

AGATHA What's he say?

CHARLES (*huddling with* AGATHA) Lion!

AGATHA Lion?

CHARLES This is what we're here for. This is what we've waited for. Boy, see where it is. I want to get a good clean shot at the blighter. (CARL *exits. Sound of roar. Scream of* CARL. *Then licking of chops*)

AGATHA Oh Charles.

CHARLES Be brave, Agatha, be brave.

AGATHA But that poor boy.

CHARLES It's all right, my dear. The natives don't feel it as much. (*Blackout*)

DOC Crocker Productions present Mr. Carl Blackbird in still another starring role. Crocker Productions present Mr. Carl Blackbird starring in a thrilling adventure. (*follow spot on sign "PORT OF INTRIGUE." Enter two spies*)

FIRST SPY (*carrying a brown suitcase*) Eet is done. I haf left ze bomb in ze train. Eet will explode in sixty seconds.

SECOND SPY You fool. You left the wrong bag. The bomb is in this one.

FIRST SPY No, eet was in the black bag.

SECOND SPY The brown one.

FIRST SPY The black one.

SECOND SPY Porter! Porter! (*enter* CARL *in porter hat*) Take this bag to the train. Quickly.

CARL Yas Sir. (*exits Explosion*)

SECOND SPY (*shrugs*) C'est la brown one. (*blackout*)

DOC Crocker Productions present Mr. Carl Blackbird in still another starring role. (*follow spot on sign: "MAGNOLIA TURF." Noise of a wild horse, and dogs barking*)

FITZ (*southern*) Colonel! Colonel, your new wild stallion, Red Lucifer, has broken his halter. The dogs are chasing him in the stable.

COLONEL Damnation! Ben! Old Ben!

FITZ No one can go in the stable now, Colonel. They'd be killed. (*enter* CARL *in hitching boy dress and pose*)

COLONEL Ben, go in there and put a bridle on Red Lucifer.

CARL Yas Sir.

COLONEL And mind you don't hurt that horse. He's worth a fortune.

FITZ But Colonel...

COLONEL Don't fret you'self. That darkey's been around horses all his... (*the horse and dog noise crescendos.* CARL *screams. A final horse snort. The men turn away*)

COLONEL It's all right, Fitz. He died doing the work he loved. (*Blackout*)

DOC (*alone in follow spot*) Now, ladies and gentlemen, Crocker Productions presents a miracle. I say it: the Miracle. In all my years of conversions to harmony, I have never had a more outstanding success. These others you see here, once too were dissatisfied men and women, but I won them. Won them with the sweetest remedy on earth. This bottle. This little bottle. However, not one of these souls, not one presented the difficult challenge of Mr. Blackbird. Not one was so hate-filled, so unwilling to see the light. But now he has tasted joy and success. Yes, and already, already, he's become a classic. I say it again, a classic. The colored man and the white man are again brothers. Dreams are fulfilled. Ladies and gentlemen, I... I... look at me... I'm crying with joy. Praise God! Ladies and gentlemen, I give you my life's work... The oldest and best-loved Negro entertainer in the world—I give you UNCLE TOM! (*lights up. Enter* CARL *in white mouth makeup and bow tie*) Come on down here, Tom. (CARL *goes downstage, doing a hambone routine*)—Say something for the folks, Tom.

CARL Watermelon!

CROCKER Isn't he a card, folks. Say something else, Tom.

CARL Shortnin' Bread!

CROCKER Isn't he great, folks? Say—you got a little song for us, Tom?

CARL Yas suh!

CROCKER Well, let's not keep those good people waiting. They came here to be entertained and we've got to give them their money's worth. Let's have it, Tom! CARL (*begins to sing "Old Black Joe" slowly.* CROCKER *tries to speed him up*) What's the matter with you, Tom? You've got to put more into it—here, let me show you. (*sings minstrel style*)

> In the evenin' by the moonlight
> You could hear those darkies singin'
> In the evenin' by the moonlight
> You could hear those banjos ringing'
> Mammyyyyy!

see what I mean, Tom—now you try it!

CARL (*humbly*) Yas suh. (*begins to sing in Tom dialect*)

> In the evenin' by the moonlight
> You could hear those darkies singin'

GIRL (*in upstage center spot*)

> No more auction block for me.

MALE CHORUS No more!
No more!

FEMALE CHORUS Steel away,
Steal away.

(*Pantomime of two slaves escaping*)

CARL (*begins to come out of the elixir's spell. He wipes of his white mouth, and throws away the bow tie. Bitterly*)

> No, Doctor Crocker, you mean like this:

(*In his natural voice*)

> In the evening, by the moonlight
> You could hear those banjos ringing

(*Indicates Chorus*)

CHORUS   O Freedom, O Freedom
We shall overcome someday.

CARL (*completely himself again*)

> But Old White Tom, he went along through life
> Thinking he was better than the black man

(*Advances on* CROCKER)

> red man, yellow man, Hot Damn!

(*He beckons and six males come forward, lift* CROCKER *for funeral procession*)

> This is the song of Old White Tom
> Who just didn't realize his time had come!

(*To background of processional music, they carry* CROCKER *center stage, placing him on the floor. They cover him with a black sheet*)

CARL (*steps forward, stands over* CROCKER *and speaks in a revivalist tone*) Brethren (*the chorus moans*)... we are gathered here to mourn (*moan*)... to mourn the loss of one we knew so well. (*moan*)

CROCKER What is this, a joke? (*they push him down*)

CARL (*continuing*)... Let no man speak against him in this hour... He was a good man. (*moans*) Too bad! (*moan*)... Too bad! (*moan*)... Too bad! (*prolonged moans*)

ALL (*singing*) "Old White Tom, he went along through life..."

(*Pallbearers begin to shovel imaginary dirt on* CROCKER)

CROCKER Stop it! Stop it! Have you all gone mad?

CHORUS (*suddenly turning on him*) Thinkin' he was better than the black man, (*he tries to escape, they chase him downstage right*) red man, yellow man, Hot Damn!

CARL This is the song of Old White Tom...

CHORUS Just didn't realize his time had come...

CARL Just didn't realize his time *has* come!

CHORUS MEMBER (*raises cane to strike* CROCKER, *Chorus stops him—he taps him gently instead, saying*) Whop!

Blackout.

(PIPER's *home. Played in front of curtain. In the blackout, the telephone can be heard ringing insistently. Lights come up as* PIPER *in bathrobe enters and answers the phone. Thunder can still be heard*)

PIPER Hello. I can't hear you. Oh, hello, Judge Crocker. The rains must have affected the wires... Yes sir, it's nearly morning. You've arrested who? But your Honor, I tell you those Chinese kids are not my people. I suggest you contact some Oriental organization: B'nai B'rith. (JOSIE *enters behind him with a book she has been reading. She too is in a robe. He doesn't see her.*) Your honor, there's absolutely nothing to worry about. I talked with young Eldridge tonight and he's going over to the studios with me tomorrow... Of course, I'm certain. You see, he's got eyes for my daughter ... He's in love with Josie. That's right. There'll be no more picketing from that boy. Yes Sir. Yes Judge. Yes sir, call me back as soon as you decide. Goodbye, your honor. (*he hangs up and discovers* JOSIE.) Josie! ... rather early for you to be up, isn't it? (*she doesn't answer, but just looks at him*) That was Judge Crocker. There's been another arrest of a picket... now don't worry yourself. Young Eldridge wasn't involved. (*he puts his arm around her*) He's a fine boy. What are you reading? (*takes the book*) Martin Luther King Jr. Well! A fine boy. I didn't know he'd written a book. (JOSIE *pulls away*)

JOSIE (*without bitterness, but with deep feeling*) Yes, sir. He's written a fine book. He's a fine man. Yes sir, your honor. Yes sir ... Yes sir! Yes sir!

PIPER Josie, things are not the same here as in the South. Josie, you may not be proud of me, but it's a white man's world and I do the best I can. Everything I've ever done, I've done for you. (*she lays her head on his shoulder. The telephone rings again. Piper looks at his daughter, then moves to the phone. He hesitates, then picks it up*) Yes sir. Yes sir. (*she exits*) Yes sir, yes sir.

(*Blackout. Final Library scene. In the blackout we hear the* LIBRARIAN *singing "Nobody Knows De Trouble I've Seen." Lights come up. Both* BROWN *and* LIBRARIAN *are bleary and aimless, beaten*)

LIBRARIAN What was it you came in here for anyway? I've forgotten.

BROWN To study for a transfer outa this district.

LIBRARIAN Oh yes. I wish I had thought. The assistant police commissioner's my uncle. I could have simply called him.

BROWN Harold Brown. (*nods*) Your uncle? ... My ... Uncle Harry Brown.

LIBRARIAN I'll call him for you. Uncle Harry'll be delighted to transfer you somewhere else. (*she takes out a phone book*)

BROWN That's real nice of you. It's kinda early in the morning.

LIBRARIAN This can't be done too soon. Goodness, look at all the Browns.

BROWN That's a lot of relatives in the twilight zone.

LIBRARIAN Wait a minute...

BROWN What?

LIBRARIAN There's Mrs. Maribelle Brown. (*laughs*)

BROWN Who's she?

LIBRARIAN President of the D.A.R.

BROWN Give her a call.

LIBRARIAN Yes, let's tell her the good news.

BROWN Look, there's Stanfield Brown. He's president of the John Birch Society in Glendale.

LIBRARIAN Call him. Call him. Look. There's Mr. Slade Brown. He's burial director at Forest dawn Cemetery.

BROWN I'll call him. There are lots of Browns, aren't there?

LIBRARIAN and BROWN Pages and pages and pages.

LIBRARIAN Cousin Brown...

BROWN Yes...

LIBRARIAN How much would a call to Sacramento* cost? (*they look at one another. Blackout. Street scene—early morning.* CARL *is picketing alone*)

JOSIE Hello, nice day. (*he ignores her*) I said nice day. (*he still ignores her. She follows him*)

JOSIE (*following him*) Step on a crack, you break your mother's back. Step in a hole, break your father's sugar bowl. Step on a stone, and you can't go home.

CARL (*stops*) What are you doing here?

JOSIE Chasing you.

CARL Look, I've made up my mind. I can't do what your father and you want me to do.

JOSIE Neither can I.

CARL You're not listening. I've sent out for the pickets. In a couple of hours, we'll all be in jail. So you better go.

---

* Brown was Governor of California.

JOSIE You're not listening to me. "Step on a stone—and you can't go home."

CARL Step off the trail... (*"Wake Up" song starts*) ... and you go to jail.

WAKE UP

Carl I do believe that the sun can shine
in the middle of the night.
We're gonna

JOSIE We're gonna walk.
We're gonna talk.
There is a new day waiting at your door.
The sun's gonna shine this morning.
The night will be no more.

I'm gonna open my window wide.
See the new day waiting at your door.
CARL We're gonna walk.
JOSIE We're gonna talk.

BOTH Sit at the table with our heads up high.
Sing, shout all about the new day
waiting at your door.
Walk! Talk! Laugh! Cry!
Sit at the table with our heads up high.
Sing! Shout! All about
The new day waiting at your door.

Wake up! The dawn is coming.
Rise up! Sleep no more!
Stand up! Meet the morning.
There's a new day waiting at your door.

Wake up! Brothers—wake up!
Rise up! Rise up!
Sleep no more! Stand up!
Sisters, stand up!
There's a new day waiting at your door.

(*Enter full Chorus down the aisles with picket signs singing "Wake up." Curtain*)

Douglas Turner Ward (1930–)

Day of Absence   1965

Until the 1960's, black playwrights were almost exclusively reviewed by white critics who, besides dispensing the usual bits of lemon with sugar, often felt compelled to wax authoritatively on what Negro Theater should be.

This condescension has been relieved by three developments: the use of black theater critics such as Clayton Rielly and Larry Neal; the development of a black audience; and an increased sensitivity on the part of white critics, who have realized that their judgments were biased by ignorance of the black experience, a commitment to traditional white aesthetics, and (in some cases) overt racial prejudices.

By 1970, if a white critic didn't like a black play, he wrote long and circuitous passages to let the reader know that the critic intended to be fair. Usually these passages boil down to either: "I don't care if he's brown, black, green or yellow, theater must . . .," or, "Maybe I'm ignorant of black experience and missing the point, but theater must . . . ."

Some of the newspaper critics who reviewed *Happy Ending* and *Day of Absence* when they premiered off-Broadway on November 15, 1965, were becoming aware that traditional criticisms did not always apply. Michael Smith of the *Village Voice* noted that in black plays "their content is all important . . .," and that "Douglas Turner Ward is writing for a black audience." Such observations may seem elementary now, but compare them to Martin Gottfried's Comments in *Women's Wear Daily*:

Douglas Turner Ward's first plays . . . are in turn derivative, contradictory, childish, dull and silly. . . . Mr. Ward's best interests are not really being served in the production of his fledgling creations.

The theatrical thematic affect of a Negro in white face is enormous and could only be conceived by a royal artist like Genet. Ward's borrowing of it was presumptuous and his application of it to a play whose attitude, basically, is peevish makes it obscene. *Day of Absence* is an elaborate pout.

Putting Mr. Gottfried's anger aside, he holds three traditional white viewpoints. First, his standard of judgment is based on Jean Genet (substitute "Shakespeare," or "the Greeks"). Second, he purports to know Mr. Ward's best interest. Third, he finds the work "dull," and "contradictory," although he acknowledges in the same review that the plays were "designed for the special taste and background of the Negro, as in 'race records'." Several other critics also noted that the Negroes in the audience "were knocking themselves out with laughter while the whites sat stone faced."

Nothing succeeds like success—especially in the commercial theater. Mr. Ward's plays were vindicated by a run of 504 performances. They have been widely produced in colleges and schools throughout the country. Finally in 1969, a Day of Absence was declared in New York City, a day in which all black people were to stay home from work. It was partially successful.

To the student of American theater it is interesting to speculate on how much of the effect of blacks in white face is gained from the over-100-year-old tradition of the American minstrel.

Day of Absence

CAST OF CHARACTERS

The play is conceived for performance by a Black cast, a reverse minstrel show done in white face.

CLEM, *a country cracker*
LUKE, *another*
MARY, *young white mother*
JOHN, *young white father*
FIRST OPERATOR
SECOND OPERATOR
THIRD OPERATOR
SUPERVISOR
MAYOR, *a small town official*
JACKSON, *his assistant*
MEN FROM THE TOWN
BUSINESSMAN
CLUBWOMAN
COURIER
CLAN, *as in KKK*
ANNOUNCER
AIDE
REB PIOUS, *a religious man*
RASTUS, *the missing man*

SCENE   *Street*
TIME   *Early morning.*

CLEM (*sitting under a sign suspended by invisible wires and bold-printed with the lettering: "STORE"*) 'Morning, Luke...
LUKE (*sitting a few paces away under an identical sign*) 'Morning, Clem...
CLEM   Go'n' be a hot day.
LUKE   Looks that way...
CLEM   Might rain though...
LUKE   Might.
CLEM   Hope it does...
LUKE   Me, too...
CLEM   Farmers could use a little wet spell for a change... How's the Missis?
LUKE   Same.
CLEM   'N' the kids?
LUKE   Them, too... How's yourns?
CLEM   Fine, thank you... (*they both lapse into drowsy silence, waving lethargically from time to time at imaginary passersby*) Hi, Joe...
LUKE   Joe...
CLEM   ...How'd it go yesterday, Luke?
LUKE   Fair.
CLEM   Same wit' me... Business don't seem to git no better or no worse. Guess we in a rut, Luke, don't it 'pear that way to you?—Morning, ma'am.
LUKE   Morning...
CLEM   Tried display, sales, advertisement, stamps—everything, yet merchandising stumbles 'round in the same old groove... But—that's better than plunging downwards, I reckon.
LUKE   Guess it is.
CLEM   Morning, Bret. How's the family?... That's good.
LUKE   Bret—
CLEM   Morning, Sue.
LUKE   How do, Sue.
CLEM   (*staring after her*) ...Fine hunk of woman.
LUKE   Sure is.
CLEM   Wonder if it's any good?
LUKE   Bet it is.
CLEM   Sure like to find out!
LUKE   So would I.
CLEM   You ever try?
LUKE   Never did...
CLEM   Morning, Gus...
LUKE   Howdy, Gus.
CLEM   Fine, thank you. (*they lapse into silence again.* CLEM *rouses himself slowly, begins to look around quizzically*) Luke...?
LUKE   Huh?
CLEM   Do you... er, er—feel anything—funny...?
LUKE   Like what?
CLEM   Like... er—something—strange?
LUKE   I dunno... haven't thought about it.

CLEM I mean... like something's wrong—outta place, unusual?

LUKE I don't know... What you got in mind?

CLEM Nothing... just that—just that—like somp'ums outta kilter. I got a funny feeling somp'ums not up to snuff. Can't figger out what it is...

LUKE Maybe it's in your haid?

CLEM No, not like that... Like somp'ums happened—or happening—gone haywire, loony.

LUKE Well, don't worry 'bout it, it'll pass.

CLEM Guess youright. (*attempts return to somnolence but doesn't succeed*)... I'm sorry, Luke, but you sure you don't feel nothing peculiar...?

LUKE (*slightly irked*) Toss it out your mind, Clem! We got a long day ahead of us. If something's wrong, you'll know 'bout it in due time. No use worrying about it 'till it comes and if it's coming, it will. Now, relax!

CLEM All right, you right... Hi, Margie...

LUKE Marge.

CLEM (*unable to control himself*) Luke, I don't give a damn what you say. Somp'ums topsy-turvy, I just know it!

LUKE (*increasingly irritated*) Now look here, Clem—it's a bright day, it looks like it's go'n' git hotter. You say the wife and kids are fine and the business is no better or no worse? Well, what else could be wrong?... If somp'ums go'n' happen, it's go'n' happen anyway and there ain't a damn fool thing you kin do to stop it! So you ain't helping me, yourself or nobody else by thinking 'bout it. It's not go'n' be no better or no worse when it gits here. It'll come to you when it gits ready to come and it's go'n' be the same whether you worry about it or not. So stop letting it upset you! (LUKE *settles back in his chair.* CLEM *does likewise.* LUKE *shuts his eyes. After a few moments, they reopen. He forces them shut again. They reopen in greater curiosity. Finally, he rises slowly to an upright position in the chair, looks around frowningly. Turns slowly to* CLEM)... Clem?... You know something?... Somp'um is peculiar...

CLEM (*vindicated*) I knew it, Luke! I just knew it! Ever since we been sitting here, I been having that feeling!

(*Scene is blacked out abruptly. Lights rise on another section of the stage where a young couple lie in bed under an invisible-wire-suspension-sign lettered: "HOME." Loud insistent sounds of baby yells are heard.* JOHN, *the husband, turns over trying to ignore the cries,* MARY, *the wife, is undisturbed.* JOHN's *efforts are futile, the cries continue until they cannot be denied. He bolts upright, jumps out of bed and disappears offstage. Returns quickly and tries to rouse* MARY)

JOHN Mary... (*nudges her, pushes her, yells into her ear, but she fails to respond*) Mary, get up... Get up!

MARY Ummm... (*shrugs away, still sleeping*)

JOHN GET UP!

MARY UMMMMMMMMM!

JOHN Don't you hear the baby bawling!... NOW GET UP!

MARY (*mumbling drowsily*)... What baby... whose baby...?

JOHN Yours!

MARY Mine? That's ridiculous... what'd you say...? Somebody's baby bawling?... How could that be so? (*hearing screams*) Who's crying? Somebody's crying!... What's crying?... WHERE'S LULA?!

JOHN I don't know. You better get up.

MARY That's outrageous!... What time is it?

JOHN Late 'nuff! Now rise up!

MARY You must be joking... I'm sure I still have four or five hours sleep in store—even more after that head-splittin' blow-out last night... (*tumbles back under covers*)

JOHN Nobody told you to gulp those last six bourbons—

MARY Don't tell me how many bourbons to swallow, not after you guzzled the whole stinking bar!... Get up?... You must be cracked... Where's Lula? She must be here, she always is...

JOHN Well, she ain't here yet, so get up and muzzle that brat before she does drive me cuckoo!

MARY (*springing upright, finally realizing gravity of situation*) Whaddaya mean Lula's not here? She's always here, she must be here... Where else kin she be? She supposed to be... She just can't *not* be here—CALL HER!

(*Blackout as* JOHN *rushes offstage. Scene shifts to a trio of* TELEPHONE OPERATORS *perched on stools before imaginary switchboards. Chaos and bedlam are taking place to the sound of buzzes. Effect of following dialogue should simulate rising pandemonium*)

FIRST OPERATOR   The line is busy—
SECOND OPERATOR   Line is busy—
THIRD OPERATOR   Is busy—
FIRST OPERATOR   Doing best we can—
SECOND OPERATOR   Having difficulty—
THIRD OPERATOR   Soon as possible—
FIRST OPERATOR   Just one moment—
SECOND OPERATOR   Would you hold on—
THIRD OPERATOR   Awful sorry, madam—
FIRST OPERATOR   Would you hold on, please—
SECOND OPERATOR   Just a second, please—
THIRD OPERATOR   Please hold on, please—
FIRST OPERATOR   The line is busy—
SECOND OPERATOR   The line is busy—
THIRD OPERATOR   The line is busy—
FIRST OPERATOR   Doing best we can—
SECOND OPERATOR   Hold on please—
THIRD OPERATOR—Can't make connections—
FIRST OPERATOR   Unable to put it in—
SECOND OPERATOR   Won't plug through—
THIRD OPERATOR   Sorry madam—
FIRST OPERATOR   If you'd wait a moment—
SECOND OPERATOR   Doing best we can—
THIRD OPERATOR   Sorry—
FIRST OPERATOR   One moment—
SECOND OPERATOR   Just a second—
THIRD OPERATOR   Hold on—
FIRST OPERATOR   YES—
SECOND OPERATOR   STOP IT!—
THIRD OPERATOR   HOW DO I KNOW—
FIRST OPERATOR   YOU ANOTHER ONE!
SECOND OPERATOR   HOLD ON DAMMIT!
THIRD OPERATOR   UP YOURS, TOO!
FIRST OPERATOR   THE LINE IS BUSY
SECOND OPERATOR   THE LINE IS BUSY—
THIRD OPERATOR   THE LINE IS BUSY—

(*The switchboard clamors a cacophony of buzzes as* OPERATORS *plug connections with the frenzy of a Chaplin movie. Their replies degenerate into a babble of gibberish. At the height of frenzy, the* SUPERVISOR *appears*)

SUPERVISOR   WHAT'S THE SNARL-UP???!!!
FIRST OPERATOR   Everybody calling at the same time, ma'am!
SECOND OPERATOR   Board can't handle it!
THIRD OPERATOR   Like everybody in big New York City is trying to squeeze a call through to li'l' ole us!
SUPERVISOR   God! . . . Somp'un terrible musta happened! . . . Buzz the emergency frequency hookup to the Mayor's office and find out what the hell's going on!

(*Scene blacks out quickly to* CLEM *and* LUKE)

CLEM (*something slowly dawning on him*) Luke . . . ?
LUKE   Yes, Clem?
CLEM (*eyes roving around in puzzlement*) Luke . . . ?
LUKE (*irked*)   I said what, Clem!
CLEM   Luke . . . ? Where—where is—the—the—?
LUKE   THE WHAT?!
CLEM   Nigras . . . ?
LUKE   ?????What . . . ?
CLEM   Nigras . . . Where is the Nigras, where is they, Luke . . . ? ALL THE NIGRAS! . . . I don't see no Nigras . . . ?!
LUKE   Whatcha mean . . . ?
CLEM (*agitatedly*)   Luke, there ain't a darkey in sight . . . And if you remember, we ain't spied a nappy hair all morning . . . The Nigras, Luke! We ain't laid eyes on nary a coon this whole morning!!!
LUKE   You must be crazy or something, Clem!
CLEM   Think about it, Luke, we been sitting here for an hour or more—try and recollect if you remember seeing jist *one* go by?!!!
LUKE (*confused*)   . . . I don't recall . . . But . . . but there musta been some . . . The heat musta got you, Clem! How in hell could that be so?!!!
CLEM (*triumphantly*)   Just think, Luke! . . . Look around ya . . . Now, every morning mosta people walkin' 'long this street is colored. They's strolling by going to work, they's waiting for the buses, they's sweeping sidewalks, cleaning stores, starting to shine shoes and wetting the mops—right?! . . . Well, look around you, Luke—where is they? (LUKE *paces up and down, checking*) I told you, Luke, they ain't nowheres to be seen.
LUKE   ???? . . . This . . . this . . . some kind of holiday for 'em—or something?
CLEM   I don't know, Luke . . . but . . . but

what I do know is they ain't here 'n' we haven't seen a solitary one . . . It's scaryfying, Luke . . . !

LUKE   Well . . . maybe they's jist standing 'n' walking and shining on other streets.—Let's go look!

(*Scene blacks out to* JOHN *and* MARY. *Baby cries are as insistent as ever*)

MARY   (*at end of patience*)   SMOTHER IT!

JOHN   (*beyond his*)   That's a hell of a thing to say 'bout your own child! You should know what to do to hush her up!

MARY   Why don't you try?!

JOHN   You had her!

MARY   You shared in borning her!!

JOHN   Possibly not!

MARY   Why, you lousy—!

JOHN   What good is a mother who can't shut up her own daughter?!

MARY   I told you she yells louder every time I try to lay hands on her.—Where's Lula? Didn't you call her?!

JOHN   I told you I can't get the call through!

MARY   Try ag'in—

JOHN   It's no use! I tried numerous times and can't even git through to the switchboard. You've got to quiet her down yourself. (*firmly*) Now, go in there and clam her up 'fore I lose my patience! (MARY *exits. Soon, we hear the yells increase. She rushes back in*)

MARY   She won't let me touch her, just screams louder!

JOHN   Probably wet 'n' soppy!

MARY   Yes! Stinks something awful! Phooooey! I can't stand that filth and odor!

JOHN   That's why she's screaming! Needs her didee changed.—Go change it!

MARY   How you 'spect me to when I don't know how?! Suppose I faint?!

JOHN   Well let her blast away. I'm getting outta here.

MARY   You can't leave me here like this!

JOHN   Just watch me! . . . See this nice split-level cottage, peachy furniture, multi-colored teevee, hi-fi set 'n' the rest? . . . Well, how you think I scraped 'em together while you curled up on your fat li'l' fanny? . . . By gitting outta here—not only *on time* . . . but EARLIER!—Beating a frantic crew of nice young executives to the punch—gitting there fustest with the mostest brown-nosing you ever saw! Now if I goof one day—just ONE DAY! —You reckon I'd stay ahead? NO! . . . There'd be a wolf-pack trampling over my prostrate body, racing to replace my smiling face against the boss' left rump! . . . NO, MAM! I'm zooming outta here on time, just as I always have and what's more—you go'n' fix me some breakfast, I'M HUNGRY!

MARY   But—

JOHN   No buts about it! (*flash blackout as he gags on a mouthful of coffee*) What you trying to do, STRANGLE ME!!! (*jumps up and starts putting on jacket*)

MARY   (*sarcastically*)   What did you expect?

JOHN   (*in biting fury*)   That you could possibly boil a pot of water, toast a few slices of bread and fry a coupler eggs! . . . It was a mistaken assumption!

MARY   So they aren't as good as Lula's!

JOHN   That is an overstatement. Your efforts don't result in anything that could possibly be digested by man, mammal, or insect! . . . When I married you, I thought I was fairly acquainted with your faults and weaknesses—I chalked 'em up to human imperfection . . . But now I know I was being extremely generous, over-optimistic and phenomenally deluded!—You have no idea how useless you really are!

MARY   Then why'd you marry me?!

JOHN   Decoration!

MARY   You shoulda married Lula!

JOHN   I might've if it wasn't 'gainst the segregation law! . . . But for the sake of my home, my child and my sanity, I will even take a chance on sacrificing my slippery grip on the status pole and drive by her shanty to find out whether she or someone like her kin come over here and prevent some ultimate disaster. (*storms toward door, stopping abruptly at exit*) Are you sure you kin make it to the bathroom wit'out Lula backing you up?!!!

(*Blackout. Scene shifts to* MAYOR's *office where a cluttered desk stands center amid papered debris*)

MAYOR   (*striding determinedly toward desk, stopping midways, bellowing*)   WOODFENCE! . . . WOODFENCE! . . . WOODFENCE! (*receiving no reply, completes distance to desk*) JACKSON! . . . JACKSON!

JACKSON   (*entering worriedly*)   Yes, sir . . . ?

MAYOR   Where's Vice-Mayor Woodfence, that no-good brother-in-law of mine?!

JACKSON Hasn't come in yet, sir.
MAYOR HASN'T COME IN?!!!... Damn bastard! Knows we have a crucial conference. Soon as he staggers through that door, tell him to shoot in here! (*angrily focusing on his disorderly desk and littered surroundings*) And git Mandy here to straighten up this mess—Rufus too! You know he shoulda been waiting to knock dust off my shoes soon as I step in. Get 'em in here!... What's the matter wit' them lazy Nigras?... Already had to dress myself because of JC, fix my own coffee without MayBelle, drive myself to work 'counta Bubber, feel my old Hag's tits after Sapphi—NEVER MIND!—Git 'em in here—QUICK!
JACKSON (*meekly*) They aren't... they aren't here, sir...
MAYOR Whaddaya mean they aren't here? Find out where they at. We got important business, man! You can't run a town wit' laxity like this. Can't allow things to git snafued jist because a bunch of lazy Nigras been out gitting drunk and living it up all night! Discipline, man, discipline!
JACKSON That's what I'm trying to tell you, sir... they didn't come in, can't be found... none of 'em.
MAYOR Ridiculous, boy! Scare 'em up and tell 'em scoot here in a hurry befo' I git mad and fire the whole goddamn lot of 'em!
JACKSON But we can't find 'em, sir.
MAYOR Hogwash! Can't nobody in this office do anything right?! Do I hafta handle every piddling little matter myself?! Git me their numbers, I'll have 'em here befo' you kin shout to—(*three men burst into room in various states of undress*)
ONE Henry—they vanished!
TWO Disappeared into thin air!
THREE Gone wit'out a trace!
TWO Not a one on the street!
THREE In the house!
ONE On the job!
MAYOR Wait a minute!!... Hold your water! Calm down—!
ONE But they've gone, Henry—GONE! All of 'em!
MAYOR What the hell you talking 'bout? Gone? Who's gone—?
ONE The Nigras, Henry! They gone!
MAYOR Gone?... Gone where?
TWO That's what we trying to tell ya—they just disappeared! The Nigras have disappeared, swallowed up, vanished! All of 'em! Every last one!
MAYOR Have everybody 'round here gone batty?... That's impossible, how could the Nigras vanish?
THREE Beats me, but it's happened!
MAYOR You mean a whole town of Nigras just evaporate like this—poof!—Overnight?
ONE Right!
MAYOR Y'all must be drunk! Why, half this town is colored. How could they just sneak out!
TWO Don't ask me, but there ain't one in sight!
MAYOR Simmer down 'n' put it to me easy-like.
ONE Well... I first suspected somp'um smelly when Sarah Jo didn't show up this morning and I couldn't reach her—
TWO Dorothy Jane didn't 'rive at my house—
THREE Georgia Mae wasn't at mine neither—and SHE sleeps in!
ONE When I reached the office, I realized I hadn't seen nary one Nigra all morning! Nobody else had either—wait a minute—Henry, have you?!
MAYOR ???Now that you mention it... no, I haven't...
ONE They gone, Henry... Not a one on the street, not a one in our homes, not a single, last living one to be found nowheres in town. What we gon' do?!
MAYOR (*thinking*) Keep heads on your shoulders 'n' put clothes on your back... They can't be far... Must be 'round somewheres ... Probably playing hide 'n' seek, that's it!... JACKSON!
JACKSON Yessir?
MAYOR Immediately mobilize our Citizens Emergency Distress Committee!—Order a fleet of sound trucks to patrol streets urging the population to remain calm—situation's not as bad as it looks—everything's under control! Then, have another squadron of squawk buggies drive slowly through all Nigra alleys, ordering them to come out wherever they are. If that don't git 'em, organize a vigilante search-squad to flush 'em outta hiding! But most important of all, track down that lazy goldbricker, Woodfence and tell him to git on top of the situation! By God, we'll find 'em

Day of Absence

even if we hafta dig 'em outta the ground!

(*Blackout. Scene shifts back to* JOHN *and* MARY *a few hours later. A funereal solemnity pervades their mood.* JOHN *stands behind* MARY *who sits, in a scene duplicating the famous "American Gothic" painting*)

JOHN ... Walked up to the shack, knocked on door, didn't git no answer. Hollered: "LULA? LULA...?—Not a thing. Went 'round the side, peeped in window—nobody stirred. Next door—nobody there. Crossed other side of street and banged on five or six other doors—not a colored person could be found! Not a man, neither woman or child—not even a little black dog could be seen, smelt or heard for blocks around ... They've gone, Mary.

MARY What does it all mean, John?

JOHN I don't know, Mary ...

MARY I always had Lula, John. She never missed a day at my side ... That's why I couldn't accept your wedding proposal until I was sure you'd welcome me and her together as a package. How am I gonna git through the day? My baby don't know *me*, I ain't acquainted wit' *it*. I've never lifted cover off pot, swung a mop or broom, dunked a dish or even pushed a dustrag. I'm lost wit'out Lula, I need her, John, I need her. (*begins to weep softly.* JOHN *pats her consolingly*)

JOHN Courage, honey ... Everybody in town is facing the same dilemma. We mustn't crack up ...

(*Blackout. Scene shifts back to* MAYOR's *office later in day. Atmosphere and tone resembles a wartime headquarters at the front.* MAYOR *is poring over huge map*)

INDUSTRIALIST Half the day is gone already, Henry. On behalf of the factory owners of this town, you've got to bail us out! Seventy-five per cent of all production is paralyzed. With the Nigra absent, men are waiting for machines to be cleaned, floors to be swept, crates lifted, equipment delivered and bathrooms to be deodorized. Why, restrooms and toilets are so filthy until they not only cannot be sat in, but it's virtually impossible to get within hailing distance because of the stench!

MAYOR Keep your shirt on, Jeb—

BUSINESSMAN Business is even in worse condition, Henry. The volume of goods moving 'cross counters has slowed down to a trickle—almost negligible. Customers are not only not purchasing—but the absence of handymen, porters, sweepers, stock-movers, deliverers and miscellaneous dirty-work doers is disrupting the smooth harmony of marketing!

CLUB WOMAN Food poisoning, severe indigestitis, chronic diarrhea, advanced diaper chafings and a plethora of unsanitary household disasters dangerous to life, limb and property! ... As a representative of the Federation of Ladies' Clubs, I must sadly report that unless the trend is reversed, a complete breakdown in family unity is imminent ... Just as homosexuality and debauchery signalled the fall of Greece and Rome, the downgrading of Southern Bellesdom might very well prophesy the collapse of our indigenous institutions ... Remember—it has always been pure, delicate, lily-white images of Dixie femininity which provided backbone, inspiration and ideology for our male warriors in their defense against the on-rushing black horde. If our gallant men are drained of this worship and idolatry—God knows! The cause won't be worth a Confederate nickel!

MAYOR Stop this panicky defeatism, y'all hear me! All machinery at my disposal is being utilized. I assure you wit' great confidence the damage will soon repair itself.—Cheerful progress reports are expected any moment now.—Wait! See, here's Jackson ... Well, Jackson?

JACKSON (*entering*) As of now, sir, all efforts are fruitless. Neither hide nor hair of them has been located. We have not unearthed a single one in our shack-to-shack search. Not a single one has heeded our appeal. Scoured every crick and cranny inside their hovels, turning furniture upside down and inside out, breaking down walls and tearing through ceilings. We made determined efforts to discover where 'bouts of our faithful uncle Toms and informers—but even they have vanished without a trace ... Searching squads are on the verge of panic and hysteria, sir, wit' hotheads among 'em campaigning for scorched earth policies. Nigras on a whole lack cellars, but there's rising sentiment favoring burning to find out whether they're underground—DUG IN!

MAYOR Absolutely counter such foolhardy

suggestions! Suppose they are tombed in? We'd only accelerate the gravity of the situation using incendiary tactics! Besides, when they're rounded up where will we put 'em if we've already burned up their shacks—IN OUR OWN BEDROOMS?!!!

JACKSON I agree, sir, but the mood of the crowd is becoming irrational. In anger and frustration, they's forgetting their original purpose was to FIND the Nigras!

MAYOR At all costs! Stamp out all burning proposals! Must prevent extremist notions from gaining ascendancy. Git wit' it... Wait—'n' for Jehovah's sake, find out where the hell is that trifling slacker, WOODFENCE!

COURIER (*rushing in*) Mr. Mayor! Mr. Mayor!... We've found some! We've found some!

MAYOR (*excitedly*) Where?!

COURIER In the—in the—(*can't catch breath*)

MAYOR (*impatiently*) Where, man? Where?!

COURIER In the colored wing of the city hospital!

MAYOR The hos—? The hospital! I shoulda known! How could those helpless, crippled, cut and shot Nigras disappear from a hospital! Shoulda thought of that!... Tell me more, man!

COURIER I—I didn't wait, sir... I—I ran in to report soon as I heard—

MAYOR WELL GIT BACK ON THE PHONE, YOU IDIOT, DON'T YOU KNOW WHAT THIS MEANS!

COURIER Yes, sir. (*races out*)

MAYOR Now we gitting somewhere!... Gentlemen, if one sole Nigra is among us, we're well on the road to rehabilitation! Those Nigras in the hospital must know somp'um 'bout the others where'bouts... Scat back to your colleagues, boost up their morale and inform 'em that things will zip back to normal in a jiffy! (*they start to file out, then pause to observe the* COURIER *reentering dazedly*) Well...? Well, man...? WHAT'S THE MATTER WIT' YOU, NINNY, TELL ME WHAT ELSE WAS SAID?!

COURIER They all... they all... they all in a—in a—coma, sir...

MAYOR They all in a what...?

COURIER In a coma, sir...

MAYOR Talk sense, man!... Whaddaya mean, they all in a coma?

COURIER Doctor says every last one of the Nigras are jist laying in bed... STILL... not moving... neither live or dead... laying up there in a coma... every last one of 'em...

MAYOR (*splutters, then grabs phone*) Get me Confederate Memorial... Put me through to the Staff Chief... YES, this is the Mayor... Sam?... What's this I hear?... But how could they be in a coma, Sam?... You don't know! Well, what the hell you think the city's paying you for!... You've got 'nuff damn hacks and quacks there to find out!... How could it be somp'um unknown? You mean Nigras know somp'um 'bout drugs your damn butchers don't?!... Well, what the crap good are they!... All right, all right, I'll be calm... Now, tell me... Uh huh, uh huh... Well, can't you give 'em some injections or somp'um ...?—You did... uh huh... DID YOU TRY A LI'L' ROUGH TREATMENT?— that too, huh... All right, Sam, keep trying... (*puts phone down delicately, continuing absently*) Can't wake em' up. Just lay there. Them that's sick won't git no sicker, them that's half-well won't git no better, babies that's due won't be born and them that's come won't show no life. Nigras wit' cuts won't bleed and them which needs blood won't be transfused... He say dying Nigras is even refusing to pass away! (*is silently perplexed for a moment, then suddenly breaks into action*) JACKSON?!... Call up the police—THE JAIL! Find out what's going on there! Them Nigras are captives! If there's one place we got darkies under control, it's there! Them sonsabitches too onery to act right either for colored or white! (JACKSON *exits. The* COURIER *follows*) Keep your fingers crossed, citizens, them Nigras in jail are the most important Nigras we got! (*All hands are raised conspicuously aloft, fingers prominently ex-ed. Seconds tick by. Soon* JACKSON *returns crestfallen*)

JACKSON Sheriff Bull says they don't know whether they still on premises or not. When they went to rouse Nigra jailbirds this morning, cell-block doors refused to swing open. Tried everything—even exploded dynamite charges— but it just wouldn't budge... Then they hoisted guards up to peep through barred windows, but couldn't see good 'nuff to tell whether Nigras was inside or not. Finally, gitting desperate, they power-hosed the cells wit' water but had to cease 'cause Sheriff Bull said he didn't wanta jeopardize drowning the Nigras since it might spoil his chance of shipping a record load of cotton pickers to the State Penitentiary for cotton-snatching jubilee ... Anyway—they ain't heard a Nigra-squeak all day.

MAYOR ???That so...? WHAT 'BOUT TRAINS 'N' BUSSES PASSING THROUGH? There must be some dinges riding through?

JACKSON We checked...not a one on board.

MAYOR Did you hear whether any other towns lost their Nigras?

JACKSON Things are status-quo everywhere else.

MAYOR (*angrily*) Then what the hell they picking on us for!

COURIER (*rushing in*) MR. MAYOR! Your sister jist called—HYSTERICAL! She says Vice-Mayor Woodfence went to bed wit' her last night, but when she woke up this morning he was gone! Been missing all day!

MAYOR ???Could Nigras be holding brother-in-law Woodfence hostage?!

COURIER No, sir. Besides him—investigations reveal that dozens or more prominent citizens—two City Council members, the chairman of the Junior Chamber of Commerce, our City College All-Southern half-back, the chairlady of the Daughters of the Confederate Rebellion, Miss Cotton-Sack Festival of the Year and numerous other miscellaneous nobodies—are all absent wit'out leave. Dangerous evidence points to the conclusion that they have been infiltrating!

MAYOR Infiltrating???

COURIER Passing all along!

MAYOR ???PASSING ALL ALONG???

COURIER Secret Nigras all the while!

MAYOR NAW! (CLUB WOMAN *keels over in faint.* JACKSON, BUSINESSMAN *and* INDUSTRIALIST *begin to eye each other suspiciously*)

COURIER Yessir!

MAYOR PASSING???

COURIER Yessir!

MAYOR SECRET NIG—!???

COURIER Yessir!

MAYOR (*momentarily stunned to silence*) The dirty mongrelizers!... Gentlemen, this is a grave predicament indeed... It pains me to surrender priority of our states' right credo, but it is my solemn task and frightening duty to inform you that we have no other recourse but to seek outside help for deliverance.

(*Blackout. Lights re-rise on Huntley-Brinkley-Murrow-Sevareid-Cronkite-Reasoner-type Announcer grasping a hand-held microphone [imaginary] a few hours later. He is vigorously, excitedly mouthing his commentary, but no sound escapes his lips... During this dumb wordless section of his broadcast, a bedraggled assortment of figures marching with picket signs occupy his attention. On their picket signs are inscribed various appeals and slogans.* "CINDY LOU UNFAIR TO BABY JOE"... "CAP'N SAM MISS BIG BOY"... "RETURN LI'L BLUE TO MARSE JIM"... "INFORMATION REQUESTED 'BOUT MAMMY GAIL"... "BOSS NATHAN PROTEST TO FAST LEROY." *Trailing behind the marchers, forcibly isolated, is a woman dressed in widow-black holding a placard which reads:* "WHY DIDN'T YOU TELL US—YOUR DEFILED WIFE AND TWO ABSENT MONGRELS")

ANNOUNCER (*who has been silently mouthing his delivery during the picketing procession, is suddenly heard as if caught in the midst of commentary*) ... Factories standing idle from the loss of non-essential workers. Stores shuttered from the absconding of uncrucial personnel. Uncollected garbage threatening pestilence and pollution... Also, each second somewheres in this former utopia below the Mason and Dixon, dozens of decrepit old men and women usually tended by faithful nurses and servants are popping off like flies—abandoned by sons, daughters and grandchildren whose refusal to provide their doddering relatives with bedpans and other soothing necessities result in their hasty, nasty, messy corpus delicties... But most critically affected of all by this complete drought of Afro-American resources are policemen and other public safety guardians denied their daily quota of Negro arrests. One officer known affectionately as "TWO-A-DAY-PETE" because of his unblemished record of TWO Negro headwhippings per day has already been carted off to the County Insane Asylum—straight-jacketed, screaming and biting, unable to withstand the shock of having his spotless slate sullied by interruption... It is feared that similar attacks are soon expected among municipal judges prevented for the first time in years of distinguished bench-sitting from sentencing one single Negro to a hoosegow or pokey... Ladies and gentlemen, as you trudge in from the joys and headaches of workday chores and dusk begins to descend on this sleepy Southern hamlet, we REPEAT—today—before early morning dew had dried upon magnolia blossoms, your comrade citizens of this lovely Dixie village awoke to the realization that some—pardon me! Not some—but ALL OF THEIR NEGROES were missing... Absent, vamoosed, departed, at bay, fugitive, away, gone and so-far unretrieved... In order to dispel your incredulity, gauge the temper of your suffering compatriots and just possibly prepare you for the likelihood of an equally nightmarish eventuality, we have gathered a cross-section of this city's most distinguished leaders for exclusive interviews... First, Mr. Council Clan, grand-dragoon of this area's most active civic organizations and staunch bell-wether of the political opposition... Mr. Clan, how do you ACCOUNT for this incredible disappearance?

CLAN A PLOT, plain and simple, that's what it is, as plain as the corns on your feet!

ANNOUNCER Whom would you consider responsible?

CLAN I could go on all night.

ANNOUNCER Cite a few?

CLAN Too numerous.

ANNOUNCER Just one?

CLAN Name names when time comes.

ANNOUNCER Could you be referring to native Negroes?

CLAN Ever try quaranteening lepers from their spots?

ANNOUNCER Their organizations?

CLAN Could you slice a nose off a mouth and still keep a face?

ANNOUNCER Commies?

CLAN Would you lop off a titty from a chest and still have a breast?

ANNOUNCER Your city government?

CLAN Now you talkin'!

ANNOUNCER State administration?

CLAN Warming up!

ANNOUNCER Federal?

CLAN Kin a blind man see?!

ANNOUNCER The Court?

CLAN Is a pig clean?!

ANNOUNCER Clergy?

CLAN Do a polecat stink?!

ANNOUNCER Well, Mr. Clan, with this massive complicity, how do you think the plot could've been prevented from succeeding?

CLAN If I'da been in office, it never woulda happened.

ANNOUNCER Then you're laying major blame at the doorstep of the present administration?

CLAN Damn tooting!

ANNOUNCER But from your oft-expressed views, Mr. Clan, shouldn't you and your followers be delighted at the turn of events? After all—isn't it one of the main policies of your society to *drive* the Negroes away? *Drive* 'em back where they came from?

CLAN DRIVVVE, BOY! DRIIIIVVVE! That's right!... When we say so and not befo'. Ain't supposed to do nothing 'til we tell 'em. Got to stay put until we exercise our God-given right to tell 'em when to git!

ANNOUNCER But why argue if they've merely jumped the gun? Why not rejoice at this premature purging of undesirables?

CLAN The time ain't ripe yet, boy... The time ain't ripe yet.

ANNOUNCER Thank you for being so informative, Mr. Clan—Mrs. Aide? Mrs. Aide? Over here, Mrs. Aide... Ladies and gentlemen, this city's Social Welfare Commissioner, Mrs. Handy Anna Aide... Mrs. Aide, with all your Negroes *AWOL*, haven't developments alleviated the staggering demands made upon your Welfare Department? Reduction of relief requests, elimination of case loads, removal of chronic welfare dependents, et cetera?

AIDE Quite the contrary. Disruption of our pilot projects among Nigras saddles our white community with extreme hardship... You see, historically, our agencies have always been foremost contributors to the Nigra Git-A-Job movement. We pioneered in enforcing social welfare theories which oppose coddling the fakers. We strenuously believe in helping Nigras help themselves by participating in meaningful labor. "Relief is Out, Work is In," is our motto. We place them as maids, cooks, butlers, and breast-feeders, cesspool-diggers, wash-basin maintainers, shoe-shine boys, and so on—mostly on a volunteer self-work basis.

ANNOUNCER Hired at prevailing salaried rates, of course?

AIDE God forbid! Money is unimportant. Would only make 'em worse. Our main goal is to improve their ethical behavior. "Rehabilitation Through Positive Participation" is another motto of ours. All unwed mothers, loose-living malingering fathers, bastard children and shiftless grandparents are kept occupied through constructive muscle-therapy. This provides the Nigra with less opportunity to indulge his pleasure-loving amoral inclinations.

ANNOUNCER They volunteer to participate in these pilot projects?

AIDE Heavens no! They're notorious shirkers. When I said the program is voluntary, I meant white citizens in overwhelming majorities do the volunteering. Placing their homes, offices, appliances and persons at our disposal for use in "Operation Uplift."... We would never dare place such a decision in the hands of the Nigra. It would never get off the ground!... No, they have no choice in the matter. "Work or Starve" is the slogan we use to stimulate Nigra awareness of what's good for survival.

ANNOUNCER Thank you, Mrs. Aide, and good luck... Rev?... Rev?... Ladies and gentlemen, this city's foremost spiritual guidance counselor, Reverend Reb Pious... How does it look to you, Reb Pious?

PIOUS (*continuing to gaze skyward*) It's in *His* hands, son, it's in *His* hand.

ANNOUNCER How would you assess the disappearance, from a moral standpoint?

PIOUS An immoral act, son, morally wrong and ethically indefensible. A perversion of Christian principles to be condemned from every pulpit of this nation.

ANNOUNCER Can you account for its occurrence after the many decades of the Church's missionary activity among them?

PIOUS It's basically a reversion of the Nigra to his deep-rooted primitivism... Now, at last, you can understand the difficulties of the Church in attempting to anchor God's kingdom among ungratefuls. It's a constant, unrelenting, no-holds-barred struggle against Satan to wrestle away souls locked in his possession for countless centuries! Despite all our aid, guidance, solace and protection, Old BeezleBub still retains tenacious grips upon the Nigras' childish loyalty—comparable to the lure of bright flames to an infant.

ANNOUNCER But actual physical departure, Reb Pious? How do you explain that?

PIOUS Voodoo, my son, voodoo... With Satan's assist, they have probably employed some heathen magic which we cultivated, sophisticated Christians know absolutely nothing about. However, before long we are confident about counteracting this evil witch-doctory and triumphing in our Holy Savior's name. At this perilous juncture, true believers of all denominations are participating in joint, 'round-the-clock observances, offering prayers for our Master's swiftest intercession. I'm optimistic about the outcome of his intervention... Which prompts me—if I may, sir—to offer these words of counsel to our delinquent Nigras... I say to you without rancor or vengeance, quoting a phrase of one of your greatest prophets, Booker T. Washington: "Return your buckets to where they lay and all will be forgiven."

ANNOUNCER A very inspirational appeal, Reb Pious. I'm certain they will find the tug of its magnetic sincerity irresistible. Thank you, Reb Pious... All in all—as you have witnessed, ladies and gentlemen—this town symbolizes the face of disaster. Suffering as severe a prostration as any city wrecked, ravaged and devastated by the holocaust of war. A vital, lively, throbbing organism brought to a screeching halt by the strange enigma of the missing Negroes... We take you now to offices of the one man into whose hands has been thrust the final responsibility of rescuing this shuddering metropolis from the precipice of destruction... We give you the honorable Mayor, Henry R. E. Lee... Hello, Mayor Lee.

MAYOR (*jovially*) Hello, Jack.

ANNOUNCER Mayor Lee, we have just concluded interviews with some of your city's leading spokesmen. If I may say so, sir, they don't sound too encouraging about the situation.

MAYOR Nonsense, Jack! The situation's well-in-hand as it could be under the circumstances. Couldn't be better in hand. Underneath every dark cloud, Jack, there's always a ray of sunlight, ha, ha, ha.

ANNOUNCER Have you discovered one, sir?

MAYOR Well, Jack, I'll tell you... Of course we've been faced wit' a little crisis, but look at it like this—we've faced 'em befo': Sherman marched through Georgia—ONCE! Lincoln freed the slaves—MOMENTARILY! Carpetbaggers even put Nigras in the Governor's mansion, state legislature, Congress and the Senate of the United States. But what happened?—Ole Dixie bounced right on back up... At this moment the Supreme Court's trying to put Nigras in our schools and the Nigra has got it in his haid to put hisself everywhere... But what you 'spect go'n' happen?—Ole Dixie will kangaroo back even higher. Southern courage, fortitude, chivalry and superiority always wins out... SHUCKS! We'll have us some Nigras befo' daylight is gone!

ANNOUNCER   Mr. Mayor, I hate to introduce this note, but in an earlier interview, one of your chief opponents, Mr. Clan, hinted at your own complicity in the affair—

MAYOR   A LOT OF POPPYCOCK! Clan is politicking! I've beaten him four times outta four and I'll beat him four more times outta four! This is not time for partisan politics! What we need now is level-headedness and across-the-board unity. This typical, rash, mealy-mouth, shooting-off-at-the-lip of Clan and his ilk proves their insincerity and voters will remember that in the next election! Won't you, voters?! (*has risen to the height of campaign oratory*)

ANNOUNCER   Mr. Mayor!... Mr. Mayor! ... Please—

MAYOR   ... I tell you, I promise you—

ANNOUNCER   PLEASE, MR. MAYOR!

MAYOR   Huh?... Oh—yes, carry on.

ANNOUNCER   Mr. Mayor, your cheerfulness and infectious good spirits lead me to conclude that startling new developments warrant fresh-found optimism. What concrete, declassified information do you have to support your claim that Negroes will reappear before nightfall?

MAYOR   Because we are presently awaiting the pay-off of a masterful five-point supra-recovery program which can't help but reap us a bonanza of Nigras 'fore sundown!... First: Exhaustive efforts to pinpoint the where'bouts of our own missing darkies continue to zero in on the bullseye... Second: The President of the United States, following an emergency cabinet meeting, has designated us the prime disaster area of the century—National Guard is already on the way... Third: In an unusual, but bold maneuver, we have appealed to the NAACP 'n' all other Nigra conspirators to help us git to the bottom of the vanishing act... Fourth: We have exercised our non-reciprocal option and requested that all fraternal Southern states express their solidarity by lending us some of their Nigras temporarily on credit... Fifth and foremost: We have already gotten consent of the Governor to round up all stray, excess and incorrigible Nigras to be shipped to us under escort of the State Militia... That's why we've stifled pessimism and are brimming wit' confidence that this fullscale concerted mobilization will ring down a jackpot of jigaboos 'fore light vanishes from sky!—

ANNOUNCER   Congratulations!   What happens if it fails?

MAYOR   Don't even think THAT! Absolutely no reason to suspect it will... (*peers over shoulder, then whispers confidentially while placing hand over mouth by* ANNOUNCER'*s imaginary mike*) ... But speculating on the dark side of your question—if we don't turn up some by nightfall, it may be all over. The harm has already been done. You see the South has always been glued together by the uninterrupted presence of its darkies. No telling how unstuck we might git if things keep on like they have.—Wait a minute, it musta paid off already! Mission accomplished 'cause here's Jackson head a time wit' the word... Well, Jackson, what's new?

JACKSON   Situation on the home front remains static, sir—can't uncover scent or shadow. The NAACP and all other Nigra front groups 'n' plotters deny any knowledge or connection wit' the missing Nigras. Maintained this even after appearing befo' a Senate Emergency Investigating Committee which subpoenaed 'em to Washington post haste and threw 'em in jail for contempt. A handful of Nigras who agreed to make spectacular appeals for ours to come back to us, have themselves mysteriously disappeared. But, worst news of all, sir, is our sister cities and counties, inside and outside the state, have changed their minds, fallen back on their promises and refused to lend us any Nigras, claiming they don't have 'nuff for themselves.

MAYOR   What 'bout Nigras promised by the Governor?!

Day of Absence

JACKSON Jailbirds and vagrants escorted here from chain-gangs and other reservations either revolted and escaped enroute or else vanished mysteriously on approaching our city limits... Deterioration rapidly escalates, sir. Estimates predict we kin hold out only one more hour before overtaken by anarchistic turmoil... Some citizens seeking haven elsewheres have already fled, but on last report were being forcibly turned back by armed sentinels in other cities who wanted no parts of 'em—claiming they carried a jinx.

MAYOR That bad, huh?

JACKSON Worse, sir... we've received at least five reports of plots on your life.

MAYOR What?!—We've gotta act quickly then!

JACKSON Run out of ideas, sir.

MAYOR Think harder, boy!

JACKSON Don't have much time, sir. One measly hour, then all hell go'n' break loose.

MAYOR Gotta think of something drastic, Jackson!

JACKSON I'm dry, sir.

MAYOR Jackson! Is there any planes outta here in the next hour?

JACKSON All transportation's been knocked out, sir.

MAYOR I thought so!

JACKSON What were you contemplating, sir?

MAYOR Don't ask me what I was contemplating! I'm still boss 'round here! Don't forgit it!

JACKSON Sorry, sir.

MAYOR ... Hold the wire!... Wait a minute...! Waaaaait a minute—GODAMMIT! All this time crapping 'round, diddling and fotsing wit' puny li'l' solutions—all the while neglecting our ace in the hole, our trump card! Most potent weapon for digging Nigras outta the woodpile!!! All the while right befo' our eyes!... Ass! Why didn't you remind me?!!!

JACKSON What is it, sir?

MAYOR ... ME—THAT'S WHAT! ME! A personal appeal from ME! *Directly to them!* ... Although we wouldn't let 'em march to the polls and express their affection for me through the ballot box, we've always known I'm held highest in their esteem. A direct address from their beloved Mayor!... If they's anywheres close within the sound of my voice, they'll shape up! Or let us know by a sign they's ready to!

JACKSON You sure *that'll* turn the trick, sir?

MAYOR As sure as my ancestors befo' me who knew that when they puckered their lips to whistle, ole Sambo was gonna come a-lickety-splitting to answer the call!... That same chips-down blood courses through these Confederate gray veins of Henry R. E. Lee!!!

ANNOUNCER I'm delighted to offer our network's facilities for such a crucial public interest address, sir. We'll arrange immediately for your appearance on an international hookup, placing you in the widest proximity to contact them wherever they may be.

MAYOR Thank you, I'm very grateful... Jackson, re-grease the machinery and set wheels in motion. Inform townspeople what's being done. Tell 'em we're all in this together. The next hour is countdown. I demand absolute cooperation, city-wide silence and inactivity. I don't want the Nigras frightened if they's nearby. This is the most important hour in town's history. Tell 'em if one single Nigra shows up during hour of decision, victory is within sight. I'm gonna git 'em that one—maybe all! Hurry and crack to it! (ANNOUNCER *rushes out, followed by* JACKSON. *Blackout. Scene re-opens, with* MAYOR *seated, eyes front, spotlight illuminating him in semi-darkness. Shadowy figures stand in the background, prepared to answer phones or aid in any other manner.* MAYOR *waits patiently until "GO!" signal is given. Then begins, his voice combining elements of confidence, tremolo and gravity*) Good evening... Despite the fact that millions of you wonderful people throughout the nation are viewing and listening to this momentous broadcast—and I thank you for your concern and sympathy in this hour of our peril—I primarily want to concentrate my attention and address these remarks solely for the benefit of our departed Nigra friends who may be listening somewheres in our farflung land to the sound of my voice... If you are—it is with heart-felt emotion and fond memories of our happy association that I ask—"Where are you...?" Your absence has left a void in the bosom of every single man, woman and child of our great city. I tell you—you don't know what it means for us to wake up in the morning and discover that your cheerful, grinning, happy-go-lucky faces are missing!... From the depths of my heart, I can only meekly, humbly suggest what it means to me personally. ... You see—the one face I will never be able to erase from my memory is the face—not of my Ma, not of Pa, neither wife or child—but the image of the first woman I came to love so well when just a wee lad—the vision of the first human I laid clear sight on at childbirth—the profile—better yet, the full face of my dear old ... Jemimah—God rest her soul... Yes! My dear ole mammy, wit' her round ebony moonbeam gleaming down upon me in the crib, teeth shining, blood-red bandana standing starched, peaked and proud, gazing down upon me affectionately as she crooned me a Southern lullaby... OH! It's a memorable picture I will eternally cherish in permanent treasure chambers of my heart, now and forever always... Well, if this radiant image can remain so infinitely vivid to me all these many years after her unfortunate demise in the Po' folks home—THINK of the misery the rest of us must be suffering after being *freshly* denied your soothing presence?! We need ya. If you kin hear me, just contact this station 'n' I will welcome you back personally. Let me just tell you that since you eloped, nothing has been the same. How could it? You're part of us, you belong to us. Just give us a sign and we'll be contented that all is well... Now if you've skipped away on a little fun-fest, we understand, ha, ha. We know you like a good time and we don't begrudge it to ya. Hell—er, er, we like a good time ourselves—who doesn't?... In fact, think of all the good times we've had together, huh? We've had some real fun, you and us, yesiree!... Nobody knows better than you and I what fun we've had together. You singing us those old Southern coon songs and dancing those Nigra jigs and us clapping, prodding 'n' spurring you on! Lots of fun, huh?!... OH BOY! The times we've had together... If you've snucked away for a bit of fun by yourself, we'll go 'long wit' ya—long as you let us know where you at so we won't be worried about you... We'll go 'long wit' you long as you don't take the joke too far. I'll admit a joke is a joke and you've played a LULU!... I'm warning you, we can't stand much more horsing 'round from you! Business is business 'n' fun is fun! You've had your fun so now let's get down to business! Come on back, YOU HEAR ME!!!... If you been hoodwinked by agents of some foreign government, I've been authorized by the President of these United States to inform you that this liberty-loving Republic is prepared to rescue you from their clutches. Don't pay no 'tention to their sireeen songs and atheistic promises! You better off under our control and you know it!... If you been bamboozled by rabble-rousing nonsense of your own so-called leaders, we prepared to offer same protection. Just call us up! Just give us a sign!... Come on, give us a sign... give us a sign—even a teeny-weeny one... ??!! (*glances around checking on possible communications. A bevy of headshakes indicate no success.* MAYOR *returns to address with desperate fervor.*) Now look—you don't know what you doing! If you persist in this disobedience, you know all too well the consequences! We'll track you to the end of the earth, beyond the galaxy, across the stars! We'll capture you and chastise you with all the vengeance we command! 'N' you know only too well how stern we kin be when double-crossed! The city, the state and the entire nation will crucify you for this unpardonable defiance! (*checks again*) No call... ? No sign... ? Time is running out! Deadline slipping past! They gotta respond! They gotta! (*resuming*) Listen to me! I'm begging y'all, you've gotta come back...! LOOK, GEORGE! (*waves dirty rag aloft*) I brought the rag you wax the car wit'. ... Don't this bring back memories, George, of all the days you spent shining that automobile to shimmering perfection... ? And you, Rufus?!... Here's the shoe polisher and the brush!... 'Member, Rufus?... Remember the happy mornings you spent popping this rag and whisking this brush so furiously 'till it created music that was sympho-nee to the ear... ? And you—MANDY?... Here's the waste-basket you didn't dump this morning. I saved it just for you!... LOOK, all y'all out there... ? (*signals and a three-person procession parades one after the other before the imaginary camera*)

DOLL WOMAN (*brandishing a crying baby* [*doll*] *as she strolls past and exits*) She's been crying ever since you left, Caldonia...

MOP MAN (*flashing mop*) It's been waiting in the same corner, Buster...

BRUSH MAN (*flagging toilet brush in one hand*

Day of Absence

and toilet plunger in other) It's been dry ever since you left, Washington...

MAYOR *(jumping in on the heels of the last exit)* Don't these things mean anything to y'all? By God! Are your memories so short?! Is there nothing sacred to ya?... Please come back, for my sake, please! All of you—even you questionable ones! I promise no harm will be done to you! Revenge is disallowed! We'll forgive everything! Just come on back and I'll git down on my knees—*(immediately drops to knees)* I'll be kneeling in the middle of Dixie Avenue to kiss the first shoe of the first one 'a you to show up... *I'll smooch any other spot you request*... Erase this nightmare 'n' we'll concede any demand you make, just come on back —please??? !!... PLEEEEEEEZE?!!!

VOICE *(shouting)* TIME!!!

MAYOR *(remaining on knees, frozen in a pose of supplication. After a brief, deadly silence, he whispers almost inaudibly)* They wouldn't answer... they wouldn't answer...

(Blackout as bedlam erupts offstage. Total blackness holds during a sufficient interval where offstage sound-effects create the illusion of complete pandemonium, followed by a diminution which trails off into an expressionistic simulation of a city coming to a strickened standstill: industrial machinery clanks to halt, traffic blares to silence, etc.... The stage remains dark and silent for a long moment, then lights re-arise on the ANNOUNCER)

ANNOUNCER A pitiful sight, ladies and gentlemen. Soon after his unsuccessful appeal, Mayor Lee suffered a vicious pummeling from the mob and barely escaped with his life. National Guardsmen and State Militia were impotent in quelling the fury of a town venting its frustration in an orgy of destruction—a frenzy of rioting, looting and all other aberrations of a town gone berserk... Then— suddenly—as if a magic wand had been waved, madness evaporated and something more frightening replaced it: Submission... Even whimperings ceased. The city: exhausted, benumbed.—Slowly its occupants slinked off into shadows, and by midnight, the town was occupied exclusively by zombies. The fight and life had been drained out... Pooped... Hope ebbed away as completely as the beloved, absent Negroes... As our crew packed gear and crept away silently, we treaded softly—as if we were stealing away from a mausoleum... The Face Of A Defeated City.

(Blackout. Lights rise slowly at the sound of rooster-crowing, signalling the approach of a new day, the next morning. Scene is same as opening of play. CLEM *and* LUKE *are huddled over dazedly, trancelike. They remain so for a long count. Finally, a figure drifts on stage, shuffling slowly)*

LUKE *(gazing in silent fascination at the approaching figure)* ... Clem...? Do you see what I see or am I dreaming...?

CLEM It's a... a Nigra, ain't it, Luke...?

LUKE Sure looks like one, Clem—but we better make sure—eyes could be playing tricks on us... Does he still look like one to you, Clem?

CLEM He still does, Luke—but I'm scared to believe—

LUKE ... Why...? It looks like Rastus, Clem!

CLEM Sure does, Luke... but we better not jump to no hasty conclusion...

LUKE *(in timid softness)* That you, Rastus...?

RASTUS *(Stepin Fetchit, Willie Best, Nicodemus, B. McQueen and all the rest rolled into one)* Why... howdy... Mr. Luke... Mr. Clem...

CLEM It is him, Luke! It is him!

LUKE Rastus?

RASTUS Yeas... sah?

LUKE Where was you yesterday?

RASTUS *(very, very puzzled)* Yes... ter... day?... Yester... day...? Why... right... here... Mr. Luke...

LUKE No you warn't, Rastus, don't lie to me! Where was you yestiddy?

RASTUS Why... I'm sure I was... Mr. Luke... Remember... I made... that... delivery for you...

LUKE That was MONDAY, Rastus, yestiddy was TUESDAY.

RASTUS Tues... day...? You don't say... Well... well... well...

LUKE Where was you 'n' all the other Nigras yesterday, Rastus?

RASTUS I... thought... yestiddy... was ... Monday, Mr. Luke—I coulda swore it...! ... See how... things... kin git all mixed up?... I coulda swore it...

LUKE TODAY is WEDNESDAY, Rastus. Where was you TUESDAY?

RASTUS Tuesday . . . huh? That's somp'um . . . I . . . don't . . . remember . . . missing . . . a day . . . Mr. Luke . . . but I guess you right . . .

LUKE Then were was you!!!???

RASTUS Don't rightly know, Mr. Luke. I didn't know I had skipped a day.—But that jist goes to show you how time kin fly, don't it, Mr. Luke . . . Uuh, uuh, uuh . . . (*he starts shuffling off, scratching head, a flicker of a smile playing across his lips.* CLEM *and* LUKE *gaze dumbfoundedly as he disappears*)

LUKE (*eyes sweeping around in all directions*) Well . . . There's the others, Clem . . . Back jist like they useta be . . . Everything's same as always . . .

CLEM ???. . . . . Is it . . . Luke . . . !

(*Slow fade. Curtain*)

II

Modern Black Women

**Lorraine Hansberry   Alice Childress   Adrienne Kennedy
Martie Charles**

Playwriting traditionally has been regarded as a man's profession. With the exception of Lillian Hellman, Mary Chase, and Jean Kerr, few women have succeeded in having their plays produced professionally. No play by a black woman had been produced on or off-Broadway before 1952, when Alice Childress' *Gold through the Trees* was presented off-Broadway. Seven years later, Lorraine Hansberry became the first black woman to have a play presented on Broadway. *A Raisin in the Sun* received unanimous critical praise and won the New York Drama Critics' Circle Award as the best play of the 1958–59 season. Besides having an excellent black cast, including Claudia McNeil, Sidney Poitier, Ruby Dee, Diana Sands, Ivan Dixon, and Louis Gossett, it was also the first play on Broadway to be directed by a black man, Lloyd Richards. Adrienne Kennedy's *Funnyhouse of a Negro* was presented in 1964, the third play by a black woman to reach professional New York theatre.

Anne Flagg, Micki Grant, Glory Van Scott, Pat Singleton, Sonia Sanchez, Salimu, Barbara Molette (who collaborates with her husband, Carlton), as well as Alice Childress, J. E. Franklin, Adrienne Kennedy, and Martie Charles, are among the black women who write today for the stage. These women, like black men, write of black life and racial injustice. But racial injustice is often on the periphery of the play, as in Anne Flagg's *Great Gettin' Up Mornin'*, which examines the anxieties of a young couple whose only child is about to become the first black to integrate a Southern public school; or in *Wine in the Wilderness*, where a recent riot provides the atmosphere in which the characters discover their true identities. In Adrienne Kennedy's avant-garde play, racism permeates the atmosphere, but the author's concern is its *effect* on her character. The plays of Sonia Sanchez, Salimu, and Martie Charles are revolutionary works written especially for black audiences. The changes demanded by these authors are not always directed toward *the man*, but often to those blacks in the community who are out of tune with the times or who have given up.

The plays in this section give the reader insight into the modern black woman from varying points of view, and in each instance she is a marked departure from the traditional stage and screen concept that we have seen in the past. No longer is she depicted as the overly devout, hard-working, suffering matriarch, the prostitute, or the faithful (and/or dumb) servant; instead she emerges as a *real* human being of dimension, having needs and desires.

Lorraine Hansberry (1931–1965)

The Drinking Gourd 1960

The Drinking Gourd, written 100 years after *The Escape* (see p. 34) examines the same subject—slavery and the flight from it. A comparison of the two plays reveals both differences and similarities.

Both authors show that the final basis of slavery was economic and that under conditions of "unopposed capitalism" any humane or moral considerations were marginal. While Mr. Brown merely points the finger at greed, Miss Hansberry adroitly traces the three financial threads of land, cotton, and labor.

Both plays consider religion. William Wells Brown presents it as an overt tool of capitalism, designed to keep the Negro content. Lorraine Hansberry represents the white preacher in *The Drinking Gourd* as an ineffective moral agent. Religious precepts without pragmatic economic power were valueless to the poor Southern white.

The differences between the two plays, aside from dramatic license, represent 100 years of research and reflection on the institution of slavery. Mr. Brown is abolitionist: no character, no feature of slavery has any redeeming quality. All white Southerners are therefore corrupt. Miss Hansberry, three generations removed, presents white characters who attempt to ameliorate the brutality of slavery, but whose "good intentions" succumb to economic reality. Her black characters, too, represent a greater range than Mr. Brown's, although they all operate from motives of self-interest.

The Drinking Gourd was written for television, which, unlike the cinema, relies heavily upon dialogue and close-ups. The visual descriptive passages in the play are important to the action, and should not be missed.

The Drinking Gourd was never produced. After the acclaim Miss Hansberry had received for the stage and film versions of *A Raisin in the Sun*, it would seem that a solid television play would have been welcomed by the networks. One can speculate, following Miss Hansberry's lead, that the financial self-interest of television would not be served in presenting a play that might alienate a large section of the audience.

The Drinking Gourd

Our new government is founded upon the great truth that the Negro is not equal to the white man—that slavery is his natural and normal condition. (Alexander H. Stephens, Vice-President of the Confederacy)

CAST OF CHARACTERS

HANNIBAL, *a slave youth of 19*
TOMMY, *white child of 10*
SOLDIER
SARAH, *a slave, age 19*
JOSHUA, *a slave child*
RISSA, *older slave woman*
HIRAM SWEET, *the master*
MARIA, *his wife*
EVERETT, *eldest son*
DR. MACON BULLETT, *white doctor*
ZEB, *small white farmer*
ELIZABETH, *his wife*
PREACHER, *white man of middle age*
COFFIN, *slave driver*

*Following preliminary production titles: introduce stark, spirited banjo themes. Main play titles and credits. Fade in: under titles: exterior two shot—*HANNIBAL*—*TOMMY*—bright day.*

HANNIBAL *is a young slave of about nineteen or twenty.* TOMMY, *about ten, is his master's son. It is* HANNIBAL *who is playing the banjo, the neck of which intrudes into close opening shot frame.*

Camera moves back to wider angle to show that TOMMY *is vigorously keeping time by clapping his hands to the beat of the music. They are seated in a tiny wooded enclosure. Sunlight and leaf shadow play on their faces, the expressions of which are animated and happy. If workable, they sing, from top.*

At completion of titles: fade out.

ACT ONE

(*Fade in: Exterior high angled panning shot—American East Coast—dusk.*

Pan down a great length of coast until definitive mood is established. Presently the lone figure of a man emerges from distance. He is tall and narrow-hipped, suggesting a certain idealized American generality. He is not Lincoln, but perhaps Lincolnesque. He wears the side whiskers of the nineteenth century and his hair is long at the neck after the manner of New England or Southern farmers of the period. He is dressed in dark military trousers and boots which are in no way recognizable as to rank or particular army. His shirt is open at the collar and rolled at the sleeves and he carries his dark tunic across his shoulders. He is not battle-scarred or dirty or in any other way suggestive of the disorder of war; but his gait is that of troubled and reflective meditation. When he speaks his voice is markedly free of identifiable regionalism. His imposed generality is to be a symbolic American specificity. He is the narrator. We come down close in his face as he turns to the sea and speaks)

SOLDIER This is the Atlantic Ocean. (*he gestures easily when he needs to*) Over there, somewhere, is Europe. And over there, down that way, I guess, is Africa. (*turning and facing inland*) And all of this, for thousands and thousands of miles in all directions, is the New World. (*he bends down and empties a pile of dirt from his handkerchief on to the sand*) And this, this is soil. Southern soil. (*opening his fist*) And this is cotton seed. Europe, Africa, the New World and Cotton. They have all gotten mixed up together to make the trouble. (*He begins to walk inland, a wandering gait full of pauses and gestures*) You see, this seed and this earth—(*gesturing now to the land around him*) only have meaning—potency—if you add a third force. That third force is labor.

(*The landscape turns to the Southern countryside.*

The Drinking Gourd

In the distance, shadowed under the incredibly beautiful willows and magnolias, is a large, magnificently columned, white manor house. As he moves close to it, the soft, indescribably sweet sound of the massed voices of the unseen slaves wafts up in the mellow, haunting organ tones of one of the most plaintive of the spirituals)

VOICES   Steal away, steal away,
Steal away to Jesus.
Steal away, steal away home—
I ain't got long to stay here.

My Lord he calls me,
He calls me by the thunder
The trumpet sounds
   within-a my soul—
I ain't got long to stay here.

Steal away, steal away, etc.

(Beyond the manor house, cotton fields, rows and rows of cotton fields. And, finally, as the narrator walks on, rows of little white painted cabins, the slave quarters.

The quarters are, at the moment, starkly deserted as though he has come upon this place in a dream only. He wanders in to what appears to be the center of the quarters with an easy familiarity at being there.

This plantation, like the matters he is going to tell us about, has no secrets from him. He knows everything we are going to see; he knows how most of us will react to what we see and how we will decide at the end of the play. Therefore, in manner and words he will try to persuade *us of nothing; he will only tell us facts and stand aside and let us see for ouselves. Thus, he almost leisurely refreshes himself with a drink from a pail hanging on a nail on one of the cabins. He wanders to the community outdoor fireplace at center and lounges against it and goes on with his telling.)*

SOLDIER   Labor so plentiful that, for a while, it might be cheaper to work a man to death and buy another one than to work the first one less harshly.

(The gentle slave hymn ends and with its end comes the arbitrarily imposed abrupt darkness of true night. Somewhere in the distance a driver's voice calls: "Quittin' time! Quittin' time!" in accompaniment to a gong or a bell. Silent indications of life begin to stir around the narrator. We become aware of points of light in some of the cabins and a great fire has begun to roar silently in the fireplace where he leans. Numbers of slaves begin to file, also silently, into the quarters; some of them immediately drop to the ground and just sit or lie perfectly still, on their backs, staring into space. Others slowly form a silent line in front of the fireplace, holding makeshift eating utensils. The narrator moves to make room for them when it is necessary and occasionally glances from them out to us, as if to see if we are truly seeing.

There is, about all of these people, a grim air of fatigue and exhaustion, reflecting the twelve to fourteen hours of almost unrelieved labor they have just completed. The men are dressed in the main in rough trousers of haphazard lengths and coarse shirts. Some have hats. The women wear single piece shifts, some of them without sleeves or collars. Some wear their hair bound in the traditional bandana of the Negro slave women of the Americas; others wear or carry the wide straw hats of the cotton fields.

SOLDIER   These people are slaves. They did not come here willingly. Their ancestors were captured, for the most part, on the West Coast of Africa by men who made such enterprise their business. *(we come in for extreme closeups of the faces of the people as he talks, moving from men to women to children with lingering intimacy)* Few of them could speak to each other. They came from many different peoples and cultures. The slavers were careful about that. Insurrection is very difficult when you cannot even speak to your fellow prisoner. All of them did not survive the voyage. Some simply died of suffocation; others of disease and still others of suicide. Others were murdered when they mutinied. And when the trade was finally suppressed—sometimes they were just dumped overboard when a British Man-o-War got after a slave ship. That was to destroy the evidence. That trade went on for three centuries. How many were stolen from their homeland? Some scholars say fifteen million. Others fifty million. No one will ever really know. In any case—today, some planters will tell you with pride that the cost of maintaining one of these human beings need not exceed seven dollars and fifty cents—a year. You see, there is no education to pay for—in fact, some of the harshest laws in the slave code are designed to keep the slave from being educated. Some of the penalties are maiming or mutilation—or death. Usually for he who is taught; but very often it is also for he who might dare to teach—including white men. There are also no minimum work hours and no guaranteed minimum wage; needless to say, there are also no trade unions. And, above all, there are no wages at all. (*As he talks a murmur of low conversation begins among the people and there is a more conspicuous stir of life among them as the* NARRATOR *now prepares, picking up his tunic and putting it across his shoulder once again, to walk out of the scene and leave it to them*) Please do not forget that this is the nineteenth century. It is a time when we still allow little children—white children—to labor twelve and thirteen hours in the factories and mines of America. We do not yet believe that women are equal citizens who should have the right to vote. It is a time when we still punish the insane for their madness. It is a time, therefore, when some men can believe and proclaim to the world that this system is the—(*enunciating carefully but without passion*) highest form of civilization in the world. (*he turns away from us and faces the now living scene in background*) *This* system:

(*The Camera immediately comes in to exclude him and down to a close-up of a large skillet suspended over the roaring fire which now crackles with live sound. Pieces of bacon and corn pone sizzle on it. A meager portion of both is lifted up and onto a plate by* RISSA, *the cook. She is a woman of late years with an expression of indifference that has already passed resignation. The slave receiving his ration from her casts a slightly hopeful glance at the balance but is waved away by the cook. He gives up easily and moves away and retires and eats his food with relish. A second and third are similarly served.*

The fourth person in line is a young girl of about nineteen. She is SARAH. *She holds out her plate for service but bends as she does so, in spite of her own weariness, to play with a small boy of about seven or eight,* JOSHUA, *who has been lingering about the cook, clutching at her skirts and getting as much in her way as he can manage.*

SARAH Hello, there, Joshua!
JOSHUA I got a stomick ache.
RISSA (*busy with her serving*) You ain't got nothing but the devil ache.
SARAH (*with mock and heavily applied sympathy to the child*) Awww, poor little thing. Show Sarah* where it hurt you, honey. (*he points his finger to a random place on his abdomen; clearly delighted to have even insincere attention*) Here? (*she pokes him to ostensibly determine the right place where the pain is, but in reality only to make him laugh, which they both seem to know*) Or, here—? Oh, I know, right here! (*she pokes him very hard with one finger and he collapses in her arms in a fit of giggling*)
RISSA If y'all don't quit that foolin' round behind me while I got all this here to do you better! (*she swings vaguely behind her with the spatula*) Stop it I say now! Sarah you worse than he is.
SARAH (*a little surreptitiously—to* JOSHUA) Where's your Uncle Hannibal? (*the child shrugs indifferently*)
RISSA (*who overhears everything that is ever spoken on the plantation*) Uh-hunh. I knew we'd get 'round to Mr. Hannibal soon enough.
SARAH (*to* RISSA) Do you know where he is?
RISSA How I know where that wild boy of mine is? If he ain't got sense enough to come for his supper, it ain't no care of mine. He's grown now. I can't be worryin' 'bout that boy. Move on out the way now. Step up here, Ben!
SARAH (*moving around to the other side and standing close*) He was out the fields again this afternoon, Aunt Rissa.
RISSA (*softly suddenly, but without breaking her working rhythm or changing her facial expression*) Coffin know?
SARAH Coffin know everything. Say he goin' to tell Marster Sweet first thing in the mornin'.
RISSA See if you can find that boy of mine, child. (SARAH *pushes the last of her food in her mouth and starts off.* RISSA *halts her and hands her a small bundle which has been lying in readiness*) His supper.

(*Cut to: exterior moonlit woods.* SARAH *emerges from the woods into a tiny clearing. She halts with a sign of exasperation when her eyes see what they are looking for.* HANNIBAL *is lying on a little hillock in deep grass with both arms folded under his head, staring up at the stars. We come down in his face as his eyes, in turn, discover* SARAH. *He*

* Invariably pronounced "Say-rah."

is a lean, vital young man with bright, commanding eyes. He smiles)

HANNIBAL (*playing the poet-fool*) And when she come to me, it were the moonrise. (HANNIBAL *holds out his hand playfully, himself mocking the spirit of the mood he was enjoying before* SARAH *appeared*) And when she touch my hand, it were the true stars fallin'. (*he takes her hand and pulls her down in the grass and kisses her. She pulls away with the urgency of her news.*)

SARAH (*handing him his food*) Coffin noticed you was gone first thing.

HANNIBAL Well, that old driver finally gettin' to be almost smart as a jackass.

SARAH Say he gona tell Marster Sweet in the mornin'. You gona catch you another whippin', boy. (*in a mood to ignore peril,* HANNIBAL *goes on eating his food*) Hannibal, why you have to run off like that all the time?

HANNIBAL Don't run off *all* the time.

SARAH Oh, Hannibal!

HANNIBAL (*finishing the meager supper and reaching out for her playfully*) "Oh, Hannibal. Oh, Hannibal!" Come here. (*he takes hold of her and kisses her once sweetly and lightly*) H'you this evenin', Miss Sarah Mae?

SARAH You don't know how mad old Coffin was today, boy, or you wouldn't be so smart. He's gona get you in trouble with Marster again.

HANNIBAL Me and you was born in trouble with Marster. (*suddenly looking up at the sky*) Hey, lookathere—

SARAH (*noting him and also looking up*) What—

HANNIBAL Lookit that big, old, fat star shining away up yonder there!

SARAH (*automatically dropping her voice and looking about a bit*) Shhh. Hannibal!

HANNIBAL (*with his hand, as though he is personally touching the stars*) 1, 2, 3, 4—they makes up the dipper. That's the Big Dipper, Sarah. The Drinking Gourd pointin' straight to the North Star!

SARAH (*knowingly*) Everybody knows that's the Big Dipper and you better hush your mouth for sure now, boy. Trees on this plantation got more ears than leaves!

HANNIBAL (*ignoring the caution*) That's the old drinkin' gourd herself! (*releasing the girl's arms and settling down, a little wistfully now*) Sure is bright tonight. Sure would make good travelin' light tonight . . .

SARAH (*with terror, clapping her hand over his mouth*) Stop it!

HANNIBAL (*moving her hand*) —up there jes pointin' away . . . *due North!*

SARAH (*regarding him sadly*) You're sure like your brother, boy. Just like him.

(HANNIBAL *ignores her and leans back in the grass in the position of the opening shot of the scene with his arms tucked under his head. He sings softly to himself*)

HANNIBAL   For the old man is a-waitin'
           for to carry you to freedom if
           you follow the drinkin' gourd.
           Follow—follow—follow . . .
           if you follow the drinking gourd . . .

SARAH (*over the song*) —look like him; talk like him; and God knows, you sure think like him. (*pause*) In time, I reckon (*very sadly*), you be gone like him.

HANNIBAL (*sitting bolt upright suddenly and peering into the woods about them*) You think Isaiah got all the way to Canada, Sarah? Mama says it's powerful far. Farther than Ohio! (*this last with true wonder*) Sure he did! I bet you old Isaiah is up there and got hisself a job and is livin' fine. I bet you that! Bet he works in a lumber yard or something and got hisself a wife and maybe even a house and—

SARAH (*quietly*) You mean if he's alive, Hannibal.

HANNIBAL Oh, he's alive all right! Catchers ain't never caught my brother. (*he whistles through his teeth*) That boy lit out of here in a way somebody go who don't mean to never be caught by nothin'! (*he waits. Then having assured himself within*) Wherever he is, he's alive. And he's free.

SARAH I can't see how his running off like. that did you much good. Or your Mama. Almost broke her heart, that's what. And worst of all, leaving his poor little baby. Leaving poor little Joshua who don't have no mother of his own as it is. Seem like your brother just went out his head when Marster sold Joshua's mother. I guess everybody on this plantation knew he wasn't gonna be here long then. Even Marster must of known.

HANNIBAL But Marster couldn't keep him

here then. Not all Marster's dogs and drivers and guns. Nothin'. (*he looks to the woods, remembering*) I met him here that night to bring him the food and a extry pair of shoes. He was standing right over there, right over there, with the moonlight streamin' down on him and he was breathin' hard, Lord, that boy was breathin' so's you could almost hear him on the other side of the woods. (*a sudden pause and then a rush in the telling*) He didn't say nothing to me, nothin' at all. But his eyes look like somebody lit a fire in 'em, they was shining so in the dark. I jes hand him the parcel and he put it in his shirt and give me a kind of push on the shoulder. (*he touches the place, remembering keenly*) Here—. And then he turned and lit out through them woods there. Like lightnin'. He was bound out this place! (*he is entirely quiet behind the completion of the narrative.* SARAH *is deeply affected by the implications of what she has heard and suddenly puts her arms around his neck and clings very tightly to him. Then she holds him back from her and looks at him for the truth*)

SARAH You aim to go, don't you, Hannibal? (*he does not answer and it is clear because of it that he intends to run off*) H'you know it's so much better to run off? (*a little desperately, near tears, thinking of the terrors involved*) Even if you make it—h'you know what's up there, what it be like to go wanderin' round by yourself in this world?

HANNIBAL I don't know. Jes know what it is to be a slave.

SARAH Where would you go—?

HANNIBAL Jes North, that's all I know. (*kind of shrugging*) Try to find Isaiah maybe. How I know what I do? (*throwing up his hands at the difficult question*) There's people up there what helps runaways.

SARAH You mean them aba-aba-litchinists? I heard Marster Sweet say once that they catches runaways and makes soap out of them.

HANNIBAL (*suddenly older and wiser*) That's slave-owner talk, Sarah. Whatever you hear Marster say 'bout slavery—you always believe the opposite. There ain't nothin' hurt slave marster so much (*savoring the notion*)—as when his property walk away from him. Guess that's the worst blow of all. Way I look at it, ever' slave ought to run off 'fore he die.

SARAH (*looking up suddenly absorbing the sense of what he has just said*) Oh, Hannibal—I couldn't go! (*she starts to shake all over*) I'm too delicate. My breath wouldn't hold out from here to the river . . .

HANNIBAL (*starting to laugh at her*) No, not you—skeerified as you is. (*he looks at her and pulls her to him*) But don't you worry, little Sarah. I'll come back. (*he smooths her hair and comforts her*) I'll come back and buy you. Mama too, if she's still livin'. (*the girl quivers in his arms and he holds her a little more tightly, looking up once again to his stars*) I surely do that thing!

(*Cut to: interior. The dining room of the "Big House."*

HIRAM SWEET *and his wife,* MARIA, *sit at either end of a well laden table, attended by two male servants. The youngest son,* TOMMY, *about ten, sits near his father and across from his older brother,* EVERETT, *who is approaching thirty. A fifth person, a dinner guest, is seated on* EVERETT'*s left. He is* DR. MACON BULLETT. *The meal has just ended but an animated conversation which characterized it lingers actively*)

EVERETT —by Heaven, I'll tell you we don't have to take any more of it! (*he hits the table with his fist for emphasis*) I say we can have 600,000 men in the field without even feeling it. The whole thing wouldn't have to last more than six months, Papa. Why can't you see that?

HIRAM (*a man in his mid-sixties, with an over-generous physique and a kind, if somewhat over-indulged face*) I see it fine! I see that it's the river of stupidity the South will eventually drown itself in.

BULLETT (*a man of a slightly quieter temperament than the other two men; with an air of deeply ingrained "refinement"*) I don't see that we have much choice, however you look at it, Hiram. They've pushed our backs against the wall. Suddenly every blubber-fronted Yankee industrialist in New England has begun to imagine himself the deliverer of the blacks; at least in public speeches. (*at the epithet,* HIRAM *looks down at his own stomach and then back at his friend with some annoyance*) The infernal hypocrites! Since all they want is the control of Congress, they ought to call a snake by its name.

EVERETT Hear, hear, sir!

HIRAM (*eating something*) The only thing is

—it doesn't make sense to fight a war you know you can't win.

(EVERETT *is so exasperated by the remark that he jumps up from the table. His mother laughs*)

EVERETT (*with genuine irritation*) Whatever are you laughing about, Mother?

MARIA Forgive me, darling. It's just that it always amuses me to see how serious you have become nowaday. (*to* BULLETT) He was so boyish and playful for so long. (*innocently*) Right up until his twenty-first birthday he used to love to have me come to him and—

EVERETT Mother, please. Papa, how can you constantly talk about our *not* winning when— (*on his fingers*)—we have the finest generals in the country and a labor force of four million who can just go on working undisturbed. Why, don't you see—if we had to, we could put every white man in the South in uniform! Will the North ever be able to boast that? (*smiling at* BULLETT) What will happen to that great rising industrial center—if its men go off to war? (*he bends close to* BULLETT *so they can laugh together*) Who will run the machines then? New England school marms? (*they laugh heartily together. Hiram watches them and folds his hands on his stomach*)

HIRAM And may I ask something of you, my son?—When *you* and the rest of the white men of the South go off to fight your half of the war, who is going to stay home and guard your slaves? Or are they simply going to stop running away because then, for the first time in history, running away will be so easy?

(EVERETT's *mouth is a little ajar from the question, though it is far from the first time he has heard it. He and* BULLETT *are merely exasperated to hear it asked again. They begin to smile at one another as though a child had once again asked a famous and tiresome riddle*)

BULLETT (*waving his hands at absurdity*) Hiram, you know perfectly well that that is not a real consideration. Abolitionist nonsense that any other slave holder should know better than worry about!

HIRAM I see. Tell me something, Macon. How many slaves did you lose off your plantation last year?

BULLETT Why—two. Prime hands, too, blast them!

HIRAM Two. And Robley hit the jackpot with his new overseer: he lost five. And one from the Davis place. And I lost one. Let's see ... two, seven, eight, nine—from this immediate district ... in spite of every single precaution that we know how to take ...

BULLETT Oh, come on now, Sweet, everyone knows that the ones who run away are the trouble-makers, the malcontents. Usually bad workers ...

HIRAM Mmm-hmm. Of course. Then why are there reward posters up on every other tree in this county? Come man, you're not talking to a starry-eyed Yankee fool! You're talking to a slaveholder!

BULLETT I don't follow your point.

HIRAM You follow my point! We all follow my point! Or else will somebody here stop laughing long enough to tell me why you and me and Robley and all the others waste all that money on armed guards and patrols and rewards and dogs? And, above all, why you and me and every other planter in the cotton South *and* the Border States tried to move heaven and earth to get the Fugitive Slave laws passed? Was it to try and guarantee the return of property that you are sitting there calmly and happily telling me doesn't run off in the first place!

EVERETT Well, Papa, of course a few—

HIRAM A few my eyelashes! What's the matter with you two! I believe in slavery! But I also understand it! I understand it well enough not to laugh at the very question that might decide this war that you are just dying to start.

EVERETT You forget, Papa, it's not going to be much of a war. And if it is, then we can always arm the *blacks*! (HIRAM *puts down his cup with astonishment and even* MACON *looks at* EVERETT *askance for his naive remark*)

HIRAM (*with undiluted sarcasm*) I have to admit that my boy here is as logical as the rest of the leaders of our cause. For what could be more logical than the idea that you can give somebody a gun and make him fight *for* what he's trying like blazes to run away *from* in the first place. (*dryly*) I salute you, Everett, you belong in Washington—immediately—among your peers.

MARIA Now, Hiram—

EVERETT You don't have to be insulting, Papa.

HIRAM   I'll be what I please in this house and you'll mind your manners to me in the face of it! (EVERETT *looks to his mother in outrage for support*)

MARIA   Well dear, you shouldn't sass your father.

EVERETT   Mother, I am not Tommy! I am a grown man. Who, incidentally, any place but this would be running his father's plantation at my age.

HIRAM   You'll run it when I can depend on you to run it in my tradition. And not before.

EVERETT   Your "tradition" is running it to ruin!

MARIA (*upset*)   Everett, I'll not have it at the table. I simply won't have it at the table. (*to the younger boy to get him away from the argument*) You may excuse yourself and go to your room if you are through, Tommy. Say goodnight to Dr. Bullett.

TOMMY   Goodnight, sir. (*he exits*)

HIRAM (*immediately*)   So I am running it to ruin am I! You hear that, Macon! This polished little pepper is now one of the new experts of the South. Knows everything. Even how to run a plantation. Studied it in Paris cafes!

BULLETT   At this point, Hiram, I hear only that you must quiet yourself. (*looking at his watch*) In fact, let's get upstairs and get it over.

HIRAM   I don't feel like going upstairs and I don't feel like being poked all over with your little sticks and tubes.

BULLETT   I came over this evening to examine you, Hiram, and I am going to examine you if we have to do it right here at the table. (*he rises and gets his black bag and* MARIA *sits nodding her appreciation of his forcefulness with the difficult man*)

MARIA   He's been eating salt again, too, Macon. I declare I can't do a thing with him.

HIRAM (*to his wife*)   Yahhhhhh.

EVERETT (*watching his father's antics*)   Stubbornness, backwardness, disorder, contempt for new ways. It's the curse of the past and it is strangling us.

HIRAM   All I can say is that if you are the spirit of the Future it sure is going to be talkative.

MARIA   Can't you ever talk nicely to him, Hiram?

EVERETT   I don't want him to talk "nice" to me. For the 80 thousandth time, I am not a little boy!

HIRAM (*to* MACON)   Isn't there something you are always quoting to me from your Shakespeare about people protesting too much? (*to* EVERETT) Seems to me, son, that I haven't done too badly with what you seem to think are my backward ways. You can testify to that, can't you, Macon? Came into this country with four slaves and fifty dollars. Four slaves and fifty dollars! (*he becomes mellow and a little grand whenever he recalls this for the world*) I planted the first seed myself and supervised my own baling. That was thirty-five years ago and I made this one of the finest, though I am the first to admit, not one of the biggest, plantations in this district. So I must know a little something about how to run it.

EVERETT   Maybe you *knew* about running it.

HIRAM   I *know* about running it!

BULLETT   Calm down now, Hiram.

HIRAM (*to* MACON)   You know what HIS idea of running this place is? It's simple. It's the "modern" way. It's what everybody does. You put the whole thing in the hands of overseers! That's all! Then you take off for Saratoga or Paris. Those aren't planters who do that—those are parasites! I'm a cotton grower, and I'll manage my own plantation until I'm put under. And that I promise God!

EVERETT   Papa, can I ask you a simple unemotional question—when is the last time our yield came anywhere near ten bales to the hand? When, Papa? You tell me.

HIRAM   Well, the land is just about finished. Five bales to the hand is pretty good for our land at this point.

EVERETT (*looking triumphantly from his father to the other*)   And when are we going to buy new land?

HIRAM (*troubled in spite of himself*)   Next year if the crop is good.

EVERETT   And if the crop is poor? Listen close to this circular conversation, Macon. (*he waves his hand to point up the absurdity*)

HIRAM   Well, we'll borrow.

EVERETT   Yes—and then what?

HIRAM   We'll buy more land.

EVERETT   And who will work the extra land? You going to buy new slaves too?

HIRAM (*rubbing his ear*)   Well, if those Virginia breeders weren't such bandits we could take on one or two more prime hands—

EVERETT But they *are* bandits, and until such time as we can get some decent legislation in this country to re-open the African slave trade we have to meet their prices. So now what?

HIRAM Don't goad me!

EVERETT Don't goad you! What do you expect me to do, sit around and watch you let this place go bankrupt! You don't seem to understand, Papa, we don't have much choice. We have got to up our yield or go under. It's as simple as that. (*to the doctor*) You know what this place is, Macon? A resort for slaves! You know what they put in the fields here? I am ashamed to tell you. Nine and one half hours!

HIRAM Nine and a half hours is plenty of labor for a hand!

EVERETT (*almost shouting*) Not on that cotton-burned land it isn't! (*then fighting to hold himself in check*) Sure, I know—there was a time when the land was pure and fertile as a dream. You hardly had to do anything but just poke something in it and it grew. But that is over with. It has to be coaxed now and you have to keep your labor in the fields a decent length of time. Nine and one half hours! Why the drivers stroll around out there as though it were all a game. (*looking at his father*) And the high water mark gets higher and higher and higher. But he doesn't care! This is his little farm, run in his little way, by his dear old friends out there who understand him and love him: Fa-la-la-la-la!

MARIA I think that will do, son.

EVERETT Yes, that will do!—That will do—! (*he jumps up as if to leave the room*)

HIRAM Where are you going?

EVERETT I am going to find John Robley and his brother and—

HIRAM —drink and gamble the night away! Is that the way you would be master here! Sit down! (EVERETT *halts with his mouth open to speak to his father in outrage.* MACON *interrupts with a deliberately quiet note*)

BULLETT (*to* MARIA) Get him to take these four times a day, if you can, Maria. (*to* HIRAM) Not three times and not five times—*four*.

MARIA (*taking the bottle and going out with it*) I will try, Macon, I will try. (*to* EVERETT *as she passes him*) Do try not to upset your father so, darling. (*she kisses him lightly and pats his cheek and exits with the bottle*)

(EVERETT *moves to a window and stands looking out at the darkness in irritation.* BULLETT *clearly waits for* MARIA's *distance and then looks at his patient as he starts to put his things away.*)

BULLETT Well, Hiram—it's all over. (*from the finality of his tone,* EVERETT *turns slowly to listen and stare at them and* HIRAM, *who also understands the opening remark, at once also winds up for a great and loud protest*) No, I mean it. There's nothing left to joke about and no more trusting to luck. It's that bad. (HIRAM *stares hard at him and the protest starts to fall away as the gravity of his friend penetrates*) As much as you hate reading, you have got to buy all the books you can and spend the rest of your life doing very little else. That's all. I absolutely insist that you stay out of the fields.

HIRAM Well, now, just a minute, Macon—

BULLETT I'm sorry, Hiram—

HIRAM Well, your being sorry doesn't help me one bit!

EVERETT Papa!

BULLETT That's all right, son.

HIRAM What do you expect me to do with my plantation. Turn it over to him so he can turn it over to a pack of overseers?

BULLETT Well, I hadn't intended to get into that, Hiram, but since you ask me. I think it would be the best thing that could happen to the Sweet plantation. (*seeing that the remark has cut the man deeply he tries to amplify in the most impartial and reasonable tone*) You and I have to face the fact that this is a new era, Hiram. Cotton is a big business in a way it never was before. If you treat it any other way, you're lost. You just have to adjust to that, Hiram. For the good of yourself and for the good of the South.

HIRAM (*bitterly*) That's easy talk for a blue-blood, Macon! We all know that you came from a long line of lace-hankied Bordeaux wine-sniffers, but I think you forget that I don't.

EVERETT (*hating most of all that he should raise the question*) Papa, please!

BULLETT (*coolly*) I cannot imagine what makes you think I have forgotten. Certainly not your manners.

EVERETT (*obligatory*) Sir, I must remind you this is my father's house.

HIRAM (*to* EVERETT) Don't you ever hush? I'm sorry, Macon, I was a little insulting and a little—

EVERETT (*almost to himself, involuntarily*) —common. (*this is clearly* EVERETT's *anguish. All three men suffer a moment of extreme discomfort and* MACON *stirs himself for departure*)

BULLETT Well, that was an extraordinary meal as usual. That Rissa of yours is an eternal wonder.

HIRAM Macon, tell me something. Don't you have the grey hours, too?

BULLETT The what?

HIRAM The grey hours, you know what I mean, don't sit there looking dumb, I call them the grey hours, you probably call them something else. That doesn't matter. I know perfectly well you have 'em, whatever you call them. I think every man that draws breath on this earth has those hours when—well—when, by God, he wonders why the stars hang out there and this planet turns and rivers run—and what he's here for.

BULLETT Yes, I suppose we all do.

HIRAM Then what happens, Macon, if it's all a lie—the way we live, the things we tell ourselves?

BULLETT Oh, come now, Hiram...

HIRAM No, I mean it—what happens if there really is some old geezer sitting up there, white beard and all—

BULLETT I don't think I'm so unready to meet my Maker, Hiram. I haven't been the worst of men on this earth—

HIRAM Macon—*you own slaves.*

BULLETT Well, that's not a sin. It was meant to be that way. That's why He made men different colors.

HIRAM Is it? I hope so, Macon, I truly hope so.

BULLETT (*rising*) Hiram, I really must get on. No, don't call Maria. Harry can see me out. Good night, Everett.

EVERETT Goodnight, sir.

BULLETT (*touching his friend on his shoulder as he exits*) Books and long afternoon naps. Goodnight, Hiram.

HIRAM (*having become strangely quiet*) Goodnight, Macon. (*the Doctor exits*)

EVERETT (*turning on him savagely as soon as the man is out of sight*) Papa, why must you insist upon eternally bringing up your "humble beginnings"—

HIRAM (*sighing*) Goodnight, son. I want to be alone. I am tired.

EVERETT (*concerned*) Are—you all right?

HIRAM Yes. Goodnight. (EVERETT *does not say another word and exits quietly from the room as the planter sits on. Presently a stir in the shadows behind him makes him turn his head*) That you, Rissa? You there.

RISSA (*coming out of the shadows as all of the Negro servants seem to do when they are called or needed*) Yessah.

HIRAM (*himself*) There wasn't enough salt in the greens.

RISSA There was all you gon a get from now on.

HIRAM Now, Rissa—

RISSA If you aiming on killin' yourself, Marster Hiram, don't be askin' 'Riss to hep you none 'cause she ain't gona do it.

HIRAM One thing about always listening to other people's conversations, Rissa, is that you hear a lot of blasted nonsense.

RISSA I don't have to lissen to no other folks' conversations to see h'you ailin'. You sittin' there now, white as cotton, sweatin' like you seen the horseman comin'. (*she stands behind him and forces him to sit back in the chair with comforting gestures*) Lord, you one stubborn man. I spec you was allus the most stubborn man I ever come across.

HIRAM Took a stubborn man to do the things I had to do. To come into the wilderness and make a plantation. Came here with four slaves and fifty dollars and made one of the finest plantations in this district.

RISSA (*attending to him, gently, patiently, mopping his brow as she stands behind his chair*) Yessah. Jes you and me and old Ezra and Zekial who run off and poor old Leo who died last year.

HIRAM (*shaking his head*) You ever expect that Ezekial would run off from me after all those years?

RISSA 'Sprise me just as much as you. Reckon I don't know what gets into some folks.

HIRAM (*suddenly breaking into laughter*) Remember that time when we were building the old barn and Zeke fell from the loft straight into that vat of molasses you had put in there to cool the day before? By God, he was a sticky boy that day! (*he roars and she does also*)

RISSA —Come flyin' to me in the kitchen screamin', "Rissa, Rissa, I'se kilt, I'se kilt!"

Me and Ezra had to tie him down to wash him he was so scared. (*a new surge of laughter*) Finally had to shave his head like a egg, 'member?

HIRAM And the time the wild hogs went after the corn in the south fields and I had to go after them with the gun and Farmer Burns thought I was shooting at him!

RISSA Do I remember?—Why we had po'k round here for months after that!

HIRAM (*feeling festive*) Fetch the gun, Rissa, go ahead let's have a look at it—

RISSA (*fussing good-naturedly as she obeys reaching for a key hanging among a dozen or so keys on her belt*) I knew it! Every time you get to thinkin' 'bout them days I have to get out, that old gun so's you kin look at it. (*she opens a long drawer and pulls the old weapon out. It is wrapped in cloth and has been kept in excellent repair*)

HIRAM (*reaching out for it eagerly as she brings it to him*) Ah!—And still shoots true as an arrow ... (*he caresses it a little*) My father gave me this gun and I remember feeling, I was fourteen, I remember feeling, "I'm a man now. A true man. I shall go into the wilderness and not seek my fortune—but *make* it!" Hah! What a cocky boy I was! ... (HIRAM *is smiling happily*)

RISSA (*clearly getting ready to remind him of something. Placing both fists on her hips*) Speakin' of boys, Marster Sweet, ain't you forgot about a certain promise in the last couple of months?

HIRAM (*frowning like a boy being reprimanded*) Oh, Rissa, Maria says she won't have it. She put up a terrible fuss about it ...

RISSA (*just as childishly—they are, in fact, very much alike*) Marster, a promise is a promise! And you promise me when that boy was born that he wasn't never gona have to be no field hand ...

HIRAM But we need all the hands in the fields we've got and Maria says there is absolutely nothing for another house servant to do around here.

(*As he is saying this* MARIA *has re-entered with a single pill and a glass of water. She stands where she is and watches the two of them*)

RISSA He kin do a little bit of everything. He kin hep me in the kitchen and Harry some in the house. He's gettin' so unruly, Marster Hiram. And you promised me—

HIRAM All right, for God's sake! Anything for peace in this house! Soon as pickin's over Hannibal is a house servant—(RISSA *sees* MARIA *and becomes quite still*. HIRAM *follows her eyes and turns to see* MARIA *as she advances toward him with the medicine and water, her face set in silent anger. Shouting at her suddenly*) Because I say so, that's why! Because I am master of this plantation and every soul on it. I am master of those fields out there and I am master of this house as well. (*she is silent*) There are some men born into this world who make their own destiny. Men who do not tolerate the rules of other men or other forces. (*he is angry at his illness and goes into a mounting rage as the camera pans away from him to the slightly nodding* RISSA *who is cut of the same cloth in her individualism; to his wife who feels in the moment only clear despair for her husband, across the floor through the open door where* EVERETT *stands listening in half-shadow*) I will not die curled up with some book! When the Maker wants me, let him come for me in the place where He should know better than all I can be found ... (EVERETT's *face turns intently as if for the first time he is hearing the essence of his father*) I have asked no man's permission for the life I have lived—and I will not start now!

(*Fade out*)

ACT TWO

(*Fade in: interior,* EVERETT'S *bedroom—afternoon. He is sitting dejectedly alone. Drinking. The door bursts open and his mother stands there with urgency in her face*)

MARIA You had better come, son!

EVERETT (*with concern*) An attack?

MARIA Yes, I've sent for Macon. (*he rushes to her and steadies her*)

EVERETT It's all right, Mother. It's going to be all right.

(*Cut to: interior* HIRAM's *bedroom. The shades have been pulled and* HIRAM *lies stretched out on his back fully dressed. A male house servant is trying to gently remove his clothes.* EVERETT *and* MARIA *enter and go directly to his bedside*)

MARIA Hiram, Macon is on his way. Everything is going to be all right.

HIRAM Saw him that time... old horseman... riding out the swamps... He was smiling at me.

MARIA (*taking over from the servant in an effort to make him comfortable*) Just lie still. Don't talk. Macon will be here in a little while and everything will be all right.

EVERETT (*aside to the servant*) When did it happen?

SERVANT Jes a little while ago, suh. They found him stretched out yonder in the fields. Eben and Jed carried him up here and me and missus got him on the bed fust thing. I think he's powaful sick this time, suh.

HIRAM Fifty dollars and four slaves... planted the first seed myself...

(MARIA *looks at her husband intently in his pain and then rises with a new air of determination and signals for her son to follow her out of the room. He obeys—a little quizzically*)

MARIA (*to servant as they go out*) We'll be right here, Harry.

SERVANT Yes m'am.

MARIA (*in the hall, in half tones and with a more precise spirit than her son has ever seen before*) Do you propose to wait any longer now, son?

EVERETT (*confused*) For what—?

MARIA To become master here.

EVERETT Oh, mother...

MARIA Everett, your father is perfectly capable of killing himself. We must become perfectly capable of stopping him from doing it.

EVERETT You heard him last week—"Some men take their destiny"—Well—

MARIA (*sharply*) I am not interested in your bitterness at this moment, Everett. You must take over the running of the plantation.—no—listen to me, and you must make him believe you have done no such thing. Every night if necessary you must sit with pencil and pad and let him tell you everything he wishes. And then —well, do as you please. You will be master then. But he will think that he is still, which is terribly important. (*with that, she turns to the door*)

EVERETT You would deceive him like that?

MARIA (*only half turning to reply*) Under the circumstances, Everett, I consider that to be the question of a weak boy, when I have clearly asked you to be a very strong man. (*looking at him*) Which is the only kind I have ever been able to truly love. (*she turns and goes and the camera lingers with* EVERETT'S *face*)

(*Dissolve to: exterior: a small farm. A lean farmer stands in a corn field between rows of feeble burnt-out looking corn. A bushel basket sits at his feet. He reaches out and twists an ear off a stalk, pulls back the green shuck and looks at the ear with anger and despair and throws it roughly into the basket where other ears like it are collected. He picks up the basket and strides angrily toward his cabin.*

Cut to: interior of the cabin. His wife is working at the stove. The farmer kicks the door open roughly with his foot and walks in and slams the basket down with fury. The woman watches him)

ZEB That's aint corn. That's sticks! (ELIZABETH *wipes her hands and comes to inspect the corn. She picks up a piece or two and drops it sadly back into the basket*) Ain't nobody going to buy that! Can't hardly get a decent price when it's good, who's going to buy that?

ELIZABETH Well, take it in anyhow. We have to try at least, Zeb.

(*Two small children stand in a corner watching them, looking as if they might welcome the corn at the moment, no matter what its condition*)

ZEB Well then—you try! (*he strides across the floor and gets a jug down from the shelf and uncorks it and drinks deeply from it*)

ELIZABETH We ain't got no choice, Zeb.

ZEB I said all right, you try! (*more quietly*) How's Timmy?

ELIZABETH (*looking into the crib in a corner of the room*) He ain't been cryin' at least.

(*The man walks over to his baby's crib and then turns away and takes another drink from the jug only to discover that it is now empty. He looks at it and suddenly smashes it on the floor. An old man has appeared at the door which* ZEB *has left open*)

PREACHER H'dy do. (*he surprises both of them a little*)

ELIZABETH Oh, hello, Preacher, come on in.

PREACHER Thought I'd pay my respects to the Dudleys and mebbe find out why they ain't made it to meetin' in the last month of Sundays. Reckon I could stand a cup of lemonade too, if you got it handy, 'Lizabeth. (*he signals the two older children over without interrupting his remarks and gives them each a candy*) Zeb, you look like a stallion somebody been whippin' with a bull whip. (ZEB *strides out of the cabin and makes splashing sounds from a basin outside the door.* ELIZABETH *puts a glass of lemonade before the* PREACHER) What's the matter with Timmy, there?

ELIZABETH Got the group all week. (*her husband comes back in stripped to the waist, dripping water from his head. She puts lemonade for him also*)

PREACHER Now, that's better. Nothing to bring temper down off a man like a little cooling water.

ZEB I'm clearin', Preacher.

PREACHER Clearin' where, son?

ZEB Don't know. The West mebbe.

PREACHER Oh, the West?

ZEB (*defensively*) Well, a lotta folks been pullin' out going West lately.

PREACHER Lookin' for the Frontier again? I kin remember when this was the Frontier.

ZEB That was a long time ago.

PREACHER A long time. Before the big plantations started gobblin' up the land and floodin' the country with slaves.

ZEB I heard me some good things 'bout the West. That if a man got a little get up in him, he still got a chance. Hear there's plenty of land still. Good land.

PREACHER Seems to be three things the South sends out more than anything else. A steady stream of cotton, fugitive slaves and poor white folks. I guess the last two is pretty much lookin' for the same thing and they both runnin' from the first.

ZEB Not me—! No sir! I ain't runnin' from cotton! I'm lookin' for some place where I can plant me some, that's what! I know 'bout plantin' and I know how to drive slaves!

PREACHER And you figger you kin get to be somebody, eh? Like the Sweets, mebbe?

ZEB If I ever got my chance, I make that Sweet plantation look like a shanty! . . . Why you laughin' like that?

PREACHER Allus been a laughin' man, allus loved a good joke.

ZEB Well, I ain't told none.

PREACHER Yep, it's a hard life.

ZEB It's a hard life if you ain't got slaves.

PREACHER That what you think, Zeb?

ZEB That's what I know.

PREACHER Your Pa managed to be a pretty good farmer without slaves, Zeb.

ZEB My Pa was a fool.

PREACHER Sure hate to hear good men called fools. He was honest and he worked hard. Didn't call nobody master and caused none to call him master. He was a farmer and a good one.

ZEB And he died eatin' dirt. (*there is a sound of reining up outside the cabin.* ELIZABETH *goes to look out*)

ELIZABETH Why it's Everett Sweet, Zeb!

ZEB Who—(*he rises from the table with a quizzical expression and goes to the door and looks out to where Everett is sitting astride his horse*)

EVERETT (*abruptly*) I'm looking for a good overseer, Zeb Dudley.

ZEB (*feeling his way*) Well, what you come here for?

EVERETT I heard you had some experience driving slaves.

PREACHER (*coming and standing behind* ZEB *in the doorway, while* ELIZABETH *looks on with interest in the background*) Well, you musta heard wrong. This boy ain't cut from what makes overseers. He's a farmer.

ZEB (*scanning* EVERETT *with his eyes, interested*) I helped out once on the Robley place. I can handle blacks if I have to. But how come you interested? You Pa don't 'low no overseer on his place.

EVERETT My father is ill in bed. I'm master at our place now and I intend to grow cotton there—a *lot* of cotton and I want and need an overseer.

PREACHER (*to* ZEB) Tell him you don't know nobody 'round here for that kind of work, Zeb.

ZEB (*shrugging the* PREACHER's *hand off his shoulder*) Leave me be, Preacher. (*to* EVERETT) How much you figger to pay?

EVERETT I'll go as high as fifteen hundred if your work is good. And if you up my yield at the end of the year, I'll give you a bonus.

ZEB Your word on that, sir?

EVERETT You heard. But I want cotton.

ZEB (*vigorously*) For two thousand dollars—I'll get them slaves of yourn to grow cotton 'tween the rows!

EVERETT You're on. Be at our place early tomorrow.

ZEB You got yourself an overseer! (EVERETT *touches his hat to them and rides off.* ZEB *gives a yell and wheels and picks up his wife and whirls her around happily. She too is very happy. The* PREACHER *watches their celebration and sits down in his defeat*) Two thousand dollars! (*he tousles the hair of his kids and gets to the* PREACHER *at the table*) You a book-learned man, Preacher, help me figger that. Fertilizer, tools on credit, so's mebbe I could put the whole two thousand t'ward two prime hands—

PREACHER (*looking at him sadly*) So that's what it's come to 'round here. Man either have to go into slavery some kind of way or pull out the South, eh?

ZEB Aw, come on, Preacher—

PREACHER You think a man's hands was made to drive slaves?

ZEB If they have to, Preacher, if they have to . . . Or mebbe you think they was made to sit idle while he watches his babies turn the color of death?

PREACHER Zeb, I seen your daddy the day he come ridin' into this here country. Perched up on his pony with a sack of flour and some seed. And he done all right with them two hands of his. He dug in the earth with 'em and he made things grow with 'em. (*he takes* ZEB*'s hands*) Your hands is the same kind, boy.

ZEB Leave me be, Preacher.

PREACHER They wasn't meant to crack no whip on no plantation. That ain't fit thing for a man to have to do, Zeb. (*pointing after* EVERETT) Them people hate our kind. Ain't I heard 'em laughin' and talkin' 'mongst themselves when they see some poor cracker walkin' down the road—about how the ne-gras was clearly put here to serve their betters but how God must of run clear out of ideas when He got to the poor white! Me and you is farmers, Zeb. Cotton and slavery has almost ruined our land. N' some of us got to try and hold out 'ginst it. Not go runnin' off to do their biddin' every time they need one of us. Them fields and swamps and pastures yonder was give to us by Him what giveth all gifts—to do right by. And we can't just give it all up to folks what hates the very sight of us—

ZEB (*frightened inside by the sense of the speech*) You talk for yourself, Preacher! You go on bein' and thinkin' what you want. But don't be 'cludin' me in on it. I ain't never found nothin' fine and noble 'bout bein' no dirt-eater. I don't aim to end up no red-neck cracker the rest of my life, out there scrappin' on that near-gravel trying to get a little corn to grow. Allus watchin' sombody else's plantation gettin' closer and closer to my land. *I'm a white man, Preacher!* And I'm going to drive slaves for Everett Sweet and he's gonna pay me for it and this time next year, Zeb Dudley aims to own himself some slaves and be a cotton planter—you hear!

PREACHER Yes . . . I hear. And I reckon I understand. And all I kin say is—God have mercy on all of us . . .

(*Cut to: interior of* RISSA*'s cabin—late. Within a collection of slaves have formed a play circle around which various individual members of the group sing and perform "Raise a Ruckus."*)

ALL Come along, little children come along!
Come where the moon is shining bright!
Get along, little children get along—
We gon a raise a ruckus tonight!

(*Outside the cabin,* HANNIBAL *and* SARAH *linger a moment before going in*)

SARAH (*with a sense of conspiracy*) I seen you this morning, Hannibal.

HANNIBAL (*who is tuning his banjo*) Where—?

SARAH You know where! Boy, you must be crazy!

(HANNIBAL *looks frightened. Then waves it away and smiles at her and takes her by the arm and leads her in to join the others.* HANNIBAL *begins to accompany on his banjo.* JOSHUA *is in the center of the singing circle, rendering the verse*)

JOSHUA My old marster promise me
Mmm Mmm Mmm
That when he died he gonna set me free
Mmm Mmm Mmm
Well, he live so long 'til his head got bald
Mmm Mmm Mmm
Then he gave up the notion of dying at all!

ALL Come along! little children come along
Come where the moon is shining bright!

Get on board, little children get on board—
We're gonna raise a ruckus tonight!

SARAH My old mistress promised me
Mmm Mmm Mmm

(*mimicked*)

"Say-rah! When I die I'm going to set you free!"
Mmm Mmm Mmm
But a dose of poison kinda helped her along
Mmm Mmm Mmm
And may the devil sing her funeral song!

(SARAH *pantomimes gleefully helping* "Mistress" *along to her grave with a shoving motion of her hand. Chorus of song is repeated by all. A man is now pushed out to the center. He gets the first line out—*)

MAN Well, the folks in the Big House all promise me—(*his eyes suddenly see the slave who has just entered the cabin. It is* COFFIN, *the driver. The others follow his gaze and the song dwindles down and goes out completely and the people start to file out of the cabin with disappointment.*)

COFFIN (*looking about at them in outrage*) Jes keep it up! That's all I got to say—jes keep on! Oughta be shamed of yourselves. Good as Marster is to y'all, can't trust none of you nary a minute what you ain't 'round singing them songs he done 'spressly f'bid on this here plantation.

(*When the last of the guests are gone, including* SARAH, HANNIBAL *settles in a corner on the floor and* COFFIN *turns his attention on* RISSA *who has been sitting apart from the festivity mending by the light of the fire*)

RISSA Spect you better get yourself to bed, Joshua. H'you this evenin', Brother Coffin?

COFFIN There ain't supposed to be no singin' of them kind of songs and you knows it good as me!

RISSA H'I'm supposed to stop folks from openin' and closin' they mouths, man?

COFFIN This here your cabin.

RISSA But it's they mouths. Joshua-lee, I told you to get yourself in the bed. Don't let me have to tell you again.

COFFIN (*to* HANNIBAL *who has been sitting watching both of them with his own amusement*) Wanna see you, boy.

HANNIBAL I'm here.

COFFIN Yes, and it's the only place you been all day where you was *supposed* to be, too. (HANNIBAL *looks uncomfortably to his mother but she studiedly does not look up from her mending*) Jes who you think pick your cotton ever'time you decides to run off?

HANNIBAL Reckon I don't worry 'bout it gettin' picked.

COFFIN (*to* RISSA) Why don't you do something 'bout this here boy! I tries to be a good driver for Marster and he the kind what makes it hard for me.

HANNIBAL And what gon' happen when you show Marster what a good, good driver you is? Marster gon' make you overseer? Maybe you think he'll jes make Coffin Marster here—

COFFIN You betta stop that sassy lip of yours with me boy or—

HANNIBAL Or what, Coffin—?

COFFIN You jes betta quit, thas all. I'm—

HANNIBAL "—one of Marster Sweet's drivers"—

COFFIN And thas a fact!

HANNIBAL Get out this cabin 'fore you get smacked upside your head.

RISSA (*looking up from her sewing*) I guess that'll be enough from you, Mr. Hannibal.

HANNIBAL I say what I please to a driver, which, as everybody know, next to a overseer be 'bout the lowest form of life known.

COFFIN Why? 'Cause I give Marster a day's work fair and square and don't fool 'round. Like you, f'instant, with all your carryin' ons. Draggin' along in the fields like you was dead; pretendin' you sick half the time. Act like you drop dead if you pick your full quota one of these days. I knows your tricks. You ain't nothin'!

HANNIBAL Coffin, how you get so mixed up in your head? Them ain't my fields yonder, man! Ain't none of it my cotton what'll rot if I leaves it half picked. They ain't my tools what I drops and breaks and loses every time I gets a chance. None of it *mine*.

COFFIN (*to* RISSA, *shaking his head ruefully*) Them was some wild boys you birthed, woman. You gona pay for it one of these days too.

RISSA (*putting down her sewing finally*) What was I supposed to do—send 'em back to the Lord? You better get on back to your cabin now, Coffin. (COFFIN *exchanges various glances of hostility with them and leaves. As soon as he is gone the mother turns on the son*) Where do you run off to all the time, son?

HANNIBAL That's Hannibal's business.

RISSA (*with quiet and deadly implications*) Who you think you sassin' now?

HANNIBAL (*intimidated by her*) I jes go off sometimes, Mama.

(*she crosses the cabin to his pallet and gets a cloth-wrapped package from under it and returns with it in her hands. She unwraps it as she advances on him: it is a Bible*)

RISSA Is that when you does your stealin'? (*he sees that the matter is exposed and is silent*) What you think the Lord think of somebody who would steal the holy book itself?

HANNIBAL If he's a just Lord—he'll think more of me than them I stole it from who don't seem to pay nothing' it says no mind.

RISSA H'long you think Marster Hiram have you 'round his house if he thinks you a thief?

HANNIBAL He ain't got me 'round his house and I ain't aimin' to be 'round his house!

RISSA Well, he's aimin' for you to. Said last night that from now on you was to work in the Big House.

HANNIBAL (*in fury*) You asked him for that, didn't you?

RISSA He promised me ever since you was a baby that you wouldn't have to work in the fields.

HANNIBAL And ever since I could talk I done told you I ain't never gon' be no house servant, no matter what! To no master. I ain't, Mama, I ain't!

RISSA What's the matter with you, Hannibal? The one thing I allus planned on was that you and Isaiah would work in the Big House where you kin get decent food and nice things to wear and learn nice mannas like a real genamun. (*pleadingly*) Why right now young Marse' got the most beautiful red broadcloth jacket that I heard him say he was tired of already—and he ain't hardly been in it. (*touching shoulders to persuade*) Fit you everwhere 'cept maybe a little in the shoulder on account you a little broader there—

HANNIBAL (*almost screaming*) I don't want Marster Everett's bright red jacket and I don't want Marster Sweet's scraps. I don't want nothin' in this whole world but to get off this plantation!

RISSA (*standing with arms still outstretched to where his shoulders were*) How come mine allcome here this way, Lord? (*she sits, wearily*) I done tol' you so many times, that you a slave, right or not, you a slave. N' you alive—you ain't dead like maybe Isaiah is—

HANNIBAL Isaiah ain't dead!

RISSA Things jes ain't that bad here. Lord, child, I been in some places (*closing her eyes at the thought of it*) when I was a young girl which was made up by the devil. I known Marsters in my time what come from hell.

HANNIBAL All marsters come from hell.

RISSA No, Hannibal, you seen what I seen you thank the good Lord for Marster Sweet. Much trouble as you been and he ain't hardly never put the whip to you more than a few times.

HANNIBAL Why he do it at all? Who he to beat me?

RISSA (*looking only at her sewing*) He's your Marster, and long as he is, he got the right, I reckon.

HANNIBAL Who give it to him?

RISSA I'm jes tryin' to tell you that life tend to be what a body make it. Some things is the way they is and that's all there is to it. You do your work and do like you tol' and you be all right.

HANNIBAL And I tell you like I tell Coffin—I am the only kind of slave I could stand to be—a bad one! Every day that come and hour that pass that I got sense to make a half step do for a whole; every day that I can pretend sickness 'stead of health; to be stupid, 'stead of smart, lazy 'stead of quick—I aims to do it. And the more pain it give *your* Marster and the more it cost him—the more Hannibal be a man!

RISSA (*very quietly from her chair*) I done spoke on the matter, Hannibal. You will work in the Big House. (*there is total quiet for a while.* HANNIBAL *having calmed a little speaks gently to his mother*)

HANNIBAL All right, Mama. (*another pause*) Mama, you ain't even asked me what I aimed to do with that Bible. (*smiling at her, wanting to cheer her up*) What you think I could do with a Bible, Mama?

RISSA (*sighing*) Sell it like everything else you gets your hands on, to them white-trash peddlers comes through here all the time.

HANNIBAL (*gently laughing*) No—I had it a

long time. I didn't take it to sell it. (*he waits, then*) Mamy, I kin read it. (RISSA *lifts her head slowly and just looks at him*) I kin. I kin read, Mama. I wasn't goin' tell you yet. (RISSA *is speechless as he gets the book and takes her hand and leads her close to a place in front of the fireplace, opening the Bible*) Listen—(*placing one finger on the script and reading painfully because of the light and the newness of the ability*) "The—Book of—Jerimiah." (*he halts and looks in her face for the wonder which is waiting there. With the wonder, water has joined the expression in her eyes, and the tears come*)

RISSA (*softly, with incredulity*) —You makin' light of your old Mama. You can't make them marks out for real—? You done memorized from prayer meetin'—

HANNIBAL (*laughing gently*) No, Mama—"And I sais...Oh, that I...had wings like ...a dove...then would I...fly away...and...be at rest..." (*he closes the book and looks at her*)

RISSA Lord, Father, bless thy holy name I seen my boy read the words of the Scripture! (*she stares at him in joy and then, suddenly the joy and the wonder are transformed to stark fear in her eyes and she snatches the book from him and hurriedly buries it and runs to the cabin door and looks about. She comes back to him, possessed by clear terror*) How you come to know this readin'?

HANNIBAL (*smiling still*) It ain't no miracle, Mama. I learned it. It took me a long time and hard work, but I learned.

RISSA That's where you go all the time—Somebody been learnin' you—(*he hangs his head in the face of the deduction*) Who—?

HANNIBAL Mama, that's one of two things I can't tell nobody...I'm learnin' to letter too. Jes started but I kin write a good number of words already.

RISSA (*dropping to her knees before him in profound fear almost involuntarily*) Don't you know what they do to you if they finds out? I seen young Marster Everett once tie a man 'tween two saplin's for that. And they run the white man what taught him out the country...

HANNIBAL (*angrily*) I took all that into account, Mama.

RISSA You got to stop. Whoever teachin' you got to stop.

HANNIBAL (*tearing free of her*) I thought you would be *proud*. But it's too late for you, Mama. You ain't fit for nothin' but slavery thinkin' no more. (*he heads for the door*)

RISSA Where you going?

HANNIBAL With all my heart I wish I could tell you, Mama. I wish to God I could believe you that much on my side! (*he steps quickly into the night and the camera comes down on* RISSA's *deeply troubled face*)

(*Dissolve to: exterior—the fields—morning. Close up of a pistol in a holster slung about a mounted man's hips. We move back to see that it is Zeb astride his horse in the fields, surrounded by the drivers. A work song surrounds the dialogue.*

ZEB (*shouting a little because he is out of doors and topping the singing*) ...the hands are to be in the fields an hour and a half before regular time and we're cuttin' the noon break in half and we'll hold 'em an hour and a half longer than the usual night quittin' time. (*the drivers look at each other with consternation*) What's the matter?

DRIVER Jes that these here people ain't used to them kinda hours, suh. Thas a powaful long set. 'Specially when you figger to cut the midday break like that, suh. The sun bad at midday, suh. They kin get to grumblin' pretty bad, suh, and makin' all kinds of trouble breakin' the tools and all.

ZEB You gonna be surprised to find out how fast these people can learn to change their ways. And any hand who don't learn fast enough will learn it fast enough when I get through with 'em.

COFFIN Yessuh! They sho' will, suh! They got inta some bad habits, though, on accounta the way this here place been run. We got some hands, suh, that jes takes advantage of po' Marster Sweet. Breakin' his tools and runnin' off all the time—

ZEB (*with incredulity*) Running off—? Who runs off?

COFFIN Oh, Lord, suh! You don't know the carryin' ons what goes on 'round this here place. Some of these here folks done got so uppity they think Marster Sweet should be out there hoein' for them, that's what. (*pointing out* HANNIBAL *in a nearby row*) There's one there, suh. Lord, that one! You'll see what I mean soon, suh. Once a week he jes pick hisself up and run off somewhere, big as he please. I done told Marster and tol him and it don't do a bit of good.

ZEB Ain't he been flogged?

COFFIN Hmmmph. Floggin' such as Marster 'low don't mount to much. That one there, shucks, he jes take his floggin' and go on off next time like befo'. He's a bad one, suh.

ZEB (*looking to* HANNIBAL *and calling to him*) Come here, boy.

HANNIBAL (*straightening up and looking around as if he is not certain who is being summoned*) Who?

ZEB WHO?—YOU, that's who! Get yourself over here! (HANNIBAL *puts down his bag with a simmering sullenness and comes to the overseer*) What's the matter with your cap there? (HANNIBAL *draws off his cap, keeping his eyes cast to the ground. The other slaves sense trouble and slow down to watch.* ZEB *notices them*) Who called a holiday around here? Get to work! (*they stir with exaggerated activity for a few minutes and gradually slow down, more interested in the incident*) Raise your eyes up there, boy! (HANNIBAL *raises his eyes and looks in the other man's eyes*) What's his name?

COFFIN This be Rissa's boy, Hannibal. He got a brother who's a runaway. (HANNIBAL *looks at* COFFIN *with overt hostility*)

ZEB (*getting down from his horse, with his whip*) Well now, is that so? Well, what you doin' still hangin' 'round here? Ain't your brother never come back and bought you and your Mama and carried you off to Paradise yet? (*one or two of the drivers giggle*) Maybe you jus' plannin' to go on off and join him some day? (*he reaches up and with the butt end of his whip turns* HANNIBAL'*s face from side to side to inspect his eyes*) You carry trouble in your eyes like a flag, boy. (*he brings the whip up with power and lands it across* HANNIBAL'*s face. An involuntary murmur rises from the watching slaves. To them all*) That's right, for nothin'! (HANNIBAL *is doubled up before him, holding his face*) I hope y'all understand it plain! From now on this here is a plantation where we plant and pick cotton! There ain't goin' to be no more foolin', no more sassin' and no more tool breakin'! This is what can happen to you when you misbehave. Now, everybody get to work! And let's have a song there!—make noise, I say! (*singing comes up. He turns to the drivers*) Keep 'em at a good pace till the break, and for God's sake keep 'em singin'! Keeps down the grumblin'! (*noticing* HANNIBAL *still clutching at his face*) And that's enough of your play actin' there, boy. Get on back to your work in the rows. (HANNIBAL *obeys and goes to his row. We come down for a medium close shot of* ZEB *remounted, one hand poised on his hip, surveying the fields before him, gun at his hip, whip still in his fingers, watching the land that is not his.*)

(*Dissolve to: exterior: the veranda.* EVERETT *is lounging in a porch chair, sipping a drink.* ZEB *stands before him with his field hat in his hand*)

EVERETT All the same, it would have been better to have picked another boy. His mother is one of my father's favorite house slaves, and they have a way of getting him to know about everything that goes on in the fields.

ZEB (*hotly*) I reckon there's some things have to be left up to me if you want this here plantation run proper, Mister Sweet.

EVERETT (*slowly turning his eyes on the man and moving them up the length of his body with inspection which overtly announces his disgust at the sight of him*) And, as you say, "I reckon" you had better reckon on knowing who is master here and who is merely overseer. Let us be very clear. You are only an instrument. Neither more nor less than that. This is my plantation. I alone am responsible, for I alone am master. Is that clear?

ZEB (*looking back at his employer with hatred in kind*) Yes sir, I reckon that's pretty clear. (*they are interrupted by* COFFIN *coming onto the veranda at a run*)

COFFIN 'Scuse me, suhs, 'scuse me, but I got somethin' most pressin' to tell you, Marster.

ZEB Now what?

COFFIN He's gone agin, suh. He's out in the fields like I told you he do all the time!

ZEB HANNIBAL!

COFFIN Yessuh! Even with what you showed him an' all the other day, he done run off from the fields again t'day. But I fix him t'day, suh! Old Coffin knowed it was time for him to pull something like this again. I followed him, suh, yessuh. Coffin know whar he be—

ZEB Well, don't stand there like a dumb ape. Fetch him and put him in the shed and strip him and—(*looking with triumph at his employer*) —I'll attend to him there. (*to* EVERETT, *bitterly again*) That is, with your permission, sir.

The Drinking Gourd

COFFIN (*truly agitated*) You don't understand. He's with young Marster, suh!

EVERETT (*sitting up with interest for the first time*) He is with *whom*?

COFFIN Young Marster Tom, suh!

EVERETT (*with incredulity*) My brother?

COFFIN Yessuh!

ZEB Let's go!

EVERETT (*rising abruptly*) I'm coming with you.

(*Cut to:* HANNIBAL'*s clearing in the woods as per opening frame before titles. Simultaneously with a close-up shot of his head framed with a banjo neck are introduced stark, spirited banjo rhythms. Now the camera moves back to show the books and papers lying about where* HANNIBAL *and* TOMMY *sit. He finishes playing with a flourish and hands the instrument to the child who puts it awkwardly in his lap and carefully begins to finger it in the quite uncertain manner of one who is learning to play. He plucks a few chords as his teacher frowns.*)

HANNIBAL Aw, come on now, Master Tommy, get yourself a little air under this finger here. You see, if the fat of your finger touch the string then the sound come out all flat like this. (*he makes an unpleasant sound on the instrument to demonstrate and to make the boy laugh, which he does*) Okay, now try again. (TOMMY *tries again and the slave nods at the minor improvement*) That's better. (*comically cheating*) That's all now, time for my lessons.

TOMMY Play me another tune first, please, Hannibal?

HANNIBAL (*boy to boy*) Aw now that ain't fair, Marse Tom. Our 'rangement allus been strictly one lesson for one lesson. Ain't that right? (*the child nods grudgingly*) And ain't a genamun supposed to keep to his 'rangement? No matter how bad he wants to do something else?

TOMMY Oh, all right. (*holding out his hand*) Did you do the composition like I told you?

HANNIBAL (*with great animation reaching into his shirt and bringing up a grimy piece of paper*) Here. I wrote me a story like you said, suh!

TOMMY (*unfolding it and reading with enormous difficulty the very crude printing*) "The—Drinking—Gourd." (*he looks at his pupil indifferently*)

HANNIBAL (*a very proud man*) Yessuh, go on, read out loud, please.

TOMMY Why—don't you know what it says?

HANNIBAL Yessuh. But I think it make me feel good inside to hear somebody else read it. T'know somebody else kin actually make sense outside of something I wrote and that I made up out my own head.

TOMMY (*sighing*) All right—"The Drinking Gourd." "When I was a boy I first come to notice (all you have to say is came, Hannibal) the Drinking Gourd. I thought (there is a 'u' and 'g' in 'thought') it was the most beautiful thing in the heavens. I do not know why—but when a man lie on his back and see the stars there is something that can happen to a man inside that be (is, Hannibal) bigger than whatever a man is." (TOMMY *frowns for the sense of the last*) "Something that makes every man feel like King Jesus on his milk white horse racing through the world telling me to stand up in the glory which is called—freedom." (HANNIBAL *sits enraptured, listening to his words*) "That is what happens to me when I lie on my back and look up at the 'Drinking Gourd.'" Well—*that*'s not a story, Hannibal.

HANNIBAL (*genuinely, but less raptured because of the remark*) Nosuh?

TOMMY No, something has to happen in a story. There has to be a beginning and an end— (*he stops mid-sentence seeing the legs of three male figures suddenly standing behind* HANNIBAL. HANNIBAL *looks in his eyes and leaps to his feet in immediate terror*)

EVERETT (*in an almost inexpressible rage*) Get back to the house, Tommy.

TOMMY (*reaching for the banjo*) Everett, you wanna hear how I can play already? I was going to surprise you! Hannibal said we should keep it a secret so I could surprise you!

EVERETT Get home, at once! (*the child looks quizzically at all the adults and gathers up his books and goes off.* HANNIBAL *backs off almost involuntarily from the men.* EVERETT *continues to* HANNIBAL) So you told him it would be your little secret.

HANNIBAL I was jes teachin' him some songs he been after me to learn, suh! (*desperately*) He beg me so.

EVERETT (*holding the composition*) Did you write this—?

HANNIBAL What's that, suh?

EVERETT (*hauling off and slapping him with all his strength.* ZEB *smiles a little to himself, watching*) THIS!... Don't stand there and try to deceive me you monkeyfaced idiot! Did you write this...?

HANNIBAL Nosuh, I don't know how to write! I swear to you I don't know how to write! Tommy wrote it...

EVERETT Tommy could print better than this when he was seven! You've had him teach you to write, haven't you...

HANNIBAL Jes a few letters, Marster. I figger I could be of more use to Marster if I could maybe read my letters and write, suh.

EVERETT (*truly outraged*) You have used your Master's own son to commit a crime against your master. How long has this been going on? Who else have you taught, boy? Even my father wouldn't like this, Hannibal. (*a close-up shot as* EVERETT'S *hand reaches out and takes* HANNIBAL's *cheeks between his fingers and turns his face from side to side to inspect his eyes*) There is only one thing I have ever heard of that was proper for an "educated" slave. It is like anything else; when a part is corrupted by disease—(*suddenly with all his energy* HANNIBAL *breaks for it*)

ZEB Get him, Coffin! (*the driver tackles* HANNIBAL *and throws him to the ground and* ZEB *comes over to help subdue him, while* EVERETT *stands immobile, slapping his leg with his riding crop*)

EVERETT ... when a part is corrupted by disease—one cuts out the disease. The ability to read in a slave is a disease—

HANNIBAL (*screaming at him, at the height of defiance in the face of hopelessness*) You can't do nothing to me to get out my head what I done learned now... I can read! And I can write! You can beat me and beat me... but I can read... (*to* ZEB) I can read and *you* can't—(ZEB *wheels in fury and raises his whip.* EVERETT *restrains his arm*)

EVERETT He has told the truth. (*to* ZEB, *coldly*) As long as he can see, he can read... (ZEB *arrests his arm slowly and slowly frowns with understanding, looking at* EVERETT *with disbelief*) You understand me perfectly. Do it now. (ZEB, *astonished and horrified, looks from the master to the slave.* EVERETT *nods at him to proceed and the man opens his mouth to protest*) Proceed.

(ZEB *looks at the master one more time, slowly takes the butt end of his whip and slowly advances toward the slave who comprehends what is to be done to him.* EVERETT *turns on his heel away from the scene, and with a traveling shot, we follow his face as he strides through the woods and as presently the tortured screams of an agonized human being surround him... Fade out*)

ACT THREE

(*Fade in: exterior—plantation grounds. Late Night.*

The shadow of a man ingeniously strung by all four limbs between two saplings, each of which are bent to the ground away from each other. Two male shadows loom near and a voice says: "All right, guess we might as well cut him down now... gangrene must've set in."

*Dissolve to: interior—*HIRAM SWEET's *bedroom where he is in bed and conducting a violent tirade. A medicine bottle smashes against the fireplace and we move across to his bed where he is in the midst of an angry denunciation of* ZEB *and* EVERETT *who both stand in the center of the floor affecting various moods of defiance, fear and impatience.* MARIA *stands near her husband's bedside, wringing her hands for fear of what the mood will do to a cardiac.* EVERETT *reaches in a restraining gesture toward his father.*

HIRAM Don't you put your murderous hands on me!

EVERETT (*to his mother quietly*) Who in the name of God told him about it?

MARIA (*shrugging*) One of the slaves, of course. (*they look at the one lone house servant in the room who casts his eyes quickly away*)

HIRAM None of your business who told me! Should have been told before of your doings. Should have been told when you hired this—this—GET THIS CREATURE OUT OF MY SIGHT AND OFF MY LAND BEFORE I SHOOT HIM!

ZEB All I got to say is that I done as I was told, sir. I was just following instructions...

SWEET Get him out of here!

MARIA Please leave, Zeb.

ZEB Yes ma'am—but you got to tell him I just done as I was told.

EVERETT Oh, get out. (ZEB *exits*)

MARIA Now, darling, just calm yourself—
HIRAM (*to his son*) So this is the way you took over the plantation.
SERVANT Dr. Bullett, suh. (MACON BULLETT *enters in jubilant mood, with a newspaper*)
BULLETT Have you all heard the news—
MARIA Why, Macon, wherever are your manners today—?
BULLETT I'm so sorry, Maria, my dear. (*he bows to her a little and greets the two men, and then resumes his excitement*) Have you heard the news?
EVERETT What news—
BULLETT Why, my dear friends, the conflict has come to life! Gentlemen, ma'am, we fired on Sumpter two days ago. The South is at war.

(*There is total silence for a second and then* EVERETT *and* MACON *whoop with joy, and* EVERETT *climbs up and pulls a scabbarded sword from above the mantelpiece and begins to wave it about, alternately embracing* MACON)

MARIA Son, will you have to go?
EVERETT Oh, mother, of course, if I am offered a commission!
MARIA (*handkerchief to eyes*) Oh, my little darling. (*then slowly, all notice* HIRAM, *who has been stricken quiet and sober by the news*)
HIRAM (*with great sadness*) You fools... you amazing fools—
MARIA Now, Hiram—
HIRAM The South is lost and you two are jumping around like butterflies in your happiness.
EVERETT Lost! The South is going to assert itself, Papa. It is going to become a nation among nations of the world—
HIRAM —Don't you know that whoever that idiot was who fired on Sumpter set the slaves free? Well, get out the liquor, gentlemen, it's all over. (*pause*) A way of life is over. The end is here and we might as well drink to what it was.
BULLETT Now look here, Hiram—
HIRAM Look where? What do you want me to see? You look. You step to the window there and look at all those people that you and your kind have just set free.
EVERETT Oh, Papa, what is all this nonsense.
HIRAM (*slowly pulling on his robe*) I give you my word that they already know about it in the quarters. (*sadly*) They do not know who or how or why this army is coming. They do not know if it is for them or indifferent to them. But they will pour out of the South by the thousands, dirty, ignorant and uncertain what the whole matter is about. But they will be against *us*. And when those Yankee maniacs up there get up one fine morning feeling heady with abolitionist zeal and military necessity and decide to arm any and every black who comes ambling across the Confederate lines—and they will—because you will put on your uniforms and fight like fiends for our lost cause. But when the Yankees give them guns and blue uniforms, gentlemen, it will all be over.

MARIA Hiram, what are you doing? Where do you think you are going?
HIRAM (*pulling himself fully out of the bed*) I am going out to see Rissa.
BULLETT As your physician, Hiram, I expressly forbid you to leave that bed.
HIRAM Macon, shut up. My time is over. I don't think I want to see that which is coming. I believed in slavery. But I understood it; it never fooled me; I always knew it for what it was. It's just as well that we die together. Get out of my way now.

(BULLETT *stands back and he exits slowly. Cut to: exterior*—RISSA's *cabin.*

HIRAM *stands outside a moment. Somewhere in the distance, a slave sings plaintively.* He goes into the cabin.* RISSA *is at the fire, boiling something in a pot.* HANNIBAL *lies flat on a bed, his eyes covered by a cloth. One or two slaves file out wordlessly as the master enters. Occasionally* HANNIBAL *cries out softly.* RISSA *methodically tastes an extract she is preparing. She then dips a fresh white cloth in a second pot and wrings it out lightly and starts toward her son. Her eyes discover the master standing clutching at the collar of his robe, himself in panting pain. He is looking down at* HANNIBAL. *She looks at the master with uncompromising indictment and he returns her gaze with one of supplication, and drops his hands in a gesture of futility. She ignores him then and goes to the boy and removes the old cover and replaces it with a fresh one. The song continues*)

HIRAM I'll send for Dr. Bullett.
RISSA I doctorin' him.

* Perhaps "Lord, How Come Me Here?" "Motherless Child," "I'm Gonna Tell God All of My Troubles."

HIRAM But fever—
RISSA I' makin' quinine. Be ready soon.
HIRAM I—are you sure . . . I think I should get Bullett.
RISSA (*without looking up*) He put his eyes back? (*silence*)
HIRAM I—I wanted to tell you, Rissa—I wanted to tell you and ask you to believe me, that I had nothing to do with this. I—some things do seem to be out of the power of my hands after all . . . Other men's rules are a part of my life . . .
RISSA (*for the first time looking up at him*) Why, ain't you *Marster*? How can a man be marster of some men and not at all of others—
HIRAM (*the depth of the question penetrates too deeply and he looks at her with sudden harshness*) You go too far—
RISSA (*with her own deadly precision*) Oh—? What will you have done to me? Will your overseer gouge out my eyes too? (*shrugging*) I don't spect blindness would matter to me. I done seen all there was worth seein' in this world—and it didn't 'mount to much. (*turning from him abruptly*) I think this talkin' disturb my boy.

(*He looks at the face which will not turn to him or comfort him in any way, and slowly rises. He starts out and we follow him into the darkness several feet, a dejected, defeated figure, which suddenly collapses. He cries out for help and one by one the lights of the cabins go out and doors close. He crawls a little on the grass, trying to get back to* RISSA's *cabin. Inside, we see her at the table again, preparing another cloth for* HANNIBAL. *She lifts her eyes and looks out of the window to see the figure of the man she can distinctly hear crying for help. She lowers her lids without expression and wrings the cloth and returns to* HANNIBAL's *bedside and places it over his eyes and sits back in her chair with her hands folded in her lap. We come down on her face as she starts to rock back and forth as* HIRAM's *cries completely cease. Fade out.*

Fade in: exterior—the veranda—evening. MARIA *sits dressed heavily in black, not moving and not looking where she stares.* EVERETT *comes up the steps, he wears a Confederate Officer's uniform and a mourning band*)
EVERETT Mother . . . (*his manner with her is that of someone seeking very hard to distract another from grief preoccupation*) What would you think if I got the carriage and took you for a nice long ride in the cool out near the pines—?
MARIA No, thank you, son.
EVERETT Oh do—it would be so refreshing and cooling for you and tomorrow I think you should treat yourself to a nice social call on the Robleys—
MARIA (*pulling her shawl about her a bit*) Thank you, Everett, but I find it chilly right here tonight. And your father never cared for the Robleys.

(*He starts to argue a little, but looks at her and changes his mind and relaxes back in his chair and lets his eyes scan the darkness in front of him where his plantation lies stretched out as a sweet, gentle hymn rises up from the quarters, the same one as in the introduction to the narrator—* "Steal Away to Jesus")

EVERETT Yes—you're right. Let's just sit here in the peace and the quiet. The singing is pretty tonight, isn't it?
MARIA (*looking dead ahead*) Peaceful? Do you really find it peaceful here, Everett?
EVERETT Sure it is, mother. (*enthusiastically*) Things are going to go well now. Zeb is beginning to understand how I want this place run; the crops are coming along as well as can be expected and the slaves have settled down nicely into the new routine of the schedule. Everything is very orderly and disciplined. (*touching her hand gently*) Above all there is nothing for you to worry about. This thing will all be over soon and I'll be home before you know it and everything will be back to normal. Only better, Mama, only better . . .

(*The camera starts to pan away from them and moves down the veranda in through the front door, into the foyer and across to the darkened dining room where it discovers, at low angles which do not show her face,* RISSA's *figure in the darkness standing before the gun cabinet which she opens with the key which hangs at her waist. She removes the gun with stealth and closes the cabinet carefully and turns as we follow her skirts and rapidly moving bare feet across the dining room into the dark kitchen and out the back way. Waiting in the darkness outside is the boy,* JOSHUA. *Still unseen above her waist, she takes him by the hand and they go at a half run toward and into the woods. We stay with them until they* come to HANNIBAL's *clearing where* SARAH *stands, poised for traveling, and trembling mightily. Just beyond her is the figure of a man, seated, waiting patiently—the blind* HANNIBAL. RISSA *locks the other woman's hand about one of those of the child and thrusts the gun in the other and moves with them to* HANNIBAL, *who rises. There is a swift embrace and the woman and the child and the blind man turn and disappear into the woods.* RISSA *watches after them and the singing of "The Drinking Gourd" goes on as we pan away from her to the quarters where the narrator last left us. Only now his musket leans against the fireplace. Once again the slaves are gone. He walks into scene with his coat on now— buttoning it with an air of decided preparation. He looks at us as he does so, as he completes the attire of a private of—the Grand Army of the Republic.*

SOLDIER Slavery is beginning to cost this nation a lot. It has become a drag on the great industrial nation we are determined to become; it lags a full century behind the great American notion of one strong federal union which our eighteenth century founders knew was the only way we could eventually become one of the most powerful nations in the world. And, now, in the nineteenth century, we are determined to hold on to that dream. (*sucking in his breath with simple determination and matter-of-factness*) And so—(*distinct military treatment of "Battle Cry of Freedom" of the period begins under—*) we must fight. There is no alternative. It is possible that slavery might destroy itself— but it is more possible that it would destroy these United States first. That it would cost our political and economic future. (*he puts on his cap and picks up his rifle*) It has already cost us, as a nation, too much of our soul.

POSTSCRIPT

Notes on two songs: "follow the drinking gourd" and "steal away"*

FOLLOW THE DRINKING GOURD The most effective weapon employed by the Negro

* From: *Songs Of The Civil War*, edited by Irwin Silber (Bonanza Books, a division of Crown Publishers, by arrangement with Columbia University Press, 1960).

slaves in the war of attrition against their white masters was escape. Each year, hundreds of thousands of dollars in valuable slave property vanished from the South—borne mysteriously on the midnight trains of the Underground Railroad. This highly secret Abolitionist organization earned its name through the extra-legal activities of thousands of Negro and white Americans who maintained a continuous line of way-stations and hiding places for fleeing Negroes. The Fugitive Slave Law came into existence in a vain effort to stem this annual floodtide of escape.

This song is based on the activities of an Underground Railroad "conductor" by the name of "Peg Leg Joe." Joe was a white sailor who wore a wooden peg in place of his right foot which had been lost in some seafaring mishap.

Peg Leg Joe would travel from plantation to plantation in the South, offering to hire out as a painter or carpenter or handyman. Once hired, Joe would quickly strike up an acquaintance with many of the young Negro men on the plantation and, in a relatively short period of time, the sailor and the slaves would be singing this strange, seemingly meaningless song. After a few weeks, Joe would hobble on and the same scene would be enacted at another plantation. Once the sailor had departed, he was never heard of again.

But the following spring, when "the sun come back and the first quail calls," scores of young Negro men from every plantation where Peg Leg Joe had stopped would disappear into the woods. Once away from the hounds and the posses, the escaping slaves would follow a carefully blazed trail—a trail marked by the symbol of a human left foot and a round spot in place of the right foot.

Traveling only at night, the fleeing man would "follow the drinking gourd," the long handle of the Big Dipper in the sky pointing steadfastly to the North Star—and freedom. Following the river bank, which "makes a mighty good road," the slave would eventually come to the place "where the great big river meets the little river"—the Ohio River. There, "the old man was a-waiting"—and Peg Leg Joe or some other agent of the Underground Railroad was ready to speed the escapee on his way to Canada.

A good story, perhaps, or is it just an old folk legend? H. B. Parks of San Antonio, Texas, onetime chief of the Division of Agriculture in the State Research Laboratory writes:

> One of my great-uncles, who was connected with the (underground) railroad movement, remembered that in the records of the Anti-Slavery Society there was a story of a peg-legged sailor, known as Peg Leg Joe, who made a number of trips through the South and induced young Negroes to run away and escape.... The main scene of his activities was in the country immediately north of Mobile, and the trail described in the song followed northward to the head waters of the Tombigee River, thence over the divide and down the Tennessee River to the Ohio.

Park's uncle went on to confirm the story of the sailor's use of the song as a guide to the escaping slaves.

STEAL AWAY It is hard to think of a melody in any music more plaintive, more fragile, less militant in spirit and tempo than this, one of the most beautiful of the old spirituals. And yet, history shows that "Steal Away" was one of the most widely used "signal" songs employed by the slaves when they wanted to hold a secret conclave somewhere off in the woods.

And on closer examination, the song is seen to abound with the subterfuge and double-meaning imagery which a secret message would require. The "green trees bending" and the "tombstones bursting" certainly might refer to specific meeting places, and it takes little imagination to visualize the lightning-struck hollow tree or abandoned barn meant by the singer as he sang out, "He calls me by the lightning."

One researcher believes that the song was written by Nat Turner, leader and organizer of one of the most famous of the early nineteenth-century slave revolts. In any event, the song has lasted as a memory of secret, clandestine revolt, and as a musical testament to the creative capacity of the people whose heritage it is.

Alice Childress (–)

Wine in the Wilderness 1969

To fully understand *Wine in the Wilderness* and the transformation that Bill Jameson undergoes in the play requires some knowledge of the historical evolution of the black middle-class in America. In *Black Bourgeoisie*, E. Franklin Frazier in 1957 traces the origin of this class from slavery through the mid-twentieth century, when "society" in the black, segregated communities became based on "conspicuous consumption," or how lavishly one lived and entertained. In the 1950's, with the advent of the Civil Rights Movement, this social striving began to diminish; emphasis shifted from the desire to be "socially elite" to the desire for unity of all blacks. Older members of the black middle-class put aside their martinis and marched along with the young; those who did not march cheered from the sidelines.

The world watched as courageous black children walked through throngs of jeering, angry whites to integrate public schools; as young college students sat-in demanding full and equal use of public facilities; as an entire black community boycotted Montgomery, Alabama's public transportation system. Many blacks became disillusioned by the slowness of change, of "tokenism," and in some instances, of no change at all. More blacks became disillusioned when Dr. Martin Luther King, leader of this non-violent movement, met a violent death. The emphasis on unity became more apparent when blacks realized that the dream they had struggled to achieve was being "deferred." When passivism failed, may blacks turned to militancy as their only alternative for survival.

Bill Jameson is the product of the old black bourgeois values. Sonny-Man and Cynthia are also victims of this old social order. They are educated; They consciously and unconsciously label themselves "better" than Tommy and Oldtimer. They are empty, artificial people, preaching blackness, brotherhood, and love simply because it is in vogue. Innately they are cold, cruel, and self-centered individuals. They are reflections of the old slave masters, imitators of white middle-class, who accept Oldtimer (they don't even know his name) because they find him amusing, and Tommy only because they feel she can be used. They are the "Oreo Cookies—black on the outside, white on the inside," that blacks talk about. Frazier states that "... members of the black bourgeoisie suffer from 'nothingness' because when Negroes attain middle-class status, their lives generally lose both content and significance." This "nothingness" is what Bill seeks to escape in his suburban life, and is what he brings with him to Harlem. His orientation is white; no matter how hard he tries to assert his blackness, it remains surface and insignificant. Tommy refers to him as a "Phoney Nigger!" Sonny-Man's facade of blackness is his constant use of "brother" and "sister"; Cynthia tends to equate being a "soul sister" with the naturalness of her hair. The only "real" people in the play are Tommy and Oldtimer. They are both honest, not living under the illusion of false reality. True, Tommy "hopes" that Bill will seriously fall for her, but if he doesn't, she is prepared to move on: "... don't nothin' happen that's not suppose to." She is a sensible woman without pretense. The beauty of *Wine in the Wilderness* is in part due to the author's sensitive treatment of Tommy, "a poor, dumb chick that's had her behind kicked until it's numb," but whose warmth, compassion, inner dignity, and pride make her more of a woman than Cynthia will ever be. She is indeed the "wine in the wilderness" that Bill has conceived; when she undergoes a metamorphosis before his eyes, he suddenly becomes aware that she is the source of inspiration that he and the others so desperately need to find themselves, and their blackness. Alice Childress has created a powerful, *new* black heroine who emerges from the depths of the black community, offering a sharp contrast to the typically strong "Mama" figure that dominates such plays as *Raisin in the Sun*.

Wine in the Wilderness

CAST OF CHARACTERS

BILL JAMESON, *an artist aged thirty-three*
OLDTIMER, *an old roustabout character in his sixties*
SONNY-MAN, *A writer aged twenty-seven*
CYNTHIA, *a social worker aged twenty-five. She is Sonny-man's wife*
TOMMY, *a woman factory worker aged thirty*

(TIME *the summer of 1964. Night of a riot.*
PLACE *Harlem, New York City, New York, U.S.A.*

SCENE: *A one room apartment in a Harlem Tenement. It used to be a three room apartment but the tenant has broken out walls and is half finished with a redecorating job. The place is now only partly reminiscent of its past tawdry days, plaster broken away and lathing exposed right next to a new brick-faced portion of wall. The kitchen is now a part of the room. There is a three-quarter bed covered with an African throw, a screen is placed at the foot of the bed to insure privacy when needed. The room is obviously* black *dominated, pieces of sculpture, wall hangings, paintings. An artist's easel is standing with a drapery thrown across it so the empty canvas beneath it is hidden. Two other canvases the same size are next to it, they too are covered and conceal paintings. The place is in a beautiful, rather artistic state of disorder. The room also reflects an interest in other darker peoples of the world . . . A Chinese incense-burner Buddha, an American Indian feathered war helmet, a Mexican serape, a Japanese fan, a West Indian travel poster. There is a kitchen table, chairs, floor cushions, a couple of box crates, books, bookcases, plenty of artist's materials. There is a small raised platform for model posing. On the platform is a backless chair.*

The tail end of a riot is going on out in the street. Noise and screaming can be heard in the distance, . . . running feet, voices shouting over loudspeakers)

OFFSTAGE VOICES Offa the street! Into your homes! Clear the street! (*the whine of a bullet is heard*) Cover that roof! It's from the roof!

(BILL *is seated on the floor with his back to the wall, drawing on a large sketch pad with charcoal pencil. He is very absorbed in his task but flinches as he hears the bullet sound, ducks and shields his head with upraised hand, . . . then resumes sketching. The telephone rings, he reaches for phone with caution, pulls it toward him by the cord in order to avoid going near window or standing up*)

BILL Hello? Yeah, my phone is on. How the hell I'm gonna be talkin' to you if it's not on? (*sound of glass breaking in the distance*) I could lose my damn life answerin' the phone. Sonny-man, what the hell you callin' me up for! I thought you and Cynthia might be downstairs dead. I banged on the floor and hollered down the air-shaft, no answer. No stuff! Thought yall was dead. I'm sittin' here drawin' a picture in your memory. In a bar! Yall sittin' in a bar? See there, you done blew the picture that's in your memory . . . No kiddin', they wouldn't let you in the block? Man, they can't keep you outta your own house. Found? You found who? Model? What model? Yeah, yeah, thanks, . . . but I like to find my own models. No! Don't bring nobody up here in the middle of a riot . . . Hey, Sonny-man! Hey! (*sound of yelling and rushing footsteps in the hall*)
WOMAN'S VOICE (*offstage*) Dammit, Bernice! The riot is over! What you hidin' in the hall for? I'm in the house, your father's in the house, . . . and you out here hidin' in the hall!
GIRL'S VOICE (*offstage*) The house might burn down!
BILL Sonny-man, I can't hear you!
WOMAN'S VOICE (*offstage*) If it do burn down, what the hell you gon' do, run off and

leave us to burn up by ourself? The riot is over. The police say it's over! Get back in the house! (*sound of running feet and a knock on the door*)

BILL They say it's over. Man, they oughta let you on your own block, in your own house ... Yeah, we still standin', this seventy year old house got guts. Thank you, yeah, thanks but I like to pick my own models. You drunk? Can't you hear when I say not to... Okay, all right, bring her... (*frantic knocking at the door*) I gotta go. Yeah, yeah, bring her. I gotta go... (*hangs up phone and opens the door for* OLDTIMER. *The old man is carrying a haul of loot... two or three bottles of liquor, a ham, a salami and a suit with price tags attached*) What's this! Oh, no, no, no, Oldtimer, not here... (*faint sound of a police whistle*) The police after you? What you bring that stuff in here for?

OLDTIMER (*runs past* BILL *to center as he looks for a place to hide the loot*) No, no, they not really after me but... I was in the basement so I could stash this stuff, ... but a fella told me they pokin' round down there... in the back yard pokin' round... the police doin' a lotta pokin' round.

BILL If the cops are searchin' why you wanna dump your troubles on me?

OLDTIMER I don't wanta go to jail. I'm too old to go to jail. What we gonna do?

BILL We can throw it the hell outta the window. Didn't you think of just throwin' it away and not worry 'bout jail?

OLDTIMER I can't do it. It's like... I'm Oldtimer but my hands and arms is somebody else that I don' know-a-tall. (BILL *pulls stuff out of* OLDTIMER's *arms and places loot on the kitchen table.* OLDTIMER's *arms fall to his sides*) Thank you, son.

BILL Stealin' ain't worth a bullet through your brain, is it? You wanna get shot down and down and drown in your own blood, ... for what? A suit, a bottle of whiskey? Gonna throw your life away for a damn ham?

OLDTIMER But I ain't really stole nothin', Bill, cause I ain' no thief. Them others, ... they smash the windows, they run in the stores and grab and all. Me, I pick up what they left scatter in the street. Things they drop... things they trample underfoot. What's in the street ain' like stealin'. This is leavin's. What I'm gon' do if the police come?

BILL (*starts to gather the things in the tablecloth that is on the table*) I'll throw it out the air-shaft window.

OLDTIMER (*places himself squarely in front of the air-shaft window*) I be damn. Uh-uh, can't let you do it, Billy-Boy. (*grabs the liquor and holds on*)

BILL (*wraps the suit, the ham and the salami in the tablecloth and ties the ends together in a knot*) Just for now, then you can go down and get it later.

OLDTIMER (*getting belligerent*) I say I ain' gon' let you do it.

BILL Sonny-man calls this "The people's revolution." A revolution should not be looting and stealing. Revolutions are for liberation. (OLDTIMER *won't budge from before the window*) Okay, man, you win, it's all yours. (*walks away from* OLDTIMER *and prepares his easel for sketching*)

OLDTIMER Don't be mad with me, Billy-Boy, I couldn't help myself.

BILL (*at peace with the old man*) No hard feelin's.

OLDTIMER (*as he uncorks bottle*) I don't blame you for bein' fed up with us, ... fella like you oughta be fed up with your people sometime. Hey, Billy, let's you and me have a little taste together.

BILL Yeah, why not.

OLDTIMER (*at table pouring drinks*) You mustn't be too hard on me. You see, you talented, you got somethin' on the ball, you gonna make it on past these white folk, ... but not me, Billy-boy, it's too late in the day for that. Time, time, time, ... time done put me down. Father Time is a bad white cat. Whatcha been paintin' and drawin' lately? You can paint me again if you wanta, ... no charge. Paint me 'cause that might be the only way I get to stay in the world after I'm dead and gone. Somebody'll look up at your paintin' and say, ... "Who's that?" And you say, ... "That's Oldtimer." (BILL *joins* OLDTIMER *at table and takes one of the drinks*) Well, here's lookin' at you and goin' down me. (*gulps drink down*)

BILL (*raising his glass*) Your health, oldtimer.

OLDTIMER My day we didn't have all this grants and scholarship like now. Whatcha been doin'?

BILL I'm working on the third part of a triptych.

OLDTIMER A what tick?

BILL A triptych.

OLDTIMER Hot-damn, that call for another drink. Here's to the trip-tick. Down the hatch. What is one-a-those?

BILL It's three paintings that make one work . . . three paintings that make one subject.

OLDTIMER Goes together like a new outfit . . . hat, shoes and suit.

BILL Right. The title of my triptych is . . . "Wine In The Wilderness" . . . Three canvases on black womanhood. . . .

OLDTIMER (*eyes light up*) Are they naked pitchers?

BILL (*crosses to paintings*) No, all fully clothed.

OLDTIMER (*wishing it was a naked picture*) Man, ain' nothin' dirty 'bout naked pitchers. That's art. What you call artistic.

BILL Right, right, right, but these are with clothes. That can be artistic too. (*uncovers one of the canvases and reveals painting of a charming little girl in Sunday dress and hair ribbon*) I call her . . . "Black girlhood."

OLDTIMER Awwwww, that's innocence! Don't know what it's all about. Ain't that the little child that live right down the street? Yeah. That call for another drink.

BILL Slow down, Oldtimer, wait till you see this. (*covers the painting of the little girl, then uncovers another canvas and reveals a beautiful woman, deep mahogany complexion, she is cold but utter perfection, draped in startling colors of African material, very "Vogue" looking. She wears a golden head-dress sparkling with brilliants and sequins applied over the paint*) There she is . . . "Wine In The Wilderness" . . . Mother Africa, regal, black womanhood in her noblest form.

OLDTIMER Hot damn. I'd die for her, no stuff, . . . oh, man. "Wine In The Wilderness."

BILL Once, a long time ago, a poet named Omar told us what a paradise life could be if a man had a loaf of bread, a jug of wine and . . . a woman singing to him in the wilderness. She is the woman, she is the bread, she is the wine, she is the singing. This Abyssinian maiden is paradise, . . . perfect black womanhood.

OLDTIMER (*pours for* BILL *and himself*) To our Abyssinian maiden.

BILL She's the Sudan, the Congo River, the Egyptian Pyramids . . . Her thighs are African Mahogany . . . she speaks and her words pour forth sparkling clear as the waters . . . Victoria Falls.

OLDTIMER Ow! Victoria Falls! She got a pretty name.

BILL (*covers her up again*) Victoria Falls is a waterfall not her name. Now, here's the one that calls for a drink. (*snatches cover from the empty canvas*)

OLDTIMER (*stunned by the empty canvas*) Your . . . your pitcher is gone.

BILL Not gone, . . . she's not painted yet. This will be the third part of the triptych. This is the unfinished third of "Wine In The Wilderness." She's gonna be the kinda chick that is grass roots, . . . no, not grass roots, . . . I mean she's underneath the grass roots. The lost woman, . . . what the society has made out of our women. She's as far from my African queen as a woman can get and still be female, she's as close to the bottom as you can get without crackin' up . . . she's ignorant, unfeminine, coarse, rude . . . vulgar . . . a poor, dumb chick that's had her behind kicked until it's numb . . . and the sad part is . . . she ain't together, you know, . . . there's no hope for her.

OLDTIMER Oh, man, you talkin' 'bout my first wife.

BILL A chick that ain' fit for nothin' but to . . . to . . . just pass her by.

OLDTIMER Yeah, later for her. When you see her, cross over to the other side of the street.

BILL If you had to sum her up in one word it would be nothin'!

OLDTIMER (*roars with laughter*) That call for a double!

BILL (*beginning to slightly feel the drinks. He covers the canvas again*) Yeah, that's a double! The kinda woman that grates on your damn nerves, And Sonny-man just called to say he found her runnin' round in the middle-a this riot, Sonny-man say she's the real thing from underneath them grass roots. A back-country chick right outta the wilds of Mississippi, . . . but she ain' never been near there. Born in Harlem, raised right here in Harlem, . . . but back country. Got the picture?

OLDTIMER (*full of laughter*) When . . . when . . . when she get here let's us stomp her to death.

BILL Not till after I paint her. Gonna put her right here on this canvas. (*pats the canvas, walks in a strut around the table*) When she gets put down on canvas, . . . then triptych will be finished.

OLDTIMER (*joins him in the strut*) Trip-tick will be finish . . . trip-tick will be finish . . .

BILL Then "Wine In The Wilderness" will go up against the wall to improve the view of some post office . . . or some library . . . or maybe a bank . . . and I'll win a prize . . . and the queen, my black queen will look down from the wall so the messed up chicks in the neighborhood can see what a woman oughta be . . . and the innocent child on one side of her and the messed up chick on the other side of her . . . MY STATEMENT.

OLDTIMER (*turning the strut into a dance*) Wine in the wilderness . . . up against the wall . . . wine in the wilderness . . . up against the wall . . .

WOMAN FROM UPSTAIRS APT (*offstage*) What's the matter! The house on fire?

BILL (*calls upstairs through the air-shaft window*) No, baby! We down here paintin' pictures! (*sound of police siren in distance*)

WOMAN FROM UPSTAIRS APT (*offstage*) So much-a damn noise! Cut out the noise! (*to her husband, hysterically*) Percy! Percy! You hear a police siren! Percy! That a fire engine?!

BILL Another messed up chick. (*gets a rope and ties it to Oldtimer's bundle*) Got an idea. We'll tie the rope to the bundle, . . . then . . . (*lowers bundle out of window*) lower the bundle outta the window . . . and tie it to this nail here behind the curtain. Now! Nobody can find it except you and me . . . Cops come, there's no loot. (*ties rope to nail under curtain*)

OLDTIMER Yeah, yeah, loot long gone 'til I want it. (*makes sure window knot is secure*) It'll be swingin' in the breeze free and easy. (*there is knocking on the door*)

SONNY-MAN Open up! Open up! Sonny-man and company.

BILL (*putting finishing touches on securing knot to nail*) Wait, wait, hold on. . . .

SONNY-MAN And-a here we come! (*pushes the door open. Enters room with his wife* CYNTHIA *and* TOMMY. SONNY-MAN *is in high spirits. He is in his late twenties, his wife* CYNTHIA *is a bit younger. She wears her hair in a natural style, her clothing is tweedy and in good, quiet taste.* SONNY-MAN *is wearing slacks and a dashiki over a shirt.* TOMMY *is dressed in a mis-matched skirt and sweater, wearing a wig that is not comical, but is wiggy looking. She has the habit of smoothing it every once in a while, patting to make sure it's in place. She wears sneakers and bobby sox, carries a brown paper sack*)

CYNTHIA You didn't think it was locked, did you?

BILL Door not locked? (*looking over* TOMMY)

TOMMY You oughta run him outta town, pushin' open people's door.

BILL Come right on in.

SONNY-MAN (*standing behind* TOMMY *and pointing down at her to draw* BILL'S *attention*) Yes, sireeeeee.

CYNTHIA Bill, meet a friend-a ours . . . This is Miss Tommy Fields. Tommy, meet a friend-a ours . . . this is Bill, Jameson . . . Bill, Tommy.

BILL Tommy, if I may call you that . . .

TOMMY (*likes him very much*) Help yourself, Bill. It's a pleasure. Bill Jameson, well, all right.

BILL The pleasure is all mine. Another friend-a ours, Oldtimer.

TOMMY (*with respect and warmth*) How are you, Mr. Timer?

BILL (*laughs along with others,* OLDTIMER *included*) What you call him, baby?

TOMMY Mr. Timer, . . . ain't that what you say? (*they all laugh expansively*)

BILL No, sugar pie, that's not his name, . . . we just say . . . "Oldtimer," that's what everybody call him . . .

OLDTIMER Yeah, they all call me that . . . everybody say that . . . OLDTIMER.

TOMMY That's cute, . . . but what's your name?

BILL His name is . . . er . . . er . . . What *is* your name?

SONNY-MAN Dog-bite, what's your name, man? (*there is a significant moment of self-consciousness as* CYNTHIA, SONNY *and* BILL *realize they don't know* OLDTIMER'S *name*)

OLDTIMER Well, it's . . . Edmond L. Matthews.

TOMMY Edmond L. Matthews. What's the L for?

OLDTIMER Lorenzo, . . . Edmond Lorenzo Matthews.

BILL AND SONNY-MAN Edmond Lorenzo Matthews.

TOMMY Pleased to meetcha, Mr. Matthews.

OLDTIMER Nobody call me that in a long, long time.

TOMMY I'll call you Oldtimer like the rest but I like to know who I'm meetin'. (OLDTIMER *gives her a chair*) There you go. He's a gentleman too. Bet you can tell my feet hurt. I got one corn... and that one is enough. Oh, it'll ask you for somethin'. (*general laughter.* BILL *indicates to* SONNY-MAN *that* TOMMY *seems right.*
CYNTHIA *and* OLDTIMER *take seats near* TOMMY)
BILL You rest yourself, baby, er... er... Tommy. You did say Tommy.
TOMMY I cut it to Tommy... Tommy-Marie, I use both of 'em sometime.
BILL How 'bout some refreshment?
SONNY-MAN Yeah, how 'bout that. (*pouring drinks*)
TOMMY Don't yall carry me too fast, now.
BILL (*indicating liquor bottles*) I got what you see and also some wine... couple-a cans-a beer.
TOMMY I'll take the wine.
BILL Yeah, I knew it.
TOMMY Don't wanta start nothin' I can't keep up. (OLDTIMER *slaps his thigh with pleasure*)
BILL That's all right, baby, you just a wine-o.
TOMMY You the one that's got the wine, not me.
BILL I use this for cookin'.
TOMMY You like to get loaded while you cook? (OLDTIMER *is having a ball*)
BILL (*as he pours wine for* TOMMY) Oh, baby, you too much.
OLDTIMER (*admiring* TOMMY) Oh, Lord, I wish, I wish, I wish I was young again.
TOMMY (*flirtatiously*) Lively as you are,... I don't know what we'd do with you if you got any younger.
OLDTIMER Oh, hush now!
SONNY-MAN (*whispering to* BILL *and pouring drinks*) Didn't I tell you! Know what I'm talkin' about. You dig? All the elements, man.
TOMMY (*worried about what the whispering means*) Let's get somethin' straight I didn't come bustin' in on the party,... I was asked. If you married and any wives or girl-friends round here... I'm innocent. Don't wanta get shot at, or jumped on. Cause I wasn't doin' a thing but mindin' my business!... (*saying the last in loud tones to be heard in other rooms*)
OLDTIMER Jus' us here, that's all.

BILL I'm single, baby. Nobody wants a poor artist.
CYNTHIA Oh, honey, we wouldn't walk you into a jealous wife or girl friend.
TOMMY You paint all-a these pitchers? (BILL *and* SONNY-MAN *hand out drinks*)
BILL Just about. Your health, baby, to you.
TOMMY (*lifts her wine glass*) All right, and I got one for you... Like my grampaw used-ta say,... Here's to the men's collars and the women's skirts,... may they never meet. (*general laughter*)
OLDTIMER But they ain't got far to go before they do.
TOMMY (*suddenly remembers her troubles*) Niggers, niggers... niggers,... I'm sick-a niggers, ain't you? A nigger will mess up everytime... Lemmie tell you what the niggers done...
BILL Tommy, baby, we don't use that word around here. We can talk about each other a little better than that.
CYNTHIA Oh, she doesn't mean it.
TOMMY What must I say?
BILL Try Afro-Americans.
TOMMY Well,... the Afro-Americans burnt down my house.
OLDTIMER Oh, no they didn't!
TOMMY Oh, yes they did... it's almost burn down. Then the firemen nailed up my door... the door to my room, nailed up shut tight with all I got in the world.
OLDTIMER Shame, what a shame.
TOMMY A *damn* shame. My clothes... Everything gone. This riot blew my life. All I got is gone like it never was.
OLDTIMER I know it.
TOMMY My transistor radio... that's gone.
CYNTHIA Ah, gee.
TOMMY The transistor... and a brand new pair-a shoes I never had on one time... (*raises her right hand*) If I never move, that's the truth ... new shoes gone.
OLDTIMER Child, when hard luck fall it just keep fallin'.
TOMMY And in my top dresser drawer I got a my-on-ase jar with forty-one dollars in it. The fireman would not let me in to get it... And it was a Afro-American fireman, don'tcha know.
OLDTIMER And you ain't got no place to stay. (BILL *is studying her for portrait possibilities*)
TOMMY (*rises and walks around room*) That's

a lie. I always got some place to go. I don't wanta boast but I ain't never been no place that I can't go back the second time. Woman I use to work for say . . . "Tommy, any time, any time you want a sleep-in place you come right here to me." . . . And that's Park Avenue, my own private bath and T.V. set . . . But I don't want that . . . so I make it on out here to the dress factory. I got friends . . . not a lot of 'em . . . but a few *good* ones. I call my friend—girl and her mother . . . they say . . . "Tommy, you come here, bring yourself over here." So Tommy got a roof with no sweat. (*looks at torn walls*) Looks like the Afro-Americans got to you too. Breakin' up, breakin' down, . . . that's all they know.

BILL   No, Tommy, . . I'm re-decorating the place . . .

TOMMY   You mean you did this to yourself?

CYNTHIA   It's gonna be wild . . . brick-face walls . . . wall to wall carpet.

SONNY-MAN   She was breakin' up everybody in the bar . . . had us all laughin' . . . crackin' us up. In the middle of a riot . . . she's gassin' everybody!

TOMMY   No need to cry, it's sad enough. They hollerin' whitey, whitey . . . but who they burn out? Me.

BILL   The brothers and sisters are tired, weary of the endless get-no-where struggle.

TOMMY   I'm standin' there in the bar . . . tellin' it like it is . . . next thing I know they talkin' bout bringin' me to meet you. But you know what I say? Can't nobody pick nobody for nobody else. It don't work. And I'm standin' there in a mis-match skirt and top and these sneaker-shoes. I just went to put my dresses in the cleaner . . . Oh, Lord, wonder if they burn down the cleaner. Well, no matter, when I got back it was all over . . . They went in the grocery store, rip out the shelves, pull out all the groceries . . . the hams . . . the . . . the . . . the can goods . . . everything . . . and then set fire . . . Now who you think live over the grocery? Me, that's who. I don't even go to the the store lookin' this way . . . but this would be the time, when . . . folks got a fella they want me to meet.

BILL   (*suddenly self-conscious*)   Tommy, they thought . . . they thought I'd like to paint you . . . that's why they asked you over.

TOMMY   (*pleased by the thought but she can't understand it*)   Paint me? For what? If he was gonna paint somebody seems to me it'd be one of the pretty girls they show in the beer ads. They even got colored on television now, . . . brushin' their teeth and smokin' cigarettes, . . . some of the prettiest girls in the world. He could get them, . . . couldn't you?

BILL   Sonny-man and Cynthia were right. I want to paint you.

TOMMY   (*suspiciously*)   Naked, with no clothes on?

BILL   No, baby, dressed just as you are now.

OLDTIMER   Wearin' clothes is also art.

TOMMY   In the cleaner I got a white dress with a orlon sweater to match it, maybe I can get it out tomorrow and pose in that. (CYNTHIA, OLDTIMER *and* SONNY-MAN *are eager for her to agree*)

BILL   No, I will paint you today, Tommy, just as you are, holding your brown paper bag.

TOMMY   Mmmmmm, me holdin' the damn bag, I don' know 'bout that.

BILL   Look at it this way, tonight has been a tragedy.

TOMMY   Sure in hell has.

BILL   And so I must paint you tonight, . . . Tommy in her moment of tragedy.

TOMMY   I'm tired.

BILL   Damn, baby, all you have to do is sit there and rest.

TOMMY   I'm hungry.

SONNY-MAN   While you're posin' Cynthia can run down to our house and fix you some eggs.

CYNTHIA   (*gives her husband a weary look*)   Oh, Sonny, that's such a lovely idea.

SONNY-MAN   Thank you, darlin', I'm in there, . . . on the beam.

TOMMY   (*ill at ease about posing*)   I don't want no eggs. I'm goin' to find me some Chinee food.

BILL   I'll go. If you promise to stay here and let me paint you, . . . I'll get you anything you want.

TOMMY   (*brightening up*)   Anything I want. Now, how he sound? All right, you comin' on mighty strong there. "Anything you want." When last you heard somebody say that? . . . I'm warnin' you, now, . . . I'm free, single and disengage, . . . so you better watch yourself.

BILL   (*keeping her away from ideas of romance*)

Now this is the way the program will go down. First I'll feed you, then I'll paint you.

TOMMY Okay, I'm game, I'm a good sport. First off, I want me some Chinee food.

CYNTHIA Order up, Tommy, the treat's on him.

TOMMY How come it is you never been married? All these girls runnin' round Harlem lookin' for husbands. (*to* CYNTHIA) I don't blame 'em, 'cause I'm lookin' for somebody myself.

BILL I've been married, married and divorced, she divorced me, Tommy, so maybe I'm not much of a catch.

TOMMY Look at it this-a-way. Some folks got bad taste. That woman had bad taste. (*all laugh except* BILL *who pours another drink*) Watch it, Bill, you gonna rust the linin' of your stomach. Ain't this a shame? The riot done wipe me out and I'm sittin' here havin' me a ball. Sittin' here ballin'! (*as* BILL *refills her glass*) Hold it, that's enough. Likker ain' my problem.

OLDTIMER I'm havin' me a good time.

TOMMY Know what I say 'bout divorce. (*slaps her hands together in a final gesture*) Anybody don' wantcha, ... later, let 'em go. That's bad taste for you.

BILL Tommy, I don't wanta ever get married again. It's me and my work. I'm not gettin' serious about anybody ...

TOMMY He's spellin' at me, now. Nigger, ... I mean Afro-American ... I ain' ask you nothin'. You hinkty, I'm hinkty too. I'm independent as a hog on ice, ... and a hog on ice is dead, cold, well-preserved ... and don't need a mother-grabbin' thing. (*all laugh heartily except* BILL *and* CYNTHIA) I know models get paid. I ain' no square but this is a special night and so this one'll be on the house. Show you my heart's in the right place.

BILL I'll be glad to pay you, baby.

TOMMY You don't really like me, do you? That's all right, sometime it happen that way. You can't pick for *nobody*. Friends get to matchin' up friends and they mess up everytime. Cynthia and Sonny-man done messed up.

BILL I like you just fine and I'm glad and grateful that you came.

TOMMY Good enough. (*extends her hand. They slap hands together*) You 'n me friends?

BILL Friends, baby, friends. (*putting rock record on*)

TOMMY (*trying out the model stand*) Okay, Dad! Let's see 'bout this *anything I want* jive. Want me a bucket-a Egg Foo Yong, and you get you a shrimp-fry rice, we split that and each have some-a both. Make him give you the soy sauce, the hot mustard and the duck sauce too.

BILL Anything else, baby?

TOMMY Since you ask, yes. If your money hold out, get me a double order egg roll. And a half order of the sweet and sour spare ribs.

BILL (*to* OLDTIMER *and* SONNY-MAN) Come on, come on. I need some strong men to help me bring back your order, baby.

TOMMY (*going into her dance ... simply standing and going through some boo-ga-loo motions*) Better go get it 'fore I think up some more to go 'long with it. (*the men laugh and vanish out of the door. Steps heard descending stairs*) Turn that off. (CYNTHIA *turns off record player*) How could I forget your name, good as you been to me this day. Thank you, Cynthia, thank you. I *like* him. Oh, I *like* him. But I don't wanta push him too fast. Oh, I got to play these cards right.

CYNTHIA (*a bit uncomfortable*) Oh, Honey, ... Tommy, you don't want a poor artist.

TOMMY Tommy's not lookin' for a meal ticket. I been doin' for myself all my life. It takes two to make it in this high-price world. A black man see a hard way to go. The both of you gotta pull together. That way you accomplish.

CYNTHIA I'm a social worker ... and I see so many broken homes. Some of these men! Tommy, don't be in a rush about the marriage thing.

TOMMY Keep it to yourself, ... but I was thirty my last birthday and haven't ever been married. I coulda been. Oh, yes, indeed, coulda been. But I don't want any and everybody. What I want with a no-good piece-a nothin'? I'll never forget what the Reverend Martin Luther King said ... "I have a dream." I liked him sayin' it 'cause truer words have never been spoke. (*straightening the room*) I have a dream, too. Mine is to find a man who'll treat me just half-way decent ... just to meet me half-way is all I ask, to smile, be kind to me. Somebody in my corner. Not to wake up by myself in the mornin' and face this world all alone.

CYNTHIA About Bill, it's best not to ever count on anything, anything at all, Tommy.

TOMMY (*this remark bothers her for a split second but she shakes it off*) Of course, Cynthia, that's one of the foremost rules of life. Don't count on *nothin'*!

CYNTHIA Right, don't be too quick to put your trust in these men.

TOMMY You put your trust in one and got yourself a husband.

CYNTHIA Well, yes, but what I mean is . . . Oh, you know. A man is a man and Bill is also an artist and his work comes before all else and there are other factors . . .

TOMMY (*sits facing* CYNTHIA) What's wrong with me?

CYNTHIA I don't know what you mean.

TOMMY Yes you do. You tryin' to tell me I'm aimin' too high by lookin' at Bill.

CYNTHIA Oh, no, my dear.

TOMMY Out there in the street, in the bar, you and your husband were so sure that he'd *like* me and want to paint my picture.

CYNTHIA But he does want to paint you, he's very eager to . . .

TOMMY But why? Somethin' don't fit right.

CYNTHIA (*feeling sorry for* TOMMY) If you don't want to do it, just leave and that'll be that.

TOMMY Walk out while he's buyin' me what I ask for, spendin' his money on me? That'd be too dirty. (*looks at books. Takes one from shelf*) Books, books, books everywhere. "Afro-American History." I like that. What's wrong with me, Cynthia? Tell me, I won't get mad with you, I swear. If there's somethin' wrong that I can change, I'm ready to do it. Eighth grade, that's all I had of school. You a social worker, I know that mean college. I come from poor people. (*examining the book in her hand*) Talkin' 'bout poverty this and poverty that and studyin' it. When you *in* it you don' be studyin' 'bout it. Cynthia, I remember my mother tyin' up her stockin's with strips-a rag 'cause she didn't have no garters. When I get home from school she'd say, . . . "Nothin' much here to eat." Nothin' much might be grits, or bread and coffee. I got sick-a all that, got me a job. Later for school.

CYNTHIA The Matriarchal Society.

TOMMY What's that?

CYNTHIA A Matriarchal Society is one in which the women rule . . . the women have the power . . . the women head the house.

TOMMY We didn't have nothin' to rule over, not a pot nor a window. And my papa picked hisself up and run off with some finger-poppin' woman and we never hear another word 'til ten, twelve years later when a undertaker call up and ask if Mama wanta come claim his body. And don'cha know, mama went on over and claim it. A woman need a man to claim, even if it's a dead one. What's wrong with me? Be honest.

CYNTHIA You're a fine person . . .

TOMMY Go on, I can take it.

CYNTHIA You're too brash. You're too used to looking out for yourself. It makes us lose our femininity . . . It makes us hard . . . it makes us seem very hard. We do for ourselves too much.

TOMMY If I don't, who's gonna do for me?

CYNTHIA You have to let the black man have his manhood again. You have to give it back, Tommy.

TOMMY I didn't take it from him, how I'm gonna give it back? What else is the matter with me? You had school, I didn't. I respect that.

CYNTHIA Yes, I've had it, the degree and the whole bit. For a time I thought I was about to move into another world, the so-called "integrated" world, a place where knowledge and know-how could set you free and open all the doors, but that's a lie. I turned away from that idea. The first thing I did was give up dating white fellas.

TOMMY I never had none to give up. I'm not soundin' on you. White folks, nothin' happens when I look at 'em. I don't hate 'em, don't love 'em, . . . just nothin' shakes a-tall. The dullest people in the world. The way they talk . . . "Oh, hooty, hooty, hoo" . . . Break it down for me to A, B, C's. That Bill . . . I like him, with his black, uppity, high-handed ways. What do you do to get a man you want? A social worker oughta tell you things like that.

CYNTHIA Don't chase him . . . at least don't let it look that way. Let him pursue you.

TOMMY What if he won't? Men don't chase me much, not the kind I like.

CYNTHIA (*rattles off instructions glibly*) Let him do the talking. Learn to listen. Stay in the background a little. Ask his opinion . . . "What do *you* think, Bill?"

TOMMY Mmmmm, "Oh, hooty, hooty, hoo."

CYNTHIA But why count on him? There are lots of other nice guys.

TOMMY You don't think he'd go for me, do you?

CYNTHIA (*trying to be diplomatic*) Perhaps you're not really his type.

TOMMY Maybe not, but he's mine. I'm so lonesome... I'm *lonesome*... I want somebody to love. Somebody to say... "That's allright," when the World treats me mean.

CYNTHIA Tommy, I think you're too good for Bill.

TOMMY I don't wanta hear that. The last man that told me I was too good for him... was tryin' to get away. He's good enough for me. (*straightening room*)

CYNTHIA Leave the room alone. What we need is a little more sex appeal and a little less washing, cooking and ironing. (TOMMY *puts down the room straightening*) One more thing, ... do you have to wear that wig?

TOMMY (*a little sensitive*) I like how *your* hair looks. But some of the naturals I don't like. Can see all the lint caught up in the hair like it hasn't been combed since know not when. You a Muslim?

CYNTHIA No.

TOMMY I'm just sick-a hair, hair, hair. Do it this way, don't do it, leave it natural, straighten it, process, no process. I get sick-a hair and talkin' 'bout it and foolin' with it. That's why I wear the wig.

CYNTHIA I'm sure your own must be just as nice or nicer than that.

TOMMY It oughta be. I only paid nineteen ninety five for this.

CYNTHIA You ought to go back to usin' your own.

TOMMY (*tensely*) I'll be givin' that some thought.

CYNTHIA You're pretty nice people just as you are. Soften up, Tommy. You might surprise yourself.

TOMMY I'm listenin'.

CYNTHIA Expect more. Learn to let men open doors for you...

TOMMY What if I'm standin' there and they don't open it?

CYNTHIA (*trying to level with her*) You're a fine person. He wants to paint you, that's all. He's doing a kind of mural thing and we thought he would enjoy painting you. I'd hate to see you expecting more out of the situation than what's there.

TOMMY Forget it, sweetie-pie, don' nothin' that's not suppose to. (*sound of laughter in the hall.* BILL, OLDTIMER *and* SONNY-MAN *enter*)

BILL No Chinese restaurant left, baby! It's wiped out. Gone with the revolution.

SONNY-MAN (*to* CYNTHIA) Baby, let's move, split the scene, get on with it, time for home.

BILL The revolution is here. Whatta you do with her? You paint her!

SONNY-MAN You write her... you write the revolution into a novel nine hundred pages long.

BILL Dance it! Sing it! "Down in the cornfield Hear dat mournful sound... (SONNY-MAN *and* OLDTIMER *harmonize*.) Dear old Massa am-a sleepin' A-sleepin' in the cold, cold ground." Now for "Wine In The Wilderness!" Triptych will be finished.

CYNTHIA (*in* BILL's *face*) "Wine In The Wilderness," huh? Exploitation!

SONNY-MAN Upstairs, all out, come on, Oldtimer. Folks can't create in a crowd. Cynthia, move it, baby.

OLDTIMER (*starting toward the window*) My things! I got a package.

SONNY-MAN (*heads him off*) Up and out. You don't have to go home, but you have to get outta here. Happy paintin', yall. (*one backward look and they are all gone*)

BILL Whatta night, whatta night, whatta night, baby. It will be painted, written, sung and discussed for generations.

TOMMY (*notices nothing that looks like Chinese food. He is carrying a small bag and a container*) Where's the Foo-Yong?

BILL They blew the restaurant, baby. All I could get was a couple-a franks and a orange drink from the stand.

TOMMY (*tersely*) You brought me a frank-footer? That's what you think-a me, a frank-footer?

BILL Nothin' to do with what I think. Place is closed.

TOMMY (*quietly surly*) This is the damn City-a New York, any hour on the clock they sellin' the chicken in the basket, barbecue ribs, pizza pie, hot pastrami samitches; and you brought me a frank-footer?

BILL Baby, don't break bad over somethin'

to eat. The smart set, the jet set, the beautiful people, kings and queens eat frankfurters.

TOMMY   If a queen sent you out to buy her a bucket-a Foo-yung, you wouldn't come back with no lonely-ass frank-footer.

BILL   Kill me 'bout it, baby! Go 'head and shoot me six times. That's the trouble with our women, yall always got your mind on food.

TOMMY   Is that our trouble? (*laughs*) Maybe you right. Only two things to do. Either eat the frankfooter or walk on outta here. You got any mustard?

BILL (*gets mustard from the refrigerator*)   Let's face it, our folks are not together. The brothers and sisters have busted up Harlem, ... no plan, no nothin'. There's your black revolution, heads whipped, hospital full and we still in the same old bag.

TOMMY (*seated at the kitchen table*)   Maybe what everybody need is somebody like you, who know how things oughta go, to get on out there and start some action.

BILL   You still mad about the frankfurter?

TOMMY   No. I keep seein' pitchers of what was in my room and how it all must be spoiled now. (*sips the orange drink*) A orange never been near this. Well, it's cold. (*looking at an incense burner*) What's that?

BILL   An incense burner, was given to me by the Chinese guy, Richard Lee. I'm sorry they blew his restaurant.

TOMMY   Does it help you to catch the number?

BILL   No, baby, I just burn incense sometime.

TOMMY   For what?

BILL   Just 'cause I feel like it. Baby, ain't you used to nothin'?

TOMMY   Ain't used to burnin' incent for nothin'.

BILL (*laughs*)   Burnin' what?

TOMMY   That stuff.

BILL   What did you call it?

TOMMY   Incent.

BILL   It's not incent, baby. It's incense.

TOMMY   Like the sense you got in your head. In-sense. Thank you. You're a very correctable person, ain't you?

BILL   Let's put you on canvas.

TOMMY (*stubbornly*)   I have to eat first.

BILL   That's another thing 'bout black women, they wanta eat 'fore they do anything else. Tommy, ... Tommy, ... I bet your name is Thomasina. You look like a Thomasina.

TOMMY   You could sit there and guess til your eyes pop out and you never would guess my first name. You might could guess the middle name but not the first one.

BILL   Tell it to me.

TOMMY   My name is Tomorrow.

BILL   How's that?

TOMMY   Tomorrow, ... like yesterday and *tomorrow*, and the middle name is just plain Marie. That's what my father name me, Tomorrow Marie. My mother say he thought it had a pretty sound.

BILL   Crazy! I never met a girl named Tomorrow.

TOMMY   They got to callin' me Tommy for short, so I stick with that. Tomorrow Marie, ... Sound like a promise that can never happen.

BILL (*straightens chair on stand. He is very eager to start painting*)   That's what Shakespeare said, ... "Tomorrow and tomorrow and tomorrow." Tomorrow, you will be on this canvas.

TOMMY (*still uneasy about being painted*)   What's the hurry? Rome wasn't built in a day, ... that's another saying.

BILL   If I finish in time, I'll enter you in an exhibition.

TOMMY (*loses interest in the food. Examines the room. Looks at portrait on the wall*)   He looks like somebody I know or maybe saw before.

BILL   That's Frederick Douglass. A man who used to be a slave. He escaped and spent his life trying to make us all free. He was a great man.

TOMMY   Thank you, Mr. Douglass. Who's the light colored man? (*indicates a frame next to the Douglass*)

BILL   He's white. That's John Brown. They killed him for tryin' to shoot the country outta the slavery bag. He dug us, you know. Old John said, "Hell no, slavery must go."

TOMMY   I heard all about him. Some folks say he was crazy.

BILL   If he had been shootin' at *us* they wouldn't have called him a nut.

TOMMY   School wasn't a great part-a my life.

BILL   If it was you wouldn't-a found out too much 'bout black history cause the books full-a nothin' but whitey, ... all except the white ones who dug us, ... they not there either. Tell me, ... who was Elijah Lovejoy?

TOMMY Elijah Lovejoy, ... Mmmmmmm. I don't know. Have to do with the Bible?

BILL No, that's another white fella, ... Elijah had a printin' press and the main thing he printed was "Slavery got to go." Well the man moved in on him, smashed his press time after time ... but he kept puttin' it back together and doin' his thing. So, one final day, they came in a mob and burned him to death.

TOMMY (*blows her nose with sympathy as she fights tears*) That's dirty.

BILL (*as* TOMMY *glances at titles in book case*) Who was Monroe Trotter?

TOMMY Was he white?

BILL No, soul brother. Spent his years tryin' to make it all right. Who was Harriet Tubman?

TOMMY I heard-a her. But don't put me through no test, Billy. (*moving around studying pictures and books*) This *room* is full-a things I don' know nothin' about. How'll I get to know?

BILL Read, go to the library, book stores, ask somebody.

TOMMY Okay, I'm askin'. Teach me things.

BILL Aw, baby, why torment yourself? Trouble with our women, ... they all wanta be great brains. Leave somethin' for a man to do.

TOMMY (*eager to impress him*) What you think-a Martin Luther King?

BILL A great guy. But it's too late in the day for the singin' and prayin' now.

TOMMY What about Malcolm X.?

BILL Great cat ... but there again ... Where's the program?

TOMMY What about Adam Powell? I voted for him. That's one thing 'bout me. I vote. Maybe if everybody vote for the right people ...

BILL The ballot box. It would take me all my life to straighten you on that hype.

TOMMY I got the time.

BILL You gonna wind up with a king size headache. The Matriarchy gotta go. Yall throw them suppers together, keep your husband happy, raise the kids.

TOMMY I don't have a husband. Course, that could be fixed. (*leaving the unspoken proposal hanging in the air*)

BILL You know the greatest thing you could do for your people? Sit up there and let me put you down on canvas.

TOMMY Bein' married and havin' a family might be good for your people as a race, but I was thinkin' bout myself a little.

BILL Forget yourself sometime, sugar. On that canvas you'll be givin' and givin' and givin' ... That's where you can do your thing best. What you stallin' for?

TOMMY (*returns to table and sits in chair*) I ... I don't want to pose in this outfit.

BILL (*patience is wearing thin*) Why, baby, why?

TOMMY I don't feel proud-a myself in this.

BILL Art, baby, we talkin' art. Whatcha want ... Ribbons? Lace? False eyelashes?

TOMMY No, just my white dress with the orlon sweater, ... or anything but this what I'm wearin'. You oughta see me in that dress with my pink linen shoes. Oh, hell, the shoes are gone. I forgot 'bout the fire ...

BILL Oh, stop fightin' me! Another thing ... our women don't know a damn thing bout bein' feminine. *Give in* sometime. It won't kill you. You tellin' me how to paint? Maybe you oughta hang out your shingle and give art lessons! You too damn opinionated. You gonna pose or you not gonna pose? Say somethin'!

TOMMY You makin' me nervous! Hollerin' at me. My mama never holler at me. Hollerin'.

BILL I'll soon be too tired to pick up the brush, baby.

TOMMY (*eye catches picture of white woman on the wall*) That's a white woman! Bet you never hollered at her and I bet she's your girlfriend ... too, and when she posed for her pitcher I bet yall was laughin' ... and you didn't buy her no frankfooter!

BILL (*feels a bit smug about his male prowess*) Awww, come on, cut that out, baby. That's a little blonde, blue-eyed chick who used to pose for me. That ain't where it's at. This is a new day, the deal is goin' down different. This is the black moment, doll. Black, black, black is bee-yoo-tee-full. Got it? *Black is beautiful.*

TOMMY Then how come it is that I don't *feel* beautiful when you *talk* to me?!!

BILL That's your hang-up, not mine. You supposed to stretch forth your wings like Ethiopia, shake off them chains that been holdin' you down. Langston Hughes said let 'em see how beautiful you are. But you determined not to ever be beautiful. Okay, that's what makes you Tommy.

TOMMY Do you *have* a girl friend? And who is she?

BILL (*now enjoying himself to the utmost*) Naw, naw, naw, doll. I *know* people, but none-a this "tie-you-up-and-I-own-you" jive. I ain't mistreatin' nobody and there's enough-a me to go around. That's another thing with our women, . . . they wanta *latch* on. Learn to play it by ear, roll with the punches, cut down on some-a this "got-you-to-the-grave" kinda relationship. Was today all right? Good, be glad, . . . take what's at hand because tomorrow never comes, it's always today. (*she begins to cry*) Awwww, I didn't mean it that way . . . I forgot your name. (*he brushes her tears away*) You act like I belong to you. You're jealous of a picture?

TOMMY That's how women are, always studyin' each other and wonderin' how they look up 'gainst the next person.

BILL (*a bit smug*) That's human nature. Whatcha call healthy competition.

TOMMY You think she's pretty?

BILL She was, perhaps still is. Long, silky hair. She could sit on her hair.

TOMMY (*with bitter arrogance*) Doesn't *everybody*?

BILL You got a head like a rock and gonna have the last word if it kills you. Baby, I bet you could knock out Mohamud Ali in the first round, then rare back and scream like Tarzan . . . "Now, I am the greatest!" (*he is very close to her and is amazed to feel a great sense of physical attraction*) What we arguin' bout? (*looks her over as she looks away. He suddenly wants to put the conversation on a more intimate level. His eye is on the bed*) Maybe tomorrow would be a better time for paintin'. Wanna freshen up, take a bath, baby? Water's nice n' hot.

TOMMY (*knows the sound and turns to check on the look. Notices him watching the bed. Starts weeping*) No, I don't! Nigger!

BILL Was that nice? What the hell, let's paint the picture. Or are you gonna hold that back too?

TOMMY I'm posin'. Shall I take off the wig?

BILL No, it's a part of your image, ain't it? You must have a reason for wearin' it. (TOMMY *snatches up her orange drink and sits in the model's chair*)

TOMMY (*with defiance*) Yes, I wear it cause you and those like you go for long, silky hair, and this is the only way I can have some without burnin' my mother-grabbin' brains out. Got it? (*she accidentally knocks over container of orange drink into her lap*) Hell, I can't wear this. I'm soaked through. I'm not gonna catch no double pneumonia sittin' up here wringin' wet while you paint and holler at me.

BILL Bitch!

TOMMY You must be talkin' bout your mama!

BILL Shut up! Aw, shut-up! (*phone rings. He finds an African throw-cloth and hands it to her*) Put this on. Relax, don't go way mad, and all the rest-a that jazz. Change, will you? I apologize. I'm sorry. (*he picks up phone*) Hello, survivor of a riot speaking. Who's calling? (TOMMY *retires behind the screen with the throw. During the conversation she undresses and wraps the throw around her. We see* TOMMY *and* BILL, *but they can't see each other*) Sure, told you not to worry. I'll be ready for the exhibit. If you don't dig it, don't show it. Not time for you to see it yet. Yeah, yeah, next week. You just make sure your exhibition room is big enough to hold the crowds that's gonna congregate to see this fine chick I got here. (*this perks* TOMMY's *ears up*) You oughta see her. The finest black woman in the world . . . No, . . . the finest *any* woman in the world . . . This gorgeous satin chick is . . . is . . . black velvet moonlight . . . an ebony queen of the universe . . . (TOMMY *can hardly believe her ears*) One look at her and you go back to Spice Islands . . . She's Mother Africa. . . . You flip, double flip. She has come through everything that has been put on her . . . (*he unveils the gorgeous woman he has painted . . . "Wine In The Wilderness."* TOMMY *believes he is talking about her*) Regal . . . grand . . . magnificent, fantastic. . . . You would vote her the woman you'd most like to meet on a desert island, or around the corner from anywhere. She's here with me now . . . and I don't know if I want to show her to you or anybody else . . . I'm beginnin' to have this deep attachment . . . She sparkles, man, Harriet Tubman, Queen of the Nile . . . sweetheart, wife, mother, sister, friend. . . . The night . . . a black diamond . . . A dark, beautiful dream . . . A cloud with a silvery lining . . . Her wrath is a storm over the Bahamas. "Wine In The Wilderness" . . . The memory of Africa... The *now* of things... but best of all and most important... She's tomorrow... she's my tomorrow... (TOMMY *is dressed in the African wrap. She is suddenly awakened to the feeling of being loved and admired. She removes the wig and fluffs her hair. Her hair under the wig must not be an accurate, well-cut Afro... but should be rather attractive natural hair. She studies herself in a mirror. We see her taller, more relaxed and sure of herself. Perhaps braided hair will go well with Afro robe*) Aw, man, later. You don't believe in nothin'! (*he covers "Wine In The Wilderness." Is now in a glowing mood*) Baby, whenever you ready. (*she emerges from behind the screen. Dressed in the wrap, sans wig. He is astounded*) Baby, what...? Where... where's the wig?

TOMMY I don't think I want to wear it, Bill.

BILL That is very becoming... the drape thing.

TOMMY Thank you.

BILL I don't know what to say.

TOMMY It's time to paint. (*steps up on the model stand and sits in the chair. She is now a queen, relaxed and smiling her appreciation for his last speech to the art dealer. Her feet are bare*)

BILL (*mystified by the change in her. Tries to do a charcoal sketch*) It is quite late.

TOMMY Makes me no difference if it's all right with you.

BILL (*wants to create the other image*) Could you put the wig back on?

TOMMY You don't really like wigs, do you?

BILL Well, no.

TOMMY Then let's have things the way you like.

BILL (*has no answer for this. He makes a haphazard line or two as he tries to remember the other image*) Tell me something about yourself, ... anything.

TOMMY (*now on sure ground*) I was born in Baltimore, Maryland and raised here in Harlem. My favorite flower is "Four O'clocks," that's a bush flower. My wearin' flower, corsage flower, is pink roses. My mama raised me, mostly by herself, God rest the dead. Mama belonged to "The Eastern Star." Her father was a "Mason." If a man in the family is a "Mason" any woman related to him can be an "Eastern Star." My grandfather was a member of "The Prince Hall Lodge." I had a uncle who was an "Elk,"... a member of "The Improved Benevolent Protective Order of Elks of the World": "The Henry Lincoln Johnson Lodge." You know, the white "Elks" are called "The Benevolent Protective Order of Elks" but the black "Elks" are called "The *Improved* Benevolent Protective Order of Elks of *the World*." That's because the black "Elks" got the copyright first but the white "Elks" took us to court about it to keep us from usin' the name. Over fifteen hundred black folk went to jail for wearin' the "Elk" emblem on their coat lapel. Years ago, ... that's what you call history.

BILL I didn't know about that.

TOMMY Oh, it's understandable. Only way I heard bout John Brown was because the black "Elks" bought his farmhouse where he trained his men to attack the government.

BILL The black "Elks" bought the John Brown Farm? What did they do with it?

TOMMY They built a outdoor theater and put a perpetual light in his memory, ... and they buildin' cottages there, one named for each state in the union and ...

BILL How do you know about it?

TOMMY Well, our "Elks" helped my cousin go through school with a scholarship. She won a speaking contest and wrote a composition titled "Onward and Upward, O, My Race." That's how she won the scholarship. Coreen knows all that Elk history.

BILL (*seeing her with new eyes*) Tell me some more about you, Tomorrow Marie. I bet you go to church.

TOMMY Not much as I used to. Early in life I pledged myself in the A.M.E. Zion Church.

BILL (*studying her face, seeing her for the first time*) A.M.E.

TOMMY A.M.E. That's African Methodist Episcopal. We split off from the white Methodist Episcopal and started our own in the year Seventeen hundred and ninety six. We built our first buildin' in the year 1800. How 'bout that?

BILL That right?

TOMMY Oh, I'm just showin' off. I taught Sunday School for two years and you had to know the history of A.M.E. Zion... or else you couldn't teach. My great, great grandparents was slaves.

BILL Guess everybody's was.

TOMMY Mine was slaves in a place called

Sweetwater Springs, Virginia. We tried to look it up one time but somebody at Church told us that Sweetwater Springs had become a part of Norfolk ... so we didn't carry it any further ... As it would be a expense to have a lawyer trace your people.

BILL (*throws charcoal pencil across room*) No good! It won't work! I can't work anymore.

TOMMY   Take a rest. Tell me about you.

BILL (*sits on bed*) Everybody in my family worked for the Post Office. They bought a home in Jamaica, Long Island. Everybody on that block bought an aluminum screen door with a duck on it, ... or was it a swan? I guess that makes my favorite flower crab grass and hedges. I have a lot of bad dreams. (TOMMY *massages his temples and the back of his neck*) A dream like suffocating, dying of suffocation. The worst kinda dream. People are standing in a weird looking art gallery, they're looking and laughing at everything I've ever done. My work begins to fade off the canvas, right before my eyes. Everything I've ever done is laughed away.

TOMMY   Don't be so hard on yourself. If I was smart as you I'd wake up singin' every mornin'. (*there is the sound of thunder. He kisses her*) When it thunders that's the angels in heaven playin', with their hoops, rollin' their hoops and bicycle wheels in the rain. My Mama told me that.

BILL   I'm glad you're here. Black *is* beautiful, you're beautiful, A.M.E. Zion, Elks, pink roses, bush flower, ... blooming out of the slavery of Sweetwater Springs, Virginia.

TOMMY   I'm gonna take a bath and let the riot and the hell of living go down the drain with the bath water.

BILL   Tommy, Tommy, Tomorrow Marie, let's save each other, let's be kind and good to each other while it rains and the angels roll those hoops and bicycle wheels.

(*They embrace. The sound of rain. Music in as lights come down. As lights fade down to darkness, music comes in louder. There is a flash of lightning. We see* TOMMY *and* BILL *in each other's arms. It is very dark. Music up louder, then softer and down to very soft. Music is mixed with the sound of rain beating against the window. Music slowly fades as gray light of dawn shows at window. Lights go up gradually. The bed is rumpled and empty.* BILL *is in the bathroom.* TOMMY *is at the stove turning off the coffee pot. She sets table with cups and saucers, spoons.* TOMMY's *hair is natural, she wears another throw [African design] draped around her. She sings and hums a snatch of a joyous spiritual.*)

TOMMY   "Great day, Great day, the world's on fire, Great day ..." (*calling out to* BILL *who is in the bath*) Honey, I found the coffee, and it's ready. Nothin' here to go with it but a cucumber and a Uneeda biscuit.

BILL (*offstage. Joyous yell from offstage*) Tomorrow and tomorrow and tomorrow! Good mornin', Tomorrow!

TOMMY (*more to herself than to* BILL) "Tomorrow and tomorrow." That's Shakespeare. (*calls to* BILL) You say that was Shakespeare?

BILL (*offstage*)   Right, baby, right!

TOMMY   I bet Shakespeare was black! You know how we love poetry. That's what give him away. I bet he was passin'. (*laughs*)

BILL (*offstage*) Just you wait, one hundred years from now all the honkeys gonna claim our poets just like they stole our blues. They gonna try to steal Paul Laurence Dunbar and LeRoi and Margaret Walker.

TOMMY (*to herself*) God moves in a mysterious way, even in the middle of a riot. (*a knock on the door*) Great day, great day the world's on fire ... (*opens the door.* OLDTIMER *enters. He is soaking wet. He does not recognize her right away*)

OLDTIMER   'Scuse me, I must be in the wrong place.

TOMMY (*patting her hair*)   This is me. Come on in, Edmond Lorenzo Matthews. I took off my hair-piece. This is me.

OLDTIMER (*very distracted and worried*) Well, howdy-do and good mornin'. (*he has had a hard night of drinking and sleeplessness*) Where Billy-boy? It pourin' down some rain out there. (*makes his way to the window*)

TOMMY   What's the matter?

OLDTIMER (*raises the window and starts pulling in the cord, the cord is weightless and he realizes there is nothing on the end of it*) No, no, it can't be. Where is it? It's gone! (*looks out the window*)

TOMMY   You gonna catch your death. You wringin' wet.

OLDTIMER   Yall take my things in? It was a bag-a loot. A suit and some odds and ends. It was my loot. Yall took it in?

TOMMY No. (*realizes his desperation. She calls to* BILL *through the closed bathroom door*) Did you take in any loot that was outside the window?
BILL (*offstage*) No.
TOMMY He said "no."
OLDTIMER (*yells out window*) Thieves, ... dirty thieves ... lotta good it'll do you ...
TOMMY (*leads him to a chair, dries his head with a towel*) Get outta the wet things. You smell just like a whiskey still. Why don't you take care of yourself. (*dries off his hands*)
OLDTIMER Drinkin' with the boys. Likker was everywhere all night long.
TOMMY You got to be better than this.
OLDTIMER Everything I ever put my hand and mind to do, it turn out wrong, ... Nothin' but mistakes ... When you don' know, you don' know. I don' know nothin'. I'm ignorant.
TOMMY Hush that talk ... You know lotsa things, everybody does. (*helps him remove wet coat*)
OLDTIMER Thanks. How's the trip-tick?
TOMMY The what?
OLDTIMER *Trip-tick*. That's a paintin'.
TOMMY See there, you know more about art than I do. What's a trip-tick? Have some coffee and explain me a trip-tick.
OLDTIMER (*proud of his knowledge*) Well, I tell you, ... a trip-tick is a paintin' that's in three parts ... but they all belong together to be looked at all at once. Now ... this is the first one ... a little innocent girl ... (*unveils picture*)
TOMMY She's sweet.
OLDTIMER And this is "Wine In The Wilderness" ... The Queen of the Universe ... the finest chick in the world.
TOMMY (TOMMY *is thoughtful as he unveils the second picture*) That's not me.
OLDTIMER No, you gonna be this here last one. The worst gal in town. A messed-up chick that—that— (*he unveils the third canvas and is face to face with the almost blank canvas, then realizes what he has said. He turns to see the stricken look on* TOMMY'*s face*)
TOMMY The messed-up chick, *that's* why they brought me here, ain't it? That's why he wanted to paint me! Say it!
OLDTIMER No, I'm lyin', I didn't mean it. It's the society that messed her up. Awwwwww, Tommy, don't look that-a-way. It's art, ... it's only art ... He couldn't mean you ... it's art

... (*the door opens.* CYNTHIA *and* SONNY-MAN *enter*)
SONNY-MAN Anybody want a ride down ... down ... down ... downtown? What's wrong? Excuse me ... (*starts back out*)
TOMMY (*blocking the exit to* CYNTHIA *and* SONNY-MAN) No, come on in. Stay with it ... "Brother" ... "Sister." Tell 'em what a trip-tick is, Oldtimer.
CYNTHIA (*very ashamed*) Oh, no.
TOMMY You don't have to tell 'em. They already know. The messed-up chick! How come you didn't pose for that, my sister? The messed-up chick lost her home last night, ... burnt out with no place to go. You and Sonny-man gave me comfort, you cheered me up and took me in, ... *took me in!*
CYNTHIA Tommy, we didn't know you, we didn't mean ...
TOMMY It's all right! I was lost but now I'm found! Yeah, the blind can see! (*she dashes behind the screen and puts on her clothing, sweater, skirt etc.*)
OLDTIMER (*goes to bathroom door*) Billy, come out!
SONNY-MAN Billy, step out here, please! (BILL *enters shirtless, wearing dungarees*) Oldtimer let it out 'bout the triptych.
BILL The rest of you move on.
TOMMY (*looking out from behind screen*) No, don't go a step. You brought me here, see me out!
BILL Tommy, let me explain it to you.
TOMMY (*coming out from behind screen*) I gotta check out my apartment, and my clothes and money. Cynthia, ... I can't wait for anybody to open the door or look out for me and all that kinda crap you talk. A bunch-a liars!
BILL Oldtimer, why you ...
TOMMY Leave him the hell alone. He ain' said nothin' that ain' so!
SONNY-MAN Explain to the sister that some mistakes have been made.
BILL Mistakes have been made, baby. The mistakes were yesterday, this is today ...
TOMMY Yeah, and I'm Tomorrow, remember? Trouble is I was Tommin' to you, to all of you, ... "Oh, maybe they gon' like me." ... I was your fool, thinkin' writers and painters know moren' me, that maybe a little bit of you would rub off on me.
CYNTHIA We are wrong. I knew it yesterday.

Tommy, I told you not to expect anything out of this . . . this arrangement.

BILL This is a relationship, not an arrangement.

SONNY-MAN Cynthia, I tell you all the time, keep outta other people's business. What the hell you got to do with who's gonna get what outta what? You and Oldtimer, yakkin' and hakkin'. (*to* OLDTIMER) Man, your mouth gonna kill you.

BILL It's me and Tommy. Clear the room.

TOMMY Better not. I'll kill him! The "black people" this and the "Afro-American" . . . that . . . You ain' got no use for none-a us. Oldtimer, you their fool too. 'Til I got here they didn't even know your damn name. There's something inside-a me that says I ain' suppose to let *nobody* play me cheap. Don't care how much they know! (*she sweeps some of the books to the floor*)

BILL Don't you have any forgiveness in you? Would I be beggin' you if I didn't care? Can't you be generous enough . . .

TOMMY Nigger, I been too damn generous with you, already. All-a these people know I wasn't down here all night posin' for no pitcher, nigger!

BILL Cut that out, Tommy, and you not going anywhere!

TOMMY You wanna bet? Nigger!

BILL Okay, you called it, baby, I did act like a low, degraded person . . .

TOMMY (*combing out her wig with her fingers while holding it*) Didn't call you no low, degraded person. Nigger! (*to* CYNTHIA *who is handing her a comb*) "Do you have to wear a wig?" Yes! To soften the blow when yall go up side-a my head with a baseball bat. (*going back to taunting* BILL *and ignoring* CYNTHIA's *comb*) Nigger!

BILL That's enough-a that. You right and you're wrong too.

TOMMY Ain't a-one-a us you like that's alive and walkin' by you on the street . . . you don't like flesh and blood niggers.

BILL Call me that, baby, but don't call yourself. That what you think of yourself?

TOMMY If a black somebody is in a history book, or printed on a pitcher, or drawed on a paintin', . . . or if they're a statue, . . . dead, and outta the way, and can't talk back, then you dig 'em and full-a so much-a damn admiration

and talk 'bout "*our*" history. But when you run into us livin' and breathin' ones, with the life's blood still pumpin' through us, . . . then you comin' on 'bout how we ain' never together. You hate us, that's what! *You hate black me!*

BILL (*stung to the heart, confused and saddened by the half truth which applies to himself*) I never hated you, I never will, no matter what you or any of the rest of you do to *make* me hate you. I won't! Hell, woman, why do you say that! Why would I hate you?

TOMMY Maybe I look too much like the mother that give birth to you. Like the Ma and Pa that worked in the post office to buy you a house and a screen door with a damn duck on it. And you so ungrateful you didn't even like it.

BILL No, I didn't, baby. I don't like screen doors with ducks on 'em.

TOMMY You didn't like who was livin' behind them screen doors. Phoney Nigger!

BILL That's all! Damnit! don't go there no more!

TOMMY Hit me, so I can tear this place down and scream bloody murder.

BILL (*somewhere between laughter and tears*) Looka here, baby, I'm willin' to say I'm wrong, even in fronta the room fulla people . . .

TOMMY (*through clenched teeth*) Nigger.

SONNY-MAN The sister is upset.

TOMMY And you stop callin' me "the" sister, . . . if you feelin' so brotherly why don't you say "*my*" sister? Ain't no we-ness in your talk. "The" Afro-American, "the" black man, there's no we-ness in you. Who you think *you* are?

SONNY-MAN I was talkin' in general er . . . *my* sister, 'bout the masses.

TOMMY There he go again. "The" masses. Tryin' to make out like we pitiful and you got it made. You the masses your damn self and don't even know it. (*another angry look at* BILL) Nigger.

BILL (*pulls dictionary from shelf*) Let's get this ignorant "nigger" talk squared away. You can stand some education.

TOMMY You *treat* me like a nigger, that's what. I'd rather be called one than treated that way.

BILL (*questions* TOMMY) What is a nigger? (*talks as he is trying to find word*) A nigger is a low, degraded person, *any* low degraded person. I learned that from my teacher in the fifth grade.

TOMMY Fifth grade is a liar! Don't pull that dictionary crap on me.

BILL (*pointing to the book*) Webster's New World Dictionary of The American Language, College Edition.

TOMMY I don't need to find out what no college white folks say nigger is.

BILL I'm tellin' you it's a low, degraded person. Listen. (*reads from the book*) Nigger, N-i-g-g-e-r, ... A Negro ... A member of any dark-skinned people ... Damn. (*amazed by dictionary description*)

SONNY-MAN Brother Malcolm *said* that's what they meant, ... nigger is a Negro, Negro is a nigger.

BILL (*slowly finishing his reading*) A vulgar, offensive term of hostility and contempt. Well, so much for the fifth grade teacher.

SONNY-MAN No, they do not call low, degraded white folks niggers. Come to think of it, did you ever hear whitey call Hitler a nigger? Now if some whitey digs us, ... the others might call him a nigger-*lover*, but they don't call him no nigger.

OLDTIMER No, they don't.

TOMMY (*near tears*) When they say "nigger," just dry-long-so, they mean educated you and uneducated me. They hate you and call you "nigger," I called you "nigger" but I love you. (*there is dead silence in the room for a split second*)

SONNY-MAN (*trying to establish peace*) There you go. There you go.

CYNTHIA (*cautioning* SONNY-MAN) Now is not the time to talk, darlin'.

BILL You love me? Tommy, that's the greatest compliment you could ...

TOMMY (*sorry she said it*) You must be runnin' a fever, nigger, I ain' said nothin' 'bout lovin' you.

BILL (*in a great mood*) You did, yes, you did.

TOMMY Well, you didn't say it to *me*.

BILL Oh, Tommy, ...

TOMMY (*cuts him off abruptly*) And don't you dare say it now. I'm tellin' you, ... it ain't to be said now. (*checks through her paper bag to see if she has everything. Starts to put on the wig, changes her mind, holds it to end of scene. Turns to the others in the room*) Oldtimer, ... my brothers and my sister.

OLDTIMER I wish I was a thousand miles away, I'm so sorry. (*he sits at the foot of the model stand*)

TOMMY I don't stay mad, it's here today and gone tomorrow. I'm sorry your feelin's got hurt, ... but when I'm hurt I turn and hurt back. Somewhere, in the middle of last night, I thought the old me was gone, ... lost forever, and gladly. But today was flippin' time, so back I flipped. Now it's "turn the other cheek" time. If I can go through life other-cheekin' the white folk, ... guess yall can be other-cheeked too. But I'm goin' back to the nitty-gritty crowd, where the talk is we-ness and us-ness. I hate to do it but I have to thank you 'cause I'm walkin' out with much more than I brought in. (*goes over and looks at the queen in the "Wine In The Wilderness" painting*) Tomorrow-Marie had such a lovely yesterday. (BILL *takes her hand, she gently removes it from his grasp*) Bill, I don't have to wait for anybody's by-your-leave to be a "Wine In The Wilderness" woman. I can be it if I wanta, ... and I *am*. I am. I am. I'm not the one you made up and painted, the very pretty lady who can't talk back, ... but I'm "Wine In The Wilderness" ... alive and kickin', me ... Tomorrow-Marie, cussin' and fightin' and lookin' out for my damn self 'cause ain' nobody else 'round to do it, dontcha know. And, Cynthia, if my hair is straight, or if it's natural, or if I wear a wig, or take it off, ... that's all right; because wigs ... shoes ... hats ... bags ... and even this ... (*she picks up the African throw she wore a few moments before ... fingers it*) They're just what what you call ... access ... (*fishing for the word*) ... like what you wear with your Easter outfit ...

CYNTHIA Accessories.

TOMMY Thank you, my sister. Accessories. Somethin' you add on or take off. The real thing is takin' place on the inside ... that's where the action is. That's "Wine In The Wilderness," ... a woman that's a real one and a good one. And yall just better believe I'm it. (*she proceeds to the door*)

BILL Tommy. (*she turns. He takes the beautiful queen, "Wine In The Wilderness" from the easel*) She's not it at all, Tommy. This chick on the canvas, ... nothin' but accessories, a dream I drummed up outta the junk room of my mind. (*places the "queen" to one side*) You are and ... (*points to* OLDTIMER) ... Edmund

Lorenzo Matthews ... the real beautiful people, ... Cynthia ...

CYNTHIA (*bewildered and unbelieving*) Who? Me?

BILL Yeah, honey, you and Sonny-man, don't know how beautiful you are. (*indicates the other side of model stand*) Sit there.

SONNY-MAN (*places cushions on the floor at the foot of the model stand*) Just sit here and be my beautiful self. (*to* CYNTHIA) Turn on, baby, we gonna get our picture took. (CYNTHIA *smiles*)

BILL Now there's Oldtimer, the guy who was here before there were scholarships and grants and stuff like that, the guy they kept outta the schools, the man the factories wouldn't hire, the union wouldn't let him join ...

SONNY-MAN Yeah, yeah, rap to me. Where you goin' with it, man? Rap on.

BILL I'm makin' a triptych.

SONNY-MAN Make it, man.

BILL (*indicating* CYNTHIA *and* SONNY-MAN) On the other side, Young Man and Woman, workin' together to do our thing.

TOMMY (*quietly*) I'm goin' now.

BILL But you belong up there in the center, "Wine In The Wilderness" ... that's who you are. (*moves the canvas of "the little girl" and places a sketch pad on the easel*) The nightmare, about all that I've done disappearing before my eyes. It was a good nightmare. I was painting in the dark, all head and no heart. I couldn't see until you came, baby. (*to* CYNTHIA, SONNY-MAN *and* OLDTIMER) Look at Tomorrow. She came through the biggest riot of all, ... somethin' called "Slavery," and she's even comin' through the "now" scene, ... folks laughin' at her, even her own folks laughin' at her. And look *how* ... with her head high like she's poppin' her fingers at the world. (*takes up charcoal pencil and tears old page off sketch pad so he can make a fresh drawing*) Aw, let me put it down, Tommy. "Wine In The Wilderness," you gotta let me put it down so all the little boys and girls can look up and see you on the wall. And you know what they're gonna say? "Hey, don't she look like somebody we know?" (TOMMY *slowly returns and takes her seat on the stand.* TOMMY *is holding the wig in her lap. Her hands are very graceful looking against the texture of the wig*) And they'll be right, you're somebody they know ... (*he is sketching hastily. There is a sound of thunder and the patter of rain*) Yeah, roll them hoops and bicycle wheels. (*music in low. Music up higher as* BILL *continues to sketch. Curtain*)

Adrienne Kennedy (1931–)

The Owl Answers   1965

Adrienne Kennedy is a poet of the theater. Unlike most black playwrights, she does not write realistic stories; she composes surreal fantasies around her characters. Her three best one-act plays—*Funnyhouse of a Negro*, *The Rat's Mass*, and *The Owl Answers*—all have at the center a young girl who is torn by the paradoxes of Spirit and Flesh; Black and White; Past and Present.

No script in this volume is as dense with images as *The Owl Answers*. And no script demands an imaginative, creative production more. Without an idea of what actual theatrical elements can do, the play may seem to some readers to be a nightmare, and in a sense, it is. Each object and character is many things, sometimes simultaneously. But, like a dream, there is a suggested literal story behind and within the kaleidoscopic visions: Child Clara is born a Bastard to a Black Mother, who cooked for the Richest White Man in the Town, Mr. William Mattheson. The mother, after bearing Clara, may have killed herself. Clara is adopted by the Reverend Passmore, a black Baptist minister, and by his frigid wife. They tell Clara that she came from the Owls. The White Father dies in Jacksonville some years later. Clara is forbidden to attend the funeral. Later, she takes leave of her job teaching English and travels to England, the beloved land of her dead White Father, the land that is the fountain of White Culture (Shakespeare, Chaucer, and Anne Boleyn) where she has a mental emotional crack-up.

Clara makes a final desperate attempt to find an identity, to resolve her love/hate for Black/White; to come to grips with her attraction for/repulsion toward purity and carnality. She picks up a Negro man on the subway and attempts to seduce him in a Harlem hotel. She fails. She remains neither spirit nor flesh, neither black nor white—an owl.

The story is told from several time positions—the present, the historical present, and the past. There is such a wealth of shifting images that the "real" story can never be certain—nor should it be. Like a rich poem, *The Owl Answers* is a storm of ambiguities that blow and swirl into a pool of liquid sunlight and shadow.

For the reader who is fascinated by the beauty, the tenderness, the horror, and the mystery of the play, reading and rereading (in the absence of a production) will be a pleasurable frustration. Many clues and many more paradoxes can be found by studying Miss Kennedy's other plays, but the beauty and the art of Adrienne Kennedy cannot be enhanced by critical analysis.

Adrienne Kennedy was born in Pittsburgh in 1931. She grew up in Cleveland and attended Ohio State University, but found the "social structure there so opposed to Negroes that she did hardly any academic work." In 1962 she joined Edward Albee's workshop. *Funnyhouse of a Negro* won her an Obie Award. She received a Guggenheim Award for creative writing in 1969.

In a tradition in which the major style has long been realism, Adrienne Kennedy has done what few black playwrights have attempted: used form to project an interior reality and thereby created a rich and demanding theatrical style.

The Owl Answers

CAST OF CHARACTERS

SHE *who is* CLARA PASSMORE *who is the* VIRGIN MARY *who is the* BASTARD *who is the* OWL
BASTARD'S BLACK MOTHER *who is the* REVEREND'S WIFE *who is* ANNE BOLEYN
GODDAM FATHER *who is the* RICHEST WHITE MAN IN THE TOWN *who is the* DEAD FATHER *who is* REVEREND PASSMORE
THE WHITE BIRD *who is* REVEREND PASSMORE'S CANARY *who is* GOD'S DOVE
THE NEGRO MAN
SHAKESPEARE
CHAUCER
WILLIAM THE CONQUEROR

The characters change slowly back and forth into and out of themselves, leaving some garment from their previous selves upon them always to remind us of the nature of SHE *who is* CLARA PASSMORE *who is the* VIRGIN MARY *who is the* BASTARD *who is the* OWL's *world.*

SCENE: A NEW YORK SUBWAY *is the* TOWER OF LONDON *is a* HARLEM HOTEL ROOM *is* ST. PETER'S.

(*The scene is shaped like a subway car. The sounds are subway sounds and the main props of a subway are visible—poles, fans, lights. Two seats on the scene are like seats on the subway, the seat in which* SHE WHO IS *sits and* NEGRO MAN's *seat. The colors of the subway props are black.*
Seated is a plain, pallid, middle-aged Negro woman, wearing a cotton summer dress that is too long, a pair of white wedged sandals. Her hair is tightly curled and exceedingly well combed in the manner a great many prim Negro women wear their hair. SHE *sits staring into space.* SHE *is* CLARA PASSMORE *who is the* VIRGIN MARY *who is the* BASTARD *who is the* OWL. *Scene moves, lights flash, a sense of exploding imprisonment.*
SHE WHO IS *speaks in a soft voice as a Negro schoolteacher from Savannah would.* SHE WHO IS *carries white handkerchiefs,* SHE WHO IS *carries notebooks that throughout the play like the handkerchiefs fall.* SHE *will pick them up, glance frienziedly at a page from a notebook, be distracted, place the notebooks in a disorderly pile, drop them again, etc.*
The scene should lurch, lights flash, hand straps move, gates slam. When THEY *come in and exit,* THEY *move in the manner of people on a train, too. There is the noise of the train, the sound of moving steel on the track.*
The WHITE BIRD's *wings should flutter loudly.*
The gates, the High Altar, the ceiling, and the Dome are like St. Peter's; the walls are like the Tower of London.
The music which SHE WHO IS *hears at the most violent times of her experience should be Haydn's Concerto for Horn in D (Third Movement).*
Objects on the stage (beards, wigs, faces) should be used in the manner that people use everyday objects such as spoons or newspapers.
The Tower Gate should be black, yet slam like a subway door.
The gates slam. FOUR PEOPLE *enter from different directions.* THEY *are* SHAKESPEARE, WILLIAM THE CONQUEROR, CHAUCER, *and* ANNE BOLEYN, *but too they are strangers entering a subway on a summer night, too they are the guards in the Tower of London. Their lines throughout the play are not spoken specifically by one person but by all or part of them*)

THEY Bastard. (THEY *start at a distance eventually crowding her. Their lines are spoken coldly.* SHE WHO IS *is only a prisoner to them*) You are not his ancestor. Keep her locked there, guard. Bastard.
SHE You must let me go down to the chapel to see him. He is my father.
THEY (*jeering*) Your father?
SHE He is my father.
THEY Keep her locked there, guard. (CHAUCER *locks the gates*)
SHE We came this morning. We were

visiting the place of our ancestors, my father and I. We had a lovely morning, we rose in darkness, took a taxi past Hyde Park through the Marble Arch to Buckingham Palace, we had our morning tea at Lyons, then came out to the Tower. We were wandering about the gardens, my father leaning on my arm, speaking of you, William the Conqueror. My father loved you, William—

THEY (*interrupting*) If you are his ancestor why are you a Negro? Yes, why is it you are a Negro if you are his ancestor? Keep her locked there.

SHE You must let me go down to the chapel to see him.

(THEY *stare coldly,* CHAUCER *and* SHAKESPEARE *exit, slamming the gate, scene moves, lights flash.* ANNE BOLEYN *and* WILLIAM THE CONQUEROR *remain staring at her.* CHAUCER *and* SHAKESPEARE *return carrying a stiff dead man in a black suit. The most noticeable thing about him is his hair—long, silky, white hair that hangs as they bring him through the gate and place him at her feet*)

THEY Here is your father.

(THEY *then all exit through various gate entrances.* SHE *picks up the dead man, drags him to a dark, carved, highback chair on the right. At the same time a dark* NEGRO MAN, *with a dark suit and black glasses on, enters from the right gate and sits on the subway seat. Flashing, movement, slamming of gate, fans twirl, The* NEGRO MAN *sits up very straight and proceeds to watch* SHE WHO IS. *Until he speaks to her, he watches her constantly with a wild, cold stare.*

The DEAD FATHER *appears dead. He is dead. Yet as* SHE *watches, he moves and comes to life. Throughout the play when the characters change and come to life it must give the impression of logic yet be understood that the other state actually existed. When the* DEAD FATHER *was dead, he was dead; when he is the* REVEREND, *he is the* REVEREND. SHE WHO IS *always watches them as they change, for this is her mental state. The* DEAD FATHER *removes his hair, takes off his white face, from the chair he takes a white church robe and puts it on. Beneath his white hair is dark Negro hair. He is now* REVEREND PASSMORE. *After he dresses he looks about as if something is missing, seizes the gate, exits, and returns with a gold bird cage that hangs near the chair and a white battered Bible. Very matter-of-factly he sits down on the chair, stares for a moment at the cage, then opens the Bible, starting to read.* SHE *watches, highly distracted, until he falls asleep. Movement, flash, twirl.*

ANNE BOLEYN *has remained behind during that time where she stands near a subway pole. She throws red rice at* SHE WHO IS *and the* DEAD FATHER *who is now* REVEREND PASSMORE. *They see her.* SHE *exits and returns with a great black gate (like the gate at Valladolid) and places the gate where the pole is. It is clear now that she has erected the gate but she cannot pass through it.* SHE WHO IS *runs to* ANNE BOLEYN)

SHE Anne, Anne Boleyn. (ANNE *throws rice at* SHE WHO IS CLARA PASSMORE *who is the* VIRGIN MARY *who is the* BASTARD *who is the* OWL) Anne, you know so much of love, won't you help me? They took my father away and will not let me see him. They locked me in this tower and I can see them taking his body across to the chapel to be buried and see his white hair hanging down. Let me into the chapel. He is my blood father. I am almost white, am I not? Let me into St. Paul's Chapel. Let me please go down to St. Paul's Chapel. I am his daughter. (ANNE *appears to listen quite attentively, but her reply is to turn into the* BASTARD'S BLACK MOTHER. *She takes off part of her own long dress and puts on a rose-colored cheap lace dress, the kind of a dress a Southern Negro woman might wear to dress up in, and anything dark on her face.* SHE WHO IS'S *reaction is to run back to her subway seat.* SHE *drops her notebooks. The* BASTARD'S BLACK MOTHER *opens her arms to* SHE WHO IS. SHE *returns to the gate*) Anne. (*as if trying to bring back* ANNE BOLEYN)

BASTARD'S BLACK MOTHER (*laughs and throws a white bridal bouquet at her*) Clara, I am not Anne. I am the Bastard's Black Mother, who cooked for somebody.

(*Still holding out her arms, she kneels by the gate, her kinky hair awry, eyes closed, she stares upward, praying. Suddenly she stops praying and pulls* SHE WHO IS *through the gate.*

The WHITE BIRD, *with very loud fluttering wings, flies down from St. Peter's Dome and goes into the cage.* REVEREND PASSMORE *gets up and closes the cage door*)

SHE Anne, it is I.

BASTARD'S BLACK MOTHER Clara, you were conceived by your Goddam Father who was the Richest White Man in the Town and somebody that cooked for him. That's why you're an owl. (*laughs*) That's why when I see you, Mary, I cry. I cry when I see Marys, cry for their deaths.

(*The* WHITE BIRD *flies in the cage.* REVEREND *reads. The* BASTARD'S BLACK MOTHER *stands at the gate, watches, then takes off rose lace dress and black face; beneath her black face is a more pallid Negro face; pulls down her hair, longer dark hair, and puts on a white dress. From a fold in the dress she takes out a picture of Christ, then kneels and stares upward. She is the* REVEREND'S WIFE. *Scene moves, flashes*)

REVEREND'S WIFE (*kneeling.* REVEREND *stands and watches her.* REVEREND'S WIFE *takes a vial from her gown and holds it up*) These are the fruits of my maidenhead, owl blood Clara who is the Bastard Clara Passmore to whom we gave our name, see the owl blood, that is why I cry when I see Marys, cry for their deaths, Owl Mary Passmore.

(SHE *gets up, exits from a side gate.* THEY *come in.* SHE WHO IS *goes to the* REVEREND *as if to implore him. He then changes into the* DEAD FATHER, *resuming his dirty white hair.* THEY *stand about*)

SHE Dear Father, my Goddam Father who was the Richest White Man in the Town, who is Dead Father—you know that England is the home of dear Chaucer, Dickens and dearest Shakespeare. Winters we spent here at the Tower, our chambers were in the Queen's House, summers we spent at Stratford with dearest Shakespeare. It was all so lovely. I spoke to Anne Boleyn, Dead Father. She knows so much of love and suffering and I believe she is going to try to help me. (*takes a sheaf of papers from her notebooks; they fall to the floor*) Communications, all communications to get you the proper burial, the one you deserve in St. Paul's Chapel. They are letting you rot, my Goddam Father who was the Richest Man in the Town—they are letting you rot in that town in Georgia. I haven't been able to see the King. I'll speak again to Anne Boleyn. She knows so much of love.

(*Shows the papers to the* DEAD FATHER *who sits with his hair hanging down, dead. She begins to unbutton her dress fitfully; naturally, since she is the black mother's bastard, her skin is black underneath. The* NEGRO MAN *continues to watch her.* SHE WHO IS *moves about, flash twirling,* REVEREND'S WIFE *prays.* SHE WHO IS *goes again to the* DEAD FATHER, *takes him by the hair, stares into his dead face.* WHITE BIRD *flies inside the cage.* REVEREND'S WIFE *stops praying, watches, smiles. Scene moves, fluttering of wings, lights flash*)

DEAD FATHER If you are my ancestor why are you a Negro, Bastard? What is a Negro doing at the Tower of London staying at the Queen's House? Clara, I am your Goddam Father who was the Richest White Man in the Town and you are a schoolteacher in Savannah who spends her summers at Teachers College. You are not my ancestor. You are my bastard. Keep her locked there, William.

(THEY *stare at her like passengers on a subway, standing, holding the hand straps*)

SHE We were wandering about the garden, you leaning on my arm, speaking of William the Conqueror. We sat on the stone bench to rest. When we stood up you stumbled and fell onto the walk—dead. Dead. I called the guard. Then I called the Warden and told him my father had just died, that we had been visiting London together, the place of our ancestors and all the lovely English, and my father just died. (*she reaches out to touch him*)

DEAD FATHER You are not my ancestor.

SHE They jeered. They brought me to this tower and locked me up. I can see they're afraid of me. From the tower I saw them drag you across the court . . . your hair hanging down. They have taken off your shoes and you are stiff. You are stiff. (*touches him*) My dear father. (*Music: Haydn*)

DEAD FATHER Daughter of somebody that cooked for me. (*Smiles*)

(*He then ignores* SHE WHO IS, *changes into the* REVEREND, *takes the Bible and starts to read. The* WHITE BIRD *flies inside the cage. Wings flutter. The* REVEREND'S WIFE *praying, lights a candle. The* REVEREND *watches the* BIRD, *sits down, watches the* BIRD *flutter, as though he expects something from him . . . as an answer,* REVEREND'S WIFE *lights another candle, then puts on her black face, rose dress. Some of the red rice has fallen near her, she says* "*Oww,*" *and starts to peck at it like a bird. She then sits up facing front on her knees, eyes wide open, very still,* "*Oww,*" *she repeats,* "*Ow.*" SHE WHO IS *wanders about, then comes to speak to the* BASTARD'S BLACK MOTHER *who remains seated like an owl. End music*)

SHE It was you the Bastard's Black Mother who told me. I asked you where did Mr. William Mattheson's family come from and you, my Black Mother, said: I believe his father came from England. England, I said. England is the Brontës' home. Did you know Black Bastard's Mother, who cooked for somebody, in the Reverend's parlor—there in a glass bookcase are books and England is the home of Chaucer, Dickens, and Shakespeare. Black Mother who cooked for somebody Mr. William Mattheson died today. I was at the College. The Reverend's Wife called me, Clara who is the Bastard who is the Virgin Mary who is the Owl, Clara, who is the Bastard who is the Virgin Mary who is the Owl, Clara she said the Reverend told me to call you and tell you Mr. William Mattheson died today or it was yesterday he died yesterday. It was yesterday. The Reverend told me to tell you it was yesterday he died and it is today they're burying him. Clara who is the Bastard, you mustn't come. Don't do anything foolish like come to the funeral, Mary. You've always been such a fool about that white man, Clara.

But I am coming, the Black Bastard's Mother. I am coming, my Goddam Father who was the Richest White Man in Jacksonville, Georgia. When I arrive in London, I'll go out to Buckingham Palace, see the Thames at dusk, and Big Ben. I'll go for lovely walks through Hyde Park, and to innumerable little tearooms with great bay windows and white tablecloths on little white tables and order tea. I will go all over and it will be June. Then I'll go out to the Tower to see you, my father.

(BASTARD'S BLACK MOTHER *has remained like an owl.* THEY *come on and stand as passengers on the subway speaking at random*)

THEY If you are his ancestor what are you doing on the subway at night looking for men? What are you doing looking for men to take to a hotel room in Harlem? Negro Men? Negro Men Clara Passmore?

(*In reply the* BASTARD'S BLACK MOTHER *laughs a bird laugh. The* WHITE BIRD *flies out of the cage*)

SHE (*runs to the* BIRD) My dead father's bird: God's Dove. My father died today.

BIRD (*mocking*) My father died today God's Dove.

SHE He was the Richest White Man in our Town. I was conceived by him and somebody that cooked for him.

BIRD What are you doing in the Tower of London then?

(*The* REVEREND *becomes the* DEAD FATHER *who comes forward, takes the* BIRD, *puts him in the cage, shuts the door*)

SHE My father. (*he turns, stares at her, and comes toward her and dies; it is his death in the gardens*) What were you saying of William, my father, you loved William so. (*she holds him in her arms. He opens his eyes*)

DEAD FATHER (*waking*) Mary, at least you are coming to me. (*Music: Haydn*)

SHE I am not Mary, I am Clara, your daughter, Reverend Passmore—I mean Dead Father. (BIRD *flies in the cage*)

DEAD FATHER Yes, my Mary, you are coming into my world. You are filled with dreams of my world. I sense it all.

(*Silence except for the wild fluttering of the* BIRD'*s wings.* NEGRO MAN *stares, lights flash, sound of steel on the track, movement*)

NEGRO MAN At last you are coming to me. (*smiles*)

DEAD FATHER Mary, come in here for eternity. Are you confused? Yes, I can see you are confused. (THEY *come on*)

THEY Are you confused?

(*One of them,* CHAUCER, *is now dressed as the* REVEREND. *He comes, falls down onto the empty high-backed chair, and sits staring into the Bible*)

DEAD FATHER So at last you are coming to me, Bastard.

(BASTARD'S BLACK MOTHER *exits from gate, returns, part owl with owl feathers upon her, dragging a great dark bed through the gate; the gate slams*)

BASTARD'S BLACK MOTHER Why be confused? The Owl was your beginning, Mary. (*begins to build with the bed and feathers the High Altar; feathers fly*)

SHE He came to me in the outhouse, he came to me under the porch, in the garden, in the fig tree. He told me you are an owl, ow, oww, I am your beginning, ow. You belong here with us owls in the fig tree not to somebody that cooks for your Goddam Father, oww, and I ran to the outhouse in the night crying oww, Bastard they say the people in the town all say Bastard, but I, I belong to God and the owls, ow and I sat in the fig tree. My Goddam Father is the Richest White Man in the Town but I belong to the owls, till Reverend Passmore adopted me they all said Bastard . . . then my father was a reverend. He preached in the Holy Baptist Church on the top of the hill, on the top of the Holy Hill, and everybody in the town knew then my name was Mary. My father was the Baptist preacher and I was Mary. (THEY *enter, slamming, lights flash, stand about passengers, the* NEGRO MAN *stares*. SHE *sits in the subway seat*)

I who am the ancestor of Shakespeare, Chaucer, and William the Conqueror, I went to London the Queen Elizabeth, London they all said who ever heard of anybody going to London but I went. I stayed in my cabin the whole crossing, solitary. I was the only Negro there. I read books on subjects like the History of London, the Life of Anne Boleyn, Mary Queen of Scots, and Sonnets. When I wasn't in the cabin I wrapped myself in a great sweater and sat over the dark desks in the writing room and wrote my father. I wrote him every day of my journey. (*pause*)

I met my father once when my mother took me to visit him and we had to go into the back door of his house. (*talking to herself.* NEGRO MAN *stares*)

I was married once briefly. On my wedding day the Reverend's Wife came to me and said when I see Marys I cry for their deaths, when I see brides, Clara, I cry for their deaths. But the past years I've spent teaching alone in Savannah. And alone I'm almost thirty-four, I who am the ancestor of somebody that cooked for somebody and William the Conqueror. (BASTARD'S BLACK MOTHER *looks more like an owl.* DEAD FATHER *dies again.* BASTARD'S BLACK MOTHER *bangs at the gate.* THEY *all laugh. The* NEGRO MAN *stands before* SHE WHO IS. SHE *screams at the* DEAD FATHER *and the* MOTHER) You must know how it is to be filled with yearning.

(THEY *laugh.* REVEREND *stares into the cage.* MOTHER *bangs at the gate*)

NEGRO MAN (*touches her*) And what exactly do you yearn for?
SHE You know.
NEGRO MAN No, what is it?
SHE I want what I think everyone wants.
NEGRO MAN And what is that?
SHE I don't know. Love or something, I guess.
NEGRO MAN Out there Owl?
DEAD FATHER In St. Paul's Chapel Owl?
THEY Keep her locked there, guard.
BASTARD'S BLACK MOTHER Is this love to come from out there?
SHE I don't know what you mean.
DEAD FATHER I know you don't.
THEY We know you don't.
SHE Call me Mary.
NEGRO MAN Mary?
THEY Keep her locked there.
DEAD FATHER If you are Mary what are you doing in the Tower of London?
NEGRO MAN Mary?

(*The* REVEREND *gets up, goes to the cage, in a silent gesture, takes the* WHITE BIRD *from the cage, holds the* BIRD *in his hand, gazes into its eyes, tugs at his beard; and gazes into the* BIRD*'s eyes. The* BASTARD'S BLACK MOTHER *reappears on the other side of the gate, owl feathers about her, bearing a vial, still wearing the long black hair of the* REVEREND'S WIFE)

BASTARD'S BLACK MOTHER When I see sweet Marys I cry for their deaths, Clara the Reverend took my maidenhead and I am not a Virgin any more and that is why you must be Mary always be Mary Clara. (*goes on building the High Altar; the* BIRD *laughs*)
SHE Mama. (*The* BASTARD'S BLACK MOTHER *stops building, stares, then turns into* ANNE BOLEYN, *while* CLARA *stands, calling*) Mama. (*watches her change to* ANNE BOLEYN, *who goes on building.* THEY *watch*)
BASTARD'S BLACK MOTHER What are you doing on the subway if you are his ancestor?
SHE I am Clara Passmore. I am not His ancestor. I ride, look for men to take to a Harlem Hotel Room, to love, dress them as my father, beg to take me.
THEY Take you?

SHE   Yes, take me Clara Passmore.
THEY   Take you, Bastard?
SHE   There is a bed there. (*the* WHITE BIRD *laughs like the* MOTHER)
WILLIAM   And do they take you?
SHE   No, William.
WILLIAM   No?
SHE   Something happens.
WILLIAM   Happens?
CHAUCER   Happens?
SHE   Something strange always happens, Chaucer.
CHAUCER   Where?
SHE   In the hotel room. It's how I've passed my summer in New York, nights I come to the subway, look for men. It's how I've passed my summer. If they would only take me? But something strange happens.
ANNE   Take you, Mary? Why, Mary?

(ANNE BOLEYN *builds.* THEY *exit,* CLARA *dressed like the* VIRGIN *in a blue crepe shawl, wanders about, then goes to* ANNE)

SHE   Anne, you must help me. They, my Black Mother and my Goddam Father and the Reverend and his wife, they and the teachers at the school where I teach, and Professor Johnson, the principal to whom I'm engaged, they all say London, who in the hell ever heard of anybody going to London. Of course I shouldn't go. They said I had lost my mind, read so much, buried myself in my books. They say I should stay and teach summer school to the kids up from Oglethorpe. But I went.

All the way from Piccadilly Circus out there in the black taxi, my cold hands were colder than ever. Then it happened no sooner than I left the taxi and passed down a gray walk through a dark gate and into a garden where there were black ravens on the grass when I broke down. I broke down and started to cry, oh the Tower, winters in Queen's House, right in front of everybody. People came and stared. I was the only Negro there. The guard came and stared, the ravens flew and finally a man with a black hat on helped me out through the gate into the street. I am never going back, Anne. Anne, I am never going back. I will not go.
THEY   Keep her locked there, guard.

(*The* NEGRO MAN *comes toward her. She dresses him as God putting a crown upon his head. The* REVEREND *watches then. A light comes into the Tower as though a cell door has been opened*)

SHE   God, do you see it? Do you see? They are opening the cell door to let me go.
NEGRO MAN   See it, Mary?
SHE   They are opening the cell door to let me go down to St. Paul's Chapel where I am yearning to go. Do you see it?
NEGRO MAN   Love? Love Mary?
SHE   Love?
NEGRO MAN   Love in St. Paul's Chapel?
SHE   No, no, the love that exists between you and me. Do you see it?
NEGRO MAN   Love Mary? (*he takes her hand; with his other hand, he tries to undress her*)
SHE   Love God.
NEGRO MAN   Love Mary?
SHE   Love God. (THEY *bring the* DEAD FATHER *and leave him at her feet*)
THEY   (*simultaneously*)   Bastard, you are not His ancestor, you are not God's ancestor.
NEGRO MAN   Love Mary?
SHE   Love God. Yes.
BASTARD'S BLACK MOTHER   (*calls*) Clara. Clara. (*The* REVEREND *watching*)
THEY   Open the door. Let her go, let her go, guards. Open the cell door.

(THEY *exit leaving the gates open.* NEGRO MAN *will not release* SHE WHO IS CLARA *who is the* BASTARD *who is the* VIRGIN MARY *who is the* OWL)

SHE   Go away. (*the* REVEREND *goes back to his chair*) Go away. (*the* NEGRO MAN *will not release her*)

(*The* REVEREND'S WIFE *goes on building the High Altar with owl feathers, prays, builds, prays, stops, holds out her hand to* SHE WHO IS, *puts up candles, puts up owl feathers, laughs, puts more candles on the High Altar*)

REVEREND'S WIFE   (*calls*) Owl, come sit by me. (*the* REVEREND'S WIFE *does not look at* SHE WHO IS *but rather stares feverishly upward, her gestures possessing the fervent quality of Biblical images. Sitting on the High Altar she holds one of her hands over her shoulder as though she drew near the fingers of a deity; suddenly her hand reaches inside her gown and she pulls up a butcher knife*) Clara. (*staring upward, holding the knife*)
SHE   Yes, the Reverend's Wife who came to me on my wedding day and said I cry for the death of brides. Yes?

REVEREND'S WIFE I told the Reverend if he ever came near me again—(*she turns the butcher knife around*)—does he not know I am Mary Christ's bride. What does he think does he think I am like your black mother who was the biggest whore in town. He must know I'm Mary, only Mary would marry the Reverend Passmore of the church on the top of the Holy Hill. (*turns the knife around, staring at it.* SHE WHO IS *goes through the gate. The* REVEREND'S WIFE *tries to get her to sit on the High Altar. When she does not the* REVEREND'S WIFE *then drags the bed, which is the High Altar through the gate to the center of the scene, arranges it, then goes on building, owls and feathers, candles*) We adopted you, took you from your bastard birth Owl. (*goes on building. The* NEGRO MAN *stands and waits for* CLARA)

SHE Home, God, we're home. Did you know we came from England, God? It's the Brontës' home too. Winters we spent here at the Tower. Our chambers were in the Queen's House. Summers we spent at Stratford. It was so lovely. God, do you remember the loveliness?

(NEGRO MAN *stares at her, green light begins coming,* WHITE BIRD *flies out, end of the lights, flashing, fans twirling, subway sounds*)

BIRD If you are the Virgin what are you doing with this Negro in a Harlem Hotel Room? Mary?
SHE My name is Clara Passmore.
BIRD Mary.

(WHITE BIRD *laughs like the* MOTHER. *The* REVEREND'S WIFE *lights candles*)

NEGRO MAN What is it?
SHE Call me Mary, God.
NEGRO MAN Mary?
SHE God, do you remember the loveliness?

(*The* REVEREND'S WIFE *lights more candles and moves closer with the butcher knife, calling*)

REVEREND'S WIFE Clara.

(*The* BIRD *flies wildly, the* REVEREND *sits in the chair reading the white tattered Bible. For an instant he seems as though he might get up and come forward but he does not, instead he smiles and goes on reading the Bible*)

NEGRO MAN What is it? What is it? What is wrong? (*he tries to undress her. Underneath, her body is black. He throws off the crown she has placed on him*) What is it? (*the* WHITE BIRD *flies toward them and about the green room*) Are you sick?

SHE (*smiles*) No, God. (SHE *is in a trance*) No, I am not sick. I only have a dream of love. A dream. Open the cell door and let me go down to St. Paul's Chapel. (*the blue crepe shawl is half about her.* SHE *shows the* NEGRO MAN *her notebooks from which a mass of papers fall.* SHE *crazily tries to gather them up*) Communications, God, communications, letters to my father. I am making it into my thesis. I write my father every day of the year.

God, I who am the Bastard who is the Virgin Mary who is the Owl, I came here this morning with my father. We were visiting England, the place of our ancestors, my father and I who am the Bastard who is the Virgin Mary who is the Owl. We had a lovely morning. We rose in darkness, took a taxi past Hyde Park, through the Marble Arch to Buckingham Palace. We had our morning tea at Lyons and then we came out to the Tower.

And I started to cry and a man with a black hat on helped me out of the gate to the street. I was the only Negro here.

They took him away and would not let me see him. They who are my Black Mother and my Goddam Father locked me in the fig tree and took his body away and his white hair hung down.

Now they my Black Mother and my Goddam Father who pretend to be Chaucer, Shakespeare, and Eliot, and all my beloved English, come to my cell and stare and I can see they despise me and I despise them.

They are dragging his body across the green, his white hair hanging down. They are taking off his shoes and he is stiff. I must get into the chapel to see him. I must. He is my blood father. God let me into his burial. (*kneeling*)

I call God and the Owl answers. (*softer*) It haunts my Tower calling, its feathers are blowing against the cell wall, speckled in the garden on the fig tree, it comes feathered great hollow-eyed with yellow skin and yellow eyes, the flying bastard. From my Tower I keep calling and the only answer is the Owl God. (*pause. Stands*)

I am only yearning for our kingdom God.

(*The* WHITE BIRD *flies back into the cage,* REVEREND *reads, smiling, the* DEAD FATHER *lies on cell floor.* THE MOTHER, *now part the* BLACK MOTHER *and part the* REVEREND'S WIFE *in a white dress, wild kinky hair, part feathered, comes closer to* CLARA)

MOTHER Owl in the fig tree, owl under the house, owl in outhouse. (*calling cheerfully the way one would call a child, kissing* SHE WHO IS) There is a way from owldom. (*kissing her again*) Clara who is the Bastard who is the Virgin who is the Owl.

SHE My Black Mother who cooked for somebody who is the Reverend's Wife. Where is Anne Boleyn?

MOTHER Owl in the fig tree do you know it? Do you? Do you know the way to St. Paul's Chapel, Clara? (*takes her hand*) I do. Kneel, Mary, by the gate and pray with me who is your black mother who is Christ's Bride. (*she holds up the butcher knife*) Kneel by the High Altar and pray with me. (*they kneel; she smiles*) Do you know it, Clara, do you Clara Bastard? (*she kisses her*) Clara, I know the way to St. Paul's Chapel. I know the way to St. Paul's Chapel, Clara.

(*Green light dims suddenly, fluttering of* WHITE BIRD's *wings, when the lights grow bright the* MOTHER *has killed herself with the butcher knife and all about is blood, flesh, and feathers, fluttering of* WHITE BIRD's *wings is loud.* SHE *and the* NEGRO MAN *stand amid blood, flesh and owl feathers, the* DEAD FATHER *stands, arises and sets fire to the High Altar with the candles. Music: Haydn*)

SHE (*the* NEGRO MAN *tries to kiss her, they are upon the burning High Altar, the* WHITE BIRD *flies out, laughs*) God, say you know I love you, Mary, yes, I love you. That love is the oldest, purest testament in my heart. Say, Mary, it was a testament imprinted on my soul long before the world began. I pray to you, Mary, God say Mary I pray to you. Darling, come to my kingdom. Mary, leave owldom—come to my kingdom. I am awaiting you.

(*The* NEGRO MAN *tries again to kiss her. The* WHITE BIRD *picks up the dead* MOTHER *and takes her to the top of St. Peter's Dome. They remain there watching. The* REVEREND *reads the Bible, smiling*)

NEGRO MAN What is wrong?
SHE Wrong, God?
NEGRO MAN God?
SHE Wrong, God?
NEGRO MAN God?

(*They are upon the burning High Altar. He tries to force her down, yet at the same time he is frightened by her. The* DEAD FATHER *who has been holding the candles, smiles, then falls dead again. The* NEGRO MAN *tries to undress* SHE WHO IS THE BASTARD, WHO IS. *When he touches her, she screams like an owl*)

SHE Negro! (*music ends*) Keep her locked there, guard. (*they struggle*) I cry for the death of Marys. (*they struggle. She screeches*) Negro! (*She tries to get out of the room but he will not let her go*) Let me go to St. Paul's Chapel. Let me go down to see my Goddam Father who was the Richest White Man in the Town. (*they struggle; he is frightened now*) God, God call me, Mary. (*she screeches louder*) God!! (*suddenly she breaks away, finds her notebook, and from it withdraws the butcher knife still with blood and feathers upon it, and very quickly tries to attack him, holds the knife up, aiming it at him, but then dropping it just as suddenly as a gesture of wild weariness. He backs away from her. She screeches. He backs further, She falls down onto the side of the burning bed. The* NEGRO MAN *backs further out through the gate.* SHE, *fallen at the side of the Altar burning, her head bowed, both hands conceal her face, feathers fly, green lights are strong, Altar burning,* WHITE BIRD *laughs from the Dome.* SHE WHO IS CLARA *who is the* BASTARD *who is the* VIRGIN MARY *suddenly looks like an owl, and lifts her bowed head, stares into space and speaks.*) Ow . . . oww.

(*Curtain*)

Martie Charles (–)

Job Security   1970

Martie Charles was one of a number of writers (Neil Harris, Ben Caldwell, Richard Wesley, Marvin X, Milburn Davis) connected with the New Lafayette Theatre in Harlem. This theater, founded in 1966 under the artistic director Robert Macbeth and resident playwright Ed Bullins, has devoted its force to creating a black theater meaningful to its own community.

With a sensitive ear for dialogue and an intuitive grasp of character, Martie Charles focuses on one of the community's most serious problems: teachers whose first commitment is to themselves instead of to their students.

Frustration, bitterness, neglect, and the need for devoted and qualified black teachers to train black students is the theme of *Job Security*. [For many years the only job offering security and respectability for black college graduates (aside from medicine, law, and the ministry), was teaching. Since only a limited number of teachers were hired each year, it was not unusual to find blacks with college degrees employed as postal workers, waiters, red caps, and pullman porters. Often individuals hired to teach had no interest in the profession but took the job because of the status and the regular salary check. The result was dissatisfied people playing roles at the expense of innocent students. The passage of fair employment laws in many areas of the country enabled blacks to take the jobs for which they had trained themselves. Now students who select teaching as a career for the most part have a genuine interest in the field.]

Martie Charles has great disdain for an educational system in which students are subjected to hatred, disinterest, and poorly qualified teachers. Ella is the victim of such a system. She is a bright, sensitive girl who has developed a tough outer skin. She yearns for the sensitive, inner Ella to be brought out; but the people who could achieve this, Mrs. Chase and Mrs. Russell, are too caught up in the mechanics of the system to help the girl. Ella is betrayed; rather than subject herself to continued disinterest and hostility, she acts. She is the anti-hero revolting against the old system with the intent of seeing a new one arise. Her action implies doom, but whatever her punishment, she has been purged; she has been truthful to herself.

The older women are also victims of the system that is operated by disinterested whites. Mrs. Johnson's position as assistant principal is obviously tokenism, since she is the last to learn what is going on in the school. She asserts her authority in the halls, checking students' passes. Mrs. Douglas aims to please her superiors—thus, the students suffer. Chase and Russell are more pathetic, reduced to playing the game in order to keep their jobs. They are miserable people filled with frustration and contempt for the system and for themselves.

In the most highly salaried school system in America, New York City, dope is sold on the playgrounds, police roam the school halls, and students graduate unable to read. Martie Charles, born and raised in Harlem, knows what happens to the students; now she shows what will happen to the system that destroys them.

Job Security

CAST OF CHARACTERS

ELLA
MRS. CHASE, *teacher*
MRS. RUSSELL, *teacher*
MRS. DOUGLAS, *parent working in the school*
MRS. JOHNSON, *assistant to the principal*

The players are black.

Scene One

(SCENE: *the stage is bare except for a desk, chair, and coat rack.* ELLA *enters*)

ELLA Miss Russell here?
CHASE Good morning, Ella.
ELLA (*urgently*) Where Miss Russell? (CHASE *waits for* ELLA's *response to her greeting.* ELLA, *looking behind her*) Come on Miss Chase! Where Miss Russell at?
CHASE What's the matter, Ella?
ELLA They won't lemme go to mah room.
CHASE Who won't?
ELLA Miss Johnson an Mr. Levy.
CHASE What did you do this time?
ELLA (*hurt*) I didn't do nothin but come to school like Miss Russell tole me. Soon's I walk in the door Miss Johnson come pushin on me talkin bout git out.

(MRS. JOHNSON *comes up behind* ELLA *and grabs her arm*)

JOHNSON How did you git in here?
ELLA Git off me!
JOHNSON Who let you in!
ELLA I walked in.
JOHNSON I told you not to enter this building.
ELLA (*trying to pull her arm free of* MRS. JOHNSON's *grasp*) Git off me! Mah mother didn't sen me to school to stan outside in the cold.
JOHNSON Should've thought of that while you were acting up in the classroom.
CHASE Mrs. Johnson . . .
JOHNSON (*interrupts*) I'll handle this, Mrs. Chase! (*to* ELLA) What are you doing inside this building?
ELLA I wanna see Miss Russell.
JOHNSON She is not your teacher, and I told you not to come to school without your mother. You are getting out right now! (*pulls* ELLA)
ELLA (*jerks her arm free*) Fuck you!
JOHNSON What did you say?
ELLA Fuck you motha fucker!
JOHNSON How dare you!
CHASE Ella!
ELLA Well, wasn't nobody botherin her! Tell Miss Russell I be back foh lunch. (*exits*)
JOHNSON (*runs to the door and calls out*) Mrs. Douglas catch that child! Don't let her get away! (*to herself*) Little animal! (*to* CHASE) I wish you wouldn't encourage that girl! (CHASE *looks at* JOHNSON) I wish you wouldn't encourage her to break the rules. She's not to enter this building until her mother comes.
CHASE Mrs. Russell saw Ella in the street a couple of times and spoke to Mr. Levy about it. Yesterday he agreed to let Ella come to school.
JOHNSON I'm the assistant to the principal and no one took the time to tell me anything about it.
CHASE She'd planned to tell you this morning.
JOHNSON Where is Mrs. Russell?
CHASE She should be here soon.
JOHNSON (*looks at her watch*) Does she always come in at this time? It's almost nine.
CHASE Mrs. Johnson, her time card *is* in the office should you care to check.
JOHNSON I think I will have a look at it, meanwhile as far as I'm concerned Ella's suspension stands (*pauses*) until I receive word to the contrary from Mr. Levy. We can no longer put up with her kind of behavior. I must talk with that child's mother.

Job Security

CHASE   Mrs. Russell is planning to make a visit to Ella's home, you might consider joining her.

JOHNSON   (*looks at* CHASE) Would you tell Mrs. Douglas to bring Ella to my office. (*exits*)

(CHASE *opens desk drawer and takes out her appointment books. She checks her schedule for the day.* RUSSELL *enters hurriedly*)

RUSSELL   Those damn trains.

CHASE   You should get a car.

RUSSELL   I can't afford no car. We still payin on the house.

CHASE   Ella and Mrs. Johnson had it this morning.

RUSSELL   What happened?

CHASE   Mrs. Johnson tried to put her out.

RUSSELL   Levy didn't speak to her?

CHASE   She said she didn't know a thing about it, and as far's she's concerned the suspension stands.

RUSSELL   I'll go and talk to her now. Did you ask her about a bigger office or another desk in here?

CHASE   I didn't get a chance to ask her much of anything she was so mad.

RUSSELL   Mad?

CHASE   She went to put Ella out and Ella turned around and called her a motha fucker.

RUSSELL   No, she didn't. (MRS. DOUGLAS *enters struggling with* ELLA)

DOUGLAS   Good mornin Miss Chase, Miss Russell, Miss Johnson not in here?

ELLA   Git off me!

RUSSELL   Good morning Mrs. Douglas. What's the problem.

ELLA   Git off mah arm.

DOUGLAS   You betta keep still foh I snap it off yoh shoulder with you nasty mouth self.

ELLA   Oh, yeah! I know one thing you betta not try.

RUSSELL   You don't have to hold her like that, let her go.

DOUGLAS   If you had uh hear what this child tell Miss Johnson, you wouldn't say that. Miss Chase know, she hear huh.

ELLA   I got a name you know.

DOUGLAS   Shut yoh mouth! I was standin right outside the door, an couldn't believe mah ears.

RUSSELL   You can let her go, Mrs. Douglas. She's not going anywhere. (DOUGLAS *releases* ELLA) Ella did you have words with Mrs. Johnson?

DOUGLAS   Words? She cuss Miss Johnson out, call her all kind uh motha fucker. This chile ain't been nothin but trouble ever since she been here. I know this one.

ELLA   You don't know me. Don't nobdy know me.

DOUGLAS   You watch how you talk to me. I ain't one uh your teachers.

ELLA   What you gonna do if I don't.

DOUGLAS   Tho you clean out the window, thas what I do foh you.

ELLA   You must be gonna pay mah doctor bill!

DOUGLAS   I pay yoh funeral bill, thas what I do foh you. I pay yoh funeral bill, you jus open up yoh mouth to me again.

ELLA   (*opens her mouth wide*) Iss open. What you gonna do?

RUSSELL   That's enough, Ella.

ELLA   Ain't "no" enough? Thas what all you grownups say. She just betta not put her hans on me again, thas all!

RUSSELL   I tole you to be quiet. Now just what happened, what did you hear Mrs. Douglas?

ELLA   Why you asking her? She wasn't here. She don't know nothing about it.

RUSSELL   Mrs. Douglas?

ELLA   She ain't gonna do nothin but lie, thas all yall know how to do is lie, lie, lie.

DOUGLAS   She know she ain't suppose to be in this building, unless her mama is wid huh.

ELLA   I be where I wanna be.

DOUGLAS   She say she was suppose to come see you and Miss Johnson ask her for her pass.

ELLA   She ain't ask me foh nothin. She just tole me to git out.

DOUGLAS   I heard her mah self, she ask you foh your pass.

ELLA   She ain't ask me foh nothin.

RUSSELL   You had a note Ella, I gave you one yesterday, what did you do with it?

ELLA   I lost it.

RUSSELL   Why didn't you tell Mrs. Johnson that.

ELLA   Ain't nobody ask her to bother me.

RUSSELL   Ella it's her job to ask for passes.

ELLA   I thought she was assistant principal.

RUSSELL   That's right.

ELLA   Then why she don't go do her job

instead uh standin round talkin and askin for passes?

RUSSELL That's not the point!

ELLA That's not the point, that's not the point, that's not the point!

RUSSELL Ella!

DOUGLAS That chile is crazy! She ought to be in a mental institution.

ELLA I am in one (*looking around*) just don't you worry bout it.

RUSSELL Why didn't you tell Mrs. Johnson I'd given you a note but you lost it.

ELLA She ain't give me no time.

DOUGLAS You had plenty time. Just ain't got no respect for nothin.

ELLA You keep messin with me an mah father come put a bullet in yoh head.

DOUGLAS What father, you ain't got none.

CHASE Oh no, Mrs. Douglas.

ELLA You don't know what I got. (*voice breaks*)

DOUGLAS (*moves in for the kill*) Thas whas wrong wid you now. Don't nobody want you. Yuh mama even sick uh you.

ELLA Jus don't worry bout it.

RUSSELL Alright Mrs. Douglas, I'll take care of everything, just tell Mrs. Johnson that Ella's in here with me.

DOUGLAS (*drunk from the smell of the child's blood*) The school don't want you. The teachers don't want you, even yuh own mama don't want you.

ELLA You don't know what my mama want. You don't know what mah mama want. You just mine your fucken business, you whitebitch.

DOUGLAS So dumb don't know white from black. (*laughing*)

CHASE Mrs. Douglas I think you'd better go.

DOUGLASS I suppose to take this chile to Miss Johnson. Pity foh anybody to have a chile like this.

ELLA I didn't come outta your belly so don't worry about it.

DOUGLAS If I had anything like you I'd stomp it to death; thas what I do stomp it to death.

ELLA You white bitch, white bitch, white bitch, white bitch.

RUSSELL Shut your mouth Ella, jus shut your mouth.

ELLA (*looks at* RUSSELL *hurt and angered*) Why you tellin me to shut mah mouth, why you didn't tell her to shut her mouth? How come you didn't tell her thas enough, like you always tellin me. How come you didn't tell her thas not the point, how come? How come? How come? How come?

CHASE Ella.

DOUGLAS Somethin gonna happen to that chile (*points*)

ELLA Don't be pointin at me.

DOUGLAS Mark mah words somethin gonna happen to her.

RUSSELL Mrs. Douglas, would you please just leave.

ELLA Yes leave, leave, all of you leave this stinkin, stinkin shit house.

DOUGLAS Miss Johnson tole me ...

RUSSELL (*interrupts*) I'll talk to Mrs. Johnson. (DOUGLAS *exits.* RUSSELL *looks at* ELLA *for a long while*)

ELLA Don't be lookin at me.

RUSSELL Did you bring the dollar?

ELLA No.

RUSSELL I thought we agreed that you were gonna pay the dollar or bring your mother.

ELLA You and Mr. Levy agreed.

RUSSELL You were there.

ELLA I'm not payin no dollar for no candy.

RUSSELL You ate the candy.

ELLA So! I eat a lot uh candy.

RUSSELL But you knew this candy was stolen from the parents room!

ELLA I didn't steal it!

RUSSELL Why did you eat the candy?

ELLA If somebody give you candy wouldn't you eat it?

RUSSELL That's not the point.

ELLA That's not the point, that's not the point, that's not the point, the ...

RUSSELL Alright Ella. You ate the candy, you pay for it!

ELLA Uh, uh, Mr. Levy make a lot uh money bein principal, let him pay for it.

RUSSELL That's not the ...

ELLA That's not the point, that's not the point, why you always say that?

RUSSELL Ella!

ELLA What?!

RUSSELL Did you tell your mother you've been suspended from school?

ELLA No!

RUSSELL Why?

ELLA She been sick. She jus got home from the hospital.
RUSSELL Did she receive the letter your teacher sent her?
ELLA He say he sent a letter to mah house.
RUSSELL Yes.
ELLA You know he lie don't you? Stupid thing don't know what he doin no how.
RUSSELL Somebody's got to talk to your mother, Ella, how long has she been home?
ELLA She just been home a couple uh days an I don't want nobody botherin her.
RUSSELL How else can I get you back into your class?
ELLA Jus don't worry bout it, cause I don't wanna go back in there no how. Ole stupid teacher don't know what he doin. He the worse teacher I ever had. Why you and Miss Chase don't have a class no more?
RUSSELL We're helping the new teachers.
ELLA Doin what?
RUSSELL We show them how to make plans for the day, how to prepare interesting lessons, how to teach them.
ELLA You must be ain't been to see mah teacher.
RUSSELL Yes I've been workin with your teacher.
ELLA Well it didn't do him no good, he still need a lot uh help, nobody lissen to him. He so stupid he don't know what he doin. We don't have no books, I'm tired uh sittin up there doin nothin, I wanna stay down here with you an Miss Chase.
RUSSELL He told me that you're very good in math so he must be doing something.
ELLA I finish those problems he give us in two minutes. I tole him to give me work that's more harder, cause I didn't wanna think bout ma mother in the hospital, all he ever say is sit down, sit down, sit down, sit down, sit down, sit down, sit down, sit down (ELLA *sings the words and does dance movements to the rhythm*)
RUSSELL Ella!
ELLA What!
RUSSELL Who gave you the candy?
ELLA I told you before, Doreen.
RUSSELL Who's Doreen, do I know her?
ELLA I don't know who you know!
RUSSELL What class is she in?
ELLA Mine. But she ain't in school now. She be here for lunch.

CHASE Ella, what happened with the candy.
ELLA I ate it.
CHASE How did you get it?
ELLA I just tole you, Doreen gave it to me.
CHASE How did Doreen get it?
ELLA Ask Doreen!
RUSSELL Answer the question, Ella!
ELLA She took it.
CHASE How did she take it?
ELLA I can't stan nosy people.
RUSSELL Ella???!
ELLA (*in a fast childlike chant*) Well you see I was with Doreen an she said I want some candy and I said, me too, I'm hungry but I ain't got no money so she said I know where some candy is. Less snatch some. So we went in the parents room an Doreen say you keep the lady busy while I take it and she took two boxes and gave me one.
CHASE For keeping the lady busy?
ELLA Thas what I said.
CHASE Ella, your mother should know!
ELLA She sick, I don't want nobody botherin her.
CHASE Who were you staying with while she was in the hospital?
ELLA My sister an she ain't got no dollar to be paying for no candy.
RUSSELL How do you suggest we get you back into your class?
ELLA I already tole you don't worry bout it cause I don't wanna go back.
RUSSELL You have to go back to your class.
ELLA Why I caint stay here wid you and Miss Chase. I be good.
RUSSELL You can't stay here, Ella.
ELLA You and Miss Chase could give me work. I like yaull, please lemme stay, I be good. I promise, I won't run out the room, I won't fight, I be good, don't make me go back to that stupid teacher.
CHASE Ella, we have nothing to do with it. (ELLA *looks*)
RUSSELL We just work here, we caint take you out of your class. You have to go back, that's where you belong, that's where Mr. Levy and Mrs. Johnson put you.
ELLA But they don't like me. They don't care where I am. (*silence*) Well, I ain't got no dollar so I caint go back no how.
RUSSELL I'm going to lend you the dollar. You just pay it back when you can. This way

we can get you out of the street and back into your classroom where you belong. (*pause*) Alright? (*goes to her purse takes out money gives it to* ELLA)

ELLA (*looks at the dollar, then at* CHASE *and* RUSSELL) I guess so.

CHASE Ella would you go next door to Mrs. Brown, and ask her if Mrs. Russell and I can have our coffee now. And be nice about it.

ELLA If she be nice to me, I be nice to her. (ELLA *leaves the dollar on the desk and exits*)

CHASE Ooo, lawd I felt bad tellin her she had to go back to that class. You think she'll stay.

RUSSELL No. She's right about him, he is stupid, and he's just in here so he can stay out of the Army.

CHASE I really felt bad tellin that child that's where she belonged.

RUSSELL Nothin we could do about it, they's have us up on insubordination charges before we know it, an I really can't afford to loose mah job, not now.

CHASE You know sometimes I'm very sorry that I don't have a class anymore. We not gettin anywhere with these people, they don't give a damned about our children.

RUSSELL I don't agree with that. We have to show them what they're doing wrong, and how to work with our children.

CHASE The only way to get a job done right and the way you want it is to do it yourself. People who have nothing to do with the training of their children are in trouble, and could be destroyed, we need to start our own schools for our black children.

RUSSELL With what? Who's gonna pay for it? Who's gonna pay us? Where else can you get the kind of job security that we have here.

CHASE Yes but while we are secure and earning a living our children are being twisted and... (RUSSELL *points to the door indicating that* ELLA *is standing outside.* ELLA *enters with a tray and two cups of coffee*)

RUSSELL Soon as I finish this, we'll see about getting you back into your class. You'll change your mind once you're back in there working. I'll see to it that you get more work.

ELLA (*picks up the dollar off the desk, examines it*) What do job security mean? (CHASE *and* RUSSELL *look at one another and then at* ELLA)

Scene Two

(*Next day*)

DOUGLAS Scuse me ladies.

RUSSELL Good morning, Mrs. Douglas.

DOUGLAS Good mornin, I just come to find out what happened with Ella.

RUSSELL She's returned to her class.

DOUGLAS She won't be there long, not if I know her.

RUSSELL Let's hope she does.

DOUGLAS I feel sorry for these teachers and what they have to put up with outta our children. Course you cain't blame half uh these kids around here when you see the kind uh homes they come outta. They ain't taught to respect nothin, just like Ella, an I know just the kinda home she come outta.

CHASE I think Ella's been upset because her mother's been in the hospital.

DOUGLAS Her mother ain't been in no hospital. She git drunk an they caint find her for days and when she come home she call them kids all kinda mothafuckers.

CHASE That's not Ella's fault.

DOUGLAS Well I seen how yaull made frens with Ella, and what not, but I tell ya, some kids just ain't no good an thas all to it. Caint nobody do nothin with Ella, she had almost every teacher in this school, and I betchu she be out that room in the next five or ten minutes. That girl been causen trouble ever since the second grade. (RUSSELL *and* CHASE *remain silent and begin to find things to do*) Well, I do know none uh the black teachers have trouble like that with they kids. If Ella was in Miss Jones class she wouldn't uh act like she did.

CHASE Mrs. Jones.

DOUGLAS Wouldn't do no harm to talk to her. See what she say. Cause if I know Ella, she ain't gonna be where she is too long any way, an' one thing 'bout Miss Jones she is really interested in everyone uh her kids like they was her own, an she got some worse'n Ella.

(ELLA *enters in a white party type dress. Her hair is dressed with white ribbons. She is carrying a small candy box*)

RUSSELL Ella!

ELLA Good mornin Miss Russell, Good morning Miss Chase. Good morning Miss

Douglas. Miss Douglas I'm sorry for what I said to you yesterday.

DOUGLAS (*looks suspiciously at* ELLA) Sorry? Oh yeah? Well alright Ella. (*starts to leave*)

ELLA Have some candy?

DOUGLAS Candy? This the candy the parents was sellin?

ELLA I know, I paid for it. Didn't I miss Russell?

RUSSELL Yes she did.

DOUGLAS I don't eat candy in the morning.

ELLA Please take a piece so I know you not mad with me no more.

DOUGLAS Alright Ella. (*looks at the candy while choosing a piece*) This candy look different from the kind I bought. (*bites into it*) It taste good.

ELLA Take another one.

DOUGLAS Believe I will. Thank you Ella. (*exits*)

CHASE Ella you look so pretty today.

ELLA Thank you. This the dress I wore to my aunt funeral.

RUSSELL Such a pretty dress for a funeral. Does your teacher know you're out of your room?

ELLA Yes, here's my pass, see.

RUSSELL How're things going?

ELLA The same.

CHASE Not even a little better?

ELLA No.

RUSSELL You certainly seemed to have made a change, Ella. I'll be up to talk with your teacher today.

CHASE Is that the same box of candy you took from the parents?

ELLA Uh, huh. Want a piece?

RUSSELL Didn't you tell me that you and Doreen ate all of that candy?

ELLA Uh, uh. She ate all uh hers. (*extends the box*) I didn't eat all uh mines.

CHASE I'm like Mrs. Douglas, I don't like to eat candy in the morning.

ELLA Jus one.

CHASE (*looking in the box*) What're these?

ELLA I put some decoration on it.

RUSSELL Decoration?

ELLA You know those lil balls like on a birthday cake? My sister work in a bakery and she always have them, so ask her to git me some.

CHASE Well Ella you look so pretty today, I'll have some just for that reason.

ELLA You don't want none Miss Russell?

RUSSELL I'll have one too.

CHASE Did your sister help you, Ella?

ELLA I did it all by my self.

RUSSELL You know those little balls really do something to the flavor.

CHASE (*reaching for another*) And they're not too sweet.

ELLA My teacher an Mr. Levy like them too.

CHASE Oh?

RUSSELL They had some candy?

ELLA Uh huh an Miss Johnson too.

CHASE Mrs. Johnson?? Mrs. Johnson?? Mr. Levy, your teacher?? (*poison begins to take effect*) and Mrs. Douglas.

RUSSELL Who else Ella?

ELLA Just you an Miss Chase thas all.

CHASE Ella?

ELLA Yes, Miss Chase?

CHASE You didn't do anything to the candy, did you?

ELLA I decorated it. (CHASE *and* RUSSELL *look at one another. By this time the poison has effected both of them*) I made it special for all yaull mothafuckers (RUSSELL *and* CHASE *begin to heave*) Yaull gone die! I tole you I didn't wanna go back to that stupid teacher. Yaull gone die! An where you goin you don't gotta worry bout no job security. Bye ladies. (*leaves them heaving and gagging.* ELLA *sings*) Glory, glory halleluiah, my teacher hit me with the ruler, the ruler turned red and the teacher dropped dead, no more school for me.

(*Lights*)

12

Black Theater for Black People

**Langston Hughes   Imamu Amiri Baraka (LeRoi Jones)
Ed Bullins   Ted Shine   Val Ferdinand**

It should be apparent to anyone who has read most of the plays in this volume that black playwrights write sometimes for whites, sometimes for whites and blacks, sometimes for blacks only.

In 1926, W. E. B. DuBois supervised the formation of the Krigwas, a theatre that was to produce plays *about* Negroes, *by* Negroes, *for* Negroes, and *near* Negroes. The white mass media did not exploit it, and white America remained unthreatened by a separatist art movement.

In 1965, LeRoi Jones demanded a theatre *about* black people, *with* black people, *for* black people, and *only* black people. This time Caucasian fears rose righteously to denounce "reverse racism." Beyond the exploitation by the news media, there were reasons for the backlash: the ungrateful Mr. Jones (who was soon to abandon even his "slave" name) was biting the hand that had given him the awards. Also, the nation had just miraculously survived the separatist threat of Malcolm X and the Black Muslims. Finally, white America had made reluctant gestures toward integration. For a suppliant to spurn the majority was too much . . . especially under the gaze of world opinion.

The authors in this section are speaking primarily to their own people in their own idiom. A white may read the plays, attend the performances, be hip and hep to ingroup life and language, but he must finally remain outside the total experience of the play. Denise Nichols of *The Free Southern Theatre* offers an explanation:

When the black artist speaks to a critical audience that is not also black, he speaks from one set of cultural and political interests and experiences to an audience with different, sometimes hostile priorities and contradicting experience. The black artist, in order to communicate across that gap, becomes an *explainer*. He must interpret how his own experience relates to the "human experience" of white people so they can understand it. . . .

The more seriously the black artist tries to affect the white consciousness, the more explicative he must become. The more explicative he becomes, the less attention he gives to the essentials of his art. A kind of negative value field is established. Racism systematically verifies itself when the slave can only break free by imitating the master, by contradicting his own reality.

The first steps of a black playwright, then, are to discover, identify, and affirm his own culture to his own culture. This is done in some black groups through plays, in others through ritual. Another face of this affirmation is the exorcism of all that is white, including the "so-called Negroes who are hopelessly grafted to integrationist ideals" Imamu Baraka writes of this exorcism in his play *Great Goodness of Life*.

Since that day in 1965 when Imamu Baraka issued his manifesto, blacks in the theater have gradually educated blacks and whites to the values of a pluralistic society versus the losses in an assimilated one—either by ignoring white protests or by counter-hostility. And in retrospect, no WASP ever expected to join the Mafia, Hadassah, or the Armenian General Benevolent Society. Why should he expect to share in black power?

Langston Hughes (1902–1967)

Little Ham 1935

Little Ham is set in the Harlem of the the 1920's. Marcus Garvey has been deported, but not the black pride he stimulated. A new middle class—mostly money from beauty and funeral parlors—has moved to Sugar Hill. (A'Leila Walker made a million dollars from beauty and hair straightening creams.) The Savoy Ballroom, where "trucking," the boogie woogie, and the Lindy Hop (named for Lindbergh's flight to Paris) originated, has opened. Wealthy whites, ballyhooed by promises of exotica (see Van Vechten's novel *Nigger Heaven*, 1927) come to The Sugar Cane, The Nest, and the Cotton Club, which excludes Negroes from its audience. Still, there is some money to be made, and an air of optimism is said to have prevailed.

Alain Locke predicted an era of "spiritual emancipation" for the New Negro. Wallace Thurman, Claude McKay, Rudolph Fisher, and Countee Cullen were writing about things black. Black musicals (*The Blackbirds of 1928*), black entertainers ("Bojangles"), and black dances (the "mess around," the "black bottom"), were in vogue. Most of this collapsed with the depression.

Although *Little Ham* premiered at the Karamu Playhouse in 1936, it is set in the late 1920's (making reference to Joe Louis, relief, and Roosevelt topical anachronisms). The play is not concerned with the pressure of the Depression. The play's concerned with the perpetual hustle for money and survival basic to a community where everybody plays the numbers so somebody can have something.

In that same decade Langston Hughes told the American Writer's Conference:

The market for Negro writers is definitely limited as long as we write about ourselves. And the more truthfully we write about ourselves, the more limited our market becomes. Those novels about Negroes that sell best, by Negroes or whites, those novels that make the best-seller lists and receive the leading prizes, are almost always books that touch very lightly upon the facts of Negro life, books that make our black ghettos in the big cities seem very happy places.... The exotic is the quaint and the happy—the pathetic or melodramatic, perhaps, but not the tragic. We are considered exotic. When we cease to be exotic, we do not sell well.

Mr. Hughes was addressing the white world. *Little Ham* is not addressed to that world. *Little Ham* is romantic but not exotic, and provides insight into the characters' will to survive. Because Mr. Hughes is writing a comedy, the characters do survive. The play is romantic because the police do not really beat up the blacks, the gangsters do not really kill the opposition, and the hustlers do not really do each other in.

Nonetheless in its many local references there is a realistic side to the play. The white gangsters run Harlem. "Dutch" is an allusion to Dutch Schultz, who ran the Cotton Club until his assassination in 1934 and whose mob strongarmed its way into the Harlem numbers racket and bars. (Malcolm X points out how few people understand the hundreds of thousands of dollars made in numbers from "nigger pennies." A penny bet, if a hit is made, brings six dollars. To win on a bet, one must duplicate the last three figures of the Stock Exchange for that day).

Mr. Hughes' Harlem canvas includes over forty characters and a plethora of religious types, including a convert to the popular Father Divine. Mr. Hughes catches the topical interest in things Abyssinian and Ethiopian. "Ethiopia shall stretch forth her hand to Harlem," the street orator exclaims. A voice from the crowd responds, "and she'll draw back a nub!" His characters play the "dozens" and they use a vernacular ("meriney") which few whites know.

As a comedy of urban life, *Little Ham* is the father to a barber shop play like *Ceremonies in*

Dark Old Men, to a barroom play like *No Place To Be Somebody*, to a romantic gambling film like *Cotton Comes to Harlem*, and to a people-drinking-on-the-stoop drama like *In the Wine Time*.

There is not much question that *Little Ham* belongs to the black theater for black people in the same way that Langston Hughes' poetry is completely understood only by the people he wrote about.

Little Ham

CAST OF CHARACTERS

MADAM LUCILLE BELL, *proprietress of Paradise Shining Parlors*
SHINGLE, *a lazy shine boy*
CUSTOMER, *on the shine stand*
JANITOR, *a numbers addict*
SUGAR LOU BIRD, *a Harlem chorus girl*
LITTLE HAM, *a sporty young shoe shiner*
MATTIE BEA, *a married woman*
OLD LADY
SHABBY MAN
BOSS LEROY, *a Harlem racketeer*
MAN IN BOOTS
TINY LEE, *a hairdresser*
LITTLE BOY
FIRST DETECTIVE
SECOND DETECTIVE
YOUTH
JASPER, *night shine boy*
WEST INDIAN
DEACONESS
TALL GUY
HOT STUFF MAN
PRETTY WOMAN
MASCULINE LADY
NEWSBOY
BUTCH, *gangster*
JIGGERS, *gang leader*
DUTCH, *gangster*
OPAL, *manicurist*
LULU, *a hairdresser*, TINY'S *sister*
MAMA, *a customer*
SNOOKS, *her child*
STAID LADY, *a customer*
MISSOURI, *her little girl*
LODGE LADY
DIVINITE
DELIVERY BOY
A COP
NELSON, *a dog*
JACK, LULU'S *boy friend*
GILBERT, TINY'S *used-to-be*
MASTER OF CEREMONIES, *at the Hello Club Ball*
BERIBBONED COMMITTEE MEMBERS
DANCERS
ORCHESTRA

ACT ONE

(TIME: *Late 1920's.*
PLACE: *Harlem.*
Late morning.
The interior of the Paradise Shining Parlors, three chairs mounted on a dais, a rack of weekly Negro newspapers and Dream Books. At opposite side of stage from door a cigar counter and cash register behind which a stately middle-aged woman called MADAM BELL *presides, a telephone booth, a closet, a gas stove, a few stools, a radio, a poster announcing the Hello Club's Social Contest and Ball.*
When the curtain rises, the radio is blaring a blues. MADAM BELL *sits behind the register taking down a number from a client, the* JANITOR *of the building, who wishes to play*)

MADAM BELL (*to one of the shine boys*) Turn that radio down, Shingle, so I can take this number. That noise gets on my nerves.
SHINGLE (*leaving customer whose shoes he is shining*) Yes, ma'am.
JANITOR (*at cigar stand*) 702 in a box. I drempt it as sure as I'm standing here, last night.
MADAM How much, a dime?
JANITOR No'm, a nickel a piece.
MADAM Thirty cents. (*opening drawer in stand*) Haven't you got any change?
JANITOR Only this here half dollar.
MADAM I wish you-all'd bring change for these numbers. Shingle, can you change this? I don't want to ring this register and get my store accounts all mixed up with the number money.
SHINGLE (*leaving customer again*) All I got is

15 cents. (*drawling*) Tips ain't amounted to nothing today.

MADAM All right, all right. (*ringing register and taking change out*) I'll have to give you some pennies.

JANITOR Well, I tell you—put ten cents on a run down, 702 to 712, 'cause I know 7 something is coming today.

MADAM Now you're talkin'. That's the way to win. Why don't you put that other dime on bolito, nickel on the first and last?

JANITOR I believe I will, 7-0 and 0-2.

MADAM (*putting the numbers down and making out a slip*) Them's good numbers, Janitor, I might play 'em myself.

JANITOR I believes they lucky.

MADAM Yes, indeed! Well, now, you don't get no change.

JANITOR That's the last cent I got till payday, so you know I believes in them numbers. I dreampt 702 just as plain last night.

SHINGLE I hope you warn't in your lickers.

JANITOR I never drinks 'cept on payday. Don't have nothing to drink on.

CUSTOMER (*on stand*) Well, I drink—and don't play. I never play numbers. I'd rather have mine in my belly than in somebody else's pocket.

JANITOR That's you. But if I ever hit, I'm gonna live on the fat o' the land. (*exits*)

SHINGLE (*pointedly, as* CUSTOMER *descends from stand*) Well, I never plays neither. I takes *my tips* home to my wife and children.

CUSTOMER (*handing him two dimes*) You're a good man. Here's a dime for yourself.

SHINGLE (*as* CUSTOMER *exits*) Thank you, sir! Thank you. (*as soon as* CUSTOMER *is gone,* SHINGLE *goes to the* MADAM, *who rings up a dime for the shine*) Here, Madam Bell, here's yo' dime, and put my ten cents on 942, will you, straight? That's the number of my new girl friend's house, where she moved in, and I knows it's lucky, 'cause I went by there last night and helped her put up the bed, and she say, "Baby, I feels like something good's gonna happen in this house!"

MADAM (*putting down numbers*) Wife and babies! Shingle, you's an awful liar!

MATTIE BEA (*sticking head in door*) S'cuse me, you all. Ain't Little Ham got here yet?

SHINGLE No'm, he ain't showed up as yet, lady.

MATTIE BEA Well, tell him I were here and'll be back directly.

SHINGLE Yes'm. (*exit* MATTIE BEA)

MADAM (*handing him paper*) Here's your slip. That makes about five numbers you played already today.

SHINGLE Yes'm. I sho' better hold on to my next tip 'cause its almost lunch time, and I's hungry.

MADAM It's about time for Ham to show up, too. He relieves you, don't he?

SHINGLE Yes'm. I wish I was as lucky as little old Ham. He sure do have plenty good womens, and he's always hittin' the numbers. For such a little man, he musta done got a charm or something 'nother.

MADAM Well, if you just work hard, Shingle, you'll have something some day, too, son.

SHINGLE What kind o' son you mean, Madam Bell?

MADAM Son of Ethiopia, my boy, waiting to stretch forth your hand. (*putting scarf about her shoulders*) Shingle, turn up that gas a little. It's getting cold. Looks like snow. And see if you can't get something good on the radio like "Trees," I hate blues.

SHINGLE Sure is cold. What month is we at now?

MADAM October.

SHINGLE (*going to the radio and monkeying with dials*) Next month's Christmas, ain't it?

MADAM No, Thanksgiving.

SHINGLE Um-uh! I hope I hits 942, by then, so's I can buy my girl friend a turkey.

MADAM Just keep on playing it. 942's bound to come out some time.

SHINGLE If I don't run out first.

(*enter good-looking chorus girl,* SUGAR LOU BIRD)

SUGAR LOU Quick shine, please. I got a rehearsal today.

SHINGLE Yes, ma'am. Just mount the chair, Miss Bird, I'll be through with this radio in a minute. (*all sorts of fantastic and discordant sounds come out of the radio as the two women try to top it with their conversation*)

SUGAR LOU (*shouting*) How you been, Madam Bell?

MADAM Not bad, not bad, Sugar Lou.

SUGAR LOU What's been running lately?

MADAM The four and sevens. 467 and 347've both come out this week.

SUGAR LOU   Well, put me a quarter straight on 744. That ought to hit it in the bread basket.

MADAM   What'd you say? (*to Shingle*) You Shingle, tone it down.

SUGAR LOU   7-4-4.

MADAM   That's a good number, girlie.

SHINGLE   (*drawling as he dials back to the records*) If I just had a dime, I'd play that number, too.

SUGAR LOU   Put a dime on it for Shingle, then—(*to him*) And that'll be your tip.

SHINGLE   Thank you! *Thank you!* I'm gonna shine 'em till you can see your pretty face in the toes.

SUGAR LOU   These are handmade shoes from abroad. They take a good shine.

SHINGLE   You been all over Europe, ain't you, Miss Bird? That's what you get for dancin' with a show.

SUGAR LOU   Yep, I been most everywhere. How about you?

SHINGLE   I been to Paris.

SUGAR LOU   Paris, Kentucky?

SHINGLE   No'm. Paris, London. And I took a train and went from there to Chicago. Then I come by zepp'lin here. (*the phone rings loudly.* SHINGLE *goes to answer*)

MADAM   (*making out slips and calling* SHINGLE *to get them*) Here, hand that to Miss Bird. (*to the girl*) How's your show doing, Sugar Lou?

SUGAR LOU   Shaping up right well. Opens next week. Looks like we might go to London after a run here. You know I was over there all last year with the Dixie Vamps, toured the Continent everywhere.

MADAM   How'd you like it?

LUGAR LOU   How'd they like me, you mean? Honey, they musta thought I was chocolate. They nearly ate me up. Looked like I'd never get out of France. (*to* SHINGLE *as he turns from phone*) Hurry up, boy. I got to get down to the theatre.

MADAM   Who was that for?

SHINGLE   Little Ham.

MADAM   Some woman, I suppose.

SHINGLE   Naturally.

SUGAR LOU   Shingle, please hurry. I've got a rehearsal.

SHINGLE   Yes'm.

MADAM   It must be nearly noon, ain't it?

SUGAR LOU   (*raising her sleeve and displaying eight or ten wrist watches*) You mean here in New York, I presume?

MADAM   Yes, darling.

SUGAR LOU   Well, it is 11:30 here.

SHINGLE   (*noticing her many watches*) Um-uh!

MADAM   Why so many watches, darling? I ain't never seen the like.

SUGAR LOU   I got one for each European capital, honey. I collected 'em while I was over there, and I wear 'em all just to tell the time o' day in each place. They came from Paris, Berlin, Monaco. Now, for instance, an Indian Prince, Naboo, gave me this little platinum thing in Paris, and I told him I'd never let it run down, nor change the hour until we met in Paris again. (*sighing*) It's 6:30 in the evening in Paris right now.

SHINGLE   Well, I be a Abyssinian! Miss Bird, what time is it in Ethiopia?

SUGAR LOU   I'm sorry, but I never met Haile Selassie.

SHINGLE   (*as he finishes with her shoes*) I knows it's lunch time in Harlem, and I ain't got nary dime to get myself a pig's foot.

SUGAR LOU   You broke?

SHINGLE   Always broke. Look like I just can't hit them numbers.

MADAM   Shingle. (*to girl*) Don't pay him no mind, Sugar Plum. That boy's always got his hand out. I'm gonna fire him if he don't watch out—asking for tips.

SUGAR LOU   That's all right! Here, Shingle, pay for my numbers and yours, and keep the change. (*hands him fifty cents*)

SHINGLE   Yes, ma'am. Thank you. Thank you.

SUGAR LOU   Be seeing you, Madam Bell. (*as she exits, she bumps into* LITTLE HAM, *who enters in a hurry—late, as usual. He steps back with a flourish, tips his hat, and bows*)

HAM   Howdy do, Miss Sugar Lou.

SUGAR LOU   Hello, Little Ham! How're you?

HAM   I'm your man! If you ain't busy after the show, lemme know.

SUGAR LOU   I might at that, Little Ham. You got any new trucking steps you can teach me?

HAM   Sure have. Look here! (*he trucks across the room toward the Madam to the music of the radio. Laughs aloud and turns and waves at* SUGAR LOU)

SUGAR LOU (*smiling*) Goodbye, boy! That sends me!

HAM (*still trucking*) I sure likes to dance, Lucille. When I'm dancing, feels like I'm loving a million women all at once!

MADAM (*peeved*) You better get here, Ham. You devil! You know you s'pose to come at eleven. Shingle, turn down that radio!

SHINGLE (*as he turns dial*) That joker can't keep time. Ham can't do nothin' but truck and love.

HAM (*in surprise*) What time is it?

SHINGLE Six o'clock in Paris.

HAM How do you know?

SHINGLE Sugar Lou just told me.

HAM You keep your mind off Sugar Lou, boy. She's got her eye on me.

SHINGLE She don't know you livin', less'n she see you.

HAM Didn't you glimpse her just givin' me that "truck on up and see me some time" look as she went out the door?

MADAM You come on in here and truck them shoebrushes. Shingle's got to go get his lunch, and some of you boys clean up that shine stand too, before Boss LeRoy comes. It's filthy.

SHINGLE Yes'm. I sure will, but just lemme play a dime on 645 first.

MADAM (*making out a slip*) 645 straight?

SHINGLE Um-um. And put this other dime on bolito, back and front.

MADAM Bolito, each way.

SHINGLE Ham, you lend me a dime to get a hot dog, please, being I ain't kicked about you being late, and tips is poor.

HAM (*tossing him a dime*) Money's nothing to me. Here, boy. Lemme see you go! Has Mattie Bea been here asking for me?

SHINGLE Some woman or 'nother stuck her head in here about half hour ago, say she'd be back.

HAM What she look like? (*beginning to unbutton his street clothes*)

SHINGLE Like a chocolate blonde with purple powder.

HAM That's Mattie Bea. She promised to bring me a muffler today. My neck is cold.

SHINGLE Why don't you buy one yourself?

HAM I likes to give the women pleasure. They loves to present me with things.

SHINGLE How come they never presents *me* with nothing, I wonder?

HAM You just not the type, Shingle, you not the type.

SHINGLE Some woman named Laura called up here, too.

HAM I ain't interested in Laura.

SHINGLE How come?

HAM She's just a used blade, and I got a new razor.

MADAM Shingle, go get your lunch.

(*Meanwhile,* HAM *has been taking off his sporty overcoat with the extra broad shoulders and removing his coat and vest, while* SHINGLE *takes his old coat out of the closet and puts it on.* HAM *dons a snappy white jacket and begins to straighten up the shoeshine stand*)

SHINGLE (*moving toward the door*) Don't you go grabbing off all the women customers this afternoon after I gets back. I wants to look at some legs, too.

HAM Aw, go on eat your pigs feet. Lemme miss you! You know you ain't no Clark Gable like I am. (SHINGLE *exits*)

MADAM Ham, you're a mess!

HAM (*coming toward her*) That's why the women like me, Lucille. You still likes me a little bit your ownself, don't you?

MADAM I let you stay around here even if you is late all the time.

HAM (*sadly*) But you done got yourself all tied up with that numbers baron now and can't go for nobody else.

MADAM We makin' money though, Ham. You know yourself, I didn't hardly make my rent out of this place before I met LeRoy, and he set me up as one of his agents for takin' bets. You must admit, LeRoy's way up yonder with the big shots when it comes to writing numbers. Why the biggest gangster in New York's behind LeRoy's outfit. Manny made LeRoy chief of this section of Harlem himself. 'Fore long you'll see me wearing more diamond wrist watches than Sugar Lou brought back from the Old Country.

HAM Well I hope you'll gimme just one to put on my big old arm so I can tell time.

MADAM I sure will, Ham, for old time's sake. (*they hold hands. She sighs*)

HAM Lucille, is there anything I can do for you?

MADAM (*coming to herself*) You might give

me a shine. (*leaves cash register and mounts shine stand*)

HAM (*suddenly busy*) You know I'll do that.

MADAM (*looking down at* HAM) Ham, honey, sometimes I worries about you. Honest I do, even if we did bust up. You fool around with too many women. And you don't take none of them serious. Someday, some one of 'em's gonna get mad and cut you from here to yonder.

HAM Not me, baby! Oh, no! When it comes to cuttin' and shootin', that's when I'm gone. Me and weapons don't mix.

MADAM That's why I couldn't let myself like you any more than I did. I'd a-been in the electric chair by now and you'd a-been in your grave.

HAM Aw, baby, don't talk so mean.

MADAM But I'm glad I didn't hurt you.

HAM Why?

MADAM You too cute, Ham, to get all cut up.

HAM You tellin' me? (*enter* MATTIE BEA)

MATTIE BEA Oh, here you is, Hamlet. I been up here three or four times tryin' to catch you. (*noticing* MADAM BELL *glaring at her*) Ham, I wants to talk to you—when you gets through.

HAM Just sit down. I'll be with you in a minute, baby. (MATTIE BEA *sits down as an* OLD LADY *enters, poorly dressed*)

OLD LADY Is I too late to play my numbers back today?

MADAM Plenty of time, plenty of time. They ain't collected yet.

OLD LADY (*as* MADAM *gets down*) I just got a few pennies my daughter give me. I wants to play 403, 862, and 919, and put . . . (*she and* MADAM *talk at the cigar counter as* HAM *and* MATTIE BEA *get together*)

HAM Girl, you oughtn't to bother me during my working hours. Don't you know I don't 'low no women to mix in with my profession?

MATTIE BEA Well, honey, I just had to see you. (*pulling out a package from beneath her coat*) Didn't you tell me your neck was cold? I done brought you this nice warm muffler. (*unwraps and offers him a bright red muffler.* HAM *tries it on*)

HAM (*looking in glass*) I reckon it'll do. It's mighty red, though. Liable to burn me up!

MATTIE BEA Don't you like red, honey?

HAM I reckon so, since you brought it to me.

MATTIE BEA Are you coming by the Silver Dollar tonight?

HAM Well, er . . . er, now my business . . .

MATTIE BEA (*impatiently*) Now, you know you ain't got no business . . .

HAM Shss—ss-s. How you know what I got?

MATTIE BEA (*loudly*) I know—you just getting tired of me, that's all, or else you actin' like it. You must think I enjoy staying home with my husband.

HAM No, baby. I don't. But can't you see this ain't no place to talk like that. (*enter a shabby but neatly dressed* MAN *who mounts the shine stand*) I got a customer.

MATTIE BEA Well, I'll be back by and by. I want you to go with me to the Hello Social Club tomorrow night, anyhow. They havin' a Charleston contest.

HAM Baby, you know you can't Charleston. (*beginning to shine the shabby* MAN'S *shoes*)

MATTIE BEA I know I can't, but we can sit there and look.

HAM Well, I wants to dance, not look, when I go to a party.

MATTIE BEA I can two-step.

HAM You can't do that good, much less Lindy hop.

MATTIE BEA Well, you goin' with me, whether you want to or not.

HAM Shss-ss! Here comes the boss, anyhow.

MATTIE BEA I'll be coming back. (*starts toward door*)

HAM O.K.

MATTIE BEA You go hang your muffler up, Ham, so you won't get it dirty. (*she exits, as* BOSS LEROY *enters and looks around importantly*)

OLD LADY (*at cigar counter*) And if I don't catch today, don't know how I'm gonna play tomorrow, but the Lawd will provide, I reckon. Fact is, I know he will.

MADAM He always does, don't he?

OLD LADY Yes, he do!

LEROY (*to* HAM) Get them papers and cigar butts off that shine stand. It looks like a pigpen in here.

HAM (*insolently*) O.K., big boy.

LEROY What'd you mean—big boy?

HAM Big boss, ain't you?

LEROY (*satisfied*) Well, all right then. (*approaches register and greets* MADAM BELL) Hello, dear. Got the slips ready for me to check up on? We ain't got much time. (*puts his arm around her as they check over the numbers. The* OLD LADY *exits*)

MADAME Hello babe! I ain't seen you all day, LeRoy, honey.

LEROY Been busy as hell, darling. Didn't get a chance to run by. One of our best writers is in jail, too. The damn fool sold a slip to a plain-clothes man. I've got to try to replace him, if I can. (*looking over the slips*) Now, let's see... (*they check up and converse as* HAM *shines the* SHABBY MAN*'s shoes*)

HAM Gettin' kinder cold, ain't it?

SHABBY MAN Yes, it is, for certain. But I had some good luck today. First time in two years.

HAM What'd you do, hit the numbers?

SHABBY MAN No, I got a job! At least, I think I did. That's why I'm getting a shine. They told me to come back at three this afternoon, dressed up. It's waiting table.

HAM Kinder hard to shine shoes as old as these is.

SHABBY MAN I know it, but they all I got. I ain't hardly got a nickel to get downtown after I pay for this shine, either.

HAM Then, that's all right, buddy. You don't have to pay, I been broke too. You just keep it. (*enter* SHINGLE)

SHABBY MAN (*getting down*) Thank you! Thank you! (*bowing as he exits*) Thank you!

SHINGLE Ham, you must-a done give the *man* a tip.

HAM I ain't give him nothin', but a shine. (*loudly*) But as long as you stayed out, you must-a done et up a whole hog, not just the feet. (BOSS *and* MADAM *both look at* SHINGLE)

LEROY I think I'll have to get a time clock in here. (*lowering his voice*) And I want you to get rid of that fresh Little Ham.

SHINGLE (*turning up the radio*) I had to drop by on Pauline a minute.

HAM I lets the women drop by on me.

SHINGLE They gonna gang up on you some day, and then you'll be sorry they knows where you at.

HAM Don't worry 'bout me, big boy.

SHINGLE (*pointing at* HAM*'s neck and the red muffler*) What's the matter, forest fire burnin' you up?

HAM (*taking off muffler*) This here's my present from Mattie Bea, so don't touch it.

SHINGLE Don't worry. I wouldn't put my neck in nothin' that red. They liable to take me for a Roosian Red.

MADAM (*loudly*) Turn down that radio so I can hear my ears.

SHINGLE (*as he takes off his overcoat*) Yes'm. (*looking at Contest poster*) Ham, what do that mean—*Social* Charleston Contest?

HAM Social—meanin' don't nobody get mad. Don't draw no guns nor knives.

SHINGLE Oh! Then I might go.

HAM Ugly as you are, though, you liable to make 'em get mad anyhow. (*phone rings*)

SHINGLE (*to* HAM) Go on! I know it's for you. (HAM *enters phone booth*)

LEROY (*putting money into a chamois bag which he secretes in an inner pocket*) Not bad, darling. But we gonna run our intake up to a hundred bucks a day, you wait and see! Now, I'll just take these duplicate tickets and run on. Also the cash. I've got to report to Manny's secretary. (*whispering*) There's a little shake-up going on in the racket today, but I reckon it'll come out all right. I'm just sitting tight. (*looking at watch*) You can let 'em play until two, then close up till the papers come out. (*a* MAN *in muddy riding boots enters and mounts the shine stand, but* SHINGLE *avoids him, lazily continuing to clean the shine stand*)

SHINGLE (*singing to himself*) *In my solitude...*

LEROY (*to* MADAM) See you later, babe. I'll drop back by and pick up the other entries in half an hour or so. (*suddenly*) Did you play today, Lucille?

MADAME My usual 6-7-8, in a box.

LEROY For how much?

MADAM Quarter apiece.

HAM (*in the phone booth, speaking loudly in a feminine voice*) I tell you Ham don't work here no more... No, indeed! There ain't nobody here by the name o' Ham. (*hangs up the receiver with a bang and emerges from the booth. To* SHINGLE) That warn't nobody but Laura, tryin' to find out is Ham here. (*mimicking her voice*) And come talkin' 'bout a winter coat somebody by the name o' Little Ham done promised to buy her a month ago, and ain't sent it to her yet.

SHINGLE (*dryly*) Here's a customer for you. (*indicating the* MAN IN BOOTS)

HAM (*noting size and dirtiness of the boots*) Go on boy, it's your turn.

SHINGLE I ain't got my cleanin' done yet.

HAM Well, I got to go to de washroom myself.

LEROY (*barking*) Give that customer service!

HAM and SHINGLE Yes, suh! (*soon as* BOSS LEROY's *back is turned,* HAM *eases toward the door, so* SHINGLE *is forced to take the hard job. Begins to wipe off the boots*)

SHINGLE (*mumbling to* HAM) All you wants to do is wait on the women.

HAM You sure is right.

SHINGLE Well, I gets tired . . . (*just then a large fat brownskin* WOMAN *enters*)

HAM Step right up, lady. (*helps her on stand, holding her hand until she is well seated*) You desires a shine?

TINY I don't want no *shampoo*!

HAM Well, I am at your service. (*as he shines*) I ain't seen you in these parts before.

TINY I just moved up this way. My business is down on 128 Street.

HAM You's a business woman?

TINY (*placidly chewing gum*) I'm a hair-dresser. And I own my own beauty parlor.

HAM Now that is what I like in a woman. That she be her own boss.

TINY That I am.

HAM You don't need nobody private-like to boss you, does you?

TINY You mean a man?

HAM That's just what I mean.

TINY I don't see nary one I could use.

HAM You must not be lookin' down then, is you?

TINY Oh, you mean yourself? I ain't acquainted with you.

HAM That's no difficulty. I'm Ham, just Little Hamlet Hitchcock Jones.

TINY And I'm Tiny Lee, that's all.

HAM Baby, you could be a Christmas doll to me.

TINY I hope you don't mean a rag doll.

HAM Woman, I mean a sugar doll. (*confidentially*) I could set you up, plump as you is. (*noise of people running down the street and shouting*)

SHINGLE What's goin' on out there? (*a* LITTLE BOY *cracks the door and sticks his head in*)

LITTLE BOY Joe Louis is goin' by down at the corner.

SHINGLE (*dropping his brushes*) Well, black my soul: Joe Louis! (*exits*)

MAN IN BOOTS I got to see him! (*exits also*)

LEROY I'm ready to go anyhow. See you later, Lucille. (*exits*)

MADAM I'd like to see that boy, too, world's greatest prize fighter. Ham, you watch the cash register. (*takes coat from closet and exits also*)

HAM Ain't nothin' in the cash register—now that LeRoy's been here.

TINY I done seen Joe Louis. I was at his last fight.

HAM You was? Who took you, high as them seats were?

TINY I took myself. I make money.

HAM Don't you need somebody to escort you places?

TINY Where'd you get that idea?

HAM A sweet little woman like you's got no business at a fight all alone by her little she-self.

TINY Now you know I ain't little. (*coyly*) Don't nobody like me 'cause I'm fat.

HAM Well, don't nobody like me 'cause I'm so young and small.

TINY You a cute little man' You mean don't *nobody* like you?

HAM (*woefully*) Nobody that amounts to nothin'.

TINY (*impulsively*) Well, from now on Tiny likes you.

HAM (*holding his shine rag*) You really gonna like me, baby?

TINY Sure I'm gonna like you, and they better not nobody else dare look at you neither.

HAM Who would want to look at me? I know I won't look at nobody myself. But, I'm gonna be the boss, ain't I, Tiny?

TINY Certainly—long as I boss you! But first, I got to know something about you. Ham, is this your place?

HAM Yes'm. (*shining shoes*)

TINY You tellin' the truth?

HAM No'm.

TINY Then this ain't your place?

HAM I mean it ain't my place.

TINY That's what I thought! Where you from?

HAM Alabam.

TINY Alabam?

HAM Yes, but I don't give a damn about it.

TINY You got any relatives?

HAM None a-tall.

TINY Neither've I. I'm all alone.

HAM You all alone?

TINY All alone.

HAM Well, from now on you ain't! Not with Ham around.

TINY Neither're you, long as Tiny's here.
HAM (*looking up soulfully*) Darling!
TINY Honey! Come on up here and kiss me, 'cause I'm too stout to get down to you. (HAM *climbs up on the stand and* TINY *takes him in her arms. Just then the door opens and* SHINGLE *and* MADAM *return*)
SHINGLE Dog take my soul!
MADAM (*acidly*) After all, Ham, you ain't John Barrymore.
TINY No, but I'm Jean Harlow, folks, and nobody yet has took a man from me.
SHINGLE Ham has met his match.
HAM (*getting down*) What you mean, match?
SHINGLE I mean a woman that can hold you down now.
HAM (*embarrassed*) I ain't had no womens before, long as you knowed me.
SHINGLE Then I was born tomorrow.
TINY Well, what he *has* had, and what he *will* have, is two different things! He belongs to Tiny now, don't you, Hamlet, honey?
HAM I sure do. (*mannishly*) That is, you belong to me. You my little Tiny.
TINY And you're Tiny's little Ham.

(*Enter* JANITOR *to play numbers again*)

JANITOR Did you all see Joe Louis passing?
SHINGLE Sure!
MADAM I not only saw him, I touched him! What a man!
JANITOR Madam, I got a penny here. Believe I'll put it on 8-8-8. Tribles. There's just 8 letters in Joe Louis' name.
MADAM (*beginning to write out slip*) Tribles is always good. I used to play 3-3-3 and 7-7-7 all the time.
HAM Babe, I sure feels lucky, findin' you. I feels so lucky I believes I sees a number in the toe of your shoe.
EVERYBODY What number?
HAM (*staring*) 1-1-6, yes sir! 116!
SHINGLE Damn if I ain't gonna play it. Is I got time, Madam?
MADAM Two minutes. I believe I'll play it myself. Ham might really be lucky.
TINY (*opening her pocketbook*) Course he's lucky. Put a dollar on it for me, straight.
JANITOR (*woefully*) I wish somebody'd lend me a dime. I come in here to get a pack o' cigarettes on credit until Sat'day, but I just got to play this one mo' number if Ham say it's good.
HAM (*tossing him a dime*) Here, buddy, try yo' luck. (*to* MADAM) And Madam, put this quarter on it for me.
TINY (*looking down*) Ain't you got no mo'n a quarter, Ham?
HAM I really ain't.
TINY (*hands him a dollar*) Here, take this buck.
HAM And right on 116 it goes. We gonna be rich tomorrow.
MADAM We gonna bust the bank.
SHINGLE I'm gonna buy my gal a hot stuff dress right straight from Fifth Avenue—by way o' some fire escape.
TINY Help me down, 'cause I got to go now. My customers is waiting to get they hair ironed out. Don't you forget, Little Ham, you mine! Here, honey, is my card, shop number, house number, telephone, and everything, written down, printed, so you can't go wrong.
HAM I couldn't never go wrong on you, sweet chile.
TINY (*pinching his cheek*) You a cute little man! You keep my slip, and if the number comes out, we share and share alike.
HAM Okeydoke! Sweetheart, I'll see you tonight.
TINY I'll see you tonight. I mean *tonight*. (*exit*)
SHINGLE (*to* MADAM) You see that Ham! He's just got a way with women, that's all!
MADAM A taking way, I'd say. If this number does hit, she'll never see Ham nor the money either. (*hands out the slips.* JANITOR *exits*)
HAM Now you all hush. (*musingly*) You know, I believes I really does like that big old fat girl.
SHINGLE For what?
HAM To boss around. The bigger the woman, the bigger boss I be's.
SHINGLE You mean the more bossed you *will* be, 'cause you really got a something on your hands now.
MADAM (*acidly*) He's got an elephant.
HAM (*hurt*) Now, Lucille, don't say that.
MADAM Well, I will say it! You got an elephant. But even at that, she looks like a better woman than that corn-colored hussy that brought you than muffler.
SHINGLE That one's married, ain't she?

Little Ham

HAM You all mean Mattie Bea? Yes, she's married—but she's broad-minded.

MADAM (*acidly*) Her mind's so broad you could lay on it!

SHINGLE Ham ain't studyin' 'bout her mind.

HAM Now, I'm studyin' 'bout Tiny now. You know, I believe I loves her.

SHINGLE You always loves the last female you just meets.

HAM Well, she's the last.

SHINGLE You don't know what love is no how.

HAM Sure I know what love is.

SHINGLE What is love?

HAM Love is taking till you can't give no mo'.

SHINGLE And what does you ever give?

HAM Myself.

SHINGLE What does you take?

MADAM He takes the soul-case out of you, that's what he takes. He drives me mad.

HAM Now, Lucille, you . . . (*enter two* WHITE MEN)

SHINGLE (*under his breath*) Uh-oh! I know these two don't want no shines.

(MADAM *begins to secrete the file of number slips hurriedly in her bosom.* HAM *is very busy with the blacking cans, hiding his slips therein.* SHINGLE *looks as if he is paralyzed. They all know the men are detectives*)

FIRST DETECTIVE I judge you give shines here?

HAM Yes, sir! Oh, yes, sir! Black or tan shoes, gray, yellow, or white.

SECOND DETECTIVE You say you shine white shoes, too?

HAM If you wants 'em shined. I'm a shiner, that's what I am.

FIRST DETECTIVE Is that all you are?

HAM Most nigh all.

SECOND DETECTIVE (*savagely*) What do you mean, most nigh?

HAM (*nonchalantly*) Don't you understand the English language? Who are you?

SHINGLE (*frightened—to* HAM) Here, here, now! Ham, hush!

SECOND DETECTIVE I guess you don't know who I am?

HAM I don't.

SECOND DETECTIVE Well, looky here! (*pulls back coat and reveals badge*)

SHINGLE I knowed it all the time.

SECOND DETECTIVE Well, come here then you, if you know so much.

(SHINGLE *approaches like molasses in the wintertime, slower than slow. Meanwhile, the other* DETECTIVE *examines the cigar stand, the cash register, etc., looking for number slips, but* MADAM *has hidden them all in her bosom*)

MADAM A poor woman can't run a decent business without being suspicioned. I never wrote a number in my life, nor played one either.

HAM Numbers? What is that? I can't even count.

SECOND DETECTIVE Never went to school, did you?

HAM I skipped that and went to barber college.

MADAM You just must look in my cash register?

FIRST DETECTIVE We just must, lady. (*Opens register, finds nothing*)

SECOND DETECTIVE (*suddenly shaking* SHINGLE *while two or three dozen number slips fall out of his pockets*) Aw, here's the evidence!

SHINGLE And all of 'em due to win today!

SECOND DETECTIVE Where'd you get 'em?

SHINGLE (*stuttering*) God knows.

FIRST DETECTIVE The judge'll find out then and not from God!

SHINGLE I-I-I was movin' and I just packed up some old papers . . .

SECOND DETECTIVE Did you play 'em here in this shine parlor?

HAM He sure didn't.

MADAM I should say not!

SHINGLE Naw, sir.

FIRST DETECTIVE Where'd you get 'em from?

SHINGLE Well, I can't tell you the name o' the place, but I can take you to the street, and see maybe can I find it.

FIRST DETECTIVE You can?

SHINGLE I reckon I can.

MADAM (*clamping her hand over her mouth as she stares at window*) LeRoy! (*nearly faints, then looks relieved as he evidently goes on*)

SECOND DETECTIVE Well, Biggs, we didn't find nothing here, so let's take this fellow and let him lead us on. And he better lead us right, or else he'll get a year in jail for every slip he's got on his person.

SHINGLE I ain't got no slips now, you all got 'em all.

HAM (*to* SHINGLE) Then they'll give the years to you—and the money to them, if any one of 'em hit.

SECOND DETECTIVE You shut up.

SHINGLE This ain't no laughin' matter. Send somebody to come and bail me out.

MADAM I will, Shingle. Don't worry.

FIRST DETECTIVE (*to the* MADAM) Don't hire boys that play the numbers, sister. It ain't wise. It's a bad habit. They're liable to steal your money to play with.

MADAM Thank you for the good advice. You all certainly gave me a shock coming in here like this. My nerves are all jittering.

SECOND DETECTIVE Next time we'll give you a warning.

MADAM (*taking them seriously*) Please do. Won't you have a cigar before you go? (*offers box*)

FIRST DETECTIVE Don't mind if I do. (*takes one. To his pal*) Go ahead, Bill.

SECOND DETECTIVE Thank you, lady.

HAM (*as they start out*) Have a shine, too?

DETECTIVES No, thanks. (*nodding at* SHINGLE) We got one, that's enough. (*they exit with* SHINGLE)

MADAM (*nearly hysterical*) Lord! Oh, my Father, oh! oh! oh! I near had heart failure! Did you see LeRoy come right there to the door and notice 'em just in time not to come in? If he'd-a come in here then, the game would've been up. They'd-a found all them slips and money and everything on him.

HAM But, Lucille, now it'll be too late to put in my 116. All them last slips we made out, Boss LeRoy done passed on by and didn't collect 'em. Now it's past the time, ain't it? Suppose my number do come out?

MADAM (*distressed*) They had to come around just before the number comes out!

HAM Just before our number got in, you mean. (*then remembering*) But this here's a depot. They oughta pay off here, anyhow. You done wrote it down.

MADAM Ham, that's got me scared. They must-a suspicioned this place, or they never would-a come here. And you know I don't want to go to jail! Oh, I don't care if we are makin' a lot o' money. I wish I'd never met LeRoy' My nerves can's stand it. He's the first racketeer I ever loved.

HAM If this had just stayed a nice little shine shop like it was when I first met you and you took me for your little Ham.

MADAM Yes, till you got wild and went runnin' off with other women! Oh, Lord, life's nothing but troubles, nothing but troubles! And oh! poor Shingle! They'll get him down to that police station maybe and beat him, and just make him tell where he played those numbers.

HAM They ain't gonna make Shingle tell nothing. He's more afraid of Boss LeRoy and the white gangsters what runs the numbers, than he is of any cops.

MADAM I'm just so distressful!

HAM I feels right blue myself. (*enter an* EFFEMINATE YOUTH)

YOUTH Can I get a polish?

HAM You mean your nails?

YOUTH I mean my slippers. (*mounting the stand*)

HAM Well, ... er, are you ... er, what nationality?

YOUTH Creole by birth, but I never draw the color line.

HAM I know you don't. Is you married?

YOUTH Oh no, I'm in vaudeville.

HAM I knowed you was in something. What do you do?

YOUTH I began in a horse-act, a comic horse-act.

HAM A who?

YOUTH A horse-act. I played the hind legs. But I got out of that. I've advanced.

HAM To what?

YOUTH I give impersonations.

HAM Is that what they call it now?

YOUTH I impersonate Mae West.

HAM Lemme see.

YOUTH Of course. (*begins to talk like Mae West, giving an amusing impersonation of that famous screen star*)

HAM You a regular moving picture!

YOUTH Indeed I am. (*enter* JASPER, *the third shine boy*)

JASPER Hello!

YOUTH Who is that?

HAM That's the night shine boy.

JASPER None o' your cracks now, Hamlet, first thing soons I get here. I know I'm dark.

HAM Who's crackin'? I'm tellin' de truth, ain't I, Jasper? You do work at night.

JASPER Yes, and I work in the daytime too,

from two o'clock on. Is the number out yet?

MADAM (*jumping*) Shss—ss! Don't mention numbers here.

JASPER How come, don't mention numbers here?

HAM Ssh-ssh! The man has been here, him and his brother.

JASPER Who?

YOUTH What man?

HAM Two bulls lookin' for numbers.

YOUTH Oh, those kind o' men!

JASPER (*frightened*) They have? If they come here again, you gonna miss me!

MADAM They arrested poor Shingle.

JASPER For what? He don't write no numbers.

HAM No, but he plays 'em.

YOUTH Can you play here?

HAM Not after two o'clock.

MADAM Not a-tall! Not a-tall! Not now! (*enter a* WEST INDIAN)

JASPER (*motioning to chair*) Right up here, sir.

WEST INDIAN I wahnt a parfick shine!

JASPER You got perfect shoes?

WEST INDIAN Naw sawh, but whan I pay me maney, I wahnt a parfick shine.

JASPER You ain't pay your money yet.

MADAM Shine the gentleman's shoes, Jasper, and don't talk so much, please. And turn down the radio, it's ruining my nerves.

WEST INDIAN Yes, 'cause I dadn't come in here to hear no tunes nor to play no number.

YOUTH (*ecstatically*) I just love that dialect.

WEST INDIAN (*glares at him*) Air you tawlkin' 'bout me?

YOUTH Oh, no. I realize you're giving an impersonation. I give impersonations too, that's why I'm interested in your art!

(*Enter a* DEACONESS *in her church bonnet and carrying a hymnbook*)

DEACONESS Gawd bless you all!

HAM Gawd bless you too, sister.

DEACONESS I would like to have a shine for the glory of Gawd.

HAM Well, get right up here and your toes'll twinkle like de mornin' star when I get through wid you.

DEACONESS (*taking chair between* YOUTH *and* WEST INDIAN) That's a precious lamb. (*as* HAM *helps her up*) We got to help one another now—because in 397 years this world will end. (HAM, JASPER, *and the* YOUTH *all draw out pencils and take that number down*)

YOUTH 3-9-7.

HAM I'm gonna play that number tomorrow, 397.

MADAM (*with a start, clasping her breast where the slips are hidden*) Don't mention numbers!

WEST INDIAN They are an abawmination, the numbers!

DEACONESS That's right! Are you a Christian?

WEST INDIAN I'm a Church of Englander, lady. Firm and true.

DEACONESS Well, I'm a Wash Foot Baptist. Touch my foot and you'll find it clean. My soul's the same way! How about you, son?

YOUTH Oh, you're speaking to me? I'm New Thought—and we don't bother with such common things as washing feet.

DEACONESS Well, you better, 'cause God ain't gonna let nobody in heaven 'thout their feet is clean. How about you, son?

HAM I was baptized and reverted when I were 10 years old, and I ain't had a dirty foot since. Amen!

JASPER Amen, hell!

DEACONESS Hallelujah! How about that other young man, so industrious here?

HAM Who? Old Jasper? He smokes reefers!

JASPER That's a damn lie.

YOUTH (*gasps*) Oh!

HAM Don't tell me you don't. 'Cause I seen you smokin'.

JASPER But I don't run with married womens.

YOUTH Neither do I.

WEST INDIAN Sister, I think you have come to a nest o' devils.

HAM That Jasper just ain't got no business o' his own to mind, that's all.

DEACONESS You all is sweet boys, and I'm gonna save your souls. Now you all listen fluently.

HAM *and* JASPER Yes'm. (*they listen and shine, tapping their cloths on the toes of the shoes in rhythm*)

DEACONESS I'm gonna recite you all a little verse, that I made up myself.

> Don't you drink no licker.
> Don't you shoot no dice.
> Don't you do nothing

You think ain't nice.
Don't you dance on Sunday.
Don't forget to pray.
An you'll get to heaven
On Judgment Day!

WEST INDIAN Amen!

HAM Hallelujah! I'm heaven bound.

JASPER The green pastures is sure gonna see a black sheep!

YOUTH Well, we believe in mind over matter, spirit over flesh.

WEST INDIAN And I believe in the Bri-tish faith.

DEACONESS And I believe in washin' feet.

JASPER And I believe in shining shoes, 'cause I got the shoeshine blues.

HAM Let's go, boy. (HAM *and* JASPER *begin to pop their rags as they shine in syncopated time, each shining three shoes at once, so that they finish with the three people on the stand the same time. Meanwhile another customer, a* TALL GUY, *comes in, and shortly after him, the* HOT STUFF MAN, *who goes across to* MADAM *and begins to show her some silk stockings he pulls from a traveling bag. As they finish shining*) Yes, sir! Yes, ma'am! (*they help the* DEACONESS *and the* YOUTH *down, and collect for their work. The* WEST INDIAN *sits there critically inspecting his shine a moment. The* TALL GUY *approaches the stand just as the* WEST INDIAN *steps down. He steps on the* TALL GUY'S *toe*)

WEST INDIAN I beg your pardon.

TALL GUY I'm just tryin' to be a gentleman. But if you want to get tough about it, then step on my corns again and see what I'll do.

DEACONESS My! My! My! He's gonna start some stuff!

WEST INDIAN What'll you do?

TALL GUY Knock you half way into next week, that's what I'll do.

WEST INDIAN (*raising his cane like a sword*) Yes, and you'll have a duel on your hands.

TALL GUY (*raising his fists*) I don't duel, I duke, and I'll choose you out.

WEST INDIAN (*contemptuously*) Aw, mawn, hush! I'll take you outside and wrop you round the downside o' that manole where the sewer run.

DEACONESS Do, Jesus!

YOUTH My dear!

TALL GUY Who you gonna wrap around the downside of a manhole?

WEST INDIAN You!

DEACONESS God don't love ugly! You boys behave!

TALL GUY Well, all right, then, start wrapping. (*they go into a clinch. The women and the* YOUTH *scream and wring their hands. The* HOT STUFF MAN *puts his suitcase down, still open.* HAM *lifts a velvet evening coat out of it*)

MADAM (*coming between them*) Stop that! Just stop! I don't allow no fighting here.

WEST INDIAN I kill you so quick you won't know the death you died, 'cause mawn, I'm a fightin' cock and my spurs is out.

TALL GUY (*his hand going toward his back pocket*) Yes, and if I draw my gun and start burnin' powder, you'll be so full o' holes your wife can use you for a tea strainer. (*at the mention of a gun the* YOUTH *and* DEACONESS *huddle near the door*)

WEST INDIAN (*hand going to back pocket also*) And if I pull mine, I'll blow you from here back before prohibition, and then some.

MADAM Jasper, call the cops! (*clutching her breast and remembering the numbers*) No, don't .... Oh, my nerves!

HAM (*with the evening coat on his arm*) You all stop that foolishness now. Here's the Hot Stuff Man and I want to pick out a present for my woman, if he got anything big enough. (*raising up the belligerents' coattails*) Ain't neither one of you all got a gun, no how.

WEST INDIAN I know it.

TALL GUY You know what?

WEST INDIAN You ain't got no gun.

TALL GUY You'd be surprised. (*pulls out a pistol*) Now get out!

WEST INDIAN (*still belligerent, but moving*) Don't tell me what to do! I don't have to do but four things—eat, sleep, stay black, and die.

TALL GUY Well, you sure will die if you fool with me. (*he raises gun and snaps it once.* MADAM *dives behind the cash register,* JASPER *behind the cigar stand, the* YOUTH *and the* DEACONESS *out the door, and the* WEST INDIAN *starts to bolt, but* HAM *grabs him by his coattail*)

HAM Pay me for that shine first.

WEST INDIAN (*running his hand in his pockets and producing a coin*) Here, mawn, here! Lemme go! (*bolts out the door, as the* TALL GUY *again clicks his gun which fails to go off*)

HAM (*looking at coin*) He gimme a Canadian dime!

JASPER (*peeping over cigar stand*) It's better'n a Canadian nickel.

TALL GUY What's the matter with this gun? It's loaded.

HAM Whatever's the matter with it, put it down, or up, one, or leave here!

MADAM (*coming out angrily*) Put that thing away! You're ruining my nerves!

JASPER (*scornfully*) Huh! I thought it would shoot!

TALL GUY (*puzzled*) I just bought it. It ought to. (*inspecting it*) Aw, no wonder! (*begins to fire, with the result that everybody goes back into hiding, and* HAM *out the door*) I had the safety on. (*ceases firing and sits calmly down on the stand to await a shine.* HAM *pokes his head back in the door*)

HAM Is you through yet?

TALL GUY Of course, of course! I knew that gun would shoot. (*the others come out of hiding,* MADAM, *the* HOT STUFF MAN, *and* JASPER. *The* YOUTH, *returning, has fainted on the footboard on the shine stand*)

HAM Get some water and throw on Mae West there.

MADAM Somebody attend to me! I can't stand it! Jasper, go get me a bucket of beer! I'm about gone.

JASPER Yes'm. (*exit* JASPER)

HAM (*to* HOT STUFF MAN) How much is this here coat? With another piece o' goods in it, 'bout two feet wide, it'd fit Tiny.

HOT STUFF MAN That's one of the finest things I've got a-hold of this season. A man that worked right in a Fifth Avenue store got me this. An inside job, wholesale. Brand new, right off the counter. I'll let you have it cheap. For a little o' nothing 'cause it's too hot for me to hold. How about ten dollars spot cash.

HAM I'll give you nine. (*the* YOUTH *begins to come to, smoothing his hair and preparing to rise*)

TALL GUY I want a shine.

HAM Jasper'll be back in a minute. I only shines white shoes. (*going on with his deal*) Is that there coat velvet?

RADIO (*suddenly loud*) Ladies, use the Venus lipstick to achieve that ravishing virginal look. (*continuing until* MADAM *turns it down*) No other lipstick on the market gives the same demure yet fascinating tint to the lips. And it cost less than any other . . .

HOT STUFF MAN Pure gelatine velvet with a Frigidaire collar, this coat is!

YOUTH (*listening to radio*) Shss-ss! You all be quiet so I can hear the beauty news.

HAM (*feeling coat again*) I might take it. That is, I think I will. Nine?

HOT STUFF MAN No. Ten. (*enter* MATTIE BEA)

MATTIE BEA Hello, there, Little Ham. I tole you I'd be back. (*sniffing*) Smells like smoke in here. Are you buyin' me a present, baby? I could go for that coat.

HAM I wouldn't want you to wear no hot stuff honey. You might get arrested. These is stolen goods.

MATTIE BEA Everything I got on is hot. Lemme try on that coat. (HOT STUFF MAN *gives her the coat. She admires herself*)

YOUTH (*hovering around*) Oh, ain't that a sweet garment!

MATTIE BEA Ham, I just got to have this.

TALL GUY (*yelling*) I want a shine!

HAM Jasper be right back. (*offers him a Dream Book*) Here, take this here Dream Book and pick out your numbers for tomorrow while you're waiting.

TALL GUY I don't believe in dreams. Gimme a *Baltimore Afro-American*. (HAM *hands him the Negro paper, for which he pays ten cents*)

MATTIE BEA Buy this coat for me, honey.

HOT STUFF MAN (*to* HAM) You said you liked it.

HAM I like it, and I'm gonna take it. But by and by, by and by. Just hold it for me.

MATTIE BEA (*returning coat*) Oh Ham, you're just too sweet. I'll wear it to the Hello Club Social tomorrow.

HAM Um-hum.

MATTIE BEA That's why I stopped by, to leave you a couple o' tickets for the Ball. One for you and one for me. I thought I'd better buy 'em in advance. Here, you keep 'em, daddy. (*reading tickets*) Hello Club Social Charleston Contest. Saturday. Tomorrow night.

HAM All right! Now you run on home, Mattie Bea, and I'll see you by and by. In the chop suey joint.

MATTIE BEA You gonna bring the coat?

HAM I'll have the coat when I come.

MATTIE BEA (*as she exits*) Goodbye, sweetheart.

HAM So long. (*after door closes*) If I ever

come! That woman's got a husband anyhow.

TALL GUY (*shouting angrily*) I'll shoot you all if I don't get a shine.

YOUTH (*nearly fainting again*) Aw-ooooo!

HAM (*to* HOT STUFF MAN) Leave me that coat. But it's not for her. (*indicating the departed* MATTIE BEA) Here's ten bucks! (*gives him the money*) And help this Creole (*pointing to the* YOUTH) out of here when you go—before he faints again.

YOUTH (*leaving on the arm of the* HOT STUFF MAN) Goodbye, Little Ham.

HAM (*to* TALL GUY) Stick 'em up—I mean your feet. (*begins to shine his shoes as* JASPER *returns with the beer*)

JASPER Refreshments is served.

MADAM Jasper, if LeRoy don't come in a few minutes, you better call him up. I want to get rid of these slips. I can't keep 'em in my bosom all day. I wonder why don't he phone, or come. He seen I was in trouble, them dicks in here. (*drinks her beer*) And he's got to go down to the station and bail out Shingle besides.

JASPER Poor Shingle! He in jail, ain't he? I tell him 'bout playing them numbers so much.

MADAM If somebody didn't play, how would we live? (JANITOR *enters*)

JASPER Go on relief, I reckon.

JANITOR Ain't the number out yet? I ain't got a cent to buy a paper to see.

HAM T'ain't out yet. 'Bout time though.

JANITOR I think I'm due to catch today on some one o' them numbers.

HAM I know we gonna catch! Ain't I done seen the number in the toe o' my baby's shoe—1-1-6, and ain't I done bought her a coat on the strength o' what I know is coming?

JANITOR What's coming?

JASPER Christmas. (*phone rings,* HAM *starts, but* MADAM *answers it*)

MADAM No, the numbers not out yet. Paper's due here any minute. (*a* PRETTY WOMAN *enters limping slightly*)

PRETTY WOMAN I've got a tack in my shoe.

HAM (*forgetting the* TALL GUY *whose shoes he is shining*) Lemme see!

PRETTY WOMAN (*mounting the shine stand*) Please do. It hurts.

HAM I certainly am sorry. (*leaving* TALL GUY *entirely*) Jasper, you finish this man's shoes, here. A lady is in trouble. (*begins to remove her shoe, fondling her foot tenderly*) You married?

PRETTY WOMAN Yes, but my husband is taking a rest cure.

HAM A who?

PRETTY WOMAN A rest cure.

HAM Rest from what?

PRETTY WOMAN He overexerted himself.

HAM Over which?

PRETTY WOMAN Exerted, overworked, tired himself out.

HAM One blip I bet he never gets rested long as he's got you. (*begins to hammer loudly on the tack in her toe*)

JASPER I bet two blips, if you was him, you'd be dead!

JANITOR (*to* MADAM) You know, lady, if I ever hit that number, I'm gonna take me a vacation. I been janitor o' this building for four years, ain't had me a week off yet.

MADAM 'Bout the only vacation you get is coming in here to play, ain't it?

JANITOR Sure is (*enter* SUGAR LOU BIRD)

SUGAR LOU Rehearsal's off until eight o'clock. Thought I'd drop by and wait for the number.

MADAM Just sit down, honey. We'll know in no time. I'm bettin' on 1-1-6 today, myself so I'm anxious, too. (*enter* OLD LADY)

OLD LADY Hit ain't out yet, is it?

JASPER Not yet, but soon.

OLD LADY (*tottering up to cigar stand*) You can't sell a body a little snuff on credit, can you?

MADAM Sorry, but we don't have snuff, Mis' Dobson.

JANITOR Why, that's out o' style now, ma.

OLD LADY Style or no style, snuff is snuff, and I likes it. (TALL GUY *leaves stand and pays* JASPER *for his shine*)

JASPER Thank you, sir.

TALL GUY I might as well wait around and see what the number is, too, so I'll know how to play tomorrow.

JASPER Sure, make yourself at home.

(TALL GUY *goes to cigar stand and buys a pack of cigarettes. Lights one and sits down on a stool with his paper. A big masculine* WOMAN *walks in and straight across to the cigar stand*)

MASCULINE LADY (*in bass voice*) Gimme a five-cent cigar. (MADAM *offers her the box and accepts payment as everybody in the shop stares*) Is the number out yet?

MADAM Not yet.

Little Ham

MASCULINE LADY Then I'll pick it up later. (*turns and strides out*)
HAM Whew! What's the world coming to?
JANITOR I don't care what it comes to, just so I hits the numbers.
MADAM Numbers! Numbers! Numbers!
SUGAR LOU That's one thing I sure miss in Europe, the numbers. They don't seem to know how to play 'em over there.
HAM They know in Harlem.
MADAM And they'll be the end of Harlem, too. They've just about whipped my nerves to a frazzle.
PRETTY WOMAN (*her shoe fixed, leaves stand, opens her purse*) Thank you! How much?
HAM Nothing a-tall! No charge—to you.
PRETTY WOMAN That's awfully nice of you.
HAM I hopes to see you again.
PRETTY WOMAN That's very possible.
HAM Then come again.
PRETTY WOMAN Maybe I will, Goodbye. (*she exits*)
HAM Goodbye.
SUGAR LOU Untrue to me already, huh, Little Ham?
HAM Untrue as I can be—at a shine stand.
JANITOR (*hearing newsboy's cry*) Listen! There they come! (*sound of* NEWSBOY *crying off stage. Enters*)
NEWSBOY Racing edition of the evening paper. Get the number.
EVERYBODY Gimme one... What's the number, boy?... Here, you got change?... Let's have a copy.
HAM (*opening paper to sporting page. Shouting*) Dog-gone my soul! I won!
JANITOR Thank God-a-mighty, I won too, then.
MADAM Ham, your number hit!
SUGAR LOU What was it?
HAM 1-1-6, folks, 116! I mean good ole 1-1-6 has done come out—that I seen in the toe o' my baby's shoe. Damn! Lemme call her up and tell her. Where is that card she gimme? (*searches in his pocket for card, finds it, and goes to phone*) Done hit the number!
JASPER You lucky rascal! You must carry a black cat's bone.
SUGAR LOU Well, it's luck for you all. Ham wins, but I lose!
OLD LADY I lose too! Lawd, I lose!
SUGAR LOU But, maybe I'll hit tomorrow.

If I don't, I'll pawn a wrist watch till that show opens.
MADAM Which watch, darling?
SUGAR LOU Oh, I think the one a duke gave me in Budapest. Nobody cares what time it is in Budapest.
JASPER Where's that, Miss Bird?
SUGAR LOU Somewhere, in... er... Norway, I believe.
OLD LADY (*weeping*) I can't never hit. My last penny, and I can't never hit. My daughter give me that money to get some matches with to light the gas.
MADAM Here, grandma, I'll give you a box of matches. (*hands her matches*)
OLD LADY But ain't you got no snuff?
MADAM No snuff! No snuff! (*exit* OLD LADY)
HAM (*at telephone*) Hello! Hello! Tiny's Hairdressin' Parlor? Well, is Tiny there?... Yes. Is this Tiny? Well, this is Little Ham! Baby, we done hit the numbers! Yeah! That number I saw in the toe o' your shoe... You's a lucky old big old sweet something, you is! Come on up here and get your money! I want to see you anyhow. I got a present for you.... Yes, I is... And two tickets to the Hello Club Ball, too. O-key-do-ky!
JASPER Some woman, as usual, on the phone.
MADAM Ham, call LeRoy, see is he coming back here. We want to collect what we won.
HAM What's his number—Edgecombe 4-1909?
MADAM That's it. (HAM *dials and listens*)
HAM Hello—er... er... (*hangs up suddenly, looks scared*)
MADAM What's the matter?
HAM I don't get nothing for a funny noise. Then somebody answers sounds like cops or gangsters, one! The toughest voice I ever heard.
MADAM (*clutching her breast*) Oh, my God!

(*Suddenly the door opens, and in comes* LEROY, *wild and disheveled. The afternoon begins to darken*)

LEROY (*hurrying across to cash register*) Lucille, baby, I got to talk to you.
HAM Man, I done hit the numbers. Stop right here!
JANITOR Me, too.
LEROY Just a minute! Just a minute! I ain't payin' off no numbers today. Harlem's all torn

up now. The Danny Jiggers gang's trying to muscle in against Manny Hudgins, and there's hell to pay. I just saw two big New Jersey cars outside my apartment, so I didn't go in.

MADAM (*as* SUGAR LOU, TALL GUY, *leave*) Oh, my nerves! My nerves!

JANITOR Well, what about my number that come out, 1-1-6?

LEROY It never went in. Didn't no numbers from my route go in today. I tell you, Harlem's on the spot. Who's gonna report numbers with the Jiggers gang in town?

HAM I just knowed something'd go wrong.

JANITOR De Lawd never intended a poor man to win money! My last fifty cents gone, and payday two weeks off yet! I tell you I want to be paid off on that number. (*hysterical*) I hit it: 1-1-6!

LEROY (*hand to pocket*) Hush, and get out of here! Or I'll blow you to bits. The gang's on my trail now, more'n likely, and you talkin' 'bout payin' off on a lousy ten-cent number.

JANITOR It's a racket! That's what it is! A racket!

LEROY Sure, we know it.

JANITOR Everyday, all my money gone on the numbers.

LEROY You have something to look forward to, don't you? Some day you might win.

JANITOR Not from lousy cheaters like you!

LEROY Get out of here! (JANITOR *exits*)

MADAM Put that gun away! If another shot's fired this afternoon, I'll die! I'll die! Here— (*reaching into her bosom*)—take these slips. I just want to get 'em out of my hands. Why did I ever go into this game? Why? Oh, why!

LEROY Quiet, Lucille, quiet! Everything'll be all right. I got three thousand dollars here, which ever way the gang war goes. That's yours and mine, darling. Understand? (*just as he is about to hand it to her, three strange* WHITE MEN *enter. They are obviously gangsters. Each has one hand in his pocket*)

BUTCH So here's where little Boss LeRoy holds forth after the number comes out?

DUTCH No wonder his apartment's empty.

JIGGERS Hand us over today's collection, you. We told that punk of a Hudgins we were taking over his field way last week. But he just kept right on, and you helpin' him. Well, now he's where the daisies'll tickle his nose when they come up in the spring. (*savagely*) And that's where you'll be if you don't act right.

MADAM (*loudly*) My heart! My nerves! My heart! (*she glares at the gangsters*)

JIGGERS Just hold tight, sister. It'll be over in a minute. (*referring to* JASPER *and* HAM) Who're these two there?

MADAM They're my shine boys.

DUTCH They look like men to me. (*to* JASPER) Who're you?

JASPER John Jasper Armstrong Smith.

DUTCH What do you do?

JASPER Shine shoes, that's all.

BUTCH (*to* HAM) How about you?

HAM Oh, I'm just here. Part of the decorations. Take the place, you take me. I just hit this afternnon for a dollar with 1-1-6.

JIGGERS One of these lucky birds, heh? Well, you're the kind of a guy we need to write for us, don't we, Butch? Fly and lucky. Folks like to play with personality lads like you. Come over here. (HAM *approaches*) What's your name?

HAM Little Ham Jones—Hamlet Hitchcock Jones.

JIGGERS Your age?

HAM Indiscrimate.

JIGGERS Well, if you're old enough to play numbers, you're old enough to write 'em. Ever do it?

HAM No, indeedy!

LEROY (*interrupting*) I always choose my own writers in this district.

JIGGERS You'll be lucky to choose yourself from here on in. We're running this racket in Harlem now.

DUTCH You're going for a ride, more'n likely.

JIGGERS (*to* HAM) Report tomorrow to our headquarters over on Lenox. (*to* MADAM BELL) Are you with us, lady? I guess you are if you want to stay in business. Keep this here Shine Parlor as your base and *keep on* writing numbers. Only we'll send *our* man to collect.

MADAM I'm with you—if my nerves'll stand it.

DUTCH You'll pull through.

JIGGERS Listen, both of you. (*to* HAM *and* MADAM) If you ever get in any trouble, just give my fixer's name to the cop, the judge, the jailer, anybody, and they'll turn you loose. We're payin' heavy protection. Just say—Schnabel.

HAM Schnabel, Schnabel, Schnabel. I sure will try to remember that.

Little Ham

JIGGERS That's it, Schnabel. He's the pay-off from now on.

DUTCH (*to the* MADAM) How about you?

MADAM I'll recall it.

JIGGERS (*to* LEROY) As for you, didn't you get word yesterday to lay off writing for Manny?

LEROY I didn't get nothing.

JIGGERS Well, come with us now, and we'll talk it over. There might be some hope for you then. But we can't use you no more, no how. You was too thick with the old crowd. (*enter* TINY *puffing and blowing*)

TINY Bless God, we won! Little Ham, I come for you and our money.

HAM You sure come at a busy time, baby.

TINY Didn't you phone for me?

HAM Yes, but that was before the crisis.

TINY What do you mean? They ain't payin' off?

JIGGERS Of course, we're paying off. Our outfit always pays off. Did you hit today, lady? Where's your slips?

TINY (*to* HAM) Ain't you give 'em the slips, baby?

HAM I ain't had time. (*fumbling in his pockets*) Here they is, one for me and one for you, 1-1-6. (*hands them to* JIGGERS)

JIGGERS Perfectly good. (*to* LEROY) Pay 'em off, you. They hit for a dollar a-piece. We're not going to start our business with no dissatisfied clients. (*as* LEROY *hesitates*) Pay 'em off!

LEROY We're short on cash. I done turned mine in.

JIGGERS (*to* DUTCH *and* BUTCH) Search him, boys! If I find a dollar on him, I'll blow his brains out.

MADAM (*screams*) Don't shoot no gun in here.

LEROY Wait, wait, wait! Here, Lemme see. I might have a few bills. (*he produces a wad of several thousand dollars*)

JIGGERS Two or three grand, that's all. Pay 'em off, and give me the rest.

LEROY (*hesitantly to* HAM) You hit for a dollar, heh?

HAM Dollar and a quarter.

LEROY Then you gets 675 dollars.

HAM I sure do. (LEROY *begins to count out the money*)

TINY You both lucky *and* cute, Ham!

HAM You tellin' me?

JIGGERS That's real money. That's just how my bank'll pay off from now on.

LEROY (*to* TINY) And you hit for a dollar?

TINY That's right.

LEROY 540 then.

TINY 540 gets it.

DUTCH If I wasn't toting a gun, I'd play these fool numbers myself.

MADAM (*to* LEROY) I had a quarter on that too, LeRoy. Here's my slip.

LEROY 135 to you then, baby.

MADAM That small change is just right.

LEROY (*sadly*) I won't have a thing left.

JIGGERS Only about two thousand bucks. Give it here! We'll use it to buy cigarettes. (LEROY *hands over the money angrily*) And come on! (*they start toward the door*)

LEROY (*looking back*) Lucille! Lucille!

MADAM My nerves won't stand it! Go on! I can't help you! (*savagely as he hesitates*) Go on! (*they exit*)

JASPER I wish I'd-a played that number—1-1-6.

TINY Baby, who's them strange men?

HAM They the new bosses o' this shop.

TINY I thought it belonged to colored folks.

HAM It do, but whites run it. How about it, Madam?

MADAM Little bit more, and they can have it! My nerves won't stand this number racket. They just won't. (*as* HAM *begins to take off his coat*) Ham, are you going off and leave me, too?

HAM I'm off at four, ain't I? Jasper's the night man. (*begins to don his street clothes*)

MADAM Come back and talk to me later. I need comfort.

TINY Not this evening, no sir. *Comfort* is with me! Come on here, boy! From now on you Tiny's Little Ham. (*as he hands her the velvet coat*) Um-huh! Is that my present? Ain't you sweet! It looks kinder small, but I'll have me a nice gold-brocaded back put in it in the morning, and wear it to the Hello Club's Ball tomorrow night. You got tickets, ain't you, sugar?

HAM Sure, I got tickets. They havin' a Charleston contest. And just like we hit that number today, we gonna win that contest tomorrow. Girl, can you Charleston?

TINY Sure, I can Charleston. Where you s'pose I been at all my life?

HAM Well, come on then. Let's dance on

away from here! (JASPER *turns up the radio and* TINY *and* HAM *dance toward the door*) Hey, now!

(*Curtain*)

ACT TWO

(*Saturday afternoon. Interior of* TINY's *Beauty Shop on Lenox Avenue. Street door center. At immediate left of door, manicurist's table. At right an overstuffed chair and a floor lamp. Two operator's booths, one on either side of door.* TINY *presides over the booth at the left.* LULU *over the booth at right. At extreme right, just outside* LULU's *booth, a radio beside a door marked "Ladies Room." At extreme left, next to* TINY's *booth, a kind of little open storeroom, sink, and closet where coats, street clothes, etc., are hung.*

As the curtain rises, both TINY *and* LULU *are busily engaged straightening heads of hair.* SUGAR LOU *is in* TINY's *chair. The manicurist,* OPAL, *is occupied applying red polish to the nails of a customer.* A LITTLE GIRL, *waiting for her* MAMA, *is in the big chair. All the women are chattering full blast, the radio going, smoke rising from oily heads, noise of traffic outside*)

TINY (*yelling to manicurist*) Opal, have you seen Bradford today?

OPEL No, Tiny, there's been not a single number writer in here today. They must be all scared out by the gang war I read about in the *News*.

CUSTOMER (*at table*) I hear they just a-switchin' and a-changin' all them writers up here in Harlem. Looks like a new lot of down-town chiselers done took over things. I hear they chased out LeRoy.

TINY Well, my new fella's writin' for the new outfit. They the ones what paid off my hit yesterday, and they give him a job right then and there. We sure knocked 1-1-6 for a row.

OPAL Did you box it?

TINY Naw, I didn't box it. Didn't need to this time.

OPAL Always box your numbers, girl. If they don't come straight they might come some other way. You're lucky you caught it right straight out like you did.

TINY You right, I'm lucky. I'm gonna play that same number back today. This time I'll box it and bolito it, too. 116's a good number! And sometimes them pari-mutuels repeats figures, you know!

LULU No, they don't either, sister. I ain't never seen a number repeat hand-running no two times yet.

SUGAR LOU Me neither.

OPAL Well, I have, girl! 417 come out twice hand-running not more'n two or three months ago.

LULU Well, I must-a been in Jalopy, cause I ain't seen it, and I play every day in the year, and ain't left New York in ten years.

OPAL I don't believe you ever leave Harlem even much, do you, Lulu?

LULU Not hardly. What business I got downtown? I can get everything I wants right here in Harlem, even to Fifth Avenue dresses so hot they just stole 'em fresh the night before.

OPAL Girl, don't believe all this stuff they call hot up here in Harlem is really stolen. They buy it at wholesale, then tell you it's stole—to make you think you're getting something worth more than it is.

LULU Cheaper than in stores though.

OPAL But if you don't know what you're buying, you can get cheated, too.

TINY Girl, my new man bought me the prettiest velveteen evening coat you ever seen yesterday from a hot selling huck.

SUGAR LOU (*in* TINY's *chair*) He did?

TINY Naturally the coat wasn't made to fit my size, exactly, but I took it early this morning to a seamster and am having a gold brocaded back put in it so I can shine like the sun at that there Hello Club Ball tonight.

OPAL Say, what time does that Charleston Contest come off?

TINY I don't know, but whatever time it comes off, me and my little short papa's gonna be there rarin' to go.

SUGAR LOU Comes off at midnight, they tell me. I'm gonna try and make it, if rehearsal's over.

LULU We gonna close up early, sis?

TINY You all can stay here if you want, but I'm gonna be gone. Stay if you need to make up that extra commission. If you don't leave early —just like me. I don't care. After I been fryin' heads all day and all week, I need myself a little recreation on Saturday nights.

OPAL Me, too.

SUGAR LOU   I sure am glad I got my appointment this afternoon. You all get so busy late on Saturdays.

TINY   Busy all day Saturdays, no matter what time you come. That's the day we really take in the money. But I just hit for 540 bucks yesterday, so you know I'm gonna have myself one *really* good time tonight.

MAMA (*in* LULU'*s chair*)   So am I, kid! I'm goin' to that Ball.

SNOOKS (*the child in the big armchair*)   Mama, hurry up!

MAMA   How can I hurry up, and one half o' my head's still looking like a gooseberry bush in August?

SNOOKS   Well, I'm tired.

MAMA   Well, get yourself a funny paper and see can't you find me a good number. Look in Popeye, or else in Skippy.

LULU   Child, I gets the best numbers out of Little Orphan Annie.

MAMA   I never win nothing on the Annie numbers.

LULU   Maybe you don't play them the right way.

MAMA   Something's wrong, something's wrong. To tell the truth, the only thing I ever catches on is funeral wreaths. Everytime I see a crape on the door, anywhere, I take down the house number. Them kind o' sad numbers is always my best bet.

OPAL (*calling*)   How about the numbers of hymns in church?

TINY   Them ain't no good. They give out too many of 'em. Seven or eight hymns every service.

MAMA   Yes, and some o' them ministers is such devils. They ain't got Christ in 'em. Naturally their numbers ain't no good.

OPAL   'Bout the best way is to pick some number that's hit good once, like Tiny's 1-1-6, and play it every day for two or three months.

LULU   No, 'taint, neither. I don't believe in them repeats, I tell you. You gotta wait too long.

TINY   Sometimes you wait that long anyhow. Turn down that radio, Lulu, so I can hear my ears.

LULU   All right, sis! (LULU *turns down radio*)

CUSTOMER (*at* OPAL'*s table*)   Well, I'm telling you, if 'twarn't for the numbers, I don't know how I'd get along. I plays six or eight dollars a week, and I always wins three or four dollars, every week.

CUSTOMER   Why, everything I own 'cept my husband I bought with my winnings. But I drempt a dream last night that I sure don't know how to play. I got to look it up. You all got a Dream Book around here?

TINY   I might have one back yonder by the sink. I'll look in a minute.

LULU   What were the dream?

CUSTOMER   I dreamt about a yellow woman washing a green dress in a white lady's back yard. Now what do that mean?

MAMA   Lemme think.

CUSTOMER   What number should I play? Any o' you all know?

MAMA   Well, er ... green is 448, if I remembers rightly.

TINY   Yes, 'tis, that's right. In Rajah Simm's Book it's 448.

LULU   Yes, but she say a *yellow* woman washing a *green* dress in a *white* lady's back yard. That's more colors than one.

SUGAR LOU   Certainly is!

CUSTOMER   Yes, and the dress faded, too.

MAMA   Do, Jesus!

CUSTOMER   When she got through washing it it weren't no color a-tall.

LULU   There now! Then you wouldn't look up green.

MAMA   No, you wouldn't.

TINY   I think you'd look up *dress*.

SUGAR LOU   I think you add all them colors together, subtract the difference, and play that.

LULU   What kind o' dress were it?

CUSTOMER   Seems like to me it were a calico dress.

OPAL   Then look up *calico*. Who knows what that would be?

TINY   I'll go see can I find that book right now. (*she leaves her booth and goes back where the shelves are. Searches until she finds the book. Meanwhile, a* STAID LADY *enters with a* LITTLE GIRL *of ten or twelve*)

STAID LADY   I want a hot-oil treatment, and I want you all to see if you can do anything with my child's hair, too, to try and bring out the Indian blood that's in her. Her head sure went back on her.

OPAL   Just have a seat. One of the operators'll take you in a minute now.

STAID LADY (*to* SNOOKS)   Get up, child, and

let me sit down. You children can sit on the arms of the chair.

SNOOKS Why don't *you* sit on the arm of the chair yourself and let us sit here?

STAID LADY Because I'm grown, that's why, and you and Missouri are nothing but tots.

SNOOKS Her name's Missouri?

STAID LADY That's it.

SNOOKS That's a state, ain't it?

MISSOURI Yes, but it's a name, too. What's your name?

SNOOKS Samantha. But they call me Snooks for short.

MISSOURI That sounds like a funny-paper name to me.

SNOOKS Well, your name sounds like mud to me.

MAMA (*yelling from* LULU's *booth*) You Snooks! Just hush. I'm ashamed o' you.

STAID LADY (*to her offspring*) Sit over here and keep still. I told you not to speak to every stranger you meet.

TINY (*returning to front with the Dream Book*) Here's the Dream Book. Now, I'd advise you to look up wash, cause that's what you was doin' in the dream, washing a dress. Lemme see what it is. (*searches in book*)

OPAL Yes, but she was washing a *green* dress, girl.

TINY Well, if it was me, I'd play the number for wash and let the colors and dress and white lady and all go. Here it is—wash—964. That's it. (*hands book to* OPAL's *customer*) Howdy-do! (*to the new arrival in chair*)

STAID LADY Howdy do! I'm in need of a hot-oil treatment. And a pull for this child.

TINY Yes'm. Just a few minutes now, and I'll be with you. (TINY *returns to* SUGAR LOU *and takes the apparatus out of her hair.* SUGAR LOU *has a beautiful croquinolle. Looks at herself in the glass*)

SUGAR LOU Honey, that's wonderful. I'll knock 'em dead at the dance tonight.

TINY You sure will. Who you goin' with, Sugar Lou?

SUGAR LOU A new hot papa I just met down at the theater—that is, if I can sneak away from my butter and egg man.

TINY What's his name?

SUGAR LOU Which one, the young one or the old one?

TINY I mean the one what pays your bills here, darling.

SUGAR LOU You ought to know him—he's the biggest undertaker in Harlem. Has three funeral parlors, and ten to twenty funerals a day.

TINY You ain't talkin' 'bout old man Willis?

SUGAR LOU That's him. He's my board and upkeep at the moment.

TINY Why he's so old his features all run together!

SUGAR LOU He's generous, though, honey. He says he's gonna gimme a half-dozen more watches for this arm.

TINY No, he ain't!

SUGAR LOU Yes, he is, too.

TINY Well, keep him, child, keep him, even if he is ninety! You ain't met my sweet papa, though, has you? I mean my real one.

SUGAR LOU Who is he?

TINY (*proudly*) His name is Little Ham.

SUGAR LOU Not little sporty Ham that shines shoes in the Paradise?

TINY That's him! And believe me, he ain't shining shoes no more. Not after last night. He's gone into business.

SUGAR LOU He has? What kind o' business?

TINY Numbers. Them new racketeers is working him right in with them. They say he's got per-son-ality.

SUGAR LOU He has that, all right. Smoothest little sawed-off pigmy this side of Abyssinia! He's got a way with the lady-folks, too.

TINY He might-a had a way—but he belongs to Tiny now.

SUGAR LOU Congratulations!

TINY Thank you.

SUGAR LOU But, say, where's Gilbert?

TINY I done put that lounge-lizard out o' my life. Gilbert warn't no good for nothing but what my white actress lady where I used to work calls "horizontal refreshment."

SUGAR LOU Gilbert always dresses nice.

TINY Yes, but on my money. I want a man what gives *me* things, like Little Ham. Besides Gilbert's a married man.

MAMA Speaking about men, you all heard about the run-in Geraldine had over her old used-to-be, ain't you?

TINY Geraldine who?

MAMA Geraldine Richards.

OPAL Not that little old scrawny mud-colored girl what comes in here every Thursday afternoon from Long Island.

MAMA   That's her. She don't get off but once a week, but that day she wants to find her man ready and waiting just for her.

OPAL   I don't blame her.

MAMA   But this time she come in from her white-folks house and the man was nowhere to be found.

TINY   What you say?

MAMA   Nowhere to be found. She went to his rooming house, and she went to the pool hall where he usually hang out, and she went to the barbecue stand—but no George.

LULU   There now!

MAMA   Then she met Gussie. You know, Gussie Mae Lewis?

TINY   Gussie's a troublemaker. Always talking.

OPAL   For sure!

LULU   Yes, she's too broadcast.

MAMA   And Gussie say she has just seen George, about two hours before going down the street with Luella Johnson.

TINY   No, he wasn't!

MAMA   Yes, he was! Gussie seen him. So what did Geraldine do but take her little scrawny self right straight to the pawnshop and buy herself a gun!

LULU   Ay! Lawd! I know she was burnt!

MAMA   And went, just as straight as she knew how, up to where Luella rooms, and caught 'em red-handed on the settee.

TINY   Naw!

MAMA   Yes, sir!

OPAL   Huh!

SNOOKS   Mama, hurry up. I wanna go out o' here.

MAMA   Shut up, and wait for me. Play with that other little girl. (STAID LADY *gathers her child to her protectively, motioning* SNOOKS *away*) Yes, ma'am, Geraldine caught that huck right in the mood for love.

TINY   And what did she do to him?

MAMA   Wore his hips out with bullets, that's what she did.

LULU   There now!

MAMA   But seem like in her excitement, she couldn't shoot very straight, so ain't none o' the bullets proved fatal. But, anyhow, George is in the hospital this week end, and they say he can't set down.

OPAL   How about that hussy of a Johnson girl?

MAMA   They say Geraldine scared Luella so bad she jumped out the window. It was just the second floor, so I reckon it didn't hurt the hellion. And ain't nobody seen her since.

TINY   (*as* SUGAR LOU *leaves the chair*)   Well, I'm a decent woman! I don't believe in no shootin' and cuttin'. When I gets mad, I just use the palm of my hand, that's all. And that's enough!

LULU   Believe me, it is! I seen Tiny slap a woman good in here one night, come startin' some stuff about she wasn't gonna pay no dollar-seventy-five—after she done had mighty nigh every treatment, shampoo, and process in the shop. She say back where she came from in North Carolina, she get all that for six bits.

TINY   Yes, child, and I say, well, in Harlem, New York, it cost just *one dollar more*. And she say, it do, huh? Well, I ain't gwine pay it! And I say, you'll pay it or else. And she say, I'll else then! And lift her dress in my face, and that is where I palmed her.

LULU   She was glad to pay to get out!

SUGAR LOU   Let me sign for my bill.

TINY   O.K., honey. (*produces pad, and* SUGAR LOU *signs, and exits*)

SUGAR LOU   Goodbye, you all. See you tonight at the Ball.

EVERYBODY   Goodbye!

TINY   (*to the* STAID LADY)   Now, I'll take you.

STAID LADY   (*to her child*)   You sit right here until they ready for you, too.

MISSOURI   Yes'm. (*her mother goes into* TINY's *booth*)

SNOOKS   (*to the other child*)   My mama don't make me sit down. (*for the moment* MISSOURI *ignores her*)

STAID LADY   (*to* TINY)   I wish there wasn't so much gossip and scandal and talk about numbers in these hairdressing parlors. It hurts my child's morals.

TINY   Your child's who?

STAID LADY   Her morals, to hear such stuff. She gets her mind full of sin.

TINY   Is that where her morals is, in her mind?

STAID LADY   I'm speaking of her soul. It's awful here in Harlem to raise a child.

TINY   I were raised here, myself.

STAID LADY   Yes, that's what I mean.

TINY   What *do* you mean?

STAID LADY   I'm sure you understand what

I mean. Let's not discuss it further. And don't burn my head.

TINY I hope not.

STAID LADY Some of these hair shops is just terrible. One of 'em gave a brownskin friend of mine a bleaching treatment and just ruined her. When they got through, she looked like she were on her last round-up. Just took all the pigment out of her skin.

TINY The pig-meat?

STAID LADY Pigment! Color! Made her a deathly gray—all chalky. Her husband liked to whipped her when he saw her, he was so mad.

TINY Some of them operators is terrible! They just dissects the hair from your scalp, their combs is so hot.

STAID LADY And they're so careless. And so immoral. Why they raided a shop near me and confiscated the hair tonic.

TINY I reckon it was licker.

STAID LADY It probably was. That little she-woman that runs it is always drunk.

TINY You don't say!

LULU A girl was in here this morning says she know where you can buy the number.

OPAL Where at?

LULU She says she knows a man, what knows a man, that is a friend of the man that works at the track and can get the number an hour or more before it comes out in Harlem. And for fifty dollars he'll phone it to anybody that wants it, in time for them to play it before the books close.

STAID LADY A racket, that's what it is.

TINY I s'pect it is, 'cause can't nobody be sure about that number till it come out.

MAMA Don't nobody know how them racing machines gonna add up.

LULU I'm just tellin' you what the girl told me. But Lawd knows I ain't gonna try it, 'cause I ain't got no fifty dollars.

CUSTOMER (*rising*) Thank you. (*yelling*) And thank you, Tiny, for the Dream Book. I'll see you all sometime next week.

TINY Thank you, and come back. I hope you hit on that *wash* number.

CUSTOMER I'm gonna play *dress* and *wash*, too.

TINY You doin' right. Good luck. Burn a black candle, and also play *green*.

OPAL Be sure and box 'em.

LULU And use lucky incense, child.

CUSTOMER Goodbye, you all. (*exits*)

EVERYBODY Goodbye.

OPAL Thank God for a minute to breathe. (*she goes to Ladies Room*)

MISSOURI (*fidgeting in chair, to* SNOOKS) Do you know any bad words?

SNOOKS I know two.

MISSOURI Tell me one of 'em.

SNOOKS Damn!

MISSOURI Aw, I know a better one than that. (*whispering*) . . . And I dare you to say it.

SNOOKS I dare you to say this one. (*whispers to* MISSOURI. MAMA *gets out of chair and pays her bill*)

MISSOURI 'Tain't as bad as mine.

SNOOKS Your word ain't as bad as mine, either.

MISSOURI Yes, it is. Mine's badder.

SNOOKS I'll be damned if it is!

STAID LADY (*shouting*) Missouri, come here!

SNOOKS I ain't gonna let her. (*blocks other child's path*)

MISSOURI Lemme by. (*pushes* SNOOKS *and* SNOOKS *grabs her.* MISSOURI *begins to cry.* MAMA *emerges from booth and shakes* SNOOKS)

MAMA I told you to behave yourself. I won't take you to the Apollo if you don't act right.

SNOOKS Well, she started it.

STAID LADY (*as* MISSOURI *comes sniffling into* TINY's *booth*) Just hush now. I tell you about fooling with strangers.

MAMA Come on, Snooks. Goodbye all (*exits*).

EVERYBODY Goodbye. (OPAL *returns to her table.* LULU *rearranges her tools.* MATTIE BEA *enters.* TINY *talks with the* STAID LADY)

MATTIE BEA Howdy.

OPAL Howdy-do!

MATTIE BEA I had an appointment with Miss Lulu for two o'clock. I'm just a little late.

LULU Just waitin' for you. I said to myself, now I know she's gonna be late.

MATTIE BEA Yes, I had to stop by the Paradise Shine Parlors to look up a friend o' mine, but he wasn't there. He's s'posed to pick me up for the dance tonight.

LULU Hello Club Ball?

MATTIE BEA Uh-hum.

LULU Everybody's going, ain't they? That Charleston Contest'll sure be hot. Do you Charleston?

MATTIE BEA Well, I ain't learned yet, but I'm gonna try. I never was much of a dancer.

You see, I was raised up in the Baptist Church and didn't get away from it till I grewed up. My Pa was a deacon.

LULU Mine was too, child, but I didn't let that hold me back.

MATTIE BEA I don't play cards till now.

LULU You don't?

MATTIE BEA Naw, child. I was taught that every card in the deck is a devil, and the aces—they is Satan's claws.

LULU Now, ain't that something? Do you play the numbers?

MATTIE BEA Oh, yes! I wasn't taught nothing about numbers when I was little.

LULU They didn't have 'em then. (*enter a large* BUXOM LADY *of commanding presence, a lodge ribbon across her breast*)

LODGE LADY Can I get a 'pointment for this afternoon? I got to have something done to this haid o' mine before tomorrow. The grand lodge's havin' a turn out, and I'm the High Grand Daughter Ruler.

OPAL Certainly, we can find a place for you today. (*looking at her appointment sheet*) How about four o'clock?

LODGE LADY Which operator's that?

OPAL Miss Tiny.

LODGE LADY All right then! I likes Tiny cause she never yet has burnt a strand o' my hair. I'll be here at four.

OPAL (*writing in book*) I'm putting you down.

LODGE LADY (*exiting*) Thank you kindly.

MATTIE BEA And they had a new shine boy at the Paradise, that's what worried me. Madam Bell say my fella's gone to writing numbers. Ain't shining shoes no more.

LULU There's been a new pay-off down at City Hall, and they say they changing lots o' writers up here. The new gang o' gangsters don't want the old crew no more. They all got bad reputations, them old writers. People would hit, then never see the runner. He'd collect the money, and keep it himself. It were awful!

MATTIE BEA Yes, it were. And half the folks in Harlem on relief, too. Don't hardly get enough money to play one number a day, let alone eat. (*they continue to talk between themselves.* OPAL *is busy polishing her own fingernails.* TINY *is working on the* STAID LADY'S *head*)

TINY I been in this business for ten years now. And when I straighten a head, it's really straight. Wait till you see what I do to your daughter's head when I get round to it. I send anybody out o' here ready to put a man in the mood for love!

STAID LADY I don't want no love for my daughter. I'm preparing her to be baptized tomorrow.

TINY Then why straighten her hair out? It'll frizzle right up again. Ain't no kind o' treatment that's water proof.

STAID LADY I want her to look her best when Reverend Hinds pushes her down in that pool to receive the spirit of the Lord.

MISSOURI Do I have to go *all* the way down in the water, mama?

STAID LADY Every inch of you's got to get wet, daughter, or you ain't baptized right. And I want *you right*. This Harlem's a place o' sin, child, and I want you protected.

TINY Religion protected me, I know. I been a Baptist for years—and ain't sinned since I was seventeen.

STAID LADY What did you do then?

TINY Told a half-lie. I told a man that Lulu was my sister and 'twarn't so. She's my half-sister.

STAID LADY Well, I ain't sinned since I were ten.

TINY What did you do?

STAID LADY Smoked a cigarette out in the barn with my brother, but the next month I was converted to Christ, and I ain't smoked since.

TINY Hallelujah!

STAID LADY Amen!

TINY Religion is a wonderful thing!

STAID LADY Yes, indeed it is! Bless God! (*a verse of "Old Time Religion" may be sung or hummed*)

TINY (*half-shouting*) Oh my! My! My! Praise the Lawd!

LULU Amen! Amen! (*enter* LITTLE HAM. *He is very sportily dressed and wears the red muffler* MATTIE BEA *gave him*)

OPAL Howdy-do!

HAM How are you?

OPAL Right well, I thank you. Did you wish to see someone?

HAM Is this the shop o' Miss Tiny Lee?

OPAL You ain't missed it.

HAM Who is in charge?

OPAL I make appointments.

HAM   Well, put me down for one.
OPAL   With me, or Miss Tiny?
HAM (*looking around*)   Where is Tiny at?
OPAL   Right there. (*indicating booth at her right*)
HAM   Oh, then put me down for Tiny. And tell her I needs to see her bad.
OPAL   Shall I interrupt her work?
HAM   Sure, tell her Little Ham is here!
OPAL   O.K. (*rises and goes to* TINY's *booth*) Here is Mr. Ham!
TINY   He is? Well, bless my soul! (*leaves the hot comb in* STAID LADY's *hair and comes out*) Hello, there, darling! Sugar lump! Sweetness! This is the first time you been in my shop, ain't it? Well, it's full o' old ladies now! Come on back here where we can talk a minute. (*takes* HAM *back to the sink and storage corner*) You little old Ham you! (*kissing*)
HAM   How's tricks?
TINY   O.K., baby! I sent my new coat over to the seamster this morning to be extended, and she say she'll have it all ready and bring it back to me this afternoon, so I can wear it to the dance tonight. It ought to be here most any time now. How's things by you?
HAM   I done wrote up most fifty dollars worth o' numbers today.
TINY   Naw you ain't.
HAM   Yes, I did, too! Folks just seem to take me for a natural-born number writer.
TINY (*worried*)   Honey, don't get pinched now.
HAM   Babe, I done been to headquarters! Them gangsters got a office over yonder in East Harlem bigger'n ten shine parlors put together, and seven hairdressing shops thrown in. And I seen the headman, the big shot, the one the G-men even never seen. I seen him! And he told me everything's all fixed with them that's in politics, and if by accident a detective or a policeman should happen to nab me by mistake, not knowin' I's one o' their men, all I got to do is say that name his first lieutenant told me last night—and the turnkey, or judge, or whoever got me locked up'll let me right out. He say just say—what were it, darling?
TINY   Snizzle, or Snopple or something like that, weren't it? You told me.
HAM   Supple, I believe.
TINY   It were something like that.
HAM   But, anyhow, I ain't gonna get locked up. I'm a fool-proof number writer, anyhow. They can't ketch me in no trap. I'm just gonna write for my friends and my friends' friends, and I got a million friends in Harlem.
TINY (*coyly*)   And who is your best friend?
HAM   You, Tiny! (*they embrace fervently*)
TINY   Then make me know it!
STAID LADY (*yelling*)   Aw-ooo! My haid is burning up! (*her hair is smoking*)
MISSOURI   Aw-ooo! Mama's burning up!
TINY   I love you, Ham.
HAM   And me you, too.
TINY   You never gonna leave me?
HAM   Never!
TINY   And you takin' me to the Ball?
HAM   *Understood.*
TINY   We's gonna strut our stuff!
HAM   Gonna dance on down!
STAID LADY (*loudly*)   Yaw-oow!
TINY   Oh, my lands! That woman's haid! (*rushes to her booth*) Darling, is you burnt?
STAID LADY (*angrily*)   Lemme out of here! Just lemme out of here!
HAM (*appearing in the door of the booth*)   Don't you want to play a number today, lady? I can still get it in for you.
STAID LADY   Jest lemme out of this place! It's possessed of the devil. (*putting her hat on angrily over her uncombed hair*)
MISSOURI   Let us out of this damn place!
TINY   Well, go on then! A little thing like a burnt haid might happen any time, specially when it's tight and dry as yours is!
STAID LADY   I thought you had religion! But I'll get back at you, Tiny Lee, don't worry! An eye for an eye and a tooth for a tooth.
TINY   Yes, and a strand for a strand. (*enter a* FEMALE MEMBER *of Father Divine's cult*)
DIVINITE   Peace, angel!
OPAL   Peace!
DIVINITE   All o' Father's beauty parlors is full to overflowin' this afternoon, so I come to you.
OPAL   We'll take you on, sister.
DIVINITE   I want my hair straightened.
OPAL   Just have a seat. One o' our operators'll take you directly. (DIVINITE *sits down*)
DIVINITE   It's truly wonderful!
STAID LADY (*going toward door*)   It's full of devils—that's what I say about Harlem. Why my head feels like I been in hell, it's so burnt up. (*exits*)

Little Ham

DIVINITE Peace!

TINY That's what I say—Peace!

HAM Peace, sister! I'm selling the numbers! Who wants one?

DIVINITE I don't need no numbers, son. I got Father and he's truly wonderful! Peace, Little Ham!

HAM (*surprised as he recognizes the* DIVINITE) Peace! Why, if it ain't Gertrude! Is you done got righteous?

DIVINITE Indeed I have, you devil you! And my name ain't Gertrude no mo'. I done took a new name in the Kingdom.

HAM What is it?

DIVINITE Sweet Delight! That's what they calls me now. Sweet Delight! (*she follows* TINY *into booth*)

HAM (*to* OPAL) I'm taking 'em down, girl, any number you want to play.

OPAL Well, put me down for—wait a minute. (*looks in Dream Book*) What's the number for *green*? Also *dress*? I wants to play 'em, boxed.

HAM I drempt you was handlin' money last night.

OPAL You drempt *I* was handlin' money last night? Why you didn't even know me last night.

HAM No, but I drempt I knowed you last night.

OPAL Well, I want to play 448 for *green* and 006 for *dress*. Put me down, papa.

HAM I sho' will, sweet.

TINY (*calling*) Opal, how many more appointments have I got before suppertime?

OPAL (*looking at book*) Four.

TINY Oh, pshaw! I thought I might get a chance to run out and have a beer or two with Little Ham. Say, Ham, what about that boy Shingle, that you told me got arrested yesterday?

HAM Aw, he's out. Five-dollar fine, that was all, for carrying concealed slips.

TINY And how about Boss LeRoy?

HAM Don't know for sure, but I hear he's been put out o' the racket. Madam's still in, though. The Shine Parlor's writing numbers today, even if Madam do say her nerves can't go it.

TINY She's just puttin' on—that old hard-fisted woman! Baby, don't you want a glass o' beer? I wish I could go out with you, Ham.

(MATTIE BEA *in other booth pricks up her ears*)

HAM I wish you could too, darling. But I know you got to work. (*to* OPAL) How much you puttin' on these numbers?

OPAL Box 'em, and put a nickel on each. That makes sixty cents, don't it?

HAM You are perzactly correct.

OPAL (*paying him*) Come around every day.

HAM As sure as the sun rises and sets and Roosevelt's a white man.

OPAL I ain't never heard o' no black Roosevelt.

HAM Neither's I. (*going toward* LULU'*s booth*) Lemme see, is there any business over here? (*looks in and sees* MATTIE BEA, *and is terribly embarrassed*) Howdy-do!

MATTIE BEA (*dryly*) So you a number writer now.

HAM I just started today!

MATTIE BEA No wonder I couldn't find you at the Paradise! I been there three times lookin' for you today. I want to know what time you coming by to get me to go to the dance tonight?

HAM That's pro-bli-ma-ti-cal.

MATTIE BEA And what's that mean?

HAM I mean—that's a problem.

MATTIE BEA What kind o' problem? You see me settin' up here getting my hair all ready to go. Now, you don't mean to say you ain't gonna take me?

HAM I mean to say that since I got to be a number writer, I works nights too. I got to count up all those numbers, and divide up all this change.

MATTIE BEA You mean you ain't goin' to the Ball?

HAM Honey, I don't see how I can.

MATTIE BEA (*leaning forward*) And me done spent *my* good money for tickets, too. And give 'em to you yesterday.

LULU Keep still, please. You'll make me burn you.

MATTIE BEA You ain't gonna pull no stuff on me, Ham! (TINY *comes out of her booth to listen*)

HAM Shss! I ain't tryin' to pull no stuff on you. I'll take you, baby, but it can't be till late.

MATTIE BEA (*delighted*) I knowed you'd take me, honey! You just wanted to tease me a little, didn't you?

HAM That's all, darling.

MATTIE BEA You little sweet ole devil you.

Come here and hold my hand. I knowed you'd take me.

TINY (*approaching*) Take *who* where?

MATTIE BEA Take *me* to the Hello Club Ball.

TINY Naw he don't! Ham's *my* man. He ain't takin you nowhere. What put that in your head? And who's you?

MATTIE BEA Who *is* you, Jumbo?

TINY (*hands on hips*) I'm a real good mama that can shake your peaches down!

MATTIE BEA Sister, my tree's too tall for you! You'd have to climb and climb again.

TINY (*loudly*) I hear you cluckin', hen, but your nest must be far away. Don't try to lay no eggs in here. (*putting her arm around* HAM) This rooster belongs to me, Miss Tiny Lee! Don't you, little Ham?

MATTIE BEA (*rising*) Take your hands off that man, you heifer, before I stomp your head!

LULU Lawd have mercy!

TINY Heifer ain't my name—but I'll take it in my left hand. If you give it to me in my right, it's your hips!

MATTIE BEA (*removing towel from neck*) Yes, you's a heifer! No other she-varmint'd try to take a woman's man away from her right under her very nose. You'll never take Ham from me. Come on, Ham, let's get out of here.

HAM Now don't act that way, Mattie Bea, you know I ain't nothin' to you.

TINY (*to* HAM) So you know the wench's name? Uh-hum! Well, I want you to forget it!

HAM All right, darling.

DIVINITE (*in* TINY's *booth*) Peace, Father!

MATTIE BEA This place's too small to whip a cat in, without getting fur in your mouth, but I'm gonna whip you, Tiny Lee.

LULU Now here, woman, don't start no ruckus in my booth, knocking over my oils and things. If you want to fight—you, Tiny, or anybody, back on out of here. (*the belligerents back on toward the entrance.* OPAL *gathers up her manicure tools and retreats toward sink. The* DIVINITE *comes out to intercede*)

TINY I'll whip you less you fly to Jesus!

DIVINITE (*touching* TINY's *sleeve*) Peace, daughter!

TINY Peace nothing! She says she's gonna take my Ham.

DIVINITE (*gently*) You can buy mo' ham in the butcher shop.

TINY But not this kind! Stand back you all.

MATTIE BEA Little Ham, get out o' the way! Don't you get hurt. (*just as they prepare to fight, in comes a* DELIVERY BOY *with a package*)

DELIVERY BOY Coat for Miss Tiny Lee.

TINY Lemme see if it's fixed right before I pay for it. Gimme it here. (*opens the box.* MATTIE BEA *recognizes it as the same coat* HAM *promised to buy for her the day before from the* HOT STUFF MAN)

MATTIE BEA That's my coat, ain't it, Ham?

HAM (*disclaiming responsibility*) It ain't none o' mine, I know that much.

TINY (*lifting out coat*) It belongs to me. Ham bought it, and it belongs to me. I paid my own money to have this solid gold extension back put in it for the Hello Club Ball tonight. (*to* HAM) And we gonna go, too, ain't we, papa? But first lemme attend to this here she-dog! (*putting down coat*)

MATTIE BEA Oh! Ham, get out of the way! (MATTIE BEA *ups with her purse and hits* TINY *on the head*)

TINY That's a dying lick. I'll limb you, woman! (TINY *reaches for* MATTIE BEA. *The* DIVINITE *runs screaming,* "Peace," *through the door, and the* DELIVERY BOY *exits as the manicure table falls.* MATTIE BEA *grabs for and secures* TINY's *hair. Just then the* LODGE LADY *enters, sees the turmoil, and rushes out calling,* "Police!")

LODGE LADY'S VOICE Police! Police! Murder! Police!

LULU Fight her to a finish, Tiny, before the cops come. Do it to her, sister! You and me had the same mama, if not the same papa—so I'm half with you.

TINY Yes, indeedy! Just get back and gimme room.

OPAL You all better stop!

HAM Do it, Tiny, cause I know you can! I'm backing you up!

MATTIE BEA Ham, you turn against me?

HAM Mattie, you small potatoes and few in the pot to me now.

MATTIE BEA After all I did for you? Take off my muffler! (*reaches out and grabs the muffler from* HAM's *throat, then resumes her struggle with* TINY)

TINY Leave him, and everything he owns, alone.

MATTIE BEA That little jiver don't own nothing. You Ham, take off that overcoat I bought you last year.

HAM What do you mean, woman?

MATTIE BEA I'll show you what I mean, if I ever get loose here. (*she grabs the collar of* HAM's *coat, and as she and* TINY *push and shove,* HAM *is almost choked. He has to struggle to get loose.* TINY *releases her grip to puff and blow a moment. And just as a* COP *comes in,* HAM *is pushing* MATTIE BEA *roughly away. It looks as if he has been beating her, so the* COP *grabs him*)

COP You dirty little woman-beater, you, come with me! You know it's against the law to hit a lady.

HAM She hit me.

COP That's no difference. Come on, now.

TINY But, officer...

COP That's all right, Miss Lee. I know you run a decent place. I'll take this little ruffian out of here.

TINY But I don't want you to take him.

MATTIE BEA Neither do I. He ain't done a thing.

HAM I sho' ain't.

TINY He sure ain't.

COP I know you women's got good hearts. (*loudly*) But I ain't got no heart for a brute that would hit a lady. (*jerks him roughly*) Come on!

HAM (*rapidly*) Shovel, Shrivel, Chapel! What's the word?

COP Is he crazy?

HAM (*frantically*) Tiny, what's the word? What's the word? What's the word?

TINY Sappy, soopy, sippy... Oh, my God, I can't remember!

COP Well, all of you all must be fools! I'm gonna call the wagon. (*roughly*) Stand up! (*drags* HAM *by the coat collar out into the street. The wails of the women follow him. At the door the* COP *turns and pushes the women back inside*) Don't bring that noise out here in the street, if you do, I'll arrest you all, too.

MATTIE BEA He ain't done nothing! Not a thing!

TINY Naw, he ain't. He's the sweetest little man in the world.

MATTIE BEA And he belongs to me.

TINY If he does, then go take him back from that cop, please.

MATTIE BEA I'll take some of your hide first.

TINY Then I'll give your collar bone a permanent wave!

MATTIE BEA You mean you'll try. Well, come on to me. (*reaches down in her stocking and produces a knife*)

TINY Uck-oh! Lulu, hand me your hot comb. (LULU *hands* TINY *a red-hot straightening comb*)

LULU (*to* MATTIE BEA) Don't you cut my sister! (MATTIE BEA *ups with the knife, but* TINY *waves the hot comb while* LULU *threatens her with a curling iron.* MATTIE BEA *shrieks and rises to run toward the door.* TINY *jabs the hot comb at her back as she escapes into the street*)

LULU Now, maybe we can have some peace in here.

TINY I hope we can. Is there anybody else wants some o' this comb? (*looks pointedly at* OPAL) I heard you talkin' to Ham. Don't think I didn't. (*mocking her*) "Come back again." Playin' numbers with my little Ham, heh?

OPAL (*pleading*) That's all I was doin', Miss Tiny.

TINY And that's all you'll ever do, too! Take yourself out of here now! Get! And take your tools. You don't work for me no more.

OPAL (*rushing into her coat*) Yes, ma'am.

TINY Anybody wants any of my Ham, they'll pay for it. Cause I'll put my brand on 'em.

OPAL I'm goin', Miss Tiny. You won't have no trouble out o' me.

TINY (*swiping at her from a distance with the hot iron*) Go!

OPAL Ow-ooo! (*exits*)

TINY There ain't no woman faithful to you —where a man is concerned.

LULU Nobody but your sister.

TINY (*bursting into tears*) Now Ham is gone, locked up, and I couldn't think o' that word for to tell the judge! Snibble, Snozzle, Snozzle! Lulu, lock the door. I can't work no more today. And turn down the radio, sister, so I can cry out loud! (*bawling*) Little Ham is gone! He's gone! Gone! (*she buries her face in the velvet coat with the golden brocaded back and weeps aloud*) Hamlet is gone!

(*Curtain*)

ACT THREE

Scene One

(*That night.*

TINY's *apartment in Harlem. Her boudoir, very*

silken and sleek, with soft lights and gay colors. Large shiny photos of Harlem theatrical celebrities all around. Big box of chocolates on the table. Radio going. Telephone by bed.

As the curtain rises, TINY, *en déshabillé, and an illegitimate part-Pekinese, named Nelson, are running wildly about the room,* TINY *evidently is in great distress*)

TINY (*to the dog*) Nelson, why don't you lay down, gettin' right under my feet all the time! Can't you see worried as I is, I'm liable to step on you and mash your gizzard out? Get from under my feet! (*goes to the telephone*) Lawd, I'm so nervous I can't hardly work this dial... Hello! Hello! That you, Lulu?... Honey, sister, I wish you'd come right on over here! ... Naw, Ham ain't out yet. Leastwise, he ain't here... Naw... Yes, I been callin' and a-callin' up de jail. And he been a-callin' me from the police station. We been tryin' to remember that name. That name the white gangster told him to say last night, and they'd let him right out. I heard it, too, but I disremembers myself. Seem like it were Snopple ... Heh? You say maybe it was Snozzel! Naw, that's Durante... It's a gangster's name. The name that works like magic down at City Hall ... Aw, Lawd, I don't know what I'm gonna do, sister. Here 'tis long past time to go to the Hello Club affair, and my Ham's in jail... Naw, I can't get nobody on the phone now, since seven o'clock. They got him up in police court, I reckon. And if he could just tell the judge that name, I know they'd let him out... Sure, I called Boss LeRoy. But he ain't boss no more in Harlem. This new gang's got a new boss up here. Some Detroit Jigaboo they imported... Yes... Please do, Lulu. Come right over... I'm liable to faint before you get here. This thing's got me so worried it's gimme nervous prostitution... The first and only man I ever really loved, and he done gone and got locked up protecting me. Honey, wasn't it marvelous the way he lit into that other woman? Ham is a man, I'm tellin' you... yes, he is... Honey, bring me a pint o' gin when you come. I don't know if I can keep my senses or not till you get here... The dance?... Naw, I ain't goin' to no dance by myself... Yes, I got my clothes all laid out, red gown and velvet coat and all, but I ain't goin' nowhere without Ham... Gilbert? Now, I ain't studyin' lettin' Gilbert take me... Should you bring him along? Gilbert? Well, bring him if you want to, but you and I know, *and he knows*, that he ain't my man no mo'. He ought to stay home with his wife. I called him up and told him so last night after Ham left here. I told him he were a good old wagon, but he done broke down—far as I'm concerned. Gilbert didn't care nothing about me no how... What you say? He says he gonna shoot Ham? He'll have me to kill if he do... Um-hum! You mean take Gilbert back just for tonight, so we can all go to this Charleston Contest?... I tell you I can't dance, worried as I is about my little, short, sweet, brand new papa... Well, yes, tell Gilbert he can come up here, but to behave himself. You say you're bringing your boy friend, too?... Well, hurry up, some o' you all and come on, 'cause I'm just about to die o' worryment. And I can't stand being alone with just a dog. Nelson ain't no company. And my *heart* is in jail... Take a taxi... Goodbye. (TINY *rises and goes to the mirror and begins to comb her hair. She takes a chocolate from a box. To dog*) Nelson, I reckon if you was a human, you'd be grayheaded by now, old as you is, and as much worryment as they is in this world! But you ain't never been in love with no man in jail, has you?... Huh? ... I wonder did you care much about that police dog you tried to reach up to last month in the hall? She were too tall for you, weren't she? Po' boy! I must take you out where some small dogs is, in the spring! Yes sir! Lawd, if I could only think of that name, to phone Ham! Snapple, snipple, snopple, skipple, bipple! Aw, hell! The devil! Shupple, maybe that were it! Naw, more like Scrappel! Scrappel! That's right, I think. Lemme see can I get the police station on the phone... (*dialing*) Plaza 3-9600 ... Hello! The Captain?... Yes, you all tell Hamlet Jones, *Scrappel* is the name... What? ... Yes, I'm the same woman done called six times, and I'll call six more times if I want to. I pays taxes for you-all bulls to live on, and I votes for aldermen, and I knows every ward boss in Harlem, knows 'em well! Was married to one of 'em—in name only—once. And I'll tell him to take your job, if you gimme any rough talk... Sure, I'd be just as brave if I was down there as I am on the phone. I knows my politics—which is Tammany!... You tell my little Ham *Scrappel* was the name... My name?... Naw! *The* name... Huh? You say you ain't got no Ham nor no Scrappel neither there?... Then where is Ham? You all discharged him?... What? Yo don't know? I have to call the night court? And they ain't got no phone? Oh, Lawd! (*hangs up receiver*) Oh, Lawd! Nelson, Ham is up before the Judge! (*praying*) Oh, Lawd, give that Judge a kind heart. Ham weren't doin' a thing but defending me. I hope he et up all them policy slips on him before they got him down to the station! (*to the dog, as the doorbell rings*) Nelson, get out of my way! (*goes to door and admits* LULU *and her boy friend,* JACK, *and also* GILBERT, *her own former flame*)

LULU Girl, I'm sorry you feelin' so bad. Maybe this gin'll cheer you up a bit. We brought lemons and ice, too. Where's your shaker?

TINY Nothin' could cheer me up tonight, Lulu, Hello, Jack. (*coldly*) Hello, Gilbert.

GILBERT Don't bass at me, woman. I ain't bit you.

TINY Now, don't start no stuff, Gilbert. We's familiar no more.

LULU Come on, Jack, let's go out in the kitchen and mix up a cocktail. We going on to the Ball, soon's we drink it. Let the other two of 'em stay here if they want to.

GILBERT Naw, we ain't gonna stay neither. Tiny's going to that dance *with me*.

TINY You got that wrong!

LULU Come on, Jack. Let's go mix the drinks. (*they exit into kitchen*)

TINY I ain't steppin' out with you *no more*, Gilbert. I done told you that by phone last night.

GILBERT I know you weigh two tons more'n a switch engine, but you can't sidetrack me like that. I'm sweet papa Gilbert from Texas where even the rabbits are too tough for stew. And I don't let no woman quit me. I quit them. Women don't quit me.

TINY Now, Gilbert, you know you ain't been a-near me for three days.

GILBERT I come up here last night and wouldn't nobody open the door. Don't think I didn't see your light. I went out in the alley and looked. Not only saw the light, but I saw shadows, too—two shadows on that back window shade—and big as you are, even you can't cast but *one*.

TINY Are you insinuating?

GILBERT Then why didn't you answer the doorbell? Or at least answer the phone? Naw, you waited till one o'clock in the morning—and then called me up to tell me you didn't want me in your life no more.

TINY And I sure don't.

GILBERT But don't think I don't know who you've taken up with? A dumb little shoeshiner named Hamlet Jones.

TINY He's no shoeshiner. Ham's a business man.

GILBERT What kind o' business man?

TINY He deals in figures.

GILBERT So do I. I play numbers, too.

TINY Well, he writes them.

GILBERT No wonder he's in jail then.

TINY He's in jail for defending me from attack.

GILBERT Who'd attack you?

TINY Don't call me out o' my name!

GILBERT Then get your clothes on and come on let's go to the dance. We liable to win that cup, good as you and I can Charleston.

TINY I'll never Charleston with you no more. Last time I went to a dance with you, you danced all night with some meriney hussy that looked like a faded-out jack-o-lantern.

GILBERT (*chucking her under the chin*) Aw, come on, baby, be sociable. I'll dance with you tonight, Tiny.

TINY After all I gived you, you come tellin' me I'm too stout to offer any competition. You wants a woman you can hold on your lap.

GILBERT Aw, sweetness, I was just kiddin'. You never forgets, do you? Just like an elephant!

TINY Naw, I don't forget! But I forgot you. Get out o' my life, Gilbert. I'm goin' and see about them cocktails. (*starts into kitchen, but backs out suddenly*) Oh, excuse me! I didn't know you all was engaged yet.

GILBERT (*harshly*) Tiny, I guess you realize I really don't give a damn about you, but I'm a man. And ain't no woman gonna quit me. When I get ready to leave you, then I leave. But you ain't gonna tell me *you* are through. No, indeed! You're gonna see plenty more of Gilbert, till *I* get good and ready to lay off.

TINY There won't be no more of *you* to see if you fool with me!

GILBERT You must forget that I carry a gun.

TINY (*as* LULU *and* JACK *enter with cocktail shaker and glasses*)   I ain't forgot nothing.
LULU   Have somethin' coolin' and refreshin'.
TINY (*pointedly to her sister*)   You all need somethin' coolin. That's what I say about love. Last week right on Lenox Avenue, I had to throw water on Nelson—that dog was so excited.
JACK   Did you all decide to go to the dance?
TINY   You all dance on down—and take Gilbert with you. I'm stayin' here.
GILBERT   We're taking Tiny too.
LULU (*pouring cocktails*)   I wish you'd come, sister.
TINY   Just wish right on, 'cause I ain't budging. (*a loud knock at the door combined with the ringing of the bell*)
LULU   What a racket!
TINY (*shouting*)   Who's there?
HAM (*voice without*)   Little Ham, that's who! Me, Ham!
LULU   Oh!
GILBERT (*sinisterly*)   Aw!
JACK   Who?
TINY (*jubilantly*)   Thank God-a-mighty! Nelson, your daddy's come home! (*rushes toward the door, then turns suddenly, recalling* GILBERT. *Whispering*) Gilbert, he might have a gun, baby. (*sweetly to her old lover*) Just step in my fur-coat closet a minute till I find out. (*sulkily* GILBERT *steps into a closet.* TINY *closes the door, locks it, and takes the key with her, as she goes to let* HAM *in*)
HAM   You took long enough to let me in! I just got out of jail, and looks like you don't want me here. Aint you glad to see me?
TINY (*ecstatically*)   Baby, I certainly are! (*takes him in her arms*) Lawd knows I are!
LULU   I'm so glad you're out, Ham.
JACK   What'd they fine you?
HAM   Not a dime.
TINY   Baby, did you ever think o' the magic name?
HAM   Never did.
LULU   Are you out on bail?
HAM   Naw, I'm freed, released, don't have to go back no more.
TINY   Ain't that wonderful! Tell us about it.
HAM   Well, as luck would have it, it were a woman judge.
LULU   A woman judge?
HAM   Yes, a woman judge! (*conceitedly*) So I just conversationed her. And she being a lady . . .
JACK   Boy, ain't you something!
HAM   I just told her any man would defend a woman, and I was a man! She say, that's right! And I say, it sure is. And smiled at her—and that were my defense.
TINY   And they ain't found no numbers on you?
HAM   Sure they found some few little slips. But I just said, now, that one there, that's my mother's telephone number what just moved to Sugar Hill. And that other one, why that's my initiation number in the Elks. They just initiated me last night, so I had to write it down to remember it. And them other slips there, the last four they found, why, that's my horoscope. I paid a astrologer ten dollars to figger that out for me and he wrote it in four pieces, what time my star comes due—at 1:16 the third month of the 47th year plus one thousand, minus 2-9-2. And the lady judge says, did I ever read Evangeline Adams, who knew all about the heavens? And I said no, but that I follows Father Divine who knows more about Heaven than anybody. So the Judge says, Peace, Father! And I said, Peace, Angel. And she lemme out.
TINY   It's truly wonderful!
LULU   Amen!
JACK   Well, now that you're here, let's go to the Ball.
HAM   Let's go. I'm ready! Honey, put on your clothes.
TINY   Give Ham a drink first. You all just turn your backs while I dress. (HAM, LULU, *and* JACK *gather round the cocktail shaker while* TINY *slips off her negligee and puts on a red lace evening gown, red slippers, and a rhinestone tiara*)
LULU (*while* TINY *dresses*)   Well, that woman what dreamed about a *colored* woman washing a green dress in a white lady's back yard was right. One of her numbers come out this afternoon.
JACK   What number?
HAM   0-0-6. That's dress! It sho' come out.
LULU   If she really played it, she caught, too.
TINY   That's a lucky lady. She catch all the time. (*pulls open drawer to get her jewels and six or eight men's pictures fall out. Looks around anxiously to see if* HAM *notices. Relieved, she picks them up quickly*)

LULU I wish it'd been me that hit today.

TINY (*still dressing*) I knowed a 6 was coming out somewhere. 0-0-6 come mighty near being our 1-1-6 again, didn't it, Ham?

HAM It sho' did. But we can't catch every day, baby.

TINY Sure can't. It's enough I caught you—and five hundred and forty dollars both—inside o' two days. (*coming toward them, dressed*)

HAM And I got you! Baby, how pretty you look! Be-ooo-ti-ful!

JACK Tons and tons of it, boy!

LULU Drink up and let's go. (*they lift their glasses and drink*)

HAM (*looking at his wrist watch*) Hurry up, and we'll be just in time for the Charleston Contest. It starts at midnight. Maybe I'll stop by my flat and put on my new suit. This one ain't been pressed today. It won't take but a minute.

TINY Sure, if you want to. I want my papa lookin' hot. (*takes her new coat and gives it to* HAM *to hold*) Jack, you see this pretty coat Ham bought me yesterday. I didn't have to do a thing to it to make it fit, but put a new back in it, and believe me, it's solid gold-brocaded Cadillac.

JACK You look like the Queen o' Sheba.

LULU You certainly look sweet, sis. I'm proud of my relative.

TINY Let's go! (*to dog*) Nelson, you stay here now, and be a nice dog.

HAM Come on.

LULU Everybody truck on down! (*opens exit door*)

GILBERT (*thumping in closet, in loud voice*) Hey! Hey! Lemme out o' here!

HAM (*stopping dead still*) What's that?

TINY Aw, come on, honey! That's some old wild man in the next apartment who's always making a lot of noise.

HAM (*doubling up his fists*) Well, if he just must get out, I'll take him on.

TINY Have you got a gun with you, darling?

HAM I ain't got no gun, but I'm *a man*.

GILBERT I'm a man, too, and I'll take you on, Ham.

HAM Sounds like he's talkin' to me.

TINY Oh, no he ain't, darlin'. Come on.

LULU Yes, for God's sake, come on.

JACK I'm going myself. (*pulls* LULU *by the arm, but she does not move from doorway*)

GILBERT Hamlet Jones, I say lemme out, you son-of-a . . .

HAM Well, hot-damn! Now, I know that's me he's calling. (*approaching closet*) Which dark horse is you? You also-ran!

GILBERT Unlock this door and you'll see! Tiny, come here and open this closet door! You know you got me locked up in here, smothered.

TINY You'll stay there, too, far as I'm concerned. Come on, Ham, let's go.

HAM Don't think I'm afraid, whoever you is. You might be bigger'n I am, but I'm every inch a man.

GILBERT I got more feet than you got inches, runt. And if you all don't lemme out o' here, you'll know it.

HAM Who you callin' runt?

GILBERT You, you stunted cockroach!

HAM (*to* TINY) Lemme at him, whoever he is!

TINY (*pleading*) Come on to the Ball, baby. We'll attend to him by and by. I don't want to get my clothes all mussed up now.

GILBERT (*angrily*) You all, none of you, didn't have no mammy!

LULU Aw-ooo!

HAM (*stepping toward door*) Well, your'n must-a been a mole, what borned you in a coal mine, 'cause even your voice sounds caved in.

GILBERT (*shooting his pistol through the door*) Take that, you so-and-so-and-so. (*fires five shots, one after another, through the door.* TINY, LULU, JACK *and* HAM *press back against the wall*) Take that! (*Bang!*) and that! (*Bang!*)

TINY (*calmly, after the shooting is over*) Well, now that's over! His kind o' gun don't carry but five bullets—and he ain't hit a thing but the other wall. Come on, you all, let's go! I don't let no Abyssinian spoil my evening. Come, Ham, let's win that Charleston cup, like we done said we would!

HAM I'll give you a taste o' my forty-four when I come back, creeper. Just stay there and breathe through them holes you done shot in the door.

GILBERT (*in closet*) Please lemme out! Tiny, please lemme out 'fore you go.

TINY (*yelling back from the doorway*) I want to spare your life, Gilbert—for your wife's sake.

I can't have no murder here, no how, 'cause little Ham would tear you to pieces, wouldn't you, Ham?

HAM   I'd limb him—limb from limb! (*taking empty gin bottle from tray and poking its neck through one of the bullet holes in the closet door*) Here, smell this through that bullet hole till I get back with *my* pistol. You might need something stronger than gin to help you, by and by.

GILBERT (*moaning*)   Tiny, help me, baby!

TINY   Help you, hell! Me and Ham's going to the Hello Club Ball. (*turns out the light*) Goodbye, Nelson, you is a sweet dog! (*all exit except the dog. Nelson remains to bark loudly in the dark as* GILBERT *yells and pounds on the locked door*)

GILBERT   Lemme out! Lemme out! Lemme out!

(*Curtain*)

Scene Two

(*Midnight.*

The Savoy Ball Room in Harlem. The orchestra may be in sight or hidden (as producer chooses), but the front of the platform should be seen. The MASTER OF CEREMONIES *stands thereon, the Grand Silver Charleston Trophy in hand, to be awarded to the winning couple of the contest about to take place. A brilliant crowd of Harlem's suavest and sportiest set, boxers, number writers, theatrical folks, hairdressers, maids, sports, and their ladies. Women in evening gowns, men in extravagantly cut suits from tuxedos to pleated backs, hair lacquered, diamonds flashing.* MADAM BELL *and* LEROY *are there together;* SUGAR LOU *and her new boy friend;* SHINGLE, *out of jail, and his company;* JASPER *and a fair young lady; the* WEST INDIAN *and a Bahama dancer—but not yet* TINY *and* HAM, *nor* JACK *and* LULU.

As the curtain rises, the orchestra is just coming to the end of a blues number to which everybody is dancing. As the piece cools off, the M.C. *signals for a loud chord to indicate that silence is desired. Everybody stops dancing*)

M.C.   Ladies and gentlemen, Lad-dees and gentel-mun! And gigolos! I have in my hand the Grand Silver Charleston Trophy engraved with the name of Harlem's most prominent, high-toned society institution, the Hello Club. Hello! Hello! Hello! (*applause*) This club has been ruling supreme amongst the Harlem Four Thousand for many years, and is known from Central Park north to the Yankee Stadium, from the Harlem River to Sugar Hill, from the Cotton Club to the Silver Dollar.

VOICE   And from the police station to Harlem Hospital.

M.C.   Also! We are known everywhere! The Hello Club leads where others follow.

VOICES   Yeah, man!... Yes, indeedy!... True! True!

M.C.   And when we give a ball, we give a ball!

VOICE   Yes, sir! (*enter* LULU *and* JACK, TINY *and* HAM, *pushing to the front*) And tonight we are presenting the Hello Club's First Annual Social Charleston Contest. This here cup I got in my hand is to be awarded to the couple that, in the opinion of the audience, and of the applause they receive, has done the best job of real righteous oh-my-soul dancing on the floor. Everybody starts at once, and the judges will go around and eliminate them that ain't got the right movements in they feet, nor Charleston in their souls. Now listen, when the man taps you on the shoulder, that means go off the floor and be audience. I don't want nobody to get bullheaded and not withdraw—'cause that would spoil the social part. (*gaily*) Everybody, now, let your spirits go to your feet, let the rhythm go to your heads, let the music move your souls, and dance on down! (*lifting his baton*) Orchestra, give it to me! (*the orchestra begins a ballroom Charleston piece, and* EVERYBODY *starts to prance, rocking and swaying in a carnival of joy. Two or three gentlemen, committee members, with ribbons across their chests, the colors of the Hello Club, are tapping those couples on the back who are dancing with the least originality and abandon. They withdraw to the sidelines. As the music goes on, finally all but four couples are eliminated. Those remaining include two unknown couples,* MADAM *and* LEROY, *and* LITTLE HAM *and* TINY. (*stopping the music*) Ladies and gentlemen! And dancers! The Contest is now reaching its final and most important stage! That of who shall win! Somebody gotta win. Now it's up to you to show, by your applause, just who deserves the cup. We'll take these last four couples in rotation, for the crowning feature of the Hello Club Ball! Couples, line up over yonder! As I give the signal, dance on out across the floor, then Charleston. First couple, let's go. (*the first couple come out and do their dance. They have probably been practicing nightly for the last three weeks at the Savoy. But it is obvious that they are trying too hard, although the crowd gives them a good hand as they finish on the opposite side of the floor*) Second couple, bring it to me! Let's go, band! (*The second couple come dancing out across the floor, bowing and tapping, parting and swaying, circling around one another like a rooster and hen, then going into the Charleston. They get a good hand, as they finish on the left in front of the* M.C.)

VOICES   Pretty good, Joe! Too tight!... Young stuff!... Oh, my!

M.C.   All right now, Madam Bell of the Paradise Shining Parlors and her pertner, Big Boss LeRoy! Let's go! (LEROY *and the* MADAM *truck out to the center of the floor and break*) Aw, Break!... Do it, Madam Lucille Bell!

MADAM   Let's go to town!

LEROY   How we gonna get there?

MADAM   Truckin' on down.

VOICES   (*and laughter*)   Do it, old folks!... Lawd, look at Madam Bell!... Aw, strut it, Boss!... Oh, my, my, my, my!...

LEROY   Let's break!

MADAM   Hey! Hey! Charleston! (*they finish up to great applause just in front of the* M.C.)

M.C.   And now for the last roundup! Come on, Little Ham! (LITTLE HAM *and* TINY *take the floor*)

VOICES   Lawd! Lawd! Lawd!... Boy, haul that load!... Tons—and tons—and tons!

HAM   All the way to town!

TINY   (*truckin*)   I'm comin', baby!

M.C.   Rock, church, rock! (TINY *and* HAM *do the most exciting, original, and jazzy dance of the whole evening, Suzy-q-ing, Lindy-hopping, Camel-walking, breaking, clutching, parting, and dancing on a dime until the entire crowd rocks with laughter, cheers, and applause*)

VOICES   That's the best!... Two tons o' rhythm!... Look at that little boy go... My! My! O my! My! (*they finish, sweating and out of breath*)

HAM   Yes, Tiny!

TINY   Yeah, man!

M.C.   That sends me! (*holding up the cup*) Now, all four couples truck around the hall, one at a time, and the applause will tell who gets the trophy. (*to the band*) Come on, boys. Let's go, truckers!

(*The band strikes up again, and in turn, the four couples dance around the hall, ending all together in a Charleston at center.* LITTLE HAM *and* TINY *get the most applause, much to the chagrin of* BOSS LEROY)

VOICES   Give it to Ham!... Yeah, man!... Ham and Tiny!...

M.C.   You all must mean Tiny and Ham! Is that right? (*to* TINY *and* HAM) Step out here in the middle of the floor. (*as they do so*) Is this who the crowd wants?

VOICES   (*and applause*) Yes!... They get it! ... Sure!... Little Ham's won!... You're right!... Give Tiny that cup!...

M.C.   They surely deserve it. My compliments! Quiet, please. (*signals the orchestra for a chord*) Ladies and partners! On behalf of the Hello Club's social committee and the entire membership of our estimable organization, I am delighted and exuberated to present this Grand Solid Silver Charleston Trophy to the winners of our contest tonight, Mr. Hamlet H. Jones and Miss Tiny Lee!

VOICES   'Ray!... Good!... Yes!... That's right!... Hurray!

(TINY *and* HAM *receive the cup amid much applause.* LULU *and* JACK *rush forward to shake their hands, also* JASPER *and* SHINGLE. LEROY *stands in a corner moping with* MADAM)

LEROY   Here I done lost my job with the numbers, and can't even win a dancing cup! When a man is down, he's down.

MADAM   Baby, you can have Little Ham's job, shining shoes. He's working in the field now.

LEROY   (*incensed, raises his arm to hit* MADAM) Woman, don't tell me...

A COMMITTEE MEMBER   (*grabs him*)   This here's a social, brother.

LEROY   Oh, all right! Then I won't fight. (*mumbling*) Come offering *me* a job shining shoes. (*to* MADAM) Come on, Lucille, let's go!

MADAM   Yes, darling, let's go. (*they start toward door, but* MADAM BELL *suddenly pauses as* MATTIE BEA *enters. Excitedly*) Look, LeRoy, there's Ham's other woman! Uh-oh!

LEROY   Who? Where? Which one?

MADAM (*pointing*)   Mattie Bea!
LEROY   Uh-oh! Watch out!
MADAM (*in anticipation*)   The fur'll fly now.

(MATTIE BEA *pauses, looks around, clenches her fists, and advances toward the bandstand with venom in her eye.* HAM *and* TINY *do not see her. Suddenly, however, the door is flung open and* GILBERT *stalks in*)

GILBERT (*loudly*)   Everybody stand back. I'm here! (*everybody turns toward the door.* TINY *and* MATTIE BEA *both scream*) I done broke down one door tonight, and I'll turn this place out, too. I'm mad!
TINY   Oh! The lion is loose!
HAM   Who? Where? What lion?
MATTIE BEA (*yells in astonishment*)   My husband! Gilbert!
HAM (*sees her for the first time and looks worried*)   Mattie Bea! (*hides behind* TINY)
GILBERT (*mollified*)   My wife! Mattie Bea, what you doin' here?
MATTIE BEA   How about you, Gilbert? I thought you said you had to work tonight?
GILBERT   I did. I just got off, honey.
MATTIE BEA   Then who are you lookin' for here?
GILBERT   You, baby, you! (HAM *and* TINY *both seem much relieved*) I thought you might be at this dance.
MATTIE BEA   Well, all right, then! I hate to be at a dance all by myself, Gilbert. But what makes you come in so loud, honey?
GILBERT   I just want everybody to know we're here, that's all—me and you. We ain't been to a dance together for so long, it's a shame, Mattie Bea.
MATTIE BEA   Sure is! (*sweetly*) But now we here, Gilbert, and you look so nice tonight, I believe I'm in love with you all over again. Take off your coat, and let's dance. (*the orchestra begins to play the* "St. Louis Blues")
GILBERT   I always was in love with you, sweetheart, even since we been married.
MATTIE BEA   Let's rest our wraps. This here's another honeymoon. (*they pull off their wraps to dance as the floor fills with dancers*)
MADAM BELL (*to* LEROY)   Sugar, let's dance one more time.
LEROY   Why not?
M.C.   All right now, everybody rock! (*entire crowd begins to dance.* TINY *places the cup in front of platform and embraces* HAM)
HAM (*while dancing*)   Tiny, is you happy, baby?
TINY   Ham, I ain't nothin' else but!
HAM   You's a dancin' thing!
TINY   And so are you, darling!
HAM   What we gonna do with this cup?
TINY   Take it to my house, and keep it there—'cause, I'm gonna keep you there, too. We going get married.
HAM   What about that man in the closet?
TINY   Who? Oh, you mean Gilbert? Honey, yonder he is dancing with Mattie Bea. He's her husband, I reckon.
HAM   So that's her husband!
TINY   He never was no headache of mine, baby.
MATTIE BEA (*dancing with* GILBERT *at the other end of the stage*)   The old love is always best, ain't it, honey?
GILBERT   Do you mean to say I'm old, darling?
MATTIE BEA   Just old enough to be sweet, that's all. Kiss me, sugar-pie. (*as they dance, they kiss. Meanwhile, the spotlight picks out the various couples dancing in the arms of love:* MADAM BELL *and* LEROY; SUGAR LOU *and her boy friend;* SHINGLE *and his lady;* JASPER *and his Harlem blonde; the* WEST INDIAN *and the Bahama girl;* JACK *and* LULU; *and at the end,* TINY *and* HAM)
TINY (*shyly, as they dance in the spotlight*)   You ain't mad about Gilbert, are you, Ham?
HAM   Naw, honey! I know things like that can happen. (*pauses*) You ain't mad about nothin' I ever did, is you?
TINY   Naw, darling. The past is past, ain't it?
HAM   Long gone!
TINY   And I don't care nothing about nobody, no how, but you. I don't want to have no more trouble today, no ways. We ain't had nothing but trouble, since we got engaged yesterday.
HAM   Trouble and luck put together! Money from the numbers, and a cup from the Charleston.
TINY   That's what life is, ain't it, baby? Trouble and luck, put together.
HAM   I reckon it is, but it's more *luck* than trouble—when a man's got the woman he loves.
TINY   Ain't it the truth! That's the way I feel about you! And you know, Little Ham, I think

you better put them numbers down. It's nothing but a racket for a good man. I'm thinking about opening a whole chain of beauty shops—and you can be my manager.

HAM We're the same as in business together.

TINY With my brains, and your personality—

HAM We'll keep them shops full of women's all the time.

(*The orchestra plays increasingly loud the sad-doleful strains of the "St. Louis Blues." SHINGLE and his lady friend dance near TINY and HAM as the lights go dim and soft colors begin to play over the dance floor*)

SHINGLE (*dancing past, yelling*) Hello, boy! You lucky dog!

HAM You see I got my arms full, don't you, Shingle? And, boy, we're dancing right on through life—happy—just like this! (*music and rose-colored darkness as the curtain falls with the spotlight on* LITTLE HAM *and* TINY)

(*Curtain*)

Imamu Amiri Baraka (LeRoi Jones) (1934–   )

The Slave   1964

The Slave is at once a highly personal work and a political statement. It is a mid-point in the purgatory of a poet's life and work; it is the Halfway House between the death of LeRoi Jones and the birth of Imamu Amiri Baraka; it is the mid-balance-point between the death of an assimilationist and the birth of a black nationalist. The play stands witness to the fury inherent in the process.

Imamu Baraka's *Dutchman* is one of the great modern one act plays. The murder in the play of Clay Williams, the young Negro from New Jersey, is the provoked ritual death of Negro integrationist fantasies. White America will seduce, tease, provoke the black man into striking out; then she will kill him (compare white and black death statistics in any riot). Clay Williams is a victim.

Walker Vessals, the black warrior in *The Slave*, is still victim, but this time he does not die—not quite. He kills the oppressor whom he loves/hates; perhaps he even kills the misceginate children he fathered. Perhaps. For the play is clearly labeled "A Fable." And fables are subject to interpretation.

To criticize the play because its naturalism is unconvincing is easy—the children would not be left alone during a bombardment; the "war" is more like 1918 than 1964. But the naturalism is of little importance. It is merely a setting, an excuse for the real drama—the ritual drama of decolonization wherein not only is the colonizer killed, but his powerful spirit that possessed the colonized is ripped out and destroyed.

The Slave was produced in December 1964 and ran 151 performances at the St. Marks Theater. Five months after its premiere Mr. Jones formed the Harlem Black Arts Repertory Theater and School, from which all whites would be excluded. (White roles would be played in white face by black actors.) The next step in the ascent to Cultural Nationalism was further exorcism of the white spirit: *Experimental Death Unit No. 1*, *Mad Heart*, *The Great Goodness of Life*, and *Black Mass*. The oppressor's presence died hard; nevertheless, Imamu Amiri Baraka grew strong and turned to the creation of Spirit House in New-Ark New Jersey, where he entered into the politics of that community. The metamorphosis of this poet has paralleled the growing consciousness of Afro-America.

It could be argued that *The Slave* speaks not only to black people but also to white. To support the inclusion of the play in this section on "Black Theater for Black People," it is enough to remind the reader that these plays are only fully understood by blacks, a fact illustrated by a white critic's observation on the premiere in 1964.

The producer-director and his three associates have done a marked disservice to the author by encouraging him to allow these inferior works [*The Toilet* was produced on the same bill] to be put on, and to the Negro cause and the Off-Broadway Theater. (George Oppenheimer, *Newsday*)

James Davis of the *Daily News* and Whitney Bolton of the *Morning Telegraph* walked out of the theater without seeing the play. But the critic for the *Journal American* wrote of the evening's experience as "the most controversial and terrifying evening in the theater this season or any other". Perhaps he came as close as a white critic can to experiencing the black poet's journey toward home.

The Slave

CHARACTERS

WALKER VESSELS, *tall, thin Negro about forty*
GRACE, *blonde woman about same age. Small, thin, beautiful*
BRADFORD EASLEY, *tall, broad white man, with thinning hair, about forty-five*

THE ACTION takes place in a large living room, tastefully furnished the way an intelligent university professor and his wife would furnish it.

ROOM is dark at the beginning of the play, except for light from explosions, which continue, sometimes close, sometimes very far away, throughout both acts, and well after curtain of each act.

PROLOGUE

WALKER (*coming out dressed as an old field slave, balding, with white hair, and an old ragged vest. Perhaps he is sitting, sleeping, initially-nodding and is awakened by faint cries, like a child's. He comes to the center of the stage slowly, and very deliberately, puffing on a pipe, and seemingly uncertain of the reaction any audience will give his speech*) Whatever the core of our lives. Whatever the deceit. We live where we are, and seek nothing but ourselves. We are liars, and we are murderers. We invent death for others. Stop their pulses publicly. Stone possible lovers with heavy worlds we think are ideas ... and we know, even before these shapes are realized, that these worlds, these depths or heights we fly to smoothly, as in a dream, or slighter, when we stare dumbly into space, leaning our eyes just behind a last quick moving bird, then sometimes the place and twist of what we are will push and sting, and what the crust of our stance has become will ring in our ears and shatter that piece of our eyes that is never closed. An ignorance. A stupidity. A stupid longing not to know ... which is automatically fulfilled. Automatically triumphs. Automatically makes us killers or foot-dragging celebrities at the core of any filth. And it is a deadly filth that passes as whatever thing we feel is too righteous to question, too deeply felt to deny. (*pause to relight pipe*) I am much older than I look ... or maybe much younger. Whatever I am or seem ... (*significant pause*) to you, then let that rest. But figure, still, that you might not be right. Figure, still, that you might be lying ... to save yourself. Or myself's image, which might set you crawling like a thirsty dog, for the meanest of drying streams. The meanest of ideas. (*gentle, mocking laugh*) Yeah. Ideas. Let that settle! Ideas. Where they form. Or whose they finally seem to be. Yours? The other's? Mine? (*shifts uneasily, pondering the last*) No, no more. Not mine. I served my slow apprenticeship ... and maybe came up lacking. Maybe. Ha. Who's to say, really? Huh? But figure, still, ideas are still in the world. They need judging. I mean, they don't come in that singular or wild, that whatever they are, just because they're beautiful and brilliant, just because they strike us full in the center of the heart.... My God! (*softer*) My God, just because, and even this, believe me, even if, that is, just because they're *right* ... doesn't mean anything. The very rightness stinks a lotta times. The very rightness. (*looks down and speaks softer and quicker*) I am an old man. An old man. (*blankly*) The waters and wars. Time's a dead thing really ... and keeps nobody whole. An old man, full of filed rhythms. Terrific, eh? That I hoarded so much dignity? An old man full of great ideas. Let's say theories. As: Love is an instrument of knowledge. Oh, not my own. Not my own ... is right. But listen now.... Brown is not brown except when used as an intimate description of personal phenomenological fields. As your brown is not my brown, et cetera, that is, we need, ahem, a meta-language. We need something not included here. (*spreads arms*) Your ideas? An old man can't be expected to be right. If I'm old. If I really claim that embarrassment. (*saddens... brightens*) A poem? Lastly, that, to distort my position? To divert you... in your hour of need. Before the thing goes on. Before you get your lousy chance. Discovering racially the funds of the universe. Discovering the last image of the thing. As the sky when the moon is broken. Or old, old blues people moaning in their sleep, singing, man, oh, nigger, nigger, you still here, as hard as nails, and takin' no shit from nobody. He say, yeah, yeah, he say yeah, yeah. He say, yeah, yeah... goin' down slow, man. Goin' down slow. He say... yeah, heh... (*running down, growing anxiously less articulate, more "field hand" sounding, blankly lyrical, shuffles slowly around, across the stage, as the lights dim and he enters the set proper and assumes the position he will have when the play starts... still moaning...*)

ACT ONE

(THE SCENE: *a light from an explosion lights the room dimly for a second and the outline of a figure is seen half sprawled on a couch. Every once in a while another blast shows the figure in silhouette. He stands from time to time, sits, walks nervously around the room examining books and paintings. Finally, he climbs a flight of stairs, stays for a few minutes, then returns. He sits smoking in the dark, until some sound is heard outside the door. He rises quickly and takes a position behind the door, a gun held out stiffly.* GRACE *and* EASLEY *open the door, turn on the light, agitated and breathing heavily.* GRACE *quiet and weary.* EASLEY *talking in harsh angry spurts*)

EASLEY   Son of a bitch. Those black son of a bitches. Why don't they at least stop and have their goddamned dinners? Goddamn son of a bitches. They're probably gonna keep that horseshit up all goddamn night. Goddamnit. Goddamn it! (*he takes off a white metal hat and slings it across the room. It bangs loudly against the brick of the fireplace*)

GRACE   Brad! You're going to wake up the children!

EASLEY   Oh, Christ!... But if they don't wake up under all that blasting, I don't think that tin hat will do it. (*he unbuttons his shirt, moves wearily across the room, still mumbling under his breath about the source of the explosions*) Hey, Grace... you want a drink? That'll fix us up. (*he moves to get the drink and spots* WALKER *leaning back against the wall, half smiling, also very weary, but still holding the gun, stomach high, and very stiffly.* EASLEY *freezes, staring at* WALKER'S *face and then the gun, and then back to* WALKER'S *face. He makes no sound. The two men stand confronting each other until* GRACE *turns and sees them*)

GRACE   Sure, I'll take a drink... one of the few real pleasures left in the Western world. (*she turns and drops her helmet to the floor, staring unbelievingly*) Ohh!

WALKER (*looks over slowly at* GRACE *and waves as from a passing train. Then he looks back at* EASLEY; *the two men's eyes are locked in the same ugly intensity.* WALKER *beckons to* GRACE)   The blinds.

GRACE   Walker! (*she gets the name out quietly, as if she is trying to hold so many other words in*) Walker... the gun!

WALKER (*half turning to look at her. He looks back at* EASLEY, *then lets the gun swing down easily toward the floor. He looks back at* GRACE, *and tries to smile*)   Hey, momma. How're you?

EASLEY (*at* WALKER, *and whatever else is raging in his own head*)   Son of a bitch!

GRACE   What're you doing here, Walker? What do you want?

WALKER (*looking at* EASLEY *from time to time*) Nothing. Not really. Just visiting. (*grins*) I was in the neighborhood; thought I'd stop by and see how the other half lives.

GRACE   Isn't this dangerous? (*she seems relieved by* WALKER'S *relative good spirits and she begins to look for a cigarette.* EASLEY *has not yet moved. He is still staring at* WALKER)

WALKER   Oh, it's dangerous as a bitch. But don't you remember how heroic I am?

EASLEY (*handing* GRACE *a cigarette, then waiting to light it*)   Well, what the hell do you want, hero? (*drawn out and challenging*)

WALKER (*with same challenge*)   Nothing you have, fellah, not one thing.

EASLEY   Oh? (*cynically*) Is *that* why you and your noble black brothers are killing what's left of this city? (*suddenly broken*) I should say... what's left of this country... or world.

WALKER   Oh, fuck you (*hotly*) fuck you...

just fuck you, that's all. Just fuck you! (*keeps voice stiffly contained, but then it rises sharply*) I mean really, just fuck you. Don't, goddamnit, don't tell me about any goddamn killing of anything. If that's what's happening. I mean if this shitty town is being flattened... let it. It needs it.

GRACE Walker, shut up, will you? (*furious from memory*) I had enough of your twisted logic in my day... you remember? I mean like your heroism. The same kind of memory. Or Lie. Do you remember which? Huh? (*starting to weep*)

WALKER (*starts to comfort her*) Grace... look... there's probably nothing I can say to make you understand me... now.

EASLEY (*steps in front of* WALKER *as he moves toward* GRACE... *feigning a cold sophistication*) Uh... no, now come, Jefe, you're not going to make one of those embrace the weeping ex-wife dramas, are you? Well, once a bad poet always a bad poet... even in the disguise of a racist murderer!

WALKER (*not quite humbled*) Yeah. (*bends head, then he brings it up quickly, forcing the joke*) Even disguised as a racist murderer... I remain a bad poet. Didn't St. Thomas say that? Once a bad poet always a bad poet... or was it Carl Sandburg, as some kind of confession?

EASLEY You're not still writing... now, are you? I should think the political, now military estates would be sufficient. And you always used to speak of the Renaissance as an evil time. (*begins making two drinks*) And now you're certainly the gaudiest example of Renaissance man I've heard of. (*finishes making drinks and brings one to* GRACE. WALKER *watches him and then as he starts to speak he walks to the cabinet, picks up the bottle, and empties a good deal of it*)

GRACE (*looking toward* WALKER *even while* EASLEY *extends the drink toward her*) Walker ... you are still writing, aren't you?

WALKER Oh, God, yes. Want to hear the first lines of my newest work? (*drinks, does a theatrical shine*) Uh, how's it go...? Oh, "Straddling each dolphin's back/And steadied by a fin,/Those innocents relive their death,/Their wounds open again."

GRACE (*staring at him closely*) It's changed quite a bit.

WALKER Yeah... it's changed to Yeats. (*laughs very loudly*) Yeah, Yeats.... Hey, professor, anthologist, lecturer, loyal opposition, et cetera, et cetera, didn't you recognize those words as being Yeats's? Goddamn, I mean if you didn't recognize them... who the hell would? I thought you knew all kinds of shit.

EASLEY (*calmly*) I knew they were Yeats'.

WALKER (*tilting the bottle again quickly*) Oh, yeah? What poem?

EASLEY The second part of "News for the Delphic Oracle."

WALKER (*hurt*) "News for the Delphic Oracle." Yeah. That's right. (*to* GRACE) You know that, Grace? Your husband knows all about everything. The second part of "News for the Delphic Oracle." (*rhetorically*) Intolerable music falls. Nymphs and satyrs copulate in the foam. (*tilts bottle again, some liquor splashes on the floor*)

EASLEY (*suddenly straightening and stopping close to* WALKER) Look... LOOK! You arrogant maniac, if you get drunk or fall out here, so help me, I'll call the soldiers or somebody ... and turn you over to them. I swear I'll do that.

GRACE Brad!

WALKER Yeah, yeah, I know. That's your job. A liberal education, and a long history of concern for minorities and charitable organizations can do that for you.

EASLEY (*almost taking hold of* WALKER'*s clothes*) No! I mean this, friend! Really! If I get the slightest advantage, some cracker soldier will be bayoneting you before the night is finished.

WALKER (*slaps* EASLEY *across the face with the back of his left hand, pulling the gun out with his right and shoving it as hard as he can against* EASLEY'*s stomach.* EASLEY *slumps, and the cruelty in* WALKER'*s face at this moment also frightens* GRACE) "My country, 'tis of thee. Sweet land of liber-ty." (*screams off key like drunken opera singer*) Well, let's say liberty and ignorant vomiting faggot professors. (*to* GRACE) Right, lady? Isn't that right? I mean you ought to know, 'cause you went out of your way to marry one. (*turns to* GRACE *and she takes an involuntary step backward. And in a cracked ghostlike voice that he wants to be loud...*) Huh? Huh? And then fed the thing my children. (*he reaches stiffly out and pushes her shoulder, intending it to be strictly a burlesque, but there is quite a bit of force in the gesture.* GRACE *falls back, just short of panic, but* WALKER *hunches his shoulders and begins to jerk his finger at the ceiling; one eye closed and one leg raised, jerking his finger absurdly at the ceiling, as if to indicate something upstairs that was to be kept secret*) Ah, yes, the children... (*affecting an imprecise "Irish" accent*) sure and they looked well enough... (*grins*) and white enough, roosting in that kennel. Hah, I hope you didn't tell Faggy, there, about those two lovely ladies. (EASLEY *is kneeling on the floor holding his stomach and shaking his head*) Ahh, no, lady, let's keep that strictly in the family. I mean among those of us who screw. (*he takes another long drink from the bottle, and "threatens"* EASLEY'*s head in a kind of burlesque*) For Lawrence, and all the cocksmen of my underprivileged youth. When we used to chase that kind of frail little sissy-punk down Raymond Boulevard and compromise his sister-in-laws in the cloak room... It's so simple to work from the bottom up. To always strike, and know, from the blood's noise that you're right, and what you're doing is right, and even *pretty*. (*suddenly more tender toward* GRACE) I swear to you, Grace, I did come into the world pointed in the right direction. Oh, shit, I learned so many words for what I've wanted to say. They all come down on me at once. But almost none of them are mine. (*he straightens up, turning quickly toward the still kneeling* EASLEY, *and slaps him as hard as he can across the face, sending his head twisting around*) Bastard! A poem for your mother!

GRACE (*lets out a short pleading cry*) Ohh! Get away from him, Walker! Get away from him, (*hysterically*) you nigger murderer!

WALKER (*has started to tilt the bottle again, after he slaps* EASLEY, *and when* GRACE *shouts at him, he chokes on the liquor, spitting it out, and begins laughing with a kind of hysterical amusement*) Oh! Ha, ha, ha... you mean... Wow! (*trying to control laughter, but it is an extreme kind of release*) No kidding? Grace, Gracie! Wow! I wonder how long you had that stored up.

GRACE (*crying now, going over to* EASLEY, *trying to help him up*) Brad. Brad. Walker, why'd you come here? Why'd you come here? Brad?

WALKER (*still laughing and wobbling clumsily around*) Nigger murderer? Wowee. Gracie, are you just repeating your faggot husband, or did you have that in you a long time? I mean ... for all the years we were together? Hooo! Yeah. (*mock seriously*) Christ, it could get to be a weight after a time, huh? When you taught the little girls to pray... you'd have to whisper, "And God bless Mommy, and God bless Daddy, the nigger murderer." Wow, that's some weight.

GRACE Shut up, Walker. Just shut up, and get out of here, away from us, please. I don't want to hear you... I don't need to hear you, again. Remember, I heard it all before, baby... you don't get me again. (*she is weeping and twisting her head, trying at the same time to fully revive* EASLEY, *who is still sitting on the floor with legs sprawled apart, both hands held to the pit of his stomach, his head nodding back and forth in pain*) Why'd you come here... just to do this? Why don't you leave before you kill somebody? (*trying to hold back a scream*) Before you kill another white person?

WALKER (*sobering, but still forcing a cynical hilarity*) Ah... the party line. Stop him before he kills another white person! Heh. Yeah. Yeah. And that's not such a bad idea, really.... I mean, after all, only you and your husband there are white in this house. Those two lovely little girls upstairs are niggers. You know, circa 1800, one drop makes you whole?

GRACE Shut up, Walker! (*she leaps to her feet and rushes toward him*) Shut your ugly head! (*he pushes her away*)

EASLEY (*raising his head and shouting as loud as he can manage*) You're filth, boy. Just filth. Can you understand that anything and everything you do is stupid, filthy, or meaningless! Your inept formless poetry. Hah. Poetry? A flashy doggerel for inducing all those unfortunate troops of yours to spill their blood in your behalf. But I guess that's something! Ritual drama, we used to call it at the university. The poetry of ritual drama. (*pulls himself up*) And even that's giving that crap the benefit of the doubt. Ritual filth would have been the right name for it.

WALKER Ritual drama... (*half musing*) yeah, I remember seeing that phrase in an old review by one of your queer academic friends... (*noticing* EASLEY *getting up*) Oh well, look at him coming up by his bootstraps. I didn't mean to hit you that hard, Professor Easley, sir... I just don't know my own strent'. (*laughs and finishes the bottle . . . starts as if he is going to throw it over his shoulder, then he places it very carefully on the table. He starts dancing around and whooping like an "Indian"*) More! Bwana, me want more fire water!

EASLEY As I said, Vessels, you're just filth. Pretentious filth.

WALKER (*dances around a bit more, then stops abruptly in front of* EASLEY; *so close they are almost touching. He speaks in a quiet menacing tone*) The liquor, turkey. The liquor. No opinions right now. Run off and get more liquor, *sabe*?

GRACE (*has stopped crying and managed to regain a cynical composure*) I'll get it, Brad. Mr. Vessels is playing the mad scene from Native Son. (*turns to go*) A second-rate Bigger Thomas.

WALKER (*laughs*) Yeah. But remember when I used to play a second-rate Othello? Oh, wow . . . you remember that, don't you, Professor No-Dick? You remember when I used to walk around wondering what that fair sister was thinking? (*hunches* EASLEY) Oh, come on now, you remember that. . . . I was Othello . . . Grace there was Desdemona . . . and you were Iago . . . (*laughs*) or at least between classes, you were Iago. Hey, who were you during classes? I forgot to find that out. Ha, the key to my downfall. I knew you were Iago between classes, when I saw you, but I never knew who you were during classes. Ah ah, that's the basis of an incredibly profound social axiom. I quote: . . . and you better write this down, Bradford, so you can pass it on to your hipper colleagues at the university . . . (*laughs*) I mean if they ever rebuild the university. What was I saying to you, enemy? Oh yeah . . . the axiom. Oh . . .

GRACE (*returning with a bottle*) You still at it, huh, Bigger?

WALKER Yeah, yeah . . . (*reaches for bottle*) Lemme see. I get it. . . . If a white man is Iago when you see him . . . uhh . . . chances are he's eviler when you don't. (*laughs*)

EASLEY Yes, that was worthy of you.

WALKER It *was* lousy, wasn't it?

GRACE Look (*trying to be earnest*) Walker, pour yourself a drink . . . as many drinks as you need . . . and then leave, will you? I don't see what you think you're accomplishing by hanging around us.

EASLEY Yes . . . I was wondering who's taking care of your mighty army while you're here in the enemy camp? How can the black liberation movement spare its illustrious leader for such a long stretch?

WALKER (*sits abruptly on couch and stretches both legs out, drinking big glass of bourbon. Begins speaking in pidgin "Japanese"*) Oh, don't worry about that, doomed American dog. Ha. You see and hear those shells beating this town flat, don't you? In fact, we'll probably be here en masse in about a week. Why don't I just camp here and wait for my brothers to get here and liberate the whole place? Huh? (*laughs*)

GRACE Walker, you're crazy!

EASLEY I think he's got more sense than that.

WALKER (*starting to make up a song*) Ohhh! I'll stay here and rape your wife . . . as I so often used to do . . . as I so often used . . .

GRACE Your mind is gone, Walker . . . completely gone. (*she turns to go upstairs. A bright blast rocks the house and she falls against the wall*)

WALKER (*thrown forward to the floor, rises quickly to see how* GRACE *is*) Hey, you all right, lady?

EASLEY Grace! (*he has also been rocked, but he gets to* GRACE *first*) Don't worry about my wife, Vessels. That's my business.

GRACE I'm O.K., Brad. I was on my way upstairs to look in on the girls. It's a wonder they're not screaming now.

WALKER They were fine when I looked in earlier. Sleeping very soundly.

EASLEY You were upstairs?

WALKER (*returning to his seat, with another full glass*) Of course I went upstairs, to see my children. In fact, I started to take them away with me, while you patriots were out. (*another close blast*) But I thought I'd wait to say hello to the mommy and step-daddy.

EASLEY You low bastard (*turning toward* WALKER *and looking at* GRACE *at the same time*)

GRACE No . . . you're not telling the truth now, Walker. (*voice quavering and rising*) You came here just to say that. Just to see what your saying that would do to me. (*turns away from him*) You're a bad liar, Walker. As always . . . a very bad liar.

WALKER You know I'm not lying. I want those children. You know that, Grace.

EASLEY I know you're drunk!

GRACE You're lying. You don't want those children. You just want to think you want them for the moment... to excite one of those obscure pathological instruments you've got growing in your head. Today, you want to feel like you want the girls. Just like you wanted to feel hurt and martyred by your misdirected cause, when you first drove us away.

WALKER Drove you away? You knew what I was in to. You could have stayed. You said you wanted to pay whatever thing it cost to stay.

EASLEY How can you lie like this, Vessels? Even I know you pushed Grace until she couldn't retain her sanity and stay with you in that madness. All the bigoted racist imbeciles you started to cultivate. Every white friend you had knows that story.

WALKER You shut up.... I don't want to hear anything you've got to say.

GRACE There are so many bulbs and screams shooting off inside you, Walker. So many lies you have to pump full of yourself. You're split so many ways... your feelings are cut up into skinny horrible strips... like umbrella struts... holding up whatever bizarre black cloth you're using this performance as your self's image. I don't even think you know who you are any more. No, I don't think you *ever* knew.

WALKER I know what I can use.

GRACE No, you never even found out who you were until you sold the last of your loves and emotions down the river... until you killed your last old friend... and found out *what* you were. My God, it must be hard being you, Walker Vessels. It must be a sick task keeping so many lying separate uglinesses together... and pretending they're something you've made and understand.

WALKER What I can use, madam... what I can use. I move now trying to be certain of that.

EASLEY You're talking strangely. What is this, the pragmatics of war? What are you saying... use? I thought you meant yourself to be a fantastic idealist? All those speeches and essays and poems... the rebirth of idealism. That the Western white man had forfeited the most impressive characteristic of his culture... the idealism of rational liberalism... and that only the black man in the West could restore that quality to Western culture, because he still understood the necessity for it. Et cetera, et cetera. Oh, look, I remember your horseshit theories, friend. I remember. And now the great black Western idealist is talking about use.

WALKER Yeah, yeah. Now you can call me the hypocritical idealist nigger murderer. You see, what I want is more titles.

GRACE And saying you want the children is another title... right? Every time you say it, one of those bulbs goes off in your head and you think you can focus on still another attribute, another beautiful quality in the total beautiful structure of the beautiful soul of Walker Vessels, sensitive Negro poet, savior of his people, deliverer of Western idealism... commander-in-chief of the forces of righteousness... Oh, God, et cetera, et cetera.

WALKER Grace Locke Vessels Easley... whore of the middle classes.

EASLEY (*turning suddenly as if to offer combat*) Go and fuck yourself.

GRACE Yes, Walker, by all means... go and fuck yourself. (*and softer*) Yes, do anything... but don't drag my children into your scheme for martyrdom and immortality, or whatever else it is makes you like you are... just don't ... don't even mention it.

EASLEY (*moving to comfort her*) Oh, don't get so worried, Grace... you know he just likes to hear himself talk... more than anything... he just wants to hear himself talk, so he can find out what he's supposed to have on his mind. (*to* WALKER) He knows there's no way in the world he could have those children. No way in the world.

WALKER (*feigning casual matter-of-fact tone*) Mr. Easley, Mrs. Easley, those girls' last name is Vessels. Whatever you think is all right. I mean I don't care what you think about me or what I'm doing... the whole mess. But those beautiful girls you have upstairs there are my daughters. They even look like me. I've loved them all their lives. Before this there was too much to do, so I left them with you. (*gets up, pours another drink*) But now... things are changed.... I want them with me. (*sprawls on couch again*) I want them with me very much.

GRACE You're lying. Liar, you don't give a shit about those children. You're a liar if you say otherwise. You never never never cared at all for those children. My friend, you have never cared for anything in the world that I know of but what's in there behind your eyes.

And God knows what ugliness that is... though there are thousands of people dead or homeless all over this country who begin to understand a little. And not just white people ... you've killed so many of your own people too. It's a wonder they haven't killed you.

EASLEY (*walks over to* WALKER) Get up and get out of here! So help me... If you don't leave here now... I'll call the soldiers. They'd just love to find you. (WALKER *doesn't move*) Really, Vessels, I'll personally put a big hole in that foul liberation movement right now... I swear it. (*he turns to go to the phone*)

WALKER (*at first as if he is good-natured*) Hey, hey... Professor Easley, I've got this gun here, remember? Now don't do that... in fact if you take another step, I'll blow your goddam head off. And I mean that, Brad, turn around and get back here in the center of the room.

GRACE (*moves for the stairs*) Ohhh!

WALKER Hey, Grace, stop... you want me to shoot this fairy, or what? Come back here!

GRACE I was only going to see about the kids.

WALKER I'm their father... I'm thinking about their welfare, too. Just come back here. Both of you sit on this couch where I'm sitting, and I'll sit in that chair over there near the ice tray.

EASLEY So now we get a taste of Vessels, the hoodlum.

WALKER Uh, yeah. Another title, boss man. But just sit the fuck down for now. (*goes to the window. Looks at his watch*) I got about an hour.

GRACE Walker, what are you going to do?

WALKER Do? Well, right now I'm going to have another drink.

EASLEY You know what she means.

GRACE You're not going to take the children, are you? You wouldn't just take them, would you? You wouldn't do that. You can't hate me so much that you'd do that.

WALKER I don't hate you at all, Grace. I hated you when I wanted you. I haven't wanted you for a long time. But I do want those children.

GRACE You're lying!

WALKER No, I'm not lying... and I guess that's what's cutting you up... because you probably know I'm not lying, and you can't understand that. But I tell you now that I'm not lying, and that in spite of all the things I've done that have helped kill love in me, I still love those girls.

EASLEY You mean, in spite of all the people you've killed.

WALKER O.K., O.K., however you want it ... however you want it, let it go at that. In spite of all the people I've killed. No, better, in spite of the fact that I, Walker Vessels, single-handedly, and with no other adviser except my own ego, promoted a bloody situation where white and black people are killing each other; despite the fact that I know that this is at best a war that will only change, ha, the complexion of tyranny... (*laughs sullenly*) in spite of the fact that I have killed for all times any creative impulse I will ever have by the depravity of my murderous philosophies... despite the fact that I am being killed in my head each day and by now have no soul or heart or warmth, even in my long killer fingers, despite the fact that I have no other thing in the universe that I love or trust, but myself... despite or in spite, the respite, my dears, my dears, hear me, O Olympus, O Mercury, God of thieves, O Damballah, chief of all the dead religions of pseudo-nigger patriots hoping to open big restaurants after de wah... har har... in spite, despite, the resistance in the large cities and the small towns, where we have taken, yes, dragged piles of darkies out of their beds and shot them for being in Rheingold ads, despite the fact that all of my officers are ignorant motherfuckers who have never read any book in their lives, despite the fact that I would rather argue politics, or literature, or boxing, or anything, with you, dear Easley, with you... (*head slumps, weeping*) despite all these things and in spite of all the drunken noises I'm making, despite... in spite of... I want those girls, very, very much. And I will take them out of here with me.

EASLEY No, you won't... not if I can help it.

WALKER Well, you can't help it.

GRACE (*jumps up*) What? Is no one to reason with you? Isn't there any way something can exist without you having the final judgment on it? Is the whole world yours... to deal with or destroy? You're right! You feel! You have the only real vision of the world. You love! No one else exists in the world except you, and those who can help you. Everyone else is nothing or else they're something to be destroyed. I'm your enemy now... right? I'm wrong. You are the children's father... but I'm no longer their mother. Every one of your yesses or nos is intended by you to reshape the world after the image you have of it. They *are* my children! I am their mother! But because somehow I've become your enemy, I suddenly no longer qualify. Forget you're their mother, Grace. Walker has decided that you're no longer to perform that function. So the whole business is erased as if it never existed. I'm *not* in your head, Walker. Neither are those kids. We are all flesh and blood and deserve to live... even unabstracted by what you think we ought to be in the general scheme of things. Even alien to it. I left you... and took the girls because you'd gone crazy. You're crazy now. This stupid ugly killing you've started will never do anything, for anybody. And you and all your people will be wiped out, you know that. And you'll have accomplished nothing. Do you want those two babies to be with you when you're killed so they can witness the death of a great man? So they can grow up and write articles for a magazine sponsored by the Walker Vessels Society?

WALKER Which is still better than being freakish mulattoes in a world where your father is some evil black thing you can't remember. Look, I was going to wait until the fighting was over... (*reflective*) until we had won, before I took them. But something occurred to me for the first time, last night. It was the idea that we might not win. Somehow it only got through to me last night. I'd sort've taken it for granted ... as a solved problem, that the fighting was the most academic of our problems, and that the real work would come necessarily after the fighting was done. But...

EASLEY Things are not going as well for you as you figured.

WALKER No. It will take a little longer, that's all. But this city will fall soon. We should be here within a week. You see, I could have waited until then. Then just marched in, at the head of the triumphant army, and seized the children as a matter of course. In fact I don't know why I didn't, except I did want to see you all in what you might call your natural habitats. I thought maybe I might be able to sneak in just as you and my ex-wife were making love, or just as you were lining the girls up against the wall to beat them or make them repeat after you, "Your daddy is a racist murderer." And then I thought I could murder both of you on the spot, and be completely justified.

GRACE You've convinced yourself that you're rescuing the children, haven't you?

WALKER Just as you convinced yourself you were rescuing them when you took them away from me.

EASLEY She was!

WALKER Now so am I.

GRACE Yes (*wearily*) I begin to get some of your thinking now. When you mentioned killing us. I'm sure you thought the whole thing up in quite heroic terms. How you'd come through the white lines, murder us, and *rescue* the girls. You probably went over that... or had it go through your head on that gray film, a thousand times until it was some kind of obligatory reality. (WALKER *laughs*)

EASLEY The kind of insane reality that brought about all the killing.

WALKER Christ, the worst thing that ever happened to the West was the psychological novel... believe me.

EASLEY When the Nazis were confronted with Freud, they claimed his work was of dubious value.

WALKER Bravo!

GRACE It's a wonder you *didn't* murder us!

WALKER (*looking suddenly less amused*) Oh ... have I forfeited my opportunity?

EASLEY (*startled reaction*) You're not serious? What reason... what possible reason would there be for killing us? I mean I could readily conceive of your killing me, but the two of us, as some kind of psychological unit. I don't understand that. You said you didn't hate Grace.

GRACE (*to press* WALKER) He's lying again, Brad. Really, most times he's not to be taken seriously. He was making a metaphor before... one of those ritual-drama metaphors... (*laughs, as does* BRAD) You said it before... just to hear what's going on in his head. Really, he's not to be taken seriously. (*she hesitates, and there is a silence*) Unless there's some way you can kill him.

WALKER (*laughs, then sobers, but begins to show the effects of the alcohol*) Oh, Grace, Grace. Now you're trying to incite your husband... which I swear is hardly Christian. I'm really surprised at you. But more so because you completely misunderstand me now ... or maybe I'm not so surprised. I guess you never did know what was going on. That's why you left. You thought I betrayed you or something. Which really knocked me on my ass, you know? I was preaching hate the white man ... get the white man off our backs ... if necessary, kill the white man for our rights ... whatever the hell that finally came to mean. And don't, now, for God's sake start thinking he's disillusioned, he's cynical, or any of the rest of these horseshit liberal definitions of the impossibility or romanticism of idealism. But those things I said ... and would say now, pushed you away from me. I couldn't understand that.

GRACE You couldn't understand it? What are you saying?

WALKER No, I couldn't understand it. We'd been together a long time, before all that happened. What I said ... what I thought I had to do ... I knew you, if any white person in the world could, I knew you would understand. And then you didn't.

GRACE You began to align yourself with the worst kind of racists and second-rate hack political thinkers.

WALKER I've never aligned myself with anything or anyone I hadn't thought up first.

GRACE You stopped telling me everything!

WALKER I never stopped telling you I loved you ... or that you were my wife!

GRACE (*almost broken*) It wasn't enough, Walker. It wasn't enough.

WALKER God, it should have been.

GRACE Walker, you were preaching the murder of all white people. Walker, I was, am, white. What do you think was going through my mind every time you were at some rally or meeting whose sole purpose was to bring about the destruction of white people?

WALKER Oh, goddamn it, Grace, are you so stupid? You were my wife ... I loved you. You mean because I loved you and was married to you ... had had children by you, I wasn't supposed to say the things I felt. I was crying out against three hundred years of oppression; not against individuals.

EASLEY But it's individuals who are dying.

WALKER It was individuals who were doing the oppressing. It was individuals who were being oppressed. The horror is that oppression is not a concept that can be specifically transferable. From the oppressed, down on the oppressor. To keep the horror where it belongs ... on those people who we can speak of, even in this last part of the twentieth century, as evil.

EASLEY You're so wrong about everything. So terribly, sickeningly wrong. What can you change? What do you hope to change? Do you think Negroes are better people than whites ... that they can govern a society *better* than whites? That they'll be more judicious or more tolerant? Do you think they'll make fewer mistakes? I mean really, if the Western white man has proved one thing ... it's the futility of modern society. So the have-not peoples become the haves. Even so, will that change the essential functions of the world? Will there be more love or beauty in the world ... more knowledge ... because of it?

WALKER Probably. Probably there will be more ... if more people have a chance to understand what it is. But that's not even the point. It comes down to baser human endeavor than any social-political thinking. What does it matter if there's more love or beauty? Who the fuck cares? Is that what the Western ofay thought while he was ruling ... that his rule somehow brought more love and beauty into the world? Oh, he might have thought that concomitantly, while sipping a gin rickey and scratching his ass ... but that was not ever the point. Not even on the Crusades. The point is that you had your chance, darling, now these other folks have theirs. (*quietly*) Now they have theirs.

EASLEY God, what an ugly idea.

WALKER (*head in hands*) I know. I know. (*his head is sagging, but he brings it up quickly. While it is down,* EASLEY *crosses* GRACE *with a significant look*) But what else you got, champ? What else you got? I remember too much horseshit from the other side for you to make much sense. Too much horseshit. The cruelty of it, don't you understand, now? The complete ugly horseshit cruelty of it is that there doesn't have to be a change. It'll be up to individuals on that side, just as it was supposed to be up to individuals on this side. Ha! ... Who failed! Just like you failed, Easley. Just like you failed.

EASLEY Failed? What are you talking about?
WALKER (*nodding*) Well, what do you think? You never did anything concrete to avoid what's going on now. Your sick liberal lip service to whatever was the least filth. Your high aesthetic disapproval of the political. Letting the sick ghosts of the thirties strangle whatever chance we had.
EASLEY What are you talking about?
WALKER What we argued about so many times... befo' de wah.
EASLEY And you see... what I predicted has happened. Now, in whatever cruel, and you said it, cruel political synapse you're taken with, or anyone else is taken with, with sufficient power I, any individual, any person who thinks of life as a purely anarchic relationship between man and God... or man and his work... any consciousness like that is destroyed... along with your *enemies*. And you, for whatever right or freedom or sickening cause you represent, kill me. Kill what does not follow.
WALKER Perhaps you're right. But I have always found it hard to be neutral when faced with ugliness. Especially an ugliness that has worked all my life to twist me.
GRACE And so you let it succeed!
WALKER The aesthete came long after all the things that really formed me. It was the easiest weight to shed. And I couldn't be merely a journalist... a social critic. No social protest... right is in the act! And the act itself has some place in the world... it makes some place for itself. Right? But you all accuse me, not understanding that what you represent, you, my wife, all our old intellectual cutthroats, was something that was going to die anyway. One way or another. You'd been used too often, backed off from reality too many times. Remember the time, remember that time long time ago, in the old bar when you and Louie Rino were arguing with me, and Louie said then that he hated people who wanted to change the world. You remember that?
EASLEY I remember the fight.
WALKER Yeah, well, I know I thought then that none of you would write any poetry either. I knew that you had moved too far away from the actual meanings of life... into some lifeless cocoon of pretended intellectual and emotional achievement, to really be able to see the world again. What was Rino writing before he got killed? Tired elliptical little descriptions of what he could see out the window.
EASLEY And how did he die?
WALKER An explosion in the school where he was teaching. (*nodding*)
EASLEY One of your terrorists did it.
WALKER Yeah, yeah.
EASLEY He was supposed to be one of your closest friends.
WALKER Yeah, yeah.
GRACE Yeah, yeah, yeah, yeah. (*with face still covered*)
WALKER We called for a strike to show the government we had all the white intellectuals backing us. (*nodding*) Hah, and the only people who went out were those tired political hacks. No one wanted to be intellectually compromised.
EASLEY I didn't go either. (*hunches* GRACE, *starts to ease out of his chair*) And it was an intellectual compromise. No one in their right mind could have backed your program completely.
WALKER No one but Negroes.
EASLEY Well, then, they weren't in their right minds. You'd twisted them.
WALKER The country twisted 'em. (*still nodding*) The country had twisted them for so long. (*head almost touching his chest*)
EASLEY (*taking very cautious step toward* WALKER, *still talking*) The politics of self-pity. (*indicates to* GRACE *that she is to talk*)
WALKER (*head down*) Yeah. Yeah.
EASLEY The politics of self-pity.
GRACE (*raising her head slowly to watch, almost petrified*) A murderous self-pity. An extraordinarily murderous self-pity. (*there is another explosion close to the house. The lights go out for a few seconds. They come on, and Easley is trying to return to his seat, but* WALKER's *head is still on his chest*)
WALKER (*mumbles*) What'd they do, hit the lights? Goddamn lousy marksmen. (EASLEY *starts again*) Lousy marksmen... and none of 'em worth shit.

(*Now, another close explosion. The lights go out again. They come on;* EASLEY *is standing almost halfway between the couch and* WALKER. WALKER's *head is still down on his chest.* EASLEY *crouches to move closer. The lights go out again. Blackout. More explosions*)

ACT TWO

(*Explosions are heard before the curtain goes up. When curtain rises, room is still in darkness, but the explosion does throw some light. Figures are still as they were at the end of first act; light from explosions outlines them briefly*)

WALKER Shit.

(*Lights come up.* WALKER's *head is still down, but he is nodding from side to side, cursing something very drunkenly.* EASLEY *stands very stiffly in the center of the room, waiting to take another step.* GRACE *sits very stiffly, breathing heavily, on the couch, trying to make some kind of conversation, but not succeeding.* WALKER *has his hand in his jacket pocket, on the gun*)

GRACE It is self-pity, and some weird ambition, Walker. (*strained silence*) But there's no reason... the girls should suffer. There's ... no reason.

(EASLEY *takes a long stride, and is about to throw himself at* WALKER, *when there is another explosion, and the lights go out again, very briefly. When they come up,* EASLEY *is set to leap, but* WALKER's *head comes abruptly up. He stares drunkenly at* EASLEY, *not moving his hand. For some awkward duration of time the two men stare at each other, in almost the same way as they had at the beginning of the play. Then* GRACE *screams*)

GRACE Walker! (WALKER *looks at her slightly, and* EASLEY *throws himself on him. The chair falls backward and the two men roll on the floor.* EASLEY *trying to choke* WALKER. WALKER *trying to get the gun out of his pocket*) Walker! Walker! (*suddenly,* WALKER *shoves one hand in* EASLEY's *face, shooting him without taking the gun from his pocket.* EASLEY *slumps backward, his face twisted, his mouth open and working.* WALKER *rolls back off* EASLEY, *pulling the gun from his pocket. He props himself against the chair, staring at the man's face*) Walker (*her shouts have become whimpers, and she is moving stiffly toward* EASLEY) Walker Walker (EASLEY's *mouth is still working... and he is managing to get a few sounds, words, out*)

WALKER (*still staring at him, pulling himself up on the chair*) Shut up, you! (*to* EASLEY) You shut up. I don't want to hear anything else from you. You just die, quietly. No more talk.

GRACE Walker! (*she is screaming again*) Walker! (*she rushes toward* EASLEY, *but* WALKER *catches her arm and pushes her away*) You're an insane man. You hear me, Walker? (*he is not looking at her, he is still staring down at* EASLEY) Walker, you're an insane man. (*she screams*) You're an insane man. (*she slumps to the couch, crying*) An insane man...

WALKER No profound statements, Easley. No horseshit like that. No elegance. You just die quietly and stupidly. Like niggers do. Like they are now. (*quieter*) Like I will. The only thing I'll let you say is, "I only regret that I have but one life to lose for my country." You can say that. (*looks over at* GRACE) Grace! Tell Bradford that he can say, "I only regret that I have but one life to lose for my country." You can say that, Easley, but that's all.

EASLEY (*straining to talk*) Ritual drama. Like I said, ritual drama... (*he dies.* WALKER *stands staring at him. The only sounds are an occasional explosion, and* GRACE's *heavy brittle weeping*)

WALKER He could have said, "I only regret that I have but one life to lose for my country." I would have let him say that... but no more. No more. There is no reason he should go out with any kind of dignity. I couldn't allow that.

GRACE You're out of your mind. (*slow, matter-of-fact*)

WALKER Meaning?

GRACE You're out of your mind.

WALKER (*wearily*) Turn to another station.

GRACE You're out of your mind.

WALKER I said, turn to another station... will you? Another station! Out of my mind is not the point. You ought to know that. (*brooding*) The way things are, being out of your mind is the only thing that qualifies you to stay alive. The only thing. Easley was in his right mind. Pitiful as he was. That's the reason he's dead.

GRACE He's dead because you killed him.

WALKER Yeah. He's dead because I killed him. Also, because he thought he ought to kill me. (*looking over at the dead man*) You want me to cover him up?

GRACE I don't want you to do anything, Walker... but leave here. (*raising her voice*) Will you do that for me... or do you want to kill me too?

WALKER Are you being ironic? Huh? (*he

grabs her arm, jerking her head up so she has to look at him) Do you think you're being ironic? Or do you want to kill me, too? . . . (*shouting*) You're mighty right I want to kill you. You're mighty goddamn right. Believe me, self-righteous little bitch, I want to kill you.

GRACE (*startled, but trying not to show it*) The cause demands it, huh? The cause demands it.

WALKER Yeah, the cause demands it.

GRACE (*she gets up and goes to* EASLEY, *kneeling beside the body*) The cause demands it, Brad. That's why Walker shot you . . . because the cause demands it. (*her head droops but she doesn't cry. She sits on her knees, holding the dead man's hand*) I guess the point is that now when you take the children I'll be alone. (*she looks up at* WALKER) I guess that's the point, now. Is that the point, Walker? Me being alone . . . as you have been now for so long? I'll bet that's the point, huh? I'll bet you came here to do exactly what you did . . . kill Brad, then take the kids, and leave me alone . . . to suffocate in the stink of my memories. (*she is trying not to cry*) Just like I did to you. I'm sure that's the point. Right? (*she leaps up suddenly at* WALKER) You scum! You murdering scum. (*they grapple for a second, then* WALKER *slaps her to the floor. She kneels a little way off from* EASLEY's *body*)

WALKER Yeh, Grace. That's the point. For sure, that's the point.

GRACE You were going to kill Brad, from the first. You knew that before you even got here.

WALKER I'd thought about it.

GRACE (*weeping, but then she stops and is quiet for a minute*) So what's supposed to happen then . . . I mean after you take the kids and leave me here alone? Huh? I know you've thought about that, too.

WALKER I have. But you know what'll happen much better than I do. But maybe you don't. What do you think happened to me when you left? Did you ever think about that? You must have.

GRACE You had your cause, friend. Your cause, remember. And thousands of people following you, hoping that shit you preached was right. I pitied you.

WALKER I know that. It took me awhile, but then I finally understood that you did pity me. And that you were somewhere, going through whatever mediocre routine you and Easley called your lives . . . pitying me. I figured that, finally, you weren't really even shocked by what was happening . . . what had happened. You were so secure in the knowledge that you were good, and compassionate . . . and right, that most of all . . . you were certain, my God, so certain . . . emotionally and intellectually, that you were right, until the only idea you had about me was to pity me. (*he wheels around to face her squarely*) God, that pissed me off. You don't really know how furious that made me. You and that closet queen, respected, weak-as-water intellectual, pitying me. God. God! (*forcing the humor*) Miss Easley, honey, I could have killed both of you every night of my life.

GRACE Will you kill me now if I say right here that I still pity you?

WALKER (*a breathless half-broken little laugh*) No. No, I won't kill you.

GRACE Well, I pity you, Walker. I really do.

WALKER Only until you start pitying yourself.

GRACE I wish I could call you something that would hurt you.

WALKER So do I.

GRACE (*wearily*) Nigger.

WALKER So do I. (*looks at his watch*) I've got to go soon.

GRACE You're still taking the girls. (*she is starting to push herself up from the floor.* WALKER *stares at her, then quickly over his shoulder at the stairway. He puts his hand in the pocket where the gun is, then he shakes his head slowly*)

GRACE (*not seeing this gesture*) You're still taking the children? (WALKER *shakes his head slowly. An explosion shakes the house a little*)

GRACE Walker. Walker. (*she staggers to her feet, shaking with the next explosion*) Walker? You shook your head? (WALKER *stands very stiffly looking at the floor.* GRACE *starts to come to him, and the next explosion hits very close or actually hits the house. Beams come down; some of the furniture is thrown around.* GRACE *falls to the floor.* WALKER *is toppled backward. A beam hits* GRACE *across the chest. Debris falls on* WALKER. *There are more explosions, and then silence*)

GRACE Walker! Walker! (*she is hurt very badly and is barely able to move the debris that is covering her*) Walker! The girls! Walker! Catherine! Elizabeth! Walker, the girls! (WALKER *finally starts to move. He is also hurt badly, but he is able to move much more freely than* GRACE. *He starts to clear away the debris and make his way to his knees*)

GRACE Walker?

WALKER Yeah? Grace?

GRACE Walker, the children . . . the girls . . . see about the girls. (*she is barely able to raise one of her arms*) The girls, Walker, see about them.

WALKER (*he is finally able to crawl over to* GRACE, *and pushes himself unsteadily up on his hands*) You're hurt pretty badly? Can you move?

GRACE The girls, Walker, see about the girls.

WALKER Can you move?

GRACE The girls, Walker . . . (*she is losing strength*) Our children!

WALKER (*he is silent for a while*) They're dead, Grace. Catherine and Elizabeth are dead. (*he starts up stairs as if to verify his statement. Stops, midway, shakes his head; retreats*)

GRACE (*looking up at him frantically, but she is dying*) Dead? Dead? (*she starts to weep and shake her head*) Dead? (*then she stops suddenly, tightening her face*) How . . . how do you know, Walker? How do you know they're dead? (WALKER's *head is drooping slightly*) How do you know they're dead, Walker? How do you . . .

(*Her eyes try to continue what she is saying, but she slumps, and dies in a short choking spasm.* WALKER *looks to see that she is dead, then resumes his efforts to get up. He looks at his watch. Listens to see if it is running. Wipes his face. Pushes the floor to get up. Another explosion sounds very close and he crouches quickly, covering his head. Another explosion. He pushes himself up, brushing sloppily at his clothes. He looks at his watch again, then starts to drag himself toward the door*)

WALKER They're dead, Grace! (*he is almost shouting*) They're dead.

(*He leaves, stumbling unsteadily through the door. He is now the old man at the beginning of the play. There are more explosions. Another one very close to the house. A sudden aggravated silence, and then there is a child heard crying and screaming as loud as it can. More explosions. Blackout. More explosions, after curtain for some time*)

Ed Bullins (1935–)

Goin' a Buffalo
1966

Drama programs in black colleges have always been in the precarious position of needing to determine their purpose in training black students. For years administrators tolerated drama because it provided a creative outlet for their otherwise "culturally deprived student bodies," and because it looked good on the record to say that "our students are *exposed* to plays." But students seeking careers in theater were discouraged, because it was highly improbable that they could earn a living in the profession. Still, drama programs emerged, debating whether or not to concentrate on preparing students to teach drama or to train them for professional work. Most schools tried to do both, although a few (such as Howard University in Washington, D.C.) are professionally oriented. The aim at Howard is to provide the student with as broad a background of production experience as possible. A typical theater season of major productions might consist of a Greek, a Shakespearean, an Irish, and a contemporary work. Plays by new black playwrights were also introduced, thanks largely to Owen Dodson's interest in playwriting, but most often these plays were received with mixed reactions because they did not deal with middle-class black life. Even though "black awareness" was in vogue during the 1960's, it was a bold step for Howard to produce *Blues for Mr. Charley* and *Dutchman* (and in both instances the language was "softened" to make it more acceptable to "sensitive young ears" and middle-class intelligentsia).

Many black colleges presented only Broadway successes, such as *Our Town*, *The Glass Menagerie*, and *The Owl and the Pussycat*, and ignored black playwrights entirely—unless they were absolutely sure that the play was "safe"—that is, would not offend the white community or the trustees. Even in literature classes, black students seldom, if ever, found black writers represented. A black teacher teaching Contemporary American Literature at a Southern college recalls that a large segment of the class was unaware of James Baldwin, even though he was at the height of his career at the time. Only a few had heard of Richard Wright or Ralph Ellison, whose *Invisible Man* was being used as a text in sociology and literature classes in many white schools. The instructor introduced a segment of black literature into the format; not only did the attitudes and interests of the students change, but so did their grades. They were able to identify with and understand the experiences that black writers had recorded, and for the first time in many of their lives literature suddenly had significance. When the instructor revealed this to the head of the department, and suggested that literature by blacks be incorporated into the course, he was dismissed with a frown and "I'll give it a thought."

Ed Bullins, Robert MacBeth, Imamu Baraka, Gilbert Moses, Thomas Dent, Val Ferdinand, Ernie McClintock, Delano Stewart, Tom Turner, Pat Curtis, Sati-Jamal, Sister Lubaba Lateef, Elma Lewis, and Vantile Whitfield are among the young black artists who have taken black theater into the black community. Their efforts, along with pressure from the students, have caused black colleges to reevaluate their drama programs and, above all, to place more emphasis on works involving the black experience.

Goin' a Buffalo is written especially for black audiences. Mr. Bullins and other black writers have expressed the tremendous elation that they feel when a black audience responds to their work. Once the audience is caught up in the production, the theater becomes electrifying. The group response is earnest—laughing, crying, commenting on the action, or sometimes talking back to the characters. It is theater in the true sense of the word—theater emotionally involving the audience, a sharp contrast to the frigid, polite response that most American theatergoers are accustomed to.

The proposition that blacks are culturally deprived is true—and will remain true until the arts are involved in *their* experiences. It is a myth that blacks do not support theater. They don't support Broadway or off-Broadway theater because it does not generally relate to them; and, too, the prices are prohibitive. But black theaters for blacks are being supported. Ed Bullins is not concerned with what white critics have to say about his plays—and why should he be? His audience is an exceptionally critical one, and he knows that only his talent as a playwright will keep them in the theater and elicit their response. He is not writing for black intelligentsia, but for the masses. His plays emerge as universal works. He is not interested in form, nor psychological, sociological, economical, or philosophical probing into the motivations of his characters. We find these elements in his play, but they are secondary. Ed Bullins' primary intent is to depict life as it is lived—*truthfully*. He comes close to fulfilling what Zola and the naturalists believed that drama should be—a slice of life, objectively presented. His characters are at once frightening and puzzling to white audiences, but blacks have no difficulty identifying and relating to them because Mr. Bullins writes about the black experience in America *as it is*. A white, middle-aged theater patron, commented that she found the play appalling; that none of the characters were admirable, and that the author had offered no "hope" at the conclusion of the play. A young black student replied, "What hope is there in a racist society?" Mr. Bullins focuses in on black life, which happens to be a reflection of the dog-eat-dog world of white society—the survival of the fittest in the march to economic success. The brothers and sisters in the play are just trying to make it in the only way they know. ("When you play the game you look for any break you can make.") His characters don't have to involve themselves in racial conflict to justify their behavior—racism surrounds the black community; it is a forever-present force.

His play seems to flow structurelessly from beginning to end, like modern jazz, but the author never deviates from his theme. The plot and the dialogue are treated with great economy. Foreshadowing is subtly done, and the play is filled with irony. The characters are all skillfully drawn, but the most memorable are Mamma Too Tight and the cold, mysterious, scheming Art, who has learned that "the whole world will come to you if you just sit back and be ready for it." Art easily replaces the old heroes of black youths—such as Buck Jones, Tim McCoy, Wild Bill Elliott, Davey Crockett—because he is a healthier idol, with whom they can identify in their daily struggle and of whom they can be proud because he comes out on top, no matter what the rest of the world thinks "tops" is. Naturalistic drama placed emphasis on heredity and environment, but this is unimportant to Mr. Bullins. His audience is aware of heredity and environment already. They *know* why Art, Curt, Pandora, and Mamma Too Tight are as they are; they don't need background exposition to enlighten them.

Ed Bullins writes for blacks, but his genius as a writer transcends racial limitations. Thus his works are read and produced internationally.

▮▮▮ Goin' a Buffalo ▮▮▮

CAST OF CHARACTERS

CURT, *29 years old*
RICH, *28 years old*
PANDORA, *22 years old. Curt's wife*
ART, *23 years old*
MAMMA TOO TIGHT, *20 years old*
SHAKY, *36 years old. Mamma Too Tight's man*
PIANO PLAYER
BASS PLAYER
DRUMMER
BARTENDER
DEENY
BOUNCER
CUSTOMERS
SHOWGIRL
VOICE

ACT ONE

Scene One

This play is about some black people: CURT, PANDORA, ART, RICH *and* SHAKY, *though* MAMMA TOO TIGHT *is white. The remainder of the cast is interracial, but two of the musicians are black and if* DEENY, *the* BOUNCER *and one of the customers are white, there might be added tensions. But it is left to the director's imagination to match the colors to the portrayals.*

TIME: *Early 1960's late evening in January.*

SCENE: *A court apartment in Los Angeles in the West Adams district. The room is done in white: white ceiling, white walls, white overly-elaborate furniture, but a red wall-to-wall carpet covers the floor. A wall bed is raised. Upstage, two doorless entrances stand on each side of the head of the bed. The right entrance is to the kitchen; the backstage area that represents the kitchen is shielded by a filmy curtain and the actors dim silhouettes are seen when the area is lighted. The left entrance will be raised and offstage right at the head of a short flight of stairs and a platform which leads into the combination bathroom-dressing room-closet. When the actors are within this area their shadows will be cast upon the wall fronting the stairs. And when the bed is lowered a scarlet spread is shown.*

Within the interior of the front room the light is a mixture of red, blues, and violet with crimson shadows bordering the edges of the stage to create the illusion of a world afire with this pocket of atmosphere an oasis.

A Telefunken, turned very low, plays the local jazz station, and CURT *and* RICH *lean over a chess board.* CURT *squats upon a stool, and facing him across the coffee table and chess board,* RICH, *a stocky brooding man, studies his next move, seated on the edge of the couch. Each has an empty beer bottle and a glass close at hand.*

CURT   I just about have you up tight, Rich.

RICH (*annoyed*) Awww... Curt, man... don't try and hustle me!

CURT (*looks at him*)   Did I say somethin' to upset you, man? (RICH *shakes his head and curses to himself. A shadow appears at head of stairs and pauses as if the figure is listening for conversation, then* PANDORA *enters, a beautiful black girl wearing tight white pants, a crimson blouse and black boots, and slowly descends the stairs while looking at the men. She crosses behind them and walks toward the kitchen.* RICH *looks a second at her behind, but drops his gaze when* CURT *begins tapping the chess board with a fingernail.* CURT *gives no discernible attention to* PANDORA. *She enters the kitchen; a light goes on.* CURT *stares at* RICH) This game's somethin' else... man.

RICH (*studies board, looks up at* CURT *and concentrates upon the board again. Mutters to himself*)   Ain't this somethin' else, though... (*looking up*) You almost got my ass, man.

CURT (*mocking*)   I have got your ass, Rich.

RICH (*half-hearted*) Awww... man... why don't you go fuck yourself? (*he places hand upon a piece*)

CURT (*warning and placing hand upon one of his pieces*) Wouldn't do that if I were you, good buddy.

RICH (*frowns and takes hand from board; he shakes head and mumbles, then curses his own caution*) Sheeet! (*he makes move*) Let's see what you're goin' ta do with that, man!

CURT (*deliberately*) Checkmate!

RICH (*half-rising*) What you say, Curt?

CURT (*toneless*) Checkmate, man. (CURT *looks toward the rear of the apartment; the faucet has been turned on, and in the kitchen* PANDORA *leisurely crosses the entrance doorway*) WE'RE READY FOR ANOTHER ONE, PANDORA!

PANDORA (*off*) Already!

CURT That's what I said, baby!

PANDORA (*re-crosses doorway*) Okay.

RICH (*mumbles and studies chess board*) Well ... I'll be goddamned. (*faucet sound goes off*)

PANDORA (*off*) You don't need fresh glasses, do ya? (*sound of refrigerator opening*)

CURT (*surly*) NO, PANDORA, JUST THE BEER!

PANDORA (*raising voice*) Okay ... Okay ... wait a fuckin' minute, will ya? Be right there! (*rattles of bottles*)

CURT (*glowering toward the kitchen, then staring at* RICH *who sits stoop-shouldered*) How 'bout another one, Rich?

RICH (*reaches into pocket and brings out a small roll and pulls off two bills and places them beside* CURT's *glass. He mutters to himself*) I wonder why in the fuck I didn't see that?

PANDORA (*with a cross expression enters carrying two bottles of Miller's Highlife*) Just because you're pissed off at the world, don't take it out on me! What'ta hell ya think ya got 'round here, maid service? (CURT *stands to meet her; she slows. Whining*) Awww ... Curt ... (*a knock comes from backstage; relieved she looks at* CURT) I wonder who would be knocking at the kitchen door, honey?

CURT (*reaches down, palms and pockets the money*) There's only one way to be sure, sugar. (*sits down, looks at* RICH) You clean, man?

RICH (*nods*) Yeah ... Curt.

CURT (*nods to* PANDORA *as the knock sounds again*) Just watch your mouth, pretty baby ... it's goin' ta get you in trouble one of these days, ya know. (PANDORA *places bottles on the edge of the table and briskly goes to open back door*)

PANDORA Maybe it's little Mamma already.

CURT (*mostly to himself*) She wouldn't come around to the back door for nobody. (CURT *disregards the noise of the kitchen door's lock snapping back and the rattle of the night chain being fixed in its hasp*) I have the blackmen this time, right, Rich?

RICH (*reaching for the beer*) Yeah.

ART (*off*) Hello, is Curt home? My name's Art. I ran into Curt this afternoon and he told me to drop by.

PANDORA (*off*) Just a minute ... I'll see. (*the sound of the door closing is heard, and* PANDORA *returns to the main room*) Curt ... Curt?

CURT (*setting up his chess pieces; in a bored voice*) Yeah, baby?

PANDORA There's a guy named Art out here who says you told him to drop around.

CURT (*not looking at her but down at the board*) Invite him in, baby. (PANDORA *exits*)

RICH Is this the guy?

CURT (*nods, in low voice*) Never a dull moment ... right, Rich?

RICH (*sarcastic*) Yeah. We're really in ta somethin', man.

(*The music changes during the remainder of this scene. "Delilah" and "Parisian Thoroughfare" as recorded by Max Roach and Clifford Brown play. These will be the theme for the scenes between* ART *and* PANDORA, *except when other music is necessary to stress altering moods. If act one extends long enough, "Sketches in Spain" by Miles Davis is to be played also, but "Delilah" should be replayed during* PANDORA's *box scene.*

Offstage, PANDORA *says*)

PANDORA Just a minute. (*and the noise of the lock and chain is followed by* ART)

ART Good evening.

(*She leads him into the living room.* RICH *has poured beer for* CURT *and himself; he stands and saunters to the radio as if to change stations, but turns after* ART *has passed behind him and sizes up the stranger from the rear*)

CURT (*stands*) Hey, good buddy! You found the place okay, huh?

ART (*pleased by greeting*) Yeah, it wasn't so hard to find but I guess I came around to the wrong door.

CURT (*with a wave*) Awww ... that's okay.

One's good as the other. It's better to come in that way if you're walkin' from Washington Boulevard. You live somewhere 'round there, don't ya?

ART (*hesitant*) Well... I did.

CURT (*gesturing*) Here, I want you to meet my wife and a buddy of mine. (*introducing* PANDORA) This is my wife, Pandora... and...

PANDORA (*smiles brightly*) We already met, kinda. He told me his name at the door.

CURT (*ignoring* PANDORA) ... and this is Rich.

RICH (*remains in same spot.* ART *turns and* RICH *gives him a casual salute*) What's happen'n, brother?

CURT (*to* PANDORA *and* RICH) This is a guy I met in jail. (*introduces* ART) Art Garrison. (*shows* ART *a seat on the couch, downstage from* RICH) Yeah, Art was one of the best young cons on Tier Three... (*to* PANDORA) Get my boy here a drink, baby.

PANDORA (*starts for kitchen*) You drink beer, Art?

ART Sure... that sounds great.

PANDORA (*over her shoulder*) We got some scotch, if you want it.

ART No, thanks. (RICH *sits, makes opening move, not looking at* ART)

CURT (*to* RICH) Yeah, if it wasn't for Art here I wouldn't be sittin' here.

RICH (*bored*) Yeah?

CURT This is the kid who banged Scooter aside the jaw during the riot last summer in the joint.

RICH (*sounding more enthused*) Yeah... you were doin' a stretch down at county jail when that happened, weren't you?

CURT Yeah, man. I was there bigger den shit. (*takes seat*) Yeah, that paddy mathafukker, Scooter, was comin' down on me with an ice pick, man... we had all been rumblin' up and down the cell block and I slipped on somethin' wet... I think it was Cory's blood 'cause Miles and his boys had stomped the mathafukker so good... (*during the telling of the incident,* PANDORA *stands framed in the kitchen doorway, watching the men*) And I went to look up and all I could see was that grey-eyed mathafukkin' Scooter comin' at me with that ice pick of his ... He reached down and grabbed my shirt front and drew back his arm and WHAMMO ... (*indicating* ART) ... just like a bat out'ta hell my boy here had scored on the sucker's jaw.

ART (*pleased*) Well... I couldn't let that white sonna bitch do you in, man.

RICH (*dryly*) What was the beef about, man?

CURT Well you know Miles goes for the Muslims though he ain't one hisself. Now the Muslims were in a hassle at the joint with the guards and the big people up top because of their religious beliefs, dig?

RICH (*interested*) What do you mean?

CURT Well, the guards didn't want them havin' their meetin's 'cause they said they were organizin' and plottin'. And the Muslims wanted some of the chow changed 'cause they don't eat the same kind'a food that we do.

RICH Yeah!

CURT So while this was all goin' on, Cory ... a young, wise nigger who thinks he's in ta somethin'... well he started agitatin' and signifyin' 'bout who the Muslims think they was. And what made it so rank was a lot of the ofays, ya know, Charles, the white man, start in sayin' things they had held back before, so Miles and some of the boys got together one day and caught that little jive sucker Cory outside his cell block and stomped him so bad the deck was greasy wit' his blood, man. That's when the shit started really goin' down, right there, man. Bumpy, Cory's cousin, come runnin' up, man, and that big nigger kicked Miles square in the nuts and laid out two of his boys before the rest of them got themselves together. By that time some of the whiteys come runnin' up and a few more of Miles' boys. Yeah, the whole shit started right there where Cory lay almost done in...

RICH Yeah... I heard a couple of cats got stabbed, man.

CURT Yeah, man, it was pretty scary for a while, mostly black cons against white ones except for the studs who just tried to stay out of the shit and the Uncle Toms... those Toms we were really out to cool.

RICH (*heated*) Yeah, you should have done those mathafukkers in!

CURT Even the guards wouldn't come into the cell block and break it up at first... a whole lot of shit went down that day. (*looking at* ART) I owe my boy here a lot for that day.

ART (*embarrassed*) Yeah, man, I would have liked to have stayed out of it but I couldn't.

CURT Yeah, Art, I us'ta wonder about that

... (*a two beat pause*) ... How could you just go about your business and stay in the middle all the time in that place when so much crap was goin' down?

ART I just stayed out of everything, that's all.

CURT But didn't you care about anything, man? Didn't you feel anything when that shit was happen'n to you?

ART Yeah, I cared but I just didn't let it bother me too much. I just froze up on everything that tried to git in and not too much touched me.

PANDORA (*from doorway*) Talk about somebody bein' cold!

CURT (*having noticed her in doorway for first time, stares at* ART) But you don't know how I appreciate what you did, man. It wasn't your fight, man. You weren't takin' sides. You were one of the quiet guys waitin' for trial who just kept his mouth shut and minded his own business.

ART I never do try and take sides in stir, just serve my time and forget about it, that's all. (PANDORA *has moved out of the doorway*)

CURT Well, I'm glad you did that time, man, and if there's anything I can ever ... (RICH *interrupts*)

RICH What were you in for, Art? (CURT *takes a drink of his beer, lights a cigarette and blows smoke across the table above the two men's heads.* PANDORA *drops something made of glass in the kitchen and curses*)

ART Well ... I was waiting for trial ... attempted murder.

RICH That's a tough one to have on your rap sheet.

ART Yeah, it doesn't do your record or you any good, especially when it ain't for money.

CURT (*finally makes answering chess move*) It was over a broad, wasn't it?

ART (*lights a cigarette, offers* RICH *a light but is refused*) Yeah. I guess girls are my main weakness.

RICH (*with unlit cigarette dangling from his lips, makes move*) How much time did you do?

ART Waited on my trial for nine months at county when the husband of the girl dropped the charges and left town.

CURT (*replies to move*) That's who you shot, the girl's husband?

ART (*his eyes following game*) Yeah.

RICH (*moves quickly*) You pretty good with a gun?

ART (*caught up in game*) I can usually hold one without it blowing my foot off.

RICH (*sharply*) Any simple ass can do that! I asked you are you any good with one!

(*The three men are fixed in tableau for a three beat interval;* ART *strains forward from his seat and is about to speak*)

CURT (*to* RICH *as he makes his move*) This move's goin' ta show ya ta stop fuckin' with Curt the Kid, good buddy. (*noise of refrigerator opening and slamming, and* PANDORA *enters with a bottle and a glass. She pours beer for* ART *and sets the glass down beside him as the men all look at the chess board*)

PANDORA (*in a light mood*) Sorry I took so long, Art. I just dropped the supper. (*to* CURT) Honey, the beans are all messed up. Little Mamma won't have anything to eat 'cept eggs.

CURT (*not looking at her*) Didn't want no fuckin' beans anyhow! And I know Mamma Too Tight don't want any either ... what kind'a shit is that ... givin' that broad beans on her first night on the streets?

PANDORA (*defensively*) That's all we got, honey ... You know we won't have any spendin' money until Deeny pays me.

RICH Why don't you have a seat, Pan?

PANDORA I gotta finish cleanin' the kitchen ... I don't want no roaches 'round here. Last place we had we had to split 'cause the roaches took it over. The little mathafukkers got mo' of the food than Curt or me. Soon as I bring in a little money to get some food with ... (CURT *looks at her sharply but she is turned toward* RICH *and* ART) ... there's mo' of them little mathafukkers there than your eyes could see. And I put too much time in fixin' this pad up nice the way it is to have them little mathafukkers move in on me and try to take it over.

CURT You better finish up, sweetcake, so I can take you to work. (*the use of the term "sweetcake" is done with derision and seldom with affection.* PANDORA *picks up* CURT'S *empty bottles and exits*) Your move, Richie.

RICH Are you sure, man?

CURT Just ask Art, he's been watchin' the game.

ART Well, I ain't in it, man.

RICH That's right, you ain't in it.

CURT (*watching* ART's *face*) Yeah, it's your move, Richie, babe.

RICH (*to* ART) That was pretty nice of that girl's ole man to let you off, Art.

ART Nawh... he wanted his ole lady to leave the state with him so he had to drop the charges against me to let her off the hook too.

RICH She was in it too, huh?

ART She shot him with me.

CURT You play this game, Art?

ART Yeah, some. But I haven't had much practice lately.

CURT Well, this one's about over.

RICH (*snorts*) Sheeet!

CURT Maybe you'd like ta play the winner.

RICH (*grimacing before making hesitant move*) Where ya livin' now, Art?

ART I just got locked out of my room.

RICH Yeah, Curt said you wanted to make some money.

ART (*intensely*) I have to, man. I'm really on my ass.

CURT Check!

RICH (*makes move*) Not yet, sucker.

ART I gotta get out of this town.

RICH You got a car, ain't ya?

CURT (*moves*) Not long now, Rich.

ART Yeah, that's about all I got. A car and a suitcase. I've also gotten more jail time in this town than in my whole life, and I've been half-way round the world and all over this country.

RICH (*moves and acts angry*) Yeah, L.A.'s no fuckin' good, man. If I was off parole now I would get the first thing on wheels out of here. How 'bout you, Curt? If you weren't out on bail wouldn't you make it?

(CURT *doesn't answer. Stage left, a knock sounds and* PANDORA *comes out of the kitchen striding toward the entrance which serves as the front door to the apartment*)

PANDORA That must be little Mamma.

CURT Sure hope it is... I would really like ta see that little broad.

PANDORA (*peers through window*) Yeah, there's that chick. (*calling outside in jocular way:*) HEY, BROAD, WHAT THEY DOIN' LETTIN' YOU OUT'TA JAIL? (*an indistinct shout and a laugh comes from outside*)

CURT (*to* RICH) Checkmate, man!

(*Lights lower to blacken the stage*)

Scene Two

(*When the lights go up* MAMMA TOO TIGHT *and* SHAKY *sit upon the lowered bed. Faintly reflecting a glow, the bed spread gives them the appearance of sitting upon smoldering coals.* MAMMA TOO TIGHT, *a small, voluptuous girl, is dressed well. Her shift complements her creamy complexion and full-blown build.* SHAKY *is nondescript but dresses in expensive casual clothes.*

CURT, RICH *and* ART *sit in the same area, stage right, facing the bed, forming the lower lip of a half-moon, and* PANDORA *has changed to a black cocktail dress and sits upon the stairs to the bathroom. She faces front with a bit of red-ruffled slip peeking beneath and around her black-stockinged legs.*

They all eat chicken from cardboard containers and reach for beers and cigarettes. The light in the kitchen is off, and the radio plays.)

ART Thanks again, Curt... if you hadn't invited me to eat I don't know what I'd do... probably had to drive downtown on what little gas I got and eat at one of those Rescue Missions.

MAMMA TOO TIGHT (*nudging* SHAKY *in the ribs*) Well, I'll be damned... Ole Curt done saved himself a soul.

SHAKY (*slow and languid*) Easy, baby, you gonna make me spill my beer.

MAMMA TOO TIGHT What you know 'bout eatin' at Rescue Missions, boy?

PANDORA (*interjecting*) You better stop callin' that guy ah boy, Mamma... ha ha... girl... you got mo' gall.

RICH (*drinking beer*) Yeah, Mamma, how fuckin' big do boys grow where you come from?

CURT (*with food in mouth*) Forget about it, Art, glad to have ya. One more don't mean a thing.

PANDORA Listen ta that, Mamma Too Tight ... (*mocking*) ... "One mo' mouf don't mean a thing." ... We eat beans all week and when you and Curt's friends come in we play big shit!... And call out for food and beer.

(CURT, SHAKY *and* ART *stop eating.* CURT *stares at* PANDORA *and* ART *holds his plate like it is hot and he is trying not to drop it on the floor.* SHAKY *eyes* MAMMA TOO TIGHT *and gives a mean scowl.* MAMMA *has seen the look on* CURT's *face before.* RICH *goes on enjoying his meal*)

MAMMA (*in a jolly tone, to* PANDORA) Girl, you don't have ta tell me a thing... these here men think that money can be just picked up off'a them pavements out there like chewin' gum paper... until they got ta get out there for themselves. (*she swings off the bed and shows flashes of lingerie*) Like this pretty boy here with the fuzz on his face. (*she approaches* ART *and stands so her hips form a prominent profile to* CURT's *line of vision*) He ain't even eatin' no mo'... and Curt's not either, honey. What I tell ya? These men are somethin' else. So weak from plottin' what we should be doin' to bring some money in that they can't eat themselves. (*puts her plate on coffee table*) I know that Curt is a big strong man... he's always lettin' Pan know. (*strong dialect*)... So he don't need no help from us frail ass women but maybe ole fuzzy wuzzy face here needs some help. (*her audience is in better humor once more. to* ART) You wants Mamma Too Tight to feeds him some food, baby boy?

SHAKY Cut out the Magnolia act. Everything wears thin, *Queenie!*

MAMMA (*sudden anger*) Don't you call me no fuckin' Queenie!

SHAKY (*sarcastic*) Anything you say, baby. (PANDORA *guffaws at* SHAKY's *tone*)

PANDORA (*mimicking* MAMMA's *drawl*) But ain't dat you name, hoon e e e?

(MAMMA *ignores* SHAKY *and* PANDORA, *picks drumstick from plate and offers it to* ART *who frowns, and she pulls it away and puts it to her mouth imitating a mother feeding a reluctant child. Finally,* ART *smiles at her as* SHAKY *speaks*)

SHAKY Why don'chou lighten up, woman!

MAMMA Lighten up?... Damn... man... I ain't here ten minutes befoe I see your face and you tell *me* to lighten up! I been with you since I hit the streets at noon and you still checkin' up on me... don't worry, man... I'm goin' ta get right ta work.

SHAKY (*slow and languid*) I know that, baby.

MAMMA (*to* PANDORA) Girl, you should of seen Shaky... ha ha ha... almost swept me off my feet, girl. Said he loved me and really missed me so much the last ninety days that he almost went out of his mind... ha ha... (*coyly*) I was so embarrassed and impressed, girl, I liked to have blushed and nearly peed on myself like a sixteen year old girl. (*change of voice*) But the ole sonna bitch didn't fool me none with that shit!... The only thing he missed was that good steady money!

CURT (*piqued*) Why don't you check yourself, Mamma!

MAMMA (*waving* CURT's *threat off and returning to the edge of the bed*) But, girl, he sho threw some lovin' on me... he heee... sheeet, I should go away again after this afternoon. (PANDORA *laughs throughout*) Ummm... chile... I nearly thought I was on that honeymoon I never had.

PANDORA You should after that routine, baby.

MAMMA And then when the sun start goin' down and things got really gettin' romantic, girl... this mathafukker says... (*lights lower; spot on bed.* SHAKY *speaks the line*)

SHAKY I want you to bring in a yard tonight, baby. (MAMMA *resumes speech. Bed spot off; colored spot on* MAMMA)

MAMMA You what, man? (*colored spot off; bed spot on*)

SHAKY A hundred stone cold dollars, baby. Tonight, baby! (*spot off; lights go up*)

MAMMA (*to* PANDORA) And girl, do you know what I said?

PANDORA Yeah, I know what you said.

MAMMA That's right, baby, I said to Shaky, "How do you want them, daddy... in fives or tens?" (*laughter halts the speeches and the glasses are filled and fingers cleaned of chicken grease and cigarettes are lit*)

CURT (*to* SHAKY) Don't let Mamma try and fool you... she wanted to see you so bad... everytime Pan us'ta go visit her she would say to Pan, "How's that ole dirty Shaky doin'?"

MAMMA Yeah, I'd ask... 'cause I'd be wonderin' why ain't the mathafukker down here.

SHAKY Now, let's not go into that again, baby.

CURT Yeah, Mamma... you know what's happen'n behind that. You know why Shaky didn't come down... you never can tell when they might have a warrant out on him or somethin' and keep him too. You remember what happened at court, don't cha?

MAMMA Yeah, I remember. How can I forget? The judge said for Shaky to leave the court 'cause everytime I'm on trial he's in the back row hangin' 'round and that last ole woman judge said she knew who Shaky was an' she'd like to put him behind bars instead of me ... but comin' down to visit me in jail is different, Curt!

SHAKY (*pleading*) Now, baby...

CURT Listen, Mamma... how old are you?

MAMMA Twenty.

CURT That means you're a big girl now, a woman who should be able to understand things, right?

MAMMA Yeah, but...

CURT (*cutting*) Right! Now listen, baby ... and listen hard ... now how many times you been busted?

MAMMA Thirty-three times ... but I only fell this once for more than ten days and that was because I got that new fuckin' woman judge. I got the best record in town of any broad on the block I know. Pandora's rap sheet is worst than mine and I was on the block two years before she was.

CURT Exactly, baby. Now if you didn't have an old man like Shaky out there workin' for you, you'd be out of business and servin' some big time ... right? Wouldn't that be a drag to be servin' some grand theft time behind givin' up a little body! Pan ain't been snatched since before we were married ... ain't that right, Pandora? See there? Now let me tell you, baby, and listen hard. (*intensely*) A self-respectin' man won't let this ole lady stay in jail. If he can't get the bail for her or the juice to pay off somebody downtown like Shaky done you to have your time cut to one-third ... (*disgust*) ... he's a punk! And any broad that even looks at the jive sucker should get her funky ass run into the ground like a piece of scum!

MAMMA (*on defensive*) I know all that, Curt, but I got so lonely down there. Nothin' down there but broads and most of them butches.

PANDORA Mamma ... don't even talk about it. Makes cold chills run up my back just thinkin' 'bout it.

CURT Yeah, we know it was hard, baby, but you can't afford to lose your old man by his gettin' busted behind a jail visit. That would be a stone trick, Mamma. Nothin' but a hammer ... Right?

MAMMA Awww ... Curt, you try and make it sound so smooth.

PANDORA He can really make it do that, girl.

RICH (*finishes drinking the last of his beer*) Hey, Shaky, I want you to take a walk with me, okay?

SHAKY (*standing slowly and visibly rocking*) Yeah, man. (*to* MAMMA) I'll see you back at the house, baby. Watch yourself.

MAMMA I'll probably be in early, Shaky. Unless I catch somethin' good. (RICH *and* SHAKY *exit by the front door.* PANDORA *accompanies them and checks the outside before they step out*) Sheet, Pandora, I thought Shaky was the Chicken Delight man when he knocked. I wasn't here ten minutes before he was knockin' on the door to see if I had my ride to the club. Didn't even think about feedin' me. (*soulful*) Just give me some good lovin' ta show me where it's at.

PANDORA These men are somethin' else, girl ... 'spect a girl to go out'ta here on an empty stomach and turn all kinds of tricks ... but Curt and me did have some beans for you, girl, but I dropped them.

MAMMA Well, I'm glad you did.

CURT (*packing away chess board*) I told her you didn't want no beans, Mamma.

MAMMA I got too many beans in the joint.

PANDORA (*peeved*) Well, that's what I had for you, chick.

MAMMA (*to* ART) Hey, pretty baby, why you so quiet?

ART Oh, I ain't got much to say, I guess.

CURT This is my boy Art, Mamma. I introduced you when you came in.

MAMMA (*sultry*) I know his name ... ha ha I just want to know his game, dat's all. Hey, fuzz face, what's yo game? Is you kinda fuzzy wuzzy 'round the edges?

ART I'm sorry ... I don't know ...

CURT Awww ... he's okay, Mamma ... he was in the joint with me. He's just quiet, that's all. Reads too much ... somethin' you should do more of.

PANDORA Why should she? Ain't heard of nobody gettin' no money readin'.

MAMMA (*to* ART) Now I know your name, fuzzy boy, now you say my name.

ART (*surprise*) Your name?

MAMMA Yeah. Say MA-MA TOO TIGHT!

ART I know your name.

MAMMA But I want you to say it.

ART I don't have to with you broadcasting it all over the place ever since you been here.

Goin' a Buffalo

MAMMA (*cross*) You must think you're wise, man.

ART (*in low, even voice*) I am, you big mouthed bitch, and I want you to stop jivin' with me. (PANDORA *giggles*. CURT *looks on enjoying the surprise showing on* MAMMA's *face*)

MAMMA Well... 'scuse me, tiger. (*walks over to* ART *and sits beside him*) Awww... forget it. I always act this way, ask Pan and Curt. 'Specially when I'm ah little bit loaded... Hey, Pandora, your friend here ain't got no sense of humor.

PANDORA Nawh... he's too much like Curt. Serious. That's why they probably get along so good, girl... they probably made for each other. (*the girls laugh*)

CURT C'mon, Pan... it's almost time for you to go to work. Deeny will be callin' nex' thing and that's one mathafukker I don't even want to see much less talk to. Go and get the stuff. (PANDORA *exits through the bathroom door*)

MAMMA (*to* ART) You want to know why they call me Mamma Too Tight, pretty baby?

CURT If Shaky ever heard you callin' my boy that, he'd break your arm, Mamma.

MAMMA Yeah, he might. But Shaky ain't where nothin's shakin' at the moment... Just out givin' Rich a fix...

CURT Both of you bitches talk too much!

MAMMA (*to* ART) You know what, fuzz wuzz? I sho wish I had a lil fuzzy wuzzy like you up there some of those cold nights in the joint. (*she gets up and walks to stand before the men. She plays it strictly for laughs, swinging her hips to the radio music and singsongs in a hearty, brazen voice like one of the old time red hot mamma's. Singing*) Why do they call me what they call me, baby? When what they call me is my name.

ART (*dryly*) I have suspicions but I'm not positive.

MAMMA (*ridiculing, but friendly*) You have suspicions as every little fuzzy wuzzy does but let me tell you... because my real name is Queenie Mack! Queenie Bell Mack! Ain't that some shit? No self-respectin' whore in the world can go 'round with a name like that unless she's in Mississippi... sheeet... QUEENIE!

ART So you named yourself Mamma Too...

MAMMA (*cutting*) No! It just happened. I don't know how. I just woke up one day with my name that way... And I like it that way ... it's me! (*turning toward* ART) Don't you think it fits, honey?

ART I think it really does.

MAMMA Damn right it does. It makes me feel so alive. That's why I'm glad to be out...

CURT (*yelling*) HEY, PANDORA!

MAMMA Man, but it's so good to be high again. It's so good to be free. (PANDORA *enters from the bathroom and descends the stairs and places a cardboard box on the table as the lights blacken briefly and the music rises*)

Scene Three

(*As the lights go up and the music lowers, the scene has shifted.* CURT *and* PANDORA *sit upon the couch, across from* ART, *and* MAMMA TOO TIGHT *has taken the stool* CURT *was seated on. Uncovered, the box waits in the center of the table.* CURT *is licking a brown cigarette as the theme plays*)

CURT Yeah. We want to make some money, Art, so we can get out of this hole. (*lights the cigarette and inhales fiercely. Drops head. Two beat pause. In strained voice, holding smoke back*) We're makin' it to Buffalo, man. You hip to Buffalo?

ART No, I don't think so...

CURT (*takes another drag*) It's a good little hustlin' town, I hear. I got a case comin' up here for passin' some bad paper, ya know, forgin' payroll checks... and when I get the money to make restitution and give the people downtown some juice, ya know, man, pay them off, I'm makin' it East. But I need some grand theft dough.

ART But won't you get some time with your record?

CURT Nawh. Probably not. You see, I'm a good thief. I take money by my wits... ya know, with a pen or by talkin' some sucker out of it. It's only seldom that I'm forced to really take any money by force. If I make full restitution for these checks and fix my lawyer up and the other people downtown, I'll get probation. They'll reduce it to a misdemeanor and breakin' probation for somethin' like that ain't nothin'... besides, Buffalo's a long way away, man.

PANDORA (*receiving cigarette from* CURT) It's supposed to be a good little town. A different scene entirely. I'm due for a good scene for a change.

CURT   Yeah, but we have to get that juice money first, baby. We gotta get us some long money.

MAMMA   Any place is better than L.A. but I heard that Buffalo is really boss.

PANDORA (*languid*)   It sho is, baby.

MAMMA   I wonder if I could get Shaky to go?

CURT   Sure you could, Mamma. He can get connections to deal his stuff there just like here. That's the idea. When we make our hit and split out of here we're goin'a take as many as we can with us. You know, set up a kinda organization.

PANDORA (*passing cigarette to* MAMMA)   They really got respect for cats from the coast back there.

ART (*getting caught up in the mood*)   Yeah, they really do . . . when I . . .

PANDORA (*cutting speech*)   With me workin' on the side and with Curt dealin' we'd be on our feet in no time.

CURT   We want to be on our feet when we get there, baby.

ART   And that's where I come in, right?

CURT   Right, good buddy.

MAMMA (*handing cigarette to* ART)   Here, baby.

ART (*waving it away*)   So what's on your mind, Curt?

MAMMA (*extending cigarette*)   I said here, baby, I just don't like to hold this thing and see all this bread go up in ashes.

ART   I don't want any.

(*A three beat stop, all caught in tableau staring at* ART, *then* PANDORA *snickers and breaks into a tittering laugh, looking at* CURT)

PANDORA (*ridicule*)   You and your friends, Curt . . . I thought . . .

CURT (*heated*)   Shut up, bitch . . . you talk too much!

PANDORA (*rising anger*)   Why shouldn't I when you bring some square-ass little . . . (CURT *slaps her; she jumps to her feet and spins to claw him but* CURT *lunges forward and slaps her again, causing her to trip backwards across the edge of the coffee table. From the floor, removing one of her shoes*) Goddamn you, Curt . . . (*she begins to crawl to her knees and* CURT *moves around the table after her. Then* ART *steps between them and pushes* CURT *backward on the couch. Surprise is upon* CURT'*s face and* MAMMA TOO TIGHT *seems frozen in place*)

CURT   WHAT THE FUCK'S GOIN' ON, MAN?

ART (*low*)   Don't hit her anymore, Curt.

CURT (*incredulous*)   What? . . . Man, are you payin' this woman's bills . . . have you got any papers on her?

PANDORA (*to* CURT)   ARE YOU PAYIN' MY BILLS, MATHAFUKKER?

CURT (*rising to attack* PANDORA; ART *blocks his way*)   I've told you to keep your mouth . . . (*to* ART *when he won't let him pass*) Now listen, Art, you're like a brother to me but you don't know what's goin' down, man.

ART   Why don't we all sit down and try and relax, Curt? Why don't you do it for me, huh? As a favor. I'm sorry for buttin' in to your business between you and your old lady but somethin' just happens to me, man, when I see a guy hit a girl. (*after a minute,* CURT *is soothed and sits upon the couch again, glaring at* PANDORA *who holds her shoe like a weapon*)

MAMMA (*partially recovered*)   Oh, man, I just hit the streets and this is what I run into . . .

CURT (*intense, to* ART)   What are you doin', man? Squarin' out on me? Man, I've went a long way . . .

ART (*leaning forward*)   Well, look, Curt . . . I can split . . . (CURT *stands and looks down on* ART. *Changing expression,* PANDORA *makes a move for the box but* CURT *waves her hand away*)

CURT   No, I don't think you better try that, Art. (*pause*) Tell me, Art. Why don't you want to smoke any marijuana?

ART   Why don't . . . I don't understand why you should ask me that.

CURT   Is your playin' hero for Pandora a game to cover up somethin', man? (MAMMA *is clutching herself as if she has returned to the womb*)

MAMMA   Oh . . . shit shit shit . . . shit . . . just today . . . just today they cut me loose . . . just today.

PANDORA (*no longer angry, placing hand on* CURT'*s arm*)   Easy, baby, I think he's okay.

CURT   You would!

ART   Now, look, man, I don't put down anybody for doin' what they want but just don't hassle me!

PANDORA (*hostile, to* ART) Cool it, baby, you're in some deep trouble now.

MAMMA Oh, goddamn... why can't I just be plain'ass Queenie Bell Mack?

CURT (*low*) What's happen'n, brother?

ART I just don't get high... that's all...

MAMMA (*nearly screaming*) Neither does J. Edgar Hoover, sucker, but he don't come in here pretend'n to be no friend!

PANDORA (*enraged, fearful of losing control, to* MAMMA) SHUT UP, BITCH! THIS IS CURT AND OUR PLACE. WE GOT MO' TO LOSE THAN JUST OUR ASS. JUST SHUT ON UP! (MAMMA *looks most like a small girl with wide, moist eyes*)

CURT For the last time, Art, tell me somethin'.

ART I just don't... (PANDORA *stands and moves in front of* CURT. *The coffee table separates them from* ART, *but she leans over*)

PANDORA (*to* CURT, *behind her*) He's alright, honey. If he were a cop he'd be smokin' stuff right along with us... you know that...

ART (*bewildered*) A cop!...

PANDORA (*sarcastic*) He's just a little square around the edges, Curt... (*silence, then: to* ART) But why, honey?

ART (*shrugging sheepishly*) I had a bad experience once behind pot, that's all. (MAMMA *chuckles until* CURT *stops her*)

MAMMA He had a bad experience... hee hee hee... ha ha ha... He had...

CURT (*menace*) Pan has already told you to check yourself, woman, he's still my friend.

PANDORA What was it all about, man... can you tell us about it?

ART I'd rather not...

CURT (*cutting*) We know you'd rather not but...

PANDORA (*cutting*) Now look, Art, you're not givin' us much of a break... we don't want to act like this but we got a lot of the future riding on what happens in the nex' few days. Why don't you tell us?

ART I would but it don't seem that much...

CURT (*not so threatening*) But it is, Art!

PANDORA C'mon, trust me. Can't you say anything? We've gone more than half-...

CURT Stop rankin' him, will ya!

PANDORA I'M ONLY DOIN' IT FOR YOU! (*silence as* CURT *and* PANDORA *stare at each other*)

ART Yeah, I'll talk about it... (CURT *sits*. PANDORA *moves around the table closer to* ART. *The cigarette has been dropped by* MAMMA *beside the box.* "Delilah" *plays*) You see... it was about three years ago. I shipped out on a freighter... ya know, one of those scows that fly the Panamanian or Liberian flag but don't really belong to any country...

MAMMA (*in small girl's voice*) Ain't they American?

ART Well, in a way. They belong to American corporations and the businessmen don't want to pay high taxes on 'em. They're pretty ratty. (PANDORA *makes a seat on the floor between the men*) Well, I went on a four month cruise, ya know, to ports around the West Indies and then to North Africa.

MAMMA Wow... that sounds gassy... I wish...

PANDORA (*cutting*) MAMMA!

ART Well, I been blowin' weed since I was about twelve...

MAMMA (*ridicule*) Ha ha ha... since he was twelve... (PANDORA *and* CURT *frown at her and she huddles in her seat and looks cold*)

ART ... and everything was cool. I smoked it when I ran into it and never thought about it much unless someone turned me on. But in Tangier it was about as easy to get as a bottle of beer. Man, I had a ball all the while I was over there and before I left I bought a big bag. (*showing with his hands*) This big for about five bucks. All the way back on my night watches I just smoked grass and just thought of what the guys on my corner back home would say when I would pull out a joint or two and just give it to them. Prices back east are about triple what they are here, so you can guess what it was worth... And all the broads I would make... you know how it goes... take a broad up to your room and smoke a little weed and if you have anything goin' for you at all, man, that's it.

PANDORA (*disgust*) Yeah, there's a lot of stupid broads in this world.

ART (*sensing the reduced tension*) And I could still sell some when my money got low and come out beautiful. I was really feeling good about that grass, Curt. Well, this tub docks in Philly about 1 A.M. and I have to leave ship and when I get to the station I find that my train don't leave until 2 the next afternoon. I got my pay and my belongings, so I stash most of my bags in a locker at the station, the bag of weed is in one but I have about half a dozen joints on me. Now I know Philly a little. I know where there's an after-hour joint so I grab a cab and go over there. The place is jumpin'... they're havin' a fish fry, and I start in drinkin' and talkin' to girls but none of them are listen'n 'cept for seven bucks for them and three for the management for rentin' one of the upstairs rooms, and I ain't buyin' no cock... not in the States...

PANDORA Well, I'm glad of that. I can take squares but not tricks, baby.

CURT (*to* PANDORA) You still runnin' your mouth, ain't you?

ART So I start talkin' with some guy and he tells me of a place he knows 'cross town that's better than this one. He looks okay to me. A blood. Dressed real sharp with a little goatee and everything. I had been talkin' to him about bein' out to sea and since he don't try and con me into a crap game and is buyin' one drink for every one of mine, I don't give a damn where we go 'cause I got the whole night to kill.

MAMMA Oh wow... I know this is the bad part...

PANDORA Listen, Mamma.

MAMMA (*turning her face away*) I don't like to hear bad things.

ART So we drinkin' bottles of beer and drivin' up Broad Street in Philly in his old wreck of a Buick and I think how it would be nice to turn on and get really loaded before we get where we're goin'. So I reach for my pocket but it's wintertime and I got on a pea jacket and sweaters and I have trouble gettin' to my pocket. And while I was lookin' I start in laughin'.

CURT Laughin'?

ART Yeah. I start wonderin' what would happen if this was a cop I was with and the idea was just too much. So funny. So I started in laughin'. And the guy asks me what I was laughin' at and I said I was just laughin' about him bein' a cop. And he said that he was and how did I know. (*two beat pause*) I don't know how I got out of that car or away from him. But soon after I was pukin' my guts up, and I threw those joints into a sewer and they wouldn't go down 'cause snow and ice was cloggin' it up. And I was stompin' on 'em so they would go down and gettin' sick and after a while my feet were all covered with ice and snow and puke and marijuana... Ya know... I had nearly twenty bucks worth of dope frozen to the soles of my shoes.

MAMMA (*seriously*) Awww... no, man... I can't stand any more.

PANDORA (*giggling*) That's the best trip I've been on this week, Art.

ART Nawh, really... baby. And the bag... I left it in a locker. Not the one I used but another empty one.

MAMMA Those janitors must'a naturally been happy the next day.

ART Yeah, they must have been but I couldn't even think of the stuff for a long time without wanting to heave up my guts.

CURT That must'a been pretty scary, man. (PANDORA *has reached over and gotten the cigarette and re-lit it*)

PANDORA (*offering it to* ART) Now it's time to get back on the horse, cowboy.

ART (*placing hand on stomach*) I don't think I can.

MAMMA You'll never think about that time in Philly again after the first drag, baby.

CURT C'mon, man, you're already one of us. Do you think I'd bring you in if I thought you'd be a square?

PANDORA Don't say that, Curt. He's not. Somethin' like what happened to him can mess up your mind about things. (*she stands over him and puffs on the cigarette. Staring at him*) Now don't think about anything... just look into my eyes. (*she inhales once more and gives the cigarette to* ART) Now, here, put it in your mouth.

ART (*takes it and puts to lips*) I can do it all right but I just don't want to.

PANDORA (*staring*) Look into my eyes and inhale. Don't think about it being in your hand. (ART *inhales and looks at her*) All the way down now and hold it.

MAMMA Don't ever say you don't believe in witches, boy.

CURT Cool it, Mamma!

PANDORA Now one more drag, Art. (ART *takes another puff and hands the reefer to* CURT. ART *has a great grin on his face*)

ART So that's what's in Pandora's box? (*lights change*)

PANDORA (*fantasy*) Among other things, Art. Among other things. But those have been lies you've been told about bad things comin' out of Pandora's box.

MAMMA Most people think that a girl's box is in other places.

PANDORA Nothin' can be found bad in there either. People only bring evil there with them. They only look for evil there. The sick . . .

ART What do you mean by sick?

PANDORA The come freaks, that's who. The queers who buy sex from a woman.

MAMMA (*bitterly*) Yeah, they say we're wrong but they're the queers . . . payin' for another person's body.

CURT (*in euphoria, musing*) Art, my man, we're goin'a Buffalo . . . goin' one day real soon.

PANDORA (*repulsion*) Some of them are real nice lookin' cats. Not old with fat greasy bellies. Real nice lookin' studs. (*bitterly*) Those are the real queers you have ta watch. They want ta hurt women.

MAMMA You hip ta that, baby? Those muscle cats, you know, muscle queens . . . always wantin' ta freak out on ya.

ART And that's all that comes out of Pandora's box? (CURT *pulls a nickel-plated revolver out of the box*)

CURT No. Right now this is the most important thing. There's always something new in there. (*handing gun to* ART) Feel it, brother. (ART *takes the gun. He is caught up in the music and with his new friends*)

ART It's a good one.

MAMMA Look how it shines. (*lights change*)

ART (*dreamlike*) Yeah . . . like Pandora's eyes. (*lights change*)

PANDORA (*fantasy*) Nothin' bad comes out of me or from my box, baby. Nothin' bad. You can believe that. It's all in what you bring to us. (*lights change*)

MAMMA That's wha's happen'n, baby.

CURT It's yours now, Art, as much yours as mine. Can you handle it, brother?

ART (*looking at* PANDORA *and taking a new reefer*) If that's my job, brother. (*the cigarette has been replaced by a new one and others are in the hands of the group;* PANDORA *drags in deeply*)

PANDORA Buffalo's goin'a be a gas. (*the phone rings from the dressing room and* CURT *goes to answer. His shadow can be seen upon the wall at the top of the stairs*)

CURT (*off*) Yeah, Deeny . . . yeah yeah yeah . . . yeah, man . . . yeah.

MAMMA Who ever heard of a telephone in the toilet?

PANDORA It's in the dressing room next to the bathroom, Mamma.

MAMMA Sho is strange . . . Hey, are you goin'a Buffalo too, fuzz wuzz?

ART It looks that way.

PANDORA (*smiling*) I think I'll like that, Art. I think that'll be nice. (*a knock sounds at the front door.* CURT'*s shadow hangs up the phone and retreats further into the area*)

CURT (*off*) PANDORA! MOVE! GOD-DAMN IT! GET A MOVE ON! (ART *stands as* PANDORA *jumps to her feet. He has a cross expression as he looks toward the dressing room entrance*)

ART (*to* PANDORA) Can I help you? (PANDORA *shakes her head*) Is there anything I can do?

PANDORA No, I don't think anybody can do anything, especially you. (*she places the gun and the marijuana in the box and hurries up the stairs. The knock comes again*)

MAMMA (*still seated, toward door*) JUST A MINUTE! (ART *watches* PANDORA *enter dressing room*) You want to get the door, Art?

ART I learned once never to open another man's door. (PANDORA *and* CURT, *in coats, come from the dressing room;* PANDORA *has her costumes in her arms.* MAMMA TOO TIGHT *gets up and walks downstage*)

CURT That fuckin' Deeny wants you to rehearse some new music before your act, Pan.

PANDORA Sonna bitch! Always late payin' somebody and always wantin' you to work your ass off.

CURT Is your car parked far, Art?

ART Not too far.

MAMMA (*looking out window*) It's only Rich.

CURT Good. He can stay here and watch the phone while we're at the club. First we'll stop and get you some gas, Art, and then you can take us to the Strip Club.

PANDORA Is your car big enough to get us all to the Strip Club on Western, Art?

ART It'll even get us as far as Buffalo, Pandora.

(*They exit.* RICH *enters, turns in doorway and is seen talking to someone outside. Then he shuts door, saunters gracefully across the room and turns the radio off. Lights dim out as he sprawls upon the couch. Curtain*)

ACT TWO

(*The curtain opens showing the Strip Club, or rather, the suggested representation of a cheap night club in the Wilshire area of Los Angeles, featuring "Bronze" strip-teasers. But the effect should be directed toward the illusions of time, place and matter. Reality is questionable here. The set should be painted in lavish phony hues except for the bare brown floor. Seeing the set, the female audience should respond: "gorgeous, lovely, marvelous, delightful," and with similar banalities. The men should wonder if the habitat of whores is not indeed the same region as their creatures of private myth, dream and fantasy.*

A rotating color-wheel, in front of the major lights, should turn constantly throughout this scene, giving an entire spectrum of altering colored shadows. Additional colored lights and spots should be used to stress mood changes and the violence of the ending scene.

A MUSICIAN *plays randomly at the piano. He is tall, wearing a dark suit with an open-necked dark shirt. The* BARTENDER, *wiry with his head shaven clean, sweeps the floor and empties ash trays. A few customers sit and watch the* MUSICIAN, *and later, the* GROUP, *as the show hasn't begun.*

The voice which is heard at the close of this act can be that of a customer.

Two other MUSICIANS *enter and climb upon the stage.*)

PIANO PLAYER (*joking, to* BASS PLAYER *seated at piano*) Hey, man, they lookin' for bass players all up and down the street but you cats are all bangin' out chords on out of tune pianos.

BASS PLAYER What's happen'n, man? Say ... listen to this ... (*he plays a couple of frames*) What about that, man ... huh?

PIANO PLAYER Man, like I said ... you're a damn good bass man ...

BASS PLAYER (*getting up*) What you say about somebody lookin' for bass men? ... Man! Turn me on. I wouldn't be here in this trap if I knew where one of those gigs were.

DRUMMER (*seated, working up a beat*) Yeah, man, they need you like they need me.

PIANO (*wryly*) How's it feel to keep gettin' replaced by a juke box? (BASS PLAYER *begins working with* DRUMMER. PIANO PLAYER *strikes a few chords then lights a cigarette*)

BASS Hey, where's Stew and Ronny? I want to practice those new charts before Pandora gets in.

PIANO (*blowing smoke out*) They quit.

BASS (*halting*) What!

DRUMMER Deeny wouldn't pay them this afternoon and pushed the new charts on them. They didn't want to learn new scores, not getting paid the money owed them, so they quit.

BASS Just like that ... they quit?

PIANO This is our last night here, too. Deeny's in trouble with the union. No more gigs here until the hearin'.

BASS Awww, man ... there's always some shit with that jive-ass sucker. Is we gettin' our bread from Deeny tonight?

DRUMMER Who knows? He don't have to pay until the last performance, and the union says stay on the gig until tonight.

BASS We always gettin' put in some cross ...

PIANO Yeah, man. But juke boxes don't go on strike and Deeny knows we know it, so let's take care of business.

BASS Man, don't tell me that ... the broads can't dance to no juke box.

PIANO (*seriously*) Why not, man?

BASS It just ain't done, man. No machine ain't never goin'a take a musician's play from him when it comes to providin' music for shows.

PIANO Don't believe it, baby ... in a couple of mo' years they'll find a way. Broads will be shakin' their cans to canned music just as good as to your playin' or mine and the customers will be payin' even higher prices ... no body wins, man. Least of all us. C'mon, let's hit it ... (*he begins playing "Delilah" as* PANDORA, MAMMA TOO TIGHT *and* CURT *make their entrances. The girls wave at the* MUSICIANS *and stop at the bar, then move to a table near the bandstand.* PANDORA *places her costumes on an empty chair of a nearby table.* CURT *stands with his back to the bar*) Okay. That's better ... c'mon ... Cook! ...

BASS (*not enthused, to* MAMMA *who waves again*) Hey, pretty girl ... (ART *walks in, saunters to the cigarette machine;* CURT *joins the girls*)

CURT Hey, I wonder where everybody's at?

DRUMMER (*stopping, followed by others*) Hey ... hey ... what's the use of this fuckin' shit? ...

PIANO What's happen'n now, man? (DRUMMER *hops from stage*)
MAMMA Damn... Stew and Ronny must be late, Pan.
PANDORA (*to* BARTENDER) What happened to your boss, Deeny, Chico? (BARTENDER *ignores her*)
DRUMMER (*to* PIANO PLAYER) Not a thing, man... everything's cool... (*goes to bar, to* BARTENDER) Hey, Chico. Give me a screwdriver and charge it to your boss.
BARTENDER Deeny ain't in the charity business, baby. (ART *sits down with his friends. One of the customers leaves*)
PANDORA (*to* BARTENDER) Yeah, baby, give me the usual and give my friends what they want. Put it on my tab.
DRUMMER (*to* BARTENDER) You let me and Deeny worry about that, cool breeze. Give me a screwdriver like I said. (BARTENDER *goes behind bar and begins mixing* DRUMMER's *drink*)
BARTENDER (*sullenly, to* PANDORA) When you gonna take care of that tab, sweetcake?
PANDORA (*angry*) When your fuckin' boss pays me, mister! Now get us our drinks, please!
CURT (*to* BASS PLAYER *who stands beside instrument*) Where's Deeny? (PIANO PLAYER *has gotten off of stage and talks to* DRUMMER *at the bar. A customer goes to jukebox and looks over the selections*)
PIANO What's happen'n, man? We got to make this gig... that's what the union says.
DRUMMER Fuck the union.
BASS (*to* CURT) It's a mystery to me, Curt.
MAMMA (*to* BASS PLAYER) That number's a gassy one, honey. Pan's gonna work by that, ain't she?
BASS Looks that way, Mamma, if anybody works at all tonight.
PIANO (*to* DRUMMER) Awww, man... you know I know how you feel...
DRUMMER Well, just don't run that crap down to me. I'm just fed up. The union screws you out of your dues and the clubs fuck you every chance they get...
PIANO It ain't exactly that way... now if...
MAMMA Don't you like Pan's new number, Art? (ART *doesn't answer. The Customer drops a coin into the jukebox and punches a selection:* "Something Cool" *sung by June Christie is played*)
PANDORA (*to* ART *and* MAMMA) Can't come in here one day without some shit goin' down. Where's the brass so I can rehearse?
MAMMA They better get here soon, honey. It'll be too late after a while.
BASS (*to* PAN) Forget about it, Pan. They ain't no brass tonight. (*to* PIANO PLAYER) Well I know all that, but it's no use rehearsin' without any brass and if this is our last night anyhow...
CURT (*rising and going to the bar*) You said this is the last night, man?
PANDORA (*to* BASS PLAYER) NO BRASS!
MAMMA (*to* ART) You hear what he said?
BASS (*putting down instrument*) Hey, fix me a C.C. and ginger ale, Chico! (*customer that played records goes to the bar and sits down*)
PANDORA (*to* BARTENDER) Hey, what about our drinks, man!
BARTENDER Okay, Pandora... just a minute.
CURT Hey, fellas... what's goin' down?

(*The* MUSICIANS *tell* CURT *about the trouble as the scene plays on in center stage at the table. The conversations should overlap as they have but become increasingly rapid and confusing if necessary.*

After the MUSICIANS *are served the* BARTENDER *takes the orders at* PANDORA's *table as* CURT *continues to talk at the bar*)

PANDORA Shit... no brass... musicians quittin'... I ain't got no job no more.
MAMMA Yeah. It don't look so good but perhaps Deeny can do somethin' when he comes in...
PANDORA Deeny... shit... Deeny... all he can do!... (*furious, searching for words*) Why, shit, woman! Deeny can't even do numbers and shit cucumbers!
ART Thanks for the drink, Pan.
PANDORA Is that all you can do, man? Say thank you!
ART No. It's not the only thing.

(MAMMA *gets up and goes over to the* BASS PLAYER *who drops out of the conversation between* CURT, *the other two* MUSICIANS *and the* BARTENDER.

Another customer leaves, leaving only one sitting upon a stool, attempting to get the BARTENDER's *attention*)

BARTENDER Well look, man, I only work here. You better settle that with Deeny. (*behind the bar the phone rings. The* BARTENDER *answers*)

CURT If that's Deeny I want to talk to him.
BARTENDER Hey, man, I'm talkin' on the phone.
DRUMMER Let me talk to the mathafukker! (*he tries to reach across the bar*)
BARTENDER (*backing off*) Hey, cool it! Wait!
PIANO (*grabbing* DRUMMER's *arm*) Hold it, man!
DRUMMER Take your fuckin' hands off me, baby!
BARTENDER Wait, I said.
CURT Tell Deeny I'm waitin' for him. (DRUMMER *breaks away from* PIANO PLAYER *and begins around the bar.* BARTENDER *reaches under bar for a weapon*)
BARTENDER (*shouts*) WAIT!!! (*the scene freezes in tableau except for the* BARTENDER, PANDORA *and* CURT. *Lights go down to purples and deep shadow shades as an eerie spot plays upon the table. Occasionally from the shadows voices are heard. In shadows*) Okay, Deeny. I'll be expectin' ya.
PANDORA (*to* ART) So he's comin'.
ART Yeah, no need to wait for very long now.
PANDORA What else can you do, Art?
ART What else can I do except say thank you, you mean?
PANDORA Yeah. That's what I mean.
ART I can wait, Pandora.
PANDORA (*jolly*) What the good of waitin' when things have ta be done? Is that why you have to eat at Rescue Missions and get favors from friends, baby? Cause you waitin'? Tell me. What are you waitin' on, Art?
ART Me? I'm just waitin' so I won't jump into somethin' too fast and I think you should do the same.
PANDORA I didn't know you gave out advice too. But I wish I could take some of it. Ya see, we're already in the middle of some deep shit... There just ain't time to sit back and cool it, honey...
ART (*disregarding the ridicule in her voice, soothing*) Yes you can... just sit back and look around and wait a while. You don't have to do anything... baby, the whole world will come to you if you just sit back and be ready for it.
PANDORA (*serious*) I wish I could. But so much has to be done and we keep fallin' behind.
BARTENDER (*in shadows*) Now what can I do, man? Deeny left with Pete and he said he'd be right back and for you guys to practice with the girls.
(*One of the customers who walked out enters with a show girl. She is dark and thin and pretty in a tinseled way. They stop in the shadows and whisper and the girl separates from him, enters the light, passes through and heads toward the dressing rooms in the rear. The customer takes a seat at the bar. He is engulfed by shadows and becomes frozen in place like the others*)
PANDORA (*nodding to show girl as she passes*) Hi, Cookie. I really dig that dress, baby.
ART Things can always get worst, Pan.
PANDORA Oh, you're one of those? How can they? Just lost my job. This was to keep us goin' until you guys turned up somethin' big and I didn't even get paid for the last two weeks so I know this just means another great big zero.
ART What do you think will happen now?
PANDORA I don't know... the job Curt's got planned can't be pulled off until three more days and in a week we got to have all our money together for the restitution and juice... not to mention the goin' away money. And I'm not even goin'a get paid for the gig.
ART Haven't you got any now?
PANDORA Just a couple of hundred but we can't go into that. Got to hold onto it. We wouldn't eat if we didn't have to. We got to hold on to every cent.
BARTENDER (*in shadows*) Do you want that scotch with anything? (DRUMMER *momentarily breaks out of position*)
DRUMMER I ain't finished talkin' yet, Chico.
BARTENDER Just a minute, man. (MAMMA *breaks out of position and goes to* PANDORA)
MAMMA Lend me a dime, Pan. I got to call Shaky.
PANDORA (*fishing in her outsized purse*) You got somethin' workin', baby?
MAMMA Yeah, Slim's gonna get somethin' from Shaky.
PANDORA That's workin'. (*she gives* MAMMA *a coin.* MAMMA *enters the shadows and walks to the rear of the club.* PANDORA *notices* ART *looking at her*) Forget about her. Shaky's got her up tight. All you could do is play young lover a little. You can't support her habit, Art.
ART She can't have a habit if she's just hit the street.

PANDORA She's got one. What do you think they came in high on? In a couple more days she'll be hooked as bad as before. Shaky'll see to that.

ART What does she do it for?

PANDORA What does...? Awww, man... what kinda question is that? I thought you knew somethin', baby.

ART I tried to ask an honest question, Pan.

PANDORA Is it an honest question when you don't have anything to go by to compare her experience with yours?

ART I don't know. Is it?

PANDORA Do you know how it feels havin' somebody paw all over you everyday?

ART Well, no...

PANDORA Then you don't know that she has to use that stuff to put off the reality of it happen'n?

ART Oh, I see.

PANDORA (*bitter*) Yeah, you see. Do you see her givin' up her body everyday and murdering herself everyday? Is that what the world has brought to her, Art? That's all she can look forward to each day... killin' herself with that needle by inches. She has her fix, and maybe a bust and she has keepin' her man. She just takes her fixes to get through the day and Shaky keeps her on it so she'll need him more.

ART That's too bad.

PANDORA Wait a minute, Art. Don't sing no sad songs for that woman, you understand? She's not askin' for your pity. She's a real woman in some ways and she won't let you take it away from her by your pity. She'd spit on your pity.

ART (*annoyed*) And you? (*lights change*)

PANDORA (*fantasy*) And me?... Well I ain't no whore... I'm just makin' this money so Curt and me can get on our feet. One day we gonna own property and maybe some businesses when we get straight... and out of this town.

ART In Buffalo?

PANDORA Maybe if we decide to stay there but I'm really an entertainer. I'll show you my act one day and Curt's got a good mind. He's a good hustler but he's givin' that up after a while. He can be anything he wants. (*lights change*)

ART What does he want?

PANDORA He wants what I want.

ART How do you know?

PANDORA He tells me... We talk about it all the time.

ART Can you be sure?

PANDORA Sure?

ART Yeah... like Mamma's sure she'll always get her fix and her bail paid.

PANDORA You little smooth faced punk... wha...

ART (*cutting*) Some guys are really lucky.

PANDORA Kiss my ass, sucker!

ART Curt and Shaky are really in to somethin'.

PANDORA Yeah! Because they're men!

ART Is that what bein' a man is, bein' lucky?

PANDORA No. It's from gettin' what you want.

ART And how do you get what you want, Pan?

PANDORA You go after it.

ART And after you have it?

PANDORA Then maybe it's yours and you can do whatever you want with it.

ART And what if I wanted you, Pandora?

PANDORA (*three beat pause*) You don't have enough to give me, Art. What could you give me that would make things better for me?

ART I'm not a giver, Pan, I'm a taker.

(*Lights go up evenly. Figures become animated and resume activities. The* BARTENDER *pours drinks and nods to grumbling* MUSICIANS *and to* CURT. *A customer goes to jukebox and drops coin in. "Parisian Thoroughfare" plays. The show girl, in thin robe, revealing skimpy costume, walks from the rear and takes seat beside customer she entered with.* MAMMA TOO TIGHT *goes to the table and sits*)

MAMMA (*brightly*) What you guys been talkin' bout so long?

PANDORA Nothin' much, why?

MAMMA Oh nothin'... just thought I'd ask. But the way you and ole fuzz wuzz was goin' at it and lookin' at each other...

PANDORA Looks can't hurt you, Mamma, but your big mouth can.

MAMMA (*fake surprise*) Pan... I didn't mean...

PANDORA I'm sure you didn't, Mamma!

MAMMA (*now hurt*) Now listen, Pan. If you can't take a little teasin'... What's wrong with you? This is my first day home and you been on my ass all the time. Girl . . . you been the best friend I ever had, but lighten up.

PANDORA Awww, Mamma . . . let's not you and me start in actin' flaky . . .

ART Would you like a drink, Mamma?

MAMMA (*pleased*) Yeah . . . but you can't pry Chico from behind that bar. (ART *stands and places hand upon* MAMMA's *shoulder*)

ART That's okay. Just sit. (*he goes to bar and stands beside* CURT *who has his back to him, drinking and brooding*)

MAMMA (*to* PANDORA) Hey, he's so nice.

PANDORA See . . . I told you I wasn't tryin' to steal your little playmate.

MAMMA (*serious*) If I didn't know you was kiddin' I wouldn't take that, Pan.

PANDORA You wouldn't? . . . Well, I wasn't kiddin', broad!

MAMMA (*half-rising*) Hey, check yourself, girl. This is me! Remember? Mamma Too Tight. Don't you know me? Lil ole Queenie Bell Mack from Biloxi, Mississippi.

PANDORA Okay, Sit down before you trip over yourself. I know who you are.

MAMMA (*sitting*) And I know you too, baby. Remember I was the one who was there those times so many yesterdays ago. Remember? I was there with you holding your hand in those dark, little lonely rooms all them nights that your man was out on a job . . . Remember how we shivered together, girl? Remember how we cried together each time he got busted and sent away again . . . I'm your friend, baby . . . and you actin' like this to me?

PANDORA (*genuine*) I'm sorry, Mamma. It's just that Art. He's different. Everything seems different when he's around.

MAMMA I think I know what you mean, Pan. I think I know . . .

(*Lights dim; color-wheel still throws pastel shadows.* CURT *and* ART *stand in spot at end of bar. In the shadows there are rustles from the other people and lighted cigarettes arc through the gloom toward mouths which suck at them like spiders draining fireflies.* CURT *turns*)

CURT Hey, Art. Sorry to put you through all this hassle but some bad shit is goin' down, man. I'm really gettin' worried . . . If things keep breakin' bad like this . . .

ART Don't worry about me, Curt. I'm just along for the ride. Try and get yourself together.

It don't matter to me what you have to go through to get yourself straight, man. Just work it on out. (*spot off* ART *and* CURT. *Spot on show girl and customer*)

CUSTOMER How 'bout it, sugar?

SHOW GIRL Are you kiddin', man?

CUSTOMER (*whining*) Well Christ . . . twenty-five bucks . . . what's it lined with . . . gold or somethin'?

SHOW GIRL You see those two broads over at that table? (*lights on* PANDORA *and* MAMMA)

CUSTOMER Yeah. You suggestin' that I hit on them?

SHOW GIRL Yeah. Do that. The one in the black dress won't even speak to you unless you're ready to leave a hundred or more . . . and besides . . . she has to like your type first. The other one might consider it for fifty.

CUSTOMER Who's the girl in the black dress?

SHOW GIRL That's *Pandora*. She headlines the Revue. You have to give her twenty bucks just to get her phone number. So why don't you go hit on her? (*lights off. Spot on* BARTENDER)

BARTENDER You call yourselves artists and then you want me to bleed for you? What kinda crap is that?

DRUMMER (*in shadows*) Listen you jive time whisky-pourer. We are artists and I don't care what you call us or how you bleed. It's cats like you and your boss who make us all the time have to act like thugs, pimps and leeches to just make it out here in this world.

BARTENDER So why ya tellin' me? So make it some other way?

PIANO PLAYER (*in shadows*) It's just impossible to talk to you people . . . it's just impossible to be heard any more. (*spot off* BARTENDER. *Spot on* CURT *and* ART)

CURT Yeah . . . when I first met her, Art. You should of seen her. It was a joint somethin' like this . . . (*lights off; spot picks up* PANDORA *standing in the door looking younger, nervous.* CURT *crosses stage to meet her as he speaks. Entering light*) She was just eighteen . . . had the prettiest little pair of tits poking right out at me . . . sharp enough to put your eyes out. (*he takes* PANDORA *in his arms and kisses her violently. She resists but he is overwhelming*)

PANDORA (*young voice*) I beg your pardon, mister.

CURT I said that you're beautiful . . . that I

want you... that you are mine forever... that it will always be this way for you, for you are mine. (*he brutally subdues her. Her hair falls across her face. Her face has that expression that prisoners sometime have when they are shifted without prior explanation from an old cell to an unfamiliar cell, equally as old*)

PANDORA   Are you the man I'm to love?

CURT (*dragging her into the shadows*)   Don't talk of something you'll never know anything about... (*they speak from the shadows now, facing the audience*)

PANDORA   I can't love you? I can't love you if I even wanted?...

CURT   You are mine... my flesh... my body... you are in my keeping.

PANDORA   Is it so much to ask for... just to be your woman?

CURT   You will do as I say... your flesh, your soul, your spirit is at my command... I possess you...

PANDORA   First there were others... now there is you... always always the same for me... (*lights change*)

CURT (*in shadows, walking toward* ART)   Yeah... she was ready... has always been. (*spot on* ART. CURT *enters light*)

ART   Pandora's a beautiful girl, Curt. You're lucky, man, to have her. I envy you.

CURT   Thanks, Art.

ART   Don't mention it, don't mention it at all. (*lights go down. Come up with* SHAKY *sitting at the table with* MAMMA *and* PANDORA)

SHAKY   What's happen'n, baby?

MAMMA   Nothin' yet, Shaky. Give me time. The joint ain't even open yet.

SHAKY   Don't take too long, woman.

MAMMA   Give me time, Shaky. Why you got to come on so strong, man? You know I always take care of business. You know I got to get used to it agin. Didn't I set up that thing between you and Slim?

SHAKY   Yeah, baby. But that's my department. You take care of business on your side of the street. (*the* BASS PLAYER *comes over to the table. To* BASS PLAYER) Let's take a walk, poppa.

BASS   After you, Shake Shake.

MAMMA   I'll be here, Shaky.

SHAKY   Let's hope you're either here or there... okay?

MAMMA   Shaky... you're goin' too fast. Don't push me so hard.

SHAKY (*leaving*)   Tonight, baby. One hundred stone cold dollars, baby. (*light on show girl and customer*)

SHOW GIRL   They're alone. Why not now?

CUSTOMER   Okay... okay... twenty-five you get... after the show tonight. (*lights off; spot on* CURT *and* ART)

CURT   When I saw you in action, Art. I said to myself I could really use that kid. Man, you're like a little brother to me now, man. I watch the way you act around people. You think on your feet and study them like a good gambler does. You're like me in a lot of ways. Man, we're a new breed, ya know. Renegades. Rebels. There's no rules for us... we make them as we break them.

ART   Sounds kind'a romantic, Curt.

CURT   And why shouldn't it? Man, this ain't a world we built so why should we try and fit in it? We have to make it over the best we can... and we are the ones to do it. We are, man, we are! (*spot on* MAMMA)

MAMMA   I don't know why I'm this way... I just am. Is it because my name is different and I am different? Is it because I talk like a spade?

PANDORA (*from shadows*)   Take a look at that! Just because this white broad's been hangin' out with us for a couple of years she's goin' ta blame that bad talk on us. (*light on table. To* MAMMA) When you brought your funky ass from Mississippi woman we couldn't even understand you... sheet... we taught you how to speak if anything!

MAMMA (*out at audience*)   All I know is that I'm here and that's where I'm at... and I'll be here until somethin' happens... I wish Shaky wouldn't push me so... I want to be good for him... I want him to be my man and care about me a little... (ART *brings* MAMMA *her drink.* CURT *sits with him at the table*)

CURT (*to* PANDORA)   Don't look so pissed off, honey.

PANDORA   Why shouldn't I? Everything's gone wrong. (CURT *stands and takes* PANDORA's *arm*)

CURT   C'mere, baby. Let me talk to you. (*they walk into the shadows*)

ART   Just saw Shaky. He didn't stay long.

MAMMA   Nawh. He's gone to take care of some business. Wants me to stay here and take care of mine.

ART   I guess that's what you should do then.

MAMMA Should I? He's rushin' me too fast, that's what he's doin'. He knows I take a little time gettin' right inside before I can go back to work but he's pushin' me. It's Curt's and Pan's fault... they're desperate for money and they're pressin' Shaky.
ART Maybe you should try and talk to him or to Curt.
MAMMA It wouldn't do any good!
ART It wouldn't? If you were my girl I'd listen to what you had to say.
MAMMA Oh, man, knock off the bullshit!
ART But I would, really.
MAMMA (*hesitant*) You would? I bet you're full of shit.
ART Sure I would. I look young but I know what you need... and I know what you want.
MAMMA (*giggling*) You do? (*peering over her glass*) What do I need and want, Fuzz Wuzz?
ART Understanding.
MAMMA What!
ART (*soft*) Understanding.
MAMMA Sheet...
ART (*softer*) Understanding. (*lights down; spot on* CURT *and* PANDORA)
PANDORA I'm gettin' fed up with all this shit, Curt. We seem to be goin' backwards, not forward.
CURT I know that, baby. But things will get straightened out. You know it has to. When the job...
PANDORA (*cutting*) The job! Yeah... it better be somethin', Curt, or you're in some big trouble... We're both in some big trouble... what'd I do without you?
CURT If anything happens, baby... let Art take care of things...
PANDORA Art?
CURT Yeah.
PANDORA (*afraid*) But I'm your woman, remember?
CURT He's like a little brother to me. I've already spoken to him about it... you can get a real gig in a show or somethin' and share an apartment with him. He'll look out for you while I'm away. Go up to Frisco and wait for me... Art's got a head and he can look after things until I get out... then things will be okay again. But that's if the worst happens and we don't get the juice money...
PANDORA (*struck*) You think that much of him, Curt?

CURT I told you he's like my brother, baby. I've been waitin' a long time for a real cat to come along... we're on our way now... (*lights lower; spot on table as* SHAKY *enters*)
SHAKY (*to* ART) Hey, what you say your name was?
ART (*smiling, holding out his hand*) It's Art, Shaky, you know I met...
SHAKY (*cutting*) Yeah, I know... what you doin' takin' up my ole lady's time? (BASS PLAYER *enters*)
ART I was only sittin' here and bought her a drink. She rode over in my car with Curt and Pan.
SHAKY That's what I mean, man... takin' up her time.
MAMMA Shaky... stop it! He wasn't doin' nothin'... he's a friend of Curt's man...
SHAKY SHUT UP!
MAMMA You don't understand... (*he slaps her.* ART *grabs his arm and pushes him sprawling across a chair.* SHAKY *regains his balance and begins to lunge but is caught by* CURT)
CURT HEY, COOL IT, MAN! What's goin' on?
SHAKY This little punk friend of yours doesn't like what I do with my woman.
BASS PLAYER Why don't you forget it, Shaky. If it had been me I would of done the same thing. Forget it. It ain't worth it.
MAMMA (*scared*) He don't understand.
SHAKY You'll see what I understand when we get home, bitch!
ART (*putting out his hand*) I'm sorry, man. It was my fault. I had... (SHAKY *knocks* ART's *hand aside and turns, being led toward the door by the* MUSICIAN)
SHAKY (*to* ART) I'll see you later.
CURT Hey, Shaky. C'mere, man. It don't mean nothin'.

(*They exit.* PANDORA *takes a seat.* CURT *goes to the bar and answers the questions of the* MUSICIANS *and the* BARTENDER. *The show girl goes to the rear of the club and the customer orders another drink*)

MAMMA He just don't understand... he can't understand and he can't give me any understanding...
PANDORA Who don't understand, Mamma?
MAMMA Shaky... he just don't understand... he should try and understand me more.

PANDORA Girl, you so stoned you're not makin' any sense. He understands, Mamma. he understands you perfectly.

MAMMA He can't, Pan. He can't or I wouldn't feel this way about him now.

ART Maybe you're changin'.

PANDORA Oh, man, you're full of it!

ART You're cynical but not that hard, Pandora.

PANDORA Man, I've seen it all. I don't have to be hard . . . I just use what I know.

ART Have you seen everything, Pan?

PANDORA Yes!

ART Then you've seen me before?

PANDORA (*staring*) Yeah . . . I've seen you before. There's a you standin' on every corner with his hands in his pockets and his fly half unzipped . . . there's a you in every drunk tank in every city . . . there's a you sniffin' around moochin' drinks and kissin' ass and thinkin' he's a make-out artist. Yeah . . . I've seen you before, punk!

MAMMA He just don't understand . . .

ART No, you've never seen me before, Pandora. I'm goin'a tell you something.

PANDORA (*sarcastic*) What are you goin'a tell me, Art?

ART That I'm goin'a change your life.

PANDORA WHAT!!!

(*Lights go up with a startling flash.* DEENY *and the bouncer,* PETE, *enter.* DEENY, *in black glasses, sports an ascot and a cummerbund under his sport coat. In the thin dress she entered in, the show girl walks from the rear and takes a seat beside the customer.* MAMMA TOO TIGHT *stands and* CURT *nearly bowls over a customer on his way to meet* DEENY *in center stage in front of* PANDORA'*s table.* PANDORA *jumps to her feet beside* MAMMA, *followed by* ART)

CURT Deeny!

(*The* BASS PLAYER *enters, and the* DRUMMER *and* PIANO PLAYER *hurry over. Behind the bar the* BARTENDER *stands tensed; the* BASS PLAYER *climbs upon the stage and begins zippering his bass fiddle into its cloth bag*)

DEENY Keep it, Curt! I don't want to hear it. I just came from the union and I've taken all the crap I'm gonna . . . the show's closed. (*chorus of yells*)

CURT Deeny, what you take us for?

PANDORA Hey, man . . . let's go in the back and talk . . .

DRUMMER (*pushing his way around the* PIANO PLAYER) Yeah, Deeny, I want to talk to you!

DEENY I just don't want to hear it from any of you. OKAY? . . . OKAY! Now everybody . . . this club is closin'. Ya hear? Everybody out inside of ten minutes . . . understand? This is my property. Get off it inside of ten minutes or I'm callin' the cops . . . your things and you out . . . hit the street . . . that means everybody! (*another chorus of yells from nearly everyone. The customers hurry out the exit and the show girl joins the group*)

BASS PLAYER (*to other* MUSICIANS) Hey, fellas, I'm splittin' . . . what about you? (MAMMA *turns and goes over to him*)

DRUMMER Man, what about my pay?

DEENY Take your bitchin' to the union, fellah. They instigated this hassle.

PANDORA We don't know nothin' bout no union, Deeny . . .

DEENY (*sarcastic*) I know you don't, sugar. But you girls should get organized . . . try to get paid hourly and get off the quota system and you'd . . .

CURT Watch your mouth, mathafukker!

BOUNCER You'd better watch yours!

DEENY (*to* BARTENDER) HEY, CHICO, CALL THE COPS! YOU JUST CAN'T REASON WITH SOME JERKS! CALL THEM NOW! (*the* BARTENDER *dials*)

PANDORA (*to* CURT) What we gonna do, baby? . . .

CURT Quiet!

PANDORA But your case, honey . . .

BARTENDER (*on phone*) Yeah . . . there's trouble at The Strip Club on Western . . . yeah . . .

(DEENY *tries to push his way past but* CURT *blocks him. The* BOUNCER *moves to shove* CURT *out of the way but* ART *steps in as the four confront each other, and the girls back off. The* PIANO PLAYER *has coaxed the* DRUMMER *to join the* BASS PLAYER *upon the stage, packing away his equipment. At a run, the show girl rushes to the rear of the club as the* BARTENDER *hangs up the phone. As the other* MUSICIANS *pack up, the* PIANO PLAYER *comes back to the group*)

PIANO Deeny, you just can't do this. This ain't right about us. We stuck by you for below scale wages, riskin' our own needs with the union to keep you in business, until you got on your feet. And still we never got paid on time. Now I hear you gonna put some names in here and clean up on the rep we made for you.

BOUNCER Shut up, mister. You're not supposed to be here right now, remember?

PANDORA (*furious*) You owe me for two and a half weeks, man!

DEENY (*trying to get by again*) Sorry, baby. Come around some time and maybe we can work out somethin'.

CURT I know why you doin' this, Deeny. Don't pull that union shit on me! You want all the girls to work for you ... on the block like tramps for ten and fifteen dollars a trick. Pan, Mamma and all the other broads. I'd die before I'd let you put my woman on the street for ten tricks a day. Why you got to be so fuckin' greedy, man? You ain't right! You already got six girls now.

BOUNCER Just say he has taste and discrimination, Curt. You know he wants your old lady because...

DEENY (*cutting*) Shut up all of you! And are you goin' to get out of my way?

MAMMA (*from bandstand*) Deeny. Who you think you are?

DEENY (*to* MAMMA) You know who I am, you stupid country cunt. And if you want to stay on the streets and keep that junkie ole man of yours cool, just keep your mouth out of this! That way you won't get your legs broke and...

CURT (*cutting*) I know why you doin' this, Deeny. (SHAKY *enters. The show girl rushes from the rear with costumes in arms and exits, speaking to no one*)

SHAKY Did I hear somebody say they gonna break Mamma's legs? (*there is general bedlam with shouts and near screaming*)

DRUMMER (*exiting*) I'm goin' ta take this farther than to the union, Deeny!

BOUNCER You can take it to your mother, punk! (DRUMMER *drops equipment and lunges toward* BOUNCER *but* PIANO PLAYER *grabs him and holds.* BASS PLAYER *helps*)

BASS PLAYER (*exiting with* DRUMMER) Hey Deeny, you're wrong! You're dead wrong, man!

PIANO (*to* CURT *and* PANDORA) Cool it. Let's all split. This ain't nothin' but a big bust. (*it becomes suddenly quiet and the* BARTENDER, *a club in hand, comes around the bar and stands behind* CURT *and* ART. SHAKY *stands to the side of* DEENY *and the* BOUNCER. MAMA *is on the bandstand, wide-eyed, and* PANDORA *is down-stage glowering at her enemies. Leaving*) I'll see you guys. (*seeing* SHAKY) Hey, man. It ain't worth it.

SHAKY I'll get in touch with you, okay?

PIANO C'mon, man. I don't like what I see.

SHAKY Make it! Be a good friend and make it. (PIANO PLAYER *exits. It is even more quiet. Very low, from somewhere outside, the theme is heard as each group eyes the other and tenses*)

PANDORA (*spitting it out, violent as unsuspected spit splattering a face*) Fuck you, Deeny! Fuck you! Fuck you! FUCK YOU!

DEENY(*frenzied*) YOU LITTLE TRAMPY BITCH... YOU...

(CURT *smashes him in the mouth as he reaches for* PANDORA. DEENY *falls back beside the table, grabs a glass and hurls it into* CURT's *face, shattering it.* CURT *launches himself upon him and pummels* DEENY *to the floor.*

Meanwhile, the BOUNCER *and* ART *fight in center stage.* SHAKY *is struck almost immediately from behind by the* BARTENDER's *club.* ART, *seeing the* BARTENDER *advancing on* CURT's *rear, breaks away and desperately kicks out at the* BARTENDER. *With a screech he doubles over and grabs his groin. The* BOUNCER *seizes* ART *from behind, about the throat, in an armlock, and begins strangling him.* PANDORA, *who has taken off her shoes after kicking* DEENY *several times as* CURT *beats him upon the floor, attacks the* BOUNCER *from behind and repeatedly strikes him about the head with her shoe heels. The* BOUNCER *loosens his grip on* ART *and grabs* PANDORA *and punches her. She falls.* ART, *gasping, reaches down for the* BARTENDER's *dropped club, picks it up and turns and beats the* BOUNCER *to the floor.*

All the while MAMMA TOO TIGHT *screams.*

With face bloodied from splintered glass, CURT *has beaten* DEENY *into unconsciousness and staggers over and pulls* PANDORA *up.*

Sirens, screeches and slamming car doors are heard from outside. Shouts)

CURT (*towing* PANDORA) C'mon, Art! Pull yourself together. The cops are here. (ART *staggers over to* SHAKY *and tries to lift him but he is too weak.* MAMMA, *crying and screaming, jumps from the bandstand and pulls at* SHAKY. *Heading for the rear*) He's too heavy, Art. Leave him. Grab Mamma and let's get out the back way. MOVE! C'MON, MAN, MOVE! (*dazed, but following orders,* ART *grabs* MAMMA'*s arms and struggles with her*)

MAMMA (*resisting*) NO! NO! I CAN'T LEAVE HIM LIKE THAT!

CURT (*exiting*) Bring her, Art. Out the back way to the car.

MAMMA (*being dragged out by* ART) My first day out . . . my first day . . . (*They exit and immediately the stage blackens, then the tumble of running feet, then*)

VOICE CHRIST! (*more heavy running, then stop*) Hey, call a couple of ambulances . . . Emergency!

(*Curtain*)

ACT THREE

Scene One

TIME: *three days later. Afternoon.*

SCENE: CURT'*s apartment. He and* RICH *play chess as in act one. The bed is lowered and* MAMMA TOO TIGHT *sleeps with the covers pulled up to her chin as if she is cold. The radio is off and the California sunshine glistens in the clean room. The room looks sterile, unlived in and motel-like without the lighting of the first act.*

CURT *wears two band-aids upon his face, one upon his forehead, the other on the bridge of his nose.*

CURT (*bored*) It'll be mate in two moves, Rich. Do you want to play it out?

RICH Nawh, man. I ain't up to it.

CURT (*sitting back*) The last three days have just taken everything out of me, man.

RICH Yeah. They been pretty rough. (CURT *stands, stretches and walks across the stage*) Hey, man. Is there any more beer?

CURT Nawh. Pan and Art's bringing some in with them when they come.

RICH (*muttering*) Yeah . . . when they get here.

CURT (*noticing* RICH'*s tone*) What did you say, man?

RICH Oh, Nothin', man.

CURT (*sharply*) You're a liar . . . I heard what you said!

RICH (*sullen*) I ain't goin'a be many more of them liars, Curt.

CURT (*gesturing*) Awww, man. Forget it . . . you know how I feel with Deeny in a coma from his concussion for the past three days and me not knowin' if he's goin' ta press charges finally or die.

RICH Yeah, man. I'm a bit edgy myself. Forget about what I said. (CURT *returns to the couch and sprawls back*)

CURT But I'd like to know what you meant by it, Rich.

RICH (*seeing no way out*) Now, Curt. You and I been friends since were young punks stealin' hub caps and tires together, right? Remember that time you, me and the guys gang banged that Pechuco broad? . . . And the Dog Town boys came up and we had that big rumble and they killed Sparky?

CURT (*sensing something coming*) How can I forget it . . . I served my first stretch behind it for stabbin' that Mexican kid, Manuel.

RICH Yeah. That was a good time ago and Manuel ain't no kid no more . . . he got killed in Korea.

CURT Yeah. But, tell me. What do you have to say, good buddy?

RICH (*pausing, then serious*) It's about this guy Art and Pandora, man.

CURT What do you mean, man?

RICH Man . . . I don't mean there's anything goin' on yet . . . but each afternoon he's taken Pandora out for the past three days they been gettin' back later . . . and . . .

CURT And what, Rich!

RICH And the way she looks at him, Curt.

CURT (*disgusted and angry*) Awww, man . . . I thought I knew you better.

RICH Well I told you that I didn't think that they were doin' anything really.

CURT But, what? That he drives her up to Sunset Strip to keep her dates with the big tricks . . . you know how much dough she brings back, man?

RICH (*resolutely*) Yeah, man. Sometimes over a hundred dollars for one trick.

CURT So you can't hurry those people for that kinda bread, man.

RICH (*trying to be understood*) But I wasn't talkin' about the tricks, Curt. I don't think they're holdin' back any money on you.

CURT Than what are you talkin' 'bout?

RICH About that little jive-ass square gettin' next to your woman, that's what!

CURT Now listen, Rich. We're friends and

all that but that little jive-ass square as you call him is just like a brother to me... and we been in some tighter things than you and me will ever be in.

RICH (*obviously hurt*) Well, forget it!

CURT No, let's not forget it. You're accusing my wife of jivin' around on me. You know that Pan's the straightest broad you'll ever find. That's why I married her. You know if we couldn't have gotten another man that she would have gone on the job and been as good as most men. She and I are a team. What could she gain by messin' 'round on me with my ace buddy?

RICH Forget it, I said.

CURT Nawh, Rich. I don't want to. I know what's really buggin' you. Ever since Shaky got busted at the Club and they found all that smack on him you been buggin' Mamma to be your woman 'cause you know that with Shaky's record he won't be hittin' the streets again for at least ten years. But you're wrong on two counts 'cause we're bailin' out Shaky tonight and takin' him with us and Mamma don't want you 'cause she wants Art but he don't go for her.

RICH (*getting to his feet*) I'll see you, man. Between your broad and that cat you can't think any more! (CURT *reaches for* RICH's *shirt front;* RICH *throws his hands off*) Take it easy, Curt. You already won a close one this week. And your guardian angel ain't around to sneak punch people. (CURT *stares at him and steps back*)

MAMMA (*from bag*) Hey, what's all that shoutin' about?

CURT Nothin', baby. Rich and I are just crackin' jokes.

MAMMA (*sitting up*) Curt, I wonder if...

CURT No, Mamma. You can't have no fix. Remember what I told you? You don't turn no tricks in town 'cause you're hot behind Shaky's bust so you don't need any heroin, right? You're on holiday and besides, you're full of codein now... that's enough...

MAMMA But I would be good if I could get some. I wouldn't worry about Shaky so much and I'd feel...

CURT You just come out of the joint clean, Mamma. You don't need anything but to keep cool.

MAMMA (*pouting*) But I got the sixteen hundred dollars that Shaky had stashed at our pad. I could buy it okay, Curt.

CURT Forget it. That money is with the other broad. We all takin' a trip with that. Besides... Shaky had over two thousand bucks worth of stuff in the pad and we sellin' it tonight so we can bail him out so he can leave with us... (MAMMA *jumps out of bed in a thin gown*)

MAMMA (*delighted*) You are? Then he'll be home soon?

CURT Yeah. Then we all make it before Deeny comes out his coma or croaks. Now get back in bed before Rich grabs you!

MAMMA (*playful*) Rich, you better not. Shaky will be home soon.

RICH (*teasing*) Sheet, woman. I don't care about old ass Shaky. C'mon, baby, why don't you get yourself a young stud?

MAMMA (*getting in bed*) When I get one it won't be you.

RICH (*serious*) Then who?

CURT (*mutters*) I told Art and Pan that we need the car this evening to drop off the stuff. After that it'll be time to get ready for the job.

RICH (*bitterly, to* MAMMA) So he's got to you, too.

MAMMA Nobody's got to me. What'chou talkin' 'bout, Rich? Art's been stayin' over to Shaky and my place for the last couple of nights while I stayed here. How can he get...

RICH (*cutting*) How did you know I was talkin' about Art?

MAMMA Cause you got Art on the brain, that's why!

CURT I thought we dropped that, Rich.

RICH (*to* MAMMA) If you're goin'a get somebody young... get a man... not some little book readin' faggot...

MAMMA (*red faced, to* RICH) Oh, go fuck yourself, man! (*she covers her head*)

RICH Okay, man. We got a lot to do tonight, so I'll lay off.

(*Through the back curtain the outside kitchen door can be seen opening. Dusk is come and* ART *enters first with a large bag;* PANDORA *follows, closes the door and purposely bumps against him as she passes. She wears dark glasses, her pants and boots*)

ART Hey, you almost made me drop this! Where should I put it? (PANDORA *enters front room smiling*)

PANDORA Hi, honey, Hello, Rich. (*She

walks over to CURT, *kisses him and places money in his hand*)

CURT Hey, pretty baby. (*he pulls her to him, gives her an extended kiss and breaks it, looking over* PANDORA's *shoulders at* RICH *who looks away*) Everything okay?

PANDORA Smooth as Silky Sullivan.

(*In the kitchen* ART *is taking items from the bag.* CURT *hands back the money to* PANDORA)

CURT Here, Pan, put this in the box with the rest.

PANDORA Okay. (*she walks past bed and looks down*) What's wrong with Mamma?

CURT Rich's been tryin' to lover her up.

RICH She won't go for my program, baby.

PANDORA (*entering the kitchen*) That's too bad... you better cultivate some charm, Rich.

RICH Yeah, that's what's happen'n. I'm not one of the lucky ones... some people don't need it.

PANDORA (*going to* ART) Let me take in the beer, Art. You put the frozen food in the refrigerator and the canned things in the cupboard. (ART *pulls her to him and kisses her. Taking breath*) Hand me the glasses, will ya? (*they kiss again, she responding this time, then she pushes him away and begins fixing beer for* CURT *and* RICH)

CURT Hey, Mamma. You want any beer?

MAMMA (*under the cover*) No, no. (PANDORA *serves* CURT *and* RICH *then climbs the stairs and enters the dressing room.* ART *comes out of the kitchen*)

RICH How you feel, Art?

ART Okay. Hollywood's an interesting place. First job I ever had just drivin' somebody around.

CURT Hope it's your last, Art. With this job tonight and my cut from sellin' Shaky's heroin we'll be just about in. Might even go into business back East.

ART Yeah? I hope so.

CURT We already got almost twenty-four hundred with Shaky's money we found at his place and the bread we've been able to hustle the last few days. After tonight we'll be set.

RICH Yeah. After tonight you'll be set.

CURT (*looking at* RICH) It's too bad you won't come with us, Rich. But your share will fix you up out here okay.

RICH Fix me up? Ha ha... I'll probably shoot that up in smack inside of several months ... but if I make it I'll probably be lookin' you up in two more years when my probation's up. No use ruin'n a good thing. When I cut this town loose I want to be clean. I just hope all goes well with you.

ART (*smiling*) Why shouldn't it?

CURT Yeah, Rich, why shouldn't it?

RICH Funny things happen to funny-style people, ya know.

CURT Yeah. Too bad you won't be comin' along... we need a clown in our show. (RICH *watches* ART *studying the chess game*)

RICH Do you see anything I missed, good buddy?

ART Oh, I don't know.

RICH You know I seldom beat Curt. Why don't you play him?

ART (*still looking at board*) Maybe I will when we find time.

CURT What would you have done from there, Art?

ART It's according to what side I'm on.

CURT You have the black. White's going to mate you in two moves.

ART He is?

RICH Yeah. He is. (ART *reaches over and picks up the black king*)

ART Most kings need a queen to be most powerful but others do the best they can. (*he places the king upon another square*) That's what I'd do, Rich.

CURT (*perceiving*) Yeah. I see... I see...

RICH Say, why'd you move there?... He can't move now... he can't put himself in check...

ART (*as* RICH *stares at him*) Yeah, Rich?

CURT (*matter-of-factly*) A stalemate.

RICH (*muttering*) I should of seen that. (*to* ART) How did you... why...

ART When you play the game you look for any break you can make.

CURT We should play sometime, Art.

ART I'm looking forward to it, Curt. But you name the time.

CURT (*standing*) I'll do that. HEY, PANDORA! We got to go! (PANDORA *comes to the top of the stairs. She has changed into a simple dress*)

PANDORA We goin' some place?

CURT I got to drop Shaky's stuff off and go down to the bail bondsman and the lawyer. I want you to drive. C'mon, Rich. Pan will sit in the car down the street in the next block and you and me will walk up the street talkin' about baseball, understand? On the corner of Adams and Crenshaw we'll meet a man and hit a grand slam.

RICH Yeah, I hope so, brother.

CURT It's trip time from here on in, baby.

PANDORA (*excited*) Wait until I get my coat.

CURT (*in good humor*) Let's go, woman. It's eighty degrees outside and we might be the hottest thing in L.A. but it just ain't that warm. Let's go, now. See you, Art. (*going to* ART) Oh, I almost forgot the car keys.

ART (*handing him the keys*) See you guys.

CURT (*hands keys to* PANDORA) You'll watch the phone, okay?

ART Sure, good buddy, I'll see to the phone.

CURT If Mamma wakes up and wants a fix don't give in to her.

ART I'll try not to.

CURT (*serious*) I mean it, Art.

ART (*smiling*) I'm dead serious, man.

PANDORA See you later, Art.

ART See you later, Pan. Good-bye, Curt. Good-bye, Rich.

(*The trio exit and* ART *goes to the radio and switches it on. It plays the theme as he enters the kitchen and gets himself a beer. He comes from the kitchen drinking from the bottle and climbs the bathroom stairs. His shadow is seen lifting and then dialing. His voice is muffled by the music and by his whisper; nothing is understood.*

After the shadow hangs up, ART *returns to the living room and descends the stairs. He sits upon the bed and shakes* MAMMA TOO TIGHT)

MAMMA (*being shaken*) Huh! I don't want any beer. (ART *shakes her once more. She uncovers her head*) Oh, Art. It's you. Where's everybody? (*he doesn't answer, looks at her. Evening comes and the room blackens*) I'm glad you woke me. I always like to talk to you but I guess I bug you since you don't say too much to me. Why ain't you sayin' nothin' now? (*three beat pause*)

ART (*laughing*) Ha ha ha...ha ha... Ma-ma Too Tight!...ha ha ha...

MAMMA You said it! Sometimes you have such a nice look on your face and now...you look different...(*pause*)...like you so happy you could scream...You never looked at me like this before, Art, never. (*in total blackness as the music plays*) You said Shaky wouldn't be back?...He won't?...I don't care as long as you don't go away...You know...you understand me. It's like you can look inside my head...Oh how did you know? Just a little bit? More? You say I can have a fix anytime I want?...Oh!...you understand me, don't cha? Don't let Curt know...you say don't worry about Curt...don't care what anybody thinks or says except you?...(*silence, pause*) Oh I feel so good now...I didn't know but I was hoping...I didn't know, honey... OH ART!...Ahhhh...now I can feel you oozing out of me...and I'm glad so glad... it's good...

Scene Two

PANDORA *leans against the kitchen door as the light go up. The atmosphere of the first act is re-created by the lights and music. The bed has been put up and* ART *sits upon the couch.* PANDORA *has been crying and what can be seen of her face around her dark glasses appears shocked. She walks to the center of the room and faces* ART)

PANDORA Art...Art...they got them. They got Curt and Rich...with all that stuff on them. The cops were waitin' on them. They busted them with all those narcotics...we'll never see them again.

ART (*rising*) We're hot, Pandora. We got to get out of town.

PANDORA They got 'em, don't you hear me, Art? What can we do?

ART Nothin'...we got to make it before Curt or Rich break and the cops are kickin' that door in.

PANDORA You said nothin'? But we... what do you mean? We got to do somethin'! (*crying*) We can't just let it happen to them... we got to do somethin' like Curt would do if it was one of us...Art! Art! DON'T JUST STAND THERE! (*he slaps her viciously, knocking off her glasses, exposing her blackened eyes*)

ART (*commanding*) Get a hold of yourself, Pandora. You've had a bad experience. (*she holds her face and looks dazed*) Now listen to me. Mamma has gone over to her place to pack and as soon as she gets back we're all leaving.

PANDORA (*dazed*) Mamma is packin'?... Did Curt tell her to pack?

ART You know he didn't. Now as soon as she gets here I want us to be packed, okay?

PANDORA But...Art...packed...where we goin'?

ART To Buffalo, baby. Where else?

PANDORA To Buffalo?

ART That's what I said. Now go up in your dressing room and get your case. (*a knock comes from the front door*) That's Mamma already...we're runnin' late, woman. C'mon, get a move on. (*he shoves her*) MOVE! GET A MOVE ON, PANDORA! (*she stumbles over the first step, catches her balance and begins climbing.* ART *looks after her*) Oh...Pandora...(*she turns and looks vacantly at him*)...Don't forget your box! (*as she turns and climbs the last steps,* ART *saunters to the radio as the knock sounds again. Instantaneously, as he switches the radio off, the stage is thrown in complete blackness*)

Ted Shine (1931–)

Herbert III

1974

Herbert III is not to be mistaken for a play about the black matriarchy. It is not. Although Margarette is concerned with the well-being of her sons, the motherly instinct that she displays is not necessarily limited to black women. The play is concerned with character rather than plot, and deals with that stage in a marriage in which man and wife find it more and more difficult to communicate. Their love has been temporarily suppressed; their interests are different, and they find each other boring. Sex is no longer important to Margarette. As a substitute she has involved herself with home, church, and her sons. Herbert is all but ignored. Husband and wife offer contrasting approaches to rearing their offspring. Herbert is more progressive, more attuned to the times; he has experienced similar frustrations in his youth and has instilled in his sons confidence in their manhood. He sees them as men. Margarette, the conservative, sees them as children whom she must continue to protect from a hostile and dangerous world. She feels that Herbert is responsible for their leaving, and subconsciously punishes him by refusing to submit to his amorous desires. Ironically, she is still sexually attracted to him, although she struggles not to be. Her concern over Herbert III's whereabouts is a normal one, but her approach is amusing. Since the play does not evolve around a tightly knit plot, what is there that sustains the reader's interest?

A prolific writer for television and stage, many of Mr. Shine's plays have been performed in Southern colleges and universities as well as off-Broadway and by the Negro Ensemble Company in New York City. A native of Dallas, Texas, Mr. Shine has taught at Dillard and Howard universities and is currently at Prairie View A & M College in Texas. He received his Master of Arts degree from the University of Iowa in playwriting and his Ph.D. from the University of California at Santa Barbara.

Herbert III

CAST

MARGARETTE, *a loving mother in her late thirties*
HERBERT, *her husband*

PLACE   Dallas, Texas. The Jackson's bedroom in their home in Oak Cliff
TIME   The present

(*It is 2:50 A.M. Night shadows fill the bedroom. Soft light spills in through a window. A double bed reveals two people.* MARGARETTE *shifts restlessly; rolls over and pulls the covers to her side revealing the body of her husband,* HERBERT. *After a moment he pulls the covers back to his side. Pause.* MARGARET *extends an arm, grasps the clock that rests on the nightstand beside the bed. She looks at it, then slowly sits up in bed. She yawns, composes herself, then climbs out of bed and exits into the hall. A light is turned on in the hallway. Pause. The sound of a toilet flushing. The offstage light is turned off. She enters the room, crosses to the window and looks out, then returns to the bed and sits. She looks at the clock again*)

MARGARETTE   Herbert? (*shakes her husband*) Her—buuuuuuuutt!

HERBERT   Huh?

MARGARETTE   You sleep?

HERBERT   Huh?

MARGARETTE   Wake up, Herbert!

HERBERT   Huh?

MARGARETTE   It's near three and Herbert the Third ain't home.

HERBERT   Ummmm-huh . . . (*he rolls over*)

MARGARETTE   (*shaking him again*) Herbert, listen to me! I'm worried. It's three o'clock and my baby ain't home yet.

HERBERT   Ummmmmmmm . . .

MARGARETTE   Don't you care what happens to your son? (*shakes him*)

HERBERT   (*half asleep*)   He's . . . okay, Margaree . . .

MARGARETTE   How you know? What's he doin' out this time-a-mornin'?

HERBERT   He say . . . he goin' bowlin'.

MARGARETTE   *This* time-a-mornin'? Somethin' musta happened to that boy!

HERBERT   He . . . alright . . .

MARGARETTE   How you know? He could be half dead somewhere—and you don't even care!

HERBERT   Gon' back to sleep . . .

MARGARETTE   How can I sleep? (*she picks up the phone, then grabs the telephone directory*)

HERBERT   (*rising slowly*)   What you doin', Margaree?

MARGARETTE   I'm gon' call the police!

HERBERT   Jesus! (*she tosses the phone book aside*)   What for, Margaree?

MARGARETTE   To see if he's in jail.

HERBERT   Damn! (*he sits up*)   That boy ain't never been in no trouble. Now gon' back to sleep!

MARGARETTE   It's dangerous out there, Herbert. Teenagers can get into all kinda trouble these days, you know that.

HERBERT   (*reclining*)   Um-huh.

MARGARETTE   He was alright 'til you bought him that car! How come you go and buy him that car?

HERBERT   *He* bought it.

MARGARETTE   *You* did. It's in your name.

HERBERT   He's payin' for it.

MARGARETTE   All he thinks about is that car. Half killin' himself to pay for it. I worked when I went to high school 'cause I *had* to, but I didn't intend for my children to.

HERBERT   Herbert the Third don't *have* to work.

MARGARETTE   He ain't got no business out slavin' for the man.

HERBERT   You usta say workin' kept boys off the street and outta trouble.

MARGARETTE   I was talkin' 'bout jobs in the summertime.

HERBERT   Tell him to quit then.

MARGARETTE Who gon' pay for that Impala? Who gon' pay for them suits he just charged?
HERBERT Lord knows I can't. That's how come he got that job.
MARGARETTE He gets off at twelve. He ought to be home by one—before that since he's drivin'.
HERBERT He told me him and some of his friends was goin' bowlin'.
MARGARETTE At this hour-a-mornin', Herbert?
HERBERT Um-huh...
MARGARETTE And you believed him?
HERBERT What would he lie for?
MARGARETTE I can't sleep 'til that boy's home in his bed. (*pause. Picks up the phone and dials*) Operator, give me the number of the police department.
HERBERT (*sitting up abruptly*) Margaree—!
MARGARETTE (*dialing*) He could be locked up—you know how the police is. They see a black boy out in the street this time-a-night, they lock him up for nothin'. Them streets is mean, Herbert... Hello...
HERBERT Damn... (*reclines again*)
MARGARETTE I want to know if you have a Herbert Jackson the Third there? (*to* HERBERT) What if he's layin' up in jail or a hospital or somethin'?
HERBERT He woulda called...
MARGARETTE (*into phone*) Oh... well... No. I don't want nobody to come out.
HERBERT See!
MARGARETTE No. He's... just a teenager, and he was at work, but he ain't home yet and— He gets off at twelve-thirty...
HERBERT Hang up that phone!
MARGARETTE (*into phone*) His daddy says he mighta gone bowlin'... I *know* teenagers ought not to be out in the streets this time-a-mornin'! That's how come I called you—
HERBERT He *ain't* out in the streets, Margaree!
MARGARETTE (*ignoring* HERBERT) You don't have to worry, once he gets home—(*she hangs up*) They talk to you like you a damn dog!
HERBERT You had no business callin' em! I tol' you!
MARGARETTE Anyway he wasn't there, thank goodness.
HERBERT You so damned dumb! Puttin' ya' business all out in the street. I tol' you he's at the Cedar Crest Lanes.
MARGARETTE (*dialing*) Operator, give me the number of Parkland Hospital—emergency ward.
HERBERT Margaree, if he was in the hospital he woulda called!
MARGARETTE How could he call if he got broke to pieces in that ol' Impala? I worked at a hospital and I saw 'em brought in—bleedin' and in shock, and—oh, Jesus!
HERBERT Damn, Margaree, will you shut the hell up and let me get some sleep?
MARGARETTE (*dialing*) I told you he didn't need that car, but can't nobody reason with you, Herbert! Your head's always been hard.
HERBERT GO TO SLEEP!
MARGARETTE He's your son too!
HERBERT But I ain't worry 'bout him!
MARGARETTE You ain't never worried 'bout nothin'! (*into phone*) Gimme emergency. (*to* HERBERT) Your *sleep* is more important to you than your son is!
HERBERT I have to be up for work at five!
MARGARETTE (*into phone*) Do you have a Herbert Jackson the Third this mornin'? (*covers receiver*) Lord, please, don't let nothin' happen to my child! (*into phone*) Herbert—H-E-R-B-E-R-T... that's right... Thank God. (*she hangs up*)
HERBERT Satisfied?
MARGARETTE Parkland ain't the only hospital in Dallas!
HERBERT It's the only one they'd take him to if somethin' had happened to him.
MARGARETTE He said the tires on that car were "may pops." Suppose he had a blowout and ran off the road and into a ditch and got all smashed up and didn't nobody see it!
HERBERT Margaree, why don't you just call the Cedar Crest Lanes and see if he's there?
MARGARETTE They may tell me anything!
HERBERT Ask to speak to him.
MARGARETTE So he can say I'm spyin' on him? That's how come mama's lose their children—by spyin' on 'em!
HERBERT Then gon' back to sleep.
MARGARETTE Your son's out in the world and you just don't care!
HERBERT *You* usta stay out 'til after three when you was his age.
MARGARETTE You *kept* me out 'til after three!

HERBERT Your mama didn't act like you're actin'.

MARGARETTE 'Cause *she* didn't know, that's why. Besides, my mama trusted you.

HERBERT She didn't know we was shackin' up at the B-Bop?

MARGARETTE No, she didn't! I wasn't the type-a-girl who'd go home an' tell my mama that I had allowed a boy to take me to a place like that! (*rises, crosses to window*) And I didn't go there that often with you! I wasn't no fast girl!

HERBERT Some things you could sho do fast.

MARGARETTE Oh dog!

HERBERT 'N you scratched my back up somethin' terrible. I was glad when our hour was up. You had wore me out, girl.

MARGARETTE Owwwwwwww, Herbert!

HERBERT I was shame to take off my undershirt at football practice.

MARGARETTE Her—buuuuuuut!

HERBERT Well, I was!

MARGARETTE Shoot! (*pause*) The onliest reason I went to the B-Bop with you was 'cause I was in love . . . then.

HERBERT You was a wild little ol' thang.

MARGARETTE Dog!

HERBERT Sho could carry on. Nelly broke my back.

MARGARETTE Shoot! You needn't pretend you wasn't experienced.

HERBERT It coulda been my first time.

MARGARETTE And I *coulda been* Lena Horne, but I wasn't.

HERBERT So?

MARGARETTE So? You was a football boy, Herbert, and yawl didn't have to ast for nothin'. You'd just walk up to a girl and take what you want.

HERBERT I do that to you?

MARGARETTE I wasn't that type-a-girl!

HERBERT How you know I was that type-a-boy?

MARGARETTE The way you shake covers?!

HERBERT I mighta been a virgin.

MARGARETTE Shoot! Is Jesus walkin' on White Rock Lake this mornin'??

HERBERT Ow, Margaree, you too cold, mama.

MARGARETTE I'm just tellin' it like it is, Herbert. I know you men. All of you dogs just want to get next to a good woman.

HERBERT What's wrong wif that?

MARGARETTE It's the woman who suffer. *She* bears yawl's children. *She* suffer the pains. *She* nurse 'em in sickness and in health, and *she* the one who worry 'bout at times like this. (*it dawns on her that* HERBERT III *may have a girl with him*) Lord! Was he takin' a girl bowlin' with him?

HERBERT He just said some friends.

MARGARETTE And you didn't ast who they was?

HERBERT Naw, mama, I didn't.

MARGARETTE Suppose he's got some woman's daughter out this time-a-mornin'! Suppose they're *not* bowlin'! Suppose they shackin' up in some motel?

HERBERT (*amused*) Like we usta do?

MARGARETTE *We* got married! I want somethin' better than that for my son. He's goin' to college. He ain't gon' ruin his life.

HERBERT I *ruin* my life?

MARGARETTE What you talkin' 'bout?

HERBERT My marryin' you.

MARGARETTE You didn't *have* to marry me, Herbert!

HERBERT You was pregnant, Margaree.

MARGARETTE So was a lot of your friend's girls, but *they* didn't marry them. You married me 'cause you loved me—I thought.

HERBERT Well . . . I wasn't expectin' to get married so young.

MARGARETTE Didn't *nobody make you* marry me, Herbert Jackson! My mama didn't come runnin' to your mama 'bout I was pregnant. *My* mama didn't even *know*! I told *you* I was and we got married, and you went to the army. That's all there was to it.

HERBERT Then how come you so down on marriage all of a sudden?

MARGARETTE I ain't down on nothin'! People *ought* to get married—they *ought* to own up to their responsibilities!

HERBERT Then if the boy wants to get married—

MARGARETTE Has he said somethin' to you 'bout gettin' married?

HERBERT Naw, but what if he did?

MARGARETTE He's too young to get married. He ain't but eighteen—

HERBERT I was eighteen when we—

MARGARETTE But *you* went to the army—that's what matured you. He don't want to be bothered with no army, and I don't blame him.

HERBERT You always talkin' 'bout not tryin' to run they lives.

MARGARETTE *Advice* never hurt nobody. 'N you know as well as I do people gon' do what they want to do. If he want's to throw his life away, that's his business. All I can do is advise him.

HERBERT What you mean "throw his life away?"

MARGARETTE You know how these fast gals are, Herbert. All they after's security—a roof over their head, and a car to ride around in—that's *all* they want.

HERBERT That all you wanted from me?

MARGARETTE I'm not talkin' about us. I'm talkin' about the young gals today. I couldn't help gettin' pregnant. I told you to get some protection, but you said the drug store was closed. I wanted to go home, but noooo, you insisted, and look what happened. But today it ain't like that. If a girl gets knocked up it's 'cause she wants to. It's 'cause she's too lazy to use the pill.

HERBERT Suppose she's a Catholic girl? 'N don't say they don't do nothin' like that.

MARGARETTE I've said all I have to say on the subject.

HERBERT (*pause*) He sho was with a fine one the other evenin'. Great big legs. Jesus! She'd make any man lose his religion.

MARGARETTE You ought to be ashamed of yourself, Herbert, thinkin' 'bout a young girl like that. You're goin' on forty and you look every minute of it.

HERBERT I can still take care of business, can't I?

MARGARETTE That's all you think about. Ol' dog! Your mind stays in the gutter. If you hadn't been so concerned with sex maybe you coulda amounted to somethin'! Here I am talkin' about a better life for your son, and you got you mind deep down in the nitty-gritty.

HERBERT He got a better life than I had.

MARGARETTE 'Cause you went and bought him that Impala?

HERBERT 'Cause he don't have to remember what I have to remember! (*gets cigarette and lights it*)

MARGARETTE Here we go again! Start with the buses.

HERBERT He don't remember the time when we used to have to sit in the back of the bus behind a sign that said "colored."

MARGARETTE No, he don't.

HERBERT He don't remember 'bout the colored drankin' fountains, or not bein' able to sit and eat at Kress and Woolsworth.

MARGARETTE That's right.

HERBERT He don't remember us not havin' a decent movie theater to go to—just the Central and the State.

MARGARETTE You could go to the Majestic.

HERBERT Yeah, bought your ticket at a side window and took the "colored" elevator up to the top balcony. The screen was so far down it looked like a postage stamp.

MARGARETTE "Nigger heaven," they used to call it.

HERBERT And the police could walk into your house, talk to you like you was a fool, beat the hell outta you—for nothin'.

MARGARETTE Still do.

HERBERT I worked out in Oak Lawn at a restaurant once. Worked overtime one night and missed the last bus back to North Dallas 'n had to walk home. The police picked me up for bein' in a white neighborhood that time-a-night. I told 'em I'd just gotten off work and had missed my bus. They told me I was lyin'. I asted 'em to call my boss. They say, "You orderin' us, nigger?" I say, "No, sir." And they say they gonna take me out to Dal High Stadium and teach me some respect. They made me take off all my clothes and them sons of bitches beat me unconscious and left me naked, layin' in the cold like a damned dog.

MARGARETTE I wish you'd cut out that kinda talk, Herbert. That's what sent Henry on the road to ruin.

HERBERT That's what made him a man.

MARGARETTE You just like the other folks 'round here—tryin' to make a hero outta that boy.

HERBERT He made a hero outta hisself, mama!

MARGARETTE You lead that boy astray. Just as sure as I'm standin' here it was you first—then them militants, and—(*she cries*) His life ruint! Twenty-two and in jail forever!!

HERBERT He'll get parolled in 'bout five years they say—maybe sooner.

MARGARETTE He ain't gonna get parolled—*ever*! Get that into your head. You talked about them police beating you ever since I can remember; how you was gonna "revenge" yourself one-a-these days. Your talk drove that boy to his—

HERBERT   A man can't let nothin' like that happen to him and not do somethin' about it.

MARGARETTE   But *you* didn't do nothin'. Poisoned that boy's mind and the first time a police stop him—

HERBERT   He wrestled that son-of-a-bitch's own gun from him, held it in his face 'n listened to him pleadin'—

MARGARETTE   Then pulled the trigger! Murder. The only reason he ain't got the 'lectric chair is cause he sick, Herbert—'n you the cause of it.

HERBERT   If they had give him the chair, them mean black boys in his organization woulda burned this town to the ground. He *told* 'em to cool it.

MARGARETTE   Now he just as wel'st be dead. He sho ain't gon' walk these sidewalks no more.

HERBERT   He maybe gone, but he ain't forgotten. His name is as big 'round here as Rap Brown's—

MARGARETTE   I don't understan' how come folks' listen to that Rap Brown and Stokley Carmichael! They partially responsible for ruinin' Henry's mind—

HERBERT   They don't even know Henry.

MARGARETTE   *He sho do know them though!*

HERBERT   Margaree—

MARGARETTE   What?

HERBERT   You done been brainwashed. You-a-victim of the establishment.

MARGARETTE   You too.

HERBERT   Naw, mama, I'm a victim of you.

MARGARETTE   I don't know what you talkin'· 'bout, Herbert!

HERBERT   Neither one of us is up with the times, but I come close to bein' than you. You got to listen to the young folks.

MARGARETTE   I always thought it was the other way 'round.

HERBERT   They *do* while we sit yackin'.

MARGARETTE   Killin' people?

HERBERT   If that's what it takes.

MARGARETTE   You just as sick as Henry!

HERBERT   I'm just as *mad* as Henry. The man lied to us, mama—all these years he been lyin' to us. Sent my ass over to Korea and tol' me when I got back democracy would be preserved, and things would be better. Shit! I couldn't even get a damned job!

MARGARETTE   Things're better now, Herbert.

HERBERT   Yeah, a little better. We accepted more promises that ain't been fulfilled, so Henry nem say to the man: "don't yawl lie no more. Put up or shut up." An' all the time it's an eye for an eye. They stan' up like men, and they die like men if need be.

MARGARETTE   You talk like one of them militants!

HERBERT   Show me a black man who ain't, and I'll show you a lie.

MARGARETTE   Well... bein' a militant ain't puttin' no money in your pocket. You won't even speak up for yourself. You been on that job for twelve years now, and in all that time you've just got two raises—once for five dollars, and once for fifteen! Have you ever got a promotion? No. But that little o' white boy come in there three years ago—you *taught him*—now he's the foreman. And you *still* doin' all the work. He bought that new house out in Richardson—complete with draperies, wall-to-wall carpeting, an all electric kitchen, and it didn't cost him but three thousand dollars more that it costed us for this shack that was worn out when they decided to let us in the section! It makes me mad, Herbert, to see you work as hard as you do and not get nowhere. Go and tell that man.

HERBERT   And risk bein' fired? This house note's still got to be paid, and we got to eat. 'N like you said, I'm hittin' forty. It ain't easy findin' a decent job at that age when you ain't skilled. Besides, I got my retirement, 'n insurance, 'n twelve years of my life wrapped up in that job.

MARGARETTE   'N your salary ain't gonna be no different the day you retire than it is now.

HERBERT   Well... we wasn't talkin' 'bout that.

MARGARETTE   No, we was talkin' 'bout Herbert the Third gettin' married, and I say he *ain't*.

HERBERT   Who said he was?

MARGARETTE   If he's out shackin' up with some little ol' fast gal and she gets messed up— that's her hard luck!

HERBERT   Suppose I had told you that?

MARGARETTE   But you *didn't* tell me that. He ain't gettin' married. I don't care *who* she is.

HERBERT (*reclining*) I gotta get some sleep.
MARGARETTE What about my baby?
HERBERT He's alright, Margaree. (*rolls over*)
MARGARETTE Talk is cheap, Herbert. I'm stubborn like the mule—you got to *show* me! *Prove* to me my baby's alright. . . . Lord, the darkness of this night . . . (*she sits for a moment on the side of the bed. Suddenly she rocks back and forth humming, then she sings*)

> Pass me not, O gentle Savior
> Hear my humble cry
> While on others Thou art calling
> Do not pass me by. . .

(*crying, she gets onto her knees.* HERBERT *grunts with disgust*) Oh, Lord. Lord, don't let my baby be somewhere dead. He's the only one *I* got. Take care of that child, Jesus. He's just a boy out havin' fun like children will do. He don't mean no harm, Lord. Touch his heart this mornin'. Reach out and touch that child and take him into your gentle arms and bring him home to me safe. Hear me, Jesus! Oh, sweet Jesus, hear my cry this morning. Please take care of my baby.
HERBERT That boy's goin' on nineteen, Margaree!
MARGARETTE He could be fifty and I'd still worry 'bout him 'long as he sleepin' under the same roof with me! (*raises her hand*) In the name of the Father, the Son, and the Holy Ghost—*Oh Jesus!* Amen. (*she climbs slowly back into bed; lies down*) Now . . . I ain't gon' worry no more. I've put him in the hands of the Lord. That's *all* I can do.
HERBERT (*half asleep*) Um-huh . . .

(*Silence.* MARGARETTE *shifts restlessly; rolls over and pulls the covers to her side revealing the body of her husband. He pulls them back. She extends an arm, grasps the clock and looks at it, sits up*)

MARGARETTE Herbert, get up!
HERBERT (*asleep*) Huuuuummmmmm . . .
MARGARETTE (*firmly*) Get up, Herbert, 'n go see if that boy's at that bowlin' alley.
HERBERT Hummmmmmmmm . . .
MARGARETTE I mean it! Get up out of this bed, Herbert, 'n go see if he's there! (*she pulls the covers off him*) I won't sleep this night 'til I know he's alright.
HERBERT Awww, hell, Margaree—
MARGARETTE If you ain't goin', I am! (*she is up and getting a dress to put on*) I will walk to that bowlin' alley through them dark streets since I don't know how to drive, but I'll get there to see about my child.
HERBERT (*sitting up*) Thought you was puttin' things in the hands of the Lord?
MARGARETTE Some times it's best to do for yourself. I was layin' there and He *tol'* me— the Lord *tol'* me to go see 'bout my baby.
HERBERT If He tol' *you* to go, how come you call me?
MARGARETTE He's your son too, but since you don't care, I'm goin' myself! Herbert the Third's the only child we got left and you act like you don't care.
HERBERT Richard and Henry ain't dead.
MARGARETTE Henry just as wel'st be—'n Richard *could be* for all we know.
HERBERT He's probably up in Canada havin' him a ball.
MARGARETTE Sometimes I wish he had gone on to the army and got it over with, but naw, he listens to them hippies—
HERBERT You said you didn't blame him for not wantin' to go to no war.
MARGARETTE Nobody *wants* to go, but you *got* to go. It's your duty. You went.
HERBERT Me'n him are different.
MARGARETTE You gon' drive over to the Cedar Crest Lanes to see 'bout that boy?
HERBERT That's the only way I'll be able to get some sleep around here.
MARGARETTE Then get on up!
HERBERT (*getting out of bed and into trousers*) Why can't we just call 'em, Margaree?
MARGARETTE I'm not gonna call that place!
HERBERT Alright, then! Alright.
MARGARETTE (*after a pause*) Herbert, I swear I can't sleep 'til I know how my baby is. (*he grunts. She begins to cry*) Oh, Jesus, Lord, please—
HERBERT (*pointing to heaven*) You that man's exadrin headache number thousand (*he is dressed now and ready to leave. He crosses to his wife*) What you want me to say to him, "Herbert, it's after three, your mama want you to come home?"
MARGARETTE I just want you to go over there and make sure he's alright. Make sure he's in there, and not in no trouble.
HERBERT He ain't no baby no more, Margaree.

MARGARETTE He's my last child, and he'll always be my baby! Now if you ain't goin', Herbert, I-a-go.

HERBERT (*starting to the door*) Damn!

MARGARETTE Herbert? (*he stops*) I wouldn't ask you to do this, but he's your son too. (*crosses to him*) The Cedar Crest Lanes ain't that far, honey. You can be over there and back before you know it.

HERBERT It'll be five o'clock before I know it too! I got a long, hard day tomorrow.

MARGARETTE Sometimes it's necessary to put your family first.

HERBERT (*grunts and crosses to the door*) You gon' be up when I get back?

MARGARETTE You think I can sleep with my child out this time-a-mornin'?

HERBERT That ain't what I'm talkin' 'bout.

MARGARETTE Just go on, Herbert.

HERBERT If I don't work a full day tomorrow 'nd my check's short, you the cause. (*exiting*)

MARGARETTE Money ain't everything.

HERBERT (*offstage*) Remember that when you astin' for new stockin's.

MARGARET Herbert, just gon'! (*the door is heard closing offstage.* MARGARETTE *crosses to the bed and sits. She is still worried. The sound of an automobile is heard starting. It drives off. She takes a cigarette from* HERBERT's *pack, lights it, but she is a non-smoker and it makes her cough. She crushes it in the ashtray, then rises and crosses to the window. She looks out, then returns to the bed, lies down and tries to relax. This is impossible. Restlessly she begins to wallow. Finally she sits up, composes herself, then picks up the phone and dials. Pause*) Mama? This is Margarette... No, we're alright... Yes'm, Herbert's alright... No'm, we ain't got no death, Mama. I called because... well... Herbert the Third ain't home, and it's almost four!... I donno where he went to, Mama... I *know* he's not at your place. Herbert went to look for him... Mama, I *know* you have to be at work in the mornin', but he's your grandson too! Ain't you worried?... I just tol' you it's nearly four and he's not in this house!... He could be dead for all I know!... Mama, I have insurance on *all* my family!... Yes, the premiums're paid! You talk like you *hope* somethin' mighta happened to your grandchild!... I know you don't want nothin' to happen, Mama, neither do I... I can't sleep... I know you was asleep, Mama, but this is important to me. Mama! Mama, don't hang up! How's Mr. Early? Don't tell me how he is tomorrow, tell me how he is *now*!... So what if I don't care for Mr. Early? I'm askin' about him for the sake of conversation... Mama, *please*... Yes'm, I'll take a dose of Sal-Ha-Patica and go to bed—I'm *already in bed*!!... Yes'm, but I'm so worried... Me and Doloris didn't make you worry *this* much, Mama! We were good girls... Well, Herbert turned out much better than you expected. I always *knew* what he had in him!... That's not the best thing he did for me, Mama! And he didn't make me leave the Catholic church! I just so happen to like the music in the Baptist church better, that's all... Mama... Mama!... No, I won't call you no more at this hour!... You've not givin' me any kind of respect,... Mama! Your language!... I'd never use that kinda language to you even if it is four o'clock in the mornin'! You're forgiven, but you ought'n to let that sinful Mr. Early put you up to sayin' nasty things like that... I'm *not* tryin' to run your business, Mama, but that man is bringing you down... No, Mama, Herbert and me're not havin' problems... He's completely satisfied, Mama... I do do that for him whenever he wants to... Whoever tol' you that just tol' a lie, and you can tell 'em I said so!... I don't care what you and Mr. Early do! Me 'n Herbert get along just fine!... Mama, a woman your age shouldn't have that on her mind... Yes, I do—whenever I'm in the mood!... Herbert stays that-a-way! If you want a granddaughter to name Tonya, tell Deloris, I don' wanna hear it... No, Mama... Mama, it's late... I know... It's after four, Mama, why don't you try'n get some sleep? (*she sighs*) Yeeeeessssss, Mama! I sent Herbert out to look for him... No, he ain't gone out chasin' no part-time broad! Herbert's a hard workin' man... I *do* satisfy him!... Mama! ... Goodnight, mama!... Goodnight, I said! ... Mama, that's a lie!... Owwwwwww!! (*she hangs up abruptly, nervously lights a cigarette, takes a drag and coughs*) Frigid! *She must be if Early don't stay home!* (*crushes out cigarette*) Herbert's *always* home. (*an ambulance is heard in the distance.* MARGARETTE *is startled*) Oh, Jesus, don't let nothin' happen to my baby! How come children have to worry you this-away? (*picks up phone, dials*) Operator, the morgue, please. That's right the city morgue. (*she gets the number and dials*) Hello? I wanna know... (*she composes herself*)... You don't happen to have a Herbert Jackson the Third there, do you?... (*relieved*) Thank you. Thank you. (*hangs up, sits on bed. A car is heard approaching, comes closer, stops, and a door is heard slamming.* MARGARETTE *rises and starts to the window, but stops midway. A door is heard opening downstairs. Then footsteps on the stairs*) Herbert? (*there is no answer*) Her-buuuuutt? (*she crosses to the door and waits*) Herbert, why don't you answer me? (HERBERT *enters without a word, removes his trousers and his coat*) Was he there?

HERBERT I tol' you that 'fore I left.

MARGARETTE Was he alright?

HERBERT Bowlin' wif his friends like I said he was.

MARGARETTE What did you say to him?

HERBERT I didn't say nothin' to him. I wasn't gon' embarrass that boy in front of his friends. (*climbing in bed*) He didn't even know I was there. (MARGARETTE *gets on her knees*)

MARGARETTE Heavenly Father—

HERBERT Why don't you come on to bed, woman, and leave that man alone?

MARGARETTE Herbert, I'm tryin' to pray. If you don't care about the blessings this family receives, I do.

HERBERT Damn!

MARGARETTE I just want to thank my Jesus. (*she is silent for a moment*) Amen. (*she rises and climbs into bed*) You don't work on Sunday, Herbert, you ought to get up out of this bed and go to church with me. (*he grunts*) No. You rather watch them football games on that television set, and pop them beer cans all day long. You ought to thank the Lord for providing you with your health, and a fine family like you got, with a wife who don't run around. Top Notch's wife is always in the street, and Lord knows where her children are—she don't care. It breaks my heart sometimes just thinkin' about it. You should get on your knees and thank the Lord—Herbert, you listenin' to me? (*he is silent*) Well... I put it all in the hands of my Lord.

(*Silence. They both are still. After a moment* HERBERT *shifts about in the bed, restlessly. He rolls over, pulls the covers to his side.* MARGARETTE *covers herself.* HERBERT *can't get back to sleep. He sits up in bed, yawns; climbs out of bed and exits into the hall. A light is turned on. Pause. A toilet flushes. He re-enters the room, climbs back into the bed. He cannot sleep*)

HERBERT Margaree? (*shakes her gently*) Margaree, baby, you sleep?

MARGARETTE Ummmmm...

HERBERT Wake up, Mama.

MARGARETTE (*pulling away in her sleep*) Ummmm...

HERBERT Come on, baby... lets play a little bit. (*touches her. Shakes her gently*) I can't get back to sleep...

MARGARETTE Ummmmm...

HERBERT (*softly*) Let's git some? (*pause*) Margaree, baby, you too tired?

MARGARETTE Ummmmm... huh...

HERBERT (*shaking her*) Margaree! Margaree!

MARGARETTE (*annoyed*) Herbert, what you want with me?

HERBERT (*embracing her*) I can't get back to sleep, baby.

MARGARETTE Herbert, please—

HERBERT You still excite me like when we was in high school.

MARGARETTE Ugh-ugh-ugh.

HERBERT Come on, Mama (*he starts to kiss her cheek*)

MARGARETTE Won't you *ever* grow up?

HERBERT Not if I got to quit this.

MARGARETTE Ugh-ugh-ugh. (*he continues to kiss her*)

HERBERT Sho is a pretty, soft, mama... so sweet... (*she begins to respond. She embraces him passionately*) Sweet Mama...

MARGARETTE Dog!

HERBERT Mama love daddy?

MARGARETTE Ummmmmmm... quit...

HERBERT Come on, baby.

MARGARETTE Her—buuuuutttt...

HERBERT Sweet, pretty, Mama...

MARGARETTE Awwwww, Herbert... mmm.

HERBERT Goddammit! (*the clock alarms. Abruptly* MARGARETTE *pushes* HERBERT *aside, rises and climbs out of bed. She turns off the alarm, then grabs her robe*) Say, Mama, ain't you comin' back?

MARGARETTE Herbert, honey, you know you got to get up—you be late for work!

HERBERT I don't give a—
MARGARETTE I'm goin' downstairs and fix you some grits 'n eggs 'n bacon, and some nice hot biscuits.
HERBERT I don't want no damned grits 'n eggs 'n bacon, and nice hot biscuits, I want me some—
MARGARETTE Now you get up from there, Herbert. You don' wanna be late this mornin'. (*crosses to door*) I'm gonna turn on the water, 'n you jump in that shower, you feel like a new man! Get on up now, baby. (*exiting*) Time slips through our fingers so fast 'til there ain't nothin' left, I swear!
HERBERT (*sitting up in bed*) Damn! I'll be goddamned! (*sound of the shower running in the bathroom*)
MARGARETTE (*singing offstage*)

> Jesus, lover of my soul,
> Let me to Thy bosom fly,
> While the nearer waters roll,
> While the tempest still is high . . .

HERBERT (*dejected, he shakes his head from side to side*) Damn! (*he continues to mumble "damn" as the curtain closes*)

Val Ferdinand (1947–)

Blk Love Song #1   1969

The Free Southern Theater was founded in 1963 by Gilbert Moses, John O'Neal, and Doris Derby in Jackson, Mississippi. They had concluded that "Mississippi's closed system effectively refuses the Negro knowledge of himself." They set out to use theater as freedom: "for thought, and involvement, and the celebration of our own culture." FST has survived, grown, and changed. One of its offshoots in New Orleans is *Blkartsouth*.

The major three playwrights for FST have been Gilbert Moses, Tom Dent, and Val Ferdinand. *Blk Love Song #1*, written and produced in 1969, is Mr. Ferdinand's play, a ritual play not unlike those produced in Spirit House and in the New Lafayette Theatre. Its form, based on verse/chant/dialogue, is designed to raise consciousness by repetition of positive and negative black images. Mr. Ferdinand explains his philosophy of theater and something of his own background in the essay that follows.

Both the essay and the play have been left as the author wrote them—unedited by arrangement of punctuation.

my slave name is vallery ferdinand iii, ain't got no free name yet, am married, got a daughter named *Asante Salaam* (which means thank you peace). my education goes or rather went like this: dropped out of carleton college in northfield, minn., served three years in the army, got kicked out of southern univ. in new o. as a result of participation in a student movement to create a black university.

i have been writing since 1962. have been with the free southern theater since summer of 68. write every and anything but mostly plays, poetry, and short stories. have written maybe 15 one act plays and have had about six of them produced. i am director of *Blkartsouth* and co-editor of *Nkombo*, a quarterly journal of *blkarts*. we want to hear from you brother/sister, write us. *Blkartsouth*, 1301 Egania Street, New Orleans, La. 70117.

Blk Love Song #1

Free Southern Theater, it's hard to really explain it. It's an idea about drama and black people's minds. An actuality sometimes. Sometimes, like when Amiri Baraka's *Slaveship* was performed in Greenville, Mississippi during the summer of 69 and literally sent the people out into the streets. Or sometimes, like when *Blkartsouth* upset the southern city of Little Rock by daring to infer that we african people were not only black and beautiful but were also now and should forever be preparing to make it on our own as a nation of black and beautiful people. It's hard to explain it. When it happens it really happens. When we get close to ourselves/our people and be for real the *Free Southern Theater* really exists. It exists when we do it. I said earlier, an idea, well . . . but not really, cause like nothing is an idea/an idea is nothing. Just nothing, not even occupying space, dreamstuff, hallucinations. An idea. No.

FST did a book that documented what FST was about for its first four years of existence. Dig that if you want to know what FST was and by extension may now be about. *FST By the FST* is a historical document. It's finished. But FST as a black theater is moving on. By the time this is in print FST (or some extension or offspring of it) will hopefully be into a better/blacker thing than we're now into. More pure. More actuality. Less ideas, theories. Real tangible alive living experiences.

We spent the first year of seventy just holding on for most of the year without funds making it totally on the voluntary commitment of a dedicated staff . . . (at times it was like voluntary slavery). The latter part of seventy was spent restructuring, evaluating, studying, and redefining. The following is from a staff paper, it explains what FST is trying to get into:

> Some define their objectives in terms of achievement in the ordinary or established realm of the theater as it exists and has existed in western culture. When we speak of Black Theater it is our intent to include only those whose primary commitment is to using the theater as an instrument to further the struggle for liberation of Black people rather than achievement in terms of traditional western or commercial theater.
>
> . . . FST is valid only in so far as it is a vehicle for our contribution to the struggle of our people for total liberation.

Like that don't have nothing to do with aesthetics. Just simply commitment, goals, aspirations, etc. But for some, that statement takes FST out of the realm of theater and sets us into something else. Which is cool. You don't really have to call what we're doing theater . . . you can call it construction work if you want to or ritual/propoganda drama or bullshit. It don't matter what you call it, not real/ity. But for sho it ain't somemore jive entertainment to win awards, we ain't just acting. We living for real.

The play you will read in here was written in *Blkartsouth*, FST's community writing/acting workshop. The audiences that saw it dug it and gave us indications of what more needed to be done. FST has a reputation of traveling around giving plays all over the south and so like even if this book sells out, more people will have seen the plays than will ever read them. And that's important to us. Frankly we hope that as a result of reading some of our work you might decide you want to perform them. That's more important than studying them for techniques and styles and methods (which is not to say that all of those things are not present). Besides you won't find even half of what we do with a play written in the script. There's hardly any of the staging we use, none of the movements hardly, not much sound, the script is a skeleton. It will give you some idea of what the play is like but only a hazy idea, a dull generality. It's left to the director and actors to put it out front, to get to the meanings. So understand that when you study say BLS #1 you won't see any stage directions or indications of who is doing what at what point. You have to do that. You got to do it to really find out what the play means. Really do it. If you are going to study this stuff at least read the play out aloud, A/LOUD. Put it in the air, put some breath into it, use your muscles and your senses. Feel it, Do it like that Study it like that. It makes a difference. Otherwise you going to miss what we're doing. You have to use more than your minds to understand/experience these plays.

We don't feel that there necessarily has to be an exact logic to what we're doing. In fact after all is said and done you *will not* really be able to get into what we're all about just by thinking about it. You might be able to catch all of the mental precepts and arguments we throw out but a lot of the stuff that hangs in the air during our performances can only be touched or felt, experienced. Much like dancing with a woman or group dancing to the other side of reality when the experience by its own weight flips the m in "me" and turns "me" into "WE!" That calls for spiritual/physical identification and tremendous releases of energy. Total acceptance. The closest thing that can be pointed to (that we know of) that will give you an idea of what black theater will be like once we get it together is negro down home church (and maybe certain black music shows, like JB or Pharoah). That's total spiritual/physical identification. The good sista sitting up and screaming in church, walking the pews, speaking in tongues and rejoicing. We want that energy/identification in our art. We want to couple that with a straight ahead pan african ideology to produce a *nation*. If a baptist preacher can build a church, buy a house and ride in a cadillac because of his ability to get people to release energy and identify then we black theater people can help build a nation.

Our writers are increasingly conscious of this direction and their work tries to move that way. We look at black people, our total make up. We try to appeal to black people, to every facet of our black peopleness. We try to fill our people's lives. Like a lot of socalled black writers aren't interested in writing about negroes or colored folks or whatever they term non-"B*L*A*C*K" black people. We feel that we have to be interested in all black people. Our motivations for writing are various but primarily we see ourselves as black artists contributing to the struggle for liberation that's trying to build a strong black nation. We know. It sounds more political than artistic . . . and a lot of it seems to be propaganda. We know. But see, drama, all art, but especially what you call drama, well that is (among other things) a very precise political/propaganda projection. Very precise. Shakespeare was an anglo-saxon english nationalist and one of the reasons they still teach his work in colleges and universities and schools period is to keep on projecting that nationalism. It don't really matter that they call it universal. That simply means that they want to be everywhere, want to push that shit on everybody regardless of whether people can identify with it or not. Cause it's universal. Like the english all ways usta say (or want to say): the sun never sets on the british empire; it was universal. But it wasn't necessarily of use to anybody but english people and people who wanted to be like them. You know like finally we believe if we be what we are, what ever we are, and be the best of it, well like that's enough.

Most of our artifacts are trivial. We can throw away statues and paintings and records. They ain't nothing but artifacts, leavings, residue. The art is in the doing, the living. And we can do it and do it and keep on doing it as long as we remain our true black selves. The impulses of creativity are even so strong in us that even in this western culture as slaves and the children of slaves (american negroes) we have been able to produce our art. See you can't equate our art with artifacts or art forms. That ain't where we at. But like that is usually where western critics look to base their arguments. Them artifacts and art forms. Them Mona Lisa's and music scores and other shit them critics and art lovers carry around in books, pictures, diagrams, and logically constructed heads. We carry ours around in our hearts. Miles shows up for a recording date with his horn. Coltrane played *kulu Se Mama* while Juno Lewis hummed it in his ear. It was transmitted like that. I mean there's a big difference.

Maybe we shouldn't use the word trivial, let's just say expendable. We don't mean to imply that the artifact is worthless, just simply that the artifact itself is not where the worth of our art resides. The essence of blackness resides in the black hearts of our people. The spiritual/physical forces that emanate from the heart. But we are conscious too that our minds have to come into play if we are to keep on keepin on, if we are to survive this western sojourn and once having survived it, journey to our nation and insure that we are never separated again. We have to develop, redevelop some things that we once took for granted. We got to lay them out. And so like our art, its essence comes from the heart (along with all that that implies) but in order for us to survive as a people in these times we must (at least some of us must) use our minds. Construct an ideology, a frame work to hang out on. Shakespeare didn't have to invent the kingship or any other social order as such, it was already invented, so he just went from within that framework. But we got to develop our own framework and at the same time that we work from within it. Many people don't understand that. We got to study ourselves, study ourselves. You can't just throw any idea out into space and say that this is a black concept, a black thing. See concepts follow actions and being. A thing is a thing. Black is a way of thing*ing* not a thing. Black is a way of arting not an art form or artifact. So the only way we can develop BLK ART concepts is to first be the concepts, is to first be the concepts we want to develop.

Something else too, we got to get our art forms and artifacts more together but we can only do this in terms of developing the artist so that the artist has capability, understanding, heart, soul, and technique enough to transmit whatever the artist wants to transmit. We don't have to work on forms no more. We got to work on the artists. If the artists feel the need for a heavier form they will create it. Witness Bird, witness Trane, Pharoah, all us can do it. An artifact can be said to be worthy based on several factors. One, that it says what the artists wants it to say; two that what it says is of some use to black people, meaning that the artifact is functional; and three that the artist had a purpose for doing it and wasn't just bullshitting. All three are important. The first is obvious. The second has to do with our particular hierarchy of values in terms of art. We're not trying to say that other people have to share this criterion. What does it matter to college english teachers (and plenty black ones for that matter) whether or not wordsworth or even ginsberg (even?) is creating an art form or artifact that is functional for black people? The third has to do with the fact that we feel that the artist can not disassociate his life as an artist from his life as a black person=people. It ain't enough to say black is beautiful. If you a black artist by what you say you are, what your art says you are, what you be telling others to be.

Now the other ways people judge art are purely subjective. They be matters of whether or not you (as an individual) agree or disagree with what is presented, how you react based on what you believe/think. The american people in general have no eye, ear, nose, heart for art. They don't know art from soup cans. They think pictures of naked ladies is art and get uptight behind African dancers. Playboy, Cavelier, et alla them is america's realest art magazines. They show what's really on the american man's mind. True confession, movie screen, mc-calls, house & yard (garden), vogue, stuff like that along with some other tripe is what american art is about. The dead cemeteries called museums, the same notes over and over again in so-called concert halls, paintings old with age and the paint peeling off, some poems that were written two hundred years ago and run off in some book, that is what americans think art is. They do. Some of you probably think this book is art. An art book or something just cause it got writing in it. The american people are un-witting dupes of faggots and circus intellectuals who are passing deadness off as art. People produce art. People are art. People art ART! If they don't they'll have to lap up some deadness or steal it if they want art. If americans want music so much let them create some instead of copying and imitating and *stealing*. We don't mean to go into a diatribe against the american people here but damn, americanism is a dumb flat kind of consciousness that ain't connected to nuthing much except money, god, the president, and phoney history. And oh yeah landing on the moon. When we say american people, we mean all people who think as americans think which includes a whole lot of black people. But anyway, meanwhile some other kind of things are happening.

We do not happen as an opposite, or a reaction, we happen because we are. This art we are doing will be just as valid, just as functional, just as beautiful after the ways of the west have past on, after new york is dust, after the nation is erected. African drums and the black art of drumming is just as valid as when the first drumbeat was sounded in the chests and breasts of our original black ancestors. If you cover both of your ears tightly with your hands and lie still you just might hear it. If you're black it just might mean that your ancestors are calling. Heed that call brothers. Sisters. Heed that call. And come on let's live.

PEACE & LIBERATION

Val Ferdinand, Director
                                    BLKARTSOUTH

BLK MAN, *dressed in blk dashiki suit, w/h liberation flag on his left shoulder like a patch*
BLK WOMAN, *dressed in long blk wrap or dress w/h liberation flag as head wrap*
CHORUS, *can be BM and BW speaking together otherwise about 6 people dressed in liberation colors*
JETHRO, *1st scene: old pants and torn shirt (slave); 2nd scene: army jacket w/h shades and boots (militant)*
SARAH, *1st scene: shapeless old time dress w/h head rag (slave); 2nd scene: modern dress w/h wig; 3rd scene: modern dress wears natural*
PEACHES, *extravagant wig (maybe blond or blond streaked), mod dress, wears bright red and boots*
SLICK, *flashy dresser wears silk scarf around his neck*
BEAT, *blue suit w/h white shirt and socks, a red tie, no shoes, wears glasses and has pencils sticking out of his front jacket pocket, holds a beat up old black hat in his hands*
Make use of mime and pantomime when BM, BW or CHORUS is speaking to give the illusion that action is still going on among the others.

(*Bareness. Open area. Use platforms or audience area for places for* BLK MAN, BLK WOMAN *and the* CHORUS. *Use lights where possible and live music although the musicians need not be visible*)

BLK WOMAN (*moves in slowly semi arcs of swaying loveliness, wears long dress*) Where is the seed of africa? Where? Where are the first men who walked the earth? Have they vanished? Has the air sucked them up into the clouds? Has the wind shook them and hung them out to dry? Where has the seed of Africa gone? What lands, what homes, where are they gone? My brother, my brothers and my father, Our fathers, Where? Where has the seed of Africa gone?
CHORUS (*flute and drums in fast rocking sand*)
They are gone to America
They are gone to the new world
They are gone to America
They are gone to the new world
They are gone to America
Into hell they have been hurled

Scene One

BLK MAN And they whipped us in America
         And seized our bodies with terrible afflictions
         And they whipped us in America
         And made us do their bidding
         And we died there, we died there in America
SARAH   Jethro ... Jethro (*she enters*)
JETHRO   I am here Sarah

SARAH Oh my man, I thought you were lost
I thought the paddy rollers done caught you sho.
I heard the dogs moaning at the new risen moon
And I reached out for you
But you were gone from your pallet on the flo
Your bed was empty and my heart became empty too
I cried. I cried and then I heard
The hound dogs baying
And I could imagine them snapping at your heels
I could imagine them dogs running dead in your tracks
Hunting you down like some wild game
And I could see you running Jethro
I could see you running
Running from the fields
Running through the thick swamps

JETHRO Sarah be quiet . . . the paddy rollers gone here us sho

SARAH Jethro is we flying to freedom
Is we gon follow the north star
Jethro is we going north

JETHRO Be quiet woman. Our home ain't north neither is it south. Our home is in the east
Way east, way across the water

SARAH Well what we gon do, Jethro
How we gon go home?

JETHRO We find a way, Sarah. We find a way.

CHORUS But is there a way for the black man
Is there a way back home
Is there a way for the black man
Is there a way back home
Is there a hope for the black man
Can someone guide him through this storm

BEAT Boy you remember this,
You is home now
Who in the hell you think you is
You young negroes

JETHRO Us young negroes, what?

BEAT Yeah, I don seen it all befo
I don seen many a young boy like you
This here world ain't big enuf to hold you
Is it boy?
Your mind is way off somewheres else

JETHRO I just ain't got no tentions of being a slave all my life.
I got other ideas, I got other things to do

BEAT What they do to you boy?

JETHRO They whipped me. They whipped me till they was tired.

BEAT What they do to you boy

JETHRO They hung me in a tree
and made me outta forbidden fruit
they stretched my body out
and ripped it open
they set me afire
and I blazed till my guts fell out. And they left me
there, to rot. They left me there
until my burnt bones dropped.

BEAT And what they do to you boy?

JETHRO They stole my woman?

SARAH (*screaming*) Jethro help me

CHORUS Can someone guide us through this storm?
Can we make it alone?

Scene Two

BEAT What they do your woman boy?

JETHRO They . . . they

SARAH (*modern dressed*) They ain't did me a damn thing
you ain't let um do.
I remember you nigger.
I remember you
Can you look at me,
you half a man.
Where were you when I screamed
Where were you?
Where were you when the
horrible weight of that
pale beast weighted mightly upon my breasts? Where
where you my man?
Where were you when that pale beast stuck himself into me.
I called you.
I called you.
Where were you.
My belly was swelling and growing, the ugly pale
seed increasing daily in me.
How could you stand to look at me then?
Where were you.
My breasts grew larger each day
more full of my life giving milk,
they grew heavy with milk
and they sagged, my breasts
and my milk for my own pale bastards.
My own.
These children, our people, One son yours and
one son, the man's. One girl calls you daddy,
the other don't know your face.
Where were you nigger.
Parading around the streets in your sharp suits
or was you hiding somewhere
your knees shaking and cracking
where were you man?

JETHRO I was here Sarah.
I been here all along.
I been here from the time
He first grabbed you.
I been here and I have suffered for it.
I been here. You don't know.
What can I tell you?
What can I say to you?
Can I tell you how it feels?
Can I tell you how it feels
to see someone else's baby

	come shootin out your body? Can I tell you how it feels to lay and listen in the night waiting for you to return from the big house can I tell you how it feels to not be able to protect you to not to be able to say: You leave my woman alone. But I done all I could, I done all I could I fought when I could and I fought and I fought and I fought even tho I knew I wasn't goin na win. I fought all I could
SARAH	But it wasn't enuf It didn't stop the white men from coming. They came anyway. They came into me What you could, wasn't enuf
JETHRO	I know. I . . . so finally I left (*he exits*)
CHORUS	(*flute and drums again*) Black men walk the streets alone Black men walk the streets alone Black men walk cause they ain't got no home Some black folks call america home Some black folks call america home But if this is home, how come black men alone

Scene Three

BEAT	I don told these young negroes that this here is our home they need to get all that talk about Africa out they head they don't know nothing about Africa They don't even know how to talk African They don't know nothing you see Africans don't no mo want to see us then we wants to see them cause they sold us to the white man to get rid of us they sold us children, yes sir And don't nobody that care for nobody by selling they own kin now how I'ma love somebody who suppose to be my brother and done went and sold me into slavery why I says them Africans is as bad as the white man, cept they don't know as much.
BLK MAN	They have told us these lies about our mother and we in turn have believed them all They have told us these lies and we have come to live them
	We have come to be the lies that they told us we were Oh we are a sad people my brothers We have denied our mother We have denied the body that borne us We have refused the milk that we grew strong on We have died the silly death Our women lost, gone, taken from us Raped and made over into the image of filth, into the image of fairy tales, into the image of a white lie And our men, our men. . . .
JETHRO	Kill the silly dilly hunky mother fuckers Stick telephone poles up between the legs of his women. Kill them. Come on brothers. What we got to lose? Come on! Now! Now! Who are we, to let the white man rule? Where are we that we swim in this shitty cesspool? Let us move. Let us be. Come. See. There is truth somewhere there is beauty and wine and women and whatever else we talk about in our lives There is all, come . . .
SARAH	You lie! You lie, man. There is only you and the whiteman. You a cheap cock hound freak and the whiteman, the devil, That is all there is. There is no beauty. There is no truth. No peace.
JETHRO	Black is beautiful.
SARAH	You lie, if it is beautiful make it so. Be that beauty. Be that beauty black . . . no, but you lie. . . .
JETHRO	I do not lie. It is just just that you are blind
SARAH	I see you! I see you, is that blindness. But then maybe I am blind for I do not see anything in you no man actions, no nation, no nothing, I do not see anything that you do. Do you do anything? Are you anything black man besides hot air, broken dreams and invalid promises. Are you anything or just a cheap 45 record cracked and warped by the sun.
JETHRO	I am your world
SARAH	Well be it!
JETHRO	I speak of the beginning, of how it was then, of how it will be again,

SARAH of how it will be again,
I speak...
SARAH Speak of the end of these white devils
who invade our flesh. Speak
of that...
JETHRO Tomorrow
SARAH Tomorrow is now.
Tomorrow is here.
JETHRO Tomorrow. There is plenty time...
we are time we are the time of this
planet...
SARAH How many white bastards must I have
before you realize that time is
now for your seed to flow into me
PEACHES (*entering*) Give it up sista that nigger
ain't gonna marry you.
And that's all you doin
Really that's all.
Just trying to runa
so-fis-ti-cated game down on this man's
head.
He don't wanta hear that.
He wants a piece of ass.
Doncha baby? Isn't that what you really
want?
Me. You want me.
You want to get into me.
Doncha baby? Ain't you crazy about
me...
SARAH Black man hear me I am calling.
Don't listen to her foolish vulgarities.
Don't listen to her marilyn monroe dream
dribblings.
I want only you. I want you to claim me.
PEACHES Yeah you sho do need a man.
Come clean bitch, admit you want a
husband....
BLK WOMAN And the world of personal encounters
becomes more and more the sordid
history
of who can fuck who
Our encounters with one another
become
sexual games and gains
BEAT Boy listen here!
Take that pussy and run.
PEACHES Buy me a drink, daddy.
Get me a mink, sugar.
Dress me in pink, honey...
And I'll give you all the love that a man
can stand.
SARAH My love is not for sale
My love is your love when you love me.
SLICK What's happenin yall?
My you women sho are looking good.

(*Coming close to* SARAH)

That's a nice looking fro baby
and yo legs is nice too.
PEACHES She don't wanta hear that, man.
She trying to find her a husband.
SLICK (*laughing wildly*) What for?
PEACHES So the nigger can stick it to her
and then run out on her ass
after the children come droppin out her
belly.
I can see her now. Ten snotty nose
kids running around the welfare office...
SARAH Why do you talk like that...
PEACHES Like what? Like "sticking it to ya"
Like that? Why? Cause I know.
I know nigger men. I know them.
I have held them close to me.
I have heard their promises
I have felt their hands on my body.
I have beared the pain of their children.
I have even washed the tears of their
manhood from their eyes.
I know them. I speak from my experience.
I speak from
lessons my life taught me.
I speak of nigger men and their in-
competence.
SLICK We are good lovers...
PEACHES You are a good lay. A wet dream.
SLICK You black bitch...
PEACHES Kiss my ass, slick.
SLICK Ain't nobody in the world got to kiss the ass
of a
funky scroungy nigger bitch...
you'd like me to do that.
You like that idea.
You want somebody to kiss your ass.
But you can hang that shit up.
BLK WOMAN Why do we talk to each other like
that?
We act like machines,
like some animal the white man
has invented. We act as if
we were made to hate each other...
SARAH Why.
SLICK Shut up bitch. What you know about life?
You still thinking about getting married.
BEAT Man the only way to get a woman
like that to respect you is to go up side her
head
ask me, man I been living a long time and
I done had to slap many a silly hoe

(SLICK *slaps* SARAH. *She screams*)

SLICK Shut up bitch. I'm just learnin you
how to be a woman.
BEAT Good work boy.
PEACHES Look at your *black man* now honey
just standing around
dumb like a manhole cover
dumb with shit in his pants
Why he don't protect you?
SLICK Why I'd cut that nigger four ways twice if
he was so much as to say boo
See he don't understand, he don't under-
stand that
If I don't hit her she'll forget that she's a
nigger bitch. If I don't hit her...
SARAH You don't have to hit me.
I know what I am
PEACHES That bitch don't even make sense man.
I know what you talkin about

Blk Love Song #1

   Will you beat me if I don't give you
    money?
   Will you beat me when I come home late?
   Will you beat me to show me your love?
SLICK I will beat you every day
   in more ways than one.
PEACHES You are a true man.
SARAH And you . . . are you a true woman?
BLK WOMAN Are we true? Where are the seeds of
    Africa?
   Are we true to ourselves? Are we
    true?
   What are our lives . . .
    sad twisted reflections . . . dead
     junk . . .
    broken window. dreams
BLK MAN Can we wake from this
   and move into something else can we grow
    into the jungles
   of life we were/we are
   can we be vast sweeping plains of
    humanity
   or is the weather too cold here for us to
    grow,
   to grow, to grow
   Let us turn to them, Let us see. . . .

(*Both the* BLK MAN *and* WOMAN *now step into the scene for the first time*)

   Peace my brothers.
   Peace my sisters.
BLK WOMAN Peace.
BEAT More of this sickness!
   What are you now
   Afro–Americans for the glorious coming
   back of ancient savage Africa
   What are you
   dream songs who call themselves
   oog-la-boog-la and other good sambo
    ancestry names
   What are you advertisements for instant
    blackness
   What are you?
BLK MAN Be quite old man
SLICK Who you think you are?
BLK MAN I'm only a man.
SLICK Yeah, well me too.
BLK WOMAN Hey my brother, how you do?
   How you be? How are you?
SLICK You da one sound sick?
BLK WOMAN I heard you talk to the sister, brother.
   Why don't you be something else
    besides a warped
   reflection of pseudo james bond
    projection. You a
   lady killer for truth brother cause I
    mean you have killed
   many sisters with your western ego
    concepts of manhood
   borrowed from the devil. Many
    sisters have died
   trying to deal with you and what
    goodness they
   thought perhaps was in you.
SLICK Bitch you sick.
BLK WOMAN Well cure me. Take me. Lead me.
   Nullify the poisons you think you see
    in me
   with the sweet antidote of your
    righteous manhood being
SLICK Bitch, I'll slap you down . . .

(*He raises his hand and the* BLK MAN *gestures and freezes* SLICK *in a sick motion of attempting to slap a woman?*)

BLK MAN My brother, your actions mark you as
    negative.
   You destroy our women with your false
    notions
   of how to relate to them.
   My brother we must stop you, we must
    be firm
   enough to stand and say no to you and
    we will.
   Leave us and return when you are willing
    to relate
   to us as a brother to his people. Go now.
BEAT Who you think you is to be coming here
    giving out orders?
   You ain't nothing but a nigger, same as
    me . . .
BLK MAN I'm the same as you, same as you used
    to be but not
   a nigger. Same as you could be, but not
    a nigger.
   Just merely the more saner same than
    your craziness.
PEACHES You motherfuckers make me sick.
BLK WOMAN Sister, your life too has to change.
   If you are not ready to be a woman
PEACHES Let me tell you something, My life is like
    it is
   because of what men are, I'm like that
    cause they
   been like that, cause if I wanted to survive
   I had no choice but to be like that.
   A man is a low down animal.
BLK WOMAN No my sister, a man is a wonderous
    creation,
   a dawn, a deep night, a whole world.
   A man is a life force born, a giver, a
    keeper, a seeker.
   A man is our hope.
PEACHES The day I hope for a nigger to . . .
BLK MAN Submit!
PEACHES Submit, shit! Submit to what,
   to your overblown talk
   you call manhood. Submit
   to a man, never. For what?
   Man, I can do everything
   you can do and most things
   better. I can be everything
   you can be.
BLK MAN Can you be a man?
PEACHES From what I done seen men be for most
    of my life
   I can be that and more. I can't give
    myself

no baby but I damn sho can out fuck any
man alive.
BLK MAN So be it. Go head on and out fuck any
man alive.
Be that perversion you think is a woman.
You must submit to yourself of yourself,
in yourself.
I can not force you to be better, but can
only be the betterness
I would like you to be. Go head on.
Dance on sister.
Dance on to the rising tom-toms of your
death
throes. Dance on, dance the spastic
dance of self
inflicted bareness. Dance my sister to the
artificial
lights of the white world. Whirl and
dance and jump.

(*The woman begins shaking lewdly to a gut bucket music, she is grinning wildly as she dances trying to entice a frozen* SLICK *into a warmness of desire for her body*)

Sister no *man* wants a thing, a toy, a sex
puppet.
Dance. You cannot warm him. Remember
even you recognized his impotence.
Remember
your love is stronger than his. You said
that.
PEACHES Come on nigger. Come on. Take me put
it in me.
Do it to me. Come on man.
BLK MAN If that is all you wish for in your life. Be
gone.

(SLICK *is still frozen and* PEACHES *falls at his feet, clutching his legs*)

BLK WOMAN Oh my sister, my sister please rise out
of
that filthiness. Be stronger than that.
BLK MAN Rise my sister. Rise.
PEACHES Slick, slick, slick, come on slick,
these niggers, they crazy, you hit me slick,
you wake me up. You beat me up. Come
on slick,
you give me money. You tell me what
to do . . .
BLK MAN You turn to the frozen man now sister
but . . .
(*He gestures and she freezes to* SLICK)
BEAT See like I ain't been saying nuthin all this
time but I
believes that you niggers is witches and such
and that you is working hoo-doo magic on that
poor boy's head. You done fixed him and
spelled him and froze her up
BLK WOMAN Negro you are the worst invention of
the centuries of
man's living. Your breath steals life
from all
those around and near you. Negro.

BLK MAN I have no hoo-doo powers. It is simply
the positive
assertion of all that I am that is freezing
them.
They the pimps and whores of our life,
they the simple
people who have been transfixed by the
whites.
They are only frozen now. But if they
want to
they can rise. They can be men and
women. They
can be everything. They can be the
original beginning.
It's there if they want it but you are
the one who we can never cure.
BLK WOMAN We cannot even call you brother.
BEAT Who are you niggers to be judging somebody.
BLK MAN We are not judging you but your life,
your actions,
all that you have been, have done. Show
us your best.
Show us that you have struggled. . . .
SARAH Jethro, what is happening?
BLK MAN The day is dawning, my sister.
JETHRO Sarah . . . I . . . I . . .
BLK WOMAN Do not be afraid, my brother. You
are a ray of this new sun.
Your heat is part of this fire
You have struggled all you could
no one can fault you.
BLK MAN Come my brother and let us try to live
our lives.
Let us try to get along with each other.
Let us be people, the people that we are.
Come my brother. The day is dawning
and we've
much work to do. We have much sickness to look into
ourselves and extract. We have studying
to do.
New ways to learn. Come my brother
and bring
your woman along to this new day.
JETHRO What . . . what do I have to do?
BLK WOMAN No matter what it is, you will be able
to do it.
Do not be afraid my brother. You are
the sun my brother
and we, your women, we are the earth.
We lay waiting
for you to rise and warm us with the
fire of your
being and nourish us with the
strength of your
manliness. We wait to grow for you a
nation.
Plant your seeds into us. We await
you. We await
your coming black man, brother.
Come on.

(*She reaches out to him*)

BLK MAN Come sister. (*they embrace. all of them*)

BEAT   What kind of shit is this. What you niggers havin, a love in?
BLK WOMAN   You are a dreamwalker, a faggot projection.
We are looking for men now. That is our search.
The sun. We need the warmth and fire and love
of the sun. Black suns. Black suns to end
this dead life we lead. What is this life,
if we do not have men, where are we to go and what are
we to do, without men. I live for a man.
Together a new nation will come.
BEAT   You niggers is sick. Listen ain't no nigger gon ever be free. And don't you forget that. You can want all you want but baby the die has
been cast a long time ago. I know what you want
but baby the man knows too and like he's not about to let you become free.
BLK MAN   We can free ourselves. . . .
BEAT   We couldn't even make enough gas right now to
start a real big fire. All we got is what the white man lets us have.
BLK MAN   And all he has he got from us.
BEAT   That may be but the point is, he got it and we ain't got it and ain't bout to get it. So you got to learn to get what you can when you can't get what you want.
BLK MAN   We can get what we want!
BLK WOMAN   Your silliness is a curse on our people. Your fear is
the death of many of our brothers. Who are you, negro?
BEAT   Rochester, Amos N'Andy, Mod Squad, Jim Brown
BLK WOMAN   No those are white projections. What is your name?
BEAT   The temptations. The supremes.
BLK MAN   No. *Your*, name.
BEAT   I have no name.
BLK MAN   Then give yourself a name.
BEAT   Negro.
BLK MAN   No, that is a name the white man gave to you.
If you have no name. Then take one.
BEAT   AMERICA!!!!!

(*He pulls an american flag out of his jacket and begins waving it*)

AMERICANAMERICANAMERICAN AMERICANAMERICAN
BLK WOMAN   Stop. Here take this, let it be your flag.
   (*unwrapping her headwrap*)   Take it.
BEAT   No no no no you crazy, you crazy crazy crazy crazy

BLK MAN   You are a creature of the mad west. We must
cast you out.

(*In slow motion, he casts* BEAT *off the stage*)

JETHRO   Why did you do that, are we not all brothers, all one?
BLK MAN   All of those who want to be one, all who want to live
in brotherhood. But because a man's skin is black that
does not mean that he is your brother. For when
a father refuses his child he is no longer a father
to that child even though he is still the father
of that child. My brother there are many among us
who play the role of brother but they are not brothers.
Do not accept an enemy as a friend simply because
he calls you brother.
JETHRO   Then how are we to know who is who?
BLK WOMAN   Check their actions, their lives
The righteous are righteous in deed,
Indeed your friends will be friends and your enemies will be enemies.
That is how it
is no matter how they say they are.
SARAH   And what of them.
BLK MAN   We shall see.

(*He motions and they move out of their freezes.* PEACHES *climbs slowly to her feet*)

BLK WOMAN   As Salaam Alaikum my brother and sister.
PEACHES   And salami to you too. Come on Slick let's go somewhere and party it's too dead around here.
BLK MAN   (*to* JETHRO)   You see my brother, many of us have no concern for liberation.

(PEACHES *and* SLICK *exit arm in arm laughing strongly*)

SARAH   They act just like nothing has happened
BLK WOMAN   Nothing has happened as far as they are concerned
their whole world never changes friday night negroes who live only to have
a good time but we've other things to do
BLK MAN   Well my brothers, we must leave
BLK WOMAN   Yes.
JETHRO   But wait. You haven't told us what to do. You haven't told us what must be done. We want to be free but we don't know how to get free.
You must tell us.
BLK WOMAN   Here take this, (*holding out headwrap*) Make this your flag.
JETHRO   A woman can not lead

BLK WOMAN   I'm not trying to lead. I do not want to lead.
            I want you to lead. Here take our flag and
            go before and claim our lives.
JETHRO   But you're . . .
SARAH   You are leading, you're telling him what to do.
BLK WOMAN   No, you lead. You tell me. You tell me the things
            to do. You tell the rest of us what to do.
            You tell the white man.
            You tell the world
            You are the one
            You are the one to tell the world
            So tell them
            You do the telling.
JETHRO   But . . . I . . . can't . . .
BLK MAN   Stop. You are a man. You can do.
JETHRO   They will kill me.
BLK MAN   They cannot kill us all
JETHRO   They have the bomb.
BLK MAN   It is only a projection of their death wishes.
          They cannot destroy what they did not create.
          They cannot kill human life. Mankind will survive
          in spite of the coldness of the West.
          This is just another ice age. We can survive this.
          Come on black man. You are drugged.
          You speak and live as if you are in a stupor,
          or a dream. Wake up. Wake up.
SARAH   Tell us what to do.
BLK WOMAN   We can not.
BLK MAN   It is not for any man to tell another what to do.
          Each man must do as he must to help his brother to
          survive. I will tell you this much:
          If you do not become the teller, the one who says what
          is, defines, best, then others will, against your interest
          They will define you out of human existence. You will
          be lost. You must examine your life. You must
          study yourself. You must be careful what you eat.
          Be careful of the friends you choose. In the
          beginning you must do much of it alone.
          And beware the white man with machines. The machines
          of the man are not evil but beware. You have much
          to do. . . .
JETHRO   But you still . . .
BLK WOMAN   We must go. But remember your woman.
            If you lose her then you will never find yourself.
            Take a woman unto you and produce. Care for the
            woman and your children by her. Teach her.
            Teach them. We must go.

(*Fast flute and drums.* BLACK MAN *and* WOMAN *back away.* JETHRO *and* SARAH *call out to them but their motions become slower and slower. Lights, and they move normally*)

JETHRO   What has happened to us?
SARAH   I'm . . . I'm . . . I'm not sure. I thought . . . but then . . . Jethro.
JETHRO   Come Sarah. Don't be afraid. There is much we
         must do. It will be hard and we'll make mistakes
         but we . . .
SARAH   We'll work it out.
JETHRO   Come let us try. (*they exit together*)

(*Flute and drums*)

BLK MAN   Where is the seed of Africa now? Will we make
          us a home?
BLK WOMAN   Will the nation rise and grow firm in the
            bodies of black women?
CHORUS   Where is the seed of Africa? When will they
         come home? Where is the seed of Africa?
         When will they come home? How long before
         from the seeds a new black nation shall bloom
         Let a new black nation bloom
         Let a new black nation bloom
         Let us a new black nation bloom!

Bibliographies

SELECTED BIBLIOGRAPHY OF PLAYS BY AUTHORS REPRESENTED IN THIS VOLUME

This list is presented to give the reader an opportunity to seek out other plays by the playwrights in this volume. If an author is not represented, it is because, as far as is known, the only play he wrote is published here.

Some playwrights have written as many as twenty or thirty plays. For a complete listing see *Black Image on the American Stage, A Bibliography of Plays and Musicals 1770–1970*, edited by James V. Hatch (New York: Drama Book Specialists, 1970).

BALDWIN, JAMES. *Blues for Mr. Charlie*. New York: Dial Press, 1964. A full-length drama of Southern race murder and corruption.

BARAKA, IMAMU AMIRI (LE ROI JONES). *Dutchman*. New York: William Morrow and Co., 1964. A one-act drama on the subway. The white girl provokes the middle-class black man to violence, then kills him.

———. *Experimental Death Unit #1*. In *Four Black Revolutionary Plays*. Indianapolis: Bobbs-Merrill, 1969. A one-act drama wherein the black army kills the whites and the blacks who "co-whort" with them.

———. *The Slave Ship*. Newark, N.J.: Jihad Productions, 1969. A short one-act depicting the brutality of the slave passage and auction.

———. *The Toilet*. New York: Grove Press, 1963. A violent one-act depicting teenage frustrations of love, race, and homosexual conflicts.

BONNER, MARITA. *Exit, An Illusion*. In *Crisis* magazine (October, 1929). This short experimental play concerns the psychological conflicts of miscegenation.

———. *The Pot-Maker*. In *Opportunity* magazine (February, 1927). This short one-act folk play is a fatalistic melodrama about Elias who is "called" to preach, and who manages the death of his wife's lover.

BRANCH, WILLIAM. *A Medal For Willie*. In *Black Drama Anthology*. Edited by Woodie King and Ron Milner. New York: New American Library, 1971. The mother of a dead black hero refuses the Army's medal and the town's honors.

BROWN, WILLIAM WELLS. *Experience: or, How To Give a Northern Man a Backbone* (1856). This play, probably never published, told the tale of a white man from the North who was sold as a slave in the South.

BROWNE, THEODORE. *The Gravy Train*. A typescript in the Schomburg Collection, New York City, 1940. This is a full-length play about a sensitive young man trying to work, go to school, and keep his wandering wife happy.

———. *A Black Woman Called Moses*. Unpublished. A full-length play on the life of Harriet Tubman.

BULLINS, ED. *Clara's Ole Man*. In *Five Plays by Ed. Bullins*. Indianapolis: Bobbs-Merrill Co., 1969. A longer one-act drama-comedy built around a college boy's calling on Clara.

———. *In the Wine Time*. In *Five Plays by Ed Bullins*. Indianapolis: Bobbs-Merrill Co., 1969. A full-length naturalistic drama of the life, struggle, and love of the people who hang out on the stoop.

———. *In New England Winter*. In *New Plays from the Black Theater*. Edited by Ed Bullins. New York: Bantam Books, 1969. A long one-act memory play.

———. *A Son Come Home*. In *Five Plays by Ed Bullins*. Indianapolis: Bobbs-Merrill Co., 1969. A one-act drama of a son who returns seeking love from his mother.

MARTIE, CHARLES. *Black Cycle*. In *Black Drama Anthology*. Edited by Woodie King and Ron Milner. New York: New America Library, 1971. A full-length drama of a black girl's rebellion against her mother and the older generation.

———. *Jamimma*. Unpublished typescript, Ron Hobbs Agency, New York City.

———. *Where We At?* Unpublished typescript New Lafayette Theater Agency, New York City. A one-act drama showing the humiliation and degradation of a black woman who refuses to help an unfortunate sister.

CHILDRESS, ALICE. *The World on a Hill*. In *Plays To Remember*. New York: MacMillan, 1968.

———. *Florence*. In *Masses and Mainstream* (October, 1950). A one-act showing a subtle confrontation between a rich white woman and a black woman in a train depot.

———. *Mojo*. New York: Dramatists Play Service, 1971. This one act is subtitled a Black Love Story; it is.

DODSON, OWEN. *The Garden of Time*. Unpublished typescript in the James Weldon Johnson Memorial Collection at Yale University.

———. *Everybody Join Hands*. In *Theater Arts Magazine* (September, 1943). The need to join China and others in the war against the Axis.

——— and CULLEN, COUNTEE. *The Third Fourth of July*. In *Theater Arts Magazine* (1946).

———. *Amistad*. Unpublished manuscript in Yale University Library (1939). The story of Cinque's rebellion aboard ship.

———. *Bayou Legend*. In *Black Drama in America: An Anthology*. Edited by Darwin T. Turner. New York: Fawcett, 1971. This is a black vagabond hero of the Peer Gynt legend set in Louisiana.

EDMONDS, RANDOLPH. *Earth and Stars*. In *Black Drama in America: An Anthology*. Edited by Darwin T. Turner. New York: Fawcett, 1971. This full-length script explores the problems of the Civil Rights Movement in the South following World War II.

———. *Silas Brown*. In *The Land of Cotton and Other Plays*. Washington, D.C.: Associated Publishers, Inc., 1943. A one-act about a stingy, cruel father who drives his son from home and lives to regret it.

———. *The Breeders*. In *Six Plays for a Negro Theater*. Boston: Walter Baker, 1934. A one-act showing slave resistance to breeding for more slaves.

———. *Nat Turner*. In *Six Plays for a Negro Theater*. Boston: Walter Baker, 1934. A one-act showing Nat Turner on the eve of the rebellion and after his defeat.

———. *The Land of Cotton*. In *The Land of Cotton and Other Plays*. Washington, D.C.: Associated Publishers, Inc., 1943. A full-length drama showing black and white sharecroppers uniting against wealthy white landowners.

FERDINAND, VAL. *Black Liberation Army*. Typescript available from *Blkartsouth*, New Orleans. A one-act of the struggle and necessity for gathering an army for revolution.

———. *Homecoming*. Typescript available from *Blkartsouth*, New Orleans. A one-act drama revealing different attitudes toward the black struggle in America.

HANSBERRY, LORRAINE. *A Raisin in the Sun*. New York: Samuel French, 1959. Story of a black family's struggle in Chicago to have dignity and the good life.

———. *Les Blancs*. In *Les Blancs: The Collected Last Plays of Lorraine Hansberry*. Edited by Robert Nemiroff. New York: Random House, 1972. A drama about a European educated African returning home to join the revolution against the colonialists.

———. *The Sign in Sidney Brustein's Window*. New York: Random House, 1965. A full-length study of white and black liberals in Greenwich Village.

———. *To Be Young Gifted, and Black*. Englewood Cliffs, N.J.: Prentice-Hall, Inc., 1969. A collage of Lorraine Hansberry's life and work.

HATCH, JAMES V., LARRY GARVIN and AIDA MORALES. *Conspiracy*. Unpublished typescript, Performing Arts Library, New York City. A ritualization from the transcript of the Chicago trial of Bobby Seale in 1969.

HATCH, JAMES V., and SAM RAPHLING. *Liar, Liar*. New York: General Music, 1972. A children's musical about the world's greatest liar.

HILL, ABRAM. *On Striver's Row*. Unpublished typescript in Schomburg Library, New York City. A full-length satire-burlesque on middle-and upper-class blacks and their striving.

——— and SILVERA, JOHN. *Liberty Deferred*. Unpublished typescript in Performing Arts Library, New York City. A complete panorama of Negro history from African slavery to 1930's. Written for, but not produced by, Federal Theater.

HUGHES, LANGSTON. *Mulatto*. In *Five Plays by Langston Hughes*. Edited by Webster Smalley. Bloomington: Indiana University Press, 1968. The mulatto son comes home to the plantation from a Northern education and tragedy follows.

———. *Soul Gone Home*. In *Five Plays by Langston Hughes*. Edited by Webster Smalley. Bloomington: Indiana University Press 1968. A one-act funeral monologue of a son for his prostitute mother.

———. *Simply Heavenly*. In *Five Plays by Langston Hughes*. Edited by Webster Smalley. Bloomington: Indiana University Press, 1968. A musical based on the adventures of Jesse B. Semple.

JACKSON, C. BERNARD. *Blood of the Lamb*. Unpublished manuscript (1964). A staged oratorio dealing with faith and skepticism.

———. *The Departure*. Unpublished manuscript (1965). A full-length musical play about man's struggle for survival.

JOHNSON, GEORGIA DOUGLAS. *Blue Blood*. In *Fifty More Contemporary One-Act Plays*. Edited by Frank Shay. New York: Appleton & Co, 1928. A drama of miscegenation with a happy ending.

———. *Frederick Douglass*. In *Negro History in Thirteen Plays*. Edited by Richardson and Miller. Washington, D.C.: Associated Publishers, 1935. The story of Douglass' escape from slavery.

———. *William and Ellen Craft*. In *Negro History in Thirteen Plays*. Edited by Richardson and Miller. Washington, D.C.: Associated Publishers, 1935. Drama of escape from slavery, structured like *Frederick Douglass*.

KENNEDY, ADRIENNE. *The Funnyhouse of a Negro*. New York: Samuel French, 1969. A surrealistic drama of miscegenation and quest for identity.

———. *A Rat's Mass*. In *New Black Playwrights*. Edited by William Couch. Baton Rouge: Louisiana State University, 1968. Brother and sister incest in a surreal one-act.

MATHEUS, JOHN. *Black Damp*. In *Carolina Magazine*. (April, 1929). Coal miners of mixed races trapped in a mine cave-in.

———. *Ti Yette*. In *Plays and Pageants from the Life of the Negro*. Edited by Willis Richardson. Washington, D.C.: Associated Publishers, 1930. Creole brother hates his sister when she dates a white man during Mardi Gras.

MILLER, MAY. *Scratches*. In *Carolina Magazine* (April, 1929). A one-act of life and love in a pool hall.

———. *Riding the Goat*. In *Plays and Pageants from the Life of the Negro*. Edited by Willis Richardson. Washington, D.C.: Associated Publishers, 1930. A comedy about a doctor who is forced to play the middle-class social game.

———. *Harriet Tubman*. In *Negro History in Thirteen Plays*. Edited by Richardson and Miller. Washington, D.C.: Associated Publishers, 1935. A historical one-act written for school children.

MITCHELL, LOFTEN. *Land Beyond The River*. In *The Black Teacher and the Dramatic Arts*. Edited by Reardon and Pawley. Westport, Conn.: Negro Universities Press, 1970. A full-length account of the Reverend De Laine's struggle to bring the "separate but equal" school laws before the Supreme Court.

———. *Tell Pharoah*. In *The Black Teacher and the Dramatic Arts*. Edited by Reardon and Pawley. Westport, Conn.: Negro Universities Press, 1970. A two-act pageant of black life, struggle, and theater in America.

———. *The Phonograph*. Unpublished. An autobiographical full-length account of the author's boyhood in Harlem.

PAWLEY, THOMAS, *Jedgement Day*. In *The Negro Caravan*. Edited by Sterling Brown. New York: Dryden Press, 1941. A one-act comedy about the guilt of a man who stays in bed instead of going to church.

———. *FFV (First Families of Virginia)*. Unpublished manuscript. A full-length drama about color prejudice within the old established black families.

PETERSON, LOUIS. *Entertain a Ghost*. Unpublished (1962).

RICHARDS, STANLEY. *Through a Glass Darky*. In *The Best Short Plays: 1947–48*. New York: Dodd, Mead & Co., 1948. A short drama dealing with religious and racial tolerance.

———. *O Distant Land*. In *The Best One-Act Plays of 1948–49*. New York: Dodd, Mead & Co., 1949.

———. *Journey to Bahia*. New York: Dramatists Play Service, Inc., 1964. A full-length play adapted from the Brazilian play *O Pagador de Promessas*.

———. *August Heat*. In *The Best One-Act Plays of 1949–50*. New York: Dodd, Mead & Co., 1950.

RICHARDSON, WILLIS. *The Broken Banjo*. In *Plays of Negro Life*. Edited by Alain Locke. New York: Harper, 1927. A "bad" man with a good heart is guilty of accidental homicide.

———. *The Chip Woman's Fortune*. In *Anthology of the American Negro in the Theater*. Edited by Lindsay Patterson. New York: The Publishers Co., 1967. This character play has an old woman giving her savings to help the family. This was the first play by a black author to be done on Broadway.

———. *The Deacon's Awakening*. In *Crisis* magazine (Nov., 1920). The Deacon learns that the women in his own family want to vote.

———. *The House of Sham*. In *Plays and Pageants from the Life of the Negro*. Edited by Willis Richardson. A middle-class family living beyond its means gets a comeuppance.

———. *Attucks the Martyr*. In *Negro History in Thirteen Plays*. Edited by Richardson and Miller. Washington, D.C.: Associated Publishers, 1935. The story of how Attucks was the first patriot killed in the American Revolution.

SÉJOUR, VICTOR. *Les Noces Vénitiennes*. Paris: M. Lévy Frères, 1855. A five-act drama written in prose. The story is the hatred and rivalry of two powerful families in Venice, the Orseoles and the Falieros.

———. *La Chute de Séjan*. Copy in Bibliothèque Nationale, Paris. A five-act verse play about the Roman emperor Tiberius and his minister Sejanus and their struggle for power; it was produced in 1849.

———. *Diégarias*. Paris: Imprimerie de Boule, 1861. A verse drama set in fifteenth century Spain. It is a revenge drama involving a disguised Jew, his daughter, and her husband Don Juan. It was produced in 1844.

———. *Richard III*. Paris: D. Giraud et J. Dagneau, 1852. A five-act prose drama; the bloody history of the rise and fall of the English king.

———. *La Tireuse de Cartes*. Paris: M. Lévy Frères, 1860. A five-act prose drama, produced in 1850. It is the story of a mother who demands the return of her daughter; when refused, she swears to kill the young husband-abductor.

SHINE, TED. *Morning, Noon, and Night*. In *The Black Teacher and the Dramatic Arts*. Edited by Reardon and Pawley. Westport, Conn.: Negro Universities Press, 1970. A full-length drama of a young boy's struggle to escape a powerful, demonic grandmother.

———. *Contribution*. In *Contributions*. New York: Dramatists Play Service, 1970. A one-act comedy of a Southern black woman who poisons her enemies.

———. *Shoes*. In *Contributions*. New York: Dramatists Play Service, 1970. A one-act about young black men to whom clothes are the ultimate sign of arrival.

———. *Plantation*. In *Contributions*. New York: Dramatists Play Service, 1970. A one-act comedy in which the black servants manage by cleverness to take over the plantation.

SPENCE, EULALIE. *Fool's Errand*. New York: Samuel French, 1927. This one-act folk comedy tells how busybody neighbors assume that the unmarried daughter of a church member is pregnant; they try to force the boyfriend to marry her.

———. *The Starter*. In *Plays of Negro Life*. Edited by Alain Locke. New York: Harper Bros., 1927. This one-act comedy is about a young woman who tries to commit her boyfriend to a promise of marriage.

WARD, DOUGLAS TURNER. *Happy Ending*. New York: Dramatists Play Service, 1966. A one-act comedy showing the cleverness of black women in dealing with white employers.

———. *The Reckoning*. New York: Dramatists play service, 1970. A long one-act comedy showing Southern corruption and how a black pimp outsmarts the governor.

———. *Brotherhood*. New York: Dramatists Play Service, 1970. A short one-act where middle-class blacks discover the prejudices of middle-class whites.

WARD, THEODORE. *Our Lan'*. In *A Theater in

Your Head. Edited by Kenneth Thrope Rowe. New York: Funk & Wagnalls, 1960. A story based on historical fact about the post–Civil War struggle of blacks to get and hold land of their own.

SELECTED BIBLIOGRAPHY OF ANTHOLOGIES CONTAINING SCRIPTS BY BLACK PLAYWRIGHTS

BARAKA, IMAMU AMIRI (LE ROI JONES). *Four Black Revolutionary Plays*. Indianapolis: Bobbs-Merrill, 1969.

Black Quartet, A. New York: New American Library, 1970.

BRASMER, WILLIAM, and DOMINICK CONSOLO. *Black Drama: An Anthology*. Columbus, Ohio: Merrill Publishing Co., 1970.

BROWN, STERLING; DAVIS, ARTHUR; and LEE, ULYSSES. *Negro Caravan*. New York: Dryden Press, Inc., 1941.

BULLINS, ED. *Five Plays by Ed Bullins*. Indianapolis: Bobbs-Merrill, 1969.

———. *Four Dynamite Plays*. New York: William Morrow and Company, 1972.

———. *New Plays from the Black Theater*. New York: Bantam Books, 1969.

———. *The Theme Is Blackness*. New York: William Morrow and Company, 1973.

———. *The Drama Review*, Vol. 12, No. 4 (Summer, 1968).

CHILDRESS, ALICE. *Black Scenes*. New York: Double Day, 1971.

COUCH, WILLIAM, JR. *New Black Playwrights*. Baton Rouge: Louisiana State University, 1968.

EDMONDS, RANDOLPH. *The Land of Cotton and Other Plays*. Washington, D.C.: Associated Publishers, 1943.

———. *Shades and Shadows*. Boston: Meador Publishing Co., 1930.

———. *Six Plays for a Negro Theater*. Boston: Walter H. Baker, 1934.

KING, WOODIE, and RON MILNER. *Black Drama Anthology*. New York: New American Library, 1971.

LOCKE, ALAIN, and GREGORY, MONTGOMERY. *Plays of Negro Life*. New York: Harper Bros., 1927.

OLIVER, CLINTON, and STEPHANIE SILLS. *Contemporary Black Drama*. New York: Charles Scribner's Sons, 1971.

PATTERSON, LINDSAY. *Black Theater*. New York: Dodd, Mead & Company, 1971.

REARDON, WILLIAM, and PAWLEY, THOMAS. *The Black Teacher and the Dramatic Arts*. Westport, Conn.: Negro Universities Press, 1970.

RICHARDSON, WILLIS. *The King's Dilemma and Other Plays for Children*. New York: Exposition Press, 1956.

———, and MILLER, MAY. *Negro History in Thirteen Plays*. Washington, D.C.: Associated Publishers, 1935.

———. *Plays and Pageants from the Life of the Negro*. Washington, D.C.: Associated Publishers, 1930.

SMALLEY, WEBSTER. *Five Plays by Langston Hughes*. Bloomington, Ind.: Indiana University Press, 1968.

TURNER, DARWIN T. *Black Drama in America: An Anthology*. New York: Fawcett Publications, 1971.

WHITE, EDGAR, *Underground, Four Plays*. New York: William Morrow and Company, 1970.

SELECTED BIBLIOGRAPHY OF BOOKS AND SOURCES ON BLACK DRAMA AND ITS THEATER ARTISTS

ABRAMSON, DORIS. *Negro Playwrights in the American Theater, 1925–1959*. New York: Columbia University Press, 1969.

ARCHER, LEONARD C. *Black Images in American Theater*. Nashville, Tenn.: Pageant Press, 1973.

BOND, FREDERICK W. *The Negro and the Drama*. Washington, D.C.: Associated Publishers, 1940.

BROWN, STERLING. *Negro Poetry and Drama*. Washington, 1937. Reprint. New York: Atheneum, 1969.

BULLINS, ED. *Black Theater* (magazine). New York: The New Lafayette Theater, 1968–1972.

DENT, THOMAS; GILBERT, MOSES; and SCHECHNER, RICHARD. *The Free Southern Theater*. Indianapolis: Bobbs-Merrill, 1969.

FLETCHER, TOM. 100 *Years of the Negro in Show Business*. New York: Burdge and Co., 1954.

HARRISON, PAUL CARTER. *The Drama of Nommo*. New York: Grove Press, Inc., 1972.

HATCH, JAMES V. *Black Image on the American Stage, A Bibliography of Plays and Musicals, 1770–1970.* New York: Drama Book Specialists, 1970.

HUGHES, LANGSTON, and MELTZER, MILTON. *Black Magic.* Englewood Cliffs, N.J.: Prentice-Hall, Inc., 1968.

ISAACS, EDITH J. *The Negro in the American Theater.* New York: Theater Arts, 1947.

JOHNSON, JAMES WELDON. *Black Manhattan.* New York: Knopf, 1930.

MARSHALL, HERBERT, and STOCK, MILDRED. *Ira Aldridge, The Negro Tragedian.* Carbondale, Ill.: Southern Illinois University Press, 1968.

MITCHELL, LOFTEN. *Black Drama: The Story of the American Negro in the Theater.* New York: Hawthorne Books, 1967.

PATTERSON, LINDSAY. *Anthology of the American Negro in the Theater.* New York: The Publishers Co., 1967.

REARDON, WILLIAM, and PAWLEY, THOMAS. *The Black Teacher and the Dramatic Arts.* Westport, Conn.: Negro Universities Press, 1970.

HATCH-BILLOPS ORAL HISTORY COLLECTION OF BLACK THEATER ARTISTS

The following is a list of interviews with black theater artists recorded on tape by James V. Hatch and his assistants at the City College of New York. These tapes, available to research students for noncommercial purposes, are stored at the Cohen Library, City College of New York and Schomburg Research Library, New York City. The project is continuing.

Osceola Archer
Charles Blackwell
Margaret Bonds
Sherri Brewer
Ivan Browning
Ed Bullins
Vinie Burrows
Anita Bush
James Butcher
Dick Campbell
Vinette Carroll
Steve Carter
Alice Childress
Ralf Coleman
Miriam Colon
Ossie Davis
Ivan Dixon
Owen Dodson
Josie Dotson
Randolph Edmonds
Lonnie Elder III
Valdo Freeman
Charles Griffin
Jester Hairston
Neil Harris
Hilda Haynes
Ida Hubbard
Eddie Hunter
Earl Hyman
Caterina Jarboro
Robert Earl Jones
Woodie King
Sister Lubaba Lateef
Rosetta LeNoire
Elma Lewis
Avon Long
Ernie McClintock
Butterfly McQueen
"Pigmeat" Markham
William Marshall
May Miller
Arthur Mitchell
Loften Mitchell
Clarence Muse
Pauline Myers
Maidie Norman
Frederick O'Neal
Juanita Oubre
Tom Pawley
Willis Richardson
Sonia Sanchez
Frank and Robert Schiffman
Charles Sebree
Noble Sissle
Eulalie Spence
Delano Stewart
Tom Turner
Joseph A. Walker
William Walker
Richard Wesley
Leigh Whipper
Vantile Whitfield
Napoleon Whiting

Index

Abolitionism, 34–35
Abramson, Doris, 35
    on *Caleb, the Degenerate*, 62
African Free School, 3
African Grove Theatre, 1, 3
African Ritual Theatre, 353
Alcott, Louisa May, 138
Aldridge, Ira, 1, 3
Ali, Muhammad, 438
All God's Chillun Got Wings (O'Neill), 100, 184
American Negro Theatre:
    early years, 437
    history of, 360, 392
Amsterdam News (newspaper), 547
Anderson, Garland, 59, 100, 101
Anicet-Bourgeois, 3
Anna Lucasta (Yordan), 438
Association for the Study of Negro History, 353
Atkinson, Brooks, 279, 583
Audience involvement, 826
Austin, Alfred, 62

Back to Africa movement, 62; *see also* Garvey, Marcus; Universal Negro Improvement Association
    in *Caleb, the Degenerate*, 63
Baldwin, James, 826
Baraka, Imamu Amiri, 241
Bearden, Romare, 618
Belasco, David, 100
Belcher, Fannin S., Jr., 62, 137
Bergson, Henri, 653
Beyond the Blues (Poole), 211
Birth Control Review (periodical), 178
Birth of a Nation (film), 61
Black artist, 773
Black Bourgeoisie (Frazier), 547, 737
Black capitalism, 280
Black consciousness, in the 1960's, 654
Black Doctor, The (Aldridge), 3
Black experience, 827
    in *Take a Giant Step*, 547
    Joseph Cotter, Sr.'s view of, 62–63

Blackface, 1–3, 618; *see also* Minstrelsy on Broadway, 100
Black image, positive heroes and, 587
Black Manhattan (Johnson), 35
Black migrations, post Civil War, 225
Black musicals, 775
    revues, 618
Black nationalism, 280, 812
    in *Big White Fog*, 279
    in U.S., 1960's, 209
Black pride, 211, 775; *see also* Back to Africa Movement; Garvey, Marcus; Universal Negro Improvement Association
Black rebellions, 135
    1917–1921, 135
    Chicago riots, 255
    Detroit and Harlem, 1943, 391, 432
    "Red Summer" of 1919, 278
Black Renaissance, *see* Negro Renaissance
Black Star Line Corporation, 278; *see also* Universal Negro Improvement Association
    history of, 279
Black Teacher and the Dramatic Arts, The (Reardon and Pawley), 671
Black theatre groups, in 1930's, 252
Bland, James, 1
Blkartsouth, 864
Brotherhood of Sleeping Car Porters, 391
Brown, Mr. (first name unknown; author of *King Shotaway*), 1
Brown, John, 34, 587
Brown, Sterling, 35, 393, 655
    on classic stereotypes, 241
Brown, William Wells, 2, 25, 34, 713
Browne, Robert, 547
Brownies Book, The (periodical), 233
Butcher, James, 321

Cabin in the Sky (film), 391
Calvi, Pietro, 3
Candidates, The (Munford), 35
Carlyle, Thomas, 59
Carmen Jones (film), 391

Carnegie, Andrew, 59; *see also The Gospel of Wealth*
Carolina Magazine, The (periodical), 192, 233
Catton, Bruce, 587
Chattanooga Daily Times (newspaper), on lynchings, 241
Chip Woman's Fortune, The (Richardson), 233
Christophe (Easton), 2
Church; *see also* Religion
   during the depression, 320
   politics in, 188
City Writers Project, W.P.A., 320
Civil Rights movement, 737
   during 1950's, 547
   sit-ins, 1960's, 671
Clansman, The (Dixon), 61
Cleaver, Eldridge, 437
Cole, Bob, 1
Comedy, 25, 775
   interracial satires, 188
   protest against racism, 1960's, 653
Communism, 279
Community theatre, 765, 826
Cook, Anne, 321
Cook, Will Marion, 1
Coolidge, Calvin, 100
Coronet Theatre (Los Angeles), 514
Cotter, Joseph, Sr., 59, 61–63
Crisis (periodical), 135, 188, 201, 255
Critics, white, of black theater, 695
Cruse, Harold, on *Raisin in the Sun*, 473
Culbertson, Ernest, 137

Daily Worker, The (newspaper), 360
Decolonization, 812
Dee, Ruby, in *Walk Hard*, 438
Deep Are the Roots (D'Usseau and Gow), 392
Dempsey, Jack, 437
Denmark Vesey (Edmonds), 241
Depression, 775
   Chicago's South Side, 278
   comparisons of blacks and whites in, 255
   reflections of, in art, 253
   religion and the church during, 320
Dessalines (Easton), 2
Dialect, 34–35; *see also* Stereotypes
   "darkey" stereotyped speech, 178
   Middle English influence on, 225
   natural speech, 210

Diégarias (Séjour), 25
Divine, Father, 775
   history of, 320
Dixon, Reverend Thomas, 61
Dodson, Owen, 514, 826
Dotson, Josie, on *Amen Corner*, 514
Douglass, Frederick, 587
Drama programs, in black colleges, 826
Dred Scott Decision, 34
DuBois, Dr. W. E. B., 135, 353, 382, 733; *see also* Krigwa Players
Dumas, Alexander, 25
Dunlap, William, 1
Dutchman (Baraka), 812

Earth and Stars (Edmonds), 242
Easton, William, 1–2
Edmonds, Randolph, 9
Ellison, Ralph, on *Big White Fog*, 279
Escape, The (Brown), 2, 25
Ethiopian Art Players, 233
Eunuch, The (Terence), 353

Fair Employment Practices Commission, 391
Federal Theatre Project, Negro Unit of, 253
Finian's Rainbow (Harburg and Saidy), 392
Flight of the Natives (Richardson), 233
Folk theatre, 209, 382
   "gettin' happy" plays in, 218
Fool, The (Pollack), 100
Foster, Stephen, 61
Frazier, Dr. E. Franklin, 475, 547, 737
Free Southern Theatre, The, 773, 864
Frolic Theatre, 100
Funnyhouse of a Negro (Kennedy), 184

Garvey, Marcus, 135, 209, 775; *see also* Back to Africa movement; United Negro Improvement Association
   imprisonment of, 278
Garveyism: *see* Back to Africa movement; United Negro Improvement Association
"Gay Nineties," 618
Georgia Minstrels, 1
Goat Alley (Culbertson), 137
Golden Boy (Odets), 437
Gospel of Wealth, The (Carnegie), 61
Gottfried, Martin, on *Day of Absence*, 695

Index

Gottschalk, Louis, 1, 25
Great Goodness of Life (Baraka), 774
Great White Hope, The (Sackler), 184, 437
Green, Doe Doe, 101
Green Pastures (Connelly), 100
Green, Paul, 393
Greenfield, Elizabeth Taylor, 1
Greenwich Mews Theatre, 587
Gregory, Lady, 209
Grimke, Angelina, 137–138

Haiti, Republic of, 3
"Halfway House," 211
Hansberry, Lorraine, 138, 393
Hapgood, Emily, 209
Harlem Black Arts Repertory Theatre and School, 812
Harlem Renaissance: *see* Negro Renaissance
Harlem Suitcase Theatre, 655
    founding of, 262
Harrigan, Nedda, 100
Harrison, Richard, 100
Hearst, William Randolph, 61
Henry, John; *see also* Stereotypes
    plays about, 360
Hewlett, James, 1, 3
Heyward, DuBose, 137
Hicks, Charles, 1
History plays, 351, 382
Howard Players, 137, 218, 233
    under Owen Dodson, 321
Howard University, 514
    Drama department of, 321, 826
Hubbard, Elbert, 59
Hudson Theatre, 100
Hughes, Langston, 279–280
Hugo, Victor, 25

Individualism, 59, 100; *see also* Self-made men
Industrial Education, 61–62; *see also* Washington, Booker T.
    in *Caleb, the Degenerate*, 63
Inner City Cultural Center, 671
Integration, 671, 774, 812
International Righteous Government, 320–321
Invisible Man, The (Ellison), 826
Ira Aldridge, the Negro Tragedian (Marshall and Stock), 3

Irish folk theater, compared to Negro Renaissance, 209

Jazz music, 618
Johnson, James Weldon:
    as Secretary of N.A.A.C.P., 137
    on William Wells Brown, 35
Jolson, Al, 100
Jones, Sissieretta, 1

Kerr, Walter:
    on *Amen Corner*, 514
    on *Take a Giant Step*, 547
Kersands, Billy, 1
King Lear (Shakespeare), 3
King Shotaway (Brown), 1
Krigwa Players, 353, 382, 773; *see also* DuBois, W. E. B.

Land of Cotton and Other Plays, The (Edmonds), 241
Law and order, 212
Lee, Canada, 393, 432
Lincoln, C. Eric, 211
Lincoln Theatre, 279
Locke, Alain, 209, 775
Lost in the Stars (Anderson), 391
Louis, Joe, 437
Lucas, Sam, 1
Lulu Belle (MacArthur and Sheldon), 100
Lynchings, 61, 137, 211, 241, 618

Macbeth (Shakespeare), 3
McClain, John, on *Amen Corner*, 514
McCullers, Carson, 658
Malcolm X, 587, 775
Marshall, Herbert, 3
Marshall, William, 587
Member of the Wedding, The (McCullers), 658
Message to Garcia (Hubbard), 59
Metro Theatre (Los Angeles), 671
Metropolitan Museum of Art, 547
Middle class values, 547, 775, 826
    versus beauties of being black, 138
    evolution of, 737
    in *Rachel*, 138
Minstrelsy, 1–2, 618; *see also* Blackface
    blacks in whiteface, effect of, and, 695
    "darkey" comedies and, 209

Miscegenation, tragic-mulatto genre of, 184
Mitchell, Loften, 35
Mitchell, Louis, 618
Mulatto (Hughes), 184

Narrative of William Wells Brown, a Fugitive Slave (Brown), 34
National Association for the Advancement of Colored People, 61
    compared with United Negro Improvement Association, 278
    drama committee of, 137
Nat Turner (Edmonds), 241
Naturalism, 812, 827
Negro Awakening: *see* Negro Renaissance
"Negro Characters as Seen by White Authors" (Brown), 393
Negro History in Thirteen Plays (Richardson and Miller), 233, 351, 353
Negro History Week, 3
Negro in Louisiana, The (Rousseve), 25
Negro in New York, The (Ottley and Weatherby), 320
Negro Pilgrimage in America, The (Lincoln), 211
Negro Playwrights in the American Theatre: 1925–1959 (Abramson), 35
Negro Playwrights Company, 279, 392
Negro Poetry and Drama (Brown), 35
Negro Renaissance, 135, 382
    "The New Negro" and, 209
"Negro's Ten Commandments, The," (Cotter), 61
New Lafayette Theatre, 765
"The New Negro" (Locke), 209
New Negro Theatre, 262
New York Black Economic Research Center, 547
New York Post (newspaper), 209
New York Public Library, 320
New York State Athletic Commission, 438
Nichols, Denise, 773
Nigger, The (Sheldon), 184
Nkombo (periodical), 864
Non-violence, vs. violence, 737; *see also* Civil Rights movement
No Place to Be Somebody (Gordone), 61
North Star, The (newspaper), 587

Octoroon, The (Boucicault), 184
"On Being Young, a Woman, and Colored" (Bonner), 201
On Strivers' Row (Hill), 360, 437
Oppenheimer, George, on *The Slave*, 812
Opportunity (periodical), 225, 655
Othello (Shakespeare), 3
Ottley, Roi, 320
Owl Answers, The (Kennedy), 184

Padlock, The (Bickerstaffe), 3
Patterson, Louise, 262
Peekskill Riot, 392
Phillips, Louis, 35
Phonograph (Mitchell), 473
Pizarro (Sheridan), 1
Plays of Negro Life (Locke and Montgomery), 137
Plays and Pageants of Negro Life (Richardson), 233
Pluralistic society, 774
Pollack, Channing, 100
Poole, Rosey, 211
Porgy (Heywood), 137
Pyramid Texts of Egypt, 353

Race prejudice, 3, 618, 711, 827
    in boxing, 437
    on Broadway, 100
    in public school teaching, 765
    in television, 713
    in theater, 1950's, 547
    of white critics, 695
"Racial tolerance," 391
Raisin in the Sun (Hansberry), 473
    compared with *Native Son*, 393
Ragtime, 618
Rand, Ayn, 59
Randolph, A. Philip, 391
Religion, 320, 713
Respectful Prostitute, The (Sartre), 241, 392
Revolution, 587; *see also* Black rebellions
Richard III (Shakespeare), 3
Richards, Beah, 514
Ritual exorcism, 773–774
    of white spirit, 812
Robertson's Playhouse (Los Angeles), 514
Robeson, Paul, 100, 392
Romantic-historical drama, 25
Romanticism, 775

Index

Roosevelt, Theodore, 61
Rousseve, Charles, 25

Sagar, Lester A., 100
Saint Marks Theatre, 812
Sandburg, Carl, 278
Sander, Alfred, 587
Sartre, Jean Paul, 241
Savoy Ballroom, 775
Scenic Designer's Guild, 514
Schomburg Research Library, 3
Schultz, Dutch, 775
Seale, Bobby, 393
Sebree, Charles, 432
Segregation, 391
    in armed forces, 432
Self-made men, 59, 100; *see also* Individualism
    in Joseph Cotter's works, 61
Separatism, in theater movements, 733
Sexual prejudice, 711
Shades and Shadows (Edmonds), 241
Shakespeare, William, 3
Shoebox Theatre (Los Angeles), 671
Sights and Sounds (periodical), 279
Silvera, Frank, 514
Six Plays for a Negro Theatre (Edmonds), 241
Slave, The (Baraka), 241
Slavery, 34, 713; *see also* Race prejudice; Lynchings
    as dramatic theme, 382
Smith, Al, 100
Smith, Michael, 695
Socialism, 280
South Pacific (Rodgers and Hammerstein), 392
Spenser, Herbert, 59
Spirit House, 812
Stereotypes, 35, 658; *see also* Dialect
    the brute, 241, 393, 437
    the contented slave, 382
    the exotic, 137, 210, 253, 775
    inferiority of blacks, 351
    Jim Crow, 438
    John Henry, 360
    mammy, 136, 737
    in motion pictures, 655
    "pity-the-poor-nigger" genre, 241
    the prostitute, 711
    the suffering Negro, 391
    Uncle Tom, 432

Stock, Mildred, 3
Student Non-Violent Coordinating Committee (SNCC), 671
Suitcase Theatre: *see* Harlem Suitcase Theatre
Sullivan, John L., 437
Surrealism, 756

Taubman, Howard, on *Amen Corner*, 514
Taylor, Clarice, 587
Théâtre Française, 25
Theatre of Being (Silvera), 514
"Three Plays for a Negro Theatre" (Torrence), 209
Titus Andronicus (Shakespeare), 3
To Be Young, Gifted, and Black (Hansberry), 473
Toilet, The (Baraka), 812
Tokenism, 737
Toomer, Jean, 209
Torrence, Ridgely, 178, 209
Trip to Coon Town, A (Cole and Johnson), 1
Trip to Niagara, A (Dunlap), 1
Truman, Harry S., 432

Uncle Tom's Cabin (Aiken), 35
Uncommon Sense (Anderson), 101
United States Supreme Court, separate but equal doctrine of, 61
Universal Negro Improvement Association; *see also* Back to Africa movement; Black pride; Garvey, Marcus
    origins and history of, 278
Urban renewal, in Washington, D.C., 211

Verse drama, 2, 25
Virginia Mummy, The, 3
Volunteers of 1814, The (Séjour), 25

Walker, A'Leila, 775
Walker, George, 618
War effort, 391
Washington, Booker T., 59, 61–62, 101, 137; *see also* Industrial Education
Watkins, Thomas, 62
Watts, Richard, on *Amen Corner*, 514
Weatherby, William, 320
Wedding Band (Childress), 184
Whitfield, Vantile, 514
Williams, Bert, 100, 618
Women's rights, c. 1919, 178

Woodson, Dr. Carter, 351, 353
Work ethic, 59, 62, 100
World War I, 135, 137
    black soldiers in, 173
    female stereotypes during, 173

Yeats, William Butler, 209

Zangwill, Israel, 62
Ziegfeld Follies, 100, 618
Zinberg, Len, 437